T0189275

Lecture Notes in Computer Science 10401

More information about this series at http://www.springer.com/series/7410

Jonathan Katz · Hovav Shacham (Eds.)

Advances in Cryptology – CRYPTO 2017

37th Annual International Cryptology Conference
Santa Barbara, CA, USA, August 20–24, 2017
Proceedings, Part I

Editors
Jonathan Katz
University of Maryland
College Park, MD
USA

Hovav Shacham
UC San Diego
La Jolla, CA
USA

ISSN 0302-9743 ISSN 1611-3349 (electronic)
Lecture Notes in Computer Science
ISBN 978-3-319-63687-0 ISBN 978-3-319-63688-7 (eBook)
DOI 10.1007/978-3-319-63688-7

Library of Congress Control Number: 2017947035

LNCS Sublibrary: SL4 – Security and Cryptology

Printed on acid-free paper

This Springer imprint is published by Springer Nature
The registered company is Springer International Publishing AG
The registered company address is: Gewerbestrasse 11, 6330 Cham, Switzerland

Preface

The 37th International Cryptology Conference (Crypto 2017) was held at the University of California, Santa Barbara, USA, during August 20–24, 2017, sponsored by the International Association for Cryptologic Research.

There were 311 submissions to Crypto 2017, a substantial increase from previous years. The Program Committee, aided by nearly 350 external reviewers, selected 72 papers to appear in the program. We are indebted to all the reviewers for their service. Their reviews and discussions, if printed out, would consume about a thousand pages.

Two papers—"Identity-Based Encryption from the Diffie-Hellman Assumption," by Nico Döttling and Sanjam Garg, and "The first Collision for Full SHA-1," by Marc Stevens, Elie Bursztein, Pierre Karpman, Ange Albertini, and Yarik Markov—were honored as best papers. A third paper—"Watermarking Cryptographic Functionalities from Standard Lattice Assumptions," by Sam Kim and David J. Wu—was honored as best paper authored exclusively by young researchers.

Crypto was the venue for the 2017 IACR Distinguished Lecture, delivered by Shafi Goldwasser. Crypto also shared an invited speaker, Cédric Fournet, with the 30th IEEE Computer Security Foundations Symposium (CSF 2017), which was held jointly with Crypto.

We are grateful to Steven Myers, the Crypto general chair; to Shai Halevi, author of the IACR Web Submission and Review system; to Alfred Hofmann, Anna Kramer, and their colleagues at Springer; to Sally Vito of UCSB Conference Services; and, of course, everyone who submitted a paper to Crypto and everyone who attended the conference.

August 2017

Jonathan Katz
Hovav Shacham

Crypto 2017

The 37th IACR International Cryptology Conference

University of California, Santa Barbara, CA, USA
August 20–24, 2017

Sponsored by the *International Association for Cryptologic Research*

General Chair

Steven Myers	Indiana University, USA

Program Chairs

Jonathan Katz	University of Maryland, USA
Hovav Shacham	UC San Diego, USA

Program Committee

Masayuki Abe	NTT Secure Platform Laboratories, Japan
Shweta Agrawal	IIT Madras, India
Adi Akavia	The Academic College of Tel Aviv-Yaffo, Israel
Elena Andreeva	KU Leuven, Belgium
Mihir Bellare	UC San Diego, USA
Dan Boneh	Stanford University, USA
Elette Boyle	IDC Herzliya, Israel
Ran Canetti	Boston University, USA, and Tel Aviv University, Israel
Jung Hee Cheon	Seoul National University, Korea
Dana Dachman-Soled	University of Maryland, USA
Ivan Damgård	Aarhus University, Denmark
Nico Döttling	UC Berkeley, USA
Orr Dunkelman	University of Haifa, Israel
Eiichiro Fujisaki	NTT Secure Platform Laboratories, Japan
Sergey Gorbunov	University of Waterloo, Canada
Vipul Goyal	Carnegie Mellon University, USA
Matthew Green	Johns Hopkins University, USA
Nadia Heninger	University of Pennsylvania, USA
Viet Tung Hoang	Florida State University, USA
Dennis Hofheinz	Karlsruhe Institute of Technology, Germany
Sorina Ionica	Université de Picardie, France

Tetsu Iwata	Nagoya University, Japan
Seny Kamara	Brown University, USA
Gaëtan Leurent	Inria, France
Rachel Lin	UC Santa Barbara, USA
Stefan Lucks	Bauhaus-Universität Weimar, Germany
Vadim Lyubashevsky	IBM Zurich, Switzerland
Mohammad Mahmoody	University of Virginia, USA
Payman Mohassel	Visa Research, USA
Claudio Orlandi	Aarhus University, Denmark
Elisabeth Oswald	University of Bristol, UK
Rafael Pass	Cornell University, USA
Gregory G. Rose	TargetProof LLC, USA
Christian Schaffner	University of Amsterdam and CWI and QuSoft, The Netherlands
Gil Segev	Hebrew University, Israel
Yannick Seurin	ANSSI, France
Douglas Stebila	McMaster University, Canada
Stefano Tessaro	UC Santa Barbara, USA
Mehdi Tibouchi	NTT Secure Platform Laboratories, Japan
Eran Tromer	Tel Aviv University, Israel, and Columbia University, USA
Dominique Unruh	University of Tartu, Estonia
Vassilis Zikas	Rensselaer Polytechnic Institute, USA

Additional Reviewers

Aysajan Abidin
Shashank Agrawal
Thomas Agrikola
Ali Akhavi
Gorjan Alagic
Martin Albrecht
Jacob Alperin-Sheriff
Joel Alwen
Joran van Apeldoorn
Daniel Apon
Gilad Asharov
Tomer Ashur
Nuttapong Attrapadung
Christian Badertscher
Saikrishna Badrinarayanan
Shi Bai
Foteini Baldimtsi
Marshall Ball
Achiya Bar-On
Razvan Barbulescu
Guy Barwell
Carsten Baum
Amin Baumeler
Fabrice Benhamouda
Daniel J. Bernstein
Jean-François Biasse
Alex Biryukov
Nir Bitansky
Olivier Blazy
Jeremiah Blocki
Andrej Bogdanov
Xavier Bonnetain
Charlotte Bonte
Carl Bootland
Christina Boura
Zvika Brakerski
Brandon Broadnax
Leon Groot Bruinderink
Benedikt Bunz
Anne Canteaut
Angelo de Caro
Ignacio Cascudo
David Cash
Wouter Castryck
Nishanth Chandran
Eshan Chattopadhyay
Binyi Chen
Jie Chen
Yilei Chen
Alessandro Chiesa
Chongwon Cho
Arka Rai Chouduhri
Heewon Chung
Kai-Min Chung
Benoit Cogliati
Aloni Cohen

Ran Cohen
Katriel Cohn-Gordon
Henry Corrigan-Gibbs
Geoffroy Couteau
Alain Couvreur
Cas Cremers
Jan Czajkowski
Wei Dai
Bernardo David
Jean Paul Degabriele
Jeroen Delvaux
Apoorvaa Deshpande
Bogdan Adrian Dina
Itai Dinur
Yevgeniy Dodis
Benjamin Dowling
Rafael Dowsley
Leo Ducas
Yfke Dulek
Tuyet Duong
Tuyet Thi Anh Duong
Fred Dupuis
Frédéric Dupuis
Alfredo Rial Duran
Sébastien Duval
Aner Moshe Ben Efraim
Maria Eichlseder
Keita Emura
Naomi Ephraim
Saba Eskandarian
Thomas Espitau
Oriol Farràs
Pooya Farshim
Sebastian Faust
Prastudy Fauzi
Nelly Fazio
Serge Fehr
Houda Ferradi
Manuel Fersch
Dario Fiore
Ben Fisch
Joseph Fitzsimons
Nils Fleischhacker
Tore Frederiksen
Rotem Arnon Friedman
Georg Fuchsbauer
Marc Fyrbiak
Tommaso Gagliardoni
Nicolas Gama
Juan Garay
Sanjam Garg
Christina Garman
Romain Gay
Peter Gazi
Alexandre Gelin
Daniel Genkin
Marios Georgiou
Benoit Gerard
Essam Ghadafi
Niv Gilboa
Dov Gordon
Rishab Goyal
Vincent Grosso
Jens Groth
Paul Grubbs
Siyao Guo
Helene Haag
Helene Haagh
Kyoohyung Han
Marcella Hastings
Carmit Hazay
Ethan Heilman
Brett Hemenway
Minki Hhan
Justin Holmgren
Akinori Hosoyamada
Yan Huang
Pavel Hubacek
Ilia Iliashenko
Vincenzo Iovino
Yuval Ishai
Joseph Jaeger
Zahra Jafragholi
Tibor Jager
Aayush Jain
Abhishek Jain
Chethan Kamath
Bhavana Kanukurthi
Angshuman Karmakar
Pierre Karpman
Stefan Katzenbeisser
Xagawa Keita
Marcel Keller
Nathan Keller
Iordanis Kerenidis
Dakshita Khurana
Andrey Kim
Dongwoo Kim
Duhyeong Kim
Eunkyung Kim
Jae-yun Kim
Jihye Kim
Jinsu Kim
Jiseung Kim
Sam Kim
Taechan Kim
Fuyuki Kitagawa
Susumu Kiyoshima
Dima Kogan
Vlad Kolesnikov
Ilan Komargodski
Venkata Koppula
Venkata Kopulla
Evgenios Kornaropoulos
Juliane Kraemer
Mukul Kulkarni
Ashutosh Kumar
Ranjit Kumaresan
Alptekin Küpçü
Lakshmi Kuppusamy
Thijs Laarhoven
Changmin Lee
Joohee Lee
Younho Lee
Nikos Leonardos
Tancrède Lepoint
Baiyu Li
Benoit Libert
Eik List
Yi-Kai Liu
Steve Lu
Yun Lu
Atul Luykx
Saeed Mahloujifar
Giulio Malavolta
Alex Malozemoff
Antonio Marcedone
Daniel P. Martin

Marco Martinoli
Daniel Masny
Takahiro Matsuda
Florian Mendel
Bart Mennink
Peihan Miao
Daniele Micciancio
Gabrielle De Micheli
Ian Miers
Andrew Miller
Kazuhiko Minematsu
Tarik Moataz
Ameer Mohammed
Hart Montgomery
Andrew Morgan
Nicky Mouha
Pratyay Mukherjee
Muhammad Naveed
María Naya-Plasencia
Kartik Nayak
Gregory Neven
Ruth Ng
Michael Nielsen
Tobias Nilges
Ryo Nishimaki
Ariel Nof
Kaisa Nyberg
Adam O'Neill
Maciej Obremski
Sabine Oechsner
Miyako Ohkubo
Rafail Ostrovsky
Daniel Page
Jiaxin Pan
Omer Paneth
Dimitris Papadopoulos
Sunno Park
Anat Paskin-Cherniavsky
Kenny Paterson
Arpita Patra
Filip Pawlega
Chris Peikert
Josef Pieprzyk
Cécile Pierrot
Krzysztof Pietrzak
Benny Pinkas
Rafael del Pino
Oxana Poburinnaya
David Pointcheval
Antigoni Polychroniadou
Raluca Ada Popa
Bart Preneel
Thomas Prest
Emmanuel Prouff
Carla Rafols
Srinivasan Raghuraman
Samuel Ranellucci
Mariana Raykova
Oded Regev
Ling Ren
Oscar Reparaz
Leo Reyzin
Silas Richelson
Matt Robshaw
Mike Rosulek
Yann Rotella
Lior Rotem
Ron Rothblum
Arnab Roy
Sujoy Sinha Roy
Olivier Ruatta
Ulrich Rührmair
Yusuke Sakai
Olivier Sanders
Yu Sasaki
Sajin Sasy
Alessandra Scafuro
Patrick Schaumont
Thomas Schneider
Peter Scholl
Gregor Seiler
Ido Shahaf
abhi shelat
Timothy Sherwood
Kyoji Shibutani
Sina Shiehian
Mark Simkin
Leonie Simpson
Maciej Skorski
Nigel Smart
Yongha Son
Fang Song
Yongsoo Song
Pratik Soni
Florian Speelman
Akshayaram Srinivasan
Martijn Stam
François-Xavier Standaert
John Steinberger
Igors Stepanovs
Noah Stephens-Davidowitz
Valentin Suder
Koutarou Suzuki
Björn Tackmann
Alain Tapp
Isamu Teranishi
Benjamin Terner
Aishwarya Thiruvengadam
Sri Aravinda Krishnan Thyagarajan
Yosuke Todo
Junichi Tomida
Luca Trevisan
Roberto Trifiletti
Daniel Tschudi
Nik Unger
Salil Vadhan
Margarita Vald
Luke Valenta
Kerem Varici
Srinivas Vivek Venkatesh
Muthuramakrishnan Venkitasubramaniam
Daniele Venturi
Damien Vergnaud
Jorge Villar
Dhinakaran Vinayagamurthy
Ivan Visconti
Damian Vizar
Christine van Vreedendal
Michael Walter
Mingyuan Wang
Xiao Wang
Yuyu Wang
Yohei Watanabe

Hoeteck Wee
Avi Weinstock
Mor Weiss
Jakob Wenzel
Daniel Wichs
David Wu
Keita Xagawa
Sophia Yakoubov
Avishay Yanay
Kan Yasuda
Donggeon Yhee
Chen Yilei
Eylon Yogev
Kazuki Yoneyama
Lanqing Yu
Thomas Zacharias
Samee Zahur
Greg Zaverucha
Mark Zhandry
Ren Zhang
Yupeng Zhang
Hong-Sheng Zhou

Platinum Sponsor

Silver Sponsors

FUJITSU

Western Digital

Contents – Part I

Bitcoin

Multiparty Computation

Award Papers

Obfuscation I

Conditional Disclosure of Secrets

Functional Encryption

Stronger Security for Reusable Garbled Circuits, General Definitions and Attacks

Shweta Agrawal(✉)

IIT Madras, Chennai, India
shweta@iitm.ac.in

Abstract. We construct a functional encryption scheme for circuits which simultaneously achieves and improves upon the security of the current best known, and incomparable, constructions from standard assumptions: reusable garbled circuits by Goldwasser, Kalai, Popa, Vaikuntanathan and Zeldovich (STOC 2013) [GKP+13] and predicate encryption for circuits by Gorbunov, Vaikuntanathan and Wee (CRYPTO 2015) [GVW15]. Our scheme is secure based on the learning with errors (LWE) assumption. Our construction implies:

1. A new construction for reusable garbled circuits that achieves stronger security than the only known prior construction [GKP+13].
2. A new construction for bounded collusion functional encryption with substantial efficiency benefits: our public parameters and ciphertext size incur an *additive* growth of $O(Q^2)$, where Q is the number of permissible queries (We note that due to a lower bound [AGVW13], the ciphertext size must necessarily grow with Q). Additionally, the ciphertext of our scheme is *succinct*, in that it does not depend on the size of the circuit. By contrast, the prior best construction [GKP+13, GVW12] incurred a *multiplicative* blowup of $O(Q^4)$ in both the public parameters and ciphertext size. However, our scheme is secure in a weaker game than [GVW12].

Additionally, we show that existing LWE based predicate encryption schemes [AFV11, GVW15] are completely insecure against a general functional encryption adversary (i.e. in the "strong attribute hiding" game). We demonstrate three different attacks, the strongest of which is applicable even to the inner product predicate encryption scheme [AFV11]. Our attacks are practical and allow the attacker to completely recover $\mathbf{x}$ from its encryption $\mathsf{Enc}(\mathbf{x})$ within a polynomial number of queries. This illustrates that the barrier between predicate and functional encryption is not just a limitation of proof techniques. We believe these attacks shed significant light on the barriers to achieving full fledged functional encryption from LWE, even for simple functionalities such as inner product zero testing [KSW08, AFV11].

Along the way, we develop a new proof technique that permits the simulator to program public parameters based on keys that will be requested in the future. This technique may be of independent interest.

J. Katz and H. Shacham (Eds.): CRYPTO 2017, Part I, LNCS 10401, pp. 3–35, 2017.
DOI: 10.1007/978-3-319-63688-7_1

1 Introduction

The last decade has witnessed important progress in the field of computing on encrypted data. Several sophisticated generalizations of encryption, such as Identity Based Encryption [BF01,Coc01,GPV08], Attribute Based Encryption [GPSW06,BSW07,GGH+13c,GVW13], Predicate Encryption [KSW08,AFV11, GVW15], Fully Homomorphic Encryption [Gen09,BV11,GSW13,BV14], Property Preserving Encryption [PR12] have burst onto the scene, significantly advancing the capabilities of modern cryptography.

These generalizations aim to provide the capability of computing "blindfolded" – namely, given an encryption of some data $\mathbf{a}$, an untrusted party should be able to perform computations on $\mathsf{Enc}(\mathbf{a})$ so that the resultant ciphertext may be decrypted meaningfully. The notion of fully homomorphic encryption permits arbitrary computation on encrypted data, but restricts decryption to be all-or-nothing, namely, the holder of the secret key may decrypt the resultant ciphertext to learn the result of the computation, but the same key also decrypts the original ciphertext revealing $\mathbf{a}$. For applications that require restricted access to results of the computation, the notion of functional encryption (FE) is more suitable. In functional encryption, a secret key is associated with a function, typically represented as a circuit C, denoted by SK_C and a ciphertext with some input $\mathbf{a}$ from the domain of C, denoted by $\mathsf{CT}_\mathbf{a}$. Given SK_C and $\mathsf{CT}_\mathbf{a}$, the user may run the decryption procedure to learn the value $C(\mathbf{a})$. Security of the system guarantees that nothing beyond $C(\mathbf{a})$ can be learned from $\mathsf{CT}_\mathbf{a}$ and SK_C. Functional encryption was formalized by Boneh et al. [BSW11] to unify and extend the notions of Identity Based Encryption, Attribute Based Encryption and Predicate Encryption, which had already appeared in the literature.

There has been considerable progress in the last several years towards constructing FE for advanced functionalities [BF01,Coc01,BW06,BW07,GPV08, CHKP10,ABB10,GPSW06,BSW07,KSW08,LOS+10,AFV11,Wat12,GVW13, GGH+13c,GGH+13b,GVW15]. For the most powerful notion of "full-fledged" functional encryption, that allows the evaluation of arbitrary efficiently-computable functions and is secure against general adversaries, the only known constructions rely on multilinear maps [GGHZ14] or indistinguishability obfuscation (iO) [GGH+13b]. However, all known candidate multi-linear map constructions [GGH13a,CLT13,GGH15] as well as some candidates of iO have been recently broken [CHL+15,CGH+15,HJ15,CJL,CFL+16,MSZ16].

From standard assumptions, the best known constructions do support general functionalities, but achieve restricted notions of security. Currently, the state-of-the-art comprises two incomparable constructions:

- The reusable garbled circuits construction of Goldwasser et al. [GTKP+13], which supports all polynomial sized Boolean circuits but restricts the attacker to only obtain a single secret key, for any circuit C of her choice. This construction can be compiled with the bounded collusion FE construction of [GVW12] to obtain a scheme which supports q queries, for any a-priori bounded q, and with a ciphertext size that grows by a multiplicative factor of $O(q^4)$. Note that the ciphertext size here does not depend on the size of the circuit C, and is thus *succinct.*

- The recent predicate encryption (PE) for circuits construction of Gorbunov et al. [GVW15], which also supports all polynomial sized Boolean circuits but restricts the attacker to only acquire keys for circuits C_i such that $C_i(\mathbf{a}) = 0$, when $\mathbf{a}$ is the vector of challenge attributes. He may not request any keys C_j such that $C_j(\mathbf{a}) = 1$. We will refer to the former as 0-keys and the latter as 1-keys. This restricted game of security is often referred to as *weak attribute hiding* in the literature.

Both constructions natively achieve the restricted *selective* notion of security, which forces the attacker to output the challenge in the very first step of the game, before seeing the public parameters.

Note that both constructions provide the functionality demanded by functional encryption, but fall short in security. Covering the distance from the restricted security definitions acheived by these constructions to full fledged functional encryption is a much sought-after goal, and one that must contend with several thorny technical issues. The former construction relies on the use of garbled circuits for decryption, which restricts the number of supported keys to 1, or, using the additional machinery of [GVW12], to some a-priori bounded q. The use of garbled circuits is central to this construction, and surmounting the bounded key limitation appears to require entirely new techniques. On the other hand, the second construction does support an unbounded number of queries, but restricts them to belong to the 0-set. It is unclear how to support even a single 1-query in this case, due to various technical hurdles that arise from the proof techniques (more on this below). Whether these techniques may be extended to support the full-fledged security game of functional encryption is an important open question, and the one we study in this work.

1.1 Our Contributions

In this work, we provide a new construction for functional encryption which simultaneously achieves and improves upon the security of the current best known, and incomparable, constructions from standard assumptions [GKP+13, GVW15]. Our scheme is secure based on the learning with errors (LWE) assumption. Our construction implies:

1. A new construction for reusable garbled circuits that achieves stronger security than the only prior construction by Goldwasser et al. (STOC 2013) [GKP+13]. In our construction, the attacker may additionally request an unbounded number of 0 keys in addition to the single arbitrary key allowed by the standard definition of reusable garbled circuits. Additionally, our construction achieves semi-adaptive security as against selective [GKP+13].
2. A new construction for bounded collusion functional encryption where the adversary is restricted to making an a-priori fixed number of queries. The ciphertext of our scheme is *succinct*, in that it does not depend on the size

of the circuit. Our public parameters and ciphertext size incur an *additive* growth of $O(Q^2)$, where Q is the number of permissible queries. By contrast, the prior best construction [GKP+13, GVW12] incurred a *multiplicative* blowup of $O(Q^4)$ in both the public parameters and ciphertext size. However, our construction is secure in a weaker game than best known [GKP+13, GVW12].

Additionally, we show that existing LWE based predicate encryption schemes [AFV11, GVW15] are completely insecure against a general functional encryption adversary (i.e. in the "strong attribute hiding" game). We demonstrate three different attacks, the strongest of which is applicable even to the inner product predicate encryption scheme [AFV11]. Our attacks are practical and allow the attacker to completely recover $\mathbf{a}$ from its encryption $\mathsf{Enc}(\mathbf{a})$ within a polynomial number of queries. This illustrates that the barrier between predicate and functional encryption is not just a limitation of proof techniques. We believe these attacks shed significant light on the barriers to achieving full fledged functional encryption for circuits from standard assumptions.

Along the way, we develop a new proof technique that permits the simulator to program public parameters based on keys that will be requested in the future. This technique may be of independent interest.

1.2 Our Techniques

Our work builds upon the constructions of Goldwasser et al. [GTKP+13] and Gorbunov et al. [GVW15]. Both these systems begin with the idea that the public attributes in an attribute based encryption scheme (ABE) may be hidden, and yet remain amenable to computation, if they are encrypted using fully homomorphic encryption. Recall that in an attribute based encryption scheme [GPSW06], a ciphertext is associated with a public attribute vector $\mathbf{a}$ and plaintext bit μ, and it hides μ, but not $\mathbf{a}$.

To hide $\mathbf{a}$, one may encrypt it using FHE to obtain $\widehat{\mathbf{a}}$, and treat this encryption as the public attribute in an ABE system. Since an ABE scheme for circuits [GVW13, BGG+14] allows for a key SK_C to evaluate an arbitrary circuit C on the attribute, the decryptor may now homomorphically compute on $\widehat{\mathbf{a}}$ using the FHE evaluation circuit. Then, given a key corresponding to the circuit $\mathsf{FHE.Eval(C, \cdot)}$, the decryptor may run the ABE decryption procedure to learn the FHE encryption of $C(\mathbf{a})$, namely $\widehat{C(\mathbf{a})}$.

This is not yet enough, as the goal is for the decryptor to learn $C(\mathbf{a})$ in the clear. To achieve this, FHE decryption must be performed on $\widehat{C(\mathbf{a})}$ in a manner that does not permit decryption of any ciphertext other than $\widehat{C(\mathbf{a})}$. The scheme of Goldwasser et al. [GTKP+13] resolves this difficulty by employing a single use garbled circuit for the FHE decryption function and using ABE to provide labels corresponding to input $\widehat{C(\mathbf{a})}$. This constrains FHE decryption, but restricts the resultant FE scheme to only be secure against a single key request. The scheme of Gorbunov et al. [GVW15] resolves this difficulty by making use of two nicely matching asymmetries:

1. *The asymmetry in computation.* To compute $C(\mathbf{a})$ using the above method, the bulk of the computation is to be performed on FHE ciphertext, namely $\mathsf{FHE.Eval}(C, \widehat{\mathbf{a}})$, where $\widehat{\mathbf{a}}$ can be public. The remainder of the computation, namely running the FHE decryption circuit on $\widehat{C(\mathbf{a})}$, is a relatively lightweight circuit.
2. *The asymmetry in attribute hiding in the ABE scheme of* [BGG+14]. There is an inherent asymmetry in the homomorphic multiplication procedure of the ABE scheme [BGG+14], so that computing a product of two ciphertexts wth attributes $\mathbf{a}_1$ and $\mathbf{a}_2$ respectively, only necessitates revealing *one* attribute (say $\mathbf{a}_1$) while the other ($\mathbf{a}_2$) can remain hidden (for addition, both $\mathbf{a}_1$ and $\mathbf{a}_2$ may remain hidden). This property is leveraged by [GVW15] to construct partially hiding predicate (or attribute) encryption (PHPE), which allows computation of an inner product of a public attribute vector corresponding to $\mathsf{FHE.Eval}(C, \widehat{\mathbf{a}})$ and a private attribute vector, corresponding to the FHE secret key. Since inner product loosely approximates FHE decryption, this allows the decryptor to obtain a plaintext value corresponding to $C(\mathbf{a})$ as desired.

While the predicate encryption scheme [GVW15] can handle an unbounded number of 0-queries from the adversary, it runs into at least three difficulties when faced with a 1-query:

1. The proof of security in the PHPE scheme uses a trapdoor puncturing technique [ABB10] in the simulation, so that the simulator has a trapdoor to sample keys for 0-queries but this trapdoor vanishes for 1-queries, disabling the simulator.
2. Given a PHPE ciphertext $\mathsf{CT}_{\widehat{\mathbf{a}}}$ with public attributes $\widehat{\mathbf{a}}$, key homomorphism [BGG+14, GVW15] enables the evaluation of a circuit C on the PHPE ciphertext resulting in a PHPE ciphertext $\mathsf{CT}_{C(\widehat{\mathbf{a}})}$ with attributes $C(\widehat{\mathbf{a}})$. By construction, this resultant ciphertext is an LWE sample with an error term which is fixed and public *linear* combination of the error terms used to construct $\mathsf{CT}_{\widehat{\mathbf{a}}}$. This error is learned by the adversary upon decryption, which creates leakage that cannot be simulated. Indeed, this leakage, when sufficient, can completely break LWE security and allow the adversary to learn $\mathbf{a}$ in the clear (see Sect. 3 for details).
3. Recall that the FHE decryption operation is a lightweight operation conducted using PHPE with the FHE secret key as the private attribute vector. While FHE decryption is lightweight, it is still not lightweight enough to be performed in its entirety while maintaining the privacy of the FHE secret. FHE decryption is an inner product followed by a threshold function, of which only the inner product can be performed securely by PHPE. The authors overcome this hurdle by making use of the "lazy OR" trick, which roughly allows the decryptor to learn not the threshold inner product, but the pure inner product, which leaks sensitive information about the noise used while encrypting $\mathbf{a}$. Again, this leakage cannot be simulated, and when sufficiently high, can lead to complete recovery of the FHE secret key.

Attacks. Interestingly, all of the above difficulties in proving security translate to polynomial time attacks that lead to complete message recovery in a game where 1-keys are permitted. Our first and strongest attack is related to the first difficulty, and is effective even against the inner product predicate encryption scheme of Agrawal et al. [AFV11]. Recall that the inner product zero test functionality of [AFV11] permits the decryptor to test whether the inner product of a vector $\mathbf{x} \in \mathbb{Z}_p^\ell$ in the ciphertext and vector $\mathbf{v} \in \mathbb{Z}_p^\ell$ in the key is zero or non-zero. We demonstrate that by requesting keys for linearly dependent functions, the attacker can construct a short basis for a matrix $\mathbf{F}$ (say) which is related to the LWE matrices used in the challenge ciphertext. By manipulating the challenge ciphertext, the attacker may recover an LWE sample of the form $\mathbf{F}^{\mathsf{T}}\mathbf{s}+\mathsf{noise}$. This LWE sample unresistingly reveals all its secrets given a trapdoor for $\mathbf{F}$, which in turn allow the attacker to recover the entire message $\mathbf{x}$ from the challenge ciphertext.

We believe this attack sheds significant light on the barriers to obtaining full fledged functional encryption even for a simple functionality such as inner product zero testing [KSW08, AFV11]. Note that full security has been achieved for a functionality that *computes* the inner product of two vectors $\mathbf{x}, \mathbf{v} \in \mathbb{Z}_p^\ell$ given $\mathsf{CT}(\mathbf{x})$ and $\mathsf{SK}(\mathbf{v})$, but it appears quite challenging to extend these techniques for the case of inner product zero testing. Intuitively, this is because the inner product zero test functionality is non-linear: 0 keys reveal almost nothing about $\mathbf{x}$ while 1 keys reveal much more. This is in contrast to the inner product computation functionality, in which all function queries, whether type 0 or type 1, reveal proportionate information about $\mathbf{x}$. Constructing functional encryption with full fledged security even for the simple functionality of [KSW08, AFV11] from lattice based assumptions appears to require fundamental new techniques.

Our second attack is against the Partially Hiding Predicate Encryption system for circuits [GVW15] and stems from the second difficulty above. This attack exploits the fact that the decryptor, given a 1-key, learns a public linear function of the error terms used in encryption. By requesting sufficient 1-keys, the attacker can solve this linear system to recover the errors used in encryption, which lead to recovery of the predicate $\mathbf{a}$ even when functionality reveals much less.

Our third attack is against the Predicate Encryption (PE) system for circuits [GVW15]. As discussed in the third difficulty above, the PE decryption key, which wishes to provide the decryptor with a threshold inner product value, instead can only provide the exact inner product value, leaving the decryptor to compute the threshold herself. This leads to an attacker learning linear equations in the errors used to construct the FHE encryption $\widehat{\mathbf{a}}$, which, when sufficiently many, let her recover the FHE secret, which in turn lets her recover $\mathbf{a}$.

We emphasize that our attacks are entirely practical and also apply to the weaker indistinguishability based security game of functional encryption [BSW11] but do not work in the "weak attribute hiding" security game considered by [AFV11, GVW15]. This suggests that using predicate encryption systems in scenarios where even a small number of arbitrary users collude is insecure in practice.

"Very-Selective" $(1, \text{poly})$-*Functional Encryption.* We provide a construction that overcomes the above vulnerabilities for the case of a single arbitrary key, whether 1 or 0, and continues to support an unbounded number of 0-keys. By restricting the attacker to any single query, this yields an alternate construction for reusable garbled circuits [GTKP+13]. We summarize the main ideas here. For clarity of exposition, we omit many details; we refer the reader to Sects. 4, 5 and 6 for the formal construction and proof.

Our starting point is the predicate encryption scheme of [GVW15], which we will hereby refer to as $(0, \text{poly})$-FE, as it supports zero 1-queries and any polynomial number of 0-queries. The construction for $(0, \text{poly})$-FE makes use of two components as described above, namely, $(0, \text{poly})$-partially hiding predicate encryption (PHPE) and fully homomorphic encryption (FHE). Our construction for $(1, \text{poly})$-FE follows the same high level template as [GVW15], and as our first step, we require $(1, \text{poly})$-PHPE. Note that the $(0, \text{poly})$-PHPE scheme does allow the key generator to release an unbounded number of both 0 and 1 queries, but as mentioned above, the proof of security breaks down if the adversary requests a 1-key. This is because the secret key corresponding to a circuit C is a low norm matrix $\mathbf{K}$ satisfying an equation of the following form:

$$\left[\, \mathbf{A} \mid \mathbf{A}_C \,\right]\mathbf{K} = \mathbf{P} \mod q$$

where the matrices $\mathbf{A}, \mathbf{P}$ are fixed and public, and the matrix $\mathbf{A}_C$ is computed by executing a homomorphic evaluation procedure [BGG+14, GVW15] corresponding to the circuit C on some public matrices. In the real system, the key generator has a trapdoor for $\mathbf{A}$, which allows it to sample $\mathbf{K}$ using known techniques [CHKP10, ABB10]. In the simulation, the matrix $\mathbf{A}_C$ has a special form, namely $\mathbf{A}_C = [\mathbf{A}\mathbf{R}_C - C(\mathbf{a}) \cdot \mathbf{G}]$ for some low norm matrix $\mathbf{R}_C$ and fixed public matrix $\mathbf{G}$. The simulator has a trapdoor for $\mathbf{G}$ which enables it to sample the required $\mathbf{K}$ also using known techniques *but only when* $C(\mathbf{a}) \neq 0$ [ABB10]. When $C(\mathbf{a}) = 0$, $\mathbf{G}$ vanishes along with its trapdoor, and the simulator has no method by which to sample $\mathbf{K}$[1].

To overcome this, we note that if the circuit C is known before the public key is generated, the simulator can instead sample $\mathbf{K}$ first and set $\mathbf{P}$ to satisfy the above equation. This is a standard trick in LWE based systems [GPV08, Pei13], and yields the same distribution of the pair $(\mathbf{K}, \mathbf{P})$ as in the real world. This allows us to take a step forward[2], but the adversary's view remains distinguishable from the real world, because decryption leaks correlated noise which is

[1] The careful reader may observe that the simulator is disabled when $C(\mathbf{a}) = 0$, not when $C(\mathbf{a}) = 1$, though we have claimed that [AFV11, GVW15] can support 0-queries and not 1 queries. This is because, traditional functional encryption literature defines decryption to be permitted when the function value is 1, and defines the function value to be 1 when $C(\mathbf{a}) = 0$. We follow this flip to be consistent with prior work.

[2] This is presently a weak security game which we term as very-selective where the circuit C as well as the challenge message is announced before the parameters are generated. This restriction will be removed subsequently.

un-simulatable, as discussed in difficulty #2 above. To overcome this, we must choose the noise in the challenge ciphertext with care so that the noise yielded by the decryption equation is statistically close to fresh and independently chosen noise. Put together, these tricks enable us to build a (1, poly)-PHPE.

However, (1, poly)-PHPE does not immediately yield (1, poly)-FE due to difficulty #3 above, namely, leakage on FHE noise. To handle this, we modify the circuit for which the PHPE key is provided so that the FHE ciphertext $\widehat{C(\mathbf{a})}$ is flooded with large noise before the inner product with the FHE secret key is computed. Now, though the attacker learns the exact noise in the evaluated FHE ciphertext $\widehat{C(\mathbf{a})}$ as before, this noise is independent of the noise used to generate $\hat{\mathbf{a}}$ and no longer leaks any sensitive information. Note that care is required in executing the noise flooding step, since correctness demands that the FHE modulus be of polynomial size and the noise to be added may be super-polynomial. To ensure this, we flood the FHE ciphertext *before* the FHE "modulus reduction" step. Now, we have at our disposal a (1, poly)-FE scheme, albeit one that is secure according to a very restricted definition of security, which requires the attacker to commit to both the challenge messages and the single arbitrary function in the first step of the game. This "very selective" definition can be upgraded to semi-adaptive, as described next.

Upgrading Very-Selective to Semi-Adaptive. We provide a method for compiling our function-selective secure PHPE construction to one that satisfies *semi-adaptive* security, in which the attacker may see the public parameters before revealing the challenge. Our transformation is generic – it applies to all constructions that satisfy certain structural properties. In more detail, we require that: (1) the PHPE ciphertext $\mathsf{CT}_{\mathbf{a}}$ be decomposable into $|\mathbf{a}|$ components CT_i, where CT_i depends only on $\mathbf{a}[i]$, and (2) CT_i is a *fixed and public* linear function of the message $\mathbf{a}[i]$ and randomness chosen for encryption.

Concretely, consider the ciphertext in the (0, poly)-PHPE of [GVW15]. For $i \in [\ell]$,

$$\mathsf{CT}_i = \mathbf{u}_i = \left(\mathbf{A}_i + \mathbf{a}[i] \cdot \mathbf{G}\right)^{\mathsf{T}} \mathbf{s} + \mathsf{noise}_i \quad \in \mathbb{Z}_q^m$$

Clearly condition (1) is satisfied – the ith component of $\mathbf{a}$ influences only $\mathbf{u}_i$. Additionally, note that

$$\mathbf{u}_i = \left\langle [\ \mathbf{A}_i^{\mathsf{T}},\ 1,\ 1\ ];\ [\ \mathbf{s},\ \mathbf{a}[i] \cdot \mathbf{G}^{\mathsf{T}}\mathbf{s},\ \mathsf{noise}_i\ ] \right\rangle \mod q$$

Here, the first vector is a fixed public vector that is known to the key generator, while the second vector is made up of components all of which are known to the encryptor.

Given these two conditions, we construct a semi-adaptive PHPE for the circuit class $\mathcal{C}$, denoted by SaPH, using two ingredients:

1. A single key fully secure[3] functional encryption scheme, denoted by FuLin, for the inner product functionality defined as:

$$F_{(\mathbf{V}_1,\ldots,\mathbf{V}_k)}(\mathbf{a}_1,\ldots,\mathbf{a}_k) = \sum_{i\in[k]} \mathbf{V}_i \cdot \mathbf{a}_i \mod q$$

   Such a scheme was recently constructed by Agrawal et al. [ALS16].
2. A $(1, \text{poly})$ selectively secure PHPE scheme for the circuit class $\mathcal{C}$, which we denote by VSelPH.

Intuitively, the idea is to nest the selective PHPE system for $\mathcal{C}$ within an adaptive FE system for inner products, so that the latter is used to generate ciphertexts of the former *on the fly*. In more detail, the public parameters of SaPH are set as the public parameters of FuLin, the secret key corresponding to C, namely SaPH.SK(C) is the tuple (VSelPH.MPK, FuLin.SK($[\ \mathbf{A}_i^{\mathsf{T}},\ 1,\ 1\ ]$), VSelPH.SK(C)) and the ciphertext is SaPH.CT $=$ FuLin.CT($[\ \mathbf{s},\ \mathbf{a}[i] \cdot \mathbf{G}^{\mathsf{T}}\mathbf{s},\ \mathsf{noise}_i\ ]$). Now, the ciphertext FuLin.CT($[\ \mathbf{s},\ \mathbf{a}[i] \cdot \mathbf{G}^{\mathsf{T}}\mathbf{s},\ \mathsf{noise}_i\ ]$) and secret key component FuLin.SK($[\ \mathbf{A}_i^{\mathsf{T}},\ 1,\ 1\ ]$) may be decrypted to obtain the VSelPH ciphertext, which may be decrypted using VSelPH.SK(C). Some care is required in ascertaining that FuLin is only invoked for a single secret key, but this can be ensured by taking multiple copies of the FuLin scheme, and using the same randomness to generate multiple copies of the same key.

The advantage to the above strategy is that the public parameters of the SaPH scheme are now set as the public parameters of the FuLin scheme, and the public parameters of the VSelPH scheme are moved into the secret keys of SaPH scheme. This enables the simulator of the SaPH scheme to provide the public parameters using the (adaptive/full) simulator for the FuLin scheme, and delay programming the PHPE public parameters until after the challenge is received, as required by the VSelPH simulator. Thus, very-selective security may be upgraded to semi-adaptive security for the circuit class $\mathcal{C}$, by leveraging adaptive security of the simpler inner product functionality. For more details, please see Sect. 5.

Generalising to Q Queries. To construct (Q, poly)-FE, we again begin by constructing (Q, poly)-PHPE, which in turn is constructed from $(1, \text{poly})$-PHPE. The $(1, \text{poly})$-PHPE scheme has the following structure: it encodes the message $\mathbf{b}$ within an LWE sample $\boldsymbol{\beta}_0 = \mathbf{P}^{\mathsf{T}}\mathbf{s} + \mathsf{noise} + \mathbf{b}$. Given other components of the ciphertext, the decryptor is able to compute a ciphertext $\mathbf{c}_{\mathsf{Eval}}$ and key generator provides as the key a short matrix $\mathbf{K}$, where

$$\mathbf{c}_{\mathsf{Eval}} = [\ \mathbf{A} \mid \mathbf{A}_C\ ]^{\mathsf{T}}\mathbf{s} + \mathsf{noise}, \quad [\ \mathbf{A} \mid \mathbf{A}_C\ ]\,\mathbf{K} = \mathbf{P} \mod q$$

By computing $\mathbf{K}^{\mathsf{T}}\mathbf{c}_{\mathsf{Eval}} - \boldsymbol{\beta}_0$ and rounding the result, the decryptor recovers $\mathbf{b}$.

---

[3] Please see Appendix 2.3 for the definition of full security.

To generalize the above to handle Q queries, a natural approach would be to encode the message Q times, using Q distinct matrices $\mathbf{P}_1, \ldots, \mathbf{P}_Q$ and have the ith key $\mathbf{K}_i$ be a short matrix satisfying $[\ \mathbf{A} \mid \mathbf{A}_{C_i}\ ]\ \mathbf{K}_i = \mathbf{P}_i \mod q$. Then, the key generator can pick $\mathbf{P}_i$ for the ith key, and sample the corresponding $\mathbf{K}_i$ as the secret key. However, this straightforward idea would require the key generator to keep track of how many keys it has produced so far and would make the key generator stateful, which is undesirable.

To get around this, we make use of a trick using cover free sets [GVW12]. The idea is to enable the key generator to generate a fresh matrix $\mathbf{P}_i^*$ for the ith key in a stateless manner, as follows. We publish a set of matrices $\{\mathbf{P}_1, \ldots, \mathbf{P}_k\}$ in the public key, for some parameter k. The key generator chooses a random subset $\Delta_i \subset [k]$ s.t. $|\Delta_i| = v$ for some suitably chosen v, and computes $\mathbf{P}_i^* = \sum_{j \in \Delta_i} \mathbf{P}_j$. It then samples $\mathbf{K}_i$ so that

$$[\ \mathbf{A} \mid \mathbf{A}_{C_i}\ ]\ \mathbf{K}_i = \mathbf{P}_i^* \mod q$$

If we choose (v, k) as functions of the security parameter κ and number of queries Q in a way that the Q subsets $\Delta_1, \ldots, \Delta_Q$ are cover free with high probability, then this ensures that the matrices $\mathbf{P}_1^*, \ldots, \mathbf{P}_Q^*$ are independent and uniformly distributed, which will enable the simulator to sample the requisite keys. This idea can be converted to a secure scheme with only an additive blowup of $O(Q^2)$ in the public key and ciphertext size. However, security is proven in a game which is weaker than [GVW12] in which the attacker may not request the 1-keys adaptively, but must announce them all at once after seeing the public parameters.

This gives us a (Q, poly)-PHPE but constructing (Q, poly)-FE requires some more work. Instead of flooding the evaluated ciphertext with a single piece of noise, we must now encode at least Q pieces of noise, to flood the ciphertext for Q decryptions. Fortunately, this can be ensured by leveraging cover-free sets again, so that the decryptor is forced to add a random cover-free subset sum of noise terms to the ciphertext before decryption. This ensures that each decryption lets the decryptor learn a fresh noise term which wipes out any troublesome noise leakage. Details are in the full version [Agr16].

Additional Related Work. We note that in an independent and concurrent work, Goyal et al. [GKW16] provide a generic method to compile selective security to semi-adaptive security for functional encryption schemes. We note that this result does not apply to our setting as-is, since our starting-point security definition is even more restricted than selective. See Sect. 2.1 for more details. In another work, Brakerski and Vaikuntanathan [BV16] achieved semi-adaptive security for "Attribute Based Encryption" using specialized techniques – these also do not apply black box to our construction.

Organization of the Paper. The paper is organized as follows. Preliminaries are provided in Sect. 2. In Sect. 3, we describe our three attacks using 1-keys against existing predicate encryption systems. In Sect. 4 we provide our construction for (1, poly) partially hiding predicate encryption. This is upgraded to achieve semi-adaptive security in Sect. 5. In Sect. 6 we provide our (1, poly) FE scheme. The generalization to (q, poly) FE is provided in the full version of the paper [Agr16].

2 Preliminaries

In this section we provide the preliminaries required for our work. For definitions of lattices and the LWE problem, we refer the reader to the full version of the paper [Agr16].

2.1 Functional Encryption

In this section, we provide the definition of functional encryption.

Definition 2.1. *A functional encryption scheme* FE *for an input universe* $\mathcal{X}$, *a circuit universe* $\mathcal{C}$ *and a message space* $\mathcal{M}$, *consists of four algorithms* FE = (FE.Setup, FE.Keygen, FE.Enc, FE.Dec) *defined as follows.*

- $\mathsf{FE.Setup}(1^\kappa)$ *is a p.p.t. algorithm takes as input the unary representation of the security parameter and outputs the master public and secret keys* (PK, MSK).
- $\mathsf{FE.Keygen}(\mathsf{MSK}, C)$ *is a p.p.t. algorithm that takes as input the master secret key* MSK *and a circuit* $C \in \mathcal{C}$ *and outputs a corresponding secret key* SK_C.
- $\mathsf{FE.Enc}(\mathsf{PK}, (\mathbf{a}, \mu))$ *is a p.p.t. algorithm that takes as input the master public key* PK *and an input message* $(\mathbf{a}, \mu) \in \mathcal{X} \times \mathcal{M}$ *and outputs a ciphertext* $\mathsf{CT}_\mathbf{a}$.
- $\mathsf{FE.Dec}(\mathsf{SK}_C, \mathsf{CT}_\mathbf{a})$ *is a deterministic algorithm that takes as input the secret key* SK_C *and a ciphertext* $\mathsf{CT}_\mathbf{a}$ *and outputs* μ *iff* $C(\mathbf{a}) = 1$, $\perp$ *otherwise.*

Note that our definition is a slightly modified, albeit equivalent version of the standard definition for FE [BSW11]. For compatibility with the definition of predicate encryption [GVW15], we define our functionality to incorporate a message bit μ which is revealed when $C(\mathbf{a}) = 1$.

Correctness. Next, we define correctness of the system.

Definition 2.2 (Correctness). *A functional encryption scheme* FE *is correct if for all* $C \in \mathcal{C}_\kappa$ *and all* $\mathbf{a} \in \mathcal{X}_\kappa$,

- *If* $C(\mathbf{a}) = 1$

$$\Pr\left[\begin{array}{l}(\mathsf{PK}, \mathsf{MSK}) \leftarrow \mathsf{FE.Setup}(1^\kappa);\\ \mathsf{FE.Dec}\Big(\mathsf{FE.Keygen}(\mathsf{MSK}, C), \mathsf{FE.Enc}(\mathsf{PK}, (\mathbf{a}, \mu))\Big) \neq \mu\end{array}\right] = \mathrm{negl}(\kappa)$$

- *If* $C(\mathbf{a}) = 0$

$$\Pr\left[\begin{array}{l}(\mathsf{PK}, \mathsf{MSK}) \leftarrow \mathsf{FE.Setup}(1^\kappa);\\ \mathsf{FE.Dec}\Big(\mathsf{FE.Keygen}(\mathsf{MSK}, C), \mathsf{FE.Enc}(\mathsf{PK}, (\mathbf{a}, \mu))\Big) \neq \perp\end{array}\right] = \mathrm{negl}(\kappa)$$

where the probability is taken over the coins of FE.Setup, FE.Keygen, *and* FE.Enc.

Security. Next, we define simulation based security for functional encryption. Note that simulation based security is impossible for functional encryption against an adversary that requests even a *single* key after seeing the challenge ciphertext [BSW11], or an unbounded number of keys before seeing the challenge ciphertext [AGVW13]. However, against an adversary who only requests an a-priori bounded number of keys *before* seeing the challenge ciphertext, simulation based security is possible but causes the ciphertext size to grow with the number of requested keys [AGVW13].

For the application of reusable garbled circuits, it suffices to construct a functional encryption scheme that supports a single key request made before seeing the challenge ciphertext. We generalize this definition to subsume the notion of *predicate encryption*, where an attacker can make an unbounded number of function queries C_i so long as it holds that the function keys do not decrypt the challenge ciphertext $\mathsf{CT}(\mathbf{a},\mu)$ to recover μ. Thus, it holds that $C_i(\mathbf{a}) = 0$ for all requested C_i. We shall refer to such C_i as 0-keys, and any C such that $C(\mathbf{a}) = 1$ as a 1-key. In our definition, the adversary can request a single arbitrary (i.e. 0 or 1) key followed by an unbounded polynomial number of 0-keys. We refer to this security notion as $(1,\text{poly})$ simulation security. The notion we achieve is semi-adaptive, in that the adversary must declare the challenge message after receiving the public key.

Definition 2.3 (**$(1,\text{poly})$-$\mathsf{SA\text{-}SIM}$ Security**)**.** *Let* FE *be a functional encryption scheme for a Boolean circuit family* $\mathcal{C}$*. For every p.p.t. adversary* Adv *and a stateful p.p.t. simulator* Sim*, consider the following two experiments:*

$\underline{\mathsf{Exp}^{\mathsf{real}}_{\mathsf{FE},\mathsf{Adv}}(1^\kappa)}$:	$\underline{\mathsf{Exp}^{\mathsf{ideal}}_{\mathsf{FE},\mathsf{Sim}}(1^\kappa)}$:
1: $(\mathsf{PK},\mathsf{MSK}) \leftarrow \mathsf{FE.Setup}(1^\kappa)$	*1:* $\mathsf{PK} \leftarrow \mathsf{Sim}(1^\kappa)$
2: $(\mathbf{a},\mu,C^*,\mathsf{st}) \leftarrow \mathsf{Adv}(1^\kappa,\mathsf{PK})$	*2:* $(\mathbf{a},\mu,C^*,\mathsf{st}) \leftarrow \mathsf{Adv}(1^\kappa,\mathsf{PK})$
3: Let $b = \mu$	*3: Let* $b = \mu$ *if* $C^*(\mathbf{a}) = 1$, $\perp$ *otherwise.*
4: $\mathsf{CT}_{\mathbf{a}} \leftarrow \mathsf{FE.Enc}(\mathsf{PK},\mathbf{a},b)$	*4:* $\mathsf{CT}_{\mathbf{a}} \leftarrow \mathsf{Sim}(1^{\lvert\mathbf{a}\rvert},C^*,b)$
5: $\mathsf{SK}_{C^*} \leftarrow \mathsf{FE.Keygen}(\mathsf{MSK},C^*)$	*5:* $\mathsf{SK}_{C^*} \leftarrow \mathsf{Sim}()$
6: $\alpha \leftarrow \mathsf{Adv}^{\mathsf{FE.Keygen}(\mathsf{MSK},\cdot)}(\mathsf{CT}_{\mathbf{a}},\mathsf{SK}_{C^*},\mathsf{st})$	*6:* $\alpha \leftarrow \mathsf{Adv}^{\mathsf{Sim}}(\mathsf{CT}_{\mathbf{a}},\mathsf{SK}_{C^*},\mathsf{st})$
7: Output $(\mathbf{a},\mu,\alpha)$	*7: Output* $(\mathbf{a},\mu,\alpha)$

We say an adversary Adv *is admissible if:*

1. *For a single query* C^**, it may hold that* $C^*(\mathbf{a}) = 1$ *or* $C^*(\mathbf{a}) = 0$.
2. *For all other queries* $C_i \neq C^*$*, it holds that* $C_i(\mathbf{a}) = 0$.

In the ideal experiment, the simulator Sim *is traditionally given access to an oracle* $U_{(\mathbf{a},\mu)}(\cdot)$*, which upon input* C *returns* $\perp$ *if* $C(\mathbf{a}) = 0$ *and* μ *if* $C(\mathbf{a}) = 1$*. However, we note that our simulator does not require access to an oracle because an admissible adversary may only make a single* 1 *query* C^**, which is provided explicitly to the simulator. Every other query* C_i *made by the adversary is a* 0 *query, hence the simulator can compare each query* C_i *with* C^**, and set* $C_i(\mathbf{a}) = 0$ *when the equality does not hold.*

The functional encryption scheme FE *is then said to be* $(1, \text{poly})$-SA-SIM-*secure if there is an admissible stateful p.p.t. simulator* Sim *such that for every admissible p.p.t. adversary* Adv, *the following two distributions are computationally indistinguishable.*

$$\left\{\mathsf{Exp}^{\mathsf{real}}_{\mathsf{FE},\mathsf{Adv}}(1^\kappa)\right\}_{\kappa\in\mathbb{N}} \overset{c}{\approx} \left\{\mathsf{Exp}^{\mathsf{ideal}}_{\mathsf{FE},\mathsf{Sim}}(1^\kappa)\right\}_{\kappa\in\mathbb{N}}$$

For the (Q, poly) version of the above game, we merely replace each occurrence of C^* with a tuple $C_1^*, \dots, C_Q^*$.

2.2 Partially Hiding Predicate Encryption

A Partially-Hiding Predicate Encryption scheme PHPE for a pair of input-universes $\mathcal{X}, \mathcal{Y}$, a predicate universe $\mathcal{C}$, a message space $\mathcal{M}$, consists of four algorithms $(\mathsf{PH.Setup}, \mathsf{PH.Enc}, \mathsf{PH.KeyGen}, \mathsf{PH.Dec})$:

$\mathsf{PH.Setup}(1^\kappa, \mathcal{X}, \mathcal{Y}, \mathcal{C}, \mathcal{M}) \to (\mathsf{PH.PK}, \mathsf{PH.MSK})$. The setup algorithm gets as input the security parameter κ and a description of $(\mathcal{X}, \mathcal{Y}, \mathcal{C}, \mathcal{M})$ and outputs the public parameter PH.PK, and the master key PH.MSK.

$\mathsf{PH.Enc}(\mathsf{PH.PK}, (\mathbf{x}, \mathbf{y}), \mu) \to \mathsf{CT}_\mathbf{y}$. The encryption algorithm gets as input PH.PK, an attribute pair $(\mathbf{x}, \mathbf{y}) \in \mathcal{X} \times \mathcal{Y}$ and a message $\mu \in \mathcal{M}$. It outputs a ciphertext $\mathsf{CT}_\mathbf{y}$.

$\mathsf{PH.KeyGen}(\mathsf{PH.MSK}, C) \to \mathsf{SK}_C$. The key generation algorithm gets as input PH.MSK and a predicate $C \in \mathcal{C}$. It outputs a secret key SK_C.

$\mathsf{PH.Dec}((\mathsf{SK}_C, C), (\mathsf{CT}, \mathbf{y})) \to \mu \vee \perp$. The decryption algorithm gets as input the secret key SK_C, a predicate C, and a ciphertext $\mathsf{CT}_\mathbf{y}$ and the public part $\mathbf{y}$ of the attribute vector. It outputs a message $\mu \in \mathcal{M}$ or $\perp$.

Correctness. We require that for all $(\mathsf{PH.PK}, \mathsf{PH.MSK}) \leftarrow \mathsf{PH.Setup}(1^\kappa, \mathcal{X}, \mathcal{Y}, \mathcal{C}, \mathcal{M})$, for all $(\mathbf{x}, \mathbf{y}, C) \in \mathcal{X} \times \mathcal{Y} \times \mathcal{C}$ and for all $\mu \in \mathcal{M}$,

- For 1-queries, namely $C(\mathbf{x}, \mathbf{y}) = 1$,

$$\left[\mathsf{PH.Dec}((\mathsf{SK}_C, C), (\mathsf{CT}_\mathbf{y}, \mathbf{y})) = \mu\right] \geq 1 - \text{negl}(\kappa)$$

- For 0-queries, namely $C(\mathbf{x}, \mathbf{y}) = 0$,

$$\left[\mathsf{PH.Dec}((\mathsf{SK}_C, C), (\mathsf{CT}_\mathbf{y}, \mathbf{y})) = \perp\right] \geq 1 - \text{negl}(\kappa)$$

Semi Adaptive SIM Security. Below, we define the SA-SIM security experiment for partially hiding predicate encryption (PHPE) that supports a single 1-query and an unbounded number of 0-queries. We denote such a scheme by $(1, \text{poly})$-PHPE scheme. We note that the scheme of Gorbunov et al. [GVW15] is a $(0, \text{poly})$-PHPE scheme.

Definition 2.4 (**$(1, \text{poly})$-SA-SIM Security**). *Let* PHPE *be a partially hiding predicate encryption scheme for a circuit family* $\mathcal{C}$. *For every stateful p.p.t. adversary* Adv *and a stateful p.p.t. simulator* Sim, *consider the following two experiments:*

$\underline{\mathsf{Exp}^{\mathsf{real}}_{\mathsf{PHPE},\mathsf{Adv}}(1^\kappa)}$:

$(\mathsf{PH.PK}, \mathsf{PH.MSK}) \leftarrow \mathsf{PH.Setup}(1^\kappa)$
$(\mathbf{x}, \mathbf{y}, C^*) \leftarrow \mathsf{Adv}(\mathsf{PH.PK})$
$\mathsf{SK}_{C^*} \leftarrow \mathsf{PH.KeyGen}(\mathsf{PH.MSK}, C^*)$
$\mu \leftarrow \mathsf{Adv}^{\mathsf{PH.KeyGen}(\mathsf{PH.MSK},\cdot)}(\mathsf{SK}_{C^*})$
Let $b = \mu$.
$\mathsf{CT}_{\mathbf{y}} \leftarrow \mathsf{PH}.\mathit{Enc}(\mathsf{PH.PK}, (\mathbf{x}, \mathbf{y}), b)$
$\alpha \leftarrow \mathsf{Adv}^{\mathsf{PH.KeyGen}(\mathsf{PH.MSK},\cdot)}(\mathsf{CT}_{\mathbf{y}})$
Output $(\mathbf{x}, \mathbf{y}, \mu, \alpha)$

$\underline{\mathsf{Exp}^{\mathsf{ideal}}_{\mathsf{PHPE},\mathsf{Sim}}(1^\kappa)}$:

$\mathsf{PH.PK} \leftarrow \mathsf{Sim}(1^\kappa)$
$(\mathbf{x}, \mathbf{y}, C^*) \leftarrow \mathsf{Adv}(\mathsf{PH.PK})$
$\mathsf{SK}_{C^*} \leftarrow \mathsf{Sim}(\mathbf{y}, 1^{|\mathbf{x}|}, C^*)$;
$\mu \leftarrow \mathsf{Adv}^{\mathsf{Sim}}(\mathsf{SK}_{C^*})$
Let $b = \mu$ *if* $C^*(\mathbf{x}, \mathbf{y}) = 1$, $\perp$ *otherwise.*
$\mathsf{CT}_{\mathbf{y}} \leftarrow \mathsf{Sim}\ (b)$
$\alpha \leftarrow \mathsf{Adv}^{\mathsf{Sim}}(\mathsf{CT}_{\mathbf{y}})$
Output $(\mathbf{x}, \mathbf{y}, \mu, \alpha)$

We say an adversary Adv *is admissible if:*

1. *For the single query* C^*, *it may hold that* $C^*(\mathbf{x}, \mathbf{y}) = 1$ *or* $C^*(\mathbf{x}, \mathbf{y}) = 0$.
2. *For all queries* $C \neq C^*$, *it holds that* $C(\mathbf{x}, \mathbf{y}) = 0$.

In the ideal experiment, the simulator Sim *is traditionally given access to an oracle* $U_{(\mathbf{x},\mathbf{y},\mu)}(\cdot)$, *which upon input* C *returns* $\perp$ *if* $C(\mathbf{x}, \mathbf{y}) = 0$ *and* μ *if* $C(\mathbf{x}, \mathbf{y}) = 1$. *However, since in our case* Sim *is provided* C^* *explicitly, and this is the only possible* 1*-query, the simulator can check whether* $C_i = C^*$ *for any query* C_i, *and if not, set* $C_i(\mathbf{x}, \mathbf{y}) = 0$. *Hence, to simplify notation, we omit the oracle in the ideal experiment above.*

The partially hiding predicate encryption scheme PHPE *is said to be* $(1, \text{poly})$*-attribute hiding if there exists a p.p.t. simulator* Sim *such that for every admissible p.p.t. adversary* Adv, *the following two distributions are computationally indistinguishable:*

$$\left\{\mathsf{Exp}^{\mathsf{real}}_{\mathsf{PHPE},\mathsf{Adv}}(1^\kappa)\right\}_{\kappa\in\mathbb{N}} \stackrel{c}{\approx} \left\{\mathsf{Exp}^{\mathsf{ideal}}_{\mathsf{PHPE},\mathsf{Sim}}(1^\kappa)\right\}_{\kappa\in\mathbb{N}}$$

Very Selective SIM Security. Next, we define a "very" selective variant of the above game, in which the adversary must announce the challenge messages as well as the challenge function C^* in the very first step of the game.

Definition 2.5 (**$(1, \text{poly})$ VSel-SIM Security**). *Let* PHPE *be a partially hiding predicate encryption scheme for a circuit family* $\mathcal{C}$. *For every p.p.t. adversary* Adv *and a stateful p.p.t. simulator* Sim, *consider the following two experiments:*

$\underline{\mathsf{Exp}^{\mathsf{real}}_{\mathsf{PHPE},\mathsf{Adv}}(1^\kappa)}$:

$(\mathbf{x}, \mathbf{y}, C^*) \leftarrow \mathsf{Adv}(\mathsf{PH.PK})$
$(\mathsf{PH.PK}, \mathsf{PH.MSK}) \leftarrow \mathsf{PH.Setup}(1^\kappa)$
$\mathsf{SK}_{C^*} \leftarrow \mathsf{PH.KeyGen}(\ \mathsf{PH.MSK}, C^*)$
$\mu \leftarrow \mathsf{Adv}^{\mathsf{PH.KeyGen}}(\mathsf{SK}_{C^*})$
Let $b = \mu$.
$\mathsf{CT}_\mathbf{y} \leftarrow \mathsf{PH}.\mathit{Enc}(\ \mathsf{PH.PK}, (\mathbf{x}, \mathbf{y}), b)$
$\alpha \leftarrow \mathsf{Adv}^{\mathsf{PH.KeyGen}(\mathsf{PH.MSK},\cdot)}(\mathsf{CT}_\mathbf{y})$
Output $(\mathbf{x}, \mathbf{y}, \mu, \alpha)$

$\underline{\mathsf{Exp}^{\mathsf{ideal}}_{\mathsf{PHPE},\mathsf{Sim}}(1^\kappa)}$:

$(\mathbf{x}, \mathbf{y}, C^*) \leftarrow \mathsf{Adv}(\mathsf{PH.PK})$
$\mathsf{PH.PK} \leftarrow \mathsf{Sim}(1^\kappa, \mathbf{y}, 1^{|\mathbf{x}|}, C^*)$
$\mathsf{SK}_{C^*} \leftarrow \mathsf{Sim}()$;
$\mu \leftarrow \mathsf{Adv}^{\mathsf{Sim}}(\mathsf{SK}_{C^*})$
Let $b = \mu$ *if* $C^*(\mathbf{x}, \mathbf{y}) = 1$, $\perp$ *otherwise.*
$\mathsf{CT}_\mathbf{y} \leftarrow \mathsf{Sim}\ (b)$
$\alpha \leftarrow \mathsf{Adv}^{\mathsf{Sim}}(\mathsf{CT}_\mathbf{y})$
Output $(\mathbf{x}, \mathbf{y}, \mu, \alpha)$

The admissibility of the adversary Adv*, the notes about the simulator and the required indistinguishability of distributions are as in Definition 2.4.*

For the definition of (Q, poly)-PHPE, where an adversary may request Q decrypting queries, we merely replace each occurence of C^* with a tuple $C_1^*, \ldots, C_Q^*$ in both the games above.

2.3 Full Security for Single Key Linear FE

Definition 2.6 (FULL-SIM **security).** *Let* FE *be a single key functional encryption scheme for a circuit family* $\mathcal{C}$. *For every p.p.t. adversary* Adv *and a stateful p.p.t. simulator* Sim, *consider the following two experiments:*

$\underline{\mathsf{Exp}^{\mathsf{real}}_{\mathsf{FE},A}(1^\kappa)}$:

$(\mathsf{PK}, \mathsf{MSK}) \leftarrow \mathsf{FE.Setup}(1^\kappa)$
$(\mathbf{a}, \mathsf{st}) \leftarrow A_1^{\mathsf{FE.Keygen}(\mathsf{MSK},\cdot)}(\mathsf{PK})$
$\mathsf{CT} \leftarrow \mathsf{FE.Enc}(\mathsf{PK}, \mathbf{a})$
$\alpha \leftarrow A_2(\mathsf{CT}, \mathsf{st})$
Output $(\mathbf{a}, \alpha)$

$\underline{\mathsf{Exp}^{\mathsf{ideal}}_{\mathsf{FE},\mathsf{Sim}}(1^\kappa)}$:

$\mathsf{PK} \leftarrow \mathsf{Sim}(1^\kappa)$
$(\mathbf{a}, \mathsf{st}) \leftarrow A_1^{\mathsf{Sim}(\cdot)}(\mathsf{PK})$
$\mathsf{CT} \leftarrow \mathsf{Sim}(\ C, C(\mathbf{a})\ )$
$\alpha \leftarrow A_2(\mathsf{CT}, \mathsf{st})$
Output $(\mathbf{a}, \mu, \alpha)$

The functional encryption scheme FE *is then said to be* FULL-SIM*-secure if there is a stateful p.p.t. simulator* Sim *such that for every p.p.t. adversary* $A = (A_1, A_2)$*, the following two distributions are computationally indistinguishable.*

$$\left\{ \mathsf{Exp}^{\mathsf{real}}_{\mathsf{FE},A}(1^\kappa) \right\}_{\kappa \in \mathbb{N}} \overset{c}{\approx} \left\{ \mathsf{Exp}^{\mathsf{ideal}}_{\mathsf{FE},\mathsf{Sim}}(1^\kappa) \right\}_{\kappa \in \mathbb{N}}$$

2.4 Algorithms Used by Our Constructions

The following algorithms will be used crucially in our construction and proof.

Trapdoor Generation. Below, we discuss two kinds of trapdoors that our construction and proof will use.

Generating Random Lattices with Trapdoors. To begin, we provide an algorithm for generating a random lattice with a trapdoor.

Theorem 2.7 [Ajt99,GPV08,MP12]. *Let q, n, m be positive integers with $q \geq 2$ and $m \geq 6n \lg q$. There is a probabilistic polynomial-time algorithm* $\mathsf{TrapGen}(q, n, m)$ *that with overwhelming probability (in n) outputs a pair ($\mathbf{A} \in \mathbb{Z}_q^{n\times m}$, $\mathbf{T} \in \mathbb{Z}^{m\times m}$) such that $\mathbf{A}$ is statistically close to uniform in $\mathbb{Z}_q^{n\times m}$ and $\mathbf{T}$ is a basis for $\Lambda_q^{\perp}((\mathbf{A}))$ satisfying*

$$\|\mathbf{T}\|_{\mathsf{GS}} \leq O(\sqrt{n \log q}\,) \quad \text{and} \quad \|\mathbf{T}\| \leq O(n \log q).$$

The Primitive Matrix $\mathbf{G}$ and its Trapdoor. The matrix $\mathbf{G} \in \mathbb{Z}_q^{n\times m}$ is the "powers-of two" matrix (see [MP12,Pei13] for the definition). The matrix $\mathbf{G}$ has a public trapdoor $\mathbf{T_G}$ such that $\|\mathbf{T_G}\|_\infty = 2$. Let $\mathbf{G}^{-1} : \mathbb{Z}_q^{n\times m} \to \mathbb{Z}_q^{n\times m}$ denote a *deterministic* algorithm which outputs a short preimage $\tilde{\mathbf{A}}$ so that $\mathbf{G}\cdot\tilde{\mathbf{A}} = \mathbf{A} \mod q$.

Three Ways of Generating a Distribution. Let $\mathbf{F} = [\ \mathbf{A}|\mathbf{AR} + \gamma\cdot\mathbf{G}\ ]$ where $\mathbf{A} \leftarrow \mathbb{Z}_q^{n\times m}$, $\mathbf{R} \leftarrow \{-1, 1\}^{m\times m}$, $\mathbf{G}$ is the primitive matrix defined above and $\gamma \in \mathbb{Z}_q$ is arbitrary (in particular, it can be 0). We are interested in the distribution $(\mathbf{F}, \mathbf{K}, \mathbf{P}) \in \mathbb{Z}_q^{n\times 2m} \times \mathbb{Z}_q^{2m\times m} \times \mathbb{Z}_q^{n\times m}$ satisfying $\mathbf{F}\,\mathbf{K} = \mathbf{P} \mod q$.

Given $\mathbf{F}$, we provide three different ways of sampling $(\mathbf{K}, \mathbf{P})$ so that the same resultant distribution is obtained.

1. The first method is to sample $\mathbf{P} \leftarrow \mathbb{Z}_q^{n\times m}$ randomly and use a trapdoor for the left matrix of $\mathbf{F}$, namely $\mathbf{A}$ to sample a low norm $\mathbf{K}$. We let $\mathbf{B} \triangleq \mathbf{AR} + \gamma\cdot\mathbf{G}$ and $\mathbf{p}$ denote a column of $\mathbf{P}$.
Algorithm $\mathsf{SampleLeft}(\mathbf{A}, \mathbf{B}, \mathbf{T_A}, \mathbf{p}, \sigma)$ [CHKP10,ABB10]:

   Inputs: a full rank matrix $\mathbf{A}$ in $\mathbb{Z}_q^{n\times m}$, a "short" basis $\mathbf{T_A}$ of $\Lambda_q^{\perp}(\mathbf{A})$, a matrix $\mathbf{B}$ in $\mathbb{Z}_q^{n\times m}$, a vector $\mathbf{p} \in \mathbb{Z}_q^n$, and a Gaussian parameter σ.

   (2.1)

   Output: The algorithm outputs a vector $\mathbf{k} \in \mathbb{Z}^{2m}$ in coset $\Lambda_q^{\mathbf{p}}(\mathbf{F})$.

Its distribution is analyzed in the following theorem.

Theorem 2.8 ([ABB10, **Theorem 17**], [CHKP10, **Lemma 3.2**]). *Let $q > 2$, $m > n$ and $\sigma > \|\mathbf{T_A}\|_{\mathsf{GS}} \cdot \omega(\sqrt{\log(2m)})$. Then* $\mathsf{SampleLeft}(\mathbf{A}, \mathbf{B}, \mathbf{T_A}, \mathbf{p}, \sigma)$ *taking inputs as in (2.1), outputs a vector $\mathbf{k} \in \mathbb{Z}^{2m}$ distributed statistically close to $\mathcal{D}_{\Lambda_q^{\mathbf{p}}(\mathbf{F}),\sigma}$ where $\mathbf{F} := (\mathbf{A} \parallel \mathbf{B})$.*

2. The second method is to again sample $\mathbf{P} \leftarrow \mathbb{Z}_q^{n\times m}$ and use a trapdoor for the right matrix $\mathbf{G}$ (when $\gamma \neq 0$) to sample $\mathbf{K}$.
Algorithm $\mathsf{SampleRight}(\mathbf{A}, \mathbf{G}, \mathbf{R}, \mathbf{T_G}, \mathbf{p}, \sigma)$*:*

   Inputs: matrices $\mathbf{A}$ in $\mathbb{Z}_q^{n\times k}$ and $\mathbf{R}$ in $\mathbb{Z}^{k\times m}$, a full rank matrix $\mathbf{G}$ in $\mathbb{Z}_q^{n\times m}$, a "short" basis $\mathbf{T_G}$ of $\Lambda_q^{\perp}(\mathbf{G})$, a vector $\mathbf{p} \in \mathbb{Z}_q^n$, and a Gaussian parameter σ.

   (2.2)

   Output: The algorithm outputs a vector $\mathbf{k} \in \mathbb{Z}^{2m}$ in coset $\Lambda_q^{\mathbf{p}}(\mathbf{F})$.

Often the matrix $\mathbf{R}$ given to the algorithm as input will be a random matrix in $\{1,-1\}^{m \times m}$. Let S^m be the m-sphere $\{\mathbf{x} \in \mathbb{R}^{m+1} : \|\mathbf{x}\| = 1\}$. We define $s_R := \|\mathbf{R}\| = \sup_{\mathbf{x} \in S^{m-1}} \|\mathbf{R} \cdot \mathbf{x}\|$.

Theorem 2.9 ([ABB10, **Theorem 19**]). *Let $q > 2, m > n$ and $\sigma > \|\mathbf{T_G}\|_{\mathsf{GS}} \cdot s_R \cdot \omega(\sqrt{\log m})$. Then* $\mathsf{SampleRight}(\mathbf{A}, \mathbf{G}, \mathbf{R}, \mathbf{T_G}, \mathbf{p}, \sigma)$ *taking inputs as in (2.2) outputs a vector $\mathbf{k} \in \mathbb{Z}^{2m}$ distributed statistically close to $\mathcal{D}_{\Lambda_q^{\mathbf{p}}(\mathbf{F}),\sigma}$ where $\mathbf{F} := (\mathbf{A} \parallel \mathbf{AR} + \gamma \cdot \mathbf{G})$.*

3. The final method is to sample $\mathbf{K} \leftarrow \left(\mathcal{D}_{\mathbb{Z}^{2m},\sigma}\right)^m$ and set $\mathbf{P} = \mathbf{F} \cdot \mathbf{K} \mod q$. We note that this method works even if $\gamma = 0$. As argued by [GPV08, Lemma 5.2], this produces the correct distribution.

Lemma 2.10. *Assume the columns of $\mathbf{F}$ generate $\mathbb{Z}_q^n$ and let $\sigma \geq \omega(\sqrt{n \log q})$. Then, for $\mathbf{k} \leftarrow \mathcal{D}_{\mathbb{Z}^{2m},\sigma}$, the distribution of the vector $\mathbf{p} = \mathbf{F} \cdot \mathbf{k} \mod q$ is statistically close to uniform over $\mathbb{Z}_q^n$. Furthermore, fix $\mathbf{p} \in \mathbb{Z}_q^n$ and let $\mathbf{t}$ be an arbitrary solution s.t. $\mathbf{F} \cdot \mathbf{t} = \mathbf{p} \mod q$. Then, the conditional distribution of $\mathbf{k} \leftarrow \mathcal{D}_{\mathbb{Z}^{2m},\sigma}$ given $\mathbf{F} \cdot \mathbf{k} = \mathbf{p} \mod q$ is $\mathbf{t} + \mathcal{D}_{\Lambda^{\perp}(\mathbf{F}),\sigma,-\mathbf{t}}$, which is precisely $\mathcal{D}_{\Lambda_q^{\mathbf{p}}(\mathbf{F}),\sigma}$.*

Public Key and Ciphertext Evaluation Algorithms. Our construction will make use of the public key and ciphertext evaluation algorithms from [BGG+14, GVW15]. Since these algorithms can be used as black boxes for our purposes, we only state their input/output behavior and properties. These algorithms were constructed by Boneh et al. [BGG+14] in the context of attribute based encryption, and extended by Gorbunov et al. [GVW15] to the setting of partially hiding predicate encryption. In this setting, the attributes are divided into a private component $\mathbf{x}$ and a public component $\mathbf{y}$, and the functionality supports computation of a lightweight inner product composed with a heavy circuit $\widehat{C}$. Formally, [GVW15] construct algorithms $\mathsf{PHPE.Eval}_{\mathsf{MPK}}$ and $\mathsf{PHPE.Eval}_{\mathsf{CT}}$ to support the following circuit family:

$$\widehat{C} \circ \mathsf{IP}(\mathbf{x}, \mathbf{y}) = \langle \mathbf{x}, \widehat{C}(\mathbf{y}) \rangle.$$

They make crucial use of the fact that $\mathsf{PHPE.Eval}_{\mathsf{CT}}$ does not need $\mathbf{x}$ for its execution since the computation involving $\mathbf{x}$ is an inner product. To compute the inner product, the multiplication may be carried out keeping $\mathbf{x}$ private and letting $\widehat{C}(\mathbf{y})$ be public, and addition may be carried out keeping both attributes private. Additionally, the circuit $\widehat{C}$ operates entirely on public attributes $\mathbf{y}$.

In more detail, [GVW15, Sect. 3.2] demonstrate the existence of the following efficient algorithms:

1. $\mathsf{Eval}_{\mathsf{MPK}}$ takes as input $\ell + t$ matrices $\{\mathbf{A}_i\}$, $\{\mathbf{B}_j\} \in \mathbb{Z}_q^{n \times m}$ and a circuit $\widehat{C} \circ \mathsf{IP} \in \mathcal{C}$ and outputs a matrix $\mathbf{A}_{\widehat{C} \circ \mathsf{IP}} \in \mathbb{Z}_q^{n \times m}$.
2. $\mathsf{Eval}_{\mathsf{CT}}$ takes as input $\ell + t$ matrices $\{\mathbf{A}_i,\}\{\mathbf{B}_j\} \in \mathbb{Z}_q^{n \times m}$, $\ell + t$ vectors $\{\mathbf{u}_i\}, \{\mathbf{v}_j\}$, the public attribute $\mathbf{y} \in \{0,1\}^{\ell}$ and a circuit $\widehat{C} \circ \mathsf{IP} \in \mathcal{C}$, and outputs a vector $\mathbf{u}_{\widehat{C} \circ \mathsf{IP}} \in \mathbb{Z}_q^m$.

3. $\mathsf{Eval_R}$ takes as input $\ell + t$ matrices $\{\mathbf{R}_i\}, \{\mathbf{R}'_j\} \in \mathbb{Z}_q^{m\times m}$, the matrix $\mathbf{A}$, the public attribute vector $\mathbf{y} \in \{0,1\}^\ell$ and a circuit $\widehat{C} \circ \mathsf{IP} \in \mathcal{C}$ and outputs a matrix $\mathbf{R}_{\widehat{C}\circ\mathsf{IP}} \in \mathbb{Z}_q^{m\times m}$.

such that the following properties hold:

$$\mathbf{u}_{\widehat{C}\circ\mathsf{IP}} = \left(\mathbf{A}_{\widehat{C}\circ\mathsf{IP}} + \widehat{C}\circ\mathsf{IP}(\mathbf{x},\mathbf{y})\cdot\mathbf{G}\right)^{\mathsf{T}}\mathbf{s} + \mathbf{e}_{\mathsf{Eval}} \tag{2.3}$$

When

$$\mathbf{A}_i = \mathbf{A}\cdot\mathbf{R}_i - \mathbf{y}[i]\cdot\mathbf{G}$$
$$\mathbf{B}_i = \mathbf{A}\cdot\mathbf{R}'_i - \mathbf{x}[i]\cdot\mathbf{G}$$
$$\text{Then } \mathbf{A}_{\widehat{C}\circ\mathsf{IP}} = \mathbf{A}\mathbf{R}_{\widehat{C}\circ\mathsf{IP}} - \widehat{C}\circ\mathsf{IP}(\mathbf{x},\mathbf{y})\cdot\mathbf{G} \tag{2.4}$$

Additionally, we may bound the norms as:

$$\|\mathbf{e}_{\mathsf{Eval}}\|_\infty \le O(\ell n\log q)^{O(d)}\cdot\max_{i\in[\ell]}\{\|\mathbf{u}_i - (\mathbf{A}_i + \mathbf{y}[i]\cdot\mathbf{G})^{\mathsf{T}}\mathbf{s}\|_\infty,\ldots\} \tag{2.5}$$

$$\|\mathbf{R}_{\widehat{C}\circ\mathsf{IP}}\|_\infty \le O(\ell n\log q)^{O(d)}\cdot\max_{i\in[\ell]}\{\|\mathbf{R}_1\|_\infty,\ldots,\|\mathbf{R}_\ell\|_\infty,\|\mathbf{R}'_1\|_\infty,\ldots,\|\mathbf{R}'_t\|_\infty\} \tag{2.6}$$

2.5 Fully Homomorphic Encryption

A leveled symmetric key fully homomorphic scheme is a tuple of P.P.T algorithms FHE.KeyGen, FHE.Enc, FHE.Eval and FHE.Dec:

$\mathsf{FHE.KeyGen}(1^\kappa, 1^d, 1^k)$: This is a probabilistic algorithm that takes as input the security parameter, the depth bound for the circuit, the message length and outputs the secret key FHE.SK.

$\mathsf{FHE.Enc}(\mathsf{FHE.SK}, \mu)$: This is a probabilistic algorithm that takes as input the secret key and message and produces the ciphertext FHE.CT.

$\mathsf{FHE.Eval}(C, \mathsf{FHE.CT})$: This is a deterministic algorithm that takes as input a Boolean circuit $C : \{0,1\}^k \to \{0,1\}$ of depth at most d and outputs another ciphertext $\mathsf{FHE.CT}'$.

$\mathsf{FHE.Dec}(\mathsf{FHE.SK}, \mathsf{FHE.CT})$: This is a deterministic algorithm that takes as input the secret key and a ciphertext and produces a bit.

Correctness. Let $\mathsf{FHE.SK} \leftarrow \mathsf{FHE.KeyGen}(1^\kappa, 1^d, 1^k)$ and C be a circuit of depth d. Then we require that

$$\Pr\Big[\mathsf{FHE.Dec}(\mathsf{FHE.SK},\ \mathsf{FHE.Eval}(C, \mathsf{FHE.Enc}(\mathsf{FHE.SK}, \mu))) = C(\mu)\Big] = 1$$

Security. Security is defined as the standard semantic security. Let $\mathcal{A}$ be an efficient, stateful adversary and $d, k = \mathrm{poly}(\kappa)$. The semantic security game is defined as follows.

1. $\mathsf{FHE.SK} \leftarrow \mathsf{FHE.Setup}(1^\kappa, 1^d, 1^k)$
2. $(\mu_0, \mu_1) \leftarrow \mathcal{A}(1^\kappa, 1^d, 1^k)$
3. $b \leftarrow \{0, 1\}$
4. $\mathsf{FHE.CT} \leftarrow \mathsf{FHE.Enc}(\mathsf{FHE.SK}, \mu_b)$
5. $b' \leftarrow \mathcal{A}(\mathsf{FHE.CT})$

We require that the advantage of $\mathcal{A}$ in the above game be negligible, namely

$$|\Pr(b' = b) - 1/2| = \mathrm{negl}(\kappa)$$

Instantiating FHE from Learning with Errors. We make use of the following instantiation of FHE from LWE.

Theorem 2.11 [BV11,BGV12,GSW13,BV14,AP14]. *There is an FHE scheme based on the LWE assumption such that, as long as $q \geq O(\kappa^2)$:*

1. $\mathsf{FHE.SK} \in \mathbb{Z}_q^t$ *for some* $t \in \mathrm{poly}(\kappa)$.
2. $\mathsf{FHE.CT}(\mu) \in \{0, 1\}^\ell$ *where* $\ell = \mathrm{poly}(\kappa, k, d, \log q)$.
3. $\mathsf{FHE.Eval}$ *outputs a ciphertext* $\mathsf{FHE.CT}' \in \{0, 1\}^\ell$.
4. *There exists an algorithm* $\mathsf{FHE.Scale}(q, p)$ *which reduces the modulus of the FHE ciphertext from q to p.*
5. *For any Boolean circuit of depth d,* $\mathsf{FHE.Eval}(C, \cdot)$ *is computed by a Boolean circuit of depth* $\mathrm{poly}(d, \kappa, \log q)$.
6. $\mathsf{FHE}.\mathit{Dec}$ *on input* $\mathsf{FHE.SK}$ *and* $\mathsf{FHE.CT}'$ *outputs a bit $b \in \{0, 1\}$. If* $\mathsf{FHE.CT}'$ *is an encryption of* 1*, then*

$$\sum_{i \in [t]} \mathsf{FHE.SK}[i] \cdot \mathsf{FHE.CT}'[i] \in [\lfloor p/2 \rfloor - B, \lfloor p/2 \rfloor + B]$$

for some fixed $B = \mathrm{poly}(\kappa)$*. If* $\mathsf{FHE.CT}'$ *is an encryption of* 0*, then*

$$\sum_{i \in [t]} \mathsf{FHE.SK}[i] \cdot \mathsf{FHE.CT}'[i] \notin [\lfloor p/2 \rfloor - B, \lfloor p/2 \rfloor + B]$$

7. *Security relies on* $\mathsf{LWE}_{\Theta(t), q, \chi}$.

3 Insecurity of Predicate Encryption Schemes Against General Adversaries

In this section, we demonstrate that known LWE based predicate encryption constructions [AFV11,GVW15] are insecure against an adversary that requests 1-keys.

3.1 Attack #1 on [AFV11] Using 1-Keys.

Warmup Attack. To begin, we show a warmup attack that results from an adversary requesting the *same* key multiple times. Since the key generation algorithm is stateless, requesting many keys for the same function results in fresh, independent keys, which may be combined to fully recover the message.

An observant reader may notice that our warmup attack may be easily prevented by derandomizing key generation (using a PRF, say) so that multiple requests of the same circuit result in the same key. However, as we show in the full version [Agr16], the attack may be generalized to an adversary requesting non-identical functions against which derandomization does not work; the warmup attack is only the simplest application of the technique.

We now describe the attack in detail. The construction of [AFV11] is described here at a high level, for more details we refer the reader to the paper.

Say the attacker requests many keys for the vector $\mathbf{v}$ such that $\langle \mathbf{x}, \mathbf{v} \rangle = 0$. Let $\mathbf{A}_{\mathbf{v}} = \sum v_i \mathbf{A}_i$. Now by construction of keys in [AFV11], we have:

$$[\mathbf{A} \mid \mathbf{A}_{\mathbf{v}}] \begin{bmatrix} \mathbf{e}_0 \\ \mathbf{f}_0 \end{bmatrix} = \mathbf{u} \pmod{q} \tag{3.1}$$

$$[\mathbf{A} \mid \mathbf{A}_{\mathbf{v}}] \begin{bmatrix} \mathbf{e}_1 \\ \mathbf{f}_1 \end{bmatrix} = \mathbf{u} \pmod{q} \tag{3.2}$$

$$\text{This implies } [\mathbf{A} \mid \mathbf{A}_{\mathbf{v}}] \begin{bmatrix} \mathbf{e}_0 - \mathbf{e}_1 \\ \mathbf{f}_0 - \mathbf{f}_1 \end{bmatrix} = \mathbf{0} \pmod{q} \tag{3.3}$$

Thus, we have a short vector in the lattice $\Lambda_q^{\perp}(\mathbf{A}|\mathbf{A}_{\mathbf{v}})$. By making many queries for the same $\mathbf{v}$, the attacker may recover a full trapdoor basis for $\Lambda_q^{\perp}(\mathbf{A}|\mathbf{A}_{\mathbf{v}})$. Now, note that the ciphertext contains $\mathbf{A}^{\mathsf{T}}\mathbf{s} + \mathsf{noise}$ as well as $(\ \mathbf{A}_i + \mathbf{x}[i]\mathbf{G}\ )^{\mathsf{T}}\mathbf{s} + \mathsf{noise}$. Since $\langle \mathbf{x}, \mathbf{v} \rangle = 0$, we can follow the decryption procedure as:

$$\begin{aligned} &\sum_i v_i (\ \mathbf{A}_i + \mathbf{x}[i]\mathbf{G}\ )^{\mathsf{T}}\mathbf{s} + \mathsf{noise} \\ &= (\ \mathbf{A}_{\mathbf{v}} + \langle \mathbf{x},\ \mathbf{v} \rangle \mathbf{G}\ )^{\mathsf{T}}\mathbf{s} + \mathsf{noise} \\ &= \mathbf{A}_{\mathbf{v}}^{\mathsf{T}}\mathbf{s} + \mathsf{noise} \quad \text{since } \langle \mathbf{x},\ \mathbf{v} \rangle = 0 \end{aligned}$$

This in turn allows the attacker to recover

$$[\mathbf{A} \mid \mathbf{A}_{\mathbf{v}}]^{\mathsf{T}}\mathbf{s} + \mathsf{noise}$$

for which he now has a trapdoor. Using the trapdoor, he can now recover the noise terms to get exact linear equations in the LWE secret $\mathbf{s}$, completely breaking LWE security. Note that by functionality, the attacker should only have been able to learn a single bit of information, namely $\langle \mathbf{x},\ \mathbf{v} \rangle = 0$.

The reason this attack works given 1-keys, i.e. in the strong attribute hiding setting, is that a particular linear relation needs to be satisfied to enable decryption, which, given a decrypting key, can be exploited to carry out the attack. Specifically, in the above attack, the decryption procedure allows the attacker to recover $[\mathbf{A}\ |\mathbf{A_v}]^\intercal \mathbf{s} + \mathsf{noise}$ which would not be possible if the decryption condition did not hold, i.e. given only 0-keys.

The generalization of the above attack, as well as the second and third attack are provided in the full version of the paper [Agr16].

4 (1, poly) Very Selective PHPE

In this section, we show that the partially hiding predicate encryption system PHPE of [GVW15] satisfies a stronger definition than described in [GVW15], namely (1, poly)-VSel-SIM security (see Definition 2.5). We emphasize that in addition to a single query of any kind, PHPE supports an unbounded number of 0-queries, as in [GVW15].

4.1 Construction

The construction of our (1, poly)-PHPE scheme is the same as in [GVW15], except the setting of certain parameters described in the full version [Agr16]. The main novelty is in the proof, which shows that in the restricted game of Definition 2.5, the attacker can obtain a key for any circuit of his choice. As in [GVW15], he can also obtain an unbounded number of 0 keys, resulting in a (1, poly)-PHPE scheme.

For completeness, we describe the construction below.

$\mathsf{PH.Setup}(1^\kappa, 1^t, 1^\ell, 1^d)$: Given as input the security parameter κ, the length of the private and public attributes, t and ℓ respectively, and the depth of the circuit family d, do the following:

1. Choose random matrices

$$\mathbf{A}_i \in \mathbb{Z}_q^{n\times m} \text{ for } i \in [\ell],\ \mathbf{B}_i \in \mathbb{Z}_q^{n\times m} \text{ for } i \in [t],\ \mathbf{P} \in \mathbb{Z}_q^{n\times m}$$

   To simplify notation, we denote by $\{\mathbf{A}_i\}$ the set $\{\mathbf{A}_i\}_{i\in[\ell]}$ and by $\{\mathbf{B}_i\}$ the set $\{\mathbf{B}_i\}_{i\in[t]}$.
2. Sample $(\mathbf{A}, \mathbf{T}) \leftarrow \mathsf{TrapGen}(1^m, 1^n, q)$.
3. Let $\mathbf{G} \in \mathbb{Z}_q^{n\times m}$ be the powers of two matrix with public trapdoor $\mathbf{T_G}$.
4. Output the public and master secret keys.

$$\mathsf{PH.PK} = \big(\{\mathbf{A}_i\}, \{\mathbf{B}_i\}, \mathbf{A}, \mathbf{P}\big),\ \ \mathsf{PH.MSK} = (\mathsf{PH.PK}, \mathbf{T})$$

$\mathsf{PH.KeyGen}(\mathsf{PH.MSK}, \widehat{\mathsf{C}} \circ \mathsf{IP}_\gamma)$: Given as input the circuit and the master secret key, do the following:

1. Let $\mathbf{A}_{\widehat{C}\circ\mathsf{IP}} = \mathsf{Eval}_{\mathsf{MPK}}\big(\{\mathbf{A}_i\}, \{\mathbf{B}_i\}, \widehat{C} \circ \mathsf{IP}\big)$.
2. Sample $\mathbf{K}$ such that

$$[\mathbf{A}|\ \mathbf{A}_{\widehat{C}\circ\mathsf{IP}} + \gamma\cdot\mathbf{G}]\ \cdot \mathbf{K} = \mathbf{P} \mod q$$

   using $\mathbf{K} \leftarrow \mathsf{SampleLeft}(\mathbf{A}, \mathbf{A}_{\widehat{C}\circ\mathsf{IP}} + \gamma\cdot\mathbf{G}, \mathbf{T}, \mathbf{P}, s)$. Here s is the standard deviation of the Gaussian being sampled (see [Agr16] for the parameters).

3. Output $\mathsf{SK}_{\widehat{C}\circ\mathsf{IP}_\gamma} = \mathbf{K}$.

$\mathsf{PH.Enc}(\mathsf{PH.PK}, (\mathbf{x}, \mathbf{y}), \mu)$: Given as input the master public key, the private attributes $\mathbf{x}$, public attributes $\mathbf{y}$ and message μ, do the following:
1. Sample $\mathbf{s} \leftarrow \mathcal{D}_{\mathbb{Z}^n, s_B}$ and error terms $\mathbf{e} \leftarrow \mathcal{D}_{\mathbb{Z}^m, s_B}$ and $\mathbf{e}' \leftarrow \mathcal{D}_{\mathbb{Z}^m, s_D}$.
2. Let $\mathbf{b} = [0, \ldots, 0, \lceil q/2 \rceil \mu]^\mathsf{T} \in \mathbb{Z}_q^m$. Set
$$\boldsymbol{\beta}_0 = \mathbf{A}^\mathsf{T}\mathbf{s} + \mathbf{e}, \quad \boldsymbol{\beta}_1 = \mathbf{P}^\mathsf{T}\mathbf{s} + \mathbf{e}' + \mathbf{b}$$
3. For $i \in [\ell]$, compute
$$\mathbf{u}_i = (\mathbf{A}_i + \mathbf{y}_i \cdot \mathbf{G})^\mathsf{T}\mathbf{s} + \mathbf{R}_i^\mathsf{T}\mathbf{e}$$
where $\mathbf{R}_i \leftarrow \{-1, 1\}^{m \times m}$.
4. For $i \in [t]$, compute
$$\mathbf{v}_i = (\mathbf{B}_i + \mathbf{x}_i \cdot \mathbf{G})^\mathsf{T}\mathbf{s} + (\mathbf{R}_i')^\mathsf{T}\mathbf{e}$$
where $\mathbf{R}_i' \leftarrow \{-1, 1\}^{m \times m}$.
5. Output the ciphertext
$$\mathsf{CT}_\mathbf{y} = (\mathbf{y}, \boldsymbol{\beta}_0, \boldsymbol{\beta}_1, \{\mathbf{u}_i\}, \{\mathbf{v}_j\})$$
for $i \in [\ell]$, $j \in [t]$.

$\mathsf{PH.Dec}(\mathsf{SK}_{\widehat{C}\circ\mathsf{IP}_\gamma}, \mathsf{CT}_\mathbf{y})$: Given as input a secret key and a ciphertext, do the following:
1. Compute
$$\mathbf{u}_{\widehat{C}\circ\mathsf{IP}} = \mathsf{Eval}_{\mathsf{CT}}\big(\{\mathbf{A}_i, \mathbf{u}_i\}, \{\mathbf{B}_j, \mathbf{v}_j\}, \widehat{C} \circ \mathsf{IP}, \mathbf{y}\big)$$
2. Compute
$$\boldsymbol{\nu} = \boldsymbol{\beta}_1 - \mathbf{K}^\mathsf{T} \begin{pmatrix} \boldsymbol{\beta}_0 \\ \mathbf{u}_{\widehat{C}\circ\mathsf{IP}} \end{pmatrix}$$
3. Round each coordinate of $\boldsymbol{\nu}$ and if $\big[\mathsf{Round}(\boldsymbol{\nu}[1]), \ldots, \mathsf{Round}(\boldsymbol{\nu}[m-1])\big] = \mathbf{0}$ then set $\mu = \mathsf{Round}(\boldsymbol{\nu}[m])$.
4. Output μ.

In the full version [Agr16], we show that the scheme is correct.

4.2 Proof of Security

Next, we argue that the above construction is secure against an adversary who requests a single key of any kind and an unbounded number of 0-keys.

Theorem 4.1. *The partially hiding predicate encryption scheme described in Sect. 4.1 is secure according in the very-selective game defined in Definition 2.5.*

Proof. We define a p.p.t. simulator Sim and argue that its output is computationally indistinguishable (under the LWE assumption) from the output of the real world. Let $b = \mu$ if $\widehat{C}^* \circ \mathsf{IP}_\gamma(\mathbf{x}, \mathbf{y}) = 1$, $\perp$ otherwise.

Simulator. $\mathsf{Sim}(\mathbf{A}_{\widehat{C}^*\circ\mathsf{IP}}, \mathbf{y}, 1^{|\mathbf{x}|}, b)$:

1. It generates all public parameters as in the real $\mathsf{PH.Setup}$ except $\mathbf{P}$. To generate $\mathbf{P}$, it computes $\mathbf{A}_{\widehat{C^*} \circ \mathsf{IP}} = \mathsf{Eval}_{\mathsf{MPK}}(\{\mathbf{A}_i\}, \{\mathbf{B}_i\}, \widehat{C^*} \circ \mathsf{IP})$, samples $\mathbf{K}^* \leftarrow (\mathcal{D}_{\mathbb{Z}^{2m},s})^m$ and sets:
$$\mathbf{P} = [\mathbf{A} \mid \mathbf{A}_{\widehat{C^*} \circ \mathsf{IP}} + \gamma \cdot \mathbf{G}]\, \mathbf{K}^* \tag{4.1}$$
2. It generates all keys using the real $\mathsf{PH.KeyGen}$ except the key for $\widehat{C^*} \circ \mathsf{IP}_\gamma$, which is set as $\mathbf{K}^*$ sampled above.
3. $\mathsf{Sim.Enc}(\widehat{C^*} \circ \mathsf{IP}_\gamma, \mathbf{y}, 1^{|\mathbf{x}|}, b)$: It takes as input the challenge circuit $\widehat{C^*} \circ \mathsf{IP}_\gamma$, the public attributes $\mathbf{y}$, the size of the private attributes $\mathbf{x}$, and the message $b = \mu$ if $\widehat{C^*} \circ \mathsf{IP}_\gamma(\mathbf{x}, \mathbf{y}) = 1$, $\perp$ otherwise. It constructs the challenge ciphertext as follows.
   - It samples $\boldsymbol{\beta}_0, \mathbf{u}_i, \mathbf{v}_i$ independently and uniformly from $\mathbb{Z}_q^m$. If $b = \perp$, it samples $\boldsymbol{\beta}_1$ also randomly from $\mathbb{Z}_q^m$.
   - If $b = \mu$, it computes $\boldsymbol{\beta}_1$ to satisfy the decryption equation corresponding to $\widehat{C^*} \circ \mathsf{IP}_\gamma$ as follows.
     - Let $\mathbf{u}_{\widehat{C^*} \circ \mathsf{IP}} = \mathsf{Eval}_{\mathsf{CT}}(\{\mathbf{A}_i, \mathbf{u}_i\}, \{\mathbf{B}_i, \mathbf{v}_i\}, \widehat{C^*} \circ \mathsf{IP}, \mathbf{y})$.
     - Sample $\mathbf{e}'' \leftarrow \mathcal{D}_{\mathbb{Z}^m, s_D}$
     - Set $\boldsymbol{\beta}_1 = (\mathbf{K}^*)^\mathsf{T} \begin{pmatrix} \boldsymbol{\beta}_0 \\ \mathbf{u}_{\widehat{C^*} \circ \mathsf{IP}} \end{pmatrix} + \mathbf{e}'' + \mathbf{b}$ where $\mathbf{b} = [0 \ldots, 0, \lceil q/2 \rceil \mu]^\mathsf{T} \in \mathbb{Z}_q^m$.
   - It outputs the challenge ciphertext
$$\mathsf{CT}^* = \Big(\{\mathbf{u}_i\}_{i \in [\ell]}, \{\mathbf{v}_i\}_{i \in [t]}, \mathbf{y}, \boldsymbol{\beta}_0, \boldsymbol{\beta}_1 \Big)$$

We argue that the output of the simulator is distributed indistinguishably from the real world. Intuitively, there are only two differences between the real world and simulated distribution. The first is that instead of choosing $\mathbf{P}$ first and sampling $\mathbf{K}^*$ to satisfy Eq. 4.1, we now choose $\mathbf{K}^*$ first and set $\mathbf{P}$ accordingly. This is a standard trick in LWE based systems (see the survey [Pei13], where this is trick 1), its first use that we are aware of appears in [GPV08].

The second difference is in how the challenge ciphertext is generated. In our challenge ciphertext the elements $(\boldsymbol{\beta}_0, \mathbf{u}_i, \mathbf{v}_i)$ are sampled uniformly at random while $\boldsymbol{\beta}_1$ which is computed using the elements $(\boldsymbol{\beta}_0, \mathbf{u}_i, \mathbf{v}_i)$ and $\mathbf{K}^*$ in order to satisfy the decryption equation for a 1 key. We note that $\boldsymbol{\beta}_1$ is the only ciphertext element that is generated differently from the challenge ciphertext in the simulator of [GVW15]. In the [GVW15] simulator, $\boldsymbol{\beta}_1$ is also sampled at random, whereas in our case, it is generated to satisfy the decryption equation involving CT^* and $\mathsf{SK}(\widehat{C^*} \circ \mathsf{IP}_\gamma)$ when $\widehat{C^*} \circ \mathsf{IP}_\gamma(\mathbf{x}, \mathbf{y}) = 1$. Enforcing this relation is necessary, as it is dictated by the correctness of the system[4].

The formal proof is provided in the full version of the paper [Agr16].

[4] Note that the step of "programming" $\boldsymbol{\beta}_1$ forces the simulator to use its knowledge of $\mathbf{y}$. On the other hand, the simulator in [GVW15] does not need to use $\mathbf{y}$ for simulation, implying that even $\mathbf{y}$ is hidden when the attacker does not request 1-keys. Since the real decryption procedure needs $\mathbf{y}$ in order to decrypt, this (in our opinion) further illustrates the weakness of the weak attribute hiding definition.

5 Upgrading Very Selective to Semi Adaptive Security for PHPE

In this section, we show how to construct a (1, poly)-Partially Hiding Predicate Encryption scheme for circuit class $\mathcal{C}$ satisfying semi adaptive security according to Definition 2.4. Our construction, which we denote by SaPH, will make use of two ingredients:

1. A single key[5], FULL-SIM secure functional encryption scheme for the following functionality:
$$F_{(\mathbf{V}_1,\ldots,\mathbf{V}_k)}(\mathbf{a}_1,\ldots,\mathbf{a}_k) = \sum_{i=1} \mathbf{V}_i \cdot \mathbf{a}_i \mod q$$
where $\mathbf{V}_i \in \mathbb{Z}_q^{m\times m}$ and $\mathbf{a}_i \in \mathbb{Z}_q^m$ for $i \in [k]$. The parameters k, q, m are input to the setup algorithm. Such a scheme was recently constructed by [ALS16][6]. We will denote this scheme by FuLin.
2. A (1, poly) very selectively secure PHPE scheme for the circuit class $\mathcal{C}$, as provided in Sect. 4. We will denote this scheme by VSelPH.

Our construction is described below.

$\mathsf{SaPH.Setup}(1^\kappa, 1^t, 1^\ell, 1^d)$: Given as input the circuit and the master secret key, do the following:
1. For $i \in [\ell]$, let $(\mathsf{FuLin.PK}_i, \mathsf{FuLin.MSK}_i) \leftarrow \mathsf{FuLin.Setup}\big(1^\kappa, (\mathbb{Z}_q^m)^3\big)$.
2. For $j \in [t]$, let $(\mathsf{FuLin.PK}'_j, \mathsf{FuLin.MSK}'_j) \leftarrow \mathsf{FuLin.Setup}\big(1^\kappa, (\mathbb{Z}_q^m)^3\big)$.
3. Let $(\mathsf{FuLin.PK}_0, \mathsf{FuLin.MSK}_0) \leftarrow \mathsf{FuLin.Setup}\big(1^\kappa, (\mathbb{Z}_q^m)^2\big)$.
4. Let $(\mathsf{FuLin.PK}'_0, \mathsf{FuLin.MSK}'_0) \leftarrow \mathsf{FuLin.Setup}\big(1^\kappa, (\mathbb{Z}_q^m)^3\big)$.
5. Let $\{\mathsf{PRG}\}_{s\in\{0,1\}^\kappa}$ be a family of PRGs with polynomial expansion. Sample a PRG seed, denoted by seed.
6. Output
$$\mathsf{PH.PK} = \big\{\mathsf{FuLin.PK}_0,\ \mathsf{FuLin.PK}'_0,\ \{\mathsf{FuLin.PK}_i\}_{i\in[\ell]},\ \{\mathsf{FuLin.PK}'_j\}_{j\in[t]}\big\}$$
$$\mathsf{PH.MSK} = \big\{\mathsf{seed},\ \mathsf{FuLin.MSK}_0,\ \mathsf{FuLin.MSK}'_0,\ \{\mathsf{FuLin.MSK}_i\}_{i\in[\ell]},\ \{\mathsf{FuLin.MSK}'_j\}_{j\in[t]}\big\}$$

$\mathsf{SaPH.Enc}\big(\mathsf{PH.PK}, (\mathbf{x},\mathbf{y}), \mu\big)$: Given as input the master public key, the private attributes $\mathbf{x}$, public attributes $\mathbf{y}$ and message μ, do the following:
1. Sample $\mathbf{s} \leftarrow \mathcal{D}_{\mathbb{Z}^n, s_B}$ and error terms $\mathbf{e} \leftarrow \mathcal{D}_{\mathbb{Z}^m, s_B}$ and $\mathbf{e}' \leftarrow \mathcal{D}_{\mathbb{Z}^m, s_D}$.
2. Let $\mathbf{b} = [0, \ldots, 0, \lceil q/2 \rceil \mu]^\mathsf{T} \in \mathbb{Z}_q^m$.
3. Sample $\mathbf{R}_i \leftarrow \{-1,1\}^{m\times m}$ for $i \in [\ell]$ and $\mathbf{R}'_j \leftarrow \{-1,1\}^{m\times m}$ for $j \in [t]$.
4. Set[7]

[5] More precisely, we require that the adversary may request the same single function any number of times, but multiple requests for the same function result in the same key.

[6] While the construction in [ALS16] has stateful KeyGen against a general adversary, we only need the single key version which is clearly stateless.

[7] Note that we are abusing notation slightly, since the message space of FuLin was set as $\mathbb{Z}_q^m$ but $\mathbf{s} \in \mathbb{Z}_q^n$. However, since $n < m$, we can pad it with zeroes to make it match. We do not explicitly state this for the sake of notational convenience.

$$\hat{\beta}_0 = \mathsf{FuLin.Enc}(\ \mathbf{s}, \mathbf{e}\ ), \qquad \hat{\mathbf{u}}_i = \mathsf{FuLin.Enc}(\ \mathbf{s},\ \mathbf{y}[i] \cdot \mathbf{G}^{\mathsf{T}}\mathbf{s},\ \mathbf{R}_i^{\mathsf{T}}\mathbf{e}\ ),$$
$$\hat{\beta}_1 = \mathsf{FuLin.Enc}(\ \mathbf{s}, \mathbf{e}', \mathbf{b}\ ), \qquad \hat{\mathbf{v}}_j = \mathsf{FuLin.Enc}(\ \mathbf{s},\ \mathbf{x}[j] \cdot \mathbf{G}^{\mathsf{T}}\mathbf{s},\ \mathbf{R}'^{\mathsf{T}}_j\mathbf{e}\ )$$

5. Output the ciphertext

$$\mathsf{CT}_{\mathbf{y}} = (\mathbf{y}, \hat{\beta}_0, \hat{\beta}_1, \{\hat{\mathbf{u}}_i\}, \{\hat{\mathbf{v}}_j\})$$

for $i \in [\ell]$, $j \in [t]$.

$\mathsf{SaPH.KeyGen}(\mathsf{PH.MSK}, \widehat{C} \circ \mathsf{IP}_\gamma)$: Given as input the circuit and the master secret key, do the following:

1. Use $\mathsf{PRG}(\mathsf{seed})$ to generate sufficient randomness rand for the $\mathsf{VSelPH.Setup}$ algorithm as well as $\{\mathsf{rand}_i\}$, $\{\mathsf{rand}'_j\}$, rand_0, rand'_0 for the $\mathsf{FuLin.KeyGen}$ algorithms.
2. Sample $(\mathsf{VSelPH.MPK}, \mathsf{VSelPH.MSK}) \leftarrow \mathsf{VSelPH.Setup}(1^\kappa, 1^t, 1^\ell, 1^d, \mathsf{rand})$.
   Parse $\mathsf{VSelPH.MPK} = (\{\mathbf{A}_i\},\ \{\mathbf{B}_j\},\ \mathbf{A},\ \mathbf{P}\ )$.
3. Let[8]

$$\mathsf{FuLin.SK}_i \leftarrow \mathsf{FuLin.KeyGen}(\ \mathsf{FuLin.MSK}_i, (\mathbf{A}_i^{\mathsf{T}}, 1, 1),\ \mathsf{rand}_i\ ) \quad \forall i \in [\ell]$$
$$\mathsf{FuLin.SK}'_j \leftarrow \mathsf{FuLin.KeyGen}(\ \mathsf{FuLin.MSK}'_j, (\mathbf{B}_j^{\mathsf{T}}, 1, 1),\ \mathsf{rand}'_j\ ) \quad \forall j \in [t]$$
$$\mathsf{FuLin.SK}_0 \leftarrow \mathsf{FuLin.KeyGen}(\ \mathsf{FuLin.MSK}_0, (\mathbf{A}^{\mathsf{T}}, 1),\ \mathsf{rand}_0\ )$$
$$\mathsf{FuLin.SK}'_0 \leftarrow \mathsf{FuLin.KeyGen}(\ \mathsf{FuLin.MSK}'_0, (\mathbf{P}^{\mathsf{T}}, 1, 1),\ \mathsf{rand}'_0\ )$$

4. Let $\mathsf{VSelPH.SK}(\widehat{C} \circ \mathsf{IP}_\gamma) \leftarrow \mathsf{VSelPH.KeyGen}(\ \mathsf{VSelPH.MSK}, \widehat{C} \circ \mathsf{IP}_\gamma\ )$.
5. Output

$$\mathsf{VSelPH.SK}(\widehat{C} \circ \mathsf{IP}_\gamma) = \Big((\mathsf{VSelPH.MPK},\ \mathsf{VSelPH.SK}(\widehat{C} \circ \mathsf{IP}_\gamma)\ ),$$
$$(\ \{\mathsf{FuLin.SK}_i\},\ \{\mathsf{FuLin.SK}'_j\},\ \mathsf{FuLin.SK}_0,\ \mathsf{FuLin.SK}'_0\ )\Big)$$

$\mathsf{SaPH.Dec}(\mathsf{SK}_{\widehat{C} \circ \mathsf{IP}_\gamma}, \mathsf{CT}_{\mathbf{y}})$: Given as input a secret key and a ciphertext, do the following:

1. Let

$$\beta_0 = \mathsf{FuLin.Dec}(\mathsf{FuLin.SK}_0, \hat{\beta}_0), \qquad \mathbf{u}_i = \mathsf{FuLin.Dec}(\mathsf{FuLin.SK}_i, \hat{\mathbf{u}}_i),$$
$$\beta_1 = \mathsf{FuLin.Dec}(\mathsf{FuLin.SK}'_0, \hat{\beta}_1), \qquad \mathbf{v}_j = \mathsf{FuLin.Dec}(\mathsf{FuLin.SK}'_j, \hat{\mathbf{v}}_j)$$

   Let $\mathsf{VSelPH.CT} = (\ \beta_0,\ \beta_1,\ \{\mathbf{u}_i\},\ \{\mathbf{v}_j\},\ \mathbf{y}\ )$.
2. Output $\mu \leftarrow \mathsf{VSelPH.Dec}(\ \mathsf{VSelPH.MPK},\ \mathsf{VSelPH.CT}, \mathsf{VSelPH.SK}\ )$.

Correctness. Correctness may be argued using the correctness of FuLin and VSelPH.

[8] Here, 1 is used to denote the $m \times m$ identity matrix.

By correctness of FuLin, the tuple $(\boldsymbol{\beta}_0, \boldsymbol{\beta}_1, \{\mathbf{u}_i\}, \{\mathbf{v}_j\})$ produced in the first step of decryption is precisely the ciphertext of the VSelPH scheme. More formally, we get:

$$\begin{aligned}
\mathbf{u}_i &= \mathsf{FuLin.Dec}(\mathsf{FuLin.SK}_i, \hat{\mathbf{u}}_i) = (\mathbf{A}_i + \mathbf{y}_i \cdot \mathbf{G})^\mathsf{T}\mathbf{s} + \mathbf{R}_i^\mathsf{T}\mathbf{e} \\
\mathbf{v}_j &= \mathsf{FuLin.Dec}(\mathsf{FuLin.SK}'_j, \hat{\mathbf{v}}_j) = (\mathbf{B}_i + \mathbf{x}_i \cdot \mathbf{G})^\mathsf{T}\mathbf{s} + (\mathbf{R}'_i)^\mathsf{T}\mathbf{e} \\
\boldsymbol{\beta}_0 &= \mathsf{FuLin.Dec}(\mathsf{FuLin.SK}_0, \hat{\boldsymbol{\beta}}_0) = \mathbf{A}^\mathsf{T}\mathbf{s} + \mathbf{e} \\
\boldsymbol{\beta}_1 &= \mathsf{FuLin.Dec}(\mathsf{FuLin.SK}'_0, \hat{\boldsymbol{\beta}}_1) = \mathbf{P}^\mathsf{T}\mathbf{s} + \mathbf{e}' + \mathbf{b}
\end{aligned}$$

Let $\mathsf{VSelPH.CT} = (\ \boldsymbol{\beta}_0, \boldsymbol{\beta}_1, \{\mathbf{u}_i\}, \{\mathbf{v}_j\}, \mathbf{y}\ )$. Then, by correctness of VSelPH, the following is correct

$$\mu = \mathsf{VSelPH.Dec}(\ \mathsf{VSelPH.MPK},\ \mathsf{VSelPH.CT}, \mathsf{VSelPH.SK}\ )$$

In the full version of the paper [Agr16], we prove the following theorem.

Theorem 5.1. *Assume that* VSelPH *satisfies* VSel-SIM *attribute hiding (Definition 2.5) and that FuLin satisfies* FULL-SIM *security (Appendix 2.3). Then the scheme SaPH satisfies* SA-SIM *attribute hiding (Definition 2.4).*

6 (1, poly)-Functional Encryption

In this section, we construct our (1, poly)-functional encryption scheme. The ciphertext of the construction is succinct, providing a unification of the results [GKP+13, GVW15]. Our construction of (1, poly)-functional encryption uses (1, poly)-partially hiding predicate encryption and fully homomorphic encryption in a manner similar to [GVW15, Sect. 4].

6.1 Construction

We begin with an overview of the main ideas in the construction. Let us recall the (0, poly)-FE scheme constructed by [GVW15]. The scheme makes use of two ingredients, namely, a (0, poly)-PHPE scheme for circuits, and a fully homomorphic encryption scheme for circuits. The ciphertext of (0, poly)-FE corresponding to an attribute $\mathbf{a}$ is a PHPE ciphertext corresponding to $(\widehat{\mathbf{a}}, \mathbf{t})$ where $\widehat{\mathbf{a}}$ is the FHE encryption of $\mathbf{a}$, and corresponds to the public attributes in PHPE, while $\mathbf{t}$ is the FHE secret key and corresponds to the private attributes in PHPE.

The secret key corresponding to circuit C in the (0, poly)-FE scheme is a set of PHPE secret keys $\{\ \widehat{C} \circ \mathsf{IP}_\gamma\ \}_{\gamma \in [\lfloor p/2 \rfloor - B, \lfloor p/2 \rfloor + B]}$ where:

$$\begin{aligned}
\widehat{C} \circ \mathsf{IP}_\gamma(\mathbf{x}, \mathbf{y}) &= 1 \ \text{ if } \langle \mathbf{x}, \widehat{C}(\mathbf{y}) \rangle = \gamma \\
&= 0 \text{ otherwise.}
\end{aligned}$$

The decryptor executes the homomorphic ciphertext evaluation procedure for circuit $\mathsf{FHE.Eval}(\cdot, C)$ on the attributes $\widehat{\mathbf{a}}$ embedded in the PHPE ciphertext as in [BGG+14] to obtain a ciphertext corresponding to public attributes

$\widehat{C(\mathbf{a})}$, where $\widehat{C(\mathbf{a})}$ is an FHE encryption of $C(\mathbf{a})$. Now, when $C(\mathbf{a}) = 1$, then by correctness of FHE, there exists a noise term $\gamma \in [\lfloor p/2 \rfloor - B, \lfloor p/2 \rfloor + B]$ such that $\langle \ \mathbf{t}, \widehat{C(\mathbf{a})} \ \rangle = \gamma$. The decryptor tries keys corresponding to all possible γ within the aforementioned range to ascertain whether $\widehat{C} \circ \mathsf{IP}_\gamma(\widehat{\mathbf{a}}, \mathbf{t}) = 1$. Note that this step makes it crucial that the FHE decryption range be polynomial in size. Fortunately, as noted by [GVW15], this can be ensured by the modulus reduction technique in FHE schemes [BGV12,GSW13,BV14], which allows a superpolynomial modulus to be scaled down to polynomial size.

The first idea in building (1, poly)-FE is to replace the use of (0, poly)-PHPE in the above transformation by the (1, poly) PHPE constructed in Sect. 4. However, as discussed in Attack #3, Sect. 3, such a straightforward adaptation leads to vulnerabilities. This is because decryption using a 1-key allows the decryptor to learn the exact inner product of the FHE ciphertext $\widehat{C(\mathbf{a})}$ and the FHE secret key $\mathbf{t}$ rather than the threshold inner product corresponding to FHE decryption. This lets her obtain leakage on the noise terms used to construct $\widehat{\mathbf{a}}$, which is problematic. We will denote the noise used in the construction of the FHE ciphertext $\widehat{\mathbf{a}}$ by $\mathsf{Noise}(\ \widehat{\mathbf{a}}\ )$.

Overcoming Leakage on FHE Noise. For a single 1-key, there is a natural way out, via "noise flooding" or "noise smudging" [Gen09,GKPV10,AJLA+12]. To prevent leakage on $\mathsf{Noise}(\ \widehat{\mathbf{a}}\ )$, we may augment the FHE evaluation circuit with a "flooding" operation, which, after computing $\mathsf{FHE.Eval}(\widehat{\mathbf{a}}, C)$ adds to it an encryption of 0 with large noise η to drown out the effects of $\mathsf{Noise}(\ \widehat{\mathbf{a}}\ )$. This idea is complicated by the fact that our construction of (1, poly)-FE must use an FHE scheme whose final modulus is polynomial in size, whereas η must be chosen to satisfy:

$$\mathsf{Noise}(\ \mathsf{FHE.Eval}(\ \widehat{\mathbf{a}}, C)\ ) + \eta \stackrel{s}{\approx} \eta \tag{6.1}$$

so that it drowns the effects of $\mathsf{Noise}(\ \widehat{\mathbf{a}}\ )$. The above constraint may necessitate η, and hence the FHE modulus, to be superpolynomial in the security parameter.

Fortunately, we can work around this difficulty by performing FHE modulus reduction after flooding. Then, η can be superpolynomial in the security parameter to obliterate the dependency of the revealed noise on the initial noise, while letting the final FHE modulus still be polynomial. Another method is to use the "sanitization" operation [DS16], which will result in better parameters for this step – however, since it does not improve our overall parameters, we do not discuss this.

Formally, we require a PHPE scheme for the circuit family $\mathcal{C}_{\mathsf{PHPE}}$ where $\widehat{C} \circ \mathsf{IP} \in \mathcal{C}_{\mathsf{PHPE}}$ is defined as follows. Let the private attributes $\mathbf{x} = \mathbf{t}$ where $\mathbf{t}$ is the FHE secret, and public attributes $\mathbf{y} = (\widehat{\mathbf{a}}, \widehat{0})$, where $\widehat{0}$ is an FHE encryption of the bit 0, with large noise η. Then, define:

$$\widehat{C}(\widehat{0}, \widehat{\mathbf{a}}) = \mathsf{FHE.Scale}_{q,p}(\ \mathsf{FHE.Eval}(\widehat{\mathbf{a}}, C) + \widehat{0})$$

$$\widehat{C} \circ \mathsf{IP}(\ \mathbf{t}, \widehat{0}, \widehat{\mathbf{a}}\ ) = \left\langle \mathbf{t},\ \widehat{C}(\widehat{0}, \widehat{\mathbf{a}}) \right\rangle \mod p$$

$$\widehat{C} \circ \mathsf{IP}_\gamma(\ \mathbf{t}, \widehat{0}, \widehat{\mathbf{a}}\ ) = 1 \text{ iff } \widehat{C} \circ \mathsf{IP}(\ \mathbf{t}, \widehat{0}, \widehat{\mathbf{a}}\ ) = \gamma, \text{ 0 otherwise.}$$

Above, FHE.Eval is the FHE ciphertext evaluation algorithm, and FHE.Scale is the modulus reduction algorithm described in Sect. 2.5. Recall that $\mathsf{FHE.Scale}_{q,p}$ takes as input an FHE ciphertext that lives modulo q and reduces it to a ciphertext that lives modulo p. For the sake of brevity, we abuse notation and do not explicitly include the inputs (q, p) in the inputs to $\widehat{C} \circ \mathsf{IP}$.

Construction. We now proceed to describe the construction.

$\mathsf{FE.Setup}(1^\kappa, 1^k, 1^d)$: The setup algorithm takes the security parameter κ, the attribute length k and the function depth d and does the following:

1. Choose the FHE modulus q in which $\mathsf{FHE.Eval}(\cdot, \cdot)$ will be computed and the FHE modulus $p \in \text{poly}(\kappa)$ in which decryption will be performed as per Sect. 2.5.
2. Invoke the setup algorithm for the PHPE scheme for family $\mathcal{C}_{\mathsf{PHPE}}$ to get:

$$(\mathsf{PH.PK}, \mathsf{PH.MSK}) \leftarrow \mathsf{PH.Setup}(1^\kappa, 1^t, 1^\ell, 1^{d'})$$

where length of private attributes $t = |\mathsf{FHE.SK}|$, length of public attributes ℓ is the length of an FHE encryption of $k+1$ bits corresponding to the attributes $\mathbf{a}$ and 0, i.e. $\ell = (k+1) \cdot |\mathsf{FHE.CT}|$ and d' is the bound on the augmented FHE evaluation circuit.
3. Output $(\mathsf{PK} = \mathsf{PH.PK},\ \mathsf{MSK} = \mathsf{PH.MSK})$.

$\mathsf{FE.Keygen}(\mathsf{MSK}, C)$: The key generation algorithm takes as input the master secret key MSK and a circuit C. It does the following:

1. Let $R \triangleq [\lfloor p/2 \rfloor - B, \lfloor p/2 \rfloor + B]$. Compute the circuit $\widehat{C} \circ \mathsf{IP}_\gamma$ as described above for $\gamma \in R$.
2. For $\gamma \in R$, compute

$$\mathsf{PH.SK}_{\widehat{C} \circ \mathsf{IP}_\gamma} \leftarrow \mathsf{PH.KeyGen}(\mathsf{PH.MSK}, \widehat{C} \circ \mathsf{IP}_\gamma)$$

3. Output the secret key as $\mathsf{SK}_C = \{\mathsf{PH.SK}_{\widehat{C} \circ \mathsf{IP}_\gamma}\}_{\gamma \in R}$.

$\mathsf{FE.Enc}(\mathsf{PK}, \mathbf{a}, \mu)$: The encryption algorithm does the following:

1. Sample a fresh FHE secret key FHE.SK, and denote it by $\mathbf{t}$.
2. Compute an FHE encryption of $\mathbf{a}$ to get $\widehat{\mathbf{a}} = \mathsf{FHE.Enc}(\ \mathbf{t}, \mathbf{a}\ )$.
3. Sample η to satisfy Eq. 6.1 and compute an FHE encryption of 0 with noise η as $\widehat{0}$.
4. Set public attributes $\mathbf{y} = (\widehat{\mathbf{a}}, \widehat{0})$ and private attributes $\mathbf{x} = \mathbf{t}$.
5. Compute $\mathsf{PH.CT}_{\widehat{\mathbf{a}},\widehat{0}} = \mathsf{PH.Enc}(\ \mathsf{PH.PK}, (\mathbf{x}, \mathbf{y}), \mu)$.
6. Output $\mathsf{CT}_{\mathbf{a}} = (\ \widehat{\mathbf{a}}, \widehat{0}, \mathsf{PH.CT}_{\widehat{\mathbf{a}},\widehat{0}}\ )$.

$\mathsf{FE.Dec}(\mathsf{SK}_C, \mathsf{CT}_{\mathbf{a}})$: Do the following:

1. Parse SK_C as the set $\{\mathsf{PH.SK}_{\widehat{C} \circ \mathsf{IP}_\gamma}\}_{\gamma \in R}$.
2. For $\gamma \in R$, let $\tau_\gamma = \mathsf{PH.Dec}(\ \mathsf{CT}_{\mathbf{a}}, \mathsf{PH.SK}_{\widehat{C} \circ \mathsf{IP}_\gamma}\ )$. If there exists some value γ' for which $\tau_{\gamma'} \neq \perp$, then output $\mu = \tau_{\gamma'}$, else output $\perp$.

Correctness. Correctness follows from correctness of PHPE and properties of FHE (see Sect. 2.5). Please see the full version [Agr16] for details.

6.2 Proof of Security

Next, we argue that the above scheme satisfies semi-adaptive security.

Theorem 6.1. *The* (1, poly) *functional encryption scheme described above is secure according to Definition 2.3.*

Proof. We construct a simulator $\mathsf{FE.Sim}$ as required by Definition 2.3 as follows.

Simulator $\mathsf{FE.Sim}(1^\kappa)$. The simulator is described as follows.

1. It invokes $\mathsf{PHPE.Sim}(1^\kappa)$ to obtain the public parameters and returns these.
2. The FE adversary outputs $(\mathbf{a}, \mu, C^*)$ upon which, $\mathsf{FE.Sim}$ obtains $(1^{|\mathbf{a}|}, \mu, C^*)$. It does the following:
   (a) It samples an FHE secret key $\mathsf{FHE.SK}$ and sets $\widehat{\mathbf{a}} = \mathsf{FHE.Enc}(\mathsf{FHE.SK}, \mathbf{0})$ and $\widehat{0} = \mathsf{FHE.Enc}(\mathsf{FHE.SK}, 0)$.
   (b) It samples γ_q to satisfy Eq. 6.1. Let γ denote its scaled down version modulo p. It computes $\widehat{C}^* \circ \mathsf{IP}_\gamma$ as described above.
   (c) It invokes $\mathsf{PHPE.Sim}\big(\ (\widehat{\mathbf{a}}, \widehat{0}), \ \ 1^{|\mathsf{FHE.SK}|}, \ \ \widehat{C}^* \circ \mathsf{IP}_\gamma, \ \ \mu \ \big)$ to obtain $\big(\,\mathsf{PH.CT}, \ \mathsf{PH.SK}(\widehat{C}^* \circ \mathsf{IP}_\gamma)\,\big)$.
   (d) For $\rho \in R \backslash \gamma$, it constructs $\widehat{C}^* \circ \mathsf{IP}_\rho$ and sends these queries to $\mathsf{PHPE.Sim}$. It receives $\mathsf{PH.SK}(\widehat{C}^* \circ \mathsf{IP}_\rho)$.
   (e) It outputs $\big(\,\mathsf{PH.CT}, \ \{\mathsf{PH.SK}(\widehat{C}^* \circ \mathsf{IP}_\rho)\}_{\rho \in R}\,\big)$.
3. When Adv makes any query C, $\mathsf{FE.Sim}$ transforms it into $\{\widehat{C} \circ \mathsf{IP}_\rho\}_{\rho \in R}$ and sends this to $\mathsf{PHPE.Sim}$. It returns the set of received keys to Adv. Note that these are 0-keys.
4. When Adv outputs α, output the same.

We argue that the simulator is correct in the full version of the paper [Agr16].

We note that the above construction is shown secure in a game which allows a single arbitrary query and other 0 queries. Circuit privacy may be obtained by using symmetric key encryption SKE to hide the key and augmenting the function circuit with SKE decryption, exactly as in [GKP+13]. The details as well as the generalization to the bounded collusion setting is provided in the full version of the paper [Agr16].

References

[ABB10] Agrawal, S., Boneh, D., Boyen, X.: Efficient lattice (H)IBE in the standard model. In: Gilbert, H. (ed.) EUROCRYPT 2010. LNCS, vol. 6110, pp. 553–572. Springer, Heidelberg (2010). doi:10.1007/978-3-642-13190-5_28

[AFV11] Agrawal, S., Freeman, D.M., Vaikuntanathan, V.: Functional encryption for inner product predicates from learning with errors. In: Lee, D.H., Wang, X. (eds.) ASIACRYPT 2011. LNCS, vol. 7073, pp. 21–40. Springer, Heidelberg (2011). doi:10.1007/978-3-642-25385-0_2

[Agr16] Agrawal, S.: Stronger security for reusable garbled circuits, general definitions and attacks. Eprint 2016/654 (2016)

[AGVW13] Agrawal, S., Gorbunov, S., Vaikuntanathan, V., Wee, H.: Functional encryption: new perspectives and lower bounds. In: Canetti, R., Garay, J.A. (eds.) CRYPTO 2013. LNCS, vol. 8043, pp. 500–518. Springer, Heidelberg (2013). doi:10.1007/978-3-642-40084-1_28

[AJLA+12] Asharov, G., Jain, A., López-Alt, A., Tromer, E., Vaikuntanathan, V., Wichs, D.: Multiparty computation with low communication, computation and interaction via threshold FHE. In: Pointcheval, D., Johansson, T. (eds.) EUROCRYPT 2012. LNCS, vol. 7237, pp. 483–501. Springer, Heidelberg (2012). doi:10.1007/978-3-642-29011-4_29

[Ajt99] Ajtai, M.: Generating hard instances of the short basis problem. In: Wiedermann, J., Emde Boas, P., Nielsen, M. (eds.) ICALP 1999. LNCS, vol. 1644, pp. 1–9. Springer, Heidelberg (1999). doi:10.1007/3-540-48523-6_1

[ALS16] Agrawal, S., Libert, B., Stehle, D.: Fully secure functional encryption for linear functions from standard assumptions. In: CRYPTO (2016)

[AP14] Alperin-Sheriff, J., Peikert, C.: Faster bootstrapping with polynomial error. In: Garay, J.A., Gennaro, R. (eds.) CRYPTO 2014. LNCS, vol. 8616, pp. 297–314. Springer, Heidelberg (2014). doi:10.1007/978-3-662-44371-2_17

[BF01] Boneh, D., Franklin, M.: Identity-based encryption from the weil pairing. In: Kilian, J. (ed.) CRYPTO 2001. LNCS, vol. 2139, pp. 213–229. Springer, Heidelberg (2001). doi:10.1007/3-540-44647-8_13

[BGG+14] Boneh, D., Gentry, C., Gorbunov, S., Halevi, S., Nikolaenko, V., Segev, G., Vaikuntanathan, V., Vinayagamurthy, D.: Fully key-homomorphic encryption, arithmetic circuit ABE and compact garbled circuits. In: Nguyen, P.Q., Oswald, E. (eds.) EUROCRYPT 2014. LNCS, vol. 8441, pp. 533–556. Springer, Heidelberg (2014). doi:10.1007/978-3-642-55220-5_30

[BGV12] Brakerski, Z., Gentry, C., Vaikuntanathan, V.: (Leveled) fully homomorphic encryption without bootstrapping. In: ITCS (2012)

[BSW07] Bethencourt, J., Sahai, A., Waters, B.: Ciphertext-policy attribute-based encryption. In: IEEE Symposium on Security and Privacy (2007)

[BSW11] Boneh, D., Sahai, A., Waters, B.: Functional encryption: definitions and challenges. In: Ishai, Y. (ed.) TCC 2011. LNCS, vol. 6597, pp. 253–273. Springer, Heidelberg (2011). doi:10.1007/978-3-642-19571-6_16

[BV11] Brakerski, Z., Vaikuntanathan, V.: Efficient fully homomorphic encryption from (standard) LWE. In: FOCS (2011)

[BV14] Brakerski, Z., Vaikuntanathan, V.: Lattice-based FHE as secure as PKE. In: ITCS (2014)

[BV16] Brakerski, Z., Vaikuntanathan, V.: Circuit-ABE from LWE: unbounded attributes and semi-adaptive security. In: Robshaw, M., Katz, J. (eds.) CRYPTO 2016. LNCS, vol. 9816, pp. 363–384. Springer, Heidelberg (2016). doi:10.1007/978-3-662-53015-3_13

[BW06] Boyen, X., Waters, B.: Anonymous hierarchical identity-based encryption (without random oracles). In: Dwork, C. (ed.) CRYPTO 2006. LNCS, vol. 4117, pp. 290–307. Springer, Heidelberg (2006). doi:10.1007/11818175_17

[BW07] Boneh, D., Waters, B.: Conjunctive, subset, and range queries on encrypted data. In: Vadhan, S.P. (ed.) TCC 2007. LNCS, vol. 4392, pp. 535–554. Springer, Heidelberg (2007). doi:10.1007/978-3-540-70936-7_29

[CFL+16] Cheon, J.H., Fouque, P.-A., Lee, C., Minaud, B., Ryu, H.: Cryptanalysis of the new CLT multilinear map over the integers. In: Fischlin, M., Coron, J.-S. (eds.) EUROCRYPT 2016. LNCS, vol. 9665, pp. 509–536. Springer, Heidelberg (2016). doi:10.1007/978-3-662-49890-3_20

[CGH+15] Coron, J.-S., Gentry, C., Halevi, S., Lepoint, T., Maji, H.K., Miles, E., Raykova, M., Sahai, A., Tibouchi, M.: Zeroizing without low-level zeroes: new MMAP attacks and their limitations. In: CRYPTO (2015)

[CHKP10] Cash, D., Hofheinz, D., Kiltz, E., Peikert, C.: Bonsai trees, or how to delegate a lattice basis. In: Gilbert, H. (ed.) EUROCRYPT 2010. LNCS, vol. 6110, pp. 523–552. Springer, Heidelberg (2010). doi:10.1007/978-3-642-13190-5_27

[CHL+15] Cheon, J.H., Han, K., Lee, C., Ryu, H., Stehlé, D.: Cryptanalysis of the multilinear map over the integers. In: Oswald, E., Fischlin, M. (eds.) EUROCRYPT 2015. LNCS, vol. 9056, pp. 3–12. Springer, Heidelberg (2015). doi:10.1007/978-3-662-46800-5_1

[CJL] Cheon, J.H., Jeong, J., Lee, C.: An algorithm for NTRU problems and cryptanalysis of the GGH multilinear map without a low level encoding of zero. Eprint 2016/139

[CLT13] Coron, J.-S., Lepoint, T., Tibouchi, M.: Practical multilinear maps over the integers. In: Canetti, R., Garay, J.A. (eds.) CRYPTO 2013. LNCS, vol. 8042, pp. 476–493. Springer, Heidelberg (2013). doi:10.1007/978-3-642-40041-4_26

[Coc01] Cocks, C.: An identity based encryption scheme based on quadratic residues. In: Honary, B. (ed.) Cryptography and Coding 2001. LNCS, vol. 2260, pp. 360–363. Springer, Heidelberg (2001). doi:10.1007/3-540-45325-3_32

[DS16] Ducas, L., Stehlé, D.: Sanitization of FHE ciphertexts. In: Fischlin, M., Coron, J.-S. (eds.) EUROCRYPT 2016. LNCS, vol. 9665, pp. 294–310. Springer, Heidelberg (2016). doi:10.1007/978-3-662-49890-3_12

[Gen09] Gentry, C.: Fully homomorphic encryption using ideal lattices. In: STOC, pp. 169–178 (2009)

[GGH13a] Garg, S., Gentry, C., Halevi, S.: Candidate multilinear maps from ideal lattices. In: Johansson, T., Nguyen, P.Q. (eds.) EUROCRYPT 2013. LNCS, vol. 7881, pp. 1–17. Springer, Heidelberg (2013). doi:10.1007/978-3-642-38348-9_1

[GGH+13b] Garg, S., Gentry, C., Halevi, S., Raykova, M., Sahai, A., Waters, B.: Candidate indistinguishability obfuscation and functional encryption for all circuits. In: FOCS (2013). http://eprint.iacr.org/

[GGH+13c] Garg, S., Gentry, C., Halevi, S., Sahai, A., Waters, B.: Attribute-based encryption for circuits from multilinear maps. In: Canetti, R., Garay, J.A. (eds.) CRYPTO 2013. LNCS, vol. 8043, pp. 479–499. Springer, Heidelberg (2013). doi:10.1007/978-3-642-40084-1_27

[GGH15] Gentry, C., Gorbunov, S., Halevi, S.: Graph-induced multilinear maps from lattices. In: Dodis, Y., Nielsen, J.B. (eds.) TCC 2015. LNCS, vol. 9015, pp. 498–527. Springer, Heidelberg (2015). doi:10.1007/978-3-662-46497-7_20

[GGHZ14] Garg, S., Gentry, C., Halevi, S., Zhandry, M.: Fully secure functional encryption without obfuscation. In: IACR Cryptology ePrint Archive, vol. 2014, p. 666 (2014)

[GKP+13] Goldwasser, S., Kalai, Y.T., Popa, R.A., Vaikuntanathan, V., Zeldovich, N.: Reusable garbled circuits and succinct functional encryption. In: STOC, pp. 555–564 (2013)

[GKPV10] Goldwasser, S., Kalai, Y.T., Peikert, C., Vaikuntanathan, V.: Robustness of the learning with errors assumption. In: ITCS (2010)

[GKW16] Goyal, R., Koppula, V., Waters, B.: Semi-adaptive security and bundling functionalities made generic and easy. In: Hirt, M., Smith, A. (eds.) TCC 2016. LNCS, vol. 9986, pp. 361–388. Springer, Heidelberg (2016). doi:10.1007/978-3-662-53644-5_14

[GPSW06] Goyal, V., Pandey, O., Sahai, A., Waters, B.: Attribute-based encryption for fine-grained access control of encrypted data. In: CCS (2006)

[GPV08] Gentry, C., Peikert, C., Vaikuntanathan, V.: Trapdoors for hard lattices and new cryptographic constructions. In: STOC (2008)

[GSW13] Gentry, C., Sahai, A., Waters, B.: Homomorphic encryption from learning with errors: conceptually-simpler, asymptotically-faster, attribute-based. In: Canetti, R., Garay, J.A. (eds.) CRYPTO 2013. LNCS, vol. 8042, pp. 75–92. Springer, Heidelberg (2013). doi:10.1007/978-3-642-40041-4_5

[GTKP+13] Goldwasser, S., Kalai, Y.T., Popa, R., Vaikuntanathan, V., Zeldovich, N.: Reusable garbled circuits and succinct functional encryption. In: Proceedings of STOC (2013)

[GVW12] Gorbunov, S., Vaikuntanathan, V., Wee, H.: Functional encryption with bounded collusions via multi-party computation. In: Safavi-Naini, R., Canetti, R. (eds.) CRYPTO 2012. LNCS, vol. 7417, pp. 162–179. Springer, Heidelberg (2012). doi:10.1007/978-3-642-32009-5_11

[GVW13] Gorbunov, S., Vaikuntanathan, V., Wee, H.: Attribute based encryption for circuits. In: STOC (2013)

[GVW15] Gorbunov, S., Vaikuntanathan, V., Wee, H.: Predicate encryption for circuits from LWE. In: Gennaro, R., Robshaw, M. (eds.) CRYPTO 2015. LNCS, vol. 9216, pp. 503–523. Springer, Heidelberg (2015). doi:10.1007/978-3-662-48000-7_25

[HJ15] Hu, Y., Jia, H.: Cryptanalysis of GGH map. Cryptology ePrint Archive: Report 2015/301 (2015)

[KSW08] Katz, J., Sahai, A., Waters, B.: Predicate encryption supporting disjunctions, polynomial equations, and inner products. In: Smart, N. (ed.) EUROCRYPT 2008. LNCS, vol. 4965, pp. 146–162. Springer, Heidelberg (2008). doi:10.1007/978-3-540-78967-3_9

[LOS+10] Lewko, A., Okamoto, T., Sahai, A., Takashima, K., Waters, B.: Fully secure functional encryption: attribute-based encryption and (hierarchical) inner product encryption. In: Gilbert, H. (ed.) EUROCRYPT 2010. LNCS, vol. 6110, pp. 62–91. Springer, Heidelberg (2010). doi:10.1007/978-3-642-13190-5_4

[MP12] Micciancio, D., Peikert, C.: Trapdoors for lattices: simpler, tighter, faster, smaller. In: Pointcheval, D., Johansson, T. (eds.) EUROCRYPT 2012. LNCS, vol. 7237, pp. 700–718. Springer, Heidelberg (2012). doi:10.1007/978-3-642-29011-4_41

[MSZ16] Miles, E., Sahai, A., Zhandry, M.: Annihilation attacks for multilinear maps: cryptanalysis of indistinguishability obfuscation over GGH13. In: Robshaw, M., Katz, J. (eds.) CRYPTO 2016. LNCS, vol. 9815, pp. 629–658. Springer, Heidelberg (2016). doi:10.1007/978-3-662-53008-5_22

[Pei13] Peikert, C.: Lattices.. to cryptography (2013). http://web.eecs.umich.edu/~cpeikert/pubs/slides-visions.pdf

[PR12] Pandey, O., Rouselakis, Y.: Property preserving symmetric encryption. In: Pointcheval, D., Johansson, T. (eds.) EUROCRYPT 2012. LNCS, vol. 7237, pp. 375–391. Springer, Heidelberg (2012). doi:10.1007/978-3-642-29011-4_23

[Wat12] Waters, B.: Functional encryption for regular languages. In: Safavi-Naini, R., Canetti, R. (eds.) CRYPTO 2012. LNCS, vol. 7417, pp. 218–235. Springer, Heidelberg (2012). doi:10.1007/978-3-642-32009-5_14

Generic Transformations of Predicate Encodings: Constructions and Applications

Miguel Ambrona[1,2(✉)], Gilles Barthe[1], and Benedikt Schmidt[3]

[1] IMDEA Software Institute, Madrid, Spain
{miguel.ambrona,gilles.barthe}@imdea.org
[2] Universidad Politécnica de Madrid, Madrid, Spain
[3] Google, Mountain View, USA
beschmidt@google.com

Abstract. Predicate encodings (Wee, TCC 2014; Chen, Gay, Wee, EUROCRYPT 2015), are symmetric primitives that can be used for building predicate encryption schemes. We give an algebraic characterization of the notion of privacy from predicate encodings, and explore several of its consequences. Specifically, we propose more efficient predicate encodings for boolean formulae and arithmetic span programs, and generic optimizations of predicate encodings. We define new constructions to build boolean combination of predicate encodings. We formalize the relationship between predicate encodings and pair encodings (Attrapadung, EUROCRYPT 2014), another primitive that can be transformed generically into predicate encryption schemes, and compare our constructions for boolean combinations of pair encodings with existing similar constructions from pair encodings. Finally, we demonstrate that our results carry to tag-based encodings (Kim, Susilo, Guo, and Au, SCN 2016).

1 Introduction

Predicate Encryption (PE) [13,25] is a form of public-key encryption that supports fine-grained access control for encrypted data. In predicate encryption, everyone can create ciphertexts while keys can only be created by the master key owner. Predicate encryption schemes use predicates to model (potentially complex) access control policies, and attributes are attached to both ciphertexts and secret keys. A predicate encryption scheme for a predicate P guarantees that decryption of a ciphertext ct_x with a secret key sk_y is allowed if and only if the attribute x associated to the ciphertext ct and the attribute y associated to the secret key sk verify the predicate P, i.e. $\mathsf{P}(x, y) = 1$. Predicate encryption schemes exist for several useful predicates, such as Zero Inner Product Encryption (ZIPE), where attributes are vectors $\boldsymbol{x}$ and $\boldsymbol{y}$ and the predicate $\mathsf{P}(\boldsymbol{x}, \boldsymbol{y})$ is defined as $\boldsymbol{x}^\top \boldsymbol{y} = 0$. Predicate encryption subsumes several previously defined notions of public-key encryption. For example, Identity-Based Encryption (IBE) [34] can be obtained by defining $\mathsf{P}(x, y)$ as $x = y$ and Attribute-Based Encryption (ABE) [33] can be obtained similarly. More concretely, for Key-Policy

J. Katz and H. Shacham (Eds.): CRYPTO 2017, Part I, LNCS 10401, pp. 36–66, 2017.
DOI: 10.1007/978-3-319-63688-7_2

ABE (KP-ABE), the attribute x is a boolean vector, the attribute y is a boolean function, and the predicate $\mathsf{P}(x, y)$ is defined as $y(x) = 1$. For Ciphertext-Policy ABE (CP-ABE), the roles of the attributes x and y are swapped.

Modular Approaches for PE. In 2014, two independent works by Wee [37] and Attrapadung [6] proposed generic and unifying frameworks for obtaining efficient fully secure PE schemes for a large class of predicates. Both works use the dual system methodology introduced by Lewko and Waters [27,36] and define a compiler that takes as input a relatively simple symmetric primitive and produces a fully secure PE construction. Wee introduced so-called *predicate encodings*, an information-theoretic primitive inspired from linear secret sharing. Attrapadung introduced so-called *pair encodings* and provided computational and information-theoretic security notions. These approaches greatly simplify the construction and analysis of predicate encryption schemes and share several advantages. First, they provide a good trade-off between *expressivity* and *performance*, while the security relies on standard and well studied assumptions. Second, they unify existing constructions into a single framework, i.e., previous PE constructions can be seen as instantiations of these new compilers with certain encodings. Third, building PE schemes by analyzing and building these simpler encodings is much easier than building PE schemes directly. Compared to full security for PE, the encodings must verify much weaker security requirements. The power of pair and predicate encodings is evidenced by the discovery of new constructions and efficiency improvements over existing ones. However, both approaches were designed over *composite order* bilinear groups. In Chen et al. [15] and Attrapadung [7] respectively extended the predicate encoding and pair encoding compiler to the *prime order* setting. Next, Agrawal and Chase [1] improved on Attrapadung's work by relaxing the security requirement on *pair encodings* and thus, capturing new constructions. In addition, their work also brings both generic approaches closer together, because like in [15], the new compiler relies (in a black-box way) on Dual System Groups (DSG) [16,17]. Additionally Kim et al. [22] recently introduced a new generic framework for modular design of predicate encryption that improves on the performance of existing compilers. Their core primitive, *tag-based encodings*, is very similar to *predicate encodings*.

1.1 Our Contributions

We pursue the study of predicate encodings and establish several general results and new constructions that broaden their scope and improve their efficiency. We also compare predicate encodings to pair and tag-based encodings.

Predicate Encodings. We show that the information-theoretic definition of α-privacy used in [15,37] is equivalent to an algebraic statement (furthermore independent of α) about the existence of solutions for a linear system of equations. Leveraging this result, we prove a representation theorem for predicate encodings: every triple of encoding functions implicitly defines a unique predicate for which it is a valid predicate encoding. Conversely, every predicate P that admits a predicate encoding is logically equivalent to the implicit predicate induced by its encoding functions. Moreover, our algebraic definition of privacy simplifies all subsequent results in the paper.

First, we define a generic optimization of predicate encodings that often leads to efficiency improvements and reduce the number of required group elements in keys and ciphertexts. We prove the soundness of the transformations and validate their benefits experimentally on examples from [15,37]; we successfully apply these simplifications to reduce the size of keys and ciphertexts by up to 50% and to reduce the number of group operations needed in some of the existing encodings.

Second, we define generic methods for combining predicate encodings. We provide encoding transformations for the *disjunction*, *conjunction* and *negation* of predicates, and for the *dual* predicate.

Tag-Based Encodings. We show that our results on predicate encodings generalize to tag-based encodings. In particular, we give a purely algebraic characterization of the hiding property of tag-based encodings. Moreover, we demonstrate that the hiding property can be strengthened without any loss of generality, by requiring equality rather than statistical closeness of distributions.

Comparison of Encodings. We compare the expressivity of the three core primitives (*predicate encodings*, *pair encodings* and *tag-based encodings*) corresponding to the three different modular frameworks. We provide an embedding that produces an information-theoretical pair encoding from every predicate encoding. Then, we use this encoding to compare our constructions to build boolean combination of predicate encodings with similar constructions for pair encodings that were introduced by [6].

In addition, we provide a transformation[1] from tag-based encodings into predicate encodings.

New Constructions. We develop several new constructions of predicate encodings and predicate encryption:

- **Combining predicates.** We show how to combine our results to build *Dual-Policy Attribute-Based Encryption (DP-ABE)* [9,10] in the frameworks of predicate encodings and tag-based encodings (Sect. 6.1). Additionally, we consider the idea of combining arbitrary encodings with a *broadcast encryption* encoding to achieve direct revocation of keys. The former encoding takes care of revocation, while the latter encodes the desired access structure.
- **Improved predicate encodings.** We provide new instances of predicate encodings that improve on best known predicate encodings proposed in [15] and have additional properties (Sect. 6.2).

[1] This transformation has side conditions, thus it is not universal, but all existing tag-based encodings (except one) satisfy these side conditions.

- **Extra features.** Finally, we show how to construct a weakly attribute-hiding predicate encoding for boolean formulas and how to enhance any predicate encoding with support for delegation (Sect. 6.3).

Implementation and Evaluation. We implement a general library for predicate encryption with support for the predicate encoding and pair encoding frameworks. Our library uses the Relic-Toolkit [5] for pairings with a 256-bits Barreto-Naehrig Curve [11]. We use our library for validating our constructions; experimental results are presented in the relevant sections. All the experiments were executed on a 8-core machine with 2.40 GHz Intel Core i7-3630QM CPU and 8 GB of RAM. Our scalability experiments show that predicate encodings can be used for real applications. The code is publicly available and open source[2].

1.2 Prior Work

Predicate encodings have been introduced in [37] and we use a refined version that is defined in [15] as our starting point. Both variants use an information-theoretic definition of the hiding while we show that there is an equivalent algebraic definition. Another related work is [20], initiating a systematic study of the communication complexity of the so-called conditional secret disclosure primitive, which is closely related to predicate encodings.

Other works also optimize existing predicate encryption schemes, for example many works focus on going from composite order constructions to the more efficient prime order ones [7,15,26]. In [15] they also propose performance improvements on dual system groups. We believe our optimizations via predicate encodings complement other possible enhancements of predicate encryption.

Boolean combinations of predicates have also been considered in the setting of pair encodings. Attrapadung [9,10] proposes generic transformations for conjunction and for the dual predicate, but neither for negation nor disjunction. We propose new transformations for conjunction and dual in the framework of predicate encodings and we also deal with negation and disjunction.

The main advantage of DP-ABE is the possibility of considering policies over *objective* attributes (associated to data) and policies over *subjective* attributes (associated to user credentials) at the same time. DP-ABE has been considered by Attrapadung in the pair encoding framework [9,10]. To the best of our knowledge, we are the first to provide DP-ABE in the predicate encoding and tag-based encoding frameworks.

Revocation is a desirable property for PE and ABE schemes that has also been considered by many works in the literature. Revocation allows to invalidate a user's secret key in such a way that it becomes useless, even if its associated attribute satisfies the policy associated to the ciphertext. Some attempts [32] propose *indirect* revocation that requires that the master secret owner periodically updates secret keys for non-revoked users. Other attempts achieve *direct* revocation [8,23,30,31], but either rely on strong assumptions or provide only

[2] Source code at https://github.com/miguel-ambrona/abe-relic.

selectively security. Our construction not only allows to achieve revocation in a *fully secure* framework, but it allows to add revocation to arbitrary predicate encodings.

Policy hiding is another property of PE, and ABE in particular, that has been broadly studied. In this context, policies associated to ciphertexts are not attached to them and therefore, unauthorized users will only learn the fact that their key does not satisfy the policy, but nothing else. Policy Hiding has been considered in several works [13,25]. The security of our construction improves on earlier works, thanks to the compiler from [15]. Our observation extends the expressivity of attribute-hiding predicate encryption for ZIPE proposed in [15] to support policy-hiding for boolean formulas.

In [15], the authors introduce the notion of *spatial encryption* predicate encodings. We generalize this notion and introduce a transformation that makes delegation possible for every predicate encoding.

Several works evaluate the suitability of ABE for different applications. For example, ABE has been used and benchmarked to enforce privacy of Electronic Medical Records (EMR) [3], in a system where healthcare organizations export EMRs to external storage locations. Other examples are Sieve [35] or Streamforce [18], systems that provide enforced access control for user data and stream data in untrusted clouds. In contrast to these works, we are the first to evaluate predicate encryption and ABE based on modern modular approaches such as the predicate encoding and pair encoding frameworks. The resulting schemes also satisfy a stronger security notion (full vs. selective security) compared to the previously mentioned evaluations. We focus on synthetic case studies, while other works analyze more realistic settings and integration of ABE into bigger systems. Combining our methods with these more practical case studies is a very interesting direction for future work.

1.3 Comparison with Agrawal and Chase (EUROCRYPT 2017)

Concurrently and independently, Agrawal and Chase [2] introduce a new security notion, which they call *symbolic property*, for pair encodings. They adapt previous generic frameworks [1,7] to define a compiler that takes pair encodings satisfying the symbolic property and produces fully secure predicate encryption schemes under the *q-ratio assumption*—a new assumption that is implied by some q-type assumptions proposed in [6,29]. Moreover, they introduce the notion of *tivially broken* pair encoding and show that any not trivially broken pair encoding must satisfy their symbolic property. Their definitions of symbolic property and trivially broken for pair encodings are closely related to our algebraic characterization of privacy of predicate encodings. However, the two results are incomparable: although pair encodings are more general than predicate encodings (see Sect. 5.1 for a more detailed comparison), their results rely of *q-type* assumption, whereas our results build on previous frameworks that rely on weaker assumptions (Matrix-DH or k-LIN).

2 Background

In this section, we first introduce some mathematical notation and then define *predicate encodings*, *tag-based encodings* and *pair encodings* the three primitives used in the three different modular frameworks for predicate encryption.

2.1 Notation

For finite sets S, we use $x \xleftarrow{\$} S$ to denote that x is uniformly sampled from S. We define $[n]$ as the range $\{1, \ldots, n\}$ for an arbitrary $n \in \mathbb{N}$. For a predicate $\mathsf{P} : \mathcal{X} \times \mathcal{Y} \to \{0, 1\}$, we use $(x, y) \in \mathsf{P}$ as a shorthand for $\mathsf{P}(x, y) = 1$. We use the same conventions for matrix-representations of linear maps on finite-dimensional spaces. We define vectors $\boldsymbol{v} \in \mathbb{F}^n$ as column matrices and denote the *transpose* of a matrix A by $A^\top$. We use $\mathsf{diag}(\boldsymbol{v})$ to denote the diagonal matrix with main diagonal $\boldsymbol{v}$. We denote the identity matrix of dimension n by I_n, a zero vector of length n by $\mathbf{0}_n$ and a zero matrix of m rows and n columns by $\mathbf{0}_{m,n}$. Let S be a set of indices and A be a matrix. A_S denotes the matrix formed from the set of columns of A with indices is in S. We define the *colspan* of a matrix $M \in \mathbb{F}^{m \times n}$ as the set of all possible linear combinations columns of M. That is $\underset{span}{col}\langle M \rangle = \{M\boldsymbol{v} : \boldsymbol{v} \in \mathbb{F}^n\} \subseteq \mathbb{F}^m$. We analogously define the *rowspan* of a matrix. We consider prime order bilinear groups $\mathcal{G} = (\mathbb{G}_1, \mathbb{G}_2, \mathbb{G}_t, e : \mathbb{G}_1 \times \mathbb{G}_2 \to \mathbb{G}_t)$ and use g_1, g_2, g_t to denote their respective generators. The map e satisfies $e(g_1^a, g_2^b) = g_t^{ab}$ for every $a, b \in \mathbb{N}$. A bilinear group is said to be symmetric if $\mathbb{G}_1 = \mathbb{G}_2$, otherwise it is called asymmetric. We abuse of notation and write $g^{\boldsymbol{v}}$ to denote $(g^{\boldsymbol{v}_1}, \ldots, g^{\boldsymbol{v}_n})$ for a group element g and a vector $\boldsymbol{v} \in \mathbb{Z}_p^n$.

2.2 Predicate Encodings

Predicate encodings are information-theoretic primitives that can be used for building predicate encryption schemes [37]. We adopt the definition from [15], but prefer to use matrix notation.

Definition 1 (Predicate encoding). *Let* $\mathsf{P} : \mathcal{X} \times \mathcal{Y} \to \{0, 1\}$ *be a binary predicate over finite sets* $\mathcal{X}$ *and* $\mathcal{Y}$. *Given a prime* $p \in \mathbb{N}$, *and* $s, r, w \in \mathbb{N}$, *a* (s, r, w)-*predicate encoding for* P *consists of five deterministic algorithms* $(\mathsf{sE}, \mathsf{rE}, \mathsf{kE}, \mathsf{sD}, \mathsf{rD})$: *the* sender encoding algorithm sE *maps* $x \in \mathcal{X}$ *into a matrix* $\mathsf{sE}_x \in \mathbb{Z}_p^{s \times w}$, *the* receiver encoding algorithm rE *maps* $y \in \mathcal{Y}$ *into a matrix* $\mathsf{rE}_y \in \mathbb{Z}_p^{r \times w}$, *the* key encoding algorithm kE *maps* $y \in \mathcal{Y}$ *into a vector* $\mathsf{kE}_y \in \mathbb{Z}_p^r$, *while the* sender *and* receiver decoding algorithms, *respectively* sD *and* rD, *map a pair* $(x, y) \in \mathcal{X} \times \mathcal{Y}$ *into vectors* $\mathsf{sD}_{x,y} \in \mathbb{Z}_p^s$ *and* $\mathsf{rD}_{x,y} \in \mathbb{Z}_p^r$ *respectively. We require that the following properties are satisfied:*

reconstructability: *for all* $(x, y) \in \mathsf{P}$, $\mathsf{sD}_{x,y}^\top \mathsf{sE}_x = \mathsf{rD}_{x,y}^\top \mathsf{rE}_y$ *and* $\mathsf{rD}_{x,y}^\top \mathsf{kE}_y = 1$;
α-privacy: *for all* $(x, y) \notin \mathsf{P}, \alpha \in \mathbb{Z}_p$,

$$\boldsymbol{w} \xleftarrow{\$} \mathbb{Z}_p^w;\ \textsf{return}\ (\mathsf{sE}_x\boldsymbol{w},\ \mathsf{rE}_y\boldsymbol{w} + \alpha \cdot \mathsf{kE}_y) \ \equiv\ \boldsymbol{w} \xleftarrow{\$} \mathbb{Z}_p^w;\ \textsf{return}\ (\mathsf{sE}_x\boldsymbol{w},\ \mathsf{rE}_y\boldsymbol{w})$$

where $\equiv$ *denotes equality of distributions.*

Reconstructability allows to recover α from $(x, y,\ \mathsf{sE}_x\boldsymbol{w},\ \mathsf{rE}_y\boldsymbol{w}+\alpha\cdot\mathsf{kE}_y)$ if $(x, y) \in \mathsf{P}$. *Privacy* ensures that α is perfectly hidden for such tuples if $(x, y) \notin \mathsf{P}$.

Example 1 (IBE predicate encoding). Let $\mathcal{X} = \mathcal{Y} = \mathbb{Z}_p$ and let $s = r = 1$, $w = 2$. We define the encoding functions as follows:

$$\mathsf{sE}_x = \begin{pmatrix} x & 1 \end{pmatrix} \qquad \mathsf{sD}_{x,y} = \begin{pmatrix} 1 \end{pmatrix}$$
$$\mathsf{rE}_y = \begin{pmatrix} y & 1 \end{pmatrix} \qquad \mathsf{rD}_{x,y} = \begin{pmatrix} 1 \end{pmatrix}$$
$$\mathsf{kE}_y = \begin{pmatrix} 1 \end{pmatrix}$$

The above is a predicate encoding for identity-based encryption, i.e., for the predicate $\mathsf{P}(x, y) = 1$ iff $x = y$. Note that $\begin{pmatrix} x & 1 \end{pmatrix} = \begin{pmatrix} y & 1 \end{pmatrix}$ when $x = y$, so reconstructability is satisfied. On the other hand, α-privacy follows from the fact that if $x \neq y$, $x \cdot w_1 + w_2$ and $y \cdot w_1 + w_2$ are pair-wise independent. ■

Predicate Encryption from Predicate Encodings. We try to provide some intuition on how predicate encodings are compiled to predicate encryption schemes by the compiler from [15]. We consider a simplified compiler (see explanations below). The master keys, ciphertexts and secret keys have the following form:

$$\mathsf{msk} = g_2^{\alpha} \qquad \mathsf{ct}_x = (g_1^s, g_1^{s\cdot\mathsf{sE}_x\boldsymbol{w}}, e(g_1, g_2)^{\alpha s} \cdot m)$$
$$\mathsf{mpk} = (g_1, g_1^{\boldsymbol{w}}, g_2, g_2^{\boldsymbol{w}}, e(g_1, g_2)^{\alpha}) \quad \mathsf{sk}_y = (g_2^r, g_2^{\alpha\cdot\mathsf{kE}_y + r\cdot\mathsf{rE}_y\boldsymbol{w}})$$

The encrypted message $m \in \mathbb{G}_t$ is blinded by a random factor $e(g_1, g_2)^{\alpha s}$. The so-called *reconstruction* property of predicate encodings ensures that this blinding factor can be recovered for a pair $(\mathsf{ct}_x, \mathsf{sk}_y)$ if $\mathsf{P}(x, y) = 1$. More concretely, for all pairs (x, y) such that $\mathsf{P}(x, y) = 1$, because multiplying by matrices $\mathsf{sD}_{x,y}$,$\mathsf{rD}_{x,y}$ is a linear operation, it is possible operate in the exponent and compute

$$g_1^{s\cdot\mathsf{sD}_{x,y}^{\top}\mathsf{sE}_x\boldsymbol{w}} \quad\text{and}\quad g_2^{\mathsf{rD}_{x,y}^{\top}(\alpha\cdot\mathsf{kE}_y + r\cdot\mathsf{rE}_y\boldsymbol{w})},$$

obtaining $g_1^{s\beta}$ and $g_2^{\alpha + r\beta}$ for $\beta = \mathsf{sD}_{x,y}^{\top}\mathsf{sE}_x\boldsymbol{w} = \mathsf{rD}_{x,y}^{\top}\mathsf{rE}_y\boldsymbol{w}$ (note that knowing the value of β is not necessary). Now, it is simple to recover $e(g_1, g_2)^{\alpha s}$ from $e(g_1^s, g_2^{\alpha + r\beta})$ and $e(g_1^{s\beta}, g_2^r)$. Security is ensured by the α-*privacy* property of the encoding together with decisional assumptions about dual system groups. Intuitively, the α-privacy property states that given certain values derived from the output of the encoding functions for random input, α remains information-theoretic hidden.

Note that the following is a simplification of their compiler, where we avoid DSG for simplicity. The real scheme produced by their compiler would have twice as many group elements (under SXDH) or three times as many (under DLIN).

2.3 Tag-Based Encodings

Tag-based encodings is a new primitive defined in a very recent work [22] that defines a new generic framework (using prime order groups) for modular design of predicate encryption.

Definition 2 (Tag-based encoding). *Let* $\mathsf{P} : \mathcal{X} \times \mathcal{Y} \to \{0,1\}$ *be a binary predicate over finite sets* $\mathcal{X}$ *and* $\mathcal{Y}$. *Given a prime* $p \in \mathbb{N}$, *and* $c, k, h \in \mathbb{N}$, *a* (c, k, h)*-tag-based encoding encoding for* P *consists of two deterministic algorithms* $(\mathsf{cE}, \mathsf{kE})$*: the* ciphertext encoding algorithm cE *maps* $x \in \mathcal{X}$ *into a matrix* $\mathsf{cE}_x \in \mathbb{Z}_p^{c \times h}$ *and the* key encoding algorithm kE *maps* $y \in \mathcal{Y}$ *into a matrix* $\mathsf{kE}_y \in \mathbb{Z}_p^{k \times h}$. *We require that the following properties are satisfied:*

reconstructability: *for all* $(x, y) \in \mathsf{P}$, *there exists an efficient algorithm that on input* (x, y) *computes vectors* $\boldsymbol{m}_c \in \mathbb{Z}_p^c$, $\boldsymbol{m}_k \in \mathbb{Z}_p^k$ *such that*

$$\boldsymbol{m}_c^\top \mathsf{cE}_x = \boldsymbol{m}_k^\top \mathsf{kE}_y \neq \boldsymbol{0}_h^\top$$

$\boldsymbol{h}$**-hiding:** *for all* $(x, y) \notin \mathsf{P}$,

$$\boldsymbol{h} \xleftarrow{\$} \mathbb{Z}_p^h;\ \textit{return}\ (\mathsf{cE}_x \boldsymbol{h},\ \mathsf{kE}_y \boldsymbol{h}) \quad \approx_s \quad \boldsymbol{h}, \boldsymbol{h}' \xleftarrow{\$} \mathbb{Z}_p^h;\ \textit{return}\ (\mathsf{cE}_x \boldsymbol{h},\ \mathsf{kE}_y \boldsymbol{h}')$$

where $\approx_s$ *denotes negligible statistical distance between distributions.*

The compiler proposed in [22] uses similar ideas to the one for predicate encodings. However, it does not rely on dual system groups and can be instantiated with symmetric bilinear maps. The message is blinded and ciphertexts and keys contain a set of group elements that are enough to recover the blinding factor only when the predicate is true. This compiler has the advantage that some elements of ciphertexts and keys are $\mathbb{Z}_p$ values and not group elements, which reduces the storage size.

2.4 Pair Encodings

Attrapadung [6,7] proposes an independent modular framework for predicate encryption, based on a primitive called *pair encoding*. For our purposes, it suffices to consider a more restrictive, information-theoretic, notion of pair encodings.

Definition 3 (Information-theoretic pair encoding). *Let* $\mathsf{P} : \mathcal{X} \times \mathcal{Y} \to \{0,1\}$ *be a binary predicate over finite sets* $\mathcal{X}$ *and* $\mathcal{Y}$. *Given a prime* $p \in \mathbb{N}$, *and* $c, k, l, m, n \in \mathbb{N}$, *let* $\boldsymbol{h} = (h_1, \ldots, h_n)$, $\boldsymbol{s} = (s_0, s_1, \ldots, s_l)$ *and* $\boldsymbol{r} = (\alpha, r_1, \ldots, r_m)$ *be sets of variables. An information-theoretic* (c, k, n)*-pair encoding scheme for* P *consists of three deterministic algorithms* $(\mathsf{Enc1}, \mathsf{Enc2}, \mathsf{Pair})$*: the* ciphertext encoding algorithm $\mathsf{Enc1}$ *maps a value* $x \in \mathcal{X}$ *into a list of polynomials* $\boldsymbol{c}_x \in \mathbb{Z}_p[\boldsymbol{s}, \boldsymbol{h}]^c$, *the* key encoding algorithm $\mathsf{Enc2}$ *maps a value* $y \in \mathcal{Y}$ *into a list of polynomials* $\boldsymbol{k}_y \in \mathbb{Z}_p[\boldsymbol{r}, \boldsymbol{h}]^k$ *and the* decoding algorithm Pair *maps a pair* $(x, y) \in \mathcal{X} \times \mathcal{Y}$ *into a matrix* $E_{x,y} \in \mathbb{Z}_p^{c \times k}$. *We require that the following properties are satisfied:*

polynomial constraints:
- *For every* $x \in \mathcal{X}$ *and every* $f \in \mathsf{Enc1}(x)$, $f = f(\boldsymbol{s}, \boldsymbol{h})$ *only contains monomials of the form* s_i *or* $s_i h_j$, $i \in [0, l]$, $j \in [n]$.

- *For every $y \in \mathcal{Y}$ and every $f \in \mathsf{Enc2}(y)$, $f = f(\boldsymbol{r}, \boldsymbol{h})$ only contains monomials of the form α, r_i or $r_i h_j$, $i \in [m]$, $j \in [n]$.*

reconstructability: *for all $(x, y) \in \mathsf{P}$ and all $\boldsymbol{c}_x \leftarrow \mathsf{Enc1}(x)$, $\boldsymbol{k}_y \leftarrow \mathsf{Enc2}(y)$, $E_{x,y} \leftarrow \mathsf{Pair}(x, y)$, the following polynomial equality holds $\boldsymbol{c}_x^\top E_{x,y} \boldsymbol{k}_y = \alpha s_0$.*

perfect security: *for all $(x, y) \notin \mathsf{P}$ and all $\boldsymbol{c}_x \leftarrow \mathsf{Enc1}(x)$, $\boldsymbol{k}_y \leftarrow \mathsf{Enc2}(y)$,*

$$\begin{array}{ll} \boldsymbol{h} \xleftarrow{\$} \mathbb{Z}_p^n;\ \boldsymbol{r} \xleftarrow{\$} (\mathbb{Z}_p^*)^m;\ \boldsymbol{s} \xleftarrow{\$} \mathbb{Z}_p^{l+1}; & \mathsf{return}\ (\boldsymbol{c}_x(\boldsymbol{s}, \boldsymbol{h}),\ \boldsymbol{k}_y(0, \boldsymbol{r}, \boldsymbol{h})) \quad \equiv \\ \boldsymbol{h} \xleftarrow{\$} \mathbb{Z}_p^n;\ \boldsymbol{r} \xleftarrow{\$} (\mathbb{Z}_p^*)^m;\ \boldsymbol{s} \xleftarrow{\$} \mathbb{Z}_p^{l+1}; \alpha \xleftarrow{\$} \mathbb{Z}_p; & \mathsf{return}\ (\boldsymbol{c}_x(\boldsymbol{s}, \boldsymbol{h}),\ \boldsymbol{k}_y(\alpha, \boldsymbol{r}, \boldsymbol{h})) \end{array}$$

where $\equiv$ denotes equality of distributions.

The compiler from pair encodings follows similar ideas to the other compilers. The message is blinded by a random factor and ciphertexts and keys contain all the information necessary to recover this blinded factor, only when the predicate holds. The compiler from pair encodings requires to compute a polynomial number of pairings during decryption, unlike the compilers for predicate encodings and tag-based encodings that need[3] 6 and 8 pairings respectively.

3 Predicate Encodings: Properties and Consequences

In this section, we present a purely algebraic (and independent of α) characterization of the α-privacy property. It simplifies both the analysis and the construction of predicate encodings. In particular, we use our characterization to define and prove a new optimization of predicate encodings, i.e., a transformation that makes the encoding functions smaller while preserving the predicate. Additionally, we unify the reconstructability and privacy properties and show that they are mutually exclusive and complementary, i.e., for every $(x, y) \in \mathcal{X} \times \mathcal{Y}$, one and only one of the two conditions holds. This unified treatment facilitates the construction and study of predicate encodings.

3.1 Algebraic Properties of Predicate Encodings

The following theorem captures two essential properties of predicate encodings: first, privacy admits a purely algebraic characterization (furthermore independent of α) given in terms of existence of solutions of a linear system of equations. Second, reconstructability and privacy, when viewed as properties of a single pair (x, y), negate each other; i.e. a pair (x, y) always satisfies exactly one of the two properties.

Theorem 1 (Algebraic characterization of privacy). *Let $p \in \mathbb{N}$ be a prime, let $s, r, w \in \mathbb{N}$ and let $S \in \mathbb{Z}_p^{s \times w}$, $R \in \mathbb{Z}_p^{r \times w}$, $\boldsymbol{k} \in \mathbb{Z}_p^r$. The following are equivalent:*

[3] Decryption in the framework of predicate encodings needs 4 pairings under SXDH assumption or 6 under DLIN, in the framework of tag-based encodings decryption requires 8 pairings and the assumption is DLIN.

- ***α-privacy*** *For every* $\alpha \in \mathbb{Z}_p$,

$$\boldsymbol{w} \overset{\$}{\leftarrow} \mathbb{Z}_p^w;\ \textsf{return}\ (S\boldsymbol{w},\ R\boldsymbol{w} + \alpha \cdot \boldsymbol{k}) \quad \equiv \quad \boldsymbol{w} \overset{\$}{\leftarrow} \mathbb{Z}_p^w;\ \textsf{return}\ (S\boldsymbol{w},\ R\boldsymbol{w})$$

- ***(algebraic) privacy*** *There exists* $\boldsymbol{w} \in \mathbb{Z}_p^w$ *such that* $S\boldsymbol{w} = \boldsymbol{0}_s$ *and* $R\boldsymbol{w} = \boldsymbol{k}$
- ***non-reconstructability*** *For every* $\boldsymbol{s} \in \mathbb{Z}_p^s$ *and* $\boldsymbol{r} \in \mathbb{Z}_p^r$, *either* $\boldsymbol{s}^\top S \neq \boldsymbol{r}^\top R$ *or* $\boldsymbol{r}^\top \boldsymbol{k} \neq 1$.

Proof. We first prove that α-privacy is equivalent to algebraic privacy. Note that the fact that $\forall\, \alpha \in \mathbb{Z}_p$,

$$\boldsymbol{w} \overset{\$}{\leftarrow} \mathbb{Z}_p^w;\ \textsf{return}\ (S\boldsymbol{w},\ R\boldsymbol{w} + \alpha \cdot \boldsymbol{k}) \quad \equiv \quad \boldsymbol{w} \overset{\$}{\leftarrow} \mathbb{Z}_p^w;\ \textsf{return}\ (S\boldsymbol{w},\ R\boldsymbol{w})$$

is equivalent to the existence of a bijection ρ_α such that for all $\boldsymbol{w} \in \mathbb{Z}_p^w$, $S\boldsymbol{w} = S \cdot \rho_\alpha(\boldsymbol{w}) \ \wedge\ R\boldsymbol{w} + \alpha \cdot \boldsymbol{k} = R \cdot \rho_\alpha(\boldsymbol{w})$. By linearity, it can be rewritten as

$$S(\rho_\alpha(\boldsymbol{w}) - \boldsymbol{w}) = \boldsymbol{0}_s \quad \wedge \quad \alpha \cdot \boldsymbol{k} = R(\rho_\alpha(\boldsymbol{w}) - \boldsymbol{w})$$

Now, the existence of such a bijection is equivalent to the existence of a solution for the following (parametric in α) linear system on $\boldsymbol{w}$: $S\boldsymbol{w} = \boldsymbol{0}_s \ \wedge\ R\boldsymbol{w} = \alpha \cdot \boldsymbol{k}$. To see this, note that if ρ_α is such a bijection, $\rho_\alpha(\boldsymbol{w}_0) - \boldsymbol{w}_0$ is a solution of the system for every $\boldsymbol{w}_0 \in \mathbb{Z}_p^w$. On the other hand, if $\boldsymbol{w}^*$ is a solution of the system, the bijection $\rho_\alpha(\boldsymbol{w}) = \boldsymbol{w} + \boldsymbol{w}^*$ satisfies the required identities. To conclude, note that the above system has a solution iff the following (independent of α) does:

$$S\boldsymbol{w} = \boldsymbol{0}_s \quad \wedge \quad R\boldsymbol{w} = \boldsymbol{k}$$

Next, we prove the equivalence between algebraic privacy and non-reconstructability. We use the following helping lemma from [12, Claim 2]: for every field $\mathbb{F}$, let $A \in \mathbb{F}^{m \times n}$ and $\boldsymbol{b} \in \mathbb{F}^n$ be matrices with coefficients in $\mathbb{F}$, the following two statements are equivalent:

- for every $\boldsymbol{a} \in \mathbb{F}^m$, $\boldsymbol{b}^\top \neq \boldsymbol{a}^\top A$;
- there exists $\boldsymbol{z} \in \mathbb{F}^n$ such that $\boldsymbol{z}^\top \boldsymbol{b} = 1$ and $A\boldsymbol{z} = \boldsymbol{0}_m$.

Assume that algebraic privacy does not hold, i.e., for every $\boldsymbol{w} \in \mathbb{Z}_p^w$, either $S\boldsymbol{w} \neq \boldsymbol{0}_s$ or $R\boldsymbol{w} \neq \boldsymbol{k}$. Equivalently, for every $\boldsymbol{w} \in \mathbb{Z}_p^w$

$$\begin{pmatrix} \boldsymbol{0}_s \\ \boldsymbol{k} \end{pmatrix} \neq \begin{pmatrix} -S \\ R \end{pmatrix} \boldsymbol{w}$$

which is equivalent (by our helping lemma) to the existence of $(\boldsymbol{z}_1, \boldsymbol{z}_2) \in \mathbb{Z}_p^s \times \mathbb{Z}_p^r$ such that

$$\begin{pmatrix} \boldsymbol{z}_1^\top\ \boldsymbol{z}_2^\top \end{pmatrix} \begin{pmatrix} \boldsymbol{0}_s \\ \boldsymbol{k} \end{pmatrix} = 1 \quad \wedge \quad \begin{pmatrix} \boldsymbol{z}_1^\top\ \boldsymbol{z}_2^\top \end{pmatrix} \begin{pmatrix} -S \\ R \end{pmatrix} = \boldsymbol{0}_w^\top$$

That is, there exists $\boldsymbol{z}_1 \in \mathbb{Z}_p^s$, $\boldsymbol{z}_2 \in \mathbb{Z}_p^r$ such that $\boldsymbol{z}_1^\top S = \boldsymbol{z}_2^\top R \ \wedge\ \boldsymbol{z}_2^\top \boldsymbol{k} = 1$, which is exactly reconstructability. The proof follows from the fact all the steps are equivalences. □

Our next result is a representation theorem. It is based on the notion of partial encoding; informally, a partial encoding consists of the first three algorithms of a predicate encoding; it is not attached to any specific predicate, nor is required to satisfy any property.

Definition 4 (Partial encoding). *Let $\mathcal{X}$ and $\mathcal{Y}$ be finite sets. Let $p \in \mathbb{N}$ be a prime and $s, r, w \in \mathbb{N}$. A (s, r, w)-partial encoding is given by three deterministic algorithms* $(\mathsf{sE}, \mathsf{rE}, \mathsf{kE})$*:* sE *maps $x \in \mathcal{X}$ into a matrix $\mathsf{sE}_x \in \mathbb{Z}_p^{s\times w}$, and* rE, kE *map $y \in \mathcal{Y}$ into a matrix $\mathsf{rE}_y \in \mathbb{Z}_p^{r\times w}$ and a vector $\mathsf{kE}_y \in \mathbb{Z}_p^r$ respectively.*

The representation theorem shows that there exists an embedding from partial encodings to predicate encodings, and that every predicate encoding lies the image of the embedding.

Theorem 2 (Representation theorem). *Let $\mathcal{X}$ and $\mathcal{Y}$ be finite sets. Let $p \in \mathbb{N}$ be a prime and $s, r, w \in \mathbb{N}$. Every (s, r, w)-partial encoding* $(\mathsf{sE}, \mathsf{rE}, \mathsf{kE})$ *for $\mathcal{X}$ and $\mathcal{Y}$ induces a predicate encoding* $(\mathsf{sE}, \mathsf{rE}, \mathsf{kE}, \mathsf{sD}, \mathsf{rD})$ *for the following predicate (henceforth coined implicit predicate):*

$$\mathsf{Pred}(x, y) \triangleq \forall \boldsymbol{w} \in \mathbb{Z}_p^w, \quad \mathsf{sE}_x \boldsymbol{w} \neq \boldsymbol{0}_s \ \vee \ \mathsf{rE}_y \boldsymbol{w} \neq \mathsf{kE}_y$$

Moreover, if $(\mathsf{sE}, \mathsf{rE}, \mathsf{kE}, \mathsf{sD}, \mathsf{rD})$ *is a predicate encoding for* P*, then for every* $(x, y) \in \mathcal{X} \times \mathcal{Y}$, $\mathsf{P}(x, y) \Leftrightarrow \mathsf{Pred}(x, y)$.

Example 2 (Implicit predicate of IBE predicate encoding). If we consider the following partial encoding functions corresponding to the encoding presented in Example 1:

$$\mathsf{sE}_x = \begin{pmatrix} x & 1 \end{pmatrix} \qquad \mathsf{rE}_y = \begin{pmatrix} y & 1 \end{pmatrix} \qquad \mathsf{kE}_y = \begin{pmatrix} 1 \end{pmatrix}$$

our Theorem 2 guarantees that it is a valid predicate encoding for the implicit predicate:

$$\mathsf{Pred}(x, y) = 1 \text{ iff } \forall (w_1, w_2) \in \mathbb{Z}_p^2, \ x \cdot w_1 + w_2 \neq 0 \ \vee \ y \cdot w_1 + w_2 \neq 1$$

A simple analysis shows that the above predicate is equivalent to $x = y$. ■

A consequence of Theorem 2 is that a predicate P over $\mathcal{X}$ and $\mathcal{Y}$ can be instantiated by a (s, r, w)-predicate encoding iff there exist $\mathcal{X}$-indexed and $\mathcal{Y}$-indexed matrices $S_x \in \mathbb{Z}_p^{s\times w}$ and $R_y \in \mathbb{Z}_p^{r\times w}$ and $\mathcal{Y}$-indexed vectors $\boldsymbol{k}_y \in \mathbb{Z}_p^r$ such that:

$$\mathsf{P}(x, y) = 1 \text{ iff } \begin{pmatrix} \boldsymbol{0}_s \\ \boldsymbol{k}_y \end{pmatrix} \notin \underset{span}{col} \left\langle \begin{matrix} S_x \\ R_y \end{matrix} \right\rangle$$

That is helpful to analyze the expressivity of predicate encodings of certain size.

Example 3. Let $\mathcal{X}$ and $\mathcal{Y}$ be finite sets, let $n \in \mathbb{N}$, we will characterize all the predicates that can be achieved from a $(1, 1, n)$-partial encoding, say $(\mathsf{sE}, \mathsf{rE}, \mathsf{kE})$.

Note that for every pair (x, y), sE_x and rE_y are vectors of length n, while kE_y is a single element. Say,

$$\mathsf{sE}_x = (f_1(x), \ldots, f_n(x)) \qquad \mathsf{rE}_y = (g_1(y), \ldots, g_n(y)) \qquad \mathsf{kE}_y = h(y)$$

for certain functions $f_i : \mathcal{X} \to \mathbb{Z}_p$, $g_i, h : \mathcal{Y} \to \mathbb{Z}_p$ for every $i \in [n]$. Theorem 2 guarantees that the above is a valid predicate encoding for the predicate

$$\mathsf{P}(x, y) = 1 \text{ iff } h(y) \neq 0 \wedge \big(\exists \beta \in \mathbb{Z}_p : \bigwedge_{i \in [n]} f_i(x) = \beta g_i(y)\big)$$

It can be shown that the predicate $\mathsf{P}((x_1, x_2), y) = 1$ iff $(x_1 = y) \vee (x_2 = y)$ cannot be captured by $(1, 1, n)$-predicate encodings, while on the contrary, the predicate $\mathsf{P}((x_1, x_2), y) = 1$ iff $(x_1 = y) \wedge (x_2 = y)$ could be instantiated. ■

3.2 Optimizing Predicate Encodings

In this section, we show that the efficiency of predicate encodings can be improved by pre- and post-processing. Specifically, we show that an (s, r, w)-encoding $(\mathsf{sE}, \mathsf{rE}, \mathsf{kE}, \mathsf{sD}, \mathsf{rD})$ for a predicate P can be transformed into a (s', r', w')-encoding $(\mathsf{sE}', \mathsf{rE}', \mathsf{kE}', \mathsf{sD}', \mathsf{rD}')$ for the same predicate, by applying a linear transformation to the matrices induced by $\mathsf{sE}, \mathsf{rE}, \mathsf{kE}$.

More precisely, if we define $\mathsf{sE}'_x = A\mathsf{sE}_x$, $\mathsf{rE}'_y = B\mathsf{rE}_y$ and $\mathsf{kE}'_y = B\mathsf{kE}_y$ for two matrices A and B, the privacy of the encoding will be preserved, but reconstructability may be destroyed. On the contrary, when we consider the partial encoding $\mathsf{sE}'_x = \mathsf{sE}_x C$, $\mathsf{rE}'_y = \mathsf{rE}_y C$ and $\mathsf{kE}'_y = \mathsf{kE}_y$ for a matrix C, reconstructability is automatically guaranteed, but privacy could not hold (for the same predicate). Intuitively, this occurs because *reconstructability* depends on the *rowspan* of the matrices $\mathsf{sE}_x, \mathsf{rE}_y$, while *privacy* depends on their *colspan*. Our following theorem imposes conditions on these matrices A, B and C so that the resulting predicate encoding is equivalent to the original one.

Theorem 3. *Let $\mathcal{X}$ and $\mathcal{Y}$ be finite sets. Let $p \in \mathbb{N}$ be a prime, $s, r, w, s', r', w' \in \mathbb{N}$, and let $(\mathsf{sE}, \mathsf{rE}, \mathsf{kE}, \mathsf{sD}, \mathsf{rD})$ be a (s, r, w)-predicate encoding for $\mathsf{P} : \mathcal{X} \times \mathcal{Y} \to \{0, 1\}$. Let A be a function that maps every element $x \in \mathcal{X}$ into a matrix $\mathsf{A}_x \in \mathbb{Z}_p^{s' \times s}$, B be a function that maps $y \in \mathcal{Y}$ into a matrix $\mathsf{B}_y \in \mathbb{Z}_p^{r' \times r}$ and let $\mathsf{C} \in \mathbb{Z}_p^{w \times w'}$ be a matrix. There exists a (s', r', w')-partial encoding $(\mathsf{sE}', \mathsf{rE}', \mathsf{kE}', \mathsf{sD}', \mathsf{rD}')$ for P, where*

$$\mathsf{sE}'_x = \mathsf{A}_x \mathsf{sE}_x \mathsf{C} \qquad \mathsf{rE}'_y = \mathsf{B}_y \mathsf{rE}_y \mathsf{C} \qquad \mathsf{kE}'_y = \mathsf{B}_y \mathsf{kE}_y$$

provided the following conditions hold:

- *For all $(x, y) \in \mathsf{P}$, $\mathsf{sD}_{x,y}^\top \in \underset{span}{\overset{row}{}} \langle \mathsf{A}_x \rangle$ and $\mathsf{rD}_{x,y}^\top \in \underset{span}{\overset{row}{}} \langle \mathsf{B}_y \rangle$;*
- *For all $(x, y) \notin \mathsf{P}$, there exists $\boldsymbol{w} \in \underset{span}{\overset{col}{}} \langle \mathsf{C} \rangle$ s.t. $\mathsf{sE}_x \boldsymbol{w} = \mathbf{0}_s$ and $\mathsf{rE}_y \boldsymbol{w} = \mathsf{kE}_y$.*

This transformation is useful to make predicate encodings simpler and more efficient in different manners. For instance, it can be used to make the matrices corresponding to encoding and decoding functions become sparser. That is, if we consider A and B as functions that apply matrix *Gaussian elimination*[4] to the matrices associated to sE and rE, kE, many entries from these matrices will be zero. Hence, fewer group operations will be performed during encryption and key generation, improving the performance. Moreover, the transformation can be used to reduce the size of mpk, ct_x and sk_y. If $w' < w$, the number of elements in mpk will decrease. This will also improve the performance of encryption and key generation (both depend directly on mpk). Additionally, if $s' < s$ or $r' < r$, the number of elements in ct_x and sk_y will also decrease respectively.

Note that a simplification from the right (multiplying by C) changes the structure of the encoding and may open the possibility of left-simplifications that were not available before and vice versa. Example 4 illustrates this idea. We optimize a predicate encoding that corresponds to the result of applying our negation transformation (from next section, Theorem 6) to the predicate encoding from Example 1.

Example 4. Let $\mathcal{X} = \mathcal{Y} = \mathbb{Z}_p$ and consider the $(2,3,4)$-predicate encoding $(\mathsf{sE}, \mathsf{rE}, \mathsf{kE}, \mathsf{sD}, \mathsf{rD})$ for $\mathsf{P}(x,y) = 1$ iff $x \neq y$, defined as

$$\mathsf{sE}_x = \begin{pmatrix} x & -1 & 0 & 0 \\ 1 & 0 & -1 & 0 \end{pmatrix} \qquad \mathsf{rE}_y = \begin{pmatrix} 0 & 1 & 0 & y \\ 0 & 0 & 1 & 1 \\ 0 & 0 & 0 & 1 \end{pmatrix} \qquad \mathsf{kE}_y = \begin{pmatrix} 0 \\ 0 \\ 1 \end{pmatrix}$$

$$\mathsf{sD}_{x,y}^\top = \begin{pmatrix} \frac{-1}{x-y} & \frac{x}{x-y} \end{pmatrix} \qquad \mathsf{rD}_{x,y}^\top = \begin{pmatrix} \frac{1}{x-y} & \frac{-x}{x-y} & 1 \end{pmatrix}$$

Note that for every pair $(x,y) \notin \mathsf{P}$, i.e. $x = y$, the single solution of the system $\mathsf{sE}_x \boldsymbol{w} = \mathbf{0}_2 \wedge \mathsf{rE}_y \boldsymbol{w} = \mathsf{kE}_y$ is $\boldsymbol{w}^\top = \begin{pmatrix} -1 & -y & -1 & 1 \end{pmatrix}$, thus the matrix

$$\mathsf{C} = \begin{pmatrix} -1 & 0 & -1 & 1 \\ 0 & 1 & 0 & 0 \end{pmatrix}^\top$$

satisfies the conditions of Theorem 3. Therefore, the $(2,3,2)$-partial encoding $(\mathsf{sE}', \mathsf{rE}', \mathsf{kE}')$, where

$$\mathsf{sE}'_x = \mathsf{sE}_x\mathsf{C} = \begin{pmatrix} -x & -1 \\ 0 & 0 \end{pmatrix} \quad \mathsf{rE}'_y = \mathsf{rE}_y\mathsf{C} = \begin{pmatrix} y & 1 \\ 0 & 0 \\ 1 & 0 \end{pmatrix} \quad \mathsf{kE}'_y = \mathsf{kE}_y = \begin{pmatrix} 0 \\ 0 \\ 1 \end{pmatrix}$$

induces a predicate encoding for the same predicate. The previous simplification, opens the possibility of applying again the theorem, with matrices A_x and B_y, obtaining a $(1,2,2)$-predicate encoding for $\mathsf{P}(x,y) = 1$ iff $x \neq y$. Concretely,

[4] Note that if matrices A_x, B_y or C are invertible, they always satisfy their respective requirements.

$$\mathsf{A}_x = \begin{pmatrix} -1 & 0 \end{pmatrix} \qquad \mathsf{sE}''_x = \begin{pmatrix} x & 1 \end{pmatrix} \qquad \mathsf{rE}''_y = \begin{pmatrix} y & 1 \\ 1 & 0 \end{pmatrix} \qquad \mathsf{rE}''_y = \begin{pmatrix} 0 \\ 1 \end{pmatrix}$$

$$\mathsf{B}_y = \begin{pmatrix} 1 & 0 & 0 \\ 0 & 0 & 1 \end{pmatrix} \qquad \mathsf{sD}''^{\top}_{x,y} = \begin{pmatrix} \frac{1}{x-y} \end{pmatrix} \qquad \mathsf{rD}''^{\top}_{x,y} = \begin{pmatrix} \frac{1}{x-y} & 1 \end{pmatrix}$$

■

The above simplifications can be successfully applied to actual predicate encodings proposed in [15]. In Sect. 6.2 we propose improved predicate encodings for *monotonic boolean formulas* and *arithmetic span programs.*

3.3 Combining Predicates

Using the new characterization of predicate encodings from the previous section, we define transformations to combine predicate encodings into new predicate encodings for more complex predicates. In particular, we define predicate encoding transformations for disjunction, conjunction, negation and the dual predicate. These combinations are useful to create new schemes that inherit different properties from the more basic building blocks. In Sect. 6, we propose several constructions that rely on these transformations.

Disjunction. We present a method to build a predicate encoding for the disjunction of P_1 and P_2 from predicate encodings for P_1 and P_2. Observe that the predicate encryption scheme obtained from the resulting predicate encoding is more efficient than the predicate encryption scheme obtained by compiling the predicate encodings of P_1 and P_2 separately, and then applying a generic transformation that builds predicate encryption schemes for a disjunction from predicate encryption schemes of its disjuncts.

Theorem 4 (Disjunction of predicate encodings). *For every (s_1, r_1, w_1)-predicate encoding $(\mathsf{sE}^1, \mathsf{rE}^1, \mathsf{kE}^1, \mathsf{sD}^1, \mathsf{rD}^1)$ for $\mathsf{P}_1 : \mathcal{X}_1 \times \mathcal{Y}_1 \to \{0,1\}$ and every (s_2, r_2, w_2)-predicate encoding $(\mathsf{sE}^2, \mathsf{rE}^2, \mathsf{kE}^2, \mathsf{sD}^2, \mathsf{rD}^2)$ for $\mathsf{P}_2 : \mathcal{X}_2 \times \mathcal{Y}_2 \to \{0,1\}$, there exists a $(s_1+s_2, r_1+r_2, w_1+w_2)$-predicate encoding $(\mathsf{sE}, \mathsf{rE}, \mathsf{kE}, \mathsf{sD}, \mathsf{rD})$ for the predicate $\mathsf{P} : (\mathcal{X}_1, \mathcal{X}_2) \times (\mathcal{Y}_1, \mathcal{Y}_2) \to \{0,1\}$ such that:*

$$\mathsf{P}((x_1, x_2), (y_1, y_2)) \Leftrightarrow \mathsf{P}_1(x_1, y_1) \vee \mathsf{P}_2(x_2, y_2)$$

Concretely,

$$\mathsf{sE}_{(x_1,x_2)} = \begin{pmatrix} \mathsf{sE}^1_{x_1} & \mathbf{0}_{s_1,w_2} \\ \mathbf{0}_{s_2,w_1} & \mathsf{sE}^2_{x_2} \end{pmatrix} \quad \mathsf{rE}_{(y_1,y_2)} = \begin{pmatrix} \mathsf{rE}^1_{y_1} & \mathbf{0}_{r_1,w_2} \\ \mathbf{0}_{r_2,w_1} & \mathsf{rE}^2_{y_2} \end{pmatrix} \quad \mathsf{kE}_{(y_1,y_2)} = \begin{pmatrix} \mathsf{kE}^1_{y_1} \\ \mathsf{kE}^2_{y_2} \end{pmatrix}$$

$$\begin{aligned} \mathsf{sD}^{\top}_{(x_1,x_2),(y_1,y_2)} &= \textit{if } \mathsf{P}_1(x_1,y_1) \textit{ then } \begin{pmatrix} \mathsf{sD}^{1\top}_{x_1,y_1} & \mathbf{0}^{\top}_{s_2} \end{pmatrix} \textit{ else } \begin{pmatrix} \mathbf{0}^{\top}_{s_1} & \mathsf{sD}^{2\top}_{x_2,y_2} \end{pmatrix} \\ \mathsf{rD}^{\top}_{(x_1,x_2),(y_1,y_2)} &= \textit{if } \mathsf{P}_1(x_1,y_1) \textit{ then } \begin{pmatrix} \mathsf{rD}^{1\top}_{x_1,y_1} & \mathbf{0}^{\top}_{r_2} \end{pmatrix} \textit{ else } \begin{pmatrix} \mathbf{0}^{\top}_{r_1} & \mathsf{rD}^{2\top}_{x_2,y_2} \end{pmatrix} \end{aligned}$$

Note that it is possible to obtain sharing between attributes, e.g., if $\mathcal{X}_1 = \mathcal{X}_2$ and the sender uses only the subset $\{(x,x) \mid x \in \mathcal{X}_1\}$ of $\mathcal{X}_1 \times \mathcal{X}_2$, the predicate becomes $\mathsf{P}(x, (y_1, y_2)) = 1$ iff $\mathsf{P}_1(x, y_1) \vee \mathsf{P}_2(x, y_2)$.

Conjunction. In contrast to disjunction, the naive solution that just concatenates secret keys fails. Given keys for attribute pairs (y_1, y_2) and (y_1', y_2'), it would be possible to recombine the components and obtain a key for (y_1, y_2') leading to collusion attacks. Our predicate encoding transformation deals with this problem by "tying" the two components together with additional randomness.

Theorem 5 (Conjunction of predicate encodings). *For every* (s_1, r_1, w_1)*-predicate encoding* $(\mathsf{sE}^1, \mathsf{rE}^1, \mathsf{kE}^1, \mathsf{sD}^1, \mathsf{rD}^1)$ *for* $\mathsf{P}_1 : \mathcal{X}_1 \times \mathcal{Y}_1 \to \{0,1\}$ *and every* (s_2, r_2, w_2)*-predicate encoding* $(\mathsf{sE}^2, \mathsf{rE}^2, \mathsf{kE}^2, \mathsf{sD}^2, \mathsf{rD}^2)$ *for* $\mathsf{P}_2 : \mathcal{X}_2 \times \mathcal{Y}_2 \to \{0,1\}$*, there exists a* $(s_1+s_2,\ r_1+r_2,\ w_1+w_2+1)$*-predicate encoding* $(\mathsf{sE}, \mathsf{rE}, \mathsf{kE}, \mathsf{sD}, \mathsf{rD})$ *for the predicate* $\mathsf{P} : (\mathcal{X}_1, \mathcal{X}_2) \times (\mathcal{Y}_1, \mathcal{Y}_2) \to \{0,1\}$ *such that:*

$$\mathsf{P}((x_1, x_2), (y_1, y_2)) \Leftrightarrow \mathsf{P}_1(x_1, y_1) \wedge \mathsf{P}_2(x_2, y_2)$$

Concretely,

$$\mathsf{sE}_{(x_1,x_2)} = \begin{pmatrix} \mathsf{sE}^1_{x_1} & \mathbf{0}_{s_1,w_2} & \mathbf{0}_{s_1} \\ \mathbf{0}_{s_2,w_1} & \mathsf{sE}^2_{x_2} & \mathbf{0}_{s_2} \end{pmatrix} \qquad \mathsf{sD}_{(x_1,x_2),(y_1,y_2)} = \frac{1}{2}\begin{pmatrix} \mathsf{sD}^1_{x_1,y_1} \\ \mathsf{sD}^2_{x_2,y_2} \end{pmatrix}$$

$$\mathsf{rE}_{(y_1,y_2)} = \begin{pmatrix} \mathsf{rE}^1_{y_1} & \mathbf{0}_{r_1,w_2} & \mathsf{kE}^1_{y_1} \\ \mathbf{0}_{r_2,w_1} & \mathsf{rE}^2_{y_2} & -\mathsf{kE}^2_{y_2} \end{pmatrix} \qquad \mathsf{rD}_{(x_1,x_2),(y_1,y_2)} = \frac{1}{2}\begin{pmatrix} \mathsf{rD}^1_{x_1,y_1} \\ \mathsf{rD}^2_{x_2,y_2} \end{pmatrix}$$

$$\mathsf{kE}_{(y_1,y_2)} = \begin{pmatrix} \mathsf{kE}^1_{y_1} \\ \mathsf{kE}^2_{y_2} \end{pmatrix}$$

Note that it is possible to combine Theorems 4 and 5 to create a predicate encoding for $\mathsf{P}_1 \bowtie \mathsf{P}_2$, where the placeholder $\bowtie \in \{\vee, \wedge\}$ can be part of keys or ciphertexts.

Negation. To obtain a functionally complete set of boolean predicate encoding transformers, we now define a transformation for negation. Our transformation unifies negated predicates like Non-zero Inner Product Encryption (NIPE) and Zero Inner Product Encryption (ZIPE). In Sect. 6.2 we use this transformation to build optimized predicate encodings. The technique works for predicate encodings where the negation transformation yields a predicate encoding that can be further simplified (using our method from Sect. 3.2).

Theorem 6 (Negation of predicate encodings). *For every* (s, r, w)*-predicate encoding* $(\mathsf{sE}, \mathsf{rE}, \mathsf{kE}, \mathsf{sD}, \mathsf{rD})$ *for* $\mathsf{P} : \mathcal{X} \times \mathcal{Y} \to \{0,1\}$ *there exists a* $(w, w+1, s+w+r)$*-predicate encoding* $(\mathsf{sE}', \mathsf{rE}', \mathsf{kE}', \mathsf{sD}', \mathsf{rD}')$ *for the predicate* $\mathsf{P}' : \mathcal{X} \times \mathcal{Y} \to \{0,1\}$ *such that* $\mathsf{P}'(x,y) \Leftrightarrow \neg\mathsf{P}(x,y)$*. Concretely,*

$$\mathsf{sE}'_x = \begin{pmatrix} \mathsf{sE}_x^\top & -I_w & \mathbf{0}_{w,r} \end{pmatrix} \quad \mathsf{rE}'_y = \begin{pmatrix} \mathbf{0}_{w,s} & I_w & \mathsf{rE}_y^\top \\ \mathbf{0}_s^\top & \mathbf{0}_w^\top & \mathsf{kE}_y^\top \end{pmatrix} \quad \mathsf{kE}'_y = \begin{pmatrix} \mathbf{0}_w \\ 1 \end{pmatrix}$$

$$\mathsf{sD}'_{x,y} = \boldsymbol{w}_{x,y} \qquad \mathsf{rD}'_{x,y} = \begin{pmatrix} -\boldsymbol{w}_{x,y} \\ 1 \end{pmatrix}$$

where for a pair $(x, y) \in \mathcal{X} \times \mathcal{Y}$ *such that* $\mathsf{P}(x, y) = 0$, $\boldsymbol{w}_{x,y}$ *is defined as the witness for algebraic privacy, i.e., a vector such that*

$$\mathsf{sE}_x \boldsymbol{w}_{x,y} = \mathbf{0}_s \quad \wedge \quad \mathsf{rE}_y \boldsymbol{w}_{x,y} = \mathsf{kE}_y$$

Note that such a vector always exists when $\mathsf{P}(x, y) = 0$. *Moreover,* sD *and* rD *do not need to be defined when* $\mathsf{P}'(x, y)$ *is not 1, that is, when* $\mathsf{P}(x, y)$ *is not* 0.

A similar construction has been considered in a posterior work [4] to this work. Specifically, they show how to transform a *conditional disclosure of secrets* (CDS) for f into a CDS for $\bar{f}$ (the complement of f).

Dual. In the literature, the notions of KP-ABE and CP-ABE are considered separately. In fact, many works are only valid for one of the two versions of Attribute Based Encryption. Our transformation unifies the notion of KP-ABE and CP-ABE in the framework of predicate encodings. In this context they should not be considered separately, because our transformation provides a Ciphertext-Policy predicate encoding from any Key-Policy predicate encoding and vice versa.

Theorem 7 (Dual predicate encoding). *For every* (s, r, w)*-predicate encoding* $(\mathsf{sE}, \mathsf{rE}, \mathsf{kE}, \mathsf{sD}, \mathsf{rD})$ *for* $\mathsf{P} : \mathcal{X} \times \mathcal{Y} \to \{0, 1\}$ *there exists a* $(r, s+1, w+1)$*-predicate encoding* $(\mathsf{sE}', \mathsf{rE}', \mathsf{kE}', \mathsf{sD}', \mathsf{rD}')$ *for the predicate* $\mathsf{P}' : \mathcal{Y} \times \mathcal{X} \to \{0, 1\}$ *such that* $\mathsf{P}'(y, x) \Leftrightarrow \mathsf{P}(x, y)$. *Concretely,*

$$\mathsf{sE}'_y = \begin{pmatrix} \mathsf{rE}_y & \mathsf{kE}_y \end{pmatrix} \qquad \mathsf{rE}'_x = \begin{pmatrix} \mathsf{sE}_x & \mathbf{0}_s \\ \mathbf{0}_w^\top & 1 \end{pmatrix} \qquad \mathsf{kE}'_x = \begin{pmatrix} \mathbf{0}_s \\ 1 \end{pmatrix}$$

$$\mathsf{sD}'_{y,x} = \mathsf{rD}_{x,y} \qquad \mathsf{rD}'_{y,x} = \begin{pmatrix} \mathsf{sD}_{x,y} \\ 1 \end{pmatrix}$$

4 Tag-Based Encodings

We show that our techniques for *predicate encodings* can be extended to the framework of *tag-based encodings*. In particular, we show a similar result to our Theorem 1, which establishes that $\boldsymbol{h}$-hiding and reconstructability are mutually exclusive and complementary.

Theorem 8. *Let* $p \in \mathbb{N}$ *be a prime, let* $k, c, h \in \mathbb{N}$ *and let* $C \in \mathbb{Z}_p^{c \times h}$, $K \in \mathbb{Z}_p^{k \times h}$. *The following are equivalent:*

- $\boldsymbol{h}$***-hiding:*** $\boldsymbol{h} \xleftarrow{\$} \mathbb{Z}_p^h$; $\mathsf{return}\ (C\boldsymbol{h}, K\boldsymbol{h}) \equiv \boldsymbol{h}, \boldsymbol{h}' \xleftarrow{\$} \mathbb{Z}_p^h$; $\mathsf{return}\ (C\boldsymbol{h}, K\boldsymbol{h}')$
- ***non-reconstructability*** *For every* $\boldsymbol{m}_c \in \mathbb{Z}_p^c$ *and very* $\boldsymbol{m}_k \in \mathbb{Z}_p^k$, *either* $\boldsymbol{m}_c^\top C \neq \boldsymbol{m}_k^\top K$ *or* $\boldsymbol{m}_c^\top C = \mathbf{0}_h^\top$.

where $\equiv$ *denotes equality of distributions.*

A consequence of Theorem 8 is that every valid tag-based encoding is perfectly hiding, or equivalently, there cannot exist a tag-based encoding where the two distributions from $\boldsymbol{h}$-hiding are negligibly close but not identical.

Thanks to the above theorem, it is possible to define *disjunction* and *conjunction* transformations for tag-based encodings along the lines of predicate encodings. We were not able to design a negation transformation for tag-based encodings and leave it for future work. On the other hand, the dual transformation is straightforward in this framework, as mentioned in [22], because the encoding primitives are completely symmetric.

Expressivity of Tag-Based Encodings vs Predicate Encodings. We propose a transformation that produces valid predicate encodings from valid tag-based encodings for the same predicate.

Theorem 9. *Given a* $(c, 1, h)$*-tag-based encoding* $(\mathsf{cE}, \mathsf{kE})$ *for* $\mathsf{P} : \mathcal{X} \times \mathcal{Y} \to \{0, 1\}$, *the* $(c, 1, h)$*-partial predicate encoding* $(\mathsf{sE}', \mathsf{rE}', \mathsf{kE}')$ *defined as* $\mathsf{sE}'_x = \mathsf{cE}_x$, $\mathsf{rE}'_y = \mathsf{kE}_y$, $\mathsf{kE}'_y = (1)$, *induces a predicate encoding for* P.

Note that because of the symmetry of tag-based encodings, Theorem 9 can be also applied to $(1, k, h)$-tag-based encodings. All the tag-based encodings proposed in [22] (except one) have either $c = 1$ or $k = 1$, so the above theorem can be applied to them.

5 Pair Encodings

In this section we provide an embedding that transforms every predicate encoding into an information-theoretic pair encoding. Consequently, we can see predicate encodings as a subclass of pair encodings. This opens the possibility of reusing the conjunction and dual transformation proposed by Attrapadung [9,10] for pair encodings, to create combinations of predicate encodings via our embedding. We show that this alternative method is fundamentally different from our direct conjunction and dual transformations on predicate encodings, where our combinations produce more efficient encodings.

5.1 Embedding Predicate Encodings into Pair Encodings

In this section we provide an embedding that produces a valid *information-theoretic pair encoding* from every valid predicate encoding (see Definitions 1 and 3 for predicate encodings and pair encodings respectively).

Definition 5 (Embedding to Pair Encodings). *Given a* (s, r, w)*-predicate encoding* $pe = (\mathsf{sE}, \mathsf{rE}, \mathsf{kE}, \mathsf{sD}, \mathsf{rD})$, *we define the embedding* $\mathsf{Emb}(pe) = (\mathsf{Enc1}_{pe}, \mathsf{Enc2}_{pe}, \mathsf{Pair}_{pe})$ *as follows:*

- $\mathsf{Enc1}_{pe}(x) = (c_0, \boldsymbol{c})$, *where* $c_0(s_0, \boldsymbol{h}) = s_0$, $\boldsymbol{c}(s_0, \boldsymbol{h}) = s_0 \cdot \mathsf{sE}_x \boldsymbol{h}$
- $\mathsf{Enc2}_{pe}(y) = (k_0, \boldsymbol{k})$, *where* $k_0(\alpha, r_1, \boldsymbol{h}) = r_1$, $\boldsymbol{k}(\alpha, r_1, \boldsymbol{h}) = \alpha \cdot \mathsf{kE}_y + r_1 \cdot \mathsf{rE}_y \boldsymbol{h}$

- $\mathsf{Pair}_{pe}(x,y) = \begin{pmatrix} 0 & \mathsf{rD}_{x,y}^{\top} \\ -\mathsf{sD}_{x,y} & \mathbf{0}_{s,r} \end{pmatrix}$

All variables $\boldsymbol{s} = (s_0)$ and $\boldsymbol{r} = (r_1)$ appear in the clear in the Enc1 and Enc2 polynomials respectively. This simplifies the pair encoding's information-theoretical security notion into one equivalent to the privacy of the predicate encoding (see proof of Theorem 10).

Theorem 10 (Correctness of the embedding). *If* $pe = (\mathsf{sE}, \mathsf{rE}, \mathsf{kE}, \mathsf{sD}, \mathsf{rD})$ *is a valid* (s, r, w)*-predicate encoding for* P*, then* $\mathsf{Emb}(pe)$ *is a valid information theoretic* $(s+1,\ r+1,\ w)$*-pair encoding for* P*.*

Our embedding shows that every predicate encoding can be transformed into a perfectly secure pair encoding. In fact, after applying the compiler from [1] to the embedding of a predicate encoding, we get the same predicate encryption scheme that the one provided by the compiler from [15].

We conclude that *predicate encodings* can be transformed into a very special class of *pair encodings*: encodings that allow decryption with 2 pairings and have only one element of randomness in both, ciphertexts and secret keys (what makes them very efficient).

5.2 Comparison Between Encoding Transformations

Attrapadung proposed generic transformations of pair encodings [9,10]. In particular, he proposed the conjunction and dual transformations. In this section we compare these transformations with the ones proposed in this work. For this, we compare the conjunction of two pair encodings, (embedded from predicate encodings) with the embedding of the conjunction of a (s_1, r_1, w_1)-predicate encoding $pe^1 = (\mathsf{sD}^1, \mathsf{rE}^1, \mathsf{kE}^1, \mathsf{sD}^1, \mathsf{rD}^1)$ and a (s_2, r_2, w_2)-predicate encoding $pe^2 = (\mathsf{sD}^2, \mathsf{rE}^2, \mathsf{kE}^2, \mathsf{sD}^2, \mathsf{rD}^2)$, i.e.,

$$\mathsf{Emb}(pe^1 \wedge_{pred} pe^2) \quad vs \quad \mathsf{Emb}(pe^1) \wedge_{pair} \mathsf{Emb}(pe^2)$$

where $\wedge_{pred}$ and $\wedge_{pair}$ are the conjunction of predicate encodings and pair encodings respectively. Note that $\wedge_{pred}$ corresponds to the transformation from our Theorem 5. On the other hand, for $\wedge_{pair}$ we use the conjunction proposed in [10].

$$\mathsf{Emb}(pe^1 \wedge_{pred} pe^2) = \begin{cases} \mathsf{Enc1}((x_1, x_2)) = (c_0, \boldsymbol{c}_1, \boldsymbol{c}_2) \\ \mathsf{Enc2}((y_1, y_2)) = (k_0, \boldsymbol{k}_1, \boldsymbol{k}_2) \\ \mathsf{Pair}((x_1, x_2), (y_1, y_2)) = E_{(x_1,x_2),(y_1,y_2)} \end{cases}$$

where $\boldsymbol{h} = (h_0, \boldsymbol{h}_1, \boldsymbol{h}_2)$ and

$$\begin{aligned} c_0(s_0, \boldsymbol{h}) &= s_0 & k_0(\alpha, r_1, \boldsymbol{h}) &= r_1 \\ \boldsymbol{c}_1(s_0, \boldsymbol{h}) &= s_0 \cdot \mathsf{sE}^1_{x_1} \boldsymbol{h}_1 & \boldsymbol{k}_1(\alpha, r_1, \boldsymbol{h}) &= (\alpha + h_0) \cdot \mathsf{kE}^1_{y_1} + r_1 \cdot \mathsf{rE}^1_{y_1} \boldsymbol{h}_1 \\ \boldsymbol{c}_2(s_0, \boldsymbol{h}) &= s_0 \cdot \mathsf{sE}^2_{x_2} \boldsymbol{h}_2 & \boldsymbol{k}_2(\alpha, r_1, \boldsymbol{h}) &= (\alpha - h_0) \cdot \mathsf{kE}^2_{y_2} + r_1 \cdot \mathsf{rE}^2_{y_2} \boldsymbol{h}_2 \end{aligned}$$

$$E_{(x_1,x_2),(y_1,y_2)} = \frac{1}{2}\begin{pmatrix} 0 & \mathsf{rD}^{1\top}_{x_1,y_1} & \mathsf{rD}^{2\top}_{x_2,y_2} \\ -\mathsf{sD}^1_{x_1,y_1} & \mathbf{0}_{s_1,r_1} & \mathbf{0}_{s_1,r_2} \\ -\mathsf{sD}^2_{x_2,y_2} & \mathbf{0}_{s_2,r_1} & \mathbf{0}_{s_2,r_2} \end{pmatrix}$$

$$\mathsf{Emb}(pe^1) \wedge_{pair} \mathsf{Emb}(pe^2) = \begin{cases} \mathsf{Enc1}((x_1,x_2)) = (c_0, \boldsymbol{c}_1, \boldsymbol{c}_2) \\ \mathsf{Enc2}((y_1,y_2)) = (k_0, \boldsymbol{k}_1, k_2, \boldsymbol{k}_3) \\ \mathsf{Pair}((x_1,x_2),(y_1,y_2)) = E_{(x_1,x_2),(y_1,y_2)} \end{cases}$$

where $\boldsymbol{h} = (\boldsymbol{h}_1, \boldsymbol{h}_2)$ and

$$\begin{aligned} c_0(s_0,\boldsymbol{h}) &= s_0 \\ \boldsymbol{c}_1(s_0,\boldsymbol{h}) &= s_0 \cdot \mathsf{sE}^1_{x_1}\boldsymbol{h}_1 \\ \boldsymbol{c}_2(s_0,\boldsymbol{h}) &= s_0 \cdot \mathsf{sE}^2_{x_2}\boldsymbol{h}_2 \end{aligned} \qquad \begin{aligned} k_0(\alpha,(r_1,r_2,r_3),\boldsymbol{h}) &= r_1 \\ \boldsymbol{k}_1(\alpha,(r_1,r_2,r_3),\boldsymbol{h}) &= r_3 \cdot \mathsf{kE}^1_{y_1} + r_1 \cdot \mathsf{rE}^1_{y_1}\boldsymbol{h}_1 \\ k_2(\alpha,(r_1,r_2,r_3),\boldsymbol{h}) &= r_2 \\ \boldsymbol{k}_3(\alpha,(r_1,r_2,r_3),\boldsymbol{h}) &= (\alpha - r_3) \cdot \mathsf{kE}^2_{y_2} + r_2 \cdot \mathsf{rE}^2_{y_2}\boldsymbol{h}_2 \end{aligned}$$

$$E_{(x_1,x_2),(y_1,y_2)} = \begin{pmatrix} 0 & \mathsf{rD}^{1\top}_{x_1,y_1} & 0 & \mathsf{rD}^{2\top}_{x_2,y_2} \\ -\mathsf{sD}^1_{x_1,y_1} & \mathbf{0}_{s_1,r_1} & \mathbf{0}_{s_1} & \mathbf{0}_{s_1,r_2} \\ \mathbf{0}_{s_2} & \mathbf{0}_{s_2,r_1} & -\mathsf{sD}^2_{x_2,y_2} & \mathbf{0}_{s_2,r_2} \end{pmatrix}$$

The resulting pair encodings are different. The first one (result of our conjunction) does not introduce new random variables and does not increase the number of pairings for decryption. On the other hand, the second conjunction adds new random variables to key generation and increases the number of pairings needed during decryption. This overhead will be amplified if nested conjunctions are used. We include a detailed comparison between the dual transformations in the full version of this paper.

6 Constructions

We provide new instances of predicate encodings to achieve predicate encryption schemes with new properties or better performance.

6.1 Combining Predicates

Dual-Policy ABE. Dual-Policy Attribute Based Encryption [9,10] has already been considered in the *pair encodings* framework. It combines KP-ABE and CP-ABE into a single construction that simultaneously allows two access control mechanisms. The main advantage is the possibility of considering policies over *objective* attributes (associated to data) and policies over *subjective* attributes (associated to user credentials) at the same time.

Our combinations of predicate encodings allow us to create predicate encryption constructions for Dual-Policy ABE in the framework of pair encodings and tag-based encodings. In particular, given an arbitrary predicate encoding for $\mathsf{P} : \mathcal{X} \times \mathcal{Y} \to \{0,1\}$, applying Theorems 7 and 5 we get an encoding for DP-ABE, i.e., for the predicate $\mathsf{P}^\star : (\mathcal{X} \times \mathcal{Y}) \times (\mathcal{Y} \times \mathcal{X}) \to \{0,1\}$ defined as

$$\mathsf{P}^\star((x,y),(y',x')) = 1 \text{ iff } \mathsf{P}(x,y) \wedge \mathsf{P}(y',x')$$

Revocation. Another application of our combinations is predicate encryption with revocation, by combining a *boolean formula predicate encoding* with a *broadcast encryption predicate encoding*. The former is used to encode the actual policy of the scheme, while the latter takes care of revocation.

Broadcast encryption has been considered in the literature to approach revocation [19,23, 30]. In broadcast encryption, a broadcasting authority encrypts a message in such a way that only authorized users will be able to decrypt it. This can be expressed with the predicate $\mathsf{P}(\boldsymbol{x}, i) = 1$ if and only if $\boldsymbol{x}_i = 1$, where $\boldsymbol{x} \in \mathcal{X} = \{0,1\}^n$ and $i \in \mathcal{Y} = [n]$. A drawback is that the number of users in the system, n, is polynomial size. Figure 1 shows the performance of predicate encryption built from a predicate encoding that combines boolean formulas with broadcast encryption. The system supports thousands of users in reasonable time.

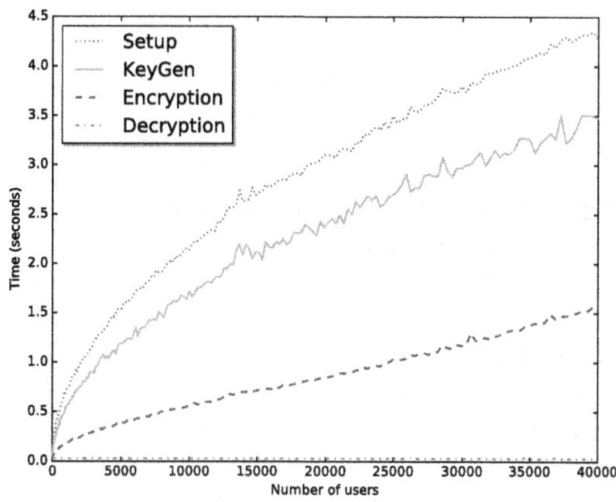

Fig. 1. Scalability of the PE for revocation

6.2 Improved Predicate Encodings

In this section we propose new predicate encodings that are more efficient than some of the encodings proposed previously in [15]. Our encodings are built by applying Theorem 6 to obtain negated encodings and observing that, in some cases, Theorem 3 can be applied to simplify the negated version into a more efficient encoding than the original one. The predicate associated to this new encoding is negated, but if inputs are also negated, the predicate will be equivalent. Figure 2 illustrates this idea. On the left, there is a boolean formula CP-ABE for 4 attributes $\{a, b, c, d\}$. On the right side, secret keys and policies are modified so that the negated version is equivalent. The attribute universe is formed by the *negated attributes*, secret keys are formed by all *negated attributes* do not appear in the original key as normal attributes, policies are negated and expressed in NNF (Negation Normal Form).

Boolean Formulas. In [15], the authors propose two predicate encoding (KP and CP versions) for monotonic boolean formulas. The predicate they consider is a particular case of a Linear Secret Sharing scheme [24]. Let $\mathcal{X} = \{0,1\}^n, \mathcal{Y} = \mathbb{Z}_p^{n \times k}$ for some $n, k \in \mathbb{N}$,

$$\mathsf{P}(\boldsymbol{x}, M) = 1 \text{ iff } \begin{pmatrix} 1 & 0 & \overset{k-1}{\cdots} & 0 \end{pmatrix} \in \underset{span}{\overset{row}{}} \langle M_{\boldsymbol{x}} \rangle$$

$$\mathsf{P}(\boldsymbol{x}, M) = 1 \text{ iff } \left(1\ 0\ \overset{k-1}{\cdots}\ 0\right) \in \underset{span}{row} \langle M_{\boldsymbol{x}} \rangle$$

P	$\bar{\mathsf{P}}$
attributes $= \{a, b, c, d\}$	attributes $= \{\bar{a}, \bar{b}, \bar{c}, \bar{d}\}$
$x = (a \wedge c) \vee d$	$x = (\bar{a} \vee \bar{c}) \wedge \bar{d}$
$y = \{a, c\}$	$y = \{\bar{b}, \bar{d}\}$
$\mathsf{P}(x, y) = 1$ iff $x(y)$	$\bar{\mathsf{P}}(x, y) = 1$ iff $\neg x(y)$

Fig. 2. Equivalent encodings of a policy using P (CP-ABE) on the left and $\bar{\mathsf{P}}$ (negated CP-ABE) on the right.

where $M_{\boldsymbol{x}}$ denotes the matrix M filtered by $\boldsymbol{x}$, i.e., $M_{\boldsymbol{x}}$ includes the i-th row of M iff $\boldsymbol{x}_i = 1$.

It has been shown [28] that for every[5] monotonic boolean formula f with attributes from $\mathcal{X}$ there exists a matrix $M \in \mathcal{Y}$ such that for every $\boldsymbol{x} \in \mathcal{X}$, $f(\boldsymbol{x}) \Leftrightarrow \mathsf{P}(\boldsymbol{x}, M)$. The key-policy predicate encoding from [15] is the following,

$$\mathsf{sE}_{\boldsymbol{x}} = \left(\mathsf{diag}(\boldsymbol{x}) \quad \mathbf{0}_{n,k-1}\right) \quad \mathsf{rE}_M = \left(\ I_n \quad M_{\{2,\dots,k\}}\right) \quad \mathsf{kE}_M = \left(M_{\{1\}}\right)$$

where $M_{\{1\}}$ denotes the first column of matrix M, $M_{\{2,\dots,k\}}$ represents the rest of the matrix. We do not include explicit decryption functions sD and rD, but they can be computed efficiently by *Gaussian elimination.*

In the above encoding, the number of elements in secret keys and ciphertexts is always maximal, it equals the number of (possibly duplicated) attributes, even for small policies. Furthermore, the maximum number of *and-gates* in a policy must be fixed a priori (because it is related the number of columns in the matrix).

We propose the following improved predicate encoding for (negated) key-policy monotonic boolean formulas, which is an equivalent predicate if instantiated with negated inputs. Let $\mathcal{X} = \{0,1\}^n$ and $\mathcal{Y} = \mathbb{Z}_p^{n \times k}$,

$$\mathsf{sE}_{\boldsymbol{x}} = I_n - \mathsf{diag}(\boldsymbol{x}) \qquad \mathsf{rE}_M = M^\top \qquad \mathsf{kE}_M = \left(1\ 0\ \overset{k-1}{\cdots}\ 0\right)^\top$$

In our encoding, the number of columns has been reduced up to half[6]. Furthermore, the size of secret keys is proportional to the complexity of policies. In particular, it is equal to the number of *and-gates* in the policy (or equivalently, the number of *or-gates* in the non-negated version). Note that our improvement also works in the ciphertext-policy case.

In Fig. 3 we present a comparison between our improved encoding for *key-policy monotonic boolean formulas* and the original one. To this end, we generate random boolean formulas for different sizes, starting from a random set of leaf

[5] Where every attribute appears at most once and the number of *and-gates* is lower than k (one could overcome the one-use restriction by considering duplicated attributes).

[6] Being half when the bound on the number of *and-gates* is maximal.

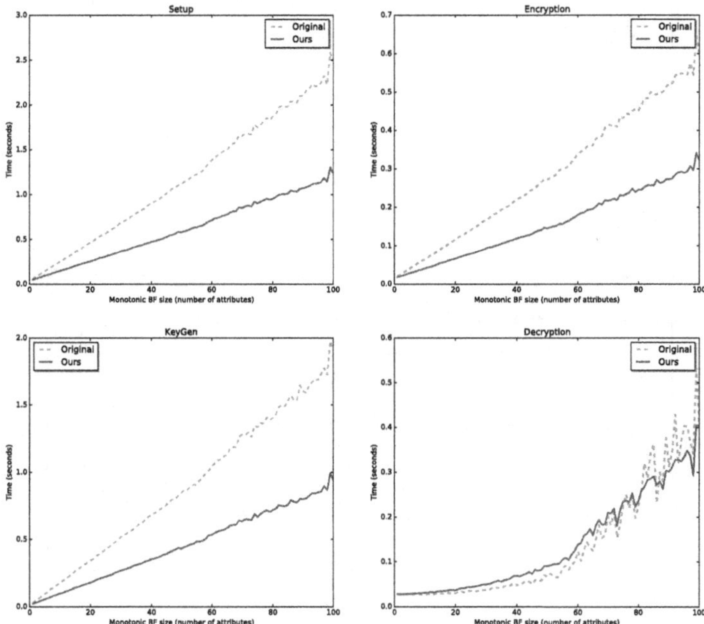

Fig. 3. Improved predicate encoding for boolean formulas vs original encoding

nodes and combining them with boolean operators $\vee$ and $\wedge$. Our tables report on the average time for each algorithm. Our encoding needs 50% less time than the original algorithms for setup, encryption and key generation. For decryption the performance is similar. All the analyzed schemes were instantiated with the same compiler, therefore all achieve the same level of security (under SXDH assumption). In terms of secret key size, our encoding is smaller in general (in the worst case, when all the gates in the policy are *or-gates*, key sizes are equal).

Arithmetic Span Programs. Chen et al. proposed in [15] a predicate encoding for *Arithmetic Span Programs (ASP)*. That is, an encoding for the predicate P defined as follows. Let $\mathcal{X} = \mathbb{Z}_p^n$, $\mathcal{Y} = \mathbb{Z}_p^{n \times k} \times \mathbb{Z}_p^{n \times k}$, for some $n, k \in \mathbb{N}$; for every $\boldsymbol{x} \in \mathcal{X}$ and every $(Y, Z) \in \mathcal{Y}$,

$$\mathsf{P}(\boldsymbol{x}, (Y, Z)) = 1 \text{ iff } \begin{pmatrix} 1 \ 0 \ \overset{k-1}{\cdots} \ 0 \end{pmatrix} \in \underset{span}{\overset{row}{}} \langle \mathsf{diag}(\boldsymbol{x}) Y + Z \rangle$$

In [21], Ishai and Wee show how to relate *Arithmetic Span Programs* computations of polynomial functions over a finite field $\mathbb{F}$, i.e., functions $f : \mathbb{F}^n \rightarrow \mathbb{F}$ that only use addition and multiplication over the field. Therefore, the above predicate can be seen as $f(\boldsymbol{x}) = 0$, where f is the polynomial function induced by (Y, Z). Let $\mathcal{X} = \mathbb{Z}_p^n$, $\mathcal{Y} = \mathbb{Z}_p^{n \times k} \times \mathbb{Z}_p^{n \times k}$, the original predicate encoding for arithmetic span programs proposed in [15] is the following:

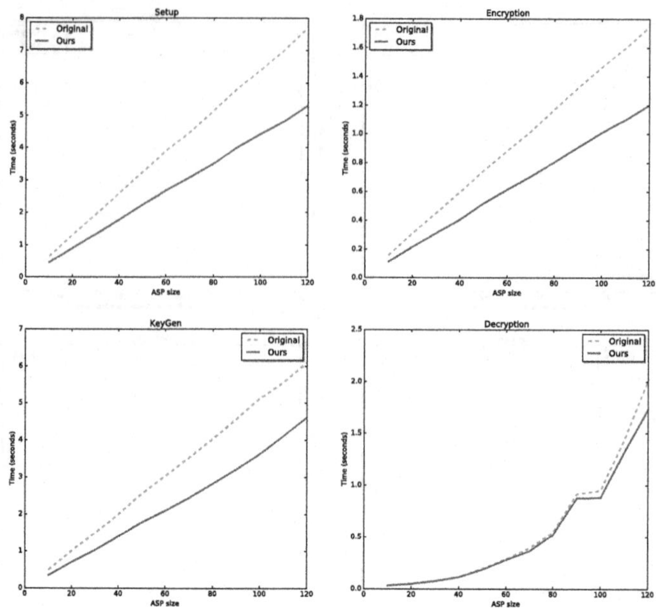

Fig. 4. Improved predicate encoding for ASP vs original encoding

$$\mathsf{sE}_x = \begin{pmatrix} \mathsf{diag}(\boldsymbol{x}) & I_n & \mathbf{0}_{n,k-1} \end{pmatrix} \quad \mathsf{rE}_{(Y,Z)} = \begin{pmatrix} I_n & \mathbf{0}_{n,n} & Y_{\{2,\dots,l\}} \\ \mathbf{0}_{n,n} & I_n & Z_{\{2,\dots,l\}} \end{pmatrix} \quad \mathsf{kE}_{(Y,Z)} = \begin{pmatrix} Y_{\{1\}} \\ Z_{\{1\}} \end{pmatrix}$$

We present a more efficient encoding for (negated[7]) arithmetic span programs:

$$\mathsf{sE}_x = \begin{pmatrix} \mathsf{diag}(\boldsymbol{x}) & -I_n \end{pmatrix} \quad \mathsf{rE}_{(Y,Z)} = \begin{pmatrix} Z^\top & Y^\top \end{pmatrix} \quad \mathsf{kE}_{(Y,Z)} = \begin{pmatrix} 1 \ 0 \overset{k-1}{\cdots} 0 \end{pmatrix}^\top$$

Figure 4 shows the performance of our new encoding for KP-ABE for Arithmetic Span Programs compared to the original encoding from [15]. As we expected, our encoding needs 66% of the time required for the original encoding for setup, encryption and key generation. Additionally, secret key size is halved with our encoding.

6.3 Extra Features

In this section we consider new theoretical results that can be proved thanks to our algebraic characterization of α-privacy and can be used to produce new predicate encodings enhanced with extra properties.

[7] In [21] there is a modification of their algorithm that produces matrices (Y, Z) such that the predicate associated is $f(\boldsymbol{x}) \neq 0$ (the double negation will cancel out).

Attribute-Hiding for Boolean Formulas. Chen et al. proposed an extension of the compiler in [15] to build weakly attribute-hiding predicate encryption schemes [13,25]. In a weakly attribute-hiding scheme, the ciphertext attribute x remains secret for unauthorized users, that only learn the fact that their secret keys are not valid. This additional compiler needs to be instantiated with *predicate encodings* satisfying additional properties. The following is a definition from [15].

Definition 6 (Attribute-Hiding Encodings). *A* (s,r,w)*-predicate encoding,* $(\mathsf{sE},\mathsf{rE},\mathsf{kE},\mathsf{sD},\mathsf{rD})$ *for* $\mathsf{P} : \mathcal{X} \times \mathcal{Y} \to \{0,1\}$ *is* attribute-hiding *if it verifies the additional requirements:*

x-oblivious reconstruction: $\mathsf{sD}_{x,y}$ *and* $\mathsf{rD}_{x,y}$ *are independent of* x.
attribute-hiding: *for all* $(x,y) \notin \mathsf{P}$,

$$\boldsymbol{w} \xleftarrow{\$} \mathbb{Z}_p^w;\ \textsf{return}\ (\mathsf{sE}_x\boldsymbol{w},\ \mathsf{rE}_y\boldsymbol{w}) \quad \equiv \quad \boldsymbol{s} \xleftarrow{\$} \mathbb{Z}_p^s; \boldsymbol{r} \xleftarrow{\$} \mathbb{Z}_p^r;\ \textsf{return}\ (\boldsymbol{s},\ \boldsymbol{r})$$

where $\equiv$ *denotes equality of distributions.*

The following theorem relates the second property with our alternative definition of predicate encodings:

Theorem 11 (Algebraic characterization of attribute-hiding). *Let* $p \in \mathbb{N}$ *be a prime, let* $s,r,w \in \mathbb{N}$ *and let* $S \in \mathbb{Z}_p^{s\times w}$, $R \in \mathbb{Z}_p^{r\times w}$, $\boldsymbol{k} \in \mathbb{Z}_p^r$. *The following are equivalent:*

- $\boldsymbol{w} \xleftarrow{\$} \mathbb{Z}_p^w;\ \textsf{return}\ (S\boldsymbol{w},\ R\boldsymbol{w}) \ \equiv\ \boldsymbol{s} \xleftarrow{\$} \mathbb{Z}_p^s;\ \boldsymbol{r} \xleftarrow{\$} \mathbb{Z}_p^r;\ \textsf{return}\ (\boldsymbol{s},\ \boldsymbol{r})$
- $\operatorname{rank}\begin{pmatrix} S \\ R \end{pmatrix} = s + r$

Note that for every (s,r,w)-predicate encoding $(\mathsf{sE},\mathsf{rE},\mathsf{kE},\mathsf{sD},\mathsf{rD})$ that is attribute-hiding, there exists an equivalent $(s,1,w)$-predicate encoding. This is because rD is independent from x and thus, we can apply our optimization Theorem 3 with matrices $\mathsf{B}_y = \mathsf{rD}_{x,y}^\top \in \mathbb{Z}_p^{1\times w}$, $\mathsf{A}_x = I_s$, $\mathsf{C} = I_w$. Therefore, the class of predicates that can be built from attribute-hiding encodings is included in the class of predicates achieved from $(s,1,w)$-predicate encodings.

Further, note that our *disjunction* and *conjunction* combinations for predicate encodings (Theorems 4 and 5 respectively) preserve the notion of attribute-hiding[8]. Exploiting this fact, we propose a Policy-Hiding ABE scheme for non-monotonic boolean formulas expressed in DNF (Disjunctive Normal Form). The inner product can be used to encode conjunctions [25]. More concretely, let $\boldsymbol{y} \in \{0,1\}^n \subseteq \mathbb{Z}_p^n$. We establish that the i-th attribute a_i appears in a secret key for $\boldsymbol{y}$ iff $\boldsymbol{y}_i = 1$. Let $S, \bar{S} \subseteq \{a_i\}_{i=1}^n$ be sets such that $S \cap \bar{S} = \emptyset$,[9]

$$\bigwedge_{a\in S} a \ \wedge \ \bigwedge_{a\in \bar{S}} \bar{a} \ \Leftrightarrow^9\ \boldsymbol{x}^\top \boldsymbol{y} = |S| \qquad \text{where } \forall i \in [n],\ \boldsymbol{x}_i = \begin{cases} 1 & \text{if } a_i \in S \\ -1 & \text{if } a_i \in \bar{S} \\ 0 & \text{otherwise} \end{cases}$$

[8] Conjunction also preserves x-oblivious reconstruction, while disjunction does not.
[9] This equivalence holds when $|S| < p$, but in practice p is a large prime.

Note that the ZIPE predicate encoding from [15, Appendix A.1] can be modified into an attribute-hiding encoding for the predicate $\mathsf{P}((\boldsymbol{x},\gamma),\boldsymbol{y}) = 1$ iff $\boldsymbol{x}^\top \boldsymbol{y} = \gamma$.

Let $\mathcal{U} = \{a,b,c\}$ be the set of attributes. We consider the predicate encoding for monotonic boolean formulas from [15]. Let $\mathcal{X} = \{0,1\}^3, \mathcal{Y} = \mathbb{Z}_p^{3\times 2}$,

$$\mathsf{sE}_{\boldsymbol{x}} = \begin{pmatrix} \mathsf{diag}(\boldsymbol{x}) & \mathbf{0}_{3,2} \end{pmatrix} \qquad \mathsf{rE}_M = \begin{pmatrix} I_3 & M_{\{2\}} \end{pmatrix} \qquad \mathsf{kE}_M = \begin{pmatrix} M_{\{1\}} \end{pmatrix}$$

The following is the encoding of a key for the formula $(a \vee c) \wedge b$, enhanced for delegation according to Theorem 12 (with $k = 1$),

$$\mathsf{rE}_M = \left(\begin{array}{cccc|c} 1&0&0&1&0\\ 0&1&0&1&0\\ 0&0&1&1&0\\ \hline 0&0&0&0&1 \end{array}\right) \qquad \mathsf{kE}_M = \left(\begin{array}{c} 1\\0\\1\\ \hline 0 \end{array}\right)$$

Let's assume we want to weaken this key to one for the formula $a \wedge b \wedge c$. Note that in this case we want to make an update of the matrix M:

$$M = \begin{pmatrix} 1&1\\0&1\\1&1 \end{pmatrix} \text{ encodes } (a \vee c) \wedge b \qquad M' = \begin{pmatrix} 1&1&1\\0&1&1\\1&1&0 \end{pmatrix} \text{ encodes } a \wedge b \wedge c$$

It can be done by multiplying rE_M from the left by A

$$\mathsf{rE}'_M = \underbrace{\begin{pmatrix} 1&0&0&1\\0&1&0&1\\0&0&1&0\\0&0&0&0 \end{pmatrix}}_{A} \cdot \underbrace{\begin{pmatrix} 1&0&0&1&0\\0&1&0&1&0\\0&0&1&1&0\\0&0&0&0&1 \end{pmatrix}}_{\mathsf{rE}_M} = \begin{pmatrix} 1&0&0&1&1\\0&1&0&1&1\\0&0&1&1&0\\0&0&0&0&0 \end{pmatrix} \qquad \mathsf{kE}'_M = A \cdot \mathsf{kE}_M = \begin{pmatrix} 1\\0\\1\\0 \end{pmatrix}$$

Fig. 5. Example of delegation of keys for monotonic boolean formulas. Since A is a linear function, it can be computed in the exponent from the given key.

Therefore, with a disjunction of k predicate encodings like the former we can encode boolean formulas that have at most k disjuncts. Note that the resulting encoding is *attribute-hiding* but it is not *x-oblivious*. However, without the knowledge of the policy x, one can guess for the disjunct his secret key satisfies (if any). In this way, a valid key will be enough to decrypt after at most k decryption tries (one for every disjunct).

Delegation. Delegation of keys is a desirable property for every predicate encryption scheme. Roughly, it allows the owner of a secret key to weaken his key creating a new one that is less powerful than the original one. This property can be used to achieve *forward secrecy* (see [14] for an application to ABE that supports delegation), where past sessions are protected from the compromise of future secret keys. More formally, we say that a predicate $\mathsf{P} : \mathcal{X} \times \mathcal{Y} \to \{0,1\}$ supports delegation if there is a partial ordering $\preceq$ on $\mathcal{Y}$ such that for every $x \in \mathcal{X}$, if $\mathsf{P}(x,y) = 1$ and $(y \preceq y')$, then $\mathsf{P}(x,y') = 1$.

Delegation has been considered in [15] as the property of some predicate encodings. We propose a generic method to convert any predicate encoding into one supporting delegation.

Theorem 12 (Delegation). *For every* (s, r, w)*-predicate encoding* $(\mathsf{sE}, \mathsf{rE}, \mathsf{kE}, \mathsf{sD}, \mathsf{rD})$ *for* $\mathsf{P} : \mathcal{X} \times \mathcal{Y} \to \{0,1\}$*, for every* $k \in \mathbb{N}$*,* $(\mathsf{sE}', \mathsf{rE}', \mathsf{kE}', \mathsf{sD}', \mathsf{rD}')$ *defined below is a valid* $(s, r+k, w+k)$*-predicate encoding for* P.

$$\mathsf{sE}'_x = \begin{pmatrix} \mathsf{sE}_x & \mathbf{0}_{s,k} \end{pmatrix} \qquad \mathsf{rE}'_y = \begin{pmatrix} \mathsf{rE}_y & \mathbf{0}_{r,k} \\ \mathbf{0}_{k,w} & I_k \end{pmatrix} \qquad \mathsf{kE}'_y = \begin{pmatrix} \mathsf{kE}_y \\ \mathbf{0}_k \end{pmatrix}$$

$$\mathsf{sD}'_{x,y} = \mathsf{sD}_{x,y} \qquad \mathsf{rD}'_{x,y} = \begin{pmatrix} \mathsf{rD}_{x,y} \\ \mathbf{0}_k \end{pmatrix}$$

The additional set of not-null rows in rE'_y can be used to weaken the linear span of rE_y, what directly modifies the predicate. In particular, this method works really well for monotonic boolean formulas (see Fig. 5 for an example).

Acknowledgements. The work presented here was supported by projects S2013/ICE-2731 N-GREENS Software-CM, ONR Grants N000141210914 and N000141512750.

A Proofs from Main Body

Proof (Of Theorem 2). The proof follows from Theorem 1 and the observation that reconstructability of predicate encodings is equivalent to Pred, while privacy of predicate encodings is equivalent to $\neg\,\mathsf{Pred}$. □

Proof (Of Theorem 3). To see correctness of the new encoding, note that for all $(x, y) \in \mathsf{P}$, since

$$\mathsf{sD}_{x,y}^{\top} \in \underset{span}{\overset{row}{}} \langle \mathsf{A}_x \rangle \;\wedge\; \mathsf{rD}_{x,y}^{\top} \in \underset{span}{\overset{row}{}} \langle \mathsf{B}_y \rangle$$

there exist $\mathsf{sD}'^{\top}_{x,y}$ and $\mathsf{rD}'^{\top}_{x,y}$ such that

$$\mathsf{sD}_{x,y}^{\top} = \mathsf{sD}'^{\top}_{x,y} \mathsf{A}_x \;\wedge\; \mathsf{rD}_{x,y}^{\top} = \mathsf{rD}'^{\top}_{x,y} \mathsf{B}_y$$

Therefore,

$$\begin{aligned} &\mathsf{sD}'^{\top}_{x,y}(\mathsf{A}_x \mathsf{sE}_x \mathsf{C}) = (\mathsf{sD}_{x,y}^{\top} \mathsf{sE}_x)\mathsf{C} = (\mathsf{rD}_{x,y}^{\top} \mathsf{rE}_y)\mathsf{C} = \mathsf{rD}'^{\top}_{x,y}(\mathsf{B}_y \mathsf{rE}_y \mathsf{C}) \\ &\mathsf{rD}'^{\top}_{x,y}(\mathsf{B}_y \mathsf{kE}_y) = \mathsf{rD}_{x,y}^{\top} \mathsf{kE}_y = 1 \end{aligned}$$

To see privacy, note that for every $(x, y) \notin \mathsf{P}$, there exists $\boldsymbol{w} \in \underset{span}{\overset{col}{}} \langle \mathsf{C} \rangle$ such that $\mathsf{sE}_x \boldsymbol{w} = \mathbf{0}_s \wedge \mathsf{rE}_y \boldsymbol{w} = \mathsf{kE}_y$. Therefore, there also exists $\boldsymbol{w}' \in \mathbb{Z}_p^{w'}$ such that $\boldsymbol{w} = \mathsf{C}\boldsymbol{w}'$. Note that,

$$\begin{aligned} \mathsf{sE}'_x \boldsymbol{w}' &= (\mathsf{A}_x \mathsf{sE}_x \mathsf{C})\boldsymbol{w}' = \mathsf{A}_x \mathsf{sE}_x \boldsymbol{w} = \mathsf{A}_x \mathbf{0}_s = \mathbf{0}_{s'} \\ \mathsf{rE}'_y \boldsymbol{w}' &= (\mathsf{B}_y \mathsf{rE}_y \mathsf{C})\boldsymbol{w}' = \mathsf{B}_y \mathsf{rE}_y \boldsymbol{w} = \mathsf{B}_y \mathsf{kE}_y = \mathsf{kE}'_y \end{aligned}$$

so algebraic privacy is satisfied. □

Proof (Of Theorem 4). Reconstructability can be seen by a simple check based on the reconstructability of the original encodings.
To see privacy, note that $\mathsf{P}_1(x_1, y_1) \vee \mathsf{P}_2(x_2, y_2) = 0$ implies $\mathsf{P}_1(x_1, y_1) = 0$ and $\mathsf{P}_2(x_2, y_2) = 0$ implies. Let $\boldsymbol{w}_1$ and $\boldsymbol{w}_2$ be witnesses of privacy of predicate encodings 1 and 2 respectively. It is easy to check that $\boldsymbol{w}^\top = \begin{pmatrix} \boldsymbol{w}_1^\top & \boldsymbol{w}_2^\top \end{pmatrix}$ is a witness of privacy of the transformed encoding. □

Proof (Of Theorem 5). A simple check shows reconstructability. To see privacy, $\mathsf{P}_1(x_1, y_1) \wedge \mathsf{P}_2(x_2, y_2) = 0$ implies $\mathsf{P}_1(x_1, y_1) = 0$ or $\mathsf{P}_2(x_2, y_2) = 0$. If the first holds, let $\boldsymbol{w}_1$ be a witness of privacy of the first encoding. Then, $\boldsymbol{w}^\top = \begin{pmatrix} 2\boldsymbol{w}_1^\top & \mathbf{0}_{w_2}^\top & -1 \end{pmatrix}$ is a witness of the algebraic privacy of the transformed encoding. If the second holds, let $\boldsymbol{w}_2$ be a witness of privacy of the second encoding. A valid witness now is $\boldsymbol{w}^\top = \begin{pmatrix} \mathbf{0}_{w_2}^\top & 2\boldsymbol{w}_2^\top & 1 \end{pmatrix}$. □

Proof (Of Theorem 6). It is not difficult to check reconstructability. Privacy holds because when $\mathsf{P}(x, y) = 1$, we can define $\boldsymbol{w}^\top = \begin{pmatrix} -\mathsf{s}\mathsf{D}_{x,y}^\top & -\mathsf{s}\mathsf{D}_{x,y}^\top \mathsf{s}\mathsf{E}_x & \mathsf{r}\mathsf{D}_{x,y}^\top \end{pmatrix}$ which can be checked to be a witness of the algebraic privacy of the transformed predicate encoding. □

Proof (Of Theorem 7). A simple check is enough to verify reconstructability. For privacy, note that when $\mathsf{P}'(y, x) = 0$, we have $\mathsf{P}(x, y) = 0$. Let $\boldsymbol{w}$ be a witness of the algebraic privacy of the original encoding. Now, $\boldsymbol{w}'^\top = \begin{pmatrix} -\boldsymbol{w}^\top & 1 \end{pmatrix}$ is a witness of the dual predicate encoding. □

Proof (Of Theorem 8). The proof follows directly from the following lemma and the observation that *(i)* is equivalent to $\boldsymbol{h}$-hiding, while *(iii)* is non-reconstructability (take $A = C$ and $B = K$). □

Lemma 1. *Let $A \in \mathbb{Z}_p^{m \times n}$ and $B \in \mathbb{Z}_p^{l \times n}$ be matrices. Let $C \in \mathbb{Z}_p^{(m+l) \times n}$ be the concatenation of A and B by rows. The following three statements are equivalent:*

(i) $\forall \boldsymbol{a} \in \mathbb{Z}_p^m, \forall \boldsymbol{b} \in \mathbb{Z}_p^l, \quad \Pr_{\boldsymbol{x} \xleftarrow{\$} \mathbb{Z}_p^n} [A\boldsymbol{x} = \boldsymbol{a} \,|\, B\boldsymbol{x} = \boldsymbol{b}] = \Pr_{\boldsymbol{x} \xleftarrow{\$} \mathbb{Z}_p^n} [A\boldsymbol{x} = \boldsymbol{a}]$

(ii) $\mathrm{rank}(C) = \mathrm{rank}(A) + \mathrm{rank}(B)$

(iii) $\forall \boldsymbol{a} \in \mathbb{Z}_p^m, \forall \boldsymbol{b} \in \mathbb{Z}_p^l, \quad \boldsymbol{a}^\top A \neq \boldsymbol{b}^\top B \ \vee \ \boldsymbol{a}^\top A = \mathbf{0}_n^\top$

Proof (Of the Lemma). Note that *(i)* holds for every $\boldsymbol{a} \in \mathbb{Z}_p^m, \boldsymbol{b} \in \mathbb{Z}_p^l$ such that $A\boldsymbol{x} = \boldsymbol{a}$ or $B\boldsymbol{x} = \boldsymbol{b}$ have no solution. Let $\boldsymbol{a} \in \mathbb{Z}_p^m, \boldsymbol{b} \in \mathbb{Z}_p^l$ be such that the systems $A\boldsymbol{x} = \boldsymbol{a}$ and $B\boldsymbol{x} = \boldsymbol{b}$ have individually at least one solution (note that such $\boldsymbol{a}$ and $\boldsymbol{b}$ always exist). We define the sets $\Omega_A = \{\boldsymbol{x} \in \mathbb{Z}_p^n : A\boldsymbol{x} = \boldsymbol{a}\}$, $\Omega_B = \{\boldsymbol{x} \in \mathbb{Z}_p^n : B\boldsymbol{x} = \boldsymbol{b}\}$, $\Omega_{AB} = \{\boldsymbol{x} \in \mathbb{Z}_p^n : A\boldsymbol{x} = \boldsymbol{a} \wedge B\boldsymbol{x} = \boldsymbol{b}\}$. By the Rouché-Capelli Theorem,

$$|\Omega_A| = p^{n - \mathrm{rank}(A)} \qquad |\Omega_B| = p^{n - \mathrm{rank}(B)} \qquad |\Omega_{AB}| = p^{n - \mathrm{rank}(C)}$$

Note that *(i)* can be expressed as $\frac{|\Omega_{AB}|}{p^n} = \frac{|\Omega_A|}{p^n} \cdot \frac{|\Omega_B|}{p^n}$ which is equivalent to the equation $p^n \cdot |\Omega_{AB}| = |\Omega_A| \cdot |\Omega_B|$, and therefore, $p^n \cdot p^{n-\mathrm{rank}(C)} = p^{n-\mathrm{rank}(A)} \cdot p^{n-\mathrm{rank}(B)}$ if and only if $\mathrm{rank}(C) = \mathrm{rank}(A) + \mathrm{rank}(B)$ which is *(ii)*.

Now, note that $\text{rank}(C) = \text{rank}(A) + \text{rank}(B)$ if and only if there is not a non-zero linear combination of rows of A that can be expressed as a linear combination of rows of B, which is equivalent to statement *(iii)*. □

Proof (Of Theorem 9). According to our Theorem 2, the partial encoding (sE', $\mathsf{rE}', \mathsf{kE}'$) induces a predicate encoding for the predicate $\mathsf{Pred}(x, y) = 1$ iff $\exists \boldsymbol{s} \in \mathbb{Z}_p^c, r \in \mathbb{Z}_p^1$ s.t. $\boldsymbol{s}^\top \mathsf{sE}'_x = r \cdot \mathsf{rE}'_y$ and $r \cdot \mathsf{kE}'_y = 1$, or equivalently, $\exists \boldsymbol{s} \in \mathbb{Z}_p^c$ s.t. $\boldsymbol{s}^\top \mathsf{cE}_x = \mathsf{kE}_y$, which is equivalent to the reconstructability of the tag-based encoding $(\mathsf{cE}, \mathsf{kE})$. According to Theorem 8 it is also equivalent to the predicate P. □

Proof (Of Theorem 10). Verifying correctness of the pair encoding is a simple check. For perfect security we need to check that, when $(x, y) \notin \mathsf{P}$, the following two distributions are identical:

$$\alpha, s_0 \xleftarrow{\$} \mathbb{Z}_p;\ r_1 \xleftarrow{\$} \mathbb{Z}_p^*;\ \boldsymbol{h} \xleftarrow{\$} \mathbb{Z}_p^w;\ \mathsf{return}\ (s_0,\ s_0 \cdot \mathsf{sE}_x \boldsymbol{h},\ r_1,\ r_1 \cdot \mathsf{rE}_y \boldsymbol{h}) \quad \equiv$$
$$s_0 \xleftarrow{\$} \mathbb{Z}_p;\ r_1 \xleftarrow{\$} \mathbb{Z}_p^*;\ \boldsymbol{h} \xleftarrow{\$} \mathbb{Z}_p^w;\ \mathsf{return}\ (s_0,\ s_0 \cdot \mathsf{sE}_x \boldsymbol{h},\ r_1,\ r_1 \cdot \mathsf{rE}_y \boldsymbol{h} + \alpha \cdot \mathsf{kE}_y)$$

Since both distributions provide s_0 and r_1 in the clear, the above checking is equivalent to the following:

$$\boldsymbol{h} \xleftarrow{\$} \mathbb{Z}_p^w;\ \mathsf{return}\ (\mathsf{sE}_x \boldsymbol{h},\ \mathsf{rE}_y \boldsymbol{h}) \quad \equiv$$
$$\alpha \xleftarrow{\$} \mathbb{Z}_p;\ r_1 \xleftarrow{\$} \mathbb{Z}_p^*;\ \boldsymbol{h} \xleftarrow{\$} \mathbb{Z}_p^w;\ \mathsf{return}\ (\mathsf{sE}_x \boldsymbol{h},\ \mathsf{rE}_y \boldsymbol{h} + \alpha / r_1 \cdot \mathsf{kE}_y)$$

but those distributions are identical due to the α-privacy of the predicate encoding[10]. □

Proof (Of Theorem 11). Given $(\boldsymbol{s}, \boldsymbol{r}) \in \mathbb{Z}_p^s \times \mathbb{Z}_p^r$, we define $\Omega_{\boldsymbol{s},\boldsymbol{r}} = \{\boldsymbol{w} \in \mathbb{Z}_p^w : S\boldsymbol{w} = \boldsymbol{s} \wedge R\boldsymbol{w} = \boldsymbol{r}\}$. The condition on the second bullet holds iff $w - s - r \geq 0$ and the cardinality of $\Omega_{\boldsymbol{s},\boldsymbol{r}}$ is p^{w-s-r}. Additionally, $|\Omega_{\boldsymbol{s},\boldsymbol{r}}|$ is independent from $\boldsymbol{r}$ and $\boldsymbol{s}$ iff the two distributions from the first bullet are identical. □

Proof (Of Theorem 12). Correctness can be easily checked. For privacy, let $(x, y) \notin \mathsf{P}$ and let $\boldsymbol{w} \in \mathbb{Z}_p^w$ be such that $\mathsf{sE}_x \boldsymbol{w} = \boldsymbol{0}_s$ and $\mathsf{rE}_y \boldsymbol{w} = \mathsf{kE}_y$. Note that $\boldsymbol{w}'^\top = \begin{pmatrix} \boldsymbol{w}^\top & \boldsymbol{0}_k^\top \end{pmatrix}$ is a witness of privacy for $(\mathsf{sE}', \mathsf{rE}', \mathsf{kE}', \mathsf{sD}', \mathsf{rD}')$. □

References

1. Agrawal, S., Chase, M.: A study of pair encodings: predicate encryption in prime order groups. In: Kushilevitz, E., Malkin, T. (eds.) TCC 2016. LNCS, vol. 9563, pp. 259–288. Springer, Heidelberg (2016). doi:10.1007/978-3-662-49099-0_10

[10] Note that $\alpha \xleftarrow{\$} \mathbb{Z}_p$, $r_1 \xleftarrow{\$} \mathbb{Z}_p^*$ and therefore, α / r_1 distributes uniformly over $\mathbb{Z}_p$, so we can apply the α-privacy property from the predicate encoding.

2. Agrawal, S., Chase, M.: Simplifying design and analysis of complex predicate encryption schemes. Cryptology ePrint Archive, Report 2017/233 (2017). EUROCRYPT (2017)
3. Akinyele, J.A., Lehmann, C.U., Green, M.D., Pagano, M.W., Peterson, Z.N.J., Rubin, A.D.: Self-protecting electronic medical records using attribute-based encryption. Cryptology ePrint Archive, Report 2010/565 (2010). http://eprint.iacr.org/2010/565
4. Applebaum, B., Arkis, B., Raykov, P., Vasudevan, P.N.: Conditional disclosure of secrets: amplification, closure, amortization, lower-bounds, and separations. In: Electronic Colloquium on Computational Complexity (ECCC), vol. 24, p. 38 (2017)
5. Aranha, D.F., Gouvêa, C.P.L.: RELIC is an Efficient LIbrary for Cryptography. https://github.com/relic-toolkit/relic
6. Attrapadung, N.: Dual system encryption via doubly selective security: framework, fully secure functional encryption for regular languages, and more. In: Nguyen, P.Q., Oswald, E. (eds.) EUROCRYPT 2014. LNCS, vol. 8441, pp. 557–577. Springer, Heidelberg (2014). doi:10.1007/978-3-642-55220-5_31
7. Attrapadung, N.: Dual system encryption framework in prime-order groups. Cryptology ePrint Archive, Report 2015/390 (2015). http://eprint.iacr.org/2015/390
8. Attrapadung, N., Imai, H.: Conjunctive broadcast and attribute-based encryption. In: Shacham, H., Waters, B. (eds.) Pairing 2009. LNCS, vol. 5671, pp. 248–265. Springer, Heidelberg (2009). doi:10.1007/978-3-642-03298-1_16
9. Attrapadung, N., Imai, H.: Dual-policy attribute based encryption. In: Abdalla, M., Pointcheval, D., Fouque, P.-A., Vergnaud, D. (eds.) ACNS 2009. LNCS, vol. 5536, pp. 168–185. Springer, Heidelberg (2009). doi:10.1007/978-3-642-01957-9_11
10. Attrapadung, N., Yamada, S.: Duality in ABE: converting attribute based encryption for dual predicate and dual policy via computational encodings. Cryptology ePrint Archive, Report 2015/157 (2015). http://eprint.iacr.org/2015/157
11. Barreto, P.S.L.M., Naehrig, M.: Pairing-friendly elliptic curves of prime order. Cryptology ePrint Archive, Report 2005/133 (2005). http://eprint.iacr.org/2005/133
12. Beimel, A.: Secret-sharing schemes: a survey. In: Chee, Y.M., Guo, Z., Ling, S., Shao, F., Tang, Y., Wang, H., Xing, C. (eds.) IWCC 2011. LNCS, vol. 6639, pp. 11–46. Springer, Heidelberg (2011). doi:10.1007/978-3-642-20901-7_2
13. Boneh, D., Waters, B.: Conjunctive, subset, and range queries on encrypted data. In: Vadhan, S.P. (ed.) TCC 2007. LNCS, vol. 4392, pp. 535–554. Springer, Heidelberg (2007). doi:10.1007/978-3-540-70936-7_29
14. Canetti, R., Halevi, S., Katz, J.: A forward-secure public-key encryption scheme. J. Cryptol. **20**(3), 265–294 (2007)
15. Chen, J., Gay, R., Wee, H.: Improved dual system ABE in prime-order groups via predicate encodings. In: Oswald, E., Fischlin, M. (eds.) EUROCRYPT 2015. LNCS, vol. 9057, pp. 595–624. Springer, Heidelberg (2015). doi:10.1007/978-3-662-46803-6_20
16. Chen, J., Wee, H.: Fully, (almost) tightly secure IBE and dual system groups. In: Canetti, R., Garay, J.A. (eds.) CRYPTO 2013. LNCS, vol. 8043, pp. 435–460. Springer, Heidelberg (2013). doi:10.1007/978-3-642-40084-1_25
17. Chen, J., Wee, H.: Dual system groups and its applications – compact hibe and more. Cryptology ePrint Archive, Report 2014/265 (2014). http://eprint.iacr.org/2014/265
18. Dinh, T.T.A., Datta, A.: Streamforce: outsourcing access control enforcement for stream data to the clouds. In: Fourth ACM Conference on Data and Application Security and Privacy, CODASPY 2014, San Antonio, TX, USA, 03–05 March 2014, pp. 13–24 (2014)

19. Garg, S., Kumarasubramanian, A., Sahai, A., Waters, B.: Building efficient fully collusion-resilient traitor tracing and revocation schemes. In: Al-Shaer, E., Keromytis, A.D., Shmatikov, V. (eds.) ACM CCS 10, pp. 121–130. ACM Press, October 2010
20. Gay, R., Kerenidis, I., Wee, H.: Communication complexity of conditional disclosure of secrets and attribute-based encryption. In: Gennaro, R., Robshaw, M. (eds.) CRYPTO 2015. LNCS, vol. 9216, pp. 485–502. Springer, Heidelberg (2015). doi:10.1007/978-3-662-48000-7_24
21. Ishai, Y., Wee, H.: Partial garbling schemes and their applications. In: Esparza, J., Fraigniaud, P., Husfeldt, T., Koutsoupias, E. (eds.) ICALP 2014. LNCS, vol. 8572, pp. 650–662. Springer, Heidelberg (2014). doi:10.1007/978-3-662-43948-7_54
22. Guo, F., Kim, J., Susilo, W., Au, M.H.: A tag based encoding: an efficient encoding for predicate encoding in prime order groups. Cryptology ePrint Archive, Report 2016/655 (2016). http://eprint.iacr.org/2016/655
23. Junod, P., Karlov, A.: An efficient public-key attribute-based broadcast encryption scheme allowing arbitrary access policies. In: Proceedings of the Tenth Annual ACM Workshop on Digital Rights Management, DRM 2010, pp. 13–24. ACM, New York (2010)
24. Karchmer, M., Wigderson, A.: On span programs. In: Proceedings of the 8th IEEE Structure in Complexity Theory, pp. 102–111. IEEE Computer Society Press (1993)
25. Katz, J., Sahai, A., Waters, B.: Predicate encryption supporting disjunctions, polynomial equations, and inner products. In: Smart, N. (ed.) EUROCRYPT 2008. LNCS, vol. 4965, pp. 146–162. Springer, Heidelberg (2008). doi:10.1007/978-3-540-78967-3_9
26. Lewko, A.B.: Tools for simulating features of composite order bilinear groups in the prime order setting. In: Pointcheval, D., Johansson, T. (eds.) EUROCRYPT 2012. LNCS, vol. 7237, pp. 318–335. Springer, Heidelberg (2012). doi:10.1007/978-3-642-29011-4_20
27. Lewko, A.B., Waters, B.: New techniques for dual system encryption and fully secure HIBE with short ciphertexts. In: Micciancio, D. (ed.) TCC 2010. LNCS, vol. 5978, pp. 455–479. Springer, Heidelberg (2010). doi:10.1007/978-3-642-11799-2_27
28. Lewko, A.B., Waters, B.: Decentralizing attribute-based encryption. In: Paterson, K.G. (ed.) EUROCRYPT 2011. LNCS, vol. 6632, pp. 568–588. Springer, Heidelberg (2011). doi:10.1007/978-3-642-20465-4_31
29. Lewko, A.B., Waters, B.: New proof methods for attribute-based encryption: achieving full security through selective techniques. In: Safavi-Naini, R., Canetti, R. (eds.) CRYPTO 2012. LNCS, vol. 7417, pp. 180–198. Springer, Heidelberg (2012). doi:10.1007/978-3-642-32009-5_12
30. Liu, Z., Wong, D.S.: Practical ciphertext-policy attribute-based encryption: traitor tracing, revocation, and large universe. In: Malkin, T., Kolesnikov, V., Lewko, A.B., Polychronakis, M. (eds.) ACNS 2015. LNCS, vol. 9092, pp. 127–146. Springer, Cham (2015). doi:10.1007/978-3-319-28166-7_7
31. Lubicz, D., Sirvent, T.: Attribute-based broadcast encryption scheme made efficient. In: Vaudenay, S. (ed.) AFRICACRYPT 2008. LNCS, vol. 5023, pp. 325–342. Springer, Heidelberg (2008). doi:10.1007/978-3-540-68164-9_22
32. Sahai, A., Seyalioglu, H., Waters, B.: Dynamic credentials and ciphertext delegation for attribute-based encryption. In: Safavi-Naini, R., Canetti, R. (eds.) CRYPTO 2012. LNCS, vol. 7417, pp. 199–217. Springer, Heidelberg (2012). doi:10.1007/978-3-642-32009-5_13

33. Sahai, A., Waters, B.: Fuzzy identity-based encryption. In: Cramer, R. (ed.) EUROCRYPT 2005. LNCS, vol. 3494, pp. 457–473. Springer, Heidelberg (2005). doi:10.1007/11426639_27
34. Shamir, A.: Identity-based cryptosystems and signature schemes. In: Blakley, G.R., Chaum, D. (eds.) CRYPTO 1984. LNCS, vol. 196, pp. 47–53. Springer, Heidelberg (1985). doi:10.1007/3-540-39568-7_5
35. Wang, F., Mickens, J., Zeldovich, N., Vaikuntanathan, V.: Sieve: cryptographically enforced access control for user data in untrusted clouds. In: 13th USENIX Symposium on Networked Systems Design and Implementation (NSDI 16), pp. 611–626, Santa Clara, CA. USENIX Association, March 2016
36. Waters, B.: Dual system encryption: realizing fully secure IBE and HIBE under simple assumptions. In: Halevi, S. (ed.) CRYPTO 2009. LNCS, vol. 5677, pp. 619–636. Springer, Heidelberg (2009). doi:10.1007/978-3-642-03356-8_36
37. Wee, H.: Dual system encryption via predicate encodings. In: Lindell, Y. (ed.) TCC 2014. LNCS, vol. 8349, pp. 616–637. Springer, Heidelberg (2014). doi:10.1007/978-3-642-54242-8_26

Practical Functional Encryption for Quadratic Functions with Applications to Predicate Encryption

Carmen Elisabetta Zaira Baltico[1(✉)], Dario Catalano[1], Dario Fiore[2], and Romain Gay[3]

[1] Dipartimento di Matematica e Informatica, Università di Catania, Catania, Italy
carmenez@hotmail.it, catalano@dmi.unict.it
[2] IMDEA Software Institute, Madrid, Spain
[3] Département d'informatique de l'ENS, École normale supérieure, CNRS, Inria, PSL Research University, 75005 Paris, France
rgay@di.ens.fr

Abstract. We present two practically efficient functional encryption schemes for a large class of quadratic functionalities. Specifically, our constructions enable the computation of so-called *bilinear maps* on encrypted vectors. This represents a practically relevant class of functions that includes, for instance, multivariate quadratic polynomials (over the integers). Our realizations work over asymmetric bilinear groups and are surprisingly efficient and easy to implement. For instance, in our most efficient scheme the public key and each ciphertext consist of $2n + 1$ and $4n + 2$ group elements respectively, where n is the dimension of the encrypted vectors, while secret keys are only two group elements. Our two schemes build on similar ideas, but develop them in a different way in order to achieve distinct goals. Our first scheme is proved (selectively) secure under standard assumptions, while our second construction is concretely more efficient and is proved (adaptively) secure in the generic group model.

As a byproduct of our functional encryption schemes, we show new predicate encryption schemes for degree-two polynomial evaluation, where ciphertexts consist of only $O(n)$ group elements. This significantly improves the $O(n^2)$ bound one would get from inner product encryption-based constructions.

1 Introduction

Traditional public key encryption allows the owner of a secret key sk to decrypt ciphertexts created with respect to a (matching) public key mpk. At the same time, without sk, ciphertexts should not reveal any non trivial information about encrypted messages. This all-or-nothing nature of encryption is becoming insufficient in applications where a more fine-grained access to data is required. Functional Encryption (FE) allows to overcome this user-centric access to data of

R. Gay—Supported by ERC Project aSCEND (639554).

J. Katz and H. Shacham (Eds.): CRYPTO 2017, Part I, LNCS 10401, pp. 67–98, 2017.
DOI: 10.1007/978-3-319-63688-7_3

encryption in a very elegant way. Intuitively, given $\mathsf{Encrypt}(m)$ and a key sk_f corresponding to some function f, the owner of sk_f learns $f(m)$ and nothing else. Apart from being an interesting theoretical object, Functional Encryption has many natural applications. Think about cloud storage scenarios where users can rely on powerful external servers to store their data. To preserve their privacy, users might want to store their files encrypted. At the same time, the users may wish to let the service providers perform basic data mining operations on this data for commercial purposes, without necessarily disclosing the whole data. Functional Encryption allows to reconcile these seemingly contradicting needs, as service providers can get secret keys that allow them to perform the desired computations while preserving, as much as possible, the privacy of users.

In terms of security, the standard notion for functional encryption is *indistinguishability.* Informally, this notion states that an adversary who is allowed to see the secret keys for functionalities $f_1, \ldots f_n$ should not be able to tell apart which of the challenge messages m_0 or m_1 has been encrypted, under the restriction that $f_i(m_0) = f_i(m_1)$, for all i. This notion was studied in [13,35] and shown inadequate for certain, complex, functionalities[1]. They also explored an alternative, simulation-based, definition, which however cannot be satisfied, in general, without resorting to the random oracle heuristic.

Background on Functional Encryption. The idea of functional encryption originates from Identity Based Encryption (IBE) [11,37] and the closely related concept of Searchable Encryption [1,10]. In IBE, the encrypted message can be interpreted as a pair (I, m), where I is a public string and m is the actual message (often called the "payload"). More in general, the index I can be interpreted as a set of attributes that can be either public or private. Public index schemes are often referred to as attribute based encryption [27,36], a primitive that is by now very well understood [25]. For private index schemes, the situation is more intricate. A first distinction is between *weakly* and *fully attribute hiding* schemes [5]. The former notion refers to schemes where the set of secret keys the adversary is allowed to see in the security games is significantly restricted. The adversary is allowed to ask only keys corresponding to functions that cannot be used to decrypt the challenge message. Examples of these schemes are Anonymous Identity based encryption [11,22], Hidden Vector Encryption [15] and (private index) predicate encryption [26,28].

Things are less well established for the setting of private index, fully attribute hiding schemes, a notion that turns out to be equivalent to full fledged functional encryption [13]. Indeed, all known constructions supporting arbitrary circuits, either work for the case of bounded collusions [23,24] or rely on powerful, but poorly understood, assumptions (e.g., [20]). Moreover, they are all terribly inefficient from a practical point of view.

---

[1] Here by complex we intend, for instance, functions that are supposed to have some computational hiding properties. In particular, Boneh *et al.* [13] argue that, in applications where security relies on such properties, indistinguishability might become problematic.

To improve efficiency, a very natural approach is to try to realize schemes using a different, bottom up, perspective. Rather than focusing on generality, one might focus on devising efficient realizations for specific functionalities of practical interest. In 2015, Abdalla *et al.* [2] addressed this question for the case of linear functionalities. In particular, they show a construction which is both very simple and relies on standard, well studied assumptions (such as LWE and DDH). The construction was proved secure in the so-called *selective* setting where the adversary is expected to choose the messages on which she wants to be challenged in advance, even before the public key is set up. Not too surprisingly, this result sparkled significant interest in this bottom-up approach, with several results proposing new schemes [6], models [4,9] and improved security [3,6].

Still, none of these results managed to efficiently support more than linear functionalities. In particular, the technical barrier is to find FE schemes in which ciphertexts have size *linear* in the number of encrypted elements, in contrast to quadratic, as it can be achieved by using a scheme for linear functions.[2] This motivates the following question:

Can we construct a practically efficient functional encryption scheme supporting more than linear functionalities?

1.1 Our Contribution

In this paper we answer the question above in the affirmative. We build two efficient functional encryption schemes for quadratic functions with linear-size ciphertexts. In terms of security, our first scheme is proven selective-secure under standard assumptions (Matrix Decisional Diffie Hellman [18] and 3-party DDH [12]), whereas our second scheme is proven adaptively secure in the generic group model, and is more efficient. In terms of functionality, to be more specific, our schemes allows to compute *bilinear maps over the integers*: messages are expressed as pairs of vectors $(\boldsymbol{x}, \boldsymbol{y}) \in \mathbb{Z}^n \times \mathbb{Z}^m$, secret keys are associated with $(n \times m)$ matrices $\mathbf{F}$, and decryption allows to compute $\boldsymbol{x}^\top \mathbf{F} \boldsymbol{y} = \sum_{i,j} f_{ij} x_i y_j$. Bilinear maps represent a very general class of quadratic functions that includes, for instance, multivariate quadratic polynomials. These functions have several practical applications. For instance, a quadratic polynomial can express many statistical functions (e.g., (weighted) mean, variance, covariance, root-mean-square), the euclidean distance between two vectors, and the application of a linear or quadratic classifier (e.g., linear or quadratic regression).

In addition to the above applications of quadratic functions, we also show that our FE for bilinear maps can be used to construct new Predicate Encryption schemes (PE for short) that satisfy the *fully attribute hiding* property, and yield efficient solutions for interesting classes of predicates, such as constant-depth

[2] Indeed, we note that a functional encryption for linear polynomials can be used to support, say, quadratic polynomials, by simply encrypting all the degree-two monomials in advance. This however leads to an inefficient solution where the size of the ciphertexts is quadratic in the number of variables.

boolean formulas and comparisons. In a nutshell, in our PE scheme ciphertexts are associated with a set of attributes $(x_1, \ldots, x_n)$ and a plaintext M, secret keys are associated with a degree-two polynomial P, and the decryption of a ciphertext $\mathsf{Ct}_{(x_1,\ldots,x_n)\in\mathbb{Z}^n}$ with a secret key $\mathsf{sk}_{P\in\mathbb{Z}[X_1,\ldots,X_n],\ \mathsf{deg}(P)\leq 2}$ recovers M if, and only if, $P(x_1, \ldots, x_n) = 1$. The attribute-hiding property refers to the fact that $\mathsf{Ct}_{(x_1,\ldots,x_n)\in\mathbb{Z}^n}$ leaks no information on its attribute $(x_1, \ldots, x_n)$, beyond what is inherently leaked by the boolean value $P(x_1, \ldots, x_n) \stackrel{?}{=} 1$. Using our new functional encryption schemes as underlying building blocks, we obtain PE constructions for quadratic polynomials where ciphertexts consist of only $O(n)$ group elements. This is in sharp contrast with the $O(n^2)$ solutions one would get via inner product encryption schemes (e.g., [28]).

An Informal Description of Our FE Schemes. Our solutions work over asymmetric bilinear groups $\mathbb{G}_1, \mathbb{G}_2, \mathbb{G}_T$ and are quite efficient. They are both essentially optimal in communication size: public key and ciphertexts are both *linear* in the size of the encrypted vectors; secret keys are only two group elements. Both our schemes share similar underlying ideas. These ideas are however developed in different ways to achieve different security and efficiency goals. Our first scheme, can be proved (selectively) secure under standard intractability assumptions but achieves somewhat worse performances in practice. The second construction, on the other hand, is (concretely) more efficient but it can be proved (adaptively) secure only in the generic group model. In what follows we will highlight some of the core ideas underlying both schemes. How these ideas are implemented and developed in the two cases will be discussed when introducing each specific scheme.

Let us recall that the functionality provided by our FE scheme is that one encrypts pairs of vectors $\boldsymbol{x}, \boldsymbol{y}$, functions are matrices $\mathbf{F}$, and decryption allows to obtain $\boldsymbol{x}^\top \mathbf{F} \boldsymbol{y}$. The initial idea of the construction is to encrypt the two vectors $\boldsymbol{x} \in \mathbb{Z}^n$ and $\boldsymbol{y} \in \mathbb{Z}^m$ in a sort of "matrix" ElGamal in the two groups $\mathbb{G}_1$ and $\mathbb{G}_2$ respectively. Namely, we set

$$\mathsf{Ct}_{(\boldsymbol{x},\boldsymbol{y})} = \{[\rho \mathbf{A} \boldsymbol{r}_i + \boldsymbol{b} x_i]_1\}_{i=1,\ldots,n}, \{[\sigma \mathbf{B} \boldsymbol{s}_j + \boldsymbol{a} y_j]_2\}_{j=1,\ldots,m}$$

where: ρ, σ are randomly chosen, $\{\mathbf{A}\boldsymbol{r}_i, \mathbf{B}\boldsymbol{s}_j\}_{i,j}$ are in the public key, and are constructed from two random matrices $\mathbf{A}$ and $\mathbf{B}$ and a collection of random vectors $\{\boldsymbol{r}_i, \boldsymbol{s}_j\}_{i,j}$, and $\boldsymbol{a}, \boldsymbol{b}$ are more carefully chosen vectors (see below) [3]. Towards finding a decryption method, we first observe that, given $\mathsf{Ct}_{(\boldsymbol{x},\boldsymbol{y})}$ and a function $\mathbf{F}$, one can use the bilinear map to compute

$$U = [(\rho\sigma)\sum_{ij} f_{ij} \boldsymbol{r}_i^\top \mathbf{A}^\top \mathbf{B} \boldsymbol{s}_j + \rho \sum_{ij} f_{ij} \boldsymbol{r}_i^\top \mathbf{A}^\top \boldsymbol{a} y_j + \sigma \sum_{ij} f_{ij} \boldsymbol{s}_j^\top \mathbf{B}^\top \boldsymbol{b} x_i + (\boldsymbol{b}^\top \boldsymbol{a}) \cdot \boldsymbol{x}^\top \mathbf{F} \boldsymbol{y}]_T.$$

Moreover, if we let $[\sum_{ij} f_{ij} \boldsymbol{r}_i^\top \mathbf{A}^\top \mathbf{B} \boldsymbol{s}_j]_1$ be the secret key for function $\mathbf{F}$ and include $[\rho\sigma]_2$ in the ciphertext, one can remove the first term in U.

---

[3] Here we adopt the, by now standard, implicit representation $[x]_s = g^x \in \mathbb{G}_s$. This notion can be easily extended to vectors and matrices (see [18]).

Our two schemes then extend this basic blueprint with additional (but different!) structure so as to enable the extraction from U of the value $[\boldsymbol{x}^\top \mathbf{F} \boldsymbol{y}]_T$. From this, in turn, the function's result can be obtained via a brute force discrete log computation[4]. At a very intuitive level (and deliberately ignoring many important details) a key difference between the two schemes lies in the way $\mathbf{A}$, $\mathbf{B}$, $\boldsymbol{a}$ and $\boldsymbol{b}$ are constructed.

In our first scheme, $\mathbf{A}$ and $\mathbf{B}$ are carefully sampled so that to be able to prove (selective) security under standard intractability assumptions (e.g. Matrix Decisional Diffie-Hellman). Moreover $\boldsymbol{a}$ and $\boldsymbol{b}$ are chosen such that $\mathbf{A}^\top \boldsymbol{a} = \mathbf{B}^\top \boldsymbol{b} = \mathbf{0}$ and $\boldsymbol{b}^\top \boldsymbol{a} = 1$. This ensures that the intermediate values $\rho \sum_{ij} f_{ij} \boldsymbol{r}_i^\top \mathbf{A}^\top \boldsymbol{a} y_j$, $\sigma \sum_{ij} f_{ij} \boldsymbol{s}_j^\top \mathbf{B}^\top \boldsymbol{b} x_i$ cancel out at decryption time.

In our second scheme, on the other hand, the public key values $\mathbf{A}\boldsymbol{r}_i$ and $\mathbf{B}\boldsymbol{s}_j$ are simple scalars, and the "canceling" is performed via an appropriate choice of vectors $\boldsymbol{a}, \boldsymbol{b}$ and simple algebraic manipulations. This makes the resulting construction (concretely) more efficient. At the same time, we lose the possibility to rely on (general) matrix assumptions and we are able to prove (adaptive) security in the generic group model. To this end, as a contribution that can be of independent interest, we state and prove a master theorem that shows hardness in the generic bilinear group model for a broad family of interactive decisional problems (notably, a family that includes our FE scheme), extending some of the tools and results of the generic group framework recently developed by Barthe et al. [8].

Concurrent and Independent Work. In concurrent and independent work, Lin [31], and Ananth and Sahai [7] present constructions of *private-key* functional encryption schemes for degree-D polynomials based on D-linear maps. As a special case for $D = 2$, these schemes support quadratic polynomials from bilinear maps, as ours. Also, in terms of security, the construction of Lin is proven selectively secure based on the SXDH assumption, while the scheme of Ananth and Sahai is selectively secure based on ad-hoc assumptions that are justified in the multilinear group model. In comparison to these works, our schemes have the advantage of working in the (arguably more challenging) *public key* setting.

We provide a summary of the existing solutions for (efficient) functional encryption for quadratic functions in Table 1.

2 Preliminaries

Notation. We denote with $\lambda \in \mathbb{N}$ a security parameter. A *probabilistic polynomial time* (PPT) algorithm $\mathcal{A}$ is a randomized algorithm for which there exists a polynomial $p(\cdot)$ such that for every input x the running time of $\mathcal{A}(x)$ is bounded by $p(|x|)$. We say that a function $\epsilon : \mathbb{N} \to \mathbb{R}^+$ is *negligible* if for every positive polynomial $p(\lambda)$ there exists $\lambda_0 \in \mathbb{N}$ such that for all $\lambda > \lambda_0$: $\epsilon(\lambda) < 1/p(\lambda)$. If S is a set, $x \leftarrow_{\mathrm{R}} S$ denotes the process of selecting x uniformly at random in S.

[4] This means that in our scheme messages and functions coefficients are assumed to be sufficiently small integers.

Table 1. Comparison between different FE schemes for quadratic functions over vectors of size n.

FE scheme	Enc. model	Security	Assumption	Ciph. size
Abdalla et al. [2]	Public-key	Selective	DDH/DCR/LWE	$O(n^2)$
Agrawal et al. [6]	Public-key	Adaptive	DDH/DCR/LWE	$O(n^2)$
Ananth-Sahai [7]	Private-key	Selective	Ad-hoc (GGM)	$O(n)$
Lin [31]	Private-key	Selective	SXDH	$O(n)$
Ours 1	Public-key	Selective	MDDH, 3-PDDH	$O(n)$
Ours 2	Public-key	Adaptive	GGM	$O(n)$

If $\mathcal{A}$ is a probabilistic algorithm, $y \leftarrow_{\mathrm{R}} \mathcal{A}(\cdot)$ denotes the process of running $\mathcal{A}$ on some appropriate input and assigning its output to y. For a positive integer n, we denote by $[n]$ the set $\{1,\ldots,n\}$. We denote vectors $\boldsymbol{x} = (x_i)$ and matrices $\mathbf{A} = (a_{i,j})$ in bold. For a set S (resp. vector $\boldsymbol{x}$) $|S|$ (resp. $|\boldsymbol{x}|$) denotes its cardinality (resp. number of entries). For any prime p and any matrix $\mathbf{A} \in \mathbb{Z}_p^{n\times m}$ with $n \geq m$, we denote by $\mathsf{orth}(\mathbf{A}) := \{\boldsymbol{a}^{\perp} \in \mathbb{Z}_p^n : \mathbf{A}^{\top}\boldsymbol{a}^{\perp} = \mathbf{0}\}$. For all square matrices $\mathbf{A} \in \mathbb{Z}_p^{n\times n}$, we denote by $\det(\mathbf{A})$ the determinant of $\mathbf{A}$. For any $n \in \mathbb{N}^*$, we denote by GL_n the general linear group of degree n, that is, the set of all $n\times n$ invertible matrices over $\mathbb{Z}_p$. By $\equiv$, we denote the equality of statistical distribution, and for any $\varepsilon > 0$, we denote by $\approx_{\varepsilon}$ the ε-statistical of two distributions.

Bilinear Groups. Let $\mathcal{G}(1^{\lambda})$ be an algorithm (that we call a *bilinear group generator*) which takes as input the security parameter and outputs the description of a bilinear group setting $\mathsf{bgp} = (p, \mathbb{G}_1, \mathbb{G}_2, \mathbb{G}_T, e, g_1, g_2)$, where $\mathbb{G}_1$, $\mathbb{G}_2$ and $\mathbb{G}_T$ are groups of the same prime order $p > 2^{\lambda}$, $g_1 \in \mathbb{G}_1$ and $g_2 \in \mathbb{G}_2$ are two generators, and $e : \mathbb{G}_1 \times \mathbb{G}_2 \to \mathbb{G}_T$ is an efficiently computable, non-degenerate, bilinear map. We define $g_T = e(g_1, g_2)$ as the canonical generator of $\mathbb{G}_T$. In the case $\mathbb{G}_1 = \mathbb{G}_2$, the groups are said *symmetric*, else they are said *asymmetric*. In this paper we work with *asymmetric* bilinear groups in which there is no efficiently computable isomorphisms between $\mathbb{G}_1$ and $\mathbb{G}_2$ (these are also known as Type-III groups [19]).

We use implicit representation of group elements as introduced in [18]. For $s \in \{1, 2, T\}$ and $x \in \mathbb{Z}_p$, we let $[x]_s = g_s^x \in \mathbb{G}_s$. This notation is extended to matrices (and vectors) as follows. For any $\mathbf{A} = (a_{i,j}) \in \mathbb{Z}_p^{m\times n}$ we define

$$[\mathbf{A}]_s = \begin{pmatrix} g_s^{a_{1,1}} & \cdots & g_s^{a_{1,n}} \\ \\ g_s^{a_{m,1}} & \cdots & g_s^{a_{m,n}} \end{pmatrix} \in \mathbb{G}_s^{m\times n}$$

Note that from an element $[x]_s \in \mathbb{G}_s$ and a scalar a it is possible to efficiently compute $[ax] \in \mathbb{G}_s$. Also, given group elements $[a]_1 \in \mathbb{G}_1$ and $[b]_2 \in \mathbb{G}_2$, one can efficiently compute $[ab]_T = e([a]_1, [b]_2)$. Furthermore, given a matrix of scalars $\mathbf{F} = (f_{i,j}) \in \mathbb{Z}_p^{n\times n}$ and two n-dimensional vectors of group elements $[\boldsymbol{a}]_1, [\boldsymbol{b}]_2$, one can efficiently compute

$$[\boldsymbol{a}^\top \mathbf{F} \boldsymbol{b}]_T = \left[\sum_{i,j \in [n]} f_{i,j} \cdot a_i \cdot b_j \right]_T = \sum_{i,j \in [n]} f_{i,j} \cdot e([a_i]_1, [b_j]_2)$$

As above, for an easier and more compact presentation, in our work we slightly abuse notation and treat all groups $\mathbb{G}_1, \mathbb{G}_2, \mathbb{G}_T$ as additive groups.

2.1 Complexity Assumptions

We recall the definitions of the Matrix Decision Diffie-Hellman (mddh) Assumption [18].

Definition 1 (Matrix Distribution). *Let $k \in \mathbb{N}$. We call $\mathcal{D}_k$ a matrix distribution if it outputs in polynomial time matrices in $\mathbb{Z}_p^{(k+1)\times k}$ of full rank k, and satisfying the following property,*

Property 1.

$$\Pr[\mathsf{orth}(\mathbf{A}) \subseteq \mathsf{span}(\mathbf{B})] = \frac{1}{\Omega(p)},$$

where $\mathbf{A}, \mathbf{B} \leftarrow_{\mathrm{R}} \mathcal{D}_k$.

Without loss of generality, we assume the first k rows of $\mathbf{A} \leftarrow_{\mathrm{R}} \mathcal{D}_k$ form an invertible matrix. Note that the basis property is not explicit in [18], but, as noted in [16, Lemma 1 (basis lemma)], all examples of matrix distribution presented in [18, Sect. 3.4], namely $\mathcal{U}_k$, $\mathcal{L}_k$, $\mathcal{SC}_k$, $\mathcal{C}_k$ and $\mathcal{IL}_k$, satisfy this property.

The $\mathcal{D}_k$-Matrix Diffie-Hellman problem in $\mathbb{G}_s$ for $s \in \{1,2,T\}$ is to distinguish the two distributions $([\mathbf{A}]_s, [\mathbf{A}\boldsymbol{w}]_s)$ and $([\mathbf{A}]_s, [\boldsymbol{u}]_s)$ where $\mathbf{A} \leftarrow_{\mathrm{R}} \mathcal{D}_k$, $\boldsymbol{w} \leftarrow_{\mathrm{R}} \mathbb{Z}_p^k$ and $\boldsymbol{u} \leftarrow_{\mathrm{R}} \mathbb{Z}_p^{k+1}$.

Definition 2 ($\mathcal{D}_k$-Matrix Diffie-Hellman Assumption $\mathcal{D}_k$-mddh). *Let $\mathcal{D}_k$ be a matrix distribution. The $\mathcal{D}_k$-Matrix Diffie-Hellman ($\mathcal{D}_k$-mddh) Assumption holds relative to $\mathcal{G}$ in $\mathbb{G}_s$, for $s \in \{1,2,T\}$, if for all PPT adversaries $\mathcal{A}$,*

$$\mathbf{Adv}_{\mathcal{G},\mathbb{G}_s,\mathcal{A}}^{\mathcal{D}_k\text{-}\mathsf{mddh}}(\lambda) := |\Pr[\mathcal{A}(\mathsf{bgp}, [\mathbf{A}]_s, [\mathbf{A}\boldsymbol{w}]_s) = 1] - \Pr[\mathcal{A}(\mathsf{bgp}, [\mathbf{A}]_s, [\boldsymbol{u}]_s) = 1]|$$

is $\mathsf{negl}(\lambda)$, where probabilities are over the choices of $\mathsf{bgp} \leftarrow_{\mathrm{R}} \mathcal{G}(1^\lambda)$, $\mathbf{A} \leftarrow_{\mathrm{R}} \mathcal{D}_k, \boldsymbol{w} \leftarrow_{\mathrm{R}} \mathbb{Z}_p^k, \boldsymbol{u} \leftarrow_{\mathrm{R}} \mathbb{Z}_p^{k+1}$.

For each $k \geq 1$, [18] specifies distributions ($\mathcal{U}_k$, $\mathcal{L}_k$, $\mathcal{SC}_k$, $\mathcal{C}_k$ and $\mathcal{IL}_k$) over $\mathbb{Z}_p^{(k+1)\times k}$ such that the corresponding $\mathcal{D}_k$-mddh assumptions are generically secure in bilinear groups and form a hierarchy of increasingly weaker assumptions. $\mathcal{L}_k$-mddh is the well known k-Linear Assumption k-Lin with 1-Lin = DDH.

Let $Q \geq 1$. For $\mathbf{W} \leftarrow_{\mathrm{R}} \mathbb{Z}_q^{k\times Q}, \mathbf{U} \leftarrow_{\mathrm{R}} \mathbb{Z}_q^{(k+1)\times Q}$, we consider the Q-fold $\mathcal{D}_k$-mddh Assumption which consists in distinguishing the distributions $([\mathbf{A}], [\mathbf{AW}])$ from $([\mathbf{A}], [\mathbf{U}])$. That is, a challenge for the Q-fold $\mathcal{D}_k$-mddh Assumption consists of Q independent challenges of the $\mathcal{D}_k$-mddh Assumption (with the same $\mathbf{A}$ but different randomness $\boldsymbol{w}$). In [18] it is shown that the two problems are equivalent.

Lemma 1 (Random self-reducibility of $\mathcal{U}_{\ell,k}$-mddh, [18]). *Let $k, Q \in \mathbb{N}$, and $s \in \{1, 2, T\}$. For any PPT adversary $\mathcal{A}$, there exists a PPT adversary $\mathcal{B}$ such that*

$$\mathbf{Adv}_{\mathcal{G},\mathbb{G}_s,\mathcal{A}}^{Q\text{-}\mathcal{D}_k\text{-mddh}}(\lambda) \leq \mathbf{Adv}_{\mathcal{G},\mathbb{G}_s,\mathcal{B}}^{\mathcal{D}_k\text{-mddh}}(\lambda) + \frac{1}{p-1}$$

where $\mathbf{Adv}_{\mathcal{G},\mathbb{G}_s,\mathcal{A}}^{Q\text{-}\mathcal{D}_k\text{-mddh}}(\lambda) := |\Pr[\mathcal{B}(\mathsf{bgp}, [\mathbf{A}]_s, [\mathbf{AW}]_s) = 1] - \Pr[\mathcal{B}(\mathsf{bgp}, [\mathbf{A}]_s, [\mathbf{U}]_s) = 1]|$ *and the probability is taken over* $\mathsf{bgp} \leftarrow_{\mathrm{R}} \mathcal{G}(1^\lambda)$, $\mathbf{A} \leftarrow_{\mathrm{R}} \mathcal{U}_k, \mathbf{W} \leftarrow_{\mathrm{R}} \mathbb{Z}_q^{k \times Q}, \mathbf{U} \leftarrow_{\mathrm{R}} \mathbb{Z}_q^{(k+1) \times Q}$.

We also recall the definition of 3-party Decision Diffie-Hellman (3-pddh) Assumption introduced in [12]. We give a variant in the asymmetric-pairing setting.

Definition 3 (3-party Decision Diffie-Hellman Assumption 3-pddh). *We say that the 3-party Decision Diffie-Hellman (3-pddh) Assumption holds relative to $\mathcal{G}$ if for all PPT adversaries $\mathcal{A}$,*

$$\begin{aligned}\mathbf{Adv}_{\mathcal{G},\mathcal{A}}^{3-\mathsf{pddh}}(\lambda) := |&\Pr[\mathcal{A}(\mathsf{bgp}, [a]_1, [b]_2, [c]_1, [c]_2, [abc]_1) = 1] \\ &- \Pr[\mathcal{A}(\mathsf{bgp}, [a]_1, [b]_2, [c]_1, [c]_2, [d]_1) = 1]| = \mathsf{negl}(\lambda)\end{aligned}$$

where the probability is taken over $\mathsf{bgp} \leftarrow_{\mathrm{R}} \mathcal{G}(1^\lambda)$, $a, b, c, d \leftarrow_{\mathrm{R}} \mathbb{Z}_p$.

2.2 Functional Encryption

We recall the definitions of Functional Encryption as given by Boneh et al. [13].

Definition 4 (Functionality). *A functionality F defined over $(\mathcal{K}, \mathcal{M})$ is a function $F : \mathcal{K} \times \mathcal{M} \to \mathcal{Y} \cup \{\perp\}$ where $\mathcal{K}$ is a key space, $\mathcal{M}$ is a message space and $\mathcal{Y}$ is an output space which does not contain the special symbol $\perp$.*

Definition 5 (Functional Encryption). *A* functional encryption *scheme* FE *for a functionality F is defined by a tuple of algorithms* FE = (Setup, KeyGen, Encrypt, Decrypt) *that work as follows.*

Setup$(1^\lambda, F)$ *takes as input a security parameter 1^λ, the functionality $F : \mathcal{K} \times \mathcal{M} \to \mathcal{Y}$, and outputs a master secret key* msk *and a master public key* mpk.

KeyGen(msk, K) *takes as input the master secret key and a key $K \in \mathcal{K}$ of the functionality (i.e., a function), and outputs a secret key* sk_K.

Encrypt(mpk, msk , M) *takes as input the master public key* mpk *and a message $M \in \mathcal{M}$, and outputs a ciphertext* Ct. *It can take as an additional input the master secret key, in which case, we talk about* private-key *functional encryption. By opposition, when* msk *is not an input of the encryption, algorithm, we say that* FE *is public-key.*

Decrypt(sk_K, Ct) *takes as input a secret key* sk_K *and a ciphertext* Ct, *and returns an output $Y \in \mathcal{Y} \cup \{\perp\}$.*

For correctness, *it is required that for all* (mpk, msk) $\leftarrow_{\mathrm{R}}$ Setup(1^λ), *all keys $K \in \mathcal{K}$ and all messages $M \in \mathcal{M}$, if* $\mathsf{sk}_K \leftarrow_{\mathrm{R}}$ KeyGen(msk, K) *and* Ct $\leftarrow_{\mathrm{R}}$ Encrypt(mpk, msk , M), *then it holds with overwhelming probability that* Decrypt(sk_K, Ct) $= F(K, M)$ *whenever* $F(K, M) \neq \perp$.

Indistinguishability-Based Security. For a functional encryption scheme FE for a functionality F over $(\mathcal{K}, \mathcal{M})$, security against chosen-plaintext attacks (IND-FE-CPA, for short) is defined via the following experiment, denoted $\mathbf{Exp}^{\text{ind-fe-cpa-}\beta}_{\mathsf{FE},\mathcal{A}}(\lambda)$, which is parametrized by an adversary $\mathcal{A}$, a bit $\beta \in \{0,1\}$, and a security parameter λ.

Setup: run $(\mathsf{mpk}, \mathsf{msk}) \leftarrow_{\mathrm{R}} \mathsf{Setup}(1^\lambda)$ and give mpk to $\mathcal{A}$.
Query: $\mathcal{A}$ adaptively makes secret key queries. At each query, $\mathcal{A}$ specifies a key K and obtains $\mathsf{sk}_K \leftarrow_{\mathrm{R}} \mathsf{KeyGen}(\mathsf{msk}, K)$ from the challenger.
Challenge: $\mathcal{A}$ chooses a pair of messages $M_0, M_1 \in \mathcal{M}$ such that $F(K, M_0) = F(K, M_1)$ holds for all keys K queried in the previous phase. The challenger computes $\mathsf{Ct}^* \leftarrow_{\mathrm{R}} \mathsf{Encrypt}(\mathsf{mpk}, M_\beta)$ and returns Ct^* to $\mathcal{A}$.
Query: $\mathcal{A}$ makes more secret key queries. At each query $\mathcal{A}$ can adaptively choose a key $K \in \mathcal{K}$, but under the requirement that $F(K, M_0) = F(K, M_1)$.
Guess: $\mathcal{A}$ eventually outputs a bit $\beta' \in \{0,1\}$, and the experiment outputs the same bit.

For any stateful adversary $\mathcal{A}$, any functional encryption scheme FE for a functionality F over $(\mathcal{K}, \mathcal{M})$, any bit $\beta \in \{0,1\}$, and any security parameter λ, we give a compact description of experiment $\mathbf{Exp}^{\text{ind-pe-cpa-}\beta}_{\mathsf{PE},\mathcal{A}}(\lambda)$, and its selective version $\mathbf{Exp}^{\text{sel-ind-pe-cpa-}\beta}_{\mathsf{PE},\mathcal{A}}(\lambda)$, in Fig. 1.

$\mathbf{Exp}^{\text{ind-fe-cpa-}\beta}_{\mathsf{FE},\mathcal{A}}(\lambda)$ (dotted), $\mathbf{Exp}^{\text{sel-ind-fe-cpa-}\beta}_{\mathsf{FE},\mathcal{A}}(\lambda)$ (solid) :	
$(M_0, M_1) \leftarrow \mathcal{A}(1^\lambda)$ (solid)	$\mathsf{EncO}(M_0, M_1)$:
$(\mathsf{mpk}, \mathsf{msk}) \leftarrow_{\mathrm{R}} \mathsf{Setup}(1^\lambda)$	Return $\mathsf{Ct}^* := \mathsf{Encrypt}(\mathsf{mpk}, \mathsf{msk}\ \text{(gray)}, M_\beta)$
$\mathsf{Ct} := \mathsf{EncO}(M_0, M_1)$ (solid)	
$\beta' \leftarrow \mathcal{A}(\mathsf{mpk}, \mathsf{Ct}\ \text{(solid)})^{\mathsf{KeyGenO}(\cdot), \mathsf{EncO}(\cdot,\cdot)\ \text{(dotted)}}$	$\mathsf{KeyGenO}(K \in \mathcal{K})$:
Return β'.	Return $\mathsf{sk}_K := \mathsf{KeyGen}(\mathsf{msk}, K)$

Fig. 1. Experiments $\mathbf{Exp}^{\text{ind-fe-cpa-}\beta}_{\mathsf{FE},\mathcal{A}}(\lambda)$ and $\mathbf{Exp}^{\text{sel-ind-fe-cpa-}\beta}_{\mathsf{FE},\mathcal{A}}(\lambda)$ for $b \in \{0,1\}$, used to define adaptive, and selective security of FE, respectively. In each procedure, the components inside a solid (dotted) frame are only present in the games marked by a solid (dotted) frame, and the components inside a gray frame only appears for private-key FE schemes. In both games, the oracle $\mathsf{EncO}(\cdot,\cdot)$ is queries at most once (by $\mathcal{A}$ or the game itself), on M_0, M_1, such that for all queries K to $\mathsf{KeyGenO}(\cdot)$, we have: $F(K, M_0) = F(K, M_1)$. Note that in the case of private-key FE, this corresponds to single-ciphertext security (which does not imply many-ciphertext security).

We define the advantage of $\mathcal{A}$ for adaptive security as:

$$\begin{aligned}
\mathbf{Adv}^{\text{ind-fe-cpa}}_{\mathsf{FE},\mathcal{A}}(\lambda) &:= \left|\Pr[\mathbf{Exp}^{\text{ind-fe-cpa-}0}_{\mathsf{FE},\mathcal{A}}(\lambda) = 1] - \Pr[\mathbf{Exp}^{\text{ind-fe-cpa-}1}_{\mathsf{FE},\mathcal{A}}(\lambda) = 1]\right| \\
&= \left|1 - 2\Pr\left[\beta' = \beta : \begin{array}{c} \beta \leftarrow_{\mathrm{R}} \{0,1\} \\ \mathbf{Exp}^{\text{ind-fe-cpa-}\beta}_{\mathsf{FE},\mathcal{A}}(\lambda) = \beta' \end{array}\right]\right|
\end{aligned}$$

We define the advantage $\mathbf{Adv}^{\mathsf{sel\text{-}ind\text{-}fe\text{-}cpa}}_{\mathsf{FE},\mathcal{A}}(\lambda)$ for selective security similarly, with respect to experiments $\mathbf{Exp}^{\mathsf{sel\text{-}ind\text{-}fe\text{-}cpa\text{-}}\beta}_{\mathsf{FE},\mathcal{A}}(\lambda)$ for $\beta \in \{0,1\}$.

Definition 6 (Indistinguishability-Based Security). *A functional encryption scheme* FE *is* adaptively *secure (resp.* selectively *secure) against chosen-plaintext attacks if for every PPT algorithm* $\mathcal{A}$, $\mathbf{Adv}^{\mathsf{ind\text{-}fe\text{-}cpa}}_{\mathsf{FE},\mathcal{A}}(\lambda)$ *(resp.* $\mathbf{Adv}^{\mathsf{sel\text{-}ind\text{-}fe\text{-}cpa}}_{\mathsf{FE},\mathcal{A}}(\lambda)$*) is negligible.*

2.3 Bilinear Maps Functionality

In this work we consider functional encryption schemes for the following *bilinear map functionality.* Let $\mathsf{bgp} = (p, \mathbb{G}_1, \mathbb{G}_2, g_1, g_2, \mathbb{G}_T, e) \leftarrow_{\mathrm{R}} \mathcal{G}(1^\lambda)$ be a bilinear group setting, and let $n, m \in \mathbb{N}^+$ be positive integers. We let the message space $\mathcal{M} := \mathbb{Z}_p^n \times \mathbb{Z}_p^m$ – every message M is a pair of vectors $(\boldsymbol{x}, \boldsymbol{y})$ – the key space $\mathcal{K} := \mathbb{Z}_p^{n\times m}$ consists of matrices – every key $K \in \mathcal{K}$ is a matrix $\mathbf{F} = (f_{i,j})$ – and the output space is $\mathcal{Y} := \mathbb{G}_T$. The functionality $F(K, M)$ is the one that computes the value $[\boldsymbol{x}^\top \mathbf{F}\, \boldsymbol{y}]_T \in \mathbb{G}_T$. As we discuss below, this functionality allows for interesting applications.

Bilinear maps over the integers. We note that for appropriate choices of $\mathcal{M} \subset \mathbb{Z}_p^n \times \mathbb{Z}_p^m$ and $\mathcal{K} \subset \mathbb{Z}_p^{n\times m}$, the output space of $F(\mathcal{K}, \mathcal{M})$ can be made of size polynomial in the security parameter. In this case, there exist efficient methods to extract $\boldsymbol{x}^\top \mathbf{F}\, \boldsymbol{y} \in \mathbb{Z}_p$ from $[\boldsymbol{x}^\top \mathbf{F}\, \boldsymbol{y}]_T \in \mathbb{G}_T$.

For example, one can fix integers $B_x, B_y, B_f \in \mathbb{N}$, and define $\mathcal{M} := \{0, \ldots, B_x\}^n \times \{0, \ldots, B_y\}^m$, $\mathcal{K} := \{0, \ldots, B_f\}^{n\times m}$. Then the quantity $B = mnB_xB_yB_f < p$ must be small enough to allow for efficient discrete logarithm computation.

Multivariate quadratic polynomials. We also note that bilinear maps over the integers capture an interesting class of quadratic functions, such *multivariate quadratic polynomials*:

$$p(\boldsymbol{m}) = p_0 + \sum_i p_i \cdot m_i + \sum_{i,j} p_{i,j} \cdot m_i \cdot m_j.$$

This can be captured by setting $\boldsymbol{x} = \boldsymbol{y} = (1, \boldsymbol{m}) \in \mathbb{Z}_p^{n+1}$ and by encoding p's coefficients in an upper triangular matrix $\mathbf{F} = (f_{i,j}) \in \mathbb{Z}_p^{(n+1)\times(n+1)}$ where: $f_{1,1} = p_0$, $f_{1,i} = p_{i-1}$ for all $i \in [2, n+1]$, $f_{i,j} = 0$ for all $i > j$, and $f_{i,j} = p_{i-1,j-1}$ for all $i \in [2, n+1]$ and $j \geq i$.

2.4 Predicate Encryption

We recall the definition of predicate encryption, as originally defined in [28,29].

Definition 7 (Predicate). *A predicate* P *defined over* $(\mathcal{X}, \mathcal{Y})$ *is a boolean function:* $\mathsf{P} : \mathcal{X} \times \mathcal{Y} \to \{0,1\}$.

Definition 8 (Predicate Encryption). *A predicate encryption (PE) scheme for a predicate* $\mathsf{P} : \mathcal{X} \times \mathcal{Y} \to \{0,1\}$ *consists of four algorithms* (Setup, Encrypt, KeyGen, Decrypt)*:*

$\mathsf{Setup}(1^\lambda, \mathsf{P}, \mathcal{M}) \to (\mathsf{mpk}, \mathsf{msk})$. *The setup algorithm gets as input the security parameter* λ*, the predicate* $\mathsf{P} : \mathcal{X} \times \mathcal{Y} \to \{0,1\}$*, the message space* $\mathcal{M}$ *and outputs the public parameter* mpk*, and the master key* msk.

$\mathsf{Encrypt}(\mathsf{mpk}, x, M) \to \mathsf{Ct}_x$. *The encryption algorithm gets as input* mpk*, an attribute* $x \in \mathcal{X}$ *and a message* $M \in \mathcal{M}$*. It outputs a ciphertext* Ct_x.

$\mathsf{KeyGen}(\mathsf{mpk}, \mathsf{msk}, y) \to \mathsf{sk}_y$. *The key generation algorithm gets as input* msk *and a value* $y \in \mathcal{Y}$*, and outputs a secret key* sk_y*. Note that* y *is public in* sk_y.

$\mathsf{Decrypt}(\mathsf{mpk}, \mathsf{sk}_y, \mathsf{Ct}_x) \to M$. *The decryption algorithm gets as input* sk_y *and* Ct_x *such that* $\mathsf{P}(x, y) = 1$*. It outputs a message* M.

For correctness, it is requires that for all $(x, y) \in \mathcal{X} \times \mathcal{Y}$ *such that* $\mathsf{P}(x, y) = 1$ *and all* $M \in \mathcal{M}$*,* $\Pr[\mathsf{Decrypt}(\mathsf{mpk}, \mathsf{sk}_y, \mathsf{Encrypt}(\mathsf{mpk}, x, M)) = M] = 1$*, where the probability is taken over* $(\mathsf{mpk}, \mathsf{msk}) \leftarrow \mathsf{Setup}(1^\lambda, \mathcal{X}, \mathcal{Y}, \mathcal{M})$*,* $\mathsf{sk}_y \leftarrow \mathsf{KeyGen}(\mathsf{mpk}, \mathsf{msk}, y)$*, and the coins of* Encrypt.

Fully Attribute-Hiding Security. We recall the notion of *fully attribute-hiding* security for predicate encryption as defined in [28]. The fully attribute hiding property refers to the fact that an adversary cannot distinguish a ciphertext for attribute $x^{(0)}$ from a ciphertext for $x^{(1)}$, as long as it only queries keys sk_y where $\mathsf{P}(x^{(0)}, y) = \mathsf{P}(x^{(1)}, y)$. This is stronger than the so-called *weakly attribute hiding* property, which requires the adversary to only query keys sk_y where $\mathsf{P}(x^{(0)}, y) = \mathsf{P}(x^{(1)}, y) = 0$.

Fully attribute hiding security is essentially the specialization of the indistinguishability based security notion for functional encryption, for the functionality $F_{\mathsf{P}}(y, (x, M))$ that outputs M if $\mathsf{P}(x, y) = 1$ and $\perp$ otherwise.

For any stateful adversary $\mathcal{A}$, any predicate encryption scheme PE, any bit $\beta \in \{0,1\}$, and any security parameter λ, we define experiments $\mathbf{Exp}^{\mathsf{ind\text{-}pe\text{-}cpa}\text{-}\beta}_{\mathsf{PE},\mathcal{A}}(\lambda)$ and $\mathbf{Exp}^{\mathsf{sel\text{-}ind\text{-}pe\text{-}cpa}\text{-}\beta}_{\mathsf{PE},\mathcal{A}}(\lambda)$ in Fig. 2. We define the advantage of $\mathcal{A}$ for adaptive security as:

$$\begin{aligned}\mathbf{Adv}^{\mathsf{ind\text{-}pe\text{-}cpa}}_{\mathsf{PE},\mathcal{A}}(\lambda) &:= \left|\Pr[\mathbf{Exp}^{\mathsf{ind\text{-}pe\text{-}cpa\text{-}0}}_{\mathsf{PE},\mathcal{A}}(\lambda) = 1] - \Pr[\mathbf{Exp}^{\mathsf{ind\text{-}pe\text{-}cpa\text{-}1}}_{\mathsf{PE},\mathcal{A}}(\lambda) = 1]\right| \\ &= \left|1 - 2\Pr\left[\beta' = \beta : \begin{array}{l}\beta \leftarrow_{\mathrm{R}} \{0,1\} \\ \mathbf{Exp}^{\mathsf{ind\text{-}pe\text{-}cpa}\text{-}\beta}_{\mathsf{PE},\mathcal{A}}(\lambda) = \beta'\end{array}\right]\right|\end{aligned}$$

We define the advantage $\mathbf{Adv}^{\mathsf{sel\text{-}ind\text{-}pe\text{-}cpa}}_{\mathsf{PE},\mathcal{A}}(\lambda)$ for selective security similarly, with respect to experiments $\mathbf{Exp}^{\mathsf{sel\text{-}ind\text{-}pe\text{-}cpa}\text{-}\beta}_{\mathsf{PE},\mathcal{A}}(\lambda)$ for $\beta \in \{0,1\}$.

Definition 9 (Fully Attribute-Hiding Security). *A predicate encryption scheme* PE *is fully attribute hiding,* adaptively *secure (resp.* selectively *secure) against chosen-plaintext attacks if for every PPT algorithm* $\mathcal{A}$*,* $\mathbf{Adv}^{\mathsf{ind\text{-}pe\text{-}cpa}}_{\mathsf{PE},\mathcal{A}}(\lambda)$ *(resp.* $\mathbf{Adv}^{\mathsf{sel\text{-}ind\text{-}pe\text{-}cpa}}_{\mathsf{PE},\mathcal{A}}(\lambda)$*) is negligible.*

$\mathbf{Exp}^{\text{ind-pe-cpa-}\beta}_{\mathsf{PE},\mathcal{A}}(\lambda)$, $\mathbf{Exp}^{\text{sel-ind-pe-cpa-}\beta}_{\mathsf{PE},\mathcal{A}}(\lambda)$:	
$(x^{(0)}, M_0, x^{(1)}, M_1) \leftarrow \mathcal{A}(1^\lambda)$	$\mathsf{EncO}(x^{(0)}, M_0, x^{(1)}, M_1)$:
$(\mathsf{mpk}, \mathsf{msk}) \leftarrow_{\mathrm{R}} \mathsf{Setup}(1^\lambda)$	Return $\mathsf{Ct}^\star := \mathsf{Encrypt}(\mathsf{mpk}, x^{(\beta)}, M_\beta)$
$\mathsf{Ct} := \mathsf{EncO}(x^{(0)}, M_0, x^{(1)}, M_1)$	$\mathsf{KeyGenO}(y \in \mathcal{Y})$:
$\beta' \leftarrow \mathcal{A}(\mathsf{mpk}, \boxed{\mathsf{Ct}})^{\mathsf{KeyGenO}(\cdot), \mathsf{EncO}(\cdot,\cdot,\cdot,\cdot)}$	Return $\mathsf{sk}_K := \mathsf{KeyGen}(\mathsf{msk}, y)$
Return β'.	

Fig. 2. Experiments $\mathbf{Exp}^{\text{ind-pe-cpa-}\beta}_{\mathsf{PE},\mathcal{A}}(\lambda)$ and $\mathbf{Exp}^{\text{sel-ind-pe-cpa-}\beta}_{\mathsf{PE},\mathcal{A}}(\lambda)$ for $b \in \{0,1\}$, used to define adaptive, and selective security of PE, respectively. In each procedure, the components inside a solid (dotted) frame are only present in the games marked by a solid (dotted) frame. In both games, the oracle $\mathsf{EncO}(\cdot,\cdot,\cdot,\cdot)$ is queried at most once (by $\mathcal{A}$ or the game itself), on $x^{(0)}, M_0, x^{(1)}, M_1$, such that for all queries y to $\mathsf{KeyGenO}(\cdot)$, we have: $\mathsf{P}(x^{(0)}, y) = P(x^{(1)}, y)$. Moreover, if $\mathsf{P}(x^{(0)}, y) = 1$ for some query y to $\mathsf{KeyGenO}(\cdot)$, then $M_0 = M_1$.

3 Our Functional Encryption for Bilinear Maps from MDDH

In this Section we present a functional encryption scheme that supports the bilinear maps functionality described in Sect. 2.3, and is proven selectively secure under standard assumptions.

To begin with, in Sect. 3.1 we describe a simple FE scheme that works in the private-key setting, and is only single-ciphertext secure.

This private-key scheme is used as a building block in the security proof of our main public-key FE scheme that we present in Sect. 3.2.

3.1 Private-Key, Single-Ciphertext Secure FE for Bilinear Maps

In this section, we present a family of private-key, single-ciphertext secure functional encryption schemes for bilinear maps, parametrized by an integer $k \geq 1$ and a matrix distribution $\mathcal{D}_k$ (see Definition 1). That is, for each $k \in \mathbb{N}$, and each matrix distribution $\mathcal{D}_k$, the scheme $\mathsf{FE}_{\mathsf{one}}(k, \mathcal{D}_k)$, presented in Fig. 3, is single-ciphertext, selectively secure under the $\mathcal{D}_k$-MDDH assumption, on asymmetric pairings.

Technical overview. Before describing the scheme in full detail in Fig. 3, we give an informal exposition of our techniques. The basic idea in our private-key, single ciphertext secure FE is to create the ciphertext and the secret keys of the form:

$$\mathsf{Ct}_{(\boldsymbol{x},\boldsymbol{y})} := \{[\mathbf{A}\boldsymbol{r}_i + \boldsymbol{b}^\perp x_i]_1\}_{i\in[n]}, \{[\mathbf{B}\boldsymbol{s}_j + \boldsymbol{a}^\perp y_j]_2\}_{j\in[m]},\ \mathsf{sk}_{\mathbf{F}} := [\sum_{i,j} f_{i,j}\boldsymbol{r}_i^\top \mathbf{A}^\top \mathbf{B}\boldsymbol{s}_j]_T,$$

where $\mathbf{A}, \mathbf{B} \leftarrow_{\mathrm{R}} \mathcal{D}_k$, and $(\mathbf{A}|\boldsymbol{b}^\perp)$, $(\mathbf{B}|\boldsymbol{a}^\perp)$ are bases of $\mathbb{Z}_p^{k+1}$ such that $\boldsymbol{a}^\perp \in \mathsf{orth}(\mathbf{A})$ and $\boldsymbol{b}^\perp \in \mathsf{orth}(\mathbf{B})$, à la [16]. The vectors $[\mathbf{A}\boldsymbol{r}_i]_1$ and $[\mathbf{B}\boldsymbol{s}_j]_2$ for $i \in [n], j \in [m]$, $\boldsymbol{a}^\perp$ and $\boldsymbol{b}^\perp$ are part of a master secret key, used to (deterministically) generate $\mathsf{Ct}_{\boldsymbol{x},\boldsymbol{y}}$ and $\mathsf{sk}_{\mathbf{F}}$. Correctness follows from the orthogonal property: decryption computes $\sum_{i,j} f_{i,j} e([\mathbf{A}\boldsymbol{r}_i + \boldsymbol{b}^\perp x_i]_1^\top, [\mathbf{B}\boldsymbol{s}_j + \boldsymbol{a}^\perp y_j]_2) = \mathsf{sk}_{\mathbf{F}} + (\boldsymbol{a}^\perp)^\top \boldsymbol{b}^\perp \cdot [F(\mathbf{F}, (\boldsymbol{x}, \boldsymbol{y}))]_T$, from which one can extract $F(\mathbf{F}, (\boldsymbol{x}, \boldsymbol{y})) = 0$ since $[(\boldsymbol{a}^\perp)^\top \boldsymbol{b}^\perp]_T$ is public. Security relies on the $\mathcal{D}_k$-MDDH Assumption [18], which stipulates that given $[\mathbf{A}]_1, [\mathbf{B}]_2$ drawn from a matrix distribution $\mathcal{D}_k$ over $\mathbb{Z}_p^{(k+1)\times k}$,

$$[\mathbf{A}\boldsymbol{r}]_1 \approx_c [\boldsymbol{u}]_1 \approx_c [\mathbf{A}\boldsymbol{r} + \boldsymbol{b}^\perp]_1 \text{ and } [\mathbf{B}\boldsymbol{s}]_2 \approx_c [\boldsymbol{v}]_2 \approx_c [\mathbf{B}\boldsymbol{s} + \boldsymbol{a}^\perp]_2,$$

where $\boldsymbol{r}, \boldsymbol{s} \leftarrow_{\mathrm{R}} \mathbb{Z}_p^k$, and $\boldsymbol{u}, \boldsymbol{v} \leftarrow_{\mathrm{R}} \mathbb{Z}_p^{k+1}$. This allows to change $\mathsf{Ct}_{(\boldsymbol{x}^{(0)},\boldsymbol{y}^{(0)})}$ into $\mathsf{Ct}_{(\boldsymbol{x}^{(1)},\boldsymbol{y}^{(1)})}$, but creates an extra term $\left[\boldsymbol{x}^{(1)\top}\mathbf{F}\boldsymbol{y}^{(1)} - \boldsymbol{x}^{(0)\top}\mathbf{F}\boldsymbol{y}^{(0)}\right]_T$ in the secret keys $\mathsf{sk}_{\mathbf{F}}$. We conclude the proof using the fact that for all $\mathbf{F}$ queried to KeyGen, $F(\mathbf{F}, (\boldsymbol{x}^{(0)}, \boldsymbol{y}^{(0)})) = F(\mathbf{F}, (\boldsymbol{x}^{(1)}, \boldsymbol{y}^{(1)}))$, as required by the security definition for FE (see Sect. 2.2 for the definition of FE), which cancels out the extra term in all secret keys.

<table>
<tr>
<td>

$\mathsf{Setup}(1^\lambda, F)$:

$\mathsf{bgp} \leftarrow_{\mathrm{R}} \mathcal{G}(1^\lambda)$, $\mathbf{A}, \mathbf{B} \leftarrow_{\mathrm{R}} \mathcal{D}_k$, $\boldsymbol{a}^\perp \leftarrow_{\mathrm{R}} \mathsf{orth}(\mathbf{A})$, $\boldsymbol{b}^\perp \leftarrow_{\mathrm{R}} \mathsf{orth}(\mathbf{B})$
For $i \in [n], j \in [m]$, $\boldsymbol{r}_i, \boldsymbol{s}_j \leftarrow_{\mathrm{R}} \mathbb{Z}_p^k$
Return $\mathsf{mpk} := (\mathsf{bgp}, [(\boldsymbol{b}^\perp)^\top \boldsymbol{a}^\perp]_T)$ and
$\mathsf{msk} := \left(\mathbf{A}, \boldsymbol{a}^\perp, \mathbf{B}, \boldsymbol{b}^\perp, \{\boldsymbol{r}_i, \boldsymbol{s}_j\}_{i\in[n],j\in[m]}\right)$

$\mathsf{KeyGen}(\mathsf{msk}, \mathbf{F} \in \mathbb{Z}_p^{n\times m})$:

$K := [\sum_{i\in[n],j\in[m]} f_{i,j} \boldsymbol{r}_i^\top \mathbf{A}^\top \mathbf{B}\boldsymbol{s}_j]_1 - [u]_1$,
$\widehat{K} := [u]_2$, where $u \leftarrow_{\mathrm{R}} \mathbb{Z}_p$
Return $\mathsf{sk}_{\mathbf{F}} := (K, \widehat{K}) \in \mathbb{G}_1 \times \mathbb{G}_2$

</td>
<td>

$\mathsf{Encrypt}(\mathsf{mpk}, \mathsf{msk}, (\boldsymbol{x}, \boldsymbol{y}) \in \mathbb{Z}_p^n \times \mathbb{Z}_p^m)$:

For $i \in [n]$: $\boldsymbol{c}_i := \mathbf{A}\boldsymbol{r}_i + \boldsymbol{b}^\perp x_i$,
For $j \in [m]$: $\widehat{\boldsymbol{c}}_j := \mathbf{B}\boldsymbol{s}_j + \boldsymbol{a}^\perp y_j$,
$\mathsf{Ct}_{(\boldsymbol{x},\boldsymbol{y})} := \{[\boldsymbol{c}_i]_1, [\widehat{\boldsymbol{c}}_j]_2\}_{i\in[n],j\in[m]}$
Return $\mathsf{Ct}_{(\boldsymbol{x},\boldsymbol{y})} \in \mathbb{G}_1^{n(k+1)} \times \mathbb{G}_2^{m(k+1)}$

$\mathsf{Decrypt}(\mathsf{mpk}, \mathsf{Ct}_{(\boldsymbol{x},\boldsymbol{y})}, \mathsf{sk}_{\mathbf{F}})$:

$D := \sum_{i\in[n],j\in[m]} f_{i,j} \cdot e([\boldsymbol{c}_i]_1, [\widehat{\boldsymbol{c}}_j]_2) - e(K, [1]_2) - e([1]_1, \widehat{K})$.
Return $v \in \mathbb{Z}_p$ such that $[v \cdot (\boldsymbol{b}^\perp)^\top \boldsymbol{a}^\perp]_T = D$.

</td>
</tr>
</table>

Fig. 3. $\mathsf{FE}_{\mathsf{one}}(k, \mathcal{D}_k)$, a family of private-key, functional encryption schemes parametrized by $k \in \mathbb{N}^*$ and a matrix distribution $\mathcal{D}_k$, single-ciphertext, selectively secure under the $\mathcal{D}_k$-MDDH assumption on asymmetric pairings.

In the following theorem we prove the correctness of the scheme $\mathsf{FE}_{\mathsf{one}}$.

Theorem 1 (Correctness). *For any $k \in \mathbb{N}^*$ and any matrix distribution $\mathcal{D}_k$, the functional encryption scheme $\mathsf{FE}_{\mathsf{one}}(k, \mathcal{D}_k)$ defined in Fig. 3 has perfect correctness.*

Proof of Theorem 1. Correctness follows from the fact that for all $i \in [n], j \in [m]$,

$$e([\boldsymbol{c}_i]_1, [\widehat{\boldsymbol{c}}_j]_2) = [\boldsymbol{r}_i^\top \mathbf{A}^\top \mathbf{B}\boldsymbol{s}_j + (\boldsymbol{b}^\perp)^\top \boldsymbol{a}^\perp x_i y_j]_T,$$

since $\mathbf{A}^\top \boldsymbol{a}^\perp = \mathbf{B}^\top \boldsymbol{b}^\perp = \mathbf{0}$. Therefore, the decryption computes

$$D := [\sum_{i,j} f_{i,j} \boldsymbol{r}_i^\top \mathbf{A}^\top \mathbf{B} \boldsymbol{s}_j + \boldsymbol{x}^\top \mathbf{F} \boldsymbol{y} \cdot (\boldsymbol{b}^\perp)^\top \boldsymbol{a}^\perp]_T - e(K, [1]_2) - e([1]_1, \widehat{K})$$
$$= \boldsymbol{x}^\top \mathbf{F} \boldsymbol{y} \cdot [(\boldsymbol{b}^\perp)^\top \boldsymbol{a}^\perp]_T.$$

Property 1 in Definition 1 implies that $(\boldsymbol{b}^\perp)^\top \boldsymbol{a}^\perp \neq 0$ with probability $1 - \frac{1}{\Omega(p)}$ over the choices of $\mathbf{A}, \mathbf{B} \leftarrow_R \mathcal{D}_k$, $\boldsymbol{a}^\perp \leftarrow_R \mathsf{orth}(\mathbf{A})$, and $\boldsymbol{b}^\perp \leftarrow_R \mathsf{orth}(\mathbf{B})$. Therefore, one can enumerate all possible $v \in \mathcal{Y}$ and check if $v \cdot [(\boldsymbol{b}^\perp)^\top \boldsymbol{a}^\perp]_T = D$. This can be done in time $|\mathcal{Y}|$, thus, we need to set $\mathcal{Y}$ to be of size $\mathsf{poly}(\lambda)$. □

Next, we show that $\mathsf{FE}_{\mathsf{one}}$ is selective-secure, for adversaries that make a single challenge encryption query, under the MDDH assumption.

Theorem 2 (Security). *For any $k \in \mathbb{N}^*$ and any matrix distribution $\mathcal{D}_k$, if the $\mathcal{D}_k$-MDDH assumptions hold in $\mathbb{G}_1$ and $\mathbb{G}_2$, then the functional encryption scheme $\mathsf{FE}_{\mathsf{one}}(k, \mathcal{D}_k)$ defined in Fig. 3 is selectively secure, in a single-ciphertext setting (see Definition 6). Namely, for any PPT adversary $\mathcal{A}$, there exist PPT adversaries $\mathcal{B}_1$ and $\mathcal{B}_2$ such that:*

$$\mathbf{Adv}^{\mathsf{sel\text{-}ind\text{-}fe\text{-}cpa}}_{\mathsf{FE}_{\mathsf{one}},\mathcal{A}}(\lambda) \leq 2 \cdot \mathbf{Adv}^{\mathcal{D}_k\text{-}\mathsf{mddh}}_{\mathcal{G},\mathbb{G}_1,\mathcal{B}_1}(\lambda) + 2 \cdot \mathbf{Adv}^{\mathcal{D}_k\text{-}\mathsf{mddh}}_{\mathcal{G},\mathbb{G}_2,\mathcal{B}_2}(\lambda) + 2^{-\Omega(\lambda)}.$$

G_0, $\boxed{G_1, \boxed{G_2}}$:

$(\boldsymbol{x}^{(0)}, \boldsymbol{y}^{(0)}), (\boldsymbol{x}^{(1)}, \boldsymbol{y}^{(1)})) \leftarrow \mathcal{A}(1^\lambda)$
$\mathbf{A}, \mathbf{B} \leftarrow_R \mathcal{D}_k$, $\boldsymbol{a}^\perp \leftarrow_R \mathsf{orth}(\mathbf{A})$, $\boldsymbol{b}^\perp \leftarrow_R \mathsf{orth}(\mathbf{B})$, $\mathsf{mpk} := \mathsf{bgp} \leftarrow_R \mathcal{G}(1^\lambda)$
For $i \in [n], j \in [m]$: $\boldsymbol{r}_i \leftarrow_R \mathbb{Z}_p^k$, $\boldsymbol{s}_j \leftarrow_R \mathbb{Z}_p^k$, $\beta \leftarrow_R \{0,1\}$
$\boldsymbol{c}_i := \mathbf{A}\boldsymbol{r}_i + x_i^{(\beta)} \boldsymbol{b}^\perp$, $\boxed{\boldsymbol{c}_i \leftarrow_R \mathbb{G}_1^{k+1}}$
$\widehat{\boldsymbol{c}}_j := \mathbf{B}\boldsymbol{s}_j + y_j^{(\beta)} \boldsymbol{a}^\perp$, $\boxed{\widehat{\boldsymbol{c}}_j \leftarrow_R \mathbb{G}_2^{k+1}}$
$\mathsf{Ct}^\star := \{[\boldsymbol{c}_i]_1, [\widehat{\boldsymbol{c}}_j]_1\}_{i \in [n], j \in [m]}$
$\beta' \leftarrow \mathcal{A}^{\mathsf{KeyGenO}(\cdot)}(\mathsf{mpk}, \mathsf{Ct}^\star)$
Return 1 if $\beta' = \beta$, 0 otherwise.

$\underline{\mathsf{KeyGenO}(\mathbf{F} \in \mathbb{Z}_p^{n \times m})}$:
$u \leftarrow_R \mathbb{Z}_p$, $K := [\sum_{i,j} f_{i,j} \boldsymbol{c}_i^\top \widehat{\boldsymbol{c}}_j]_1 - [\boldsymbol{x}^{\top(\beta)} \mathbf{F} \boldsymbol{y}^{(\beta)} (\boldsymbol{b}^\perp)^\top \boldsymbol{a}^\perp]_1 - [u]_1$, $\widehat{K} := [u]_2$
Return $\mathsf{sk}_{\mathbf{F}} := (K, \widehat{K})$

Fig. 4. Games G_0, G_1, G_2, for the proof of selective security of $\mathsf{FE}_{\mathsf{one}}(k, \mathcal{D}_k)$ in Fig. 3. In each procedure, the components inside a solid (dotted) frame are only present in the games marked by a solid (dotted) frame.

Proof of Theorem 2. We prove the security of $\mathsf{FE}_{\mathsf{one}}(k, \mathcal{D}_k)$ via a series of games that is compactly presented in Fig. 4. Before going to the details of the proof and proving the indistinguishability of each consecutive pair of games, we provide below a high level view of the game transitions:

Game G_0 is the selective security experiment for scheme $\mathsf{FE}_{\mathsf{one}}$ with only some syntactic changes. This is shown in Lemma 2.

Game G_1 is the same as game G_0 except that the $\boldsymbol{c}_i$ ciphertext components are uniformly random over $\mathbb{G}_1^{k+1}$. In Lemma 3 we show that G_0 is computationally indistinguishable from G_1 under the MDDH assumption.

Game G_2 is the same as game G_1 except that the $\widehat{\boldsymbol{c}}_j$ ciphertext components are uniformly random over $\mathbb{G}_2^{k+1}$. In Lemma 4 we show that G_1 is computationally indistinguishable from G_2 under the MDDH assumption. Finally, we show in in Lemma 5 that the adversary's view in this game is independent of the bit β, and thus the adversary's advantage in this game is zero.

More formally, in what follows, we use Adv_i to denote the advantage of $\mathcal{A}$ in game G_i, that is $\mathsf{Adv}_i := |1 - 2\Pr[G_i \text{ returns } 1]|$.

Lemma 2 **(G_0).** $\mathsf{Adv}_0 = \mathbf{Adv}^{\mathsf{ind\text{-}fe\text{-}cpa}}_{\mathsf{FE}_{\mathsf{one}},\mathcal{A}}(\lambda)$.

Proof of Lemma 2. We show that G_0 corresponds to the game for selective security of the functional encryption scheme, in the private-key, single-ciphertext setting, as defined in Definition 6. It is clear that the output of the Setup algorithm is identically distributed in both of these games. We show that this is also the case for the outputs of the $\mathsf{KeyGenO}$ oracle. Indeed, for all $i \in [n]$, $j \in [m]$, we have:

$$\boldsymbol{c}_i^\top \widehat{\boldsymbol{c}}_j = \boldsymbol{r}_i^\top \mathbf{A}^\top \mathbf{B} \boldsymbol{s}_j + x_i^{(\beta)} y_j^{(\beta)} (\boldsymbol{b}^\perp)^\top \boldsymbol{a}^\perp.$$

Thus, in game G_0, for all $\mathbf{F} \in \mathbb{Z}_p^{n \times m}$, $\mathsf{KeyGenO}(\mathbf{F})$ computes:

$$\begin{aligned}
K &:= \sum_{i,j} f_{i,j} [\boldsymbol{c}_i^\top \widehat{\boldsymbol{c}}_j]_1 - [\boldsymbol{x}^{(\beta)\top} \mathbf{F} \boldsymbol{y}^{(\beta)} (\boldsymbol{b}^\perp)^\top \boldsymbol{a}^\perp]_1 - [u]_1 \\
&= \sum_{i,j} f_{i,j} [\boldsymbol{r}_i^\top \mathbf{A}^\top \mathbf{B} \boldsymbol{s}_j]_1 + [\boldsymbol{x}^{(\beta)\top} \mathbf{F} \boldsymbol{y}^{(\beta)} (\boldsymbol{b}^\perp)^\top \boldsymbol{a}^\perp]_1 - [\boldsymbol{x}^{(\beta)\top} \mathbf{F} \boldsymbol{y}^{(\beta)} (\boldsymbol{b}^\perp)^\top \boldsymbol{a}^\perp]_1 - [u]_1 \\
&= \sum_{i,j} f_{i,j} [\boldsymbol{r}_i^\top \mathbf{A}^\top \mathbf{B} \boldsymbol{s}_j]_1 - [u]_1
\end{aligned}$$

which is exactly as in the security game for selective security. □

Lemma 3 **(G_0 to G_1).** *There exists a PPT adversary $\mathcal{B}_0$ such that*

$$|\mathsf{Adv}_0 - \mathsf{Adv}_1| \leq 2 \cdot \mathbf{Adv}^{\mathcal{D}_k\text{-}\mathsf{mddh}}_{\mathcal{G},\mathbb{G}_1,\mathcal{B}_0}(\lambda) + 2^{-\Omega(\lambda)}.$$

Proof of Lemma 3. Here, we use the MDDH assumption on $[\mathbf{A}]_1$ to change the distribution of the challenge ciphertext, after arguing that one can simulate the game without knowing $\boldsymbol{a}^\perp$ or $[\mathbf{A}]_2$.

Namely, we build a PPT adversary $\mathcal{B}'_0$ against the n-fold $\mathcal{D}_k$-MDDH assumption in $\mathbb{G}_1$ such that $|\mathsf{Adv}_0 - \mathsf{Adv}_1| \leq 2 \cdot \mathbf{Adv}^{n\text{-}\mathcal{D}_k\text{-}\mathsf{mddh}}_{\mathcal{G},\mathbb{G}_1,\mathcal{B}'_0}(\lambda) + 2^{-\Omega(\lambda)}$. Then, by Lemma 1, this implies the existence of a PPT adversary $\mathcal{B}_0$ such that $|\mathsf{Adv}_0 - \mathsf{Adv}_1| \leq 2 \cdot \mathbf{Adv}^{\mathcal{D}_k\text{-}\mathsf{mddh}}_{\mathcal{G},\mathbb{G}_1,\mathcal{B}_0}(\lambda) + 2^{-\Omega(\lambda)}$.

Adversary $\mathcal{B}'_0$ simulates the game to $\mathcal{A}$ as described in Fig. 5. Finally, it outputs 1 if the bit β' output by the adversary $\mathcal{A}$ is equal to β, 0 otherwise. We show that when $\mathcal{B}'_0$ is given a real MDDH challenge, that is, $[\boldsymbol{h}_1|\cdots|\boldsymbol{h}_n]_1 := \mathbf{AR}$ for $\mathbf{R} \leftarrow_{\mathrm{R}} \mathbb{Z}_p^{k\times n}$, then it simulates the game G_0, whereas it simulates the game G_1 when given a fully random challenge, i.e. when $[\boldsymbol{h}_1|\cdots|\boldsymbol{h}_n]_1 \leftarrow_{\mathrm{R}} \mathbb{G}_1^{(k+1)\times n}$, which implies the lemma.

$\mathcal{B}'_0(\mathsf{bgp}, [\mathbf{A}]_1, [\boldsymbol{h}_1|\cdots|\boldsymbol{h}_n]_1)$:
$((\boldsymbol{x}^{(0)}, \boldsymbol{y}^{(0)}), (\boldsymbol{x}^{(1)}, \boldsymbol{y}^{(1)})) \leftarrow \mathcal{A}(1^\lambda)$
$\mathbf{B} \leftarrow_{\mathrm{R}} \mathcal{D}_k$, $\beta \leftarrow_{\mathrm{R}} \{0,1\}$, $\boldsymbol{b}^\perp \leftarrow_{\mathrm{R}} \mathsf{orth}(\mathbf{B})$, For $j \in [m]$: $\boldsymbol{s}_j \leftarrow_{\mathrm{R}} \mathbb{Z}_p^k$, $\boldsymbol{z} \leftarrow_{\mathrm{R}} \mathbb{Z}_p^{k+1}$
$\boldsymbol{c}_i := \boldsymbol{h}_i + x_i^{(\beta)} \boldsymbol{b}^\perp$
$\widehat{\boldsymbol{c}}_j := \mathbf{B}\boldsymbol{s}_j + y_j^{(\beta)} \boldsymbol{z}$;
Return $\mathsf{mpk} := (\mathsf{bgp}, [(\boldsymbol{b}^\perp)^\top \boldsymbol{z}]_T)$ and $\mathsf{Ct} := \{[\boldsymbol{c}_i]_1, [\widehat{\boldsymbol{c}}_j]_2\}_{i\in[n],j\in[m]}$

$\mathsf{KeyGenO}(\mathbf{F} \in \mathbb{Z}_p^{n\times m})$:
$u \leftarrow_{\mathrm{R}} \mathbb{Z}_p$, $K := \sum_{i,j} f_{i,j}[\boldsymbol{c}_i^\top \widehat{\boldsymbol{c}}_j]_1 - [u]_1 - \boldsymbol{x}^{(\beta)\top}\mathbf{F}\boldsymbol{y}^{(\beta)} \cdot [(\boldsymbol{b}^\perp)^\top \boldsymbol{z}]_1$, $\widehat{K} := [u]_2$
Return $\mathsf{sk}_{\mathbf{F}} := (K, \widehat{K})$

Fig. 5. Adversary $\mathcal{B}'_0$ against the n-fold $\mathcal{D}_k$-mddh assumption, for the proof of Lemma 3.

We use the following facts.

1. For all $\boldsymbol{s} \in \mathbb{Z}_p^k$, $\mathbf{B} \in \mathbb{Z}_p^{(k+1)\times k}$, $\boldsymbol{b}^\perp \in \mathsf{orth}(\mathbf{B})$, and $\boldsymbol{a}^\perp \in \mathbb{Z}_p^{k+1}$, we have:
$$(\boldsymbol{b}^\perp)^\top \boldsymbol{a}^\perp = (\boldsymbol{b}^\perp)^\top(\mathbf{B}\boldsymbol{s} + \boldsymbol{a}^\perp).$$
2. For all $y_j^{(\beta)} \in \mathbb{Z}_p$, $\boldsymbol{s} \in \mathbb{Z}_p^k$:
$$\left(\{\boldsymbol{s}_j\}_{j\in[m]}\right)_{\boldsymbol{s}_j \leftarrow_{\mathrm{R}} \mathbb{Z}_p^k} \equiv \left(\{\boldsymbol{s}_j + y_j^{(\beta)}\boldsymbol{s}\}_{j\in[m]}\right)_{\boldsymbol{s}_j \leftarrow_{\mathrm{R}} \mathbb{Z}_p^k}.$$
3. $$\left(\mathbf{B}\boldsymbol{s} + \boldsymbol{a}^\perp\right)_{\mathbf{A},\mathbf{B}\leftarrow_{\mathrm{R}}\mathcal{D}_k, \boldsymbol{a}^\perp \leftarrow_{\mathrm{R}} \mathsf{orth}(\mathbf{A}), \boldsymbol{s}\leftarrow_{\mathrm{R}}\mathbb{Z}_p^k} \approx_{\frac{1}{\Omega(p)}} (\boldsymbol{z})_{\boldsymbol{z}\leftarrow_{\mathrm{R}}\mathbb{Z}_p^{k+1}},$$
since $(\mathbf{B}|\boldsymbol{a}^\perp)$ is a basis of $\mathbb{Z}_p^{k+1}$, with probability $1 - \frac{1}{\Omega(p)}$ over the choices of $\mathbf{A}, \mathbf{B}$, and $\boldsymbol{a}^\perp$ (this is implied by Property 1).

Therefore, we have for all $\boldsymbol{y}^{(\beta)} \in \mathbb{Z}_p^m$:

$$\left(\mathbf{A}, \boldsymbol{b}^\perp, \{\mathbf{B}\boldsymbol{s}_j + y_j^{(\beta)}\boldsymbol{a}^\perp\}_{j\in[m]}, (\boldsymbol{b}^\perp)^\top \boldsymbol{a}^\perp\right)$$
where $\mathbf{A}, \mathbf{B} \leftarrow_{\mathrm{R}} \mathcal{D}_k$, $\boldsymbol{a}^\perp \leftarrow_{\mathrm{R}} \mathsf{orth}(\mathbf{A})$, $\boldsymbol{b}^\perp \leftarrow_{\mathrm{R}} \mathsf{orth}(\mathbf{B})$, $\boldsymbol{s}_j \leftarrow_{\mathrm{R}} \mathbb{Z}_p^k$
$$\equiv \left(\mathbf{A}, \boldsymbol{b}^\perp, \{\mathbf{B}\boldsymbol{s}_j + y_j^{(\beta)}\boldsymbol{a}^\perp\}_{j\in[m]}, (\boldsymbol{b}^\perp)^\top(\mathbf{B}\boldsymbol{s} + \boldsymbol{a}^\perp)\right)$$

where $\mathbf{A}, \mathbf{B} \leftarrow_{\mathrm{R}} \mathcal{D}_k, \boldsymbol{a}^{\perp} \leftarrow_{\mathrm{R}} \mathsf{orth}(\mathbf{A}), \boldsymbol{b}^{\perp} \leftarrow_{\mathrm{R}} \mathsf{orth}(\mathbf{B}),\ \boldsymbol{s} \leftarrow_{\mathrm{R}} \mathbb{Z}_p^k, \boldsymbol{s}_j \leftarrow_{\mathrm{R}} \mathbb{Z}_p^k$ (by 1.)

$$\equiv \left(\mathbf{A}, \boldsymbol{b}^{\perp}, \{\mathbf{B}\boldsymbol{s}_j + y_j^{(\beta)}(\mathbf{B}\boldsymbol{s} + \boldsymbol{a}^{\perp})\}_{j\in[m]}, (\boldsymbol{b}^{\perp})^{\top}(\mathbf{B}\boldsymbol{s} + \boldsymbol{a}^{\perp})\right)$$

where $\mathbf{A}, \mathbf{B} \leftarrow_{\mathrm{R}} \mathcal{D}_k, \boldsymbol{a}^{\perp} \leftarrow_{\mathrm{R}} \mathsf{orth}(\mathbf{A}), \boldsymbol{b}^{\perp} \leftarrow_{\mathrm{R}} \mathsf{orth}(\mathbf{B}), \boldsymbol{s}, \boldsymbol{s}_j \leftarrow_{\mathrm{R}} \mathbb{Z}_p^k$ (by 2.)

$$\approx_{\frac{1}{\Omega(p)}} \left(\mathbf{A}, \boldsymbol{b}^{\perp}, \{\mathbf{B}\boldsymbol{s}_j + y_j^{(\beta)}\boldsymbol{z}\}_{j\in[m]}, (\boldsymbol{b}^{\perp})^{\top}\boldsymbol{z}\right)$$

where $\mathbf{A}, \mathbf{B} \leftarrow_{\mathrm{R}} \mathcal{D}_k, \boldsymbol{a}^{\perp} \leftarrow_{\mathrm{R}} \mathsf{orth}(\mathbf{A}), \boldsymbol{b}^{\perp} \leftarrow_{\mathrm{R}} \mathsf{orth}(\mathbf{B}),\ \boldsymbol{z} \leftarrow_{\mathrm{R}} \mathbb{Z}_p^{k+1}, \boldsymbol{s}_j \leftarrow_{\mathrm{R}} \mathbb{Z}_p^k$ (by 3.)

When $\mathcal{B}'_0$ is given a real MDDH challenge, i.e., when for all $i \in [n]$, $\boldsymbol{h}_i := \mathbf{A}\boldsymbol{r}_i$, for $\boldsymbol{r}_i \leftarrow_{\mathrm{R}} \mathbb{Z}_p^k$, we have $\boldsymbol{c}_i := \mathbf{A}\boldsymbol{r}_i + x_i^{(\beta)}\boldsymbol{b}^{\perp}$, exactly as in game G_0, whereas $\boldsymbol{c}_i$ is uniformly random over $\mathbb{Z}_p^{k+1}$ when $\mathcal{B}'_0$ is given a random challenge, i.e., when for all $i \in [n]$, $\boldsymbol{h}_i \leftarrow_{\mathrm{R}} \mathbb{Z}_p^{k+1}$, as in game G_1. As shown in the equation above, the rest of $\mathcal{A}$'s view, namely, mpk, $\{\widehat{\boldsymbol{c}}_j\}_{j\in[m]}$ computed by $\mathcal{B}'_0$, and its simulation of $\mathsf{KeyGenO}$, are statistically close to those of G_0 (resp. G_1) when $\mathcal{B}'_0$ is given a real MDDH challenge (resp. a uniformly random challenge). □

Lemma 4 **(G_1 to G_2).** *There exists a PPT adversary $\mathcal{B}_1$ such that*

$$|\mathsf{Adv}_1 - \mathsf{Adv}_2| \leq 2 \cdot \mathbf{Adv}^{\mathcal{D}_k\text{-}\mathsf{mddh}}_{\mathcal{G},\mathbb{G}_2,\mathcal{B}_1}(\lambda) + \frac{2}{p-1}.$$

Proof of Lemma 4. Here, we use the MDDH assumption on $[\mathbf{B}]_2$ to change the distribution of the challenge ciphertext, after arguing that one can simulate the game without knowing $\boldsymbol{b}^{\perp}$ or $[\mathbf{B}]_1$.

Namely, we build a PPT adversary $\mathcal{B}'_1$ against the m-fold $\mathcal{D}_k$-MDDH assumption in $\mathbb{G}_2$ such that $|\mathsf{Adv}_1 - \mathsf{Adv}_2| \leq 2 \cdot \mathbf{Adv}^{m\text{-}\mathcal{D}_k\text{-}\mathsf{mddh}}_{\mathcal{G},\mathbb{G}_2,\mathcal{B}'_1}(\lambda)$. Then, by Lemma 1, this implies the existence of a PPT adversary $\mathcal{B}_1$ such that $|\mathsf{Adv}_1 - \mathsf{Adv}_2| \leq 2 \cdot \mathbf{Adv}^{\mathcal{D}_k\text{-}\mathsf{mddh}}_{\mathcal{G},\mathbb{G}_2,\mathcal{B}_1}(\lambda) + \frac{2}{p-1}$.

Adversary $\mathcal{B}'_1$ simulates the game to $\mathcal{A}$ as described in Fig. 6. Finally, it outputs 1 if the bit β' output by the adversary $\mathcal{A}$ is equal to β, 0 otherwise. We show that when $\mathcal{B}'_1$ is given a real MDDH challenge, that is, $[\boldsymbol{h}_1|\cdots|\boldsymbol{h}_m]_2 := [\mathbf{BS}]_2$ for $\mathbf{S} \leftarrow_{\mathrm{R}} \mathbb{Z}_p^{k\times m}$, then it simulates the game G_1, whereas it simulates the game G_2 when given a uniformly random challenge, i.e. when $[\boldsymbol{h}_1|\cdots|\boldsymbol{h}_m]_2 \leftarrow_{\mathrm{R}} \mathbb{G}_2^{(k+1)\times m}$, which implies the lemma.

We use the fact that for all $\mathbf{A}, \mathbf{B} \in \mathbb{Z}_p^{(k+1)\times k}$,

$$(\mathbf{B}, \boldsymbol{a}^{\perp}, (\boldsymbol{b}^{\perp})^{\top}\boldsymbol{a}^{\perp})_{\boldsymbol{a}^{\perp}\leftarrow_{\mathrm{R}}\mathsf{orth}(\mathbf{A}), \boldsymbol{b}^{\perp}\leftarrow_{\mathrm{R}}\mathsf{orth}(\mathbf{B})} \equiv (\mathbf{B}, \boldsymbol{a}^{\perp}, v)_{v\leftarrow_{\mathrm{R}}\mathbb{Z}_p)}.$$

Note that the leftmost distribution corresponds to mpk, $\{\boldsymbol{c}_i\}_{i\in[n]}$, and $\mathsf{KeyGenO}$ distributed as in games G_1 or G_2 (these are identically distributed in these two games), while the last distribution corresponds to mpk, $\{\boldsymbol{c}_i\}_{i\in[n]}$, and $\mathsf{KeyGenO}$ simulated by $\mathcal{B}'_1$.

Finally, when $\mathcal{B}'_1$ is given a real MDDH challenge, i.e., when for all $j \in [m]$, $\boldsymbol{h}_j := \mathbf{B}\boldsymbol{s}_j$, for $\boldsymbol{s}_j \leftarrow_{\mathrm{R}} \mathbb{Z}_p^k$, we have $\widehat{\boldsymbol{c}}_j := \mathbf{B}\boldsymbol{s}_j + y_j^{(\beta)}\boldsymbol{a}^{\perp}$, exactly as in game G_1,

$\underline{\mathcal{B}_1(\mathsf{bgp}, [\mathbf{B}]_2, [\boldsymbol{h}_1|\cdots|\boldsymbol{h}_m]_2):}$
$((\boldsymbol{x}^{(0)}, \boldsymbol{y}^{(0)}), (\boldsymbol{x}^{(1)}, \boldsymbol{y}^{(1)})) \leftarrow \mathcal{A}(1^\lambda)$
$\mathbf{A} \leftarrow_{\mathrm{R}} \mathcal{D}_k$, $\beta \leftarrow_{\mathrm{R}} \{0,1\}$, $\boldsymbol{a}^\perp \leftarrow_{\mathrm{R}} \mathsf{orth}(\mathbf{A})$, $v \leftarrow_{\mathrm{R}} \mathbb{Z}_p$
$\boldsymbol{c}_i \leftarrow_{\mathrm{R}} \mathbb{Z}_p^{k+1}$
$\widehat{\boldsymbol{c}}_j := \boldsymbol{h}_j + y_j^{(\beta)} \boldsymbol{a}^\perp$;
Return $\mathsf{mpk} := (\mathsf{bgp}, [v]_T)$ and $\mathsf{Ct} := \{[\boldsymbol{c}_i]_1, [\widehat{\boldsymbol{c}}_j]_2\}_{i \in [n], j \in [m]}$

$\underline{\mathsf{KeyGenO}(\mathbf{F} \in \mathbb{Z}_p^{n \times m}):}$
$u \leftarrow_{\mathrm{R}} \mathbb{Z}_p$, $\widehat{K} := \sum_{i,j} f_{i,j} [\boldsymbol{c}_i^\top \widehat{\boldsymbol{c}}_j]_2 - [u]_2 - \boldsymbol{x}^{(\beta)\top} \mathbf{F} \boldsymbol{y}^{(\beta)} \cdot [v]_1$, $K := [u]_1$
Return $\mathsf{sk}_{\mathbf{F}} := (K, \widehat{K})$

Fig. 6. Adversary $\mathcal{B}_1$ against the $\mathcal{D}_k$-MDDH assumption, for the proof of Lemma 4.

whereas $\widehat{\boldsymbol{c}}_j$ is uniformly random over $\mathbb{Z}_p^{k+1}$ when $\mathcal{B}_1'$ is given a random challenge, i.e., when for all $j \in [m]$, $\boldsymbol{h}_j \leftarrow_{\mathrm{R}} \mathbb{Z}_p^{k+1}$, as in game G_2. □

Lemma 5 (G_2). $\mathsf{Adv}_2 = 0$.

Proof of Lemma 5. By definition of the security game, for all $\mathbf{F}$ queried to $\mathsf{KeyGenO}$, we have: $\boldsymbol{x}^{(\beta)\top} \mathbf{F} \boldsymbol{y}^{(\beta)} = \boldsymbol{x}^{(0)\top} \mathbf{F} \boldsymbol{y}^{(0)}$. Therefore, the view of the adversary in G_2 is completely independent from the random bit $\beta \leftarrow_{\mathrm{R}} \{0,1\}$. □

Combining Lemmas 3, 4, and 5 gives Theorem 2. □

3.2 Public-Key FE for Bilinear Maps

In this section, we propose a family of public-key functional encryption schemes for the bilinear map functionality, that is $F : \mathcal{K} \times \mathcal{M} \rightarrow \mathcal{Y}$, where $\mathcal{K} := \mathbb{Z}_p^{n \times m}$, $\mathcal{M} := \mathbb{Z}_p^n \times \mathbb{Z}_p^m$, and $\mathcal{Y} := \mathbb{G}_T$. The family of schemes is parametrized by an integer $k \geq 1$ and a matrix distribution $\mathcal{D}_k$ (see Definition 1) so that, for each $k \in \mathbb{N}$, and each matrix distribution $\mathcal{D}_k$, the scheme $\mathsf{FE}(k, \mathcal{D}_k)$, presented in Fig. 7, is selectively secure under the $\mathcal{D}_k$-MDDH and the 3-pddh assumptions, on asymmetric pairings.

TECHNICAL OVERVIEW. We first give a high level view of our techniques. Our public-key FE builds on the private-key, single ciphertext secure FE presented in Sect. 3.1, but differs from it in the following essential way.

- In the public-key setting, for the encryption to compute $[\mathbf{A}\boldsymbol{r}_i + \boldsymbol{b}^\perp x_i]$ and $[\mathbf{B}\boldsymbol{s}_j + \boldsymbol{a}^\perp y_j]$ for $i \in [n], j \in [m]$ and any $\boldsymbol{x} \in \mathbb{Z}_p^n, \boldsymbol{y} \in \mathbb{Z}_p^m$, the vectors $[\boldsymbol{a}^\perp]_2$ and $[\boldsymbol{b}^\perp]_1$ would need to be part of the public key, which is incompatible with the MDDH assumption on $[\mathbf{A}]_1$ or $[\mathbf{B}]_2$. To solve this problem, we add an extra dimension, namely, we use bases $\left(\begin{array}{c|c} \mathbf{A}|\boldsymbol{b}^\perp & 0 \\ \hline \mathbf{0} & 1 \end{array}\right)$ and $\left(\begin{array}{c|c} \mathbf{B}|\boldsymbol{a}^\perp & 0 \\ \hline \mathbf{0} & 1 \end{array}\right)$ where the extra dimension will be used for correctness, while $(\mathbf{A}|\boldsymbol{b}^\perp)$ and $(\mathbf{B}|\boldsymbol{a}^\perp)$ will be used for security (using the MDDH assumption, since $\boldsymbol{a}^\perp$ and $\boldsymbol{b}^\perp$ are not part of the public key anymore).

- To avoid mix and match attacks, the encryption randomizes the bases

$$\begin{pmatrix} \mathbf{A} | \boldsymbol{b}^{\perp} & 0 \\ \mathbf{0} & 1 \end{pmatrix} \text{ and } \begin{pmatrix} \mathbf{B} | \boldsymbol{a}^{\perp} & 0 \\ \mathbf{0} & 1 \end{pmatrix}$$

into

$$\mathbf{W}^{-1} \begin{pmatrix} \mathbf{A} | \boldsymbol{b}^{\perp} & 0 \\ \mathbf{0} & 1 \end{pmatrix} \text{ and } \mathbf{W}^{\top} \begin{pmatrix} \mathbf{B} | \boldsymbol{a}^{\perp} & 0 \\ \mathbf{0} & 1 \end{pmatrix}$$

for $\mathbf{W} \leftarrow_{\mathrm{R}} \mathsf{GL}_{k+2}$ a random invertible matrix. This "glues" the components of a ciphertext that are in $\mathbb{G}_1$ to those that are in $\mathbb{G}_2$.
- We randomize the ciphertexts so as to contain $[\mathbf{A}\boldsymbol{r}_i \cdot \gamma]_1$ and $[\mathbf{B}\boldsymbol{s}_j \cdot \sigma]_2$, where $\gamma, \sigma \leftarrow_{\mathrm{R}} \mathbb{Z}_p$ are the same for all $i \in [n]$, and $j \in [m]$, but fresh for each ciphertext. The ciphertexts also contain $[\gamma \cdot \sigma]_1$, for correctness.

$\underline{\mathsf{Setup}(1^\lambda, F)}$:
$\mathsf{bgp} \leftarrow_{\mathrm{R}} \mathcal{G}(1^\lambda)$, $\mathbf{A}, \mathbf{B} \leftarrow_{\mathrm{R}} \mathcal{D}_k$;
For $i \in [2n], j \in [2m]$, $\boldsymbol{r}_i, \boldsymbol{s}_j \leftarrow_{\mathrm{R}} \mathbb{Z}_p^k$.
Return $\mathsf{mpk} := \{[\mathbf{A}\boldsymbol{r}_i]_1, [\mathbf{B}\boldsymbol{s}_j]_2\}_{i\in[2n], j\in[2m]}$
and $\mathsf{msk} := \big(\mathbf{A}, \mathbf{B}, \{\boldsymbol{r}_i, \boldsymbol{s}_j\}_{i\in[2n], j\in[2m]}\big)$

$\underline{\mathsf{KeyGen}(\mathsf{msk}, \mathbf{F} \in \mathbb{Z}_p^{n\times m})}$:
$K := [\sum_{i\in[n], j\in[m]} f_{i,j}(\boldsymbol{r}_i^\top \mathbf{A}^\top \mathbf{B}\boldsymbol{s}_j + \boldsymbol{r}_{i+n}^\top \mathbf{A}^\top \mathbf{B}\boldsymbol{s}_{j+m})]_1 - [u]_1 \in \mathbb{G}_1$
$\widehat{K} := [u]_2 \in \mathbb{G}_2$, where $u \leftarrow_{\mathrm{R}} \mathbb{Z}_p$.
Return $\mathsf{sk}_{\mathbf{F}} := (K, \widehat{K}) \in \mathbb{G}_1 \times \mathbb{G}_2$

$\underline{\mathsf{Encrypt}(\mathsf{mpk}, (\boldsymbol{x}, \boldsymbol{y}) \in \mathbb{Z}_p^n \times \mathbb{Z}_p^m)}$:
$\mathbf{W}, \mathbf{V} \leftarrow_{\mathrm{R}} \mathsf{GL}_{k+2}$, $\gamma \leftarrow_{\mathrm{R}} \mathbb{Z}_p$; $c_0 = \widehat{c}_0 := \gamma$; for all $i \in [n], j \in [m]$:
$$\boldsymbol{c}_i := \begin{pmatrix} \gamma \cdot \mathbf{A}\boldsymbol{r}_i \\ x_i \end{pmatrix}^\top \mathbf{W}^{-1}, \ \boldsymbol{c}_{n+i} := \begin{pmatrix} \gamma \cdot \mathbf{A}\boldsymbol{r}_{n+i} \\ 0 \end{pmatrix}^\top \mathbf{V}^{-1},$$
$$\widehat{\boldsymbol{c}}_j := \mathbf{W} \begin{pmatrix} \mathbf{B}\boldsymbol{s}_j \\ y_j \end{pmatrix}, \ \widehat{\boldsymbol{c}}_{m+j} := \mathbf{V} \begin{pmatrix} \mathbf{B}\boldsymbol{s}_{m+j} \\ 0 \end{pmatrix}$$
$\mathsf{Ct}_{(\boldsymbol{x},\boldsymbol{y})} := \{[c_0]_1, [\widehat{c}_0]_2, [\boldsymbol{c}_i]_1, [\widehat{\boldsymbol{c}}_j]_2\}_{i\in[2n], j\in[2m]} \in \mathbb{G}_1^{2n(k+2)+1} \times \mathbb{G}_2^{2m(k+2)+1}$

$\underline{\mathsf{Decrypt}(\mathsf{mpk}, \mathsf{Ct}_{(\boldsymbol{x},\boldsymbol{y})}, \mathsf{sk}_{\mathbf{F}})}$:
Return $\sum_{i\in[n], j\in[m]} f_{i,j}(e([\boldsymbol{c}_i]_1, [\widehat{\boldsymbol{c}}_j]_2) + e([\boldsymbol{c}_{n+i}]_1, [\widehat{\boldsymbol{c}}_{m+j}]_2)) - e([c_0]_1, \widehat{K}) - e(K, [\widehat{c}_0]_2)$.

Fig. 7. $\mathrm{FE}(k, \mathcal{D}_k)$, a family of functional encryption schemes parametrized by $k \in \mathbb{N}^*$ and a matrix distribution $\mathcal{D}_k$, selectively secure under the $\mathcal{D}_k$-mddh and 3-pddh assumptions.

Discussion on the Techniques. We note that the techniques used here share some similarities with Dual Pairing Vector Space constructions (e.g., [17,30,32, 33]). In particular, our produced ciphertexts and private keys are distributed as in their corresponding counterparts in [32]. The similarities end here though. These previous constructions all rely on the Dual System Encryption paradigm

[39], where the security proof uses a hybrid argument over all secret keys, leaving the distribution of the public key untouched. Our approach, on the other hand, manages to avoid this inherent security loss by changing the distributions of *both* the secret and public keys. Our approach also differs from [12] and follow-up works [14,21] in that they focus on the comparison predicate (see Sect. 5), a function that can be expressed via a quadratic function that is significantly simpler than those considered here. Indeed, for the case of comparisons predicates it is enough to consider vectors of the form: $[\mathbf{A}\boldsymbol{r}_i + x_i \boldsymbol{b}^\perp]_1, [\mathbf{B}\boldsymbol{s}_j + y_j \boldsymbol{a}^\perp]_2$, where x_i and y_j are either 0, or some random value (fixed at setup time, and identical for all ciphertexts and secret keys), or are just random garbage.

In the following theorem we show that the scheme satisfies correctness.

Theorem 3 (Correctness). *For any $k \in \mathbb{N}^*$ and any matrix distribution $\mathcal{D}_k$, the functional encryption scheme $\mathsf{FE}(k, \mathcal{D}_k)$ defined in Fig. 7 has perfect correctness.*

Proof of Theorem 3. Correctness follows from the facts that for all $i \in [n]$, $j \in [m]$:

$$e([\boldsymbol{c}_i]_1, [\widehat{\boldsymbol{c}}_j]_2) = [\gamma \boldsymbol{r}_i^\top \mathbf{A}^\top \mathbf{B}\boldsymbol{s}_j + x_i y_j]_T \text{ and } e([\boldsymbol{c}_{n+i}]_1, [\widehat{\boldsymbol{c}}_{m+j}]_2) = [\gamma \boldsymbol{r}_{n+i}^\top \mathbf{A}^\top \mathbf{B}\boldsymbol{s}_{m+j}]_T.$$

Therefore, the decryption gets

$$\begin{aligned}
&[\sum_{i\in[n],j\in[m]} f_{i,j}\gamma(\boldsymbol{r}_i^\top \mathbf{A}^\top \mathbf{B}\boldsymbol{s}_j + \boldsymbol{r}_{n+i}^\top \mathbf{A}^\top \mathbf{B}\boldsymbol{s}_{m+j})]_T \\
&+ [\sum_{i\in[n],j\in[m]} f_{i,j} x_i y_j]_T - e([\boldsymbol{c}_0]_1, \widehat{K}) - e(K, [\widehat{\boldsymbol{c}}_0]_2) \\
&= [\sum_{i\in[n],j\in[m]} f_{i,j} x_i y_j]_T.
\end{aligned}$$

□

Next, in the following theorem we prove that the scheme satisfies indistinguishability based security in a selective sense.

Theorem 4 (Security). *For any $k \in \mathbb{N}^*$ and any matrix distribution $\mathcal{D}_k$, if the $\mathcal{D}_k$-MDDH and the* 3-pddh *assumptions hold relative to $\mathcal{G}$, then the functional encryption scheme $\mathsf{FE}(k, \mathcal{D}_k)$ defined in Fig. 7 is selectively secure. Precisely, for any PPT adversary $\mathcal{A}$, there exists PPT adversaries $\mathcal{B}$ and $\mathcal{B}'$ such that:*

$$\mathbf{Adv}_{\mathsf{FE},\mathcal{A}}^{\mathsf{sel\text{-}ind\text{-}fe\text{-}cpa}}(\lambda) \leq 16 \cdot \mathbf{Adv}_{\mathcal{G},\mathcal{B}}^{\mathcal{D}_k\text{-}\mathsf{mddh}}(\lambda) + 4 \cdot \mathbf{Adv}_{\mathcal{G},\mathcal{B}'}^{3\text{-}\mathsf{pddh}}(\lambda) + 2^{-\Omega(\lambda)}.$$

We prove the security of $\mathsf{FE}(k, \mathcal{D}_k)$ via a series of games that are compactly presented in Fig. 8. The complete details of the proof are given in the full version; here we give an intuitive description of each game transition:

Game G_0 is the selective security experiment for scheme FE. For the sake of the proof, we look at the public key elements $\{[\mathbf{A}\boldsymbol{r}_i]_1, [\mathbf{B}\boldsymbol{s}_j]_2\}_{i\in[2n],j\in[2m]}$ as a ciphertext of the $\mathsf{FE}_{\mathsf{one}}$ scheme encrypting vectors $(\mathbf{0}, \mathbf{0}) \in \mathbb{Z}_p^{2n} \times \mathbb{Z}_p^{2m}$.

G_0, $\boxed{\mathrm{G}_1, \mathrm{G}_2, \mathrm{G}_3, \mathrm{G}_4}$, G_5:

$((\boldsymbol{x}^{(0)}, \boldsymbol{y}^{(0)}), (\boldsymbol{x}^{(1)}, \boldsymbol{y}^{(1)})) \leftarrow \mathcal{A}(1^\lambda)$

$\mathsf{bgp} \leftarrow_{\mathrm{R}} \mathcal{G}(1^\lambda)$; $\mathbf{A}, \mathbf{B} \leftarrow_{\mathrm{R}} \mathcal{D}_k$; $\beta \leftarrow_{\mathrm{R}} \{0,1\}$; $\boxed{\boldsymbol{a}^\perp \leftarrow_{\mathrm{R}} \mathsf{orth}(\mathbf{A}), \boldsymbol{b}^\perp \leftarrow_{\mathrm{R}} \mathsf{orth}(\mathbf{B})}$

For $i \in [2n], j \in [2m]$: $\boldsymbol{r}_i \leftarrow_{\mathrm{R}} \mathbb{Z}_p^k$, $\boldsymbol{s}_j \leftarrow_{\mathrm{R}} \mathbb{Z}_p^k$

$\mathsf{mpk} := \left\{ \left[\mathbf{A}\boldsymbol{r}_i + \boxed{x_i^{(\beta)}\boldsymbol{b}^\perp}\right]_1, \left[\mathbf{A}\boldsymbol{r}_{n+i} - \boxed{x_i^{(0)}\boldsymbol{b}^\perp}\right]_1, \left[\mathbf{B}\boldsymbol{s}_j + \boxed{y_j^{(\beta)}\boldsymbol{a}^\perp}\right]_2, \left[\mathbf{B}\boldsymbol{s}_{m+j} + \boxed{y_j^{(0)}\boldsymbol{a}^\perp}\right]_2 \right\}_{i\in[n], j\in[m]}$

$\mathbf{W} \leftarrow_{\mathrm{R}} \mathsf{GL}_{k+2}$, $\gamma \leftarrow_{\mathrm{R}} \mathbb{Z}_p$; $\boxed{v \leftarrow_{\mathrm{R}} \mathbb{Z}_p}$; $c_0 = \widehat{c}_0 := \gamma$

$$\boldsymbol{c}_i := \begin{pmatrix} \gamma\mathbf{A}\boldsymbol{r}_i + \boxed{\gamma x_i^{(\beta)}\boldsymbol{b}^\perp} + \boxed{v x_i^{(\beta)}\boldsymbol{b}^\perp} \\ x_i^{(\beta)} - \boxed{x_i^{(\beta)}} \end{pmatrix}^\top \mathbf{W}^{-1}$$

$$\boldsymbol{c}_{n+i} := \begin{pmatrix} \gamma\mathbf{A}\boldsymbol{r}_{n+i} - \boxed{\gamma x_i^{(0)}\boldsymbol{b}^\perp} - \boxed{v x_i^{(0)}\boldsymbol{b}^\perp} \\ 0 + \boxed{x_i^{(0)}} \end{pmatrix}^\top \mathbf{V}^{-1}$$

$$\widehat{\boldsymbol{c}}_j := \mathbf{W}\begin{pmatrix} \mathbf{B}\boldsymbol{s}_j + \boxed{y_j^{(\beta)}\boldsymbol{a}^\perp} \\ y_j^{(\beta)} - \boxed{y_j^{(\beta)}} \end{pmatrix}; \quad \widehat{\boldsymbol{c}}_{m+j} := \mathbf{V}\begin{pmatrix} \mathbf{B}\boldsymbol{s}_{m+j} + \boxed{y_j^{(0)}\boldsymbol{a}^\perp} \\ 0 + \boxed{y_j^{(0)}} \end{pmatrix}$$

$\mathsf{Ct}^\star := \{[c_0]_1, [\widehat{c}_0]_2, [\boldsymbol{c}_i]_1, [\widehat{\boldsymbol{c}}_j]_2\}_{i\in[2n], j\in[2m]}$

$\beta' \leftarrow \mathcal{A}^{\mathsf{KeyGenO}(\cdot)}(\mathsf{mpk}, \mathsf{Ct}^\star)$

Return 1 if $\beta' = \beta$, 0 otherwise.

$\underline{\mathsf{KeyGenO}(\mathbf{F} \in \mathbb{Z}_p^{n\times m})}$:

$u \leftarrow_{\mathrm{R}} \mathbb{Z}_p$

$K := [\sum_{i\in[n], j\in[m]} f_{i,j}(\boldsymbol{r}_i^\top \mathbf{A}^\top \mathbf{B}\boldsymbol{s}_j + \boldsymbol{r}_{n+i}^\top \mathbf{A}^\top \mathbf{B}\boldsymbol{s}_{m+j})]_1 - [u]_1 \in \mathbb{G}_1$

$\widehat{K} := [u]_2 \in \mathbb{G}_2$

Return $\mathsf{sk}_{\mathbf{F}} := (K, \widehat{K}) \in \mathbb{G}_1 \times \mathbb{G}_2$

Fig. 8. Games G_i, $i = 0, \ldots, 5$ for the proof of selective security of $\mathsf{FE}(k, \mathcal{D}_k)$ in Fig. 7. In each procedure, the components inside a solid (dotted, gray) frame are only present in the games marked by a solid (dotted, gray) frame.

Game G_1: with the above observation in mind, in this game we change the distribution of the public key elements so as to be interpreted as an $\mathsf{FE}_{\mathsf{one}}$ ciphertext encrypting the vectors

$$(\widetilde{\boldsymbol{x}}, \widetilde{\boldsymbol{y}}) = \left(\begin{pmatrix} \boldsymbol{x}^{(\beta)} \\ -\boldsymbol{x}^{(0)} \end{pmatrix}, \begin{pmatrix} \boldsymbol{y}^{(\beta)} \\ \boldsymbol{y}^{(0)} \end{pmatrix} \right) \in \mathbb{Z}_p^{2n} \times \mathbb{Z}_p^{2m}$$

In the full version we show how to argue the indistinguishability of G_1 from G_0 based on the selective, single-ciphertext security of $\mathsf{FE}_{\mathsf{one}}$ (that in turn reduces to $\mathcal{D}_k$-MDDH).

Game G_2: in this game we change the distribution of the $\boldsymbol{c}_i$ components of the challenge ciphertext. We switch from using $\{\gamma\mathbf{A}\boldsymbol{r}_i + \widetilde{x}_i \cdot \gamma\boldsymbol{b}^\perp\}_{i\in[2n]}$ to

$\{\gamma \mathbf{A} \boldsymbol{r}_i + \widetilde{x}_i \cdot (\gamma + v)\boldsymbol{b}^{\perp}\}_{i \in [2n]}$, for a random $v \leftarrow_{\mathrm{R}} \mathbb{Z}_p$. In the full version we argue the indistinguishability of this change under the 3-pddh assumption.

Game G_3: by using a statistical argument we show that in this game the challenge ciphertexts can be rewritten as

$$\boldsymbol{c}_i := \begin{pmatrix} \gamma \mathbf{A} \boldsymbol{r}_i + (\gamma + v) x_i^{(\beta)} \boldsymbol{b}^{\perp} \\ 0 \end{pmatrix}^{\top} \mathbf{W}^{-1};$$

$$\boldsymbol{c}_{n+i} := \begin{pmatrix} \gamma \mathbf{A} \boldsymbol{r}_{n+i} - (\gamma + v) x_i^{(0)} \boldsymbol{b}^{\perp} \\ x_i^{(0)} \end{pmatrix}^{\top} \mathbf{V}^{-1};$$

$$\widehat{\boldsymbol{c}}_j := \mathbf{W} \begin{pmatrix} \mathbf{B} \boldsymbol{s}_j + y_j^{(\beta)} \boldsymbol{a}^{\perp} \\ 0 \end{pmatrix}; \widehat{\boldsymbol{c}}_{m+j} := \mathbf{V} \begin{pmatrix} \mathbf{B} \boldsymbol{s}_{m+j} + y_j^{(0)} \boldsymbol{a}^{\perp} \\ y_j^{(0)} \end{pmatrix}.$$

This step essentially shows that the change in game G_2 made the ciphertexts less dependent on the bit β.

Game G_4: in this game we change again the distribution of the challenge ciphertext components $\boldsymbol{c}_i$ switching from using $\{\gamma \mathbf{A} \boldsymbol{r}_i + \widetilde{x}_i \cdot (\gamma + v)\boldsymbol{b}^{\perp}\}_{i \in [2n]}$ to $\{\gamma \mathbf{A} \boldsymbol{r}_i + \widetilde{x}_i \cdot \gamma \boldsymbol{b}^{\perp}\}_{i \in [2n]}$. This change is analogous to that introduced in game G_2, and its indistinguishability follows from the 3-pddh assumption.

The crucial observation is that the public key in this game can be seen as an $\mathsf{FE}_{\mathsf{one}}$ ciphertext encrypting vector $(\widetilde{\boldsymbol{x}}, \widetilde{\boldsymbol{y}})$, while the challenge ciphertext of game G_4 can be seen as an encryption of vectors

$$\left(\begin{pmatrix} \mathbf{0} \\ \hline \boldsymbol{x}^{(0)} \end{pmatrix}, \begin{pmatrix} \mathbf{0} \\ \hline \boldsymbol{y}^{(0)} \end{pmatrix} \right) \in \mathbb{Z}_p^{2n} \times \mathbb{Z}_p^{2m}$$

using such public key. At a high level, the idea is that we moved to a game in which the dependence on the challenge messages $(\boldsymbol{x}^{(\beta)}, \boldsymbol{y}^{(\beta)})$ is only in the public key.

Game G_5: in this game we change back the distribution of the public key elements so as to be interpreted as an $\mathsf{FE}_{\mathsf{one}}$ ciphertext encrypting vectors $(\mathbf{0}, \mathbf{0})$. The indistinguishability of this game from game G_4 can be argued based on the selective, single-ciphertext security of the $\mathsf{FE}_{\mathsf{one}}$ scheme.

The proof is concluded by arguing that in this game the view of the adversary is independent of the bit β.

4 Our Efficient Functional Encryption for Bilinear Maps in the GGM

In this section, we present a functional encryption scheme, $\mathsf{FE}_{\mathsf{GGM}}$, that supports the *bilinear map functionality*, and is proven secure against adaptive adversaries in the generic group model. In addition to be proven adaptive secure, this scheme enjoys a simpler structure, and is more efficient, as it admits shorter ciphertexts that comprise $2(n + m + 1)$ group elements (as opposed to $6n + 6m + 2$ in the SXDH instantiation of the scheme of Sect. 3.2). For ease of exposition, the scheme is presented for the case in which the functions act over vectors of the same dimension n. It is easy to see that the case in which $(\boldsymbol{x}, \boldsymbol{y}) \in \mathbb{Z}_p^n \times \mathbb{Z}_p^m$ with $n > m$ can be captured by padding $\boldsymbol{y}$ with zero entries.[5]

Technical Overview. We first provide a high-level view of the techniques used in this construction. The initial idea of the construction is to encrypt the two vectors $\boldsymbol{x}$ and $\boldsymbol{y}$ à la ElGamal in the two groups $\mathbb{G}_1$ and $\mathbb{G}_2$ respectively, i.e., the ciphertext includes $\boldsymbol{c} = [r \cdot \boldsymbol{a} + \boldsymbol{x}]_1$ and $\boldsymbol{d} = [s \cdot \boldsymbol{b} + \boldsymbol{y}]_2$ where r, s are randomly chosen and the vectors $([\boldsymbol{a}]_1, [\boldsymbol{b}]_2)$ are in the public key. At this point, we observe that, given $\boldsymbol{c}, \boldsymbol{d}$ and a function $\mathbf{F}$, one can use the bilinear map to compute $U = [(r \cdot \boldsymbol{a} + \boldsymbol{x})^\top \mathbf{F}(s \cdot \boldsymbol{b} + \boldsymbol{y})]_T$. This basic idea is similar to that of the scheme of Sect. 3.2. However, here we develop a different technique to enable decryption.

The basic scheme presented above is extended as follows. First, we let the secret key for function $\mathbf{F}$ be the element $[\boldsymbol{a}^\top \mathbf{F} \boldsymbol{b}]_1$. Now, if in the ciphertext we include the element $[rs]_2$, one can extract

$$[s\boldsymbol{x}^\top \mathbf{F}\boldsymbol{b} + r\boldsymbol{a}^\top \mathbf{F}\boldsymbol{y} + \boldsymbol{x}^\top \mathbf{F}\boldsymbol{y}]_T = U \cdot e([\boldsymbol{a}^\top \mathbf{F}\boldsymbol{b}]_1, [rs]_2)^{-1}.$$

Above the function's result is still "blinded" by cross terms $s(\boldsymbol{x}^\top \mathbf{F}\boldsymbol{b}) + r(\boldsymbol{a}^\top \mathbf{F}\boldsymbol{y})$. Our second idea, to solve this issue and enable full decryption, is to add to the ciphertext the ElGamal encryptions of the vectors $s \cdot \boldsymbol{x}$ and $r \cdot \boldsymbol{y}$. Namely, we add to the ciphertext the elements $\widehat{\boldsymbol{c}} = [t \cdot \boldsymbol{a} + s \cdot \boldsymbol{x}]_1$ and $\widehat{\boldsymbol{d}} = [z \cdot \boldsymbol{b} + r \cdot \boldsymbol{y}]_2$ for random t, z, and the element $[rs - t - z]_2$ (instead of $[rs]_2$). With all this information, one can compute the value U in the same way as above, and then use the public key $([\boldsymbol{a}]_1, [\boldsymbol{b}]_2)$ and the ciphertext components $\widehat{\boldsymbol{c}}, \widehat{\boldsymbol{d}}$ to compute

$$U' = [(t \cdot \boldsymbol{a} + s \cdot \boldsymbol{x})^\top \mathbf{F}\boldsymbol{b} + \boldsymbol{a}^\top \mathbf{F}(z \cdot \boldsymbol{b} + r \cdot \boldsymbol{y})]_T.$$

By a simple calculation, the function's result can be finally computed as

$$[\boldsymbol{x}^\top \mathbf{F}\boldsymbol{y}]_T = U \cdot U'^{-1} \cdot e([\boldsymbol{a}^\top \mathbf{F}\boldsymbol{b}]_1, [rs - z - t]_2)^{-1}.$$

As a final note, in the full scheme secret keys are slightly different, we randomize them in order to achieve collusion resistance.

Below we present our second FE scheme in detail.

$\mathsf{Setup}(1^\lambda, n)$ runs the bilinear group generator $\mathsf{bgp} \leftarrow_{\mathrm{R}} \mathcal{G}(1^\lambda)$ to obtain parameters $\mathsf{bgp} = (p, \mathbb{G}_1, \mathbb{G}_2, \mathbb{G}_T, g_1, g_2, e)$. Next, the algorithm samples a scalar $w \leftarrow_{\mathrm{R}} \mathbb{Z}_p$ and two vectors $\boldsymbol{a}, \boldsymbol{b} \leftarrow_{\mathrm{R}} \mathbb{Z}_p^n$ uniformly at random. The message space is $\mathcal{M} \subseteq \mathbb{Z}_p^n \times \mathbb{Z}_p^n$ and the key space is the set of matrices $\mathcal{K} \subseteq \mathbb{Z}_p^{n \times n}$. It returns the master secret key $\mathsf{msk} := (w, \boldsymbol{a}, \boldsymbol{b})$, and the master public key $\mathsf{mpk} := (\mathsf{bgp}, [\boldsymbol{a}]_1, [\boldsymbol{b}]_2, [w]_2)$.

[5] Furthermore, with a close look one can see that the last $n - m$ components of the vectors $[\boldsymbol{b}]_2$, $\boldsymbol{d}$ and $\widehat{\boldsymbol{d}}$ would become useless and thus can be discarded.

$\mathsf{KeyGen}(\mathsf{msk}, \mathbf{F})$ takes as input the master secret key msk and a matrix $\mathbf{F} \in \mathcal{K}$ and it returns a secret key $\mathsf{sk}_{\mathbf{F}} := (S_1, S_2, \mathbf{F}) \in \mathbb{G}_1^2 \times \mathcal{K}$ where S_1, S_2 are computed as follows. It samples a random $\gamma \leftarrow_{\mathrm{R}} \mathbb{Z}_p$ and computes

$$(S_1, S_2) := ([\boldsymbol{a}^\top \mathbf{F}\, \boldsymbol{b} + \gamma \cdot w]_1, [\gamma]_1).$$

$\mathsf{Encrypt}(\mathsf{mpk}, (\boldsymbol{x}, \boldsymbol{y}))$ takes as input the master public key and a message consisting of two vectors $\boldsymbol{x}, \boldsymbol{y} \in \mathcal{M}$, and returns a ciphertext $\mathsf{Ct} := (\boldsymbol{c}, \widehat{\boldsymbol{c}}, \boldsymbol{d}, \widehat{\boldsymbol{d}}, E, \widehat{E})$ computed as follows.

Choose $r, s, t, z \in \mathbb{Z}_p$ uniformly at random and compute

$$\begin{aligned} \boldsymbol{c} &:= [r \cdot \boldsymbol{a} + \boldsymbol{x}]_1, & \widehat{\boldsymbol{c}} &:= [t \cdot \boldsymbol{a} + s \cdot \boldsymbol{x}]_1 \\ \boldsymbol{d} &:= [s \cdot \boldsymbol{b} + \boldsymbol{y}]_2, & \widehat{\boldsymbol{d}} &:= [z \cdot \boldsymbol{b} + r \cdot \boldsymbol{y}]_2 \\ E &:= [rs - z - t]_2 & \widehat{E} &:= [w(rs - z - t)]_2 \end{aligned}$$

$\mathsf{Decrypt}(\mathsf{sk}_{\mathbf{F}}, \mathsf{Ct})$ parsing $\mathsf{sk}_{\mathbf{F}} := (S_1, S_2, \mathbf{F})$ and $\mathsf{Ct} := (\boldsymbol{c}, \widehat{\boldsymbol{c}}, \boldsymbol{d}, \widehat{\boldsymbol{d}}, E, \widehat{E})$, it computes and outputs

$$V := \mathbf{c}^\top \mathbf{F}\, \boldsymbol{d} - [\boldsymbol{a}]_1{}^\top \mathbf{F}\, \widehat{\boldsymbol{d}} - \widehat{\boldsymbol{c}}^\top \mathbf{F}\, [\boldsymbol{b}]_2 - e(S_1, E) + e(S_2, \widehat{E}) \in \mathbb{G}_T.$$

Correctness. To see the correctness of our scheme, let

$$\begin{aligned} A &= \mathbf{c}^\top \mathbf{F}\, \boldsymbol{d} = [r \cdot \boldsymbol{a} + \boldsymbol{x}]_1^\top \mathbf{F}\, [s \cdot \boldsymbol{b} + \boldsymbol{y}]_2 \\ &= [(rs) \cdot \boldsymbol{a}^\top \mathbf{F}\, \boldsymbol{b} + r \cdot \boldsymbol{a}^\top \mathbf{F}\, \boldsymbol{y} + s \cdot \boldsymbol{x}^\top \mathbf{F}\, \boldsymbol{b} + \boldsymbol{x}^\top \mathbf{F}\, \boldsymbol{y}]_T \\ B &= [\boldsymbol{a}]_1{}^\top \mathbf{F}\, \widehat{\boldsymbol{d}} + \widehat{\boldsymbol{c}}^\top \mathbf{F}\, [\boldsymbol{b}]_2 = [\boldsymbol{a}]_1^\top \mathbf{F}\, [z \cdot \boldsymbol{b} + r \cdot \boldsymbol{y}]_2 + [t \cdot \boldsymbol{a} + s \cdot \boldsymbol{x}]_1^\top \mathbf{F}\, [\boldsymbol{b}]_2 \\ &= [z \cdot \boldsymbol{a}^\top \mathbf{F}\, \boldsymbol{b} + r \cdot \boldsymbol{a}^\top \mathbf{F}\, \boldsymbol{y} + t \cdot \boldsymbol{a}^\top \mathbf{F}\, \boldsymbol{b} + s \cdot \boldsymbol{x}^\top \mathbf{F}\, \boldsymbol{b}]_T \end{aligned}$$

and note that

$$\begin{aligned} A - B &= [(rs - t - z) \cdot \boldsymbol{a}^\top \mathbf{F}\, \boldsymbol{b} + \boldsymbol{x}^\top \mathbf{F}\, \boldsymbol{y}]_T = e(S_1 - [w \cdot \gamma]_1, E) + [\boldsymbol{x}^\top \mathbf{F}\, \boldsymbol{y}]_T \\ &= e(S_1, E) - e(S_2, \widehat{E}) + [\boldsymbol{x}^\top \mathbf{F}\, \boldsymbol{y}]_T \end{aligned}$$

Since $V = A - B - e(S_1, E) + e(S_2, \widehat{E})$ it is easy to see that $V = [\boldsymbol{x}^\top \mathbf{F}\, \boldsymbol{y}]_T$.

Security of $\mathsf{FE}_{\mathsf{GGM}}$. In this section we state the security of the functional encryption scheme $\mathsf{FE}_{\mathsf{GGM}}$ of Sect. 4 in the generic group model.

Theorem 5. *The functional encryption scheme $\mathsf{FE}_{\mathsf{GGM}}$ described in Sect. 4 satisfies security against chosen-plaintext attacks (i.e., indistinguishability-based security) in the generic bilinear group model. Precisely, for every adversary $\mathcal{A}$ which makes at most Q key derivation oracle queries and $\widetilde{Q}$ generic group oracle queries its advantage is*

$$\mathbf{Adv}^{\mathsf{ind\text{-}fe\text{-}cpa}}_{\mathsf{FE}_{\mathsf{GGM}}, \mathcal{A}}(\lambda) \leq \frac{5(6n + 6 + \widetilde{Q} + 2Q)^2}{p}$$

The full proof of security is deferred to the full version. Here we only provide an overview of the strategy.

At an intuitive level, the proof consists of two main steps. We first state and prove a master theorem that shows hardness in the generic bilinear group model for a broad family of interactive decisional problems, notably a family which includes the indistinguishability-based experiment for our functional encryption scheme. Slightly more in detail, our master theorem states that these problems are generically hard under a certain algebraic side condition on the distribution of the elements received by the adversary. These results and techniques are rather general and can be of independent interest.

Second, following the guidelines of our master theorem, the second step of the proof consists in showing that the scheme $\mathsf{FE}_{\mathsf{GGM}}$ meets the algebraic side condition of our master theorem. This is the core part of the proof. Very intuitively, we look at the structure of the scheme's group elements seen by the adversary – public key, ciphertext, secret keys for a bunch of functions – for which the matching of the side condition means that the only information extractable from them is the functions' outputs. So, if the adversary issues only "legitimate" queries (i.e., queries for functions that produce the same results on the two challenge messages), it will not be able to understand which pair of vectors was encrypted.

5 Predicate Encryption for Bilinear Maps Evaluation

Here we show how to use our functional encryption schemes to build a Predicate Encryption (PE) scheme for the evaluation of bilinear maps over attributes (for lack of space, the definition of PE is recalled in Sect. 2.4). Specifically, we give a scheme for the predicate $\mathsf{P} : \mathcal{X} \times \mathcal{Y} \to \{0,1\}$ where $\mathcal{X} \subset \mathbb{Z}_p^n \times \mathbb{Z}_p^m$, $\mathcal{Y} \subset \mathbb{Z}_p^{n \times m}$, and for all $(\boldsymbol{x}, \boldsymbol{y}) \in \mathcal{X}$ and $\mathbf{F} \in \mathcal{Y}$:

$$\boldsymbol{x}^\top \mathbf{F} \boldsymbol{y} \in \{0,1\} \text{ and } \mathsf{P}((\boldsymbol{x}, \boldsymbol{y}), \mathbf{F}) = 1 \text{ iff } \boldsymbol{x}^\top \mathbf{F} \boldsymbol{y} = 1.$$

In Fig. 9, we present a generic construction of PE for P from any functional encryption scheme FE for the bilinear maps functionality $F : \mathcal{K} \times \mathcal{M}' \to \mathcal{Y}'$, where $\mathcal{M}' := \mathbb{Z}_p^n \times \mathbb{Z}_p^m$, $\mathcal{K} := \mathbb{Z}_p^{n \times m}$, $\mathcal{Y}' := \mathbb{G}_T$ and for all $(\boldsymbol{x}, \boldsymbol{y}) \in \mathcal{M}'$, $\mathbf{F} \in \mathcal{K}$

$$F(\mathbf{F}, (\boldsymbol{x}, \boldsymbol{y})) = [\boldsymbol{x}^\top \mathbf{F} \boldsymbol{y}]_T\,.$$

The PE scheme can be instantiated by using one of our FE constructions presented in Sects. 3 and 4. We compare our constructions with previous PE that support the evaluation of bilinear maps in Fig. 2.

Theorem 6 (Correctness). *If* $\mathsf{FE} := (\mathsf{Setup}_{\mathsf{FE}}, \mathsf{KeyGen}_{\mathsf{FE}}, \mathsf{Encrypt}_{\mathsf{FE}}, \mathsf{Decrypt}_{\mathsf{FE}})$ *is a perfectly correct functional encryption scheme for functionality* F*, then so is the predicate encryption scheme* PE *defined in Fig. 9.*

Proof of Theorem 6. By correctness of FE, we have for all $(\boldsymbol{x}, \boldsymbol{y}) \in \mathcal{X}$, $w \in \mathbb{Z}_p$, $\mathbf{F} \in \mathcal{Y}$:

$$F(\mathbf{F}, (w \cdot \boldsymbol{x}, \boldsymbol{y})) = [w \cdot \boldsymbol{x}^\top \mathbf{F} \boldsymbol{y}]_T = [w \cdot \mathsf{P}((\boldsymbol{x}, \boldsymbol{y}), \mathbf{F})]_T\,.$$

Thus, when $\mathsf{P}((\boldsymbol{x}, \boldsymbol{y}), \mathbf{F}) = 1$, decryption recovers the encapsulation key $[w]_T$.

Table 2. Comparison between different PE for bilinear maps evaluation.

PE scheme	Security	Assumption	Ciph. size
KSW08 [28]	Selective	Composite	$O(n^2)$
OT09 [33]	Selective	RDSP,IDSP	$O(n^2)$
AFV11 [5]	Selective	LWE	$O(n^2)$
OT11 [34]	Adaptive	DLIN	$O(n^2)$
Ours 1	Selective	MDDH, 3-PDDH	$O(n)$
Ours 2	Adaptive	GGM	$O(n)$

$\underline{\mathsf{Setup}(1^\lambda, \mathcal{X}, \mathcal{Y}, 1^k, \mathcal{M} := \mathbb{G}_T)}$:
Return $(\mathsf{mpk}, \mathsf{msk}) \leftarrow_{\mathrm{R}} \mathsf{Setup}_{\mathsf{FE}}(1^\lambda, F)$

$\underline{\mathsf{KeyGen}(\mathsf{msk}, \mathbf{F} \in \mathcal{Y})}$:
Return $\mathsf{sk}_{\mathbf{F}} := \mathsf{KeyGen}_{\mathsf{FE}}(\mathsf{msk}, \mathbf{F})$

$\underline{\mathsf{Encrypt}(\mathsf{mpk}, (\boldsymbol{x}, \boldsymbol{y}) \in \mathcal{X}, M \in \mathbb{G}_T)}$:
$w \leftarrow_{\mathrm{R}} \mathbb{Z}_p$; $C_0 := [w]_T + M$
$C_1 := \mathsf{Encrypt}_{\mathsf{FE}}(\mathsf{mpk}, (w \cdot \boldsymbol{x}, \boldsymbol{y}))$
Return $\mathsf{Ct}_{(\boldsymbol{x},\boldsymbol{y})} := (C_0, C_1)$

$\underline{\mathsf{Decrypt}(\mathsf{mpk}, \mathsf{Ct}_{(\boldsymbol{x},\boldsymbol{y})} := (C_0, C_1), \mathsf{sk}_{\mathbf{F}})}$:
$K := \mathsf{Decrypt}_{\mathsf{FE}}(\mathsf{mpk}, C_1, \mathsf{sk}_{\mathbf{F}})$
Return $C_0 - K$.

Fig. 9. PE, a predicate encryption scheme, selectively (resp. adaptively) secure if the underlying FE scheme ($\mathsf{Setup}_{\mathsf{FE}}, \mathsf{KeyGen}_{\mathsf{FE}}, \mathsf{Encrypt}_{\mathsf{FE}}, \mathsf{Decrypt}_{\mathsf{FE}}$) is selectively (resp. adaptively) secure.

Theorem 7 (Security). *If* $\mathsf{FE} := (\mathsf{Setup}_{\mathsf{FE}}, \mathsf{KeyGen}_{\mathsf{FE}}, \mathsf{Encrypt}_{\mathsf{FE}}, \mathsf{Decrypt}_{\mathsf{FE}})$ *is an adaptively (resp. selectively) secure encryption scheme for F, then so is the predicate encryption scheme* PE *defined in Fig. 9. Namely, for any PPT adversary $\mathcal{A}$, there exists a PPT adversary $\mathcal{B}$ such that:*

$$\mathbf{Adv}^{\mathsf{ind\text{-}pe\text{-}cpa}}_{\mathsf{PE},\mathcal{A}}(\lambda) \leq 4 \cdot \mathbf{Adv}^{\mathsf{ind\text{-}fe\text{-}cpa}}_{\mathsf{FE},\mathcal{B}}(\lambda).$$

Similarly, in the selective case, for any PPT adversary $\mathcal{A}$, there exists a PPT adversary $\mathcal{B}$ such that:

$$\mathbf{Adv}^{\mathsf{sel\text{-}ind\text{-}pe\text{-}cpa}}_{\mathsf{PE},\mathcal{A}}(\lambda) \leq 4 \cdot \mathbf{Adv}^{\mathsf{sel\text{-}ind\text{-}fe\text{-}cpa}}_{\mathsf{FE},\mathcal{B}}(\lambda).$$

Proof of Theorem 7, Adaptive Security. We prove the adaptive security of PE via a series of games described in Fig. 10 and we use Adv_i to denote the advantage of $\mathcal{A}$ in game G_i, that is $\mathsf{Adv}_i := |1 - 2\Pr[\mathrm{G}_i \text{ returns } 1]|$. G_0 is defined as:

$$\begin{aligned} & \beta \leftarrow_{\mathrm{R}} \{0,1\} \\ \mathrm{G}_0 : \ & \beta' \leftarrow \mathbf{Exp}^{\mathsf{ind\text{-}pe\text{-}cpa\text{-}}\beta}_{\mathsf{PE},\mathcal{A}}(\lambda) \\ & \text{Return } 1 \text{ if } \beta' = \beta, 0 \text{ otherwise.} \end{aligned}$$

Where $\mathbf{Exp}^{\mathsf{ind\text{-}pe\text{-}cpa\text{-}}\beta}_{\mathsf{PE},\mathcal{A}}(\lambda)$ is the experiment used in Definition 9 of fully attribute-hiding security for predicate encryption. In particular, we have that

G_0, $\boxed{\mathrm{G}_1, \mathrm{G}_2}$:

$\beta \leftarrow_{\mathrm{R}} \{0,1\}$, $(\mathsf{mpk}, \mathsf{msk}) \leftarrow_{\mathrm{R}} \mathsf{Setup}_{\mathsf{FE}}(1^\lambda, F)$
$\beta' \leftarrow \mathcal{A}^{\mathsf{KeyGenO}(\cdot),\mathsf{EncO}(\cdot,\cdot,\cdot,\cdot)}(\mathsf{mpk})$
Return 1 if $\beta' = \beta$, 0 otherwise.

$\underline{\mathsf{EncO}((\boldsymbol{x}^{(0)}, \boldsymbol{y}^{(0)}), M_0, (\boldsymbol{x}^{(1)}, \boldsymbol{y}^{(1)}), M_1)}$:
$w \leftarrow_{\mathrm{R}} \mathbb{Z}_p$, $C_0 := [w]_T + M_\beta$, $C_1 := \mathsf{Encrypt}_{\mathsf{FE}}(\mathsf{mpk}, (w \cdot \boldsymbol{x}^{(\beta)}, \boldsymbol{y}^{(\beta)}))$
$\boxed{\text{If } M_0 \neq M_1,\ C_1 := \mathsf{Encrypt}_{\mathsf{FE}}(\mathsf{mpk}, (\mathbf{0}, \mathbf{0}))}$
If $M_0 = M_1$, $C_1 := \mathsf{Encrypt}_{\mathsf{FE}}(\mathsf{mpk}, (w \cdot \boldsymbol{x}^{(0)}, \boldsymbol{y}^{(0)}))$
Return $\mathsf{Ct} := (C_0, C_1)$

$\underline{\mathsf{KeyGenO}(\mathbf{F} \in \mathbb{Z}_p^{n \times m})}$:
Return $\mathsf{sk}_{\mathbf{F}} := \mathsf{KeyGen}_{\mathsf{FE}}(\mathsf{msk}, \mathbf{F})$

Fig. 10. Games G_i, for $i = 0, 1, 2$ for the proof of adaptive security of PE in Fig. 9. In each procedure, the components inside a solid (dotted) frame are only present in the games marked by a solid (dotted) frame.

$\mathsf{Adv}_0 = \mathbf{Adv}^{\mathsf{ind\text{-}pe\text{-}cpa}}_{\mathsf{PE},\mathcal{A}}(\lambda)$. We explain in Remark 1 how to obtain the same results for selective security.

Lemma 6 (G_0 **to** G_1). *There exists a PPT adversary* $\mathcal{B}_0$:

$$|\mathsf{Adv}_0 - \mathsf{Adv}_1| \leq 2 \cdot \mathbf{Adv}^{\mathsf{ind\text{-}fe\text{-}cpa}}_{\mathsf{FE},\mathcal{B}_0}(\lambda).$$

Proof of Lemma 6. By definition of the security game, we know that if $M_0 \neq M_1$, then it must be that for all queries $\mathbf{F}$ to $\mathsf{KeyGenO}(\cdot)$, $\boldsymbol{x}^{(\beta)\top}\mathbf{F}\boldsymbol{y}^{(\beta)} = 0$ (i.e., the predicate over the challenge attributes is false). Therefore, using the adaptive security of the underlying FE scheme, we can switch: $\mathsf{Encrypt}(\mathsf{mpk}, (w \cdot \boldsymbol{x}^{(\beta)}, \boldsymbol{y}^{(\beta)}))$, computed by EncO when $M_0 \neq M_1$, to $\mathsf{Encrypt}(\mathsf{mpk}, (\mathbf{0}, \mathbf{0}))$. □

Lemma 7 (G_1 **to** G_2). *There exists a PPT adversary* $\mathcal{B}_1$:

$$|\mathsf{Adv}_1 - \mathsf{Adv}_2| \leq 2 \cdot \mathbf{Adv}^{\mathsf{ind\text{-}fe\text{-}cpa}}_{\mathsf{FE},\mathcal{B}_1}(\lambda).$$

Proof of Lemma 7. By definition of the security game, we know that for all queries $\mathbf{F}$ to $\mathsf{KeyGenO}(\cdot)$, $\mathsf{P}((\boldsymbol{x}^{(0)}, \boldsymbol{y}^{(0)}), \mathbf{F}) = \mathsf{P}((\boldsymbol{x}^{(1)}, \boldsymbol{y}^{(1)}), \mathbf{F})$. Together with the fact that for all $(\boldsymbol{x}, \boldsymbol{y}) \in \mathcal{X}$ and $\mathbf{F} \in \mathcal{Y}$: $\boldsymbol{x}^\top \mathbf{F} \boldsymbol{y} \in \{0,1\}$, we obtain that: $\boldsymbol{x}^{(0)\top}\mathbf{F}\boldsymbol{y}^{(0)} = \boldsymbol{x}^{(1)\top}\mathbf{F}\boldsymbol{y}^{(1)}$. Therefore, using the adaptive security of the underlying FE scheme, we can switch: $\mathsf{Encrypt}(\mathsf{mpk}, (w \cdot \boldsymbol{x}^{(\beta)}, \boldsymbol{y}^{(\beta)}))$, computed by EncO when $M_0 = M_1$, to $\mathsf{Encrypt}(\mathsf{mpk}, (w \cdot \boldsymbol{x}^{(0)}, \boldsymbol{y}^{(0)}))$. □

Lemma 8 (G_2). $\mathsf{Adv}_2 = 0$.

Proof of Lemma 8. We show that the $\mathcal{A}$'s view is independent of $\beta \leftarrow_{\mathrm{R}} \{0,1\}$ in this game. If $M_0 \neq M_1$, the challenge ciphertext is of the form (C_0, C_1) where $C_0 := [w]_T + M_\beta$ for $w \leftarrow_{\mathrm{R}} \mathbb{Z}_p$, and C_1 is independent of w and β. Thus, the message M_β is completely hidden by the one-time pad $[w]_T$, and the ciphertext is independent of β.

If $M_0 = M_1$, the challenge ciphertext is of the form (C_0, C_1) where $C_0 := [w]_T + M_\beta$ for $w \leftarrow_{\mathrm{R}} \mathbb{Z}_p$, which is independent of β since $M_0 = M_1$; and $C_1 := \mathsf{Encrypt}(\mathsf{mpk}, (w \cdot \boldsymbol{x}^{(0)}, \boldsymbol{y}^{(0)}))$, which is also independent of β. □

Theorem 7 follows readily from Lemmas 6, 7, and 8. □

Remark 1 (Selective FE ⇒ selective PE). We can adapt straightforwardly the proof of Theorem 7, to the selective setting, simply by constructing PPT adversaries $\mathcal{B}_0$ and $\mathcal{B}_1$ against the selective security of the underlying FE, exactly as those in Lemmas 6 and 7, except that those adversaries first receive a challenge $(\boldsymbol{x}^{(0)}, \boldsymbol{y}^{(0)}), (\boldsymbol{x}^{(1)}, \boldsymbol{y}^{(1)})$ from the adversary $\mathcal{A}$, playing against the selective security of the PE, upon which they sample $w \leftarrow_{\mathrm{R}} \mathbb{Z}_p$, and send $(w \cdot \boldsymbol{x}^{(0)}, \boldsymbol{y}^{(0)}), (w \cdot \boldsymbol{x}^{(1)}, \boldsymbol{y}^{(1)})$ as their selective challenge. Finally, we use the statistical argument from Lemma 8, which works exactly in the same way for the selective setting.

5.1 Applications of PE for Bilinear Maps Evaluation

In this section, we discuss two applications of our fully attribute-hiding PE scheme supporting bilinear maps evaluation.

PE for Constant Depth Boolean Formulas. As a first application, we can use the PE scheme in Fig. 9 to handle boolean functions of constant degree d in n variables. This yields a solution where ciphertexts comprise $O(n^{d/2})$ group elements, in contrast to $O(n^d)$ group elements in [28] (the asymptotic is taken for large n, constant d).

The idea is to encode a predicate for boolean formulas into a predicate for bilinear maps evaluation. This can be done as follows. Consider the following predicate $\mathsf{P} : \mathcal{X} \times \mathcal{Y} \to \{0,1\}$, with $\mathcal{X} := \mathbb{Z}_2^n$ and $\mathcal{Y} := \{T \in \mathbb{Z}_2[X_1, \ldots, X_n], \deg(T) \leq d\}$, such that for all $\boldsymbol{x} \in \mathcal{X}$, $T \in \mathcal{X}$, $\mathsf{P}(\boldsymbol{x}, T) = 1$ iff $T(\boldsymbol{x}) = 1$. Below we describe how to encode $\boldsymbol{x} \in \mathcal{X}$ and $T \in \mathcal{Y}$ into a vector $\widetilde{\boldsymbol{x}}$ and a matrix $\widetilde{\mathbf{T}}$ such that $\mathsf{P}(\boldsymbol{x}, T) = 1$ iff $\widetilde{\boldsymbol{x}}^\top \widetilde{\mathbf{T}} \widetilde{\boldsymbol{x}} = 1$.

To see this, assume for simplicity that d is even, and let us consider the setting where $n \geq \frac{d}{2}$. First, we map every $\boldsymbol{x} \in \mathcal{X}$ to $\widetilde{\boldsymbol{x}} := (M_1(\boldsymbol{x}), \ldots, M_{\widetilde{d}}(\boldsymbol{x})) \in \mathbb{Z}_2^{\widetilde{d}}$, where $\widetilde{d} := \sum_{i=0}^{\frac{d}{2}} \binom{n}{i}$, and for all $j \in \left[\binom{n}{\frac{d}{2}}\right]$, M_j is the j-th monomial of degree at most $\frac{d}{2}$ on n variables (there are exactly $\widetilde{d}$ such monomials, which we order arbitrarily). Second, we write every $T \in \mathcal{Y}$ as $\sum_{i,j \in [\widetilde{d}]} T_{i,j} M_i M_j$, where for all $i, j \in [\widetilde{d}]$, $T_{i,j} \in \mathbb{Z}_2$, and we map $T \in \mathcal{Y}$ to $\widetilde{\mathbf{T}} \in \mathbb{Z}_2^{\widetilde{d} \times \widetilde{d}}$ such that for all $i, j \in [\widetilde{d}]$, $\widetilde{T}_{i,j} := T_{i,j}$. This way, for all $\boldsymbol{x} \in \mathcal{X}$ and $T \in \mathcal{Y}$, we have $\mathsf{P}(\boldsymbol{x}, T) = 1$ iff $\widetilde{\boldsymbol{x}}^\top \widetilde{\mathbf{T}} \widetilde{\boldsymbol{x}} = T(\boldsymbol{x}) = 1$.

Therefore, using the PE which supports bilinear maps evaluation presented in Sect. 5, we obtain a PE for boolean formulas with ciphertexts of size $O(\widetilde{d})$. Using a similar encoding to the PE from [28] that support linear maps evaluation yields a solution with ciphertexts of dimension $O(\widehat{d})$ where $\widehat{d} := \sum_{i=0}^{d} \binom{n}{i}$. When considering asymptotic for large n, constant d, our ciphertext size is $O(n^{d/2})$, against $O(n^d)$ for [28].

Finally, we note that boolean formulas can be arithmetized into a polynomial over $\mathbb{Z}_2$, à la [38]. Namely, for boolean variables $x, y \in \mathbb{Z}_2$, $\mathsf{AND}(x, y)$ is encoded as $x \cdot y$, $\mathsf{OR}(x, y)$ is encoded as $x + y - xy$, and $\mathsf{NOT}(x) = 1 - x$.

PE for Comparison. Let us consider the comparison predicate $\mathsf{P}_{\leq} : [N] \times [N] \rightarrow \{0, 1\}$ that for all $x, y \in [N]$ is defined by

$$\mathsf{P}_{\leq}(x, y) = 1 \text{ iff } x \leq y.$$

We can reduce this predicate to a polynomial of degree two, as done (implicitly) in [12], as follows. First, any integer $x \in [N]$ is canonically mapped to the lexicographically ordered pair $(x_1, x_2) \in [\sqrt{N}] \times [\sqrt{N}]$ (we assume $\sqrt{N}$ is an integer for simplicity). Then x_1 is mapped to vectors $\widetilde{\boldsymbol{x}} := \begin{pmatrix} \mathbf{0}^{x_1} \\ \mathbf{1}^{\sqrt{N}-x_1} \end{pmatrix} \in \{0, 1\}^{\sqrt{N}}$ where $\mathbf{1}^{\ell}$, $\mathbf{0}^{\ell}$ denote the all-one and all-zero vectors in $\{0, 1\}^{\ell}$, respectively; and $\widehat{\boldsymbol{x}} := \boldsymbol{e}_{x_1} \in \{0, 1\}^{\sqrt{N}}$, where for all $i \in [\sqrt{N}]$, $\boldsymbol{e}_i$ denotes the i'th vector of the canonical basis of $\mathbb{Z}_p^{\sqrt{N}}$. Finally, $x_2 \in [\sqrt{N}]$ is mapped to $\bar{\boldsymbol{x}} := \begin{pmatrix} \mathbf{0}^{x_2-1} \\ \mathbf{1}^{\sqrt{N}-x_2+1} \end{pmatrix}$. For all $(x_1, x_2), (y_1, y_2) \in [\sqrt{N}] \times [\sqrt{N}]$:

$$\mathsf{P}_{\leq}((x_1, x_2), (y_1, y_2)) = 1 \text{ iff } \widetilde{x}_{y_1} + \widehat{x}_{y_1} \cdot \bar{x}_{y_2} = 1,$$

where for any vector $\boldsymbol{z} \in \mathbb{Z}_p^{\sqrt{N}}$, and any $i \in [\sqrt{N}]$, we denote by $z_i \in \mathbb{Z}_p$ the i-th coordinate of $\boldsymbol{z}$.

This means that by using the above encoding, for an integer attribute $x \in [N]$ one can use a PE for bilinear maps evaluation to encrypt the pair of vectors

$$\left(\begin{pmatrix} \widetilde{\boldsymbol{x}} \\ \widehat{\boldsymbol{x}} \end{pmatrix}, \begin{pmatrix} 1 \\ \bar{\boldsymbol{x}} \end{pmatrix} \right) \in \mathbb{Z}_p^{2\sqrt{N}} \times \mathbb{Z}_p^{1+\sqrt{N}}$$

Table 3. Summary of different fully-attribute hiding PE schemes for comparison.

PE scheme	Security	Assumption	Ciph. size
BSW06 [12]	Selective	Composite	$O(\sqrt{N})$
GKSW10 [21]	Selective	SXDH	$5\sqrt{N} \cdot \lvert\mathbb{G}_1\rvert + 4\sqrt{N} \cdot \lvert\mathbb{G}_2\rvert + \lvert\mathbb{G}_T\rvert$
Ours 1	Selective	MDDH, 3-PDDH	$(12\sqrt{N} + 1) \cdot \lvert\mathbb{G}_1\rvert + (6\sqrt{N} + 7) \cdot \lvert\mathbb{G}_2\rvert$
Ours 2	Adaptive	GGM	$(4\sqrt{N} + 1) \cdot \lvert\mathbb{G}_1\rvert + (2\sqrt{N} + 3) \cdot \lvert\mathbb{G}_2\rvert$

This gives a PE for comparison with ciphertexts of $O(\sqrt{N})$ group elements, as in [12,21]. A more precise comparison is given in Table 3.

Acknowledgements. The research of Dario Fiore is partially supported by the European Union's Horizon 2020 Research and Innovation Programme under grant agreement 688722 (NEXTLEAP), the Spanish Ministry of Economy under project references TIN2015-70713-R (DEDETIS), RTC-2016-4930-7 (DataMantium), and under a Juan de la Cierva fellowship to Dario Fiore, and by the Madrid Regional Government under project N-Greens (ref. S2013/ICE-2731).

References

1. Abdalla, M., et al.: Searchable encryption revisited: consistency properties, relation to anonymous IBE, and extensions. In: Shoup, V. (ed.) CRYPTO 2005. LNCS, vol. 3621, pp. 205–222. Springer, Heidelberg (2005). doi:10.1007/11535218_13
2. Abdalla, M., Bourse, F., Caro, A., Pointcheval, D.: Simple functional encryption schemes for inner products. In: Katz, J. (ed.) PKC 2015. LNCS, vol. 9020, pp. 733–751. Springer, Heidelberg (2015). doi:10.1007/978-3-662-46447-2_33
3. Abdalla, M., Bourse, F., De Caro, A., Pointcheval, D.: Better security for functional encryption for inner product evaluations. Cryptology ePrint Archive, Report 2016/011 (2016). http://eprint.iacr.org/2016/011
4. Abdalla, M., Raykova, M., Wee, H.: Multi-input inner-product functional encryption from pairings. IACR Cryptology ePrint Archive, 2016:425 (2016)
5. Agrawal, S., Freeman, D.M., Vaikuntanathan, V.: Functional encryption for inner product predicates from learning with errors. In: Lee, D.H., Wang, X. (eds.) ASIACRYPT 2011. LNCS, vol. 7073, pp. 21–40. Springer, Heidelberg (2011). doi:10.1007/978-3-642-25385-0_2
6. Agrawal, S., Libert, B., Stehlé, D.: Fully secure functional encryption for inner products, from standard assumptions. In: Robshaw, M., Katz, J. (eds.) CRYPTO 2016. LNCS, vol. 9816, pp. 333–362. Springer, Heidelberg (2016). doi:10.1007/978-3-662-53015-3_12
7. Ananth, P., Sahai, A.: Projective arithmetic functional encryption and indistinguishability obfuscation from degree-5 multilinear maps. In: Coron, J.-S., Nielsen, J.B. (eds.) EUROCRYPT 2017. LNCS, vol. 10210, pp. 152–181. Springer, Cham (2017). doi:10.1007/978-3-319-56620-7_6
8. Barthe, G., Fagerholm, E., Fiore, D., Mitchell, J.C., Scedrov, A., Schmidt, B.: Automated analysis of cryptographic assumptions in generic group models. In: Garay, J.A., Gennaro, R. (eds.) CRYPTO 2014. LNCS, vol. 8616, pp. 95–112. Springer, Heidelberg (2014). doi:10.1007/978-3-662-44371-2_6
9. Bishop, A., Jain, A., Kowalczyk, L.: Function-hiding inner product encryption. In: Iwata, T., Cheon, J.H. (eds.) ASIACRYPT 2015. LNCS, vol. 9452, pp. 470–491. Springer, Heidelberg (2015). doi:10.1007/978-3-662-48797-6_20
10. Boneh, D., Di Crescenzo, G., Ostrovsky, R., Persiano, G.: Public key encryption with keyword search. In: Cachin, C., Camenisch, J.L. (eds.) EUROCRYPT 2004. LNCS, vol. 3027, pp. 506–522. Springer, Heidelberg (2004). doi:10.1007/978-3-540-24676-3_30
11. Boneh, D., Franklin, M.K.: Identity-based encryption from the weil pairing. In: Kilian, J. (ed.) CRYPTO 2001. LNCS, vol. 2139, pp. 213–229. Springer, Heidelberg (2001). doi:10.1007/3-540-44647-8_13

12. Boneh, D., Sahai, A., Waters, B.: Fully collusion resistant traitor tracing with short ciphertexts and private keys. In: Vaudenay, S. (ed.) EUROCRYPT 2006. LNCS, vol. 4004, pp. 573–592. Springer, Heidelberg (2006). doi:10.1007/11761679_34
13. Boneh, D., Sahai, A., Waters, B.: Functional encryption: definitions and challenges. In: Ishai, Y. (ed.) TCC 2011. LNCS, vol. 6597, pp. 253–273. Springer, Heidelberg (2011). doi:10.1007/978-3-642-19571-6_16
14. Boneh, D., Waters, B.: A fully collusion resistant broadcast, trace, and revoke system. In: Juels, A., Wright, R.N., Vimercati, S. (eds.) ACM CCS 2006, pp. 211–220. ACM Press, October/November 2006
15. Boneh, D., Waters, B.: Conjunctive, subset, and range queries on encrypted data. In: Vadhan, S.P. (ed.) TCC 2007. LNCS, vol. 4392, pp. 535–554. Springer, Heidelberg (2007). doi:10.1007/978-3-540-70936-7_29
16. Chen, J., Gay, R., Wee, H.: Improved dual system ABE in prime-order groups via predicate encodings. In: Oswald, E., Fischlin, M. (eds.) EUROCRYPT 2015. LNCS, vol. 9057, pp. 595–624. Springer, Heidelberg (2015). doi:10.1007/978-3-662-46803-6_20
17. Chen, J., Lim, H.W., Ling, S., Wang, H., Wee, H.: Shorter IBE and signatures via asymmetric pairings. In: Abdalla, M., Lange, T. (eds.) Pairing 2012. LNCS, vol. 7708, pp. 122–140. Springer, Heidelberg (2013). doi:10.1007/978-3-642-36334-4_8
18. Escala, A., Herold, G., Kiltz, E., Ràfols, C., Villar, J.: An algebraic framework for Diffie-Hellman assumptions. In: Canetti, R., Garay, J.A. (eds.) CRYPTO 2013. LNCS, vol. 8043, pp. 129–147. Springer, Heidelberg (2013). doi:10.1007/978-3-642-40084-1_8
19. Galbraith, S.D., Paterson, K.G., Smart, N.P.: Pairings for cryptographers. Discrete Appl. Math. **156**(16), 3113–3121 (2008)
20. Garg, S., Gentry, C., Halevi, S., Raykova, M., Sahai, A., Waters, B.: Candidate indistinguishability obfuscation and functional encryption for all circuits. In: 54th FOCS, pp. 40–49. IEEE Computer Society Press, October 2013
21. Garg, S., Kumarasubramanian, A., Sahai, A., Waters, B.: Building efficient fully collusion-resilient traitor tracing and revocation schemes. In: Al-Shaer, E., Keromytis, A.D., Shmatikov, V. (eds.) ACM CCS 2010, pp. 121–130. ACM Press, October 2010
22. Gentry, C.: Practical identity-based encryption without random oracles. In: Vaudenay, S. (ed.) EUROCRYPT 2006. LNCS, vol. 4004, pp. 445–464. Springer, Heidelberg (2006). doi:10.1007/11761679_27
23. Goldwasser, S., Kalai, Y.T., Popa, R.A., Vaikuntanathan, V., Zeldovich, N.: Reusable garbled circuits and succinct functional encryption. In: Boneh, D., Roughgarden, T., Feigenbaum, J. (eds.) 45th ACM STOC, pp. 555–564. ACM Press, June 2013
24. Gorbunov, S., Vaikuntanathan, V., Wee, H.: Functional encryption with bounded collusions via multi-party computation. In: Safavi-Naini, R., Canetti, R. (eds.) CRYPTO 2012. LNCS, vol. 7417, pp. 162–179. Springer, Heidelberg (2012). doi:10.1007/978-3-642-32009-5_11
25. Gorbunov, S., Vaikuntanathan, V., Wee, H.: Attribute-based encryption for circuits. In: Boneh, D., Roughgarden, T., Feigenbaum, J. (eds.) 45th ACM STOC, pp. 545–554. ACM Press, June 2013
26. Gorbunov, S., Vaikuntanathan, V., Wee, H.: Predicate encryption for circuits from LWE. In: Gennaro, R., Robshaw, M. (eds.) CRYPTO 2015. LNCS, vol. 9216, pp. 503–523. Springer, Heidelberg (2015). doi:10.1007/978-3-662-48000-7_25

27. Goyal, V., Pandey, O., Sahai, A., Waters, B.: Attribute-based encryption for fine-grained access control of encrypted data. In: Juels, A., Wright, R.N., Vimercati, S. (eds.) ACM CCS 2006, pp. 89–98. ACM Press, October/November 2006. Available as Cryptology ePrint Archive Report 2006/309
28. Katz, J., Sahai, A., Waters, B.: Predicate encryption supporting disjunctions, polynomial equations, and inner products. In: Smart, N. (ed.) EUROCRYPT 2008. LNCS, vol. 4965, pp. 146–162. Springer, Heidelberg (2008). doi:10.1007/978-3-540-78967-3_9
29. Katz, J., Sahai, A., Waters, B.: Predicate encryption supporting disjunctions, polynomial equations, and inner products. J. Cryptol. **26**(2), 191–224 (2013)
30. Lewko, A.B.: Tools for simulating features of composite order bilinear groups in the prime order setting. In: Pointcheval, D., Johansson, T. (eds.) EUROCRYPT 2012. LNCS, vol. 7237, pp. 318–335. Springer, Heidelberg (2012). doi:10.1007/978-3-642-29011-4_20
31. Lin, H.: Indistinguishability obfuscation from DDH on 5-linear maps and locality-5 PRGs. In: CRYPTO 2017 (to appear). Also available at Cryptology ePrint Archive, Report 2016/1096 (2016). http://eprint.iacr.org/2016/1096
32. Okamoto, T., Takashima, K.: Homomorphic encryption and signatures from vector decomposition. In: Galbraith, S.D., Paterson, K.G. (eds.) Pairing 2008. LNCS, vol. 5209, pp. 57–74. Springer, Heidelberg (2008). doi:10.1007/978-3-540-85538-5_4
33. Okamoto, T., Takashima, K.: Hierarchical predicate encryption for inner-products. In: Matsui, M. (ed.) ASIACRYPT 2009. LNCS, vol. 5912, pp. 214–231. Springer, Heidelberg (2009). doi:10.1007/978-3-642-10366-7_13
34. Okamoto, T., Takashima, K.: Fully secure functional encryption with general relations from the decisional linear assumption. In: Rabin, T. (ed.) CRYPTO 2010. LNCS, vol. 6223, pp. 191–208. Springer, Heidelberg (2010). doi:10.1007/978-3-642-14623-7_11
35. O'Neill, A.: Definitional issues in functional encryption. Cryptology ePrint Archive, Report 2010/556 (2010). http://eprint.iacr.org/2010/556
36. Sahai, A., Waters, B.: Fuzzy identity-based encryption. In: Cramer, R. (ed.) EUROCRYPT 2005. LNCS, vol. 3494, pp. 457–473. Springer, Heidelberg (2005). doi:10.1007/11426639_27
37. Shamir, A.: Identity-based cryptosystems and signature schemes. In: Blakley, G.R., Chaum, D. (eds.) CRYPTO 1984. LNCS, vol. 196, pp. 47–53. Springer, Heidelberg (1985). doi:10.1007/3-540-39568-7_5
38. Shamir, A.: IP=PSPACE. In: 31st FOCS, pp. 11–15. IEEE Computer Society Press, October 1990
39. Waters, B.: Dual system encryption: realizing fully secure IBE and HIBE under simple assumptions. In: Halevi, S. (ed.) CRYPTO 2009. LNCS, vol. 5677, pp. 619–636. Springer, Heidelberg (2009). doi:10.1007/978-3-642-03356-8_36

Foundations I

Memory-Tight Reductions

Benedikt Auerbach[1(✉)], David Cash[2], Manuel Fersch[1], and Eike Kiltz[1]

[1] Horst Görtz Institute for IT Security, Ruhr University Bochum, Bochum, Germany
{benedikt.auerbach,manuel.fersch,eike.kiltz}@rub.de
[2] Rutgers University, New Brunswick, NJ, USA
david.cash@cs.rutgers.edu

Abstract. Cryptographic reductions typically aim to be *tight* by transforming an adversary A into an algorithm that uses essentially the same resources as A. In this work we initiate the study of *memory efficiency* in reductions. We argue that the amount of working memory used (relative to the initial adversary) is a relevant parameter in reductions, and that reductions that are inefficient with memory will sometimes yield less meaningful security guarantees. We then point to several common techniques in reductions that are memory-inefficient and give a toolbox for reducing memory usage. We review common cryptographic assumptions and their sensitivity to memory usage. Finally, we prove an impossibility result showing that reductions between some assumptions must *unavoidably* be either memory- or time-inefficient. This last result follows from a connection to data streaming algorithms for which unconditional memory lower bounds are known.

Keywords: Memory · Tightness · Provable security · Black box reduction

1 Introduction

Cryptographic reductions support the security of a cryptographic scheme S by showing that any attack against S can be transformed into an algorithm for solving a problem P. The *tightness* of a reduction is in general some measure of how closely the reduction relates the resources of attacks against S to the resources of the algorithm for P. A tighter reduction gives a better algorithm for P, ruling out a larger class of attacks against S. Typically one considers resources like runtime, success probability, and sometimes the number of queries (to oracles defined in P) of the resultant algorithm when evaluating the tightness of a reduction.

This work revisits how we measure the resources of the algorithm produced by a reduction. We observe that *memory usage* is an often important but overlooked metric in evaluating cryptographic reductions. Consider typical "tight" reductions from the literature, which start with an attack against a scheme S that uses (say) time t_S to achieve success probability ε_S, and transform the

J. Katz and H. Shacham (Eds.): CRYPTO 2017, Part I, LNCS 10401, pp. 101–132, 2017.
DOI: 10.1007/978-3-319-63688-7_4

attack into an algorithm for problem P running in time $t_P \approx t_S$ and succeeding with probability $\varepsilon_P \approx \varepsilon_S$. We observe that reductions tight in this sense are sometimes highly *memory-loose*: If the attack against S used m_S bits of working memory, the reduction may produce an algorithm using $m_P \gg m_S$ bits of memory to solve P. Depending on P, this changes the conclusions we can draw about the security of the scheme.

In this paper we investigate memory-efficiency in cryptographic reductions in various settings. We show that some standard decisions in security definitions have a bearing on memory efficiency of possible reductions. We give several simple techniques for improving memory efficiency of certain classes of reductions, and finally turn to a connection between streaming algorithms and memory/time-efficient reductions.

TIGHTNESS, MEMORY-TIGHTNESS, AND SECURITY. Reductions between a problem P and a cryptographic scheme S that approximately preserve runtime and success probability are usually called *tight* (c.f. [6,8,17]). Tight reductions are preferred because they provide stronger assurance for the security of S. Specifically, let us call an algorithm running in time t and succeeding with probability ε a (t, ε)-algorithm (for a given problem, or to attack a given scheme). Suppose that a reduction converts a (t_S, ε_S)-adversary against scheme S into a (t_P, ε_P)-algorithm for P where (t_P, ε_P) are functions of the first two. If it is believed that no (t_P, ε_P) algorithm should exist for P, then one concludes that no (t_S, ε_S) adversary can exist against S.

If a reduction is not tight, then in order to conclude that scheme S is secure against (t_S, ε_S)-adversaries one must adjust the parameters of the instance of P on which S is built, leading to a less efficient construction. In some extreme cases, obtaining a reasonable security level for a scheme with a non-tight reduction leads to an impractical construction. Addressing this issue has become an active area of research in the last two decades (e.g. [4–6,8,11,12,18]).

In this work we keep track of the amount of memory used in reductions. To see when memory usage becomes relevant, let a (t, m, ε)-algorithm use t time steps, m bits of memory, and succeed with probability ε. A tight reduction from S to P transforms $(t_S, m_S, \varepsilon_S)$-adversaries into $(t_P, m_P, \varepsilon_P)$-algorithms, where "tight" guarantees $t_S \approx t_P$ and $\varepsilon_S \approx \varepsilon_P$, but permits $m_P \gg m_S$, up to the worst-case $m_P \approx t_P$.

Now, suppose concretely that we want S to be secure against $(2^{256}, 2^{128}, O(1))$-adversaries, based on very conservative estimates of the resources available to a powerful government. Consider two possible "tight" reductions: One that is additionally "memory-tight" and transforms a $(2^{256}, 2^{128}, O(1))$-adversary A against S into a $(2^{256}, 2^{128}, O(1))$-algorithm B_{mt} for P, and one that is "memory-loose" and instead only yields a $(2^{256}, 2^{256}, O(1))$-algorithm B_{nmt} for P.

The crucial point is that some problems P can be solved faster when larger amounts of memory are used. In our example above, it may be that P is impossible to solve with 2^{256} time and 2^{128} memory for some specific security parameter λ. But with both time and memory up to 2^{256} bits, the best algorithm may be able to solve instances of P with security parameter λ, and with even larger parameters up to some $\lambda' > \lambda$. The memory-looseness of the reduction now bites, because to achieve the original security goal for S we must use the larger parameter λ' for P, resulting in a slower instantiation of the scheme. When P is a problem involving a symmetric primitive where the "security parameter" cannot be changed the issue is more difficult to address.

We now address two points in turn: If P is easier to solve when large memory is available, what does this mean for memory-tight reductions? And when are reductions "memory-loose"?

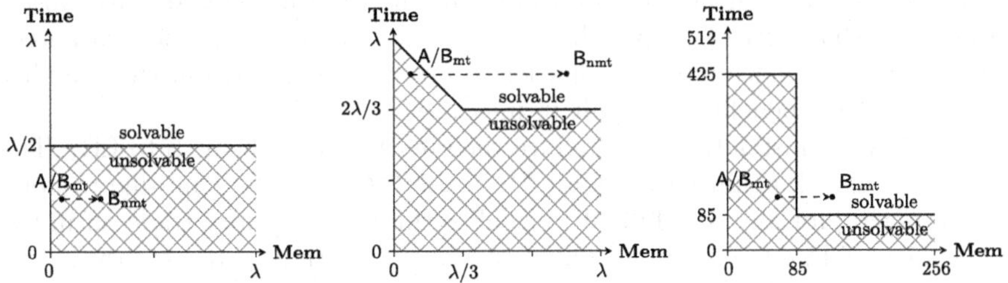

Fig. 1. Time/memory trade-off plots for collision-resistance (CR_2, left), triple collision-resistance (CR_3, middle) and LPN with dimension 1024 and error rate 1/4 (right). All plots are log-log and the axes on the right plot are not to scale.

MEMORY-SENSITIVE PROBLEMS AND MEMORY-TIGHTNESS. Many, but not all, problems P relevant to cryptography can be solved more quickly with large memory than with small. In the public-key realm these include factoring, discrete-logarithm in prime fields, Learning Parities with Noise (LPN), Learning With Errors (LWE), approximate Shortest Vector Problem, and Short Integer Solution (SIS). In symmetric-key cryptography such problems include key-recovery against multiple-encryption, finding multi-collisions in hash functions, and computation of memory-hard functions. We refer to problems like these as *memory-sensitive.* (We refer to Sect. 6 for more discussion.)

On the other hand, problems P exist where the best known algorithm also uses small memory: Discrete-logarithm in elliptic curve groups over prime-fields [16], finding (single) collisions in hash functions [23], finding a preimage in hash functions (exhaustive search), and key recovery against block-ciphers (also exhaustive search).

Let us consider some specific examples to illustrate the impact of a memory-loose reduction to a non-memory-sensitive versus a memory-sensitive problem. Let CR_k be the problem of finding a k-way collision in a hash function H with λ output bits, that is, finding k distinct domain points $x_1, \ldots, x_k$ such that $\mathsf{H}(x_1) = \mathsf{H}(x_2) = \cdots = \mathsf{H}(x_k)$ for some fixed $k \geq 2$.

First suppose we reduce the security of a scheme S to CR_2, which is standard collision-resistance. The problem CR_2 is not memory-sensitive, and the best known attack is a $(2^{\lambda/2}, O(1), O(1))$-algorithm. In the left plot of Fig. 1 we visualize the "feasible" region for CR_2, where the shaded region is unsolvable. Now we consider two possible reductions. One is a memory-tight reduction which maps an adversary A (with some time and memory complexity, with possibly much less memory than time) to an algorithm B_{mt} for CR_2 with the same time and memory. The other reduction is memory-loose (but time-tight) and maps A to an adversary $\mathsf{B}_{\mathrm{nmt}}$ that uses time and memory approximately equal to the time of A. We plot the effect of these reductions in the left part of the figure. A tight reduction leaves the point essentially unchanged, while a memory-loose reduction moves the point horizontally to the right. Both reductions will produce a $\mathsf{B}_{\mathrm{nmt}}$ in the region not known to be solvable, thus giving a meaningful security statement about A that amounts to ruling out the shaded region of adversaries. We do note that there is a possible quantitative difference in the guarantees of the reductions, since it is only harder to produce an algorithm with smaller memory, but this benefit is difficult to measure.

Now suppose instead that we reduce the security of a scheme S to CR_3. The best known attack against CR_3 is a $(2^{(1-\alpha)\lambda}, 2^{\alpha\lambda}, O(1))$-algorithm due to Joux and Lucks [20], for any $\alpha \leq 1/3$. We visualize this time-memory trade-off in the middle plot of Fig. 1, and again any adversary with time and memory in the shaded region would be a cryptanalytic advance. We again consider a memory-tight versus a memory-loose reduction. The memory-tight reduction preserves the point for the adversary A in the plot and thus rules out $(t_S, m_S, O(1))$ adversaries for any t_S, m_S in the shaded region. A memory-loose (but time-tight) reduction mapping A to $\mathsf{B}_{\mathrm{nmt}}$ for CR_3 that blows up memory usage up to time usage will move the point horizontally to the right. We can see that there are drastic consequences when the original adversary A lies in the triangular region with time $>2\lambda/3$ and memory $<\lambda/3$, because the reduction produces an adversary $\mathsf{B}_{\mathrm{nmt}}$ using resources for which CR_3 is known to be broken. In summary, the reduction only rules out adversaries A below the horizontal line with time $= 2\lambda/3$.

Finally we consider an example instantiation of parameters for the *learning parities with noise* (LPN) problem, which is memory-sensitive, where a memory-loose reduction would diminish security guarantees. In Sect. 6 we recall this problem and the best attacks, and in the right plot of Fig. 1 the shaded region represents the infeasible region for the problem in dimension 1024 and error rate 1/4. (For simplicity, all hidden constants are ignored in the plot.) In this problem the effect of memory-looseness is more stark. Despite using a large dimension, a memory-loose reduction can only rule out attacks running in time $<2^{85}$. A memory-tight reduction, however, gives a much stronger guarantee for adversaries with memory less than 2^{85}.

Memory-loose reductions. Reductions are often memory-loose, and small decisions in definitions can lead to memory usage being artificially high. We start with an illustrative example.

Suppose we have a tight security reduction (in the traditional sense) in the random oracle model [7] between a problem P and some cryptographic scheme S. More concretely, suppose a reduction transforms a $(t_S, m_S, \varepsilon_S)$-adversary A_S in the random-oracle model into a $(t_P, m_P, \varepsilon_P)$-algorithm A_P for P. A typical reduction has A_P simulate a security game for A_S, including the random oracle, usually via a table that stores responses to queries issued by A_S. Naively removing the table from storage usually is not an option for various reasons: For example, if A_S queries the oracle on the same input twice, then it expects to see the same output twice, or perhaps the reduction needs to "program" the random oracle with responses that must be remembered.

Storing a table for the random oracle may dramatically increase memory usage of the algorithm A_P. If adversary A_S makes q_H queries to the random oracle, then A_P will store $\Omega(q_H)$ bits of memory, plus the internal memory m_S of A_S during the simulation, which gives

$$m_P = m_S + \Omega(q_H).$$

In the worst case, A_S could run in constant memory and make one random oracle query per time unit, meaning that A_P requires as much memory as its running time. Thus the reduction may be "tight" in the traditional sense with $t_P \approx t_S, \varepsilon_P \approx \varepsilon_S$, but also have

$$m_P = m_S + t_S. \tag{1}$$

Thus A_P may use an enormous amount of memory m_P even if A_S satisfied $m_S = O(1)$.

This example is only the start. Memory-looseness is sometimes, but not always, easily fixed, and seems to occur because it was not measured in reductions. Below we will furnish examples of other reductions that are (sometimes implicitly) memory-loose. We will also discuss some decisions in definitions and modeling that dramatically effect memory usage but are not usually stressed.

1.1 Our Results

Even though there exists an extensive literature on tightness of cryptographic security reductions (e.g. [5,8,11,12]), memory has, to the best of our knowledge, not been considered in the context of security reductions. In this paper we first identify the problems related to non-memory-tight security reductions. To overcome the problems, we initiate a systematic study on how to make known security reductions memory-tight. Concretely, we provide several techniques to obtain memory-efficient reductions and give examples where they can be applied. Our techniques can be used to make many security reductions memory-tight, but not all of them. Furthermore, we show that this is inherent, i.e., that there exist natural cryptographic problems that do not have a fully tight security reduction. Finally, we examine various memory-sensitive problems such as the learning parity with noise (LPN) problem, the factoring problem, and the discrete logarithm problem over finite fields.

The Random Oracle technique. Recall that a classical simulation of the random oracle using the lazy sampling technique requires the reduction to store $O(q_H)$ values. The idea is to replace the responses $H(x)$ to a random oracle query x by $\mathsf{PRF}(k, x)$, where PRF is a pseudo-random function and k is its key. The limitation of this technique is that it can only be applied to very restricted cases of a programmable random oracle.

THE REWINDING TECHNIQUE. The idea of the rewinding technique is to use the adversary as a "memory device." Concretely, whenever the reduction would like to access values previously output by the adversary that it did not store in its memory, it simply rewinds the adversary which is executed with the same random coins and with the same input. This way the reduction's running time doubles, but (unlike previous applications of the rewinding technique in cryptography, e.g., [22]) the overall success probability does not decrease. The rewinding technique can be applied multiple times providing a trade-off between memory efficiency and running time of the reduction. To exemplify the techniques, we show a memory-tight security reduction to the RSA full-domain hash signature scheme in the appendix.

A LOWER BOUND. Some reductions appear (to us at least) to inherently require increased memory. We take a first step towards formalizing this intuition by proving a lower bound on the memory usage of a class of black-box reductions in two scenarios.

First, we revisit a reduction implicitly used to justify the standard unforgeability notion for digital signatures, which reduces a game with several chances to produce a valid forgery to the standard game with only one chance. One can take this as a possible indication that signatures with memory-tight reductions in the more permissive model may be preferred. Second, we prove a similar lower bound on the memory usage of a class of reductions between a "multi-challenge" variant of collision resistance and standard collision resistance.

Interestingly, our lower bound follows from a result on *streaming algorithms*, which are designed to use small space while working with sequential access to a large stream of data.

OPEN PROBLEMS. This work initiates the study of memory-tight reductions in cryptography. We give a number of techniques to obtain such reductions, but many open problems remain. There are likely other reductions in the literature that we have not covered, and to which our techniques do not apply. It is even unclear how one should consider basic definitions, like unforgeability for signatures, since the generic reductions from more complicated (but more realistic) definitions may be tight but not memory-tight.

One reduction we did consider, but could not improve, is the IND-CCA security proof for Hash ElGamal in the random oracle model [1] under the gap Diffie-Hellman assumption. This reduction (and some others that use "gap" assumptions) use their random oracle table in a way that our techniques cannot address. We conjecture that a memory-tight reduction does not exist in this case, and leave it as an open problem to (dis)prove our conjecture.

2 Complexity Measures

We denote random sampling from a finite set A according to the uniform distribution with $a \xleftarrow{\$} A$. By $\mathrm{Ber}(\alpha)$ we denote the Bernoulli distribution for parameter α, i.e., the distribution of a random variable that takes value 1 with probability α and value 0 with probability $1-\alpha$; by $\mathbb{P}_\ell$ the set of primes of bit size ℓ and by log the logarithm with base 2.

2.1 Computational Model

COMPUTATIONAL MODEL. All *algorithms* in this paper are taken to be RAMs. These programs have access to memory with words of size λ, along with a constant number of registers that each hold one word. In this paper λ will always be the security parameter of a construction or a problem under consideration.

We define *probabilistic algorithms* to be RAMs with a special instruction that fills a distinguished register with random bits (independent of other calls to the special instruction). We note that this instruction does not allow for rewinding of the random bits, so if the algorithm wants to access previously used random bits then it must store them. *Running* an algorithm A means executing a RAM machine with input written in its memory (starting at address 0). If A is randomized, we write $y \xleftarrow{\$} \mathsf{A}(I)$ to denote the random variable y that is obtained by running A on input I (which may consist of a tuple $I = (I_1, \ldots, I_n)$). If A is deterministic, we write $\leftarrow$ instead of $\xleftarrow{\$}$. We sometimes give an algorithm A access to *stateful oracles* $\mathsf{O}_1, \mathsf{O}_2, \ldots, \mathsf{O}_n$. Each O_i is defined by a RAM M_i. We also define an associated string st_O called the *oracle state* that is stored in a protected region of the memory of A that can only be read by the oracles. Initially st_O is defined to be empty. An algorithm A *calls an oracle* O_i via a special instruction, which runs the corresponding RAM on input from a fixed region of memory of A along with the oracle state st_O. The RAM M_i uses its own protected working memory, and finally its output is written into a fixed region of memory for A, the updated state is written to st_O, and control is transferred back to A.

GAMES. Most of our security definitions and proofs use *code-based games* [9]. A game G consists of a RAM defining an Init oracle, zero or more stateful oracles $\mathsf{O}_1, \ldots, \mathsf{O}_n$, and a Fin RAM oracle. An adversary A is said to play game G if its first instruction calls Init (handing over its own input) and its last instruction calls Fin, and in between these calls it only invokes $\mathsf{O}_1, \ldots, \mathsf{O}_n$ and performs local computation. We further require that A outputs whatever Fin outputs.

Executing game G *with* A is formally just running A with input λ, the security parameter. Keeping with convention, we denote the random variable induced by executing G with A as G^A (where the sample space is the randomness of A and the associated oracles). By $\mathsf{G}^\mathsf{A} \Rightarrow \mathtt{out}$ we denote the event that G executed with A outputs $\mathtt{out}$. In our games we sometimes denote a "Stop" command that takes an argument. When Stop is invoked, its argument is considered the output of the game (and the execution of the adversary is halted). If a game description omits the Fin procedure, it means that when A calls Fin on some input x, Fin simply invokes Stop with argument x. By default, integer variables are initialized to 0, set variables to $\emptyset$, strings to the empty string and arrays to the empty array.

2.2 Complexity Measures

This work is concerned with measuring the resource consumption of an adversary in a way that allows for meaningful conclusions about security. Success probabilities and time are widely used in the cryptographic literature with general agreement on the details, which we recall first. Memory consumption of reductions is however new, so we next discuss the possible options in measuring memory and the implications.

SUCCESS PROBABILITY. We define the *success probability of* A *playing game* G *as* $\mathbf{Succ}(\mathsf{G}^{\mathsf{A}}) := \Pr[\mathsf{G}^{\mathsf{A}} \Rightarrow 1]$.

RUNTIME. Let A be an algorithm (RAM) with no oracles. The runtime of A, denoted $\mathbf{Time}(\mathsf{A})$, is the worst-case number of computation steps of A over all inputs of bit-length λ and all possible random choices. Now let G be a game and A be an adversary that plays game G. The runtime of executing G with A is usually taken to be the number of computation steps of A plus the number of computation steps of each RAM used to respond to oracle queries: We denote this as $\mathbf{TotalTime}(\mathsf{G}^{\mathsf{A}})$ or $\mathbf{TotalTime}(\mathsf{A})$. One may prefer not to include the time used by the oracles, and in this case we denote $\mathbf{LocalTime}(\mathsf{G}^{\mathsf{A}})$ or $\mathbf{LocalTime}(\mathsf{A})$ to be the number of steps of A only.

MEMORY. We define the memory consumption of a RAM program A without oracles, denoted $\mathbf{Mem}(\mathsf{A})$, to be size (in words of length λ) of the code of A plus the worst-case number of registers used in memory at any step in computation, over all inputs of bit-length λ and all random choices. Now let G be a game and A be an adversary that plays game G. The memory required to execute game G with A includes the memory needed to input and output to A, as well as input and output to each oracle, along with the working memory and state of each oracle. We denote this as $\mathbf{TotalMem}(\mathsf{G}^{\mathsf{A}})$ or $\mathbf{TotalMem}(\mathsf{A})$. Alternatively, one may measure only the code and memory consumed by A, but not its oracles. We denote this measure by $\mathbf{LocalMem}(\mathsf{A})$.

One advantage of the **LocalMem** measure is that it can avoid small details of security definitions drastically changing the meaning of memory-tightness in reductions.

Sometimes it will be convenient to measure the memory consumption in bits, in which case we use $\mathbf{Mem}_2(\mathsf{A})$, $\mathbf{LocalMem}_2(\mathsf{A})$, and $\mathbf{TotalMem}_2(\mathsf{A})$.

2.3 Case Study I: Unforgeability of Digital Signatures

Let (Gen, Sign, Ver) be a digital signature scheme (see Sect. 5 for the exact syntax of signatures, which is standard). On the left side of Fig. 2 we recall the game UFCMA that defines the standard notion of (existential) unforgeability under chosen-message attacks. The advantage of an adversary A is

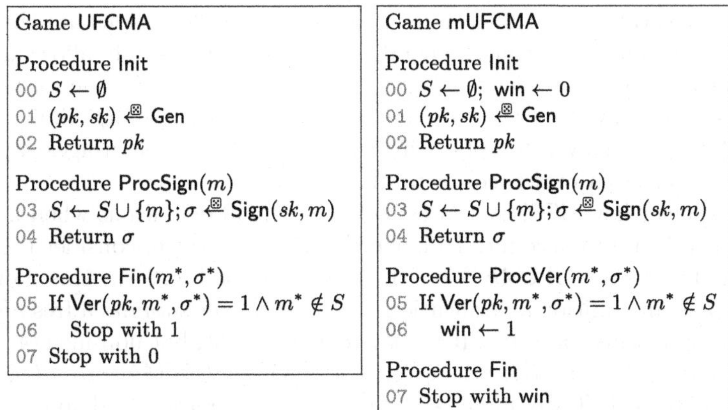

Fig. 2. Games UFCMA, mUFCMA.

defined by $\mathbf{Adv}(\mathsf{UFCMA}^{\mathsf{A}}) = \mathbf{Succ}(\mathsf{UFCMA}^{\mathsf{A}})$, and a signature scheme where $\mathbf{Adv}(\mathsf{UFCMA}^{\mathsf{A}})$ is "small" for some class of adversaries is usually defined to be "secure". In order for the definition to be meaningful, the game UFCMA checks that the signature σ^* on m^* is valid, and also that m^* was not queried to the signing oracle. In our version of the definition, the signing oracle maintains a set S of messages that were queried, and the game uses S to check if m^* was queried.

The UFCMA game is an example where we prefer **LocalMem** to **TotalMem**. Any adversary A playing UFCMA will always have $\mathbf{TotalMem}(\mathsf{A}) = \Omega(q_S)$, where q_S is the number of signature queries it issues, while it may have $\mathbf{LocalMem}(\mathsf{A})$ much smaller. Restricting the number of signing queries q_S is an option but weakens the definition.

An alternative style of definition for unforgeability is to limit the class of adversaries A considered to those that are "well behaved" in that they never submit an m^* that was previously queried. The game no longer needs to track which messages were queried to the signing oracle in order to be meaningful. This definition is equivalent up to a small increase in (local) running time, but it is not clear if the same is true for memory. To convert *any* adversary to be well behaved, natural approaches mimic our version of the game, storing a set S and checking the final forgery locally before submitting.

We contend that there is good reason to prefer our definition over the version that only quantifies over well-behaved adversaries. In principle, it is possible that a signature construction is secure against a class of well-behaved adversaries (say, running in a bounded amount of time and memory) but not against general adversaries running with the same time/memory. Counter-intuitively, such a general adversary might produce a forgery without knowing itself if the forgery is fresh and thus wins the game. Since we cannot rule this out, we prefer our stronger definition.

STRONGER UNFORGEABILITY. Games in many crypto-definitions are chosen to be simple and compact but also general. The game UFCMA only allows a single attempt at a forgery in order to shorten proofs, but the definition also tightly implies (up to a small increase in runtime) a version of unforgeability where the attacker gets many attempts, which more closely models usages where an attacker will have many chances to produce a forgery.

It is less clear how UFCMA relates to more general definitions when memory tightness is taken into account. To make this more concrete, consider the game mUFCMA (for "many UFCMA") on the right side of Fig. 2. In this game the adversary has an additional verification oracle. If it ever submits a fresh forgery to this oracle, it wins the game. It is easy to give a tight, but non-memory-tight, reduction converting any (t, m, ε)-adversary playing mUFCMA into a (t', m', ε)-adversary playing UFCMA for $t' \approx t$ but $m' \gg m$. Other trade-offs are also possible but achieving tightness in all three parameters seems difficult.

For the reasons described in the introduction, a memory-tight reduction from winning mUFCMA to winning UFCMA is desirable. In Sect. 4, we show that a certain class of black-box reductions for these problems in fact cannot be simultaneously tight in runtime, memory, and success probability. We conclude that signatures with dedicated memory-tight proofs against adversaries in the mUFCMA may provide stronger security assurance, especially when security is reduced to a memory-sensitive problem like RSA.

We remark that the common reduction from multi-challenge to single-challenge IND-CPA/IND-CCA security for public-key encryption is memory tight (but not tight in terms of the success probability).

2.4 Case Study II: Collision-Resistance Definitions

Collision-resistance, and multi-collision-resistance of hash functions, is used for security reductions in many contexts. Let H be a keyed hash function (with κ-bit keys), with standard syntax. On the left side of Fig. 3 we recall the game CR_t used to define t-collision resistance. The game provides no extra oracles, and A wins if it can find t domain points that are mapped to the same point by H.

As we will see in later sections, it is sometimes feasible to fix typical memory-tight reductions to CR_t. We however now consider using collision-resistance (for $t = 2$) for *domain extension of pseudorandom functions*. Let $\mathsf{F} : \{0,1\}^\kappa \times \{0,1\}^\delta \rightarrow \{0,1\}^\rho$ be a keyed function with input-length δ which should have random looking input/output behavior to some class of adversaries (see Sect. 3.1 for a formal definition of PRFs). We can define a new keyed function F^* that takes arbitrary-length inputs by

$$\mathsf{F}^* : \{0,1\}^{2\kappa} \times \{0,1\}^* \rightarrow \{0,1\}^\rho,$$
$$\mathsf{F}^*((k, k_h),\ x) = \mathsf{F}(k,\ \mathsf{H}(k_h, x)).$$

The proof that F^* is a PRF is an easy hybrid argument. One first bounds the probability that an adversary submits two inputs that collide in H. Once this probability is known to be small, the memory-tight reduction to the pseudorandomness of F is immediate.

Naive attempts at the reduction to collision-resistance are however not memory-tight. One can run the adversary attacking F^* and record its queries, checking for any collisions, but this increases memory usage.

To model what such a proof is trying to do, we formulate a new game for t-collision resistance called mCR_t in the right side of Fig. 3. In the game, the adversary has an oracle ProcInput that takes a message and adds it to a set S. At the end of the game, the adversary wins if S contains any t inputs that are mapped to the same point. The game implements this check using counters stored in a dictionary.

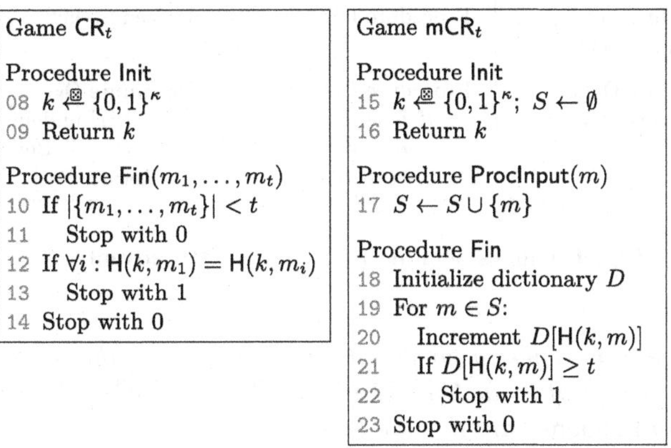

Fig. 3. Games $\mathsf{CR}_t, \mathsf{mCR}_t$.

Returning to the proof for F^*, one can easily construct an adversary to play mCR_2 using any PRF adversary. The resulting reduction will be memory-tight. Thus it would be desirable to have a memory-tight reduction from mCR_2 to CR_2 to complete the proof. This however seems difficult or even impossible, and in Sect. 4 we show that a class of black-box reductions cannot be memory-tight. As discussed in the introduction, t-collision-resistance is not memory sensitive for $t = 2$, and thus the meaning of a memory-tight reduction is somewhat diminished (i.e. it does not justify more aggressive parameter settings). For $t > 2$ the effect of memory-tightness is more significant.

3 Techniques to Obtain Memory Efficiency

In this section we describe four techniques to obtain memory-efficient reductions. In Sect. 5 we show how to apply those techniques to memory-tightly prove the security of the RSA Full Domain Hash signature scheme [7]. Using this example we also point to technical challenges that may arise when applying multiple techniques in the same proof.

3.1 Pseudorandom Functions

First, we formally define pseudorandom functions. They are the main tool used in this section to make reductions memory efficient.

Definition 1. *Let κ, δ and ρ be integers. Further let* $\mathsf{F}\colon \{0,1\}^\kappa \times \{0,1\}^\delta \to \{0,1\}^\rho$ *be a deterministic algorithm and let* A *be an adversary that is given access to an oracle and outputs a single bit. The* PRF advantage *of* A *is defined as* $\mathbf{Adv}(\mathsf{PRF}^{\mathsf{A}}) := |\mathbf{Succ}(\mathsf{Real}^{\mathsf{A}}) - \mathbf{Succ}(\mathsf{Random}^{\mathsf{A}})|$*, where* Real *and* Random *are the games depicted in Fig. 4.*

Game Real	Game Random	Game Random_α
Procedure Init	Procedure Init	Procedure Init
$k \xleftarrow{\$} \{0,1\}^\kappa$		
Procedure $\mathsf{O_F}(x)$	Procedure $\mathsf{O_F}(x)$	Procedure $\mathsf{O_F}(x)$
Return $\mathsf{F}(k,x)$	If $R[x]$ undefined:	If $R[x]$ undefined:
	$R[x] \xleftarrow{\$} \{0,1\}^\rho$	$R[x] \xleftarrow{\$} \mathrm{Ber}(\alpha)$
	Return $R[x]$	Return $R[x]$

Fig. 4. Games defining PRF and α-PRF advantage.

If the range of F *is just a single bit $\{0,1\}$, we define the α-*PRF advantage *with bias $0 \le \alpha \le 1$ of* A *as* $\mathbf{Adv}(\mathsf{PRF}_\alpha^{\mathsf{A}}) := |\mathbf{Succ}(\mathsf{Real}^{\mathsf{A}}) - \mathbf{Succ}(\mathsf{Random}_\alpha^{\mathsf{A}})|$*, where* Real *and* Random_α *are the games in Fig. 4.*

Note that a $2^{-\rho}$-PRF can be easily constructed from a standard PRF with range $\{0,1\}^\rho$ by mapping 1^ρ to 1 and all other values to 0. A $1/q$-PRF for arbitrary q can be constructed in a similar way from a standard PRF with sufficiently large image size ρ.

3.2 Generating (Pseudo)random Coins

Our first technique is the simplest, where we observe random coins used by adversaries can be replaced with pseudorandom coins, and that this substitution will save memory in certain reductions.

Consider a security game G and an adversary A. Both are probabilistic processes and therefore require randomness. When considering memory efficiency details on storing random coins could come to dominate memory usage. Specifically, some reductions run an adversary multiple times with the same random tape, which must be stored in between runs. One possibility to do this is by sampling all randomness required in game G^{A} (including the randomness used by A) in advance. More formally let $L \le 2^\lambda$ be an upper bound on the amount of executions of the instruction filling an register with random bits in G^{A}. Then the sampling of random coins can be replaced filling and storing L registers (memory units) with random bits at the beginning of Init and in the rest of the game replacing the ith call to the instruction with a procedure Coins returning the contents of the ith register. This is formalized in game G_0 of Fig. 5.

The game can be simulated in a memory-efficient way by replacing the random bits used by G and A with pseudorandom bits generated by a PRF $\mathsf{F}\colon \{0,1\}^\kappa \times \{0,1\}^\delta \to \{0,1\}^\lambda$, as described in Game G_1 of Fig. 5. In this variant the game sets up the counter i in the usual way. Then a PRF key k is sampled from a key space $\{0,1\}^\kappa$ and calls to Coins are simulated by returning the pseudorandom bits $\mathsf{F}(k,i)$. We now compare the two ways of executing the game in terms of success probability, running time, and memory consumption.

G_0: **Standard Coin Generation**	G_1: **Memory-Efficient Coin Generation**
Procedure Init	Procedure Init
$r \xleftarrow{\$} (\{0,1\}^\lambda)^L$	$k \xleftarrow{\$} \{0,1\}^\kappa$
Procedure Coins	Procedure Coins
$i \leftarrow i+1$	$i \leftarrow i+1$
Return r_i	Return $\mathsf{F}(k,i)$

Fig. 5. Generating (pseudo)random coins in a memory-efficient way. By r_i we denote the ith block of λ bits of the string r.

Success Probability. By a simple reduction to the security of the PRF, there exists an adversary B with $\textbf{LocalTime}(\mathsf{B}) = \textbf{LocalTime}(\mathsf{A})$, $\textbf{LocalMem}(\mathsf{B}) = \textbf{LocalMem}(\mathsf{A}) + 1$ such that

$$\left|\textbf{Succ}(\mathsf{G}_0^{\mathsf{A}})] - \textbf{Succ}(\mathsf{G}_1^{\mathsf{A}})\right| \leq \textbf{Adv}(\mathsf{PRF}^{\mathsf{B}})$$

(see Definition 1). Observe that B perfectly simulates the Coins oracle as follows. For A's i^{th} query to Coins, it queries O_F of the PRF games on i and relays its response back to A. To do this, it needs to store a counter of $\log L$ bits. All other procedures are simulated as specified in G_1.

Running Time. Game G_1 needs to evaluate the PRF (via algorithm F) L times, hence we have $\textbf{TotalTime}(\mathsf{G}_1^{\mathsf{A}}) \leq \textbf{TotalTime}(\mathsf{G}_0^{\mathsf{A}}) + L \cdot \textbf{Time}(\mathsf{F})$.

Memory. Both games have to store a counter i of size $\log L \leq \lambda$ bits, which equals one memory unit. But while game G_0 needs memory for storing L strings, the memory-efficient game G_1 only needs additional memory $\textbf{Mem}(\mathsf{F})$. Note that the PRF key is included in the memory of F. So overall, we have

$$\textbf{TotalMem}(\mathsf{G}_0^{\mathsf{A}}) = \textbf{LocalMem}(\mathsf{A}) + 1 + L,$$
$$\textbf{TotalMem}(\mathsf{G}_1^{\mathsf{A}}) = \textbf{LocalMem}(\mathsf{A}) + 1 + \textbf{Mem}(\mathsf{F}).$$

Note that when applying this (and the following) techniques in a larger environment, special care has to be taken to keep the entire game consistent with the components changed by the technique. In particular, all intermediate reductions in a sequence of games have to be memory efficient to yield an overall memory-efficient reduction.

3.3 Random Oracles

Suppose a security game G is defined in the random oracle model, that is one of the game's procedures models a random oracle

$$H\colon \{0,1\}^{\delta} \rightarrow \{0,1\}^{\lambda}.$$

The standard way of implementing this is via a technique called lazy sampling [9], meaning that when an adversary A queries H on some value x, the game has to check if $H(x)$ is already defined, and if not, it samples $H(x)$ from some distribution and stores the value in a list, see G_0 in Fig. 6. This means that in the worst case, it needs to store as many strings as the number of adversarial queries.

However, there are several settings where the random oracle can be implemented by a PRF $\mathsf{F}\colon \{0,1\}^{\kappa} \times \{0,1\}^{\delta} \rightarrow \{0,1\}^{\lambda}$ as described in G_1 of Fig. 6, thus making G more memory-efficient. Among these settings are the non-programmable random oracle model and certain random oracles, where only values obtained or computed during the Init procedure are used to program them.

G_0: **Standard Random Oracle**	G_1: **Memory-Efficient Random Oracle**
Procedure Init	Procedure Init
	$k \xleftarrow{\$} \{0,1\}^{\kappa}$
Procedure $\mathsf{RO}(x_i)$	Procedure $\mathsf{RO}(x_i)$
If $H[x_i]$ undefined:	Return $\mathsf{F}(k, x_i)$
$\quad H[x_i] \xleftarrow{\$} \{0,1\}^{\lambda}$	
Return $H[x_i]$	

Fig. 6. The Random Oracle technique to simulate RO in a memory-efficient way. Here x_i denotes the ith query to RO. Note that the queries $x_1, \ldots, x_q$ are not necessarily distinct.

In the following paragraph we analyze how success probability, running time and memory consumption change if we apply this technique.

SUCCESS PROBABILITY. There exists an adversary B with **LocalTime**(A) = **LocalTime**(B) and **LocalMem**(A) = **LocalMem**(B) such that

$$\left|\mathbf{Succ}(\mathsf{G}_0^{\mathsf{A}}) - \mathbf{Succ}(\mathsf{G}_1^{\mathsf{A}})\right| \leq \mathbf{Adv}(\mathsf{PRF}^{\mathsf{B}}).$$

B perfectly simulates the RO by relaying all of A's queries to O_F of the PRF games and forwarding the responses back to A. All other procedures are simulated as specified in G_1. When B is run with respect to game Random of Definition 1 it provides A with a perfect simulation of G_0, if it is run with respect to game Real with a perfect simulation of game G_1.

RUNNING TIME. Let q_H be the number of random oracle queries posed by the adversary. Then game G_1 needs to evaluate the PRF q_H times, hence we have $\mathbf{TotalTime}(\mathsf{G}_1^{\mathsf{A}}) \leq \mathbf{TotalTime}(\mathsf{G}_0^{\mathsf{A}}) + q_H \cdot \mathbf{Time}(\mathsf{F})$.

MEMORY. Game G_0 needs to store an array H of size at least $q_H \cdot \lambda$ bits ($= q_H$ memory units), while the memory-efficient game only needs memory to execute the PRF via algorithm F. So overall, we have

$$\mathbf{TotalMem}(\mathsf{G}_0^{\mathsf{A}}) \geq \mathbf{LocalMem}(\mathsf{A}) + q_H,$$
$$\mathbf{TotalMem}(\mathsf{G}_1^{\mathsf{A}}) = \mathbf{LocalMem}(\mathsf{A}) + \mathbf{Mem}(\mathsf{F}).$$

3.4 Random Oracle Index Guessing Technique

This technique is used when random oracle queries are answered in two different ways, e.g. in a reduction where challenge values, like a discrete logarithm challenge $X = g^x$, are embedded in the programmable random oracle. Usually this is done by guessing some index i^* between 1 and q_H in the beginning, where q_H is the number of random oracle queries posed by the adversary. During the simulation, the challenge value is then embedded in the reduction's response to the $i^{*\text{th}}$ random oracle query.

To do this, the game needs to keep a list of all queries and responses. Independently of the way the game answers all the other queries except for the $i^{*\text{th}}$ one, simply keeping a counter is not sufficient, since an adversary posing the same query all the time would then receive two different responses and the random oracle thus wouldn't be well defined anymore. An example of such a game using the index guessing technique is game G_0 of Fig. 7, where two deterministic procedures P_0 and P_1 are used to program H depending on i^*.

To make games of this kind memory-efficient, one can use a $1/q_H$-PRF (see Definition 1) $\mathsf{F}\colon \{0,1\}^\kappa \times \{0,1\}^\delta \to \{0,1\}$, associating to each value of the domain of the random oracle a bit 0 with probability $1 - 1/q_H$ or 1 with probability $1/q_H$ and then programming the random oracle accordingly as described in game G_1 of Fig. 7. This method of using a biased bit goes back to Coron [14].

G_0: **Standard Index Guessing**	G_1: **Memory-Efficient Index Guessing**
Procedure Init	Procedure Init
$i^* \xleftarrow{\$} \{1, \ldots, q_H\}$	$k \xleftarrow{\$} \{0,1\}^\kappa$
Procedure $\mathsf{RO}(x_i)$	Procedure $\mathsf{RO}(x_i)$
If $H[x_i]$ undefined:	If $\mathsf{F}(k, x_i) = 0$: Return $\mathsf{P}_0(x_i)$
If $i = i^*$: $H[x_i] \leftarrow \mathsf{P}_0(x_i)$	Else: Return $\mathsf{P}_1(x_i)$
Else: $H[x_i] \leftarrow \mathsf{P}_1(x_i)$	
Return $H[x_i]$	

Fig. 7. The random oracle index guessing technique. By x_i we denote the ith query to RO. F is a $1/q_H$-PRF. Note that the queries to RO are not necessarily distinct.

We now compare the two games in terms of success probability, running time and memory efficiency.

SUCCESS PROBABILITY. Let A be an adversary that is executed in G_0. We define an intermediate game G_0', as depicted in Fig. 8, in which the index guessing is replaced by tossing a biased coin for each query.

```
G'_0

Procedure RO(x_i)
If c[x_i] undefined: c[x_i] <-$ Ber(1/q_H)
If c[x_i] = 0: Return P_0(x_i)
Else: Return P_1(x_i)
```

Fig. 8. Intermediate game for the transition to memory-efficient index guessing.

These games are identical if $c[x_{i^*}] = 0$ and $c[x_i] = 1$ for all $i \neq i^*$. Hence,

$$\mathbf{Succ}((\mathsf{G}_0')^{\mathsf{A}}) \geq (1 - {}^1\!/_{q_H})^{q_H - 1} \cdot \mathbf{Succ}(\mathsf{G}_0^{\mathsf{A}}) \geq e^{-1} \cdot \mathbf{Succ}(\mathsf{G}_0^{\mathsf{A}}).$$

Now it is easy to construct an adversary B against F with $\mathbf{LocalTime}(\mathsf{B}) = \mathbf{LocalTime}(\mathsf{A})$ and $\mathbf{LocalMem}(\mathsf{B}) = \mathbf{LocalMem}(\mathsf{A})$ that provides A with a perfect simulation of $\mathsf{G}_{0'}$ when interacting with game Random_α of Fig. 4 or respectively with a perfect simulation of G_1 when interacting with Real. Hence $|\mathbf{Succ}((\mathsf{G}_0')^{\mathsf{A}}) - \mathbf{Succ}(\mathsf{G}_1^{\mathsf{A}})| \leq \mathbf{Adv}(\mathsf{PRF}^{\mathsf{B}}_{1/q_H})$. So overall, we have

$$\mathbf{Succ}(\mathsf{G}_1^{\mathsf{A}}) \geq e^{-1} \cdot \mathbf{Succ}(\mathsf{G}_0^{\mathsf{A}}) - \mathbf{Adv}(\mathsf{PRF}^{\mathsf{B}}_{1/q_H}).$$

RUNNING TIME. Game G_1 needs to evaluate the ${}^1\!/_{q_H}$-PRF q_H times, hence we have $\mathbf{TotalTime}(\mathsf{G}_1^{\mathsf{A}}) = \mathbf{TotalTime}(\mathsf{G}_0^{\mathsf{A}}) + q_H \cdot \mathbf{Time}(\mathsf{F})$.

MEMORY. The standard game needs to store an array of size at least $q_H \cdot \lambda$ bits and the integer i^*, while the memory-efficient game only needs additional memory $\mathbf{Mem}(\mathsf{F})$. So overall, we have

$$\mathbf{TotalMem}(\mathsf{G}_0^{\mathsf{A}}) \geq \mathbf{LocalMem}(\mathsf{A}) + q_H + 1,$$
$$\mathbf{TotalMem}(\mathsf{G}_1^{\mathsf{A}}) = \mathbf{LocalMem}(\mathsf{A}) + \mathbf{Mem}(\mathsf{F}).$$

Note that for simplicity we ignored the memory consumption and running time for procedures P_0 and P_1.

3.5 Single Rewinding Technique

This technique can be used for games containing a procedure Query, which can be called by an adversary A up to q times on inputs $x_1, \ldots, x_q$. When A terminates, it queries Fin on a value x^*. Procedure Fin then checks whether there exists $i \in \{1, \ldots, q\}$ such that $\mathsf{R}(x_i, x^*) = 1$, where R is an efficiently computable relation specific to the game. If so, it invokes Stop with 1. If no such i exists it invokes Stop with 0. Note that we do not specify how queries to Query are answered since it is not relevant here. To be able to check whether there exists an i such that $\mathsf{R}(x_i, x^*) = 1$, the game usually stores the values $x_1, \ldots, x_q$ as described in G_0 in Fig. 9.

However it is possible to make the game memory efficient as described in G_1 of Fig. 9. In this variant the game no longer stores all the x_i's. Instead, it only stores the adversarial input x^* to Fin and then *rewinds* A to the start, i.e., it runs it a second time providing it with the *exact same input and random coins*, and responding to queries to Query with the *same values* as in the first run. This means that from the adversary's view, the second run is an exact replication of the first one. Whenever A calls Query on a value x_i, the game checks whether $\mathsf{R}(x^*, x_i) = 1$ and—if so—invokes Stop with 1. Note that it is necessary to store the random coins given to A as well as random coins potentially used to answer queries to Query to be able to rewind. This can be done memory-efficiently with the technique of Sect. 3.2.

Standard Game $\mathsf{G}_0^{\mathsf{A}}$	**Memory-efficient Game $\mathsf{G}_1^{\mathsf{A}}$**
Procedure Query(x_i)	Procedure Query(x_i)
$X_i \leftarrow x_i$	During rewinding:
...	If $\mathsf{R}(X^*, x_i) = 1$: Stop with 1
	...
Procedure Fin(x^*)	Procedure Fin(x^*)
For $i = 1$ to q	$X^* \leftarrow x^*$
If $\mathsf{R}(x^*, X_i) = 1$: Stop with 1	Rewind A to start
Stop with 0	Stop with 0

Fig. 9. The single rewinding technique.

Success Probability. Since after rewinding, G_1 provides A with the exact same input as in the first execution, all values x_i are the same in both executions of A, so

$$\mathbf{Succ}(\mathsf{G}_0^{\mathsf{A}}) = \mathbf{Succ}(\mathsf{G}_1^{\mathsf{A}}).$$

Running Time. G_0 runs A once, while G_1 runs A twice. Both games invoke the relation algorithm R a total number of q times, so overall we obtain

$$\mathbf{TotalTime}(\mathsf{G}_1^{\mathsf{A}}) \leq 2 \cdot \mathbf{TotalTime}(\mathsf{G}_0^{\mathsf{A}}).$$

Memory. $\mathsf{G}_0^{\mathsf{A}}$ stores all values $x_1, \ldots, x_q, x^*$ while $\mathsf{G}_1^{\mathsf{A}}$ only stores x^* and one of the $x_i, 1 \leq i \leq q$ at a time. Assuming each of the values $x_1, \ldots, x_q, x^*$ takes one memory unit, we obtain

$$\mathbf{TotalMem}(\mathsf{G}_0^{\mathsf{A}}) = \mathbf{LocalMem}(\mathsf{A}) + \mathbf{Mem}(\mathsf{R}) + q + 1,$$
$$\mathbf{TotalMem}(\mathsf{G}_1^{\mathsf{A}}) = \mathbf{LocalMem}(\mathsf{A}) + \mathbf{Mem}(\mathsf{R}) + 2.$$

We remark that the single rewinding technique can be extended to a multiple-rewinding technique, in which the reduction runs the adversary m times (on the same random coins and with the same input). For example, in Theorem 4 we consider a reduction between t-multi-collision-resistance and t-collision-resistance that rewinds the adversary several times.

4 Streaming Algorithms and Memory-Efficiency

In this section we prove two lower bounds on the memory usage of black-box reductions between certain problems. The first shows that any reduction from mUFCMA to UFCMA must either use more memory, run the adversary many times, or obey some tradeoff between the two options. The second gives a similar result for mCR_t to CR_t reductions. We start by recalling results from the data-stream model of computation which will provide the principle tools for our lower bounds.

In this section we also deal with bit-memory ($\mathbf{Mem}_2$) which measures the number of bits used, rather than **Mem** which measures the number of λ-bit words used.

4.1 The Data Stream Model

The *data stream model* is typically used to reason about algorithmic challenges where a very large input can only be accessed in discrete pieces in a given order, possibly over multiple passes. For instance, data from a high-rate network connection may often be too large to store and thus only accessed in sequence.

STREAMING FORMALIZATION. We adopt the following notation for a streaming problem: An input is a vector $\mathbf{y} \in U^n$ of dimension n over some finite universe U. We say that the number of elements in the stream is n. An algorithm B accesses $\mathbf{y}$ via a stateful oracle $\mathsf{O}_\mathbf{y}$ that works as follows: On the first call it saves an initial state $i \leftarrow 0$ and returns $\mathbf{y}[0]$. On future calls, $\mathsf{O}_\mathbf{y}$ sets $i \leftarrow (i+1 \mod n)$, and returns $\mathbf{y}[i]$. The oracle models accessing a stream of data, one entry at a time. When the counter i is set to 0 (either at the start or by wrapping modulo n), the algorithm B is said to be initiating a *pass* on the data. The *number of passes* during a computation $\mathsf{B}^{\mathsf{O}_\mathbf{y}}$ is thus defined as $p = \lceil q/n \rceil$, where q is the number of queries issued by B to its oracle.

A STREAMING LOWER BOUND. Below we will use a well-known result lower bounding the trade-off between the number of passes and memory required to determining the most frequent element in a stream. We will also use a lower bound on a related problem that can be proven by the same techniques.

For a vector $\mathbf{y} \in U^n$, define $F_\infty(\mathbf{y})$ as

$$F_\infty(\mathbf{y}) = \max_{s \in U} |\{i : \mathbf{y}[i] = s\}|.$$

That is, $F_\infty(\mathbf{y})$ is the number of appearances of the most frequent value in $\mathbf{y}$. Our results will use the following modified version of F_∞, denoted $F_{\infty,t}$ that only checks if the most frequent value appears t times or not:

$$F_{\infty,t}(\mathbf{y}) = \begin{cases} 1 & \text{if } F_\infty(\mathbf{y}) \geq t \\ 0 & \text{otherwise} \end{cases}$$

We also define the function $G(\mathbf{y})$ as follows. It divides its input into two equal-length halves $\mathbf{y} = \mathbf{y}_1 \| \mathbf{y}_2$, each in $U^{n/2}$. We let

$$G(\mathbf{y}_1 \| \mathbf{y}_2) = \begin{cases} 1 & \text{if } \exists j \; \forall i : \mathbf{y}_2[j] \neq \mathbf{y}_1[i] \\ 0 & \text{otherwise} \end{cases}.$$

In words, G outputs 1 whenever $\mathbf{y}_2$ contains an entry that is not in $\mathbf{y}_1$.

Theorem 1 (Corollary of [21,24]). *Let t be a constant and B be a randomized algorithm such that for all $\mathbf{y} \in U^n$,*

$$\Pr[\mathsf{B}^{\mathsf{O}_\mathbf{y}}(|U|, n) = F_{\infty,t}(\mathbf{y}))] \geq c,$$

where $1/2 < c \leq 1$ is a constant. Then $\mathbf{LocalMem}_2(\mathsf{B}) = \Omega(\min\{n/p, |U|/p\})$, *where p is the number of passes B makes in the worst case. The same statement holds if $F_{\infty,t}$ is replaced with G.*

This theorem is actually a simple corollary of a celebrated result on the communication complexity of the disjointness problem, which has several other applications. See also the lecture notes by Roughgarden [25] that give an accessible theorem statement and discussion after Theorem 4.11 of that document.

The standard version of this theorem only states that computing F_∞ requires the stated space, so we sketch how to obtain our easy corollary. The full proof is omitted from this version due to the page limit. The proof for F_∞ works by showing that any p-pass streaming algorithm with local memory m can be used to construct a p-round two-party protocol to compute whether sets S_1, S_2 held by the parties are disjoint. One then proves a communication lower bound on any protocol to test for disjointness.

A simple modification of this argument shows that computing G also gives such a protocol: It easily allows two parties to compute if $S_1 \setminus S_2$ is empty, which is equivalent to computing if $\overline{S_1}$ and S_2 are disjoint. Thus one can reduce disjointness to this problem by having the first party take the compliment of its set.

The modification for $F_{\infty,t}$ is slightly more subtle. The essential idea is that one party can copy its set $t-1$ times when feeding it to the streaming algorithm. Then if the parties' sets are not disjoint, we will have $F_{\infty,t}$ equal to 1 and 0 otherwise. Since t is a constant this affects the lower bound by only a constant factor.

4.2 mUFCMA-to-UFCMA Lower Bound

BLACK-BOX REDUCTIONS FOR mUFCMA TO UFCMA. Let R be an algorithm playing the UFCMA game. Recall that R receives input pk and has access to an oracle $\mathsf{ProcSign}$, and stops the game by querying $\mathsf{Fin}(m^*, \sigma^*)$. Below for an adversary A playing mUFCMA, we write R^{A} to mean that R has additionally "oracle access to A", which means an oracle $\mathsf{NxtQ}_{\mathsf{A}}$ that returns the "next query" of A after accepting a response to the previous query from R. When A halts (i.e. $\mathsf{NxtQ}_{\mathsf{A}}$ returns a query to Fin), the oracle resets itself to start again with the same random tape and input pk.

Definition 2. *A* restricted black-box reduction from mUFCMA to UFCMA *for signature scheme* $(\mathsf{Gen}, \mathsf{Sign}, \mathsf{Ver})$ *is an oracle algorithm* R*, playing* UFCMA*, that respects the following restrictions for any* A*:*

1. R^{A} *starts by forwarding its initial input (consisting of the security parameter and public key) to* $\mathsf{NxtQ}_{\mathsf{A}}$.
2. *When the oracle* $\mathsf{NxtQ}_{\mathsf{A}}$ *emits a query for* $\mathsf{ProcSign}(m)$, R *forwards* m *to its own signing oracle* $\mathsf{ProcSign}$ *and returns the result to* $\mathsf{NxtQ}_{\mathsf{A}}$*, possibly after some computation.*
3. *When* $\mathsf{NxtQ}_{\mathsf{A}}$ *emits a query for* $\mathsf{ProcVer}(m^*, \sigma^*)$, R *performs some computation then returns an empty response to* $\mathsf{NxtQ}_{\mathsf{A}}$.
4. *When* R *queries* $\mathsf{Fin}(m^*, \sigma^*)$*, the value* (m^*, σ^*) *will be amongst the values that* $\mathsf{NxtQ}_{\mathsf{A}}$ *returned as a query to* $\mathsf{ProcVer}$.

Finally we say that R *is* advantage-preserving *if there exists an absolute constant* $1/2 < c \leq 1$ *such that for all adversaries* A *and all random tapes* r *for* A,

$$\mathbf{Succ}(\mathsf{UFCMA}^{\mathsf{R}^{\mathsf{A}}} \mid r) \geq c \cdot \mathbf{Succ}(\mathsf{mUFCMA}^{\mathsf{A}} \mid r), \tag{2}$$

where $\mathbf{Succ}(\cdot \mid r)$ *is exactly* $\mathbf{Succ}(\cdot)$ *conditioned on the tape of* A *being fixed to* r.

These restrictions force R to behave in a combinatorial manner that is amenable to a connection to streaming lower bounds. The final condition, requiring R to preserve the advantage of A for all random tapes, is especially restrictive. At the end of the section we discuss directions for considering more general R.

Theorem 2. *Let* $(\mathsf{Gen}, \mathsf{Sign}, \mathsf{Ver})$ *be any signature scheme with message length* $\delta = \lambda$*. Let* R *be a restricted black-box reduction from* mUFCMA *to* UFCMA *that is advantage-preserving, and let* p *be the number of times* R *runs* A*. Then for any*[1] $q = q(\lambda)$ *there exists an adversary* A^* *making* q *signing queries, and using memory* $\mathbf{LocalMem}_2(\mathsf{A}^*) = O(\mathbf{LocalMem}_2(\mathsf{Ver}))$*, such that* $\mathbf{LocalMem}_2(\mathsf{R}^{\mathsf{A}^*}) =$

$$\Omega(\min\{\frac{q}{p+1}, \frac{2^\lambda}{p+1}\}) - O(\log q) - \max\{\mathbf{LocalMem}_2(\mathsf{Gen}), \mathbf{LocalMem}_2(\mathsf{Ver})\}.$$

Proof. Let R be a restricted black-box reduction for $(\mathsf{Gen}, \mathsf{Sign}, \mathsf{Ver})$ that is advantage-preserving for some $c \geq 1/2$. We proceed fixing an adversary A^* and using $\mathsf{R}^{\mathsf{A}^*}$ to construct a streaming algorithm B, making $p+1$ passes on its stream, such that

$$\Pr[\mathsf{B}^{\mathsf{O}_{\mathbf{y}}}(2^\delta, n) = G(\mathbf{y})] \geq c \tag{3}$$

[1] We assume that q is linear-space constructible.

for all n and all $\mathbf{y} \in (\{0,1\}^\lambda)^n$. We will apply the streaming lower bound on computing G (Theorem 1) to B, and then relate the memory used by B to that of $\mathsf{R}^{\mathsf{A}^*}$ to obtain the theorem.

We start by fixing the adversary A^*. It takes as input the security parameter λ and public key pk. Then A^* selects q random messages $m_1, \ldots, m_q$, and queries them to $\mathsf{ProcSign}$, and ignores the outputs. Next A^* selects q more random messages $m'_1, \ldots, m'_q$, and for each m'_j it forges a signature σ'_j by brute force and queries (m'_j, σ'_j) to $\mathsf{ProcVer}$. After the verification queries, it halts.

We record two facts about A^*. Let $\mathbf{y} \in (\{0,1\}^\lambda)^{2q}$ the vector consisting of all of its queried messages, in order (the first q to $\mathsf{ProcSign}$, and the second q to $\mathsf{ProcVer}$ along with signatures). First, if $G(\mathbf{y}) = 0$, then $\mathbf{Succ}(\mathsf{mUFCMA}^{\mathsf{A}^*} \mid \mathbf{y}) = 0$ because A^* will not issue any queries with a fresh forgery. If however $G(\mathbf{y}) = 1$, then $\mathbf{Succ}(\mathsf{mUFCMA}^{\mathsf{A}^*} \mid \mathbf{y}) = 1$ because A^* will issue at least one fresh forgery to the verification oracle.

Algorithm $\mathsf{B}^{\mathsf{O}_\mathbf{y}}$ will run $\mathsf{R}^{\mathsf{A}^*}$, which expects input pk, oracles for $\mathsf{ProcSign}$, Fin (for the UFCMA game) and oracle $\mathsf{NxtQ}_{\mathsf{A}^*}$ for an adversary. $\mathsf{B}^{\mathsf{O}_\mathbf{y}}$ works as follows, on input $(2^\lambda, n := 2q)$:

- B starts by initializing a $\log n$-bit counter $i \leftarrow 0$, running $(pk, sk) \xleftarrow{\$} \mathsf{Gen}(\lambda)$, and running R on input pk.
- B responds the oracle query $\mathsf{ProcSign}(m)$ from R by returning $\mathsf{Sign}(sk, m)$.
- When R queries $\mathsf{NxtQ}_{\mathsf{A}^*}$, B ignores the input and responds as follows:
  - If $i < n/2$, then B queries $\mathsf{O}_\mathbf{y}$, which returns $\mathbf{y}_1[i]$, and has $\mathsf{NxtQ}_{\mathsf{A}^*}$ return $\mathsf{ProcSign}(\mathbf{y}_1[i])$ as the next query.
  - If $i \geq n/2$, it queries $\mathsf{O}_\mathbf{y}$ to get $\mathbf{y}_2[j]$ (where $j = i - n/2$). Then B computes a valid signature σ_j by brute force, and increments i modulo n. It then has $\mathsf{NxtQ}_{\mathsf{A}^*}$ return $\mathsf{ProcVer}(\mathbf{y}_2[j], \sigma)$ as the next query.
- When R queries $\mathsf{Fin}(m^*, \sigma^*)$, B performs another pass on its stream and checks if m^* appears anywhere in $\mathbf{y}_1$. If it does, then it outputs 0 and otherwise it outputs 1.

We now verify (3). If $G(\mathbf{y}) = 0$ then $\mathsf{B}^{\mathsf{O}_\mathbf{y}}$ will output 0 with probability 1. This is because our restrictions on R, which restricts it to outputting a value m^* that was queried by A^* to $\mathsf{ProcVer}$. On the other hand, if $G(\mathbf{y}) = 1$ then $\mathsf{B}^{\mathsf{O}_\mathbf{y}}$ will output 1 with probability at least c. This is because A^* will have success probability 1 when such a $\mathbf{y}$ is fixed, so by (2) $\mathsf{R}^{\mathsf{A}^*}$ has success probability at least c, and B outputs 1 whenever R succeeds in the simulated mUFCMA game.

It is clear that B makes $p+1$ passes on its stream, where p is the number of times $\mathsf{R}^{\mathsf{A}^*}$ runs A^*. Applying Theorem 1 to B we have

$$\mathbf{LocalMem}_2(\mathsf{B}) = \Omega(\min\{n/(p+1), 2^\lambda/(p+1)\}).$$

On the other hand, by the construction of B we have that $\mathbf{LocalMem}_2(\mathsf{B})$

$$= O(\mathbf{LocalMem}_2(\mathsf{R}^{\mathsf{A}^*})) + \max\{\mathbf{LocalMem}_2(\mathsf{Gen}), \mathbf{LocalMem}_2(\mathsf{Ver})\})$$

Combining the two bounds on $\mathbf{LocalMem}_2(\mathsf{B})$, and noting that $q = \Theta(n)$, gives the theorem. □

4.3 mCR_t-to-CR_t Lower Bound

BLACK-BOX REDUCTIONS FOR mCR_t TO CR_t. Similar to the case with signatures, we formalize a class of reductions from mCR_t to CR_t for a hash function H. Let R be an oracle algorithm R^{A} that play the CR_t game (with the only oracle being Fin), and additionally has access to an oracle $\mathsf{NxtQ}_{\mathsf{A}}$ that returns the next query or some adversary playing the game mCR_t. The only oracles in mCR_t are $\mathsf{ProcInput}$ and Fin, so $\mathsf{NxtQ}_{\mathsf{A}}$ either returns a domain point m or halts A. As before, the oracle resets itself after the last query by A, with the same input and random tape.

Definition 3. *A* restricted black-box reduction from mCR_t to CR_t *for a hash function* H *is an oracle algorithm* R*, playing* CR_t*, that respects the following restrictions for any* A*:*

1. R^{A} *starts by forwarding its initial input (consisting of the security parameter and hashing key) to* $\mathsf{NxtQ}_{\mathsf{A}}$*.*
2. *When* R *queries* $\mathsf{Fin}(m_1, \ldots, m_t)$*, the values* $m_1, \ldots, m_t$ *will be amongst the values that* $\mathsf{NxtQ}_{\mathsf{A}}$ *returned as a query to* $\mathsf{ProcInput}$*.*

Finally we say that R *is* advantage-preserving *if there exists an absolute constant* $1/2 < c \le 1$ *such that for all adversaries* A *and all random tapes* r *for* A*,*

$$\mathbf{Succ}(\mathsf{mCR}_t^{\mathsf{R}^{\mathsf{A}}} \mid r) \ge c \cdot \mathbf{Succ}(\mathsf{CR}_t^{\mathsf{A}} \mid r), \tag{4}$$

where $\mathbf{Succ}(\cdot \mid r)$ *is exactly* $\mathbf{Succ}(\cdot)$ *conditioned on the tape of* A *being fixed to* r*.*

Theorem 3. *Let* H *be the function (with empty hash key) that truncates the last* λ *bits of its input. Let* R *be a restricted black-box reduction from* mCR_t *to* CR_t *that is advantage-preserving and let* p *be the number of times* R *runs* A*. Then for any*[2] $q = q(\lambda) \le 2^\lambda$ *there exists an adversary* A^* *making* q *signing queries, and using memory* $\mathbf{LocalMem}_2(\mathsf{A}^*) = O(\lambda)$*, such that*

$$\mathbf{LocalMem}_2(\mathsf{R}^{\mathsf{A}^*}) = \Omega(\min\{q/p, 2^\lambda/p\}).$$

Proof. We proceed similarly to the proof of Theorem 2, but we now construct a streaming algorithm $\mathsf{B}^{\mathsf{O}_{\mathbf{y}}}$ for $F_{\infty,t}$ instead of G. Let R be a restricted black-box reduction for H that is advantage-preserving for some $c \ge 1/2$. We will fix an adversary A^* and use $\mathsf{R}^{\mathsf{A}^*}$ to construct a streaming algorithm B, making p passes on its stream, such that

$$\Pr[\mathsf{B}^{\mathsf{O}_{\mathbf{y}}}(2^\delta, n) = F_{\infty,t}(\mathbf{y})] \ge c \tag{5}$$

for all n and all $\mathbf{y} \in (\{0,1\}^\lambda)^n$.

[2] We again assume that q is linear-space constructible.

The adversary A^* works as follows: On input λ (and empty hash key), it chooses q random messages $m_1, \ldots, m_q$ and queries $m_i \| i$ to its $\mathsf{ProcInput}$ oracle, where i is encoded in λ bits. It then queries Fin and halts.

Let $\mathbf{y} \in (\{0,1\}^\lambda)^q$ be the vector consisting of all of messages queried to $\mathsf{ProcInput}$. If $F_{\infty,t}(\mathbf{y}) = 0$, then $\mathbf{Succ}(\mathsf{mCR}_t^{\mathsf{A}^*} | \mathbf{y}) = 0$ because there will be no t-collision in the queries of A^*. If however $F_{\infty,t}(\mathbf{y}) = 1$, then $\mathbf{Succ}(\mathsf{mUFCMA}^{\mathsf{A}^*} | \mathbf{y}) = 1$ because A^* there will be a t-collision, as the hash function H is defined to truncate the final λ bits of its inputs, which consist of the counter value.

The streaming algorithm $\mathsf{B}^{\mathsf{O}_\mathbf{y}}(2^\lambda, q)$ works as follows. It initializes a counter i to 0 and runs R. When R requests an input from $\mathsf{NxtQ}_{\mathsf{A}^*}$, $\mathsf{B}^{\mathsf{O}_\mathbf{y}}$ queries its oracle for $\mathbf{y}[i]$ and returns $\mathbf{y}[i] \| i$ to R. When R halts by calling $\mathsf{Fin}(m_1, \ldots, m_t)$, $\mathsf{B}^{\mathsf{O}_\mathbf{y}}$ simply checks if the messages are all of the form $y \| i$ for a fixed y and different values of i. If so, it outputs 1 and otherwise it outputs 0.

It is easy to verify that B satisfies (5) and that it makes p passes on its input stream. Therefore by Theorem 1 we have

$$\mathbf{LocalMem}_2(\mathsf{B}) = \Omega(\min\{q/p, 2^\lambda/p\}).$$

By construction we also have

$$\mathbf{LocalMem}_2(\mathsf{B}) = O(\mathbf{LocalMem}_2(\mathsf{R}^{\mathsf{A}^*})).$$

Combining these inequalities gives the theorem. □

Sharpness of the bounds. We observe that when one is not concerned with memory-tightness then it is trivial to reduce t-multi-collision-resistance to t-collision-resistance, by simply storing all inputs to $\mathsf{ProcInput}$ and checking for collisions. This will however be non-tight if the mCR_t adversary uses small memory but produces a large number of domain points (i.e. q is large). Memory tightness can be achieved via rewinding $O(q)$ times, but this increases the run-time of the reduction.

Theorem 4. *Let* $\mathsf{H}\colon \{0,1\}^\kappa \times \{0,1\}^\lambda \to \{0,1\}^\lambda$ *be a hash function and let* t *be a fixed natural number. Then for all adversaries* A *in the* mCR_t *game with parameter* λ *making* q *queries to* $\mathsf{ProcInput}$ *and for all natural numbers* $1 \leq c, p, m \leq q < 2^\lambda$ *such that* $c \cdot p \cdot m = q$ *there exists an adversary* B *in the* CR_t *game such that*

$$\begin{aligned}
\mathbf{Succ}(\mathsf{CR}_t^{\mathsf{B}}) &\geq \frac{1}{2c} \cdot \mathbf{Succ}(\mathsf{mCR}_t^{\mathsf{A}}),\\
\mathbf{LocalTime}(\mathsf{B}) &\leq (2p+1) \cdot \mathbf{LocalTime}(\mathsf{A}) + (mp(q+1)+q) \cdot \mathbf{Time}(\mathsf{H})\\
\mathbf{LocalMem}(\mathsf{B}) &= \mathbf{LocalMem}(\mathsf{A}) + \mathbf{Mem}(\mathsf{H}) + 3m + t + 3.
\end{aligned}$$

If we choose $c = 1$ and $m = q/p$, this theorem proves that the lower bound from Theorem 3 is sharp.

```
Adversary B
00 k ←$ Init_CRt
01 FOR ℓ = 1 to p:
02    sample distinct i_1, ..., i_m from {1, ..., q}
03    run A on input k
04    FOR j = 1 to m:
05       x_j ← H(k, A(i_j))
06    run A on input k
07    FOR i = 1 to q:
08       FOR j = 1 to m:
09          IF x_j = H(k, A(i)) ∧ i_j ≠ i:
10             c_j ← c_j + 1
11             IF c_j = t:
12                run A on input k
13                store all of A's t outputs y_1 ... y_t such that H(y_α) = x_j
14                Stop with y_1 ... y_t
```

Fig. 10. Adversary B in the CR_t game. By $\mathsf{A}(j)$ we denote the j-th out of q inputs of A to ProcInput.

Proof. By assumption $m = q/cp$. Let A be an adversary in the mCR_t game. For simplicity we assume that A is deterministic, otherwise we can apply the PRF coin fixing technique from Sect. 3.2.

Consider adversary B as defined in Fig. 10. First, B stores the hash values of m out of the q inputs of A to ProcInput. Note that A only needs to be run once to perform these operations in line 05, as the indices i_1 to i_m can be sorted. Then it rewinds A to the start and checks for collisions of the stored hash values with all of the hash values of A's inputs to ProcInput. Assume that at least t of A's inputs have the same hash value. Then in each execution of the loop starting in line 01 B succeeds in finding the colliding messages if it stored the corresponding hash value. The probability of this event is bounded from below by $m/q = 1/cp$. The loop is repeated p times with freshly sampled $i_1, \ldots, i_m$. Thus

$$\Pr[\mathsf{CR}_t^{\mathsf{B}} \Rightarrow 1 \mid \mathsf{mCR}_t^{\mathsf{A}} \Rightarrow 1] \geq 1 - (1 - {}^{1}\!/_{cp})^p \geq 1 - e^{-{}^{1}\!/_{c}} \geq 1/2c.$$

This implies $\mathbf{Succ}(\mathsf{CR}_t^B) \geq {}^{1}\!/_{2c} \cdot \mathbf{Succ}(\mathsf{mCR}_t^A)$. When B finds a collision, it rewinds A one last time to obtain the preimages of the t colliding values.

So overall, B runs A at most $2p + 1$ times and the hash algorithm H at most $p(m + mn) + q$ times. It needs to store $2m + 3$ counters of size $\log q \leq \lambda$ (i.e. $2m + 3$ memory units), m values from H's range $\{0, 1\}^\rho$ (i.e. m memory units) and the t elements from $\{0, 1\}^\delta$ that collide under H (i.e. t memory units) and provide memory for A and H. □

Limitations, extensions, and open problems. Our notion of black-box reductions assumes that the reduction will only run the adversary A from beginning to end, each time with the same random tape. It would be interesting to generalize the reduction to allow for partial rewinding of A, and also for saving "snapshots" of the state of A that allow for rewinding.

Our restrictions on black-box reductions confine them to essentially work like combinatorial streaming algorithms. It seems likely that these restrictions can be greatly relaxed by using a different notion of black-box reduction and using pathological (unbounded) signature schemes and hash functions to enforce the combinatorial behavior of the reduction with high probability. We pursued our version of the results for simplicity.

5 Memory-Tight Reduction for RSA Full Domain Hash Signatures

This section gives an example of a memory-tight reduction obtained via the techniques of Sect. 3. We first recall the syntax of signature schemes and recall the RSA assumption. Then we show how the RSA Full Domain Hash signature scheme can be shown secure in the random oracle model using coin replacement, random oracle replacement, single rewinding, and the random oracle index guessing technique. For subtle reasons we implement all techniques using a single PRF to obtain a memory tight reduction.

Signature schemes. A *signature scheme* consists of algorithms Gen,Sign,Ver such that: algorithm Gen generates a verification key pk and a signing key sk; on input of a signing key sk and a message m algorithm Sign generates a signature σ or the failure indicator $\perp$; on input of a verification key pk, a message m, and a candidate signature σ, deterministic algorithm Ver outputs 0 or 1 to indicate rejection and acceptance, respectively. A signature scheme is correct if for all sk, pk, m, if $\mathsf{Sign}(sk, m)$ outputs a signature then Ver accepts it. Recall that the standard security notion of existential unforgeability against chosen message attacks is defined in Sect. 2.3 via the game of Fig. 2.

RSA assumption. Let GenRSA_λ be an algorithm that returns $(N = pq, e, d)$, where p and q are distinct primes of bit size $\lambda/2$ and e, d are such that $e = d^{-1} \bmod \Phi(N)$.

Definition 4 (RSA Assumption). *Game* RSA_λ *defining the hardness of RSA relative to* GenRSA_λ *is depicted in Fig. 11.*

Game RSA_λ

Procedure Init	Procedure $\mathsf{Fin}(x^*)$
$(N, e, d) \xleftarrow{\$} \mathsf{GenRSA}_\lambda$	If $x = x^*$:
$x \xleftarrow{\$} \mathbb{Z}_N$	Stop with 1
$y \leftarrow x^e \bmod N$	Stop with 0
Return (N, e, y)	

Fig. 11. The RSA_λ game relative to algorithm GenRSA_λ.

RSA-FDH. The RSA Full Domain Hash (RSA-FDH) signature scheme [7] is defined in Fig. 12. Its security can be reduced to the RSA assumption in the random oracle model (see [8,14]). In the usual proof the reduction interacting with an adversary against RSA-FDH's existential unforgeability making up to q_H hash queries and up to q_s signing queries simulates the random oracle using lazy sampling and therefore has to store up to $(q_H + q_s)$ messages making the reduction highly non-memory-tight. However, the proof can be made memory-efficient by using the coin replacement technique of Sect. 3.2, the random oracle technique of Sect. 3.3, the random oracle index guessing technique of Sect. 3.4, and the single rewinding technique of Sect. 3.5.

Gen	$\mathsf{Sign}(sk, m)$	$\mathsf{Ver}(pk, m, \sigma)$
$(N, e, d) \xleftarrow{\$} \mathsf{GenRSA}_\lambda$	$(N, d) \leftarrow sk$	$(N, e) \leftarrow pk$
$pk \leftarrow (N, e)$, $sk \leftarrow (N, d)$	$\sigma \leftarrow \mathsf{H}(m)^d \bmod N$	If $\sigma^e = \mathsf{H}(m) \bmod N$:
Pick RO $\mathsf{H}\colon \{0,1\}^\lambda \to \mathbb{Z}_N$	Return σ	Return 1
Return (pk, sk)		Return 0

Fig. 12. The RSA-FDH signature scheme for parameter λ.

Theorem 5. *Let* $\mathsf{F}\colon \{0,1\}^\lambda \times \{0,1\}^\lambda \to \{0,1\}^{2\lambda+1}$ *be a PRF. Then for every adversary* A *in the* UFCMA *game for RSA-FDH with parameter* λ *that poses* q_H *queries to the* Hash, q_s *queries to the* $\mathsf{ProcSign}$ *oracle, and samples at most* $L \leq 2^\lambda$ *memory units of randomness, in the random oracle model there exist an adversary* B_1 *against the* RSA_λ *game, an adversary* B_2 *against the* PRF *game such that*

$$\mathbf{Succ}(\mathsf{UFCMA}^{\mathsf{A}}) \leq e\, q_s\, \mathbf{Succ}(\mathsf{RSA}_\lambda^{\mathsf{B}_2}) + e\, q_s\, \mathbf{Adv}(\mathsf{PRF}^{\mathsf{B}_1}).$$

Further it holds that

$$\begin{aligned}
\mathbf{LocalMem}(\mathsf{B}_1) &= \mathbf{LocalMem}(\mathsf{A}) + \mathbf{Mem}(\mathsf{GenRSA}_\lambda) + 6,\\
\mathbf{LocalMem}(\mathsf{B}_2) &= \mathbf{LocalMem}(\mathsf{A}) + \mathbf{Mem}(\mathsf{F}) + 6,\\
\mathbf{LocalTime}(\mathsf{B}_1) &\approx 2\mathbf{LocalTime}(\mathsf{A}) + \mathbf{Time}(\mathsf{RSA}_\lambda),\\
\mathbf{LocalTime}(\mathsf{B}_2) &\approx \mathbf{LocalTime}(\mathsf{A}) + (q_H + q_s + L) \cdot \mathbf{Time}(\mathsf{F}).
\end{aligned}$$

Note that in the proof of Theorem 5 it is necessary to apply the random coins technique and the random oracle technique in the same step. Otherwise one obtains an intermediate reduction that is not memory-tight: the reduction either *has to simulate the random oracle by lazy sampling (in case the random coins technique is applied first)* or, *since rewinding is impossible, it has to store the messages asked to the signing oracle (if the random oracle technique is applied first).*

Proof. Consider the sequence of games of Fig. 13. For computations in $\mathbb{Z}_N$ we omit writing $\bmod N$ if it is clear from the context. We assume without loss of

G_0 / G_1

```
Procedure Init
00 (N,e,d) <-$ GenRSA_λ
01
02
03 r <-$ ({0,1}^λ)^L
04 Return (N,e)

Procedure Hash(m_i)
05 If H[m_i] undefined:
06    H[m_i] <-$ Z_N
07
08
09 Return H[m_i]                (G0)
10 Return H[m_i]^e              (G1)

Procedure ProcSign(m_i)
11 M <- M ∪ {m_i}
12
13 Return Hash(m_i)^d           (G0)
14 Return Hash(m_i)             (G1)

Procedure Coins
15 j <- j+1
16 Return r_j

Procedure Fin(m*, σ*)
17
18
19 If m* ∈ M:
20    Stop with 0
21 If (σ*)^e = Hash(m*):
22    Stop with 1
23 Stop with 0
```

G_2

```
Procedure Init
00 (N,e,d) <-$ GenRSA_λ
01 x <-$ Z_N
02 y <- x^e
03 r <-$ ({0,1}^λ)^L
04 Return (N,e)

Procedure Hash(m_i)
05 If H[m_i] undefined:
06    H[m_i] <-$ Z_N
07    B[m_i] <-$ Ber(1/q_s)
08 If B[m_i] = 1:
09    Return H[m_i]^e y
10 Else: Return H[m_i]^e

Procedure ProcSign(m_i)
11 M <- M ∪ {m_i}
12 If B[m_i] = 1:
13    Abort
14 Return Hash(m_i)

Procedure Coins
15 j <- j+1
16 Return r_j

Procedure Fin(m*, σ*)
17 If B[m*] = 0:
18    Stop with 0
19 If m* ∈ M:
20    Stop with 0
21 If (σ*)^e = Hash(m*):
22    Stop with 1
23 Stop with 0
```

G_3

```
Procedure Init
00 (N,e,d) <-$ GenRSA_λ
01 x <-$ Z_N
02 y <- x^e
03 k <-$ {0,1}^κ(N)
04 Return (N,e)

Procedure Hash(m_i)
05
06
07
08 If F2(k, m_i) = 1:
09    Return F1(k, m_i)^e y
10 Return F1(k, m_i)^e

Procedure ProcSign(m_i)
11 M <- M ∪ {m_i}
12 If F2(k, m_i) = 1:
13    Abort
14 Return Hash(m_i)

Procedure Coins
15 j <- j+1
16 Return F0(k, j)

Procedure Fin(m*, σ*)
17 If F2(k, m_i) = 0:
18    Stop with 0
19 If m* ∈ M:
20    Stop with 0
21 If (σ*)^e = Hash(m*):
22    Stop with 1
23 Stop with 0
```

Fig. 13. Games G_0 to G_3 for the proof of Theorem 5.

generality that any message procedures ProcSign or Fin are queried on was before already queried to Hash.

Game G_0 is the standard UFCMA game as in Fig. 2 instantiated with the RSA-FDH algorithms and with the randomness for adversary A provided via procedure Coins, so

$$\mathbf{Succ}(\mathsf{UFCMA}^{\mathsf{A}}) = \mathbf{Succ}(\mathsf{G}_0^{\mathsf{A}}). \tag{6}$$

In G_1, instead of returning $\mathsf{H}(m)$, the Hash procedure returns $\mathsf{H}(m)^e$ and the ProcSign procedure computes signatures as $(\mathsf{H}(m)^e)^d = \mathsf{H}(m)$ accordingly. This doesn't change the distribution of the hash values and the signatures, so

$$\mathbf{Succ}(\mathsf{G}_0^{\mathsf{A}}) = \mathbf{Succ}(\mathsf{G}_1^{\mathsf{A}}). \tag{7}$$

Game G_2 introduces a couple of aborting conditions. With probability $1/q_s$ abort condition $B[m^*] = 0$ of line 17 does not occur. Furthermore, for each message

m_i the probability that abort condition $B[m_i] = 1$ of line 12 does not occur is given by $1 - 1/q_s$. Adversary A makes at most q_s queries to $\mathsf{ProcSign}$. Hence,

$$\mathbf{Succ}(\mathsf{G}_2^{\mathsf{A}}) \geq {}^{1}\!/_{q_s}(1 - {}^{1}\!/_{q_s})^{q_s} \cdot \mathbf{Succ}(\mathsf{G}_1^{\mathsf{A}}) \geq {}^{1}\!/_{(eq_s)} \cdot \mathbf{Succ}(\mathsf{G}_1^{\mathsf{A}}). \tag{8}$$

In Game G_3 randomness is replaced by PRF F, whose range we split into $\mathsf{F} = \mathsf{F}_0||\mathsf{F}_1||\mathsf{F}_2 \in \{0,1\}^\lambda \times \{0,1\}^\lambda \times \{0,1\}$. Sampling of random coins is replaced in Game G_3 by evaluating F_0 on counter j, sampling the values $H[m_i]$ and $B[m_i]$ is replaced by evaluating F_1 and F_2 on m_i, respectively. For simplicity we assume that F_2 is a pseudorandom function that outputs elements in $\mathbb{Z}_N \approx \{0,1\}^\lambda$ and that F_2 is a α-biased pseudorandom function with $\alpha := 1/q_s$. (This is formally not correct but we do not want to distract from the main points of our proof, which is about memory-tightness.) We proceed by constructing an adversary B_1 against the PRF game such that

$$\mathbf{Adv}(\mathsf{PRF}^{\mathsf{B}_1}) \geq |\mathbf{Succ}(\mathsf{G}_2^{\mathsf{A}}) - \mathbf{Succ}(\mathsf{G}_3^{\mathsf{A}})|, \tag{9}$$

$$\mathbf{LocalTime}(\mathsf{B}_1) \approx 2\mathbf{LocalTime}(\mathsf{A}) + \mathbf{Time}(\mathsf{RSA}_\lambda), \tag{10}$$

$$\mathbf{LocalMem}(\mathsf{B}_1) = \mathbf{LocalMem}(\mathsf{A}) + \mathbf{Mem}(\mathsf{GenRSA}_\lambda) + 6. \tag{11}$$

The definition of B_1 is in Fig. 14. Adversary B_1 sets up the values (N, e, d) using GenRSA, samples $x \xleftarrow{\$} \mathbb{Z}_N$, sets $y \leftarrow x^e$ and runs A on input (N, e). It simulates the procedures Hash, $\mathsf{ProcSign}$ and Coins by invoking its PRF oracle O_F. When A calls Fin on message-signature pair (m^*, σ^*) adversary B_1 rewinds A to line 03, answering all of its queries in the same way. Note that this is possible, since all replies to queries on Hash, $\mathsf{ProcSign}$ and Coins are derived using O_F. During the rewinding B_1 raises a flag coll if A queries procedure $\mathsf{ProcSign}$ on m^*. Hence the event $\{\mathsf{coll} = 1\}$ is equivalent to condition $m^* \in M$ of line 19 of games G_2 and G_3. When A calls Fin a second time on (m^*, σ^*), adversary B_1 stops with 0 or 1 according to the message-signature pair. If B_1 interacts with PRF-game Random it provides A with a perfect simulation of game G_2, if it interacts with Real with a perfect simulation of game G_3. Hence Eq. (9) follows. We now analyze B_1's running time and memory consumption. B_1 runs GenRSA_λ

```
B1

Procedure Init
00 (N, e, d) <-$ GenRSA_λ      (1)
01 x <-$ Z_N                   (1)
02 y <- x^e                    (1)
03 Invoke A on (N, e)

Procedure Coins
04 j <- j + 1
05 Return O_F0(j))

Procedure Hash(m_i)
06 If O_F2(m_i) = 1:
07     Return (O_F1(m_i))^e · y
08 Return (O_F1(m_i))^e

Procedure ProcSign(m_i)
09 If m_i = m*:                (2)
10     coll <- 1               (2)
11 If O_F2(m_i) = 1:
12     Abort
13 Return Hash(m_i)

Procedure Fin(m*, σ*)
14 Store m*, rewind A          (1)
15 If O_F2(m_i) = 0:           (2)
16     Stop with 0             (2)
17 If coll = 1:                (2)
18     Stop with 0             (2)
19 If (σ*)^e = Hash(m*):       (2)
20     Stop with 1             (2)
21 Stop with 0                 (2)
```

Fig. 14. Adversary B_1 against the PRF game for the proof of Theorem 5 in Sect. 5. B_1 rewinds A once on the same inputs. Lines marked with (i) are only executed during the i-th invocation.

once and A twice and performs some minor bookkeeping. It furthermore has to store the code of A and GenRSA_λ as well as at any point in time 6λ bits which equals 6 memory units (i.e., the three integers (N, e, y) of size 3λ, up to two messages of length λ each and a counter of size $\log_2(L) \le \lambda$.

```
Adversary B2
Procedure Init
(N, e, y) ←$ Init_RSA
k ←$ {0,1}^κ(N)
Invoke A on (N, e)
Procedure Coins
j ← j + 1
Return F1(k, j)

Procedure Hash(m_i)
If F2(k, m_i) = 1:
    Return F1(k, m_i)^e y
Return F1(k, m_i)^e
Procedure ProcSign(m_i)
If F2(k, m_i) = 1:
    Abort
Return Hash(m_i)

Procedure Fin(m*, σ*)
If F2(k, m*) = 0:
    Abort
If (σ*)^e = Hash(m*):
    x* ← σ*/F1(k, m*)
Call Fin_RSA(x*)
```

Fig. 15. Adversary B_2 against the RSA_λ game for the proof of Theorem 5 in Sect. 5.

We conclude the proof by giving an adversary B_2 against the RSA_λ game such that

$$\mathbf{Succ}(\mathsf{RSA}_\lambda^{\mathsf{B}_2}) \ge \mathbf{Succ}(\mathsf{G}_3^{\mathsf{A}}), \tag{12}$$

$$\mathbf{LocalTime}(\mathsf{B}_2) \approx \mathbf{LocalTime}(\mathsf{A}) + (q_H + q_s + L)\mathbf{Time}(\mathsf{F}) \tag{13}$$

$$\mathbf{LocalMem}(\mathsf{B}_2) = \mathbf{LocalMem}(\mathsf{A}) + \mathbf{Mem}(\mathsf{GenRSA}_\lambda) + 6. \tag{14}$$

Then the claim of the theorem follows from Eq. (7) to (9) and Sect. 5. The definition of B_2 is in Fig. 15. It queries $\mathsf{Init}_{\mathsf{RSA}}$ to receive an RSA challenge (N, e, y) and samples a PRF key k. Then it invokes A on input (N, e) providing it with a perfect simulation of the procedures Hash, ProcSign and Coins. When A invokes procedure Fin on message-signature pair (m^*, σ^*), adversary B_2 checks whether $\mathsf{F}_2(k, m^*) = 0$ and—if so—aborts. Note that by definition of procedure Hash adversary B_2 not aborting implies that $\mathsf{Hash}(m^*) = (\mathsf{F}_1(k, m^*))^e y$. Hence if B_2 does not abort and if the signature is valid, i.e. $(\sigma^*)^e = \mathsf{Hash}(m^*)$ holds, then B_2's answer $x^* = \sigma/\mathsf{F}_1(k, m^*)$ to the RSA challenge is valid. Since A succeeding in game G_3 implies both aforementioned conditions Sect. 5 follows. We conclude the proof by analyzing B_2's running time and memory consumption. B_2 runs A once and F up to $(q_H + q_s + L)$ times and performs some minor bookkeeping. Furthermore it has to store the code of A and F as well as at any point in time 6λ bits which equals 6 additional memory units (i.e., a counter of bit-size $\log_2(L) \le \lambda$, a PRF key of bit-size $\kappa \le \lambda$, a message of bit-size λ and three integers of size λ). □

6 Memory-Sensitive Problems

In this section we discuss the memory sensitivity of two cryptographic problems, multi-collision-resistance and learning parities with noise. In the full version of this paper [3], we will also analyze the memory sensitivity of the discrete logarithm problem in prime fields and of the factoring problem.

To quantify the memory sensitivity of a problem P we plot time/memory trade-offs as in the Fig. 1. The horizontal axis is memory consumption and the vertical axis is running time, both on a log scale. A point (x, y) is either labeled with "solvable" or "unsolvable", where solvable means that there exists an algorithm with running time at most 2^x and memory consumption at most 2^y that solves the problem. We refer to the boundary between the solvable and unsolvable regions as the *transition line.*

A time/memory trade-off plot of a non-memory-sensitive problem typically has an (approximately) horizontal transition line, and as discused in Sect. 1, a non-memory-tight reduction has less impact. The steeper the slope of the transition line, the more memory-sensitive the problem is. We refer for the introduction for an example with concrete numbers for.

k-WAY COLLISION RESISTANCE. The k-way collision problem CR_k is to find a k-collision in a hash function with λ output bits. The following table provides an overview over known algorithms to solve CR_k with constant success probability for $k \in \{2, 3\}$.

Algorithm A	$\mathbf{Mem}(\mathsf{CR}_t^{\mathsf{A}})$	$\mathbf{Time}(\mathsf{CR}_t^{\mathsf{A}})$
Birthday ($k = 2$)	$O(1)$	$2^{\lambda/2}$
Joux-Lucks [20] ($k = 3$)	2^α	$2^{\lambda(1-\alpha)}$ ($\alpha \leq 1/3$)

From the table we derive the time/memory graph of CR_k in Fig. 16. CR_3 is memory sensitive, whereas CR_2 is not (as it has a horizontal transition line).

LEARNING PARITY WITH NOISE. Another example of a memory sensitive problem is the well-known *Learning Parity with Noise (LPN)* problem. Let $\lambda \in \mathbb{N}$ be the dimension and $\tau \in [0, 1/2)$ be a constant that defines the error probability. The problem $\mathsf{LPN}_{\lambda,\tau}$ is to compute a random secret $s \xleftarrow{\$} \mathbb{F}_2^\lambda$, given "noisy" random inner products with s, i.e. samples (a_i, ν_i) where $a_i \xleftarrow{\$} \mathbb{F}_2^\lambda$, and $\nu_i = \langle a_i, s \rangle + e_i$ for $e_i \xleftarrow{\$} Ber(\tau)$.

Memory usage and running time of the best known algorithms for $\mathrm{LPN}_{\lambda,\tau}$ with constant success probability are given in the following table.

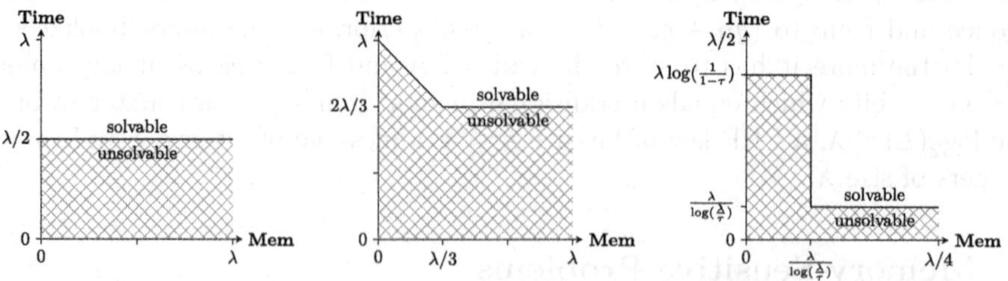

Fig. 16. Time memory graphs of CR_k for $k = 2$ (left) and $k = 3$ (middle) and of $\mathrm{LPN}_{\lambda,\tau}$ for $\lambda = 1024$ and $\tau = 1/4$ (right). Both **Time** and **Mem** are in log scale.

Algorithm A	**LocalMem**($\mathsf{LPN}^{\mathsf{A}}_{\lambda,\tau}$)	**LocalTime**($\mathsf{LPN}^{\mathsf{A}}_{\lambda,\tau}$)
BKW [10]	$2^{\lambda/\log(\lambda/\tau)}$	$2^{\lambda/\log(\lambda/\tau)}$
Gauss [15]	$O(1)$	$2^{\lambda \log(1/1-\tau)}$

Figure 16 provides the corresponding time/memory graph. Note that the recent work [15] also considers a hybrid algorithm between Well-Pooled Gauss and BKW, but the interval where the hybrid algorithm actually has better performance is so small that we decided to ignore it.

We note that the situation with the Learning with Errors (LWE), the Shortest Integer Solution (SIS), and the approximate SVP problem is similar to that of the LPN problem [2,13,19].

Acknowledgments. The motivation of considering memory in the context of security reductions stems from the talk "Practical LPN Cryptanalysis", given by Alexander May at the Dagstuhl Seminar 16371 on Public-Key Cryptography. We thank Elena Kirshanova, Robert Kübler, and Alexander May for their help with assessing the memory-sensitivity of a number of hard problems. Finally, we are grateful to one of the CRYPTO 2017 reviewers for his/her very detailed and thoughtful review.

Auerbach was supported by the NRW Research Training Group SecHuman; Cash was supported in part by NSF grant CNS-1453132; Fersch and Kiltz were supported in part by ERC Project ERCC (FP7/615074) and by DFG SPP 1736 Big Data.

References

1. Abdalla, M., Bellare, M., Rogaway, P.: The oracle Diffie-Hellman assumptions and an analysis of DHIES. In: Naccache, D. (ed.) CT-RSA 2001. LNCS, vol. 2020, pp. 143–158. Springer, Heidelberg (2001). doi:10.1007/3-540-45353-9_12
2. Albrecht, M.R., Player, R., Scott, S.: On the concrete hardness of learning with errors. J. Math. Cryptol. **9**(3), 169–203 (2015). http://www.degruyter.com/view/j/jmc.2015.9.issue-3/jmc-2015-0016/jmc-2015-0016.xml
3. Auerbach, B., Cash, D., Fersch, M., Kiltz, E.: Memory-tight reductions. Cryptology ePrint Archive, Report 2017/??? (2017). http://eprint.iacr.org/2017/???
4. Bader, C., Jager, T., Li, Y., Schäge, S.: On the impossibility of tight cryptographic reductions. In: Fischlin, M., Coron, J.-S. (eds.) EUROCRYPT 2016. LNCS, vol. 9666, pp. 273–304. Springer, Heidelberg (2016). doi:10.1007/978-3-662-49896-5_10
5. Bellare, M., Boldyreva, A., Micali, S.: Public-key encryption in a multi-user setting: security proofs and improvements. In: Preneel, B. (ed.) EUROCRYPT 2000. LNCS, vol. 1807, pp. 259–274. Springer, Heidelberg (2000). doi:10.1007/3-540-45539-6_18
6. Bellare, M., Ristenpart, T.: Simulation without the artificial abort: simplified proof and improved concrete security for waters' IBE scheme. In: Joux, A. (ed.) EUROCRYPT 2009. LNCS, vol. 5479, pp. 407–424. Springer, Heidelberg (2009). doi:10.1007/978-3-642-01001-9_24
7. Bellare, M., Rogaway, P.: Random oracles are practical: a paradigm for designing efficient protocols. In: Ashby, V. (ed.) ACM CCS 1993, Fairfax, Virginia, USA, 3–5 November 1993, pp. 62–73. ACM Press (1993)

8. Bellare, M., Rogaway, P.: The exact security of digital signatures-how to sign with RSA and rabin. In: Maurer, U. (ed.) EUROCRYPT 1996. LNCS, vol. 1070, pp. 399–416. Springer, Heidelberg (1996). doi:10.1007/3-540-68339-9_34
9. Bellare, M., Rogaway, P.: The security of triple encryption and a framework for code-based game-playing proofs. In: Vaudenay, S. (ed.) EUROCRYPT 2006. LNCS, vol. 4004, pp. 409–426. Springer, Heidelberg (2006). doi:10.1007/11761679_25
10. Blum, A., Kalai, A., Wasserman, H.: Noise-tolerant learning, the parity problem, and the statistical query model. J. ACM **50**(4), 506–519 (2003). http://doi.acm.org/10.1145/792538.792543
11. Chatterjee, S., Koblitz, N., Menezes, A., Sarkar, P.: Another look at tightness II: practical issues in cryptography. Cryptology ePrint Archive, Report 2016/360 (2016). http://eprint.iacr.org/2016/360
12. Chatterjee, S., Menezes, A., Sarkar, P.: Another look at tightness. In: Miri, A., Vaudenay, S. (eds.) SAC 2011. LNCS, vol. 7118, pp. 293–319. Springer, Heidelberg (2012). doi:10.1007/978-3-642-28496-0_18
13. Chen, Y., Nguyen, P.Q.: BKZ 2.0: better lattice security estimates. In: Lee, D.H., Wang, X. (eds.) ASIACRYPT 2011. LNCS, vol. 7073, pp. 1–20. Springer, Heidelberg (2011). doi:10.1007/978-3-642-25385-0_1
14. Coron, J.-S.: On the exact security of full domain hash. In: Bellare, M. (ed.) CRYPTO 2000. LNCS, vol. 1880, pp. 229–235. Springer, Heidelberg (2000). doi:10.1007/3-540-44598-6_14
15. Esser, A., Kübler, R., May, A.: LPN decoded. In: Katz, J., Shacham, H. (eds.) CRYPTO 2017. LNCS, vol. 10402, pp. 486–514. Springer, Cham (2017)
16. Galbraith, S.D., Gaudry, P.: Recent progress on the elliptic curve discrete logarithm problem. Cryptology ePrint Archive, Report 2015/1022 (2015). http://eprint.iacr.org/2015/1022
17. Galindo, D.: The exact security of pairing based encryption and signature schemes. In: Based on a talk at Workshop on Provable Security, INRIA, Paris (2004). http://www.dgalindo.es/galindoEcrypt.pdf
18. Gay, R., Hofheinz, D., Kiltz, E., Wee, H.: Tightly CCA-secure encryption without pairings. In: Fischlin, M., Coron, J.-S. (eds.) EUROCRYPT 2016. LNCS, vol. 9665, pp. 1–27. Springer, Heidelberg (2016). doi:10.1007/978-3-662-49890-3_1
19. Herold, G., Kirshanova, E., May, A.: On the asymptotic complexity of solving LWE. Des. Codes Crypt. 1–29 (2017). http://dx.doi.org/10.1007/s10623-016-0326-0
20. Joux, A., Lucks, S.: Improved generic algorithms for 3-collisions. In: Matsui, M. (ed.) ASIACRYPT 2009. LNCS, vol. 5912, pp. 347–363. Springer, Heidelberg (2009). doi:10.1007/978-3-642-10366-7_21
21. Kalyanasundaram, B., Schnitger, G.: The probabilistic communication complexity of set intersection. SIAM J. Discrete Math. **5**(4), 545–557 (1992). http://dx.doi.org/10.1137/0405044
22. Pointcheval, D., Stern, J.: Security arguments for digital signatures and blind signatures. J. Cryptol. **13**(3), 361–396 (2000)
23. Pollard, J.M.: A monte carlo method for factorization. BIT Numer. Math. **15**(3), 331–334 (1975). http://dx.doi.org/10.1007/BF01933667
24. Razborov, A.A.: On the distributional complexity of disjointness. Theor. Comput. Sci. **106**(2), 385–390 (1992). http://dx.doi.org/10.1016/0304-3975(92)90260-M
25. Roughgarden, T.: Communication complexity (for algorithm designers) (2015). http://theory.stanford.edu/~tim/w15/l/w15.pdf

Be Adaptive, Avoid Overcommitting

Zahra Jafargholi[1(✉)], Chethan Kamath[2], Karen Klein[2], Ilan Komargodski[3], Krzysztof Pietrzak[2], and Daniel Wichs[4]

[1] Aarhus University, Aarhus, Denmark
zahra@au.cs.dk
[2] IST Austria, Am Campus 1, 3400 Klosterneuburg, Austria
{ckamath,karen.klein,pietrzak}@ist.ac.at
[3] Weizmann Institute of Science, 76100 Rehovot, Israel
ilan.komargodski@weizmann.ac.il
[4] Northeastern University, Boston, USA
wichs@ccs.neu.edu

Abstract. For many cryptographic primitives, it is relatively easy to achieve *selective security* (where the adversary commits a-priori to some of the choices to be made later in the attack) but appears difficult to achieve the more natural notion of *adaptive security* (where the adversary can make all choices on the go as the attack progresses). A series of several recent works shows how to cleverly achieve adaptive security in several such scenarios including *generalized selective decryption* (Panjwani, TCC '07 and Fuchsbauer et al., CRYPTO '15), *constrained PRFs* (Fuchsbauer et al., ASIACRYPT '14), and *Yao garbled circuits* (Jafargholi and Wichs, TCC '16b). Although the above works expressed vague intuition that they share a common technique, the connection was never made precise. In this work we present a new framework that connects all of these works and allows us to present them in a unified and simplified fashion. Moreover, we use the framework to derive a new result for adaptively secure *secret sharing over access structures defined via monotone circuits.* We envision that further applications will follow in the future.

Underlying our framework is the following simple idea. It is well known that selective security, where the adversary commits to n-bits of information about his future choices, automatically implies adaptive security at the cost of amplifying the adversary's advantage by a factor of up to 2^n. However, in some cases the proof of selective security proceeds via a sequence of hybrids, where each pair of adjacent hybrids locally only

Z. Jafargholi—Supported by The Danish National Research Foundation and The National Science Foundation of China (under the grant 61061130540) for the Sino-Danish Center for the Theory of Interactive Computation, within which part of this work was performed; and by the Advanced ERC grant MPCPRO.

C. Kamath—Supported by the European Research Council, ERC consolidator grant (682815 - TOCNeT).

I. Komargodski—Supported by a Levzion fellowship and by a grant from the Israel Science Foundation.

D. Wichs—Research supported by NSF grants CNS-1314722, CNS-1413964.

J. Katz and H. Shacham (Eds.): CRYPTO 2017, Part I, LNCS 10401, pp. 133–163, 2017.
DOI: 10.1007/978-3-319-63688-7_5

requires some smaller partial information consisting of $m \ll n$ bits. The partial information needed might be completely different between different pairs of hybrids, and if we look across all the hybrids we might rely on the entire n-bit commitment. Nevertheless, the above is sufficient to prove adaptive security, at the cost of amplifying the adversary's advantage by a factor of only $2^m \ll 2^n$.

In all of our examples using the above framework, the different hybrids are captured by some sort of a *graph pebbling game* and the amount of information that the adversary needs to commit to in each pair of hybrids is bounded by the maximum number of pebbles in play at any point in time. Therefore, coming up with better strategies for proving adaptive security translates to various pebbling strategies for different types of graphs.

1 Introduction

Many security definitions come in two flavors: a stronger "adaptive" flavor, where the adversary can arbitrarily make various choices during the course of the attack, and a weaker "selective" flavor where the adversary must commit to some or all of his choices a-priori. For example, in the context of *identity-based encryption*, selective security requires the adversary to decide on the identity of the attacked party at the very beginning of the game whereas adaptive security allows the attacker to first see the master public key and some secret keys before making this choice. Often, it appears to be much easier to achieve selective security than it is to achieve adaptive security.

A series of recent works achieves adaptive security in several such scenarios where we previously only knew how to achieve selective security: *generalized selective decryption (GSD)* [8,23], *constrained PRFs* [9], and *garbled circuits* [16]. Although some of these works suggest a vague intuition that there is a general technique at play, there was no attempt to make this precise and to crystallize what the technique is or how these results are connected. In this work we present a new framework that connects all of these works and allows us to present them in a unified and simplified fashion. Moreover, we use the framework to derive a new result for adaptively secure secret sharing over access structures defined via monotone circuits.

At a high level, our framework carefully combines two basic tools commonly used throughout cryptography: *random guessing* (of the adaptive choices to be made by the adversary)[1] and *the hybrid argument.* Firstly, "random guessing" gives us a generic way to qualitatively upgrade selective security to adaptive security at a quantitative cost in the amount of security. In particular, assume

[1] In many previous works – including [8,9,16], and by the authors of this paper – this random guessing was referred to as "complexity leveraging", but this seems to be an abuse of the term. Instead, complexity leveraging [7] refers to the use of two different schemes, S_1, S_2, where the two schemes are chosen with different values of the security parameter, k_1 and k_2, where $k_1 < k_2$ and such that an adversary against S_2 (or perhaps even the honest user of S_2) can break the security of S_1.

we can prove the security of a selective game where the adversary commits to n-bits of information about his future choices. Then, we can also prove adaptive security by guessing this commitment and taking a factor of 2^n loss in the security advantage. However, this quantitative loss is often too high and hence we usually wish to avoid it or at least lower it. Secondly, the hybrid argument allows us to prove the indistinguishability of two games G_L and G_R by defining a sequence of hybrid games $\mathsf{G}_\mathsf{L} \equiv \mathsf{H}_0, \mathsf{H}_1, \ldots, \mathsf{H}_\ell \equiv \mathsf{G}_\mathsf{R}$ and showing that each pair of neighboring hybrids H_i and H_{i+1} are indistinguishable.

Our Framework. Our framework starts with two adaptive games G_L and G_R that we wish to show indistinguishable but we don't initially have any direct way of doing so. Let H_L and H_R be selective versions of the two games respectively, where the adversary initially has to commit to some information $w \in \{0,1\}^n$ about his future choices. Furthermore, assume there is some sequence of selective hybrids $\mathsf{H}_\mathsf{L} = \mathsf{H}_0, \mathsf{H}_1, \ldots, \mathsf{H}_\ell \equiv \mathsf{H}_\mathsf{R}$ such that we can show that H_i and H_{i+1} are indistinguishable. A naïve combination of the hybrid argument and random guessing shows that G_L and G_R are indistinguishable at a factor of $2^n \cdot \ell$ loss in security, but we want to do better.

Recall that the hybrids H_i are selective and require the adversary to commit to w. However, it might be the case that for each i we can prove that H_i and H_{i+1} would be indistinguishable even if the adversary didn't have to commit to all of w but only some partial-information $h_i(w) \in \{0,1\}^m$ for $m \ll n$ (formalizing this condition precisely requires great care and is the major source of subtlety in our framework). Notice that the partial information that we need to know about w may be completely different for different pairs of hybrids, and if we look across all hybrids then we may need to know all of w. Nevertheless, we prove that this suffices to show that the adaptive games G_L and G_R are indistinguishable with only a $2^m \cdot \ell \ll 2^n \cdot \ell$ loss of security.

Applications of Our Framework. We show how to understand all of the prior works mentioned above as applications of our framework. In many cases, this vastly simplifies prior works. We also use the framework to derive a new result, proving the adaptive security of Yao's secret sharing scheme for access structures defined via monotone circuits.

In all of the examples, we get a series of selective hybrids $\mathsf{H}_1, \ldots, \mathsf{H}_\ell$ that correspond to *pebbling configurations* in some graph pebbling game. The amount of information needed to show that neighboring hybrids H_i and H_{i+1} are indistinguishable only depends on the configuration of the pebbles in the i'th step of the game. Therefore, using our framework, we translate the problem of coming up with adaptive security proofs to the problem of coming up with pebbling strategies that only require a succinct representation of each pebbling configuration.

We now proceed to give a high level overview of each of our results applying our general framework to specific problems, and refer to the main body for technical details.

1.1 Adaptive Secret Sharing for Monotone Circuits

Secret sharing schemes, introduced by Blakley [4] and Shamir [27], are methods that enable a dealer, that has a secret piece of information, to distribute this secret among n parties such that a "qualified" subset of parties has enough information to reconstruct the secret while any "unqualified" subset of parties learns nothing about the secret. The monotone collection of "qualified" subsets is known as an *access structure*. Any access structure admits a secret sharing scheme but the share size could be exponential in n [14]. We are interested in efficient schemes in which the share size is polynomial (in n and possibly in a security parameter).

Many of the classical schemes for secret sharing are *perfectly* (information theoretically) secure. The largest class of access structures that admit such a (perfect and efficient) scheme was obtained by Karchmer and Wigderson [18] for the class of all functions that can be computed by monotone span programs. This result generalized a previous work of Benaloh and Leichter [3] (which, in turn, improved a result of Ito et al. [14]) that showed the same result but for a smaller class of access structures: those functions that can be computed by monotone Boolean formulas. Under cryptographic hardness assumptions, efficient schemes for more general access structures are known (but security is only for bounded adversaries). In particular, in an unpublished work (mentioned in [1], see also Vinod et al. [28]), Yao showed how to realize schemes for access structures that are described by monotone *circuits*. This construction could be used for access structures which are known to be computed by monotone circuits but are not known to be computed by monotone span programs, e.g., directed connectivity [17,24].[2] Komargodski et al. [21] showed how to realize the class of access structures described by monotone functions in NP[3] under the assumption that witness encryption for NP [10] and one-way functions exist.[4,5]

Selective vs. Adaptive Security. All of the schemes described above guarantee security against static adversaries, where the adversary chooses a subset of parties it controls before it sees any of the shares. A more natural security guarantee would be to require that even an adversary that chooses its set of parties in an *adaptive* manner (i.e., based on the shares it has seen so far) is unable to learn the secret (or any partial information about it).

It is known that the schemes that satisfy perfect security (including the works [3,14,18] mentioned above) actually satisfy this stronger notion of adaptive

[2] In the access structure for directed connectivity, the parties correspond to an edge in the complete *directed* graph and the "qualified" subsets are those edges that connect two distinguished nodes s and t.

[3] For access structures in NP, a qualified set of parties needs to know an NP witness that they are qualified.

[4] Witness encryption for a language $L \in \mathsf{NP}$ allows to encrypt a message relative to a statement $x \in L$ such that anyone holding a witness to the statement can decrypt the message, but if $x \notin L$, then the message is computationally hidden.

[5] One can relax the additional assumption of one-way functions to an average-case hardness assumption in NP [20].

security. However, the situation for the schemes that are based on cryptographic assumptions (including Yao's scheme and the scheme of [21]) is much less clear. Using random guessing (see Lemma 1) it can be shown that these schemes are adaptively secure, but this reduction loses an exponential (in the number of parties) factor in the security of the scheme. Additionally, as noted in [21], their scheme can be shown to be adaptively secure if the witness encryption scheme is *extractable*.[6] The latter is a somewhat controversial assumption that we prefer to avoid.

Our Results. We analyze the adaptive security of Yao's scheme under our framework and show that in some cases the security loss is much smaller than 2^n. Roughly, we show that if the access structure can be described by a monotone circuit of depth d and s gates (with unbounded fan-in and fan-out) the security loss is proportional to $s^{O(d)}$. Thus, for shallow circuits our analysis shows that an exponential loss is avoidable.

To exemplify the usefulness of the result, consider, for instance, the directed st-connectivity access structure mentioned in Footnote 6. It is known that it can be computed by a monotone circuit of size $O(n^3 \log n)$ and depth $O(\log^2 n)$, but its monotone formula and span-program complexity is $2^{\Omega(\log^2 n)}$ [17,24]. Thus, no efficient perfectly secure scheme is known, and our proof shows that Yao's scheme for this access structure is secure based on the assumption that quasi-polynomially-secure one-way functions exist.

Yao's Scheme. In this scheme, an access structure is described by a monotone circuit. The sharing procedure first labels the output wire of the circuit with the shared secret and then proceeds to assign labels to all wires of the circuit; in the end the label on each input wire is included in the share of the corresponding party. The procedure for assigning labels is recursive and in each step it labels the input wires of a gate g assuming its output wires are already labeled (recall that we assume unbounded fan-in and fan-out so there are many input and output wires). To do so, we first sample a fresh encryption key s for a symmetric-key encryption scheme. If the gate is an AND gate, then we label each input wire with a random string conditioned on their XOR being s, and if the gate is an OR gate, then we label each input wire with s. In either case, we encrypt the labels of the output wires under s and include these ciphertexts associated with the gate g as part of ever party's share. The reconstruction of the scheme works by reversing the above procedure from the leaves to the root. This scheme is indeed efficient for access structures that have polynomial-size monotone circuits.

Security Proof. Our goal is to show that as long as an adversary controls an unqualified set, he cannot learn anything about the secret. We start by outlining the selective security proof (following the argument of [28]), where the adversary first commits to the "corrupted" set. The proof is via a series of hybrids in

[6] This is a knowledge assumption that says that if an adversary can decrypt a witness encryption ciphertext, then it must *know* a witness which can be extracted from it.

which we slowly replace the ciphertexts associated with various gates g with bogus ciphertexts. Once we do this for the output gate, the shares become independent of the secret which proves security. The gates for which we can replace the ciphertexts with bogus ones are the gates for which the adversary cannot compute the corresponding encryption key. Since the adversary controls an unqualified set, a sequence which eventually results with replacing the encryption of the root gate must exist. Since in every hybrid we "handle" one gate and never consider it again, the number of hybrids is at most the number of gates in the circuit.

The problem with lifting this proof to the adaptive case is that it seems inherent to know the corrupted set of parties in order to know for which gates g to switch the ciphertexts from real to bogus (and in what order). However, in the adaptive game this set is not known during the sharing procedure. A naïve use of random guessing would result in an exponential security loss 2^n, where n is the number of parties.

To overcome this we associate each intermediate hybrid H_i with a *pebbling configuration* in which each gate in the circuit is either pebbled (ciphertexts are bogus) or unpebbled (ciphertexts are real). The pebbling rules are:

1. Can place or remove a pebble on any AND gate for which (at least) one input wire is either *not* corrupted or comes out of a gate with a pebble on it.
2. Can place or remove a pebble on any OR gate for which all of the incoming wires are either non-corrupted input wires or come out of gates all of which have pebbles on them.

The initial hybrid corresponds to the case in which all gates are unpebbled and the final hybrid corresponds to the case in which all gates are unpebbled except the root gate which has a pebble. Now, any pebbling strategy that takes us from the initial configuration to the final one, corresponds to a sequence of selective hybrids H_i. Furthermore, to prove indistinguishability of neighboring hybrids $\mathsf{H}_i, \mathsf{H}_{i+1}$ we don't need the adversary to commit to the entire set of corrupted parties ahead of time but it suffices if the adversary only commits to the pebble configuration in steps i and $i+1$. Therefore, if the pebbling strategy has the property that each configuration requires few bits to describe, then we would be able to use our framework. We show that for every corrupted set and any monotone circuit of depth d and s gates, there exists such a pebbling strategy, where the number of moves is roughly $2^{O(d)}$ and each configuration has a very succinct representation: roughly $d \cdot \log s$ bits. Plugging this into our framework, we get a proof of adaptive security with security loss proportional to $s^{O(d)}$. We refer to Sect. 4 for the precise details.

1.2 Generalized Selective Decryption

Generalized Selective Decryption (GSD), introduced by Panjwani [23], is a game that captures the difficulty of proving adaptive security of certain protocols, most notably the Logical Key Hierarchy (LKH) multicast encryption protocol. On a high level, it deals with scenario where we have many secret keys k_i and various ciphertexts encrypting one key under another (but no cycles). We will discuss this problem in depth in the full version [15], here giving a high level overview on how our framework applies to this problem.

Let $(\mathsf{Enc}, \mathsf{Dec})$ be a CPA-secure symmetric encryption scheme with (probabilistic) $\mathsf{Enc}\colon \mathcal{K}\times\mathcal{M} \rightarrow \mathcal{C}$ and $\mathsf{Dec}\colon \mathcal{K}\times\mathcal{C} \rightarrow \mathcal{M}$. We assume $\mathcal{K} \subseteq \mathcal{M}$, i.e., we can encrypt keys. In the game, the challenger—either $\mathsf{G_L}$ or $\mathsf{G_R}$—picks $n+1$ random keys $k_0, \ldots, k_n \in \mathcal{K}$, and the adversary A is then allowed to make three types of queries:[7]

- Encryption query: on input $(\mathtt{encrypt}, i, j)$ receives $\mathsf{Enc}(k_i, k_j)$.
- Corruption queries: on input $(\mathtt{corrupt}, i)$ receives k_i.
- Challenge query, only one is allowed: on input $(\mathtt{challenge}, i)$ receives k_i in the real game $\mathsf{G_L}$, and a random value in the random game $\mathsf{G_R}$.

We think of this game as generating a directed graph, with vertex set $\mathcal{V} = \{0, \ldots, n\}$, where every $(\mathtt{encrypt}, i, j)$ query adds a directed edge (i, j), and we say a vertex v_i is corrupted if a query $(\mathtt{corrupt}, i)$ was made, or v_i can be reached from a corrupted vertex. The goal of the adversary is to distinguish the games $\mathsf{G_L}$ or $\mathsf{G_R}$, with the restriction that the constructed graph has no cycles, and the challenge vertex is a sink. To prove security, i.e., reduce the indistinguishability of $\mathsf{G_L}$ or $\mathsf{G_R}$ to the security of Enc, we can consider a selectivized version of this game where A must commit to the graph as described above (which uses $<n^2$ bits). The security of this selectivized game can then be reduced to the security of Enc by a series of $<n^2$ hybrids, where a distinguisher for any two consecutive hybrids can be used to break the security of Enc with the same advantage. Using random guessing followed by a hybrid argument we conclude that if Enc is δ-secure, the GSD game is $\delta \cdot n^2 \cdot 2^{n^2}$-secure. Thus, we lose an exponential in n^2 factor in the reduction.

Fortunately, if we look at the actual protocols that GSD is supposed to capture, it turns out that the graphs that A can generate are not totally arbitrary. Two interesting cases are given by GSD restricted to graphs of bounded depth, and to trees. For these cases better reductions exist. Panjwani [23] shows that if the adversary is restricted to play the game such that the resulting graph is of depth at most d, a reduction losing a factor $(2n)^d$ exists. Moreover, Fuchsbauer et al. [8] give a reduction losing a factor $n^{3 \log n}$ when the underlying graph is a tree. In the full version we prove these results in our framework. Our proofs are much simpler than the original ones, especially than the proof of [23] which is very long and technical. This is thanks to our modular approach, where our general framework takes care of delicate probabilistic arguments, and basically just leaves us with the task of designing pebbling strategies, where each pebbling configuration has a succinct description, for various graphs, which is a clean combinatorial problem. The generic connection between adaptive security proofs of the GSD problem and graph pebbling is entirely new to this work.

[7] In the actual game the adversary can also make standard CPA encryption queries $\mathsf{Enc}(k_i, m)$ for chosen m, i. As this doesn't meaningfully change the security proof we ignore this here.

GSD on a Path. Let us sketch the proof idea for the [8] result, but for an even more restricted case where the graph is a path visiting every node exactly once. In other words there is a permutation σ over $\{0, \ldots, n\}$ and the adversary's queries are of the form $(\texttt{encrypt}, \sigma(i-1), \sigma(i))$ and $(\texttt{challenge}, \sigma(n))$. We first consider the selective game where A must commit to this permutation σ ahead of time. Let $\mathsf{H_L}, \mathsf{H_R}$ be the selectivized versions of $\mathsf{G_L}$, $\mathsf{G_R}$ respectively.

To prove selective security, we can define a sequence of hybrid games $\mathsf{H_L} = \mathsf{H}_0, \ldots, \mathsf{H}_\ell = \mathsf{H_R}$. Each hybrid is defined by a path, $0 \to 1 \to \ldots \to n$, with a subset of the edges holding a black pebble. In the hybrid games, a pebble on $(i, i+1)$ means that instead of answering the query $(\texttt{encrypt}, \sigma(i), \sigma(i+1))$ with the "real" answer $\mathsf{Enc}(k_{\sigma(i)}, k_{\sigma(i+1)})$, we answer it with a "fake" answer $\mathsf{Enc}(k_{\sigma(i)}, r)$ for a random r. The goal is to move from a hybrid with no pebbles (this corresponds to $\mathsf{H_L}$) to one with a single black pebble on the "sink" edge $(n-1, n)$ (this corresponds to $\mathsf{H_R}$). We can prove that neighboring hybrids are indistinguishable via a reduction from CPA-security as long as the pebbling configurations are only modified via the following legal moves:

1. We can put/remove a pebble on the source edge $(0, 1)$ at any time.
2. We can put/remove a pebble on an edge $(i, i+1)$ if the preceding edge $(i-1, i)$ has a pebble.

This is because adding/removing a pebble $(i, i+1)$ means changing what we encrypt under key $k_{\sigma(i)}$ and therefore we need to make sure that either the edge is a source edge or there is already a pebble on the preceding edge to ensure that the key $k_{\sigma(i)}$ is never being encrypted under some other key.

The simplest "basic pebbling strategy" consists of $2n$ moves where we add pebbles on the path $0 \to 1 \to \ldots \to n$, one by one starting on the left and then remove one by one starting on the right, keeping only the pebble on the sink edge $(n-1, n)$. This is illustrated in Fig. 1(a) for $n = 8$. The strategy uses n pebbles. However, there are other pebbling strategies that allow us to trade off more moves for fewer pebbles. For example there is a "recursive strategy" (recursively pebble the middle vertex, then recursively pebble the right-most vertex, then recursively remove the pebble from the middle vertex) that uses at most $\log n + 1$ pebbles (instead of n), but requires $3^{\log n} + 1$ moves (instead of just $2n$). This is illustrated in Fig. 1(b).

As we described, each pebbling strategy with ℓ moves gives us a sequence of hybrids $\mathsf{H_L} = \mathsf{H}_0, \ldots, \mathsf{H}_\ell = \mathsf{H_R}$ that allows us to prove selective security. Furthermore, we can prove relatively easily that neighboring hybrids $\mathsf{H}_j, \mathsf{H}_{j+1}$ are indistinguishable even if the adversary doesn't commit to the entire permutation σ but only to the value $\sigma(i)$ of vertices i where either H_j or H_{j+1} has a pebble on the edge $(i-1, i)$. Using our framework, we therefore get a proof of adaptive security where the security loss is $\ell \cdot n^p$ where p is the maximum number of pebbles used and ℓ is the number of pebbling moves. In particular, if we use the recursive pebbling strategy described above we only suffer a quasipolynomial security loss $3^{\log n} \cdot n^{\log n + 1}$, as compared with $2n \cdot (n+1)!$ for naïve random guessing where the adversary commits to the entire permutation σ.

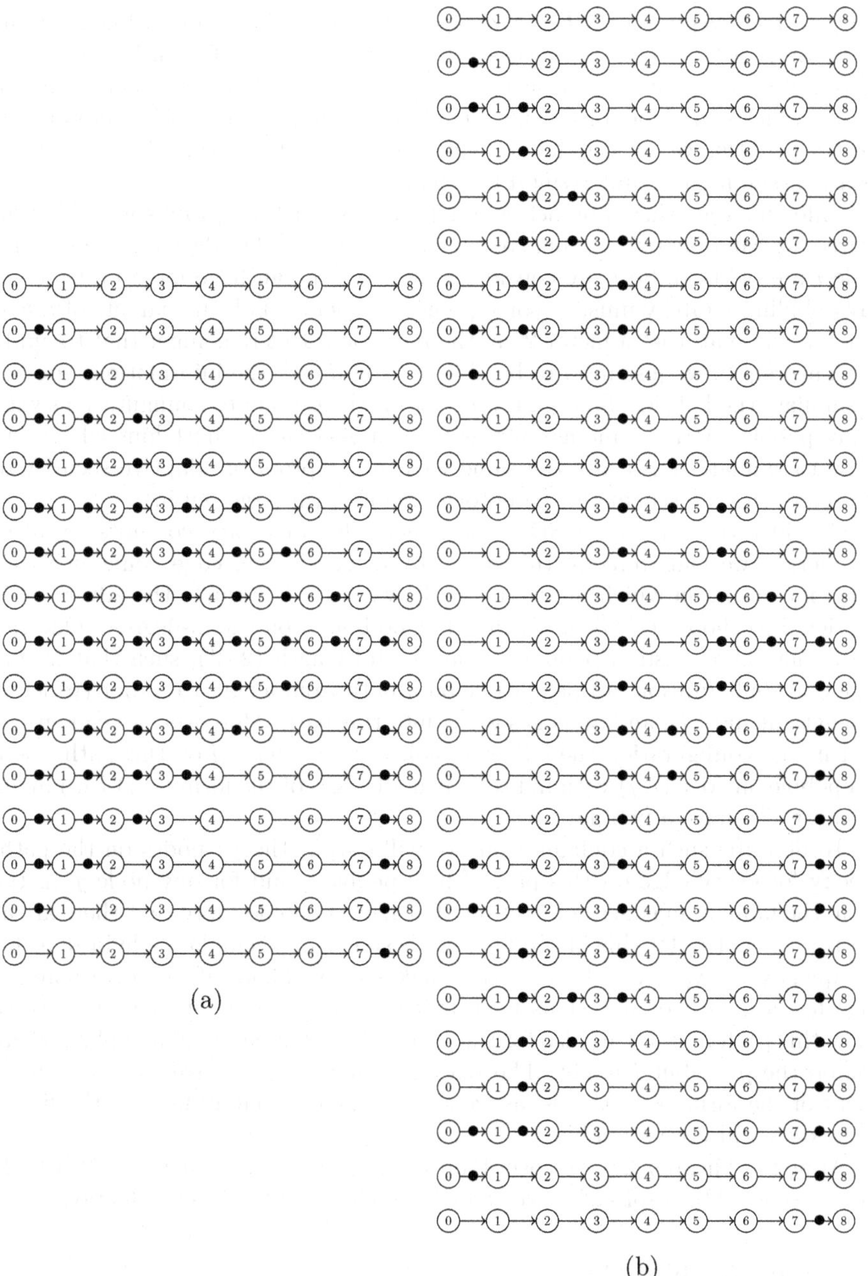

Fig. 1. "Classical" hybrid argument vs. improved hybrid argument. In both diagrams, the edges that carry a pebble are faked. (a) Illustration of the classical hybrids $\mathsf{H}_0, \ldots, \mathsf{H}_{15}$ for GSD on a path graph with $n = 8$ edges: the number of hybrids is $2n = 16$, and the number of fake edges is at most n. (b) A sequence of hybrids $\tilde{\mathsf{H}}_0, \ldots, \tilde{\mathsf{H}}_{27}$ that use fewer fake edges: even though the number of hybrids is $3^{\log n} + 1 = 28$, the number of fake edges is at most $\log n + 1 = 4$. The argument on the right is identical to the one using nested hybrids in [8].

GSD on Low Depth and Other Families of Graphs. The proof outline for GSD on paths is just a very special case of our general result for GSD for various classes of graphs, which we discuss in the full version. If we consider a class of graphs which can be pebbled using ℓ pebbling configurations, each containing at most q pebbles, we get a reduction showing that GSD for this class is $\delta \cdot \ell \cdot 2^q$ secure, assuming the underlying Enc scheme is δ-secure.

Unfortunately, this approach will not gain us much for graphs with high in-degree: we can only put a pebble on an edge (i, j) if all the edges $(*, i)$ going into node i are pebbled. So if we consider graphs which can have large in-degree d, any pebbling strategy must at some point have pebbled all the parents of i, and thus we'll lose at least a factor 2^d in the reduction. But remember that to apply our Theorem 2, we just need to be able to "compress" the information required to simulate the hybrids. So even if the hybrids correspond to configurations with many pebbles, that is fine as long as we can generate a short hint which will allow to emulate it (we use the same idea in the proof of adaptive security of the secret sharing scheme for monotone circuits with large fan-in).

Consider the selective GSD game, where the adversary commits to all of its queries, we can think of this as a DAG, where each edge comes with an index indicating in which query this node was added. Assume the adversary is restricted to choose DAGs of depth l (but no bound on the in-degree). One can show that there exists a pebbling sequence (of length $(2n)^l$), such that in any pebbling configuration, all pebbles lie on a path from a sink to a root (which is of length at most l), and on edges going into this path. Moreover, we can ensure that in any configuration the following holds: if for a node j on this path, there is a pebble on edge (i, j) with index t, then all edges of the form $(*, j)$ with index $<t$ must also have a pebble.

To describe such a configuration, we will output the $\leq l$ nodes on the path, specify for every edge on this path if it is pebbled, and for any node j on the path, the number of edges going into j that have a pebble (note that there are at most $2^l n^{2l}$ choices for this hint). The hint is sufficient to emulate a hybrid, as for any query $(\texttt{encrypt}, i, j)$ the adversary makes, we will know if the corresponding edge has a pebble or not. This is clear if the edge (i, j) is on the path, as we know this path in full. But also for the other edges that can hold a pebble, where j is on the path but i is not. The reason is that we just have to count which query of the form $(*, j)$ this is, as we got a number c telling us that the first c such edges will have a pebble.

Applying Theorem 2, we recover Panjwani's result [23] showing that if the GSD game restricted to graphs of depth l only loses a factor $n^{O(l)}$ in the reduction.

1.3 Yao's Garbled Circuits

Garbled circuits, introduced by Yao in (oral presentations of) [29,30], can be used to garble a circuit C and an input x in a way that reveals $C(x)$ but hides everything else. More precisely, a garbling scheme has three procedures; one to garble the circuit C and produce a garbled circuit $\widetilde{C}$, one to garble the input x and produce a garbled input $\widetilde{x}$, and one that evaluates the garbled circuit $\widetilde{C}$ on the garbled input $\widetilde{x}$ to get $C(x)$. Furthermore, to prove security, there must be a simulator that only gets the output of the computation $C(x)$ and can simulate the garbled circuit $\widetilde{C}$ and input $\widetilde{x}$, such that no PPT adversary can distinguish them from the real garbling.

Adaptive vs. Selective Security. In the adaptive setting, the adversary A first chooses the circuit C and gets back the garbled circuit $\widetilde{C}$, then chooses the input x, and gets back garbled input $\widetilde{x}$. The adversary's goal is to decide whether he was interacting with the real garbling scheme or the simulator. In the selective setting, the adversary has to choose the circuit C as well as the input x at the very beginning and only then gets back $\widetilde{C}, \widetilde{x}$.

Prior Work. The work of Bellare et al. [2] raised the question of whether Yao's construction or indeed any construction of garbled circuits achieves adaptive security. The work of Hemenway et al. [12] gave the first construction of non-trivial adaptively secure garbled circuits based on one-way functions, by modifying Yao's construction with an added layer of encryption having some special properties. Most recently, the work of Jafargholi and Wichs [16] gives the first analysis of adaptive security for Yao's unmodified garbled circuit construction which significantly improves on the parameters of trivial random guessing. See [16] for a more comprehensive introduction and broader background on garbled circuits and adaptive security.

Here, we present the work of [16] as a special case of our general framework. Indeed, the work of [16] already implicitly follows our general framework fairly closely and therefore we only give a high level overview of how it fits into it.

Selective Hybrids. We start by outlining the selective security proof for Yao's garbled circuits, following the presentation of [12,16] which is in turn based on the proof of Lindell and Pinkas [22]. Essentially the proof proceeds via series of hybrids which modify one garbled gate at a time from the Real distribution to a $\mathsf{Simulated}$ one. However, this cannot be done directly in one step and instead requires going through an intermediate distribution called $\mathsf{InputDep}$ (we explain the name later). There are important restrictions on the order in which these steps can be taken:

1. We can switch a gate from Real to $\mathsf{InputDep}$ (and vice versa) if it is at the input level or if its predecessor gates are already $\mathsf{InputDep}$.
2. We can switch a gate from $\mathsf{InputDep}$ to $\mathsf{Simulated}$ (and vice versa) if it is at the output level or if its successor gates are already $\mathsf{Simulated}$.

The simplest strategy to switch all gates from Real to $\mathsf{Simulated}$ is to start with the input level and go up one level at a time switching all gates to $\mathsf{InputDep}$. Then start with the output level and go down one level at a time switching all gates to $\mathsf{Simulated}$. This corresponds to the basic proof of selective security of Yao garbled circuits.

However, the above is not the only possibility. In particular, any strategy for switching all gates from Real to $\mathsf{Simulated}$ following rules (1) and (2) corresponds to a sequence of hybrid games for proving selective security. We can identify the above with a *pebbling game* where one can place pebbles on the gates of the circuit. The Real distribution corresponds to not having a pebble and there are two types of pebbles corresponding to the InputDep and Simulated distributions. The goal is to start with no pebbles and finish by placing a Simulated pebble on every gate in the circuit while only performing legal moves according to rules (1) and (2) above. Every pebbling strategy gives rise to a sequence of hybrid games $\mathsf{H}_0, \mathsf{H}_1, \ldots, \mathsf{H}_\ell$ for proving selective security, where the number of hybrids ℓ corresponds to the number of moves and each hybrid H_i is defined by the configuration of pebbles after i moves.

From Selective to Adaptive. The problem with translating selective security proofs into the adaptive setting lies with the InputDep distribution of a gate. This distribution depends on the input x (hence the name) and, in the adaptive setting, the input x that the adversary will choose is not yet known at the time when the garbled circuit is created. To be more precise, the InputDep distribution of a gate i only depends on the 1-bit value going over the output wire of that gate during the computation $C(x)$. Moreover, if we take any two fixed hybrid games $\mathsf{H}_i, \mathsf{H}_{i+1}$ corresponding to two neighboring pebble configurations (ones which differ by a single move) we can prove indistinguishability even if the adversary does not commit to the entire n-bit input x ahead of time but only commits to the bits going over the output wires of all gates i that are in InputDep mode in either configuration. This means that as long as the pebbling strategy only uses m pebbles of the InputDep type at any point in time, each pair of hybrids $\mathsf{H}_i, \mathsf{H}_{i+1}$ can proved indistinguishable in a partially selective setting where the adversary only commits to m bits of information about his input ahead of time, rather than committing to the entire n bit input x. Using our framework, this shows that whenever there is a pebbling strategy for the circuit C that requires ℓ moves and uses at most m pebbles of the InputDep type, we can translate the selective hybrids into a proof of adaptive security where the security loss is $\ell \cdot 2^m$.

It turns out that for any graph of depth d there is a pebbling strategy that uses $O(d)$ pebbles and $\ell = 2^{O(d)}$ moves, meaning that we can prove adaptive security with a $2^{O(d)}$ security loss. This leads to a proof of adaptive security for NC^1 circuits where the reduction has only polynomial security loss, but more generally we can often get a much smaller security loss than the trivial 2^n bound achieved by naïve random guessing.[8]

[8] The presentation in [16] follows the above outline fairly closely and the reader can easily match it with our general framework. The one conceptual difference is that we think of all the hybrids H_i as existing in the selective setting where the adversary commits to the entire input but then we analyze indistinguishability of neighboring hybrids in a partially selective setting. The work of [16] thought of the hybrids H_i as already being partially selective, which made it difficult to compare neighboring hybrids, since the adversary was expected to commit to different information in each one. We view our new framework as being conceptually simpler.

1.4 Constrained Pseudorandom Functions

Goldreich et al. [11] introduced the notion of a pseudorandom function (PRF). A PRF is an efficiently computable keyed function $\mathsf{F}\colon \mathcal{K} \times \mathcal{X} \to \mathcal{Y}$, where $\mathsf{F}(k, \cdot)$, instantiated with a random key $k \leftarrow \mathcal{K}$, cannot be distinguished from a function randomly chosen from the set of all functions $\mathcal{X} \to \mathcal{Y}$ with non-negligible probability. More recently, the notion of constrained pseudorandom functions (CPRF) was introduced as an extension of PRFs, by Boneh and Waters [5], Boyle et al. [6] and Kiayias et al. [19], independently. Informally, a constrained PRF allows the holder of a master key to derive keys which are constrained to a set, in the sense that such a key can be used to evaluate the PRF on that set, while the outputs on inputs outside of this set remain indistinguishable from random.

Goldreich et al., in addition to formally defining PRFs, gave a construction of a PRF from any length doubling pseudorandom generator (PRG). Their construction is depicted in Fig. 2. All three of the aforementioned results [5,6,19] show that this GGM construction already gives a so-called "prefix-constrained" PRF, which is a CPRF where for any $x \in \{0,1\}^*$, one can give out keys which allow to evaluate the PRF on all inputs whose prefix is x. This is a simple but already very interesting class of CPRFs as it can be used to construct a punctured PRF, which in turn is a major tool in constructing various sophisticated primitives based on indistinguishability obfuscation (see, for example, [5,13,26]).

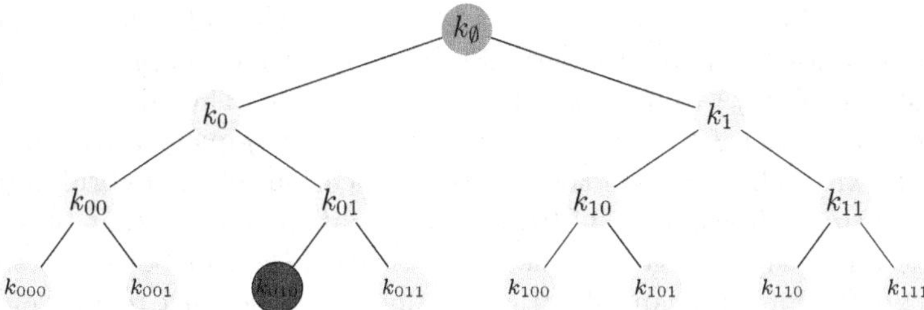

Fig. 2. Illustration of the GGM PRF. Every left child $k_{x\|0}$ of a node k_x is defined as the first half of $\mathsf{PRG}(k_x)$, the right child $k_{x\|1}$ as the second half. The circled node corresponds to $\mathsf{GGM}(k_\emptyset, 010)$.

Prior Work. To show that the GGM construction is a prefix-constrained PRF one must show how to transform an adversary that breaks GGM as a prefix-constrained PRF into a distinguisher for the underlying PRG. The proofs in [5,6,19] only show selective security, where the adversary must initially commit to the output he wants to be challenged on in the security game. There is a loss in tightness by a factor of $2n$. This can then be turned into a proof against adaptive adversaries via random guessing, losing an additional exponential factor 2^n in the input length n.

Fuchsbauer et al. [9] showed that it is possible to achieve adaptive security by losing only factor of $(3q)^{\log n}$, where q denotes the number of queries made by the adversary—if q is polynomial, the loss is not exponential as before, but just quasi-polynomial. The bound relies on the so-called "nested hybrids" technique. Informally, the idea is to iterate random guessing and hybrid arguments several times. The random guessing is done in a way where one only has to guess some tiny amount of information, which although insufficient to get a full reduction using the hybrid argument, nevertheless reduces the complexity of the task significantly. Every such iteration "cuts" the domain in half, so after logarithmically many iterations the reduction is done. If the number of iterations is small, and the amount of information guessed in each iteration tiny, this can still lead to a reduction with much smaller loss than "single shot" random guessing.

Our Results. We cast the result in [9] in our framework, giving an arguably simpler and more intuitive proof. To this aim, we first describe the GGM construction and sketch its security proof.

Given a $\mathsf{PRG}\colon \{0,1\}^m \to \{0,1\}^{2m}$, the PRF $\mathsf{GGM}\colon \{0,1\}^m \times \{0,1\}^n \to \{0,1\}^m$ is defined recursively as

$$\mathsf{GGM}(k,x) = k_x \text{ where } k_\emptyset = k \text{ and } k_{x\|0}\|k_{x\|1} = \mathsf{PRG}(k_x).$$

The construction is also a prefix-constrained PRF: given a key k_x for any $x \in \{0,1\}^*$, one can evaluate $\mathsf{GGM}(k,x')$ for all x' whose prefix is x.

The security of the GGM as a PRF is given in [11]. In particular, they show that if an adversary exists who distinguishes $\mathsf{GGM}(k,\cdot)$ (real experiment) from a uniformly random function (random experiment) with advantage ϵ making q (adaptive) queries, then an adversary of roughly the same complexity exists who distinguishes $\mathsf{PRG}(U_m)$ from U_{2m} with advantage ϵ/nq. Thus if we assume that PRG is δ-secure, then GGM is δnq-secure against any q-query adversary of the same complexity. This is one of the earliest applications of the hybrid argument.

The security definition for CPRFs is quite different from that of standard PRFs: the adversary will get to query the CPRF $\mathsf{F}(k,\cdot)$ in both, the real and random experiment (and can ask for constrained keys, not just regular outputs), and only at the very end the adversary will choose a challenge query x^*, which is then answered with either the correct CPRF output $\mathsf{F}(k,x^*)$ (in the real experiment) or a random value (in the random experiment). In the selective version of these security experiments, the adversary has to choose the challenge x^* before making any queries. In particular, for the case of prefix-constrained PRFs, the experiment is as follows. The challenger samples $k \in \{0,1\}^n$ uniformly at random. The adversary $\mathcal{A}$ first commits to some $x^* \in \{0,1\}^n$. Then it can make *constrain* queries $x \in \{0,1\}^*$ for any x which is not a prefix of x^*, and receives the constrained key k_x in return. Finally, $\mathcal{A}$ gets either $\mathsf{GGM}(k,x^*)$ (in the real game) or a random value, and must guess which is the case.

Selective Hybrids. A naïve sequence of selective hybrids, which is of length $2n$, relies just on the knowledge of x^*. For $n = 8$ the corresponding 16 hybrid games are illustrated in Fig. 1a. Each path $\mathrm{C}(n)$ corresponds to a hybrid, and it "encodes" how the value of the function F is computed on the challenge input

x^* (and this determines how the function is computed on the rest of the inputs too). An edge that does not carry a pebble is computed, normally, as defined in GGM—i.e., if the ith edge is not pebbled then $k_{x^*[1,i-1]\|0}\|k_{x^*[1,i-1]\|1}$ is set to $\mathsf{PRG}(k_{x[1,i-1]})$, where for $x \in \{0,1\}^n$, $x[1,i]$ denotes its i bit prefix. On the other hand, for an edge with a pebble, we replace the PRG output with a random value—i.e., $k_{x^*[1,i-1]\|0}\|k_{x^*[1,i-1]\|1}$ is set to a uniformly random string in $\{0,1\}^{2m}$. It's not hard to see that any distinguisher for two consecutive hybrids can be directly used to break the PRG with the same advantage by embedding the PRG-challenge – which is either U_{2m} or $\mathsf{PRG}(U_m)$ – at the right place. Using random guessing we can get adaptive security losing an additional factor 2^n in the distinguishing advantage by initially guessing $x^* \in \{0,1\}^n$.

From Selective to Adaptive. Before we explain the improved reduction, we take a step back and consider an even more selective game where A must commit, in addition to the challenge query $x_q = x^*$, also to the constrain queries $\{x_1, \ldots, x_{q-1}\}$. We can use the knowledge of $x_1, \ldots, x_{q-1}$ to get a better sequence of hybrids: this requires two tricks. First, as in GSD on a path, instead of using the pebbling strategy in Fig. 1a, we switch to the recursive pebbling sequence in Fig. 1b. Second, we need a more concise "indexing" for the pebbles: unlike in the proof for GSD, here we can't simply give the positions of the (up to $\log n + 1$) pebbles as hint to simulate the hybrids, as the graph has exponential size, thus even the position of a single pebble would require as many bits to encode as the challenge x^*. Instead, we assume there's an upper bound q on the number of queries made by the adversary. For a pebble on the ith edge, we just give the index of the first constrain query whose i bit prefix coincides with x^*, i.e., the minimum j such that $x_j[1,i] = x^*[1,i]$. This information is sufficient to tell when exactly during the experiment we have to compute a value that corresponds to a pebbled edge.

As there are $3^{\log n}$ hybrids, and each hint comes from a set of size $q^{\log n}$ (i.e., a value $\leq q$ for every pebble), our Theorem 2 implies that GGM is a $\delta(3q)^{\log n}$ secure prefix-constrained PRF if PRG is δ secure. Details are given in the full version [15].

2 Notation

Throughout, we use λ to denote the security parameter. We use capital letters like X to denote variables, small letters like x to denote concrete values, calligraphic letters like $\mathcal{X}$ to denote sets and sans-serif letters like X to denote algorithms. Our algorithms can all be modelled as (potentially interactive, probabilistic, polynomial time) Turing machines. With $\mathsf{X} \equiv \mathsf{Y}$ we denote that X has exactly the same input/output distribution as Y, and $X \sim Y$ denotes that X and Y have the same distributions. $U_{\mathcal{X}}$ denotes the uniform distribution over $\mathcal{X}$. In particular, U_n denotes the uniform distribution over $\{0,1\}^n$. For a set $\mathcal{X}$, $s_{\mathcal{X}}$ denotes the complexity of sampling uniformly at random from $\mathcal{X}$. For $a, b \in \mathbb{N}$, $a \geq b$, by $[a,b]$ we denote the set $\{a, a+1, \ldots, b\}$. For $x \in \{0,1\}^n$ we'll denote with $x[1,i]$ its i bit prefix.

3 The Framework

We consider a game described via a challenger G which interacts with an adversary A. At the end of the interaction, G outputs a decision bit b and we let $\langle \mathsf{A}, \mathsf{G} \rangle$ denote the random variable corresponding to that bit.

Definition 1. *We say that two games defined via challengers G_0 and G_1 are (s, ε)-indistinguishable if for any adversary A of size at most s:*

$$|\Pr[\langle \mathsf{A}, \mathsf{G}_0 \rangle = 1] - \Pr[\langle \mathsf{A}, \mathsf{G}_1 \rangle = 1]| \leq \varepsilon.$$

We say that two games are perfectly indistinguishable and write $\mathsf{G}_0 \equiv \mathsf{G}_1$ if they are $(\infty, 0)$-indistinguishable.

Selectivized Games. We define two operations that convert adaptive or partially selective games into further selective games.

Definition 2 (Selectivized Game). *Given an (adaptive) game G and some function $g\colon \{0,1\}^* \to \mathcal{W}$ we define the selectivized game $\mathsf{H} = \mathsf{SEL}_{\mathcal{W}}[\mathsf{G}, g]$ which works as follows. The adversary A first sends a commitment $w \in \mathcal{W}$ to H. Then H runs the challenger G against A, at the end of which G outputs a bit b'. Let $\mathsf{transcript}$ denote all communication exchanged between G and A. If $g(\mathsf{transcript}) = w$ then H outputs the bit b' and else it outputs 0. See Fig. 3(a).*

Note that the selectivized game gets a commitment w from the adversary but essentially ignores it during the rest of the game. Only, at the very end of the game, it checks that the commitment matches what actually happened during the game.

Definition 3 (Further Selectivized Game). *Assume $\hat{\mathsf{H}}$ is a (partially selective) game which expects to receive some commitment $u \in \mathcal{U}$ from the adversary in the first round. Given functions $g\colon \{0,1\}^* \to \mathcal{W}$ and $h\colon \mathcal{W} \to \mathcal{U}$ we define the further selectivized game $\mathsf{H} = \mathsf{SEL}_{\mathcal{U} \to \mathcal{W}}[\hat{\mathsf{H}}, g, h]$ as follows. The adversary A first sends a commitment $w \in \mathcal{W}$ to H and H begins running $\hat{\mathsf{H}}$ and passes it $u = h(w)$. It then continues running the game between $\hat{\mathsf{H}}$ and A at the end of which $\hat{\mathsf{H}}$ outputs a bit b'. Let $\mathsf{transcript}$ denote all communication exchanged between $\hat{\mathsf{H}}$ and A. If $g(\mathsf{transcript}) = w$ then H outputs the bit b' and else it outputs 0. See Fig. 3(b).*

Note that if $\hat{\mathsf{H}}$ is a (partially selective) game where the adversary sends some commitment u, then in the further selectivized game the adversary might have to commit to more information w. The further selectivized game essentially ignores w and only relies on the partial information $u = h(w)$ during the course of the game but only at the very end is still checks that the full commitment w matches what actually happened during the game.

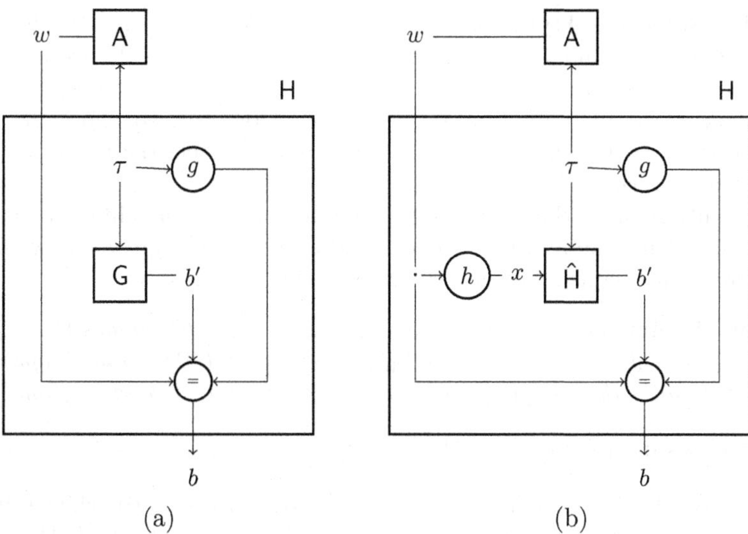

Fig. 3. *Selectivizing.* (a): $\mathsf{SEL}_{\mathcal{W}}[\mathsf{G}, g]$, and (b): $\mathsf{SEL}_{\mathcal{U}\to\mathcal{W}}[\hat{\mathsf{H}}, g, h]$. The symbol τ is short for $\mathsf{transcript}$, the nodes with g and h compute the respective functions, whereas the node with $=$ outputs a bit b as prescribed in the consistency check.

Random Guessing. We first present the basic reduction using random guessing.

Lemma 1. *Assume we have two games defined via challengers G_0 and G_1 respectively. Let $g\colon \{0,1\}^* \to \mathcal{W}$ be an arbitrary function and define the selectivized games $\mathsf{H}_b = \mathsf{SEL}_{\mathcal{W}}[\mathsf{G}_b, g]$ for $b \in \{0,1\}$. If H_0, H_1 are (s,ε)-indistinguishable then G_0, G_1 are $(s - s_{\mathcal{W}}, \varepsilon \cdot |\mathcal{W}|)$-indistinguishable, where $s_{\mathcal{W}}$ denotes the complexity of sampling uniformly at random from $\mathcal{W}$.*

Proof. We prove the contrapositive. Assume that there is an adversary A of size $s' = s - s_{\mathcal{W}}$ such that

$$|\Pr[\langle \mathsf{A}, \mathsf{G}_0\rangle = 1] - \Pr[\langle \mathsf{A}, \mathsf{G}_1\rangle = 1]| > \varepsilon \cdot |\mathcal{W}|.$$

Let A^* be the adversary that first chooses a uniformly random $w \leftarrow \mathcal{W}$ and then runs A. Then for $b \in \{0,1\}$:

$$\Pr[\langle \mathsf{A}^*, \mathsf{H}_b\rangle = 1] = \Pr[\langle \mathsf{A}, \mathsf{G}_b\rangle = 1]/|\mathcal{W}|$$

and therefore

$$|\Pr[\langle \mathsf{A}^*, \mathsf{H}_0\rangle = 1] - \Pr[\langle \mathsf{A}^*, \mathsf{H}_1\rangle = 1]| > \varepsilon.$$

Moreover, since A^* is of size $s' + s_{\mathcal{W}} = s$ this shows that H_0 and H_1 are not (s,ε)-indistinguishable.

Partially Selective Hybrids. Consider the following setup. We have two adaptive games $\mathsf{G_L}$ and $\mathsf{G_R}$. For some function $g\colon \{0,1\}^* \to \mathcal{W}$ we define the selectivized games $\mathsf{H_L} = \mathsf{SEL}_{\mathcal{W}}[\mathsf{G_L}, g]$, $\mathsf{H_R} = \mathsf{SEL}_{\mathcal{W}}[\mathsf{G_R}, g]$ where the adversary commits to some information $w \in \mathcal{W}$. Moreover, to show the indisitinguishability of $\mathsf{H_L}, \mathsf{H_R}$ we have a sequence of ℓ (selective) hybrid games $\mathsf{H_L} = \mathsf{H}_0, \mathsf{H}_1, \ldots, \mathsf{H}_\ell = \mathsf{H_R}$.

If we only assume that neighboring hybrids $\mathsf{H}_i, \mathsf{H}_{i+1}$ are indistinguishable then by combining the hybrid argument and random guessing we know that $\mathsf{G_L}$ and $\mathsf{G_R}$ are indistinguishable at a security loss of $\ell \cdot |\mathcal{W}|$.

Theorem 1. *Assume that for each $i \in \{0, \ldots, \ell-1\}$, the games $\mathsf{H}_i, \mathsf{H}_{i+1}$ are (s, ε)-indistinguishable. Then $\mathsf{G_L}$ and $\mathsf{G_R}$ are $(s - s_{\mathcal{W}}, \varepsilon \cdot \ell \cdot |\mathcal{W}|)$-indistinguishable, where $s_{\mathcal{W}}$ denotes the complexity of sampling uniformly at random from $\mathcal{W}$.*

Proof. Follows from Lemma 1 and the hybrid argument.

Our goal is to avoid the loss of $|\mathcal{W}|$ in the above theorem. To achieve this, we will assume a stronger condition: not only are neighboring hybrids $\mathsf{H}_i, \mathsf{H}_{i+1}$ indistinguishable, but they are selectivized versions of less selective games $\hat{\mathsf{H}}_{i,0}, \hat{\mathsf{H}}_{i,1}$ which are already indistinguishable. In particular, we assume that for each pair of neighboring hybrids $\mathsf{H}_i, \mathsf{H}_{i+1}$ there exist some less selective hybrids $\hat{\mathsf{H}}_{i,0}, \hat{\mathsf{H}}_{i,1}$ where the adversary only commits to much less information $h_i(w) \in \mathcal{U}$ instead of $w \in \mathcal{W}$. In more detail, for each i there is some function $h_i\colon \mathcal{W} \to \mathcal{U}$ that lets us interpret H_{i+b} as a selectivized version of $\hat{\mathsf{H}}_{i,b}$ via $\mathsf{H}_{i+b} \equiv \mathsf{SEL}_{\mathcal{U}\to\mathcal{W}}[\hat{\mathsf{H}}_{i,b}, g, h_i]$. In that case, the next theorem shows that we only get a security loss proportional to $|\mathcal{U}|$ rather than $|\mathcal{W}|$. Note that different pairs of "less selective hybrids" $\hat{\mathsf{H}}_{i,0}, \hat{\mathsf{H}}_{i,1}$ rely on completely different partial information $h_i(w)$ about the adversary's choices. Moreover, the "less selective" hybrid that we associate with each H_i can be different when we compare $\mathsf{H}_{i-1}, \mathsf{H}_i$ (in which case it is $\hat{\mathsf{H}}_{i-1,1}$) and when we compare H_i and H_{i+1} (in which case it is $\hat{\mathsf{H}}_{i,0}$).

Theorem 2 (main). *Let $\mathsf{G_L}$ and $\mathsf{G_R}$ be two adaptive games. For some function $g\colon \{0,1\}^* \to \mathcal{W}$ we define the selectivized games $\mathsf{H_L} = \mathsf{SEL}_{\mathcal{W}}[\mathsf{G_L}, g]$, $\mathsf{H_R} = \mathsf{SEL}_{\mathcal{W}}[\mathsf{G_R}, g]$. Let $\mathsf{H_L} = \mathsf{H}_0, \mathsf{H}_1, \ldots, \mathsf{H}_\ell = \mathsf{H_R}$ be some sequence of hybrid games.*

Assume that for each $i \in \{0, \ldots, \ell-1\}$, there exists a function $h_i\colon \mathcal{W} \to \mathcal{U}$ and games $\hat{\mathsf{H}}_{i,0}, \hat{\mathsf{H}}_{i,1}$ such that:

$$\mathsf{H}_i \equiv \mathsf{SEL}_{\mathcal{U}\to\mathcal{W}}[\hat{\mathsf{H}}_{i,0}, g, h_i], \quad \mathsf{H}_{i+1} \equiv \mathsf{SEL}_{\mathcal{U}\to\mathcal{W}}[\hat{\mathsf{H}}_{i,1}, g, h_i]. \tag{1}$$

Furthermore, assume that $\hat{\mathsf{H}}_{i,0}, \hat{\mathsf{H}}_{i,1}$ are (s, ε)-indistinguishable. Then $\mathsf{G_L}$ and $\mathsf{G_R}$ are $(s - s_{\mathcal{U}}, \varepsilon \cdot \ell \cdot |\mathcal{U}|)$-indistinguishable, where $s_{\mathcal{U}}$ denotes the complexity of sampling uniformly at random from $\mathcal{U}$.

Proof. Assume that A is an adaptive distinguisher for $\mathsf{G_L}$ and $\mathsf{G_R}$ of size s' such that

$$|\Pr[\langle \mathsf{A}, \mathsf{G_L} \rangle = 1] - \Pr[\langle \mathsf{A}, \mathsf{G_R} \rangle = 1]| > \varepsilon'.$$

Let A^* be a fully selective distinguisher that guesses $w \leftarrow \mathcal{W}$ uniformly at random in the first round and then runs A. By the same argument as in Lemma 1 and Theorem 1 we know that there exists some $i \in [0, \ell)$ such that:

$$|\Pr[\langle \mathsf{A}^*, \mathsf{H}_i \rangle = 1] - \Pr[\langle \mathsf{A}^*, \mathsf{H}_{i+1} \rangle = 1]| \geq \varepsilon'/(\ell \cdot |\mathcal{W}|) \tag{2}$$

Let A' be a partially selective distinguisher that guesses $u \leftarrow \mathcal{U}$ uniformly at random in the first round and then runs A. We want to relate the probabilities $\Pr[\langle \mathsf{A}^*, \mathsf{H}_{i+b} \rangle = 1]$ and $\Pr[\langle \mathsf{A}', \hat{\mathsf{H}}_{i,b} \rangle = 1]$.

Recall that the game $\langle \mathsf{A}^*, \mathsf{H}_{i+b} \rangle$ consists of A^* selecting a uniformly random value $w \leftarrow \mathcal{W}$ (which we denote by the random variable W) and then we run A against $\hat{\mathsf{H}}_{i,b}(u)$ (denoting the challenger $\hat{\mathsf{H}}_{i,b}$ that gets a commitment u in first round) which results in some $\mathsf{transcript}$ and an output bit b^*; if $g(\mathsf{transcript}) = w$ the final output is b^* else 0.

Similarly, the game $\langle \mathsf{A}', \hat{\mathsf{H}}_{i,b} \rangle$ consists of A' selecting a uniformly random value $u \leftarrow \mathcal{U}$ (which we denote by the random variable U) and then we run A against $\hat{\mathsf{H}}_{i,b}(u)$. Therefore:

$$\begin{aligned}
&\Pr[\langle \mathsf{A}^*, \mathsf{H}_{i+b} \rangle = 1] \\
&\quad= \sum_{u \in \mathcal{U}} \Pr[\underbrace{h_i(W) = u}_{\mathrm{I}}] \cdot \Pr[\underbrace{\langle \mathsf{A}, \hat{\mathsf{H}}_{i,b}(u) \rangle = 1}_{\mathrm{II}}] \cdot \Pr[W = g(\mathsf{transcript}) | \mathrm{I}, \mathrm{II}] \\
&\quad= \sum_{u \in \mathcal{U}} \frac{|h_i^{-1}(u)|}{|\mathcal{W}|} \cdot \Pr[\langle \mathsf{A}, \hat{\mathsf{H}}_{i,b}(u) \rangle = 1] \cdot \frac{1}{|h_i^{-1}(u)|} \\
&\quad= \frac{1}{|\mathcal{W}|} \cdot \sum_{u \in \mathcal{U}} \Pr[\langle \mathsf{A}, \hat{\mathsf{H}}_{i,b}(u) \rangle = 1] \\
&\quad= \frac{|\mathcal{U}|}{|\mathcal{W}|} \cdot \sum_{u \in \mathcal{U}} \Pr[\langle \mathsf{A}, \hat{\mathsf{H}}_{i,b}(u) \rangle = 1] \cdot \Pr[U = u] \\
&\quad= \frac{|\mathcal{U}|}{|\mathcal{W}|} \cdot \Pr[\langle \mathsf{A}', \hat{\mathsf{H}}_{i,b} \rangle = 1]
\end{aligned}$$

Combining the above with Eq. 2 we get:

$$|\Pr[\langle \mathsf{A}', \hat{\mathsf{H}}_{i,0} \rangle = 1] - \Pr[\langle \mathsf{A}', \hat{\mathsf{H}}_{i,1} \rangle = 1]| \geq \varepsilon'/(\ell \cdot |\mathcal{U}|)$$

Since by assumption $\hat{\mathsf{H}}_{i,0}, \hat{\mathsf{H}}_{i,1}$ are (s, ε)-indistinguishable and A' is of size $s' + s_{\mathcal{U}}$ this shows that when $s' = s - s_{\mathcal{U}}$ then $\varepsilon' \leq \varepsilon \cdot \ell \cdot |\mathcal{U}|$ which proves the theorem.

3.1 Example: GSD on a Path

As an example, we consider the problem of generalised selective decryption (GSD) on a path graph with n edges, where n is a power of two.

Let $(\mathsf{Enc}, \mathsf{Dec})$ be a symmetric encryption scheme with (probabilistic) $\mathsf{Enc}\colon \mathcal{K} \times \mathcal{M} \to \mathcal{C}$ and $\mathsf{Dec}\colon \mathcal{K} \times \mathcal{C} \to \mathcal{M}$. We assume $\mathcal{K} \subseteq \mathcal{M}$ so that we can encrypt keys, and that the encryption scheme is (s,δ)-indistinguishable under chosen-plaintext attack.[9] In the game, the challenger—either $\mathsf{G_L}$ or $\mathsf{G_R}$—picks $n+1$ random keys $k_0,\ldots,k_n \in \mathcal{K}$, and the adversary A is then allowed to make two types of queries:

- Encryption queries, $(\mathtt{encrypt}, v_i, v_j)$: it receives back $\mathsf{Enc}(k_i, k_j)$.
- Challenge query, $(\mathtt{challenge}, v_{i^*})$: here the answer differs between $\mathsf{G_L}$ and $\mathsf{G_R}$, with $\mathsf{G_L}$ answering with k_{i^*} (real key) and $\mathsf{G_R}$ answering with $r \leftarrow \mathcal{K}$ (random, "fake" key).

A cannot ask arbitrary queries: it is restricted to encryption queries that form a path graph with the challenge query as the sink. That is, a valid attacker A is allowed exactly n encryption queries $(\mathtt{encrypt}, v_{i_t}, v_{j_t})$, for $t = 1,\ldots,n$, and a single $(\mathtt{challenge}, v_{i^*})$ query such that the directed graph $\mathsf{G}_\mathcal{K} = (\mathcal{V},\mathcal{E})$ with $\mathcal{V} = \{v_0,\ldots,v_n\}$ and $\mathcal{E} = \{(v_{i_1}, v_{j_1}),\ldots,(v_{i_n}, v_{j_n})\}$ forms a path with sink v_{i^*}.

Fully Selective Hybrids. Let's look at a naïve sequence of intermediate hybrids $\mathsf{H}_0,\ldots,\mathsf{H}_{2n-1}$. The fully selective challenger H_I receives as commitment the exact permutation σ that A will query—i.e., $v_{\sigma(i)}$ is the ith vertex on the path. Therefore, $\mathcal{W} = S_{n+1}$ (the symmetry group over $0,\ldots,n$) and g is the function that outputs the observed permutation from $\mathsf{transcript}$. Next, H_I samples $2(n+1)$ keys $k_0,\ldots,k_n,r_0,\ldots,r_n$, and when A makes a query $(\mathtt{encrypt}, v_{\sigma(i)}, v_{\sigma(i+1)})$, it returns

for $0 \le I \le n$:

$$\begin{array}{lll} \mathsf{Enc}(k_{\sigma(i)}, r_{\sigma(i+1)}) & \textbf{if } (0 \le i \le I) & \text{(Fake edge)} \\ \mathsf{Enc}(k_{\sigma(i)}, k_{\sigma(i+1)}) & \textbf{otherwise.} & \text{(Real edge)} \end{array}$$

for $n < I \le 2n-1$:

$$\begin{array}{lll} \mathsf{Enc}(k_{\sigma(i)}, r_{\sigma(i+1)}) & \textbf{if } (0 \le i \le 2n-1-I) \vee (i = n-1) & \text{(Fake edge)} \\ \mathsf{Enc}(k_{\sigma(i)}, k_{\sigma(i+1)}) & \textbf{otherwise.} & \text{(Real edge)} \end{array} \tag{3}$$

Thus, in the sequence $\mathsf{H}_0,\ldots,\mathsf{H}_{2n-1}$, edges are "faked" sequentially down the path, and then "restored", except for the last edge, in the reverse order up the path—see Fig. 1a. By definition, $\mathsf{H}_0 = \mathsf{G_L}$ and $\mathsf{H}_{2n-1} = \mathsf{G_R}$. Moreover, H_I and H_{I+1} can be shown (s,δ)-indistinguishable: when A queries for $(\mathtt{encrypt}, v_{\sigma(I)}, v_{\sigma(I+1)})$, the reduction R_I returns the challenge ciphertext

$$\begin{array}{lll} \mathsf{C}(\cdot, k_{\sigma(I+1)}, r_{\sigma(I+1)}) & \textbf{if } (I \le n) & \text{(Real to fake)} \\ \mathsf{C}(\cdot, r_{\sigma(I+1)}, k_{\sigma(I+1)}) & \textbf{otherwise.} & \text{(Fake to real)} \end{array} \tag{4}$$

For the rest of the queries, R_I works as prescribed in Eq. 3.[10] It is easy to see that R_I simulates H_I when the ciphertext corresponds to the first message, and

[9] To be precise, we only need the encryption scheme to be secure in a weaker model where encryptions of two random messages $m_0, m_1 \in \mathcal{K}$ under a random key $k \in \mathcal{K}$ are (s,δ)-indistinguishable, with the adversary having access to ciphertexts on random messages from $\mathcal{K}$.

[10] Even though R_I does not know the key $k_{\sigma(I)}$, the query $(\mathtt{encrypt}, v_{\sigma(I-1)}, v_{\sigma(I)})$ does not cause a problem as its response is $\mathsf{Enc}(k_{\sigma(I)}, r_{\sigma(I-1)})$.

H_{I+1} otherwise. By Theorem 1, $(s - n \cdot s_{\mathsf{Enc}}, \delta(2n+1)(n+1)!)$-indistinguishability of G_L and G_R follows, where s_{Enc} is the complexity of the Enc algorithm and the $(n+1)!$ factor is the size of the set $\mathcal{W} = S_{n+1}$.

Partially Selective Hybrids. In order to simulate according to the strategy just described, it *suffices* for the hybrid (as well as the reduction) to guess the edges that are faked—however, this number can be at most n (e.g., in the middle hybrids) and, therefore, the simulator guesses the whole path anyway. Intuitively, this is where the overall looseness of the bound stems from. Now, consider the alternative sequence of hybrids $\tilde{\mathsf{H}}_0, \ldots, \tilde{\mathsf{H}}_{27}$ given in Fig. 1b: the edges in this sequence are faked and restored, *one* at a time, in a recursive manner to ensure that at most four edges end up fake per hybrid. In particular, the new hybrid $\tilde{\mathsf{H}}_I$, fakes all the edges that belong to a set $\mathcal{P}_I \subseteq \mathcal{E}$. That is, when A makes a query $(\mathtt{encrypt}, v_i, v_j)$—instead of following Eq. 3,—$\tilde{\mathsf{H}}_I$ returns

$$\begin{array}{ll} \mathsf{Enc}(k_i, r_j) \textbf{ if } ((v_i, v_j) \in \mathcal{P}_I) & \text{(Fake edge)} \\ \mathsf{Enc}(k_i, k_j) \textbf{ otherwise}. & \text{(Real edge)} \end{array} \tag{5}$$

This strategy can be extended to arbitrary n, and there exists such a sequence of sets $\mathcal{P}_0, \ldots, \mathcal{P}_{3^{\log n}}$ where the sets are of size at most $\log n + 1$.[11]

$\tilde{\mathsf{H}}^{\mathsf{A}}_{I+b}$
Obtain $\sigma \in S_{n+1}$ from A
Compute $\mathcal{P} := \mathcal{P}_0, \ldots, \mathcal{P}_\ell$
Run $\hat{\mathsf{H}}_{I,b}((\mathcal{P}_I, \mathcal{P}_{I+1}))$
if $g(\mathsf{transcript}) = \sigma$ **then**
  return $\hat{\mathsf{H}}_{I,b}$'s output
else return 0
end if

$\hat{\mathsf{H}}^{\mathsf{A}}_{I,b}((\mathcal{P}_I, \mathcal{P}_{I+1}))$
Choose $2n$ keys $r_1, \ldots, r_n, k_1, \ldots, k_n \leftarrow \mathcal{K}$
Whenever A queries $(\mathtt{encrypt}, v_i, v_j)$:
if $(v_i, v_j) \in \mathcal{P}_{I+b}$ **then return** $\mathsf{Enc}(k_i, r_j)$
else return $\mathsf{Enc}(k_i, k_j)$
end if
return A's output

Algorithm 1: $\tilde{\mathsf{H}}_{I+b} = \mathsf{SEL}_{\mathcal{U} \to \mathcal{W}}[\hat{\mathsf{H}}_{I,b}, g, h_I]$

Next, we show that the above simulation strategy satisfies the requirements for applying Theorem 2. Firstly, as shown in Algorithm 1, the strategy is partially selective—i.e., $\tilde{\mathsf{H}}_{I+b} = \mathsf{SEL}_{\mathcal{U} \to \mathcal{W}}[\hat{\mathsf{H}}_{I,b}, g, h_I]$, where, for $I \in [0, \ell = 3^{\log n}]$, the function $h_I : S_{n+1} \to \mathcal{E}^{\log n + 1}$ computes $\mathcal{P}_I$. Secondly, as the simulation in $\hat{\mathsf{H}}_{I,0}$ and $\hat{\mathsf{H}}_{I,1}$ differ by exactly one edge—which is real in one and fake in the other—they can be shown to be (s, δ)-indistinguishable. To be precise, if $(v_{i^*}, v_{j^*}) := \mathcal{P}_I \triangle \mathcal{P}_{I+1}$, where $\triangle$ denotes the symmetric difference, when A queries for $(\mathtt{encrypt}, v_{i^*}, v_{j^*})$, the reduction $\tilde{\mathsf{R}}_I$ returns

$$\begin{array}{ll} \mathsf{C}(\cdot, k_{j^*}, r_{j^*}) \textbf{ if } (\mathcal{P}_I \subset \mathcal{P}_{I+1}) & \text{(Real to fake)} \\ \mathsf{C}(\cdot, r_{j^*}, k_{j^*}) \textbf{ otherwise}. & \text{(Fake to real)} \end{array} \tag{6}$$

with the rest of the queries answered as in Eq. 5.

[11] In the full version, one can see that the sequence $\mathcal{P}_0, \ldots, \mathcal{P}_{3^{\log n}}$ corresponds to an "edge-pebbling" of the path graph.

Although, the number of hybrids is greater than in the previous sequence, the number of fake edges in any hybrid is at most $\log n + 1$. Thus, the reduction can work with less information than earlier. By Theorem 2, $(s - n \cdot s_{\mathsf{Enc}} - s_{\mathcal{P}}, \delta \cdot 3^{\log n} \cdot n^{2(\log n+1)})$-indistinguishability of $\mathsf{G_L}$ and $\mathsf{G_R}$ follows, where $s_{\mathcal{P}}$ is the size of the algorithm that generates the set $\mathcal{P} = \{\mathcal{P}_0, \ldots, \mathcal{P}_\ell\}$, and the $n^{2(\log n+1)}$ factor results from the fact that the compressed set $\mathcal{U} = \mathcal{E}^{\log n+1}$. Thus, the bound is improved considerably from exponential to quasi-polynomial. A more formal treatment is given in the full version [15].

4 Adaptive Secret Sharing for Monotone Circuits

Throughout history there have been many formulations of secret sharing schemes, each providing a different notion of correctness or security. We focus here on the computational setting and adapt the definitions of [21] for our purposes. Rogaway and Bellare [25] survey many different definitions, so we refer there for more information.

A computational secret sharing scheme involves a dealer who has a secret, a set of n parties, and a collection M of "qualified" subsets of parties called the access structure.

Definition 4 (Access structure). *An* access structure *M on parties $[n]$ is a monotone set of subsets of $[n]$. That is, $M \subseteq 2^{[n]}$ and for all $X \in M$ and $X \subseteq X'$ it holds that $X' \in M$.*

We sometimes think of M as a characteristic function $M : 2^{[n]} \to \{0,1\}$ that outputs 1 on input X if and only if X is in the access structure. Here, we mostly consider access structures that can be described by a *monotone Boolean circuit.* These are directed acyclic graphs (DAGs) in which leaves are labeled by input variables and every internal node is labeled by an OR or AND operation. We assume that the circuit has fan-in k_{in} and fan-out (at most) k_{out}. The computation is done in the natural way from the leaves to the root which corresponds to the output of the computation. A circuit in which every gate has fan-out $k_{\mathsf{out}} = 1$ is called a *formula.*

A secret sharing scheme for M is a method by which the dealer efficiently distributes shares to the parties such that (1) any subset in M can efficiently reconstruct the secret from its shares, and (2) any subset not in M cannot efficiently reveal any partial information on the secret. We denote by Π_i the share of party i and by Π_X the joint shares of parties $X \subseteq [n]$.

Definition 5 (Secret sharing). *Let $M : 2^{[n]} \to \{0,1\}$ be an access structure. A secret sharing scheme for M consists and secret space $\mathcal{S}$ of efficient sharing and reconstruction procedures S and R, respectively, that satisfy the following requirements:*

1. *$\mathsf{S}(1^\lambda, n, S)$ gets as input the unary representation of a security parameter, the number of parties and a secret $S \in \mathcal{S}$, and generates a share for each party.*

2. $\mathsf{R}(1^\lambda, \Pi_X)$ *gets as input the unary representation of a security parameter, the shares of a subset of parties* X*, and outputs a string* S'*.*
3. Completeness: *For a qualified set* $X \in M$ *the reconstruction procedure* R *outputs the shared secret:*

$$\Pr\left[\mathsf{R}(1^\lambda, \Pi_X) = S\right] = 1,$$

where the probability is over the randomness of the sharing procedure $\Pi_1, \ldots, \Pi_n \leftarrow \mathsf{S}(1^\lambda, n, S)$*.*
4. Adaptive security: *For every adversary* A *of size* s *it holds that*

$$|\Pr[\langle \mathsf{A}, \mathsf{G}_0 \rangle = 1] - \Pr[\langle \mathsf{A}, \mathsf{G}_1 \rangle = 1]| \le \epsilon,$$

where the challenger G_b *is defined as follows:*
   (a) *The adversary* A *specifies a secret* $S \in \mathcal{S}$*.*
      i. *If* $b = 0$*: the challenger generate shares* $\Pi_1, \ldots, \Pi_n \leftarrow \mathsf{S}(1^\lambda, n, S)$*.*
      ii. *If* $b = 1$*: the challenger samples a random* $S' \in \mathcal{S}$ *and generate shares* $\Pi_1, \ldots, \Pi_n \leftarrow \mathsf{S}(1^\lambda, n, S')$*.*
   (b) *The adversary* adaptively *specifies an index* $i \in [n]$ *and if the set of parties he requested so far is unqualified, he gets back* Π_i*, the share of the i-th party.*
   (c) *Finally, the adversary outputs a bit* b'*, which is the output of the experiment.*

The selective security variant is obtained by changing item 4b in the definition of the challenger G_b so that the adversary first sends a commitment to the set of shares X he wants to see ahead of time before seeing any share. We denote this challenger by $\mathsf{H}_b = \mathsf{SEL}_{2^{[n]}}[\mathsf{G}_b, X]$.

4.1 The Scheme of Yao

Here we describe the scheme of Yao (mentioned in [1], see also Vinod et al. [28]). The access structure M is given by a monotone Boolean circuit that is composed of AND and OR gates with fan-in k_{in} and fan-out (at most) k_{out}. Each leaf in the circuit is associated with an input variable $x_1, \ldots, x_n$ (there may be multiple inputs corresponding to the same input variable). During the sharing process, each wire in the circuit is assigned a label and the shares of party $i \in [n]$ corresponds to the labels of the wires corresponding to the input variable x_i. The sharing is done from the output wire to the leaves. The reconstruction is done in reverse: using the shares of the parties (that correspond to labels of the input wires), we recover the label of the output wire which will correspond to the secret.

The scheme (S, R) uses a symmetric-key encryption scheme $\mathsf{SKE} = (\mathsf{Enc}, \mathsf{Dec})$ in which keys are uniformly random strings in $\{0,1\}^\lambda$ and is ϵ-secure: any polynomial-time adversary cannot distinguish the encryption of $m_1 \in \{0,1\}^\lambda$ from an encryption of $m_2 \in \{0,1\}^\lambda$ with probability larger than ϵ. The sharing procedure S is described in Fig. 4.

The sharing procedure S**:**

Input: A secret $S \in \{0,1\}^\lambda$.

1. Initialize $\Pi(S,i) = \emptyset$ for every $i \in [n]$.
2. Label the output wire ow with the secret $\ell_{ow} = S$.
3. Repeat the following until all input wires of the circuit are labeled.
   (a) Let g be a gate with k_{in} input wires and (at most) k_{out} output wires. Let $w'_1,\ldots,w'_{k_{\mathsf{out}}}$ be the output wires of g having labels $\ell_{w'_1},\ldots,\ell_{w'_{k_{\mathsf{out}}}}$ and $w_1,\ldots,w_{k_{\mathsf{in}}}$ be the input wires. Associate with g a fresh encryption key $s_g \leftarrow \{0,1\}^\lambda$.
   (b) If $g =$ AND, assign the label of $w_1,\ldots,w_{k_{\mathsf{in}}}$ to be random conditioned on $\ell_{w_1} \oplus \cdots \oplus \ell_{w_{k_{\mathsf{in}}}} = s_g$.
   (c) If $g =$ OR, assign the label of $w_1,\ldots,w_{k_{\mathsf{in}}}$ to be s_g.
   (d) For every $i \in [n]$, add to the share of the ith party an encryption of the labels of the w'_i's under s_g. That is,
   $$\Pi(S,i) = \Pi(S,i) \cup \{(g, \mathsf{Enc}_{s_g}(\ell_{w'_1}),\ldots,\mathsf{Enc}_{s_g}(\ell_{w'_{k_{\mathsf{out}}}}))\}.$$
4. For every input wire w associated with the input variable x_i, add to the share of the ith party the tuple that consists of the name of the wire and its label:
   $$\Pi(S,i) = \Pi(S,i) \cup \{(w, \ell_w)\}.$$
5. Output $\Pi(S,1),\ldots,\Pi(S,n)$.

Fig. 4. Yao's secret sharing scheme (S,R) for an access structure M described by a monotone Boolean circuit.

The reconstruction procedure R of the scheme is essentially applying the reverse operations from the leaves of the circuit to the root. Given the labels of the input wires of an AND gate g, we recover the key associated with g by applying a XOR operation on the labels of the input wires, and then recover the labels of the output wires by decrypting the corresponding ciphertexts. Given the labels of the input wires of an OR gate g, we recover the key associated with g by setting it to be the label of any input wire, and then recover the labels of the output wires by decrypting the corresponding ciphertexts. The label of the output wire of the root gate is the recovered secret.

The scheme is efficient in the sense that the share size of each party is bounded by $k_{\mathsf{out}} \cdot \lambda \cdot s$, where s is the number of gates in the circuit. So, if the circuit is of polynomial-size (in n), then the share size is also polynomial (in n and in the security parameter).

Correctness of the scheme follows by an induction on the depth of the circuit and we omit further details here. Vinod et al. [28] proved that this scheme[12] is selectively secure by a sequence of roughly s hybrid arguments, where s is the

[12] To be more precise, the scheme that Vinod et al. presented and analyzed is slightly different. Specifically, they considered AND and OR gates with fan-out 1 and showed how to separately handle FAN-OUT gates (gates that have fan-in 1 and fan-out 2). Their analysis can be modified to handle our scheme.

number of gates in the circuit representation of M. By the basic random guessing lemma (Lemma 1), this scheme is also adaptively secure but the security loss is exponential in the number of players the adversary requests to see. The later can be exponential in $O(n)$ so for our scheme to be adaptively secure, we need the encryption scheme to be exponentially secure.

Theorem 3 [28]. *Assume that* SKE *is a* ϵ*-secure symmetric-key encryption scheme. Then, for any polynomial-time adversary* A *and any access structure on* n *parties described by a monotone circuit with* s *gates, it holds that*

$$|\Pr[\langle \mathsf{A}, \mathsf{H}_0 \rangle = 1] - \Pr[\langle \mathsf{A}, \mathsf{H}_1 \rangle = 1]| \leq k_{\mathsf{out}} \cdot s \cdot \epsilon,$$

and (using Lemma 1),

$$|\Pr[\langle \mathsf{A}, \mathsf{G}_0 \rangle = 1] - \Pr[\langle \mathsf{A}, \mathsf{G}_1 \rangle = 1]| \leq 2^n \cdot k_{\mathsf{out}} \cdot s \cdot \epsilon,$$

In the following subsection we prove that the scheme is adaptively secure and the security loss is roughly $2^{d \cdot \log s}$, where d and s are the depth and number of gates, respectively, in the circuit representing the access structure.

Theorem 4. *Assume that* SKE *is* ϵ*-secure. Then, for any polynomial-time adversary* A *and any access structure on* n *parties described by a monotone circuit of depth* d *and* s *gates with fan-in* k_{in} *and fan-out* k_{out}*, it holds that*

$$|\Pr[\langle \mathsf{A}, \mathsf{G}_0 \rangle = 1] - \Pr[\langle \mathsf{A}, \mathsf{G}_1 \rangle = 1]| \leq 2^{d \cdot (\log s + \log k_{\mathsf{in}} + 2)} \cdot (2k_{\mathsf{in}})^{2d} \cdot k_{\mathsf{out}} \cdot \epsilon.$$

4.2 Hybrids and Pebbling Configurations

To prove Theorem 4 we rely on the framework introduced in Theorem 2 that we briefly recall here. Our goal is to prove that an adversary cannot distinguish the challengers $\mathsf{G}_{\mathsf{L}} = \mathsf{G}_0$ and $\mathsf{G}_{\mathsf{R}} = \mathsf{G}_1$, corresponding to the adaptive game. We define the selective version of the games $\mathsf{H}_{\mathsf{L}} = \mathsf{SEL}_{2^{[n]}}[\mathsf{G}_{\mathsf{L}}, X]$ and $\mathsf{H}_{\mathsf{R}} = \mathsf{SEL}_{2^{[n]}}[\mathsf{G}_{\mathsf{R}}, X]$, where the adversary has to commit to the whole set of shares it wished to see ahead of time. We construct a sequence of ℓ selective hybrid games $\mathsf{H}_{\mathsf{L}} = \mathsf{H}_0, \mathsf{H}_1, \ldots, \mathsf{H}_{\ell-1}, \mathsf{H}_\ell = \mathsf{H}_{\mathsf{R}}$. For each H_i we define two selective games $\hat{\mathsf{H}}_{i,0}$ and $\hat{\mathsf{H}}_{i,1}$ and show that for every $i \in \{0, \ldots, \ell-1\}$, there exists a mapping h_i such that the games H_{i+b} and $\hat{\mathsf{H}}_{i,b}$ (for $b \in \{0,1\}$) are equivalent up to the encoding of the inputs to the games (given by h_i). Then, we can apply Theorem 2 and obtain our result.

The Fully-Selective Hybrids. The sequence of fully selective hybrids $\mathsf{H}_{\mathsf{L}} = \mathsf{H}_0$, $\mathsf{H}_1, \ldots, \mathsf{H}_{\ell-1}, \mathsf{H}_\ell = \mathsf{H}_{\mathsf{R}}$ is defined such that each experiment is associated with a pebbling configuration. In a pebbling configuration, each gate is either pebbled or unpebbled. A configuration is specified by a compressed string that fully specifies the names of the gates which have a pebble on them (and the rest of the gates implicitly do not). We will define the possible pebbling configurations later but for now let us denote by Q the number of possible pebbling configurations.

We define for every $j \in [Q]$, a hybrid experiment H_j in which the adversary first commits to the set X of parties it wishes to see their shares, and then the challenger executes a *new sharing procedure* S^j that depends on the j-th pebbling configuration. Roughly, this sharing procedure acts exactly as the original sharing procedure S, but whenever it encounters a gate with a pebble it generates bogus ciphertexts rather than the real ones. This sharing procedure is described in Fig. 5.

The sharing procedure S^j:

Input: A secret $S \in \{0,1\}^\lambda$.

1. Initialize $\Pi_i = \emptyset$ for every $i \in [n]$.
2. Label the output wire ow with the secret $\ell_{ow} = S$.
3. Repeat the following until all input wires of the circuit are labeled.
   (a) Let g be a gate with k_{in} input wires and (at most) k_{out} output wires. Let $w'_1, \ldots, w'_{k_{\mathsf{out}}}$ be the output wires of g having labels $\ell_{w'_1}, \ldots, \ell_{w'_{k_{\mathsf{out}}}}$ and $w_1, \ldots, w_{k_{\mathsf{in}}}$ be the input wires. Associate with g a fresh encryption key $s_g \leftarrow \{0,1\}^\lambda$.
   (b) If g = AND, assign the label of $w_1, \ldots, w_{k_{\mathsf{in}}}$ to be random conditioned on $\ell_{w_1} \oplus \cdots \oplus \ell_{w_{k_{\mathsf{in}}}} = s_g$.
   (c) If g = OR, assign the label of $w_1, \ldots, w_{k_{\mathsf{in}}}$ to be s_g.
   (d) If g has no pebble on it: For every $i \in [n]$, add to the share of the ith party an encryption of the labels of the w'_i's under s_g. That is,
   $$\Pi_i = \Pi_i \cup \left(g, \mathsf{Enc}_{s_g}(\ell_{w'_1}), \ldots, \mathsf{Enc}_{s_g}(\ell_{w'_{k_{\mathsf{out}}}})\right).$$
   (e) If g has a pebble on it: Sample fresh random strings $r_1, \ldots, r_{k_{\mathsf{out}}}$ and for every $i \in [n]$, add to the share of the ith party an encryption of r_i and under s_g. That is,
   $$\Pi_i = \Pi_i \cup \{(g, \mathsf{Enc}_{s_g}(r_1), \ldots, \mathsf{Enc}_{s_g}(r_{k_{\mathsf{out}}}))\}.$$
4. For every input wire w associated with the input variable x_i, add to the share of the ith party the tuple that consists of the name of the wire and its label:
   $$\Pi_i = \Pi_i \cup \{(w, \ell_w)\}.$$
5. Output $\Pi_1, \ldots, \Pi_n$.

Fig. 5. The sharing procedure S^j for an access structure M, described by a monotone Boolean circuit, and the j-th pebbling configuration which encodes the color of the pebble on each gates.

Observe that the hybrid that corresponds to the configuration in which all gates are unpebbled is identical to the experiment H_L and the configuration in which there is a pebble only on the root gate corresponds to the experiment H_R.

Pebbling Rules and Strategies. The rules of the pebbling game depend on the subset of parties whose shares the adversary sees. The rules are:

1. Can place or remove a pebble on any AND gate for which (at least) one input wire is either *not* in X or comes out of a gate with a pebble on it.
2. Can place or remove a pebble on any OR gate for which all of the incoming wires are either input wires *not* in X or come out of gates all of which have pebbles on them.

Our goal is to find a sequence of pebbling rules so that starting with the initial configuration (in which there are no pebbles at all) will end up with a pebbling configuration in which only the root has a pebble. Jumping ahead, we would like for the sequence of pebbling rules to have the property that each configuration is as short to describe as possible (i.e., minimize Q). One way to achieve this is to have at any configuration along the way, as few pebbles as possible. An even more succinct representation can be obtained if we allow many pebbles but have a way to succinctly represent their location. This is what we achieve in the following lemma.

Lemma 2. *For every subset of parties X and any monotone circuit of depth d, fan-in k_{in}, and s gates, there exists a sequence of $(2k_{\mathsf{in}})^{2d}$ pebbling rules such that every pebbling configuration can be uniquely described by at most $d \cdot (\log s + \log k_{\mathsf{in}} + 1)$ bits.*

Proof. A pebbling configuration is described by a list of pairs (gate name, counter), where the counter is a number between 1 and k_{in}, and another bit b to specify whether the root gate has a pebble or not. The counter will represent the number of predecessors, ordered from left to right, that have a pebble on them. Any encoding uniquely defines a pebbling configuration (but notice that the converse is not true).

Denote by $T_X(d)$ the number of pebbling rules needed (i.e., the length of the sequence) and by $P_X(d)$ the maximum size of the description of the pebbling configuration during the sequence. The sequence of pebbling rules is defined via a recursive procedure in the depth d. We first pebble each of the k_{in} predecessors of the root *from left to right* and add a pair (root gate, counter) to the configuration. After we finish pebbling each predecessor we increase the counter by 1 to keep track of how many predecessors have been pebbled. To pebble all predecessors we used $k_{\mathsf{in}} \cdot T_X(d-1)$ pebbling rules and the maximal size of a configuration is at most $P_X(d-1) + (\log s + \log k_{\mathsf{in}} + 1)$. The $\log s$ term comes from specifying the name of the root gate, the $\log k_{\mathsf{in}}$ term come from the number of predecessors of the root gate that have a pebble on them, and the single bit is to signal whether the root gate is pebbled or not.

After this recursive pebbling each of the predecessors have a pebble only at their root gate and the root (of the depth d circuit) has no pebble. Now, we need to remove the pebble from the root of every predecessor of the root gate and put a pebble on the root gate. For the latter we apply one pebbling rule and put a pebble on the root gate. To remove the pebbles from the predecessors of the root gate we reverse the recursive pebbling procedure (by "unpebbling" from right to left and updating the counter appropriately), resulting in the application of additional $k_{\mathsf{in}} \cdot T_X(d-1)$ pebbling rules. When we finish unpebbling, since the root has no predecessors with pebbles, we remove from the description of the configuration the pair corresponding to the root gate. Thus, we get that the maximum size of a pebbling configuration at any point in time is

$$P_X(d) \leq P_X(d-1) + (\log s + \log k_{\mathsf{in}} + 1) \Rightarrow P_X(d) \leq d \cdot (\log s + \log k_{\mathsf{in}} + 1).$$

The total number of pebbling rules we apply is

$$T_X(d) \leq 2k_{\mathsf{in}} \cdot T_X(d-1) + 1 \Rightarrow T_X(d) \leq (2k_{\mathsf{in}})^{2d}.$$

This completes the proof of the lemma.

Recall that we denote by Q the number of possible pebbling configurations. Using the pebbling strategy from Lemma 2, we get that

$$Q \leq 2^{d\cdot(\log s + \log k_{\mathsf{in}} + 1)}.$$

The Partially-Selective Hybrids. We define the partially selective hybrids $\hat{\mathsf{H}}_{j,0}$ and $\hat{\mathsf{H}}_{j,1}$ for every H_j and $j \in [Q]$. In both hybrid games $\hat{\mathsf{H}}_{j,0}$ and $\hat{\mathsf{H}}_{j,1}$, the adversary first commits to the *j-th pebbling configuration* and *the next pebbling rule to apply.* Denote by $j' \in [Q]$ the index of the pebbling configuration resulting from applying the next configuration rule to the j-th pebbling configuration. In $\hat{\mathsf{H}}_{j,0}$ the challenger samples the shares from S^j and in $\hat{\mathsf{H}}_{j,1}$ the challenger samples the shares from $\mathsf{S}^{j'}$ (but other than this the games do not change).

Denote by $\mathcal{U}$ the space of messages that the adversary has to commit in the partially selective hybrids $\hat{\mathsf{H}}_{j,b}$. This space includes all tuples of pebbling configurations and an additional valid pebbling rule. First, recall that there are Q possible pebbling configurations. Seocnd, observe that a pebbling rule can be described by a gate name: a pebbling rule is just flipping the color of the pebble on that gate. For a circuit with s gates this requires additional $\log s$ bits. Thus, $\mathcal{U} = \{(i,g) \mid i \in [Q], g \in [s]\}$ and this means that the size of $\mathcal{U}$ is bounded by

$$|\mathcal{U}| \leq Q \cdot s \leq 2^{d\cdot(\log s + \log k_{\mathsf{in}} + 1)} \cdot s.$$

By semantic security of the symmetric-key encryption scheme and the fact that we replace k_{out} ciphertexts with bogus ones, we have that the games $\hat{\mathsf{H}}_{j,0}$ and $\hat{\mathsf{H}}_{j,1}$ are indistinguishable. The proof is by planting the challenge ciphertext as the ciphertext in the gate where the "next pebbling rule" is applied. In $\hat{\mathsf{H}}_{j,0}$ it is a "real" ciphertext while in $\hat{\mathsf{H}}_{j,1}$ it is a bogus one.

Lemma 3. *Assume that* SKE *is* ϵ*-secure. Then, for any polynomial-time adversary* A *and any access structure on* n *parties described by a monotone circuit it holds that*

$$|\Pr[\langle \mathsf{A}, \hat{\mathsf{H}}_{j,0}\rangle = 1] - \Pr[\langle \mathsf{A}, \hat{\mathsf{H}}_{j,1}\rangle = 1]| \leq k_{\mathsf{out}} \cdot \epsilon.$$

Applying Theorem 2 with the fact that $\ell \leq (2k_{\mathsf{in}})^{2d}$ and $|\mathcal{U}| \leq 2^{d\cdot(\log s+\log k_{\mathsf{in}}+1)} \cdot s$, we get that if SKE is ϵ-secure, then for any polynomial-time adversary A and any access structure on n parties described by a monotone circuit of depth d and s gates of fan-in k_{in} and fan-out k_{out}, it holds that

$$\begin{aligned} |\Pr[\langle \mathsf{A}, \mathsf{G}_0\rangle = 1] - \Pr[\langle \mathsf{A}, \mathsf{G}_1\rangle = 1]| &\leq 2^{d\cdot(\log s+\log k_{\mathsf{in}}+1)} \cdot s \cdot (2k_{\mathsf{in}})^{2d} \cdot k_{\mathsf{out}} \cdot \epsilon \\ &\leq 2^{d\cdot(\log s+\log k_{\mathsf{in}}+2)} \cdot (2k_{\mathsf{in}})^{2d} \cdot k_{\mathsf{out}} \cdot \epsilon. \end{aligned}$$

5 Open Problems

In this work we presented a framework for proving adaptive security of various schemes including secret sharing over access structures defined via monotone circuits, generalized selective decryption, constrained PRFs, and Yao's garbled circuits. The most natural future direction is to find more applications where our framework can be used to prove adaptive security with better security loss than using the standard random guessing. Also, improving our results in terms of security loss is an open problem.

In all of our applications of the framework, the security loss of a scheme is captured by the existence of some pebbling strategy. Does there exist a connection in the opposite direction between the security loss of a scheme and possible pebbling strategies? That is, is it possible to use lower bounds for pebbling strategies to show that various security losses are necessary?

Acknowledgments. The fourth author thanks his advisor Moni Naor for asking whether Yao's secret sharing scheme is adaptively secure and for his support.

References

1. Beimel, A.: Secret-sharing schemes: a survey. In: Chee, Y.M., Guo, Z., Ling, S., Shao, F., Tang, Y., Wang, H., Xing, C. (eds.) IWCC 2011. LNCS, vol. 6639, pp. 11–46. Springer, Heidelberg (2011). doi:10.1007/978-3-642-20901-7_2
2. Bellare, M., Hoang, V.T., Rogaway, P.: Adaptively secure garbling with applications to one-time programs and secure outsourcing. In: Wang, X., Sako, K. (eds.) ASIACRYPT 2012. LNCS, vol. 7658, pp. 134–153. Springer, Heidelberg (2012). doi:10.1007/978-3-642-34961-4_10
3. Benaloh, J.C., Leichter, J.: Generalized secret sharing and monotone functions. In: Goldwasser, S. (ed.) CRYPTO 1988. LNCS, vol. 403, pp. 27–35. Springer, New York (1990). doi:10.1007/0-387-34799-2_3
4. Blakley, G.R.: Safeguarding cryptographic keys. In: Proceedings of AFIPS 1979 National Computer Conference, vol. 48, pp. 313–317 (1979)
5. Boneh, D., Waters, B.: Constrained pseudorandom functions and their applications. In: Sako, K., Sarkar, P. (eds.) ASIACRYPT 2013. LNCS, vol. 8270, pp. 280–300. Springer, Heidelberg (2013). doi:10.1007/978-3-642-42045-0_15
6. Boyle, E., Goldwasser, S., Ivan, I.: Functional signatures and pseudorandom functions. In: Krawczyk, H. (ed.) PKC 2014. LNCS, vol. 8383, pp. 501–519. Springer, Heidelberg (2014). doi:10.1007/978-3-642-54631-0_29

7. Canetti, R., Goldreich, O., Goldwasser, S., Micali, S.: Resettable zero-knowledge (extended abstract). In: 32nd ACM STOC, pp. 235–244. ACM Press, May 2000
8. Fuchsbauer, G., Jafargholi, Z., Pietrzak, K.: A quasipolynomial reduction for generalized selective decryption on trees. In: Gennaro, R., Robshaw, M. (eds.) CRYPTO 2015. LNCS, vol. 9215, pp. 601–620. Springer, Heidelberg (2015). doi:10.1007/978-3-662-47989-6_29
9. Fuchsbauer, G., Konstantinov, M., Pietrzak, K., Rao, V.: Adaptive security of constrained PRFs. In: Sarkar, P., Iwata, T. (eds.) ASIACRYPT 2014. LNCS, vol. 8874, pp. 82–101. Springer, Heidelberg (2014). doi:10.1007/978-3-662-45608-8_5
10. Garg, S., Gentry, C., Sahai, A., Waters, B.: Witness encryption and its applications. In: Boneh, D., Roughgarden, T., Feigenbaum, J. (eds.) 45th ACM STOC, pp. 467–476. ACM Press, June 2013
11. Goldreich, O., Goldwasser, S., Micali, S.: On the cryptographic applications of random functions (extended abstract). In: Blakley, G.R., Chaum, D. (eds.) CRYPTO 1984. LNCS, vol. 196, pp. 276–288. Springer, Heidelberg (1985). doi:10.1007/3-540-39568-7_22
12. Hemenway, B., Jafargholi, Z., Ostrovsky, R., Scafuro, A., Wichs, D.: Adaptively secure garbled circuits from one-way functions. In: Robshaw, M., Katz, J. (eds.) CRYPTO 2016, Part III. LNCS, vol. 9816, pp. 149–178. Springer, Heidelberg (2016). doi:10.1007/978-3-662-53015-3_6
13. Hohenberger, S., Sahai, A., Waters, B.: Replacing a random oracle: full domain hash from indistinguishability obfuscation. In: Nguyen, P.Q., Oswald, E. (eds.) EUROCRYPT 2014. LNCS, vol. 8441, pp. 201–220. Springer, Heidelberg (2014). doi:10.1007/978-3-642-55220-5_12
14. Ito, M., Saito, A., Nishizeki, T.: Secret sharing schemes realizing general access structure. In: Proceedings of IEEE Global Telecommunication Conference (Globecom 1987), pp. 99–102 (1987)
15. Jafargholi, Z., Kamath, C., Klein, K., Komargodski, I., Pietrzak, K., Wichs, D.: Be adaptive, avoid overcommitting. Cryptology ePrint Archive, Report 2017/515 (2017). http://eprint.iacr.org/2017/515
16. Jafargholi, Z., Wichs, D.: Adaptive security of Yao's garbled circuits. In: Hirt, M., Smith, A. (eds.) TCC 2016-B. LNCS, vol. 9985, pp. 433–458. Springer, Heidelberg (2016). doi:10.1007/978-3-662-53641-4_17
17. Karchmer, M., Wigderson, A.: Monotone circuits for connectivity require super-logarithmic depth. In: 20th ACM STOC, pp. 539–550. ACM Press, May 1988
18. Karchmer, M., Wigderson, A.: On span programs. In: Proceedings of Structures in Complexity Theory, pp. 102–111 (1993)
19. Kiayias, A., Papadopoulos, S., Triandopoulos, N., Zacharias, T.: Delegatable pseudorandom functions and applications. In: Sadeghi, A.R., Gligor, V.D., Yung, M. (eds.) ACM CCS 2013, pp. 669–684. ACM Press, November 2013
20. Komargodski, I., Moran, T., Naor, M., Pass, R., Rosen, A., Yogev, E.: One-way functions and (im)perfect obfuscation. In: 55th FOCS, pp. 374–383. IEEE Computer Society Press, October 2014
21. Komargodski, I., Naor, M., Yogev, E.: Secret-sharing for NP. J. Cryptol. **30**(2), 444–469 (2017). http://dx.doi.org/10.1007/s00145-015-9226-0
22. Lindell, Y., Pinkas, B.: A proof of security of Yao's protocol for two-party computation. J. Cryptol. **22**(2), 161–188 (2009)
23. Panjwani, S.: Tackling adaptive corruptions in multicast encryption protocols. In: Vadhan, S.P. (ed.) TCC 2007. LNCS, vol. 4392, pp. 21–40. Springer, Heidelberg (2007). doi:10.1007/978-3-540-70936-7_2

24. Robere, R., Pitassi, T., Rossman, B., Cook, S.A.: Exponential lower bounds for monotone span programs. In: 57th FOCS, pp. 406–415. IEEE Computer Society Press (2016)
25. Rogaway, P., Bellare, M.: Robust computational secret sharing and a unified account of classical secret-sharing goals. In: Ning, P., di Vimercati, S.D.C., Syverson, P.F. (eds.) ACM CCS 2007, pp. 172–184. ACM Press, October 2007
26. Sahai, A., Waters, B.: How to use indistinguishability obfuscation: deniable encryption, and more. In: Shmoys, D.B. (ed.) 46th ACM STOC, pp. 475–484. ACM Press, May/Jun 2014
27. Shamir, A.: How to share a secret. Commun. ACM **22**(11), 612–613 (1979)
28. Vinod, V., Narayanan, A., Srinathan, K., Rangan, C.P., Kim, K.: On the power of computational secret sharing. In: Johansson, T., Maitra, S. (eds.) INDOCRYPT 2003. LNCS, vol. 2904, pp. 162–176. Springer, Heidelberg (2003). doi:10.1007/978-3-540-24582-7_12
29. Yao, A.C.C.: Protocols for secure computations (extended abstract). In: 23rd FOCS, pp. 160–164. IEEE Computer Society Press, November 1982
30. Yao, A.C.C.: How to generate and exchange secrets (extended abstract). In: 27th FOCS, pp. 162–167. IEEE Computer Society Press, October 1986

Two-Party Computation

The TinyTable Protocol for 2-Party Secure Computation, or: Gate-Scrambling Revisited

Ivan Damgård[1(✉)], Jesper Buus Nielsen[1], Michael Nielsen[1], and Samuel Ranellucci[2,3]

[1] Department of Computer Science, Aarhus University, Aarhus, Denmark
ivan@cs.au.dk
[2] George Mason University, Fairfax, USA
[3] University of Maryland, College Park, USA

Abstract. We propose a new protocol, nicknamed TinyTable, for maliciously secure 2-party computation in the preprocessing model. One version of the protocol is useful in practice and allows, for instance, secure AES encryption with latency about 1 ms and amortized time about 0.5 μs per AES block on a fast cloud set-up. Another version is interesting from a theoretical point of view: we achieve a maliciously and unconditionally secure 2-party protocol in the preprocessing model for computing a Boolean circuit, where both the communication complexity and preprocessed data size needed is $O(s)$ where s is the circuit size, while the computational complexity is $O(k^{\epsilon}s)$ where k is the statistical security parameter and $\epsilon < 1$ is a constant. For general circuits with no assumption on their structure, this is the best asymptotic performance achieved so far in this model.

1 Introduction

In 2-party secure computation, two parties A and B want to compute an agreed function securely on privately held inputs, and we want to construct protocols ensuring that the only new information a party learns is the intended output.

In this paper we will focus on malicious security: one of the parties is under control of an adversary and may behave arbitrarily. As is well known, this means that we cannot guarantee that the protocol always gives output to the honest party, but we can make sure that the output, if delivered, is correct. It is also well known that we cannot accomplish this task without using a computational assumption, and in fact heavy public-key machinery must be used to some extent.

However, as observed in several works [BDOZ11, DPSZ12, NNOB12, DZ13], one can confine the use of cryptography to a preprocessing phase where the inputs need not be known and can therefore be done at any time prior to the actual computation. The preprocessing produces "raw material" for the on-line phase which is executed once the inputs are known, and this phase can be information theoretically secure, and usually has very small computational and communication complexity, but round complexity proportional to the depth of the computation in question. An alternative (which is not our focus here) is to use

J. Katz and H. Shacham (Eds.): CRYPTO 2017, Part I, LNCS 10401, pp. 167–187, 2017.
DOI: 10.1007/978-3-319-63688-7_6

Yao-garbled circuits. This approach is incomparable even in the case we consider here where the function to compute is known in advance. This is because malicious security requires many garbled circuit to be stored and evaluated in the on-line phase. Hence, the round and communication complexity is smaller than for information theoretic protocols, but the storage and computational complexity is larger.

We will focus on the case where the desired computation is specified as a Boolean circuit. The case of arithmetic circuits over large fields was handled in [DPSZ12] which gave a solution where communication and computational complexities as well as the size of the preprocessed data (called data complexity in the following) are proportional to the circuit size. The requirement is that the field has $2^{\Omega(k)}$ elements where k is the security parameter and the allowed error probability is $2^{-\Omega(k)}$.

On the other hand, for Boolean circuits, state of the art is the protocol from [DZ13], nick-named MiniMac which achieves data and communication complexity $O(s)$ where s is the circuit size, and computational complexity $O(k^{\epsilon} s)$, where $\epsilon < 1$ is a constant. For an alternative variant of the protocol, all complexities are $O(\text{polylog}(k)s)$. However, the construction only works for circuits with a sufficiently nice structure, called "well formed" circuits in [DZ13]. Informally, a well-formed circuit allows a modest amount of parallelization throughout the computation – for instance, very tall and skinny circuits are not allowed. If well-formedness is not assumed, both complexities would be $\Omega(ks)$ using known protocols.

On the practical side, many of the protocols in the preprocessing model are potentially practical and several of them have been implemented. In particular, implementations of the MiniMac protocol were reported in [DLT14, DZ16]. In [DLT14], MiniMac was optimised and used for computing many instances of the same Boolean circuit in parallel, while in [DZ16] the protocol was adapted specifically for computing the AES circuit, which resulted in an implementation with latency about 6 ms and an amortised time of 0,4 ms per AES block.

Our Contribution. In this paper, we introduce a new protocol for the preprocessing model, nick-named TinyTable. The idea is to implement each (non-linear) gate by a scrambled version of its truthtable. Players will do look-ups in the tables using bits that are masked by uniformly random bits chosen in the preprocessing phase, together with the tables.

The idea of gate-scrambling goes back at least to [CDvdG87] where a (much less efficient) approach based on the quadratic residuosity problem was proposed. Scrambled truth tables also appear more recently in [IKM+13], but here the truthtable for the entire function is scrambled, leading to a protocol with complexity exponential in the length of the inputs (but very small communication). Even more recently, in [DZ16], a (different form of) table look-up was used to implement the AES S-boxes.

What we do here is to observe that the idea of scrambled truth tables makes especially good sense in the preprocessing model and, more importantly, if we combine this with the "right" authentication scheme, we get an extremely practical and maliciously secure protocol. This first version of our protocol has communication complexity $O(s)$ and data and computational complexity $O(ks)$. Although the computational complexity is asymptotically inferior to previous protocols when counting elementary bit operations, it works much better in practice: XOR and NOT gates require no communication, and for each non-linear gate, each player sends and receives 1 bit and XORs 1 word from memory into a register. This means that TinyTable saves a factor of at least 2 in communication in comparison to standard *passively* secure protocols in the preprocessing model, such as GMW with precomputed OT's or the protocol using circuit randomization via Beaver-triples.

We implemented a version of this protocol that was optimised for AES computation, by using tables for each S-box. This is more costly in preprocessing but, compared to a Boolean circuit implementation, it reduces the round complexity of the on-line phase significantly (to about 10). On a fast cloud set-up, we obtain on-line latency of 1 ms and amortized time about 0.5 µs per AES block for an error probability of 2^{-64}. To the best of our knowledge, this is the fastest on-line time obtained for secure two-party AES with malicious security. To illustrate what we gain from the AES specific approach, we also implemented the version that works for any Boolean circuit and applied it to an AES circuit computing the same function as the optimized protocol does. On the same cloud set-up and same security level, we obtained a latency of 2.4 ms and amortized time about 10 µs per AES block.

We describe how one can do the preprocessing we require based on the preprocessing phase of the TinyOT protocol from [NNOB12]. This protocol is basically maliciously secure OT extension with some extra processing on top. In the case of Boolean circuits, the work needed to preprocess an AND gate roughly equals the work we would need per AND gate in TinyOT. For the case of AES S-box tables, we show how to use a method from [DK10] to preprocess such tables. This requires 7 *binary* multiplications per table entry and local computation.

As for the speeds of preprocessing one can obtain, the best approaches and implementations of this type of protocol are from [FKOS15]. They do not have an implementation of the exact case we need here (2-party TinyOT) but they estimate that one can obtain certainly more than 10.000 AND gates per second and most likely up to 100.000 per second [Kel]. This would mean that we could preprocess a binary AES circuits in about 40 ms.

Our final contribution is a version of our protocol that has better asymptotic performance. We get data and communication complexity $O(s)$, and computational complexity $O(k^{\epsilon}s)$, where $\epsilon < 1$ is a constant. Alternatively we can also have all complexities be $O(\text{polylog}(k)s)$. While this is the same result that was obtained for the MiniMac protocol, note that we get this for *any* circuit, not just for well-formed ones. Roughly speaking, the idea is to use the MiniMac protocol to authenticate the bits that players send during the on-line phase. This task is very simple: it parallelizes easily and can be done in constant depth. Therefore we get a better result than if we had used MiniMac directly on the circuit in question.

2 Construction

We show a 2PC protocol for securely computing a Boolean circuit C for two players A and B. The circuit may contain arbitrary gates taking two inputs and giving one output. We let $G_1, \ldots, G_N$ be the gates of the circuit, and let $w_1, \ldots, w_W$ be the wires. We note that arbitrary fan-out is allowed, and we do not assume special fan-out gates for this, we simply allow that an arbitrary number of copies of a wire leave a gate, and all these copies are assigned the same wire index. We assume for simplicity that both parties are to learn the output.

We will fix some arbitrary order in which the circuit can be evaluated gate by gate, such that the output gates come last, and such that when we are about to evaluate gate i, its inputs have already been computed. We assume throughout that the indexing of the gates satisfy this constraint. We call the wires coming out of the output gates the *output wires*.

We first specify a functionality for preparing preprocessing material that will allow computation of the circuit with semi-honest security, see Fig. 1[1].

The idea behind the construction of the tables is that when the time comes to compute gate G_i, both players will know "encrypted bits" $e_u = b_u \oplus r_u$ and $e_v = b_v \oplus r_v$, for the input wires, where b_u, b_v are the actual "cleartext" bits going into G_i, and r_u, r_v are random masking bits that are chosen in the preprocessing. In addition, the preprocessing sets up two tables A_i, B_i for each gate, one held by A and one held by B. These tables are used to get hold of a similar encrypted bit for the output wire: $e_o = b_o \oplus r_o$, where $b_o = G_i(b_u, b_v)$. This works because the tables are set up such that $A_i[e_u, e_v], B_i[e_u, e_v]$ is an additive sharing of $b_o \oplus r_o$, i.e.,

$$A_i[b_u \oplus r_u, b_v \oplus r_v] \oplus B_i[b_u \oplus r_u, b_v \oplus r_v] = b_o \oplus r_o \ .$$

These considerations lead naturally to the protocol for computing C securely shown in Fig. 2. For the security of this construction, note that since the masking bits for the wires are uniformly random, each bit e_u is random as well (except when w_u is an output wire), and so the positions in which we look up in the tables are also random. With these observations, it is easy to see that we have:

Proposition 1. *F_{sem}^{pre} composed with π_{sem} implements (with perfect semi-honest security) the ideal functionality F_{SFE} for secure function evaluation.*

[1] For this functionality as well as for the other preprocessing functionalities we define, whenever players are to receive shares of a secret value, the functionality lets the adversary choose shares for the corrupt player. This is a standard trick to make sure that the functionality is easier to implement: the simulator can simply run a fake instance of the protocol with the adversary and give to the functionality the shares that the corrupt player gets out of this. If we had let the functionality make all the choices, the simulator would have to force the protocol into producing the shares that the functionality wants. This weaker functionality is still useful: as long as the shared secret is safe, we don't care which shares the corrupt player gets.

Preprocessing Functionality F_{sem}^{pre}.

1. On input C from both players, do the following: For each wire w_u, choose a random masking bit r_u. This bit will be used to mask the bit b_u that will actually be on w_u when we do the computation, i.e., $e_u = b_u \oplus r_u$ will become known to the players. If w_u is an input wire, give r_u to the player who owns w_u.
2. For each gate G_i, with input wires w_u, w_v and output wire w_o, we will construct two tables A_i, B_i each with 4 entries, indexed by bits (c, d). This is done as follows: for each of the 4 possible values of bits (c, d), do:
   (a) If both player are honest, choose a random bit $s_{c,d}$. Otherwise take $s_{c,d}$ as input from the adversary. Let $G_i(\cdot, \cdot)$ denotes the function computed by gate G_i.
   (b) If both parties are honest, or if A is corrupt, set $A_i[c, d] = s_{c,d}$ and $B_i[c, d] = s_{c,d} \oplus (r_o \oplus G_i(c \oplus r_u, d \oplus r_v))$.
   (c) If B is corrupt, set $B_i[c, d] = s_{c,d}$ and $A_i[c, d] = s_{c,d} \oplus (r_o \oplus G_i(c \oplus r_u, d \oplus r_v))$.
3. For each gate G_i, hand A_i to player A and B_i to player B. For each output wire w_u, send r_u to both players.

Fig. 1. Functionality for preprocessing, semi-honest security.

Protocol π_{sem}.

1. A and B send C as input to F and get a set of tables $\{A_i, B_i | \; i = 1 \ldots N\}$, as well as a bit b_u for each input wire w_u.
2. For each input wire w_u, if A holds input x_u for this wire, send $e_u = x_u \oplus b_u$ to B. If B holds input x_u, send $e_u = x_u \oplus b_u$ to A.
3. For $i = 1$ to N, do: Let G_i have input wires w_u, w_v and output wire w_o (so that e_u, e_v have been computed). A sends $A_i[e_u, e_v]$ to B, and B sends $B_i[e_u, e_v]$ to A. Set $e_o = A_i[e_u, e_v] \oplus B_i[e_u, e_v]$.
4. The parties output the bits $\{e_o \oplus r_o | \; w_o \text{ is an output wire}\}$.

Fig. 2. Protocol for semi-honest security.

Here, F_{SFE} is a standard functionality that accepts C as input from both parties, then gets x from A, y from B and finally outputs $C(x, y)$ to both parties, in case of semi-honest corruption. In case of malicious corruption, it will send the output to the corrupted party and let the adversary decide whether to abort or not. Only in the latter case will it send the output to the honest party. We assume that the communication is not secret, even when both players are honest, so the protocol does not have to keep the output secret in this case. We give a precise specification in Fig. 4.

It is also very natural that we can get malicious security if we assume instead a functionality that commits A and B to the tables. We can get this effect by letting the functionality also store the tables and outputting bits from them to the other party on request. In other words, what we need is a functionality that

Functionality F^{pre}_{mal}.

1. On input C from both players, execute the same algorithm as F^{pre}_{sem} would on input C.
2. In addition, for $i = 1, \ldots, N$ and for all 4 values of (c, d), do:
   If both players are honest, select random k-bit strings $a^0_{i,c,d}, a^1_{i,c,d}, b^0_{i,c,d}, b^1_{i,c,d}$.
   If player A is corrupt, take $b^0_{i,c,d}, b^1_{i,c,d}$ as input from the adversary and choose $a^0_{i,c,d}, a^1_{i,c,d}$ at random.
   If player B is corrupt, take $a^0_{i,c,d}, a^1_{i,c,d}$ as input from from the adversary and choose $b^0_{i,c,d}, b^1_{i,c,d}$ at random.
3. Hand $a^0_{i,c,d}, a^1_{i,c,d}$ to B and $b^0_{i,c,d}, b^1_{i,c,d}$ to A.
   Hand $a^{A_i[c,d]}_{i,c,d}$ to A, and $b^{B_i[c,d]}_{i,c,d}$ to B.

Fig. 3. Preprocessing functionality, malicious security.

Functionality F_{SFE}.

1. On input C from both players, and inputs strings x_A from A and x_B from B compute the output string $y = C(x_A, x_B)$. If both players are honest, send y to both players and the adversary.
2. On input "compute function" from the adversary, send y to the adversary.
3. On input "deliver output" from the adversary, send y to the honest player.
4. If a player is corrupted and at any point, the adversary sends "abort", stop.

Fig. 4. Secure function evaluation functionality, malicious security.

allows us to commit players to correlated bit strings such that they can later open a subset of the bits. Note that the subset cannot be known in advance, which makes it more difficult to implement efficiently. Indeed, if we go for the simplest information theoretically secure solution in the preprocessing model, the storage requirement will be $O(\ell k)$ bits where ℓ is the string length and k is the security parameter. This is achieved, essentially by committing to each bit individually, we give more details on this below. In contrast, if we just need to open the entire string or nothing, $O(\ell + k)$ bits is sufficient using standard techniques. However, this difference is not inherent: as we discuss in more detail in Sect. 6, one can in fact achieve both storage and communication complexity $O(\ell + k)$ bits also for opening a subset that is unknown a priori. On the other hand, the simple bit-by-bit solution works better in practice.

In Fig. 3, we show a functionality that does preprocessing as in the semi-honest case, but in addition commits players bit by bit to the content of the tables. The idea is that, for entry $A_i[c, d]$ in a table, A is also given a random string $a^{A_i[c,d]}_{i,c,d}$ which serves as an authentication code that A can use to show that he sends the correct value of $A_i[c, d]$, while B is given the pair $a^0_{i,c,d}, a^1_{i,c,d}$ serving as a key that B can use to verify that he gets the correct value. Of course, using the authentication codes directly in this way, we would have to

Protocol π_{mal}.

1. A and B send C as input to F^{pre}_{mal} and get a set of tables $\{A_i, B_i | \ i = 1 \dots N\}$, as well as masking bits for input and output wires. In addition, for all values of (i, c, d), A receives strings $b^0_{i,c,d}, b^1_{i,c,d}$ and $a^{A_i[c,d]}_{i,c,d}$. These are stored for later. (Symmetrically, B gets and stores a corresponding set of strings.)
2. Initialize variables: A sets $m_A = t_A = 0^k$, and B sets $m_B = t_B = 0^k$. Here m_A is an accumulative MAC on the values that A sends and t_B is a value held by B that should equal m_A if A was honest. A symmetric condition applies to m_B and t_A.
3. For each input wire w_u, if A holds input x_u for this wire, send $e_u = x_u \oplus b_u$ to B. If B holds input x_u, send $e_u = x_u \oplus b_u$ to A.
4. Define M such that the last $N - M$ gates are output gates. For $i = 1$ to M do:
   (a) Let G_i have input wires w_u, w_v and output wire w_o (so that e_u, e_v have been computed).
   (b) A sends $e_A = A_i[e_u, e_v]$ to B, and sets $m_A = m_A \oplus a^{e_A}_{i,e_u,e_v}$. B sets $t_B = t_B \oplus a^{e_A}_{i,e_u,e_v}$. Note that B can do this, as he has both strings $a^0_{i,e_u,e_v}, a^1_{i,e_u,e_v}$.
   (c) B sends $e_B = B_i[e_u, e_v]$ to A, and sets $m_B = m_B \oplus b^{e_B}_{i,e_u,e_v}$. A sets $t_A = t_A \oplus b^{e_B}_{i,e_u,e_v}$.
   (d) Both parties set $e_o = e_A \oplus e_B$.

   Check if all bits opened until now were correct: A sends m_A to B and B sends m_B to A. A verify that $t_A = m_B$ and B verify that $t_B = m_A$. The parties abort if this is not the case.
6. Reveal the outputs. For $i = M + 1$ to N do:
   (a) Let G_i have input wires w_u, w_v and output wire w_o (so that e_u, e_v have been computed).
   (b) A sends $e_A = A_i[e_u, e_v]$ and $a^{e_A}_{i,e_u,e_v}$ to B. B checks that $a^{e_A}_{i,e_u,e_v}$ is correct. Note that B can do this, as he has both strings $a^0_{i,e_u,e_v}, a^1_{i,e_u,e_v}$.
   (c) B sends $e_B = B_i[e_u, e_v]$ and $b^{e_B}_{i,e_u,e_v}$ to A. A checks that $b^{e_B}_{i,e_u,e_v}$ is correct.
   (d) Both parties set $e_o = e_A \oplus e_B$.

   If there are many outputs, the correctness of the sent information can be checked via an accumulative MAC as in Step 3
7. The parties output the bits $\{e_o \oplus r_o | \ w_o$ is an output wire$\}$.

Fig. 5. Protocol for malicious security.

send k bits to open each bit. However, in our application, we can bring down the communication needed to (essentially) $\ell + k$ bits, because we can delay verification of most of the bits opened. The idea is that, instead of sending the authentication codes, players will accumulate the XOR of all of them and check for equality later at the end. The protocol shown in Fig. 5 uses this idea to implement maliciously secure computation.

Theorem 1. *F^{pre}_{mal} composed with π_{mal} implements F_{SFE} with statistical security against malicious and static corruption.*

Proof. We will show security in the UC model (in the variant where the environment also plays the role of the adversary), which means we need to exhibit a simulator S such that no (unbounded) environment Z can distinguish F_{mal}^{pre} composed with π_{mal} from S composed with F_{SFE}. The case where no player is corrupt is trivial to simulate since messages sent contain uniformly random bits, with the only exception of the output stage where the shares sent determine the outputs - which the simulator knows, and hence these shares are also easy to simulate. We now describe the simulation for the case where A is corrupt (the other case where B is corrupt is similar).

Set-up. S runs internally copies of F_{mal}^{pre} and π_{mal} where it corrupts A, and gives B a default input, say all zeros. It will let Z play the role of the corrupt A. We assume that both players send the same circuit C to be computed (otherwise there is nothing to simulate) and S will send C to F_{SFE}.

Input. In the input stage of the protocol, when Z (corrupt A) sends e_u for an input wire, S computes $b_u = e_u \oplus r_u$ and sends it to F_{SFE}. This is the extracted input of A for this wire, note that S knows r_u from (its copy of) F_{mal}^{pre}.

Computing stage. For the first M gates, S will simply let its copy of B run the protocol with Z acting as corrupt A. If B aborts, S sends "abort" to F_{SFE} and stops, otherwise it sends "compute result".

Output stage. S gets the outputs from F_{SFE}, i.e., b_o for each output wire w_o. S modifies the table inside its copy of B such that for each output gate G_i with input wires w_u, w_v and output w_o, $B_i[e_u, e_v]$ satisfies $b_o = r_o \oplus A_i[e_u, e_v] \oplus B_i[e_u, e_v]$. Note that S knows r_o and $A_i[e_u, e_v]$ from its copy of F_{mal}^{pre}. S now runs the output stage according to the protocol. If Z lets the protocol finish normally, S sends "deliver output" to F_{SFE}, otherwise it sends "abort".

To show that this simulation is statistically good, observe first that the simulation up until the point where the outputs are opened is perfect: this follows since in the computation phase of the protocol, the honest player sends only uniformly random bits that are independent of anything else in the environment's view. Therefore this also holds for the simulated honest player, even if he runs with a default input. The reason why only random bits are sent is as follows: whenever the honest player sends a bit, it can be assigned to a particular wire, say w_v that has not been handled before. Therefore no information about the wire mask r_v was released before. The bit sent by the honest player can be written as r_v xored with other bits and since r_v was chosen independently of anything else, the bit sent is also random in the adversary's view.

In the verification step (last part of Item 4 of the protocol), the honest player sends the correct verification value m_B that can be computed from what the environment has already seen. The correct verification value $m_A = t_B$ to be sent by A is well defined (it can be computed easily from the view of the environment), and if the value actually sent is incorrect, the protocol will abort in both the real and the simulated process.

Now, if the protocol proceeds to the output step, the only new information the environment sees is, for each output gate G_i with input wires w_u, w_v and output w_o: the output b_o as well as B's share $e_B = B_i[e_u, e_v]$ and the verification value $b_{i,e_u,e_v}^{e_B}$. Note the latter two values are determined from b_o and the environment's view so far: e_B is determined by $b_o = e_A \oplus e_B$ and then $b^{e_B}_{i,e_u,e_v}$ is determined by what A received from the preprocessing initially. It follows that the entire simulation is perfect given the event that the output generated is the same in the real as in the simulated process.

Now, in the simulation the output is always the correct output based on the inputs determined in the input stage. Therefore, to argue statistically close simulation, it is sufficient to show that the real protocol completes with incorrect output except with probability 2^{-k}. This in turn follows easily from the fact that if A always sends correct shares from the tables, the output is always correct. And if he does not, the verification value corresponding to the incorrect message is completely unknown to A and can be guessed with probability at best 2^{-k}. Hence B will abort in any such case, except with probability 2^{-k}.

This theorem can quite easily be extended to adaptive corruption (of one player). For this case, the simulator would start running internally a copy of the protocol where A, B are honest and use default inputs. When A (or B) will be corrupted, one observes that the internal view of A can easily be modified so it is consistent with the real input of A (which the simulator is now given). The simulator gives this modified view of A to the environment and continues as described in the proof of the above theorem.

2.1 Free XOR

It is easy to modify our construction to allow non-interactive processing of XOR gates. For simplicity, we only show how this works for the case of semi-honest security, malicious security is obtained in exactly the same way as in the previous section (Fig. 6).

The idea is to select the wire masks in a different way, exploiting the homomorphic properties of XOR gates. Basically, if we encounter a NOT gate, we make sure the output wire mask is equal the input wire mask. For XOR gates we set the output wire mask to the XOR of the input wires masks. We ensure this invariant by traversing the circuit, since the wire masks can no longer be sampled independently at random. One could set the output wire mask to zero for all output gates and traverse the gates backwards $G_N, \ldots, G_1$ ensuring the invariant on the wire masks. Another approach, which is the one we use in the following, is to traverse the gates forwardly $G_1, \ldots, G_N$ ensuring the invariants and then give output wire masks to the parties, who will then remove the mask before returning the actual output. In the online phase, we can now process XOR and NOT gates locally by computing the respective function directly on masked values. The resulting protocol is shown in Fig. 7.

2.2 Removing NOT-Gates

A slight change in the preprocessing allows us to completely remove the on-line operations associated with NOT gates. Namely, when preprocessing a NOT gate G_i, we will set $r_o = 1 - r_v$, where w_u, w_o are the input and output wires, anything else remains unchanged. Then, in the on-line phase, we can simply ignore the NOT gates, or in other words, by convention we will set $e_o = e_u$.

Preprocessing Functionality $F^{pre}_{freeXOR,sem}$.

1. On input C from both players, for each input wire w_u, choose a random bit r_u, and if w_u is an input wire, give r_u to the player who owns that wire.
For $i = 1$ to N, do: Let w_u, w_v be the input wires of G_i and w_o the output wire. Note that we have already chosen masking bits r_u, r_v for w_u, w_v. If G_i is an XOR gate, set $r_o = r_u \oplus r_v$. If G_i is a NOT gate (so that w_u is the only input wire), set $r_o = r_u$ If G_i is any other gate, choose r_o at random.
2. For each gate G_i which is not an XOR or NOT gate, with input wires w_u, w_v and output wire w_o, we will construct two tables A_i, B_i each with 4 entries, indexed by bits (c, d). This is done as follows: for each of the 4 possible values of bits (c, d), do:
   (a) If both player are honest, choose a random bit $s_{c,d}$. Otherwise take $s_{c,d}$ as input from the adversary. Let $G_i(\cdot, \cdot)$ denote the function computed by gate G_i.
   (b) If both parties are honest, or if A is corrupt, set
   $A_i[c, d] = s_{c,d}$ and $B_i[c, d] = s_{c,d} \oplus (r_o \oplus G_i(c \oplus r_u, d \oplus r_v))$.
   (c) If B is corrupt, set
   $B_i[c, d] = s_{c,d}$ and $A_i[c, d] = s_{c,d} \oplus (r_o \oplus G_i(c \oplus r_u, d \oplus r_v))$.
3. For each gate G_i, where we built tables, hand A_i to player A and B_i to player B. Send wire masks for the output wires to both players.

Fig. 6. Functionality for preprocessing, semi-honest security with free XOR.

Protocol π_{sem}.

1. A and B send C as input to F and get a set of tables $\{A_i, B_i |\ i = 1 \ldots N\}$, as well as a bit b_u for each input wire w_u.
2. For each input wire w_u, if A holds input x_u for this wire, send $e_u = x_u \oplus b_u$ to B. If B holds input x_u, send $e_u = x_u \oplus b_u$ to A.
3. For $i = 1$ to N, do: Let G_i have input wires w_u, w_v and output wire w_o (so that e_u, e_v have been computed). If G_i is an XOR gate, set $e_o = e_u \oplus e_v$. If G_i is a NOT gate (so that w_u is the only input wire), set $e_o = 1 - e_u$. Otherwise (we have tables for this gate): A sends $A_i[e_u, e_v]$ to B, and B sends $B_i[e_u, e_v]$ to A. Both set $e_o = A_i[e_u, e_v] \oplus B_i[e_u, e_v]$.
4. The parties output the bits $\{e_o \oplus r_o |\ w_o \text{ is an output wire}\}$.

Fig. 7. Protocol for semi-honest security, free XOR.

2.3 Generalisation to Bigger Tables

If the circuit contains a part that evaluates a non-linear function f on a small input, it is natural to implement computation of this function as a table. If the input is small, such a table is not prohibitively large. Suppose, for instance, that the input and output is 8 bits, as is the case for the AES S-Box. Then we will store tables A_f, B_f each indexed by 8-bit value M such that $A_f[M] \oplus B_f[M] = f(x \oplus M) \oplus O$, where O is an 8-bit output mask chosen in the preprocessing. We make sure in the preprocessing that the i'th bit of B denoted $B[i]$ equals the wire mask for the i'th wire going into the evaluation of f, whereas $O[i]$ equals the wire mask for the i'th wire receiving output from f. We can then use the table for f exactly as we use the tables for the AND gates.

To get malicious security we must note that the simple authentication scheme we used in the binary case will be less practical here: as we have 256 possible output values, each party would need to store 256 strings per table entry. It turns out this can be optimized considerably using a different MAC scheme, as described in the following section.

3 The Linear MAC Scheme

In this section, we describe some variations over a well-known information theoretically secure MAC scheme that can be found, e.g., in [NNOB12]. We optimise it to be efficient on modern Intel processors, this requires some changes in the construction and hence we need to specify and reprove the scheme. It is intended to be used in conjunction with the generalisation to bigger tables described in the previous section.

There is a committer C, a verifier V and a preprocessor P. There is a security parameter k. Some of the computations are done over the finite field $\mathbb{F} = \mathrm{GF}(2^k)$. Let $p(\mathtt{X})$ be the irreducible polynomial of degree k used to do the computation in $\mathbb{F} = \mathrm{GF}(2^k)$, i.e., elements $x, y \in \mathbb{F}$ are polynomials of degree at most $k-1$ and multiplication is computed as $z = xy \bmod p$. We will also be doing computations in the finite field $\mathbb{G} = \mathrm{GF}(2^{2k-1})$. Let $q(\mathtt{X})$ be the irreducible polynomial of degree $2k-1$ used to do the computation in $\mathbb{G}$. Notice that elements $x, y \in \mathbb{F}$ are polynomials of degree at most $k-1$, so xy is a polynomial of degree at most $2k-2$. We can therefore think of xy as an element of $\mathbb{G}$. Note in particular that $xy \bmod q = xy$ when $x, y \in \mathbb{F}$.

3.1 Basic Version

The MAC scheme has message space $\mathbb{F}$. We denote a generic message by $x \in \mathbb{F}$. The MAC scheme has key space $\mathbb{F} \times \mathbb{G}$. We denote a generic key by $K = (\alpha, \beta) \in \mathbb{F} \times \mathbb{G}$. The tag space is $\mathbb{G}$. We denote a generic tag by $y \in \mathbb{G}$. The tag is computed as $y = \mathrm{mac}_K(x) = \alpha x + \beta$. Note that $\alpha \in \mathbb{F}$ and $x \in \mathbb{F}$, so $\alpha x \in \mathbb{G}$ as described above and hence can be added to β in $\mathbb{G}$. We use this particular scheme because it can be computed very efficiently using the `PCLMULQDQ` instruction on modern Intel processors. With one `PCLMULQDQ` instruction we can compute αx from which we can compute $\alpha x + \beta$ using one additional XOR.

The intended use of the MAC scheme is as follows. The preprocessor samples a message x and a uniformly random key K and computes $y = \mathrm{mac}_K(x)$. It gives K to V and gives (x, y) to C. To reveal the message C sends (x, y) to V who accepts if and only if $y = \mathrm{mac}_K(x)$. Since K is sampled independently of x, the scheme is clearly hiding in the sense that V gets no information on x before receiving the opening information. We now show that the scheme is binding.

Let $\mathcal{A}$ be an unbounded adversary. Run $\mathcal{A}$ to get a message $x \in \mathbb{F}$. Sample a uniformly random key $(\alpha, \beta) \in \mathbb{F} \times \mathbb{G}$ and compute $y = \alpha x + \beta$. Given y to $\mathcal{A}$. Run $\mathcal{A}$ to get an output $(y', x') \in \mathbb{G} \times \mathbb{F}$. We say that $\mathcal{A}$ wins if $x' \neq x$ and $y' = \text{mac}_K(x')$. We can show that no $\mathcal{A}$ wins with probability better than 2^{-k}. To see this, notice that if $\mathcal{A}$ wins then he knows x, y, x', y' such that $y = \alpha x + \beta$ and $y' = \alpha x' + \beta$. This implies that $y' - y = \alpha(x' - x)$, from which it follows that $\alpha = (y' - y)(x' - x)^{-1}$. This means that if $\mathcal{A}$ can win with probability r then $\mathcal{A}$ can guess α with probability at least r. It is then sufficient to prove that no adversary can guess α with probability better than 2^{-k}. This follows from the fact that α is uniformly random given $\alpha x + \beta$, because αx is some element of $\mathbb{G}$ and β is a uniformly random element of $\mathbb{G}$ independent of αx.

3.2 The Homomorphic Vector Version

We now describe a vector version of the scheme which allows to commit to multiple message using a single key.

The MAC scheme has message space $\mathbb{F}^\ell$. We denote a generic message by $\boldsymbol{x} \in \mathbb{F}^\ell$. The MAC scheme has key space $\mathbb{F} \times \mathbb{G}^\ell$. We denote a generic key by $K = (\alpha, \boldsymbol{\beta}) \in \mathbb{F} \times \mathbb{G}^\ell$. The tag space is $\mathbb{G}^\ell$. We denote a generic tag by $\boldsymbol{y} \in \mathbb{G}^\ell$. The tag is computed as $\boldsymbol{y} = \text{mac}_K(\boldsymbol{x}) = \alpha \boldsymbol{x} + \boldsymbol{\beta}$, i.e., $y_i = \alpha x_i + \beta_i$. Note that $\alpha \in \mathbb{F}$ and $x_i \in \mathbb{F}$, so $\alpha x_i \in \mathbb{G}$.

The intended use of the MAC scheme is as follows. The preprocessor samples a message $\boldsymbol{x}$ and a uniformly random key K and computes $\boldsymbol{y} = \text{mac}_K(\boldsymbol{x})$. It gives K to V and gives $(\boldsymbol{x}, \boldsymbol{y})$ to C. To reveal the message x_i the comitter C sends (x_i, y_i) to V, who accepts if and only if $y_i = \alpha x_i + \beta_i$.

The preprocessed information also allows to open to any sum of a subset of the x_i's. Let $\boldsymbol{\lambda} \in \mathbb{F}^\ell$ with $\lambda_i \in \{0, 1\}$. Let $x_\lambda = \sum_i \lambda_i x_i \pmod{\mathbb{F}}$, let $y_\lambda = \sum_i \lambda_i y_i \pmod{\mathbb{G}}$, and let let $\beta_\lambda = \sum_i \lambda_i \beta_i \pmod{\mathbb{G}}$. To reveal x_λ the committer C sends (x_λ, y_λ) and the verifier V checks that $y_\lambda = \alpha x_\lambda + \beta_\lambda$. If both players are honest, this is clearly the case. The only non-trivial thing to notice is that since $\sum_i \lambda_i x_i \pmod{\mathbb{F}}$ does not involve any reduction modulo p we have that $\sum_i \lambda_i x_i \pmod{\mathbb{F}} = \sum_i \lambda_i x_i = \sum_i \lambda_i x_i \pmod{\mathbb{G}}$.

The scheme is hiding in the sense that after a number of openings to elements x_λ the verifier learns nothing more than what can be computed from the received values x_λ. To see this notice that K is independent of $\boldsymbol{x}$ and hence could be simulated by V. Also the openings can be simulated. Namely, whenever V received an opening (x_λ, y_λ) from an honest C, we know that $y_\lambda = \alpha x_\lambda + \beta_\lambda$, so V could have computed y_λ itself from x_λ and K. Hence no information extra to x_λ is transmitted by transmitting (x_λ, y_λ).

We then prove that the scheme is binding. Let $\mathcal{A}$ be an unbounded adversary. Run $\mathcal{A}$ to get a message $\boldsymbol{x} \in \mathbb{F}^\ell$. Sample a uniformly random key $(\alpha, \boldsymbol{\beta}) \in \mathbb{F} \times \mathbb{G}^\ell$ and compute $y_i = \alpha x_i + \beta_i$ for $i = 1, \ldots, \ell$. Give $\boldsymbol{y}$ to $\mathcal{A}$. Run $\mathcal{A}$ to get an output $(y', x', \boldsymbol{\lambda}) \in \mathbb{G} \times \mathbb{F} \times \{0, 1\}^\ell$. We say that $\mathcal{A}$ wins if $x' \neq x_\lambda$ and $y' = \alpha x' + \beta_\lambda$. We can show that no $\mathcal{A}$ wins with probability better than 2^{-k}. To see this, notice that if $\mathcal{A}$ wins then he knows x' and y' such that $y' = \alpha x' + \beta_\lambda$. He also knows x_λ and y_λ as these can be computed from $\boldsymbol{x}$, $\boldsymbol{y}$ and $\boldsymbol{\lambda}$, which he knows already.

And, it holds that $y_\lambda = \alpha x_\lambda + \beta_\lambda$. Therefore $y' - y_\lambda = \alpha(x' - x_\lambda)$, and it follows as above that $\mathcal{A}$ can compute α. Since no information is leaked on α by the value $\alpha\boldsymbol{x} + \boldsymbol{\beta}$ given to $\mathcal{A}$ it follows that it is uniform in $\mathbb{F}$ in the view of $\mathcal{A}$. Therefore $\mathcal{A}$ can compute α with probability at most 2^{-k}.

We note for completeness that the scheme could be extended to arbitrary linear combinations. In that case one would however have to send $x_\lambda = \sum_i \lambda_i x_i \pmod{\mathbb{F}}$ and $y_\lambda = \sum_i \lambda_i x_i \pmod{\mathbb{F}}$ which would involve doing reductions modulo p. The advantage of the above scheme where $\lambda_i \in \{0, 1\}$ is that no polynomial reductions are needed, allowing full use of the efficiency of the `PCLMULQDQ` instruction.

3.3 Batched Opening

We now present a method to open a large number of commitments in an amortised efficient way, by sending only k bits.

For notational simplicity we assume that C wants to reveal all the values $(x_1, \ldots, x_n)$, but the scheme trivially extends to opening arbitrary subsets and linear combinations. To reveal $(x_1, \ldots, x_n)$ as described above, C would send $Y^{\mathsf{C}} = (y_1, \ldots, y_n)$ and V would compute $y_i^{\mathsf{V}} = \alpha x_i + \beta_i$ for $i = 1, \ldots, n$ and $Y^{\mathsf{V}} = (y_1^{\mathsf{V}}, \ldots, y_n^{\mathsf{V}})$ and check that $Y^{\mathsf{V}} = Y^{\mathsf{C}}$. Consider now the following optimization where C and V is given a function H that outputs (at least) k bits. They could then compare Y^{C} and Y^{V} by sending $h^{\mathsf{C}} = H(Y^{\mathsf{C}})$ and checking that $h^{\mathsf{C}} = H(Y^{\mathsf{V}})$.

We saw above that if C sends $(x_1', \ldots, x_n')$ and $(y_1', \ldots, y_n')$ where $x_i' \neq x_i$ for some i, then C can guess y_i^{V} with probability at most 2^{-k}, so that $Y^{\mathsf{C}} \neq Y^{\mathsf{V}}$ with overwhelming probability. We could therefore let H be any collision resistant hash function, but we want something that can be implemented very efficiently on modern processors. So we will instead define H as follows:

$$H(d_1, \ldots, d_n) = \bigoplus_{i=1}^{n} F(d_i)$$

where we think of F as a random oracle that outputs k bits.

This is clearly secure in the random oracle model: by what we saw above, if $x_i' \neq x_i$ then with overwhelming probability, C has not been able to call the oracle on input y_i^{V}. Assuming he has not, he has no information on the value of $F(y_i^{\mathsf{V}})$, and hence the probability that h^{C} happens to be equal to $H(Y^{\mathsf{V}})$ is 2^{-k}.

Recall that we are going to use the MAC scheme outlined here for the case where we use bigger tables than for Boolean gates, such as the AES S-box, and that in such a case the preprocessing will produce this type of linear MACs. This means that if we use the batch opening method, we will need to compute H in the on-line phase. Our definition of H is well suited for this on modern Intel processors: macs will typically be of size at most 128 bits, so as F we can use AES encryption under a fixed key that is chosen for each protocol execution. We will make the heuristic assumption that we can model this as a random permutation. Then, assuming we will be calling the function much less than $\sqrt{2^{128}} = 2^{64}$ times (which should certainly be true in practice) such a permutation is well known to be statistically indistinguishable from a random function.

4 Preprocessing

In this section we show how to securely implement the preprocessing for Boolean circuits. The idea is to generate the tables by a computation on linear secret shared values, which in case of malicious security also include MACs. We will consider an additive secret sharing of x where A hold $x_A \in \{0,1\}$ and B hold $x_B \in \{0,1\}$ such that $x = x_A + x_B$.

In the case of malicious security the MACs are elements in a finite field $\mathbb{F}$ of characteristic 2 and size at least 2^k where k is the security parameter. Here A hold a key $\alpha_A \in \mathbb{F}$ and B a key $\alpha_B \in \mathbb{F}$. We denote a secret shared value with MACs $[\![x]\!]$ where A hold (x_A, y_A, β_A) and B hold (x_B, y_B, β_B) such that $y_A = \alpha_B x_A + \beta_B$ and $y_B = \alpha_A x_B + \beta_A$. If a value is to be opened the MAC is checked, e.g. if x is opened to A she receives x_B and y_B and checks that indeed $y_B = \alpha_A x_B + \beta_A$ or abort otherwise. This is also the format used in the TinyOT protocol [NNOB12], so we can use the preprocessing protocol from there to produce single values $[\![a]\!]$ for random a and triples of form $[\![x]\!], [\![y]\!], [\![z]\!]$ where x, y are random bits and $z = xy$. Any other preprocessing producing the same data format will of course also be OK, for instance, the protocols presented in [FKOS15] will give better speeds than original TinyOT.

Note that, by a standard protocol [Bea91], we can use one triple to produce from any $[\![a]\!], [\![b]\!]$ the product $[\![ab]\!]$, this just requires opening $a+x, b+y$ and local computation. Also, we can compute the sum $[\![a+b]\!]$ by only local computation.

In Fig. 8, we describe a protocol that implements the preprocessing functionality F^{pre}_{mal} assuming a secure source of triples and single random values as described here, and also assuming that the circuit contains only AND, XOR and NOT gates. We use a function F that we model as a random oracle.

For simplicity the protocol is phrased as a loop that runs through all gates of the circuit, but we stress that it can be executed in constant round: we can execute step 3 in the protocol by first doing all the XOR and NOT gates, using only local operations. At this point wire masks have been chosen for all input and output wires of all AND gates, and they can now all be done in parallel.

Preprocessing for AES. To preprocess an AES Sbox table, we can again make use of the TinyOT preprocessing. This can be combined with a method from [DK10]. Here, it is shown how to compute the Sbox function securely using 7 binary multiplications and local operations. We can then make the table by simply computing each entry (in parallel). It is also possible to compute the Sbox using arithmetic in $\mathbb{F}_{256}$, but if we have to build such multiplications from binary ones, as we would if using TinyOT, this most likely does not pay off.

Protocol π^{pre}_{mal}.

1. Invoke the TinyOT preprocessing such that for each AND gate we have a triple secret of shared values $[\![x]\!]$, $[\![y]\!]$ and $[\![z]\!]$ such that $xy = z$.
2. Also using the TinyOT preprocessing, for each wire w_i that is an input wire, or an output wire from an AND gate, the players assign a random $[\![r_i]\!]$ to w_i, r_i will serve as the masking bit for w_i.
3. For each gate G_i with where masking bits $[\![r_u]\!], [\![r_v]\!]$ have been assigned to the input wires w_u, w_v the players do as follows, depending on the type of gate:
   NOT: Set the output wire mask $[\![r_o]\!] = [\![r_u]\!]$
   XOR: Set the output wire mask $[\![r_o]\!] = [\![r_u]\!] + [\![r_v]\!]$
   AND:
   - Compute $[\![r_u r_v]\!]$ from $[\![r_u]\!]$ and $[\![r_v]\!]$ using the triple assigned to this AND gate, using the protocol from [Bea91].
   - For all $c, d \in \{0, 1\}$ define $t_{c,d} = (r_u + c)(r_v + d) + r_o$ and compute a secret sharing of it as follows: $[\![t_{c,d}]\!] = [\![r_u r_v]\!] + c[\![r_v]\!] + d[\![r_u]\!] + [\![cd]\!] + [\![r_o]\!]$. This requires only local computation.

   Note that $t_{c,d}$ is the bit that needs to be additively secret shared for entry (c, d) in the table for gate G_i.
   A sets $A_i[c, d]$ to be his share of $t_{c,d}$ (which he knows from $[\![t_{c,d}]\!]$), B defines $B_i[c, d]$ similarly.
   Note further that from his part of $[\![t_{c,d}]\!]$, A can compute valid MACs $mac^0_{i,c,d}, mac^1_{i,c,d}$ for both possible values of B's additive share in $t_{c,d}$.
   A sets $a^0_{i,c,d} = F(mac^0_{i,c,d})$, $a^1_{i,c,d} = F(mac^1_{i,c,d})$, while B defines $b^0_{i,c,d}, b^1_{i,c,d}$ similarly[a].
4. For each output gate open the wire mask r_o to both players. For each input wire w_i, open r_i to the player who owns that wire.
5. The parties return the opened input masks, output masks as well as tables A_i, B_i and verifications strings $a^0_{i,c,d}, a^1_{i,c,d}, b^0_{i,c,d}, b^1_{i,c,d}$ for each AND gate.

[a] We need to apply F because we want the verification strings to be independent, and this is not the case if we use the macs directly.

Fig. 8. Protocol for preprocessing with malicious security

5 Implementation

We implement two clients, Alice and Bob, securely evaluating the AES-128 encryption function. Alice inputs the message, Bob inputs the *expanded* key and both parties learns the ciphertext. This function contains several operations where all operations except SUBBYTES are linear. We first implement an optimized version where all linear operations are computed locally using the AES-NI/SSE instruction set, and every non-linear Sbox lookup is replaced with a tinytable lookup and opening. Afterwards we implement a binary version with free XOR gates and no NOT gates using the AES-EXPANDED circuit from [TS]. For both implementations we benchmark a passively secure version and maliciously secure versions all providing statistical security 2^{-k}. Here we test the linear MAC scheme with $k = 64$ and the lookup table MAC scheme with $k = 64$ and $k = 32$.

In the protocol the parties receive preprocessed data generated by a trusted party. We assume this data is present in memory and reuse the same instance for our benchmark. The parties proceed to compute the encryption function on a set of test vectors and verify correctness. We test the implementation on two setups: a basic LAN setup and on a cloud. The LAN setup consist of two PCs connected via 1 GbE, where each machine has a i7-3770K CPU at 3.5 GHz and 32 GB RAM. For our cloud setup we use Amazon EC2 with two C4.8XLARGE instances locally connected via 10 GbE with 36 vCPUs (hyperthreads). The parties communicate over the TCP protocol.

We now analyse the size of the preprocessed data - we concentrate on the tables and ignore the size of the input and output bit masks. For the optimized version, we need 40 KiB of preprocessing data for one passively secure evaluation (160 tiny tables with 2^8 entries of one byte each). For the binary version we need 2.7 KiB (5440 tiny tables with 4 entries of one bit each). For malicious security we add MACs. The simple lookup MAC scheme use $k + 256k$ bits extra per table entry. The linear MAC scheme reuse a k bit key and use $2k$ bits extra per table entry. Beside the input phase, the optimized version has 10 rounds of communication for the passive version and 12 rounds for the active version, i.e. two more rounds for MAC checking before and after opening the result. Similarly the binary version have 41 rounds of communication (layers in the circuit) for the passive version and 43 for the active. The size of the preprocessed data can be seen in Table 1.

Table 1. Size of preprocessed data

	Optimized	Binary
Linear-64	760.0 KiB	342.7 KiB
Lookup-64	80.4 MiB	512.7 KiB
Lookup-32	40.2 MiB	257.7 KiB
Passive	40.0 KiB	2.7 KiB

The results measured as the average over 30 s. For the sequential tests in both the optimized and binary version, the network delay is the major factor. For the amortized tests of the optimized version, the bandwidth is the limiting factor on the LAN setup, whereas computation takes over on the cloud setup as we raise the security parameter. For the amortized binary version the computation is the limiting factor on both setups. The timings for the optimized implementation are summarized in Table 2 and the binary version in Table 3.

Table 2. Execution times for optimized version

	LAN		Cloud	
	Sequential	Parallel	Sequential	Parallel
Linear-64	1.03 ms	3.15 µs	1.09 ms	0.47 µs
Lookup-64	1.03 ms	3.01 µs	1.05 ms	0.45 µs
Lookup-32	1.02 ms	2.95 µs	1.05 ms	0.32 µs
Passive	0.88 ms	2.89 µs	0.97 ms	0.29 µs

Table 3. Execution times for binary version

	LAN		Cloud	
	Sequential	Parallel	Sequential	Parallel
Linear-64	4.92 ms	75.36 µs	2.37 ms	19.19 µs
Lookup-64	4.38 ms	54.72 µs	2.22 ms	11.90 µs
Lookup-32	4.18 ms	40.81 µs	2.18 ms	9.98 µs
Passive	3.94 ms	25.50 µs	1.84 ms	6.73 µs

6 An Asymptotically Better Solution

Recall that the main problem we have with obtaining malicious security is that we must make sure that players reveal correct bits from the tables they are given, but on the other hand only the relevant bits should be revealed.

In this section we show an asymptotically better technique for committing players to their tables such that we can open only the relevant bits.

The idea is as follows: if player A is to commit to string $\boldsymbol{s}$, that is known at preprocessing time, then the preprocessing protocol will establish a (verifiable) secret sharing of $\boldsymbol{s}$ among the players. Concretely, we will use the representation introduced for the so-called MiniMac protocol in [DZ13]: we choose an appropriate linear error correcting (binary) code C. This code should be able to encode strings of length k bits, and have length and minimum distance linear in k.[2]

For a string $\boldsymbol{s}$ of length ℓ (comparable to the circuit size, so $\ell >> k$) we define the encoding $C(\boldsymbol{s})$ by splitting $\boldsymbol{s}$ in k-bit blocks, encoding each block in C and concatenating the encodings. The preprocessing will share $C(\boldsymbol{s})$ additively among the players.

The preprocessing also chooses a random string $\boldsymbol{a}$, unknown to both players, and both $\boldsymbol{a}$ and $\boldsymbol{a} * C(\boldsymbol{s})$ are additively secret shared. Here $*$ denotes the bitwise (Schur) product. We will use the notation $[\boldsymbol{s}]$ as shorthand for all the additive shares of $\boldsymbol{s}$, $\boldsymbol{a}$ and $\boldsymbol{a} * C(\boldsymbol{s})$. The idea is that $\boldsymbol{a} * C(\boldsymbol{s})$ serves as a message authentication code for authenticating $\boldsymbol{s}$, where $\boldsymbol{a}$ is the key. We note that, as

[2] Furthermore its Schur transform should also have minimum distance linear in k. The Schur transform is the code obtained as the linear span of all vectors in the set $\{\boldsymbol{c} * \boldsymbol{d} |\ \boldsymbol{c}, \boldsymbol{d} \in C\}$. See [DZ13] for further details on existence of such codes.

Functionality $F^{pre}_{MiniMac}$.

1. On input a circuit $Circ$ from both players, execute the same algorithm as F^{pre}_{sem} would on input $Circ$.
2. Let $\boldsymbol{s}_A$ be the string obtained by concatenating all tables $\{A_i\}$ created for A. Similarly $\boldsymbol{s}_B$ contains all B's tables. Create MiniMac representations $[\boldsymbol{s}_A], [\boldsymbol{s}_B]$ and give the resulting additive shares to A and B.
3. Create correlated random strings $data_A, data_B$ that will enable the MiniMac protocol to do $\lceil \ell/k \rceil$ multiplications of blocks, and hand $data_A$ to A and $data_B$ to B.

Fig. 9. Preprocessing functionality using the MiniMac protocol

in [DZ13], $\boldsymbol{a}$ is in fact a global key that is also used for other data represented in this same format.

Functionality F_{Table}.

1. On input a circuit $Circ$ from both players, execute the same algorithm as F^{pre}_{sem} would on input $Circ$.
2. Let $\boldsymbol{s}_A$ be the string obtained by concatenating all tables $\{A_i\}$ created for A. Similarly $\boldsymbol{s}_B$ contains all B's tables. At any later point, whenever both players input an index set pointing to a substring of $\boldsymbol{s}_A$ or $\boldsymbol{s}_B$, output the substring to both players.

Fig. 10. Functionality giving on-line access to tables

Based on this preprocessing, we can design a protocol that allows A to open any desired substring of $\boldsymbol{s}$, as follows: let I denote the characteristic vector of the substring, i.e., it is an ℓ bit string where the i'th bit is 1 if A is to reveal the i'th bit of $\boldsymbol{s}$ and 0 otherwise.

We then compute a representation $[I]$ (which is trivial using the additive shares of $\boldsymbol{a}$), use the MiniMac protocol to compute $[I * \boldsymbol{s}]$ and then open this representation to reveal $I * \boldsymbol{s}$ which gives B the string he needs to know and nothing more. This is possible if we let the preprocessing supply appropriate correlated randomness for the multiplication of I and $\boldsymbol{s}$. The protocol we just sketched here will be called $\pi_{MiniMac}$ in the following.

In Fig. 9 we specify the preprocessing functionality $F^{pre}_{MiniMac}$ we assumed in $\pi_{MiniMac}$, i.e., it outputs the tables as well as MiniMac representations of them. Now consider the functionality F_{table} from Fig. 10 that simply stores the tables and outputs bits from them on request. By trivial modification of the security proof for MiniMac, we have

Lemma 1. *The protocol $\pi_{MiniMac}$ composed with $F^{pre}_{MiniMac}$ implements F_{table} with statistical security against a malicious adversary.*

Protocol π_{mal}^{table}.

1. A and B send circuit $Circ$ as input to F_{table} and get a set of tables $\{A_i, B_i | \ i = 1 \dots N\}$, as well as a bit b_u for each input wire w_u.
2. For each input wire w_u, if A holds input x_u for this wire, send $e_u = x_u \oplus b_u$ to B. If B holds input x_u, send $e_u = x_u \oplus b_u$ to A.
3. Define M such that the last $N - M$ gates are output gates. For $i = 1$ to M do:
   (a) Let G_i have input wires w_u, w_v and output wire w_o (so that e_u, e_v have been computed).
   (b) A sends $e_A = A_i[e_u, e_v]$ to B.
   (c) B sends $e_B = B_i[e_u, e_v]$ to A.
   (d) Both parties set $e_o = e_A \oplus e_B$.
   Check if all bits opened until now were correct: A and B both ask F_{table} for the substring of A's tables that she was supposed to reveal in the previous steps. B checks against what he received from A and aborts if there is a mismatch. Symmetrically, A and B also ask F_{table} for the substring of B's tables that she was supposed to reveal in the previous steps. A checks against what he received from B and aborts if there is a mismatch.
4. Reveal the outputs. For $i = M + 1$ to N do:
   (a) Let G_i have input wires w_u, w_v and output wire w_o (so that e_u, e_v have been computed).
   (b) A sends $e_A = A_i[e_u, e_v]$ to B.
   (c) B sends $e_B = B_i[e_u, e_v]$ to A.
   (d) Both parties set $e_o = e_A \oplus e_B$.
5. The parties use F_{table} to confirm that the bits sent in the previous step were correct, in the same way as in Step 4. If there was no abort, the parties output the bits $\{e_o | \ G_o \text{ is an output gate}\}$.

Fig. 11. Simple protocol for malicious security.

As for the on-line efficiency of $\pi_{MiniMac}$, note that in [DZ13] the MiniMac protocol is claimed to be efficient only for so-called well-formed circuits, but this is not a problem here since the circuit we need to compute is a completely regular depth 1 circuit. Indeed, bit-wise multiplication of strings is exactly the operation MiniMac was designed to do efficiently. Therefore, simple inspection of [DZ13] shows that the preprocessing data we need will be of size $O(\ell) = O(s)$, where s is the circuit size, and this is also the communication complexity. The computational complexity is dominated by the time spent on encoding in C. Unfortunately, we do not know codes with the right algebraic properties that also have smart encoding algorithms, so the only approach known is to simply multiply by the generator matrix. We can optimize by noting that if $\ell > k^2$ we will always be doing many encodings in parallel, so we can collect all vectors to encode in a matrix and use fast matrix multiplication. With current state of the art, this leads to computational complexity $O(sk^{\epsilon})$ where $\epsilon \approx 0.3727$.

Alternatively, we can let C be a Reed-Solomon code over an extension field with $\Omega(k)$ elements. We can then use FFT algorithms for encoding and then all complexities will be $O(\text{polylog}(k)s)$.

As a final step, consider the protocol π_{mal}^{table} from Fig. 11. By trivial adaptation of the proof for semi-honest security, we get that

Lemma 2. *The protocol* π_{mal}^{table} *composed with* F_{table} *implements* F_{SFE} *with malicious and statistical security.*

We can then combine Lemmas 1 and 2 to get a protocol for F_{SFE} in the preprocessing model, which together with the efficiency consideration above gives us:

Theorem 2. *There exists 2-party protocol in the preprocessing model (using* $F_{MiniMac}^{pre}$*) for computing any Boolean circuit of size s with malicious and statistical security, where the preprocessed data size and communication complexity are* $O(s)$ *and the computational complexity is* $O(k^\epsilon s)$ *where k is the security parameter and* $\epsilon < 1$*. There also exists a protocol for which all complexities are* $O(\text{polylog}(k)s)$*.*

Acknowledgements. The first and third authors were supported by advanced ERC grant MPCPRO.

References

[BDOZ11] Bendlin, R., Damgård, I., Orlandi, C., Zakarias, S.: Semi-homomorphic encryption and multiparty computation. In: Paterson, K.G. (ed.) EUROCRYPT 2011. LNCS, vol. 6632, pp. 169–188. Springer, Heidelberg (2011). doi:10.1007/978-3-642-20465-4_11

[Bea91] Beaver, D.: Efficient multiparty protocols using circuit randomization. In: Feigenbaum, J. (ed.) CRYPTO 1991. LNCS, vol. 576, pp. 420–432. Springer, Heidelberg (1992). doi:10.1007/3-540-46766-1_34

[CDvdG87] Chaum, D., Damgård, I.B., Graaf, J.: Multiparty computations ensuring privacy of each party's input and correctness of the result. In: Pomerance, C. (ed.) CRYPTO 1987. LNCS, vol. 293, pp. 87–119. Springer, Heidelberg (1988). doi:10.1007/3-540-48184-2_7

[DK10] Damgård, I., Keller, M.: Secure multiparty AES. In: Sion, R. (ed.) FC 2010. LNCS, vol. 6052, pp. 367–374. Springer, Heidelberg (2010). doi:10.1007/978-3-642-14577-3_31

[DLT14] Damgård, I., Lauritsen, R., Toft, T.: An empirical study and some improvements of the MiniMac protocol for secure computation. In: Abdalla, M., Prisco, R. (eds.) SCN 2014. LNCS, vol. 8642, pp. 398–415. Springer, Cham (2014). doi:10.1007/978-3-319-10879-7_23

[DPSZ12] Damgård, I., Pastro, V., Smart, N., Zakarias, S.: Multiparty computation from somewhat homomorphic encryption. In: Safavi-Naini, R., Canetti, R. (eds.) CRYPTO 2012. LNCS, vol. 7417, pp. 643–662. Springer, Heidelberg (2012). doi:10.1007/978-3-642-32009-5_38

[DZ13] Damgård, I., Zakarias, S.: Constant-overhead secure computation of boolean circuits using preprocessing. In: Sahai, A. (ed.) TCC 2013. LNCS, vol. 7785, pp. 621–641. Springer, Heidelberg (2013). doi:10.1007/978-3-642-36594-2_35

[DZ16] Damgård, I., Zakarias, R.W.: Fast oblivious AES a dedicated application of the MiniMac protocol. In: Pointcheval, D., Nitaj, A., Rachidi, T. (eds.) AFRICACRYPT 2016. LNCS, vol. 9646, pp. 245–264. Springer, Cham (2016). doi:10.1007/978-3-319-31517-1_13

[FKOS15] Frederiksen, T.K., Keller, M., Orsini, E., Scholl, P.: A unified approach to MPC with preprocessing using OT. In: Iwata, T., Cheon, J.H. (eds.) ASIACRYPT 2015. LNCS, vol. 9452, pp. 711–735. Springer, Heidelberg (2015). doi:10.1007/978-3-662-48797-6_29

[IKM+13] Ishai, Y., Kushilevitz, E., Meldgaard, S., Orlandi, C., Paskin-Cherniavsky, A.: On the power of correlated randomness in secure computation. In: Sahai, A. (ed.) TCC 2013. LNCS, vol. 7785, pp. 600–620. Springer, Heidelberg (2013). doi:10.1007/978-3-642-36594-2_34

[Kel] Keller, M. Private Communication

[NNOB12] Nielsen, J.B., Nordholt, P.S., Orlandi, C., Burra, S.S.: A new approach to practical active-secure two-party computation. In: Safavi-Naini, R., Canetti, R. (eds.) CRYPTO 2012. LNCS, vol. 7417, pp. 681–700. Springer, Heidelberg (2012). doi:10.1007/978-3-642-32009-5_40

[TS] Tillich, S., Smart, N.: Circuits of Basic Functions Suitable For MPC and FHE. https://www.cs.bris.ac.uk/Research/CryptographySecurity/MPC/

Privacy-Free Garbled Circuits for Formulas: Size Zero and Information-Theoretic

Yashvanth Kondi[1(✉)] and Arpita Patra[2]

[1] International Institute of Information Technology Bangalore, Bangalore, India
yashvanth.kondi@iiitb.org

[2] Indian Institute of Science, Bangalore, India
arpita@csa.iisc.ernet.in

Abstract. Garbled circuits are of central importance in cryptography, finding widespread application in secure computation, zero-knowledge (ZK) protocols, and verifiable outsourcing of computation to name a few. We are interested in a particular kind of garbling scheme, termed *privacy-free* in the literature. We show that Boolean formulas can be garbled *information-theoretically* in the privacy-free setting, producing *no* ciphertexts at all. Existing garbling schemes either rely on cryptographic assumptions (and thus require cryptographic operations to construct and evaluate garbled circuits), produce garbled circuits of non-zero size, or are restricted to low depth formulaic circuits. Our result has both theoretical and practical implications for garbled circuits as a primitive. On the theory front, our result breaks the known theoretical lower bound of one ciphertext for garbling an AND gate in this setting. As an interesting implication of producing size zero garbled circuits, our scheme scores adaptive security for free. On the practical side, our garbling scheme involves only cheap XOR operations and produces size zero garbled circuits. As a side result, we propose several interesting extensions of our scheme. Namely, we show how to garble threshold and high fan-in gates.

An aspect of our garbling scheme that we believe is of theoretical interest is that it does *not* maintain the invariant that the garbled circuit evaluator must not at any point be in possession of both keys of any wire in the garbled circuit.

Our scheme directly finds application in ZK protocols where the verification function of the language is representable by a formulaic circuit. Such examples include Boolean formula satisfiability. The ZK protocols obtained by plugging in our scheme in the known paradigm of building ZK protocols from garbled circuits offer better proof size, while relying on standard assumptions. Furthermore, the adaptivity of our garbling scheme allows us to cast our ZK protocols in the offline-online setting and offload circuit dependent communication and computation to the offline phase. As a result, the online phase enjoys communication and computation (in terms of number of symmetric key operations) complexity that are linearly proportional to the witness size alone.

Y. Kondi—This work is supported by the Infosys Foundation.

A. Patra—This work is partially supported by INSPIRE Faculty Fellowship (DST/INSPIRE/04/2014/015727) from Department of Science & Technology, India.

J. Katz and H. Shacham (Eds.): CRYPTO 2017, Part I, LNCS 10401, pp. 188–222, 2017.
DOI: 10.1007/978-3-319-63688-7_7

Keywords: Garbled circuits · Privacy-free · Formula · Information-theoretic · Authenticity

1 Introduction

Garbled circuits (GC) are of paramount importance in cryptographic protocol theory, lending their power in building vital cryptographic primitives such as secure computation in two party [Yao86,LP07,LP11,LR15] and multiparty [BELO16,CKMZ14,MRZ15] settings, zero-knowledge protocols [JKO13,FNO15, ZRE15], verifiable outsourcing of computation [GGP10], and functional encryption [SS10] to name a few. Roughly speaking, a GC allows evaluation of a circuit in its encoded form on an encoded input, and produces an encoded output. Based on the application that a GC serves, the information required to decode the output may be provided to the evaluator, or retained by the GC constructor if she wishes to keep the function output private. GCs first made their appearance in Yao's secure two-party computation protocol [Yao86]. Following multiple optimizations [BMR90,MNPS04,NPS99,PSSW09,BHKR13,GLNP15, ZRE15,KMR14,KS08], GCs today are an indispensable primitive used in various secure protocols. Their theoretical importance and potential to serve as a cryptographic primitive has been recognized by Bellare *et al.* [BHR12b], who elevate GCs from a technique to be used in other protocols, to a cryptographic primitive. To facilitate abstraction as a primitive, the fundamental work of Bellare *et al.* [BHR12b] formalizes three notions of security that a garbling scheme may achieve; namely privacy, obliviousness, and authenticity, and shows separation between them. Informally, privacy aims to protect the privacy of encrypted inputs, while obliviousness hides both the input and the output when the output decoding information is withheld. However once the output decoding information is revealed, obliviousness does not necessarily imply privacy of inputs. Lastly, authenticity captures the unforgeability of the output of a garbled circuit evaluation. Different applications of GC often use different combinations of the above properties of garbling schemes. Majority of the schemes in the literature, including the classical scheme of Yao [Yao86], satisfy all the three aforementioned properties.

In the original scheme of Yao [Yao86], each wire in the GC was assigned two strings called "keys", each corresponding to bit values zero and one on that wire. A garbled gate in the circuit was represented by ciphertexts encrypting its output wire keys using the corresponding input wire keys as per the gate's truth table. A garbled gate for a gate with fan-in two is thus constituted of four ciphertexts. An evaluator who knows one key for each input wire can only open one of the ciphertexts and therefore obtain only one key for the gate output wire, corresponding to the bit output of the gate. The final garbled circuit was a composition of the garbled gates, and its size was defined as the number of bits of ciphertext needed overall. The encoded input consisted of the keys on the input wires corresponding to the input bits. On receiving an encoded input, an evaluator evaluates the gates topologically, finding the output key for every gate, and stops when the keys for the output gates are obtained. The efficiency of a GC is determined by the computation cost (for the constructor and the evaluator) and its size. The latter directly impacts the communication complexity of protocols that employ the GC. Towards making secure computation practically efficient, tremendous efforts have been made in boosting the performance and efficiency of GCs. Some of the outstanding lines of work are highlighted below.

The work of the evaluator is significantly cut down via a technique called point-and-permute [BMR90, MNPS04]. Specifically, it cuts down the computation cost of an evaluator to one quarter, by introducing a pointing mechanism for every gate that imparts to the evaluator the knowledge of the particular ciphertext that she needs to decrypt in order to evaluate a garbled gate. Put differently, an evaluator simply decrypts the relevant ciphertext, skipping the remaining three for a two-input gate. Next, the celebrated Free-XOR technique [KS08] shows a simple yet brilliant way of garbling and evaluating XOR gates with zero ciphertexts and no cryptographic operations. Garbled Row Reduction (GRR) techniques [NPS99, PSSW09, GLNP15, ZRE15] are devoted towards making concise garbled gates by fixing some of the ciphertexts to constant values (therefore removing the need to transmit them). Both free-XOR and GRR techniques are instrumental in reducing the size of GCs. To date, the best known garbling scheme can garble an XOR gate with zero ciphertexts, and an AND gate with just two ciphertexts using free-XOR and clever GRR techniques [ZRE15]. Precluding further improvement in this domain, the work of [ZRE15] shows optimality of two ciphertexts (or $2\,\mu$ bits; μ is the computational security parameter) for garbling an AND gate. Specifically, the lower bound holds true for any scheme that is captured by their characterization of linear garbling techniques. Informally, a garbling scheme qualifies to be linear when the circuit constructor and evaluator need to perform linear operations apart from making random oracle calls. Several other techniques for improving the computation cost of the constructor and evaluator are reported in [BHR12b, BHKR13]. The efficiency study of GCs are further enriched and extended by considering a number of interesting relaxations that lead to further optimizations. In one, some of the security properties of GCs are compromised. In the others, specific classes of circuits are used for garbling. As we discuss below, these relaxed notions of GCs are not only interesting from an application perspective, but they also show significant savings in terms of both size and computation cost. Since our work makes further inroad in the study of the GCs exploiting some relaxations, we take a detailed look at the relevant literature in order to set the stage for our contribution.

Privacy-Free Garbling. In a breakthrough result, Jawurek *et al.* [JKO13] show that efficient zero knowledge (ZK) protocols for non-algebraic languages can be constructed based on garbling schemes achieving only authenticity. Frederiksen *et al.* [FNO15] termed this class of garbling schemes as *privacy-free*. There has since been significant interest in garbled circuit based ZK protocols [CGM16, HMR15]. A privacy-free garbling scheme does not need to satisfy privacy nor obliviousness, instead it only requires authenticity and a notion of *verifiability*. Informally, verifiability ensures that even a malicious constructor cannot create a garbled circuit that can be evaluated to different garbled output values, for inputs which when applied to the circuit in clear give the same output. This property is needed to mitigate selective failure attacks that a malicious verifier could possibly mount in a ZK protocol. Though as of writing this paper, the primary motivation of work in privacy-free garbling is to plug into the GC based ZK protocols which can prove that a 'prover' knows x such that $f(x) = 1$ in zero knowledge efficiently for non-algebraic f, verifiable outsourcing of computation provides another potential application for privacy-free GCs [BHR12b,BHR12a]. Motivated by the important use-cases of privacy-free garbling schemes, [FNO15,ZRE15] study the efficiency of privacy-free garbling. Both works show that more efficient GCs than the most optimized Yao's GC can be constructed by leveraging privacy-freeness. In terms of individual gate garbling computation and communication cost in the privacy-free setting, the Half Gates approach [ZRE15] which is currently the most efficient, requires one ciphertext per garbled AND gate, and no ciphertexts to garble XOR gates (with two calls to a hash function H per AND gate). Zahur *et al.* [ZRE15] also argue a lower bound of one ciphertext (or μ bits; μ is the computational security parameter) required to garble an AND gate for any linear scheme, and conclude optimality of their privacy-free construction.

Garbling for Formulaic Circuits. Formulaic circuits or formulas, informally, are circuits comprised solely of gates with fan-out of one. Formulaic circuits have several use-cases, such as Boolean formula satisfiability and membership in a language to name a few. By Cook's theorem, there exists a Boolean formula of size polynomial in $|x|$ that can verify an NP-witness of membership of x in language L. Formula satisfiability and language membership are well studied languages in the study of ZK protocols [CD97,KR06,Gro10,Lip12,GGPR13]. There are examples abound showing that treating Boolean formulas as a separate case from a general circuit may be apt [Kol05,KR06,KKKS15]. In the context of garbling, Kempka *et al.* [KKKS15] show how to garble a formulaic circuit with just four bits to represent each garbled gate. In contrast, even the best known garbling scheme for general circuits [ZRE15] needs $\mathcal{O}(\mu)$ bits where μ denotes computational security parameter. However, the garbling scheme of Kempka *et al.* [KKKS15] requires expensive public-key operations (which also disqualifies it from being a linear scheme). In yet another attempt, Kolesnikov [Kol05] shows how to garble a formula information-theoretically under the umbrella of "Gate Evaluation Secret Sharing", or *GESS*. The underlying garbling scheme achieves privacy (and though not explicitly proven or defined, authenticity) using only information-theoretic operations and produces a GC of size *zero*. On the down side, the keys associated with the wires have their length dependent on the depth of the circuit. Specifically, for a circuit of depth d and a statistical security parameter κ, a key on an input wire can be of size $\mathcal{O}(d(\kappa + d))$. Thus the input circuit needs to be of low depth, apart from being formulaic. The blow-up in key size also means that it does not meet the requirement of linearity as per [ZRE15]. Information-theoretic schemes are attractive in practice due to their highly efficient computation cost.

The schemes reported in [FNO15,ZRE15,KKKS15] are neither information-theoretic nor do they produce size-zero GCs. On the other hand, while the scheme of [Kol05] produces size-zero GCs, it is restricted to low-depth formulaic circuits. This leaves open the question of achieving best of the both worlds and sets the stage for our contribution.

1.1 Our Contribution

In this work, we explore privacy-free garbling for formulas (of arbitrary depth). Our findings are presented below.

Privacy-Free Garbling for Formulas with Size-Zero GCs and Information-Theoretic Security. The main contribution in this paper is to present a privacy-free garbling scheme for formulas of arbitrary depth that achieves information-theoretic security, size-zero GCs, and circuit-depth independence for the keys. Unlike in the information-theoretic scheme of [Kol05], the key length for the wires in our scheme is independent of the circuit depth. Unlike the schemes of [FNO15, ZRE15, KKKS15], ours is information-theoretic and is extremely fast due to the usage of cheap XOR operations. A couple of interesting theoretical implications of our result are given below.

- ***Breaking the lower bound of*** [ZRE15]**.** The proven lower bound on the number of ciphertexts (bits) for garbling an AND gate is one (μ bits; μ is a security parameter) as per any linear garbling scheme. We show that our scheme is linear and yet requires *no* ciphertext at all to garble any gate. This breaks the lower bound shown in [ZRE15] for linear garbling schemes in the privacy-free setting.
- ***Achieving Adaptive Security for Free.*** A garbling scheme is said to achieve static security if its security properties are guaranteed as long as the choice of input to the circuit is not allowed to depend on the garbled circuit itself. A scheme is adaptively secure when there is no such restriction. Several applications, notably one-time programs [GKR08], secure outsourcing [GGP10], and ZK protocols cast in offline-online setting [KR06] need adaptive security, where the input may depend on the garbled circuit. An interesting implication of size-zero GC is that, in the terminology of Bellare *et al.* [BHR12b, BHR12a] achieving static security for our construction is equivalent to achieving adaptive security[1].

Several works confirm that privacy-freeness brings along efficiency both in terms of size and computation complexity of garbled circuits. We reaffirm this belief. Specifically, garbling an XOR gate requires three XOR operations (which can be improved in the multi-fan-in setting), while garbling an AND gate requires only one XOR operation. Evaluating any gate requires at most one XOR operation. Interestingly, contrary to the norm in secure multiparty computation, AND gates are handled (garbled, evaluated, and verified) more efficiently than XOR gates in our construction. Furthermore, our scheme requires only one κ-bit random string to generate all keys for both incoming wires to an AND or XOR gate.

[1] Specifically, our scheme achieves `aut1` security in the terminology of [BHR12a].

In Table 1, we compare our work against other schemes operating in the privacy-free setting to garble formulaic circuits, namely with [FNO15, ZRE15, Kol05]. The performance is measured with respect to a statistical security parameter κ for the information-theoretic constructions and with respect to a computational security parameter μ for cryptographic constructions, for a formulaic circuit of depth d. For most of the practical purposes, the value of μ can be taken as 128, while the value of κ can be taken as 40. Apart from usual measures (size and computation cost) of GCs, we also take into account the input key length of the GCs resulted from various schemes for comparison. The input key length impacts the communication required in the input encoding phase, which is frequently done by expensive Oblivious Transfer (OT) [EGL85] instances.

Table 1. Performance and security comparison of various privacy-free garbling schemes for formulaic circuits. Calls to H refers to the number of hash function invocations. μ and κ refer to the computational and the statistical parameter respectively. d is circuit depth.

Garbling scheme	Cost per gate						Input key size	Security
	Size (in bits)		Computation (calls to H)					
	XOR	AND	Constructor		Evaluator			
			XOR	AND	XOR	AND		
Row reduction (GRR1) [FNO15]	μ	μ	0	3	0	1	μ	Static computational
freeXOR+GRR2 [FNO15]	0	2μ	0	3	0	1	μ	Static computational
Half gates [ZRE15]	0	μ	0	2	0	1	μ	Static computational
GESS [Kol05]	0	0	0	0	0	0	$\mathcal{O}(d(\kappa + d))$	Adaptive unconditional
This work	**0**	**0**	**0**	**0**	**0**	**0**	κ	**Adaptive unconditional**

Technically, our scheme is very simple. We garble "upwards" from the output wire similar to the garbling schemes of [Kol05, KKKS15]. As with many secure computation protocols, at the heart of our scheme is our method for handling AND gates. Here, we provide a preview of how our scheme garbles an AND gate g. Denote the keys corresponding to bit b on the left and right incoming wires, and the gate output wire, as L^b, R^b, and K^b respectively. Our garbling scheme proceeds as follows. L^1 and R^1 are defined as additive shares of K^1 so that $L^1 \oplus R^1 = K^1$. Therefore, an evaluator can derive $K^1 = L^1 \oplus R^1$ only if she has both L^1 and R^1. We then copy the value of K^0 to the zero keys of both incoming wires; $L^0 = R^0 = K^0$. An evaluator hence has the output key corresponding to bit value zero if she has a zero key on either incoming wire. Note that in the case that the left incoming wire has value 0 flowing on it, and the right incoming wire 1, an evaluator will effectively possess both keys R^0 and R^1 on the right incoming wire; R^1 obtained legitimately, and R^0 as it is equal to L^0. We show that our scheme tolerates the leakage of certain keys within the garbled circuit (both directly and indirectly due to the observation above), at no cost of security.

The above aspect of our scheme is of theoretical interest as we do not maintain the invariant that an evaluator is allowed to know only one key on each wire. Our scheme achieves authenticity despite conceding both keys to an evaluator on certain wires. In fact, this property is taken advantage of in order to gain much in terms of efficiency. To the best of our knowledge, ours is the first garbling scheme where this invariant is not maintained. A direct implication of violating this invariant is that the standard proof paradigms for garbled circuits (which assume the invariant to hold) are not applicable here. We exploit the fact that the only gate that is necessarily "uncompromised" is the circuit output gate, and reduce (with no security loss) the authenticity of the circuit output gate in the context of an arbitrarily large circuit, to the authenticity of a single-gate circuit.

Extensions for High Fan-In Gates and General Circuits. To optimize our garbling scheme, we propose efficient garbling of ℓ-fan-in gates. Apart from handling ℓ-fan-in XOR and AND gates, we consider *threshold* gates and provide a new garbling scheme for them. A threshold gate with fan-in ℓ and threshold t with $\ell > t$ outputs 1 when at least $t + 1$ inputs carry the bit 1, and zero otherwise. The threshold range $1 < t < \ell - 1$ is of interest to us, as the gate otherwise degenerates into an ℓ-fan-in AND or NAND gate, which can be handled more efficiently by our scheme. Boolean threshold gates are considered and motivated by Ball *et al.* [BMR16], who construct a scheme to garble them natively (generating $\mathcal{O}\left(\log^3 \ell / \log\log \ell\right)$ ciphertexts) as opposed to garbling a composition of AND, XOR and NOT gates (yielding $\mathcal{O}\left(\ell \log \ell\right)$ ciphertexts using the best known garbling scheme of [ZRE15]). Here, we present a method of garbling Boolean threshold gates (embedded in formulaic circuits) directly in privacy-free setting, producing no ciphertext, and using only information-theoretic operations; specifically two independent instances of Shamir secret sharing [Sha79] per threshold gate.

The power of threshold gates is brought out in the fact that $\mathsf{NC}^0 \subsetneq \mathsf{AC}^0 \subsetneq \mathsf{TC}^0$, where circuits deciding languages in TC^0 contain majority gates in addition to AND, OR and NOT. More practically, threshold gates implement natural expressions in the settings of zero-knowledge [JKO13] and attribute-based credentials [KKL+16]. In the former case, threshold gates can implement statements of the form, "I have witnesses for at least t out of these ℓ statements", without revealing for which statements the prover has witnesses. In the case of attribute-based credentials, one can prove that her attributes satisfy at least t criteria out of ℓ in a policy, without revealing which ones, or how many exactly.

We show how to garble and evaluate ℓ fan-in XOR and AND gates with fewer XOR operations than are needed when we express such gates in terms of two fan-in XOR and AND gates respectively. Specifically, garbling an ℓ-fan-in XOR gate directly takes 2ℓ XOR operations, as opposed to $3(\ell-1)$ XOR operations to garble $\ell - 1$ XOR gates individually. Evaluating an ℓ-fan-in AND gate, in $2^\ell - 1$ cases out of 2^ℓ, will take zero XOR operations. In the final case, the evaluation is done at the same cost as evaluating $\ell - 1$ individual AND gates.

For completeness, we describe how to adapt our scheme to garble generic circuits in the privacy-free setting in the full version of the paper. While the adaptation itself is not generally efficient for circuits that are not largely formulaic, it establishes the feasibility of violating the single-key invariant when garbling any generic circuit, at least in the privacy-free setting. Our approach relies on cryptographic assumptions. For generic circuits that are not largely formulaic in nature, the construction of [FNO15, ZRE15] can be used. However, both the constructions rely on non-standard assumptions. In [FNO15], it is a customized notion of key derivation function (KDF) where random oracle can be shown to be a secure KDF. In [ZRE15], the construction needs a circular correlation robust hash function. We take a look at the scheme of [GLNP15] which works under standard pseudo-random function (PRF) assumption and propose several optimizations in privacy-free setting in the full version of the paper.

Application to ZK Protocols. Lately, ZK protocols from garbled circuits has gained a lot of momentum [JKO13, FNO15, CGM16], with applications such as attribute-based key exchange built on top of them [KKL+16]. We apply our garbling scheme to the domain of ZK protocols where the verification function of the language is representable by an almost formulaic circuit such as Boolean formula satisfiability. When we plug in our scheme in the paradigm of [JKO13] (with a slight tweak), we get ZK protocols that rely on standard assumption (PRG) in the OT-hybrid model and results in a better proof size for right choice of the security parameters than the known instantiations in the same paradigm. The best known GC-based ZK instantiation that results from the composition of the privacy-free construction of [ZRE15] and the ZK protocols of [JKO13] needs to rely on KDF and circular correlation-robust hash function.

Leveraging the adaptivity of our garbling scheme, we cast our ZK protocols in the offline-online paradigm and offload circuit dependent expensive communication and computation to the offline phase. As a result, the witness size alone linearly impacts the communication and computation (in terms of number of symmetric key operations) complexities of the online phase. The existing ZK protocols relying on statically secure garbling schemes cannot match the online complexities of our protocol as the garbled circuit needs to be sent in the online phase. In contrast to the garbled circuit based ZK protocols (including ours) where public key operations are proportional to the witness size, the theoretically interesting ZK proofs/arguments [CD97, KR06, Gro10, Lip12, GGPR13] for satisfiability employ public key operations proportional to the circuit size. We focus on the protocols that are practically relevant. A practical non-interactive alternative can be found in ZKBoo [GOM16], however at the cost of a large proof size; the proof is linear in the size of the statement, and computed (and communicated) only after the witness is available. A comparison of our ZK protocol for Boolean formula satisfiability with [JKO13] instantiated in the offline-online paradigm with the state of the art privacy-free garbling scheme [ZRE15] is provided in Table 2.

1.2 Organization

In Sect. 2, we recall the necessary definitions. In Sect. 3, we present our privacy-free information-theoretic garbling scheme for formulas. The full proof of security appears in Sect. 4. The definition of a privacy-free linear garbling scheme and the proof that our scheme qualifies to be a linear scheme is presented in Sect. 5. We

Table 2. Complexities of GC based ZK for Boolean formula satisfiability. The last two rows correspond to the protocols in offline-online setting. The computational and statistical security parameters are μ and κ respectively, and the size of the statement is m, while the size of the witness is n.

Protocol	Communication		Computation (input encoding and GC evaluation)	
	Offline	Online	Offline	Online
[JKO13] + [ZRE15]	0	$\mathcal{O}(\mu m + \kappa n)$	0	$\mathcal{O}(n)$ PKE + $\mathcal{O}(m)$ hash invocations
Our protocol	0	$\boldsymbol{\mathcal{O}(\kappa m + \kappa n)}$	0	$\boldsymbol{\mathcal{O}(n)}$ **PKE +** $\boldsymbol{\mathcal{O}(m)}$ **XORs**
[JKO13] + [ZRE15] (offline-online)	$\mathcal{O}(\mu n)$	$\mathcal{O}(\mu m)$	$\mathcal{O}(n)$ PKE	$\mathcal{O}(m)$ hash invocations
Our protocol (offline-online)	$\mathcal{O}(\kappa m)$	$\boldsymbol{\mathcal{O}(\mu n)}$	$\mathcal{O}(n)$ PKE	$\boldsymbol{\mathcal{O}(n)}$ **PRG invocations +** $\boldsymbol{\mathcal{O}(m)}$ **XORs**

present the optimizations for ℓ fan-in gates in Sect. 6. Our ZK protocol appears in Sect. 7 and the required functionalities are recalled in Appendix A.

2 Preliminaries

We use $a \leftarrow \{0,1\}^n$ to denote that a is assigned a uniformly random n-bit string, and $a \leftarrow \mathsf{alg}(x)$ to denote that a is assigned the value output by randomized algorithm alg when supplied the input x. We use $b := a$ to denote that b is deterministically assigned the value a. The operator $a||b$ denotes the concatenation of a and b. PPT denotes probabilistic polynomial time. The value κ is used throughout this paper to denote the statistical security parameter, which is reflected in the key length of the instance of the garbling scheme. For all practical purposes, the value of κ can be taken as 40. We also use the terms "zero key" and "key corresponding to bit value zero" interchangeably. In what follows, we present the required definitions. We denote by $[x]$, the set of elements $\{1,\ldots,x\}$.

2.1 Formulaic Circuits

Informally, a formula is a circuit which has a fan-out of one for every gate. The implication of this is that a gate's output wire can either be a circuit output wire, or an input wire for only one other gate. Formally, we use a modified version of the syntax for circuits in [BHR12b]. In GC based ZK protocols [JKO13], the verification circuit that needs to be garbled has one bit output. The output zero indicates that the proof is rejected, whereas the output one indicates that the proof is accepted.

Definition 1. *A formulaic circuit is characterized by a tuple $f = (n, q, A, B, G)$. The parameters n, q define the number of input, and non-input wires respectively. Wires are indexed from 1 to $n + q$, with 1 to n being input wires, and $n + q$ being the output wire. A gate is identified by its outgoing wire index. For a gate $g \in [n + 1, n + q]$, $A(g)$ and $B(g)$ are* injective *functions that map to left and right incoming wire indices respectively*[2]*. We have $B(g) \in [1, n + q - 1]$,*

[2] This is a departure from the [BHR12b] definition for conventional circuits. The injection property required here ensures that every gate in the circuit has a fan-out of one.

and $A(g) \in [0, n+q-1]$*;* $A(g) = 0$ *if* g *has fan-in of 1. We also require that* $A(g) < B(g) < g$*. Additionally, we require that for every gate* g*, if* $\exists g', A(g') = g$*, then* $\nexists g'', B(g'') = g$*, and vice versa. This is to ensure that a gate can be an incoming wire to at most one other gate. The gate functionality* $G(g)$ *is a map* $G(g) : \{0,1\}^2 \mapsto \{0,1\}$.

The terms "wire" and "gate" are used interchangeably throughout the paper, as a gate is identified by the index of its outgoing wire.

2.2 Privacy-Free Garbling Scheme

A garbling scheme, as defined in [BHR12b], is defined by a tuple $(\mathsf{Gb}, \mathsf{En}, \mathsf{De}, \mathsf{Ev})$. Their arguments and outputs are as follows:

- Gb: $(f, 1^\kappa) \mapsto (F, e, d)$. Given the function f to garble, the PPT algorithm Gb outputs the garbled circuit F, encoding information e, and decoding information d.
- En: $(x, e) \mapsto X$. Given clear function input x and valid encoding information e, the deterministic algorithm En outputs garbled input X.
- Ev: $(F, X) \mapsto Y$. Given a garbled circuit F and garbled input X for that circuit, Ev deterministically outputs garbled output Y.
- De: $(Y, d) \mapsto y$. Given garbled output Y, and valid decoding information d, De deterministically outputs the clear function output y. If Y is not consistent with d, then De outputs $\perp$.

Definition 2 (Correctness). *A garbling scheme satisfies* correctness *if for every valid circuit* f *and its input* x*, we have*

$$\forall (F, e, d) \leftarrow \mathsf{Gb}(f, 1^\kappa),\ \mathsf{De}(\mathsf{Ev}(F, \mathsf{En}(x, e)), d) = f(x)$$

We consider only *projective* garbling schemes, where the encoding information e is of the form $\left(\left(k_i^0, k_i^1\right)_{i \in [n]}\right)$. We refer the reader to [BHR12b] for a formal treatment and discussion.

In [BHR12b], definitions for the security notions of privacy, obliviousness, and authenticity are provided. However, as we are not interested in achieving privacy or obliviousness, we will only consider authenticity, and the notion of verifiability defined in [JKO13].

Definition 3 (Authenticity). *A garbling scheme satisfies* unconditional authenticity *if for every computationally unbounded* $\mathcal{A}$*, and for every* $f : \{0,1\}^n \mapsto \{0,1\}$ *and* $x \leftarrow \{0,1\}^n$*, we have*

$$\Pr\left[(Y \neq \mathsf{Ev}(F, X)) \ \wedge\ (\mathsf{De}(Y, d) \neq \perp)\ :\ Y \leftarrow \mathcal{A}(F, X)\right] \leq 2^{-\kappa}$$

where $(F, e, d) \leftarrow \mathsf{Gb}(f, 1^\kappa)$*, and* $X := \mathsf{En}(e, x)$.

The definition for unconditional authenticity in Definition 3 is stronger than that of Bellare *et al.* [BHR12b], as it places no bound on the computational power of the adversary, and specifies that no such adversary should be able to perform better than randomly guessing a garbled output. Intuitively, schemes delivering such guarantees should rely only on information theoretic operations.

Finally, we also consider the property of *verifiability* introduced in [JKO13]. A privacy-free garbling scheme that can be plugged into their ZK protocol must have an additional 'verification function' $\mathsf{Ve} : (F, f, e) \mapsto b$. The purpose of this function is to enable the Prover (who evaluates the garbled circuit) to verify that the garbled circuit that she was given was legitimately constructed, which is important in ensuring that the garbled output obtained upon evaluation doesn't reveal any input bits, i.e. the Prover's witness. This function outputs a single bit b, given a garbled circuit F, the underlying clear function f, and encoding information e. Informally, when Ve outputs 1 for a certain F, f, e, then evaluating F on garbled input X corresponding to x such that $f(x) = 1$ will produce garbled output that matches the expected garbled output that can be extracted given F, e.

Definition 4 (Verifiability). *A verifiable garbling scheme contains a poly-time computable function* Ve *such that there exists a poly-time algorithm* Ext, *which for every computationally unbounded adversary* $\mathcal{A}$, *function* f *within the domain of* Gb, *input* x *where* $f(x) = 1$, *ensures the following,*

$$\Pr\left[\mathsf{Ext}(F, e) = \mathsf{Ev}\left(F, \mathsf{En}(e, x)\right)\right] = 1, \textit{ when } \mathsf{Ve}\left(F, f, e\right) = 1; \; (F, e) \leftarrow \mathcal{A}\left(1^{\kappa}, f\right)$$

For completeness, we require: $\forall (F, e, d) \leftarrow \mathsf{Gb}\left(f, 1^{\kappa}\right), \; \mathsf{Ve}\left(F, f, e\right) = 1.$

Note that like Definition 3 the above definition for verifiability is stronger than the original one in [JKO13], owing to the fact that our Definition 4 does not place a bound on the running time of the adversary, and does not permit even a negligible error for the Ext algorithm.

An unconditionally secure privacy-free garbling scheme is defined by a tuple $\mathcal{G} = (\mathsf{Gb}, \mathsf{En}, \mathsf{Ev}, \mathsf{De}, \mathsf{Ve})$, and satisfies the correctness, authenticity, and verifiability properties detailed in Definitions 2, 3, and 4.

3 Privacy-Free Garbling for Formulas

In this section, we define our construction for an unconditionally secure, verifiable privacy-free garbling scheme whose domain of circuits that can be garbled are formulaic. As per previous paradigms of garbling formulaic circuits in [Kol05, KKKS15], our garbling scheme proceeds upwards from the output wire.

3.1 Garbling Individual Gates

As per Yao's paradigm of garbling circuits [Yao86], every wire in the circuit is assigned two κ-bit string tokens, called "keys"; one each for bit values zero and one on that wire. For a gate g, let the output wire keys corresponding to zero and one be K^0 and K^1 respectively. The zero and one keys of the left incoming wire are L^0, L^1 respectively, and those of the right incoming wire are R^0, R^1 respectively. The bit value flowing on wire w is b_w. A gate garbling routine is a randomized algorithm that accepts the gate keys K^0, K^1 as arguments, and returns constructed keys L^0, L^1, R^0, R^1 for the gate's input wires. A gate evaluation routine deterministically returns a key $K^{G_g(b_L, b_R)}$ where G_g is the gate functionality, upon being supplied with input wire keys L^{b_L}, R^{b_R} (and possibly input bits b_L, b_R). In this section, we define gate garbling and evaluation routines for XOR, AND, and NOT gates.

Garbling XOR Gates. Garbling and evaluation of XOR gates is relatively simple. Our garbling scheme for XOR gates is similar to that of Kolesnikov's [Kol05]. The wire keys produced by our garbling scheme maintain the same relation, namely $L^{b_L} \oplus R^{b_R} = K^{b_L \oplus b_R}$. However, while the construction of [Kol05] requires four XOR operations to garble an XOR gate, our construction requires only three (tending to two in the l-fan-in setting), hence saving on computation cost.

First, K^0 is split into two additive shares, assigned to L^1 and R^1 respectively. Therefore, $L^1 \oplus R^1 = K^0$. Next, K^1 is masked with R^1 and assigned to L^0, and independently masked with L^1 and assigned to R^0. I.e. $L^0 := K^1 \oplus R^1$ and $R^0 := K^1 \oplus L^1$. This ensures that $L^0 \oplus R^1 = R^0 \oplus L^1 = K^1$. Conveniently, $L^0 \oplus R^0 = L^1 \oplus R^1 = K^0$.

Evaluation can hence be defined as follows: if the evaluator has keys L^{b_L} and R^{b_R}, corresponding to bits b_L and b_R on the left and right wires respectively, she can obtain the output key as $K^{b_L \oplus b_R} = L^{b_L} \oplus R^{b_R}$. Correctness of evaluating an XOR gate as per this scheme is implicit.

The VeXOR routine defined in Fig. 1 ensures that any combination of L^{b_L}, R^{b_R} taken from L^0, L^1, R^0, R^1 consistently evaluates to a $K^{b_L \oplus b_R}$. This can be considered a "consistency check", that a given tuple of keys (L^0, L^1, R^0, R^1) maintain correctness of a garbled XOR gate.

Garbling AND Gates. Our construction for garbling AND gates is as simple as the one defined for XOR gates, however the proof of authenticity is not as straightforward. Interestingly, our scheme requires only one XOR operation to garble an AND gate, and at most one XOR operation to evaluate a garbled AND gate (in three out of four cases, evaluation is completely free). This makes garbling, evaluation, and verification of AND gates cheaper than that of XOR gates. Figure 2 formalizes the construction discussed in the Introduction.

Correctness of evaluating an AND gate as per this scheme is hence implicit. Note that if an evaluator has key L^0, she will be missing L^1, therefore making whatever key she has on the right incoming wire irrelevant; K^1 remains completely hidden unless both L^1 and R^1 are available. A similar argument applies in case she has R^0. Additionally, if she is able to derive K^1 during evaluation, it implies that she started with L^1 and R^1, keeping K^0 inaccessible for the lack of

GbXOR $(K^0, K^1, 1^\kappa)$

The zero and one keys of the left and right incoming wires will be L^0, R^0 and L^1, R^1 respectively

1. Split K^0 into additive secret shares, $L^1 \leftarrow \{0,1\}^\kappa$; $R^1 := K^0 \oplus L^1$
2. Mask K^1 for the incoming zero keys, $L^0 := K^1 \oplus R^1$; $R^0 := K^1 \oplus L^1$
3. **return** L^0, L^1, R^0, R^1

EvXOR (L^{b_L}, R^{b_R})

1. **return** $L^{b_L} \oplus R^{b_R}$

VeXOR (L^0, L^1, R^0, R^1)

1. Generate both output keys in all combinations
   i. $K^{00} := L^0 \oplus R^0$; $K^{01} := L^0 \oplus R^1$
   ii. $K^{11} := L^1 \oplus R^1$; $K^{10} := L^1 \oplus R^0$
2. **if** $K^{00} \neq K^{11}$ **or** $K^{10} \neq K^{01}$ **then** the keys are inconsistent, **return** 0, $\perp$, $\perp$. **else return** 1, K^{00}, K^{01}

Fig. 1. Garbling, evaluation and verification of an XOR gate

L^0 and R^0. Therefore, during an evaluation of the gate for the first time (when no gate $g' > g$ has been evaluated yet), the evaluator will be unable to forge the output key that she is missing.

It can be observed that knowledge of L^0 implies knowledge of R^0. Due to the earlier argument regarding K^1 being perfectly hidden unless both L^1 and R^1 are known, this does not pose a problem. Intuitively, the worst that an adversary could do with this knowledge (eg. given L^0 and R^1) is obtain both keys on the right incoming wire, but the damage is "contained"; wires occurring after this gate are not affected. Examining what an adversarial evaluator is capable of doing with this information (beyond just one 'pass' of evaluation) requires a more comprehensive analysis, which we defer to Sect. 4. We show that despite the information leaked by the key structure of the AND gates, our scheme achieves unconditional authenticity.

The routine VeAND defined in Fig. 2 verifies that both incoming wires of a gate g have the same zero key, which will also be the zero key for g. The key corresponding to bit value one for wire g is defined such that it requires no consistency checking with respect to its incoming wires' keys. This routine can hence be considered a "consistency check" that a given tuple of keys (L^0, L^1, R^0, R^1) maintain correctness of a garbled AND gate.

Garbling NOT Gates. NOT gates can be garbled for free, like in [Kol05], by switching the association of the zero and one keys. If wire w has keys K_w^0, K_w^1

$\mathsf{GbAND}\left(K^0, K^1, 1^\kappa\right)$

The zero and one keys of the left and right incoming wires are L^0, R^0 and L^1, R^1 respectively

1. Set both zero keys, $L^0 := K^0;\ R^0 := K^0$
2. Split K^1 into additive secret shares, $L^1 \leftarrow \{0,1\}^\kappa;\ R^1 := K^1 \oplus L^1$
3. **return** L^0, L^1, R^0, R^1

$\mathsf{EvAND}\left(L^{b_L}, R^{b_R}, b_L, b_R\right)$

Note that we require the bit values on the incoming wires to evaluate AND gates

1. **if** $b_L = 0$ **then return** L^{b_L}
2. **else if** $b_R = 0$ **then return** R^{b_R}
3. **else return** $L^{b_L} \oplus R^{b_R}$

$\mathsf{VeAND}\left(L^0, L^1, R^0, R^1\right)$

1. **if** $L^0 \neq R^0$ **then** zero keys are inconsistent, **return** $0, \perp, \perp$. **else return** $1, L^0, L^1 \oplus R^1$

Fig. 2. Garbling, evaluation and verification of an AND gate

corresponding to bit values zero and one respectively, and is input to a NOT gate g, the outgoing wire of g will have keys $K_g^0 = K_w^1$, $K_g^1 = K_w^0$ corresponding to values 0 and 1 respectively.

Note that none of the above schemes require ciphertexts to be published. Given that XOR, NOT, and AND gates can be garbled without ciphertexts, we therefore have a scheme to garble any formula without ciphertexts in the information-theoretic, privacy-free setting. Note that unlike the GESS construction of [Kol05], in our scheme the key size on every wire is the same (κ bits), hence allowing the online communication complexity of encoding the input x to be dependent only on the size of the input x, and not circuit depth of f.

3.2 Garbling an Entire Circuit

We can combine the routines defined in Figs. 1 and 2 in order to construct a garbling scheme for an entire formulaic circuit. Our garbling scheme $\mathcal{G}$ is defined by the tuple $\mathcal{G} = (\mathsf{Gb}, \mathsf{En}, \mathsf{Ev}, \mathsf{De}, \mathsf{Ve})$, as detailed in Figs. 3, 4, 5, 4, and 6 respectively.

We can further optimize our scheme to handle ℓ-fan-in gates with better concrete efficiency. A detailed discussion is deferred to Sect. 6. The full proof of security appears in the next section.

$\mathsf{Gb}\left(f, 1^{\kappa}\right)$

- Parse n, q from f
- Denote the keys on wire w as K_w^0, K_w^1 corresponding to bit values 0 and 1 respectively

1. Start with the the circuit output gate, $g = n + q$
2. Set circuit output gate keys, $K_g^0 \leftarrow \{0,1\}^{\kappa}$; $K_g^1 \leftarrow \{0,1\}^{\kappa}$
3. **while** $g > n$ **do**
   i. $\alpha := A(g)$; $\beta := B(g)$
   ii. **if** g is an XOR Gate **then** $K_\alpha^0, K_\alpha^1, K_\beta^0, K_\beta^1 \leftarrow \mathsf{GbXOR}\left(K_g^0, K_g^1, 1^{\kappa}\right)$
   iii. **else if** g is an AND Gate **then** $K_\alpha^0, K_\alpha^1, K_\beta^0, K_\beta^1 \leftarrow \mathsf{GbAND}\left(K_g^0, K_g^1, 1^{\kappa}\right)$
   iv. **else** g is a NOT gate, $K_\beta^0 := K_g^1$; $K_\beta^1 := K_g^0$
   v. Proceed to the previous gate, $g := g - 1$
4. Prepare encoding information, $e := \left(\left(K_i^0, K_i^1\right)_{i \in [n]}\right)$
5. Prepare decoding information, $d := \left(K_{n+q}^0, K_{n+q}^1\right)$
6. **return** $\varnothing$, e, d

Fig. 3. Garbling an entire circuit

$\mathsf{En}\left(x, e\right)$

Let x_i denote the ith bit of x

1. Parse e into keys, $\left(\left(K_i^0, K_i^1\right)_{i \in [n]}\right) := e$
2. **return** $\left(K_i^{x_i} \| x_i\right)_{i \in [n]}$

$\mathsf{De}\left(Y, d\right)$

1. **if** $Y = d[0]$ **then return** 0
2. **else if** $Y = d[1]$ **then return** 1
3. **else return** $\perp$

Fig. 4. Encoding a clear function input and decoding a garbled output

4 Full Proof of Security

Theorem 1. *The garbling scheme $\mathcal{G}$ is an unconditionally secure privacy-free garbling scheme.*

Correctness follows from the correctness of the garbling schemes for individual gates, discussed in Sect. 3.1. Verifiability follows from the consistency-checks of individual gates conducted in the Ve algorithm, discussed in Sect. 3.1.

We now construct a proof of authenticity by reducing the authenticity of our scheme for a generic formulaic circuit to the authenticity of a single garbled

Ev (F, X)

- The clear circuit f is assumed to be known
- Let K_w, b_w denote the key obtained on wire w, and the bit on that wire respectively

1. Parse $(K_w || b_w)_{i \in [n]} := X$
2. Start with the first input gate $g := n + 1$
3. **while** $g \leq n + q$ **do**
   i. $\alpha := A(g)$; $\beta := B(g)$
   ii. **if** g is an XOR Gate **then** compute $b_g := b_\alpha \oplus b_\beta$ and $K_g \leftarrow \mathsf{EvXOR}(K_\alpha, K_\beta)$
   iii. **else if** g is an AND Gate **then** compute $b_g := b_\alpha \wedge b_\beta$ and $K_g \leftarrow \mathsf{EvAND}(K_\alpha, K_\beta, b_\alpha, b_\beta)$
   iv. **else** g is a NOT gate, $b_g := \neg b_\beta$
   v. Proceed to the next gate, $g := g + 1$
4. The key on the last wire is the garbled output, **return** K_{n+q}

Fig. 5. Evaluating a garbled circuit on garbled input

Ve (F, f, e)

- The consistency of each gate is verified, and if found to be consistent, the corresponding keys are derived
- Let K_w^0, K_w^1 denote the keys corresponding to values 0 and 1 respectively on wire w
- Parse n, q from f

1. Parse e into keys $\left(\left(K_i^0, K_i^1\right)_{i \in [n]}\right) := e$
2. Start with the first gate, $g := n + 1$
3. **while** $g \leq n + q$ **do**
   i. $\alpha := A(g)$; $\beta := B(g)$
   ii. **if** g is an XOR gate **then**
      - $b, K_g^0, K_g^1 := \mathsf{VeXOR}\left(K_\alpha^0, K_\alpha^1, K_\beta^0, K_\beta^1\right)$
      - **if** $b = 0$ **then return** 0

   iii. **else if** g is an AND gate **then**
      - $b, K_g^0, K_g^1 := \mathsf{VeAND}\left(K_\alpha^0, K_\alpha^1, K_\beta^0, K_\beta^1\right)$
      - **if** $b = 0$ **then return** 0

   iv. **else** g is a NOT gate, $K_g^0 := K_\beta^1$; $K_g^1 := K_\beta^0$
   v. Proceed to the next gate, $g := g + 1$
4. All keys are consistent, **return** 1

Fig. 6. Verifying a garbled circuit

gate. We start by showing that a garbling of a circuit consisting of one gate is authentic. We then show that forging an output for an n-input garbled formulaic circuit is exactly as hard as forging an output for the same circuit with one of its gates deleted, when garbled with the same randomness[3]. The "hidden core" of our argument is that any compromise in the keys of a gate *allowed* by our scheme will not concede the gate's child's keys; the damage will only spread 'upward' to its incoming wires. We denote an adversary wishing to compromise the authenticity of a circuit with n inputs as $\mathcal{A}_n$.

4.1 Single Gate Case

Lemma 1. *The garbling scheme $\mathcal{G}$ achieves unconditional authenticity as per Definition 3 when the domain is restricted to circuits f with input size $n = 2$.*

Proving that an adversarial evaluator will be unable to forge an output key, given her requested input keys for any single gate will prove Lemma 1. This can be done by considering the garbling of AND and XOR gates, as per Figs. 2 and 1 respectively.

Let the keys on the left input wire be L^0, L^1, right input wire be R^0, R^1, and output wire be K^0, K^1. The evaluator has input bits b_L and b_R on the left and right input wires respectively. Consequently, she is given the keys L^{b_L} and R^{b_R}. We denote the adversarial evaluator as $\mathcal{A}_2$, and show that she can not forge the key $K^{\neg b_K}$, where b_K is the output bit (either $b_L \wedge b_R$ or $b_L \oplus b_R$ as per the case).

XOR Gate. The authenticity of XOR gate garbling is relatively straightforward. As per the output of the GbXOR routine, we have,

$$L^0 \oplus R^0 = L^1 \oplus R^1 = K^0, \text{ and } L^1 \oplus R^0 = L^0 \oplus R^1 = K^1$$

Let $b_K = b_L \oplus b_R$. The evaluator computes $K^{b_K} = L^{b_L} \oplus R^{b_R}$. The adversarial evaluator $\mathcal{A}_2$ wishing to forge $K^{\neg b_K}$ will notice that the only relations connecting her input keys to $K^{\neg b_K}$ are as follows: $K^{\neg b_K} = L^{\neg b_L} \oplus R^{b_R} = L^{b_L} \oplus R^{\neg b_R}$. Clearly, she will be unable to forge $K^{\neg b_K}$ without guessing either $L^{\neg b_L}$ or $R^{\neg b_R}$.

AND Gate. To show authenticity of a garbled AND gate, we have to take into account that one of the input wires may compromise both keys. We analyze all four cases, based on the input bits. Keep in mind that $L^0 = R^0 = K^0$, and $L^1 \oplus R^1 = K^1$.

1. $b_L = b_R = 0$: In this case, $\mathcal{A}_2$ has absolutely no information about K^1, and can do no better than directly guessing it.
2. $b_L = b_R = 1$: In this case, $\mathcal{A}_2$ has absolutely no information about K^0, and can do no better than directly guessing it.
3. $b_L = 1$, $b_R = 0$, $b_K = b_L \wedge b_R = 0$: $\mathcal{A}_2$ has $K^0 = R^0$, as well as L^1. Due to the key structure, she also obtains $L^0 = R^0$. However, this information is useless, as the missing output key $K^1 = L^1 \oplus R^1$ requires knowledge of R^1, which $\mathcal{A}_2$ does not have.
4. $b_L = 0$, $b_R = 1$, $b_K = b_L \wedge b_R = 0$: This case is identical to Case 3, as the left and right input wires are treated symmetrically.

[3] I.e. the random tapes used in the garbling of f and f' are identical.

NOT Gate. A NOT gate may be added on or removed from any wire at will, with no implications for authenticity, as the distributions of input and output keys for the individual gates remain unchanged.

Hence, we have shown on a case-by-case basis that there exists no gate or input combination in which an adversary $\mathcal{A}_2$ can do better than guessing the output key $K^{\neg b_K}$ that she is missing. Therefore, even a computationally unbounded adversary will be successful in forging a gate output with probability no greater than $2^{-\kappa}$, which proves Lemma 1.

4.2 Reduction Step

In this section, we perfectly reduce the authenticity of the garbling of an n-input formulaic circuit to that of an $(n-1)$-input one. We denote the garbling (i.e. collection of keys on each wire, generated within Gb) of a function f as $\mathcal{K} = \left(K_i^0, K_i^1\right)_{i\in[1,n+q]}$.

Simply put, given that garbling an n-input formulaic circuit f produces $\mathcal{K}$, an adversary loses no advantage by deleting an input gate g (gate fed only by circuit input wires), as Lemma 1 demonstrates that the keys on input wires $A(g)$ and $B(g)$ are completely useless in forging an unknown key for g. Hence, an adversary $\mathcal{A}_n$ wishing to forge an output key as per $\mathcal{K}$ will be as successful in forging an output key as per $\mathcal{K}'$, a garbling of f with any input gate g deleted. An adversary for the latter procedure is denoted by $\mathcal{A}_{n-1}$. As there is no security loss in the reduction from $\mathcal{A}_n$ to $\mathcal{A}_{n-1}$, we finally conclude that $\mathcal{A}_n$ is as successful in forging an output as per $\mathcal{K}$ as $\mathcal{A}_2$ is in forging an output for a single-gate circuit. We know from Lemma 1 that no such computationally unbounded $\mathcal{A}_2$ succeeds with probability greater than $2^{-\kappa}$.

Given an adversary $\mathcal{A}_n$ that can forge an output for an n-input formulaic circuit f, we construct adversary $\mathcal{A}_{n-1}$ (in Fig. 7), that can forge an output for an $(n-1)$-input formulaic circuit f' with the same probability of success. For readability, for a scheme $\mathcal{G}$, denote the event that a computationally unbounded adversary $\mathcal{A}$ succeeds in forging a garbled output Y given F, X for some f, x (where $(F, e, d) \leftarrow \mathsf{Gb}(f, 1^\kappa); X \leftarrow \mathsf{En}(e, x)$), by the outcome of $\mathsf{Aut}_\mathcal{G}(\mathcal{A}, 1^\kappa)$. Specifically,

$$\mathsf{Aut}_\mathcal{G}(\mathcal{A}, 1^\kappa) = \begin{cases} 1 & \text{if } \mathcal{A}(F, X) = Y; Y \neq \mathsf{Ev}(F, X), \mathsf{De}(Y, d) \neq \perp \\ 0 & \text{otherwise} \end{cases}$$

It is clear to see that a garbling scheme $\mathcal{G}$ is authentic if, and only if, $\Pr\left[\mathsf{Aut}_\mathcal{G}(\mathcal{A}, 1^\kappa) = 1\right] \leq 2^{-\kappa}$, $\forall \mathcal{A}$. Therefore, as there is no security loss in our reduction from $\mathcal{A}_n$ to $\mathcal{A}_{n-1}$, we have:

$$\Pr\left[\mathsf{Aut}_\mathcal{G}(\mathcal{A}_n, 1^\kappa) = 1\right] = \Pr\left[\mathsf{Aut}_\mathcal{G}(\mathcal{A}_{n-1}, 1^\kappa) = 1\right] = \\ \cdots = \Pr\left[\mathsf{Aut}_\mathcal{G}(\mathcal{A}_2, 1^\kappa) = 1\right] \leq 2^{-\kappa}$$

Note that the reduction from $\mathcal{A}_n$ to $\mathcal{A}_{n-1}$ detailed in Fig. 7 only works for formulaic circuits; deleting a gate with fan-out of l will produce l different input

$\mathcal{A}_{n-1}$

- $\mathcal{A}_{n-1}$ has black-box access to $\mathcal{A}_n$, which is capable of forging Y for the garbled circuit F and corresponding encoded input X for a certain formulaic circuit f and corresponding n-bit input x.
- Using $\mathcal{A}_n$, $\mathcal{A}_{n-1}$ forges garbled output Y' for a (F', X'), for some formulaic circuit f' and corresponding $(n-1)$-bit input x'.
- f', x' are derived from f, x as follows:
   i. Choose some gate g from f such that both parents $A(g)$ and $B(g)$ are input wires[a].
   ii. Construct f' identical to f, with the exception that $g, A(g), B(g)$ are replaced with a single input wire numbered g'.
   iii. Parse x into bits $x_1 x_2 \cdots x_i \cdots x_n$, copy them to create x', with the exception of $x_{A(g)}$ and $x_{B(g)}$, which are replaced with $x'_{g'} = G_g\left(x_{A(g)}, x_{B(g)}\right)$[b]
   iv. f', x' are now an $(n-1)$-input function and its corresponding input such that $f(x) = f'(x')$

1. Parse X' into keys $X'_1 X'_2 \cdots X'_{n-1}$, and copy them into X at the appropriate locations.
2. X will be missing keys at locations $A(g)$ and $B(g)$. They can be generated as follows[c]:
   - **if** g was an XOR gate **then** $X_{A(g)} \leftarrow \{0,1\}^\kappa$; $X_{B(g)} := X_{A(g)} \oplus X'_{g'}$
   - **else if** g was an AND gate **then**
      i. **if** $x_{A(g)} = x_{B(g)} = 0$ **then** $X_{A(g)} := X_{B(g)} := X'_{g'}$
      ii. **else if** $x_{A(g)} = x_{B(g)} = 1$ **then** $X_{A(g)} \leftarrow \{0,1\}^\kappa$, $X_{B(g)} := X_{A(g)} \oplus X'_{g'}$
      iii. **else if** $x_{A(g)} = 0$ **then** $X_{A(g)} := X'_{g'}$, $X_{B(g)} \leftarrow \{0,1\}^\kappa$
      iv. **else** $X_{B(g)} := X'_{g'}$, $X_{A(g)} \leftarrow \{0,1\}^\kappa$
3. Send X to $\mathcal{A}_n$ and output the response, **output** $\mathcal{A}_n\left(\varnothing, X, 1^\kappa\right)$

[a] Even g such that its parent is a NOT gate $A(g)$ with its parent as an input wire $w = B(A(g)) < n$ will work. In this case, consider $\neg x_w$ in place of x_w wherever relevant in this algorithm.

[b] G_g is the gate functionality of gate g, ie. XOR or AND

[c] This subroutine effectively garbles the missing gate g such that the keys for parents $A(g), B(g)$ consistently evaluate to the keys on wire g'. Note that this leaves all the original keys generated when garbling f' undisturbed, hence implying that a forged key returned by $\mathcal{A}_n$ for its garbling of f can directly be output as a forged key for the garbling of f' given to $\mathcal{A}_{n-1}$. Also note a minor technical detail, that we ignore that X_i is actually $K_i||b_i$ on an input wire, for readability.

Fig. 7. Constructing adversary $\mathcal{A}_{n-1}$ given $\mathcal{A}_n$

wires, each with its own independent pair of keys. For $\mathcal{A}_{n-1}$ to ensure that the deleted gate's keys are consistent with l different outgoing wires is undefined as per our garbling scheme.

Hence, there exists no computationally unbounded adversary that succeeds in forging an output for a formulaic circuit of any size when garbled by $\mathcal{G}$, with probability greater than $2^{-\kappa}$. This proves Theorem 1.

4.3 Adaptive Security

We had mentioned in an earlier section that our scheme achieves adaptive security, or $\mathsf{aut1}$ in the terminology of [BHR12a], as opposed to Definition 3 which they term static security, or aut.

We show this by illustrating that an adversary in the $\mathsf{Aut1}_{\mathcal{G}}$ game (which forms the basis for the definition of adaptive security) is at no advantage in forging a garbled output, as compared to an adversary wishing to break the 'static' authenticity of our scheme as per Definition 3.

In the $\mathsf{Aut1}_{\mathcal{G}}$ game, the adversary is allowed to request from the game the garbled circuit F for her function f *before* she chooses x for which she receives encoded input $X = \mathsf{En}(e, x)$. The $\mathsf{Aut1}_{\mathcal{G}}$ game consists of three stages:

1. The GARBLE stage accepts from $\mathcal{A}$ a circuit f, computes $(F, e, d) \leftarrow \mathsf{Gb}(1^\kappa, f)$, and returns F to $\mathcal{A}$.
2. The INPUT stage accepts from $\mathcal{A}$ an input x, outputs $\perp$ if it is not in the domain of f, otherwise returns $X = \mathsf{En}(e, x)$ to $\mathcal{A}$.
3. The FINALIZE stage accepts from $\mathcal{A}$ a garbled output Y, and outputs 1 if $Y \neq \mathsf{Ev}(F, X)$ while still being a valid garbled output (i.e. $\mathsf{De}(Y, d) \neq \perp$), and 0 otherwise.

The output of the experiment $\mathsf{Aut1}_{\mathcal{G}}(\mathcal{A}, 1^\kappa)$ is the value output by the FINALIZE stage. An unconditionally adaptively authentic scheme will ensure that $\Pr[\mathsf{Aut1}_{\mathcal{G}}(\mathcal{A}, 1^\kappa) = 1] \leq 2^{-\kappa}$ for all computationally unbounded $\mathcal{A}$.

It is immediately evident that this extra concession granted to the adversary is useless in our setting, as our scheme does not produce any ciphertexts to represent a garbled circuit. An adversary $\mathcal{A}'$ for the $\mathsf{Aut1}_{\mathcal{G}}$ game can be given a null string to serve as the garbled circuit F of any function f that it may submit to the GARBLE stage. Therefore, $\mathcal{A}'$ is forced to choose x completely independently of the garbling of f, effectively having to commit to f, x simultaneously. Hence, the task of $\mathcal{A}'$ is equivalent to that of a static adversary $\mathcal{A}(F, X)$ attempting to forge a garbled output as per Definition 3, which is proven not to succeed with probability better than $2^{-\kappa}$ by Theorem 1.

5 Breaking the Lower Bound of [ZRE15]

Zahur *et al.* [ZRE15] observe that most known garbling schemes fit into their characterization of *linear* garbling techniques. Informally, a linear garbling scheme proceeds gate by gate, at each gate generating a vector $\mathbf{S} = (R_1, \cdots, R_r, Q_1, \cdots, Q_q)$, where R_is are fresh random values, and Q_is are obtained by independent calls to a random oracle (queries may depend on R_i values). The gate ciphertexts as well as the keys on each wire touching the gate are derived by linearly combining the values in $\mathbf{S}$. The only non-linearity allowed in their model is through the random oracle invocations, and permutation bits. All elements are μ bits long, where μ is the security parameter. They prove that an ideally secure garbling scheme that is linear as per their characterization must adhere to certain lower bounds in terms of bits of ciphertext produced when garbling a *single atomic* AND gate. An ideally secure garbling scheme ensures that no computationally unbounded adversary (with bounded calls to the random oracle) will have advantage better than $\mathsf{poly}(\mu)/2^{\mu}$ in the security games of Bellare *et al.* [BHR12b]. The following are the bounds in the private and privacy-free settings respectively, as argued by Zahur *et al.* [ZRE15].

Lower Bound for Garbling Schemes Achieving Privacy. Linear garbling schemes are shown to require at least 2μ bits of ciphertext to garble an AND gate privately. This bound was circumvented (but not contradicted) in the works of Ball *et al.* [BMR16] and Kempka *et al.* [KKS16] by a different treatment of permutation bits. Both schemes garble a single AND gate privately but non-composably with just one ciphertext.

Lower Bound for Privacy-Free Garbling Schemes. Linear garbling schemes achieving authenticity are argued to require at least μ bits of ciphertext to garble an AND gate. To the best of our knowledge, this bound is currently unchallenged. Our scheme is clearly linear (with no requirement of a random oracle) and yet garbles AND gates with *no ciphertexts* for any μ. Moreover, our scheme composes to garble a non-trivial class of circuits (i.e. formulas) with no ciphertexts.

5.1 Linear Garbling

We recall the formal definition of linear garbling [ZRE15], but simplified for the privacy-free setting. Specifically, we enforce that the permutation bit always be 0, as there is no reason for the semantic value of a wire key to be hidden from an evaluator in this setting. Indeed, both previous privacy-free schemes [ZRE15, FNO15] rely on an evaluator knowing the semantic value of the key she has. A garbling scheme $\mathcal{G}$ is linear if its routines are of the form described in Fig. 8.

Claim ([ZRE15]). Every linear ideally secure privacy-free garbling scheme for AND gates must have $p \geq 1$. The garbled gate consists of at least μ bits.

Our privacy-free garbling scheme is a linear garbling scheme with the following parameters for an AND gate and with $\mu = \kappa$:

- Number of ciphertexts $p = 0$, random values $r = 3$ and random oracle queries $q = 0$.
- The same vector to obtain all zero keys, $\mathbf{L}_0 = \mathbf{R}_0 = \mathbf{K}_0 = [1\ 0\ 0]$
- Vectors to select independent input 1-keys, $\mathbf{L}_1 = [0\ 1\ 0]$, $\mathbf{R}_1 = [0\ 0\ 1]$
- Output 1-key vector as the sum of both input 1-keys, $\mathbf{K}_1 = \mathbf{L}_1 + \mathbf{R}_1 = [0\ 1\ 1]$
- $(C^i)_{i\in[p]}$ is an empty set as there are no ciphertexts required.
- Evaluation vectors $(\mathbf{V}_{\alpha,\beta})_{\alpha,\beta\in\{0,1\}}$ as follows:
  - When the evaluator has a zero key, output the zero key. So, $V_{0,0} = V_{0,1} = [1\ 0]$, $V_{1,0} = [0\ 1]$.
  - When both keys correspond to 1, output their sum. So $V_{1,1} = [1\ 1]$.

- We describe here a simplified characterization of linear garbling [ZRE15] for the privacy-free setting. Note that garbling by default is for a single gate.
- The integers p, q, r, and vectors $\mathbf{L}_0, \mathbf{L}_1, \mathbf{R}_0, \mathbf{R}_1, \mathbf{K}_0, \mathbf{K}_1, \left(\mathbf{C}^i\right)_{i\in[p]}, \left(\mathbf{V}_{\alpha,\beta}\right)_{\alpha,\beta\in\{0,1\}}$ parameterize garbling scheme $\mathcal{G} = (\mathsf{Gb}, \mathsf{En}, \mathsf{Ev}, \mathsf{De})$. p denotes the number of ciphertexts. r and q denote the number of uniformly random elements and the number of random oracle calls needed. Each of the above vectors is of size $r + q$ (except $\mathbf{V}_{\alpha,\beta}$ which is of size $p + q + 2$) with entries in $GF\left(2^\mu\right)$.

$\mathsf{Gb}\left(\cdot, 1^\mu\right)$

1. **for** $i \in [r]$ **do** Choose $R_i \leftarrow GF\left(2^\mu\right)$
2. **for** $i \in [q]$ **do** Make a query to the random oracle, store the response in Q_i
3. Construct $\mathbf{S} = (R_1, \cdots, R_r, Q_1, \cdots, Q_q)$
4. **for** $i \in \{0, 1\}$ **do** Corresponding to semantic value i, compute keys on the two input wires as $L_i := \langle \mathbf{L}_i, \mathbf{S}\rangle$ and $R_i := \langle \mathbf{R}_i, \mathbf{S}\rangle$, and the output wire as $K_i := \langle \mathbf{K}_i, \mathbf{S}\rangle$
5. **for** $i \in [p]$ **do** Compute the ith gate ciphertext $C_i := \langle \mathbf{C}^i, \mathbf{S}\rangle$
6. Construct and output encoding information $e := \left(\left(L_0, L_1\right), \left(R_0, R_1\right)\right)$, and gate ciphertexts $F = \left(C_i\right)_{i\in[p]}$

$\mathsf{En}\left(x, e\right)$

1. Parse $(x_0, x_1) := x$, and $\left(\left(L_0, L_1\right), \left(R_0, R_1\right)\right) := e$
2. Output $X = \left(L_{x_0}||x_0, R_{x_1}||x_1\right)$

$\mathsf{Ev}\left(F, X\right)$

1. Parse input labels $\left(L_\alpha||\alpha, R_\beta||\beta\right) := X$, and ciphertexts $\left(C_i\right)_{i\in[p]} := F$
2. **for** $i \in [q]$ **do** Make a query to the random oracle, store the response in Q'_i
3. Construct $\mathbf{T} = \left(L_\alpha, R_\beta, Q'_1, \cdots, Q'_q, C_1, \cdots, C_p\right)$
4. Output $\langle \mathbf{V}_{\alpha,\beta}, \mathbf{T}\rangle$

Fig. 8. Form of linear garbling schemes

Succinctness of Our Garbling Scheme. As Zahur *et al.* [ZRE15] note, almost all practical techniques so far for garbling Boolean circuits qualify as linear as per their characterization. If we use their parameters to define $s = p + r + q$ as a measure of 'program succinctness' of a linear garbling scheme, then we observe that our garbling scheme has the most succinct program ($s = 3$) of all garbling schemes in the literature.

5.2 Where the [ZRE15] Technique for Bounding Privacy-Free Garbling Fails

As illustrated above, our garbling scheme is clearly linear and achieves ideal security, but can still garble an AND gate in the privacy-free setting with *no* ciphertext. Our scheme is therefore a simple and direct counterexample to the argument of Zahur *et al.* [ZRE15] that a linear garbling scheme achieving ideal authenticity must produce at least μ bits of ciphertext when garbling and AND gate.

In more detail, the ciphertext generating $\mathbb{G}_{a,b}$ becomes a dimension 0 matrix. At the core of the linear garbling model is that the evaluator's behaviour must depend only on the public α, β 'signal' bits, a property which is adhered to by our privacy-free scheme. In our setting, the signal bits convey the actual semantic values with which the keys are associated. However, the lower bound proof in [ZRE15] relies on the property that changing a 'permute' bit a/b which is defined when garbling, must also change the corresponding signal bit on which the evaluator acts. In our setting it is immediate that this assumption does not need to hold (as α, β are not tied to a, b), and our scheme takes advantage of this to break the claimed lower bound.

6 ℓ-fan-in Gates

In this section, we describe how to handle ℓ-fan-in gates efficiently. We first provide a new garbling scheme for *threshold* gates in Sect. 6.1, then describe how to save computation in garbling and evaluating ℓ-fan-in XOR and AND gates respectively in Sects. 6.2 and 6.3.

6.1 Threshold Gates

An ℓ-input threshold gate, parameterized by a threshold t, realizes the following function:

$$f_t(x_1, \cdots, x_i, \cdots, x_\ell) = \begin{cases} 1, & \text{if} \sum_{i=1}^{\ell} x_i > t \\ 0, & \text{otherwise} \end{cases}$$

The threshold range $1 < t < \ell - 1$ is of interest to us, as the gate otherwise degenerates into an ℓ-fan-in AND or NAND gate, which can be handled more efficiently by our scheme. Boolean threshold gates are considered and motivated by Ball *et al.* [BMR16], who construct a scheme to garble them natively (generating $\mathcal{O}\left(\log^3 \ell / \log\log \ell\right)$ ciphertexts) as opposed to garbling a composition of AND, XOR and NOT gates (yielding $\mathcal{O}\left(\ell \log \ell\right)$ ciphertexts using the best known garbling scheme of [ZRE15]). Here, we present a method of garbling Boolean threshold gates (embedded in formulaic circuits) directly, producing no ciphertext, and using only information-theoretic operations; specifically two independent instances of Shamir secret sharing [Sha79] per threshold gate assuming the underlying field to be $GF(2^\kappa)$.

The idea is as follows; an evaluator having inputs $x_1 \cdots x_\ell$ to the threshold gate computing f_t, such that $\sum_{i=1}^{\ell} x_\ell = m$, will possess m input 1-keys, and $\ell - m$ input 0-keys. Let the gate output keys be denoted as K^0 and K^1, and denote the

$\mathsf{GbTHR}\left(\ell, t, K^0, K^1, 1^\kappa\right)$

The zero and one keys of the ith incoming wire will be K_i^0, K_i^1. We denote the set of all t-degree polynomials with constant s as $\mathcal{P}^{s,t}$.

1. Choose a uniformly random t-degree polynomial with K^1 as its constant, $h_{K^1} \leftarrow \mathcal{P}^{K^1,t}$
2. Generate the input 1-keys to be Shamir shares of K^1, **for all** $i \in [\ell]$ **do** $K_i^1 := h_{K^1}(i)$
3. Choose a uniformly random $(\ell - (t+1))$-degree polynomial with K^0 as its constant, $h_{K^0} \leftarrow \mathcal{P}^{K^0,(\ell-(t+1))}$
4. Generate the input 0-keys to be Shamir shares of K^0, **for all** $i \in [\ell]$ **do** $K_i^0 := h_{K^0}(i)$.
5. **return** $\left(K_i^0, K_i^1\right)_{i\in[1,\ell]}$

$\mathsf{EvTHR}\left(t', (j_i, K_i)_{i\in[t+1]}\right)$

1. The input to this routine is assumed to be a set of $t'+1$ unique (index, key) pairs, where each key corresponds to the same value. Note that t' may be t or $\ell - (t+1)$ depending on the gate output.
2. Using Lagrange interpolation, we obtain the unique t-degree polynomial h, such that $h(j_i) = K_i, \forall i \in [t+1]$.
3. Compute the output key by retrieving the constant of h; $K := h(0)$.
4. **return** K

$\mathsf{VeTHR}\left(t, \left(K_i^0, K_i^1\right)_{i\in[\ell]}\right)$

1. Using Lagrange interpolation, we obtain the unique t-degree polynomial h_{K^1}, such that $h_{K^1}(i) = K_i^1, \forall i \in [t+1]$.
2. **if** $\exists j \in [t+2, \ell]$ such that $h_{K^1}(j) \neq K_j^1$ **then return** $0, \bot, \bot$
3. Using Lagrange interpolation, we obtain the unique $(\ell - (t+1))$-degree polynomial h_{K^0}, such that $h_{K^0}(i) = K_i^0, \forall i \in [\ell - t]$.
4. **if** $\exists j \in [\ell - t + 1, \ell]$ such that $h_{K^0}(j) \neq K_j^0$ **then return** $0, \bot, \bot$
5. The input 0-keys and 1-keys each define unique polynomials of degrees $\ell - (t+1)$ and t respectively. Compute the output keys to be the constants of the curves, $K^0 := h_{K^0}(0)$ and $K^1 := h_{K^1}(0)$
6. **return** $1, K^0, K^1$

Fig. 9. Garbling, evaluation and verification of a threshold gate

keys on the ith input wire as K_i^0, K_i^1. As the requirement of the threshold gate is that more than t of the evaluator's inputs must be 1 in order to output 1, we need to devise a garbled evaluation scheme which allows the evaluator to obtain K^1 when she has more than t K_i^1s. A natural candidate for this construction is a threshold secret sharing scheme, where the K_i^1s form a t-out-of-l sharing of K^1; i.e. any $t+1$ of the K_i^1s are sufficient to reconstruct K^1, while having t or fewer K_i^1s renders K^1 unconditionally hidden except with a probability of $2^{-\kappa}$.

Note that in order to correctly realise f_t, our garbled gate evaluation scheme also needs to ensure that if (and only if) the evaluator has fewer than $(t+1)$ input values equal to 1, she should obtain K^0. In this case, her $\ell - m$ zero keys K_i^0 should be sufficient to reconstruct K^0. Therefore, we define the K_i^0s to form an $(\ell - (t+1))$-out-of-l sharing of K^0, i.e. any $(\ell - t)$ of the K_i^0s are sufficient to reconstruct K^0. This also ensures that when $m > t$ (i.e. $f_t(x_1 \cdots x_\ell) = 1$), she will be unable to reconstruct K^0, as $(\ell - m) < (\ell - t)$, and she only has $(\ell - m)$ K_i^0s.

We formalize the described scheme in Fig. 9. It is evident how to invoke the GbTHR, EvTHR, and VeTHR routines within the Gb, Ev, and Ve algorithms respectively. To formally prove the authenticity of our threshold gate garbling routine, we describe how the adversary $\mathcal{A}_{n-\ell+1}$, given black-box access to $\mathcal{A}_n$, can forge an output for an $n-\ell+1$ input formula obtained by deleting an ℓ-fan-in input threshold gate from an n-input formula used by $\mathcal{A}_n$, in Fig. 10.

$$\mathcal{A}_{n-\ell+1}(f', x', F', X')$$

- This procedure is a modification of the adversary from Fig. 7, to accommodate threshold gates.
- Without loss of generality, f' was generated by deleting an input threshold gate g from f, which was fed by input bits $x_1 \cdots x_\ell$.
- This routine adds a clause to Step 2 of the original $\mathcal{A}_{n-1}$ to detail how to generate $X_1 \cdots X_\ell$ for $\mathcal{A}_n$, given the input key X'_g on wire g'.

2. - **else if** g was a threshold gate f_t **then**
    i. $b := f_t(x_1 \cdots x_\ell)$
    ii. **if** $b = 1$ **then** Choose a uniformly random t-degree polynomial with X'_g as its constant, $h \leftarrow \mathcal{P}^{X'_g, t}$
    iii. **else** Choose a uniformly random $(\ell - (t+1))$-degree polynomial with X'_g as its constant, $h \leftarrow \mathcal{P}^{X'_g, (\ell-(t+1))}$
    iv. **for** $i \in [1, \ell]$ **do**
        - **if** $x_i = b$ **then** $X_i := h(i)$
        - **else** $X_i \leftarrow \{0,1\}^\kappa$

Fig. 10. Deleting a threshold gate to reduce $\mathcal{A}_n$ to $\mathcal{A}_{n-\ell+1}$ as per the gate deletion proof strategy

Security. As discussed earlier, the unconditional authenticity of our threshold gate garbling in the single gate case is implied by the unconditional security of Shamir's secret sharing [Sha79]. Observe that our threshold gate garbling scheme is also made possible by the violation of Yao's invariant; the nature of threshold secret sharing is such that once the curve is reconstructed, the missing shares can be computed as well. Specifically, possessing the 1-key on $t+1$ input wires to an ℓ-fan-in threshold gate computing f_t, allows the reconstruction of the 1-keys on the remaining $\ell - (t+1)$ input wires in addition to the gate output 1-key. However, this information is useless in reconstructing the 0-key of the gate, and hence has no impact on authenticity.

Extension to Circuits. It is easy to see that our threshold gate garbling gadget can be used to augment any privacy-free circuit garbling scheme $\mathcal{G}_c$, at the cost of cryptographic assumptions no stronger than required by $\mathcal{G}_c$. Every input key k_i^b to the threshold gate g can be mapped to a corresponding K_i^b output by GbTHR. During evaluation, K_i^b is made accessible given k_i^b by means of a ciphertext $T[g]_{i,b} = H(g,i,k_i^b,b) \oplus K_i^b$, where H is the cryptographic primitive used to implement encryption in $\mathcal{G}_c$, eg. PRF [GLNP15], KDF [FNO15], circular correlation robust hash [ZRE15].

While this gadget costs only 2ℓ ciphertexts to implement, we can additionally optimize this construction to cut down the ciphertexts by half. Intuitively, we can set the curves h_{K^1} and h_{K^0} pseudorandomly rather than uniformly at random. Specifically, the polynomial h_{K^1} in GbTHR (Fig. 9) can be set by fixing $t-1$ points as $h_{K^1}(i) = H(g,i,1,k_i^1)$, $\forall i \in [t-1]$, so that cipherexts are needed to convey only the remaining $\ell - t + 1$ points. The same optimization applied to h_{K^0} yields that the total number of ciphertexts that need to be communicated for this gadget is now $\ell + 2$.

Performance. Our base construction for formulas is significantly more efficient than a naive approach, as representing threshold gates in a formula is highly non-trivial, with upper bounds of $\mathcal{O}\left(\ell^{3.04}\right)$ [Ser14]. As for general circuits, the construction of Ball *et al.* [BMR16] will cost $\mathcal{O}\left(\log^3 \ell / \log\log \ell\right)$ more ciphertexts than our construction when embedded directly in a Boolean circuit (accounting for ℓ 'projection' gates) despite relying on a circular correlation robust hash function.

6.2 Improved ℓ-fan-in XOR

The routine to garble an individual XOR gate described in Fig. 1 performs 3 XOR operations in order to derive the incoming wire keys corresponding to a given pair of gate keys. Hence, in order to garble ℓ XOR gates, repeating this routine $\ell - 1$ times will cost $3(\ell - 1)$ XOR operations.

Consider a subtree (with ℓ leaves) consisting only of XOR gates, contained within the tree representation of a formulaic circuit. Note that there are $\ell - 1$ gates in this subtree. Without loss of generality, let the subtree be collapsed into a single gate accepting ℓ incoming wires. For convenience, the incoming wires (leaves of the subtree) are assumed to be numbered consecutively from w to $w + \ell - 1$, with the final XOR gate itself (root of the subtree) being numbered g such that the internal nodes of the subtree are numbered consecutively from $w + \ell$ to $g - 1$. As usual, the keys on wire i are denoted K_i^0, K_i^1, corresponding to bit values 0 and 1 respectively.

Consider the keys $\left(K_i^0, K_i^1\right)_{i \in [w,g]}$ to be produced by $\ell - 1$ instances of the GbXOR routine from Fig. 1; starting from the root K_g^0, K_g^1 and ending at the leaves to produce $(K_i^0, K_i^1)_{i \in [w, w+\ell-1]}$. Observe that the zero and one keys on each wire differ by the same offset; i.e. $\forall i \in [w, g]$:

$$K_w^0 \oplus K_w^1 = \cdots = K_i^0 \oplus K_i^1 = \cdots = K_g^0 \oplus K_g^1 \quad (1)$$

We make use of the property observed in Eq. (1) in order to garble such an ℓ-fan-in XOR gate more efficiently. Essentially, the 0-keys of the incoming wires are chosen so as to form an additive secret sharing of the gate's 0-key. The 1-keys are then generated by offsetting the 0-keys by the same offset as the gate key pair (i.e. $K_g^0 \oplus K_g^1$). The formal description is given in Fig. 11.

$\mathsf{GbXOR}\left(\ell, K^0, K^1, 1^\kappa\right)$

- We have to generate ℓ key pairs, which will produce either K^0 or K^1 appropriately upon being combined by XORing
- The resultant keys are locally indexed here as $K_i^0, K_i^1, i \in [1, \ell]$

1. Calculate the offset, $\Delta := K^0 \oplus K^1$
2. Choose the 0-keys on all but one wire randomly, **for all** $i \in [1, \ell - 1]$ **do** $K_i^0 \leftarrow \{0, 1\}^\kappa$
3. Set the final 0-key so that all the incoming wires' 0-keys form an additive secret sharing of K^0, $K_\ell^0 := \left(\bigoplus_{i=1}^{\ell-1} K_i^0\right) \oplus K^0$
4. Offset the 0-keys to generate the 1-keys on the incoming wires. **for all** $i \in [1, \ell]$ **do** $K_i^1 = K_i^0 \oplus \Delta$
5. **return** $(K_i^0, K_i^1)_{i \in [1, \ell]}$

Fig. 11. Garbling an ℓ-fan-in XOR gate

The routine detailed in Fig. 11 produces keys that adhere to the exact same distribution as the result of invoking the original GbXOR routine $\ell - 1$ times in an appropriate sequence. The evaluation and verification algorithms for garbled XOR gates (Fig. 1) are directly compatible. A separate proof of authenticity is therefore not required.

As for the computation cost, the new GbXOR routine of Fig. 11 requires one XOR operation to find the gate offset, $\ell - 1$ XOR operations to additively secret share one of the gate keys, and ℓ XOR operations to offset each of the 1-keys on the incoming wires, bringing the total to 2ℓ. This beats the $3(\ell - 1)$ cost of using multiple instances of the original routine when $\ell > 3$.

6.3 Improved ℓ-fan-in AND

The cost of garbling an AND gate is already minimal, at a single XOR operation per gate. Instead, we focus on optimizing the evaluation of AND gates.

Similar to the ℓ-fan-in case of XOR gates, consider a subtree consisting solely of AND gates, contained in a formulaic circuit. The gates in the subtree are numbered as described in the ℓ-fan-in XOR section; w to $w+\ell-1$ for the inputs, $w+\ell$ to g for the intermediate gates, and g for the root of the subtree. The subtree is collapsed into a single ℓ-fan-in AND gate. We follow the standard naming convention for wire keys and bit values.

Observe that if any of the bit values on wires w to $w+\ell-1$ are 0, then the entire subtree (the ℓ-fan-in AND gate) will evaluate to 0, as $b_g = b_w \wedge \cdots \wedge b_{w+\ell-1}$. Also observe that as per the GbAND routine defined in Fig. 2, the following relation holds:

$$K_w^0 = \cdots = K_i^0 = \cdots = K_g^0, \quad \forall i \in [w, g] \tag{2}$$

We exploit the above relation in order to save time during evaluation; if a wire $j \in [w, w+\ell-1]$ is found to be carrying a bit value of 0, then the ℓ-fan-in AND gate output is set to 0, with the key K_j being assigned to the gate output key K_g. The routine is formally detailed in Fig. 12.

EvAND $\left((K_i, b_i)_{i\in[1,\ell]}, 1^\kappa\right)$

- We have to process ℓ (key, bit value) pairs that effectively correspond to an ℓ-fan-in AND gate.
- The incoming wire keys and bit values are locally indexed as K_i, b_i, where $i \in [1, \ell]$, and the resultant key and bit value are locally indexed as K_g, b_g.

1. **if** $\exists j \in [1, \ell]$ such that $b_j = 0$ **then** Gate output is zero, K_j is also the output key. $K_g := K_j$
2. **else** Gate output is 1, XOR all input keys. $K_g := \bigoplus_{i=1}^{\ell} K_i$
3. **return** K_g, b_g

Fig. 12. Evaluating an l-fan-in AND gate

The only case where XOR operations are performed in the EvAND routine in Fig. 12 is when all input bit values are 1; i.e. $b_i = 1, \forall i \in [w, w+\ell-1]$. Even so, only $\ell-1$ XOR operations are performed, which is the same as when $\ell-1$ instances of the original EvAND routine from Fig. 2 are executed. However, if there exists at least one incoming wire carrying bit value 0, i.e. $\exists j \in [w, w+\ell-1], b_j = 0$, no XOR operations are performed to evaluate the entire ℓ-fan-in AND gate. This occurs for $2^\ell - 1$ out of the 2^ℓ input cases. The number of XOR operations saved will be equal to the number of gates in the (now collapsed) subtree that evaluate to bit value 1. As there is no modification to the garbling routine, there is no additional proof of authenticity required here.

7 Online-Efficient Zero-Knowledge

Privacy-free GCs are motivated by applications to ZK protocols. Specifically, when plugged into the ZK protocol of [JKO13], a privacy-free GC yields an efficient method to prove non-algebraic statements. In this section, we show that when instantiated with our scheme, we obtain a ZK protocol for Boolean formula satisfiability (SAT) statements in the online-offline paradigm, where the communication in the online phase is linearly proportional only to the size of the witness.

A SAT verification function can be realised by a formula. A witness bit may occur a number of times in the formula. While realizing the formula as a formulaic circuit, each occurrence of a witness bit in the formula is treated as a separate input wire. Denoting the ith witness bit of the formula to be represented by input wires $\mathbf{I}_i = \{i_0, i_1, \cdots i_l\}$ in the formulaic circuit, in order for the formula to correctly check a witness $w = (w_i)_{i\in[n]}$ we must ensure that $\forall j \in \mathbf{I}_i$, $x_j = w_i$. We stress that the cumulative size of the $\mathbf{I}_i$s may be much bigger than the witness length. We denote the size of $\cup_i^n \mathbf{I}_i$ as n'. We denote the size of the (formulaic) circuit by m and the size of the witness w as n. So we have $n \leq n' \leq m$.

Our ZK protocol $\pi = (\pi_{\mathsf{off}}, \pi_{\mathsf{on}})$ is described in Fig. 13. Informally, protocol π is a direct adaptation of the ZK protocol in [JKO13] to the online-offline setting, by shifting the public-key operations (OTs) to the offline phase. However, we observe that the same witness bit is used to select multiple GC keys, and accordingly use a domain extension technique for the OTs in order to encode n' garbled inputs with just n OT instances. This is the core of why the communication required in π_{on} is only proportional to the witness size, and not the size of the statement. The proof of security appears in the full version of the paper and the formal definitions of the necessary ideal functionalities $\mathcal{F}_{\mathsf{COM}}, \mathcal{F}_{\mathsf{COT}}, \mathcal{F}_{\mathsf{ZK}}^{\mathsf{R}}$ are postponed to Appendix A.

Computation Cost. The offline phase will require $\mathcal{O}(n)$ PRG invocations by $\mathcal{V}$, and $\mathcal{O}(n)$ public key operations (OTs) by both $\mathcal{P}$ and $\mathcal{V}$. The online phase will require $\mathcal{O}(n)$ PRG invocations by $\mathcal{P}$ to unmask the input keys, $\mathcal{O}(m)$ XORs to evaluate the GC, and another $\mathcal{O}(n)$ public key operations to verify that the GC is valid. $\mathcal{V}$ need only perform $\mathcal{O}(n)$ XOR operations in the online phase, and open one commitment.

Communication Cost. The preprocessing phase will require $\mathcal{O}(m)$, and the online phase will require $\mathcal{O}(n)$ bits of communication. The ZK protocol when instantiated with a statically secure garbling scheme can not possibly yield an online phase which is independent of the size of the statement. This is because the garbled circuit will necessarily have to be sent after the evaluator commits to her input.

Our ZK Protocol Without Offline Phase. Our protocol in Fig. 13 in its monolithic form can be obtained by running the OTs in an online fashion where the inputs of $\mathcal{V}$ are the seeds of the PRG and the inputs of $\mathcal{P}$ are the witness bits directly. We

- The witness checking formulaic circuit f is the only input available during π_{off}. During π_{on}, the prover $\mathcal{P}$ additionally has her witness $w = w_1 w_2 \cdots w_n$ as input.
- $G(\cdot)$ is a length-expanding PRG.
- The protocol is in the $(\mathcal{F}_{\mathsf{COT}}, \mathcal{F}_{\mathsf{COM}})$-hybrid model (formal definitions of these functionalities appear in Appendix A).

π_{off}

1. $\mathcal{V}$ garbles the circuit, $\left(\emptyset, \left(K_i^0, K_i^1\right)_{i\in[n']}, Z\right) \leftarrow \mathsf{Gb}\left(1^\kappa, f\right)^a$ and groups together input keys for the same witness bit as $\boldsymbol{K}_i^b = \left(K_j^b\right)_{j\in \mathbf{I}_i}$ for all $i \in [n]$ and $b \in \{0,1\}$.
2. For all $i \in [n]$ and $b \in \{0,1\}$, $\mathcal{V}$ samples seeds $S_i^b \leftarrow \{0,1\}^\mu$, computes $T_i^b := \boldsymbol{K}_i^b \oplus G(S_i^b)$ and sends T_i^b to $\mathcal{P}$.
3. For all $i \in [n]$, $\mathcal{P}$ samples $r_i \leftarrow \{0,1\}$ and sends $(\texttt{choose}, id, r_i)$ to $\mathcal{F}_{\mathsf{COT}}$.
4. On receiving messages $(\texttt{chosen}, id)$ for $i \in [n]$ from $\mathcal{F}_{\mathsf{COT}}$, $\mathcal{V}$ samples $R_i^0, R_i^1 \leftarrow \{0,1\}^\mu$ and sends $\left(\texttt{transfer}, id, R_i^0, R_i^1\right)$ as input to $\mathcal{F}_{\mathsf{COT}}$ for all $i \in [n]$.
5. $\mathcal{P}$ receives $(\texttt{transferred}, id, R_i^{r_i})$, for $i \in [n]$ from $\mathcal{F}_{\mathsf{COT}}$.

π_{on}

6. For all $i \in [n]$, $\mathcal{P}$ computes $d_i := r_i \oplus w_i$ and sends d_i to $\mathcal{V}$.
7. For all $i \in [n]$, $\mathcal{V}$ computes $M_i^0 := S_i^0 \oplus R_i^{d_i}$, $M_i^1 := S_i^1 \oplus R_i^{\neg d_i}$, and sends $\left(M_i^0, M_i^1\right)$ to $\mathcal{P}$.
8. $\mathcal{P}$ does the following:
   i. computes $S_i^{w_i} := M_i^{w_i} \oplus R_i^{r_i}$ for all $i \in [n]$
   ii. computes $\boldsymbol{K}_i^{w_i} := T_i^{w_i} \oplus G\left(S_i^{w_i}\right)$ for all $i \in [n]$
   iii. parses $\{K_i^{w_i}\}_{i\in[n']}$ from $\{\boldsymbol{K}_i^{w_i}\}_{i\in[n]}$
   iv. evaluates the garbled circuit to obtain $Z' := \mathsf{Ev}\left(\emptyset, \{K_i^{w_i}\}_{i\in[n']}\right)$
   v. sends $(\texttt{commit}, id, Z')$ to $\mathcal{F}_{\mathsf{COM}}$.
9. On receiving $(\texttt{committed}, id, |Z'|)$ from $\mathcal{F}_{\mathsf{COM}}$, $\mathcal{V}$ sends the message $(\texttt{open-all}, id)$ to $\mathcal{F}_{\mathsf{COT}}$.
10. On receiving $\left(\texttt{transfer}, id, R_i^0, R_i^1\right)$ for all $i \in [n]$ from $\mathcal{F}_{\mathsf{COT}}$, $\mathcal{P}$ does the following
    i. computes S_i^0, S_i^1 for all $i \in [n]$ using M_i^0, M_i^1 and R_i^0, R_i^1
    ii. computes $\boldsymbol{K}_i^b := T_i^b \oplus G(S_i^b)$ for all $i \in [n]$ and $b \in \{0,1\}$
    iii. and parses $\left\{K_i^b\right\}_{i\in[n']}$ from $\{\boldsymbol{K}_i^b\}_{i\in[n]}$ for $b \in \{0,1\}$
    iv. aborts if $\mathsf{Ve}\left(\emptyset, f, \left\{K_i^0, K_i^1\right\}_{i\in[n']}\right) \neq 1$, sends $(\texttt{reveal}, id)$ to $\mathcal{F}_{\mathsf{COM}}$ otherwise.
11. On receiving the message $(\texttt{reveal}, id, Z')$ from $\mathcal{F}_{\mathsf{COM}}$, $\mathcal{V}$ outputs $\texttt{accept}$ if $Z = Z'$.

[a] Instead of returning d, Gb is tweaked to return the 1-key on the output wire.

Fig. 13. Online-efficient ZK from our privacy-free garbling scheme

compare this protocol with that of [JKO13] composed with [ZRE15]. While our protocol offers the qualitative advantage of relying on weaker primitives (PRGs), we also note that since our garbling scheme is instantiated with a statistical security parameter, it can offer a better proof size.

A Zero-Knowledge from Garbled Circuits: Required Functionalities

Here we describe the required ideal functionalities. The Zero-knowledge functionality is detailed in Fig. 14. The $\mathcal{F}_{\mathsf{COT}}$ and $\mathcal{F}_{\mathsf{COM}}$ functionalities are provided in Figs. 15 and 16 respectively. The $\mathcal{F}_{\mathsf{COT}}$ functionality can be securely realised in the framework of [PVW08] with an augmentation for the **Open-all** property, as discussed in [JKO13]. The $\mathcal{F}_{\mathsf{COM}}$ functionality can be securely and efficiently realised as well [Lin11].

- This is the ideal functionality for proving in zero-knowledge to a Verifier $\mathcal{V}$ that a Prover $\mathcal{P}$ possesses a witness w for instance x as per relation R. As in [JKO13] we use an ideal functionality to succinctly capture our requirements of a zero-knowledge protocol.

1. Receive $(\texttt{prove}, sid, x, w)$ from P and $(\texttt{verify}, sid, x')$ from V
2. **if** $x = x'$ and $R(x, w) = 1$ **then** output $(\texttt{verified}, x)$ to V

Fig. 14. The zero-knowledge functionality

- This is the ideal functionality for Committing Oblivious Transfer, borrowed from [JKO13]. A Sender S provides two messages, of which a Receiver R chooses to receive one. S doesn't know which message R chose, and R has no information about the message it didn't choose. Upon receiving a signal from S, the functionality reveals both messages to R.

$\mathcal{F}_{\mathsf{COT}}$

1. **Choose:** Receive $(\texttt{choose}, id, b)$ from R, where $b \in \{0, 1\}$. If no message of the form $(\texttt{choose}, id, \cdot)$ exists in memory, store $(\texttt{choose}, id, b)$ and send $(\texttt{chosen}, id)$ to S.
2. **Transfer:** Receive $(\texttt{transfer}, id, tid, m_0, m_1)$ from S, where $m_0, m_1 \in \{0, 1\}^\kappa$. If no message of the form $(\texttt{transfer}, id, tid, \cdot, \cdot)$ exists in memory, and a message of the form $(\texttt{choose}, id, b)$ exists in memory, then send $(\texttt{transferred}, id, tid, m_b)$ to R.
3. **Open-all:** Receive $(\texttt{open-all})$ from the S. Send all messages of the form $(\texttt{transfer}, id, tid, m_0, m_1)$ to R.

Fig. 15. The ideal committing OT functionality

- The ideal commitment functionality, borrowed from [JKO13].
- A Sender S commits to a message m, which she later reveals to the receiver R. S is 'bound' to only the message that she committed, while the message is hidden from R until S opens her commitment.

$\mathcal{F}_{\mathsf{COM}}$

1. **Commit:** Receive $(\texttt{commit}, id, m)$ from the sender, where $m \in \{0,1\}^*$. If no such message already exists in memory, then store $(\texttt{commit}, id, m)$ and send $(\texttt{committed}, id, |m|)$ to R.
2. **Reveal:** Receive $(\texttt{reveal}, id)$ from S, send $(\texttt{reveal}, id, m)$ to R if corresponding $(\texttt{commit}, id, m)$ exists in memory.

Fig. 16. The ideal commitment functionality

References

[BELO16] Ben-Efraim, A., Lindell, Y., Omri, E.: Optimizing semi-honest secure multiparty computation for the internet. In: Proceedings of the 2016 ACM SIGSAC Conference on Computer and Communications Security, CCS 2016, pp. 578–590. ACM, New York (2016)

[BHKR13] Bellare, M., Hoang, V.T., Keelveedhi, S., Rogaway, P.: Efficient garbling from a fixed-key blockcipher. In: IEEE Symposium on Security and Privacy (SP) 2013, pp. 478–492. IEEE (2013)

[BHR12a] Bellare, M., Hoang, V.T., Rogaway, P.: Adaptively secure garbling with applications to one-time programs and secure outsourcing. In: Wang, X., Sako, K. (eds.) ASIACRYPT 2012. LNCS, vol. 7658, pp. 134–153. Springer, Heidelberg (2012). doi:10.1007/978-3-642-34961-4_10

[BHR12b] Bellare, M., Hoang, V.T., Rogaway, P.: Foundations of garbled circuits. In: ACM CCS 2012, pp. 784–796. ACM (2012)

[BMR90] Beaver, D., Micali, S., Rogaway, P.: The round complexity of secure protocols. In: Proceedings of the Twenty-Second Annual ACM Symposium on Theory of Computing (STOC 1990), pp. 503–513. ACM (1990)

[BMR16] Ball, M., Malkin, T., Rosulek, M.: Garbling gadgets for Boolean and arithmetic circuits. In: ACM CCS 2016, pp. 565–577. ACM (2016)

[CD97] Cramer, R., Damgård, I.: Linear zero-knowledge - a note on efficient zero-knowledge proofs and arguments. In: Proceedings of the Twenty-Ninth Annual ACM Symposium on the Theory of Computing, El Paso, TX, USA, 4–6 May 1997, pp. 436–445 (1997)

[CGM16] Chase, M., Ganesh, C., Mohassel, P.: Efficient zero-knowledge proof of algebraic and non-algebraic statements with applications to privacy preserving credentials. In: Robshaw, M., Katz, J. (eds.) CRYPTO 2016. LNCS, vol. 9816, pp. 499–530. Springer, Heidelberg (2016). doi:10.1007/978-3-662-53015-3_18

[CKMZ14] Choi, S.G., Katz, J., Malozemoff, A.J., Zikas, V.: Efficient three-party computation from cut-and-choose. In: Garay, J.A., Gennaro, R. (eds.) CRYPTO 2014. LNCS, vol. 8617, pp. 513–530. Springer, Heidelberg (2014). doi:10.1007/978-3-662-44381-1_29

[EGL85] Even, S., Goldreich, O., Lempel, A.: A randomized protocol for signing contracts. Commun. ACM **28**(6), 637–647 (1985)

[FNO15] Frederiksen, T.K., Nielsen, J.B., Orlandi, C.: Privacy-free garbled circuits with applications to efficient zero-knowledge. In: Oswald, E., Fischlin, M. (eds.) EUROCRYPT 2015. LNCS, vol. 9057, pp. 191–219. Springer, Heidelberg (2015). doi:10.1007/978-3-662-46803-6_7

[GGP10] Gennaro, R., Gentry, C., Parno, B.: Non-interactive verifiable computing: outsourcing computation to untrusted workers. In: Rabin, T. (ed.) CRYPTO 2010. LNCS, vol. 6223, pp. 465–482. Springer, Heidelberg (2010). doi:10.1007/978-3-642-14623-7_25

[GGPR13] Gennaro, R., Gentry, C., Parno, B., Raykova, M.: Quadratic span programs and succinct NIZKs without PCPs. In: Johansson, T., Nguyen, P.Q. (eds.) EUROCRYPT 2013. LNCS, vol. 7881, pp. 626–645. Springer, Heidelberg (2013). doi:10.1007/978-3-642-38348-9_37

[GKR08] Goldwasser, S., Kalai, Y.T., Rothblum, G.N.: One-time programs. In: Wagner, D. (ed.) CRYPTO 2008. LNCS, vol. 5157, pp. 39–56. Springer, Heidelberg (2008). doi:10.1007/978-3-540-85174-5_3

[GLNP15] Gueron, S., Lindell, Y., Nof, A., Pinkas, B.: Fast garbling of circuits under standard assumptions. In: ACM CCS 2015, pp. 567–578. ACM (2015)

[GOM16] Giacomelli, I., Orlandi, C., Madsen, J.: ZKBoo: faster zero-knowledge for Boolean circuits. In: 25th USENIX Security Symposium (USENIX Security 2016). USENIX Association (2016)

[Gro10] Groth, J.: Short pairing-based non-interactive zero-knowledge arguments. In: Abe, M. (ed.) ASIACRYPT 2010. LNCS, vol. 6477, pp. 321–340. Springer, Heidelberg (2010). doi:10.1007/978-3-642-17373-8_19

[HMR15] Hu, Z., Mohassel, P., Rosulek, M.: Efficient zero-knowledge proofs of non-algebraic statements with sublinear amortized cost. In: Gennaro, R., Robshaw, M. (eds.) CRYPTO 2015. LNCS, vol. 9216, pp. 150–169. Springer, Heidelberg (2015). doi:10.1007/978-3-662-48000-7_8

[JKO13] Jawurek, M., Kerschbaum, F., Orlandi, C.: Zero-knowledge using garbled circuits: how to prove non-algebraic statements efficiently. In: ACM CCS 2013, pp. 955–966. ACM (2013)

[KKKS15] Kempka, C., Kikuchi, R., Kiyoshima, S., Suzuki, K.: Garbling scheme for formulas with constant size of garbled gates. In: Iwata, T., Cheon, J.H. (eds.) ASIACRYPT 2015. LNCS, vol. 9452, pp. 758–782. Springer, Heidelberg (2015). doi:10.1007/978-3-662-48797-6_31

[KKL+16] Kolesnikov, V., Krawczyk, H., Lindell, Y., Malozemoff, A.J., Rabin, T.: Attribute-based key exchange with general policies. In: Proceedings of 2016 ACM SIGSAC Conference on Computer and Communications Security, Vienna, Austria, 24–28 October 2016, pp. 1451–1463 (2016)

[KKS16] Kempka, C., Kikuchi, R., Suzuki, K.: How to circumvent the two-ciphertext lower bound for linear garbling schemes. In: Cheon, J.H., Takagi, T. (eds.) ASIACRYPT 2016. LNCS, vol. 10032, pp. 967–997. Springer, Heidelberg (2016). doi:10.1007/978-3-662-53890-6_32

[KMR14] Kolesnikov, V., Mohassel, P., Rosulek, M.: FleXOR: flexible garbling for XOR gates that beats free-XOR. In: Garay, J.A., Gennaro, R. (eds.) CRYPTO 2014. LNCS, vol. 8617, pp. 440–457. Springer, Heidelberg (2014). doi:10.1007/978-3-662-44381-1_25

[Kol05] Kolesnikov, V.: Gate evaluation secret sharing and secure one-round two-party computation. In: Roy, B. (ed.) ASIACRYPT 2005. LNCS, vol. 3788, pp. 136–155. Springer, Heidelberg (2005). doi:10.1007/11593447_8

[KR06] Kalai, Y.T., Raz, R.: Succinct non-interactive zero-knowledge proofs with preprocessing for LOGSNP. In: Proceedings of 47th Annual IEEE Symposium on Foundations of Computer Science (FOCS 2006), Berkeley, California, USA, 21–24 October 2006, pp. 355–366 (2006)

[KS08] Kolesnikov, V., Schneider, T.: Improved garbled circuit: free XOR gates and applications. In: Aceto, L., Damgård, I., Goldberg, L.A., Halldórsson, M.M., Ingólfsdóttir, A., Walukiewicz, I. (eds.) ICALP 2008. LNCS, vol. 5126, pp. 486–498. Springer, Heidelberg (2008). doi:10.1007/978-3-540-70583-3_40

[Lin11] Lindell, Y.: Highly-efficient universally-composable commitments based on the DDH assumption. In: Paterson, K.G. (ed.) EUROCRYPT 2011. LNCS, vol. 6632, pp. 446–466. Springer, Heidelberg (2011). doi:10.1007/978-3-642-20465-4_25

[Lip12] Lipmaa, H.: Progression-free sets and sublinear pairing-based non-interactive zero-knowledge arguments. In: Cramer, R. (ed.) TCC 2012. LNCS, vol. 7194, pp. 169–189. Springer, Heidelberg (2012). doi:10.1007/978-3-642-28914-9_10

[LP07] Lindell, Y., Pinkas, B.: An efficient protocol for secure two-party computation in the presence of malicious adversaries. In: Naor, M. (ed.) EUROCRYPT 2007. LNCS, vol. 4515, pp. 52–78. Springer, Heidelberg (2007). doi:10.1007/978-3-540-72540-4_4

[LP11] Lindell, Y., Pinkas, B.: Secure two-party computation via cut-and-choose oblivious transfer. In: Ishai, Y. (ed.) TCC 2011. LNCS, vol. 6597, pp. 329–346. Springer, Heidelberg (2011). doi:10.1007/978-3-642-19571-6_20

[LR15] Lindell, Y., Riva, B.: Blazing fast 2PC in the offline/online setting with security for malicious adversaries. In: ACM CCS 2015, pp. 579–590. ACM (2015)

[MNPS04] Malkhi, D., Nisan, N., Pinkas, B., Sella, Y.: Fairplay-secure two-party computation system. In: USENIX Security Symposium 2004, vol. 4 (2004)

[MRZ15] Mohassel, P., Rosulek, M., Zhang, Y.: Fast and secure three-party computation: the garbled circuit approach. In: ACM CCS 2015, pp. 591–602. ACM (2015)

[NPS99] Naor, M., Pinkas, B., Sumner, R.: Privacy preserving auctions and mechanism design. In: Proceedings of the 1st ACM Conference on Electronic Commerce, pp. 129–139. ACM (1999)

[PSSW09] Pinkas, B., Schneider, T., Smart, N.P., Williams, S.C.: Secure two-party computation is practical. In: Matsui, M. (ed.) ASIACRYPT 2009. LNCS, vol. 5912, pp. 250–267. Springer, Heidelberg (2009). doi:10.1007/978-3-642-10366-7_15

[PVW08] Peikert, C., Vaikuntanathan, V., Waters, B.: A framework for efficient and composable oblivious transfer. In: Wagner, D. (ed.) CRYPTO 2008. LNCS, vol. 5157, pp. 554–571. Springer, Heidelberg (2008). doi:10.1007/978-3-540-85174-5_31

[Ser14] Sergeev, I.S.: Upper bounds for the formula size of symmetric Boolean functions. Russ. Math. **58**(5), 30–42 (2014)

[Sha79] Shamir, A.: How to share a secret. Commun. ACM **22**(11), 612–613 (1979)

[SS10] Sahai, A., Seyalioglu, H.: Worry-free encryption: functional encryption with public keys. In: ACM CCS 2010, pp. 463–472. ACM (2010)

[Yao86] Yao, A.C.-C.: How to generate and exchange secrets (extended abstract). In: 27th Annual Symposium on Foundations of Computer Science, pp. 162–167. IEEE (1986)

[ZRE15] Zahur, S., Rosulek, M., Evans, D.: Two halves make a whole. In: Oswald, E., Fischlin, M. (eds.) EUROCRYPT 2015. LNCS, vol. 9057, pp. 220–250. Springer, Heidelberg (2015). doi:10.1007/978-3-662-46803-6_8

Secure Arithmetic Computation with Constant Computational Overhead

Benny Applebaum[1(✉)], Ivan Damgård[2], Yuval Ishai[3], Michael Nielsen[2], and Lior Zichron[1]

[1] Tel Aviv University, Tel Aviv, Israel
bennyap@post.tau.ac.il, liorzichron@mail.tau.ac.il
[2] Aarhus University, Aarhus, Denmark
{ivan,mic}@cs.au.dk
[3] Technion and UCLA, Haifa, Israel
yuvali@cs.technion.ac.il

Abstract. We study the complexity of securely evaluating an arithmetic circuit over a finite field $\mathbb{F}$ in the setting of secure two-party computation with semi-honest adversaries. In all existing protocols, the number of arithmetic operations per multiplication gate grows either linearly with $\log|\mathbb{F}|$ or polylogarithmically with the security parameter. We present the first protocol that only makes a *constant* (amortized) number of field operations per gate. The protocol uses the underlying field $\mathbb{F}$ as a black box, and its security is based on arithmetic analogues of well-studied cryptographic assumptions.

Our protocol is particularly appealing in the special case of securely evaluating a "vector-OLE" function of the form $\boldsymbol{a}x + \boldsymbol{b}$, where $x \in \mathbb{F}$ is the input of one party and $\boldsymbol{a}, \boldsymbol{b} \in \mathbb{F}^w$ are the inputs of the other party. In this case, which is motivated by natural applications, our protocol can achieve an asymptotic rate of 1/3 (i.e., the communication is dominated by sending roughly $3w$ elements of $\mathbb{F}$). Our implementation of this protocol suggests that it outperforms competing approaches even for relatively small fields $\mathbb{F}$ and over fast networks.

Our technical approach employs two new ingredients that may be of independent interest. First, we present a general way to combine any linear code that has a fast encoder and a cryptographic ("LPN-style") pseudorandomness property with another linear code that supports fast encoding *and erasure-decoding*, obtaining a code that inherits both the pseudorandomness feature of the former code and the efficiency features of the latter code. Second, we employ local *arithmetic* pseudo-random generators, proposing arithmetic generalizations of boolean candidates that resist all known attacks.

1 Introduction

There are many situations in which computations are performed on sensitive *numerical* data. A computation on numbers can usually be expressed

J. Katz and H. Shacham (Eds.): CRYPTO 2017, Part I, LNCS 10401, pp. 223–254, 2017.
DOI: 10.1007/978-3-319-63688-7_8

as a sequence of arithmetic operations such as addition, subtraction, and multiplication.[1]

In cases where the sensitive data is distributed among multiple parties, this calls for *secure arithmetic computation*, namely secure computation of functions defined by arithmetic operations. It is convenient to represent such a function by an *arithmetic circuit*, which is similar to a standard boolean circuit except that gates are labeled by addition, subtraction, or multiplication. It is typically sufficient to consider such circuits that evaluate the operations over a large *finite field* $\mathbb{F}$, since arithmetic computations over the integers or (bounded precision) reals can be reduced to this case. Computing over finite fields (as opposed to integers or reals) can also be a feature, as it is useful for applications in threshold cryptography (see, e.g., [15,26]). In the present work we are mainly interested in the case of secure arithmetic *two-party* computation in the presence of *semi-honest* adversaries.[2] From here on, the term "secure computation" will refer specifically to this case.

Oblivious Linear-Function Evaluation. A natural complete primitive for secure arithmetic computation is Oblivious Linear-function Evaluation (OLE). OLE is a two-party functionality that receives a field element $x \in \mathbb{F}$ from Alice and field elements $a, b \in \mathbb{F}$ from Bob and delivers $ax + b$ to Alice. OLE can be viewed as the arithmetic analogue of 1-out-of-2 Oblivious Transfer of bits (bit-OT) [22]. In the binary case, every boolean circuit C can be securely evaluated with perfect security by using $O(|C|)$ invocations of an ideal bit-OT oracle via the "GMW protocol" [27,30]. A simple generalization of this protocol can be used to evaluate any arithmetic circuit C over $\mathbb{F}$ using $O(|C|)$ invocations of OLE and $O(|C|)$ field operations [35].

The Complexity of Secure Arithmetic Computation. The goal of this work is to minimize the complexity of secure arithmetic computation. In light of the above, this reduces to efficiently realizing multiple instances of OLE. We start by surveying known approaches. The most obvious is a straightforward reduction to standard secure computation methods by emulating field operations using bit operations. This approach is quite expensive both asymptotically and in terms of concrete efficiency. In particular, it typically requires many "cryptographic" operations for securely emulating each field operation.

A more direct approach is via *homomorphic encryption*. Since OLE is a degree-1 function, it can be directly realized by using "linear-homomorphic" encryption schemes (that support addition and scalar multiplication). This approach can be instantiated using Paillier encryption [18,26,48] or using encryption schemes based on (ring)-LWE [19,43]. While these techniques can be optimized to achieve good communication complexity, their concrete computational cost is

[1] More complex numerical computations can typically be efficiently reduced to these simple ones, e.g., by using suitable low-degree approximations.

[2] Our results extend naturally to the case of secure multi-party computation with no honest majority. We restrict the attention to the two-party case for simplicity.

quite high. In asymptotic terms, the best instantiations of this approach have *computational overhead* that grows polylogarithmically with the security parameter k. That is, the computational complexity of such secure computation protocols (in any standard computational model) is bigger than the computational complexity of the insecure computation by at least a polylogarithmic factor in k.

Another approach, first suggested by Gilboa [26] and recently implemented by Keller et al. [37], is to use a simple information-theoretic reduction of OLE to string-OT. By using a bit-decomposition of Alice's input x, an OLE over a field $\mathbb{F}$ with ℓ-bit elements can be perfectly reduced to ℓ instances of OT, where in each OT one of two field elements is being transferred from Bob to Alice. Using fast methods for OT extension [12,31], the OTs can be implemented quite efficiently. However, even when neglecting the cost of OTs, the communication involves 2ℓ field elements and the computation involves $O(\ell)$ field operations per OLE. This overhead can be quite large for big fields $\mathbb{F}$ that are often useful in applications.

A final approach, which is the most relevant to our work, uses a computationally secure reduction from OLE to string-OT that assumes the peudorandomness of noisy random codewords in a linear code. This approach was first suggested by Naor and Pinkas [46] and was further developed by Ishai et al. [35]. The most efficient instantiation of these protocols relies on the assumption that a noisy random codeword of a Reed-Solomon code is pseudorandom, provided that the noise level is sufficiently high to defeat known list-decoding algorithms. In the best case scenario, this approach has polylogarithmic computational overhead (using asymptotically fast FFT-based algorithms for encoding and decoding Reed-Solomon codes). See Sect. 1.3 for a more detailed overview of existing approaches and [35] for further discussion of secure arithmetic computation and its applications.

The above state of affairs leaves the following question open:

> *Is it possible to realize secure arithmetic computation with* constant computational overhead*?*

To be a bit more precise, by "constant computational overhead" we mean that there is a protocol which can securely evaluate any arithmetic circuit C over any finite field $\mathbb{F}$, with a computational cost (on a RAM machine) that is only a constant times bigger than the cost of performing $|C|$ field operations with no security at all. Here we make the standard convention of viewing the size of C also as a security parameter, namely the view of any adversary running in time poly($|C|$) can be simulated up to a negligible error (in $|C|$). In the boolean case, Ishai et al. [34] showed that secure computation with constant computational overhead can be based on the conjectured existence of a local polynomial-stretch pseudo-random generator (PRG). In contrast, in all known protocols for the arithmetic case the computational overhead either grows linearly with $\log|\mathbb{F}|$ or polylogarithmically with the security parameter.

1.1 Our Contribution

We improve both the asymptotic and the concrete efficiency of secure arithmetic computation. On the asymptotic efficiency front, we settle the above open question in the affirmative under plausible cryptographic assumptions. More concretely, our main result is a protocol that securely evaluates any arithmetic circuit C over $\mathbb{F}$ using only $O(|C|)$ field operations, independently of the size of $\mathbb{F}$. The protocol uses the underlying field $\mathbb{F}$ as a black box, where the number of field operations depends only on the security parameter and not on the field size.[3] The security of the protocol is based on arithmetic analogues of well-studied cryptographic assumptions: concretely, an arithmetic version of an assumption due to Alekhnovich [1] (or similar kinds of "LPN-style" assumptions) and an arithmetic version of a local polynomial-stretch PRG [4,11,34].[4]

On the concrete efficiency front, our approach is particularly appealing for a useful subclass of arithmetic computations that efficiently reduce to a multi-output extension of OLE that we call *vector-OLE*. A vector-OLE of width w is a two-party functionality that receives a field element $x \in \mathbb{F}$ from Alice and a pair of *vectors* $\boldsymbol{a}, \boldsymbol{b} \in \mathbb{F}^w$ from Bob and delivers $\boldsymbol{a}x + \boldsymbol{b}$ to Alice. We obtain a secure protocol for vector-OLE with constant computational overhead and with an asymptotic communication rate of 1/3 (i.e., the communication is dominated by sending roughly $3w$ elements of $\mathbb{F}$). Our implementation of this protocol suggests that it outperforms competing approaches even for relatively small fields $\mathbb{F}$ and over fast networks. The protocol is also based on more conservative assumptions, namely it can be based only on the first of the two assumptions on which our more general result is based. This assumption is arguably more conservative than the assumption on noisy Reed-Solomon codes used in [35,46], since the underlying codes do not have an algebraic structure that gives rise to efficient (list-)decoding algorithms.

Vector-OLE can be viewed as an arithmetic analogue of string-OT. Similarly to the usefulness of string-OT for garbling schemes [54], vector-OLE is useful for *arithmetic garbling* [5,10] (see Sect. 4). Moreover, there are several natural secure computation tasks that can be directly and efficiently realized using vector-OLE. One class of such tasks are in the domain of secure linear algebra [17]. As a simple example, the secure multiplication of an $n \times n$ matrix by a length-n vector easily reduces to n instances of vector-OLE of width n. Another class of applications is in the domain of securely searching for nearest neighbors, e.g., in the context of secure face recognition [21]. The goal is to find in a database of n vectors of dimension d the vector which is closest in Euclidean distance to a given target vector. This task admits a simple reduction to d instances of width-n vector OLE, followed by non-arithmetic secure computation of a simple function (minimum) of n integers whose size is independent of d. The cost of such a protocol is

[3] The protocol additionally uses standard "bit-operations," but their complexity is dominated by the field operations for every field size.

[4] More precisely, we need a polynomial-stretch PRG with constant locality and *constant degree*, or equivalently, a polynomial-stretch PRG which can be computed by a constant-depth ($\mathbf{NC^0}$) arithmetic circuit. For brevity, through the introduction we refer to such a PRG as being *local* and implicitly assume the additional constant-degree requirement.

dominated by the cost of vector-OLE. See Sect. 5 for a more detailed discussion of these applications.

1.2 Overview of Techniques

Our constant-overhead protocol for a general circuit C is obtained in three steps. The first step is a reduction of the secure computation of C to $n = O(|C|)$ instances of OLE via an arithmetic version of the GMW protocol.

The second step is a reduction of n instances of OLE to roughly $\sqrt{n}$ instances of vector-OLE of width $w = O(\sqrt{n})$. This step mimics the approach for constant-overhead secure computation of boolean circuits taken in [34], which combines a local polynomial-stretch PRGs with an information-theoretic garbling scheme [32,54]. To extend this approach from the boolean to the arithmetic case, two changes are made. First, the information-theoretic garbling scheme for NC^0 is replaced by an arithmetic analogue [10]. More interestingly, the polynomial-stretch PRGs in NC^0 needs to be replaced by an arithmetic analogue. We propose candidates for such arithmetic PRGs that generalize the boolean candidates from [11,28] and can be shown to resist known classes of attacks. While the security of these PRG candidates remains to be further studied, there are no apparent weaknesses that arise from increasing the field size.

The final, and most interesting, step is a constant-overhead protocol for vector-OLE. As noted above, the protocol obtained in this step is independently useful for applications, and our implementation of this protocol beats competing approaches not only asymptotically but also in terms of its concrete efficiency.

Our starting point is the code-based OLE protocol from [35,46]. This protocol can be based on any randomized linear encoding scheme E over $\mathbb{F}$ that has a the following "LPN-style" pseudorandomness property: If we encode a message $x \in \mathbb{F}$ and replace a small random subset of the symbols by uniformly random field elements, the resulting noisy codeword is pseudorandom. For most linear encoding schemes this appears to be a conservative assumption, since there are very few linear codes for which efficient decoding techniques are known. The OLE protocol proceeds by having Alice compute a random encoding $\boldsymbol{y} = E(x)$ and send a noisy version $\boldsymbol{y}'$ of $\boldsymbol{y}$ to Bob. Bob returns $\boldsymbol{c}' = a\boldsymbol{y}' + \boldsymbol{b}$ to Alice, where $\boldsymbol{b} = E(b)$ is a random linear encoding of b. Knowing the noise locations, Alice can decode $c = ax + b$ from $\boldsymbol{c}'$ via erasure-decoding in the linear code defined by E. If we ignore the noise coordinates, $\boldsymbol{c}'$ does not reveal to Alice any additional information about (a, b) except the output $ax + b$. However, the noise coordinates can reveal more information. To prevent this information from being leaked, Alice uses oblivious transfer (OT) to selectively learn only the non-noisy coordinates of $\boldsymbol{c}'$.

An attempt to extend the above protocol to the case of vector-OLE immediately encounters a syntactic difficulty. If the single value a is replaced by a vector $\boldsymbol{a}$, it is not clear how to "multiply" $\boldsymbol{y}'$ by $\boldsymbol{a}$. A workaround taken in [35] is to use a "multiplicative" encoding scheme E based on Reed-Solomon codes. The encoding and decoding of these codes incurs a polylogarithmic computational overhead, and the high noise level required for defeating known list-decoding algorithms results in a poor concrete communication rate. The algebraic nature of the codes also makes the underlying intractability assumption look quite strong. It is therefore desirable to base a similar protocol on other types of linear codes.

Our first idea for using general linear codes is to apply "vector-OLE reversal." Concretely, we apply a simple protocol for reducing vector-OLE to the computation of $\boldsymbol{a}x + \boldsymbol{b}$ where $\boldsymbol{a}$ is the input of Bob, x and $\boldsymbol{b}$ the are the inputs of Alice, and the output is delivered to Bob. Now a general linear encoding E can be used by Bob to encode its input $\boldsymbol{a}$, and since x is a scalar Alice can multiply the encoding by x and add an encoding of $\boldsymbol{b}$. If we base E on a linear-time encodable and decodable code, such as the code of Spielman [51], the protocol can be implemented using only $O(w)$ field operations. The problem with this approach the is that the pseudorandomness assumption looks questionable in light of the existence of an efficient decoding algorithm for E. Even if the noise level can chosen in a way that still respects linear-time erasure-decoding but makes error-correction intractable (which is not at all clear), this would require a high noise rate and hurt the concrete efficiency.

Our final idea, which may be of independent interest, is that instead of requiring a single encoding E to simultaneously satisfy both "hardness" and "easiness" properties, we can combine two types of encoding to enjoy the best of both worlds. Concretely, we present a general way to combine any linear code C_1 that has a fast encoder and a cryptographic ("LPN-style") pseudorandomness property with another linear code C_2 that supports fast encoding and erasure-decoding (but has no useful hardness properties) to get a randomized linear encoding E that inherits the pseudorandomness feature from C_1 and the efficiency features from C_2. This is achieved by using a noisy output of C_1 to mask the output of C_2, which we pad with a sufficient number of 0s. Given the knowledge of the noise locations in the padding zone, the entire C_1 component can be recovered in a "brute-force" way via Gaussian elimination, and one can then compute and decode the output of C_2. When the expansion of E is sufficiently large, the Gaussian elimination is only applied to a short part of the encoding length and hence does not form an efficiency bottleneck. Using these ideas, we obtain a constant-overhead vector-OLE protocol under a seemingly conservative assumption, namely a natural arithmetic analogue of an assumption due to Alekhnovich [1] or a similar assumption for other linear-time encodable codes that do not have the special structure required for fast erasure-decoding.

1.3 Related Work

We first give an overview of known techniques for OLE (with semi-honest security) and compare to what can be obtained using our approach.

First, the work of Gilboa [26] (see also [37]) implements OLE in a field with n-bit elements using n oblivious transfers of field elements. The asymptotic communication complexity of this approach is larger than ours by a factor $\Omega(n)$.

In particular, if the goal is to implement vector-OLE, we can say something more concrete. Our vector-OLE implementation sends n/r bits to do 1 OLE on n-bit field elements, where r is the rate, which is between $1/5$ and $1/10$ for our implementation. The OT based approach will need to send at least n^2 bits to do the same. So in cases where network bandwidth is the bottleneck, we can expect to be faster than the OT based approach by a factor nr. Our experiments indicate that this happens for network speeds around 20–50 Mbits/sec. Actually, also at large network speeds, our vector-OLE implementation outperforms the OT based approach: The latest timings for semi-honest string OT on the type of architecture we used (2 desktop computers connected by a LAN) are from [12] (see also [37]) and indicate that one OT can be done in amortised time about 0.2 µs, so that 0.2 nµs would an estimate for the time needed for one OLE. In contrast, our times (for 100-bit security) are much smaller, even for the smallest case we considered ($n = 32$) we have 0.7 µs amortised time per OLE. For larger fields, the picture is similar, for instance for $n = 1024$, we obtain 19.5 µs per OLE, where the estimate for the OT based technique is about 200 µs.

A second class of OLE protocols can be obtained from homomorphic encryption schemes: one party encrypts his input under his own key and sends the ciphertext to the other party. He can now multiply his input "into the ciphertext" and randomize it appropriately before returning it for decryption. This will work based on Paillier encryption (see, e.g., [21] for an application of this) but will be very slow because exponentiation is required for the plaintext multiplication. A more efficient approach is to use (ring)-LWE based schemes, as worked out in [19] by Damgård et al. Here the asymptotic communication overhead is worse than ours by a poly-logarithmic factor, at least for prime fields if one uses the so-called SIMD variant where the plaintext is a vector of field elements. However, the approach becomes very problematic for extension fields of large degree because key generation requires that we find a cyclotomic polynomial that splits in a very specific way modulo the characteristic, and one needs to go to very large keys before this happens. Quantifying this precisely is non-trivial and was not done in [19], but as an example, the overhead in ciphertext size is a factor of about 7 for a 64-bit prime fields, but is 1850 for $\mathbb{F}_{2^8}$. Also, the computational overhead for ring-LWE based schemes is much higher than ours: even if we pack as many field elements, say λ, into a ciphertext as possible, the overhead involved in encryption and decryption is superlinear in λ. Further λ needs to grow with the field size, again the asymptotic growth is hard to quantify exactly, but it is definitely super logarithmic. In more concrete terms, the computational overhead of homomorphic encryption makes these protocols slower in practice than the pure OT-based approach (see [37]), which is in turn generally slower than our approach for the case of vector-OLE.

A final class of protocols is more closely related to ours, namely the code-based approach of Naor and Pinkas [46] and its generalizations from [35]. The most efficient instantiation of these protocols is based on an assumption on pseudo-randomness of noisy Reed-Solomon codewords, whereas we use codes generated from sparse matrices. Because encoding and decoding Reed-Solomon codes is not known to be in linear time, these protocols are asymptotically slower that ours by a poly-logarithmic factor. As for the communication, we obtain an asymptotic rate of 1/3 and can obtain a practical rate of around 1/4. The rate of the protocol from [35] is also constant but much smaller: one loses a factor 2 because the protocol involves point-wise multiplication of codewords, so codewords need to be long enough to allow decoding of a Reed-Solomon code based on polynomials of double degree. Even more significantly, on top of the above, the distance needs to be increased (so the rate decreases) to protect against attacks that rely on efficient list-decoding algorithms for Reed-Solomon codes. This class of attacks does not apply to our approach, since it does not require the code for which the pseudorandomness assumption holds to have any algebraic structure.

2 Preliminaries

2.1 The Arithmetic Setting

Our formalization of secure arithmetic computation follows the one from [35], but simplifies it to account for the simpler setting of security against semi-honest adversaries. We also refine the computational model to allow for a more concrete complexity analysis. We refer the reader to [35] for more details.

Functionalities. We represent the functionalities that we want to realize securely via a multi-party variant of arithmetic circuits.

Definition 1 (Arithmetic circuits). *An* arithmetic circuit C *has the same syntax as a standard boolean circuit, except that the gates are labeled by '+' (addition), '−' (subtraction) or '*' (multiplication). Each input wire can be labeled by an input variable x_i or a constant $c \in \{0,1\}$. Given a finite field $\mathbb{F}$, an arithmetic circuit C with n inputs and m outputs naturally defines a function $C^{\mathbb{F}} : \mathbb{F}^n \to \mathbb{F}^m$. An arithmetic* functionality circuit *is an arithmetic circuit whose inputs and outputs are labeled by party identities. In the two-party case, such a circuit C naturally defines a two-party functionality $C^{\mathbb{F}} : \mathbb{F}^{n_1} \times \mathbb{F}^{n_2} \to \mathbb{F}^{m_1} \times \mathbb{F}^{m_2}$. We denote by $C^{\mathbb{F}}(x_1, x_2)_P$ the output of Party P on inputs (x_1, x_2).*

Protocols and Complexity. To allow for a concrete complexity analysis, we view a protocol as a finite object that is generated by a protocol compiler (defined below). We assume that field elements have an adversarially chosen representation by ℓ-bit strings, where the protocol can depend on ℓ (but not on the representation). The representation is needed for realizing our protocols in the plain model. When considered as protocols in the OT-hybrid model, our protocols can be cast in the more restrictive arithmetic model of Applebaum et al. [5], where the parties do not have access to the bit-length of field elements or their representation, but can still perform field operations and communicate field elements over the OT channel. Protocols in this model have the feature that the number of field operations is independent of the field size.

By default, we model a protocol by a RAM program.[5] The choice of computational model does not change the number of field operations, which anyway

[5] This choice is related to our use of the linear-time decoding algorithm of Spielman [51], which can only be implemented in linear time in the RAM model (and requires quasi-linear circuit size).

dominates the overall cost as the field grows. In our theorem statements we will only refer to the number of field operations T, with the implicit understanding that all other computations can be implemented using $O(T\ell)$ bit operations. (Note that $T\ell$ bit operations are needed just for writing the outputs of T field operations.)

Protocol Compiler. A *protocol compiler* $\mathcal{P}$ takes a security parameter 1^k, an arithmetic (two-party) functionality circuit C and bit-length parameter ℓ as inputs, and outputs a protocol Π that realizes C given an oracle to any field $\mathbb{F}$ whose elements are represented by ℓ-bit strings. It should satisfy the following correctness and security requirements.

- Correctness: For every choice of $k, C, \mathbb{F}, \ell$, any representation of elements of $\mathbb{F}$ by ℓ-bit strings, and every possible pair of inputs (x_1, x_2) for C, the execution of Π on (x_1, x_2) ends with the parties outputting $C(x_1, x_2)$, except with negligible probability in k.
- Security: For every polynomial-size non-uniform $\mathcal{A}$ there is a negligible function ϵ such that the success probability of $\mathcal{A}$ in the following game is bounded by $1/2 + \epsilon(k)$:
  - On input 1^k, the adversary $\mathcal{A}$ picks a functionality circuit C, positive integer ℓ and field $\mathbb{F}$ whose elements are represented by ℓ-bit strings. The representation of field elements and field operations are implemented by a circuit $\mathcal{F}$ output by $\mathcal{A}$. (Note that all of the above parameters, including the complexity of the field operations, are effectively restricted to be polynomial in k.)
  - Let $\Pi^{\mathcal{F}}$ be the protocol returned by the compiler $\mathcal{P}$ on $1^k, C, \ell$, instantiating the field oracle $\mathbb{F}$ using $\mathcal{F}$.
  - $\mathcal{A}$ picks a corrupted party $P \in \{1, 2\}$ and two input pairs $x^0 = (x_1^0, x_2^0)$, $x^1 = (x_1^1, x_2^1)$ such that $C^{\mathbb{F}}(x^0)_P = C^{\mathbb{F}}(x^1)_P$.
  - Challenger picks a random bit b.
  - $\mathcal{A}$ is given the view of Party P in $\Pi^{\mathcal{F}}(x^b)$ and outputs a guess for b.

OLE and Vector OLE. We will be particularly interested in the following two arithmetic computations: an OLE takes an input $x \in \mathbb{F}$ from Alice and a pair $a, b \in \mathbb{F}$ from Bob and delivers $ax + b$ to Alice. Vector OLE of width w is similar, except that the input of Bob is a pair of vectors $\boldsymbol{a}, \boldsymbol{b} \in \mathbb{F}^w$ and the output is $\boldsymbol{a}x + \boldsymbol{b}$. OLE and vector OLE can be viewed as arithmetic analogues of bit-OT and string-OT, respectively. Indeed, in the case $\mathbb{F} = \mathbb{F}_2$, the OLE functionalities coincide with the corresponding OT functionalities up to a local relabeling of the inputs. An arithmetic generalization of the standard "GMW Protocol" [30, 35] compiles any arithmetic circuit functionality C into a perfectly secure protocol that makes $O(s_\times)$ calls to an ideal OLE functionality, where $s_\times$ is the number of multiplication gates, and $O(|C|)$ field operations. Hence, to securely compute C with $O(|C|)$ field operations in the plain model it suffices to realize n instances of OLE using $O(n)$ field operations.

2.2 Decomposable Affine Randomized Encoding (DARE)

Let $f : \mathbb{F}^\ell \to \mathbb{F}^m$ where $\mathbb{F}$ is some finite field.[6] We say that a function $\hat{f} : \mathbb{F}^\ell \times \mathbb{F}^\rho \to \mathbb{F}^m$ is a *perfect randomized encoding* [8,32] of f if for every input $x \in \mathbb{F}^\ell$, the distribution $\hat{f}(x;r)$ induced by a uniform choice of $r \stackrel{\$}{\leftarrow} \mathbb{F}^\rho$, "encodes" the string $f(x)$ in the following sense:

1. (Correctness) There exists a decoding algorithm Dec such that for every $x \in \mathbb{F}^\ell$ it holds that
$$\Pr_{r \stackrel{\$}{\leftarrow} \mathbb{F}^\rho} [\mathsf{Dec}(\hat{f}(x;r)) = f(x)] = 1.$$
2. (Privacy) There exists a randomized algorithm $\mathcal{S}$ such that for every $x \in \mathbb{F}^\ell$ and uniformly chosen $r \stackrel{\$}{\leftarrow} \mathbb{F}^\rho$ it holds that
$$\mathcal{S}(f(x)) \quad \text{is distributed identically to} \quad \hat{f}(x;r).$$

We say that $\hat{f}(x;r)$ is decomposable and affine if $\hat{f}$ can be written as $\hat{f}(x;r) = (\hat{f}_0(r), \hat{f}_1(x_1;r), \ldots, \hat{f}_n(x_\ell;r))$ where $\hat{f}_i$ is linear in x_i, i.e., it can be written as $\boldsymbol{a}_i x_i + \boldsymbol{b}_i$ where the vectors $\boldsymbol{a}_i$ and $\boldsymbol{b}_i$ arbitrarily depend on the randomness r.

It follows from [33] (cf. [10]) that every single-output function $f : \mathbb{F}^d \to \mathbb{F}$ which can be computed by constant-depth circuit (aka $\mathbf{NC^0}$ function) admits a decomposable encoding which can be encoded and decoded by an arithmetic circuit of finite complexity D which depends only in the circuit depth. Note that any multi-output function can be encoded by concatenating independent randomized encodings of the functions defined by its output bits. Thus, we have the following:

Fact 1. *Let $f : \mathbb{F}^\ell \to \mathbb{F}^m$ be an $\mathbf{NC^0}$ function. Then, f has a DARE $\hat{f}$ which can be encoded, decoded and simulated by an arithmetic circuit of size $O(m)$ where the constant in the big-O notation depends on the circuit depth.*[7]

We mention that the circuits for the encoding, decoder, and simulator can be all constructed efficiently given the circuit for f.

3 Vector OLE of Large Width

In this section, our goal is to construct a semi-honest secure protocol for Vector OLE of width w over the field $\mathbb{F} = \mathbb{F}_p$ for parties Alice and Bob.

As a stepping stone, we will first implement a "reversed" version of this that can easily be turned into what we actually want: for the Reverse vector OLE functionality, Bob has input $\boldsymbol{a} \in \mathbb{F}^w$, while Alice has input $x \in \mathbb{F}, \boldsymbol{b} \in \mathbb{F}^w$, and the functionality outputs nothing to Alice and $\boldsymbol{a} \cdot x + \boldsymbol{b}$ to Bob. The latter will

[6] The following actually holds even for the case of general rings.

[7] This hidden constant corresponds to the maximal complexity of encoding an output of f. The latter is at most cubic in the size of the branching program that computes f_i (and can be even smaller for some concrete useful special cases).

be based on a special gadget (referred to as *fast hard/easy code*) that allows fast encoding and decoding under erasures but semantically hides the encoded messages in the presence of noise. We describe first this gadget and then give the protocol.

3.1 Ingredients

The main ingredient we need is a public matrix M over $\mathbb{F}$ with the following pseudorandomness property: If we take a random vector $\boldsymbol{y}$ in the image of M, and perturb it with "noise", the resulting vector $\hat{\boldsymbol{y}}$ is computationally indistinguishable from a truly random vector over $\mathbb{F}$. Our noise distribution corresponds to the p-ary symmetric channel with crossover over probability μ, that is, $\hat{\boldsymbol{y}} = \boldsymbol{y} + \boldsymbol{e}$ where for each coordinate of $\boldsymbol{e}$ we assign independently the value zero with probability $1 - \mu$ and a uniformly chosen non-zero element from $\mathbb{F}$ with probability $1 - \mu$. We let $\mathcal{D}(\mathbb{F})^t_\mu$ denote the corresponding noise distributions for vectors of length t (and occasionally omit the parameters $\mathbb{F}, \mu$ and t when they are clear from the context). For concreteness, the reader may think of μ as 1/4. The properties needed for our protocol are summarized in the following assumption, that will be discussed in Sect. 7.

Assumption 2 (Fast pseudorandom matrix). *There exists a constant $\mu < 1/2$ and an efficient randomized algorithm $\mathcal{M}$ that given a security parameter 1^k and a field representation $\mathbb{F}$, samples a $k^3 \times k$ matrix M over $\mathbb{F}$ such that the following holds:*

1. *(Linear-time computation) The mapping $f_M : \boldsymbol{x} \mapsto M\boldsymbol{x}$ can be computed in linear-time in the output length. Formally, we assume that the sampler outputs a description of an $O(k^3)$-size arithmetic circuit over $\mathbb{F}$ for computing f_M.*
2. *(Pseudorandomness) The following ensembles (indexed by k) are computationally indistinguishable for* poly(k) *adversaries*

$$(M, M\boldsymbol{r} + \boldsymbol{e}) \qquad \text{and} \qquad (M, \boldsymbol{z}),$$

where $M \xleftarrow{\$} \mathcal{M}(1^k, p)$, $\boldsymbol{r} \xleftarrow{\$} \mathbb{F}_p^k$, $\boldsymbol{e} \xleftarrow{\$} \mathcal{D}_\mu(\mathbb{F}_p)^\ell$ and $\boldsymbol{z} \xleftarrow{\$} \mathbb{F}_p^{k^3}$.

3. *(Linear independence) If we sample $M \xleftarrow{\$} \mathcal{M}(1^k, \mathbb{F})$ and keep each of the first $k \log^2 k$ rows independently with probability μ (and remove all other rows), then, except with negligible probability in k, the resulting matrix has full rank.*

We will also need a linear error correcting code Ecc over $\mathbb{F}$ with constant rate R and linear time encoding and decoding, where we only need decoding from a constant fraction of erasures μ' which is slightly larger than the noise rate μ. (For $\mu = 1/4$ we can take $\mu' = 1/3$.) Such codes are known to exist (cf. [51]) and can be efficiently constructed given a black-box access to $\mathbb{F}$.

Fast Hard/Easy Code. We combine the "fast code" Ecc and the "fast pseudorandom code" $\mathcal{M}$ into a single gadget that provides fast encoding and decoding under erasures, but hides the encoded message when delivered through a noisy channel. The gadget supports messages of length $w = \Theta(k^3)$. Our gadget is initialized by sampling a $k^3 \times k$ matrix M over $\mathbb{F}$ using the randomized algorithm $\mathcal{M}$ promised in Assumption 2. We view the matrix M as being composed of two matrices M^{top} with $u = 2k \log^2 k$ rows and k columns, placed above M^{bottom} which has $v = k^3 - u$ rows and k columns. Let $w = Rv = \Theta(k^3)$ be a message length parameter (corresponding to the width of the vector-OLE). Note that our Ecc encodes vectors of length w into vectors of length v.

For a message $\boldsymbol{a} \in \mathbb{F}^w$, and random vector $\boldsymbol{r} \in \mathbb{F}^k$, define the mapping

$$E_{\boldsymbol{r}}(\boldsymbol{a}) = M\boldsymbol{r} + (0^u \circ \mathsf{Ecc}(\boldsymbol{a})),$$

where $\circ$ denotes concatenation (and so $(0^u \circ \mathsf{Ecc}(\boldsymbol{a}))$ is a vector of length $u+v$). We will make use of the following useful properties of E:

1. (Fast and Linear) The mapping $E_{\boldsymbol{r}}(\boldsymbol{a})$ can be computed by making only $O(k^3)$ arithmetic operations. Moreover, it is a linear function of $(\boldsymbol{r}, \boldsymbol{a})$ and so $E_{\boldsymbol{r}}(\boldsymbol{a}) + E_{\boldsymbol{r}'}(\boldsymbol{a}') = E_{\boldsymbol{r}+\boldsymbol{r}'}(\boldsymbol{a} + \boldsymbol{a}')$.
2. (Hiding under errors) For any message $\boldsymbol{a}$ and $\boldsymbol{r} \xleftarrow{\$} \mathbb{F}^k$ $\boldsymbol{e} \xleftarrow{\$} \mathcal{D}(\mathbb{F})_{\mu}^{k^3}$, the vector $E_{\boldsymbol{r}}(\boldsymbol{a}) + \boldsymbol{e}$ is pseudorandom and, in particular, it computationally hides $\boldsymbol{a}$.
3. (Fast decoding under erasures) Given a random $(1-\mu)$-subset I of the coordinates of $\boldsymbol{z} = E_{\boldsymbol{r}}(\boldsymbol{a})$ (i.e., each coordinate is erased with independently probability μ) it is possible to recover the vector $\boldsymbol{a}$, with negligible error probability, by making only $O(|\boldsymbol{z}|) = O(k^3)$ arithmetic operations. Indeed, letting I_0 (resp., I_1) denote the coordinates received from the u-prefix of $\boldsymbol{z}$ (resp., v-suffix of $\boldsymbol{z}$), we first recover $\boldsymbol{r}$ by solving the linear system $\boldsymbol{z}_{I_0} = (M^{\mathsf{top}}\boldsymbol{r})_{I_0}$ via Gaussian elimination in $O(k^3)$ arithmetic operations. By Assumption 2 (property 3) the system is likely to have a unique solution. Then we compute $(M^{\mathsf{bottom}}\boldsymbol{r})_{I_1}$ in time $O(k^3)$, subtract from $(E_{\boldsymbol{r}}(\boldsymbol{a}))_{I_1}$ to get $\mathsf{Ecc}(\boldsymbol{a})_{I_1}$, from which $\boldsymbol{a}$ can be recovered by erasure decoding in time $O(k^3)$.

3.2 From Fast Hard/Easy Code to Reverse Vector-OLE

Our protocol uses the gadget E to implement a reversed vector-OLE. In the following we assume that the parties have access to a variant Oblivious Transfer of field elements which we assume (for now) is given as an ideal functionality. To be precise, the variant we need is one where Alice sends a field element f, Bob chooses to receive f, or to receive nothing, while Alice learns nothing new.

We describe the protocol under the assumption that the width w is taken to be $\Theta(k^3)$. A general value of w will be treated either by padding or by partitioning into smaller blocks of size $O(k^3)$ each. (See the proof of Theorem 3.)

Construction 1 (Reverse Vector OLE protocol). *To initialize the protocol one of the parties samples the matrix $M \xleftarrow{\$} \mathcal{M}(1^k, \mathbb{F})$ and publish it. The gadget E (and the parameters u, v and w) are now defined based on M and k as described above.*

1. *Bob has input* $\boldsymbol{a} \in \mathbb{F}^w$. *He selects random* $\boldsymbol{r} \in \mathbb{F}^k$, *chooses* $\mathbf{e}$ *according to* $\mathcal{D}(\mathbb{F})_\mu^{u+v}$ *and sends to Alice the vector* $\mathbf{c} = E_{\boldsymbol{r}}(\boldsymbol{a}) + \mathbf{e}$.
2. *Alice has input* $x, \boldsymbol{b}$. *She chooses* $\mathbf{r}' \in \mathbb{F}^k$ *at random and computes* $\mathbf{d} = x \cdot \mathbf{c} + E_{\boldsymbol{r}'}(\boldsymbol{b})$.
3. *Let* I *be an index set that contain those indices* i *for which* $\mathbf{e}_i = 0$. *These are called the noise free positions in the following. The parties now execute, for each entry* i *in* $\mathbf{d}$, *an OT where Alice sends* $\mathbf{d}_i$. *If* $i \in I$, *Bob chooses to receive* $\mathbf{d}_i$, *otherwise he chooses to receive nothing.*
4. *Notice that, since the function* E *is linear, we have*

$$\boldsymbol{d} = E_{x\boldsymbol{r}+\boldsymbol{r}'}(x\boldsymbol{a} + \boldsymbol{b}) + x\boldsymbol{e}.$$

Using subscript-I to denote restriction to the noise-free positions, what Bob has just received is

$$\boldsymbol{d}_I = (E_{\boldsymbol{s}}(x\boldsymbol{a} + \boldsymbol{b}))_I,$$

where $\boldsymbol{s} = x\boldsymbol{r} + \boldsymbol{r}'$. *Using the fast-decoding property of* E *(property 3), Bob recovers the vector* $x\boldsymbol{a} + \boldsymbol{b}$ *(by making* $O(k^3)$ *arithmetic operations) and outputs* $x\boldsymbol{a} + \boldsymbol{b}$.

We are now ready to show that the reverse vector OLE protocol works:

Lemma 1. *Suppose that Assumption 2 holds. Then Construction 1 implements the Reverse Vector-OLE functionality of width* $w = \Theta(k)$ *over* $\mathbb{F}$ *with semi-honest and computational security in the OT-hybrid model. Furthermore, ignoring the cost of initialization, the arithmetic complexity of the protocol is* $O(w)$.

Proof. The running time follows easily by inspection of the protocol. We prove correctness. By Assumption 2 (property 3), except with negligible probability Bob recovers the vector $\boldsymbol{s}$ correctly. Also, by a Chernoff bound, the v-suffix of the error vector $\boldsymbol{e}$ contains at most $\mu' v$ non-zero coordinates. Therefore, the decoding procedure of the error-correcting code succeeds.

As for privacy, consider first the case where Alice is corrupt. We can then simulate Bob's message with a random vector in $\mathbb{F}^{u+v}$ which will be computationally indistinguishable by Assumption 2. If Bob is corrupt, we can simulate what Bob receives in OTs given Bob's output $x\boldsymbol{a} + \boldsymbol{b}$, namely we compute $\boldsymbol{f} = E_{\boldsymbol{s}}(x\boldsymbol{a} + \boldsymbol{b})$ for a random $\boldsymbol{s}$ and sample a set I as in the protocol (each coordinate $i \in [k^3]$ is chosen with probability $1 - \mu$). Then for the OT in position i, we let Bob receive $\boldsymbol{f}_i$ if $i \in I$ and nothing otherwise. This simulates Bob's view perfectly, since in the real protocol $\boldsymbol{s} = x\boldsymbol{r} + \boldsymbol{r}'$ is indeed uniformly random, and the received values for positions in I do not depend on x or $\boldsymbol{e}$, only on $\boldsymbol{s}$ and Bob's output. □

3.3 From Reverse Vector-OLE to Vector-OLE

Finally, to get a protocol for the vector OLE Functionality, note that we can get such a protocol from the Reverse vector OLE functionality:

Construction 2 (vector-OLE Protocol). *Given an input $\boldsymbol{a}, \boldsymbol{b} \in \mathbb{F}^w$ for Bob, and $x \in \mathbb{F}$ for Alice, the parties do the following:*

1. *Call the Reverse Vector-OLE functionality, where Bob uses input $\boldsymbol{a}$ and Alice uses input x and a randomly chosen $\boldsymbol{b}' \xleftarrow{\$} \mathbb{F}^w$. As a result, Bob will receive $x\boldsymbol{a} + \boldsymbol{b}'$.*
2. *Bob sends $\boldsymbol{b}+(x\boldsymbol{a}+\boldsymbol{b}')$ to Alice. Now, Alice outputs $(\boldsymbol{b}+(x\boldsymbol{a}+\boldsymbol{b}')-\boldsymbol{b}' = x\boldsymbol{a}+\boldsymbol{b}$.*

It is trivial to show that this implements the vector-OLE functionality with perfect security. Combining the above with Lemma 1, we derive the following theorem.

Theorem 3. *Suppose that Assumption 2 holds. Then, there exists a protocol that implements the vector-OLE functionality of width w over $\mathbb{F}$ with semi-honest computational security in the OT-hybrid model with arithmetic complexity of $O(w) + \mathrm{poly}(k)$.*

Proof. For $w < k^3$, the theorem follows directly from Construction 2 and Lemma 1 (together with standard composition theorem for secure computation). The more general case (where w is larger) follows by reducing long w-vector OLE's into t calls to w_0-vector OLE for $w_0 = \Theta(k^3)$ and $t = w/w_0$. Since initialization is only performed once (with a one-time $\mathrm{poly}(k)$ cost) and M is re-used, the overall complexity is $\mathrm{poly}(k) + O(tw_0) = \mathrm{poly}(k) + O(w)$ as claimed. □

Remark 1 (Implementing the OTs). First, note that the OT variant we need can be implemented efficiently for large fields as follows: Alice chooses a short *seed* for a PRG and to send field element f, she sends $f \oplus PRG(seed)$ and then does an OT where she offers Bob *seed* and a random value. If Bob wants to receive f, he chooses to get *seed*, otherwise he choose the random value.

Our protocol employs $O(w)$ such OTs on field elements, or equivalently, on strings of length $\log|\mathbb{F}|$ bits. For sufficiently long strings (i.e., $w = \mathrm{poly}(k)$ for sufficiently large polynomial) one can get these OT very cheaply both practically and theoretically.

Indeed, the implementation we described (which is similar to an observation from [34]), can be done with optimal asymptotic complexity of $O(w \log|\mathbb{F}|)$ bit operations assuming the existence of a linear-stretch pseudorandom generator $G : \{0,1\}^k \to \{0,1\}^{2k}$ which is computable in linear-time $O(k)$. Moreover, such a generator can be based on the binary version of Assumption 2, as follows from [9]. In practice, we can get the OT's very efficiently via OT extension and perhaps (for very large fields) using a PRG based on AES which is extremely efficient on modern Intel CPUs.

Remark 2 (On the achievable rate). Note that the full vector OLE protocol communicates $u+v$ field elements, does $u+v$ OTs and finally sends w field elements. The rate is defined as the size of the output (w) divided by the communication complexity. Now, asymptotically, we can ignore u since it is $o(v)$. Furthermore, v is the length of the code Ecc, which needs to be about $w/(1-\mu)$ to allow for erasure decoding w values from a fraction of μ random erasures. By the previous remark, an OT can be done at rate 1, so it counts as 1 field element. So we find that the rate asymptotically at best approaches $(1-\mu)/(3-\mu)$ (i.e., $3/11 \approx 1/4$ for $\mu = 1/4$). If we are willing to believe that Assumption 2 holds for any constant error rate (and large enough code length k) then we can obtain rate approaching $1/3 - \epsilon$ for any constant $\epsilon > 0$.

4 Batch-OLEs

In this section we implement n copies of OLE (of width 1) with constant computational overhead based on vector-OLE with constant computational overhead and a polynomial-stretch arithmetic pseudorandom generator of constant depth. The transformation is similar to the one described in [34] for the binary setting, and is based on a combination Beaver's OT extension [13] with a decomposable randomized encoding.

4.1 From Vector-OLE to $\mathbf{NC^0}$ Functionalities

We begin by observing that local functionalities can be reduced to vector-OLE with constant computational overhead. This follows from an arithmetic variant of Yao's protocol [54] where the garbled circuit is replaced with fully-decomposable randomized encoding. For simplicity, we restrict our attention to functionalities in which only the first party Alice gets the input.

Lemma 2. *Let $\mathbb{F}$ be a finite field and let f be a two-party $\mathbf{NC^0}$ functionality that takes ℓ_1 field elements from the sender, ℓ_2 field elements from the receiver, and delivers m field elements to the receiver. Then, we can securely compute f with an information-theoretic security in the semi-honest model with arithmetic complexity of $O(m)$ and by making $O(\ell_2)$ calls to ideal $O(m/\ell_2)$-width OLE.*

The constant in the big-O notation depends on the circuit depth of f.

Proof. View f as a function over $\mathbb{F}^\ell$ where $\ell = \ell_1 + \ell_2$. By Fact 1, there exists a DARE $\hat{f}$ which can be encoded and decoded by an $O(m)$-size arithmetic circuit. Recall, that

$$\hat{f}(x;r) = (\hat{f}_0(r), (\hat{f}_i(x_i;r))_{i\in[\ell]}), \quad \text{where } \hat{f}_i(x_i;r) = x_i\boldsymbol{a}_i(r) + \boldsymbol{b}_i(r).$$

Since the encoding is computable by $O(m)$-size circuit, it is also possible to take r and collectively compute $(\boldsymbol{a}_i(r), \boldsymbol{b}_i(r))_{i\in[\ell]}$ by $O(m)$ arithmetic operations. Also, the total length of these vectors is $O(m)$.

Let us denote by $A \cup B$ the partition of $[\ell]$ to the inputs given to Alice and the inputs given to Bob, and so $|A| = \ell_1$ and $|B| = \ell_2$. Let $w = m/\ell_2$ and assume an ideal vector OLE of width w. Given an input x_A for Alice and x_B for Bob, the parties use Yao's garbled-circuit protocol to compute f as follows:

- Bob selects randomness $r \xleftarrow{\$} \mathbb{F}^\rho$ for the encoding and sends $\hat{f}_0(r)$ together with $(\hat{f}_i(x_i;r))_{i\in B}$.

- For every $i \in A$ the parties invoke width w-OLE where Alice uses x_i as her input and Bob uses $(\boldsymbol{a}_i(r), \boldsymbol{b}_i(r))$ as his inputs. If the length W_i of $\boldsymbol{a}_i(r)$ and $\boldsymbol{b}_i(r)$ is larger than w, the vectors are partitioned to w-size blocks and the parties use $\lceil (W_i/w) \rceil$ calls to w-width OLE. (In the j-th call Bob uses the j-th block of $(\boldsymbol{a}_i(r), \boldsymbol{b}_i(r))$ as his input and Alice uses x_i as her input.)
- Finally, Alice aggregates the encoding $\hat{f}(x; r)$, applies the decoder and recovers the output $f(x)$.

It is not hard to verify that both parties can be implemented by making at most $O(\ell)$ arithmetic operations. (In fact, they can be implemented by $O(\ell)$-size arithmetic circuits). Moreover, the number of call to the w vector-OLE is $\sum_{i \in A} \lceil W_i/w \rceil = O(m/w) = O(\ell_2)$. The correctness of the protocol follows from the correctness of the DARE. Assuming perfect OLE, the protocol provides perfect security for Bob (who gets no message during the protocol) and for Alice (whose view can be trivially simulated using the perfect simulator of the DARE). □

4.2 From Pseudorandom-OLE to OLE

The following lemma is an arithmetic variant of Beaver's reduction from batch-OT to OT with "pseudorandom" selection bits.

Lemma 3. *Let $G : \mathbb{F}^k \to \mathbb{F}^n$ be a pseudorandom generator. Consider the two-party functionality g that takes a seed $\boldsymbol{s} \in \mathbb{F}^k$ from Alice and n pairs of field elements $(a_i, b_i), i \in [n]$ from Bob and delivers to Alice the value $y_i a_i + b_i$ where $\boldsymbol{y} = G(\boldsymbol{s})$. Then, in the g-hybrid model it is possible to securely compute n copies of OLE of width 1 with semi-honest computational security and complexity of $O(n)$ arithmetic operations and a single call to g.*

Proof. Let $\boldsymbol{x} = (x_i)_{i \in [n]}$ be Alice's input and let $(a_i, b_i), i \in [n]$ be Bob's input.

1. Alice and Bob call the protocol for g where Alice uses a random seed $s \xleftarrow{\$} \mathbb{F}^k$ as an input and Bob uses the pairs $(a_i, c_i), i \in [n]$ where $c_i \xleftarrow{\$} \mathbb{F}$ are chosen uniformly at random. Alice gets back the value $u_i = y_i a_i + c_i$ for $i \in [n]$.
2. Alice sends to Bob the values $\Delta_i = x_i - y_i$, for every $i \in [n]$.
3. Bob responds with $v_i = \Delta_i a_i + (b_i - c_i)$ for every $i \in [n]$.
4. Alice outputs $z_i = u_i + v_i$ for every $i \in [n]$.

It is not hard to verify that correctness holds, i.e., $z_i = x_i a_i + b_i$. To prove security, observe that Alice's view, which consists of $(\boldsymbol{x}, \boldsymbol{s}, \boldsymbol{u}, \boldsymbol{v})$, can be perfectly simulated. Indeed, given an input $\boldsymbol{x}$ and an output $\boldsymbol{z}$: Sample $\boldsymbol{s} \xleftarrow{\$} \mathbb{F}^k$ together with $\boldsymbol{u} \xleftarrow{\$} \mathbb{F}^n$ and set $\boldsymbol{v} = \boldsymbol{z} - \boldsymbol{u}$. As for Bob, his view consists of $\boldsymbol{a}, \boldsymbol{b}, \boldsymbol{c}$ and a pseudorandom string $\boldsymbol{\Delta}$. We can therefore simulate Bob's view by sampling $\boldsymbol{\Delta}$ (and $\boldsymbol{c}$) uniformly at random. □

4.3 From $\mathbf{NC}^0$ PRG to Batch-OLE

To get our final result, we need a polynomial-stretch $\mathbf{NC}^0$ arithmetic pseudorandom generator. In fact, it suffices to have a collection of such PRG's.

Assumption 4 (polynomial-stretch $\mathbf{NC}^0$ PRG (arithmetic version)). *There exists a polynomial-time algorithm that given* 1^k *and a field representation* $\mathbb{F}$ *samples an* $\mathbf{NC}^0$ *mapping* $G : \mathbb{F}^k \to \mathbb{F}^{k^2}$ *(represented by a circuit) such that with all but negligible probability* G *is a pseudorandom generator against* $\mathrm{poly}(k)$ *adversaries.*

Assumption 4 is discussed in Sect. 7. For now, let us mention that similar assumptions were made in the binary setting and known binary candidates have natural arithmetic variants.

Combining Lemmas 2 with 3, we get the following theorem.

Theorem 5. *Suppose that Assumption 4 holds. Then, it is possible to securely compute* n *copies of OLE over* $\mathbb{F}$ *in the semi-honest model by making* $O(n/k)$ *calls to ideal* $O(k)$*-width OLE and* $O(n) + \mathrm{poly}(k)$ *additional arithmetic operations.*

Proof. Let $t = n/k^2$. Implement the OLE's using t batches each of size k^2. By Lemmas 2 and 3, each such batch can be implemented by making k calls to ideal $O(k)$-width OLE and $O(k^2)$ additional arithmetic operations. Since the initialization of the pseudorandom generator has a one-time $\mathrm{poly}(k)$ cost, we get the desired complexity. □

Combining Theorems 3 and 5, together with an optimal OT implementation (which by Remark 1 follows from standard OT), and plugging in standard composition theorem for secure computation, we derive the following theorem.

Corollary 1 (main result). *Suppose that Assumptions 2 and 4 hold, and a standard binary OT exists. Then, there exists a protocol for securely computing* n *copies of OLE over* $\mathbb{F}$ *with semi-honest computational security, and arithmetic complexity of* $O(n) + \mathrm{poly}(k)$.

5 Applications of Vector-OLE

In the previous section we used vector-OLE only as a tool to obtain OLE. However, there are applications where vector-OLE is precisely what we need.

First, it is easy to see that a secure multiplication of an $n \times n$ matrix by a length-n vector reduces to n instances of width-n vector-OLE. Therefore, using our implementation of vector-OLE, it is straightforward to multiply a matrix by a vector with $O(n^2)$ field operations, which is asymptotically optimal, and with a small concrete overhead. This can be used as a building block for other natural secure computation tasks, such as matrix multiplication and other instances of secure linear algebra; see [17,44] for other examples and motivating applications.

Another class of applications is where a party holds some object that needs to be compared to entries in a database held by another party. The characteristic property is that the input of party is fixed whereas the input from the other party varies (as we run through the database). A good example is secure face recognition, where a face has been measured in some location and we now want to securely test if the measurement is close to an object in a database – containing, say, suspects of some kind. This reduces to computing the Euclidean distance from one point in a space of dimension m (say) to n points in the same space, and then comparing these distances, perhaps to some threshold. It is clearly sufficient to compute the square distance, so this means that what we need to compute will numbers of form

$$\sum_i (x_i - y_i^j)^2 = \sum_i x_i^2 + (y_i^j)^2 - 2x_i y_i^j,$$

where $(x_1, ..., x_m)$ is the point held by the client, and $(y_1^j, ..., y_m^j)$ is the $j'th$ point in the database. Clearly, additive shares of x_i^2 and $(y_i^j)^2$ can be computed locally, while additive shares of $2x_i y_i^j$ can be done using vector-OLE, namely we fix i and compute $2x_i \cdot (y_i^1, ..., y_i^n)$.

Once we have additive shares of the square distances, the comparisons can be done using standard Yao-garbling. Since this only requires small circuits whose size is independent of the dimension m, this can be expected to add negligible overhead.

We note that the secure face recognition problem was considered in [21], where a solution based on Paillier encryption was proposed (see [50] for optimizations). This adds a very large computational overhead compared our solution, since an exponentiation is required for each product $2x_i y_i^j$.

Similar applications of vector-OLE can apply in many other contexts of securely computing on numerical data that involve computations of low-degree polynomials. See, e.g., [16,24] and references therein for some recent relevant works in the context of secure machine learning.

6 Implementation

We have implemented the vector-OLE protocol. This is the most practical of our constructions and, as we explained in the previous section, it has applications of its own, even without the conversion to OLEs of width 1.

6.1 Choice of the Matrix M

For the vector OLE protocol, we need a fast pseudorandom matrix M (see Assumption 2). For this, we have chosen to use a random d-sparse matrix for a suitable constant d. This means we are basing ourselves on Assumption 6 from Sect. 7, which essentially just says that a random d-sparse matrix is likely to satisfy a good "expansion" property which leads to pseudorandomness (i.e., satisfy Assumption 2). In particular, to get b bits of security, we select the size of M, such that, except with tiny probability, every set S of at most b rows have joint support which is larger than $|S|$ (i.e., S is non-shrinking). This level of expansion is somewhat optimistic, but still seems to defend against known attacks. (See the discussion in Sect. 7.)

In the earlier theory sections we have assumed that the number rows in M is $\Theta(k^3)$. This was because we wanted to amortize away the $O(k^3)$ amount of work needed to do Gaussian elimination using the top part of the matrix. However, to achieve this number of rows in the concrete security analysis we would need to go to rather large values of k, and this would create some issues with memory management. Hence, to get a more practical version with a relatively small footprint, we chose to settle for $O(k^2)$ rows. Then, for 80-bit security and $d = 10$ it turns out that we will need approximately $k = 182$ columns and k^2 rows, while for 100-bit security we need $k = 240$.

Note that once the number of rows and columns is fixed, this also fixes the parameters u, v from the vector OLE protocol.

6.2 ECC: Using Luby Transform Codes

It remains to consider the erasure correcting code ECC. For this, we want to use Luby Transform (LT) codes [42]. LT codes have extremely simple and efficient en- and decoding algorithms, using only field addition and subtraction, no multiplications or inversions are needed. On the other hand, LT codes were designed for a streaming scenario, where one continues the stream until the receiver has enough data to decode. In our case, we must stop at some finite codeword size, and this means we will have a non-negligible probability that decoding fails. In practice, one can think of this as a small but constant error probability, say 1%. On the other hand, this be detected, and the event that decoding fails only depends on the concrete choice of LT code and the choice of the noiseless positions.

Since the player A knows the LT code to be used and is also the one who chooses the noise pattern, he can simply choose a random noise pattern subject to the condition that decoding succeeds.

The protocol will then always terminate successfully, but we need to make a slightly stronger computational assumption to show that the protocol is secure: the pseudorandomness condition for the matrix M must hold even if we exclude, say 1% of the possible noise patterns. It turns out that, given the known attacks, excluding any 1% of the noise patterns makes no significant difference.[8]

More concretely we instantiate the encoding function $\mathsf{Ecc} : \mathbb{F}^w \to \mathbb{F}^v$ over the *Robust Soliton distribution* also defined in [42]. One generates a output symbol

[8] Indeed, since we remove a *small* subset of all possible noise patterns, the remaining patterns cannot be linearized, i.e., cannot be written as a low-degree function of few fresh variables, and so known attacks do not seem to apply. Of course, one should make sure that the excluded noise patterns do not correlate somehow with the choice of the "pseudorandom" matrix M (say in a way that leaves few "special" coordinates of the secret random seed, r, uncovered). However, in our case, the matrix M is chosen at random independently of the choice of the LT-code (which determines the excluded noise patterns). See also the discussion in Sect. 7.

by sampling a degree *dec* from that distribution and defining the symbol as the sum of *dec* input symbols chosen uniformly among alle the input symbols. This distribution is defined over two constant parameters δ and c. Here δ denotes the probability of failed decoding, which together with c adds extra weight to the probability of smaller degree encoding symbols. The two parameters also determine a constant β for which $v = w\beta$, but since v and w is fixed in our construction, β is also fixed, and we have one degree of freedom less. Thus we instantiate the distribution with parameters w, v and δ and let those determine c such that $\beta = v/w$.

Note that δ may deviate from the actual probability of failed decoding λ depending on the concrete code. We estimate λ by testing our code on 50.000 random codewords. Note that we fixed the value of v earlier, as a result of choosing M. Given this, we tested different combinations of w and δ to achieve a code decodes $w/4$ errors with probability λ. Our concrete parameters are shown in Table 1. Here is presented different choices for w and δ that shows how one may trade width for failure probability. In the implementation we will use the codes corresponding to $\delta = 0.01$ for both security parameters.

Table 1. Implementation parameters

k	u	v	w	δ	λ
182	244	33.124	5.000	0.001	0.0017
			10.000	0.01	0.016
			14.000	0.1	0.095
240	320	57.600	10.000	0.001	0.0003
			20.000	0.01	0.015
			23.000	0.1	0.069

6.3 Doing Oblivious Transfers

In the vector OLE protocol we need 1 OT for each row of M. It is natural to implement this via OT extension which can be done very efficiently in a situation like ours where we need a substantial number of OTs. For instance, in [12,36], an amortised time of about 0.2 µs per semi-honestly secure string OT was obtained, when generating enough of them in one go. Note that in the protocol specification, we required a special OT variant where one message is sent and the receiver chooses to get it or not. But this can of course be implemented using standard 1–2 string OT where the sender offers the message in question and a dummy.

In order to not require a specific relation between the number of OTs produced by one run of an OT extension and what our protocol requires, we have assumed that we precompute a number of random OTs, which we then adjust to the actual values using standard techniques. The adjustment requires one message in both directions where the first one can be sent in parallel with the message in the Vector OLE protocol, so we get a protocol with a total of 3 messages.

We have not implemented the OT extension itself, instead we simulate the data and communication needed when using the preprocessed OTs. The hypothesis is that that time required to create the random OTs in the first place is insignificant compared to the rest of the computation required. We discuss below the extent to which this turned out to be true.

6.4 Communication Overhead

Having fixed the parameter choices, we can already compute the communication we will need: we can ignore the communication relating to the top part of the matrix M as this is responsible for less than 1% of the communication. Then, by simple inspection of the protocol, one sees that we need to send $v + w$ field element and do v OTs. We implement the OTs directly from 1–2 OT which means an OT costs communication of 2 field elements and 1 bit. So we get a total of $3v + w$ field elements (plus v bits, which we can ignore when the field is large). With our choice of LT code, v is roughly $3w$, so we have $10w$ field elements to send. Hence the rate is indeed constant, as expected, namely 1/10. Accepting a larger failure probability for LT decoding, we could get a rate of roughly 1/7. As explained in Remark 2, the best we can hope for asymptotically is about 1/4 when the noise rate is 1/4.

There are two reasons why we do not reach this goal: first, we chose to use LT codes for erasure correction to optimize the computational overhead, but this comes at the price of a suboptimal rate. Second we implement the OTs at rate 1/2. As explained in Remark 1, rate (almost) 1 is possible, but only for large fields. So for fields of size 1000 bits or more, we believe the rate of our implementation can be pushed to about 1/5 without significantly affecting its concrete computational overhead.

6.5 Test Set-Up and Results

Our set-up consists of two identical machines, each with 32 GB RAM and a 64-bit i7-3770K CPU running at 3.5 GHz. The machines are connected on a 1 GbE network with 0.15 ms delay.

A b-bit field is instantiated by choosing $\mathbb{F}_p$ for the largest prime $p < 2^b$. All matrix operations are optimized to that of sparse matrices except for the Gaussian elimination, where we construct an augmented matrix and do standard row reduction. All parameters are loaded into memory prior to the protocol execution including the matrix M, the LT code and a finite set of test vectors.

First a version is implemented using the GNU Multiple Precision Arithmetic Library for finite field arithmetic. We benchmark this version with b-bit field for $b \in \{32, 64, \ldots, 2048\}$. In this setting we allocate $2b$ bits for each element once, such that we never have to allocate more e.g. at multiplication operations, which consists of a MUL and MOD GMP call. We further replace the MOD call after addition and subtraction with a conditional sum.

Since most computation in the protocol includes field operations, we optimized the finite field for 32-bit and 64-bit versions. Here the 32-bit version only use half of the machine's word size, but offers fast modulo operation after a multiplication with the DIV instruction. The 64-bit version utilizes the full word size, but relies on the compiler's implementation of the modulo operation for UINT128_T as supported in GCC-based compilers. For random number generation, we use the Mersenne Twister SFMT variant instead of GMP.

In Tables 2 and 3 it is shown how the GMP and the optimized version compare for respectively $k = 182$ and $k = 240$. Here, we measure the amortized time per single OLE, or more precisely, since the protocol securely computes the multiplication of a scalar by a vector of length w, we divide the time for this by w to get the time per oblivious multiplication. We obtain these times by having as many threads as possible run the protocol in a loop and counting only successful executions. These amortized timings are also depicted in Fig. 1. Afterwards we run the protocol sequentially in a single thread and measure how fast we can execute one instance of the protocol. This indicates the latency, i.e., the time taken from the protocol starts until data is ready. Finally, since we use much less network speed than what is available, we present the network bandwidth we actually use, as this may become a limiting factor in low-bandwidth networks. The reason why the optimized versions use more bandwidth than corresponding GMP versions is that they are computationally faster, so the network is forced to handle the same amount of communication in shorter time. Then for larger fields, bandwidth usage increases because larger field elements need to be sent, but for the largest field size (2048 bits) we see a decrease because computation now has slowed down to the extent that there is more than twice the time to send field elements of double size (compared to 1024 bits).

Table 2. Benchmark of the vector-OLE protocol for $k = 182$

Field size	Version	OLE time	Latency	Network
32 bit	Optimized	0.56 µs	0.04 s	45.53 MB/s
64 bit	Optimized	1.00 µs	0.14 s	50.83 MB/s
32 bit	GMP	3.65 µs	0.26 s	6.98 MB/s
64 bit	GMP	3.66 µs	0.27 s	13.92 MB/s
128 bit	GMP	4.24 µs	0.31 s	24.03 MB/s
256 bit	GMP	6.37 µs	0.47 s	31.98 MB/s
512 bit	GMP	9.58 µs	0.64 s	42.50 MB/s
1024 bit	GMP	18.29 µs	1.15 s	44.53 MB/s
2048 bit	GMP	50.85 µs	2.87 s	32.04 MB/s

Table 3. Benchmark of the vector-OLE protocol for $k = 240$

Field size	Version	OLE time	Latency	Network
32 bit	Optimized	0.70 µs	0.12 s	31.70 MB/s
64 bit	Optimized	1.14 µs	0.25 s	38.86 MB/s
32 bit	GMP	3.96 µs	0.48 s	5.57 MB/s
64 bit	GMP	3.97 µs	0.48 s	11.12 MB/s
128 bit	GMP	4.52 µs	0.56 s	19.56 MB/s
256 bit	GMP	6.61 µs	0.82 s	26.75 MB/s
512 bit	GMP	9.93 µs	1.15 s	35.59 MB/s
1024 bit	GMP	19.48 µs	2.22 s	36.29 MB/s
2048 bit	GMP	51.73 µs	5.45 s	27.34 MB/s

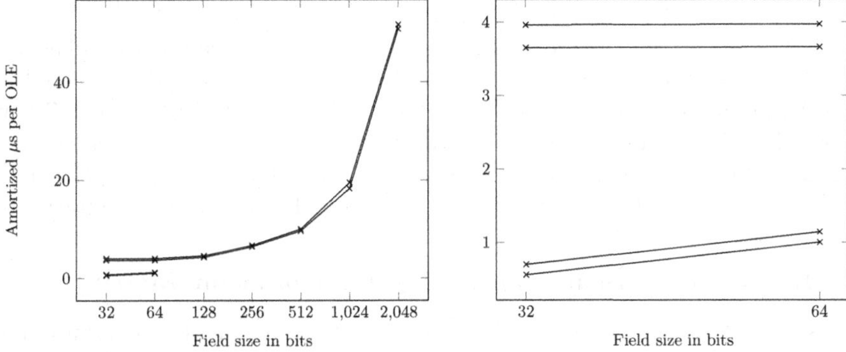

Fig. 1. Amortized time per OLE compared to field size

We note the protocol latency for 100-bit security is about 2–3 times that of 80-bit security. But for the amortized times the increase in security parameter comes cheaply because we double w in going from 80 to 100-bit security.

In our setup, we need to execute between 2 and 3 OTs per single OLE. Given the results from [12] which were obtained on an architecture similar to ours, we can expect these to take an amortised time of 0.6 µs, which as expected becomes insignificant as the field size grows, but cannot be ignored for the optimized version on smaller fields.

As computation is the bottleneck compared to network bandwidth, we identify which part of the computation is the most expensive. We test the optimized 32-bit version for $k = 182$ and focus on the Gaussian elimination, the Luby encoding and decoding and a matrix-vector product $c = M \cdot r$. This is presented in Table 4 as an index set. Here the Gaussian elimination acts as base value and takes 45% of the total protocol time including communication.

Since the Gaussian elimination costs more than other parts of the protocol, this means that one would need to increase w for the amortization to work.

Table 4. Timing of computation

Operation	Index
Gauss elimination	100
Luby decoding	22
Luby encoding (Ecc)	3
Encode $c = M \cdot r$	13

However one could replace this step with any algorithm for solving linear systems, in particular algorithms taking advantage of matrix sparsity such as [53]. Finally one may take advantage of specific constructions of finite fields allowing for even faster arithmetic operations.

7 About the Assumptions

Our results rely on two types of assumptions, both of which can be viewed as natural arithmetic analogues of assumptions that have been studied in the boolean case. We discuss our instantiations of these assumptions below. In Sect. 7.1 we discuss the assumption we use for instantiating our constant-overhead vector-OLE protocol, whereas in Sect. 7.2 we discuss the additional assumption used for obtaining constant-overhead protocol for general arithmetic computations.

7.1 Instantiating Assumption 2 (Fast Pseudorandom Matrix)

An distribution ensemble $\mathcal{M} = \{\mathcal{M}_k\}$ over $m(k) \times k$ matrices is pseudorandom for noise rate μ if it satisfies property 2 of Assumption 2. It is natural to assume that, for every $m = \mathrm{poly}(k)$, a random $m \times k$ matrix is pseudorandom over any finite field. (This is the arithmetic analogue of the Decisional-Learning-Parity-with-Noise assumption [14,29,49]). However, Assumption 2 requires the corresponding linear map to be computable in $O(m)$ arithmetic operations (together with an additional linear-independency condition). We suggest two possible instantiations for this assumption.

The Druk-Ishai Ensemble. Druk and Ishai [20] constructed, for any finite field $\mathbb{F}$ and any code length $m \in \mathrm{poly}(k)$, an ensemble $\mathcal{M}$ of linear-time computable (m, k) error-correcting code over $\mathbb{F}$ whose distance approaches the Gilbert-Varshamov bound [25,52] with overwhelming probability. It was further conjectured that, over the binary field, the ensemble is pseudorandom for arbitrary polynomial $m(k)$.[9] The assumption seems to hold for arbitrary finite

[9] The basic construction is described for codes with codeword of length $m = O(k)$; however, one can extend it for codes with codeword of polynomial length $m(k)$, by independently sampling polynomially many $O(k) \times k$ generating matrixes and placing them one on top of the other to get a $\mathrm{poly}(k) \times k$ matrix. The pseudorandomness assumption of [20, Sect. 5.1] applies to this variant for arbitrary polynomial number of samples.

fields as well. Moreover, the ensemble satisfies Condition 3 of Assumption 2 since, by [20, Theorem 5], every subset of $m' = \omega(k)$ rows of the code generates, except with negligible probability, a code of distance $1 - 1/|\mathbb{F}| - o(1)$.

Alechnovich's Ensemble. Alekhnovich [1, Remark 1] conjectured that sparse binary matrices which are "well expanding" are pseudorandom for constant noise rate. We will use the arithmetic version of this assumption. For this we will need the following definition.

Definition 2. *Let $G = (S_1, \ldots, S_m)$ as a d-uniform hypergraph with m hyperedges over k nodes (hereafter referred to as (k, m, d)-hypergraph). We say that G is expanding with* threshold r *and* expansion factor c *(in short G is (r, c)-expanding) if the union of every set of $\ell \leq r$ hyperedges $S_{i_1}, \ldots, S_{i_\ell}$ contains at least $c\ell$ nodes. For a field $\mathbb{F}$ and (k, m, d)-hypergraph G we define a probability distribution $\mathcal{M}(G, \mathbb{F})$ over $m \times k$ matrices as follows: Take $M_{i,j}$ to be a fresh random non-zero field element if j appears in the i-th hyperedge of G; otherwise, set $M_{i,j}$ to zero.*

Assumption 6 (Arithmetic version of Alekhnovich's assumption). *For every constant $d > 3$, $m = \text{poly}(k)$, real $\mu \in (0, 1/2)$ and finite field $\mathbb{F}$, the following holds for all sufficiently large k's. If G is a (k, m, d)-hypergraph which is $(t, 2d/3)$-expanding then any circuit of size $T = \exp(\Omega(t))$ cannot distinguish with advantage better than 1/T between $(M, \boldsymbol{v})$ and $(M, M\boldsymbol{r} + \boldsymbol{e})$ where $M \xleftarrow{\$} \mathcal{M}(G, \mathbb{F})$, $\boldsymbol{v} \xleftarrow{\$} \mathbb{F}^m$, $\boldsymbol{r} \xleftarrow{\$} \mathbb{F}^k$ and $\boldsymbol{e} \xleftarrow{\$} \mathcal{D}_\mu(\mathbb{F}_p)^\ell$.*

Remarks:

1. (Expansion vs. Security) The assumption says that the level of security is exponential in the size of the smallest expanding set. In particular, an expansion threshold of (k^ϵ) guarantees sub-exponential hardness.[10] This bound is consistent with the best known attacks, and, over the binary field, can be analytically established for a large family of algorithms including myopic algorithms, semi-definite programs, linear-tests, low-degree polynomials, and constant depth circuits (see [6] and references therein). Many of these results can be established for the arithmetic setting as well. The constant $2d/3$ (and the hidden constant in the Omega notation), determine the exact relation between expansion and security. The choice of $2d/3$ is somewhat arbitrary, and it may be the case that an absolute expansion factor (which does not grow with d) suffice. For our practical implementation, we take an "optimistic" estimate and require an expansion factor slightly larger than 1, which guarantees that the support of r-size sets do not shrink.
2. (Variants) One may conjecture that the assumption holds with probability 1 over the choice of M. That is, any matrix (including 0–1 matrix) whose underlying graph is expanding is pseudorandom.

[10] An exponential level of security requires expansion threshold of $\Omega(k)$ which can be achieved only when the number of rows is linearly larger than the number of columns.

3. (Efficiency) Observe that since G is (k, m, d)-hypergraph any matrix in the support of $\mathcal{M}(G, \mathbb{F}_p)$ is d-sparse in the sense that each of its rows has exactly d non-zero elements. The linear mapping $f_M : \boldsymbol{x} \mapsto M\boldsymbol{x}$ can be therefore computed by performing $O(dm) = O(m)$ arithmetic operations.
4. (Linear Independency) Recall that Assumption 2 requires that a random subset of $k \log^2 k$ of the rows of M have, except with negligible probability, full rank. In Lemma 5 we show that this condition holds as long as G is *semi-regular* in the sense that each of its nodes participates in at least $\Omega(m/k)$ hyperedges.
5. (Different noise distributions) The choice of i.i.d based noise is somewhat arbitrary and it seems likely that other noise distributions can be used. In fact, it seems plausible that one can use any noise distribution which has high entropy and cannot be approximated by a low-degree function of few fresh variables (and thus is not subject to linearization attacks).

Given the above discussion, Assumption 2 now follows from Assumption 6 and the existence of an explicit family of expanders. The latter point is discussed in Sect. 7.2.

7.2 Instantiating Assumption 4 ($\mathbf{NC^0}$ Polynomial-Stretch PRG)

In the binary setting, the existence of locally-computable polynomial-stretch PRG was extensively studied in the last decade. (See [4] and references therein.) Let $f : \mathbb{F}^k \rightarrow \mathbb{F}^m$ be a d-local function which maps a k-long vector x into an m-long vector $(P_1(x_{S_1}), \ldots, P(x_{S_m}))$ where $S_i \in [k]^d$ is a d-tuple and P_i is a d-variate multi-linear polynomial. Over the binary field, it is conjectured that as long as the (k, m, d) hypergraph $G = (S_1, \ldots, S_m)$ is expanding and the P_i's are sufficiently "non-degenerate" the function forms a good pseudorandom generator. (This is an extension of Goldreich's original one-wayness conjecture [28].) In fact, this is conjectured to be the case even if all the polynomials $P_1, \ldots, P_m$ are taken to be the same polynomial P. We denote the resulting function by $f_{G,P}$ and make the analog arithmetic assumption. In the following we say that a function $f : \mathbb{F}^k \rightarrow \mathbb{F}^m$ is T-pseudorandom if every circuit of size at most T cannot distinguish $f(x), x \xleftarrow{\$} \mathbb{F}^k$ from $y \xleftarrow{\$} \mathbb{F}^m$ with advantage better than $1/T$.

Assumption 7. *For every finite field $\mathbb{F}$ and every polynomial $m(k)$ there exists a constant d and a d-variate multi-linear polynomial $P : \mathbb{F}^d \rightarrow \mathbb{F}$ such that for every (k, m, d) hypergraph G which is $(t, 2d/3)$-expanding the function $f_{G,P}$: $\mathbb{F}^k \rightarrow \mathbb{F}^m$ is $\exp(\Omega(t))$-pseudorandom over $\mathbb{F}$.*

As in the case of Alechnovich's assumption, the constant $2/3$ is somewhat arbitrary and a smaller constant may suffice. (A lower-bound of $1/d$ can be established.) In the binary setting, security was reduced to one-wayness assumption [3] and was analytically established for a large family of algorithms including myopic algorithms, linear tests, statistical algorithms, semi-definite programs and algebraic attacks [6,7,11,23,38,47]. Some of these results can be extended to the arithmetic setting as well.

On Explicit Unbalanced Constant-Degree Expanders. In order to employ Assumptions 6 and 7 one needs an explicit family of $(k, m = k^{1+\delta}, d = O(1))$ hypergraphs which are $(k^{\epsilon}, (1+\Omega(1))d)$-expanding.[11] This assumption is known to be necessary for the existence of d-local (binary) PRG that stretches k bits to m bits [9], and so it was used (either explicitly or implicitly) in previous works who employed such a local PRG (e.g., [2,34,39–41]).

While recent advances in the theory of pseudorandomness have come close to generating such explicit highly-expanding hypergraphs, in our regime of parameters ($m = \omega(k)$ and $d = O(1)$), an explicit *provable* construction is still unknown. It is important to mention that, by a standard calculation (cf. [45]), a uniformly chosen hypergraph G (i.e., each hyperedge contains a random d-subset of the nodes) is likely to be $(r = \text{poly}(k), 2d/3)$-expanding except with some inverse polynomial failure probability $\epsilon(k)$. Moreover, we can reduce the failure probability to $1/k^c$ for an arbitrary (predetermined) constant c at the expense of increasing the sampling complexity to k^{b_c}, where the constant b grows with c. (This can be done by rejecting hypergraphs which fail to expand for sets of size at most b_c, and re-sampling the hypergraph if needed). As a result one gets a protocol that fails with "tunable" inverse polynomial probability which is *independent* of the running-time of the adversary. Moreover, the failure event is restricted to a one-time setup phase and its probability does not increase with the number of times the protocol is executed. Such a guarantee seems to be satisfactory in most practical scenarios. Finally, we mention that there are several heuristic approaches for constructing unbalanced constant-degree expanding hypergraphs. For example, by using some fixed sequence of bits (e.g., the binary expansion of π) and interpreting it as an (k, m, d)-hypergraph via some fixed translation. Assuming such a heuristic to give an explicit construction can be viewed as being a conservative "combinatorial" assumption, in the spirit of standard cryptographic assumptions.

Acknowledgements. The first and fifth authors were supported by the European Union's Horizon 2020 Programme (ERC-StG-2014-2020) under grant agreement no. 639813 ERC-CLC, by an ICRC grant and by the Check Point Institute for Information Security. The third author was supported in part by NSF-BSF grant 2015782, BSF grant 2012366, ISF grant 1709/14, DARPA/ARL SAFEWARE award, NSF Frontier Award 1413955, NSF grants 1619348, 1228984, 1136174, and 1065276, a Xerox Faculty Research Award, a Google Faculty Research Award, an equipment grant from Intel, and an Okawa Foundation Research Grant. This material is based upon work supported by the DARPA through the ARL under Contract W911NF-15-C-0205. The views expressed are those of the authors and do not reflect the official policy or

[11] One can always increase the number of hyperedges to arbitrary polynomial $m = k^a$ at the expense of a minor loss in the other parameters. This can be done by taking a sequence of hypergraphs $G_1, \ldots, G_c$ where G_i is a $(k^{(1+\delta)^{i-1}}, k^{(1+\delta)^i}, d)$-hypergraphs which is (r, bd)-expanding and compose them together (by treating the hyperedges of the i-th graph as the nodes of the $(i+1)$-th hypergraph) and get a $(k, k^{(1+\delta)^i}, D = d^c)$-hypergraph which is $(r/(bd)^{c-1}, bD)$-expanding. Taking c to be a sufficiently large constant (i.e., $\log_{1+\delta} a$), yields the required result.

position of the DoD, the NSF, or the U.S. Government. The second and forth author were supported by the advanced ERC grant MPCPRO.

A The Rank of Sparse Matrices

In this section we analyze the rank of matrices which are sampled from the distribution $\mathcal{M}(G, \mathbb{F}_p)$ where G is a hypergraph with m hyperedges and k. We begin with the following key observation.

Lemma 4. *Let $\mathbb{F}$ be a field of cardinality $p > 2$ and let G be a hypergraph over k nodes and ℓ hyperedges with the property that every set of nodes S appears in at least $t|S|$ hyperedges for $t = \omega(\log k)$. Then, a random matrix $M \xleftarrow{\$} \mathcal{M}(G, \mathbb{F}_p)$ will have full rank except with probability* $\exp(-\Omega(t))$.

Proof. To prove the claim it suffices to show that

$$\Pr_M[\exists v \neq 0^k \text{ s.t } Mv = 0^\ell] = \exp(-\Omega(t))$$

For a non-empty subset $S \subseteq [k]$, let V_S be the set of all vectors $v \in \mathbb{F}^k$ whose support (set of non-zero coordinates) equals to S. By a union-bound, it suffices to upper-bound

$$\sum_{S \neq \emptyset} q_S, \quad \text{where } q_S = \Pr[\exists v \in V_S \text{ s.t } Mv = 0^\ell]. \tag{1}$$

We will later show that

$$q_S \leq 2^{-|S|(t-1)\log(p-1)} = 2^{-\Omega(|S|t)} \tag{2}$$

Hence we can upper-bound (1) by

$$\sum_{w=1}^{k} \sum_{S:|S|=w} q_S \leq \sum_{w=1}^{k} k^w 2^{-\Omega(wt)} \leq \sum_{w=1}^{k} 2^{-\Omega(wt)} \leq 2^{-\Omega(t)}.$$

It is left to prove (2). Fix a set S of cardinality w, and let us assume without loss of generality that the first t hyperedges of G touch S. Fix some vector $v \in V_S$ and recall that the vector $r_i, i \in [t]$ is sampled by assigning a random non-zero field element to every $j \in [k]$ that participates in the i-th hyperedges. Therefore, every such row is orthogonal to v independently with probability at most $1/(p-1)$. We conclude that, for every $v \in V_S$, we have that

$$\Pr_M[Mv = 0^\ell] \leq (p-1)^{-tw}.$$

By a union-bound, we conclude that

$$q_S \leq \sum_{v \in V_S} \Pr[Mv = 0^\ell] \leq (p-1)^{-w(t-1)},$$

as required. □

Lemma 5. *Let G be a (k, m, d) hypergraph with $m = \omega(kr)$ where $d = O(1)$ and $r = \omega(k \log k)$. Assume that each node of G participates in at least $\Omega(m/k)$ hyperedges. Then, for any field $\mathbb{F}$ of size larger than 2, if we sample $M \xleftarrow{\$} \mathcal{M}(G, \mathbb{F})$ and sub-sample r rows from M, then the resulting matrix M' will have full rank except with negligible probability. Moreover, the above is true even if the rows of M' are sampled from M with replacement.*

For $m = k^3$ and $r = k \log^2 k$, we conclude that the distribution $\mathcal{M}(G, \mathbb{F})$ satisfies the linear-independence condition from Assumption 2.

Proof. Let us describe the sampling procedure in an equivalent way: First sample a hypergraph G' by sub-sampling r hyperedges from G, and then sample M' from $\mathcal{M}(G', \mathbb{F})$. By Lemma 4, it suffices to show that, except with negligible probability, every set S of nodes in G' participates in at least $\omega(\log k)|S|$ hyperedges. Below, we will show that each fixed subset S participates in at least $\omega(\log k)|S|$ hyperedges except with probability $\exp(-\omega(k))$. The theorem therefore follows by a union bound over all 2^k possible subsets.

Fix some non-empty set of nodes S. By assumption, the number of "good" hyperedges in G that touch S is at least $m_0 = |S|\Omega(m/(dk))$. Observe that whenever we sample an hyperedge from M the probability of hitting a good hyperedge is at least $q = (m_0 - r)/m$, regardless of the "history" of the previous samples. (This is true for both sampling with or without replacement.) Therefore, the probability of "failure", i.e., hitting less than $qr/2$ good hyperedges, is upper-bounded by the probability of failure in a binomial experiment where we sample r hyperedges where is good independently with probability q. By a multiplicative Chernoff bound, the probability of seeing less that $qr/2$ successes is at most $\exp(-\Omega(qr))$. Noting that $qr = \Omega(\frac{r|S|}{dk}) - \frac{r^2}{m} = |S|\Omega(r/k) = |S|\omega(\log^2 k)$, concludes the proof. □

By taking G to be the complete $(k, m = \binom{k}{d}, d)$ hypergraph, we derive the following lemma.

Lemma 6. *Let $\mathbb{F}$ be a field of cardinality $p > 2$, and let d be a constant. Then, except with negligible probability in k, a random d-sparse $k \log^2 k \times k$ matrix M over $\mathbb{F}$ has full rank.*

Proof. Let G the complete $(k, m = \binom{k}{d}, d)$ hypergraph and note that the distribution of M can be obtained by sampling $T \xleftarrow{\$} \mathcal{M}(G, \mathbb{F})$ and then sub-sampling $k \log^2 k$ rows from T. The lemma follows from Lemma 5. □

References

1. Alekhnovich, M.: More on average case vs approximation complexity. Comput. Complex. **20**(4), 755–786 (2011)
2. Ananth, P., Sahai, A.: Projective arithmetic functional encryption and indistinguishability obfuscation from degree-5 multilinear maps. IACR Cryptology ePrint Archive 2016:1097 (2016)

3. Applebaum, B.: Pseudorandom generators with long stretch and low locality from random local one-way functions. SIAM J. Comput. **42**(5), 2008–2037 (2013)
4. Applebaum, B.: Cryptographic hardness of random local functions - survey. Comput. Complex. **25**(3), 667–722 (2016)
5. Applebaum, B., Avron, J., Brzuska, C.: Arithmetic cryptography: extended abstract. In: Proceedings of the 2015 Conference on Innovations in Theoretical Computer Science, ITCS 2015, Rehovot, Israel, 11–13 January 2015, pp. 143–151 (2015)
6. Applebaum, B., Barak, B., Wigderson, A.: Public-key cryptography from different assumptions. In: STOC, pp. 171–180 (2010)
7. Applebaum, B., Bogdanov, A., Rosen, A.: A dichotomy for local small-bias generators. In: Cramer, R. (ed.) TCC 2012. LNCS, vol. 7194, pp. 600–617. Springer, Heidelberg (2012). doi:10.1007/978-3-642-28914-9_34
8. Applebaum, B., Ishai, Y., Kushilevitz, E.: Cryptography in NC^0. SIAM J. Comput. **36**(4), 845–888 (2006)
9. Applebaum, B., Ishai, Y., Kushilevitz, E.: On pseudorandom generators with linear stretch in NC^0. Comput. Complex. **17**(1), 38–69 (2008)
10. Applebaum, B., Ishai, Y., Kushilevitz, E.: How to garble arithmetic circuits. SIAM J. Comput. **43**(2), 905–929 (2014)
11. Applebaum, B., Lovett, S.: Algebraic attacks against random local functions and their countermeasures. In: STOC, pp. 1087–1100 (2016)
12. Asharov, G., Lindell, Y., Schneider, T., Zohner, M.: More efficient oblivious transfer extensions. Cryptology ePrint Archive, Report 2016/602 (2016). http://eprint.iacr.org/2016/602
13. Beaver, D.: Correlated pseudorandomness and the complexity of private computations. In: STOC, pp. 479–488 (1996)
14. Blum, A., Furst, M., Kearns, M., Lipton, R.J.: Cryptographic primitives based on hard learning problems. In: Stinson, D.R. (ed.) CRYPTO 1993. LNCS, vol. 773, pp. 278–291. Springer, Heidelberg (1994). doi:10.1007/3-540-48329-2_24
15. Boneh, D., Franklin, M.K.: Efficient generation of shared RSA keys. J. ACM **48**(4), 702–722 (2001)
16. Bost, R., Popa, R.A., Tu, S., Goldwasser, S.: Machine learning classification over encrypted data. In: 22nd Annual Network and Distributed System Security Symposium, NDSS 2015, San Diego, California, USA, 8–11 February 2015
17. Cramer, R., Damgård, I.: Secure distributed linear algebra in a constant number of rounds. In: Kilian, J. (ed.) CRYPTO 2001. LNCS, vol. 2139, pp. 119–136. Springer, Heidelberg (2001). doi:10.1007/3-540-44647-8_7
18. Damgård, I., Jurik, M.: A generalisation, a simplification and some applications of Paillier's probabilistic public-key system. In: Kim, K. (ed.) PKC 2001. LNCS, vol. 1992, pp. 119–136. Springer, Heidelberg (2001). doi:10.1007/3-540-44586-2_9
19. Damgård, I., Pastro, V., Smart, N., Zakarias, S.: Multiparty computation from somewhat homomorphic encryption. In: Safavi-Naini, R., Canetti, R. (eds.) CRYPTO 2012. LNCS, vol. 7417, pp. 643–662. Springer, Heidelberg (2012). doi:10.1007/978-3-642-32009-5_38
20. Druk, E., Ishai, Y.: Linear-time encodable codes meeting the Gilbert-Varshamov bound and their cryptographic applications. In: ITCS, pp. 169–182 (2014)
21. Erkin, Z., Franz, M., Guajardo, J., Katzenbeisser, S., Lagendijk, I., Toft, T.: Privacy-preserving face recognition. In: Goldberg, I., Atallah, M.J. (eds.) PETS 2009. LNCS, vol. 5672, pp. 235–253. Springer, Heidelberg (2009). doi:10.1007/978-3-642-03168-7_14

22. Even, S., Goldreich, O., Lempel, A.: A randomized protocol for signing contracts. CACM **28**(6), 637–647 (1985)
23. Feldman, V., Perkins, W., Vempala, S.: On the complexity of random satisfiability problems with planted solutions. In: STOC, pp. 77–86 (2015)
24. Gilad-Bachrach, R., Dowlin, N., Laine, K., Lauter, K.E., Naehrig, M., Wernsing, J.: Cryptonets: applying neural networks to encrypted data with high throughput and accuracy. In: Proceedings of the 33rd International Conference on Machine Learning, ICML 2016, New York, NY, USA, 19–24 June 2016, pp. 201–210 (2016)
25. Gilbert, E.N.: A comparison of signalling alphabets. Bell Syst. Tech. J. **31**(3), 504–522 (1952)
26. Gilboa, N.: Two party RSA key generation. In: Wiener, M. (ed.) CRYPTO 1999. LNCS, vol. 1666, pp. 116–129. Springer, Heidelberg (1999). doi:10.1007/3-540-48405-1_8
27. Goldreich, O.: Foundations of Cryptography: Basic Applications, vol. 2. Cambridge University Press, Cambridge (2004)
28. Goldreich, O.: Candidate one-way functions based on expander graphs. In: Goldreich, O. (ed.) Studies in Complexity and Cryptography. Miscellanea on the Interplay between Randomness and Computation. LNCS, vol. 6650, pp. 76–87. Springer, Heidelberg (2011). doi:10.1007/978-3-642-22670-0_10
29. Goldreich, O., Krawczyk, H., Luby, M.: On the existence of pseudorandom generators. SIAM J. Comput. **22**(6), 1163–1175 (1993)
30. Goldreich, O., Micali, S., Wigderson, A.: How to play any mental game or a completeness theorem for protocols with honest majority. In: Proceedings of the 19th Annual ACM Symposium on Theory of Computing, New York, NY, USA, pp. 218–229 (1987)
31. Ishai, Y., Kilian, J., Nissim, K., Petrank, E.: Extending oblivious transfers efficiently. In: Boneh, D. (ed.) CRYPTO 2003. LNCS, vol. 2729, pp. 145–161. Springer, Heidelberg (2003). doi:10.1007/978-3-540-45146-4_9
32. Ishai, Y., Kushilevitz, E.: Randomizing polynomials: a new representation with applications to round-efficient secure computation. In: FOCS (2000)
33. Ishai, Y., Kushilevitz, E.: Perfect constant-round secure computation via perfect randomizing polynomials. In: Widmayer, P., Eidenbenz, S., Triguero, F., Morales, R., Conejo, R., Hennessy, M. (eds.) ICALP 2002. LNCS, vol. 2380, pp. 244–256. Springer, Heidelberg (2002). doi:10.1007/3-540-45465-9_22
34. Ishai, Y., Kushilevitz, E., Ostrovsky, R., Sahai, A.: Cryptography with constant computational overhead. In: STOC, pp. 433–442 (2008)
35. Ishai, Y., Prabhakaran, M., Sahai, A.: Secure arithmetic computation with no honest majority. In: Reingold, O. (ed.) TCC 2009. LNCS, vol. 5444, pp. 294–314. Springer, Heidelberg (2009). doi:10.1007/978-3-642-00457-5_18
36. Keller, M., Orsini, E., Scholl, P.: Actively secure OT extension with optimal overhead. Cryptology ePrint Archive, Report 2015/546 (2015). http://eprint.iacr.org/2015/546
37. Keller, M., Orsini, E., Scholl, P.: MASCOT: faster malicious arithmetic secure computation with oblivious transfer. In: Proceedings of the 2016 ACM SIGSAC Conference on Computer and Communications Security, Vienna, Austria, 24–28 October 2016, pp. 830–842 (2016)
38. Kothari, P.K., Mori, R., O'Donnell, R., Witmer, D.: Sum of squares lower bounds for refuting any CSP (2017). CoRR, abs/1701.04521
39. Lin, H.: Indistinguishability obfuscation from constant-degree graded encoding schemes. In: Fischlin, M., Coron, J.-S. (eds.) EUROCRYPT 2016. LNCS, vol. 9665, pp. 28–57. Springer, Heidelberg (2016). doi:10.1007/978-3-662-49890-3_2

40. Lin, H.: Indistinguishability obfuscation from DDH on 5-linear maps and locality-5 PRGs. IACR Cryptology ePrint Archive 2016:1096 (2016)
41. Lin, H., Vaikuntanathan, V.: Indistinguishability obfuscation from DDH-like assumptions on constant-degree graded encodings. In: FOCS, pp. 11–20 (2016)
42. Luby, M.: LT codes. In: FOCS, p. 271. IEEE Computer Society (2002)
43. Lyubashevsky, V., Peikert, C., Regev, O.: On ideal lattices and learning with errors over rings. In: Gilbert, H. (ed.) EUROCRYPT 2010. LNCS, vol. 6110, pp. 1–23. Springer, Heidelberg (2010). doi:10.1007/978-3-642-13190-5_1
44. Mohassel, P., Weinreb, E.: Efficient secure linear algebra in the presence of covert or computationally unbounded adversaries. In: Wagner, D. (ed.) CRYPTO 2008. LNCS, vol. 5157, pp. 481–496. Springer, Heidelberg (2008). doi:10.1007/978-3-540-85174-5_27
45. Mossel, E., Shpilka, A., Trevisan, L.: On epsilon-biased generators in NC^0. Random Struct. Algorithms **29**(1), 56–81 (2006)
46. Naor, M., Pinkas, B.: Oblivious polynomial evaluation. SIAM J. Comput. **35**(5), 1254–1281 (2006)
47. O'Donnell, R., Witmer, D.: Goldreich's PRG: evidence for near-optimal polynomial stretch. In: CCC, pp. 1–12 (2014)
48. Paillier, P.: Public-key cryptosystems based on composite degree residuosity classes. In: Stern, J. (ed.) EUROCRYPT 1999. LNCS, vol. 1592, pp. 223–238. Springer, Heidelberg (1999). doi:10.1007/3-540-48910-X_16
49. Regev, O.: On lattices, learning with errors, random linear codes, and cryptography. J. ACM **56**(6), 34:1–34:40 (2009)
50. Sadeghi, A.-R., Schneider, T., Wehrenberg, I.: Efficient privacy-preserving face recognition. In: Lee, D., Hong, S. (eds.) ICISC 2009. LNCS, vol. 5984, pp. 229–244. Springer, Heidelberg (2010). doi:10.1007/978-3-642-14423-3_16
51. Spielman, D.A.: Linear-time encodable and decodable error-correcting codes. IEEE Trans. Inf. Theory **42**(6), 1723–1731 (1996)
52. Varshamov, R.R.: Estimate of the number of signals in error correcting codes. In: Doklady Akademii Nauk SSSR, no. 117, pp. 739–741 (1957)
53. Wiedemann, D.H.: Solving sparse linear equations over finite fields. IEEE Trans. Inf. Theory **32**(1), 54–62 (1986)
54. Yao, A.C.-C.: How to generate and exchange secrets (extended abstract). In: FOCS, pp. 162–167 (1986)

Encryption Switching Protocols Revisited: Switching Modulo p

Guilhem Castagnos[1(✉)], Laurent Imbert[2], and Fabien Laguillaumie[2,3]

[1] IMB UMR 5251, Université de Bordeaux, LFANT/INRIA, Bordeaux, France
guilhem.castagnos@math.u-bordeaux.fr
[2] CNRS, Université Montpellier/CNRS LIRMM, Montpellier, France
[3] Université Claude Bernard Lyon 1, CNRS/ENSL/INRIA/UCBL LIP, Lyon, France

Abstract. At CRYPTO 2016, Couteau, Peters and Pointcheval introduced a new primitive called *encryption switching protocols*, allowing to switch ciphertexts between two encryption schemes. If such an ESP is built with two schemes that are respectively additively and multiplicatively homomorphic, it naturally gives rise to a secure 2-party computation protocol. It is thus perfectly suited for evaluating functions, such as multivariate polynomials, given as arithmetic circuits. Couteau et al. built an ESP to switch between Elgamal and Paillier encryptions which do not naturally fit well together. Consequently, they had to design a clever variant of Elgamal over $\mathbf{Z}/n\mathbf{Z}$ with a costly shared decryption.

In this paper, we first present a conceptually simple generic construction for encryption switching protocols. We then give an efficient instantiation of our generic approach that uses two well-suited protocols, namely a variant of Elgamal in $\mathbf{Z}/p\mathbf{Z}$ and the Castagnos-Laguillaumie encryption which is additively homomorphic over $\mathbf{Z}/p\mathbf{Z}$. Among other advantages, this allows to perform all computations modulo a prime p instead of an RSA modulus. Overall, our solution leads to significant reductions in the number of rounds as well as the number of bits exchanged by the parties during the interactive protocols. We also show how to extend its security to the malicious setting.

1 Introduction

Through interactive cryptographic protocols, secure multi-party computation (MPC) allows several parties to compute the image of a pre-agreed function of their private inputs. At the end of the interaction, anything that a party (or a sufficiently small coalition of parties) has learned from the protocol could have been deduced from its public and secret inputs and outputs. In other words, the adversary's view can be efficiently forged by a simulator that has only access to the data publicly known by the adversary. This important area of research emerged in the 80s with the works of Yao [46] and Goldreich et al. [22]. Formal security notions can be found in [4,8,34]. Initially considered as a theoretical subject due to overly inefficient protocols, MPC has nowadays reached a reasonable complexity and has became relevant for practical purposes [6] especially in the 2-party case [31,33,40]. Several techniques may be used to design secure

J. Katz and H. Shacham (Eds.): CRYPTO 2017, Part I, LNCS 10401, pp. 255–287, 2017.
DOI: 10.1007/978-3-319-63688-7_9

multi-party computation. Some recently proposed solutions use or combine tools from oblivious transfer [3,30], secret sharing with pre-processing [16,37], garbled circuits [31], homomorphic encryption [11,15], and somewhat or fully homomorphic encryption [2,5].

In [10], Couteau et al. formalized an innovative technique to securely compute functions between two players, thanks to interactive cryptographic protocols called *encryption switching protocols* (ESP). This mechanism permits secure 2-party computations against semi-honest adversaries (honest-but-curious) as well as malicious adversaries, i.e. opponents which might not follow the specifications of the protocol. Couteau et al.'s proposal relies on a pair of encryption schemes $(\Pi_+, \Pi_\times)$ which are respectively additively and multiplicatively homomorphic and which share a common message space. Furthermore, there exists switching algorithms to securely convert ciphertexts between Π_+ and $\Pi_\times$. More precisely, there exists a protocol $\mathsf{Switch}_{+\to\times}$ which takes as input an encryption C_m^+ of a message m under Π_+, and returns a ciphertext $C_m^\times$ of the same message m under $\Pi_\times$. Symmetrically, there exists a second protocol $\mathsf{Switch}_{\times\to+}$ which computes a ciphertext for m under Π_+ when given a ciphertext for m under $\Pi_\times$. The advantage of this construction is that it benefits from the intrinsic efficiency of multiplicatively homomorphic encryption like Elgamal [18] or additively homomorphic encryption like Paillier [38]. In [10], Couteau et al. present a natural construction for secure 2-party computation from any ESP.

Applications. Two-party computation is the most important application of an ESP. In [11], an MPC protocol is built from only an additively homomorphic encryption scheme which is a natural alternative to an ESP. The round complexity of their protocol is in $\mathcal{O}(d)$, where d is the depth of the circuit $\mathcal{C}$ to be evaluated, and if we suppose that the multiplicative gates can be evaluated in parallel at each level. With an ESP, gathering the additive and multiplicative gates separately would imply a dramatic improvement. Fortunately, the result by Valiant et al. from [45, Theorem 3], states that for any circuit $\mathcal{C}$ of size s and degree d computing a polynomial f, there is another circuit $\mathcal{C}'$ of size $\mathcal{O}(s^3)$ and depth $\mathcal{O}(\log(s)\log(d))$ which computes the same polynomial f. Moreover, Allender et al. showed that the circuit $\mathcal{C}'$ is by construction layered (see [1]), in the sense that it is composed of layers whose gates are all the same and alternatively $+$ and $\times$. Roughly speaking, $\mathcal{C}'$ is of the form $(\sum\prod)^{\mathcal{O}(\log(s)\log(d))}$ where $\sum$ has only additive gates and $\prod$ has only multiplicative gates. In other words, the polynomial f can be written as a composition of $\mathcal{O}(\log(s)\log(d))$ polynomials written in a sparse representation. The ESP allows to treat each $\sum$ and $\prod$ independently, so that the number of switches and therefore the number of rounds is essentially $\mathcal{O}(\log(s)\log(d))$, instead of $\mathcal{O}(d)$ for [11]. Any enhancement of an ESP will naturally improve any protocol which requires to evaluate on encrypted data a polynomial given in the form of a sum of monomials. Especially it is well-suited to oblivious evaluation of multivariate polynomials [27,36,42] or private disjointness testing [47].

Related Works. The idea of switching between ciphertexts for different homomorphic encryption schemes was first proposed by Gavin and Minier in [20] in the context of oblivious evaluation of multivariate polynomials. They proposed to combine a variant of Elgamal over $(\mathbf{Z}/N\mathbf{Z})^*$ (where N is an RSA modulus) with a Goldwasser-Micali encryption protocol [23]. Unfortunately, as noticed by Couteau et al. [10], their design contains a serious flaw which renders their scheme insecure (the public key contains a square root of unity with Jacobi symbol -1, which exposes the factorization of N). Another attempt was proposed in [44] with a compiler designed to embed homomorphic computation into C programs to operate on encrypted data. The security of this construction relies on a very strong assumption since switching between the encryption schemes is done using a secure device which decrypts and re-encrypts using the secret key. In [29], Lim et al. proposed a primitive called *switchable homomorphic encryption* implemented using Paillier and Elgamal, in the context of computation on encrypted data. Again, this proposal uses an insecure version of Elgamal, which does not satisfy the indistinguishability under a chosen plaintext attack. It is indeed very difficult to design two compatible encryption schemes from unrelated protocols like Paillier and Elgamal. Couteau et al. managed to tune Elgamal so that it can switch with Paillier, but their construction remains fairly expensive. In particular, they constructed a variant of Elgamal over $(\mathbf{Z}/n\mathbf{Z})^*$, where n is an RSA modulus, which is the same as the Paillier modulus. As Elgamal is secure only in the subgroup $\mathbf{J}_n$ of $(\mathbf{Z}/n\mathbf{Z})^*$ of elements of Jacobi symbol $+1$, they need a careful encoding of the group $(\mathbf{Z}/n\mathbf{Z})^*$. The security relies on the DDH assumption in $\mathbf{J}_n$ and the quadratic residuosity assumption in $(\mathbf{Z}/n\mathbf{Z})^*$. Because their Elgamal variant does not support a simple 2-party decryption (a Paillier layer has to be added to Elgamal in order to simulate a threshold decryption), the switching protocols are intricate and specific to their construction.

Our Contributions and Overview of Our Results. In this paper, we first propose a generic ESP inspired by Couteau et al.'s solid basis. Our construction relies on the existence of an additively homomorphic encryption Π_+ and a multiplicatively homomorphic encryption $\Pi_\times$ which support a 1-round threshold decryption and achieve classical security properties (IND-CPA and zero-knowledge of the 2-party decryption). Because the message spaces must be compatible, we suppose that Π_+ works over a ring $\mathcal{R}$ and $\Pi_\times$ over a monoid $\mathcal{M}$ with $\mathcal{R} \cap \mathcal{M} = \mathcal{R}^*$ where $\mathcal{R}^*$ is the set of invertible elements of $\mathcal{R}$. A major issue when designing an ESP is to embed the zero message[1] into the message space for $\Pi_\times$, while preserving the homomorphic and security properties. In Sect. 4.2, we propose a generic technique to do so, inspired by the approach employed in [10]. Contrary to their construction, our switching protocols over $\mathcal{R}^*$ (i.e. without the zero-message) are symmetrical, i.e. both $\mathsf{Switch}_{+\to\times}$ and $\mathsf{Switch}_{\times\to+}$ follow the same elementary description given in Fig. 3. This is possible for two reasons: first because we suppose that both Π_+ and Π_+ admit a single round 2-party

[1] The zero message has to be taken into account since it can arise easily by homomorphically subtracting two equivalent ciphertexts of the same message.

decryption, and second because they both possess a $\mathsf{ScalMul}$ algorithm which takes as input a ciphertext of m and a plaintext α and outputs a ciphertext of $\alpha \times m$ (which is why we consider a ring as the message space for Π_+ instead of an additive group).

Besides, they are very efficient: as detailed in Sect. 5.3, they only require 2 rounds, whereas Couteau et al.'s $\mathsf{Switch}_{\times\to+}$ needs 6. Our full switching protocols work over $\mathcal{R}^* \cup \{0\}$. They are built on top of the switching protocols over $\mathcal{R}^*$ (i.e. without 0), plus some additional tools like 2-party re-encryption, encrypted zero test, and a 2-party protocol to homomorphically compute a product under Π_+ (see Fig. 1). Our security proofs are simpler than Couteau et al.'s. In terms of round complexity, the savings are substantial: our full ESP protocols require 7 and 4 rounds respectively, whereas Couteau et al's ESP need 7 and 11.

In a second part, we propose an efficient instantiation of our generic protocol over the field $\mathbf{Z}/p\mathbf{Z}$. Working over $\mathbf{Z}/p\mathbf{Z}$ has several advantages compared to $\mathbf{Z}/n\mathbf{Z}$ (for an RSA modulus n): it means true message space equality, instead of computational equality. It also means faster arithmetic by carefully choosing the prime p. Our instantiation combines a variant of Elgamal together with the Castagnos-Laguillaumie additively homomorphic encryption from [9]. Because Elgamal is only secure in the subgroup of squares modulo p, our variant over $\mathbf{Z}/p\mathbf{Z}^*$, denoted Eg^*, encodes the messages into squares and adds the encryption of a witness bit (i.e. the Legendre Symbol) under Goldwasser-Micali [23] for its homomorphic properties modulo 2. For Π_+, we use a variant of the Castagnos-Laguillaumie encryption scheme (CL) described in [9, Sect. 4]. We work over (subgroups of) the class group of an order of a quadratic field of discriminant $\Delta_p = -p^3$. Computations are done in this class group. The elements are represented by their unique reduced representative, i.e. by two integers of size $\sqrt{|\Delta_p|}$. Thus, an element of the class group requires $3 \log p$ bits. Under slightly different security assumptions, it is possible to further reduce the size of the elements and to achieve a better bit complexity. We discuss these implementation options in Sect. 5.3 and compare their costs with the ESP from Couteau et al. [10]. Our ESP protocol reduces the round complexity by a factor of almost 3 in the $\times \to +$ direction, while remaining constant in the other direction. Using the variant of CL optimized for size, the bit complexity is also significantly reduced in the $\times \to +$, while remaining in the same order of magnitude in the other.

We also propose improvements on CL that can be on independent interest. That system makes exponentiations in a group whose order is unknown but where a bound is known. We show that using discrete Gaussian distribution instead of uniform distribution improves the overall computational efficiency of the scheme. Moreover in order to use our generic construction, we devise a 2-party decryption for CL.

Eventually we discuss in Sect. 6 how to adapt our generic construction and our instantiation against malicious adversaries.

2 Cryptographic Building Blocks

In this section, we recall some classical definitions and operations that will be useful in the rest of the paper.

2.1 Homomorphic Encryption Schemes

In Sect. 3, we will give a definition of *Encryption Switching Protocols (ESP)*, previously proposed in [10]. An ESP allows to switch a ciphertext under an encryption protocol Π_1 into a ciphertext under another encryption protocol Π_2, and vice versa. ESP require the protocols Π_1 and Π_2 to be (partially) homomorphic. In this paper, we consider ESP between an additively homomorphic encryption Π_+ and a multiplicatively homomorphic encryption $\Pi_\times$.

In Definitions 1 and 2 below, we define Π_+ and $\Pi_\times$ formally in a generic context. An additive homomorphic encryption is most commonly defined over a group. In our setting, Π_+ is defined over a ring $\mathcal{R}$ to guarantee that for $m, m' \in \mathcal{R}$, the product $m \times m'$ is well defined. For genericity $\Pi_\times$ is defined over an algebraic structure with a single associative binary operation (denoted $\times$) and an identity element; i.e. a monoid. By doing so, our definition encapsulates encryption schemes over $(\mathbf{Z}/pq\mathbf{Z})^* \cup \{0\}$ (with p, q primes) such as [10], as well as our instantiation over $\mathbf{Z}/p\mathbf{Z}$ presented in Sect. 5.

Definition 1 (Additively homomorphic encryption). *Let $(\mathcal{R}, +, \times, 1_\mathcal{R}, 0_\mathcal{R})$ be a ring. An* additively homomorphic encryption scheme *over the message space $\mathcal{R}$ is a tuple $\Pi_+ = (\mathsf{Setup}, \mathsf{KeyGen}, \mathsf{Encrypt}, \mathsf{Decrypt}, \mathsf{Hom}_+, \mathsf{ScalMul})$ such that:*

Setup *is a PPT algorithm which takes as input a security parameter 1^λ and outputs public parameters* params *(these public parameters will be omitted in the algorithms' inputs).*

KeyGen *is a PPT algorithm taking public parameters as inputs and outputting a pair of public and secret key (pk, sk).*

$\mathsf{Encrypt}$ *is a PPT algorithm which takes as input some public parameters, a public key pk and a message $m \in \mathcal{R}$, and outputs an encryption c.*

$\mathsf{Decrypt}$ *is a PPT algorithm which takes as input public parameters, a public key pk (omitted in* $\mathsf{Decrypt}$*'s input), a secret key sk and a ciphertext c, and outputs a message $m \in \mathcal{R}$.*

Hom_+ *is a PPT algorithm which takes as inputs some public parameters, a public key pk and two ciphertexts c and c' of $m \in \mathcal{R}$ and $m' \in \mathcal{R}$ respectively, and outputs a ciphertext c'' such that $\Pi_+.\mathsf{Decrypt}(sk, c'') = m + m' \in \mathcal{R}$.*

$\mathsf{ScalMul}$ *is a PPT algorithm which takes as inputs some public parameters, a public key pk, a ciphertext c of $m \in \mathcal{R}$ and a plaintext $\alpha \in \mathcal{R}$, and outputs a ciphertext c' such that $\Pi_+.\mathsf{Decrypt}(sk, c') = \alpha \times m \in \mathcal{R}$.*

Remark 1. A generic algorithm for computing $\Pi_+.\mathsf{ScalMul}(pk, c, \alpha)$ is given by $\mathsf{2Mul}_+(c, \Pi_+.\mathsf{Encrypt}(\alpha))$, where $\mathsf{2Mul}_+$ is an interactive PPT algorithm which computes homomorphically the product of two ciphertexts for Π_+. $\mathsf{2Mul}_+$ is defined more formally in Sect. 2.3. For our instantiation we provide a non-interactive, more efficient version over $\mathbf{Z}/p\mathbf{Z}$ (see Sect. 5).

Definition 2 (Multiplicatively homomorphic encryption). *Let* $(\mathcal{M}, \times, 1_{\mathcal{M}})$ *be a monoid. A* multiplicatively homomorphic encryption scheme *over the message space* $\mathcal{M}$ *is* $\Pi_\times = (\mathsf{Setup}, \mathsf{KeyGen}, \mathsf{Encrypt}, \mathsf{Decrypt}, \mathsf{Hom}_\times, \mathsf{ScalMul})$ *such that:*

Setup, KeyGen, Encrypt *and* Decrypt *as in Definition 1 except that* Encrypt *and* Decrypt *receives the input messages from* $\mathcal{M}$ *instead of* $\mathcal{R}$.

$\mathsf{Hom}_\times$ *is a PPT algorithm which takes as input some public parameters, a public key* pk *and two ciphertexts* c *and* c' *of* $m \in \mathcal{M}$ *and* $m' \in \mathcal{M}$ *respectively, and outputs a ciphertext* c'' *such that* $\Pi_\times.\mathsf{Decrypt}(sk, c'') = m \times m' \in \mathcal{M}$.

ScalMul *is a PPT algorithm which takes as inputs some public parameters, a public key* pk*, a ciphertext* c *of* $m \in \mathcal{M}$ *and a plaintext* $\alpha \in \mathcal{M}$*, and outputs a ciphertext* c' *such that* $\Pi_\times.\mathsf{Decrypt}(sk, c') = \alpha \times m \in \mathcal{M}$.

Remark 2. A generic algorithm for computing $\Pi_\times.\mathsf{ScalMul}(pk, c, \alpha)$ is given by $\Pi_\times.\mathsf{Hom}_\times(pk, c, c')$, where $c' = \Pi_\times.\mathsf{Encrypt}(pk, \alpha)$. In Sect. 5, we provide a more efficient version over $(\mathbf{Z}/p\mathbf{Z})^*$.

The above encryption schemes must be correct in the usual sense. Moreover, we consider as a security requirement the indistinguishability under a chosen plaintext attack (IND-CPA). We refer the reader to e.g., [25] for the standard definition of IND-CPA.

2.2 One Round 2-Party Decryption

A crucial feature of the encryption protocols which are used in the ESP is the fact that they support a 2-party decryption (threshold cryptosystems were introduced in [17]). These encryption schemes are equipped with a Share procedure that is run by a trusted dealer, which works as follows: it takes as input a pair of keys (sk, pk) obtained from the KeyGen algorithm and produces two shares sk_A and sk_B of the secret key sk. It outputs (sk_A, sk_B) and an updated public part still denoted pk. Its decryption procedure is an interactive protocol denoted 2Dec which takes as inputs the public parameters, a ciphertext c, and the secret key of each participant sk_A and sk_B and outputs a plaintext m which would have been obtained as $\mathsf{Decrypt}(sk, c)$.

Contrary to the classical definition of threshold decryption, we suppose that the protocol is in a *single* round. The protocol $\mathsf{2Dec}(pk, c; sk_A; sk_B)$ is supposed as follows: Alice starts the protocol and sends her information in one flow to Bob which ends the computation and gets the plaintext. This is because in our context, we do not decrypt plaintexts but plaintexts which are masked by a random element. For example, protocols whose decryption only performs exponentiations with secret exponents gives one round 2-party decryption by sharing the exponentiations. This is the case for many cryptosystems.

The semantic security is adapted from the standard IND-CPA notion by giving the adversary one of the two secret keys, as well as a share decryption oracle which simulate the party with the other secret key. A formal definition can be found for instance in [11,41].

We need as an additional security requirement the notion of zero-knowledge defined in Appendix A, which means that no information on the secret keys are leaked during an interaction with a curious adversary. Cryptosystems like Elgamal [17] or Paillier [19] satisfy all these properties. We will propose a variant of Elgamal and a variant of Castagnos-Laguillaumie [9] that satisfy also these properties in Sect. 5.

2.3 Homomorphically Computing a Product with Π_+

A core routine of our protocol is the computation of a Π_+-encryption of a product XY given Π_+-encryptions of X and Y (this is why we assume that Π_+ has a ring $\mathcal{R}$ as message space). We describe in Fig. 1 a protocol which is implicitly used in [10]. It is a simplified variant of a protocol proposed by Cramer et al. from [11]: the main difference comes from the fact that the result of this 2-party computation is obtained only by one of the user, who can forward the result to the other. This leads to the use of a single randomness on Alice's side, instead of one on each side. We will denote by $\mathsf{2Mul}_+(pk, C_X^+, C_Y^+; sk_A; sk_B)$ a call to this protocol. Again, this protocol will be a 2-round protocol since the shared decryption is single round, and the first ciphertext can be sent along with the shared decryption. This protocol has to be zero-knowledge in the sense similar to those of Definitions 5 and 7 (we do not write down this definition which can be readily adapted).

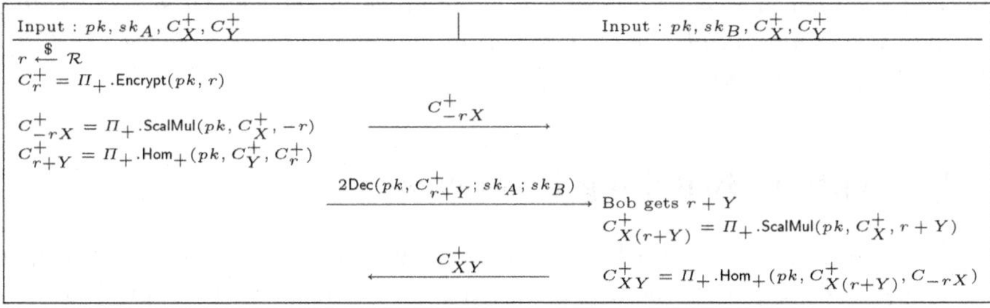

Fig. 1. $\mathsf{2Mul}_+$: 2-party protocol to compute C_{XY}^+ from C_X^+ and C_Y^+

Theorem 1. *Let Π_+ be an additively homomorphic encryption scheme with a zero-knowledge one round 2-party decryption. Then, the protocol described in Fig. 1 is correct and zero-knowledge.*

Proof. The correctness follows from the correctness of the encryption scheme and its homomorphic properties. Let us prove first that it is zero-knowledge for Alice. We describe a simulator Sim whose behavior is indistinguishable from Alice's behavior in front of an adversarial Bob. The simulator receives as input the public key pk_+ and will set $\mathsf{Sim}_{\mathsf{Share}}$ as follows: it calls out $\mathsf{Sim}^{2d}_{\mathsf{Share}}$ procedure of the zero-knowledge property of 2-party decryption for Π_+ with pk_+ as input. It obtains a simulated share $sk_B = x_B^+$ and feeds the adversary with it. When Sim is requested for the 2-party computation of C^+_{XY} from C^+_X and C^+_Y, it receives a pair of $((C^+_X, C^+_Y), \bar{C})$ where $\bar{C}$ is a ciphertext of XY, it does the following to simulate C^+_{-rX}, C^+_{r+Y} and C_A: First, It picks R at random in the plaintext space and sets $C^+_{r+Y} = \mathsf{Encrypt}(pk, R)$. Then it uses the simulator for the zero-knowledge for Alice of the 2-party decryption $\mathsf{Share}^{2d}_A(C^+_{r+Y}, R, x^+_B)$ so that Bob decrypts R (which is equivalent to $\mathsf{Decrypt}(sk, C^+_{r+Y})$). Eventually, it sets $C_{-rX} = \mathsf{Hom}_+(\bar{C}, \mathsf{ScalMul}(C^+_X, -R))$. This ciphertext encrypts $XY - RX$ so that Bob's final Hom_+ evaluation will cancel out the RX part and lead to $\bar{C}$.

The simulated view is the same as a genuine one with $R = r + Y$, which means that they are indistinguishable, and the protocol is zero-knowledge for Alice. The protocol is obviously zero-knowledge for Bob: Bob's contribution is simulated by just sending $\bar{C}$. □

2.4 2-Party Re-encryption

The final tool we need to build our encryption switching protocol is an interactive 2-party protocol to re-encrypt a ciphertext from an encryption scheme Π_+ intended to pk into a ciphertext of the same encryption scheme of the same message, but intended to another key pk'. This protocol is depicted in Fig. 2. Note that the initial ciphertext to be transformed is not known to Bob. This protocol readily extends to the multiplicative case, which is useless for our purpose. With a proof similar to the proof of Theorem 1, we showed that

Theorem 2. *Let Π_+ be an additively homomorphic encryption scheme with a zero-knowledge one round 2-party decryption then the protocol described in Fig. 2 is correct and zero-knowledge.*

3 Encryption Switching Protocols

The global scenario is established as follows: two semantically secure threshold homomorphic encryption schemes, one additive, and the other multiplicative, are at the disposal of two players. A public key is provided for each protocols, and the matching secret key is shared among the players by a trusted dealer. Ideally, these two encryption schemes should have the same plaintext space, which is assumed to be a ring or a field. An encryption switching protocols makes it possible to interactively transform a ciphertext from a source encryption scheme into a ciphertext for the other encryption scheme (the target one) and *vice versa*. The formal definitions are given in the following paragraphs.

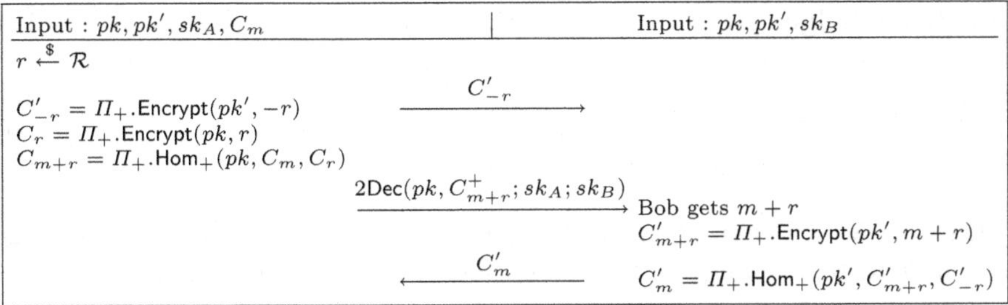

Fig. 2. 2-party ReEnc_+

Definition 3 (Twin ciphertexts). *Let Π_+ and $\Pi_\times$ be two different encryption schemes with plaintext and ciphertext spaces respectively $\mathcal{M}_+, \mathcal{C}_+$ and $\mathcal{M}_\times, \mathcal{C}_\times$. If $C_m^+ \in \mathcal{C}_+$ and $C_m^\times \in \mathcal{C}_\times$ are two encryptions of the same message $m \in \mathcal{M}_+ \cap \mathcal{M}_\times$, they are said to be* twin ciphertexts.

We will say that two ciphertexts from the same encryption scheme which decrypt to the same plaintext are *equivalent.*

Definition 4 (Encryption Switching Protocols). *An encryption switching protocol (ESP) between Π_+ and $\Pi_\times$, denoted $\Pi_+ \rightleftharpoons \Pi_\times$, is a protocol involving three parties: a trusted dealer $\mathcal{D}$ and two users A and B. It uses common* Setup *and* KeyGen *algorithms to set the message space between Π_+ and $\Pi_\times$ and keys. It is a pair of interactive protocols* (Share, Switch) *defined as follows:*

- $\mathsf{Share}((pk_+, sk_+), (pk_\times, sk_\times)) \rightarrow (pk, sk_A, sk_B)$*: It is a protocol (run by $\mathcal{D}$) which takes as input two pairs of keys (pk_+, sk_+) and $(pk_\times, sk_\times)$ produced from Π_+.*KeyGen*, $\Pi_\times$.*KeyGen *and* Setup. *It outputs the shares sk_A (sent to A) and sk_B (sent to B) of $(sk_+, sk_\times)$ and updates the public key pk.*
- $\mathsf{Switch}_{\mathsf{way}}((pk, sk_A, c), (pk, sk_B, C)) \rightarrow C'$ *or $\perp$: It is an interactive protocol in the direction* $\mathsf{way} \in \{+ \rightarrow \times, \times \rightarrow +\}$ *which takes as common input the public key and a ciphertext C under the source encryption scheme and as secret input the secret shares sk_A and sk_B. The output is a twin ciphertext C' of C under the target encryption scheme or $\perp$ if the execution encountered problems.*

Correctness. An encryption switching protocols $\Pi_+ \rightleftharpoons \Pi_\times$ is *correct* if for any $\lambda \in \mathbf{N}$, $(\mathsf{params}_+, \mathsf{params}_\times) \leftarrow \mathsf{Setup}(1^\lambda)$, for any pair of keys $(pk_+, sk_+) \leftarrow \Pi_+.\mathsf{KeyGen}(1^\lambda, \mathsf{params}_+)$ and $(pk_\times, sk_\times) \leftarrow \Pi_\times.\mathsf{KeyGen}(1^\lambda, \mathsf{params}_\times)$, for any shares $(pk, sk_A, sk_B) \leftarrow \mathsf{Share}((pk_+, sk_+), (pk_\times, sk_\times))$, for any twin ciphertext pair $(C_m^+, C_m^\times)$ of a message $m \in \mathcal{M}_+ \cap \mathcal{M}_\times$,

$$\Pi_+.\mathsf{Decrypt}(sk_+, \mathsf{Switch}_{\times \rightarrow +}((pk, sk_A, C_m^\times), (pk, sk_B, C_m^\times))) = m$$
$$\Pi_\times.\mathsf{Decrypt}(sk_\times, \mathsf{Switch}_{+ \rightarrow \times}((pk, sk_A, C_m^+), (pk, sk_B, C_m^+))) = m.$$

Zero-Knowledge. An ESP has to satisfy a notion of zero-knowledge similar to the notion of zero-knowledge for threshold decryption (see Definition 7). This property means that an adversary will not learn any other information on the secret share of a participant that he can learn from his own share, the input, and the output of the protocol.

Definition 5. *An encryption switching protocols* $\Pi_+ \rightleftharpoons \Pi_\times$ *is* zero-knowledge for A *if there exists an efficient simulator* $\mathsf{Sim} = (\mathsf{Sim}_{\mathsf{Share}}, \mathsf{Sim}_A)$ *which simulates the sharing phase and the player* A.

The subroutine $\mathsf{Sim}_{\mathsf{Share}}$ *takes as input a public key* $(pk_+, pk_\times)$ *and outputs* (pk', sk'_B) *that simulates the public key obtained from the* Share *algorithm and Bob's share of the secret key.*

The subroutine Sim_A *takes as input a direction* $\mathsf{way} \in \{+ \to \times, \times \to +\}$, *a source ciphertext* C, *a twin ciphertext* $\bar{C}$ *and a flow* flow. *It emulates the output of an honest player* A *would answer upon receiving the flow* flow *when running the protocol* $\mathsf{Switch}_{\mathsf{way}}((pk, sk_A, C), (pk, sk_B, C))$ *without* sk_A *but possibly* sk_B, *and forcing the output to be a ciphertext* C' *which is equivalent to* $\bar{C}$.

Then, for all $\lambda \in \mathbf{N}$, *for any parameters* $(\mathsf{params}_+, \mathsf{params}_\times) \leftarrow \mathsf{Setup}(1^\lambda)$, *for any pairs of keys* $(pk_+, sk_+) \leftarrow \Pi_+.\mathsf{KeyGen}(1^\lambda, \mathsf{params}_+)$ *and* $(pk_\times, sk_\times) \leftarrow \Pi_\times.\mathsf{KeyGen}(1^\lambda, \mathsf{params}_\times)$, $(pk, sk_A, sk_B) \leftarrow \mathsf{Share}((pk_+, sk_+), (pk_\times, sk_\times))$ *or for any* simulated *share* $(pk', sk'_B) \leftarrow \mathsf{Sim}_{\mathsf{Share}}(pk)$, *and for any adversary* $\mathcal{D}$ *playing the role of* B, *the advantage*

$$\mathsf{Adv}^{zk}_{A,\Pi_+ \rightleftharpoons \Pi_\times}(\mathcal{D}) = \left|\Pr[1 \leftarrow \mathcal{D}^{A}(pk, sk_B)] - \Pr[1 \leftarrow \mathcal{D}^{\mathsf{Sim}_A()}(pk', sk'_B)]\right|$$

is negligible.

We define similarly an encryption switching protocols $\Pi_+ \rightleftharpoons \Pi_\times$ *that is* zero-knowledge for B. *It is* zero-knowledge *if it is zero-knowledge for* A *and* B.

4 Generic Construction of an ESP on a Ring

We describe in this section a generic construction of an encryption switching protocol in the semi-honest model. Even though an ESP could allow to switch between any encryption schemes, its main interest is when its implemented with homomorphic encryptions. Therefore, we start with an additively homomorphic encryption Π_+ and a multiplicatively homomorphic encryption $\Pi_\times$ whose message space is respectively a ring $\mathcal{R}$ and a monoid $\mathcal{M}$. To fit most of the applications, we will make the assumption that $\mathcal{M} = \mathcal{R}^*$, the subgroup of invertible elements of $\mathcal{R}$, since in general the multiplicative homomorphic encryption will have a group as message space. In particular, this means that the intersection over which the switches are defined is $\mathcal{R} \cap \mathcal{M} = \mathcal{R}^*$.

As in [10], in the first place, we are going to describe how we can switch between Π_+-encryptions and $\Pi_\times$-encryptions over $\mathcal{R}^*$. Then we will show how to modify $\Pi_\times$ in order to extend its message space to $\mathcal{R}^* \cup \{0\}$.

Definition 6 (Compatible encryption protocols). *Let $(\mathcal{R}, +, \times)$ be a ring. Let Π_+ and $\Pi_\times$ be an additively and multiplicatively homomorphic encryption in the sense of Definitions 1 and 2. They are said to be* compatible *if Π_+ and $\Pi_\times$ have respectively $\mathcal{R}$ and $\mathcal{R}^*$ as message space, both of them admit a one-round 2-party decryption as defined in Sect. 2.2, there exists a common setup algorithm* Setup *and common* KeyGen *which allows to set common parameters.*

Remark 3. To illustrate this, our instantiation (resp. Couteau et al.'s instantiation) switches between an additively homomorphic encryption whose message space is the field $(\mathbf{Z}/p\mathbf{Z}, +, \times)$ (resp. the ring $(\mathbf{Z}/N\mathbf{Z}, +, \times)$) and a multiplicative homomorphic encryption whose message space is the group $((\mathbf{Z}/p\mathbf{Z})^*, \times)$ (resp. $((\mathbf{Z}/N\mathbf{Z})^*, \times)$) and the former is modified so that its message space is the monoid $(\mathbf{Z}/p\mathbf{Z}, \times)$ (resp. $((\mathbf{Z}/N\mathbf{Z})^* \cup \{0\}, \times)$). In particular, Couteau et al.'s make the additional algorithmic assumption that $(\mathbf{Z}/N\mathbf{Z})^*$ is computationally equal to $\mathbf{Z}/N\mathbf{Z}$.

Share Protocol of the ESP. The keys of Π_+ and $\Pi_\times$ are first shared by a trusted dealer, this corresponds to the Share algorithm from Definition 4. From public parameters generated using the common Setup algorithm and two pairs of keys (pk_+, sk_+) and $(pk_\times, sk_\times)$ it outputs the secret share $sk_A = (sk_A^+, sk_A^\times)$ for Alice and $sk_B = (sk_B^+, sk_B^\times)$ for Bob using the Share procedures of the 2-party decryption of Π_+ and $\Pi_\times$.

4.1 Switching Protocols over $\mathcal{R}^*$

We describe here the two 2-party switching protocols from an additive homomorphic encryption of m to a multiplicative one and *vice versa.* Contrary to Couteau *et al.*'s protocol [10], the two protocols are actually the *same* since both the additive and the multiplicative scheme support a ScalMul operation and a *single-round* 2-party decryption. It is important to note that in our instantiation, the round complexity is only 2, since the first ciphertext $C_{R^{-1}}^{(2)}$ can be sent within the flow of the 2-party decryption which is only one round (cf. Sect. 2.2 or Figs. 9 and 11). We suppose that $m \neq 0$ here, and more precisely the message to be switched lies in $\mathcal{R} \cap \mathcal{M} = \mathcal{R}^*$.

Switching Protocols Between Π_1.Encrypt(m) and Π_2.Encrypt(m). In Fig. 3, as our switching protocols in the two directions are the same, the pair (Π_1, Π_2) is either $(\Pi_+, \Pi_\times)$ or $(\Pi_\times, \Pi_+)$.

The correctness of these two protocols is clear. They are generic and the switch from $\Pi_\times$ to Π_+ is highly simpler than the one in [10] (ours is 2-round instead of 6-round) and our instantiation will keep this simplicity. We prove in the following theorem that they are zero-knowledge, and the security proof itself is also very simple. It only relies on the zero-knowledge property of the shared decryptions.

Input : $pk^1, pk^2, sk_A^1, C_m^{(1)}$		Input : $pk^1, pk^2, sk_B^1, C_m^{(1)}$
$R \xleftarrow{\$} \mathcal{R}^*$		
$C_{mR}^{(1)} = \Pi_1.\mathsf{ScalMul}(pk^1, C_m^{(1)}, R)$		
$C_{R^{-1}}^{(2)} = \Pi_2.\mathsf{Encrypt}(pk^2, R^{-1})$	$\xrightarrow{C_{R^{-1}}^{(2)}}$	
	$\xrightarrow{\mathsf{2Dec}(pk^1, C_{mR}^{(1)}; sk_A^1; sk_B^1)}$	Bob gets mR
	$\xleftarrow{C_m^{(2)}}$	$C_m^{(2)} = \Pi_2.\mathsf{ScalMul}(pk^2, C_{R^{-1}}^{(2)}, mR)$

Fig. 3. 2-party $\mathsf{Switch}_{1\to 2}$ from Π_1 to Π_2 where $(\Pi_1, \Pi_2) \in \{(\Pi_+, \Pi_\times), (\Pi_\times, \Pi_+)\}$.

Theorem 3. *The ESP between Π_+ and $\Pi_\times$, whose switching routines are described in Fig. 3, is zero-knowledge if Π_+ and $\Pi_\times$ are two compatible encryption schemes which have zero-knowledge one round 2-party decryptions.*

Proof. The proof consists in proving that after a share of the secret keys, both switching procedures are zero-knowledge for Alice and Bob. Let us start with the proof that the ESP is zero-knowledge for Alice. We are going to describe a simulator Sim whose behavior is indistinguishable from Alice's behavior in front of an adversarial Bob.

$\mathsf{Sim}_{\mathsf{Share}}$: The simulator receives as input the public key $(pk_+, pk_\times)$ and simulates the Share procedure as follows: it calls out the $\mathsf{Sim}^{2d}_{\mathsf{Share}}$ procedures of the zero-knowledge property of Alice for 2-party decryption of respectively Π_+ and $\Pi_\times$ with pk_+ and $pk_\times$ as input. In particular it obtains $sk'_B = (x_B^+, x_B^\times)$ it can feed the adversary with. When Sim is requested for a switch, it receives a pair of twin ciphertexts $(C, \bar{C})$.

Game G_0. This game is the real game. The simulator generates all the secret shares in an honest way and gives his share to Bob. It plays honestly any switching protocols on an input $(C, \bar{C})$ using Alice's secret key.

Game G_1. The first modification concerns the *additive to multiplicative* direction. The setup and key generation are the same as in the previous game. When requested to participate to a $\mathsf{Switch}_{+\to\times}$, with $(C, \bar{C})$ as input, the simulator picks uniformally at random $x \in \mathcal{R}^*$ and sets $C_{mR}^+ = \Pi_+.\mathsf{Encrypt}(x)$ and $C_{R^{-1}}^\times = \Pi_\times.\mathsf{ScalMul}(\bar{C}, x^{-1})$. The simulator then concludes the protocol honestly. This game is indistinguishable from the previous since, as x is random, it is equivalent to a genuine protocol using $R = x/m$, where m is the plaintext under C and $\bar{C}$.

Game G_2. In this game, we modify the shared decryption for Π_+ using the simulator of 2-party decryption. First, the simulation gives the key x_B^+ obtained by the simulation of the shares to Bob. Then after Sim simulated the pair $(C_{mR}^+, C_{R^{-1}}^\times)$ as above, it uses the simulator $\mathsf{Sim}_A^{2d}(C_{mR}^+, x, x_B^+, \cdot)$ for the 2-party decryption of Π_+ to interact with Bob, where C_{mR}^+ is an encryption of x. Thanks to the property of this simulator this game is indistinguishable from the previous one (note that the key x_B^+ is only used in that part of the protocol). Eventually,

the last computation done by Bob, $\Pi_\times$.ScalMul$(C^\times_{R^{-1}}, x)$ gives a multiplicative ciphertext of m equivalent to $\bar{C}$.
Game G_3. In this game, we address the *multiplicative to additive* way. The setup and key generation are the same as in the previous games. As in Game G_1, when requested to participate to a $\mathsf{Switch}_{\times\to+}$, with $(C, \bar{C})$ as input, the simulator picks uniformally at random $x \in \mathcal{R}^*$ and sets $C^\times_{mR} = \Pi_\times.\mathsf{Encrypt}(x)$ and $C^+_{R^{-1}} = \Pi_+.\mathsf{ScalMul}(\bar{C}, x^{-1})$. Then, Sim continues honestly the protocol. This game is indistinguishable from the previous one.
Game G_4. The shared $\Pi_\times$ decryption is modified as in Game G_2. The simulation now gives the simulated key $x^\times_B$ to Bob and then uses the simulator for the 2-party decryption of $\Pi_\times$ with ciphertext $C^\times_{mR}$ and corresponding plaintext x. Thanks to the property of this simulator this game is indistinguishable from the previous one. Again, Bob's last computation $\Pi_+.\mathsf{ScalMul}(C^+_{R^{-1}}, x)$ gives a ciphertext equivalent to $\bar{C}$.

In conclusion, the advantage of the attacker is negligible.

We now prove that the ESP is zero-knowledge for Bob, by describing a simulator Sim whose behavior is indistinguishable from Bob's behavior in front of an adversarial Alice. The simulator receives as input the public key $pk = (pk_+, pk_\times)$ and simulates the Share procedure as above and feed the adversary (Alice) with the corresponding secret key. When Sim is requested for a switch, it receives a pair of twin ciphertexts $(C, \bar{C})$. In both directions, the simulation is trivial, since Bob's only flow is the final forward of the twin ciphertext (we have suppose that the 2-party decryption has only one round from Alice to Bob), which is done by sending the $\bar{C}$ ciphertext. This is indistinguishable from a true execution since $\bar{C}$ is a random ciphertext which encrypts the same plaintext that C. $\square$

4.2 Modification of $\Pi_\times$ to Embed the Zero Message

One technical issue to design switching protocols between Π_+ and $\Pi_\times$ is to embed the zero message into $\Pi_\times$'s message space so that the message spaces match. To do so, we need to modify the $\Pi_\times$ encryption. We will use a technique quite similar to those in [10]: During their encryption, if the message m is equal to 0, a bit b is set to 1. It is set to 0 for any other message. Then, the message $m + b$ (which is never 0) is encrypted using their Elgamal encryption. As this encryption scheme is no longer injective, to discriminate an encryption of 0, the ciphertext is accompanied by two encryptions under classical Elgamal of T^b and T'^b where T, T' are random elements. We note that these two encryptions are in fact encryptions of b which are homomorphic for the or gate: If $b = 0$, we get an Elgamal encryption of 1 and if $b = 1$, an Elgamal encryption of a random element (which is equal to 1 only with negligible probability). Thanks to the multiplicativity of Elgamal, if we multiply an encryption of b and an encryption of b', we get an Elgamal encryption of 1 only if $b = b' = 0$ and an Elgamal encryption of a random element otherwise. In [10] the second encryption of b is actually an extractable commitment, the corresponding secret key is only known by the simulator in the security proof.

In our case, we use the additively homomorphic encryption Π_+ to discriminate the zero message: Π_+ is used to encrypt a random element r if $m = 0$ and 0 otherwise. As a consequence, it will be possible to directly obtain an encryption of $\bar{b}$ (the complement of the bit b used during encryption) under Π_+ using the zero-testing procedure during the switch from $\Pi_\times^0$ to Π_+ (see Fig. 7). This gives a real improvement compared to [10] when we instantiate our generic protocols. As in [10] we add a useless second encryption of r to be used by the simulation in the security proof. Our modification is formally described in Fig. 4. The $\mathsf{Hom}_\times$ procedure is obtained by applying the $\mathsf{Hom}_\times$ procedures of $\Pi_\times$, and Π_+. For the $\mathsf{ScalMul}$ procedure, which corresponds to a multiplication by a plaintext α, it applies the $\mathsf{ScalMul}$ procedure of $\Pi_\times$ if $\alpha \neq 0$ and add an encryption of 0 to the additive part. If $\alpha = 0$, it outputs an encryption of 0.

Algo. $(\Pi_+ \rightleftharpoons \Pi_\times^0).\mathsf{KeyGen}(1^\lambda)$

1. $\mathsf{params} \leftarrow (\Pi_+ \rightleftharpoons \Pi_\times).\mathsf{Setup}(1^\lambda)$
2. $((pk^\times, sk^\times), (pk^+, sk^+)) \leftarrow (\Pi_+ \rightleftharpoons \Pi_\times).\mathsf{KeyGen}(1^\lambda, \mathsf{params})$
3. $(pk', sk') \leftarrow \Pi_+.\mathsf{KeyGen}(1^\lambda, \mathsf{params})$
4. Set $pk \leftarrow (pk^\times, pk^+, pk')$ and $sk \leftarrow (sk^\times, sk^+, sk')$
5. Return (pk, sk)

Algo. $\Pi_\times^0.\mathsf{Encrypt}(pk, m)$

1. Parse pk as $(pk^\times, pk^+, pk')$
2. If $m = 0$ set $b \leftarrow 1$ and $r \xleftarrow{\$} \mathcal{R}^*$ otherwise set $b \leftarrow 0$ and $r \leftarrow 0$
3. $C_{m+b}^\times \leftarrow \Pi_\times.\mathsf{Encrypt}(pk^\times, m + b)$
4. $C_r^+ \leftarrow \Pi_+.\mathsf{Encrypt}(pk^+, r)$
5. $C_r' \leftarrow \Pi_+.\mathsf{Encrypt}(pk', r)$
6. Return $(C_{m+b}^\times, C_r^+, C_r')$

Algo. $\Pi_\times^0.\mathsf{Decrypt}(sk, (C_{m+b}^\times, C_r^+, C_r'))$

1. Parse sk as $(sk^\times, sk^+, sk')$
2. $B \leftarrow \Pi_+.\mathsf{Decrypt}(sk^+, C_r^+)$
3. If $B \neq 0$ return 0
   else
   return $\Pi_\times.\mathsf{Decrypt}(sk^\times, C_{m+b}^\times)$

Fig. 4. $\Pi_\times$ over $\mathcal{R}$: $\Pi_\times^0$

The protocol $\Pi_\times^0$ directly inherits the indistinguishability under a chosen message attack from those of $\Pi_\times$ and Π_+. By a standard hybrid argument, we can prove the following theorem, whose proof is omitted.

Theorem 4. *If Π_+ and $\Pi_\times$ are IND-CPA, then $\Pi_\times^0$ is also IND-CPA.*

4.3 Full Switching Protocols

Encrypted Zero-Test. In [10] an encrypted zero test (EZT) to obliviously detect the zero messages during switches is presented. In our case, EZT takes as input a ciphertext C_m^+ from the additively homomorphic encryption Π_+ of a message m and outputs a Π_+ ciphertext C_b^+ of a bit b equals to 1 if $m = 0$ and equals to 0 otherwise. The EZT has to be zero-knowledge in the sense that there exists an efficient simulator for each player which, on input a pair of twin ciphertext $(C, \bar{C})$, is indistinguishable from these honest players. This simulator runs without the secret share of the user it simulates.

During the security proof, the simulator will obtain the bit b thanks to the knowledge of the secret key which decrypts the additional encryption of r appended during encryption (see Fig. 4).

This EZT protocol is done using garbled circuits techniques. An alternative would be to use techniques based on homomorphic encryption [32]. The resulting protocol is described in Fig. 5. The function $H : \mathcal{R}^* \longrightarrow \{0,1\}^\kappa$ (for a security parameter κ) belongs to a universal hash function family (in practice, this will be a reduction modulo 2^κ of the integer representation of an element of $\mathcal{R}$). We denote by eq the function that on input $(u, v) \in \{0,1\}^\kappa$ outputs 1 if $u = v$ and 0 otherwise and we denote by Garble(f) the computation of a garbled circuit evaluating the function f.

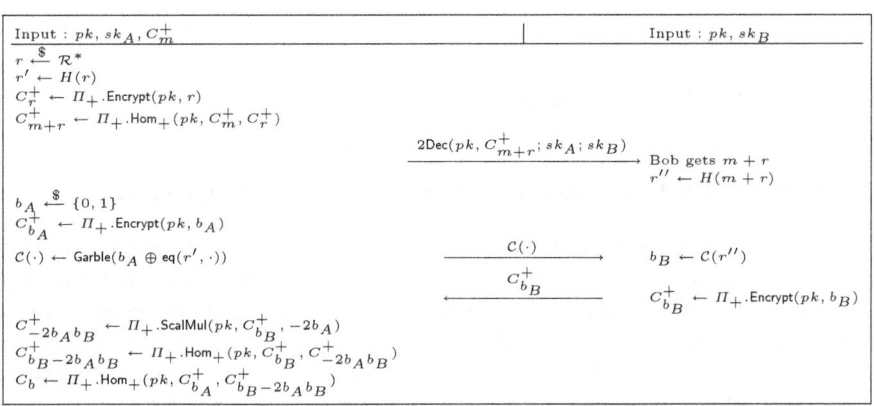

Fig. 5. EZT: 2-party protocol to compute C_b^+ from C_m^+

The correctness of the protocol comes from the fact that the last three lines of the protocol compute the encryption of $b_A \oplus b_B$ by homomorphically evaluating $b_A + b_B - 2b_Ab_B$ from the encryptions of b_A and b_B. By construction, $b_A \oplus b_B = \mathsf{eq}(r', r'')$ which is equals to 1 if $m = 0$ and 0 otherwise, with probability $1 - 2^{-\kappa}$. This is exactly the encryption of the bit b. This protocol is zero-knowledge (see [10]). Using [28], the communication needed is $8\kappa^2$ bits of preprocessing for the garbled circuit and κ^2 bits and κ oblivious transfers for the online phase (cf. [10, Fig. 4]).

Input : $(pk^\times, pk^+, pk'), sk_A, C_m^+$		Input : $(pk^\times, pk^+, pk'), sk_B, C_m^+$
Alice gets C_b^+	$\xleftrightarrow{\mathsf{EZT}(C_m^+)}$	
Alice gets C'_b	$\xleftrightarrow{\mathsf{ReEnc}_+(pk^+, pk', C_b^+)}$	Bob gets C'_b
$C_{m+b}^+ = \Pi_+.\mathsf{Hom}_+(pk^+, C_m^+, C_b^+)$	$\xrightarrow{C_{m+b}^+}$	
Alice gets $C_{m+b}^\times$	$\xleftrightarrow{\mathsf{Switch}_{+\to\times}(C_{m+b}^+)}$	Bob gets $C_{m+b}^\times$
$r, r' \xleftarrow{\$} \mathcal{R}^*$ $C_{rb}^+ = \Pi_+.\mathsf{ScalMul}(pk^+, C_b^+, r)$ $C'_{r'b} = \Pi_+.\mathsf{ScalMul}(pk', C'_b, r')$		
$C_m^\times = (C_{m+b}^\times, C_{rb}^+, C'_{r'b})$	$\xrightarrow{C_m^\times}$	

Fig. 6. 2-party $\mathsf{Switch}_{+\to\times}$ from Π_+ to $\Pi_\times^0$ over $\mathcal{R}^* \cup \{0\}$

Input : $pk, sk_A, C_m^\times = (C_{m+b}^\times, C_r^+, C'_r)$		Input : $pk, sk_B, C_m^\times = (C_{m+b}^\times, C_r^+, C'_r)$
Alice gets C_{m+b}^+	$\xleftrightarrow{\mathsf{Switch}_{\times\to+}(C_{m+b}^\times)}$	Bob gets C_{m+b}^+
Alice gets $C_{\bar{b}}^+$	$\xleftrightarrow{\mathsf{EZT}(C_r^+)}$	
Alice gets $C_{\bar{b}(m+b)}^+ = C_m^+$	$\xleftrightarrow{\mathsf{2Mul}_+(C_{m+b}^+, C_{\bar{b}}^+; sk_A; sk_B)}$	Bob gets $C_{\bar{b}(m+b)}^+ = C_m^+$

Fig. 7. 2-party $\mathsf{Switch}_{\times\to+}$ from $\Pi_\times^0$ to Π_+ over $\mathcal{R}^* \cup \{0\}$

4.4 2-Party ESP Between Π_+.Encrypt(m) and $\Pi_\times^0$.Encrypt(m)

The protocol of Fig. 6 is quite similar to the one of [10]. First we use the EZT sub-protocol to get a Π_+ encryption of the bit b. A notable difference with the protocol of [10] is that this encryption of b can be used directly to set an element of the ciphertext for Π_+^0, which saves many rounds in the interaction. Since the bit b is encrypted twice (this second encryption is only used during the security proof), the ReEnc_+ protocols allows to re-encrypt the output of EZT to the right public key. Then, thanks to the homomorphic property of the Π_+ scheme, Alice can construct an additive encryption of $m + b$ and the $\mathsf{Switch}_{+\to\times}$ protocol of Fig. 3 is used to get the Π_+-encryption of $m + b$. The two ciphertexts of b are randomized to get a proper multiplicative ciphertext.

In Fig. 7, starting from a multiplicative ciphertext of m, we run an $\mathsf{Switch}_{\times\to+}$ with the first component of $C_m^\times$, which is a $\Pi_\times$-encryption of $m + b$. Hence, we get C_{m+b}^+. Then, we run the EZT protocol on the second component C_r^+ and the output the encryption of a bit b' whose value is 1 when $r = 0$, i.e., when $b = 0$ and 0 otherwise. Therefore $b' = \bar{b}$ and EZT actually outputs an encryption of $\bar{b}$. It is now possible to homomorphically remove the bit b remaining in the Π_+-encryption of $m + b$, C_{m+b}^+. Inspired by the implicit technique used in [10], we use the $\mathsf{2Mul}_+$ protocol to obtain, from $C_{\bar{b}}^+$ and C_{m+b}^+, a Π_+-encryption of $(m + b)\bar{b}$ which is equal to a Π_+-encryption of m.

Note that we can not simply use the fact that $m + b + \bar{b} - 1 = m$ over $\mathbf{Z}$ to get m: The expression $m + b$ is really equal to the message m plus the bit b only for fresh multiplicative ciphertexts. After an homomorphic multiplication between a ciphertext of a non zero message with a ciphertext of zero it becomes something random. As a result, we have to multiply it by $\bar{b}$ to get 0.

The zero-knowledge property of our ESP essentially comes from the fact that each routine (ReEnc_+ and $\mathsf{2Mul}_+$) is individually zero-knowledge, inherited from the zero-knowledge of the 2-party decryption of the encryption protocols. We also use the fact that the encryption schemes are IND-CPA, in order to be able to simulate intermediate ciphertexts. This means that the assumptions in our theorem are weak and very natural.

Theorem 5. *The ESP between Π_+ and $\Pi^0_\times$ whose routines are described in Figs. 6 and 7 is zero-knowledge if Π_+ and $\Pi_\times$ are two compatible encryptions that are IND-CPA and whose 2-party decryptions are zero-knowledge, and* EZT *is zero-knowledge.*

Proof (sketch). The full proof of this theorem can be found in Appendix B. This proof can be sketched as follows: First we give the secret key sk' to the simulation. From a pair of twin ciphertexts, it allows the simulation to know the bit that encode the fact that the plaintext is 0 or not. With that knowledge, the simulation can retrieve the ciphertexts that constitute the input and the output of each building block, and use their zero-knowledge simulator to emulate them. Then, we remove the knowledge of sk' from the simulation which replaces each input and output by random ciphertexts. Thanks to the IND-CPA property of the encryption schemes this is indistinguishable from the previous step. As a result, the whole protocol is simulated without knowing any secret. □

5 Instantiation of Our Generic Construction on $\mathbf{Z}/p\mathbf{Z}$

In this section we provide an instantiation of our generic construction on a field $\mathbf{Z}/p\mathbf{Z}$ for a prime p, by describing an additively homomorphic encryption and a multiplicatively homomorphic one. Both schemes enjoy an Elgamal structure. For the additively homomorphic encryption scheme, we will use as a basis the scheme introduced in [9] (denoted CL in the following). It uses the notion of a DDH *group with an easy* DL *subgroup*, which is instantiated using class groups of quadratic fields. For the multiplicatively homomorphic scheme, we devise a variant of the traditional Elgamal encryption over the whole group $(\mathbf{Z}/p\mathbf{Z})^*$. Both schemes are described in the next subsection. We also describe their 2-party decryption, since it is required by the generic construction.

5.1 Additively Homomorphic Scheme over $\mathbf{Z}/p\mathbf{Z}$

Castagnos-Laguillaumie Encryption. The encryption scheme from [9] is additively homomorphic modulo a prime p. The general protocol is well suited for relatively small p. For the ESP context, we need a large message space as p

must be at least of 2048 bits for the security of the Elgamal protocol. As a result, we use the first variant of CL described in [9, Sect. 4]. This variant is defined with subgroups of the class group of an order of a quadratic field of discriminant $\Delta_p = -p^3$. Thus all computations are done in this class group. Note that elements are classes of ideals, that can be represented by their unique reduced elements, i.e., by two integers of roughly the size of $\sqrt{|\Delta_p|}$. As a consequence, a group element can be represented with $3 \log p$ bits.

We provide some improvements detailed in the following. The CL scheme does exponentiations to some random powers in a cyclic group of unknown order. Let us denote by $\mathfrak{g}$ a generator of this group. Only an upper bound B on this order is known. In order to make the result of these exponentiations look like uniform elements of the cyclic group, the authors of [9] choose to sample random exponents from a large enough uniform distribution, and more precisely over $\{0, \ldots, B'\}$ where $B' = 2^{\lambda-2}B$, so that the resulting distribution is as distance to uniform less than $2^{-\lambda}$.

However, it is more efficient to use a folded discrete Gaussian Distribution instead of a folded uniform distribution. Let $z \in \mathbf{Z}$ and $\sigma > 0$ a real number and let us denote by $\rho_\sigma(z) = \exp(-\pi z^2/\sigma^2)$ a Gaussian centered function and define the probability mass function $\mathcal{D}_\sigma$ over $\mathbf{Z}$ by $\mathcal{D}_\sigma(z) := \rho_\sigma(z)/\sum_{z \in \mathbf{Z}} \rho_\sigma(z)$.

If z is sampled from $\mathcal{D}_\sigma$, we have $|z| > \tau\sigma$ with probability smaller than $\sqrt{2\pi e}\tau \exp(-\pi\tau^2)$ (cf. [35, Lemma 2.10]). We denote by $\tau(\lambda)$ the smallest τ such that this probability is smaller than $2^{-\lambda}$.

If we set $\sigma = \sqrt{\ln(2(1+2^{\lambda+1}))/\pi}B$, Lemma 1 of Appendix C of the long version shows that the distribution obtained by sampling z from $\mathcal{D}_\sigma$ and computing $\mathfrak{g}^z$ is at distance less than $2^{-\lambda}$ to the uniform distribution in $\langle \mathfrak{g} \rangle$.

For instance for $\lambda = 128$, we only add, in the worst case, 6 iterations in the square and multiply algorithm to compute $\mathfrak{g}^z$, whereas one has to add 126 iterations with a folded uniform distribution.

Description of the Scheme. We denote by CL.Gen a parameter generator for CL. It takes as input 1^λ and outputs a tuple $(p, \mathfrak{g}, \mathfrak{f}, \sigma)$. This tuple is such that p is a prime satisfying $p \equiv 3 \pmod 4$ so that computing discrete logarithms in $C(-p)$, the ideal class group of the quadratic order of discriminant $-p$, takes 2^λ times. Then $\mathfrak{g} \in C(-p^3)$ is a class of order ps where s is unknown and expected to be of the order of magnitude of the class number of $C(-p)$: a concrete implementation for $\mathfrak{g}$ is given in [9, Fig. 2]. It consists in generating a random ideal of the maximal order of discriminant $-p$, and lifting it in the order of discriminant $-p^3$. Eventually, $\mathfrak{f} \in C(-p^3)$ is the class of the ideal $p^2\mathbf{Z} + ((-p + \sqrt{-p^3})/2)\mathbf{Z}$ and σ will be the standard deviation of the Gaussian Distribution discussed before: $\sigma = \sqrt{\ln(2(1+2^{\lambda+1}))/\pi}B$, with $B = \log(p)p^{3/2}/(4\pi)$.

The scheme relies on the notion of a DDH group with an easy DL subgroup. It is IND-CPA under the DDH assumption in the group generated by $\mathfrak{g}$. On the other hand, in the subgroup of order p generated by $\mathfrak{f}$, there is a polynomial time algorithm, denoted CL.Solve which takes as input an element of $\langle \mathfrak{f} \rangle$ and which outputs its discrete logarithm in basis $\mathfrak{f}$. We refer the reader to [9] for concrete implementation of CL.Gen and CL.Solve. The resulted scheme is given in Fig. 8.

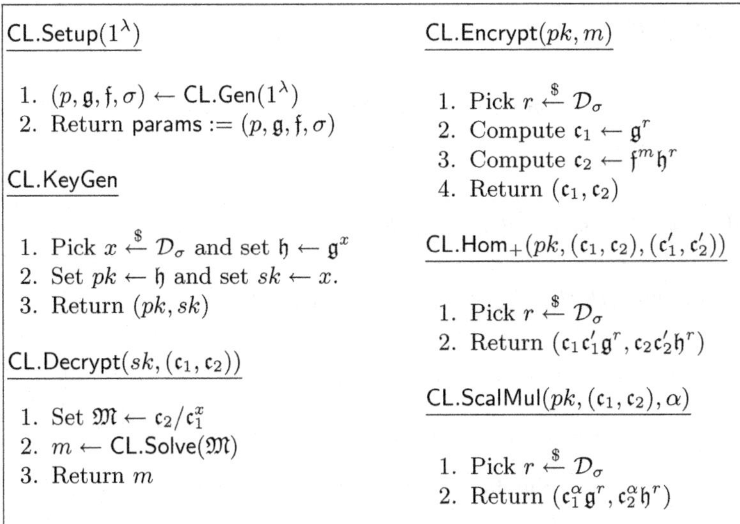

Fig. 8. Castagnos-Laguillaumie over $\mathbf{Z}/p\mathbf{Z}$: CL

Theorem 6 [9]. *The* CL *scheme of Fig. 8 is an additively homomorphic encryption scheme over* $\mathbf{Z}/p\mathbf{Z}$*, IND-CPA under the* DDH *assumption in the ideal class group of the quadratic order of discriminant* $-p^3$.

One Round 2-Party Decryption for CL**.** We now devise in Fig. 9 a one round 2-party decryption for CL as defined in Sect. 2.2, i.e. subroutines to share the secret key and the interactive protocol for decryption. As the scheme has an Elgamal structure, it can be readily adapted from the threshold variant of the original Elgamal scheme (cf. [39] for instance) with a simple additive secret sharing of the key $x = x_A + x_B$. However, as the group order is unknown, this secret sharing must be done over the integers. This kind of sharing has been addressed before (cf. [14, Sect. 4] for instance).

As x is sampled from $\mathcal{D}_\sigma$, we saw before that $x \in [-\tau(\lambda)\sigma, \tau(\lambda)\sigma]$ for a small $\tau(\lambda)$ except with negligible probability. Then the integer x_A is taken uniformly at random in the interval $[-\tau(\lambda)\sigma 2^\lambda, \tau(\lambda)\sigma 2^\lambda]$, and $x_B = x - x_A$. This choice makes the secret sharing private. Note that in that case, there is no gain in using a Gaussian Distribution to generate the shares. We refer the interested reader to Appendix D of the long version for details.

Theorem 7. *The 2-party Decryption for* CL *described in Fig. 9 is correct and zero-knowledge.*

Proof. Correctness follows from the shared exponentiation. Let us prove first that the protocol is zero-knowledge for Alice (see Definition 7 in Appendix A).

For the secret key shares, the simulator $\mathsf{Sim}^{2d}_{\mathsf{Share}}$ picks x' from $\mathcal{D}_\sigma$, $x'_A \xleftarrow{\$} \{-\tau(\lambda)\sigma 2^\lambda, \ldots, \tau(\lambda)\sigma 2^\lambda\}$ and set $x'_B = x' - x'_A$. As the secret sharing is private,

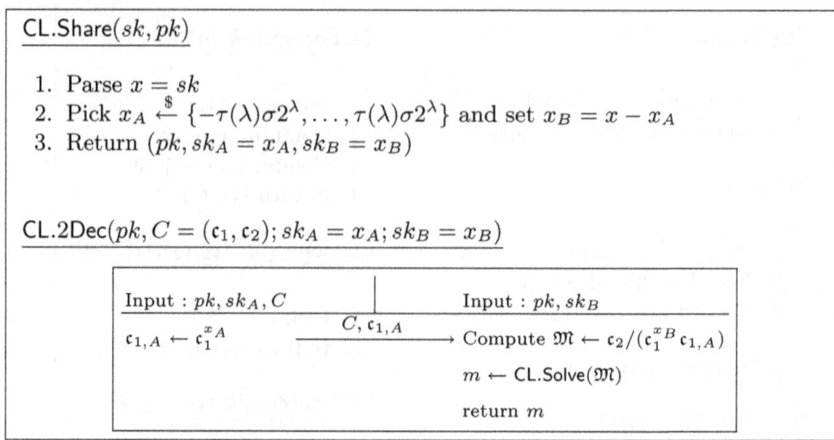

Fig. 9. 2-party decryption for CL

the distribution of x'_B is statistically indistinguishable from the distribution of the real x_B (see Appendix D of the long version for the computation of the statistical distance).

Then we describe the simulator Sim_A^{2d} which emulates Alice. From a ciphertext C, a plaintext m, it computes $\mathfrak{M} = \mathfrak{f}^m$. Then it simulates $\mathfrak{c}_{1,A}$ by setting $\mathfrak{c}_{1,A} = \mathfrak{c}_2/(\mathfrak{M}\mathfrak{c}_1^{x'_B})$, so that Bob's computations leads to $\mathfrak{M}$. The value sent by the simulation is thus perfectly indistinguishable from the real one.

It is straightforward to see that the protocol is zero-knowledge for Bob: secret key shares are simulated as previously, and x'_A is obviously indistinguishable from the real x_A, and then Bob sends nothing during the protocol. □

5.2 Multiplicatively Homomorphic Scheme over $\mathbf{Z}/p\mathbf{Z}$

Elgamal over $(\mathbf{Z}/p\mathbf{Z})^*$. Let q be an odd Sophie Germain prime, and let us denote by p the associated prime, *i.e.*, $p = 2q + 1$. The DDH assumption is widely supposed to hold in the subgroup of order q of $(\mathbf{Z}/p\mathbf{Z})^*$ which is the subgroup of quadratic residues modulo p, denoted S_p. The Elgamal cryptosystem defined in S_p is multiplicatively homomorphic and semantically secure if the DDH assumption holds in that subgroup.

It is well-known that the DDH assumption does not hold in the whole group $(\mathbf{Z}/p\mathbf{Z})^*$. As a result, in order to extend the message space to $(\mathbf{Z}/p\mathbf{Z})^*$, we need to encode elements of $(\mathbf{Z}/p\mathbf{Z})^*$ as quadratic residues. The situation is quite similar to the Elgamal over $(\mathbf{Z}/n\mathbf{Z})^*$ of [10], but actually simpler to handle since we work modulo a prime p and not modulo an RSA integer n (in particular, we can publicly compute square roots or distinguish quadratic and non quadratic residues and we do not have to hide the factorization of n).

Since $p = 2q + 1$, we have $p \equiv 3 \pmod 4$, and -1 is not a quadratic residue modulo p. Let $m \in (\mathbf{Z}/p\mathbf{Z})^*$, let us denote by (m/p) the Legendre symbol of m

modulo p. Then $(m/p) \times m$ is a quadratic residue mod p. Let L be the group morphism from $((\mathbf{Z}/p\mathbf{Z})^*, \times)$ to $(\mathbf{Z}/2\mathbf{Z}, +)$ that maps m to 0 (resp. to 1) if m is a quadratic residue (resp. is a non quadratic residue). The map

$$\begin{array}{ccc} ((\mathbf{Z}/p\mathbf{Z})^*, \times) & \longrightarrow & (S_p, \times) \times (\mathbf{Z}/2\mathbf{Z}, +) \\ m & \longmapsto & ((m/p) \times m,\ L(m)) \end{array}$$

is a group isomorphism. As a consequence we can encode elements of $(\mathbf{Z}/p\mathbf{Z})^*$ as a square plus one bit. The square can be encrypted with the traditional Elgamal encryption, and the bit $L(m)$ has to be encrypted separately. In order to have a multiplicatively homomorphic encryption, $L(m)$ has to be encrypted with a scheme that is homomorphic for the addition in $\mathbf{Z}/2\mathbf{Z}$. We choose Goldwasser-Micali encryption [23] for that. The drawback is that we need an additional assumption, namely the Quadratic Residuosity assumption (QR) for the security of our protocol. To avoid that, an idea could have been to encrypt $L(m)$ as an integer in the exponent with another Elgamal scheme or with the additive scheme of the previous Subsection. However, after computing the product of ℓ messages $m_1, \ldots, m_\ell$ over encrypted data, the decryption would give more information than the Legendre symbol of the product of the m_i's, namely $\sum_{i=1}^{n} L(m_i)$ in the integers, instead of modulo 2. Moreover, this extra information has to be taken into account to devise a zero-knowledge 2-party decryption. As this information can not be simulated, this gives a complex 2-party protocol, perhaps by using an extra homomorphic encryption scheme like in [10]. Note that a solution consisting in randomizing $L(m)$ by adding a (small) even integer, with a Gaussian Distribution, for instance, still leaks the number ℓ of multiplications that have been made. As a result, it seems to be an interesting open problem to devise an encryption scheme that allows homomorphic addition in $\mathbf{Z}/2\mathbf{Z}$, or that simulates it without leaks, without relying on a factorization-based assumption (in [10], the same problem was handled more smoothly thanks to the fact that the authors worked with a composite modulus).

Description of the Scheme. Let λ be a security parameter. Let $\mathsf{GM.Gen}$ be a parameter generator for the Goldwasser-Micali encryption scheme. It takes as input 1^λ and outputs (N, p', q') such that $p', q' \equiv 3 \pmod 4$ are primes and $N = p'q'$ is such that factoring N takes 2^λ time. We use the threshold variant of Goldwasser-Micali described in [26] to define a suitable 2-party decryption.

We also define $\mathsf{Eg}^*.\mathsf{Gen}$ a parameter generator for Elgamal. It takes as input 1^λ and outputs (p, q, g) such that q is a prime, $p = 2q + 1$ is a prime such that computing discrete logarithms in $(\mathbf{Z}/p\mathbf{Z})^*$ takes 2^λ times, and g a generator of S_p, *i.e.*, and element of $(\mathbf{Z}/p\mathbf{Z})^*$ of order q. We depict in Fig. 10, the adaptation of Elgamal over the whole multiplicative group $(\mathbf{Z}/p\mathbf{Z})^*$, denoted Eg^*.

The following theorem is a consequence of the previous discussion and the properties of the Goldwasser-Micali variant. Note that modulo N, $c_3^{(N-p'-q'+1)/4}$ equals 1 if c_3 is a quadratic residue, and -1 if c_3 has Jacobi symbol 1 and is not a quadratic residue.

Eg*.Setup(1^λ)

1. Set $(p, q, g) \leftarrow$ Eg*.Gen(1^λ)
2. Return params := (p, q, g)

Eg*.KeyGen

1. Set $(N, p', q') \leftarrow$ GM.Gen(1^λ)
2. Add N to params
3. Pick $x \xleftarrow{\$} \{0, \ldots, q-1\}$
4. Set $h \leftarrow g^x$
5. Set $pk \leftarrow h$
6. Set $sk \leftarrow (x, p', q')$
7. Return (pk, sk)

Eg*.Decrypt($sk, (c_1, c_2, c_3)$)

1. Set $M \leftarrow c_2/c_1^x \pmod p$
2. Set $L \leftarrow c_3^{(N-p'-q'+1)/4} \pmod N$
3. If $L = 1$ return M else return $-M$

Eg*.Encrypt(pk, m)

1. Pick $r \xleftarrow{\$} \{1, \ldots, q-1\}$
2. Pick $r' \xleftarrow{\$} \{1, \ldots, N-1\}$
3. Set $c_1 \leftarrow g^r \pmod p$
4. Set $c_2 \leftarrow (m/p)mh^r \pmod p$
5. Set $c_3 \leftarrow (-1)^{L(m)}r'^2 \pmod N$
6. Return (c_1, c_2, c_3)

Eg*.Hom$_\times$($pk, (c_1, c_2, c_3), (c_1', c_2', c_3')$)

1. Pick $r \xleftarrow{\$} \{0, \ldots, q-1\}$
2. Pick $r' \xleftarrow{\$} \{1, \ldots, N-1\}$
3. Return $(c_1c_1'g^r, c_2c_2'h^r, c_3c_3'r'^2)$

Eg*.ScalMul($pk, (c_1, c_2, c_3), \alpha$)

1. Pick $r \xleftarrow{\$} \{0, \ldots, q-1\}$
2. Pick $r' \xleftarrow{\$} \{1, \ldots, N-1\}$
3. Set $c_1' \leftarrow c_1 g^r \pmod p$
4. Set $c_2' \leftarrow (\alpha/p)\alpha c_2 h^r \pmod p$
5. Set $c_3' \leftarrow (-1)^{L(\alpha)}c_3 r'^2 \pmod N$
6. Return (c_1', c_2', c_3')

Fig. 10. Elgamal over $(\mathbf{Z}/p\mathbf{Z})^*$: Eg*

Theorem 8. *The* Eg* *scheme of Fig. 10 is multiplicatively homomorphic over* $(\mathbf{Z}/p\mathbf{Z})^*$, *and it is IND-CPA under the* DDH *assumption in the subgroup of quadratic residues of* $(\mathbf{Z}/p\mathbf{Z})^*$ *and the* QR *assumption in* $(\mathbf{Z}/N\mathbf{Z})^\times$.

One Round 2-Party Decryption for Eg***.** We describe in Fig. 11 a one round 2-party decryption for Eg*. This protocol is adapted from the threshold variant of the original Elgamal scheme and the basic threshold Goldwasser-Micali of [26, Subsect. 3.1].

This simple protocol gives a huge performance improvement compared to the Elgamal over $(\mathbf{Z}/n\mathbf{Z})^*$ of [10]: in that work, after the exponentiations, a CRT reconstruction is needed to recover m, and a quantity that leads to the factorization of n must be shared. To make this 2-party reconstruction zero-knowledge, the authors use an additional additively homomorphic encryption, and have to do the reconstruction over encrypted data. As a result, the protocol is very complex (implicitly described in [10, Fig. 2]) with 5 rounds instead of 1.

Theorem 9. *The 2-party Decryption for* Eg* *described in Fig. 11 is correct and zero-knowledge.*

Eg*.Share(sk, pk)

1. Parse $(x, p', q') = sk$
2. Pick $x_A \xleftarrow{\$} \{0, \ldots, q-1\}$ and set $x_B \equiv x - x_A \pmod{q}$
3. Pick $p_A, p_B, q_A, q_B \xleftarrow{\$} \{0, \ldots, N\}$ such that $p_A \equiv p_B \equiv q_A \equiv q_B \equiv 0 \pmod{4}$
4. Set $p_0 = p' - p_A - p_B$ and $q_0 = q' - q_A - q_B$
5. Set $pk \leftarrow (pk, N_0 = (N - p_0 - q_0)/4)$
6. Return $(pk, sk_A = (x_A, x'_A), sk_B = (x_B, x'_B))$

Eg*.2Dec($pk, C = (c_1, c_2, c_3); sk_A = (x_A, p_A, q_A); sk_B = (x_B, p_B, q_B)$)

Input : pk, sk_A, C		Input : pk, sk_B
$c_{1,A} \leftarrow c_1^{x_A} \pmod{p}$		
$c_{3,A} \leftarrow c_3^{(-p_A-q_A)/4} \pmod{N}$		
	$\xrightarrow{C, c_{1,A}, c_{3,A}}$	Set $M \leftarrow c_2/(c_1^{x_B} c_{1,A}) \pmod{p}$
		Set $L \leftarrow c_{3,A} c_3^{(-p_B-q_B)/4} c_3^{N_0} \pmod{N}$
		If $L = 1$ return M else return $-M$

Fig. 11. 2-party decryption for Eg*

Proof. The proof is similar to the proof of Theorem 7. For the Elgamal part of the protocol, secret key shares are simply taken uniformly at random in $\{0, \ldots, q-1\}$, and the value sent by Alice is computed as $c_{1,A} = c_2/(Mc_1^{x_B})$, where $M = (m/p)m$. The Goldwasser-Micali part of the protocol is also simulated in a similar fashion from c_3 and $L(m)$ and the key share from a fake factorization of N just as in [26, Subsect. 3.1] □

Extension of the Message Space from $(\mathbf{Z}/p\mathbf{Z})^*$ to $\mathbf{Z}/p\mathbf{Z}$. We use the generic construction depicted in Fig. 4 with the additively homomorphic scheme described in the previous subsection. We denote by Eg_p.Gen, a group generator which combines the generators for Eg* and CL: on input 1^λ, it first runs Eg*.Gen, which outputs (p, q, g). The prime p equals 3 mod 4 and is such that computing discrete logarithms in $(\mathbf{Z}/p\mathbf{Z})^*$ takes time 2^λ. As the best algorithms for computing such discrete logarithms are faster than the algorithms for computing discrete logarithms in the class group $C(-p)$ (the sub-exponential complexity is respectively $L_p[1/3, (64/9)^{1/3} + o(1)]$ and $L_p[1/2, 1 + o(1)]$, see [24,43]), this prime p is compatible with the prime generated by CL.Gen. As a result Eg_p.Gen executes CL.Gen by setting this prime p and adapts the others quantities accordingly. The resulting scheme is described in Fig. 12 for completeness.

$\mathsf{Eg}_p.\mathsf{Setup}(1^\lambda)$

1. Set $(p, q, g, \mathfrak{g}, \mathfrak{f}, \sigma) \leftarrow \mathsf{Eg}^*.\mathsf{Gen}(1^\lambda)$
2. Return params $:= (p, q, g, \mathfrak{g}, \mathfrak{f}, \sigma)$

$\mathsf{Eg}_p.\mathsf{KeyGen}$

1. Set $(N, p', q') \leftarrow \mathsf{GM.Gen}(1^\lambda)$
2. Add N to params
3. Pick $x^\times \xleftarrow{\$} \{0, \ldots, q-1\}$
4. Set $h^\times \leftarrow g^{x^\times}$
5. Pick $x^+ \xleftarrow{\$} \mathcal{D}_\sigma$ and set $\mathfrak{h}^+ \leftarrow \mathfrak{g}^{x^+}$
6. Pick $x' \xleftarrow{\$} \mathcal{D}_\sigma$ and set $\mathfrak{h}' \leftarrow \mathfrak{g}^{x'}$
7. Set $pk \leftarrow (h^\times, \mathfrak{h}^+, \mathfrak{h}')$
8. Set $sk \leftarrow (x^\times, p', q', x^+, x')$
9. Return (pk, sk)

$\mathsf{Eg}_p.\mathsf{Decrypt}(sk, (c_1, c_2, c_3))$

1. Set $\mathfrak{M} \leftarrow \mathfrak{c}_2/\mathfrak{c}_1^{x^+}$
2. Set $B \leftarrow \mathsf{CL.Solve}(\mathfrak{M})$
3. If $B \neq 0$ return 0
4. Set $M \leftarrow c_2/c_1^{x^\times} \pmod p$
5. Set $L \leftarrow c_3^{(N-p'-q'+1)/4} \pmod N$
6. If $L = 1$ return M else return $-M$

$\mathsf{Eg}_p.\mathsf{Encrypt}(pk, m)$

1. If $m = 0$ set $b \leftarrow 1$ and $r \xleftarrow{\$} (\mathbf{Z}/p\mathbf{Z})^*$ otherwise set $b \leftarrow 0$ and $r \leftarrow 0$
2. Pick $r^\times \xleftarrow{\$} \{1, \ldots, q-1\}$
3. Pick $r^{\times\prime} \xleftarrow{\$} \{1, \ldots, N-1\}$
4. Set $c_1 \leftarrow g^{r^\times} \pmod p$
5. Set $c_2 \leftarrow ((m+b)/p)(m+b)h^{\times^{r^\times}} \pmod p$
6. Set $c_3 \leftarrow (-1)^{L(m+b)} r^{\times\prime 2} \pmod N$
7. Pick $r^+ \xleftarrow{\$} \mathcal{D}_\sigma$
8. Compute $\mathfrak{c}_1 \leftarrow \mathfrak{g}^{r^+}, \mathfrak{c}_2 \leftarrow \mathfrak{f}^r \mathfrak{h}^{+^{r^+}}$
9. Pick $r' \xleftarrow{\$} \mathcal{D}_\sigma$
10. Compute $\mathfrak{c}_1' \leftarrow \mathfrak{g}^{r'}, \mathfrak{c}_2' \leftarrow \mathfrak{f}^r \mathfrak{h}'^{r'}$
11. Return $(c_1, c_2, c_3, \mathfrak{c}_1, \mathfrak{c}_2, \mathfrak{c}_1', \mathfrak{c}_2')$

Fig. 12. Elgamal over $\mathbf{Z}/p\mathbf{Z}$: Eg_p

5.3 ESP over $\mathbf{Z}/p\mathbf{Z}$: Efficiency and Comparisons

In Table 1 we give the round complexity (*rc*) and bit complexity (*bc*) of our algorithms and we compare our full ESP protocols with that of Couteau et al. [10]. For sake of clarity, and because it is identical to that of [10], we omit the complexities resultant from the garbled circuit-based EZT protocols. Our 2-party decryption algorithms (both for CL and Eg^*) only require 1 round. Note that we carefully analyzed the interactive algorithms so as to gather consecutive flows when possible within a single round. For example our $\mathsf{2Mul}_+$ and ReEnc_+ protocols (see Figs. 1 and 2) require only 2 rounds since Alice can send C^+_{rX} (resp. C'_{-r}) and her 2Dec data simultaneously. For the same reason, our generic switches in $\mathcal{R}^*$ also require 2 rounds. Therefore, our $(\Pi_+ \rightleftharpoons \Pi^0_\times).\mathsf{Switch}_{+\to\times}$ needs 7 rounds: 2 for the initial EZT, 2 for ReEnc_+, 2 for sending C^+_{m+b} and the $\mathsf{Switch}_{+\to\times}$, and 1 for sending the final result to Bob. In the other direction, the initial $\mathsf{Switch}_{\times\to+}$ and the EZT are independent and can thus be processed simultaneously in 2 rounds. Adding 2 rounds for the $\mathsf{2Mul}_+$, the round complexity for $(\Pi_+ \rightleftharpoons \Pi^0_\times).\mathsf{Switch}_{\times\to+}$ adds up to 4 rounds only. In comparison, and using the same optimizations, the ESP switches from Couteau et al. requires 7 and 11 rounds respectively.

We express the communication cost in terms of the number of bits exchanged between the parties. The bit complexity (bc) is given as a function of the ring/field size. Observe that although, the best (conjectured) asymptotic complexity to compute a discrete logarithm in the ideal class group used in CL is in $L_p[1/2, 1 + o(1)]$ (see [24]), one must consider a prime p that is large enough to guarantee that the DLP over $(\mathbf{Z}/p\mathbf{Z})^*$ is hard, i.e. such that $L_p[1/3, (64/9)^{1/3} + o(1)] > 2^\lambda$ (see e.g. [43]). In Table 1, ℓ, represents the bit length of p for our protocol over $\mathbf{Z}/p\mathbf{Z}$ and of n for Couteau et al.'s protocol over $\mathbf{Z}/n\mathbf{Z}$.

For our protocols, we give the bit complexities for two variants: for the version of CL used in this paper bc is the cost deduced from Fig. 8. The drawback of this scheme is that ciphertexts are represented with 2 elements of $C(-p^3)$ which gives $2 \times 2 \times \frac{3}{2} \times \ell = 6\ell$ against 2ℓ for Paillier. Therefore, we include a column with the cost bc' that correspond to the so-called "faster variant" of CL from [9, Sect. 4]. This variant defines ciphertexts in $C(-p) \times C(-p^3)$, represented with $\ell + 3\ell = 4\ell$ elements. Moreover, for 2-party decryption we only have to share an exponentiation in $C(-p)$ instead of $C(-p^3)$ so the cost drops from $6\ell + 3\ell = 9\ell$ to $4\ell + \ell = 5\ell$.

Table 1. Comparisons of the round complexities and bit complexities of our protocols (v1 and v2) with that of Couteau et al. [10]. (*) For the EZT protocol the communication cost for the garbled circuit is omitted as it is the same for v1, v2 and [10] (cf. Subsect. 4.3 for the cost).

	Round complexity		Bit complexity		
	This work	[10]	v1	v2	[10]
Algorithms					
$\mathsf{Eg}^*.\mathsf{2Dec}$	1	n/a	5ℓ	5ℓ	n/a
$\mathsf{CL.2Dec}$	1	n/a	9ℓ	5ℓ	n/a
$\mathsf{CL.EZT}(*)$	2	n/a	15ℓ	9ℓ	n/a
$\mathsf{CL.2Mul}_+$	2	n/a	21ℓ	13ℓ	n/a
$\mathsf{CL.ReEnc}_+$	2	n/a	21ℓ	13ℓ	n/a
$(\Pi_+ \rightleftharpoons \Pi_\times).\mathsf{Switch}_{+\to\times}$	2	2	15ℓ	11ℓ	10ℓ
$(\Pi_+ \rightleftharpoons \Pi_\times).\mathsf{Switch}_{\times\to+}$	2	6	17ℓ	13ℓ	36ℓ
ESP protocols					
$(\Pi_+ \rightleftharpoons \Pi^0_\times).\mathsf{Switch}_{+\to\times}$	7	7	69ℓ	45ℓ	37ℓ
$(\Pi_+ \rightleftharpoons \Pi^0_\times).\mathsf{Switch}_{\times\to+}$	4	11	53ℓ	35ℓ	61ℓ

For the former variant, the security depends upon DDH in $C(-p^3)$ whereas for the faster variant it is based upon the following indistinguishability argument: Let $\mathfrak{g}$ be a generator of a subgroup of $C(-p)$. After having chosen m, the adversary is asked to distinguished the following distributions: $\{(\mathfrak{g}^x, \mathfrak{g}^y, \psi(\mathfrak{g}^{xy})), x, y \leftarrow \mathcal{D}_{\sigma/p}\}$ and $\{(\mathfrak{g}^x, \mathfrak{g}^y, \psi(\mathfrak{g}^{xy})\mathfrak{f}^m), x, y \leftarrow \mathcal{D}_{\sigma/p}\}$, where $\mathcal{D}_\sigma$ is the Gaussian Discrete distribution defined in Subsect. 5.1 and ψ is a lifting map from $C(-p)$ to $C(-p^3)$, defined in [9, Lemma 3]. We denote LDDH by the corresponding assumption. The algorithmic assumptions required for each protocol are presented in Table 2.

Table 2. Algorithmic assumptions

This work (v1)	This work (v2)	[10]
DDH in $C(-p^3)$	LDDH in $C(-p^3)$	DCR
DDH in S_p	DDH in S_p	DDH in S_n
QR	QR	QR

6 ESP Secure Against Malicious Adversaries

To reach the security against malicious adversaries, it is necessary to add zero-knowledge proofs by all parties that every computation is done correctly with the knowledge of every plaintext. In [10], the zero-knowledge proofs are classical Schnorr-like proofs and range proofs, but they need also to design a new strong primitive called *twin ciphertext proof* (TCP) to prove that a pair of ciphertexts from two different encryption schemes is actually a pair of twin ciphertexts. This allows to avoid generic circuit-based zero-knowledge proofs, but still requires a costly cut-and-choose technique (which can be amortized). This proof consists first in gathering a large pool of random genuine twin ciphertexts (proved thanks to the knowledge of the plaintext and the randomness, and of the homomorphic property of the encryption schemes). This part is done once for all. During an ESP, each time a twin ciphertext proof is needed, a fresh twin ciphertext pair is taken from the pool to perform a simple co-linearity proof.

To enhance our generic construction against malicious adversaries, we use the same method. In fact, the additional properties needed for the homomorphic encryption schemes are the same as in [11]: the Π_+ and the $\Pi_\times$ encryption schemes must support zero-knowledge proof of plaintext knowledge, proof that the ScalMul operation has been performed correctly and also support a 2-party decryption in the malicious setting. Then we use the TCP technique as in [10] for twin ciphertext proofs.

As a result, we modify our generic construction by adding such proofs in each step of the switching protocols. This ensures honest behavior and thus make the ESP secure in the malicious settings. In particular this brings soundness in the sense of [10]: no malicious player can force the output of an ESP not to be a twin ciphertext.

The protocols Π_+ and $\Pi_\times$ described in the instantiation from the previous section support the required features. For the $\Pi_\times$ encryption scheme, we need zero knowledge proofs and 2-party decryption secure against malicious adversary for the classical Elgamal and for the Goldwasser-Micali encryption scheme. This can be done with classical methods: zero-knowledge proof *á la* Schnorr, adding verification keys to the public keys for 2-party decryption and proof of exponentiations to the same power. Note that for Goldwasser-Micali, we need to modify key generation to use strong primes p' and q' as in [26].

For the Π_+ encryption scheme which is based on the Castagnos-Laguillaumie encryption scheme, we need proofs for an Elgamal variant in a group of unknown order, namely a class group of a quadratic order. Then 2-party decryption secure against malicious adversary is obtained as for the $\Pi_\times$ scheme.

Generalizations of Schnorr proofs in group of unknown orders have been addressed extensively in [7]. In this framework, a generalized Schnorr proof can be used if the cyclic group considered is what is called a *safeguard group*, which is roughly a group whose set of small orders elements is small and known, and for which it is hard to find roots of elements. The case of class groups has been explicitly taken in account for example in [12,13], where it is argue in particular that class groups of discriminant $-p$, $C(-p)$, can be considered to have the properties of safeguard groups. As a result, we can apply directly the framework of [7] for the faster variant of CL mentioned in Subsect. 5.3 as exponentiations are defined in $C(-p)$ for this variant.

7 Conclusion

The encryption switching protocol is a promising cryptographic primitive formalized by Couteau et al. in [10]. We propose in this article a generic framework to build such an ESP. Our approach makes the design of an ESP simple and efficient. In particular, we propose an instantiation whose round complexity is dramatically improved compared to Couteau et al., since we reduce by a factor 3 the number of round in the multiplicative to additive direction (while we have the same number of rounds in the other way). Again, in terms of bit complexity, our switching protocol in the multiplicative to additive direction gains a factor almost 1.7, while in the other direction Couteau et al.'s switch is smaller by a factor 1.2. This is essentially because in our case, the additively homomorphic encryption has large ciphertexts. In particular, any additively homomorphic encryption satisfying the conditions of our construction with smaller elements will allow to gain in terms of bit complexity. Our instantiation, which is secure in the semi-honest model under classical assumptions can be extended to the malicious case. We believe that it is possible to improve our instantiation by deviating a bit more from the generic construction. Moreover, an interesting open problem is to design an encryption scheme which is homomorphic for the $+$ in $\mathbf{F}_2$ without the factorization assumption. A consequence could be to have an ESP whose security relies only on a discrete logarithm related assumption. Designing a more efficient encrypted zero-test is also a direction which will allow a significant improvement in the protocol.

Acknowledgments. The authors would like to thank Geoffroy Couteau for fruitful discussions, careful reading and constructive comments on the preliminary version of this work. We also express our thanks to Bruno Grenet, Romain Lebreton, Benoît Libert and Damien Stehlé for their feedbacks.

The authors are supported in part by the French ANR ALAMBIC project (ANR-16-CE39-0006), by the "Investments for the future" Programme IdEx Bordeaux - CPU (ANR-10-IDEX-03-02), and by ERC Starting Grant ERC-2013-StG-335086-LATTAC.

A 2-Party Decryption: Zero-Knowledge

Definition 7. *An encryption scheme Π supporting 2-party decryption is* zero-knowledge for A *if there exists an efficient simulator* $\mathsf{Sim}^{2d} = (\mathsf{Sim}^{2d}_{\mathsf{Share}}, \mathsf{Sim}^{2d}_A)$ *which simulates the sharing phase and the player A.*

The subroutine $\mathsf{Sim}^{2d}_{\mathsf{Share}}$ *takes as input a public key pk and outputs* (pk', sk'_B) *that simulates the public key obtained from the* Share *algorithm and Bob's share of the secret key.*

The subroutine Sim^{2d}_A *takes as input a public key pk a ciphertext c, a plaintext m, possibly* sk_B *and a flow* flow. *It emulates honest player A's answer upon receiving the flow* flow *when running the protocol* $\mathsf{2Dec}(pk, c; sk_A; sk_B)$ *without* sk_A*, and forcing the output to be m.*

Then, for all $\lambda \in \mathbf{N}$*, for any* $(\mathsf{params} \leftarrow \mathsf{Setup}(1^\lambda)$*, for any pair of keys* $(pk, sk) \leftarrow \Pi.\mathsf{KeyGen}(1^\lambda, \mathsf{params})$*, for any shares* $(pk, sk_A, sk_B) \leftarrow \mathsf{Share}(pk, sk)$ *or for any* simulated *share* $(pk', sk'_B) \leftarrow \mathsf{Sim}^{2d}_{\mathsf{Share}}(pk)$*, and for any adversary* $\mathcal{D}$ *playing the role of B, the advantage*

$$\mathsf{Adv}^{zk}_{A,\Pi}(\mathcal{D}) = \left|\Pr[1 \leftarrow \mathcal{D}^A(pk, sk_B)] - \Pr[1 \leftarrow \mathcal{D}^{\mathsf{Sim}^{2d}_A()}(pk', sk'_B)]\right|$$

is negligible. We define similarly that Π is zero-knowledge for B. *It is* zero-knowledge *if it is zero-knowledge for A and B.*

B Proof of Theorem 5

Proof. Once again, the proof consists in proving that after a share of the secret keys, both switching procedures are zero-knowledge for Alice and Bob. As both switches consist in a sequence of protocols that have been independently proved secure, the main issue in the proof consists in showing that their sequential combination is still secure. The reduction will get a pair $(C, \bar{C})$ of input and output of the whole switches, and the main idea is to construct such intermediate pairs for each independent subroutines using random ciphertexts.

ZK for Alice. Let us start with the proof that the ESP is zero-knowledge for Alice. We describe a simulator Sim whose behavior is indistinguishable from Alice's behavior in front of an adversarial Bob.

$\mathsf{Sim}_{\mathsf{Share}}$: The simulator receives the public key $(pk_+, pk_\times)$ and sets $\mathsf{Sim}_{\mathsf{Share}}$ as follows: it calls out the $\mathsf{Sim}^{2d}_{\mathsf{Share}}$ procedures of the zero-knowledge property of Alice for 2-party decryption of respectively Π_+ and $\Pi_\times$ with pk_+ and $pk_\times$ as input. In particular it gets $sk'_B = (x_B^+, x_B^\times)$ it feeds the adversary with. When Sim is requested for a switch, it receives a pair of twin ciphertexts $(C, \bar{C})$.

Game G_0. This game is the real game. The simulator simulates all the secrets in an honest way and gives his share to Bob. It plays honestly any switching protocols on an input $(C, \bar{C})$ using Alice's secret key.

Game G_1. Each time Sim is requested for a switch ($\mathsf{Switch}_{\times\to+}$ or $\mathsf{Switch}_{+\to\times}$) it is given as input $(C, \bar{C})$ and one of the two is an encryption of m under $\Pi_\times^0$, which contains an Π_+-encryption under pk' of the bit b. The simulation uses its knowledge of the secret key sk' to decrypt the bit b. This game is indistinguishable from the previous one.

Game G_2. A modification is done for the *additive to multiplicative* case. The setup and key generation are the same as in the previous game. When requested to participate to a $\mathsf{Switch}_{+\to\times}$, with $(C, \bar{C})$ as input, the simulator uses its knowledge of b to query the EZT's simulator for Alice with $(C, \Pi_+.\mathsf{Encrypt}(pk^+, b))$ as input. By definition of the simulator for the EZT, this game is indistinguishable from the previous one.

Game G_3. After the simulation of the EZT procedure, Alice and Bob gets C_b^+. The simulation now uses the ReEnc_+'s simulator for Alice with this C_b^+ and $\Pi_+.\mathsf{Encrypt}(pk', b)$ as input, once again thanks to the knowledge of b. Thanks to the zero-knowledge property of ReEnc_+, this game is indistinguishable from the previous one.

Game G_4. Now the simulation uses the simulator for the $\mathsf{Switch}_{+\to\times}$. As the simulation knows $\bar{C}$, it can extract its first component which is a $\Pi_\times$-encryption of $m+b$. Therefore, it calls $\mathsf{Switch}_{+\to\times}$'s simulator for Alice with C_{m+b}^+ (obtained by genuinely computing the Hom_+ after the re-encryption) and $\bar{C}$'s first component. Because we proved that the $\mathsf{Switch}_{+\to\times}$ procedure is zero-knowledge in Theorem 3, this game is indistinguishable from the previous one.

Game G_5. The final flow from the switching protocols is simply the forward of $\bar{C}$ since it is a twin ciphertext of C: this game is indistinguishable from the previous one.

Game G_6. The modification now concerns the *multiplicative to additive* case. The simulation has as input $(C, \bar{C})$ where C is an encryption of a message m under $\Pi_\times^0$ and $\bar{C}$ is a twin ciphertext. Sim still knows the bit b. To simulate the switch, it uses the corresponding simulator for Alice with, as input the first component of C which is an encryption using $\Pi_\times$ of $m + b$ and $\Pi_+.\mathsf{Hom}_+(pk^+, \bar{C}, \Pi_+.\mathsf{Encrypt}(pk^+, b))$ which is an encryption $m+b$ under Π_+. Because of the zero-knowledge property of this switch proved in Theorem 3, this game is indistinguishable from the previous one.

Game G_7. The simulation now simulates the EZT procedure: it feeds the corresponding simulator with the second component of C (which is an encryption of a random element under Π_+) and $\Pi_+.\mathsf{Encrypt}(pk^+, \bar{b})$, which is a valid input. The EZT being zero-knowledge, this game is indistinguishable from the previous.

Game G_8. The last step of the switch in the multiplicative to additive direction is the computation of the Π_+ encryption of a product. The simulation makes a call to the simulator of the $\mathsf{2Mul}_+$ protocol with as input: the output of the first switch, the output of the EZT and $\bar{C}$. As this is a genuine input, this game is indistinguishable from the previous.

Game G_9. From now on, the simulation will not use its knowledge of b and of the secret key sk'. To do so, in the additive to multiplicative direction, the simulation will feed the EZT simulator with (C, C'), where C' is a ciphertext of a random element in $\mathcal{R}$ under pk, instead of an encryption of b (see Game G_2.). Thanks to the IND-CPA property of Π_+, this game is indistinguishable from the previous one.

Game G_{10}. The simulation runs the simulator for the re-encryption process with C_b^+ and a ciphertext of random element in $\mathcal{R}$ under pk', instead of an encryption of b, and again, because Π_+ is IND-CPA, this game is indistinguishable from the previous one.

Game G_{11}. In the multiplicative to additive direction, the simulator of the first ESP is run with the first component of C and a ciphertext of a random element in $\mathcal{R}^*$ under $pk^\times$. Since $\Pi_\times$ is IND-CPA, this game is indistinguishable from the previous one.

Game G_{12}. The simulation now runs the EZT simulator with the second component of C and a ciphertext of a random element of $\mathcal{R}$ instead of an encryption of $\bar{b}$. Because Π_+ is IND-CPA, this game is indistinguishable from the previous.

Game G_{13}. The simulation now uses the procedure $\mathsf{Sim}_{\mathsf{Share}}$ to simulates Bob's keys. By the zero-knowledge property of the 2-party decryption, this game is indistinguishable from the previous one and the adversary is in an environment completely simulated by Sim.

ZK for Bob. The proof that the protocols are zero-knowledge for Bob follows the same lines. It is a bit simpler since Bob has less contribution in the additive to multiplicative direction and the switch the other way around is essentially symmetric. □

References

1. Allender, E., Jiao, J., Mahajan, M., Vinay, V.: Non-commutative arithmetic circuits: depth reduction and size lower bounds. Theor. Comput. Sci. **209**(1), 47–86 (1998)
2. Asharov, G., Jain, A., López-Alt, A., Tromer, E., Vaikuntanathan, V., Wichs, D.: Multiparty computation with low communication, computation and interaction via threshold FHE. In: Pointcheval, D., Johansson, T. (eds.) EUROCRYPT 2012. LNCS, vol. 7237, pp. 483–501. Springer, Heidelberg (2012). doi:10.1007/978-3-642-29011-4_29
3. Asharov, G., Lindell, Y., Schneider, T., Zohner, M.: More efficient oblivious transfer extensions with security for malicious adversaries. In: Oswald, E., Fischlin, M. (eds.) EUROCRYPT 2015. LNCS, vol. 9056, pp. 673–701. Springer, Heidelberg (2015). doi:10.1007/978-3-662-46800-5_26
4. Beaver, D.: Foundations of secure interactive computing. In: Feigenbaum, J. (ed.) CRYPTO 1991. LNCS, vol. 576, pp. 377–391. Springer, Heidelberg (1992). doi:10.1007/3-540-46766-1_31

5. Bendlin, R., Damgård, I., Orlandi, C., Zakarias, S.: Semi-homomorphic encryption and multiparty computation. In: Paterson, K.G. (ed.) EUROCRYPT 2011. LNCS, vol. 6632, pp. 169–188. Springer, Heidelberg (2011). doi:10.1007/978-3-642-20465-4_11
6. Bogetoft, P., Damgård, I., Jakobsen, T., Nielsen, K., Pagter, J., Toft, T.: A practical implementation of secure auctions based on multiparty integer computation. In: Di Crescenzo, G., Rubin, A. (eds.) FC 2006. LNCS, vol. 4107, pp. 142–147. Springer, Heidelberg (2006). doi:10.1007/11889663_10
7. Camenisch, J., Kiayias, A., Yung, M.: On the portability of generalized Schnorr proofs. In: Joux, A. (ed.) EUROCRYPT 2009. LNCS, vol. 5479, pp. 425–442. Springer, Heidelberg (2009). doi:10.1007/978-3-642-01001-9_25
8. Canetti, R.: Security and composition of multiparty cryptographic protocols. J. Cryptol. **13**(1), 143–202 (2000)
9. Castagnos, G., Laguillaumie, F.: Linearly homomorphic encryption from DDH. In: Nyberg, K. (ed.) CT-RSA 2015. LNCS, vol. 9048, pp. 487–505. Springer, Cham (2015). doi:10.1007/978-3-319-16715-2_26
10. Couteau, G., Peters, T., Pointcheval, D.: Encryption switching protocols. In: Robshaw, M., Katz, J. (eds.) CRYPTO 2016. LNCS, vol. 9814, pp. 308–338. Springer, Heidelberg (2016). doi:10.1007/978-3-662-53018-4_12
11. Cramer, R., Damgård, I., Nielsen, J.B.: Multiparty computation from threshold homomorphic encryption. In: Pfitzmann, B. (ed.) EUROCRYPT 2001. LNCS, vol. 2045, pp. 280–300. Springer, Heidelberg (2001). doi:10.1007/3-540-44987-6_18
12. Damgård, I., Fujisaki, E.: A statistically-hiding integer commitment scheme based on groups with hidden order. In: Zheng, Y. (ed.) ASIACRYPT 2002. LNCS, vol. 2501, pp. 125–142. Springer, Heidelberg (2002). doi:10.1007/3-540-36178-2_8
13. Damgård, I., Koprowski, M.: Generic lower bounds for root extraction and signature schemes in general groups. In: Knudsen, L.R. (ed.) EUROCRYPT 2002. LNCS, vol. 2332, pp. 256–271. Springer, Heidelberg (2002). doi:10.1007/3-540-46035-7_17
14. Damgård, I., Mikkelsen, G.L.: Efficient, robust and constant-round distributed RSA key generation. In: Micciancio, D. (ed.) TCC 2010. LNCS, vol. 5978, pp. 183–200. Springer, Heidelberg (2010). doi:10.1007/978-3-642-11799-2_12
15. Damgård, I., Nielsen, J.B.: Universally composable efficient multiparty computation from threshold homomorphic encryption. In: Boneh, D. (ed.) CRYPTO 2003. LNCS, vol. 2729, pp. 247–264. Springer, Heidelberg (2003). doi:10.1007/978-3-540-45146-4_15
16. Damgård, I., Zakarias, S.: Constant-overhead secure computation of boolean circuits using preprocessing. In: Sahai, A. (ed.) TCC 2013. LNCS, vol. 7785, pp. 621–641. Springer, Heidelberg (2013). doi:10.1007/978-3-642-36594-2_35
17. Desmedt, Y., Frankel, Y.: Threshold cryptosystems. In: Brassard, G. (ed.) CRYPTO 1989. LNCS, vol. 435, pp. 307–315. Springer, New York (1990). doi:10.1007/0-387-34805-0_28
18. ElGamal, T.: A public key cryptosystem and a signature scheme based on discrete logarithms. IEEE Trans. Inf. Theory **31**, 469–472 (1985)
19. Fouque, P.-A., Poupard, G., Stern, J.: Sharing decryption in the context of voting or lotteries. In: Frankel, Y. (ed.) FC 2000. LNCS, vol. 1962, pp. 90–104. Springer, Heidelberg (2001). doi:10.1007/3-540-45472-1_7
20. Gavin, G., Minier, M.: Oblivious multi-variate polynomial evaluation. In: Roy, B., Sendrier, N. (eds.) INDOCRYPT 2009. LNCS, vol. 5922, pp. 430–442. Springer, Heidelberg (2009). doi:10.1007/978-3-642-10628-6_28

21. Gentry, C., Peikert, C., Vaikuntanathan, V.: Trapdoors for hard lattices and new cryptographic constructions. In: 40th ACM STOC, pp. 197–206. ACM Press (2008)
22. Goldreich, O., Micali, S., Wigderson, A.: How to play any mental game or a completeness theorem for protocols with honest majority. In: 19th ACM STOC, pp. 218–229. ACM Press (1987)
23. Goldwasser, S., Micali, S.: Probabilistic encryption. J. Comput. Syst. Sci. **28**(2), 270–299 (1984)
24. Jacobson, M.J.: Computing discrete logarithms in quadratic orders. J. Cryptol. **13**(4), 473–492 (2000)
25. Katz, J., Lindell, Y.: Introduction to Modern Cryptography, 2nd edn. Chapman & Hall/CRC, Boca Raton (2014)
26. Katz, J., Yung, M.: Threshold cryptosystems based on factoring. In: Zheng, Y. (ed.) ASIACRYPT 2002. LNCS, vol. 2501, pp. 192–205. Springer, Heidelberg (2002). doi:10.1007/3-540-36178-2_12
27. Kiayias, A., Yung, M.: Secure games with polynomial expressions. In: Orejas, F., Spirakis, P.G., van Leeuwen, J. (eds.) ICALP 2001. LNCS, vol. 2076, pp. 939–950. Springer, Heidelberg (2001). doi:10.1007/3-540-48224-5_76
28. Kolesnikov, V., Schneider, T.: Improved garbled circuit: free XOR gates and applications. In: Aceto, L., Damgård, I., Goldberg, L.A., Halldórsson, M.M., Ingólfsdóttir, A., Walukiewicz, I. (eds.) ICALP 2008. LNCS, vol. 5126, pp. 486–498. Springer, Heidelberg (2008). doi:10.1007/978-3-540-70583-3_40
29. Lim, H.W., Tople, S., Saxena, P., Chang, E.C.: Faster secure arithmetic computation using switchable homomorphic encryption. Cryptology ePrint Archive, Report 2014/539 (2014)
30. Lindell, Y., Pinkas, B.: Secure two-party computation via cut-and-choose oblivious transfer. In: Ishai, Y. (ed.) TCC 2011. LNCS, vol. 6597, pp. 329–346. Springer, Heidelberg (2011). doi:10.1007/978-3-642-19571-6_20
31. Lindell, Y., Pinkas, B., Smart, N.P.: Implementing two-party computation efficiently with security against malicious adversaries. In: Ostrovsky, R., De Prisco, R., Visconti, I. (eds.) SCN 2008. LNCS, vol. 5229, pp. 2–20. Springer, Heidelberg (2008). doi:10.1007/978-3-540-85855-3_2
32. Lipmaa, H., Toft, T.: Secure equality and greater-than tests with sublinear online complexity. In: Fomin, F.V., Freivalds, R., Kwiatkowska, M., Peleg, D. (eds.) ICALP 2013. LNCS, vol. 7966, pp. 645–656. Springer, Heidelberg (2013). doi:10.1007/978-3-642-39212-2_56
33. Malkhi, D., Nisan, N., Pinkas, B., Sella, Y.: Fairplay - secure two-party computation system. In: Proceedings of the 13th USENIX Security Symposium, San Diego, CA, USA, 9–13 August 2004, pp. 287–302. USENIX (2004)
34. Micali, S., Rogaway, P.: Secure computation. In: Feigenbaum, J. (ed.) CRYPTO 1991. LNCS, vol. 576, pp. 392–404. Springer, Heidelberg (1992). doi:10.1007/3-540-46766-1_32
35. Micciancio, D., Regev, O.: Worst-case to average-case reductions based on Gaussian measures. SIAM J. Comput. **37**(1), 267–302 (2007)
36. Naor, M., Pinkas, B.: Oblivious polynomial evaluation. SIAM J. Comput. **35**(5), 1254–1281 (2006)
37. Nielsen, J.B., Nordholt, P.S., Orlandi, C., Burra, S.S.: A new approach to practical active-secure two-party computation. In: Safavi-Naini, R., Canetti, R. (eds.) CRYPTO 2012. LNCS, vol. 7417, pp. 681–700. Springer, Heidelberg (2012). doi:10.1007/978-3-642-32009-5_40

38. Paillier, P.: Public-key cryptosystems based on composite degree residuosity classes. In: Stern, J. (ed.) EUROCRYPT 1999. LNCS, vol. 1592, pp. 223–238. Springer, Heidelberg (1999). doi:10.1007/3-540-48910-X_16
39. Pedersen, T.P.: A threshold cryptosystem without a trusted party. In: Davies, D.W. (ed.) EUROCRYPT 1991. LNCS, vol. 547, pp. 522–526. Springer, Heidelberg (1991). doi:10.1007/3-540-46416-6_47
40. Pinkas, B., Schneider, T., Smart, N.P., Williams, S.C.: Secure two-party computation is practical. In: Matsui, M. (ed.) ASIACRYPT 2009. LNCS, vol. 5912, pp. 250–267. Springer, Heidelberg (2009). doi:10.1007/978-3-642-10366-7_15
41. Shoup, V., Gennaro, R.: Securing threshold cryptosystems against chosen ciphertext attack. J. Cryptol. **15**(2), 75–96 (2002)
42. Tassa, T., Jarrous, A., Ben-Ya'akov, Y.: Oblivious evaluation of multivariate polynomials. J. Math. Cryptol. **7**(1), 1–29 (2013)
43. Thomé, E.: Algorithmic number theory and applications to the cryptanalysis of cryptographical primitives. Habilitation à diriger des recherches, Université de Lorraine (2012)
44. Tople, S., Shinde, S., Chen, Z., Saxena, P.: AUTOCRYPT: enabling homomorphic computation on servers to protect sensitive web content. In: ACM CCS 2013, pp. 1297–1310. ACM Press (2013)
45. Valiant, L.G., Skyum, S., Berkowitz, S., Rackoff, C.: Fast parallel computation of polynomials using few processors. SIAM J. Comput. **12**(4), 641–644 (1983)
46. Yao, A.C.C.: Protocols for secure computations (extended abstract). In: 23rd FOCS, pp. 160–164. IEEE Computer Society Press, November 1982
47. Ye, Q., Wang, H., Pieprzyk, J., Zhang, X.-M.: Efficient disjointness tests for private datasets. In: Mu, Y., Susilo, W., Seberry, J. (eds.) ACISP 2008. LNCS, vol. 5107, pp. 155–169. Springer, Heidelberg (2008). doi:10.1007/978-3-540-70500-0_12

Bitcoin

The Bitcoin Backbone Protocol with Chains of Variable Difficulty

Juan Garay[1(✉)], Aggelos Kiayias[2], and Nikos Leonardos[3]

[1] Yahoo Research, Sunnyvale, CA, USA
juan.a.garay@gmail.com
[2] University of Edinburgh and IOHK, Edinburgh, UK
akiayias@inf.ed.ac.uk
[3] National and Kapodistrian University of Athens, Athens, Greece
nikos.leonardos@gmail.com

Abstract. Bitcoin's innovative and distributedly maintained *blockchain* data structure hinges on the adequate degree of difficulty of so-called "proofs of work," which miners have to produce in order for transactions to be inserted. Importantly, these proofs of work have to be hard enough so that miners have an opportunity to unify their views in the presence of an adversary who interferes but has bounded computational power, but easy enough to be solvable regularly and enable the miners to make progress. As such, as the miners' population evolves over time, so should the difficulty of these proofs. Bitcoin provides this adjustment mechanism, with empirical evidence of a constant block generation rate against such population changes.

In this paper we provide the first formal analysis of Bitcoin's target (re)calculation function in the cryptographic setting, i.e., against all possible adversaries aiming to subvert the protocol's properties. We extend the q-bounded synchronous model of the *Bitcoin backbone protocol* [Eurocrypt 2015], which posed the basic properties of Bitcoin's underlying blockchain data structure and shows how a robust public transaction ledger can be built on top of them, to environments that may introduce or suspend parties in each round.

We provide a set of necessary conditions with respect to the way the population evolves under which the "Bitcoin backbone with chains of variable difficulty" provides a robust transaction ledger in the presence of an actively malicious adversary controlling a fraction of the miners

The full version of this paper can be found at the Cryptology ePrint Archive [12].

J. Garay—Part of this work was done while the authors were visiting the Simons Institute for the Theory of Computing, supported by the Simons Foundation and by the DIMACS/Simons Collaboration in Cryptography through NSF grant #CNS-1523467.

A. Kiayias—Work partly performed at the National and Kapodistrian University of Athens, supported by ERC project CODAMODA #259152. Work partly supported by H2020 Project #653497, PANORAMIX.

N. Leonardos—Research supported by ERC project CODAMODA, # 259152. Work partly done while at LIAFA, Université Paris Diderot–Paris 7.

J. Katz and H. Shacham (Eds.): CRYPTO 2017, Part I, LNCS 10401, pp. 291–323, 2017.
DOI: 10.1007/978-3-319-63688-7_10

strictly below 50% at each instant of the execution. Our work introduces new analysis techniques and tools to the area of blockchain systems that may prove useful in analyzing other blockchain protocols.

1 Introduction

The Bitcoin backbone [11] extracts and analyzes the basic properties of Bitcoin's underlying *blockchain* data structure, such as "common prefix" and "chain quality," which parties ("miners") maintain and try to extend by generating "proofs of work" (POW, aka "cryptographic puzzles" [1,8,14,23])[1]. It is then formally shown in [11] how fundamental applications including consensus [17,22] and a robust public transaction ledger realizing a decentralized cryptocurrency (e.g., Bitcoin [20]) can be built on top of them, assuming that the hashing power of an adversary controlling a fraction of the parties is strictly less than 1/2.

The results in [11], however, hold for a static setting, where the protocol is executed by a *fixed* number of parties (albeit not necessarily known to the participants), and therefore with POWs (and hence blockchains) of fixed difficulty. This is in contrast to the actual deployment of the Bitcoin protocol where a "target (re)calculation" mechanism adjusts the hardness level of POWs as the number of parties varies during the protocol execution. In more detail, in [11] the target T that the hash function output must not exceed, is set and hardcoded at the beginning of the protocol, and in such a way that a specific relation to the number of parties running the protocol is satisfied, namely, that a ratio f roughly equal to $qnT/2^{\kappa}$ is small, where q is the number of queries to the hash function that each party is allowed per round, n is the number of parties, and κ is the length of the hash function output. Security was only proven when the number of parties is n and the choice of target T is never recalculated, thus leaving as open question the full analysis of the protocol in a setting where, as in the real world, parties change dynamically over time.

In this paper, we abstract for the first time the target recalculation algorithm from the Bitcoin system, and present a generalization and analysis of the Bitcoin backbone protocol with chains of variable difficulty, as produced by an evolving population of parties, thus answering the aforementioned open question.

In this setting, there is a parameter m which determines the length of an "epoch" in number of blocks.[2] When a party prepares to compute the j-th block of a chain with $j \bmod m = 1$, it uses a target calculation algorithm that determines the proper target value to use, based on the party's local view about the total number of parties that are present in the system, as reflected by the rate of blocks that have been created so far and are part of the party's chain. (Each block contains a timestamp of when it was created; in our synchronous setting, timestamps will correspond to the round numbers when blocks are created—see

[1] In Bitcoin, solving a proof of work essentially amounts to brute-forcing a hash inequality based on SHA-256.

[2] In Bitcoin, m is set to 2016 and roughly corresponds to 2 weeks in real time—assuming the number of parties does not change much.

Sect. 2.) To accomodate the evolving population of parties, we extend the model of [11] to environments that are free to introduce and suspend parties in each round. In other respects, we follow the model of [11], where all parties have the same "hashing power," with each one allowed to pose q queries to the hash function that is modeled as a "random oracle" [3]. We refer to our setting as the *dynamic q-bounded synchronous setting.*

In order to give an idea of the issues involved, we note that without a target calculation mechanism, in the dynamic setting the backbone protocol is not secure *even if all parties are honest* and follow the protocol faithfully. Indeed, it is easy to see that a combination of an environment that increases the number of parties and adversarial network conditions can lead to substantial divergence (a.k.a. "forks") in the chains of the honest parties, leading to the violation of the agreement-type properties that are needed for the applications of the protocol, such as maintaining a robust transaction ledger. The attack is simple: the environment increases the number of parties constantly so that the block production rate per round increases (which is roughly the parameter f mentioned above); then, adversarial network conditions may divide the parties into two sets, A and B, and schedule message delivery so that parties in set A receive blocks produced by parties in A first, and similarly for set B. According to the Bitcoin protocol, parties adopt the block they see first, and thus the two sets will maintain two separate blockchains.

While this specific attack could in principle be thwarted by modifying the Bitcoin backbone (e.g., by randomizing which block a party adopts when they receive in the same round two blocks of the same index in the chain), it certainly would not cope with all possible attacks in the presence of a full-blown adversary and target recalculation mechanism. Indeed, such an attack was shown in [2], where by mining "privately" with timestamps in rapid succession, corrupt miners are able to induce artificially high targets in their private chain; even though such chain may grow slower than the main chain, it will still make progress and, via an anti-concentration argument, a sudden adversarial advance that can break agreement amongst honest parties cannot be ruled out.

Given the above, our main goal is to show that the backbone protocol with a Bitcoin-like target recalculation function satisfies the common prefix and chain quality properties, as an intermediate step towards proving that the protocol implements a robust transaction ledger. Expectedly, the class of protocols we will analyze will not preserve its properties for arbitrary ways in which the number of parties may change over time. In order to bound the error in the calibration of the block generation rate that the target recalculation function attempts, we will need some bounds on the way the number of parties may vary. For $\gamma \in \mathbb{R}^+$ and $s \in \mathbb{N}$, we will call a sequence $(n_r)_{r\in\mathbb{N}}$ of parties *(γ, s)-respecting* if it holds that in a sequence of rounds S with $|S| \leq s$, $\max_{r\in S} n_r \leq \gamma \cdot \min_{r\in S} n_r$, and will determine for what values of these parameters the backbone protocol is secure.

After formally describing blockchains of variable difficulty and the Bitcoin backbone protocol in this setting, at a high level our analysis goes as follows. We first introduce the notion of *goodness* regarding the approximation that is performed on f in an epoch. In more detail, we call a round r (η, θ)-*good*, for some parameters $\eta, \theta \in \mathbb{R}^+$, if the value f_r computed for the actual number of parties and target used in round r by some honest party, falls in the range $[\eta f, \theta f]$, where f is the initial block production rate (note that the first round is always assumed good). Together with "goodness" we introduce the notion of *typical* executions, in which, informally, for any set S of consecutive rounds the successes of the adversary and the honest parties do not deviate too much from their expectations as well as no "bad" event concerning the hash function occurs (such as a collision). Using a martingale bound we demonstrate that almost all polynomially bounded (in κ) executions are typical.

Next, we proceed to show that in a typical execution any chain that an honest party adopts (1) contains timestamps that are approximately accurate (i.e., no adversarial block has a timestamp that differs too much from its real creation time), and (2) it has a target such that the probability of block production remains near the fixed constant f, i.e., it is "good." Finally, these properties allow us to demonstrate that a typical execution enjoys the common prefix and chain quality properties, which is a stepping stone towards the ultimate goal, that of establishing that the backbone protocol with variable difficulty implements a robust transaction ledger. Specifically, we show the following:

Main Result. (Informal—see Theorems 4 and 5). The Bitcoin backbone protocol with chains of variable difficulty, suitably parameterized, satisfies with overwhelming probability in m and κ the properties of (1) *persistence*—if a transaction tx is confirmed by an honest party, no honest party will ever disagree about the position of tx in the ledger, and (2) *liveness*—if a transaction tx is broadcast, it will eventually become confirmed by all honest parties.

Remark. Regarding the actual parameterization of the Bitcoin system (that uses epochs of $m = 2016$ blocks), even though it is consistent with all the constraints of our theorems (cf. Remark 3 in Sect. 6.1), it cannot be justified by our martingale analysis. In fact, our probabilistic analysis would require much longer epochs to provide a sufficiently small probability of attack. Tightening the analysis or discovering attacks for parameterizations beyond our security theorems is an interesting open question.

Finally, we note that various extensions to our model are relevant to the Bitcoin system and constitute interesting directions for further research. Importantly, a security analysis in the "rational" setting (see, e.g., [9,15,24]), and in the "partially synchronous," or "bounded-delay" network model [7,21][3].

2 Model and Definitions

We describe our protocols in a model that extends the synchronous communication network model presented in [10,11] for the analysis of the Bitcoin backbone

[3] In the latest version of [10], we show that in the case of fixed difficulty, the analysis of the Bitcoin backbone in the synchronous model extends with relative ease to partial synchrony. We leave the extension of the variable-difficulty case for future work.

protocol in the static setting with a fixed number of parties (which in turn is based on Canetti's formulation of "real world" notion of protocol execution [4–6] for multi-party protocols) to the dynamic setting with a varying number of parties. In this section we provide a high-level overview of the model, highlighting the differences that are intrinsic to our dynamic setting.

Round Structure and Protocol Execution. As in [10], the protocol execution proceeds in rounds with inputs provided by an environment program denoted by $\mathcal{Z}$ to parties that execute the protocol Π, and our adversarial model in the network is "adaptive," meaning that the adversary $\mathcal{A}$ is allowed to take control of parties on the fly, and "rushing," meaning that in any given round the adversary gets to see all honest players' messages before deciding his strategy. The parties' access to the hash function and their communication mechanism are captured by a joint random oracle/diffusion functionality which reflects Bitcoin's peer structure. The diffusion functionality, [10], allows the order of messages to be controlled by $\mathcal{A}$, i.e., there is no atomicity guarantees in message broadcast [13], and, furthermore, the adversary is allowed to spoof the source information on every message (i.e., communication is not authenticated). Still, the adversary cannot change the contents of the messages nor prevent them from being delivered. We will use DIFFUSE as the message transmission command that captures this "send-to-all" functionality.

The parties that *may* become active in a protocol execution are encoded as part of a control program C and come from a universe $\mathcal{U}$ of parties.

The protocol execution is driven by an environment program $\mathcal{Z}$ that interacts with other instances of programs that it spawns at the discretion of the control program C. The pair $(\mathcal{Z}, C)$ forms of a *system of interactive Turing machines* (ITM's) in the sense of [5]. The execution is with respect to a program Π, an adversary $\mathcal{A}$ (which is another ITM) and the universe of parties $\mathcal{U}$. Assuming the control program C allows it, the environment $\mathcal{Z}$ can activate a party by writing to its input tape. Note that the environment $\mathcal{Z}$ also receives the parties' outputs when they are produced in a standard subroutine-like interaction. Additionally, the control program maintains a flag for each instance of an ITM, (abbreviated as ITI in the terminology of [5]), that is called the `ready` flag and is initially set to false for all parties.

The environment $\mathcal{Z}$, initially is restricted by C to spawn the adversary $\mathcal{A}$. Each time the adversary is activated, it may send one or more messages of the form $(\mathsf{Corrupt}, P_i)$ to C and C will mark the corresponding party as corrupted.

Functionalities Available to the Protocol. The ITI's of protocol Π will have access to a joint ideal functionality capturing the random oracle and the diffusion mechanism which is defined in a similar way as [10] and is explained below.

- The random oracle functionality. Given a query with a value x marked for "calculation" for the function $H(\cdot)$ from an honest party P_i and assuming

x has not been queried before, the functionality returns a value y which is selected at random from $\{0,1\}^{\kappa}$; furthermore, it stores the pair (x, y) in the table of $H(\cdot)$, in case the same value x is queried in the future. Each honest party P_i is allowed to ask q queries in each round as determined by the diffusion functionality (see below). On the other hand, each honest party is given unlimited queries for "verification" for the function $H(\cdot)$. The adversary $\mathcal{A}$, on the other hand, is given a bounded number queries in each round as determined by diffusion functionality with a bound that is initialized to 0 and determined as follows: whenever a corrupted party is activated, the party can ask the bound to be increased by q; each time a query is asked by the adversary the bound is decreased by 1. No verification queries are provided to $\mathcal{A}$. Note that the value q is a polynomial function of κ, the security parameter. The functionality can maintain tables for functions other than $H(\cdot)$ but, by convention, the functionality will impose query quotas to function $H(\cdot)$ only.

- The diffusion functionality. This functionality keeps track of rounds in the protocol execution; for this purpose it initially sets a variable *round* to be 1. It also maintains a RECEIVE() string defined for each party P_i in $\mathcal{U}$. A party that is activated is allowed to query the functionality and fetch the contents of its personal RECEIVE() string. Moreover, when the functionality receives a message (Diffuse, m) from party P_i it records the message m. A party P_i can signal when it is complete for the round by sending a special message (RoundComplete). With respect to the adversary $\mathcal{A}$, the functionality allows it to receive the contents of all contents sent in Diffuse messages for the round and specify the contents of the RECEIVE() string for each party P_i. The adversary has to specify when it is complete for the current round. When all parties are complete for the current round, the functionality inspects the contents of all RECEIVE() strings and includes any messages m that were diffused by the parties in the current round but not contributed by the adversary to the RECEIVE() tapes (in this way guaranteeing message delivery). It also flushes any old messages that were diffused in previous rounds and not diffused again. The variable *round* is then incremented.

The Dynamic q-Bounded Synchronous Setting. Consider $\mathbf{n} = \{n_r\}_{r \in \mathbb{N}}$ and $\mathbf{t} = \{t_r\}_{r \in \mathbb{N}}$ two series of natural numbers. As mentioned, the first instance that is spawned by $\mathcal{Z}$ is the adversary $\mathcal{A}$. Subsequently the environment may spawn (or activate if they are already spawned) parties $P_i \in \mathcal{U}$. The control program maintains a counter in each sequence of activations and matches it with the current round that is maintained by the diffusion functionality. Each time an honest party diffuses a message containing the label "`ready`" the control program C increases the ready counter for the round. In round r, the control program C will enable the adversary $\mathcal{A}$ to complete the round, only provided that (i) exactly n_r parties have transmitted `ready` message, (ii) the number of ("corrupt") parties controlled by $\mathcal{A}$ should match t_r.

Parties, when activated, are able to read their input tape INPUT() and communication tape RECEIVE() from the diffusion functionality. Observe that parties are unaware of the set of activated parties. The Bitcoin backbone protocol requires from parties (miners) to calculate a POW. This is modeled in [11] as parties having access to the oracle $H(\cdot)$. The fact that (active) parties have limited ability to produce such POWs, is captured as in [11] by the random oracle functionality and the fact that it paces parties to query a limited number of queries *per round*. The bound, q, is a function of the security parameter κ; in this sense the parties may be called q-bounded[4]. We refer to the above restrictions on the environment, the parties and the adversary as the *dynamic q-bounded synchronous setting.*

The term $\{\text{VIEW}^{P,\mathbf{t},\mathbf{n}}_{\Pi,\mathcal{A},\mathcal{Z}}(z)\}_{z\in\{0,1\}^*}$ denotes the random variable ensemble describing the view of party P after the completion of an execution running protocol Π with environment $\mathcal{Z}$ and adversary $\mathcal{A}$, on input $z \in \{0,1\}^*$. We will only consider a "standalone" execution without any auxiliary information and we will thus restrict ourselves to executions with $z = 1^\kappa$. For this reason we will simply refer to the ensemble by $\text{VIEW}^{P,\mathbf{t},\mathbf{n}}_{\Pi,\mathcal{A},\mathcal{Z}}$. The concatenation of the view of all parties ever activated in the execution is denoted by $\text{VIEW}^{\mathbf{t},\mathbf{n}}_{\Pi,\mathcal{A},\mathcal{Z}}$.

Properties of Protocols. In our theorems we will be concerned with *properties* of protocols Π running in the above setting. Such properties will be defined as predicates over the random variable $\text{VIEW}^{\mathbf{t},\mathbf{n}}_{\Pi,\mathcal{A},\mathcal{Z}}$ by quantifying over all possible adversaries $\mathcal{A}$ and environments $\mathcal{Z}$. Note that all our protocols will only satisfy properties with a small probability of error in κ as well as in a parameter k that is selected from $\{1,\ldots,\kappa\}$ (with foresight we note that in practice would be able to choose k to be much smaller than κ, e.g., $k = 6$).

The protocol class that we will analyze will not be able to preserve its properties for arbitrary sequences of parties. To restrict the way the sequence $\mathbf{n}$ is fluctuating we will introduce the following class of sequences.

Definition 1. *For* $\gamma \in \mathbb{R}^+$, *we call a sequence* $(n_r)_{r\in\mathbb{N}}$ (γ, s)-respecting *if for any set* S *of at most* s *consecutive rounds,* $\max_{r\in S} n_r \le \gamma \cdot \min_{r\in S} n_r$.

Observe that the above definition is fairly general and also can capture exponential growth; e.g., by setting $\gamma = 2$ and $s = 10$, it follows that every 10 rounds the number of ready parties may double. Note that this will not lead to an exponential running time overall since the total run time is bounded by a polynomial in κ, (due to the fact that $(\mathcal{Z}, C)$ is a system of ITM's, $\mathcal{Z}$ is locally polynomial bounded, C is a polynomial-time program, and thus [5, Proposition 3] applies).

More formally, a protocol Π would satisfy a property Q for a certain class of sequences $\mathbf{n}, \mathbf{t}$, provided that for all PPT $\mathcal{A}$ and locally polynomial bounded $\mathcal{Z}$, it holds that $Q(\text{VIEW}^{\mathbf{t},\mathbf{n}}_{\Pi,\mathcal{A},\mathcal{Z}})$ is true with overwhelming probability of the coins of $\mathcal{A}, \mathcal{Z}$ and the random oracle functionality.

In this paper, we will be interested in (γ, s)-respecting sequences $\mathbf{n}$, sequences $\mathbf{t}$ suitably restricted by $\mathbf{n}$, and protocols Π suitably parameterized given $\mathbf{n}, \mathbf{t}$.

[4] In [11] this is referred to as the "flat-model" in terms of computational power, where all parties are assumed equal. In practice, different parties may have different "hashing power"; note that this does not sacrifice generality since one can imagine that real parties are simply clusters of some arbitrary number of flat-model parties.

3 Blockchains of Variable Difficulty

We start by introducing blockchain notation; we use similar notation to [10], and expand the notion of blockchain to explicitly include *timestamps* (in the form of a round indicator). Let $G(\cdot)$ and $H(\cdot)$ be cryptographic hash functions with output in $\{0,1\}^\kappa$. A *block with target* $T \in \mathbb{N}$ is a quadruple of the form $B = \langle r, st, x, ctr \rangle$ where $st \in \{0,1\}^\kappa, x \in \{0,1\}^*$, and $r, ctr \in \mathbb{N}$ are such that they satisfy the predicate $\mathsf{validblock}_q^T(B)$ defined as

$$(H(ctr, G(r, st, x)) < T) \wedge (ctr \leq q).$$

The parameter $q \in \mathbb{N}$ is a bound that in the Bitcoin implementation determines the size of the register *ctr*; as in [10], in our treatment we allow q to be arbitrary, and use it to denote the maximum allowed number of hash queries in a round (cf. Sect. 2). We do this for convenience and our analysis applies in a straightforward manner to the case that *ctr* is restricted to the range $0 \leq ctr < 2^{32}$ and q is independent of *ctr*.

A *blockchain*, or simply a *chain* is a sequence of *blocks*. The rightmost block is the *head* of the chain, denoted $\text{head}(\mathcal{C})$. Note that the empty string ε is also a chain; by convention we set $\text{head}(\varepsilon) = \varepsilon$. A chain $\mathcal{C}$ with $\text{head}(\mathcal{C}) = \langle r, st, x, ctr \rangle$ can be extended to a longer chain by appending a valid block $B = \langle r', st', x', ctr' \rangle$ that satisfies $st' = H(ctr, G(r, st, x))$ and $r' > r$, where r' is called the *timestamp* of block B. In case $\mathcal{C} = \varepsilon$, by convention any valid block of the form $\langle r', st', x', ctr' \rangle$ may extend it. In either case we have an extended chain $\mathcal{C}_{\mathsf{new}} = \mathcal{C}B$ that satisfies $\text{head}(\mathcal{C}_{\mathsf{new}}) = B$.

The *length* of a chain $\text{len}(\mathcal{C})$ is its number of blocks. Consider a chain $\mathcal{C}$ of length ℓ and any nonnegative integer k. We denote by $\mathcal{C}^{\lceil k}$ the chain resulting from "pruning" the k rightmost blocks. Note that for $k \geq \text{len}(\mathcal{C})$, $\mathcal{C}^{\lceil k} = \varepsilon$. If $\mathcal{C}_1$ is a prefix of $\mathcal{C}_2$ we write $\mathcal{C}_1 \preceq \mathcal{C}_2$.

Given a chain $\mathcal{C}$ of length $\text{len}(\mathcal{C}) = \ell$, we let $\mathbf{x}_\mathcal{C}$ denote the vector of ℓ values that is stored in $\mathcal{C}$ and starts with the value of the first block. Similarly, $\mathbf{r}_\mathcal{C}$ is the vector that contains the timestamps of the blockchain $\mathcal{C}$.

For a chain of variable difficulty, the target T is recalculated for each block based on the round timestamps of the previous blocks. Specifically, there is a function $D : \mathbb{Z}^* \to \mathbb{R}$ which receives an arbitrary vector of round timestamps and produces the next target. The value $D(\varepsilon)$ is the initial target of the system. The *difficulty* of each block is measured in terms of how many times the block is harder to obtain than a block of target T_0. In more detail, the difficulty of a block with target T is equal to T_0/T; without loss of generality we will adopt the simpler expression $1/T$ (as T_0 will be a constant across all executions). We will use $\text{diff}(\mathcal{C})$ to denote the difficulty of a chain. This is equal to the sum of the difficulties of all the blocks that comprise the chain.

The Target Calculation Function. Intuitively, the target calculation function $D(\cdot)$ aims at maintaining the block production rate constant. It is parameterized by $m \in \mathbb{N}$ and $f \in (0,1)$; Its goal is that m blocks will be produced every

m/f rounds. We will see in Sect. 6 that the probability $f(T,n)$ with which n parties produce a new block with target T is approximated by

$$f(T,n) \approx \frac{qTn}{2^\kappa}.$$

(Note that $T/2^\kappa$ is the probability that a single player produces a block in a single query.)

To achieve the above goal Bitcoin tries to keep $qTn/2^\kappa$ close to f. To that end, Bitcoin waits for m blocks to be produced and based on their difficulty and how fast these blocks were computed it computes the next target. More specifically, say the last m blocks of a chain $\mathcal{C}$ are for target T and were produced in $\varDelta$ rounds. Consider the case where a number of players

$$n(T,\varDelta) = \frac{2^\kappa m}{qT\varDelta}$$

attempts to produce m blocks of target T; note that it will take them approximately $\varDelta$ rounds in expectation. Intuitively, the number of players at the point when m blocks were produced is estimated by $n(T,\varDelta)$; then the next target T' is set so that $n(T,\varDelta)$ players would need m/f rounds in expectation to produce m blocks of target T'. Therefore, it makes sense to set

$$T' = \frac{\varDelta}{m/f} \cdot T,$$

because if the number of players is indeed $n(T,\varDelta)$ and remains unchanged, it will take them m/f rounds in expectation to produce m blocks. If the initial estimate of the number parties is n_0, we will assume T_0 is appropriately set so that $f \approx qT_0n_0/2^\kappa$ and then

$$T' = \frac{n_0}{n(T,\varDelta)} \cdot T_0.$$

Remark 1. Recall that in the flat q-bounded setting all parties have the same hashing power (q-queries per round). It follows that n_0 represents the estimated initial hashing power while $n(T,\varDelta)$ the estimated hashing power during the last m blocks of the chain $\mathcal{C}$. As a result the new target is equal to the initial target T_0 multiplied by the factor $n_0/n(T,\varDelta)$, reflecting the change of hashing power in the last m blocks.

Based on the above we give the formal definition of the target (re)calculation function, which is as follows.

Definition 2. *For fixed constants $\kappa, \tau, m, n_0, T_0$, the target calculation function $D : \mathbb{Z}^* \to \mathbb{R}$ is defined as*

$$D(\varepsilon) = T_0 \quad \text{and} \quad D(r_1,\ldots,r_v) = \begin{cases} \frac{1}{\tau}\cdot T & \text{if } \frac{n_0}{n(T,\varDelta)} \cdot T_0 < \frac{1}{\tau}\cdot T; \\ \tau \cdot T & \text{if } \frac{n_0}{n(T,\varDelta)} \cdot T_0 > \tau \cdot T; \\ \frac{n_0}{n(T,\varDelta)} \cdot T_0 & \text{otherwise,} \end{cases}$$

where $n(T, \Delta) = 2^{\kappa} m/qT\Delta$, *with* $\Delta = r_{m'} - r_{m'-m}$, $T = D(r_1, \ldots, r_{m'-1})$, *and* $m' = m \cdot \lfloor v/m \rfloor$.

In the definition, $(r_1, \ldots, r_v)$ corresponds to a chain of v blocks with r_i the timestamp of the ith block; m', Δ, and T correspond to the last block, duration, and target of the last completed epoch, respectively.

Remark 2. A remark is in order about the case $\frac{n_0}{n(T,\Delta)} \cdot T_0 \notin [\frac{1}{\tau}T, \tau T]$, since this aspect of the definition is not justified by the discussion preceeding Definition 2. At first there may seem to be no reason to introduce such a "dampening filter" in Bitcoin's target recalculation function and one should let the parties to try collectively to approximate the proper target. Interestingly, in the absence of such dampening, an efficient attack is known [2] (against the common-prefix property). As we will see, this dampening is sufficient for us to prove security against all attackers, including those considered in [2] (with foresight, we can say that the attack still holds but it will take exponential time to mount).

4 The Bitcoin Backbone Protocol with Variable Difficulty

In this section we give a high-level description of the Bitcoin backbone protocol with chains of variable difficulty; a more detailed description, including the pseudocode of the algorithms, is given in the full version. The presentation is based on the description in [11]. We then formulate two desired properties of the blockchain—*common prefix* and *chain quality*—for the dynamic setting.

4.1 The Protocol

As in [11], in our description of the backbone protocol we intentionally avoid specifying the type of values/content that parties try to insert in the chain, the type of chain validation they perform (beyond checking for its structural properties with respect to the hash functions $G(\cdot), H(\cdot)$), and the way they interpret the chain. These checks and operations are handled by the external functions $V(\cdot), I(\cdot)$ and $R(\cdot)$ (the *content validation function*, the *input contribution function* and the *chain reading function*, resp.) which are specified by the application that runs "on top" of the backbone protocol. The Bitcoin backbone protocol in the dynamic setting comprises three algorithms.

Chain Validation. The validate algorithm performs a validation of the structural properties of a given chain $\mathcal{C}$. It is given as input the value q, as well as hash functions $H(\cdot), G(\cdot)$. It is parameterized by the content validation predicate predicate $V(\cdot)$ as well as by $D(\cdot)$, the *target calculation function* (Sect. 3). For each block of the chain, the algorithm checks that the proof of work is properly solved (with a target that is suitable as determined by the target calculation function), and that the counter *ctr* does not exceed q. Furthermore it collects the inputs from all blocks, $\mathbf{x}_{\mathcal{C}}$, and tests them via the predicate $V(\mathbf{x}_{\mathcal{C}})$. Chains that fail these validation procedure are rejected.

Chain Comparison. The objective of the second algorithm, called maxvalid, is to find the "best possible" chain when given a set of chains. The algorithm is straightforward and is parameterized by a $\mathsf{max}(\cdot)$ function that applies some ordering to the space of blockchains. The most important aspect is the chains' difficulty in which case $\mathsf{max}(\mathcal{C}_1, \mathcal{C}_2)$ will return the most *difficult* of the two. In case $\text{diff}(\mathcal{C}_1) = \text{diff}(\mathcal{C}_2)$, some other characteristic can be used to break the tie. In our case, $\mathsf{max}(\cdot, \cdot)$ will always return the first operand to reflect the fact that parties adopt the first chain they obtain from the network.

Proof of Work. The third algorithm, called pow, is the proof of work-finding procedure. It takes as input a chain and attempts to extend it via solving a proof of work. This algorithm is parameterized by two hash functions $H(\cdot), G(\cdot)$ as well as the parameter q. Moreover, the algorithm calls the target calculation function $D(\cdot)$ in order to determine the value T that will be used for the proof of work. The procedure, given a chain $\mathcal{C}$ and a value x to be inserted in the chain, hashes these values to obtain h and initializes a counter ctr. Subsequently, it increments ctr and checks to see whether $H(ctr, h) < T$; in case a suitable ctr is found then the algorithm succeeds in solving the POW and extends chain $\mathcal{C}$ by one block.

The Bitcoin Backbone Protocol. The core of the backbone protocol with variable difficulty is similar to that in [11], with several important distinctions. First is the procedure to follow when the parties become active. Parties check the `ready` flag they possess, which is false if and only if they have been inactive in the previous round. In case the `ready` flag is false, they diffuse a special message '**Join**' to request the most recent version of the blockchain(s). Similarly, parties that receive the special request message in their RECEIVE() tape broadcast their chains. As before parties, run "indefinitely" (our security analysis will apply when the total running time is polynomial in κ). The input contribution function $I(\cdot)$ and the chain reading function $R(\cdot)$ are applied to the values stored in the chain. Parties check their communication tape RECEIVE() to see whether any necessary update of their local chain is due; then they attempt to extend it via the POW algorithm pow. The function $I(\cdot)$ determines the input to be added in the chain given the party's state st, the current chain $\mathcal{C}$, the contents of the party's input tape INPUT() and communication tape RECEIVE(). The input tape contains two types of symbols, READ and (INSERT, *value*); other inputs are ignored. In case the local chain $\mathcal{C}$ is extended the new chain is diffused to the other parties. Finally, in case a READ symbol is present in the communication tape, the protocol applies function $R(\cdot)$ to its current chain and writes the result onto the output tape OUTPUT().

4.2 Properties of the Backbone Protocol with Variable Difficulty

Next, we define the two properties of the backbone protocol that the protocol will establish. They are close variants of the properties in [11], suitably modified for the dynamic q-bounded synchronous setting.

The *common prefix* property essentially remains the same. It is parameterized by a value $k \in \mathbb{N}$, considers an arbitrary environment and adversary, and it holds as long as any two parties' chains are different only in their most recent k blocks. It is actually helpful to define the property between an honest party's chain and another chain that may be adversarial. The definition is as follows.

Definition 3 (Common-Prefix Property). *The* common-prefix *property* Q_{cp} *with parameter* $k \in \mathbb{N}$ *states that, at any round of the execution, if a chain* $\mathcal{C}$ *belongs to an honest party, then for any valid chain* $\mathcal{C}'$ *in the same round such that either* $\text{diff}(\mathcal{C}') > \text{diff}(\mathcal{C})$, *or* $\text{diff}(\mathcal{C}') = \text{diff}(\mathcal{C})$ *and* $\text{head}(\mathcal{C}')$ *was computed no later than* $\text{head}(\mathcal{C})$, *it holds that* $\mathcal{C}^{\lceil k} \preceq \mathcal{C}'$ *and* $\mathcal{C}'^{\lceil k} \preceq \mathcal{C}$.

The second property, called *chain quality*, expresses the number of honest-party contributions that are contained in a sufficiently long and continuous part of a party's chain. Because we consider chains of variable difficulty it is more convenient to think of parties' contributions in terms of the total difficulty they add to the chain as opposed to the number of blocks they add (as done in [11]). The property states that adversarial parties are bounded in the amount of difficulty they can contribute to any sufficiently long segment of the chain.

Definition 4 (Chain-Quality Property). *The* chain quality *property* Q_{cq} *with parameters* $\mu \in \mathbb{R}$ *and* $\ell \in \mathbb{N}$ *states that for any party* P *with chain* $\mathcal{C}$ *in* $\text{VIEW}^{\mathbf{t,n}}_{\Pi,\mathcal{A},\mathcal{Z}}$, *and any segment of that chain of difficulty* d *such that the timestamp of the first block of the segment is at least* ℓ *smaller than the timestamp of the last block, the blocks the adversary has contributed in the segment have a total difficulty that is at most* $\mu \cdot d$.

4.3 Application: Robust Transaction Ledger

We now come to the (main) application the Bitcoin backbone protocol was designed to solve. A *robust transaction ledger* is a protocol maintaining a ledger of transactions organized in the form of a chain $\mathcal{C}$, satisfying the following two properties.

- *Persistence:* Parameterized by $k \in \mathbb{N}$ (the "depth" parameter), if an honest party P, maintaining a chain $\mathcal{C}$, reports that a transaction tx is in $\mathcal{C}^{\lceil k}$, then it holds for every other honest party P' maintaining a chain $\mathcal{C}'$ that if $\mathcal{C}'^{\lceil k}$ contains tx, then it is in exactly the same position.
- *Liveness:* Parameterized by $u, k \in \mathbb{N}$ (the "wait time" and "depth" parameters, resp.), if a transaction tx is provided to all honest parties for u consecutive rounds, then it holds that for any player P, maintaining a chain $\mathcal{C}$, tx will be in $\mathcal{C}^{\lceil k}$.

We note that, as in [11], Liveness is applicable to either "neutral" transactions (i.e., those that they are never in "conflict" with other transactions in the ledger), or transactions that are produced by an oracle Txgen that produces honestly generated transactions.

5 Overview of the Analysis

Our main goal is to show that the backbone protocol satisfies the properties common prefix and chain quality (Sect. 4.2) in a (γ, s)-respecting environment as an intermediate step towards proving, eventually, that the protocol implements a robust transaction ledger. In this section we present a high-level overview of our approach; the full analysis is then presented in Sect. 6. To prove the aforementioned properties we first characterize the set of *typical* executions. Informally, an execution is typical if for any set S of consecutive rounds the successes of the adversary and the honest parties do not deviate too much from their expectations and no bad event occurs with respect to the hash function (which we model as a "random oracle"). Using the martingale bound of Theorem 6 we demonstrate that almost all polynomially bounded executions are typical. We then proceed to show that in a typical execution any chain that an honest party adopts (1) contains timestamps that are approximately accurate (i.e., no adversarial block has a timestamp that differs too much by its real creation time) and (2) has a target such that the probability of block production remains near a fixed constant f. Finally, these properties of a typical execution will bring us to our ultimate goal: to demonstrate that a typical execution enjoys the common prefix and the chain quality properties, and therefore one can build on the blockchain a robust transaction ledger (Sect. 4.3). Here we highlight the main steps and the novel concepts that we introduce.

"Good" Executions. In order to be able to talk quantitatively about typical executions, we first introduce the notion of (η, θ)-*good* executions, which expresses how well the parties approximate f. Suppose at round r exactly n parties query the oracle with target T. The probability at least one of them will succeed is

$$f(T, n) = 1 - \left(1 - \frac{T}{2^\kappa}\right)^{qn}.$$

For the initial target T_0 and the initial estimate of the number of parties n_0, we denote $f_0 = f(T_0, n_0)$. Looking ahead, the objective of the target recalculation mechanism is to maintain a target T for each party such that $f(T, n_r) \approx f_0$ for all rounds r. (For succintness, we will drop the subscript and simply refer to it as f.)

Now, at a round r of an execution E the honest parties might be querying the random oracle for various targets. We denote by $T_r^{\min}(E)$ and $T_r^{\max}(E)$ the minimum and maximum over those targets. We say r is a target-recalculation point of a valid chain $\mathcal{C}$, if there is a block with timestamp r and m exactly divides the number of blocks up to (and including) this block. Consider constants $\eta \in (0, 1]$ and $\theta \in [1, \infty)$ and an execution E:

Definition 5 **(Abridged).** A round r is (η, θ)-*good* in E if $\eta f \leq f(T_r^{\min}(E), n_r)$ and $f(T_r^{\max}(E), n_r) \leq \theta f$. An execution E is (η, θ)-*good* if every round of E was (η, θ)-good.

We are going to study the progress of the honest parties only when their targets lie in a reasonable range. It will turn out that, with high probability, the honest parties always work with reasonable targets. The following bound will be useful because it gives an estimate of the progress the honest parties have made in an (η, θ)-good execution. We will be interested in the progress coming from *uniquely successful rounds*, where exactly one honest party computed a POW. Let Q_r be the random variable equal to the (maximum) difficulty of such rounds (recall a block with target T has difficulty $1/T$); 0 otherwise. We refer to Q_r also as "unique" difficulty. We are able to show the following.

Proposition 2 (Informal). If r is an (η, θ)-good round in an execution E, then $\mathbf{E}[Q_r(E_{r-1})] \geq (1-\theta f)pn_r$, where $Q_r(E_{r-1})$ is the unique difficulty conditioned on the execution so far, and $p = \frac{q}{2^\kappa}$.

"Per round" arguments regarding relevant random variables are not sufficient, as we need executions with "good" behavior over a sequence of rounds—i.e., variables should be concentrated around their means. It turns out that this is not easy to get, as the probabilities of the experiments performed per round depend on the history (due to target recalculation). To deal with this lack of concentration/variance problem, we introduce the following measure.

Typical Executions. Intuitively, the idea that this notion captures is as follows. Note that at each round of a given execution E the parties perform Bernoulli trials with success probabilities possibly affected by the adversary. Given the execution, these trials are determined and we may calculate the expected progress the parties make given the corresponding probabilities. We then compare this value to the actual progress and if the difference is "reasonable" we declare E *typical*. Note, however, that considering this difference by itself will not always suffice, because the variance of the process might be too high. Our definition, in view of Theorem 6 (Appendix A), says that either the variance is high with respect to the set of rounds we are considering, or the parties have made progress during these rounds as expected. A bit more formally, for a given random oracle query in an execution E, the history of the execution just before the query takes place, determines the parameters of the distribution that the outcome of this query follows as a POW (a Bernoulli trial). For the queries performed in a set of rounds S, let $V(S)$ denote the sum of the variances of these trials.

Definition 8 (Abridged). An execution E is (ϵ, η, θ)-*typical* if, for any given set S of consecutive rounds such that $V(S)$ is appropriately bounded from above:

- The average unique difficulty is *lower*-bounded by $\frac{1}{|S|}(\sum_{r\in S}\mathbf{E}[Q_r(E_{r-1})] - \epsilon(1-\theta f)p\sum_{r\in S} n_r)$;
- the average maximum difficulty is *upper*-bounded by $\frac{1}{|S|}(1+\epsilon)p\sum_{r\in S} n_r$;
- the adversary's average difficulty of blocks with "easy" targets is *upper*-bounded by $\frac{1}{|S|}(1+\epsilon)p\sum_{r\in S} t_r$, while the *number* of blocks with "hard" targets is bounded below m by a suitable constant; and
- no "bad events" with respect to the hash function occur (e.g., collisions).

The following is one of the main steps in our analysis.

Proposition 4 (Informal). Almost all polynomially bounded executions (in κ) are typical. The probability of an execution not being typical is bounded by $\exp(-\Omega(\min\{m,\kappa\}) + \ln L)$ where L is the total run-time.

Recall (Remark 2) that the dynamic setting (specifically, the use of target recalculation functions) offers more opportunities for adversarial attacks [2]. The following important intermediate lemma shows that if a typical execution is good up to a certain point, chains that are privately mined for long periods of time by the adversary will not be adopted by honest parties.

Lemma 2 (Informal). Let E be a typical execution in a (γ, s)-respecting environment. If E_r is (η, θ)-good, then, no honest party adopts at round $r+1$ a chain that has not been extended by an honest party for at least $O(\frac{m}{\tau f})$ consecutive rounds.

An easy corollary of the above is that in typical executions, the honest parties' chains cannot contain blocks with timestamps that differ too much from the blocks' actual creation times.

Corollary 1 (Informal). Let E be a typical execution in a (γ, s)-respecting environment. If E_{r-1} is (η, θ)-good, then the timestamp of any block in E_r is at most $O(\frac{m}{\tau f})$ away from its actual creation time (cf. the notion of *accuracy* in Definition 6).

Additional important results we obtain regarding (η, θ)-good executions are that their epochs last about as much as they should (Lemma 3), as well as a "self-correcting" property, which essentially says that if every chain adopted by an honest party is $(\eta\gamma, \frac{\theta}{\gamma})$-good in E_{r-1} (cf. the notion of a *good chain* in Definition 5), then E_r is (η, θ)-good (Corollary 2). The above (together with several smaller intermediate steps that we omit from this high-level overview) allow us to conclude:

Theorem 1 (Informal). A typical execution in a (γ, s)-respecting environment is $O(\frac{m}{\tau f})$-accurate and (η, θ)-good.

Common Prefix and Chain Quality. Typical executions give us the two desired low-level properties of the blockchain:

Theorems 2 and 3 (Informal). Let E be a typical execution in a (γ, s)-respecting environment. Under the requirements of Table 1 (Sect. 6.1), common prefix holds for any $k \geq \theta\gamma m/8\tau$ and chain quality holds for $\ell = m/16\tau f$ and $\mu \leq 1 - \delta/2$, where for all r, $t_r < n_r(1-\delta)$.

Robust Transaction Ledger. Given the above we then prove the properties of the robust transaction ledger:

Theorems 4 and 5 (Informal). Under the requirements of Table 1, the backbone protocol satisfies persistence with parameter $k = \Theta(m)$ and liveness with wait time $u = \Omega(m + k)$ for depth k.

We refer to Sect. 6 for the full analysis of the protocol.

6 Full Analysis

In this section we present the full analysis and proofs of the backbone protocol and robust transaction ledger application with chains of variable difficulty. The analysis follows at a high level the roadmap presented in Sect. 5.

6.1 Additional Notation, Definitions, and Preliminary Propositions

Our probability space is over all executions of length at most some polynomial in κ. Formally, the set of elementary outcomes can be defined as a set of strings that encode every variable of every party during each round of a polynomially bounded execution. We won't delve into such formalism and leave the details unspecified. We will denote by Pr the probability measure of this space. Define also the random variable $\mathcal{E}$ taking values on this space and with distribution induced by the random coins of all entities (adversary, environment, parties) and the random oracle.

Suppose at round r exactly n parties query the oracle with target T. The probability at least one of them will succeed is

$$f(T, n) = 1 - \left(1 - \frac{T}{2^\kappa}\right)^{qn}.$$

For the initial target T_0 and the initial estimate of the number of parties n_0, we denote $f_0 = f(T_0, n_0)$. Looking ahead, the objective of the target recalculation mechanism would be to maintain a target T for each party such that $f(T, n_r) \approx f_0$ for all rounds r. For this reason, we will drop the subscript from f_0 and simply refer to it as f; to avoid confusion, whenever we refer to the function $f(\cdot, \cdot)$, we will specify its two operands.

Note that $f(T, n)$ is concave and increasing in n and T. In particular, Fact 2 applies. The following proposition provides useful bounds on $f(T, n)$. For convenience, define $p = q/2^\kappa$.

Proposition 1. *For positive integers κ, q, T, n and $f(T, n)$ defined as above,*

$$\frac{pTn}{1 + pTn} \leq f(T, n) \leq pTn \leq \frac{f(T, n)}{1 - f(T, n)}, \quad \text{where } p = \frac{q}{2^\kappa}.$$

Proof. The bounds can be obtained using the inequalities $(1 - x)^\alpha \geq 1 - x\alpha$, valid for $x \leq 1$ and $\alpha \geq 1$, and $e^{-x} \leq \frac{1}{1+x}$, valid for $x \geq 0$. □

At a round r of an execution E the honest parties might be querying the random oracle for various targets. We denote by $T_r^{\min}(E)$ and $T_r^{\max}(E)$ the minimum and maximum over those targets. We say r is a target-recalculation point of a valid chain $\mathcal{C}$, if there is a block with timestamp r and m exactly divides the number of blocks up to (and including) this block.

We now define two desirable properties of executions which will be crucial in the analysis. We will show later that most executions have these properties.

Definition 5. *Consider an execution E and constants $\eta \in (0,1]$ and $\theta \in [1,\infty)$. A target-recalculation point r in a chain $\mathcal{C}$ in E is* (η,θ)-good *if the new target T satisfies $\eta f \le f(T,n_r) \le \theta f$. A chain $\mathcal{C}$ in E is* (η,θ)-good *if all its target-recalculation points are* (η,θ)-good. *A round r is* (η,θ)-good *in E if $\eta f \le f(T_r^{\min}(E),n_r)$ and $f(T_r^{\max}(E),n_r) \le \theta f$. We say that E is* (η,θ)-good *if every round of E was (η,θ)-good.*

For a round r, the following set of chains is of interest. It contains, besides the chains that the honest parties have, those chains that could potentially belong to an honest party.

$$\mathcal{S}_r = \left\{ \mathcal{C} \in E_r \;\middle|\; \begin{array}{l} \text{“}\mathcal{C}\text{ belongs to an honest party” or} \\ \text{“for some chain } \mathcal{C}' \text{ of an honest party diff}(\mathcal{C}) > \text{diff}(\mathcal{C}')\text{” or} \\ \text{“for some chain } \mathcal{C}' \text{ of an honest party diff}(\mathcal{C}) = \text{diff}(\mathcal{C}') \text{ and} \\ \qquad\qquad \text{head}(\mathcal{C}) \text{ was computed no later than head}(\mathcal{C}')\text{”} \end{array} \right\},$$

where $\mathcal{C} \in E_r$ means that $\mathcal{C}$ exists and is valid at round r.

Definition 6. *Consider an execution E. For $\epsilon \in [0,\infty)$, a block created at round r is* ϵ-accurate *if it has a timestamp r' such that $|r'-r| \le \epsilon\frac{m}{f}$. We say that E_r is* ϵ-accurate *if no chain in $\mathcal{S}_r$ contains a block that is not ϵ-accurate. We say that E is* ϵ-accurate *if for every round r in the execution, E_r is ϵ-accurate.*

Our next step is to define the typical set of executions. To this end we define a few more quantities and random variables.

In an actual execution E the honest parties may be split across different chains with possibly different targets. We are going to study the progress of the honest parties only when their targets lie in a reasonable range. It will turn out that, with high probability, the honest parties always work with reasonable targets. For a round r, a set of consecutive rounds S, and constant $\eta \in (0,1)$, let

$$T^{(r,\eta)} = \frac{\eta f}{p n_r} \quad \text{and} \quad T^{(S,\eta)} = \min_{r \in S} T^{(r,\eta)}.$$

To expunge the mystery from the definition of $T^{(r,\eta)}$, note that in an (η,θ)-good round all honest parties query for target at least $T^{(r,\eta)}$. We now define for each round r a real random variable D_r equal to the *maximum difficulty* among all blocks with targets at least $T^{(r,\eta)}$ computed by honest parties at round r. Define also Q_r to equal D_r when exactly one block was computed by an honest party and 0 otherwise.

Regarding the adversary, we are going to be interested in periods of time during which he has gathered a number of blocks in the order of m. Given that the targets of blocks are variable themselves, it is appropriate to consider the difficulty acquired by the adversary not in a set of consecutive rounds but rather in a set of consecutive adversarial queries that may span a number of rounds but do are not necessarily a multiple of q.

For a set of consecutive queries indexed by a set J, we define the following value that will act as a threshold for targets of blocks that are attempted adversary.

$$T^{(J)} = \frac{\eta(1-\delta)(1-2\epsilon)(1-\theta f)}{32\tau^3\gamma} \cdot \frac{m}{|J|} \cdot 2^{\kappa}.$$

Given the above threshold, for $j \in J$, if the adversary computed at his j-th query a block of difficulty at most $1/T^{(J)}$, then let the random variable $A_j^{(J)}$ be equal to the difficulty of this block; otherwise, let $A_j^{(J)} = 0$. The above definition suggests that we collect in $A_j^{(J)}$ the difficulty acquired by the adversary as long as it corresponds to blocks that are not too difficult (i.e., those with targets less than $T^{(J)}$). With foresight we note that this will enable a concentration argument for random variable $A_j^{(J)}$. We will usually drop the superscript (J) from A.

Let $\mathcal{E}_{r-1}$ contain the information of the execution just before round r. In particular, a value E_{r-1} of $\mathcal{E}_{r-1}$ determines the targets against which every party will query the oracle at round r, but it does not determine D_r or Q_r. If E is a fixed execution (i.e., $\mathcal{E} = E$), denote by $D_r(E)$ and $Q_r(E)$ the value of D_r and Q_r in E. If a set of consecutive queries J is considered, then, for $j \in J$, $A_j^{(J)}(E)$ is defined analogously. In this case we will also write $\mathcal{E}_j^{(J)}$ for the execution just before the j-th query of the adversary.

With respect to the random variables defined above, the following bound will be useful because it gives an estimate of the progress the honest parties have made in an (η,θ)-good execution. Note that we are interested in the progress coming from *uniquely successful rounds*, where exactly one honest party computed a POW. The expected difficulty that will be computed by the n_r honest parties at round r is pn_r. However, the easier the POW computation is, the smaller $\mathbf{E}[Q_r|\mathcal{E}_{r-1} = E_{r-1}]$ will be with respect to this value. Since the execution is (η,θ)-good, a POW is computed by the honest parties with probability at most θf. This justifies the appearance of $(1-\theta f)$ in the bound.

Proposition 2. *If round r is (η,θ)-good in E, then* $\mathbf{E}[Q_r|\mathcal{E}_{r-1} = E_{r-1}] \geq (1-\theta f)pn_r$.

Proof. Let us drop the subscript r for convenience. Suppose that the honest parties were split into k chains with corresponding targets $T_1 \leq T_2 \leq \cdots \leq T_k = T^{\max}$. Let also $n_1, n_2, \ldots, n_k$, with $n_1 + \cdots + n_k = n$, be the corresponding number of parties with each chain. First note that

$$\prod_{j\in[k]} [1 - f(T_j, n_j)] \geq \prod_{j\in[k]} [1 - f(T^{\max}, n_j)] = 1 - f(T^{\max}, n) \geq 1 - \theta f,$$

where the first inequality holds because $f(T,n)$ is increasing in T. Proposition 1 now gives

$$\mathbf{E}[Q_r|\mathcal{E}_{r-1}=E_{r-1}] = \sum_{i\in[k]} \frac{f(T_i,n_i)/T_i}{1-f(T_i,n_i)} \cdot \prod_{j\in[k]} [1-f(T_j,n_j)] \geq (1-\theta f) \sum_{i\in[k]} pn_i.$$

□

The properties we have defined will be shown to hold in a (γ,s)-respecting environment, for suitable γ and s. The following simple fact is a consequence of the definition.

Fact 1. *In a (γ,s)-respecting environment, for any set S of consecutive rounds with $|S|\leq s$, any $S'\subseteq S$, and any $n\in\{n_r : r\in S\}$,*

$$\frac{1}{\gamma}\cdot n \leq \frac{1}{|S'|}\cdot \sum_{r\in S'} n_r \leq \gamma\cdot n.$$

Proof. The average of several numbers is bounded by their min and max. Furthermore, the definition of (γ,s)-respecting implies $\min_{r\in S} n_r \geq \frac{1}{\gamma}\max_{r\in S} n_r \geq \frac{1}{\gamma}n$ and $\max_{r\in S} n_r \leq \gamma \min_{r\in S} \leq \gamma n$. Thus,

$$\frac{1}{\gamma}\cdot n \leq \min_{r\in S} n_r \leq \min_{r\in S'} n_r \leq \frac{1}{|S'|}\cdot \sum_{r\in S'} n_r \leq \max_{r\in S'} n_r \leq \max_{r\in S} n_r \leq \gamma\cdot n.$$

□

Our analysis involves a number of parameters that are suitably related. Table 1 summarizes them, recalls their definitions and lists all the constraints that they should satisfy.

Remark 3. We remark that for the actual parameterization of the parameters τ, m, f of Bitcoin[5], i.e., $\tau = 4, m = 2016, f = 0.03$, vis-à-vis the constraints of Table 1, they can be satisfied for $\delta = 0.99, \eta = 0.268, \theta = 1.995, \epsilon = 2.93\cdot 10^{-8}$, for $\gamma = 1.281$ and $s = 2.71\cdot 10^5$. Given that s measures the number of rounds within which a fluctuation of γ may take place, we have that the constraints are satisfiable for a fluctuation of up to 28% every approximately 2 months (considering a round to last 18 s).

[5] Note that in order to calculate f, we can consider that a round of full interaction lasts 18 s; If this is combined with the fact that the target is set for a POW to be discovered approximately every 10 min, we have that $18/600 = 0.3$ is a good estimate for f.

Table 1. System parameters and requirements on them. The parameters are as follows: positive integers s, m, L; positive reals $f, \gamma, \delta, \epsilon, \tau, \eta, \theta$, where $f, \epsilon, \delta \in (0,1)$, and $0 < \eta \leq 1 \leq \theta$.

n_r: number of honest parties mining in round r
t_r: number of activated parties that are corrupted
δ: advantage of honest parties, $\forall r (t_r/n_r < 1-\delta)$
(γ, s): determines how the number of parties fluctuates across rounds, cf. Definition 1
f: probability at least one honest party succeeds in a round assuming n_0 parties and target T_0 (the protocol's initialization parameters)
τ: the dampening filter, see Definition 2
(η, θ): lower and upper bound determining the goodness of an execution, cf. Definition 5
ϵ: quality of concentration of random variables in typical executions, cf. Definition 8
m: the length of an epoch in number of blocks
L: the total run-time of the system
[(R0)] $\forall r : t_r < (1-\delta) n_r$
[(R1)] $s \geq \frac{\tau m}{f} + \frac{m}{8\tau f}$
[(R2)] $\frac{\delta}{2} \geq 2\epsilon + \theta f$
[(R3)] $\tau - {}^1\!/_{8\tau} > 1/(1-\epsilon)(1-\theta f)\eta$
[(R4)] $17(1+\epsilon)\theta \leq 8\tau(\gamma - \theta f)$
[(R5)] $9(1+\epsilon)\eta\gamma^2 \leq 4(1-\eta\gamma f)$
[(R6)] $7\theta(1-\epsilon)(1-\theta f) \geq 8\gamma^2$

6.2 Chain-Growth Lemma

We now prove the Chain-growth lemma. This lemma appears already in [11], but it refers to number of blocks instead of difficulty. In [16] the name "chain growth" appears for the first time and the authors explicitly state a chain-growth property.

Informally, this lemma says that honest parties will make as much progress as how many POWs they obtain. Although simple to prove, the chain-growth lemma is very important, because it shows that no matter what the adversary does the honest parties will advance (in terms of accumulated difficulty) by at least the difficulty of the POWs they have acquired.

Lemma 1. *Let E be any execution. Suppose that at round u an honest party has a chain of difficulty d. Then, by round $v+1 \geq u$, every honest party will have received a chain of difficulty at least $d + \sum_{r=u}^{v} D_r(E)$.*

Proof. By induction on $v-u$. For the basis, $v+1 = u$ and $d + \sum_{r=u}^{v} D_r(E) = d$. Observe that if at round u an honest party has a chain $\mathcal{C}$ of difficulty d, then that party broadcast $\mathcal{C}$ at a round earlier than u. It follows that every honest party will receive $\mathcal{C}$ by round u.

For the inductive step, note that by the inductive hypothesis every honest party has received a chain of difficulty at least $d' = d + \sum_{r=u}^{v-1} D_r$ by round v. When $D_v = 0$ the statement follows directly, so assume $D_v > 0$. Since every honest party queried the oracle with a chain of difficulty at least d' at round v, if follows that an honest party successful at round v broadcast a chain of difficulty at least $d' + D_v = d + \sum_{r=u}^{v} D_r$. □

6.3 Typical Executions: Definition and Related Proofs

We can now define formally our notion of *typical* executions. Intuitively, the idea that this definition captures is as follows. Suppose that we examine a certain execution E. Note that at each round of E the parties perform Bernoulli trials with success probabilities possibly affected by the adversary. Given the execution, these trials are determined and we may calculate the expected progress the parties make given the corresponding probabilities. We then compare this value to the actual progress and if the difference is reasonable we declare E *typical.* Note, however, that considering this difference by itself will not always suffice, because the variance of the process might be too high. Our definition, in view of Theorem 6, says that either the variance is high with respect to the set of rounds we are considering, or the parties have made progress during these rounds as expected.

Beyond the behavior of random variables described above, a typical execution will also be characterized by the absence of a number of bad events about the underlying hash function $H(\cdot)$ which is used in proofs of work and is modeled as a random oracle. The bad events that are of concern to us are defined as follows; (recall that a block's creation time is the round that it has been successfully produced by a query to the random oracle either by the adversary or an honest party).

Definition 7. *An* insertion *occurs when, given a chain $\mathcal{C}$ with two consecutive blocks B and B', a block B^* created after B' is such that B, B^*, B' form three consecutive blocks of a valid chain. A* copy *occurs if the same block exists in two different positions. A* prediction *occurs when a block extends one with later creation time.*

Given the above we are now ready to specify what is a typical execution.

Definition 8 (Typical execution). *An execution E is (ϵ, η, θ)-*typical *if the following hold:*

(a) If, for any set S of consecutive rounds, $pT^{(S,\eta)} \sum_{r \in S} n_r \geq \frac{\eta m}{16\tau\gamma}$, then

$$\sum_{r \in S} Q_r(E) \geq \sum_{r \in S} \mathbf{E}[Q_r | \mathcal{E}_{r-1} = E_{r-1}] - \epsilon(1 - \theta f)p \sum_{r \in S} n_r$$
$$\text{and} \sum_{r \in S} D_r(E) \leq (1 + \epsilon)p \sum_{r \in S} n_r.$$

(b) *For any set J indexing a set of consecutive queries of the adversary we have*

$$\sum_{j \in J} A_j(E) \leq (1+\epsilon)2^{-\kappa}|J|$$

and during these queries the blocks with targets (strictly) less than $\tau T^{(J)}$ that the adversary has acquired are (strictly) less than $\frac{\eta(1-\epsilon)(1-\theta f)}{32\tau^2\gamma} \cdot m$.

(c) *No insertions, no copies, and no predictions occurred in E.*

Remark 4. Note that if J indexes the queries of the adversary in a set S of consecutive rounds, then $|J| = q\sum_{r \in S} t_r$ and the inequality in Definition 8(b) reads $\sum_{j \in J} A_j(E) \leq (1+\epsilon)p\sum_{r \in S} t_r$.

The next proposition simplify our applications of Definition 8(a).

Proposition 3. *Assume E is a typical execution in a (γ, s)-respecting environment. For any set S of consecutive rounds with $|S| \geq \frac{m}{16\tau f}$,*

$$\sum_{r \in S} D_r \leq (1+\epsilon)p\sum_{r \in S} n_r.$$

If in addition, E is (η, θ)-good, then

$$\sum_{r \in S} Q_r \geq (1-\epsilon)(1-\theta f)p\sum_{r \in S} n_r$$

and any block computed by an honest party at any round r corresponds to target at least $T^{(r,\eta)}$, and so contributes to the random variables D_r and Q_r (if the r was uniquely successful).

Proof. We first partition S into several parts with size at least $\frac{m}{16\tau f}$ and at most s. In view of Proposition 2, for both of the inequalities, we only need to verify the 'if' part of Definition 8(a) for each part S' of S. Indeed, by the definition of $T^{(S',\eta)}$ and Fact 1, $pT^{(S',\eta)}\sum_{r \in S'} n_r \geq \eta f|S'|/\gamma \geq \frac{\eta m}{16\tau\gamma}$. The last part, in view of the definition of $T^{(r,\eta)}$, is equivalent to r being (η, θ)-good. □

Almost all polynomially bounded executions (in κ) are typical:

Proposition 4. *Assuming the ITM system $(\mathcal{Z}, C)$ runs for L steps, the event "$\mathcal{E}$ is not typical" is bounded by $\exp(-\Omega(\min\{m, \kappa\}) + \ln L)$. Specifically, the bound is $\exp\{-\frac{\eta\epsilon^2(1-2\delta)m}{64\tau^3\gamma} + 2(\ln L + \ln 2)\} + 2^{-\kappa+1+2\log L}$.*

Proof. See the full version. □

6.4 Typical Executions are Good and Accurate

Lemma 2. *Let E be a typical execution in a (γ, s)-respecting environment. If E_r is (η, θ)-good, then $\mathcal{S}_{r+1}$ contains no chain that has not been extended by an honest party for at least $\frac{m}{16\tau f}$ consecutive rounds.*

Proof. Suppose—towards a contradiction—$\mathcal{C} \in \mathcal{S}_{r+1}$ and has not been extended by an honest party for at least $\frac{m}{16\tau f}$ rounds. Without loss of generality we may assume that $r+1$ is the first such round.

Let $r^* \leq r$ denote the greatest timestamp among the blocks of $\mathcal{C}$ computed by honest parties ($r^* = 0$ if none exists). Define $S = \{r^*+1, \ldots, r\}$ with $|S| \geq \frac{m}{16\tau f}$ and the index-set of the corresponding set of queries $J = \{1, \ldots, q\sum_{r\in S} t_r\}$. Suppose that the blocks of $\mathcal{C}$ with timestamps in S span k epochs with corresponding targets $T_1, \ldots, T_k$. For $i \in [k]$ let m_i be the number of blocks with target T_i and set $M = m_1 + \cdots + m_k$.

Our plan is to contradict the assumption that $\mathcal{C} \in \mathcal{S}_{r+1}$, by showing that the honest parties have accumulated more difficulty than the adversary. To be precise, note that the blocks $\mathcal{C}$ has gained in S sum to $\sum_{i\in[k]} \frac{m_i}{T_i}$ difficulty. On the other hand, by the Chain-Growth Lemma 1, all the honest parties have advanced during the rounds in S by $\sum_{r\in S} D_r(E) \geq \sum_{r\in S} Q_r(E)$. Since $|S| \geq \frac{m}{16\tau f}$, Proposition 3 implies that $\sum_{r\in S} Q_r(E)$ is at least $(1-\epsilon)(1-\theta f)p\sum_{r\in S} n_r$. Therefore, to obtain a contradiction, it suffices to show that

$$\sum_{i\in[k]} \frac{m_i}{T_i} < (1-\epsilon)(1-\theta f)p\sum_{r\in S} n_r. \tag{1}$$

We proceed by considering cases on M.

First, suppose $M \geq 2M'$, where $M' = \frac{\eta(1-\epsilon)(1-\theta f)}{32\tau^2\gamma} \cdot m$ (see Definition 8(b)). Partition the part of $\mathcal{C}$ with these M blocks into ℓ parts, so that each part has the following properties: (1) it contains at most one target-calculation point, and (2) it contains at least M' blocks with the same target. Note that such a partition exists because $M \geq 2M'$ and $M' < m$. For $i \in [\ell]$, let $j_i \in J$ be the index of the query during which the last block of the i-th part was computed. Set $J_i = \{j_{i-1}+1, \ldots, j_i\}$, with $j_0 = 0$. Note that Definition 8(c) implies $j_{i-1} < j_i$, and this is a partition of J. Recalling Definition 8(b), the sum of the difficulties of all the blocks in the i-th part is at most $\sum_{j\in J_i} A_j(E)$. This holds because one of the targets is at least $\tau T^{(J_i)}$ (since more than M' blocks have been computed in J_i with this target) and so both are at least $T^{(J_i)}$ (since targets with at most one calculation point between them can differ by a factor at most τ). Thus,

$$\sum_{i\in[k]} \frac{m_i}{T_i} \leq \sum_{\substack{i\in[\ell]\\ j\in J_i}} A_j(E) \leq \sum_{i\in[\ell]} \frac{1+\epsilon}{2^\kappa}|J_i| = (1+\epsilon)p\sum_{r\in S} t_r < (1+\epsilon)(1-\delta)p\sum_{r\in S} n_r,$$

where in the last step we used Requirement (R0). Requirement (R1) implies $(1+\epsilon)(1-\delta) \leq (1-\epsilon)(1-\theta f))$; thus, Eq. (1) holds concluding the case $M \geq 2M'$.

Otherwise, $k \leq 2$ and $m_1 + m_2 < 2M'$. Let S' consist of the first $\frac{m}{16\tau f}$ rounds of S. We are going to argue that in this case Eq. (1) holds even for S' in the place of S. Since we are in a (γ, s)-respecting environment, by Fact 1, $\gamma \sum_{r \in S'} n_r \geq n_{r^*}|S'|$. Furthermore, since r^* is (η, θ)-good, $T_1 \geq T^{(r^*,\eta)} = \eta f / p n_{r^*}$. Recalling also that $T_2 \geq T_1/\tau$, we have $\frac{m_1}{T_1} + \frac{m_2}{T_2} \leq \frac{m_1 + \tau m_2}{T_1}$, which in turn is at most

$$\frac{\tau M}{T^{(r^*,\eta)}} < \frac{2\tau M' p n_{r^*}}{\eta f} \leq \frac{2\tau\gamma M' p \sum_{r \in S'} n_r}{\eta f |S'|} \leq \frac{32\tau^2 \gamma M' p \sum_{r \in S} n_r}{\eta m}$$

and, after substituting M', Eq. (1) holds concluding this case and the proof. □

Corollary 1. *Let E be a typical execution in a (γ, s)-respecting environment. If E_{r-1} is (η, θ)-good, then E_r is $\frac{m}{16\tau f}$-accurate.*

Proof. Suppose—towards a contradiction—that, for some $r^* \leq r$, $\mathcal{C} \in \mathcal{S}_{r^*}$ contains a block which is not $\frac{m}{16\tau f}$-accurate and let $u \leq r^* \leq r$ be the timestamp of this block and v its creation time. If $u - v > \frac{m}{16\tau f}$, then every honest party would consider $\mathcal{C}$ to be invalid during rounds $v, v+1, \ldots, u$. If $v - u > \frac{m}{16\tau f}$, then in order for $\mathcal{C}$ to be valid it should not contain any honest block with timestamp in $u, u+1, \ldots, v$. (Note that we are using Definition 8(c) here as a block could be inserted later.) In either case, $\mathcal{C} \in \mathcal{S}_{r^*}$, but has not been extended by an honest party for at least $\frac{m}{16\tau f}$ rounds. Since E_{r^*-1} is (η, θ)-good, the statement follows from Lemma 2. □

Lemma 3. *Let E be a typical execution in a (γ, s)-respecting environment and r^* an $(\eta\gamma, \frac{\theta}{\gamma})$-good target-recalculation point of a valid chain $\mathcal{C}$. For $r > r^* + \frac{\tau m}{f}$, assume E_{r-1} is (η, θ)-good. Then, either the duration Δ of the epoch of $\mathcal{C}$ starting at r^* satisfies*

$$\frac{m}{\tau f} \leq \Delta \leq \frac{\tau m}{f},$$

or $\mathcal{C} \notin \mathcal{S}_u$ for each $u \in \{r^* + \frac{\tau m}{f}, \ldots, r\}$.

Proof. Let T be the target of the epoch in question.

For the upper bound, assume $\Delta > \frac{\tau m}{f}$. We show first that in the rounds $S = \{r^* + \frac{m}{16\tau f}, \ldots, r^* + \frac{\tau m}{f} - \frac{m}{16\tau f}\}$ the honest parties have acquired more than $\frac{m}{T}$ difficulty. Note that the rounds of S are (η, θ)-good as they come before r. Thus, by Proposition 3, the difficulty acquired in S by the honest parties is at least

$$(1-\epsilon)(1-\theta f)p \sum_{r \in S} n_r \geq (1-\epsilon)(1-\theta f)p \cdot \frac{|S| n_{r^*}}{\gamma} \geq (1-\epsilon)(1-\theta f)|S| \frac{\eta f}{T} > \frac{m}{T}.$$

For the first inequality, we used Fact 1. For the second, recall that r^* is $(\eta\gamma, \theta/\gamma)$-good and so $pTn_{r^*} \geq f(T, n_{r^*}) \geq \eta\gamma f$. For the last inequality observe that $|S| = \frac{m}{f}(\tau - 1/8\tau)$ and thus follows from Requirement (R3).

Next, we observe that chain $\mathcal{C}$ either has a block within the epoch in question that is computed by an honest party in a round within the period $[r^*, r^* + \frac{m}{16\tau f})$, or by Lemma 2, $\mathcal{C} \notin \mathcal{S}_u$ for each $u \in \{r^* + \frac{m}{16\tau f}, \ldots, r\} \supseteq \{r^* + \frac{\tau m}{f}, \ldots, r\}$. Assuming the first happens, it follows that by round $r^* + \frac{\tau m}{f} - \frac{m}{16\tau f}$ the honest parties' chains have advanced by an amount of difficulty which exceeds the total difficulty of the epoch in question. This means that no honest party will extend $\mathcal{C}$ during the rounds $\{r^* + \frac{\tau m}{f} - \frac{m}{16\tau f} + 1, \ldots, \Delta\}$. Since it is assumed $\Delta > r^* + \frac{\tau m}{f}$, Lemma 2 can then be applied to imply that $\mathcal{C} \notin \mathcal{S}_u$ for $u \in \{r^* + \frac{\tau m}{f}, \ldots, r\}$.

For the lower bound, we assume $\Delta < \frac{m}{\tau f}$ and that $\mathcal{C} \in \mathcal{S}_u$ for some $u \in \{r^* + \Delta + 1, \ldots, r\}$, and seek a contradiction. Clearly, the honest parties contributed only during the set of rounds $S = \{r^*, \ldots, r^* + \Delta\}$. The adversary, by Lemma 2, may have contributed only during $S' = \{r^* - \frac{m}{16\tau f}, \ldots, r^* + \Delta + \frac{m}{16\tau f}\}$. Let J be the set of queries available to the adversary during the rounds in S'. We show that in a typical execution the honest parties together with the adversary cannot acquire difficulty $\frac{m}{T}$ in the rounds in the sets S and S' respectively. With respect to the honest parties, Proposition 3 applies. Regarding the adversary, assume first $T \geq T^{(J)}$ (it is not hard to verify that the case $T < T^{(J)}$ leads to a more favorable bound). It follows that the total difficulty contributed to the epoch is at most

$$(1+\epsilon)p\Big(\sum_{r\in S} n_r + \sum_{r \in S'} t_r\Big) \leq (1+\epsilon)p\gamma n_{r^*}(|S| + |S'|) < (1+\epsilon)p\gamma n_{r^*} \cdot \frac{17m}{8\tau f}.$$

The first inequality follows from Fact 1 using $t_r < (1-\delta)n_r$. For the second substitute the upper bounds on the sizes of S and S'. Next, note that r^* is an $(\eta\gamma, \theta/\gamma)$-good recalculation point and so $f(T, n_{r^*}) \leq \theta f/\gamma$. By Proposition 1, $pTn_{r^*} < f(T, n_{r^*})/(1 - f(T, n_{r^*})) \leq (\theta f/\gamma)/(1 - \theta f/\gamma)$. It follows that the last displayed quantity is at most $\frac{17(1+\epsilon)\theta}{8\tau(\gamma - \theta f)} \cdot \frac{m}{T}$ and recalling Requirement (R4) this less than $\frac{m}{T}$ as desired. $\square$

Proposition 5. *Assume E is a typical execution in a (γ, s)-respecting environment. Consider a round r and a set of consecutive rounds S with $|S| \geq \frac{m}{32\tau^2 f}$. If E_{r-1} is (η, θ)-good, then the adversary, during the rounds in S, has contributed at most $(1-\delta)(1+\epsilon)p\sum_{r\in S} n_r$ difficulty to $\mathcal{S}_r$.*

Proof. Without loss of generality, we will assume in this proof that $t_r = (1-\delta)n_r$ for each $r \in S$. Furthermore, we assume $|S| \leq \frac{\tau m}{f}$. If this is not the case, then we can partition S to parts of appropriate sizes and apply the arguments that follow to each sum. The statement will follow upon summing over all parts.

By Lemma 2, for any block B in $\mathcal{S}_r$, there is a block in the same chain and computed at most $\frac{m}{16\tau f}$ rounds earlier than it. By Lemma 3, there is at most one recalculation point between them. Let u be the round the honest party computed this block and T its target. Note that since E is (η, θ)-good, $T \geq T^{(u,\eta)} = \frac{\eta f}{pn_u}$ and the target of B is at least $\tau^{(-1)}T$. We are going to show that, with J the set of queries that correspond to S, we have $\tau^{-1}T \geq T^{(J)}$. This will suffice, because $(1-\delta)(1+\epsilon)p\sum_{r\in S} n_r \geq (1+\epsilon)p\sum_{r\in S} t_r$, and this is at least $\sum_{j\in J} A_j$ in a typical execution (Definition 8(b)).

Note first that, using Fact 1 and the lower-bound on $|S|$,

$$2^{-\kappa}|J| = (1-\delta)p\sum_{r\in S} n_r \geq (1-\delta)p\frac{|S|n_u}{\gamma} \geq (1-\delta)p\frac{mn_u}{32\tau^3 f\gamma}.$$

Recalling the definition of $T^{(J)}$ and using this bound,

$$T^{(J)} = \frac{\eta(1-\delta)(1-2\epsilon)(1-\theta f)}{32\tau^3\gamma} \cdot \frac{m}{|J|} \cdot 2^\kappa \leq \frac{\eta f(1-2\epsilon)(1-\theta f)}{\tau p n_u} < \frac{T^{(u,\eta)}}{\tau} \leq \frac{T}{\tau},$$

as desired. □

Lemma 4. *Let E be a typical execution in a (γ, s)-respecting environment and assume E_{r-1} is (η, θ)-good. If $\mathcal{C} \in \mathcal{S}_r$, then $\mathcal{C}$ is $(\eta\gamma, \theta/\gamma)$-good in E_r.*

Proof. Note that it is our assumption that every chain is $(\eta\gamma, \theta/\gamma)$-good at the first round. Therefore, to prove the statement, it suffices to show that if a chain is $(\eta\gamma, \theta/\gamma)$-good at a recalculation point r^*, then it will also be $(\eta\gamma, \theta/\gamma)$-good at then next recalculation point $r^* + \Delta$.

Let r^* and $r^* + \Delta \leq r$ be two consecutive target-calculation points of a chain $\mathcal{C}$ and T the target of the corresponding epoch. By Lemma 3 and Definition 2 of the target-recalculation function, the new target will be

$$T' = \frac{\Delta}{m/f} \cdot T,$$

where Δ is the duration of the epoch.

We wish to show that

$$\eta\gamma f \leq f(T', n_{r^*+\Delta}) \leq \theta f/\gamma.$$

To this end, let $S = \{r^*, \ldots, r^* + \Delta\}$, $S' = \{\max\{0, r^* - \frac{m}{16\tau f}\}, \ldots, \min\{r^* + \Delta + \frac{m}{16\tau f}, r\}\}$, and let J index the queries available to the adversary in S'. Note that, by Corollary 1, every block in the epoch was computed either by an honest party during a round in S or by the adversary during a round in S'.

Suppose—towards a contradiction—that $f(T', n_{r^*+\Delta}) < \eta\gamma f$. Using the definition of $f(T, n)$, this implies $q n_{r^*+\Delta} \ln(1 - \frac{T'}{2^\kappa}) > \ln(1 - \eta\gamma f)$. Applying the inequality $-\frac{x}{1-x} < \ln(1-x) < -x$, valid for $x \in (0, 1)$, substituting the expression for T' above and rearranging, we obtain

$$\frac{m}{T} > \frac{1 - \eta\gamma f}{\eta\gamma} \cdot p\Delta n_{r^*+\Delta}.$$

By Propositions 3 and 5 it follows that

$$\frac{m}{T} \leq 2(1+\epsilon)p \sum_{r \in S'} n_r \leq 2(1+\epsilon)p \cdot \frac{\Delta + \frac{m}{8\tau f}}{|S'|} \cdot \sum_{r \in S'} n_r.$$

By Lemma 3, $\Delta \geq \frac{m}{\tau f}$. Thus, $\frac{\Delta + \frac{m}{8\tau f}}{\Delta} \leq \frac{9}{8}$. Using this, Requirement (R5), and combining the inequalities on $\frac{m}{T}$,

$$\gamma n_{r^*+\Delta} < \frac{9(1+\epsilon)\eta\gamma^2}{4(1-\eta\gamma f)} \cdot \frac{1}{|S'|} \sum_{r \in S'} n_r \leq \frac{1}{|S'|} \sum_{r \in S'} n_r,$$

contradicting Fact 1.

For the upper bound, assume $f(T', n_{r^*+\Delta}) > \theta f/\gamma$, which (see Proposition 1) implies

$$\frac{m}{T} < \frac{\gamma}{\theta} \cdot p\Delta n_{r^*+\Delta}.$$

Set $S = \{r^* + \frac{m}{16\tau f}, \ldots, r^* + \Delta - \frac{m}{16\tau f}\}$. Since an honest party posses $\mathcal{C}$ at round r, it follows by Lemma 2 that there is a block computed by an honest party in $\mathcal{C}$ during $\{r^*, \ldots, r^* + \frac{m}{16\tau f} - 1\}$ and one during $\{r^* + \Delta - \frac{m}{16\tau f} + 1, \ldots, r^* + \Delta\}$. By the Chain-Growth Lemma 1, it follows that the honest parties computed less than $\frac{m}{T}$ difficulty during S. In particular,

$$\frac{m}{T} > (1-\epsilon)(1-\theta f)p \sum_{r \in S} n_r \geq (1-\epsilon)(1-\theta f)p \cdot \frac{\Delta - \frac{m}{8\tau f}}{|S|} \cdot \sum_{r \in S} n_r.$$

By Lemma 3, $\Delta \geq \frac{m}{\tau f}$. Thus, $\frac{\Delta - \frac{m}{8\tau f}}{\Delta} \geq \frac{7}{8}$. Using this, Requirement (R6), and combining the inequalities on $\frac{m}{T}$,

$$\frac{n_{r^*+\Delta}}{\gamma} > \frac{7\theta}{8\gamma^2}(1-\epsilon)(1-\theta f) \cdot \frac{1}{|S|} \sum_{r \in S} n_r \geq \frac{1}{|S|} \sum_{r \in S} n_r,$$

contradicting Fact 1. □

Corollary 2. *Let E be a typical execution in a (γ, s)-respecting environment and E_{r-1} be (η, θ)-good. If every chain in $\mathcal{S}_{r-1}$ is $(\eta\gamma, \frac{\theta}{\gamma})$-good, then E_r is (η, θ)-good.*

Proof. We use notations and definitions of Lemma 3. Let $\mathcal{CS}_r$ and let r^* be its last recalculation point in E_{r-1}. Let T be the target after r^* and T' the one at r. We need to show that $f(T', n_r) \in [\eta f, \theta f]$. Note that if r is a recalculation point, this follows by Lemma 4. Otherwise, $T' = T$ and $\eta\gamma \leq f(T, n_{r^*}) \leq \theta f/\gamma$. Using Lemma 3, $r - r^* \leq \Delta \leq \frac{\tau m}{f}$. Thus, $\frac{1}{\gamma} n_{r^*} \leq n_r \leq \gamma n_{r^*}$. By Fact 2 we have $f(T, n_r) \leq f(T, \gamma n_{r^*}) \leq \gamma f(T, n_{r^*}) \leq \theta f$ and $f(T, n_r) \geq f(T, \frac{1}{\gamma} n_{r^*}) \geq \frac{1}{\gamma} f(T, n_{r^*}) \geq \eta f$. □

Corollary 3. *Let E be a typical execution in a (γ, s)-respecting environment. Then every round is (η, θ)-good in E.*

Proof. For the sake of contradiction, let r be the smallest round of E that is not (η, θ)-good. This means that there is a chain $\mathcal{C}$ and an honest party that possesses this chain in round r and the corresponding target T is such that $f(T, n_r) \notin [\eta f, \theta f]$. Note that E_{r-1} is (η, θ)-good, and so, by Corollary 1, E_r is $\frac{m}{16\tau f}$-accurate. Let $r^* < r$ be the last $(\eta\gamma, \theta/\gamma)$-good recalculation point of $\mathcal{C}$ (let r^* be 0 in case there is no such point).

First suppose that there is another recalculation point $r' \in (r^*, r]$. By the definition of r^*, r' is not $(\eta\gamma, \theta/\gamma)$-good. However, the assumptions of Lemma 4 hold, implying that $\mathcal{C}$ is $(\eta\gamma, \theta/\gamma)$-good. We have reached a contradiction.

We may now assume that there is no recalculation point in $(r^*, r]$ and so the points r^* and r correspond to the same target T with $\eta\gamma \leq f(T, n_{r^*}) \leq \theta f/\gamma$. Note that since r^* is an $(\eta\gamma, \theta/\gamma)$-good recalculation point and E_{r-1} is (η, θ)-good, we have $r - r^* \leq \frac{\tau m}{f}$. This follows from Lemma 3, because $\mathcal{C}$ belongs to an honest party at round r. Thus, $\frac{1}{\gamma} n_{r^*} \leq n_r \leq \gamma n_{r^*}$, and so (by Fact 2) $f(T, n_r) \leq f(T, \gamma n_{r^*}) \leq \gamma f(T, n_{r^*}) \leq \theta f$ and $f(T, n_r) \geq f(T, \frac{1}{\gamma} n_{r^*}) \geq \frac{1}{\gamma} f(T, n_{r^*}) \geq \eta f$. □

Theorem 1. *A typical execution in a (γ, s)-respecting environment is $\frac{m}{16\tau f}$-accurate and (η, θ)-good.*

Proof. This follows from Corollaries 3 and 1. □

6.5 Common Prefix and Chain Quality

Proposition 6. *Let E be a typical execution in a (γ, s)-respecting environment. Any $\frac{\theta\gamma m}{8\tau}$ consecutive blocks in an epoch of a chain $\mathcal{C} \in \mathcal{S}_r$ have been computed in at least $\frac{m}{16\tau f}$ rounds.*

Proof. Suppose—towards a contradiction—that the blocks of $\mathcal{C}$ where computed during the rounds in S^*, for some S^* such that $|S^*| < \frac{m}{16\tau f}$. Consider an S such that $S^* \subseteq S$ and $|S| = \frac{m}{16\tau f}$ and the property that a block of target T in $\mathcal{C}$ was computed by an honest party in some round $v \in S$. Such an S exists by Lemmas 2 and 3. By Propositions 3 and 5, the number of blocks of target T computed in S is at most

$$(1+\epsilon)(2-\delta)pT \sum_{u \in S} n_u \leq (1+\epsilon)(2-\delta)pT\gamma n_v |S| \leq \frac{(1+\epsilon)(2-\delta)\gamma |S| \theta f}{1-\theta f} \leq \frac{\theta\gamma m}{8\tau}.$$

For the first inequality we used Fact 1, for the second Fact 1 and that round v is (η, θ)-good, and for the last one Requirement (R2). □

Let us say that two chains $\mathcal{C}$ and $\mathcal{C}'$ *diverge* before round r, if the timestamp of the last block on their common prefix is less than r.

Lemma 5. *Let E be a typical execution in a (γ, s)-respecting environment. Any $\mathcal{C}, \mathcal{C}' \in \mathcal{S}_r$ do not diverge before round $r - \frac{m}{16\tau f}$.*

Proof. Consider the last block on the common prefix of $\mathcal{C}$ and $\mathcal{C}'$ that was computed by an honest party and let r^* be the round on which it was computed (set $r^* = 0$ if no such block exists). Denote by $\mathcal{C}^*$ the common part of $\mathcal{C}$ and $\mathcal{C}'$ up to (and including) this block and let $d^* = \mathrm{diff}(\mathcal{C}^*)$ and $S = \{i : r^* < u < r\}$. We claim that

$$(1+\epsilon)(1-\delta)p \sum_{u \in S} n_u \geq \sum_{u \in S} Q_u. \tag{2}$$

In view of Proposition 5, it suffices to show that the difficulty which the adversary contributed to $\mathcal{C}$ and $\mathcal{C}'$ is at least the right-hand side of (2). The proof of this rests on the following observation.

Consider any block B extending a chain $\mathcal{C}_1$ that was computed by an honest party in a uniquely successful round $u \in S$. Consider also an arbitrary $d \in \mathbb{R}$ such that $\mathrm{diff}(\mathcal{C}_1) \leq d < \mathrm{diff}(\mathcal{C}_1 B)$. We are going to argue that if another chain of difficulty at least d exists, then the block that "contains" the point of difficulty d was computed by the adversary. More formally, suppose a chain $\mathcal{C}_2 B'$ exists such that $B' \neq B$ and $\mathrm{diff}(\mathcal{C}_2) \leq d < \mathrm{diff}(\mathcal{C}_2 B')$. We observe that B' was computed by the adversary. This is because no honest party would extend $\mathcal{C}_2$ at a round later than u since $\mathrm{diff}(\mathcal{C}_2) \leq d < \mathrm{diff}(\mathcal{C}_1 B)$; on the other hand, if an honest party computed B' at some round $u' < u$, then no honest party would have extended $\mathcal{C}_1$ at round u since $\mathrm{diff}(\mathcal{C}_1) \leq d < \mathrm{diff}(\mathcal{C}_2 B')$; finally, note that u is also ruled out since it was a uniquely successful round by assumption.

Returning to the proof of (2) note that, by the Chain-Growth Lemma 1, $\mathrm{diff}(\mathcal{C}')$ and $\mathrm{diff}(\mathcal{C})$ are at least $d^* + \sum_{u \in S} Q_u$. To show (2) it suffices to argue that for all $d \in (d^*, \sum_{u \in S} Q_u]$ there is always a B' as above that lies either on $\mathcal{C}$, or on $\mathcal{C}'$, or on their common prefix. But this is always possible since B cannot be both on $\mathcal{C}$ and $\mathcal{C}'$ (note that by the definition of r^*, B cannot be on their common prefix). To finish the proof note that (2) contradicts Proposition 3 for large enough S. □

Theorem 2 (Common Prefix). *Let E be a typical execution in a (γ, s)-respecting environment. For any round r and any two chains in $\mathcal{S}_r$, the common-prefix property holds for $k \geq \frac{\theta\gamma m}{4\tau}$.*

Proof. Suppose common prefix fails for two chains $\mathcal{C}$ and $\mathcal{C}'$ at round r. At least $k/2$ of the blocks in each chain after their common prefix, lie in a single epoch. Proposition 6 implies that $\mathcal{C}$ and $\mathcal{C}'$ diverge before round $r - \frac{m}{16\tau f}$, contradicting Lemma 5. □

Theorem 3 (Chain Quality). *Suppose E is a typical execution in a (γ, s)-respecting environment. For the chain of any honest party at any round in E, the chain-quality property holds with parameters $\ell = \frac{m}{16\tau f}$ and $\mu = (1 + \delta/2)\lambda < (1 - \delta/2)$, where $\lambda = \max\{t_r/n_r\} < (1 - \delta)$.*

Proof. Let us denote by B_i the i-th block of $\mathcal{C}$ so that $\mathcal{C} = B_1 \ldots B_{\mathrm{len}(\mathcal{C})}$ and consider L consecutive blocks $B_u, \ldots, B_v$. Define L' as the least number of consecutive blocks $B_{u'}, \ldots, B_{v'}$ that include the L given ones (i.e., $u' \leq u$ and $v \leq v'$) and have the properties (1) that the block $B_{u'}$ was computed by an honest party or is B_1 in case such block does not exist, and (2) that there exists a round at which an honest party was trying to extend the chain ending at block $B_{v'}$. Observe that number L' is well defined since $B_{\mathrm{len}(\mathcal{C})}$ is at the head of a chain that an honest party is trying to extend. Denote by d' the total difficulty of these L' blocks. Define also r_1 as the round that $B_{u'}$ was created (set $r_1 = 0$ if $B_{u'}$ is the genesis block), r_2 as the first round that an honest party attempts to extend $B_{v'}$, and let $S = \{r : r_1 \leq r \leq r_2\}$. Note that $|S| \geq \frac{m}{16\tau f}$.

Now let x denote the total difficulty of all the blocks from honest parties that are included in the L blocks and—towards a contradiction—assume that

$$x < \left[1 - \left(1 + \frac{\delta}{2}\right)\lambda\right] d \leq \left[1 - \left(1 + \frac{\delta}{2}\right)\lambda\right] d'. \tag{3}$$

Suppose first that all the L' blocks $\{B_j : u' \leq j \leq v'\}$ have been computed during the rounds in the set S. Recalling Proposition 5, we now argue the following sequence of inequalities.

$$(1+\epsilon)(1-\delta)p\sum_{u\in S} n_u \geq d' - x \geq \Big(1+\frac{\delta}{2}\Big)\lambda d' \geq \Big(1+\frac{\delta}{2}\Big)\lambda\sum_{u\in S} Q_u. \quad (4)$$

The first inequality follows from the definition of x and d' and Proposition 5. The second one comes from the relation between x and d' outlined in (3). To see the last inequality, assume $\sum_{u\in S} Q_u > d'$. But then, by the Chain-Growth Lemma 1, the assumption than an honest party is on $B_{v'}$ at round r_2 is contradicted as all honest parties should be at chains of greater length. We now observe that (4) contradicts Proposition 3, since

$$\Big(1+\frac{\delta}{2}\Big)\lambda\sum_{u\in S} Q_u > (1-\epsilon)(1-\theta f)\Big(1-\frac{\delta}{2}\Big)p\sum_{u\in S} n_u \geq (1+\epsilon)(1-\delta)p\sum_{u\in S} n_u,$$

where the middle inequality follows by Requirement (R2).

To finish the proof we need to consider the case in which these L' blocks contain blocks that the adversary computed in rounds outside S. It is not hard to see that this case implies either a prediction or an insertion and cannot occur in a typical execution. □

6.6 Persistence and Liveness

Theorem 4. *Let E be a typical execution in a (γ, s)-respecting environment. Persistence is satisfied with depth $k \geq \frac{\theta\gamma m}{4\tau}$.*

Proof. Suppose an honest party P has at round r a chain $\mathcal{C}$ such that $\mathcal{C}^{\lceil k}$ contains a transaction tx.

We first show that the $k \geq \frac{\theta\gamma m}{4\tau}$ blocks of $\mathcal{C}$ cannot have been computed in less than $\frac{m}{16\tau f}$ rounds. Suppose—towards a contradiction—that this was the case. By Lemma 3, at least $\frac{\theta\gamma m}{8\tau}$ of the k blocks belong to a single epoch and Proposition 6 is contradicted.

To show persistence, note that if any party $P' \neq P$ has a chain $\mathcal{C}'$ at round r and $\mathcal{C}^{\lceil k}$ is not a prefix of $\mathcal{C}'$, then Lemma 5 is contradicted. Next, let $r' > r$ be the first round after r such that an honest party P' has a chain $\mathcal{C}'$ such that $\mathcal{C}^{\lceil k}$ is not a prefix of $\mathcal{C}'$. By the note above and the minimality of r' it follows that no honest party had a prefix of $\mathcal{C}'$ at round $r' - 1$. Thus, $\mathcal{C}'$ existed at round $r' - 1$ and P' had another chain $\mathcal{C}''$ at that round such that $\mathcal{C}^{\lceil k} \preceq \mathcal{C}''$ and $\operatorname{diff}(\mathcal{C}'') < \operatorname{diff}(\mathcal{C}')$. We now observe that $\mathcal{C}'$ and $\mathcal{C}''$ contradict Lemma 5 at round $r' - 1$. □

Theorem 5. *Let E be a typical execution in a (γ, s)-respecting environment. Liveness is satisfied for depth k with wait-time $\frac{m}{16\tau f} + \frac{\gamma k}{\eta f(1-\epsilon)(1-\theta f)}$.*

Proof. Suppose a transaction tx is included in any block computed by an honest party for $\frac{m}{16\tau f}$ consecutive rounds and let S denote the set of $\frac{\gamma k}{\eta f(1-\epsilon)(1-\theta f)}$ rounds that follow these rounds. Consider now the chain $\mathcal{C}$ of an arbitrary honest party after the rounds in S. By Lemma 2, $\mathcal{C}$ contains an honest block computed in the $\frac{m}{16\tau f}$ rounds. This block contains tx. Furthermore, after the rounds in the set S, on top of this block there has been accumulated at least $\sum_{r\in S} Q_r$ amount of difficulty. We claim that this much difficulty corresponds to at least k blocks. To show this, assume $|S| \leq s$ (or consider only the first s rounds of S). Let T be the smallest target computed by an honest party during the rounds in S and let u be such a round. It suffices to show $T\sum_{r\in S} Q_r \geq k$. Indeed,

$$T\sum_{r\in S} Q_r \geq (1-\epsilon)(1-\theta f)pT\sum_{r\in S} n_r \geq (1-\epsilon)(1-\theta f)\frac{pTn_u|S|}{\gamma} \geq k.$$

The first inequality follows from Proposition 3, the second by Fact 1, and for the last one we substitute the size of S and use that $pTn_u \geq f(T, n_u) \geq \eta f$ (since u is (η, θ)-good). □

A Martingale Sequences and Other Mathematical Facts

Definition 9 [19, Chap. 12]. *A sequence of random variables $X_0, X_1, \ldots$ is a martingale with respect to the sequence $Y_0, Y_1, \ldots$, if, for all $n \geq 0$, (1) X_n is a function of $Y_0, \ldots, Y_n$, (2) $\mathbf{E}[|X_n|] < \infty$, and (3) $\mathbf{E}[X_{n+1}|Y_0, \ldots, Y_n] = X_n$.*

Theorem 6 [18, Theorem 3.15]. *Let $X_0, X_1, \ldots$ be a martingale with respect to the sequence $Y_0, Y_1, \ldots$. For $n \geq 0$, let*

$$V = \sum_{i=1}^{n} \mathrm{var}(X_i - X_{i-1}|Y_0, \ldots, Y_{i-1}) \text{ and } b = \max_{1\leq i\leq n} \sup(X_i - X_{i-1}|Y_0, \ldots, Y_{i-1}),$$

where sup is taken over all possible assignments to $Y_0, \ldots, Y_{i-1}$. Then, for any $t, v \geq 0$,

$$\Pr\big[(X_n \geq X_0 + t) \wedge (V \leq v)\big] \leq \exp\left\{-\frac{t^2}{2v + 2bt/3}\right\}.$$

Fact 2. *Suppose $f : \mathbb{R}_{\geq 0} \to \mathbb{R}_{\geq 0}$ is concave and $f(0) \geq 0$. Then, for any $x, y \in [0, \infty)$ and $\lambda \in [1, \infty)$, $f(x/\lambda) \geq f(x)/\lambda$, $f(\lambda x) \leq \lambda f(x)$, $f(x+y) \leq f(x)+f(y)$.*

The following well-known inequalities may be used without reference.

Fact 3. *(1) $1 + x < e^x$, for all x. (2) $-\frac{x}{1-x} < \ln(1-x)$, for $x \in (0, 1)$. (3) $\frac{x}{1+x/2} < \ln(1+x) < x$, for $x > 0$.*

References

1. Back, A.: Hashcash (1997). http://www.cypherspace.org/hashcash
2. Bahack, L.: Theoretical bitcoin attacks with less than half of the computational power (draft). IACR Cryptology ePrint Archive 2013, 868 (2013). http://eprint.iacr.org/2013/868
3. Bellare, M., Rogaway, P.: Random oracles are practical: a paradigm for designing efficient protocols. In: Denning, D.E., Pyle, R., Ganesan, R., Sandhu, R.S., Ashby, V. (eds.) Proceedings of the 1st ACM Conference on Computer and Communications Security, CCS 1993, Fairfax, Virginia, USA, 3–5 November 1993, pp. 62–73. ACM (1993). http://doi.acm.org/10.1145/168588.168596
4. Canetti, R.: Security and composition of multiparty cryptographic protocols. J. Cryptol. **13**(1), 143–202 (2000)
5. Canetti, R.: Universally composable security: a new paradigm for cryptographic protocols. Cryptology ePrint Archive, Report 2000/067 (2000). http://eprint.iacr.org/2000/067
6. Canetti, R.: Universally composable security: a new paradigm for cryptographic protocols. In: 42nd Annual Symposium on Foundations of Computer Science, FOCS 2001, 14–17 October 2001, Las Vegas, Nevada, USA, pp. 136–145. IEEE Computer Society (2001). http://dx.doi.org/10.1109/SFCS.2001.959888
7. Dwork, C., Lynch, N.A., Stockmeyer, L.J.: Consensus in the presence of partial synchrony. J. ACM **35**(2), 288–323 (1988). http://doi.acm.org/10.1145/42282.42283
8. Dwork, C., Naor, M.: Pricing via processing or combatting junk mail. In: Brickell, E.F. (ed.) CRYPTO 1992. LNCS, vol. 740, pp. 139–147. Springer, Heidelberg (1993). doi:10.1007/3-540-48071-4_10
9. Eyal, I., Sirer, E.G.: Majority is not enough: bitcoin mining is vulnerable. In: Christin, N., Safavi-Naini, R. (eds.) FC 2014. LNCS, vol. 8437, pp. 436–454. Springer, Heidelberg (2014). doi:10.1007/978-3-662-45472-5_28
10. Garay, J.A., Kiayias, A., Leonardos, N.: The bitcoin backbone protocol: analysis and applications. IACR Cryptology ePrint Archive 2014, 765 (2014). http://eprint.iacr.org/2014/765
11. Garay, J., Kiayias, A., Leonardos, N.: The bitcoin backbone protocol: analysis and applications. In: Oswald, E., Fischlin, M. (eds.) EUROCRYPT 2015. LNCS, vol. 9057, pp. 281–310. Springer, Heidelberg (2015). doi:10.1007/978-3-662-46803-6_10
12. Garay, J.A., Kiayias, A., Leonardos, N.: The bitcoin backbone protocol with chains of variable difficulty. IACR Cryptology ePrint Archive 2016, 1048 (2016). http://eprint.iacr.org/2016/1048
13. Hadzilacos, V., Toueg, S.: A modular approach to fault-tolerant broadcasts and related problems. Technical report (1994)
14. Juels, A., Brainard, J.G.: Client puzzles: a cryptographic countermeasure against connection depletion attacks. In: NDSS, The Internet Society (1999)
15. Kiayias, A., Koutsoupias, E., Kyropoulou, M., Tselekounis, Y.: Blockchain mining games. In: Conitzer, V., Bergemann, D., Chen, Y. (eds.) Proceedings of the 2016 ACM Conference on Economics and Computation, EC 2016, Maastricht, The Netherlands, 24–28 July 2016, pp. 365–382. ACM (2016). http://doi.acm.org/10.1145/2940716.2940773
16. Kiayias, A., Panagiotakos, G.: Speed-security tradeoffs in blockchain protocols. IACR Cryptology ePrint Archive 2015, 1019 (2015). http://eprint.iacr.org/2015/1019

17. Lamport, L., Shostak, R.E., Pease, M.C.: The byzantine generals problem. ACM Trans. Program. Lang. Syst. **4**(3), 382–401 (1982)
18. McDiarmid, C.: Concentration. In: Habib, M., McDiarmid, C., Ramirez-Alfonsin, J., Reed, B. (eds.) Probabilistic Methods for Algorithmic Discrete Mathematics. Algorithms and Combinatorics, vol. 16, pp. 195–248. Springer, Heidelberg (1998). doi:10.1007/978-3-662-12788-9_6
19. Mitzenmacher, M., Upfal, E.: Probability and Computing - Randomized Algorithms and Probabilistic Analysis. Cambridge University Press, Cambridge (2005)
20. Nakamoto, S.: Bitcoin open source implementation of P2P currency. http://p2pfoundation.ning.com/forum/topics/bitcoin-open-source
21. Pass, R., Seeman, L., Shelat, A.: Analysis of the blockchain protocol in asynchronous networks. In: Coron, J.-S., Nielsen, J.B. (eds.) EUROCRYPT 2017. LNCS, vol. 10211, pp. 643–673. Springer, Cham (2017). doi:10.1007/978-3-319-56614-6_22
22. Pease, M.C., Shostak, R.E., Lamport, L.: Reaching agreement in the presence of faults. J. ACM **27**(2), 228–234 (1980)
23. Rivest, R.L., Shamir, A., Wagner, D.A.: Time-lock puzzles and timed-release crypto. Technical report, Cambridge, MA, USA (1996)
24. Sapirshtein, A., Sompolinsky, Y., Zohar, A.: Optimal selfish mining strategies in bitcoin. CoRR abs/1507.06183 (2015). http://arxiv.org/abs/1507.06183

Bitcoin as a Transaction Ledger: A Composable Treatment

Christian Badertscher[1(✉)], Ueli Maurer[1], Daniel Tschudi[1], and Vassilis Zikas[2]

[1] ETH Zurich, Zurich, Switzerland
{christian.badertscher,maurer,tschudid}@inf.ethz.ch
[2] RPI, Troy, USA
vzikas@cs.rpi.edu

Abstract. Bitcoin is one of the most prominent examples of a distributed cryptographic protocol that is extensively used in reality. Nonetheless, existing security proofs are property-based, and as such they do not support composition.

In this work we put forth a universally composable treatment of the Bitcoin protocol. We specify the goal that Bitcoin aims to achieve as a ledger functionality in the (G)UC model of Canetti et al. [TCC'07]. Our ledger functionality is weaker than the one recently proposed by Kiayias, Zhou, and Zikas [EUROCRYPT'16], but unlike the latter suggestion, which is arguably not implementable given the Bitcoin assumptions, we prove that the one proposed here is securely UC realized under standard assumptions by an appropriate abstraction of Bitcoin as a UC protocol. We further show how known property-based approaches can be cast as special instances of our treatment and how their underlying assumptions can be cast in (G)UC without restricting the environment or the adversary.

1 Introduction

Since Nakamoto first proposed Bitcoin as a decentralized cryptocurrency [28], several works have focused on analyzing and/or predicting its behavior under different attack scenarios [4,14,15,18,30,33,34]. However, a core question remained:

What security goal does Bitcoin achieve under what assumptions?

An intuitive answer to this question was already given in Nakamoto's original white paper [28]: Bitcoin aims to achieve some form of consensus on a set of valid transactions. The core difference of this consensus mechanism with traditional consensus [24–26,31] is that it does not rely on having a known (permissioned) set of participants, but everyone can join and leave at any point in time. This is often referred to as the *permissionless* model. Consensus in this model is achieved by shifting from the traditional assumptions on the fraction of cheating versus honest participants, to assumptions on the collective computing power of the

---

The full version of this paper can be found at the Cryptology ePrint Archive [6].
V. Zikas—Research supported in part by IOHK.

J. Katz and H. Shacham (Eds.): CRYPTO 2017, Part I, LNCS 10401, pp. 324–356, 2017.
DOI: 10.1007/978-3-319-63688-7_11

cheating participants compared to the total computing power of the parties that support the consensus mechanism. The core idea is that in order for a party's action to affect the system's behavior, it needs to prove that it is investing sufficient computing resources. In Bitcoin, these resources are measured by means of solutions to a presumably computation-intensive problem.

Although the above idea is implicit in [28], a formal description of Bitcoin's goal had not been proposed or known to be achieved (and under what assumptions) until the recent works of Garay et al. [16] and Pass et al. [29]. In a nutshell, these works set forth models of computation and, in these models, an abstraction of Bitcoin as a distributed protocol, and proved that the output of this protocol satisfies certain security properties, for example the *common prefix* [16] or consistency [29] property. This property confirms—under the assumption that not too much of the total computing power of the system is invested in breaking it—a heuristic argument used by the Bitcoin specification: if some block makes it deep enough into the blockchain of an honest party, then it will eventually make it into the blockchain of every honest party and will never be reversed.[1] In addition to the common prefix property, other quality properties of the output of the abstracted blockchain protocol were also defined and proved. A more detailed description of the security properties in [16,29] is included in Sect. 4.4.

Bitcoin as a Service for Cryptographic Protocols. The main use of the Bitcoin protocol is as a decentralized monetary system with a payment mechanism, which is what it was designed for. And although the exact economic forces that guide its sustainability are still being researched, and certain rational models predict it is not a stable solution, it is a fact that Bitcoin has not met any of these pessimistic predictions for several years and it is not clear it ever will do. And even if it does, the research community has produced and is testing several alternative decentralized cryptocurrencies, e.g., [7,9,27], that are more functional and/or resilient to theoretic attacks than Bitcoin. Thus, it is reasonable to assume that decentralized cryptocurrencies are here to stay.

This leads to the natural questions of how one can use this new reality to improve the security and/or efficiency of cryptographic protocols? First answers to this question were given in [1–3,8,20–23] where it was shown how Bitcoin can be used as a punishment mechanism to incentivize honest behavior in higher level cryptographic protocols such as fair lotteries, poker, and general multiparty computation. But in order to formally define and prove the security of the above constructions in a widely accepted cryptographic framework for multiparty protocols, one needs to define what it means for these protocols to be run in a world that gives them access to the Bitcoin network as a resource to improve their security. In other words, the question now becomes:

What functionality can Bitcoin provide to cryptographic protocols?

[1] In the original Bitcoin heuristic "deep enough" is defined as six blocks, whereas in these works it is defined as linear in an appropriate security parameter.

To address this question, Bentov and Kumaresan [8] introduced a model of computation in which protocols can use a punishment mechanism to incentivize adversaries to adhere to their protocol instructions. As a basis, they use the universal composition framework of Canetti [10], but the proposed modifications do not support composition and it is not clear how standard UC cryptographic protocols can be cast as protocols in that model.

In a different direction, Kiayias et al. [19] connected the above question with the original question of Bitcoin's security goal. More concretely, they proposed identifying the resource that Bitcoin (or other decentralized cryptocurrencies) offers to cryptographic protocols as its security goal, and expressing it in a standard language compatible with the existing literature on cryptographic multi-party protocols. More specifically, they modeled the ideal guarantees as a transaction-ledger functionality in the universal composition framework. To be more precise, the ledger of [19] is formally a global setup in the (extended) GUC framework of Canetti et al. [11].

In a nutshell, the ledger proposed by [19] corresponds to a trusted party which keeps a state of blocks of transactions and makes it available, upon request, to any party. Furthermore, it accepts transactions from any party and records them as long as they pass an appropriate validation procedure that depends on the above publicly available state as well as other registered messages. Periodically, this ledger puts the transactions that were recently registered into a block and adds them into the state. As proved in [19], giving multi-party protocols access to such a transaction-ledger functionality allows for formally capturing, within the composable (G)UC framework, the mechanism of leveraging security loss with coins. The proposed ledger functionality guarantees all properties that one could expect from Bitcoin and encompasses the properties in [16,29]. Therefore, it is natural to postulate that it is a candidate for defining the security goal of Bitcoin (and potentially other decentralized cryptocurrencies). However, the ledger functionality proposed by [19] was not accompanied by a security proof that any of the known cryptocurrencies implements it.

However, as we show, despite being a step in the right direction, the ledger proposed in [19] cannot be realized under standard assumptions about the Bitcoin network. On the positive side, we specify a new transaction ledger functionality which still guarantees all properties postulated in [16,29], and prove that a reasonable abstraction of the Bitcoin protocol implements this ledger. In our construction, we describe Bitcoin as a UC protocol which generalizes both protocols proposed in [16,29]. Along the way we devise a compound way of capturing in UC assumptions like the ones in [16,29], which enables us to compare the strengths of these models.

Related Literature. The security of Bitcoin as a cryptographic protocol was previously studied by Garay et al. [16] and by Pass et al. [29] who proposed and analyzed an abstraction of the core of the Bitcoin protocol in a *property-based* manner. The treatment of [16,29] does not offer composable security guarantees. More recently, Kiayias et al. [19] proposed capturing the security goal and resource implemented by Bitcoin by means of a shared transaction-ledger functionality in the universal composition with global setup (GUC) framework of Canetti et al. [11]. However, the proposed ledger-functionality is too strong to be implementable by Bitcoin. We refer the interested reader to the full version [6] for the basic elements of these works and a discussion on simulation-based security in general. A formal comparison of our treatment with [16,29], which indicates how both these protocols and definitions can be captured as special cases of our security definition, is given in Sect. 4.4.

Our Results. We put forth the first universally composable (simulation-based) proof of security of Bitcoin in the (G)UC model of Canetti et al. [11]. We observe that the ledger functionality proposed by Kiayas et al. [19] is too strong to be implemented by the Bitcoin protocol—in fact, by any protocol in the permissionless setting, which uses network assumptions similar to Bitcoin. Intuitively, the reason is that the functionality allows too little interference of the simulator with its state, making it impossible to emulate adversarial attacks that result, e.g., in the adversary inserting only transactions coming from parties it wants or that result in parties holding chains of different length.

Therefore, we propose an alternative ledger functionality $\mathcal{G}_{\text{LEDGER}}$ which shares certain design properties with the proposal in [19] but which can be provably implemented by the Bitcoin protocol. As in [19], our proposed functionality can be used as a global setup to allow protocols with different sessions to make use of it, thereby enabling the ledger to be cast as shared among any protocol that wants to use it. The ledger is parametrized by a generic transaction validation predicate which enables it to capture decentralized blockchain protocols beyond Bitcoin. Our functionality allows for parties/miners to join and or leave the computation and allows for adaptive corruption.

Having defined our ledger functionality we next prove that for an appropriate validation predicate $\mathcal{G}_{\text{LEDGER}}$ is implemented by Bitcoin assuming that miners which deviate from the Bitcoin protocol do not control a majority of the total hashing power at any point. To this end, we describe an abstraction of the Bitcoin protocol as a synchronous UC protocol. Our protocol generalizes both [16,29]—as we argue, the protocols described in these works can be captured as instances of our protocols. The difference between these two instances is the network assumption that is used—more precisely, the assumption about knowledge on the network delay—and the assumption on the number of queries per round. To capture these assumptions in UC, we devise a methodology to formulate functionality wrappers to capture assumptions, and discuss the implications of such a method in preserving universal composability.

Our protocol works over a network of bounded-delay channels, where similar to [29], the miners are not aware of (an upper bound on) the actual delay that the network induces. We argue that such a network is strictly weaker than a network with known bounded delay, which is implicit in the synchrony assumptions of [16] (cf. Remark 1). Notwithstanding, unlike previous works, instead of starting from a complete network that offers multicast, we explain how such a network could be implemented by running the message-diffusion mechanism of the Bitcoin network (which is run over a lower level network of unicast channels). Intuitively, this network is built by every miner, upon joining the system, choosing some existing miners of its choice to use them as relay-nodes.

Our security proof proposes a useful modularization of the Bitcoin protocol. Concretely, we first identify the part of the Bitcoin code which intuitively corresponds to the lottery aspect, provide an ideal UC functionality that reflects this lottery aspect, and prove that this part of the Bitcoin code realizes the proposed functionality. We then analyze the remainder of the protocol in the simpler world where the respective code that implements the lottery aspect is replaced by invocations of the corresponding functionality. Using the composition theorem, we can then immediately combine the two parts into a proof of the full protocol.

Similarly to the *backbone* protocol from [16] our above UC protocol description of Bitcoin relies only on proofs of work and not on digital signatures. As a result, it implements a somewhat weaker ledger, which does not guarantee that transactions submitted by honest parties will eventually make it into the blockchain.[2] As a last result, we show that (similarly to [16]) by incorporating public-key cryptography, i.e., taking signatures into account in the validation predicate, we can implement a stronger ledger that ensures that transactions issued by honest users—i.e., users who do not sign contradicting transactions and who keep their signing keys for themselves—are guaranteed to be eventually included into the blockchain. The fact that our protocol is described in UC makes this a straight-forward, modular construction using the proposed transaction ledger as a hybrid. In particular, we do not need to consider the specifics of the Bitcoin protocol in the proof of this step. This also allows us to identify the maximum (worst-case) delay a user needs to wait before being guaranteed to see its transaction on the blockchain and be assured that it will not be inverted.

2 A Composable Model for Blockchain Protocols in the Permissionless Model

In this section we describe our (G)UC-based model of execution for the Bitcoin protocol. We remark that providing such a formal model of execution forces us to make explicit all the implicit assumptions from previous works. As we lay down the theoretical framework, we will also discuss these assumptions along with their strengths and differences.

Bitcoin miners are represented as players—formally Interactive Turing Machine instances (ITIs)—in a multi-party computation. They interact which each other by exchanging messages over an unauthenticated multicast network with eventual delivery (see below) and might make queries to a common random oracle. We will assume a central adversary $\mathcal{A}$ who gets to corrupt miners and might use them to attempt to break the protocol's security. As is common in (G)UC, the resources available to the parties are described as hybrid functionalities. Before we provide the formal specification of such functionalities, we

[2] We formulate a weakened guarantee, which we then amplify using digital signatures.

first discuss a delicate issue that relates to the set of parties (ITIs) that might interact with an ideal functionality.

Functionalities with Dynamic Party Sets. In many UC functionalities, the set of parties is defined upon initiation of the functionality and is not subject to change throughout the lifecycle of the execution. Nonetheless, UC does provide support for functionalities in which the set of parties that might interact with the functionality is dynamic. This dynamic nature is an inherent feature of the Bitcoin protocol—where miners come and go at will. In this work we make this explicit by means of the following mechanism: All the functionalities considered here include the following three instructions that allow honest parties to join or leave the set $\mathcal{P}$ of players that the functionality interacts with, and inform the adversary about the current set of registered parties:[3]

- Upon receiving ($\text{REGISTER}, \mathsf{sid}$) from some party p_i (or from $\mathcal{A}$ on behalf of a corrupted p_i), set $\mathcal{P} = \mathcal{P} \cup \{p_i\}$. Return ($\text{REGISTER}, \mathsf{sid}, p_i$) to the caller.
- Upon receiving (DE-REGISTER, sid) from some party $p_i \in \mathcal{P}$, set $\mathcal{P} := \mathcal{P} \setminus \{p_i\}$. Return ($\text{DE-REGISTER}$, sid, p_i) to p_i.
- Upon receiving (GET-REGISTERED, sid) from the adversary $\mathcal{A}$, the functionality returns (GET-REGISTERED, $\mathsf{sid}, \mathcal{P}$) to $\mathcal{A}$.

For simplicity in the description of the functionalities, for a party $p_i \in \mathcal{P}$ we will use p_i to refer to this party's ID.

In addition to the above registration instructions, global setups, i.e., shared functionalities that are available both in the real and in the ideal world and allow parties connected to them to share state [11], allow also UC functionalities to register with them.[4] Concretely, global setups include, in addition to the above party registration instructions, two registration/de-registration instructions for functionalities:

- Upon receiving ($\text{REGISTER}, \mathsf{sid}_C$) from a functionality $\mathcal{F}$, set $F := F \cup \{\mathcal{F}\}$.
- Upon receiving (DE-REGISTER, sid_C) from a functionality $\mathcal{F}$, set $F := F \setminus \{\mathcal{F}\}$.
- Upon receiving (GET-REGISTERED-F, sid_C) from the adversary $\mathcal{A}$, the functionality returns (GET-REGISTERED-F, sid_C, F) to $\mathcal{A}$.

The above three (or six in case of global setups) instructions will be part of the code of *all* ideal functionalities considered in this work. However, to keep the description simpler we will omit these instructions from the formal descriptions. We are now ready to formally describe each of the available functionalities.

[3] Note that making the set of parties dynamic means that the adversary needs to be informed about which parties are currently in the computation so that he can chose how many (and which) parties to corrupt.

[4] Although we allow no communication between functionalities, we will allow functionalities to communicate with global setups. (They can use the interface of global setups to additional honest parties, which is anyway open to the environment.)

The Communication Network. In Bitcoin, parties/miners communicate over an incomplete network of asynchronous unauthenticated unidirectional channels. Concretely, every miner chooses a set of other miners as its immediate neighbors—typically by using some public information on IP addresses of existing miners—and uses its neighbors to send messages to all the miners in the Bitcoin network. This corresponds to multicasting the message[5]. This is achieved by a standard diffusion mechanism: The sender sends the message it wishes to multicast to all its neighbors who check that a message with the same content was not received before, and if this is the case forward it to their neighbors, who then do the same check, and so on. We make the following two assumptions about the communication channels in the above diffusion mechanism/protocol:

- They guarantee (reliable) delivery of messages within a delay parameter Δ, but are otherwise specified to be of asynchronous nature (see below) and hence no protocol can rely on timings regarding the delivery of messages. The adversary might delay any message sent through such a channel, but at most by Δ. In particular, the adversary cannot block messages. However, he can induce an arbitrary order on the messages sent to some party.
- The receiver gets no information other than the messages themselves. In particular, a receiver cannot link a message to its sender nor can he observe whether or not two messages were sent from the same sender.
- The channel offers no privacy guarantees. The adversary is given read access to all messages sent on the network.

Our formal description of communication with eventual delivery within the UC framework builds on ideas from [5,13,17]. In particular, we capture such communication by assuming for each miner $p_j \in \mathcal{P}$ a multi-use *unicast* channel $\mathcal{F}_{\text{U-CH}}$ with receiver p_j, to which any miner $p_i \in \mathcal{P}$ can connect and input messages to be delivered to $p_j \in \mathcal{P}$. A miner connecting to the unicast channel with receiver p_j corresponds to the above process of looking up p_j and making him one of its access points. The unicast channel does not provide any information to its receiver about who else is using it. In particular, messages are buffered but the information of who is the sender is deleted; instead, the channel creates unique independent message-IDs that are used as handles for the messages. Furthermore, the adversary—who is informed about both the content of the messages and about the handles—is allowed to delay messages by any finite amount, and allowed to deliver them in an arbitrary out-of-order manner.

To ensure that the adversary cannot arbitrarily delay the delivery of messages submitted by honest parties, we use the following idea: We first turn the UC channel-functionality to work in a "fetch message" mode, where the channel delivers the message to its intended recipient p_j if and only if p_j asks to receive it by issuing a special "fetch" command. If the adversary wishes to delay the delivery of some message with message ID mid, he needs to submit to the channel

[5] In [16] this mechanism is referred to as "broadcast"; here, we use multicast to make explicit the fact that this primitive is different from a standard Byzantine-agreement-type broadcast, in that it does not guarantee any consistency for a malicious sender.

functionality an integer value T_{mid}—the *delay* for message with ID mid. This will have the effect that the channel ignores the next T_{mid} fetch attempts, and only then allows the receipt of the sender's message. Importantly, we require that the channel does not accept more than Δ accumulative delay on any message. To allow the adversary freedom in scheduling the delivery of messages, we allow him to input delays more than once, which are added to the current delay amount. If the adversary wants to deliver the message in the next activation, all he needs to do is submit a negative delay. Furthermore, we allow the adversary to schedule more than one messages to be delivered in the same "fetch" command. Finally, to ensure that the adversary is able to re-order such batches of messages arbitrarily, we allow $\mathcal{A}$ to send special $(\mathtt{swap}, \mathsf{mid}, \mathsf{mid}')$ commands that have as an effect to change the order of the corresponding messages. The detailed specification of the described channels, denoted $\mathcal{F}_{\text{U-CH}}$ is provided in the full version [6]. Note that in the descriptions throughout the paper, for a vector $\vec{M}$ we denote by the symbol $||$ the operation which adds a new element to $\vec{M}$.

From Unicast to Multicast. As already mentioned, the Bitcoin protocol uses the above asynchronous-and-bounded-delay unicast network as a basis to achieve a multicast mechanism. A multicast functionality with bounded delay can be defined similarly to the above unicast channel. The main difference is that once a message is inserted it is recorded once for each possible receiver. The adversary can add delays to any subset of messages, but again for any message the cumulative delay cannot exceed Δ. He is further allowed to do partial and inconsistent multicasts, i.e., where different messages are sent to different parties. This is the main difference of such a multicast network from a broadcast network. The detailed specification of the corresponding functionality $\mathcal{F}_{\text{N-MC}}$ is similar to that of $\mathcal{F}_{\text{U-CH}}$ and is provided in the full version [6]. There we also show how the simple round-based diffusion mechanism can be used to implement a multicast mechanism from unicast channels as long as the corresponding network among honest parties stays strongly connected. (A network graph is strongly connected if there is a directed path between any two nodes in the network, where the unicast channels are seen as the directed edges from sender to receiver.)

The Random Oracle. As usual in cryptographic proofs, the queries to the hash function are modeled by assuming access to a random oracle (functionality) $\mathcal{F}_{\text{RO}}$. This functionality is specified as follows: upon receiving a query $(\text{EVAL}, \mathsf{sid}, x)$ from a registered party, if x has not been queried before, a value y is chosen uniformly at random from $\{0,1\}^\kappa$ (for security parameter κ) and returned to the party (and the mapping (x, y) is internally stored). If x has been queried before, the corresponding y is returned.

Synchrony. Katz et al. [17], proposed a methodology for casting synchronous protocols in UC by assuming they have access to an ideal functionality $\mathcal{G}_{\text{CLOCK}}$, *the clock*, that allows parties to ensure that they proceed in synchronized rounds.

Informally, the idea is that the clock keeps track of a round variable whose value the parties can request by sending it (CLOCK-READ, sid_C). This value is updated only once all honest parties sent the clock a (CLOCK-UPDATE, sid_C) command.

Given such a clock, the authors of [17] describe how synchronous protocols can maintain their necessary round structure in UC: For every round ρ each party first executes all its round-ρ instructions and then sends the clock a CLOCK-UPDATE command. Subsequently, whenever activated, it sends the clock a CLOCK-READ command and does not advance to round $\rho+1$ before it sees the clocks variable being updated. This ensures that no honest party will start round $\rho+1$ before every honest party has completed round ρ. In [19], this idea was transfered to the (G)UC setting, by assuming that the clock is a global setup. This allows for different protocols to use the same clock and is the model we will also use here. The detailed specification of $\mathcal{G}_{\text{CLOCK}}$ is given in the full version [6].

As argued in [17], in order for an eventual-delivery (aka guaranteed termination) functionality to be UC implementable by a synchronous protocol, it needs to keep track of the number of activations that an honest party gets—so that it knows when to generate output for honest parties. This requires that the protocol itself, when described as a UC interactive Turing-machine instance (ITI), has a predictable behavior when it comes to the pattern of activations that it needs before it sends the clock an update command. We capture this property in a generic manner in Definition 1.

In order to make the definition better accessible, we briefly recall the mechanics of activations in UC. In a UC protocol execution, an honest party (ITI) gets activated either by receiving an input from the environment, or by receiving a message from one of its hybrid-functionalities (or from the adversary). Any activation results in the activated ITI performing some computation on its view of the protocol and its local state and ends with either the party sending a message to some of its hybrid functionalities or sending an output to the environment, or not sending any message. In either of this case, the party loses the activation.[6]

For any given protocol execution, we define the *honest-input sequence* $\vec{\mathcal{I}}_H$ to consist of all inputs that the environment gives to honest parties in the given execution (in the order that they were given) along with the identity of the party who received the input. For an execution in which the environment has given m inputs to the honest parties in total, $\vec{\mathcal{I}}_H$ is a vector of the form $((x_1, \mathtt{pid}_1), \ldots, (x_m, \mathtt{pid}_m))$, where x_i is the i-th input that was given in this execution, and $\mathtt{pid}_i$ is the corresponding party who received this input. We further define the *timed honest-input sequence*, denoted as $\vec{\mathcal{I}}_H^T$, to be the honest-input sequence augmented with the respective clock time when an input was given. If the timed honest-input sequence of an execution is $\vec{\mathcal{I}}_H^T = ((x_1, \mathtt{pid}_1, \tau_1), \ldots, (x_m, \mathtt{pid}_m, \tau_m))$, this means that $((x_1, \mathtt{pid}_1), \ldots, (x_m, \mathtt{pid}_m))$ is the honest-input sequence corresponding to this execution, and for each $i \in [n]$, τ_i is the time of the global clock when input x_i was handed to $\mathtt{pid}_i$.

[6] In the latter case the activation goes to the environment by default.

Definition 1. *A $\mathcal{G}_{\text{CLOCK}}$-hybrid protocol Π has a* predictable synchronization pattern *iff there exist an algorithm* $\texttt{predict-time}_{\Pi}(\cdot)$ *such that for any possible execution of Π (i.e., for any adversary and environment, and any choice of random coins) the following holds: If $\vec{\mathcal{I}}_H^T = ((x_1, \texttt{pid}_1, \tau_1), \ldots, (x_m, \texttt{pid}_m, \tau_m))$ is the corresponding timed honest-input sequence for this execution, then for any $i \in [m-1] : \texttt{predict-time}_{\Pi}((x_1, \texttt{pid}_1, \tau_1), \ldots, (x_i, \texttt{pid}_i, \tau_i)) = \tau_{i+1}$.*

As we argue, all synchronous protocol described in this work are designed to have a predictable synchronization pattern.

Assumptions as UC Functionality Wrappers. In order to prove statements about cryptographic protocols one often makes assumptions about what the environment can or cannot do. For example, a standard assumption in [16,29] is that in each round the adversary cannot do more calls to the random oracle than what the honest parties (collectively) can do. This can be captured by assuming a restricted environment and adversary which balances the amount of times that the adversary queries the random oracle. In a property-based treatment such as [16,29] this assumptions is typically acceptable.

However, in a simulation-based definition, restricting the class of adversaries and environments in a security statement means that we can no longer generically apply the composition theorem, which dismisses one of the major advantages of using simulation-based security in the first place. Therefore, instead of restricting the class of environments/adversaries, here we take a different approach to capture the fact that the adversary's access to the RO is restricted with respect to that of honest parties. In particular, we capture this assumption by means of a functionality wrapper that wraps the RO functionality and forces the above restrictions on the adversary, for example by assigning to each corrupted party at most q activations per round for a parameter q. To keep track of rounds the functionality registers with the global clock $\mathcal{G}_{\text{CLOCK}}$. We refer the reader to [6] for a detailed specification of such a wrapped random-oracle functionality $\mathcal{W}^q(\mathcal{F}_{\text{RO}})$.

Remark 1 (Functionally Black-box Use of the Network (Delay)). A key difference between the models in [16,29] is that in the latter the parties do not know any bound on the delay of the network. In particular, although both models are in the synchronous setting, in [29] a party in the protocol does not know when to expect a message which was sent to it in the previous round. Using terminology from [32], the protocol uses the channel in a *functionally black-box* manner. Restricting to such protocols—a restriction which we also adopt in this work—is in fact implying a weaker assumption on the protocol than standard (known) bounded-delay channel. Intuitively the reason is that no such protocol can realize a bounded-delay network with a known upper bound (unless it sacrifices termination) since the protocol cannot decide whether or not the bound has been reached.

3 The Transaction-Ledger Functionality

In this section we describe our ledger functionality, denoted as $\mathcal{G}_{\text{LEDGER}}$, which can, for example, be achieved by (a UC version) of the Bitcoin protocol. As in [19], our ledger is parametrized by certain algorithms/predicates that allow us to capture a more general version of a ledger which can be instantiated by various cryptocurrencies. Since our abstraction of the Bitcoin protocol is in the synchronous model of computation (this is consistent with known approaches in the cryptographic literature), our ledger is also designed for this synchronous model. Nonetheless, several of our modeling choices are made with the foresight of removing or limiting the use of the clock and leaving room for less synchrony.

At a high level, our ledger $\mathcal{G}_{\text{LEDGER}}$ has a similar structure as the ledger proposed in [19]. Concretely, anyone (whether an honest miner or the adversary) might submit a transaction which is validated by means of a predicate Validate, and if it is found valid it is added to a buffer buffer. The adversary $\mathcal{A}$ is informed that the transaction was received and is given its contents.[7] Informally, this buffer also contains transactions that, although validated, are not yet deep enough in the blockchain to be considered out-of-reach for a adversary.[8] Periodically, $\mathcal{G}_{\text{LEDGER}}$ fetches some of the transactions in the buffer, and using an algorithm Blockify creates a block including these transactions and adds this block to its permanent state state, which is a data structure that includes the part of the blockchain the adversary can no longer change. This corresponds to the *common prefix* in [16,29]. Any miner or the adversary is allowed to request a read of the contents of the state.

This sketched specification is simple, but in order to have a ledger that can be implemented by existing blockchain protocols, we need to relax this functionality by giving the adversary more power to interfere with it and influence its behavior. Before sketching the necessary relaxations we discuss the need for a new ledger definition and it potential use as a global setup.

Remark 2 (Impossibility to realize the ledger of [19]*).* The main reasons why the ledger in [19] is not realizable by known protocols under reasonable assumptions are as follows: first, their ledger guarantees that parties always obtain the same common state. Even with strong synchrony assumptions, this is not realizable since an adversary, who just mined a new block, is not forced to inform each party instantaneously (or at all) and thus could, e.g., make parties observe different lengths of the same prefix. Second, the adversarial influence is restricted to permuting the buffer. This is too optimistic, as in reality the adversary can try to mine a new block and possibly exclude certain transactions. Also, this excludes any possibility to quantify quality. Third, letting the update rate be fixed does not adequately reflect the probabilistic nature of blockchain protocols.

---

7 This is inevitable since we assume non-private communication, where the adversary sees any message as soon as it is sent, even if the sender and receiver are honest.

8 E.g., in [19] the adversary is allowed to permute the contents of the buffer.

Remark 3 (On the sound usage of a ledger as a global setup). As presented in [19], a UC ledger functionality $\mathcal{G}_{\text{LEDGER}}$ can be cast as a global setup [11] which allows different protocols to share state. This is true for any UC functionality as stated in [11,12]. Nonetheless, as pointed out in the recent work of Canetti et al. [12], one needs to be extra careful when replacing a global setup by its implementation, e.g., in the case of $\mathcal{G}_{\text{LEDGER}}$ by the UC Bitcoin protocol of Sect. 4. Indeed, such a replacement does not, in general, preserve a realization proof of some ideal functionality $\mathcal{F}$ that is conducted in a ledger-hybrid world, because the simulator in that proof might rely on specific capabilities that are not available any more after replacement (as the global setup is also replaced in the ideal world). The authors of [12] provide a sufficient condition for such a replacement to be sound. This condition is generally too strong to be satisfied by any natural ledger implementation, which opens the question of devising relaxed sufficient conditions for sound replacements in an MPC context. As this work focuses on the realization of ledger functionalities per se, we can treat $\mathcal{G}_{\text{LEDGER}}$ as a standard UC functionality.

In the following, we review the necessary relaxations to obtain a realizable ledger. We conclude this section with the specification of our generic ledger functionality.

State-Buffer Validation. The first relaxation is with respect to the invariant that is enforced by the validation predicate $\mathsf{Validate}$. Concretely, in [19] it is assumed that the validation predicate enforces that the buffer does not include conflicting transactions, i.e., upon receipt of a transaction, $\mathsf{Validate}$ checks that it is not in conflict with the state and the buffer, and if so the transaction is added to the buffer. However, in reality we do not know how to implement such a strong filter, as different miners might be working on different, potentially conflicting sets of transactions. The only time when it becomes clear which of these conflicting transactions will make it into the state is once one of them has been inserted into a block which has made it deep enough into the blockchain (i.e., has become part of state). Hence, given that the buffer includes all transactions that might end up in the state, it might at some point include both conflicting transactions.

To enable us for a provably implementable ledger, in this work we take a different approach. The validate predicate will be less restrictive as to which transactions make it into the buffer. Concretely, at the very least, $\mathsf{Validate}$ will enforce the invariant that no single transaction in the buffer contradicts the state state, while different transactions in buffer might contradict each other. Looking ahead, a stronger version that is achievable by employing digital signatures (presented in Sect. 5), could enforce that no submitted transaction contradicts other submitted transactions. As in [19], whenever a new transaction x is submitted to $\mathcal{G}_{\text{LEDGER}}$, it is passed to $\mathsf{Validate}$ which takes as input a transaction and the current state and decides if x should be added to the buffer. Additionally, as buffer might include conflicts, whenever a new block is added to the state, the buffer (i.e., every single transaction in buffer) is re-validated using $\mathsf{Validate}$ and invalid transactions in buffer are removed. To allow for this re-validation to be generic, transactions that are added to the buffer are accompanied by certain metadata, i.e., the identity of the submitter, a unique transaction ID `txid` [9], or the time τ when x was received.

State Update Policies and Security Guarantees. The second relaxation is with respect to the rate and the form and/or origin of transactions that make it into a block. Concretely, instead of assuming that the state is extended in fixed time intervals, we allow the adversary to define when this update occurs. This is done by allowing the adversary, at any point, to propose what we refer to as the next-block candidate `NxtBC`. This is a data structure containing the contents of the next block that $\mathcal{A}$ wants to have inserted into the state. Leaving `NxtBC` empty can be interpreted as the adversary signaling that it does not want the state to be updated in the current clock tick.

Of course allowing the adversary to always decide what makes it into the state `state`, or if anything ever does, yields a very weak ledger. Intuitively, this would be a ledger that only guarantees the common prefix property [16] but no liveness or chain quality. Therefore, to enable us to capture also stronger properties of blockchain protocols we parameterize the ledger by an algorithm `ExtendPolicy` that, informally, enforces a state-update policy restricting the freedom of the adversary to choose the next block and implementing an appropriate compliance-enforcing mechanism in case the adversary does not follow the policy. This enforcing mechanism simply returns a default policy-complying block using the current contents of the buffer. We point out that a good simulator for realizing the ledger will avoid triggering this compliance-enforcing mechanism, as this could result in an uncontrolled update of the state which would yield a potential distinguishing advantage. In other words, a good simulator, i.e., ideal-world adversary, always complies with the policy.

In a nutshell, `ExtendPolicy` takes the current contents of the buffer `buffer`, along with the adversary's recommendation `NxtBC`, and the *block-insertion times vector* $\vec{\tau}_{\mathtt{state}}$. The latter is a vector listing the times when each block was inserted into `state`. The output of `ExtendPolicy` is a vector including the blocks to be appended to the state during the next state-extend time-slot (where again, `ExtendPolicy` outputting an empty vector is a signal to not extend). To ensure that `ExtendPolicy` can also enforce properties that depend on who inserted how many (or which) blocks into the state—e.g. the so-called *chain quality* property from [16]—we also pass to it the timed honest-input sequence $\vec{\mathcal{I}}_H^T$ (cf. Sect. 2).

Some examples of how `ExtendPolicy` allows us to define ways that the protocol might restrict the adversary's interference in the state-update include the following properties from [16]:

- *Liveness* corresponds to `ExtendPolicy` enforcing the following policy: If the state has not been extended for more that a certain number of rounds and the

[9] In Bitcoin, `txid` would be the hash-pointer corresponding to this transaction. Note that the generic ledger can capture explicit guarantees on the ability or disability to link transactions, as this crucially depends on the concrete choice of an ID mechanism.

simulator keeps recommending an empty NxtBC, ExtendPolicy can choose some of the transactions in the buffer (e.g., those that have been in the buffer for a long time) and add them to the next block. Note that a good ideal-world adversary will never allow for this automatic update to happen and will make sure that he keeps the state extend rate within the right amount.

- *Chain quality* corresponds to ExtendPolicy enforcing the following policy: ExtendPolicy looks into the blocks of state for a special type of transaction (corresponding to a so-called coinbase transaction) and parses the state (using the sequence of honest inputs $\vec{\mathcal{I}}_H^T$ and the block-insertion times vector $\vec{\tau}_{\texttt{state}}$) to see how long ago (in time or block-number) the last block that gave a block-mining reward to some honest party was inserted into the state. If this happened "too long" ago (this will be a parameter of this ExtendPolicy), then ExtendPolicy forces the coinbase transaction of the next block to have as the miner ID the ID submitted by some honest miner.

In addition to the above standard properties, ExtendPolicy allows us to also capture additional security properties of various blockchain protocols, e.g., the fact that honest transactions eventually make it into a block and the fact that transactions with higher rewards make it into a block faster than others.

In Sect. 4 where we prove the security of Bitcoin, we will provide the concrete specification of Validate and ExtendPolicy for which the Bitcoin protocol realizes our ledger.

Output Slackness and Sliding Window of State Blocks. The common prefix property guarantees that blocks which are sufficiently deep in the blockchain of an honest miner will eventually be included in the blockchain of every honest miner. Stated differently, if an honest miner receives as output from the ledger a state state, every honest miner will eventually receive state as its output. However, in reality we cannot guarantee that at any given point in time all honest miners see exactly the same blockchain length; this is especially the case when network delays are incorporated into the model, but it is also true in the zero-delay model of [16]. Thus it is unclear how state can be defined so that at any point all parties have the same view on it.

Therefore, to have a ledger implementable by standard assumptions we make the following relaxation: We interpret state as the view of the state of the miner with the longest blockchain. And we allow the adversary to define for every honest miner p_i a subchain $\texttt{state}_i$ of state of length $|\texttt{state}_i| = \texttt{pt}_i$ that corresponds to what p_i gets as a response when he reads the state of the ledger (formally, the adversary can fix a pointer $\texttt{pt}_i$). For convenience, we denote by $\texttt{state}|_{\texttt{pt}_i}$ the subchain of state that finishes in the $\texttt{pt}_i$-th block. Once again, to avoid over-relaxing the functionality to an unuseful setup, our ledger allows the adversary to only move the pointers forward and it forbids the adversary to define pointers for honest miners that are too far apart, i.e., more than windowSize state blocks. The parameter $\texttt{windowSize} \in \mathbb{N}$ denotes a core parameter of the ledger. In particular, the parameter windowSize reflects the similarity of the blockchain to the dynamics of a so-called *sliding window*, where the window of size windowSize contains the possible views of honest miners onto state and where the head of the window advances with the head of the state. In addition, it is convenient to express security properties of concrete blockchain protocols, including the properties discussed above, as assertions that hold within such a sliding window (for any point in time).

Synchrony. In order to keep the ideal execution indistinguishable from the real execution, the adversary should be unable to use the clock for distinguishing. Since in the ideal world when a dummy party receives a CLOCK-UPDATE-message for $\mathcal{G}_{\text{CLOCK}}$ it will forward it, the ledger needs to be responsible that the clock counter does not advance before all honest parties have received sufficiently many activations. This is achieved by the use of the function `predict-time`($\vec{\mathcal{I}}_H^T$) (see Definition 1), which, as we show, is defined for our ledger protocol. This function allows $\mathcal{G}_{\text{LEDGER}}$ to predict when the protocol would update the round and ensure that it only allows the clock to advance if and only if the protocol would. Observe that the ledger sees all protocol-relevant inputs/activations to honest parties and can therefore easily keep track of the honest inputs sequence $\vec{\mathcal{I}}_H^T$.

A final observation is with respect to guarantees that the protocol (and therefore also the ledger) can give to recently registered honest parties. Consider the following scenario: An honest party registers as miner in round r and waits to receive from honest parties the transactions to mine and the current longest blockchain. In Bitcoin, upon joining, the miner sends out a special request—we denote this here as a special NEW-MINER-message—and as soon as any party receives it, it responds with the set of transactions and longest blockchain it knows. Due to the network delay, the parties might take up to Δ rounds to receive the NEW-MINER notification, and their response might also take up to Δ rounds before it arrives to the new miner. However, because we do not make any assumption on honest parties knowing Δ (see Remark 1) they need to start mining as soon as a message arrives (otherwise they might wait indefinitely). But now the adversary, in the worst case, can make these parties mine on any block he wants and have them accept any valid chain he wants as the current state while they wait for the network's response: simply delay everything sent to these parties by honest miners by the maximum delay Δ, and instead, immediately deliver what you want them to work on. Thus, for the first `Delay` $:= 2\Delta$ rounds[10] (where `Delay` is a parameter of our ledger) these parties are practically in the control of the adversary and their computing power is contributed to his. We will call such miners *de-synchronized* and denote the set of such miners by $\mathcal{P}_{DS}$. The formal specification of our ledger functionality $\mathcal{G}_{\text{LEDGER}}$ is given in the following. Using standard notation, we write $[n]$ to denote the set $\{1, \ldots, n\}$.

[10] For technical reasons described in Sect. 4.1, Δ rounds in the protocol correspond to 2Δ clock-ticks.

Functionality $\mathcal{G}_{\text{LEDGER}}$

$\mathcal{G}_{\text{LEDGER}}$ is parametrized by four algorithms, Validate, ExtendPolicy, Blockify, and predict-time$_{BC}$, along with two parameters: windowSize, Delay $\in \mathbb{N}$. The functionality manages variables state, NxtBC, buffer, τ_L, and $\vec{\tau}_{\text{state}}$, as described above. The variables are initialized as follows: state $:= \vec{\tau}_{\text{state}} :=$ NxtBC $:= \varepsilon$, buffer $:= \emptyset$, $\tau_L = 1$.

The functionality maintains the set of registered parties $\mathcal{P}$, the (sub-)set of honest parties $\mathcal{H} \subseteq \mathcal{P}$, and the (sub-set) of de-synchronized honest parties $\mathcal{P}_{DS} \subset \mathcal{H}$. The set $\mathcal{P}, \mathcal{H}, \mathcal{P}_{DS}$ are all initially set to $\emptyset$. When a new honest party is registered, it is added to all $\mathcal{P}_{DS}$ (hence also to $\mathcal{H}$ and $\mathcal{P}$) and the current time of registration is also recorded; similarly, when a party is deregistered, it is removed from both $\mathcal{P}$ and $\mathcal{P}_{DS}$.

For each party $p_i \in \mathcal{P}$ the functionality maintains a pointer pt_i (initially set to 1) and a current-state view $\text{state}_i := \varepsilon$ (initially set to empty). The functionality also keeps track of the timed honest-input sequence in a vector $\vec{\mathcal{I}}_H^T$ (initially $\vec{\mathcal{I}}_H^T := \varepsilon$).

Upon receiving any input I from any party or from the adversary, send (CLOCK-READ, sid$_C$) to $\mathcal{G}_{\text{CLOCK}}$ and upon receiving response (CLOCK-READ, sid$_C, \tau$) set $\tau_L := \tau$ and do the following:

1. If I was received by an honest party $p_i \in \mathcal{P}$:
   (a) Set $\vec{\mathcal{I}}_H^T := \vec{\mathcal{I}}_H^T || (I, p_i, \tau_L)$;
   (b) Compute $\vec{N} = (\vec{N}_1, \ldots, \vec{N}_\ell) :=$ ExtendPolicy($\vec{\mathcal{I}}_H^T$, state, NxtBC, buffer, $\vec{\tau}_{\text{state}}$) and if $\vec{N} \neq \varepsilon$ set state := state||Blockify($\vec{N}_1$)||...||Blockify($\vec{N}_\ell$) and $\vec{\tau}_{\text{state}} := \vec{\tau}_{\text{state}} || \tau_L^\ell$, where $\tau_L^\ell = \tau_L || \ldots, || \tau_L$.
   (c) For each BTX $\in$ buffer: if Validate(BTX, state, buffer) $= 0$ then delete BTX from buffer.
   (d) If there exists $j \in [\ell]$ with $p_{i_j} \in \mathcal{H} \setminus \mathcal{P}_{DS}$: $|\text{state}| - \hat{\text{pt}}_i \leq$ windowSize or $\hat{\text{pt}}_{i_j} \geq |\text{state}_{i_j}|$, then for every $j \in [\ell]$ set $\text{pt}_i := |\text{state}| - |\vec{\mathbf{N}}|$ for every $p_i \in \mathcal{P}$.
2. Let $\hat{\mathcal{P}} \subseteq \mathcal{P}_{DS}$ denote the set of desynchronized honest parties that were registered at time $\tau' \leq \tau_L -$ Delay. Set $\mathcal{P}_{DS} := \mathcal{P}_{DS} \setminus \hat{\mathcal{P}}$.
3. Depending on the above input I and its sender's ID, $\mathcal{G}_{\text{LEDGER}}$ executes the corresponding code from the following list:
   - *Submiting a transaction:*
     If $I =$ (SUBMIT, sid, x) and is received from a party $p_i \in \mathcal{P}$ or from $\mathcal{A}$ (on behalf of a corrupted party p_i) do the following:
     (a) Choose a unique transaction ID txid and set BTX $:= (x, \text{txid}, \tau_L, p_i)$
     (b) If Validate(BTX, state, buffer) $= 1$, then buffer := buffer $\cup$ {BTX}.
     (c) Send (SUBMIT, BTX) to $\mathcal{A}$.
   - *Reading the state:*
     If $I =$ (READ, sid) is received from a party $p_i \in \mathcal{P}$ then set $\text{state}_i := \text{state}|_{\min\{\text{pt}_i, |\text{state}|\}}$ and return (READ, sid, state$_i$) to the requestor. If the requestor is $\mathcal{A}$ then send (state, buffer, $\vec{\mathcal{I}}_H^T$) to $\mathcal{A}$.

- *Updating the state:*
  If $I = (\text{MAINTAIN-LEDGER}, \mathsf{sid}, \mathsf{minerID})$ is received by an honest party $p_i \in \mathcal{P}$ and (after updating $\vec{\mathcal{I}}_H^T$ as above) $\mathtt{predict\text{-}time}(\vec{\mathcal{I}}_H^T) = \hat{\tau} > \tau_L$ then send $(\text{CLOCK-UPDATE}, \mathsf{sid}_C)$ to $\mathcal{G}_{\text{CLOCK}}$. Else send I to $\mathcal{A}$.
- *The adversary proposing the next block:*
  If $I = (\text{NEXT-BLOCK}, (\mathtt{txid}_1, \ldots, \mathtt{txid}_\ell))$ is sent from the adversary, update $\mathtt{NxtBC}$ as follows:
  (a) Set $\mathtt{NxtBC} := \varepsilon$.
  (b) For $i = 1, \ldots, \ell$ do: if there exists $\mathtt{BTX} := (x, \mathtt{txid}, \mathsf{minerID}, \tau_L, p_i) \in \mathsf{buffer}$ with ID $\mathtt{txid} = \mathtt{txid}_i$ then set $\mathtt{NxtBC} := \mathtt{NxtBC}||\mathtt{txid}_i$.
  (c) Output $(\text{NEXT-BLOCK}, ok)$ to $\mathcal{A}$.
- *The adversary setting state-slackness:*
  If $I = (\text{SET-SLACK}, (p_{i_1}, \hat{\mathtt{pt}}_{i_1}), \ldots, (p_{i_\ell}, \hat{\mathtt{pt}}_{i_\ell}))$, with $\{p_{i_1}, \ldots, p_{i_\ell}\} \subseteq \mathcal{H} \setminus \mathcal{P}_{DS}$ is received from the adversary $\mathcal{A}$ do the following:
  (a) If for all $j \in [\ell] : |\mathsf{state}| - \hat{\mathtt{pt}}_{i_j} \leq \mathtt{windowSize}$ and $\hat{\mathtt{pt}}_{i_j} \geq |\mathsf{state}_{i_j}|$, set $\mathtt{pt}_{i_1} := \hat{\mathtt{pt}}_{i_1}$ for every $j \in [\ell]$ and return $(\text{SET-SLACK}, ok)$ to $\mathcal{A}$.
  (b) Otherwise set $\mathtt{pt}_{i_j} := |\mathsf{state}|$ for all $j \in [\ell]$.
- *The adversary setting the state for desychronized parties:*
  If $I = (\text{DESYNC-STATE}, (p_{i_1}, \mathsf{state}'_{i_1}), \ldots, (p_{i_\ell}, \mathsf{state}'_{i_\ell}))$, with $\{p_{i_1}, \ldots, p_{i_\ell}\} \subseteq \mathcal{P}_{DS}$ is received from the adversary $\mathcal{A}$, set $\mathsf{state}_{i_j} := \mathsf{state}'_{i_j}$ for each $j \in [\ell]$ and return $(\text{DESYNC-STATE}, ok)$ to $\mathcal{A}$.

4 Bitcoin as a Transaction Ledger Protocol

In this section we prove our main theorem, namely that, under appropriate assumptions, Bitcoin realizes an instantiation of the ledger functionality from the previous section. More concretely, we cast the Bitcoin protocol as a UC protocol, where consistent with the existing methodology we assume that the protocol is synchronous, i.e., parties can keep track of the current round by using an appropriate global clock functionality. We first describe the UC protocol, denoted Ledger-Protocol, in Sect. 4.1 which abstracts the components of Bitcoin that are relevant for the construction of such a ledger—similar to how the backbone protocol [16] captures core Bitcoin properties in their respective model of computation. Later, in Sect. 4.2, we specify the ledger functionality $\mathcal{G}_{\text{LEDGER}}^{\text{B}}$ that is implemented by the UC ledger protocol as an instance of our general ledger functionality, i.e., by providing appropriate instantiations of algorithms Validate, Blockify, and ExtendPolicy. In fact, for the sake of generality, we specify generic classes of Validate and Blockify and parameterize our Ledger-Protocol with these classes, so that the security statement still stays generic. We then prove our main theorem (Theorem 1) which can be described informally as follows:

Theorem (*informal*). *Let Validate be the class of predicates that only take into account the current state and a transaction (i.e., no transaction IDs, time, or party IDs), and let* windowSize $= \omega(\log \kappa)$, *κ being the length of the outputs of the random oracle. Then, for an appropriate* ExtendPolicy *and for any function* Blockify, *the protocol* Ledger-Protocol *instantiated with algorithms* Validate *and* $\mathsf{Blockify}$ *securely realizes a ledger functionality* $\mathcal{G}_{\text{LEDGER}}^{\mathcal{B}}$ *(the generic ledger instantiated with the above functions) under the following assumptions on network delays and mining power, where mining power is roughly understood as the ability to find proofs of work via queries to the random oracle (and will be formally defined later):*

- *In any round of the protocol execution, the collective mining power of the adversary, contributed by corrupted and temporarily de-synchronized miners, does not exceed the mining power of honest (and synchronized) parties in that round. The exact relation additionally captures the (negative) impact of network delays on the coordination of mining power of honest parties.*
- *No message can be delayed in the network by more than* $\Delta = O(1)$ *rounds.*

We prove the above theorem via what we believe is a useful modularization of the Bitcoin protocol (cf. Fig. 1). Informally, this modularization distills out form the protocol a reactive *state-extend* subprocess which captures the lottery that decides which miner gets to advance the blockchain next and additionally the process of propagating this state to other miners. Lemma 1 shows that the state-extend module/subprocess implements an appropriate reactive UC functionality $\mathcal{F}_{\text{STX}}$. We can then use the UC composition theorem which allows us to argue security of Ledger-Protocol in a simpler hybrid world where, instead of using this subprocess, parties make calls to the functionality $\mathcal{F}_{\text{STX}}$. We conclude this section (Subsect. 4.4) by showing how both the GKL and PSs protocols can be cast as special cases of our protocol which provides the basis for comparing the different models and their respective assumptions.

4.1 The Bitcoin Ledger as a UC Protocol

In the following we provide the formal description of protocol Ledger-Protocol. The protocol assumes as hybrids the multi-cast network $\mathcal{F}_{\text{N-MC}}$ (recall that we assume that this network does have an upper bound Δ on the delay unknown to the protocol) and a random oracle functionality $\mathcal{F}_{\text{RO}}$. Before providing the detailed specification of our ledger protocol, we establish some useful notation and terminology that we use throughout this section. For compatibility with existing work, wherever it does not overload notation, we use some of the terminology and notation from [16].

Blockchain. A *blockchain* $\mathcal{C} = \mathbf{B}_1, \ldots, \mathbf{B}_n$ is a (finite) sequence of blocks where each *block* $\mathbf{B}_i = \langle \mathsf{s}_i, \mathtt{st}_i, \mathsf{n}_i \rangle$ is a triple consisting of the *pointer* s_i, the *state block* $\mathtt{st}_i$, and the *nonce* n_i. A special block is the *genesis block* $\mathbf{G} = \langle \bot, \mathtt{gen}, \bot \rangle$ which contains the genesis state $\mathtt{gen}$. The *head* of chain $\mathcal{C}$ is the block $\mathsf{head}(\mathcal{C}) := \mathbf{B}_n$ and the *length* $\mathsf{length}(\mathcal{C})$ of the chain is the number of blocks, i.e., $\mathsf{length}(\mathcal{C}) = n$. The chain $\mathcal{C}^{\lceil k}$ is the (potentially empty) sequence of the first $\mathsf{length}(\mathcal{C}) - k$ blocks of $\mathcal{C}$. The *state* $\vec{\mathtt{st}}$ corresponding to $\mathcal{C}$ is defined as a sequence of the corresponding state blocks, i.e., $\vec{\mathtt{st}} := \mathtt{st}_1 || \ldots || \mathtt{st}_n$. In other words, one should think of the blockchain $\mathcal{C}$ as an encoding of its underlying state $\vec{\mathtt{st}}$; such an encoding might, e.g., organize $\mathcal{C}$ is an efficient searchable data structure as is

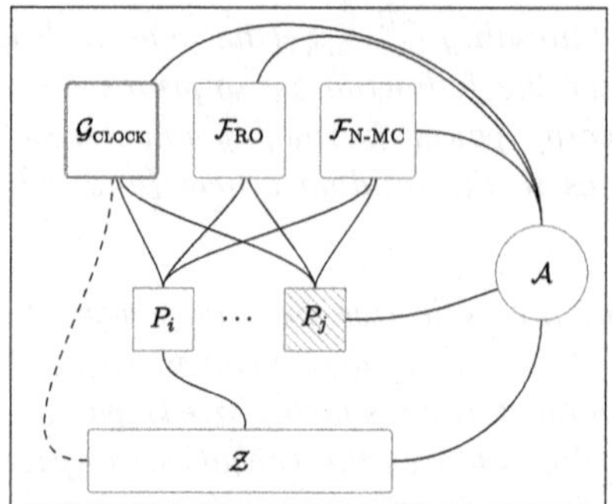

(a) In the real world parties have access to the global clock $\mathcal{G}_{\text{CLOCK}}$, the random oracle $\mathcal{F}_{\text{RO}}$, and network $\mathcal{F}_{\text{N-MC}}$. Here, parties execute the Bitcoin protocol Ledger-Protocol

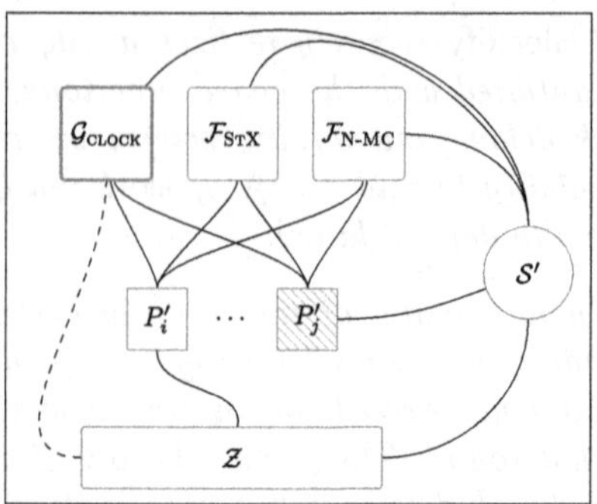

(b) In the hybrid world parties have access to the state-exchange functionality $\mathcal{F}_{\text{STX}}$ (instead of the random oracle). Here, parties execute the modularized protocol Modular-Ledger-Protocol

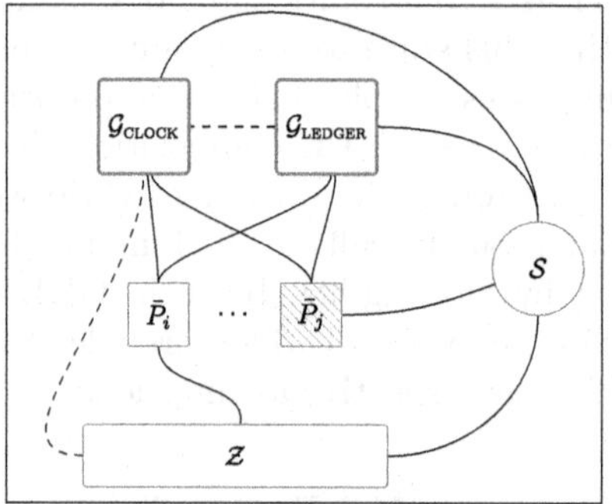

(c) In the ideal world, dummy parties have access to the global clock $\mathcal{G}_{\text{CLOCK}}$ and the ledger $\mathcal{G}_{\text{LEDGER}}$

Fig. 1. Modularization of the Bitcoin protocol.

the case in the Bitcoin protocol where a blockchain is a linked list implemented with hash-pointers.

In the protocol, the blockchain is the data structure storing a sequence of entries, often referred to as transactions. Furthermore, as in [19], in order to capture blockchains with syntactically different state encoding, we use an algorithm $\text{blockify}_{\mathcal{B}}$ to map a vector of transactions into a state block. Thus, each block $\mathtt{st} \in \vec{\mathtt{st}}$ (except the genesis state) of the state encoded in the blockchain has the form $\mathtt{st} = \text{Blockify}(\vec{N})$ where $\vec{N}$ is a vector of transactions.

For a blockchain $\mathcal{C}$ to be considered a valid blockchain, it needs to satisfy certain conditions. Concretely, the validity of a blockchain $\mathcal{C} = \mathbf{B}_1, \ldots, \mathbf{B}_n$ where $\mathbf{B}_i = \langle \mathsf{s}_i, \mathtt{st}_i, \mathsf{n}_i \rangle$ depends on two aspects: *chain-level* validity, also referred to as syntactic validity, and a *state-level* validity also referred to as semantic validity. Syntactic validity is defined with respect to a difficulty parameter $\mathsf{D} \in [\kappa]$, where

κ is the security parameter, and a given hash function $H(\cdot) : \{0,1\}^* \to \{0,1\}^\kappa$; it requires that, for each $i > 1$, the value s_i contained in $\mathbf{B}_i$ satisfies $\mathsf{s}_i = H[\mathbf{B}_{i-1}]$ and that additionally $H[\mathbf{B}_i] < \mathsf{D}$ holds.

The semantic validity on the other hand is defined on the state $\vec{\mathtt{st}}$ encoded in the blockchain $\mathcal{C}$ and specifies whether this content is valid (which might depend on a particular application). The validation predicate Validate defined in the ledger functionality (cf. Sect. 3) plays a similar role. In fact, the semantic validity of the blockchain can be defined using an algorithm that we denote isvalidstate which is builds upon the Validate predicate. The idea is that for any choice of Validate, the blockchain protocol using isvalidstate for semantic validation of the chain implements the ledger parametrized with Validate. More specifically, algorithm isvalidstate checks that a given blockchain state can be built in an iterative manner, such that each contained transaction is considered valid according to Validate upon insertion. It further ensures that the state starts with the genesis state and that state blocks contain a special *coin-base* transaction $\mathsf{x}^{\text{coin-base}}_{\text{minerID}}$ which assigns them to a miner. We remark that this only works for predicates Validate which ignore all information other than the state and transaction that is being validated.[11] To avoid confusion, throughout this section we use $\mathsf{ValidTx}_{\text{B}}$ to refer to the validate predicate with the above restriction. The pseudo-code of the algorithm isvalidstate which builds upon $\mathsf{ValidTx}_{\text{B}}$ is provided in the full version [6]. We succinctly denote by $\mathsf{isvalidchain}_D(\mathcal{C})$ the predicate that returns true iff chain $\mathcal{C}$ satisfies syntactic and semantic validity as defined above.

The Ledger Protocol. We are now ready to formally define our blockchain protocol $\mathsf{Ledger\text{-}Protocol}_{q,\mathsf{D},T}$ (we usually omit the parameters when clear from the context). The protocol allows an arbitrary number of parties/miners to communicate by means of a multicast network $\mathcal{F}_{\text{N-MC}}$. Note that this means that the adversary can send different messages to different parties. New miners might dynamically joint or leave the protocol by means of the registration/de-registration commands: when they join they register with all associated functionalities and when they leave they deregister.[12]

Each party maintains a local blockchain which initially consists of the genesis block. The chains of honest parties might differ (but as we will prove, it will have a common prefix which will define the ledger state). New transactions are added in a 'mining process'. First, a party collects valid transactions (according to $\mathsf{ValidTx}_{\text{B}}$) and creates a new state block $\mathtt{st}$ using $\mathsf{blockify}_{\text{B}}$. Next, the party attempts to mine a new block which can be validly added to their local blockchain. The mining is done using the $\mathsf{extendchain}_D$ algorithm which takes as inputs a chain $\mathcal{C}$, a state block $\mathtt{st}$, and the number q of attempts. The core

[11] Recall that in the general ledger description, Validate might depend on some associated metadata; although this might be useful to capture alternative blockchains, it is not the case for Bitcoin.

[12] Note that when a party registers to a local functionality such as the network or the random oracle it does not lose its activation token. This is a subtle point to ensure that the real and ideal worlds are in-sync regarding activations.

idea of the algorithm is to find a proof-of-work which allows to extend $\mathcal{C}$ by a block which encodes st. The pseudo-code of this algorithm is provided in the full version [6]. After each mining attempt parties will multicast their current chain. A party will replace its local chain if it receives a longer chain. When queried to output the state of the ledger, Ledger-Protocol outputs the state of its longest chain, where it first chops-off the most recent T blocks. This behavior will ensure that all honest parties output a consistent ledger state.

As already mentioned, our Bitcoin-Ledger protocol proceeds in rounds which are implemented by using a global synchronization clock $\mathcal{G}_{\text{CLOCK}}$. For formal reasons that have to do with how activations are handled in UC, we have each round correspond to two sub-rounds (also known as mini-rounds). To avoid confusion we refer to clock rounds as *clock-ticks.* We say that a protocol is in round r if the current time of the clock is $\tau \in \{2r-1, 2r\}$. In fact, having two clock-ticks per round is the way to ensure in synchronous UC that messages (e.g., a block) sent within a round are delivered at the beginning of the next round. The idea is that each round is divided into two mini-rounds, where each mini-round corresponds to a clock tick, and treat the first mini-round as a *working mini-round* where parties might mine new blocks and submit them to the multicast network for delivery, and in the second *reading mini-round* they simply fetch messages from the network to obtain messages sent in the previous round. The pseudo-code of this UC blockchain protocol, denoted as Ledger-Protocol, is provided in the full version [6], where we also argue that the protocol satisfies Definition 1.

4.2 The Bitcoin Ledger

We next show how to instantiate the ledger functionality from Sect. 3 with appropriate parameters so that it is implemented by protocol Ledger-Protocol. To define this Bitcoin ledger $\mathcal{G}^{\text{B}}_{\text{LEDGER}}$, we need to give specific instantiations of the three functions Validate, Blockify, and ExtendPolicy.

As mentioned above, in case of Validate we use the same predicate as the protocol uses to validate the states: For a given transaction x and a given state state, the predicate decides whether this transaction is valid with respect to state. Given such a validation predicate, the ledger validation predicate takes a specific simple form which, excludes dependency on anything other than the transaction x and the state state, i.e., for any values of txid, τ_L, p_i, and buffer:

$$\mathsf{Validate}((\mathtt{x}, \mathtt{txid}, \tau_L, p_i), \mathsf{state}, \mathsf{buffer}) := \mathsf{ValidTx}_{\text{B}}(\mathtt{x}, \mathsf{state}).$$

Blockify can be an arbitrary algorithm, and if the same algorithm is used in Ledger-Protocol the security proof will go through. However, as discussed below (in Definition 2), a meaningful Blockify should be in certain relation with the ledger's Validate predicate. (This relation is satisfied by the Bitcoin protocol.)

Finally, we define ExtendPolicy. At a high level, upon receiving a list of possible candidate blocks which should go into the state of the ledger, ExtendPolicy does the following: for each block it first verifies that the blocks are valid with respect to the state they extend. (Only valid blocks might be added to the state.) Moreover, ExtendPolicy ensures the following property:

1. The speed of the ledger is not too fast. This is implemented by defining a bound $\texttt{minTime}_{\text{window}}$ on the time (number of rounds) within which no more than windowSize state blocks can be added.
2. The speed of the ledger is not too slow. This is implemented by defining a bound $\texttt{maxTime}_{\text{window}}$ within which at least windowSize state blocks have to be added. This is known as minimal chain-growth.
3. The adversary cannot claim too many block for parties it is corrupting. This is formally enforced by defining an upper bound η on the number of these so-called adversarial blocks within a sequence of state blocks. This is known as chain quality. Formally, this is enforced by requiring that a certain fraction of blocks need to start with a coinbase transaction that is associated with an actual honest and synchronized party.
4. Last but not least, ExtendPolicy guarantees that if a transaction is "old enough", and still valid with respect to the actual state, then it is included into the state. This is a weak form of guaranteeing that a transaction will make it into the state unless it is in conflict. As we show in Sect. 5, this guarantee can be amplified by using digital signatures.

In order to enforce these policies, ExtendPolicy first defines an alternative block, which satisfies all of the above criteria in an ideal way, and whenever it catches the adversary in trying to propose blocks that do not obey the policies, it punishes the adversary by proposing its own generated block. The formal description of the extend policy (as pseudo-code) for $\mathcal{G}^{\text{B}}_{\text{LEDGER}}$ is given in the full version [6].

On the Relation Between Blockify and Validate. As already discussed above, ExtendPolicy guarantees that the adversary cannot block the extension of the state indefinitely, and that occasionally an honest miner will receive the block reward (via the coin-base) transaction. These correspond to the chain-growth and chain-quality properties from [16]. However, our generic ExtendPolicy makes explicit that a priori, we cannot exclude that the chain always extends with blocks that include a coin-base transaction only, i.e., any submitted transaction is ignored and never inserted into a new blocks. This issue is an orthogonal one to ensuring that honest transactions are not invalidated by adversarial interaction—which, as argued in [16], is achieved by adding digital signatures.

To see where this could be problematic in general, consider a blockify that, at a certain point, creates a block that renders all possible future transactions invalid. Observe that this does not mean that our protocol is insecure and that this is as well possible for the protocols of [16,29]; indeed our proof shows that the protocol will give exactly the same guarantees as an $\mathcal{G}_{\text{LEDGER}}$ parametrized with such an algorithm Blockify.

Nonetheless, a look in reality indicates that this situation never occurs with Bitcoin. To capture that this is the case, Validate and Blockify need to be in a certain relation with each other. Informally, this relation should ensure that the above sketched situation never occurs. A way to ensure this, which is already implemented by the Bitcoin protocol, is by restricting Blockify to only make an invertible manipulation of the blocks when they are inserted into the state—e.g., be an encoding function of a code—and define Validate to depend on the inverse of Blockify. This is captured in the following definition.

Definition 2. *A co-design of* Blockify *and* Validate *is* non-self-disqualifying *if there exists an efficiently computable function* Dec *mapping outputs of* Blockify *to vectors* $\vec{N}$ *such that there exists a validate predicate* Validate′ *for which the following properties hold for any possible state* state $= st_1||\ldots||st_\ell$, *buffer* buffer, *vectors* $\vec{N} := (x_1, \ldots, x_m)$, *and transaction* x:

1. $\mathsf{Validate}(x, \mathsf{state}, \mathsf{buffer}) = \mathsf{Validate}'(x, \mathsf{Dec}(st_1)||\ldots||\mathsf{Dec}(st_\ell), \mathsf{buffer})$
2. $\mathsf{Validate}(x, \mathsf{state}||\mathsf{Blockify}(\vec{N}), \mathsf{buffer})$
$$= \mathsf{Validate}'(x, \mathsf{Dec}(st_1)||\ldots||\mathsf{Dec}(st_\ell)||\vec{N}, \mathsf{buffer})$$

We remark that the actual validation of Bitcoin does satisfy the above definition, since a transaction is only rendered invalid with respect to the state if the coins it is trying to spend have already been spent, and this only depends on the transactions in the state and not the metadata added by Blockify. Hence, in the following, we assume that $\mathsf{ValidTx}_{\text{B}}$ and $\mathsf{blockify}_{\text{B}}$ satisfy the relation in Definition 2.

4.3 Security Analysis

We next turn to the security analysis of our protocol. As already mentioned, we argue security in two step. In a first step, we distill out from the protocol Ledger-Protocol a state-extend subprocess, denoted as StateExchange-Protocol, and devise an alternative, modular description of the Ledger-Protocol protocol in which every party makes invocations of this subprocess. We denote this modularized protocol by Modular-Ledger-Protocol. By a game-hopping argument, we prove that the original protocol Ledger-Protocol and the modularized protocol Modular-Ledger-Protocol are in fact functionally equivalent. The advantage of having such a modular description is that we are now able to define an appropriate ideal functionality $\mathcal{F}_{\text{STX}}$ that is realized by StateExchange-Protocol. Using the universal composition theorem we can deduce that Ledger-Protocol UC emulates Modular-Ledger-Protocol where invocations of StateExchange-Protocol are replaced by invocations of $\mathcal{F}_{\text{STX}}$. The second step of the proof consists of proving that, under appropriate assumptions, Modular-Ledger-Protocol, where invocations of StateExchange-Protocol are replaced by invocations of $\mathcal{F}_{\text{STX}}$, implements the Bitcoin ledger described in Sect. 4.2.

Step 1. The state-exchange functionality $\mathcal{F}_{\text{STX}}$ allows parties to submit ledger states which are accepted with a certain probability. Accepted states are then multicast to all parties. Informally, it can be seen as lottery on which (valid) states are exchanged among the participants. Parties can use $\mathcal{F}_{\text{STX}}$ to multicast a valid state, but instead of accepting any submitted state and sending it to all (registered) parties, $\mathcal{F}_{\text{STX}}$ keeps track of all states that it ever saw, and implements the following mechanism upon submission of a new ledger state $\vec{\mathtt{st}}$ and a state block $\mathtt{st}$ from any party: If $\vec{\mathtt{st}}$ was previously submitted to $\mathcal{F}_{\text{STX}}$ and $\vec{\mathtt{st}}||\mathtt{st}$ is a valid state, then $\mathcal{F}_{\text{STX}}$ accepts $\vec{\mathtt{st}}||\mathtt{st}$ with probability p_H (resp. p_A

for dishonest parties); accepted states are then sent to all registered parties. The formal specification follows:

Functionality $\mathcal{F}_{\text{STX}}^{\Delta,p_H,p_A}$

The functionality is parametrized with a set of parties $\mathcal{P}$. Any newly registered (resp. deregistered) party is added to (resp. deleted from) $\mathcal{P}$. For each party $p \in \mathcal{P}$ the functionality manages a tree $\mathcal{T}_p$ where each rooted path corresponds to a valid state the party has received. Initially each tree contains the genesis state. Finally, it manages a buffer $\vec{M}$ which contains successfully submitted states which have not yet been delivered to (some) parties in $\mathcal{P}$.

Submit/receive new states:

- Upon receiving $(\text{SUBMIT-NEW}, \mathsf{sid}, \vec{\mathtt{st}}, \mathtt{st})$ from some participant $p_s \in \mathcal{P}$, if $\mathsf{isvalidstate}(\vec{\mathtt{st}}||\mathtt{st}) = 1$ and $\vec{\mathtt{st}} \in \mathcal{T}_p$ do the following:
  1. Sample B according to a Bernoulli-Distribution with parameter p_H (or p_A if p_s is dishonest).
  2. If $B = 1$, set $\vec{\mathtt{st}}_{new} \leftarrow \vec{\mathtt{st}}||\mathtt{st}$ and add $\vec{\mathtt{st}}_{new}$ to $\mathcal{T}_{p_s}$. Else set $\vec{\mathtt{st}}_{new} \leftarrow \vec{\mathtt{st}}$.
  3. Output $(\text{SUCCESS}, \mathsf{sid}, B)$ to p_s.
  4. On response $(\text{CONTINUE}, \mathsf{sid})$ where $\mathcal{P} = \{p_1, \ldots, p_n\}$ choose n new unique message-IDs $\mathsf{mid}_1, \ldots, \mathsf{mid}_n$, initialize n new variables $D_{\mathsf{mid}_1} := D_{\mathsf{mid}_1}^{MAX} := \ldots := D_{\mathsf{mid}_n} := D_{\mathsf{mid}_n}^{MAX} := 1$ set $\vec{M} := \vec{M}||(\vec{\mathtt{st}}_{new}, \mathsf{mid}_1, D_{\mathsf{mid}_1}, p_1)|| \ldots ||(\vec{\mathtt{st}}_{new}, \mathsf{mid}_n, D_{\mathsf{mid}_n}, p_n)$, and send $(\text{SUBMIT-NEW}, \mathsf{sid}, \vec{\mathtt{st}}_{new}, p_s, (p_1, \mathsf{mid}_1), \ldots, (p_n, \mathsf{mid}_n))$ to the adversary.
- Upon receiving $(\text{FETCH-NEW}, \mathsf{sid})$ from a party $p \in \mathcal{P}$ or $\mathcal{A}$ (on behalf of p), do the following:
  1. For all tuples $(\vec{\mathtt{st}}, \mathsf{mid}, D_{\mathsf{mid}}, p) \in \vec{M}$ set $D_{\mathsf{mid}} := D_{\mathsf{mid}} - 1$.
  2. Let $\vec{M}_0^p$ denote the subvector of $\vec{M}$ including all tuples of the form $(\vec{\mathtt{st}}, \mathsf{mid}, D_{\mathsf{mid}}, p)$ where $D_{\mathsf{mid}} = 0$ (in the same order as they appear in $\vec{M}$). For each tuple $(\vec{\mathtt{st}}, \mathsf{mid}, D_{\mathsf{mid}}, p) \in \vec{M}_0^p$ add $\vec{\mathtt{st}}$ to $\mathcal{T}_p$. Delete all entries in $\vec{M}_0^p$ from $\vec{M}$ and send $\vec{M}_0^p$ to p.
- Upon receiving $(\text{SEND}, \mathsf{sid}, \vec{\mathtt{st}}, p')$ from $\mathcal{A}$ on behalf some *corrupted* $p \in \mathcal{P}$, if $p' \in \mathcal{P}$ and $\vec{\mathtt{st}} \in \mathcal{T}_p$, choose a new unique message-ID mid, initialize $D := 1$, add $(\vec{\mathtt{st}}, \mathsf{mid}, D_{\mathsf{mid}}, p')$ to $\vec{M}$, and return $(\text{SEND}, \mathsf{sid}, \vec{\mathtt{st}}, p', \mathsf{mid})$ to $\mathcal{A}$.

Further adversarial influence on the network:

- Upon receiving $(\text{SWAP}, \mathsf{sid}, \mathsf{mid}, \mathsf{mid}')$ from $\mathcal{A}$, if mid and mid' are message-IDs registered in the current $\vec{M}$, swap the corresponding tuples in $\vec{M}$. Return $(\text{SWAP}, \mathsf{sid})$ to $\mathcal{A}$.
- Upon receiving $(\text{DELAY}, \mathsf{sid}, T, \mathsf{mid})$ from $\mathcal{A}$, if T is a valid delay, mid is a message-ID for a tuple $(\vec{\mathtt{st}}, \mathsf{mid}, D_{\mathsf{mid}}, p)$ in the current $\vec{M}$ and $D_{\mathsf{mid}}^{MAX} + T \leq \Delta$, set $D_{\mathsf{mid}} := D_{\mathsf{mid}} + T$ and set $D_{\mathsf{mid}}^{MAX} := D_{\mathsf{mid}}^{MAX} + T$.

The Modular-Ledger-Protocol uses the same hybrids as Ledger-Protocol but abstracts the lottery implemented by the mining process by making calls to the above state exchange functionality $\mathcal{F}_{\mathrm{STX}}^{\Delta,p_H,p_A}$. The detailed specification of the Modular-Ledger-Protocol protocol can be found in the full version [6]. Note that the only remaining parameter of Modular-Ledger-Protocol is the chop-off parameter T, the rest is part of $\mathcal{F}_{\mathrm{STX}}^{\Delta,p_H,p_A}$. The following Lemma states that our Bitcoin protocol implements the above modular ledger protocol. The proof appears in [6].

Lemma 1. *The UC blockchain protocol* Ledger-Protocol$_{q,D,T}$ *UC emulates the protocol* Modular-Ledger-Protocol$_T$ *that runs in a hybrid world with access to the functionality* $\mathcal{F}_{\mathrm{STX}}^{\Delta,p_H,p_A}$ *with* $p_A := \frac{D}{2^\kappa}$ *and* $p_H = 1 - (1 - p_A)^q$, *and* Δ *denotes the network delay.*

Step 2. We are now ready to complete the proof of our main theorem. Before providing the formal statement it is useful to discuss some of the key properties used in both, the statement and the proof. The security of the Bitcoin protocol depends on various key properties of an execution. This means that its security depends on the number of random oracle queries (or, in the $\mathcal{F}_{\mathrm{STX}}$ hybrid world, the number of submit-queries) by the pool of corrupted miners. Therefore it is important to capture the relevant properties of such a UC execution. In the following we denote by upper-case R the number of rounds of a given protocol execution.

Capturing Query Power in an Execution. In an execution, we measure the query power per logical round r, which can be conveniently captured as a function $\mathsf{T}_{qp}(r)$. We observe that in an interval of, say, t_{rc} rounds, the total number of queries is

$$Q_{t_{rc}}^{r'} = \sum_{r=r'}^{r'+t_{rc}-1} \mathsf{T}_{qp}(r).$$

In each round $r \in [R]$, each honest miner gets a certain number $q_i^{(r)}$ of activations from the environment to maintain the ledger (i.e., to try to extend the state). Let

$$q_H^{(r)} := \sum_{p_i \text{ honest in round r}} q_i^{(r)}.$$

Also, the adversary makes a certain number $q_A^{(r)}$ of queries to $\mathcal{F}_{\mathrm{STX}}$. We get

$$\mathsf{T}_{qp}(r) = q_A^{(r)} + q_H^{(r)}.$$

Quantifying Total Mining Power in an Execution. Mining power is the expected number of successful state extensions, i.e., the number of times a new state block is successfully mined. The mining power of round r is therefore

$$\mathsf{T}_{mp}(r) := q_A^{(r)} \cdot p_A + q_H^{(r)} \cdot p_H.$$

Recall that p_H is the success probability per query of an honest miner and p_A is the success probability per query of a corrupted miner. If $p_A = p$ and $p_H = 1-(1-p)^q$, it is convenient to consider $(q_A^{(r)} + q \cdot q_H^{(r)}) \cdot p$ as the total mining power (by applying Bernoulli's inequality). Within an interval of t_{rc} rounds, we can for example quantify the overall expectation by $\mathsf{T}_{mp}^{\text{total}}(t_{rc}) := \sum_{r=1}^{t_{rc}} \mathsf{T}_{mp}(r)$. This allows to formulate the goal of a re-calibration of the difficulty parameter as requiring that this value should be 2016 blocks for t_{rc} corresponding a desired time bound (such as roughly two weeks), which is part of future work.

Quantifying Adversarial Mining Power in an Execution. The *adversarial mining power* $\mathsf{mp}_A(r)$ per round is made up of two parts: first, queries by corrupted parties, and second, queries by honest, but de-synchronized miners.

$$\mathsf{mp}_A(r) := p_A \cdot q_A^{(r)} + p_H \cdot \sum_{p_i \text{ is de-sync}} q_i^{(r)}.$$

Recall that a party is considered desynchronized for 2Δ rounds after its registration.

It is convenient to measure the adversary's contribution to the mining power as the fraction of the overall mining power. In particular, we assume there is a parameter $\rho \in (0, 1)$ such that in any round r, the relation $\mathsf{mp}_A(r) \le \rho \cdot \mathsf{T}_{mp}(r)$ holds. We then define $\beta_r := \rho \cdot \mathsf{T}_{mp}(r)$. Looking ahead, if a model is flat, then the fraction $(1 - \rho)$ corresponds to the fraction of users that are honest and synchronized.

Quantifying Honest and Synchronized Mining Power in an Execution. In each round $r \in [R]$, each honest miner gets a certain number $q_{i,r}$ of activations from the environment, where it can submit one new state to $\mathcal{F}_{\text{STX}}$. This state is accepted with probability p_H. We define the vector $\vec{q_r}$ such that for any honest miner p_i in round r, $\vec{q_r}[i] = q_{i,r}$. The probability that a miner p_i is successful to extend the state by at least one block is $\alpha_{i,r} := 1 - (1 - p_H)^{q_{i,r}}$ and the probability that at least one *registered and synchronized*, uncorrupted miner successfully queries $\mathcal{F}_{\text{STX}}$ to extend its local longest state is

$$\alpha_r := 1 - \prod_{\text{honest sync } p_i} (1 - \alpha_{i,r}) = 1 - \prod_{\text{honest sync } p_i} (1 - p_H)^{q_{i,r}}.$$

Looking ahead, in existing flat models of Bitcoin, parties are expected to be synchronized and are otherwise counted as dishonest and the quantity $(1 - \rho)$ is the fraction of honest and synchronized miners.

Worst-Case Analysis. We analyze Bitcoin in a worst-case fashion. Let us assume that the protocol runs for $[R]$ rounds, then

$$\alpha := \min \{\alpha_r\}_{r \in [R]}, \text{ and } \beta := \max \{\beta_r\}_{r \in [R]}.$$

Remark 4. This view on Bitcoin gives already a glimpse for the relevance of the re-calibration sub-protocol which is considered as part of future work. Ideally, we would like the variation among the values α_r and among the values β_r to be small, which needs an additional assumption on the increase of computing power per round. Thanks to the re-calibration phase, such a bound can exist at all. If no re-calibration phase would happen, any strictly positive gradient of the computing power development would eventually provoke Bitcoin failing, as the value β (as a fraction of the total mining power) could not be reasonably bounded. We are now ready to state the main theorem. The proof of the theorem can be found in the full version [6].

Theorem 1. *Let the functions $\mathsf{ValidTx}_{\mathcal{B}}$, $\mathsf{blockify}_{\mathcal{B}}$, and* `ExtendPolicy` *be as defined above. Let $p \in (0, 1)$, integer $q \geq 1$, $p_H = 1 - (1 - p)^q$, and $p_A = p$. Let $\Delta \geq 1$ be the upper bound on the network delay. Consider $\mathsf{Modular\text{-}Ledger\text{-}Protocol}_T$ in the $(\mathcal{G}_{\text{CLOCK}}, \mathcal{F}_{\text{STX}}^{\Delta,p_H,p_A}, \mathcal{F}_{\text{N-MC}}^{\Delta})$-hybrid world. If, for some $\lambda > 1$, the relation*

$$\alpha \cdot (1 - 2 \cdot (\Delta + 1) \cdot \alpha) \geq \lambda \cdot \beta \tag{1}$$

is satisfied in any real-world execution, where α and β are defined as above, then the protocol $\mathsf{Modular\text{-}Ledger\text{-}Protocol}_T$ UC-realizes $\mathcal{G}_{\text{LEDGER}}^{\mathcal{B}}$ for any parameters in the range

$$\texttt{windowSize} = T \quad \text{and} \quad \texttt{Delay} = 4\Delta,$$

$$\texttt{maxTime}_{\text{window}} \geq \frac{\texttt{windowSize}}{(1-\delta)\cdot\gamma} \quad \text{and} \quad \texttt{minTime}_{\text{window}} \leq \frac{\texttt{windowSize}}{(1+\delta)\cdot\max_r \mathsf{T}_{mp}(r)},$$

$$\eta > (1+\delta)\cdot\texttt{windowSize}\cdot\frac{\beta}{\gamma},$$

where $\gamma := \frac{\alpha}{1+\Delta\alpha}$ and $\delta > 0$ is an arbitrary constant. In particular, the realization is perfect except with probability $R \cdot \mathsf{negl}(T)$, where R denotes the upper bound on the number of rounds, and $\mathsf{negl}(T)$ denotes a negligible function in T.

Remark 5. It is worth noting the implications of Eq. 1. In practice, typically p is small such that α (and thus γ) can be approximated using Bernoulli's inequality to be $(1-\rho)mp$, where m is the estimated number of hash queries in the Bitcoin network per round. Hence, by canceling out the term mp and letting p be sufficiently small (compared to $\frac{1}{\Delta m}$), Eq. 1 collapses roughly to the condition that $(1-\rho)(1-\epsilon) \geq (1+\delta)\rho$, which basically relates the fractions of adversarial vs. honest mining power. Also, as pointed out by [29], for too large values of p in the order of $p > \frac{1}{mp}$, Eq. 1 is violated for any constant fraction ρ of corrupted miners and they present an attack in this case.

Proof (Overview). To show the theorem we specify a simulator for the ideal world that internally runs the round-based mining procedure of every honest party. Whenever the real world parties complete a working round, then the simulator has to assemble the views of all honest (and synchronized) miners that it simulates and determine their common prefix of states, i.e., the longest state stored or received by each simulated party when chopping off T blocks. The adversary will then propose a new block candidate, i.e., a list of transactions, to the ledger to announce that the common prefix has increased. To reflect that not all parties have the same view on this common prefix, the simulator can adjust the state pointers accordingly. This simulation is perfect and corresponds to an emulation of real-world processes. What possibly prevents a perfect simulation is the requirement of a consistent prefix and the restrictions imposed by `ExtendPolicy`. In order to show that these restrictions do not forbid a proper simulation, we have to justify why the choice of the parameters in the theorem statement is acceptable. To this end, we analyze the real-world execution to bound the corresponding bad events that prevent a perfect simulation. This can be done following the detailed analysis provided by Pass et al. [29] which includes the necessary claims for lower and upper on chain growth, chain quality, and prefix consistency. From these claims, it follows that our simulator can simulate the real-world, since the restrictions imposed by the ledger prohibit a prefect simulation only with probability $R \cdot \mathsf{negl}(T)$. This is an upper bound on the distinguishing advantage of the real and ideal world. The detailed proof is found in [6]. □

Note that the theorem statement a-priori holds for any environment (but simply yields a void statement if the conditions are not met). In order to turn this into a composable statement, we follow the approach proposed in Sect. 2 and model restrictions as wrapper functionalities to ensure the condition of the theorem. We review two particular choices in Sect. 4.4. The general conceptual principle behind this is the following: For the hybrid world, that consists of a network $\mathcal{F}_{\text{N-MC}}$, a clock $\mathcal{G}_{\text{CLOCK}}$ and a random oracle $\mathcal{F}_{\text{RO}}$ with output length κ (or alternatively the state-exchange functionality $\mathcal{F}_{\text{STX}}$ instead of the random oracle), define a wrapper functionality $\mathcal{W}$ which ensures the condition in Eq. 1 and (possibly) additional conditions on minimal (honest) and maximal (dishonest) mining power. This can be done by enforcing appropriate restrictions along the lines of the basic example in Sect. 2 (e.g., imposing an upper bound on parties, or RO queries per round etc.). We provide the details and the specification of such a general random-oracle wrapper $\mathcal{W}^{\Delta,\lambda,\mathsf{T}_{mp}}_{\alpha,\beta,\mathsf{D}}(\mathcal{F}_{\text{RO}})$ with its parameters[13] in the full version of this work [6]. For this wrapper we have the following desired corollary to Theorem 1 and Lemma 1. This statement is guaranteed to compose according to the UC composition theorem.

Corollary 1. *The UC blockchain protocol* $\mathsf{Ledger\text{-}Protocol}_{q,D,T}$ *that is executed in the* $(\mathcal{G}_{\text{CLOCK}}, \mathcal{F}^{\Delta}_{\text{N-MC}}, \mathcal{W}^{\Delta,\lambda,T_{mp}}_{\alpha,\beta,D}(\mathcal{F}_{\text{RO}}))$*-hybrid world, UC-realizes functionality* $\mathcal{G}^{\mathcal{B}}_{\text{LEDGER}}$ *(with the respective parameters assured by Theorem 1).*

[13] The parameters are the ones introduced in this section: a lower bound on honest mining power (per round) α, an upper bound on adversarial mining power (per round) β, the total mining power (per round) T_{mp}, the network delay Δ, the difficulty parameter D (that influences the probability of a successful PoW), and finally a value $\lambda > 1$ describing the required gap between honest and dishonest mining power.

4.4 Comparison with Existing Work

We demonstrate how the protocols, assumptions, and results from the two existing works analyzing security of Bitcoin (in a property based manner) can be cast as special cases of our construction.

We start with the result in [16], which is the so-called flat and synchronous model[14] with instant delivery and a constant number of parties n (i.e., Bitcoin is seen as an n-party MPC protocol).[15] Consider the concrete values for α and β as follows:

- Let n denote the number of parties. Each corrupted party gets at most q activations to query the $\mathcal{F}_{\text{STX}}$ per round. Each honest party is activated exactly once per round.
- In the model of GKL, we have $q \geq 1$. Thus, we get $p_H = 1 - (1-p)^q$ and $p_A = p$. We can further conclude that $\mathsf{T}_{mp}^{\text{GKL}}(r) \leq p \cdot q \cdot n$.
- The adversary gets (at most) q queries per corrupted party with probability $p_A = p$ and one query per honest but desynchronized party with success probability $p_H = 1 - (1-p)^q$. If t_r denotes the number of corrupted or desynchronized parties in round r, we get $\mathsf{mp}_A^{\text{GKL}}(r) \leq t_r \cdot q \cdot p$ and thus $\beta_r^{\text{GKL}} = p \cdot q \cdot (\rho \cdot n)$, where ρn is the (assumed) upper bound on the number of miners contributing to the adversarial mining power (independent of r).
- Each honest and synchronized miner gets exactly one activation per round, i.e., $q_{i,r} := 1$, with $p_H = 1-(1-p)^q \in (0,1)$, for some integer $q > 0$. Inserting it into the general equation yields $\alpha_r^{\text{GKL}} = 1 - (1-p)^{q(1-\rho)\cdot n}$ (independent of r). Note that since n is assumed to be fixed in their model, $q(1-\rho) \cdot n$ is in fact a lower bound on the honest and synchronized hashing power.

We can now easily specify a wrapper $\mathcal{W}_{\text{GKL}}$ as special case of the above general wrapper. In the hybrid world $(\mathcal{G}_{\text{CLOCK}}, \mathcal{W}_{\text{GKL}}(\mathcal{F}_{\text{STX}}^{\Delta,p_H,p_A}), \mathcal{F}_{\text{N-MC}}^{\Delta})$ this ensures the condition of Theorem 1 and we arrive at the following composable statement:

Corollary 2. *The protocol* Modular-Ledger-Protocol$_{\mathcal{T}}$ *UC-realizes the functionality* $\mathcal{G}_{\text{LEDGER}}^{\mathcal{B}}$ *in the* $(\mathcal{G}_{\text{CLOCK}}, \mathcal{W}_{\text{GKL}}(\mathcal{F}_{\text{STX}}^{1,p_H,p_A}), \mathcal{F}_{\text{N-MC}}^{1})$*-hybrid model (setting delay* $\Delta = 1$*) for the parameters assured by Theorem 1 for the above choice:*

$$\alpha^{\text{GKL}} = 1 - (1-p)^{(1-\rho)\cdot q \cdot n} \quad \textit{and} \quad \beta^{\text{GKL}} = p \cdot q \cdot (\rho \cdot n).$$

Similarly, we can instantiate the above values with the assumptions of [29]:

- For each corrupted (and desynchronized) party, the adversary gets at most one query per round. Each honest miner makes exactly one query per round. This means that $q_A^{(r)} + q_H^{(r)} = n_r$.

[14] The flat model means that every party gets the same number of hash queries in every round.

[15] In a recent paper, the authors of [16] propose an analysis of Bitcoin for a variable number of parties. Capturing the appropriate assumptions for this case, as a wrapper in our composable setting, is part of future work.

- In the PSs model, $p_H = p_A = p$ and hence $\mathsf{T}_{mp}^{\mathrm{PSs}}(r) \leq p \cdot n_r = p \cdot n$, where n is as above. With these values we get $\mathsf{mp}_A^{\mathrm{PSs}}(r) = p \cdot n_r^{\mathrm{corr}}$ and consequently $\beta_r^{\mathrm{PSs}} = p \cdot (\rho \cdot n)$, where ρn denotes the upper bound on corrupted parties in any round. Putting things together, we also have $\alpha_r^{\mathrm{PSs}} = 1 - (1-p)^{(1-\rho)\cdot n}$. Note that since n is assumed to be fixed in their model, $(1-\rho)\cdot n$ is in fact a lower bound on the honest and synchronized hashing power.

We can again specify a wrapper functionality $\mathcal{W}_{\mathrm{PSs}}$ as above (where the restriction is 1 query per corrupted instead of q). We again have that the hybrid world $(\mathcal{G}_{\mathrm{CLOCK}}, \mathcal{W}_{\mathrm{PSs}}(\mathcal{F}_{\mathrm{STX}}^{\Delta,p,p}), \mathcal{F}_{\mathrm{N\text{-}MC}}^{\Delta})$ will ensure the condition of the theorem and directly yields the following composable statement.

Corollary 3. *The protocol Modular-Ledger-Protocol$_T$ UC-realizes $\mathcal{G}_{\mathrm{LEDGER}}^{\text{₿}}$ in the $(\mathcal{G}_{\mathrm{CLOCK}}, \mathcal{W}(\mathcal{F}_{\mathrm{STX}}^{\Delta,p,p}), \mathcal{F}_{\mathrm{N\text{-}MC}}^{\Delta})$-hybrid model (with network delay $\Delta \geq 1$) for the parameters assured by Theorem 1 for the above choice:*

$$\alpha^{\mathrm{PSs}} = 1 - (1-p)^{(1-\rho)\cdot n} \quad \textit{and} \quad \beta^{\mathrm{PSs}} = p \cdot (\rho \cdot n).$$

5 Implementing a Stronger Ledger

As already observed in [16], the Bitcoin protocol makes use of digital signatures to protect transactions which allows it to achieve stronger guarantees. Informally, the stronger guarantee ensures that every transaction submitted by an honest miner will eventually make it into the state. Using our terminology, this means that by employing digital signatures, Bitcoin implements a stronger ledger. In this section we present this stronger ledger and show how such an implementation can be captured as a UC protocol which makes black-box use of the Ledger-Protocol to implement this ledger. The UC composition theorem makes such a proof immediate, as we do not need to think about the specifics of the invoked ledger protocol, and we can instead argue security in a world where this protocol is replaced by $\mathcal{G}_{\mathrm{LEDGER}}^{\text{₿}}$.

Protection of Transactions Using Accounts. In Bitcoin, a miner creates an account ID AccountID by generating a signature key pair and hashing the public key. Any transaction of this party includes this account ID, i.e., $\mathtt{x} = (\mathsf{AccountID}, \mathtt{x}')$. An important property is that a transaction of a certain account cannot be invalidated by a transaction with a different account ID. Hence, to protect the validity of a transaction, upon submitting $\mathtt{x}$, party p_i has to sign it, append the signature and verification key to get a transaction $((\mathsf{AccountID}, \mathtt{x}'), vk, \sigma)$. The validation predicate now additionally has to check that the account ID is the hash of the public key and that the signature σ is valid with respect to the verification key vk. Roughly, an adversary can invalidate $\mathtt{x}$, only by either forging a signature relative to vk, or by possessing key pair whose hash of the public key collides with the account ID of the honest party. The details of the protocol and the validate predicate as pseudo-code are provided in the full version [6].

Realized Ledger. The realized ledger abstraction, denoted by $\mathcal{G}^{\text{B}+}_{\text{LEDGER}}$, is formally specified in [6]. Roughly, it is a ledger functionality as the one from the previous section, but which additionally allows parties to create unique accounts. Upon receiving a transaction from party p_i, $\mathcal{G}^{\text{B}+}_{\text{LEDGER}}$ only accepts a transaction containing the AccountID that was previously associated to p_i and ensures that parties are restricted to issue transactions using their own accounts.

Amplification of Transaction Liveness. In Bitcoin a given transaction can only be invalidated due to another one with the same account. By definition of the enhanced ledger, this means that no other party can make a transaction of p_i not enter the state. The liveness guarantee for transactions specified by `ExtendPolicy` in the previous chapter implies captures that if a valid transaction is in the buffer for long enough then it eventually enters the state. For $\mathcal{G}^{\text{B}+}_{\text{LEDGER}}$, this implies that if p_i submits a single transaction which is valid according to the current state, then this transaction will eventually be contained in the state. More precisely, we can conclude that this happens within the next $2 \cdot \texttt{windowSize}$ new state blocks in the worst case. Relative to the current view of p_i this is no more than within the next $3 \cdot \texttt{windowSize}$ blocks as argued in [6].

References

1. Andrychowicz, M., Dziembowski, S.: PoW-based distributed cryptography with no trusted setup. In: Gennaro, R., Robshaw, M. (eds.) CRYPTO 2015. LNCS, vol. 9216, pp. 379–399. Springer, Heidelberg (2015). doi:10.1007/978-3-662-48000-7_19
2. Andrychowicz, M., Dziembowski, S., Malinowski, D., Mazurek, Ł.: Fair two-party computations via bitcoin deposits. In: Böhme, R., Brenner, M., Moore, T., Smith, M. (eds.) FC 2014. LNCS, vol. 8438, pp. 105–121. Springer, Heidelberg (2014). doi:10.1007/978-3-662-44774-1_8
3. Andrychowicz, M., Dziembowski, S., Malinowski, D., Mazurek, L.: Secure multi-party computations on bitcoin. In: 2014 IEEE Symposium on Security and Privacy, pp. 443–458. IEEE Computer Society Press, May 2014
4. Babaioff, M., Dobzinski, S., Oren, S., Zohar, A.: On bitcoin and red balloons. SIGecom Exch. **10**(3), 5–9 (2011)
5. Backes, M., Hofheinz, D., Müller-Quade, J., Unruh, D.: On fairness in simulatability-based cryptographic systems. In: FMSE 2005 (2005)
6. Badertscher, C., Maurer, U., Tschudi, D., Zikas, V.: Bitcoin as a transaction ledger: a composable treatment. Cryptology ePrint Archive, Report 2017/149 (2017)
7. Ben-Sasson, E., Chiesa, A., Garman, C., Green, M., Miers, I., Tromer, E., Virza, M.: Zerocash: decentralized anonymous payments from bitcoin. In: 2014 IEEE Symposium on Security and Privacy, pp. 459–474. IEEE Computer Society Press, May 2014
8. Bentov, I., Kumaresan, R.: How to use bitcoin to design fair protocols. In: Garay, J.A., Gennaro, R. (eds.) CRYPTO 2014. LNCS, vol. 8617, pp. 421–439. Springer, Heidelberg (2014). doi:10.1007/978-3-662-44381-1_24
9. Buterin, V.: A next-generation smart contract and decentralized application platform (2013). https://github.com/ethereum/wiki/wiki/White-Paper

10. Canetti, R.: Universally composable security: a new paradigm for cryptographic protocols. In: 42nd FOCS, pp. 136–145. IEEE Computer Society Press, October 2001
11. Canetti, R., Dodis, Y., Pass, R., Walfish, S.: Universally composable security with global setup. In: Vadhan, S.P. (ed.) TCC 2007. LNCS, vol. 4392, pp. 61–85. Springer, Heidelberg (2007). doi:10.1007/978-3-540-70936-7_4
12. Canetti, R., Shahaf, D., Vald, M.: Universally composable authentication and key-exchange with global PKI. In: Cheng, C.-M., Chung, K.-M., Persiano, G., Yang, B.-Y. (eds.) PKC 2016. LNCS, vol. 9615, pp. 265–296. Springer, Heidelberg (2016). doi:10.1007/978-3-662-49387-8_11
13. Coretti, S., Garay, J., Hirt, M., Zikas, V.: Constant-round asynchronous multi-party computation based on one-way functions. In: Cheon, J.H., Takagi, T. (eds.) ASIACRYPT 2016. LNCS, vol. 10032, pp. 998–1021. Springer, Heidelberg (2016). doi:10.1007/978-3-662-53890-6_33
14. Eyal, I.: The miner's dilemma. In: 2015 IEEE Symposium on Security and Privacy, pp. 89–103. IEEE Computer Society Press, May 2015
15. Eyal, I., Sirer, E.G.: Majority is not enough: bitcoin mining is vulnerable. In: Christin, N., Safavi-Naini, R. (eds.) FC 2014. LNCS, vol. 8437, pp. 436–454. Springer, Heidelberg (2014). doi:10.1007/978-3-662-45472-5_28
16. Garay, J., Kiayias, A., Leonardos, N.: The bitcoin backbone protocol: analysis and applications. In: Oswald, E., Fischlin, M. (eds.) EUROCRYPT 2015. LNCS, vol. 9057, pp. 281–310. Springer, Heidelberg (2015). doi:10.1007/978-3-662-46803-6_10
17. Katz, J., Maurer, U., Tackmann, B., Zikas, V.: Universally composable synchronous computation. In: Sahai, A. (ed.) TCC 2013. LNCS, vol. 7785, pp. 477–498. Springer, Heidelberg (2013). doi:10.1007/978-3-642-36594-2_27
18. Kiayias, A., Koutsoupias, E., Kyropoulou, M., Tselekounis, Y.: Blockchain mining games. In: EC (2016)
19. Kiayias, A., Zhou, H.-S., Zikas, V.: Fair and robust multi-party computation using a global transaction ledger. In: Fischlin, M., Coron, J.-S. (eds.) EUROCRYPT 2016. LNCS, vol. 9666, pp. 705–734. Springer, Heidelberg (2016). doi:10.1007/978-3-662-49896-5_25
20. Kumaresan, R., Bentov, I.: How to use bitcoin to incentivize correct computations. In: Ahn, G.-J., Yung, M., Li, N. (eds.) ACM CCS 2014, pp. 30–41. ACM Press, November 2014
21. Kumaresan, R., Bentov, I.: Amortizing secure computation with penalties. In: Weippl, E.R., Katzenbeisser, S., Kruegel, C., Myers, A.C., Halevi, S. (eds.) ACM CCS 2016, pp. 418–429. ACM Press, October 2016
22. Kumaresan, R., Moran, T., Bentov, I.: How to use bitcoin to play decentralized poker. In: Ray, I., Li, N., Kruegel, C. (eds.) ACM CCS 15, pp. 195–206. ACM Press, October 2015
23. Kumaresan, R., Vaikuntanathan, V., Vasudevan, P.N.: Improvements to secure computation with penalties. In: Weippl, E.R., Katzenbeisser, S., Kruegel, C., Myers, A.C., Halevi, S. (eds.) ACM CCS 2016, pp. 406–417. ACM Press, October 2016
24. Lamport, L.: The part-time parliament. ACM Trans. Comput. Syst. **16**(2), 133–169 (1998)
25. Lamport, L.: Paxos made simple, fast, and byzantine. In: OPODIS (2002)
26. Lamport, L., Shostak, R.E., Pease, M.C.: The byzantine generals problem. ACM Trans. Program. Lang. Syst. **4**(3), 382–401 (1982)

27. Miers, I., Garman, C., Green, M., Rubin, A.D.: Zerocoin: anonymous distributed e-cash from bitcoin. In: 2013 IEEE Symposium on Security and Privacy, pp. 397–411. IEEE Computer Society Press, May 2013
28. Nakamoto, S.: Bitcoin: a peer-to-peer electronic cash system (2008). http://bitcoin.org/bitcoin.pdf
29. Pass, R., Seeman, L., Shelat, A.: Analysis of the blockchain protocol in asynchronous networks. In: Coron, J.-S., Nielsen, J.B. (eds.) EUROCRYPT 2017. LNCS, vol. 10211, pp. 643–673. Springer, Cham (2017). doi:10.1007/978-3-319-56614-6_22
30. Pass, R., Shi, E.: FruitChains: a fair blockchain. Cryptology ePrint Archive, Report 2016/916 (2016)
31. Rabin, M.O.: Randomized byzantine generals. In: FOCS (1983)
32. Rosulek, M.: Must you know the code of f to securely compute f? In: Safavi-Naini, R., Canetti, R. (eds.) CRYPTO 2012. LNCS, vol. 7417, pp. 87–104. Springer, Heidelberg (2012). doi:10.1007/978-3-642-32009-5_7
33. Sompolinsky, Y., Zohar, A.: Secure high-rate transaction processing in bitcoin. In: Böhme, R., Okamoto, T. (eds.) FC 2015. LNCS, vol. 8975, pp. 507–527. Springer, Heidelberg (2015). doi:10.1007/978-3-662-47854-7_32
34. Zohar, A.: Bitcoin: under the hood. Commun. ACM **58**(9), 104–113 (2015)

Ouroboros: A Provably Secure Proof-of-Stake Blockchain Protocol

Aggelos Kiayias[1(✉)], Alexander Russell[2], Bernardo David[3], and Roman Oliynykov[4]

[1] University of Edinburgh and IOHK, Edinburgh, UK
akiayias@inf.ed.ac.uk
[2] University of Connecticut, Storrs, CT, USA
acr@cse.uconn.edu
[3] Tokyo Institute of Technology and IOHK, Tokyo, Japan
bernardo.david@iohk.io
[4] IOHK, Kiev, Ukraine
roman.oliynykov@iohk.io

Abstract. We present "Ouroboros", the first blockchain protocol based on *proof of stake* with rigorous security guarantees. We establish security properties for the protocol comparable to those achieved by the bitcoin blockchain protocol. As the protocol provides a "proof of stake" blockchain discipline, it offers qualitative efficiency advantages over blockchains based on proof of physical resources (e.g., proof of work). We also present a novel reward mechanism for incentivizing Proof of Stake protocols and we prove that, given this mechanism, honest behavior is an approximate Nash equilibrium, thus neutralizing attacks such as selfish mining.

1 Introduction

A primary consideration regarding the operation of blockchain protocols based on proof of work (PoW)—such as bitcoin [18]—is the energy required for their execution. At the time of this writing, generating a single block on the bitcoin blockchain requires a number of hashing operations exceeding 2^{60}, which results in striking energy demands. Indeed, early calculations indicated that the energy requirements of the protocol were comparable to that of a small country [20].

This state of affairs has motivated the investigation of alternative blockchain protocols that would obviate the need for proof of work by substituting it with another, more energy efficient, mechanism that can provide similar guarantees.

A. Kiayias—Work partly performed while at the National and Kapodistrian University of Athens, supported by ERC project CODAMODA #259152. Work partly supported by H2020 Project #653497, PANORAMIX.

A. Russell—Research partially supported by National Science Foundation grant #1407205.

B. David—Work partly supported by European Research Council Starting Grant #279447.

J. Katz and H. Shacham (Eds.): CRYPTO 2017, Part I, LNCS 10401, pp. 357–388, 2017.
DOI: 10.1007/978-3-319-63688-7_12

It is important to point out that the proof of work mechanism of bitcoin facilitates a type of randomized "leader election" process that elects one of the miners to issue the next block. Furthermore, provided that all miners follow the protocol, this selection is performed in a randomized fashion proportionally to the computational power of each miner. (Deviations from the protocol may distort this proportionality as exemplified by "selfish mining" strategies [10, 25].)

A natural alternative mechanism relies on the notion of "proof of stake" (PoS). Rather than miners investing computational resources in order to participate in the leader election process, they instead run a process that randomly selects one of them proportionally to the *stake* that each possesses according to the current blockchain ledger.

In effect, this yields a self-referential blockchain discipline: maintaining the blockchain relies on the stakeholders themselves and assigns work to them (as well as rewards) based on the amount of stake that each possesses as reported in the ledger. Aside from this, the discipline should make no further "artificial" computational demands on the stakeholders. In some sense, this sounds ideal; however, realizing such a proof-of-stake protocol appears to involve a number of definitional, technical, and analytic challenges.

Previous Work. The concept of PoS has been discussed extensively in the bitcoin forum.[1] Proof-of-stake based blockchain design has been more formally studied by Bentov et al., both in conjunction with PoW [4] as well as the sole mechanism for a blockchain protocol [3]. Although Bentov et al. showed that their protocols are secure against some classes of attacks, they do not provide a formal model for analysing PoS based protocols or security proofs relying on precise definitions. Heuristic proof-of-stake based blockchain protocols have been proposed (and implemented) for a number of cryptocurrencies.[2] Being based on heuristic security arguments, these cryptocurrencies have been frequently found to be deficient from the point of view of security. See [3] for a discussion of various attacks.

It is also interesting to contrast a PoS-based blockchain protocol with a classical consensus blockchain that relies on a *fixed* set of authorities (see, e.g., [8]). What distinguishes a PoS-based blockchain from those which assume static authorities is that stake changes over time and hence the trust assumption evolves with the system.

Another alternative to PoW is the concept of *proof of space* [1,9], which has been specifically investigated in the context of blockchain protocols [21]. In a proof of space setting, a "prover" wishes to demonstrate the utilization of space (storage/memory); as in the case of a PoW, this utilizes a physical resource but can be less energy demanding over time. A related concept is *proof of space-time* (PoST) [16]. In all these cases, however, an expensive physical resource (either storage or computational power) is necessary.

[1] See "Proof of stake instead of proof of work", Bitcoin forum thread. Posts by user "QuantumMechanic" and others. (https://bitcointalk.org/index.php?topic=27787.0.).

[2] A non-exhaustive list includes NXT, Neucoin, Blackcoin, Tendermint, Bitshares.

The PoS Design Challenge. A fundamental problem for PoS-based blockchain protocols is to simulate the leader election process. In order to achieve a fair randomized election among stakeholders, entropy must be introduced into the system, and mechanisms to introduce entropy may be prone to manipulation by the adversary. For instance, an adversary controlling a set of stakeholders may attempt to simulate the protocol execution trying different sequences of stakeholder participants so that it finds a protocol continuation that favors the adversarial stakeholders. This leads to a so called "grinding" vulnerability, where adversarial parties may use computational resources to bias the leader election.

Our Results. We present "Ouroboros", a provably secure proof of stake system. To the best of our knowledge this is the first blockchain protocol of its kind with a rigorous security analysis. In more detail, our results are as follows.

First, we provide a model that formalizes the problem of realizing a PoS-based blockchain protocol. The model we introduce is in the spirit of [12], focusing on *persistence* and *liveness*, two formal properties of a robust transaction ledger. *Persistence* states that once a node of the system proclaims a certain transaction as "stable", the remaining nodes, if queried and responding honestly, will also report it as stable. Here, stability is to be understood as a predicate that will be parameterized by some security parameter k that will affect the certainty with which the property holds. (E.g., "more than k blocks deep".) *Liveness* ensures that once an honestly generated transaction has been made available for a sufficient amount of time to the network nodes, say u time steps, it will become stable. The conjunction of liveness and persistence provides a robust transaction ledger in the sense that honestly generated transactions are adopted and become immutable. Our model is suitably amended to facilitate PoS-based dynamics.

Second, we describe a novel blockchain protocol based on PoS. Our protocol assumes that parties can freely create accounts and receive and make payments, and that stake shifts over time. We utilize a (very simple) secure multiparty implementation of a coin-flipping protocol to produce the randomness for the leader election process. This distinguishes our approach (and prevents so called "grinding attacks") from other previous solutions that either defined such values deterministically based on the current state of the blockchain or used collective coin flipping as a way to introduce entropy [3]. Also, unique to our approach is the fact that the system ignores round-to-round stake modifications. Instead, a snapshot of the current set of stakeholders is taken in regular intervals called *epochs*; in each such interval a secure multiparty computation takes place utilizing the blockchain itself as the broadcast channel. Specifically, in each epoch a set of randomly selected stakeholders form a committee which is then responsible for executing the coin-flipping protocol. The outcome of the protocol determines the set of next stakeholders to execute the protocol in the next epoch as well as the outcomes of all leader elections for the epoch.

Third, we provide a set of formal arguments establishing that no adversary can break persistence and liveness. Our protocol is secure under a number of plausible assumptions: (1) the network is synchronous in the sense that an upper bound can be determined during which any honest stakeholder is able to communicate with any other stakeholder, (2) a number of stakeholders drawn from the honest majority is available as needed to participate in each epoch, (3) the stakeholders do not remain offline for long periods of time, (4) the adaptivity of corruptions is subject to a small delay that is measured in rounds linear in the security parameter (or alternatively, the players have access to a sender-anonymous broadcast channel). At the core of our security arguments is a probabilistic argument regarding a combinatorial notion of "forkable strings" which we formulate, prove and also verify experimentally. In our analysis we also distinguish *covert attacks*, a special class of general forking attacks. "Covertness" here is interpreted in the spirit of covert adversaries against secure multiparty computation protocols, cf. [2], where the adversary wishes to break the protocol but prefers not to be caught doing so. We show that covertly forkable strings are a subclass of the forkable strings with much smaller density; this permits us to provide two distinct security arguments that achieve different trade-offs in terms of efficiency and security guarantees. Our forkable string analysis is a natural and fairly general tool that can be applied as part of a security argument the PoS setting.

Fourth, we turn our attention to the incentive structure of the protocol. We present a novel reward mechanism for incentivizing the participants to the system which we prove to be an (approximate) Nash equilibrium. In this way, attacks like *block withholding* and *selfish-mining* [10,25] are mitigated by our design. The core idea behind the reward mechanism is to provide positive payoff for those protocol actions that cannot be stifled by a coalition of parties that diverges from the protocol. In this way, it is possible to show that, under plausible assumptions, namely that certain protocol execution costs are small, following the protocol faithfully is an equilibrium when all players are rational.

Fifth, we introduce a stake delegation mechanism that can be seamlessly added to our blockchain protocol. Delegation is particularly useful in our context as we would like to allow our protocol to scale even in a setting where the set of stakeholders is highly fragmented. In such cases, the delegation mechanism can enable stakeholders to delegate their "voting rights", i.e., the right of participating in the committees running the leader selection protocol in each epoch. As in *liquid democracy*, (a.k.a. delegative democracy [11]), stakeholders have the ability to revoke their delegative appointment when they wish independently of each other.

Given our model and protocol description we also explore how various attacks considered in practice can be addressed within our framework. Specifically, we discuss double spending attacks, transaction denial attacks, 51% attacks, nothing-at-stake, desynchronization attacks and others. Finally, we present evidence regarding the efficiency of our design. First we consider double spending attacks. For illustrative purposes, we perform a comparison with Nakamoto's analysis for bitcoin regarding transaction confirmation time with assurance 99.9%. Against covert adversaries, the transaction confirmation time is from 10 to 16 times faster than that of bitcoin, depending on the adversarial hashing power; for general adversaries confirmation time is from 5 to 10 times faster.

Moreover, our concrete analysis of double-spending attacks relies on our combinatorial analysis of forkable and covertly forkable strings and applies to a much broader class of adversarial behavior than Nakamoto's more simplified analysis.[3] We then survey our prototype implementation and report on benchmark experiments run in the Amazon cloud that showcase the power of our proof of stake blockchain protocol in terms of performance. Due to lack of space we present the above in the full version [14].

Related Work. In parallel to the development of Ouroboros, a number of other protocols were developed targeting various positions in the design space of distributed ledgers based on PoS. Sleepy consensus [5] considers a fixed stakeholder distribution (i.e., stake does not evolve over time) and targets a "mixed" corruption setting, where the adversary is allowed to perform fail-stop and recover corruptions in addition to Byzantine faults. It is actually straightforward to extend our analysis in this mixed corruption setting, cf. Remark 2; nevertheless, the resulting security can be argued only in the "corruptions with delay" setting that we introduce, and thus is not fully adaptive. Snow White [6] addresses an evolving stakeholder distribution and uses a corruption delay mechanism similar to ours for arguing security. Nevertheless, contrary to our protocol, the Snow White design is susceptible to a "grinding" type of attack that can bias high probability events in favor of the adversary. While this does not hurt security asymptotically, it prevents a concrete parameterisation that does not take into account adversarial computing power. Algorand, [15], provides a distributed ledger following a Byzantine agreement *per block* approach that can withstand adaptive corruptions. Given that agreement needs to be reached for each block, such protocols will produce blocks at a rate substantially slower than a PoS blockchain (where the slow down matches the length of the execution of the Byzantine agreement protocol). In this respect, despite the existence of forks, blockchain protocols enjoy the flexibility of permitting the clients to set the level of risk that they are willing to undertake, allowing low risk profile clients to enjoy faster processing times. Finally, Fruitchain, [23], provides a reward mechanism and an approximate Nash equilibrium proof for a PoW-based blockchain. We use a similar reward mechanism at the blockchain level, nevertheless our underlying mechanics are different since we have to operate in a PoS setting. The core of the idea is to provide a PoS analogue of "endorsing" inputs in a *fair proportion* using the same logic as the PoW-based byzantine agreement protocol for honest majority from [12].

2 Model

Time, Slots, and Synchrony. We consider a setting where time is divided into discrete units called *slots*. A ledger, described in more detail below, associates

[3] Nakamoto's simplifications are pointed out in [12]: the analysis considers only the setting where a block withholding attacker acts without interaction as opposed to a more general attacker that, for instance, tries strategically to split the honest parties in more than one chains during the course of the double spending attack.

with each time slot (at most) one ledger *block*. Players are equipped with (roughly synchronized) clocks that indicate the current slot. This will permit them to carry out a distributed protocol intending to collectively assign a block to this current slot. In general, each slot sl_r is indexed by an integer $r \in \{1, 2, \ldots\}$, and we assume that the real time window that corresponds to each slot has the following properties.

- The current slot is determined by a publicly-known and monotonically increasing function of current time.
- Each player has access to the current time. Any discrepancies between parties' local time are insignificant in comparison with the length of time represented by a slot.
- The length of the time window that corresponds to a slot is sufficient to guarantee that any message transmitted by an honest party at the beginning of the time window will be received by any other honest party by the end of that time window (even accounting for small inconsistencies in parties' local clocks). In particular, while network delays may occur, they never exceed the slot time window.

Transaction Ledger Properties. A protocol Π implements a robust transaction ledger provided that the ledger that Π maintains is divided into "blocks" (assigned to time slots) that determine the order with which transactions are incorporated in the ledger. It should also satisfy the following two properties.

- **Persistence.** Once a node of the system proclaims a certain transaction tx as *stable*, the remaining nodes, if queried, will either report tx in the same position in the ledger or will not report as stable any transaction in conflict to tx. Here the notion of stability is a predicate that is parameterized by a security parameter k; specifically, a transaction is declared *stable* if and only if it is in a block that is more than k blocks deep in the ledger.
- **Liveness.** If all honest nodes in the system attempt to include a certain transaction, then after the passing of time corresponding to u slots (called the transaction confirmation time), all nodes, if queried and responding honestly, will report the transaction as stable.

In [13,22] it was shown that persistence and liveness can be derived from the following three elementary properties provided that protocol Π derives the ledger from a data structure in the form of a blockchain.

- **Common Prefix (CP); with parameters** $k \in \mathbb{N}$. The chains $\mathcal{C}_1, \mathcal{C}_2$ possessed by two honest parties at the onset of the slots $sl_1 < sl_2$ are such that $\mathcal{C}_1^{\lceil k} \preceq \mathcal{C}_2$, where $\mathcal{C}_1^{\lceil k}$ denotes the chain obtained by removing the last k blocks from $\mathcal{C}_1$, and $\preceq$ denotes the prefix relation.
- **Chain Quality (CQ); with parameters** $\mu \in (0, 1] \rightarrow (0, 1]$ **and** $\ell \in \mathbb{N}$. Consider any portion of length at least ℓ of the chain possessed by an honest party at the onset of a round; the ratio of blocks originating from the adversary is at most $1 - \mu$. We call μ the chain quality coefficient.

- **Chain Growth (CG); with parameters $\tau \in (0,1], s \in \mathbb{N}$.** Consider the chains $\mathcal{C}_1, \mathcal{C}_2$ possessed by two honest parties at the onset of two slots sl_1, sl_2 with sl_2 at least s slots ahead of sl_1. Then it holds that $\text{len}(\mathcal{C}_2) - \text{len}(\mathcal{C}_1) \geq \tau \cdot s$. We call τ the speed coefficient.

Some remarks are in place. Regarding common prefix, we capture a strong notion of common prefix, cf. [13]. Regarding chain quality, the function μ satisfies $\mu(\alpha) \geq \alpha$ for protocols of interest. In an ideal setting, μ would be the identity function: in this case, the percentage of malicious blocks in any sufficiently long chain segment is proportional to the cumulative stake of a set of (malicious) stakeholders.

It is worth noting that for bitcoin we have $\mu(\alpha) = \alpha/(1-\alpha)$, and this bound is in fact tight—see [12], which argues this guarantee on chain quality. The same will hold true for our protocol construction. As we will show, this will still be sufficient for our incentive mechanism to work properly.

Finally chain growth concerns the rate at which the chain grows (for honest parties). As in the case of bitcoin, the *longest* chain plays a preferred role in our protocol; this provides an easy guarantee of chain growth.

Security Model. We adopt the model introduced by [12] for analysing security of blockchain protocols enhanced with an ideal functionality $\mathcal{F}$. We denote by $\mathsf{VIEW}^{P,\mathcal{F}}_{\Pi,\mathcal{A},\mathcal{Z}}(\kappa)$ the view of party P after the execution of protocol Π with adversary $\mathcal{A}$, environment $\mathcal{Z}$, security parameter κ and access to ideal functionality $\mathcal{F}$. We note that multiple different "functionalities" can be encompassed by $\mathcal{F}$.

We stress that contrary to [12], our analysis is in the "standard model", and without a random oracle functionality. Nevertheless we do employ a "diffuse" and "Key and Transaction" functionality with the following interfaces described below.

- Diffuse functionality. It maintains a incoming string for each party U_i that participates. A party, if activated, is allowed at any moment to fetch the contents of its incoming string hence one may think of this as a mailbox. Furthermore, parties can give the instruction to the functionality to diffuse a message. The functionality keeps rounds (called slots) and all parties are allowed to diffuse once in a round. Rounds do not advance unless all parties have diffused a message. The adversary, when activated, can also interact with the functionality and is allowed to read all inboxes and all diffuse requests and deliver messages to the inboxes in any order it prefers. At the end of the round, the functionality will ensure that all inboxes contain all messages that have been diffused (but not necessarily in the same order they have been requested to be diffused). The current slot index may be requested at any time by any party. If a stakeholder does not fetch in a certain slot the messages written to its incoming string, they are flushed.
- Key and Transaction functionality. The key registration functionality is initialized with n users, $U_1, \ldots, U_n$ and their respective stake $s_1, \ldots, s_n$; given such initialization, the functionality will consult with the adversary and will

accept a (possibly empty) sequence of (Corrupt, U) messages and mark the corresponding users U as corrupt. For the corrupt users without a public-key registered the functionality will allow the adversary to set their public-keys while for honest users the functionality will sample public/secret-key pairs and record them. Public-keys of corrupt users will be marked as such. Subsequently, any sequence of the following actions may take place: (i) A user may request to retrieve its public and secret-key, whereupon, the functionality will return it to the user. (ii) The whole directory of public-keys may be required in whereupon, the functionality will return it to the requesting user. (iii) A new user may be requested to be created by a message (Create, $U, \mathcal{C}$) from the environment, in which case the functionality will follow the same procedure as before: it will consult the adversary regarding the corruption status of U and will set its public and possibly secret-key depending on the corruption status; moreover it will store $\mathcal{C}$ as the suggested initial state. The functionality will return the public-key back to the environment upon successful completion of this interaction. (iv) A transaction may be requested on behalf of a certain user by the environment, by providing a template for the transaction (which should contain a unique nonce) and a recipient. The functionality will adjust the stake of each stakeholder accordingly. (v) An existing user may be requested to be corrupted by the adversary via a message (Corrupt, U). A user can only be corrupted after a delay of D slots; specifically, after a corruption request is registered the secret-key will be released after D slots have passed according to the round counter maintained in the Diffuse interface.

Given the above we will assume that the execution of the protocol is with respect to a functionality $\mathcal{F}$ that is incorporating the above two functionalities as well as possibly additional functionalities to be explained below. Note that a corrupted stakeholder U will relinquish its entire state to $\mathcal{A}$; from this point on, the adversary will be activated in place of the stakeholder U. Beyond any restrictions imposed by $\mathcal{F}$, the adversary can only corrupt a stakeholder if it is given permission by the environment $\mathcal{Z}$ running the protocol execution. The permission is in the form of a message (Corrupt, U) which is provided to the adversary by the environment. In summary, regarding activations we have the following.

- At each slot sl_j, the environment $\mathcal{Z}$ is allowed to activate any subset of stakeholders it wishes. Each one of them will possibly produce messages that are to be transmitted to other stakeholders.
- The adversary is activated at least as the last entity in each sl_j, (as well as during all adversarial party activations).

It is easy to see that the model above confers such sweeping power on the adversary that one cannot establish any significant guarantees on protocols of interest. It is thus important to restrict the environment suitably (taking into account the details of the protocol) so that we may be able to argue security. With foresight, the restrictions we will impose on the environment are as follows.

Restrictions Imposed on the Environment. The environment, which is responsible for activating the honest parties in each round, will be subject to the following constraints regarding the activation of the honest parties running the protocol.

- In each slot there will be at least one honest activated party (independently of whether it is a slot leader).
- There will be a parameter $k \in \mathbb{Z}$ that will signify the maximum number of slots that an honest shareholder can be offline. In case an honest stakeholder is spawned after the beginning of the protocol via $(\mathsf{Create}, U, \mathcal{C})$ its initialization chain $\mathcal{C}$ provided by the environment should match an honest parties' chain which was active in the previous slot.
- In each slot sl_r, and for each active stakeholder U_j there will be a set $\mathbb{S}_j(r)$ of public-keys and stake pairs of the form $(\mathsf{vk}_i, s_i) \in \{0,1\}^* \times \mathbb{N}$, for $j = 1, \ldots, n_r$ where n_r is the number of users introduced up to that slot. Public-keys will be marked as "corrupted" if the corresponding stakeholder has been corrupted. We will say the adversary is restricted to less than 50% relative stake if it holds that the total stake of the corrupted keys divided by the total stake $\sum_i s_i$ is less than 50% in all possible $\mathbb{S}_j(r)$. In case the above is violated an event $\mathsf{Bad}^{1/2}$ becomes true for the given execution.

We note that the offline restriction stated above is very conservative and our protocol can tolerate much longer offline times depending on the way the course of the execution proceeds; nevertheless, for the sake of simplicity, we use the above restriction. Finally, we note that in all our proofs, whenever we say that a property Q holds with high probability over all executions, we will in fact argue that $Q \vee \mathsf{Bad}^{1/2}$ holds with high probability over all executions. This captures the fact that we exclude environments and adversaries that trigger $\mathsf{Bad}^{1/2}$ with non-negligible probability.

3 Our Protocol: Overview

We first provide a general overview of our protocol design approach. The protocol's specifics depend on a number of parameters as follows: (i) k is the number of blocks a certain message should have "on top of it" in order to become part of the immutable history of the ledger, (ii) ϵ is the advantage in terms of stake of the honest stakeholders against the adversarial ones; (iii) D is the corruption delay that is imposed on the adversary, i.e., an honest stakeholder will be corrupted after D slots when a corrupt message is delivered by the adversary during an execution; (iv) L is the lifetime of the system, measured in slots; (v) R is the length of an epoch, measured in slots.

We present our protocol description in four *stages* successively improving the adversarial model it can withstand. In all stages an "ideal functionality" $\mathcal{F}_{\mathsf{LS}}^{\mathcal{D},\mathsf{F}}$ is available to the participants. The functionality captures the resources that are available to the parties as preconditions for the secure operation of the protocol (e.g., the genesis block will be specified by $\mathcal{F}_{\mathsf{LS}}^{\mathcal{D},\mathsf{F}}$).

Stage 1: Static stake; $D = L$. In the first stage, the trust assumption is static and remains with the initial set of stakeholders. There is an initial stake distribution which is hardcoded into the genesis block that includes the public-keys of the stakeholders, $\{(\mathsf{vk}_i, s_i)\}_{i=1}^{n}$. Based on our restrictions to the environment, honest majority with advantage ϵ is assumed among those initial stakeholders. Specifically, the environment initially will allow the corruption of a number of stakeholders whose relative stake represents $\frac{1-\epsilon}{2}$ for some $\epsilon > 0$. The environment allows party corruption by providing tokens of the form $(\mathsf{Corrupt}, U)$ to the adversary; note that due to the corruption delay imposed in this first stage any further corruptions will be against parties that have no stake initially and hence the corruption model is akin to "static corruption." $\mathcal{F}_{\mathsf{LS}}^{\mathcal{D},\mathsf{F}}$ will subsequently sample ρ which will seed a "weighted by stake" stakeholder sampling and in this way lead to the election of a subset of m keys $\mathsf{vk}_{i_1}, \ldots, \mathsf{vk}_{i_m}$ to form the committee that will possess honest majority with overwhelming probability in m, (this uses the fact that the relative stake possessed by malicious parties is $\frac{1-\epsilon}{2}$; a linear dependency of m to ϵ^{-2} will be imposed at this stage). In more detail, the committee will be selected implicitly by appointing a stakeholder with probability proportional to its stake to each one of the L slots. Subsequently, stakeholders will issue blocks following the schedule that is determined by the slot assignment. The longest chain rule will be applied and it will be possible for the adversary to fork the blockchain views of the honest parties. Nevertheless, we will prove with a Markov chain argument that the probability that a fork can be maintained over a sequence of n slots drops exponentially with at least $\sqrt{n}$, cf. Theorem 1 against general adversaries.

Stage 2: Dynamic state with a beacon, epoch period of R slots, $D = R \ll L$. The central idea for the extension of the lifetime of the above protocol is to consider the sequential composition of several invocations of it. We detail a way to do that, under the assumption that a trusted beacon emits a uniformly random string in regular intervals. More specifically, the beacon, during slots $\{j \cdot R + 1, \ldots, (j+1)R\}$, reveals the j-th random string that seeds the leader election function. The critical difference compared to the static state protocol is that the stake distribution is allowed to change and is drawn from the blockchain itself. This means that at a certain slot sl that belongs to the j-th epoch (with $j \geq 2$), the stake distribution that is used is the one reported in the most recent block with time stamp less than $j \cdot R - 2k$.

Regarding the evolving stake distribution, transactions will be continuously generated and transferred between stakeholders via the environment and players will incorporate posted transactions in the blockchain based ledgers that they maintain. In order to accommodate the new accounts that are being created, the $\mathcal{F}_{\mathsf{LS}}^{\mathcal{D},\mathsf{F}}$ functionality enables a new $(\mathsf{vk}, \mathsf{sk})$ to be created on demand and assigned to a new party U_i. Specifically, the environment can create new parties who will interact with $\mathcal{F}_{\mathsf{LS}}^{\mathcal{D},\mathsf{F}}$ for their public/secret-key in this way treating it as a trusted component that maintains the secret of their wallet. Note that the adversary can interfere with the creation of a new party, corrupt it, and supply its own (adversarially created) public-key instead. As before, the environment, may request transactions between accounts from stakeholders and it can also generate transactions in collaboration with the adversary on behalf of the corrupted accounts. Recall that our assumption is that at any slot, in the view of any honest player, the stakeholder distribution satisfies honest majority with advantage ϵ (note that different honest players might perceive a different stakeholder distribution in a certain slot). Furthermore, the stake can shift by at most σ statistical distance over a certain number of slots. The statistical distance here will be measured considering the underlying distribution to be the weighted-by-stake sampler and how it changes over the specified time interval. The security proof can be seen as an induction in the number of epochs L/R with the base case supplied by the proof of the static stake protocol. In the end we will argue that in this setting, a $\frac{1-\epsilon}{2} - \sigma$ bound in adversarial stake is sufficient for security of a single draw (and observe that the size of committee, m, now should be selected to overcome also an additive term of size $\ln(L/R)$ given that the lifetime of the systems includes such a number of successive epochs). The corruption delay remains at $D = R$ which can be selected arbitrarily smaller than L, thus enabling the adversary to perform adaptive corruptions as long as this is not instantaneous.

Stage 3: Dynamic state without a beacon, epoch period of R slots, $R = \Theta(k)$ and delay $D \in (R, 2R) \ll L$. In the third stage, we remove the dependency to the beacon, by introducing a secure multiparty protocol with "guaranteed output delivery" that simulates it. In this way, we can obtain the long-livedness of the protocol as described in the stage 2 design but only under the assumption of the stage 1 design, i.e., the mere availability of an initial random string and an initial stakeholder distribution with honest majority. The core idea is the following: given we guarantee that an honest majority among elected stakeholders will hold with very high probability, we can further use this elected set as participants to an instance of a secure multiparty computation (MPC) protocol. This will require the choice of the length of the epoch to be sufficient so that it can accommodate a run of the MPC protocol. From a security point of view, the main difference with the previous case, is that the output of the beacon will become known to the adversary before it may become known to the honest parties. Nevertheless, we will prove that the honest parties will also inevitably learn it after a short number of slots. To account for the fact that the adversary gets this headstart (which it may exploit by performing adaptive corruptions) we increase the wait time for corruption from R to a suitable value in $(R, 2R)$ that negates this advantage and depends on the secure MPC design. A feature of this stage from a cryptographic design perspective is the use of the ledger itself for the simulation of a reliable broadcast that supports the MPC protocol.

Stage 4: Input endorsers, stakeholder delegates, anonymous communication. In the final stage of our design, we augment the protocol with two new roles for the entities that are running the protocol and consider the benefits of anonymous communication. Input-endorsers create a second layer of transaction endorsing prior to block inclusion. This mechanism enables the protocol to withstand deviations such as selfish mining and enables us to show that honest behaviour is an approximate Nash equilibrium under reasonable assumptions regarding the costs of running the protocol. Note that input-endorsers are assigned to slots in the same way that slot leaders are, and inputs included in blocks are only acceptable if they are endorsed by an eligible input-endorser. Second, the *delegation* feature allows stakeholders to transfer committee participation to selected delegates that assume the responsibility of the stakeholders in running the protocol (including participation to the MPC and issuance of blocks). Delegation naturally gives rise to "stake pools" that can act in the same way as mining pools in bitcoin. Finally, we observe that by including an anonymous communication layer we can remove the corruption delay requirement that is imposed in our analysis. This is done at the expense of increasing the online time requirements for the honest parties. Due to lack of space we refer to the full version for more details, [14].

4 Our Protocol: Static State

4.1 Basic Concepts and Protocol Description

We begin by describing the blockchain protocol π_{SPoS} in the "static stake" setting, where leaders are assigned to blockchain slots with probability proportional to their (fixed) initial stake which will be the effective stake distribution throughout the execution. To simplify our presentation, we abstract this leader selection process, treating it simply as an "ideal functionality" that faithfully carries out the process of randomly assigning stakeholders to slots. In the following section, we explain how to instantiate this functionality with a secure computation.

We remark that—even with an ideal leader assignment process—analyzing the standard "longest chain" preference rule in our PoS setting appears to require significant new ideas. The challenge arises because large collections of slots (epochs, as described above) are assigned to stakeholders at once; while this has favorable properties from an efficiency (and incentive) perspective, it furnishes the adversary a novel means of attack. Specifically, an adversary in control of a certain population of stakeholders can, at the beginning of an epoch, choose when standard "chain update" broadcast messages are delivered to honest parties with full knowledge of future assignments of slots to stakeholders. In contrast, adversaries in typical PoW settings are constrained to make such decisions in an online fashion. We remark that this can have a dramatic effect on the ability of an adversary to produce alternate chains; see the discussion on "forkable strings" below for detailed discussion.

In the static stake case, we assume that a fixed collection of n stakeholders $U_1, \ldots, U_n$ interact throughout the protocol. Stakeholder U_i possesses s_i stake before the protocol starts. For each stakeholder U_i a verification and signing key pair $(\mathsf{vk}_i, \mathsf{sk}_i)$ for a prescribed signature scheme is generated; we assume without loss of generality that the verification keys $\mathsf{vk}_1, \ldots$ are known by all stakeholders. Before describing the protocol, we establish basic definitions following the notation of [12].

Definition 1 (Genesis Block). *The* genesis block B_0 *contains the list of stakeholders identified by their public-keys, their respective stakes* $(\mathsf{vk}_1, s_1), \ldots, (\mathsf{vk}_n, s_n)$ *and auxiliary information* ρ.

With foresight we note that the auxiliary information ρ will be used to seed the slot leader election process.

Definition 2 (State). *A* state *is a string* $st \in \{0,1\}^\lambda$.

Definition 3 (Block). *A* block B *generated at a slot* $sl_i \in \{sl_1, \ldots, sl_R\}$ *contains the current state* $st \in \{0,1\}^\lambda$, *data* $d \in \{0,1\}^*$, *the slot number* sl_i *and a signature* $\sigma = \mathsf{Sign}_{\mathsf{sk}_i}(st, d, sl)$ *computed under* sk_i *corresponding to the stakeholder* U_i *generating the block.*

Definition 4 (Blockchain). *A* blockchain *(or simply* chain*) relative to the genesis block* B_0 *is a sequence of blocks* $B_1, \ldots, B_n$ *associated with a strictly increasing sequence of slots for which the state* st_i *of* B_i *is equal to* $H(B_{i-1})$, *where* H *is a prescribed collision-resistant hash function. The* length *of a chain* $\mathrm{len}(\mathcal{C}) = n$ *is its number of blocks. The block* B_n *is the* head *of the chain, denoted* $\mathrm{head}(\mathcal{C})$. *We treat the empty string* ε *as a legal chain and by convention set* $\mathrm{head}(\varepsilon) = \varepsilon$.

Let $\mathcal{C}$ be a chain of length n and k be any non-negative integer. We denote by $\mathcal{C}^{\lceil k}$ the chain resulting from removal of the k rightmost blocks of $\mathcal{C}$. If $k \geq \mathrm{len}(\mathcal{C})$ we define $\mathcal{C}^{\lceil k} = \varepsilon$. We let $\mathcal{C}_1 \preceq \mathcal{C}_2$ indicate that the chain $\mathcal{C}_1$ is a prefix of the chain $\mathcal{C}_2$.

Definition 5 (Epoch). *An* epoch *is a set of* R *adjacent slots* $S = \{sl_1, \ldots, sl_R\}$.

(The value R is a parameter of the protocol we analyze in this section.)

Definition 6 (Adversarial Stake Ratio). *Let* $U_\mathcal{A}$ *be the set of stakeholders controlled by an adversary* $\mathcal{A}$. *Then the* adversarial stake ratio *is defined as*

$$\alpha = \frac{\sum_{j \in U_\mathcal{A}} s_j}{\sum_{i=1}^{n} s_i},$$

where n *is the total number of stakeholders and* s_i *is stakeholder* U_i*'s stake.*

Slot Leader Selection. In the protocol described in this section, for each $0 < j \leq R$, a *slot leader* E_j is determined who has the (sole) right to generate a block at sl_j. Specifically, for each slot a stakeholder U_i is selected as the slot leader with probability p_i proportional to its stake registered in the genesis block B_0; these assignments are independent between slots. In this static stake case, the genesis block as well as the procedure for selecting slot leaders are determined by an ideal functionality $\mathcal{F}_{\mathsf{LS}}^{\mathcal{D},\mathsf{F}}$, defined in Fig. 1. This functionality is parameterized by the list $\{(\mathsf{vk}_1, s_1), \ldots, (\mathsf{vk}_n, s_n)\}$ assigning to each stakeholder its respective stake, a distribution $\mathcal{D}$ that provides auxiliary information ρ and a *leader selection function* F defined below.

Definition 7 (Leader Selection Process). *A leader selection process with respect to stakeholder distribution* $\mathbb{S} = \{(\mathsf{vk}_1, s_1), \ldots, (\mathsf{vk}_n, s_n)\}$, $(\mathcal{D}, \mathsf{F})$ *is a pair consisting of a distribution and a deterministic function such that, when* $\rho \leftarrow \mathcal{D}$ *it holds that for all* $sl_j \in \{sl_1, \ldots, sl_R\}$, $\mathsf{F}(\mathbb{S}, \rho, sl_j)$ *outputs* $U_i \in \{U_1, \ldots, U_n\}$ *with probability*

$$p_i = \frac{s_i}{\sum_{k=1}^{n} s_k}$$

where s_i *is the stake held by stakeholder* U_i *(we call this "weighing by stake"); furthermore the family of random variables* $\{\mathsf{F}(\mathbb{S}, \rho, sl_j)\}_{j=1}^{R}$ *are independent.*

We note that sampling proportional to stake can be implemented in a straightforward manner. For instance, a simple process operates as follows. Let $\tilde{p}_i = s_i / \sum_{j=i}^{n} s_j$. For each $i = 1, \ldots, n-1$, provided that no stakeholder has yet been selected, the process flips a $\tilde{p}_i$-biased coin; if the result of the coin is 1, the party U_i is selected for the slot and the process is complete. (Note that $\tilde{p}_n = 1$, so the process is certain to complete with a unique leader.) When we implement this process as a function $F(\cdot)$, sufficient randomness must be allocated to simulate the biased coin flips. If we implement the above with λ precision for each individual coin flip, then selecting a stakeholder will require $n\lceil \log \lambda \rceil$ random bits in total. Note that using a pseudorandom number generator (PRG) one may use a shorter "seed" string and then stretch it using the PRG to the appropriate length.

Functionality $\mathcal{F}_{\mathsf{LS}}^{\mathcal{D},\mathsf{F}}$

$\mathcal{F}_{\mathsf{LS}}^{\mathcal{D},\mathsf{F}}$ incorporates the diffuse and key/transaction functionality from Section 2 and is parameterized by the public keys and respective stakes of the initial stakeholders $\mathbb{S}_0 = \{(\mathsf{vk}_1, s_1), \ldots, (\mathsf{vk}_n, s_n)\}$, a distribution $\mathcal{D}$ and a function F so that $(\mathcal{D}, \mathsf{F})$ is a leader selection process. In addition, $\mathcal{F}_{\mathsf{LS}}^{\mathcal{D},\mathsf{F}}$ interacts with stakeholders as follows:

- Upon receiving $(\mathsf{genblock\_req}, U_i)$ from stakeholder U_i, $\mathcal{F}_{\mathsf{LS}}^{\mathcal{D},\mathsf{F}}$ proceeds as follows. If ρ has not been set, $\mathcal{F}_{\mathsf{LS}}^{\mathcal{D},\mathsf{F}}$ samples $\rho \leftarrow \mathcal{D}$. In any case, $\mathcal{F}_{\mathsf{LS}}^{\mathcal{D},\mathsf{F}}$ sends $(\mathsf{genblock}, \mathbb{S}_0, \rho, \mathsf{F})$ to U_i.

Fig. 1. Functionality $\mathcal{F}_{\mathsf{LS}}^{\mathcal{D},\mathsf{F}}$.

A Protocol in the $\mathcal{F}_{\mathsf{LS}}^{\mathcal{D},\mathsf{F}}$*-Hybrid Model.* We start by describing a simple PoS based blockchain protocol considering static stake in the $\mathcal{F}_{\mathsf{LS}}^{\mathcal{D},\mathsf{F}}$-hybrid model, i.e., where the genesis block B_0 (and consequently the slot leaders) are determined by the ideal functionality $\mathcal{F}_{\mathsf{LS}}^{\mathcal{D},\mathsf{F}}$. The stakeholders $U_1, \ldots, U_n$ interact among themselves and with $\mathcal{F}_{\mathsf{LS}}^{\mathcal{D},\mathsf{F}}$ through Protocol π_{SPoS} described in Fig. 2.

The protocol relies on a $\mathsf{maxvalid}_S(\mathcal{C}, \mathbb{C})$ function that chooses a chain given the current chain $\mathcal{C}$ and a set of valid chains $\mathbb{C}$ that are available in the network. In the static case we analyze the simple "longest chain" rule. (In the dynamic case the rule is parameterized by a common chain length; see Sect. 5.)

Function $\mathsf{maxvalid}(\mathcal{C}, \mathbb{C})$: Returns the longest chain from $\mathbb{C} \cup \{\mathcal{C}\}$. Ties are broken in favor of $\mathcal{C}$, if it has maximum length, or arbitrarily otherwise.

Protocol π_{SPoS}

π_{SPoS} is a protocol run by stakeholders $U_1, \ldots, U_n$ interacting among themselves and with $\mathcal{F}_{\mathsf{LS}}^{\mathcal{D},\mathsf{F}}$ over a sequence of slots $S = \{sl_1, \ldots, sl_R\}$. π_{SPoS} proceeds as follows:

1. **Initialization** Stakeholder $U_i \in \{U_1, \ldots, U_n\}$, receives from the key registration interface its public and secret key. Then it receives the current slot from the diffuse interface and in case it is sl_1 it sends $(\mathsf{genblock\_req}, U_i)$ to $\mathcal{F}_{\mathsf{LS}}^{\mathcal{D},\mathsf{F}}$, receiving $(\mathsf{genblock}, \mathbb{S}_0, \rho, \mathsf{F})$ as answer. U_i sets the local blockchain $\mathcal{C} = B_0 = (\mathbb{S}_0, \rho)$ and the initial internal state $st = H(B_0)$. Otherwise, it receives from the key registration interface the initial chain $\mathcal{C}$, sets the local blockchain as $\mathcal{C}$ and the initial internal state $st = H(\mathrm{head}(\mathcal{C}))$.
2. **Chain Extension** For every slot $sl_j \in S$, every online stakeholder U_i performs the following steps:
   (a) Collect all valid chains received via broadcast into a set $\mathbb{C}$, verifying that for every chain $\mathcal{C}' \in \mathbb{C}$ and every block $B' = (st', d', sl', \sigma') \in \mathcal{C}'$ it holds that $\mathsf{Vrf}_{\mathsf{vk}'}(\sigma', (st', d', sl')) = 1$, where vk' is the verification key of the stakeholder $U' = \mathsf{F}(\mathbb{S}_0, \rho, sl')$. U_i computes $\mathcal{C}' = \mathsf{maxvalid}(\mathcal{C}, \mathbb{C})$, sets $\mathcal{C}'$ as the new local chain and sets state $st = H(\mathrm{head}(\mathcal{C}'))$.
   (b) If U_i is the slot leader determined by $\mathsf{F}(\mathbb{S}_0, \rho, sl_j)$, it generates a new block $B = (st, d, sl_j, \sigma)$ where st is its current state, $d \in \{0,1\}^*$ is the transaction data and $\sigma = \mathsf{Sign}_{\mathsf{sk}_i}(st, d, sl_j)$ is a signature on (st, d, sl_j). U_i computes $\mathcal{C}' = \mathcal{C}|B$, broadcasts $\mathcal{C}'$, sets $\mathcal{C}'$ as the new local chain and sets state $st = H(\mathrm{head}(\mathcal{C}'))$.

Fig. 2. Protocol π_{SPoS}.

4.2 Forkable Strings

In our security arguments we routinely use elements of $\{0,1\}^n$ to indicate which slots—among a particular window of slots of length n—have been assigned to adversarial stakeholders. When strings have this interpretation we refer to them as *characteristic strings.*

Definition 8 (Characteristic String). *Fix an execution with genesis block B_0, adversary $\mathcal{A}$, and environment $\mathcal{Z}$. Let $S = \{sl_{i+1}, \ldots, sl_{i+n}\}$ denote a sequence of slots of length $|S| = n$. The* characteristic string *$w \in \{0,1\}^n$ of S is defined so that $w_k = 1$ if and only if the adversary controls the slot leader of slot sl_{i+k}. For such a characteristic string $w \in \{0,1\}^*$ we say that the index i is* adversarial *if $w_i = 1$ and* honest *otherwise.*

We start with some intuition on our approach to analyze the protocol. Let $w \in \{0,1\}^n$ be a characteristic string for a sequence of slots S. Consider two observers that (i) go offline immediately prior to the commencement of S, (ii) have the same view $\mathcal{C}_0$ of the current chain prior to the commencement of S, and (iii) come back online at the last slot of S and request an update of their chain. A fundamental concern in our analysis is the possibility that such observers can be presented with a "diverging" view over the sequence S: specifically, the possibility that the adversary can force the two observers to adopt two different chains $\mathcal{C}_1, \mathcal{C}_2$ whose common prefix is $\mathcal{C}_0$.

We observe that not all characteristic strings permit this. For instance the (entirely honest) string 0^n ensures that the two observers will adopt the same chain $\mathcal{C}$ which will consist of n new blocks on top of the common prefix $\mathcal{C}_0$. On the other hand, other strings do not guarantee such common extension of $\mathcal{C}_0$; in the case of 1^n, it is possible for the adversary to produce two completely different histories during the sequence of slots S and thus furnish to the two observers two distinct chains $\mathcal{C}_1, \mathcal{C}_2$ that only share the common prefix $\mathcal{C}_0$. In the remainder of this section, we establish that strings that permit such "forkings" are quite rare—indeed, we show that they have density $2^{-\Omega(\sqrt{n})}$ so long as the fraction of adversarial slots is $1/2 - \epsilon$.

To reason about such "forkings" of a characteristic string $w \in \{0,1\}^n$, we define below a formal notion of "fork" that captures the relationship between the chains broadcast by *honest* slot leaders during an execution of the protocol π_{SPoS}. In preparation for the definition, we recall that honest players always choose to extend a maximum length chain among those available to the player on the network. Furthermore, if such a maximal chain $\mathcal{C}$ includes a block B previously broadcast by an honest player, the prefix of $\mathcal{C}$ prior to B must entirely agree with the chain (terminating at B) broadcast by this previous honest player. This "confluence" property follows immediately from the fact that the state of any honest block effectively commits to a unique chain beginning at the genesis block. To conclude, any chain $\mathcal{C}$ broadcast by an honest player must begin with a chain produced by a previously honest player (or, alternatively, the genesis block), continue with a possibly empty sequence of adversarial blocks and, finally, terminate with an honest block. It follows that the chains broadcast by honest players form a natural directed tree. The fact that honest players reliably broadcast their chains and always build on the longest available chain introduces a second important property of this tree: the "depths" of the various honest blocks added by honest players during the protocol must all be distinct.

Of course, the actual chains induced by an execution of π_{SPoS} are comprised of blocks containing a variety of data that are immaterial for reasoning about forking. For this reason the formal notion of fork below merely reflects the directed tree formed by the relevant chains and the *identities of the players*—expressed as indices in the string w—responsible for generating the blocks in these chains.

Forks and Forkable Strings. We define, below, the basic combinatorial structures we use to reason about the possible views observed by honest players during a protocol execution with this characteristic string.

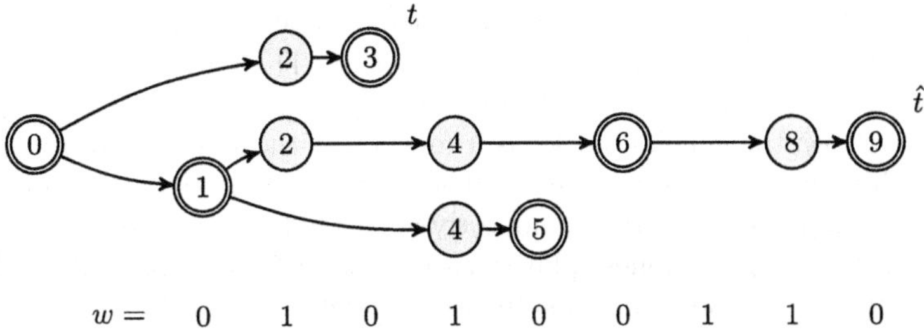

Fig. 3. A fork F for the string $w = 010100110$; vertices appear with their labels and honest vertices are highlighted with double borders. Note that the depths of the (honest) vertices associated with the honest indices of w are strictly increasing. Two tines are distinguished in the figure: one, labeled $\hat{t}$, terminates at the vertex labeled 9 and is the longest tine in the fork; a second tine t terminates at the vertex labeled 3. The quantity $\text{gap}(t)$ indicates the difference in length between t and $\hat{t}$; in this case $\text{gap}(t) = 4$. The quantity $\text{reserve}(t) = |\{i \mid \ell(v) < i \leq |w| \text{ and } w_i = 1\}|$ indicates the number of adversarial indices appearing after the label of the last honest vertex v of the tine; in this case $\text{reserve}(t) = 3$. As each leaf of F is honest, F is closed.

Definition 9 (Fork). *Let $w \in \{0,1\}^n$ and let $H = \{i \mid w_i = 0\}$ denote the set of honest indices. A* fork *for the string w is a directed, rooted tree $F = (V, E)$ with a labeling $\ell : V \to \{0, 1, \ldots, n\}$ so that*

- *each edge of F is directed away from the root;*
- *the root $r \in V$ is given the label $\ell(r) = 0$;*
- *the labels along any directed path in the tree are strictly increasing;*
- *each honest index $i \in H$ is the label of exactly one vertex of F;*
- *the function $\mathbf{d} : H \to \{1, \ldots, n\}$, defined so that $\mathbf{d}(i)$ is the depth in F of the unique vertex v for which $\ell(v) = i$, is strictly increasing. (Specifically, if $i, j \in H$ and $i < j$, then $\mathbf{d}(i) < \mathbf{d}(j)$.)*

As a matter of notation, we write $F \vdash w$ to indicate that F is a fork for the string w. We say that a fork is trivial *if it contains a single vertex, the root.*

Definition 10 (Tines and height). *A path in a fork F originating at the root is called a* tine*. For a tine t we let* length(t) *denote its* length, *equal to the number of edges on the path. The* height *of a fork (as usual for a tree) is defined to be the length of the longest tine. For two tines t_1 and t_2 of a fork F, we write $t_1 \sim t_2$ if they share an edge. Note that $\sim$ is an equivalence relation on the set of nontrivial tines; on the other hand, if t_ϵ denotes the "empty" tine consisting solely of the root vertex then $t_\epsilon \not\sim t$ for any tine t.*

If a vertex v of a fork is labeled with an adversarial index (i.e., $w_{\ell(v)} = 1$) we say that the vertex is *adversarial*; otherwise, we say that the vertex is *honest*. For convenience, we declare the root vertex to be honest. We extend this terminology to tines: a tine is *honest* if it terminates with an honest vertex and *adversarial* otherwise. By this convention the empty tine t_ϵ is honest.

See Fig. 3 for an example, which also demonstrates some of the quantities defined above and in the remainder of this section. The fork shown in the figure reflects an execution in which *(i)* the honest player associated with the first slot builds directly on the genesis block (as it must), *(ii)* the honest player associated with the third slot is shown a chain of length 1 produced by the adversarial player of slot 2 (in addition to the honestly generated chain of step *(i)*), which it elects to extend, *(iii)* the honest player associated with slot 5 is shown a chain of length 2 building on the chain of step *(i)* augmented with a further adversarial block produced by the player of slot 4, etc.

Definition 11. *We say that a fork is* flat *if it has two tines $t_1 \not\sim t_2$ of length equal to the height of the fork. A string $w \in \{0,1\}^*$ is said to be* forkable *if there is a flat fork $F \vdash w$.*

Note that in order for an execution of π_{SPoS} to yield two entirely disjoint chains of maximum length, the characteristic string associated with the execution must be forkable. Our goal is to establish the following upper bound on the number of forkable strings.

Theorem 1. *Let $\epsilon \in (0,1)$ and let w be a string drawn from $\{0,1\}^n$ by independently assigning each $w_i = 1$ with probability $(1-\epsilon)/2$. Then* $\Pr[w$ *is forkable*$] = 2^{-\Omega(\sqrt{n})}$.

In subsequent work, Russell et al. [24] improved this bound to $2^{-\Omega(n)}$.

Structural Features of Forks: Closed Forks, Prefixes, Reach, and Margin. We begin by defining a natural notion of inclusion for two forks:

Definition 12 (Fork prefixes). *If w is a prefix of the string $w' \in \{0,1\}^*$, $F \vdash w$, and $F' \vdash w'$, we say that F is a* prefix *of F', written $F \sqsubseteq F'$, if F is a consistently-labeled subgraph of F'. Specifically, every vertex and edge of F appears in F' and, furthermore, the labels given to any vertex appearing in both F and F' are identical.*

If $F \sqsubseteq F'$, each tine of F appears as the prefix of a tine in F'. In particular, the labels appearing on any tine terminating at a common vertex are identical and, moreover, the depth of any honest vertex appearing in both F and F' is identical.

In many cases, it is convenient to work with forks that do not "commit" anything beyond final honest indices.

Definition 13 (Closed forks). *A fork is* closed *if each leaf is honest. By convention the trivial fork, consisting solely of a root vertex, is closed.*

Note that a closed fork has a unique longest tine (as all maximal tines terminate with an honest vertex, and these must have distinct depths). Note, additionally, that if w is a prefix of w' and $F' \vdash w'$, then there is a unique closed fork $F \vdash w$ for which $F \sqsubseteq F'$.

Definition 14 (Gap, reserve and reach). *Let $F \vdash w$ be a closed fork and let $\hat{t}$ denote the (unique) tine of maximum length in F. We define the* gap *of a tine t, denoted* gap(t)*, to be the difference in length between $\hat{t}$ and t; thus*

$$\text{gap}(t) = \text{length}(\hat{t}) - \text{length}(t).$$

We define the reserve *of a tine t to be the number of adversarial indices appearing in w after the last index in t; specifically, if t is given by the path $(r, v_1, \ldots, v_k)$, where r is the root of F, we define*

$$\text{reserve}(t) = |\{i \mid w_i = 1 \textit{ and } i > \ell(v_k)\}|.$$

We remark that this quantity depends both on F and the specific string w associated with F. Finally, for a tine t we define

$$\text{reach}(t) = \text{reserve}(t) - \text{gap}(t).$$

Definition 15 (Margin). *For a closed fork $F \vdash w$ we define $\lambda(F)$ to be the maximum reach taken over all tines in F:*

$$\lambda(F) = \max_t \text{reach}(t).$$

Likewise, we define the margin *of F, denoted $\mu(F)$, to be the "penultimate" reach taken over edge-disjoint tines of F: specifically,*

$$\text{margin}(F) = \mu(F) = \max_{t_1 \not\sim t_2} \Big(\min\{\text{reach}(t_1), \text{reach}(t_2)\}\Big). \tag{1}$$

We remark that the maxima above can always obtained by honest tines. Specifically, if t is an adversarial tine of a fork $F \vdash w$, $\text{reach}(t) \leq \text{reach}(\overline{t})$, where $\overline{t}$ is the longest honest prefix of t.

As $\sim$ is an equivalence relation on the nonempty tines, it follows that there is always a pair of (edge-disjoint) tines t_1 and t_2 achieving the maximum in the defining Eq. (1) which satisfy $\text{reach}(t_1) = \lambda(F) \geq \text{reach}(t_2) = \mu(F)$.

The relevance of margin to the notion of forkability is reflected in the following proposition.

Proposition 1. *A string w is forkable if and only if there is a closed fork $F \vdash w$ for which* $\text{margin}(F) \geq 0$.

Proof. If w has no honest indices, then the trivial fork consisting of a single root node is flat, closed, and has non-negative margin; thus the two conditions are equivalent. Consider a forkable string w with at least one honest index and let $\hat{i}$ denote the largest honest index of w. Let F be a flat fork for w. As mentioned above, there is a unique closed fork $\overline{F} \vdash w$ obtained from F by removing any adversarial vertices from the ends of the tines of F. Note that the tine $\hat{t}$ containing $\hat{i}$ is the longest tine in $\overline{F}$, as this is the largest honest index of w. On the other hand, F is flat, in which case there are two edge-disjoint tines t_1 and t_2 with length at least that of $\hat{t}$. The prefixes of these two tines in $\overline{F}$ must clearly have reserve no less than gap (and hence non-negative reach); thus margin$(\overline{F}) \geq 0$ as desired.

On the other hand, suppose w has a closed fork with margin$(F) \geq 0$, in which case there are two edge-disjoint tines of F, t_1 and t_2, for which reach$(t_i) \geq 0$. Then we can produce a flat fork by simply adding to each t_i a path of gap(t_i) vertices labeled with the subsequent adversarial indices promised by the definition of reserve().

In light of this proposition, for a string w we focus our attention on the quantities

$$\lambda(w) = \max_{\substack{F \vdash w, \\ F \text{ closed}}} \lambda(F), \qquad \mu(w) = \max_{\substack{F \vdash w, \\ F \text{ closed}}} \mu(F),$$

and, for convenience,

$$\mathbf{m}(w) = (\lambda(w), \mu(w)).$$

Note that this overloads the notation $\lambda(\cdot)$ and $\mu(\cdot)$ so that they apply to both forks and strings, but the setting will be clear from context. We remark that the definitions do not guarantee a priori that $\lambda(w)$ and $\mu(w)$ can be achieved by the same fork, though this is established by the full treatment in [14]. In any case, it is clear that $\lambda(w) \geq 0$ and $\lambda(w) \geq \mu(w)$ for all strings w; furthermore, by Proposition 1 a string w is forkable if and only if $\mu(w) \geq 0$. We refer to $\mu(w)$ as the *margin* of the string w.

With these definitions in place, we are prepared to survey the proof of Theorem 1.

Proof (of Theorem 1; high level survey). The proof proceeds by establishing a recursive description of $\mathbf{m}(w0)$ and $\mathbf{m}(w1)$ in terms of $\mathbf{m}(w)$ and providing an analysis of the Markov chain that arises by considering $\mathbf{m}(\cdot)$ for strings drawn from a binomial distribution. This yields an upper bound on the probability that $\mu(w) \geq 0$ and hence the event that w is forkable. The full proof appears in the e-print version of the paper [14].

Covert Adversaries. Observe that an adversary that broadcasts *two distinct* blocks for a particular slot leaves behind a suspicious "audit trail"—multiple signed blocks for the same slot—which conspicuously deviates from the protocol. This may be undesirable for certain practical adversaries, who wish to maintain the facade of honesty. We say that such an adversary is "covert" and note that such adversaries have reduced power to disrupt the protocol. We discuss this in detail and consider the probability of forkability with these weakened adversaries in the full version of the paper [14].

4.3 Common Prefix

Recall that the chains constructed by honest players during an execution of π_{SPoS} correspond to tines of a fork, as defined and studied in the previous sections.

The random assignment of slots to stakeholders given by $\mathcal{F}_{\mathsf{LS}}^{\mathcal{D},\mathsf{F}}$ guarantees that the coordinates of the associated characteristic string w follow the binomial distribution with probability equal to the adversarial stake. Thus Theorem 1 establishes that no execution of the protocol π_{SPoS} can induce two tines (chains) of maximal length with no common prefix.

In the context of π_{SPoS}, however, we wish to establish a much stronger common prefix property: The chains reported by any two honest players must have a "recent" common prefix, in the sense that removing a small number of blocks from the shorter chain results in a prefix of the longer chain.

Theorem 2. *Let $k, R \in \mathbb{N}$ and $\epsilon \in (0,1)$. The probability that the π_{SPoS} protocol, when executed with a $(1-\epsilon)/2$ fraction of adversarial stake, violates the common prefix property with parameter k throughout an epoch of R slots is no more than $\exp(-\Omega(\sqrt{k}) + \ln R)$; the constant hidden by the $\Omega()$ notation depends only on ϵ.*

Proof (sketch). The full proof (see [14]) proceeds by showing that if common prefix with parameter k is violated for a particular fork, then the underlying characteristic string must have a forkable substring of length k. Thus

$$\begin{aligned}\Pr[\text{common prefix violation}] &\leq \Pr\begin{bmatrix}\exists \alpha, \beta \in \{1, \ldots, R\} \text{ so that } \alpha + k - 1 \leq \beta \\ \text{and } w_\alpha \ldots w_\beta \text{ is forkable}\end{bmatrix} \\ &\leq \sum_{1 \leq \alpha \leq R} \underbrace{\sum_{\alpha+k-1 \leq \beta \leq R} \Pr[w_\alpha \ldots w_\beta \text{ is forkable}]}_{(*)}.\end{aligned}$$

Recall that the characteristic string $w \in \{0,1\}^R$ for such an execution of π_{SPoS} is determined by assigning each $w_i = 1$ independently with probability $(1-\epsilon)/2$. According to Theorem 1 the probability that a string of length t drawn from this distribution is forkable is no more than $\exp(-c\sqrt{t})$ for a positive constant c. Note that for any $\alpha \geq 1$,

$$\sum_{t=\alpha+k-1}^{R} e^{-c\sqrt{t}} \leq \int_{k-1}^{\infty} e^{-c\sqrt{t}}\, dt = (2/c^2)(1 + c\sqrt{k-1})e^{-c\sqrt{k-1}} = e^{-\Omega(\sqrt{k})}$$

and it follows that the sum $(*)$ above is $\exp(-\Omega(\sqrt{t}))$. Thus

$$\Pr[\text{common prefix violation}] \leq R \cdot \exp(-\Omega(\sqrt{k})) \leq \exp(\ln R - \Omega(\sqrt{k})),$$

as desired.

4.4 Chain Growth and Chain Quality

Anticipating these two proofs, we record an additive Chernoff–Hoeffding bound. (See, e.g., [17] for a proof.)

Theorem 3 (Chernoff–Hoeffding bound). *Let $X_1, \ldots, X_T$ be independent random variables with $\mathbb{E}[X_i] = p_i$ and $X_i \in [0,1]$. Let $X = \sum_{i=1}^{T} X_i$ and $\mu = \sum_{i=1}^{T} p_i = \mathbb{E}[X]$. Then, for all $\delta \geq 0$,*

$$\Pr[X \geq (1+\delta)\mu] \leq e^{-\frac{\delta^2}{2+\delta}\mu} \quad \text{and} \quad \Pr[X \leq (1-\delta)\mu] \leq e^{-\frac{\delta^2}{2+\delta}\mu}.$$

We will start with the chain growth property.

Theorem 4. *The π_{SPoS} protocol satisfies the chain growth property with parameters $\tau = 1 - \alpha, s \in \mathbb{N}$ throughout an epoch of R slots with probability at least $1 - \exp(-\Omega(\epsilon^2 s) + \ln R)$ against an adversary holding an $\alpha - \epsilon$ portion of the total stake.*

Proof (sketch). The proof proceeds by applying the Chernoff bound to ensure that with high probability a characteristic string drawn from the binomial distribution has a $\approx \tau = (1 - \alpha)$ fraction of honest indices. Note that each honest player will force the length of the resulting chain to increase by one in any execution of π_{SPoS}. See [14] for a complete presentation.

Having established chain growth we now turn our attention to chain quality. Recall that the chain quality property with parameters μ and ℓ asserts that among every ℓ consecutive blocks in a chain (possessed by an honest user), the fraction of adversarial blocks is no more than μ.

Theorem 5. *Let $\alpha - \epsilon$ be the adversarial stake ratio. The π_{SPoS} protocol satisfies the chain quality property with parameters $\mu(\alpha - \epsilon) = \alpha/(1 - \alpha)$ and $\ell \in \mathbb{N}$ throughout an epoch of R slots with probability at least*

$$1 - \exp\bigl(-\Omega(\epsilon^2 \alpha \ell) + \ln R\bigr).$$

Proof (sketch). This likewise follows from appropriate application of the Chernoff bound. See [14] for full discussion.

5 Our Protocol: Dynamic Stake

5.1 Using a Trusted Beacon

In the static version of the protocol in the previous section, we assumed that stake was static during the whole execution (i.e., one epoch), meaning that stake changing hands inside a given epoch does not affect leader election. Now we put forth a modification of protocol π_{SPoS} that can be executed over multiple epochs in such a way that each epoch's leader election process is parameterized by the stake distribution at a certain designated point of the previous epoch, allowing for change in the stake distribution across epochs to affect the leader election process. As before, we construct the protocol in a hybrid model, enhancing the $\mathcal{F}_{\mathsf{LS}}^{\mathcal{D},\mathsf{F}}$ ideal functionality to now provide randomness and auxiliary information for the leader election process throughout the epochs (the enhanced functionality will be called $\mathcal{F}_{\mathsf{DLS}}^{\mathcal{D},\mathsf{F}}$). We then discuss how to implement $\mathcal{F}_{\mathsf{DLS}}^{\mathcal{D},\mathsf{F}}$ using only $\mathcal{F}_{\mathsf{LS}}^{\mathcal{D},\mathsf{F}}$ and in this way reduce the assumption back to the simple common random string selected at setup.

Before describing the protocol for the case of dynamic stake, we need to explain the modification of $\mathcal{F}_{\mathsf{LS}}^{\mathcal{D},\mathsf{F}}$ so that multiple epochs are considered. The resulting functionality, $\mathcal{F}_{\mathsf{DLS}}^{\mathcal{D},\mathsf{F}}$, allows stakeholders to query it for the leader selection data specific to each epoch. $\mathcal{F}_{\mathsf{DLS}}^{\mathcal{D},\mathsf{F}}$ is parameterized by the initial stake of each stakeholder before the first epoch e_1 starts; in subsequent epochs, parties will take into consideration the stake distribution in the latest block of the previous epoch's first $R - 2k$ slots. Given that there is no predetermined view of the stakeholder distribution, the functionality $\mathcal{F}_{\mathsf{DLS}}^{\mathcal{D},\mathsf{F}}$ will provide only a random string and will leave the interpretation according to the stakeholder distribution to the party that is calling it. The effective stakeholder distribution is the sequence $\mathbb{S}_1, \mathbb{S}_2, \ldots$ defined as follows: $\mathbb{S}_1$ is the initial stakeholder distribution; for slots $\{(j-1)R+1, \ldots, jR\}$ for $j \geq 2$ the effective stakeholder $\mathbb{S}_j$ is determined by the stake allocation that is found in the latest block with time stamp at most $(j-1)R - 2k$, provided all honest parties agree on it, or is undefined if the honest parties disagree on it. The functionality $\mathcal{F}_{\mathsf{DLS}}^{\mathcal{D},\mathsf{F}}$ is defined in Fig. 4.

Functionality $\mathcal{F}_{\mathsf{DLS}}^{\mathcal{D},\mathsf{F}}$

$\mathcal{F}_{\mathsf{DLS}}^{\mathcal{D},\mathsf{F}}$ incorporates the diffuse and key/transaction functionality from Section 2 and is parameterized by the public keys and respective stakes of the initial (before epoch e_1 starts) stakeholders $\mathbb{S}_0 = \{(\mathsf{vk}_1, s_1^0), \ldots, (\mathsf{vk}_n, s_n^0)\}$ a distribution $\mathcal{D}$ and a leader selection function F. In addition, $\mathcal{F}_{\mathsf{DLS}}^{\mathcal{D},\mathsf{F}}$ operates as follows:

- Upon receiving $(\mathsf{genblock\_req}, U_i)$ from stakeholder U_i it operates as functionality $\mathcal{F}_{\mathsf{LS}}^{\mathcal{D},\mathsf{F}}$ on that message.
- Upon receiving $(\mathsf{epochrnd\_req}, U_i, e_j)$ from stakeholder U_i, if $j \geq 2$ is the current epoch, $\mathcal{F}_{\mathsf{DLS}}^{\mathcal{D},\mathsf{F}}$ proceeds as follows. If ρ^j has not been set, $\mathcal{F}_{\mathsf{DLS}}^{\mathcal{D},\mathsf{F}}$ samples $\rho^j \leftarrow \mathcal{D}$. Then, $\mathcal{F}_{\mathsf{DLS}}^{\mathcal{D},\mathsf{F}}$ sends $(\mathsf{epochrnd}, \rho^j)$ to U_i.

Fig. 4. Functionality $\mathcal{F}_{\mathsf{DLS}}^{\mathcal{D},\mathsf{F}}$.

We now describe protocol π_{DPoS}, which is a modified version of π_{SPoS} that updates its genesis block B_0 (and thus the leader selection process) for every new epoch. The protocol also adopts an adaptation of the static $\mathsf{maxvalid}_S$ function, defined so that it narrows selection to those chains which share common prefix. Specifically, it adopts the following rule, parameterized by a prefix length k:

> Function $\mathsf{maxvalid}(\mathcal{C}, \mathbb{C})$. Returns the longest chain from $\mathbb{C} \cup \{\mathcal{C}\}$ that does not fork from $\mathcal{C}$ more than k blocks. If multiple exist it returns $\mathcal{C}$, if this is one of them, or it returns the one that is listed first in $\mathbb{C}$.

Protocol π_{DPoS} is described in Fig. 5 and functions in the $\mathcal{F}_{\mathsf{DLS}}^{\mathcal{D},\mathsf{F}}$-hybrid model.

Protocol π_{DPoS}

π_{DPoS} is a protocol run by a set of stakeholders, initially equal to $U_1, \ldots, U_n$, interacting among themselves and with $\mathcal{F}_{\mathsf{DLS}}^{\mathcal{D},\mathsf{F}}$ over a sequence of L slots $S = \{sl_1, \ldots, sl_L\}$. π_{DPoS} proceeds as follows:

1. **Initialization** Stakeholder $U_i \in \{U_1, \ldots, U_n\}$, receives from the key registration interface its public and secret key. Then it receives the current slot from the diffuse interface and in case it is sl_1 it sends $(\mathsf{genblock\_req}, U_i)$ to $\mathcal{F}_{\mathsf{LS}}^{\mathcal{D},\mathsf{F}}$, receiving $(\mathsf{genblock}, \mathbb{S}_0, \rho, \mathsf{F})$ as the answer. U_i sets the local blockchain $\mathcal{C} = B_0 = (\mathbb{S}_0, \rho)$ and the initial internal state $st = H(B_0)$. Otherwise, it receives from the key registration interface the initial chain $\mathcal{C}$, sets the local blockchain as $\mathcal{C}$ and the initial internal state $st = H(\text{head}(\mathcal{C}))$.
2. **Chain Extension** For every slot $sl \in S$, every online stakeholder U_i performs the following steps:
   (a) If a new epoch e_j, with $j \geq 2$, has started, U_i defines $\mathbb{S}_j$ to be the stakeholder distribution drawn from the most recent block with time stamp less than $jR - 2k$ as reflected in $\mathcal{C}$ and sends $(\mathsf{epochrnd\_req}, U_i, e_j)$ to $\mathcal{F}_{\mathsf{LS}}^{\mathcal{D},\mathsf{F}}$, receiving $(\mathsf{epochrnd}, \rho^j)$ as answer.
   (b) Collect all valid chains received via broadcast into a set $\mathbb{C}$, verifying that for every chain $\mathcal{C}' \in \mathbb{C}$ and every block $B' = (st', d', sl', \sigma') \in \mathcal{C}'$ it holds that $\mathsf{Vrf}_{\mathsf{vk}'}(\sigma', (st', d', sl')) = 1$, where vk' is the verification key of the stakeholder $U' = \mathsf{F}(\mathbb{S}_{j'}, \rho^{j'}, sl')$ with $e_{j'}$ being the epoch in which the slot B' belongs (as determined by sl'). U_i computes $\mathcal{C}' = \mathsf{maxvalid}(\mathcal{C}, \mathbb{C})$, sets $\mathcal{C}'$ as the new local chain and sets state $st = H(\text{head}(\mathcal{C}'))$.
   (c) If U_i is the slot leader determined by $\mathsf{F}(\mathbb{S}_j, \rho^j, sl)$ in the current epoch e_j, it generates a new block $B = (st, d, sl, \sigma)$ where st is its current state, $d \in \{0,1\}^*$ is the data and $\sigma = \mathsf{Sign}_{\mathsf{sk}_i}(st, d, sl)$ is a signature on (st, d, sl). U_i computes $\mathcal{C}' = \mathcal{C}|B$, broadcasts $\mathcal{C}'$, sets $\mathcal{C}'$ as the new local chain and sets state $st = H(\text{head}(\mathcal{C}'))$.

Fig. 5. Protocol π_{DPoS}

Remark 1. The modification to $\mathsf{maxvalid}(\cdot)$ to not diverge more than k blocks from the last chain possessed will require stakeholders to be online at least every k slots. The relevance of the rule comes from the fact that as stake shifts over time, it will be feasible for the adversary to corrupt stakeholders that used to possess a stake majority at some point without triggering $\mathsf{Bad}^{1/2}$ and thus any adversarial chains produced due to such an event should be rejected. It is worth noting that this restriction can be easily lifted if one can trust honest stakeholders to securely erase their memory; in such case, a forward secure signature can be employed to thwart any past corruption attempt that tries to circumvent $\mathsf{Bad}^{1/2}$.

5.2 Simulating a Trusted Beacon

While protocol π_{DPoS} handles multiple epochs and takes into consideration changes in the stake distribution, it still relies on $\mathcal{F}_{\mathsf{DLS}}^{\mathcal{D},\mathsf{F}}$ to perform the leader selection process. In this section, we show how to implement $\mathcal{F}_{\mathsf{DLS}}^{\mathcal{D},\mathsf{F}}$ through

Protocol π_{DLS}, which allows the stakeholders to compute the randomness and auxiliary information necessary in the leader election.

Recall, that the only essential difference between $\mathcal{F}_{\mathsf{LS}}^{\mathcal{D},\mathsf{F}}$ and $\mathcal{F}_{\mathsf{DLS}}^{\mathcal{D},\mathsf{F}}$ is the continuous generation of random strings $\rho^2, \rho^3, \ldots$ for epochs $e_2, e_3, \ldots$. The idea is simple, protocol π_{DLS} will use a coin tossing protocol to generate unbiased randomness that can be used to define the values $\rho^j, j \geq 2$ bootstrapping on the initial random string and initial honest stakeholder distribution. However, notice that the adversary could cause a simple coin tossing protocol to fail by aborting. Thus, we build a coin tossing scheme with "guaranteed output delivery."

Protocol π_{DLS} is described in Fig. 6 and uses a publicly verifiable secret sharing (PVSS) [26] (we defer to the full version the full description of the scheme).

The assumption we will use about the PVSS scheme is that the resulting coin-flipping protocol simulates a perfect beacon with distinguishing advantage ϵ_{DLS}. Simulation here suggests that, in the case of honest majority, there is a simulator that interacts with the adversary and produces indistinguishable protocol transcripts when given the beacon value after the commitment stage. We remark that using [26] as a PVSS, a simulator can achieve simulatability in the random oracle model by taking advantage of the programmability of the oracle. Using a random oracle is by no means necessary though and the same benefits may be obtained by a CRS embedded into the genesis block.

5.3 Robust Transaction Ledger

We are now ready to state the main result of the section that establishes that the π_{DPOS} protocol with the protocol π_{DLS} as a sub-routine implements a robust transaction ledger under the environmental conditions that we have assumed. Recall that in the dynamic stake case we have to ensure that the adversary cannot exploit the way stake changes over time and corrupt a set of stakeholders that will enable the control of the majority of an elected committee of stakeholders in an epoch. In order to capture this dependency on stake "shifts", we introduce the following property.

Definition 16. *Consider two slots sl_1, sl_2 and an execution $\mathcal{E}$. The stake shift between sl_1, sl_2 is the maximum possible statistical distance of the two weighted-by-stake distributions that are defined using the stake reflected in the chain $\mathcal{C}_1$ of some honest stakeholder active at sl_1 and the chain $\mathcal{C}_2$ of some honest stakeholder active at sl_2 respectively.*

Given the definition above we can now state the following theorem.

Theorem 6. *Fix parameters $k, R, L \in \mathbb{N}, \epsilon, \sigma \in (0,1)$. Let $R = 10k$ be the epoch length and L the total lifetime of the system. Assume the adversary is restricted to $\frac{1-\epsilon}{2} - \sigma$ relative stake and that the π_{SPOS} protocol satisfies the common prefix property with parameters R, k and probability of error ϵ_{CP}, the chain quality property with parameters $\mu \geq 1/k, k$ and probability of error ϵ_{CQ} and the chain*

Protocol π_{DLS}

π_{DLS} is a protocol run by a subset of elected stakeholders each one corresponding to a slot during an epoch e_j that lasts $R = 10k$ slots, without loss of generality denoted by $U_1, \ldots, U_R$ (which are not necessarily distinct), and entails the following phases.

1. **Commitment Phase** ($4k$ slots) When epoch e_j starts, for $1 \leq i \leq n$, stakeholder U_i samples a uniformly random string u_i and randomness r_i for the underlying commitment scheme, generates shares $\sigma_1^i, \ldots, \sigma_n^i \leftarrow \mathsf{Deal}(n, u_i)$ and encrypts each share σ_k^i under stakeholder U_k's public-key. Finally, U_i posts the encrypted shares and commitments $\mathsf{Com}(r_i, u_i)$ to the blockchain.
2. **Reveal Phase** ($4k$ slots) After slot $4k$, for $1 \leq i \leq n$, stakeholder U_i opens its commitment by posting $\mathsf{Open}(r_i, u_i)$ to the blockchain provided that the blockchain contain valid shares from the majority of $U_1, \ldots, U_R$; if not, each U_i terminates.
3. **Recovery Phase** ($2k$ slots) After slot $8k$, for any stakeholder U^a that has not participated in the reveal phase, i.e., it has not posted in $\mathcal{C}^{\lceil k}$ an $\mathsf{Open}(r_a, u_a)$ message, for $1 \leq i \leq R$, U_i submits its share σ_i^a for insertion to the blockchain. When all shares $\sigma_1^a, \ldots, \sigma_n^a$ are available, each stakeholder U_i can compute $\mathsf{Rec}(\sigma_1^a, \ldots, \sigma_n^a)$ to reconstruct u_a (independently of whether U^a opens the commitment or not).

   The simulation of $\mathsf{epochrnd\_req}$ is then as follows.
   - Given input $(\mathsf{genblock\_req}, U_i, e_j, \mathbb{S}_j)$, the stakholder uses the commitment values in the blockchain to compute $\rho^j = \sum_{l \in \mathbb{L}} u_l$ where $\mathbb{L}$ is the subset of stakeholders that were elected in epoch e_j. It returns $(\mathsf{genblock}, B_0, \mathbb{S}_j)$ with $B_0 = (\mathbb{S}_j, \rho^j)$.

Fig. 6. Protocol π_{DLS}.

growth property with parameters $\tau \geq 1/2, k$ and probability of error ϵ_{CG}. Furthermore, assume that π_{DLS} simulates a perfect beacon with distinguishing advantage ϵ_{DLS}.

Then, the π_{DPOS} protocol satisfies persistence with parameters k and liveness with parameters $u = 2k$ throughout a period of L slots (or $\mathsf{Bad}^{1/2}$ happens) with probability $1 - (L/R)(\epsilon_{\mathsf{CQ}} + \epsilon_{\mathsf{CP}} + \epsilon_{\mathsf{CG}} + \epsilon_{\text{DLS}})$, assuming that σ is the maximum stake shift over $10k$ slots, corruption delay $D \geq 2R - 4k$ and no honest player is offline for more than k slots.

Proof. (sketch) Let us first consider the execution of π_{DPOS} when $\mathcal{F}_{\mathsf{DLS}}^{\mathcal{D},\mathsf{F}}$ is used instead of π_{DLS}. Let BAD_r be the event that any of the three properties $\mathsf{CP}, \mathsf{CQ}, \mathsf{CG}$ is violated at round $r \geq 1$ while no violation of any of them occurred prior to r. It is easy to see that $\Pr[\cup_{r \leq R} \mathsf{BAD}_r] \leq \epsilon_{\mathsf{CQ}} + \epsilon_{\mathsf{CP}} + \epsilon_{\mathsf{CG}}$. Conditioning now on the negation of this event, we can repeat the argument for the second epoch, since $D \geq R$ and thus the adversary cannot influence the stakeholder selection for the second epoch. It follows that $\Pr[\cup_{r \leq L} \mathsf{BAD}_r] \leq (L/R)(\epsilon_{\mathsf{CQ}} + \epsilon_{\mathsf{CP}} + \epsilon_{\mathsf{CG}})$. It is easy now to see that persistence and liveness hold conditioning on the negation of the above event: a violation of persistence would violate common prefix. On the other hand, a violation of liveness would violate either chain growth or chain quality for the stated parameters.

Observe that the above result will continue to hold even if $\mathcal{F}_{\mathsf{DLS}}^{\mathcal{D},\mathsf{F}}$ was weakened to allow the adversary access to the random value of the next epoch $6k$ slots ahead of the end of the epoch. This is because the corruption delay $D \geq 2R - 4k = 16k$.

Finally, we examine what happens when $\mathcal{F}_{\mathsf{DLS}}^{\mathcal{D},\mathsf{F}}$ is substituted by $\mathcal{F}_{\mathsf{LS}}^{\mathcal{D},\mathsf{F}}$ and the execution of protocol π_{DLS}. Consider an execution with environment $\mathcal{Z}$ and adversary $\mathcal{A}$ and event BAD that happens with some probability β in this execution. We construct an adversary $\mathcal{A}^*$ that operates in an execution with $\mathcal{F}_{\mathsf{DLS}}^{\mathcal{D},\mathsf{F}}$, weakened as in the previous paragraph, and induces the event BAD with roughly the same probability β. $\mathcal{A}^*$ would operate as follows: in the first $4k$ slots, it will use an honest party to insert in the blockchain the simulated commitments of the honest parties; this is feasible for $\mathcal{A}^*$ as in $4k$ slots, chain growth will result in the blockchain growing by at least $2k$ blocks and thus in the first k blocks there will be at least a single honest block included. Now $\mathcal{A}^*$ will obtain from $\mathcal{F}_{\mathsf{DLS}}^{\mathcal{D},\mathsf{F}}$ the value of the beacon and it will simulate the opening of all the commitments on behalf of the honest parties. Finally, in the last $2k$ slots it will perform the forced opening of all the adversarial commitments that were not opened. The protocol simulation will be repeated for each epoch and the statement of the theorem follows. □

Remark 2. We note that it is easy to extend the adversarial model to include fail-stop (and recover) corruptions in addition to Byzantine corruptions. The advantage of this mixed corruption setting, is that it is feasible to prove that we can tolerate a large number of fail-stop corruptions (arbitrarily above 50%). The intuition behind this is simple: the forkable string analysis still applies even if an arbitrary percentage of slot leaders is rendered inactive. The only necessary provision for this would be expand the parameter k inverse proportionally to the rate of non-stopped parties. We omit further details.

6 Incentives

So far our analysis has focused on the cryptographic adversary setting where a set of honest players operate in the presence of an adversary. In this section we consider the setting of a coalition of rational players and their incentives to deviate from honest protocol operation.

Input Endorsers. In order to address incentives, we modify further our basic protocol to assign two different roles to stakeholders. As before in each epoch there is a set of elected stakeholders that runs the secure multiparty coin flipping protocol and are the slot leaders of the epoch. Together with those there is a (not necessarily disjoint) set of stakeholders called the endorsers. Now each slot has two types of stakeholders associated with it; the slot leader who will issue the block as before and the slot *endorser* who will endorse the input to be included in the block. Moreover, contrary to slot leaders, we can elect multiple slot endorsers for each slot, nevertheless, without loss of generality we just assume a single input endorser per slot in this description. While this seems like an insignificant modification it gives us a room for improvement because of the following reason: endorsers' contributions will be acceptable even if they are d slots late, where $d \in \mathbb{N}$ is a parameter.

The enhanced protocol, π_{DPOSwE}, can be easily seen to have the same persistence and liveness behaviour as π_{DPOS}: the modification with endorsers does not provide any possibility for the adversary to prevent the chain from growing, accepting inputs, or being consistent. However, if we measure chain quality in terms of number of *endorsed inputs* included this produces a more favorable result: it is easy to see that the number of endorsed inputs originating from a set of stakeholders S in any k-long portion of the chain is proportional to the relative stake of S with high probability. This stems from the fact that it is sufficient that a single honest block is created for all the endorsed inputs of the last d slots to be included in it. Assuming $d \geq 2k$, any set of stakeholders S will be an endorser in a subset of the d slots with probability proportional to its cumulative stake, and thus the result follows.

A Suitable Class of Reward Mechanisms. The reward mechanism that we will pair with input endorsers operates as follows. First we set the endorsing acceptance window, d to be $d = 2k$. Let $\mathcal{C}$ be a chain consisting of blocks $B_0, B_1, \ldots$. Consider the sequence of blocks that cover the j-th epoch denoted by $B_1, \ldots, B_s$ with timestamps in $\{jR+1, \ldots, (j+1)R+2k\}$ that contain an $r \geq 0$ sequence of endorsed inputs that originate from the j-th epoch (some of them may be included as part of the $j+1$ epoch). We define the total reward pool P_R to be equal to the sum of the transaction fees that are included in the endorsed inputs that correspond to the j-th epoch. If a transaction occurs multiple times (as part of different endorsed inputs) or even in conflicting versions, only the first occurrence of the transaction is taken into account (and is considered to be part of the ledger at that position) in the calculation of P, where the total order used is induced by the order the endorsed inputs that are included in $\mathcal{C}$. In the sequence of these blocks, we identify by $L_1, \ldots, L_R$ the slot leaders corresponding to the slots of the epoch and by $E_1, \ldots, E_r$ the input endorsers that contributed the sequence of r endorsed inputs. Subsequently, the i-th stakeholder U_i can claim a reward up to the amount $(\beta \cdot |\{j \mid U_i = E_j\}|/r + (1-\beta) \cdot |\{j \mid U_i = L_j\}|/R)P$ where $\beta \in [0,1]$. Claiming a reward is performed by issuing a "coinbase" type of transaction at any point after $4k$ blocks in a subsequent epoch to the one that a reward is being claimed from.

Observe that the above reward mechanism has the following features: (i) it rewards elected committee members for just being committee members, independently of whether they issued a block or not, (ii) it rewards the input endorsers with the inputs that they have contributed. (iii) it rewards entities for epoch j, after slot $jR + 4k$.

We proceed to show that our system is a δ-Nash (approximate) equilibrium, cf. [19, Sect. 2.6.6]. Specifically, the theorem states that any coalition deviating from the protocol can add at most an additive δ to its total rewards.

A technical difficulty in the above formulation is that the number of players, their relative stake, as well as the rewards they receive are based on the transactions that are generated in the course of the protocol execution itself. To simplify the analysis we will consider a setting where the number of players is static, the stake they possess does not shift over time and the protocol has negligible cost to be executed. We observe that the total rewards (and hence also utility by our assumption on protocol costs) that any coalition V of honest players are able extract from the execution lasting $L = tR + 4k + 1$ slots, is equal to

$$\mathcal{R}_V(\mathcal{E}) = \sum_{j=1}^{t} P_{\mathsf{all}}^{(j)} \left(\beta \frac{IE_V^j(\mathcal{E})}{R} + (1-\beta)\frac{SL_V^j(\mathcal{E})}{r_j} \right)$$

for any execution $\mathcal{E}$ where common prefix holds with parameter k, where r_j is the total endorsed inputs emitted in the j-th epoch (and possibly included at any time up to the first $2k$ slots of epoch $j+1$), $P_{\mathsf{all}}^{(j)}$ is the reward pool of epoch j, $SL_V^j(\mathcal{E})$ is the number of times a member of V was elected to be a slot leader in epoch j and $IE_V^j(\mathcal{E})$ the number of times a member of V was selected to endorse an input in epoch j.

Observe that the actual rewards obtained by a set of rational players V in an execution $\mathcal{E}$ might be different from $\mathcal{R}_V(\mathcal{E})$; for instance, the coalition of V may never endorse a set of inputs in which case they will obtain a smaller number of rewards. Furthermore, observe that we leave the value of $\mathcal{R}_V(\mathcal{E})$ undefined when $\mathcal{E}$ is an execution where common prefix fails: it will not make sense to consider this value for such executions since the view of the protocol of honest parties can be divergent; nevertheless this will not affect our overall analysis since such executions will happen with sufficiently small probability.

We will establish the fact that our protocol is a δ-Nash equilibrium by proving that the coalition V, even deviating from the proper protocol behavior, it cannot obtain utility that exceeds $\mathcal{R}_V(\mathcal{E}) + \delta$ for some suitable constant $\delta > 0$.

Theorem 7. *Fix any $\delta > 0$; the honest strategy in the protocol is a δ-Nash equilibrium against any coalition commanding a proportion of stake less than $(1-\epsilon)/2 - \sigma$ for some constants $\epsilon, \sigma \in (0,1)$ as in Theorem 6, provided that the maximum total rewards P_{all} provided in all possible protocol executions is bounded by a polynomial in λ, while $\epsilon_{\mathsf{CQ}} + \epsilon_{\mathsf{CP}} + \epsilon_{\mathsf{CG}} + \epsilon_{\mathsf{DLS}}$ is negligible in λ.*

We refer to the full version of the paper, [14], for the proof.

Remark 3. In the above theorem, for simplicity, we assumed that protocol costs are not affective the final utility (in essence this means that protocol costs are assumed to be negligible). Nevertheless, it is straightforward to extend the proof to cover a setting where a negative term is introduced in the payoff function for each player proportional to the number of times inputs are endorsed and the number of messages transmitted for the MPC protocol. The proof would be resilient to these modifications because endorsed inputs and MPC protocol messages cannot be stifled by the adversary and hence the reward function can be designed with suitable weights for such actions that offsets their cost. Still note that the rewards provided are assumed to be "flat" for both slots and endorsed inputs and thus the costs would also have to be flat. We leave for future work the investigation of a more refined setting where costs and rewards are proportional to the actual computational steps needed to verify transactions and issue blocks.

7 Stake Delegation

In this section we introduce a *delegation scheme* whereby the stakeholders of the PoS protocol can delegate the protocol execution rights to another set of parties, the *delegates*. A delegate may participate in the protocol only if it represents a certain number of stakeholders whose aggregate stake exceeds a given threshold. Such a participation threshold ensures that a "fragmentation" attack, that aims to increase the delegate population in order to hurt the performance of the protocol, cannot incur a large penalty as it is capable to force the size of the committee that runs the protocol to be small (it is worth noting that the delegation mechanism is similar to *mining pools* in proof-of-work blockchain protocols).

Delegation Scheme. The concept of delegation is simple: any stakeholder can allow a *delegate* to generate blocks on her behalf. In the context of our protocol, where a slot leader signs the block it generates for a certain slot, such a scheme can be implemented in a straightforward way based on *proxy signatures* [7].

A stakeholder can transfer the right to generate blocks by creating a *proxy signing key* that allows the delegate to sign messages of the form (st, d, sl_j) (i.e., the format of messages signed in Protocol π_{DPoS} to authenticate a block). In order to limit the delegate's block generation power to a certain range of epochs/slots, the stakeholder can limit the proxy signing key's valid message space to strings ending with a slot number sl_j within a specific range of values. The delegate can use a proxy signing key from a given stakeholder to simply run Protocol π_{DPoS} on her behalf, signing the blocks this stakeholder was elected to generate with the proxy signing key. This simple scheme is secure due to the *Verifiability* and *Prevention of Misuse* properties of proxy signature schemes, which ensure that any stakeholder can verify that a proxy signing key was actually issued by a specific stakeholder to a specific delegate and that the delegate can only use these keys to sign messages inside the key's valid message space, respectively. We remark that while proxy signatures can be described as a high level generic primitive, it is easy to construct such schemes from standard digital signature schemes through delegation-by-proxy as shown in [7]. In this construction, a stakeholder signs a certificate specifying the delegates identity (e.g., its public key) and the valid message space. Later on, the delegate can sign messages within the valid message space by providing signatures for these messages under its own public key along with the signed certificate. As an added advantage, proxy signature schemes can also be built from aggregate signatures in such a way that signatures generated under a proxy signing key have essentially the same size as regular signatures [7].

An important consideration in the above setting is the fact that a stakeholder may want to withdraw her support to a stakeholder prior to its proxy signing key expiration. Observe that proxy signing keys can be uniquely identified and thus they may be revoked by a certificate revocation list within the blockchain.

Eligibility Threshold. Delegation as described above can ameliorate fragmentation that may occur in the stake distribution. Nevertheless, this does not prevent a malicious stakeholder from dividing its stake to multiple accounts and, by refraining from delegation, induce a very large committee size. To address this, as mentioned above, a threshold T, say 1%, may be applied. This means that any delegate representing less a fraction less than T of the total stake is automatically barred from being a committee member. This can be facilitated by redistributing the voting rights of delegates representing less than T to other delegates in a deterministic fashion (e.g., starting from those with the highest stake and breaking ties according to lexicographic order). Suppose that a committee has been formed, $C_1, \ldots, C_m$, from a total of k draws of weighing by stake. Each committee member will hold k_i such votes where $\sum_{i=1}^{m} k_i = k$. Based on the eligibility threshold above it follows that $m \leq T^{-1}$ (the maximum value is the case when all stake is distributed in T^{-1} delegates each holding T of the stake).

References

1. Ateniese, G., Bonacina, I., Faonio, A., Galesi, N.: Proofs of space: when space is of the essence. In: Abdalla, M., de Prisco, R. (eds.) SCN 2014. LNCS, vol. 8642, pp. 538–557. Springer, Cham (2014). doi:10.1007/978-3-319-10879-7_31
2. Aumann, Y., Lindell, Y.: Security against covert adversaries: efficient protocols for realistic adversaries. J. Cryptol. **23**(2), 281–343 (2010)
3. Bentov, I., Gabizon, A., Mizrahi, A.: Cryptocurrencies without proof of work. CoRR, abs/1406.5694 (2014)
4. Bentov, I., Lee, C., Mizrahi, A., Rosenfeld, M.: Proof of activity: extending bitcoin's proof of work via proof of stake [extended abstract]. SIGMETRICS Perform. Eval. Rev. **42**(3), 34–37 (2014)
5. Bentov, I., Pass, R., Shi, E.: The sleepy model of consensus. IACR Cryptology ePrint Archive 2016:918 (2016)
6. Bentov, I., Pass, R., Shi, E.: Snow white: provably secure proofs of stake. IACR Cryptology ePrint Archive 2016:919 (2016)
7. Boldyreva, A., Palacio, A., Warinschi, B.: Secure proxy signature schemes for delegation of signing rights. J. Cryptol. **25**(1), 57–115 (2012)
8. Danezis, G., Meiklejohn, S.: Centrally banked cryptocurrencies. In: 23rd Annual Network and Distributed System Security Symposium, NDSS 2016, San Diego, California, USA, 21–24 February 2016. The Internet Society (2016)
9. Dziembowski, S., Faust, S., Kolmogorov, V., Pietrzak, K.: Proofs of space. In: Gennaro, R., Robshaw, M. (eds.) CRYPTO 2015. LNCS, vol. 9216, pp. 585–605. Springer, Heidelberg (2015). doi:10.1007/978-3-662-48000-7_29

10. Eyal, I., Sirer, E.G.: Majority is not enough: Bitcoin mining is vulnerable. In: Christin, N., Safavi-Naini, R. (eds.) FC 2014. LNCS, vol. 8437, pp. 436–454. Springer, Heidelberg (2014). doi:10.1007/978-3-662-45472-5_28
11. Ford, B.: Delegative democracy (2002). http://www.brynosaurus.com/deleg/deleg.pdf
12. Garay, J., Kiayias, A., Leonardos, N.: The Bitcoin backbone protocol: analysis and applications. In: Oswald, E., Fischlin, M. (eds.) EUROCRYPT 2015. LNCS, vol. 9057, pp. 281–310. Springer, Heidelberg (2015). doi:10.1007/978-3-662-46803-6_10
13. Kiayias, A., Panagiotakos, G.: Speed-security tradeoffs in blockchain protocols. Cryptology ePrint Archive, Report 2015/1019 (2015). http://eprint.iacr.org/2015/1019
14. Kiayias, A., Russell, A., David, B., Oliynykov, R.: Ouroboros: a provably secure proof-of-stake blockchain protocol. Cryptology ePrint Archive, Report 2016/889 (2017). http://eprint.iacr.org/2016/889
15. Micali, S.: ALGORAND: the efficient and democratic ledger. CoRR, abs/1607.01341 (2016)
16. Moran, T., Orlov, I.: Proofs of space-time and rational proofs of storage. Cryptology ePrint Archive, Report 2016/035 (2016). http://eprint.iacr.org/2016/035
17. Motwani, R., Raghavan, P.: Randomized Algorithms. Cambridge University Press, New York (1995)
18. Nakamoto, S.: Bitcoin: a peer-to-peer electronic cash system (2008). http://bitcoin.org/bitcoin.pdf
19. Nisan, N., Roughgarden, T., Tardos, E., Vazirani, V.V.: Algorithmic Game Theory. Cambridge University Press, New York (2007)
20. O'Dwyer, K.J., Malone, D.: Bitcoin mining and its energy footprint. ISSC 2014/CIICT 2014, Limerick, 26–27 June 2014
21. Park, S., Pietrzak, K., Kwon, A., Alwen, J., Fuchsbauer, G., Gazi, P.: Spacemint: a cryptocurrency based on proofs of space. IACR Cryptology ePrint Archive 2015:528 (2015)
22. Pass, R., Seeman, L., Shelat, A.: Analysis of the blockchain protocol in asynchronous networks. IACR Cryptology ePrint Archive 2016:454 (2016)
23. Pass, R., Shi, E.: Fruitchains: a fair blockchain. IACR Cryptology ePrint Archive 2016:916 (2016)
24. Russell, A., Moore, C., Kiayias, A., Quader, S.: Forkable strings are rare. Cryptology ePrint Archive, Report 2017/241, March 2017. http://eprint.iacr.org/2017/241
25. Sapirshtein, A., Sompolinsky, Y., Zohar, A.: Optimal selfish mining strategies in bitcoin. CoRR, abs/1507.06183 (2015)
26. Schoenmakers, B.: A simple publicly verifiable secret sharing scheme and its application to electronic voting. In: Wiener, M. (ed.) CRYPTO 1999. LNCS, vol. 1666, pp. 148–164. Springer, Heidelberg (1999). doi:10.1007/3-540-48405-1_10

Multiparty Computation

Robust Non-interactive Multiparty Computation Against Constant-Size Collusion

Fabrice Benhamouda(✉), Hugo Krawczyk, and Tal Rabin

IBM Research, Yorktown Heights, USA
fabrice.benhamouda@normalesup.org,
hugo@ee.technion.ac.il, talr@us.ibm.com

Abstract. Non-Interactive Multiparty Computations (Beimel et al., Crypto 2014) is a very powerful notion equivalent (under some corruption model) to garbled circuits, Private Simultaneous Messages protocols, and obfuscation. We present robust solutions to the problem of Non-Interactive Multiparty Computation in the computational and information-theoretic models. Our results include the first efficient and robust protocols to compute any function in NC^1 for constant-size collusions, in the information-theoretic setting and in the computational setting, to compute any function in P for constant-size collusions, assuming the existence of one-way functions. Our constructions start from a Private Simultaneous Messages construction (Feige, Killian Naor, STOC 1994 and Ishai, Kushilevitz, ISTCS 1997) and transform it into a Non-Interactive Multiparty Computation for constant-size collusions.

We also present a new Non-Interactive Multiparty Computation protocol for symmetric functions with significantly better communication complexity compared to the only known one of Beimel et al.

Keywords: Non-interactive multiparty computation · Private Simultaneous Messages

1 Introduction

A non-interactive multiparty computation enables n parties $P_1, \ldots, P_n$, each holding a private input, and a special party P_0, called an evaluator, to compute a joint function of the n parties' inputs so that the evaluator learns the output. The communication structure in this setting is that each party sends a single message to the evaluator. This is a highly desired mode of interaction as the required connectivity between the parties is extremely simple, yet it enables to carry out natural computations such as voting and auctions.

Feige et al. [4] were first to study such a model, referred to as the *Private Simultaneous Messages (PSM)*[1] model. They considered information-theoretic security, namely, in a PSM protocol for a function f, the evaluator of the function learns the output of the function on the parties' inputs and *nothing else.*

[1] Name given by Ishai and Kushilevitz [9].

J. Katz and H. Shacham (Eds.): CRYPTO 2017, Part I, LNCS 10401, pp. 391–419, 2017.
DOI: 10.1007/978-3-319-63688-7_13

Essential to their solutions was the assumption that the evaluator does not collude with any of the n parties. If such collusions were possible, even with a single misbehaving party, their protocols would lose the privacy guarantee.

Beimel et al. [3] generalized the PSM model to what they call *Non-Interactive Multiparty Computation (NIMPC)*, by considering the possibility of collusions between parties and the evaluator. In this setting the notion of security needs to be modified as clearly we cannot prevent the evaluator from computing the function on all possible inputs of the colluding parties. Thus, they define the notion of "best possible security" by utilizing the residual function [8] for a set of colluding parties T. The residual function of f is all the values $f(y_1, \ldots, y_n)$ where $y_i = x_i$ if $P_i \notin T$ (x_i being the input of the non-colluding party P_i) and $y_i \in \{0, 1\}$ for $P_i \in T$. A secure protocol would enable the adversary to learn the residual function and nothing more. An NIMPC protocol that can withstand collusions of up to t parties is called *t-robust.* If $t = n$ the protocol is said to be *fully robust.*

Due to their very restricted communication pattern, both PSM and NIMPC require some form of setup arrangement. PSM assumes a common random string shared by the parties while NIMPC allows for a setup phase where parties are provided with *correlated randomness.* The latter models an offline stage run independently of the parties' inputs with the actual computation of the function happening in a later online phase.

We note that while the above notions were introduced in the information-theoretic setting, they apply to the computational case as well. The notion of NIMPC turns out to be extremely powerful both in the computational and information-theoretic setting, and for a wide range of applications. It generalizes such notions as obfuscation and garbling schemes, and is a weaker variant of multi-input functional encryption. At the same time, in more practical settings, NIMPC can be used for voting, auctions, or distributed computations on bulletin boards.

The wide applicability of the NIMPC abstraction is also reflected in the wide range of results (and open questions) for what is computable in this model. In the information-theoretic setting, Feige et al. [4] show that *any* function can be computed with *exponential size* messages sent from parties to evaluator. At the same time, they show that any function in NC^1 can be computed with polynomial-size messages. Ishai and Kushilevitz [9] further expanded the class of functions that can be computed by PSM protocols to log-space language classes such as $\text{mod}_p L$ and to log-space counting classes such as $\#L$.

Not surprisingly, the NIMPC model proves to be more challenging, even for restricted robustness. Beimel et al. [3] prove that some non-trivial functions can be computed with information-theoretic security in this model. They showed that the iterated product function $f(x_1, \ldots, x_n) = x_1 \cdots x_n$ over a group $\mathbb{G}$ can be computed efficiently with a collusion of any size. In addition, for any function f, they exhibit a solution that can tolerate arbitrary collusions but is exponential in the total bit-length of the inputs. Their strongest result shows that symmetric functions over a domain $\mathcal{X}_1 \times \cdots \times \mathcal{X}_n$ where each $\mathcal{X}_i$ is of constant-size admits a t-robust NIMPC with polynomial complexity for constant t.

Can these information-theoretic NIMPC results be extended to a larger class, e.g., NC^1, as in the PSM case? A negative result follows from Goldwasser and Rothblum [6] implicitly stating that the existence of an efficient protocol for NC^1 that can tolerate a polynomial-size collusion (i.e., of size $t = \Omega(n^\alpha)$, with $\alpha > 0$ being constant) in the information-theoretic setting would imply the collapse of the polynomial-time hierarchy. This still leaves the possibility that robust NIMPC with restricted, say constant-size, collusions are still possible for NC^1. Yet, Beimel et al. show evidence that even achieving 1-robustness, i.e., security against a collusion of one party with the evaluator, may require a new technical approach (they show that natural approaches to realize NIMPC based on known PSM or garbling techniques fail even for $t = 1$). They leave this question open.

In the computational setting the situation is strikingly different. First of all, in the PSM model or the equivalent 0-robust NIMPC, one can compute any polynomial-time computable function with polynomial-size messages under the sole assumption of the existence of one-way functions. Indeed, note that a Yao garbled circuit is a 0-robust NIMPC. At the other end, fully-robust NIMPC for any polynomial function can be constructed using multi-input functional encryption which Goldwasser et al. [5] build on the basis of indistinguishability obfuscation (iO) and one-way functions. Actually, the existence of efficient NIMPC protocols for P that can tolerate a polynomial-size collusion implies iO.

The above results leave two wide gaps in our knowledge regarding the feasibility of constructing robust NIMPC protocols. In the information-theoretic setting, PSM exists for at least all of NC^1 while NIMPC with non-zero robustness is only known for a handful of simple functions [3]. In the computational setting, one-way functions suffice for 0-robust NIMPC for all polynomial functions, and under iO fully-robust NIMPC for all P is possible.
This raises two important questions:

1. Do information-theoretic robust NIMPC protocols exist, even for 1-robustness, for a class of functions covered by PSM, e.g., NC^1?
2. Do computational robust NIMPC protocols exist for P, with restricted robustness, under weaker assumptions than iO?

These are open questions postulated in the work of Beimel et al. [3] and the ones that we set to answer.

1.1 Our Results

From PSM to NIMPC. Our main theorem shows an information-theoretic transformation which takes any PSM (or 0-robust NIMPC) construction and transforms it into a t-robust NIMPC protocol. The resultant protocol has complexity that is, roughly, $n^{O(t)}$ times that of the given PSM protocol. Furthermore, if the original PSM relied on some assumptions the new protocol relies on the same assumptions without needing to introduce any further assumptions.

This single theorem is extremely powerful and its corollaries give an affirmative answer to the two questions raised above.

In the information-theoretic setting we have that for constant t, there exist efficient t-robust protocols for the same class of functions for which efficient PSM protocols exist, in particular for the whole class NC^1 and the classes shown in [9], namely, $\text{mod}_p L$ and log-space counting classes such as $\#L$.

In the computational setting, we achieve robust NIMPC solutions for constant-size collusions for any polynomial-time function, solely based on one way functions. That is, we narrow the gap between the PSM solutions based on one-way functions that tolerate no collusions, and the solutions based on iO, that can tolerate any number of collusions. Recall that robust NIMPC solutions for any polynomial-time function, even for polynomial-size collusions, implies iO.

Design. The idea governing our result was to directly find a solution to the problem identified by Beimel et al. [3, Sect. 6]. The essence of the problem can be understood by considering a Yao garbled circuit. The circuit is set up so that each input wire i has two possible labels $m'_{i,0}, m'_{i,1}$ one of which will be used by party P_i to convey its input to the evaluator. The problem arises when P_i colludes with the evaluator providing both labels for input wire i. One might hope that this would only enable the evaluator to compute the residual function, i.e., $f(x_1, \ldots, x_{i-1}, 0, x_{i+1}, \ldots, x_n)$ and $f(x_1, \ldots, x_{i-1}, 1, x_{i+1}, \ldots, x_n)$, which is allowed. However, the above paper shows that in fact more is exposed via the knowledge of both labels, thus violating the security of the computation. This problem also arises in similar constructions based on Barrington theorem [2] and Kilian randomization [12], or the Ishai-Kushilevitz protocol in [9].

The issue is that the adversary can learn two different labels $m'_{i,0}$ and $m'_{i,1}$ for the same input wire i, when P_i is colluding. If we could prevent it, this would resolve the problem described above. Yet, this seems challenging as we need to enable P_i to still have a message for a possible input of 0 and a message for a possible input of 1, otherwise it will render the computation impossible. But maybe this counter-intuitive approach can be achieved?

Given a function f, n parties, $P_1, \ldots, P_n$, holding inputs $x_1, \ldots, x_n$ (resp.), an evaluator P_0, and a PSM which computes the function we will do the following. We duplicate the PSM a number of times (this number is a function of the number of colluding parties; we denote it for now by κ), creating the copies $\mathcal{PSM}_1, \ldots, \mathcal{PSM}_\kappa$. Each PSM will have a fresh set of labels for its input wires. Concretely, $\mathcal{PSM}_{\boldsymbol{\sigma}}$ will have labels $m'_{\boldsymbol{\sigma},i,0}, m'_{\boldsymbol{\sigma},i,1}$ for $i = \{1, \ldots, n\}$. On top of these copies of the PSM we will put NIMPC protocols which we call *selectors*. There will be n selectors $\mathcal{S}el_1, \ldots, \mathcal{S}el_n$, one for each party. The input wires for all the selectors will be labeled by $m_{i,0}, m_{i,1}$ for $i = \{1, \ldots, n\}$. The selector $\mathcal{S}el_i$ is expected to output a label $m'_{\boldsymbol{\sigma},i,x_i}$ for exactly one index $\boldsymbol{\sigma}$. Each selector will have one output wire for a total of n output wires for all the selectors combined.

Clearly, the adversary can still utilize both $m_{i,0}, m_{i,1}$ of a colluding party on the input wires to the selectors. But the selectors will be sophisticated. Given a specific set of labels for the inputs wires, they will provide a full set of labels for only one of the copies of the PSM. Given a different set of input wire labels, they will provide a full set of labels for a different PSM. So for the example above, on input the set of labels $m_{1,x_1}, \ldots, m_{i-1,x_{i-1}}, m_{i,0}, m_{i+1,x_{i+1}}, \ldots, m_{n,x_n}$, the adversary will receive the labels for $\mathcal{PSM}_{\sigma}$ and on input the set of labels $m_{1,x_1}, \ldots, m_{i-1,x_{i-1}}, m_{i,1}, , m_{i+1,x_{i+1}}, \ldots, m_{n,x_n}$ it will receive the labels for $\mathcal{PSM}_{\sigma'}$. Thus, effectively disarming the adversary from the ability to learn two different labels for the same input of the *same* PSM. Note, that the adversary can still run the selectors multiple times on different inputs, in fact, on 2^t if there are t colluding parties. But the selectors can "tolerate" such behavior without violating the privacy of the inputs of the non-colluding parties.

Thus we have achieved that the combination of selectors $\mathcal{S}el_i$ and κ copies of the original PSM yield a t-robust NIMPC for the function computed by the PSM. See Fig. 1.

Example for One Colluding Party. In the following, we give a flavor of the ideas of our protocols in the specific case where only one party is colluding with the evaluator. In this case we would need two copies of the PSM, $\mathcal{PSM}_1$ and $\mathcal{PSM}_2$ with labels $m'_{1,i,0}, m'_{1,i,1}$ and $m'_{2,i,0}, m'_{2,i,1}$ (resp.) for the input wire corresponding to party P_i. Thus, we want the selectors either to provide a full set of labels for one or the other of the two PSMs.

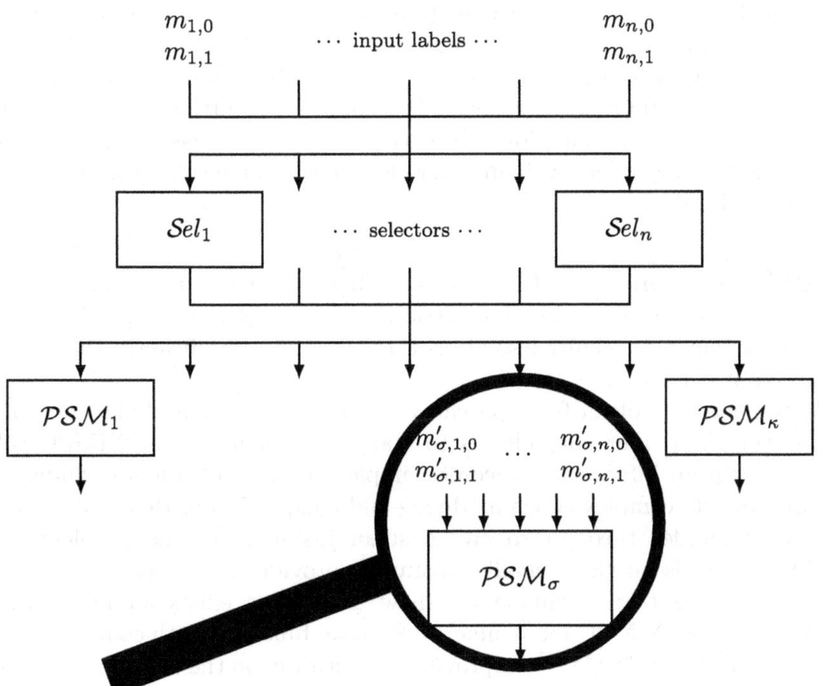

Given input labels $m_{1,x_1}, \ldots, m_{n,x_n}$, the selectors choose an index σ and output the labels $m'_{\sigma,1,x_1}, \ldots, m'_{\sigma,n,x_n}$ for the instance $\mathcal{PSM}_{\sigma}$. For different input labels (that a collusion of t users can obtain), a different index σ' is chosen.

Fig. 1. NIMPC transformation

We define Sel_i, the algorithm used by the evaluator to derive exactly one of the labels $m'_{1,i,x_i}, m'_{2,i,x_i}$ from the input labels $m_{1,x_1}, \ldots, m_{n,x_n}$, as:

$$Sel_i(m_{1,x_1}, \ldots, m_{n,x_n}) = \begin{cases} m'_{1,i,0} & \text{if } \sum_{j=1}^{n} x_j = 0 \bmod 2 \text{ and } x_i = 0, \\ m'_{1,i,1} & \text{if } \sum_{j=1}^{n} x_j = 0 \bmod 2 \text{ and } x_i = 1, \\ m'_{2,i,0} & \text{if } \sum_{j=1}^{n} x_j = 1 \bmod 2 \text{ and } x_i = 0, \\ m'_{2,i,1} & \text{if } \sum_{j=1}^{n} x_j = 1 \bmod 2 \text{ and } x_i = 1. \end{cases}$$

We assume that x_i can be implicitly obtained from m_{i,x_i}. Things will be made more formal later.

Let us examine the output of the selector and see that it works properly. W.l.o.g., assume that P_i is the colluding party and that the evaluator first uses the message corresponding to an input of 0 for P_i and that this sets the sum of all the parties' inputs to 0. In this case the selector for all parties, colluding or not, will output one of the values from the two top rows depending on the party's individual input. These are all labels for $\mathcal{PSM}_1$. Now, if the evaluator flips the input value of the colluding party to be 1, this causes the sum of all the parties' inputs to flip to 1, resulting in the selector outputting a value from the bottom two rows of the function. Those outputs are all labels of $\mathcal{PSM}_2$. Thus, we manage to prevent the evaluator from learning two labels for the same input of the same PSM.

NIMPC for Symmetric Functions. While our above result and also [3] provide NIMPC protocols for symmetric functions (both of complexity $n^{O(t)}$), here we present a specialized solution that improves significantly the level of robustness it can offer.

A symmetric Boolean function can be seen as a function of the sum of its inputs over $\mathbb{Z}_{n+1}$. Our core idea is to start with an inefficient NIMPC solution based on an information-theoretic implementation of Yao's garbling and then improve its complexity via a "divide-and-conquer" approach that uses the Chinese remainder theorem to create small instances of the problem. The NIMPC protocols on these smaller instances provide much stronger collusion resistance. Using this technique we show that there exists an information-theoretic t-robust NIMPC for symmetric Boolean functions with communication complexity $n^{\log\log n+\log t+O(1)}$, improving significantly on the best prior protocol in [3, Theorem 4.17] that has communication complexity $\binom{n}{t} \cdot O(2^t \cdot n^4)$.

1.2 Related Work

Halevi et al. [8] wanted to avoid the need for a fresh common or correlated randomness string for each execution. However, their model requires the parties to sequentially interact with the evaluator. They provide solutions for very specific patterns of interaction, assuming a public-key infrastructure (PKI).

Halevi et al. [7] expand the graphs of interaction patterns that can be handled in [8] to directed graphs, chains, and star. They examine which functions can be computed under these communication patterns and show that any interaction pattern can be reduced via an information theoretic protocol to a star, while providing the best possible security that can be achieved. Note that a star communication pattern is equivalent to the pattern presented in NIMPC. Using our new t-robust NIMPC protocols for the star communication pattern can enable a constant number of colluding parties for general communication patterns without relying on strong assumptions such as iO.

In [16] the authors provide an exponential lower bound of the communication complexity of NIMPC protocols for arbitrary functions, and improve the polynomial factors of the communication complexity of the NIMPC protocol for arbitrary functions of Beimel et al. They further extend their result in [14] improved complexity of the previous NIMPC protocol for arbitrary function with multi-bit inputs, yet it still has exponential complexity.

1.3 Organization of the Paper

In Sect. 2, we start by an extensive overview to provide intuition for the techniques we use in our transformation of PSM into t-robust NIMPC. After some formal preliminaries in Sect. 3, we present one of the main components of the transformation and of our NIMPC protocol for symmetric functions, namely selectors, in Sect. 4. In Sect. 5, we define and construct another component of the transformation, namely admissible linear indexing function. The transformation itself is formally described and proven in Sect. 6. Finally, in Sect. 7, we show our new NIMPC protocol for symmetric functions.

2 Overview

In this section we provide an extensive overview of the techniques we use in our transformation from PSM to t-robust NIMPC with emphasis on ideas and intuition at the expense of formalism. For the sake of simplicity, we assume that the inputs of the parties are bits.

2.1 Defining the Indexing Function

In the Introduction we showed that we need selectors that, for every given set of inputs of the parties, choose a different PSM, and then output a consistent set of labels for the input wires of the chosen PSM. In this section, we explain how to choose the PSM. This is done via what we call an indexing function ind.

The indexing function ind takes as input a vector $\boldsymbol{x}$, which reflects the inputs of the parties. The entry for a non-colluding P_i will be set to its actual input, x_i and the rest of the entries are fixed by the adversary. When the adversary controls t parties it can create 2^t distinct vectors $\boldsymbol{x}$, running over all possible inputs of the colluding parties. These 2^t vectors can in fact be reflected in 2^t evaluations of the selectors. Thus, we want to have (at least) 2^t PSM and in return require that the indexing function, ind, will map each one of the possible vectors into a different PSM. We will index the PSM by $\boldsymbol{\sigma}$ in some set $\mathcal{S}$.

We now build the indexing function ind. Let ind be a function that on input $\boldsymbol{x} = (x_1, \ldots, x_n)$ outputs an index $\boldsymbol{\sigma} \in \mathcal{S}$. The function ind should have the property that if a party P_i is colluding then any input $\boldsymbol{x}$ to ind that has $x_i = 0$ should produce a different $\boldsymbol{\sigma}$ than the same $\boldsymbol{x}$ but with $x_i = 1$. In general, no coalition of t colluding parties should be able to choose their inputs so that two different inputs lead to the selection of the same index $\boldsymbol{\sigma}$. Note that this does not mean that ind should be injective but rather that if one fixes the inputs of the non-colluding parties, then any two assignments of the remaining t inputs should result in a different value $\boldsymbol{\sigma}$ output by ind. Going back to the example from the Introduction, for $t = 1$ we implicitly defined $\mathsf{ind}(\boldsymbol{x}) = x_1 + \cdots + x_n$ and obtained the desired property. Indeed, if all the inputs are fixed except the one of a single colluding party P_i, each input x_i of P_i yields a different value $\mathsf{ind}(\boldsymbol{x})$ (note that this property assumes a single colluding party but does not require to know who this party is).

For the general case of t colluding parties we build ind using a linear code. We first observe that for any value $\boldsymbol{\sigma}$ in the range of ind, it should be that the set $\mathsf{ind}^{-1}(\boldsymbol{\sigma})$ forms a code of distance at least $t+1$. Indeed, assume that two different elements $\boldsymbol{x_1}, \boldsymbol{x_2}$ in the set $\mathsf{ind}^{-1}(\boldsymbol{\sigma})$ have Hamming distance $\leq t$ and let $T \subseteq \{1, \ldots, n\}$ be the set of entries where the two differ. Choosing T as the set of colluding parties, we have that $\boldsymbol{x_1}, \boldsymbol{x_2}$ coincide in all the honest parties' inputs, differ on the colluding parties' inputs, yet they are mapped to the same value $\boldsymbol{\sigma}$. This contradicts our requirement from ind. We can thus define ind via a linear code of distance $t+1$ over a linear space $\mathbb{F}_q^n$ (for some prime power q) as follows. Let $H \in \mathbb{F}_q^{\ell \times n}$ be the parity-check matrix of such a code, namely, the code is formed by all vectors $\boldsymbol{x} \in \mathbb{F}_q^n$ for which $H \cdot \boldsymbol{x} = 0$. This means that $H^{-1}(0)$ is a code of distance $t+1$ and the same is also true, by linearity, for $H^{-1}(\boldsymbol{\sigma})$ for any other $\boldsymbol{\sigma}$ in the range of H. Thus, defining $\mathsf{ind}(\boldsymbol{x}) = H \cdot \boldsymbol{x}$ we get the property we needed. See Sect. 5 for the details.

We note that using such an H, we get that the set of possible values $\boldsymbol{\sigma}$ (i.e., the range of the function ind) is of size q^ℓ ($\ell = t$ in our implementation, for well-chosen prime powers q) and that is also the number of PSMs. This is the source of exponential complexity in our construction and the reason for why we are polynomial-time only for constant t.

2.2 Reduction of $\mathcal{S}el_i$ to Message-Outputting Protocols

Given an indexing function $\mathsf{ind}\colon \boldsymbol{x} \mapsto H \cdot \boldsymbol{x} \in \mathbb{F}_q^\ell$ as above, our goal is now to construct the selector $\mathcal{S}el_i$ which is an NIMPC protocol for the following functions:

$$h_i \colon \boldsymbol{x} \in \{0,1\}^n \mapsto m'_{\mathsf{ind}(\boldsymbol{x}), i, x_i}. \tag{1}$$

where messages $m'_{\boldsymbol{\sigma},i,b}$ are implicit secret parameters of the NIMPC. The message $m'_{\boldsymbol{\sigma},i,b}$ is the message that party P_i would send on input b in the PSM $\mathcal{PSM}_{\boldsymbol{\sigma}}$. We recall that the selector $\mathcal{S}el_i$ ensures that an adversary should not be able to obtain two messages $m'_{\boldsymbol{\sigma},i,b}$ and $m'_{\boldsymbol{\sigma},i,1-b}$ for the same $\boldsymbol{\sigma}$ and i.

We can reduce the construction of such selectors $\mathcal{S}el_i$ to the construction of an NIMPC for the following functions:

$$h_{\boldsymbol{\sigma},i,b} \colon \boldsymbol{x} \in \mathbb{F}_q^n \mapsto \begin{cases} m'_{\boldsymbol{\sigma},i,b} & \text{if } \mathsf{ind}(\boldsymbol{x}) = \boldsymbol{\sigma} \text{ and } x_i = b, \\ \bot & \text{otherwise.} \end{cases} \tag{2}$$

The idea consists in running all the NIMPC protocols for all the functions $h_{\boldsymbol{\sigma},i,b}$, for each $\boldsymbol{\sigma} \in \mathcal{S}$ and each $b \in \{0,1\}$, in parallel, to get the selector $\mathcal{S}el_i$. Exactly one of them will have a non-$\bot$ output. To avoid leaking the value $b = x_i$ and $\boldsymbol{\sigma} = \mathsf{ind}(\boldsymbol{x})$, these protocols are randomly permuted.

As the condition "$\mathsf{ind}(\boldsymbol{x}) = \boldsymbol{\sigma}$ and $x_i = b$" in Eq. (2) is linear, we can rewrite these functions in terms of matrix-vector operations, a representation that will facilitate the design of NIMPC protocols for such functions. We first define the following generic family of functions indexed by a public matrix M in $\mathbb{F}_q^{k \times n}$ (for our constructions, $k = \ell + 1$), a secret vector $\boldsymbol{u}$ in $\mathbb{F}_q^k$, and a secret message $\tilde{m}$ in $\mathbb{F}_q$:

$$h_{M,\boldsymbol{u},\tilde{m}} \colon \boldsymbol{x} \in \mathbb{F}_q^n \mapsto \begin{cases} \tilde{m} \in \mathbb{F}_q & \text{if } \boldsymbol{u} = M \cdot \boldsymbol{x}, \\ \bot & \text{otherwise.} \end{cases}$$

An NIMPC for such a function is called a *message-outputting protocol.*

Now, assuming w.l.o.g. that $m'_{\boldsymbol{\sigma},i,b} \in \mathbb{F}_q$,[2] we can represent the above functions $h_{\boldsymbol{\sigma},i,b}$ as special cases of $h_{M,\boldsymbol{u},\tilde{m}}$ by setting

$$M = M^{(i)} = \begin{pmatrix} H \\ \boldsymbol{e}_i^{\mathsf{T}} \end{pmatrix}, \qquad \boldsymbol{u} = \boldsymbol{u}^{(\boldsymbol{\sigma},b)} = \begin{pmatrix} \boldsymbol{\sigma} \\ b \end{pmatrix}, \qquad \tilde{m} = m'_{\boldsymbol{\sigma},i,b},$$

where $\boldsymbol{\sigma} \in \mathbb{F}_q^{\ell}$, and $\boldsymbol{e}_i$ is the i-th vector of the canonical basis of $\mathbb{F}_q^n$.

To sum up, we have reduced the task of designing the selectors $\mathcal{S}el_i$ to the task of designing outputting-message protocols, i.e., NIMPC for $h_{M,\boldsymbol{u},\tilde{m}}$. At this point, we can completely ignore the process that lead us to considering these functions $h_{M,\boldsymbol{u},\tilde{m}}$.

2.3 Robust Message-Outputting Protocols

Let us now design robust message-outputting protocols, i.e., NIMPC for $h_{M,\boldsymbol{u},\tilde{m}}$. We note that while in our application M is public and $\boldsymbol{u}$ and $\tilde{m}$ are to remain hidden, here our presentation treats $\boldsymbol{u}$ as public. A full description of the NIMPC protocol for $h_{M,\boldsymbol{u},\tilde{m}}$, including addressing the secrecy of $\boldsymbol{u}$, is presented in Sect. 4.2.

[2] We can always represent the message $m'_{\boldsymbol{\sigma},i,b}$ as a tuple of elements in $\mathbb{F}_q$, and use an independent message-outputting protocol for each of these elements.

Linear Secret Sharing Scheme. We start by recalling the following linear secret sharing scheme LSSS [11], a variant of which is at the core of our construction.

The scheme is specified for n parties and an access structure defined on the basis of a matrix $M \in \mathbb{F}_q^{k \times n}$ and vector $\boldsymbol{v}$ in $\mathbb{F}_q^k$. Parties P_i, for i in some set $I \subseteq \{1, \ldots, n\}$, can reconstruct the secret message $\tilde{m}$ if and only if:

$$\boldsymbol{v} \in \operatorname{Span}((M_{\cdot,i})_{i \in I}), \tag{3}$$

where $M_{\cdot,i}$ denotes the i-th column of M, in which case, we say that the set I is *authorized.*

The scheme provides each party P_i with a share s'_i defined as:

$$s'_i = \boldsymbol{s}^\intercal \cdot M_{\cdot,i},$$

where $\boldsymbol{s}$ is a randomly chosen vector in F_q^k. In addition, the scheme publishes (or gives to each party)

$$s'_0 = \tilde{m} - \boldsymbol{s}^\intercal \cdot \boldsymbol{v},$$

where $\tilde{m}$ is the secret being shared.

An authorized set I can recover the secret $\tilde{m}$ as follows. Since I is authorized, there exist scalars $\lambda_i \in \mathbb{F}_q$ for $i \in I$ so that $\sum_{i \in I} \lambda_i \cdot M_{\cdot,i} = \boldsymbol{v}$. Thus, parties P_i for $i \in I$ recover the secret $\tilde{m}$ as:

$$\tilde{m} = s'_0 + \sum_{i \in I} \lambda_i \cdot s'_i.$$

Conversely, if I is not an authorized set, the values s'_i only define the linear form $\boldsymbol{v} \in \mathbb{F}_q^k \mapsto \boldsymbol{s}^\intercal \cdot \boldsymbol{v}$ for vectors $\boldsymbol{v}$ in the span of the columns $M_{\cdot,i}$, for $i \in I$. As $\boldsymbol{v}$ is not in this span, the value $\boldsymbol{s}^\intercal \cdot \boldsymbol{v}$ is uniformly random from the point of view of the parties, and $\tilde{m}$ is completely masked.

NIMPC for When $h_{M,\boldsymbol{u},\tilde{m}}(\boldsymbol{x}) = \tilde{m}$. Back to our NIMPC construction for the family $h_{M,\boldsymbol{u},\tilde{m}}$, we want that the adversary can reconstruct $\tilde{m}$ if and only if it has access to a vector $\boldsymbol{x} \in \mathbb{F}_q^n$ such that

$$\boldsymbol{u} = M \cdot \boldsymbol{x}.$$

More precisely, let $T \subseteq \{1, \ldots, n\}$ be the set of colluding parties. For any vector $\boldsymbol{x} \in \mathbb{F}_q^n$, let $\boldsymbol{x}_T$ and $\boldsymbol{x}_{\bar{T}}$ be the two vectors in $\mathbb{F}_q^n$ defined as:

$$x_{T,i} = \begin{cases} x_i & \text{if } i \in T, \\ 0 & \text{otherwise,} \end{cases} \quad \text{and} \quad x_{\bar{T},i} = \begin{cases} 0 & \text{if } i \in T, \\ x_i & \text{otherwise.} \end{cases}$$

In other words, $\boldsymbol{x}_T$ corresponds to the inputs that the adversary can control[3] while $\boldsymbol{x}_{\bar{T}}$ corresponds to the inputs fixed by the honest parties. Each vector $\boldsymbol{x}_T$

[3] Note that while the honest parties' inputs are from $\{0, 1\}$, we cannot control the inputs the adversary uses. The adversary can choose inputs from $\mathbb{F}_q$.

is related to one value of the residual function that the adversary is allowed to compute. We have:

$$\boldsymbol{x} = \boldsymbol{x}_T + \boldsymbol{x}_{\bar{T}}.$$

With this terminology, we have that the adversary should be able to reconstruct $\tilde{m}$ if and only if there exists a vector $\boldsymbol{x}_T$ such that

$$\boldsymbol{u} = M \cdot \boldsymbol{x} = M \cdot (\boldsymbol{x}_T + \boldsymbol{x}_{\bar{T}}),$$

or, equivalently,

$$\boldsymbol{u} - M \cdot \boldsymbol{x}_{\bar{T}} \in \mathrm{Span}((M_{\cdot,i})_{i \in T}).$$

This corresponds exactly to the definition of the access structure for the above LSSS scheme where $\boldsymbol{v} = \boldsymbol{u} - M \cdot \boldsymbol{x}_{\bar{T}}$. We adapt this scheme to our NIMPC setting as follows (see Fig. 2 in Sect. 4.2 for the details).

Recall that an NIMPC protocol starts with a setup phase (a.k.a. offline pre-processing) in order to generate the correlated randomness. It is indeed impossible to achieve any reasonable security notion without correlated randomness in this non-interactive setting.

In this setup phase, we first generate a uniform vector $\boldsymbol{s} \in \mathbb{F}_q^k$ and give to each party P_i the share of the above secret sharing scheme, namely, $s'_i = \boldsymbol{s}^\intercal \cdot M_{\cdot,i}$, as part of its correlated randomness. Assuming we know $\boldsymbol{x}_{\bar{T}}$, we could define the following value

$$s'_0 = \tilde{m} - \boldsymbol{s}^\intercal \cdot \boldsymbol{u} + \boldsymbol{s}^\intercal \cdot M \cdot \boldsymbol{x}_{\bar{T}}$$

that would correspond to the value s'_0 in the secret sharing scheme when $\boldsymbol{v} = \boldsymbol{u} - M \cdot \boldsymbol{x}_{\bar{T}}$. Yet, this value (as well as $\boldsymbol{v}$) depends on the set T and $\boldsymbol{x}_{\bar{T}}$ that is unknown at the time of sharing. Thus, the correlated randomness (and thus the messages sent by the parties) needs to contain additional information to allow authorized reconstruction of s'_0 and, as a result, $\tilde{m}$.

To achieve this, in the setup phase, we also generate independent uniform scalars $r_1, \ldots, r_n \in \mathbb{F}_q$, compute $r_0 = \sum_{i=1}^{n} r_i$, publish (in lieu of s'_0):

$$\mu_0 = \tilde{m} - \boldsymbol{s}^\intercal \cdot \boldsymbol{u} - r_0,$$

and give to each party P_i the scalar r_i as part of its correlated randomness. Finally, party P_i on input x_i outputs the message:

$$\mu_{i,x_i} = r_i + s'_i \cdot x_i.$$

With these values, message $\tilde{m}$ can be reconstructed in case that $M \cdot \boldsymbol{x} = \boldsymbol{u}$ through the following computation:

$$\tilde{m} = \mu_0 + \sum_{i=1}^{n} \mu_{i,x_i}.$$

(this equality is obtained by developing the right-hand term as $\mu_0 + r_0 + \sum s'_i x_i = \tilde{m} - \boldsymbol{s}^\intercal \cdot \boldsymbol{u} + \sum s_i M_{\cdot,i} x_i = \tilde{m} - \boldsymbol{s}^\intercal \cdot \boldsymbol{u} + \sum s_i u_i = \tilde{m}$).

The above shows correctness of the NIMPC scheme for the family $h_{M,\boldsymbol{u},\tilde{m}}$. We now argue robustness, namely, only $\tilde{m}$ is disclosed and only in case that $M \cdot \boldsymbol{x} = \boldsymbol{u}$. All other information remains (information-theoretically) hidden.

Note that when the set of colluding parties is T, the adversary's view (in collusion with P_0) consists of:

$$\begin{aligned} \mu_0 &= \tilde{m} - \boldsymbol{s}^\intercal \cdot \boldsymbol{u} - r_0 && \\ \mu_{i,x_i} &= r_i + \boldsymbol{s}^\intercal \cdot M_{\cdot,i} \cdot x_i && \text{for } i \in \bar{T} = \{1,\ldots,n\} \setminus T \\ r_i & && \text{for } i \in T \\ s'_i &= \boldsymbol{s}^\intercal \cdot M_{\cdot,i} && \text{for } i \in T. \end{aligned}$$

The proof of robustness follows by showing that all these values can be simulated given only

$$s'_0 = \tilde{m} - \boldsymbol{s}^\intercal \cdot \boldsymbol{u} + \boldsymbol{s}^\intercal \cdot M \cdot \boldsymbol{x}_{\bar{T}} \quad \text{and} \quad s'_i = \boldsymbol{s}^\intercal \cdot M_{\cdot,i} \text{ for } i \in T, \tag{4}$$

which correspond to the shares of parties P_i, for $i \in T$, for the access structure defined by Eq. (3) of the LSSS scheme when $\boldsymbol{v} = \boldsymbol{u} - M \cdot \boldsymbol{x}_{\bar{T}}$. This shows that the above view of the adversary contains no more information than the LSSS shares hence implying the secrecy of $\tilde{m}$ in case that the equality $\boldsymbol{u} = M \cdot \boldsymbol{x}$ does not hold.

Detecting When $h_{M,\boldsymbol{u},\tilde{m}}(\boldsymbol{x}) = \perp$. The above NIMPC protocol is almost a protocol for $h_{M,\boldsymbol{u},\tilde{m}}$, except that it always outputs something even when it should output $\perp$. To finish the construction, we need to add a way to detect whether $h_{M,\boldsymbol{u},\tilde{m}}(\boldsymbol{x}) = \perp$ or not, i.e., whether $M \cdot \boldsymbol{x} = \boldsymbol{u}$ or not.

This is simple to achieve: in the setup phase, we just pick uniform independent vectors $\boldsymbol{r}'_1, \ldots, \boldsymbol{r}'_n \in \mathbb{F}_q^n$, compute $\boldsymbol{r}'_0 = \sum_{i=1}^n \boldsymbol{r}'_i$, publish $\boldsymbol{\nu}_0 = \boldsymbol{u} + \boldsymbol{r}'_0$, and give to each party P_i the vector $\boldsymbol{r}'_i$ as part of its correlated randomness.

Then, on input x_i, party P_i outputs (in addition to μ_{i,x_i}):

$$\boldsymbol{\nu}_{i,x_i} = \boldsymbol{r}'_i + M_{\cdot,i} \cdot x_i.$$

In other words, on input x_i, P_i outputs the message $m_{i,x_i} = (\mu_{i,x_i}, \boldsymbol{\nu}_{i,x_i})$.

To check whether $M \cdot \boldsymbol{x} = \boldsymbol{u}$, it is then sufficient to check whether:

$$\boldsymbol{\nu}_0 = \sum_{i=1}^{n} \boldsymbol{\nu}_{i,x_i}.$$

Robustness and correctness are straightforward.

2.4 Putting It All Together

We now summarize the steps in our transformation from a PSM for a function f to a t-robust NIMPC for the same function f. Full and formal details are presented in Sects. 4.2, 5, and 6 (see Fig. 4).

First, we choose a linear code of length n and of distance at least $t+1$, for a well-chosen prime power q. Let $H \in \mathbb{F}_q^{\ell \times n}$ be its parity-check matrix (we can choose q as the smallest prime power greater or equal to n, and $\ell = t$). We define the indexing function as $\mathsf{ind}\colon \boldsymbol{x} \mapsto H \cdot \boldsymbol{x} \in \mathbb{F}_q^\ell$.

Second, in the setup phase, we consider q^ℓ copies of the PSM, indexed by elements $\boldsymbol{\sigma}$ of $\mathbb{F}_q^\ell$. We generate the correlated randomness of all these PSMs, and denote by $m'_{\boldsymbol{\sigma},i,b}$ the message that party P_i would send on input b in the PSM $\mathcal{PSM}_{\boldsymbol{\sigma}}$ of index $\boldsymbol{\sigma}$, for $\boldsymbol{\sigma} \in \mathbb{F}_q^\ell$, $i \in \{1,\dots,n\}$, and $b \in \{0,1\}$.

Third, we construct the n NIMPC protocols, $\mathcal{S}el_1,\dots,\mathcal{S}el_n$ (the linear selectors), for the functions $h_1,\dots,h_n$ (resp.) defined in Eq. (1):

$$h_i\colon \boldsymbol{x} \in \{0,1\}^n \mapsto m'_{\mathsf{ind}(\boldsymbol{x}),i,x_i}.$$

As explained in Sect. 2.2, these selectors are constructed as parallel composition of outputting-message protocols, described in Sect. 2.3.

The correlated randomness of the resulting t-robust NIMPC protocol just consists in the concatenation of the correlated randomness of $\mathcal{S}el_1,\dots,\mathcal{S}el_n$. The message that party P_i sends on input x_i is the concatenation of the ones it would send in $\mathcal{S}el_1,\dots,\mathcal{S}el_n$ on input x_i. To compute the output, the evaluator first simulates the evaluators of $\mathcal{S}el_1,\dots,\mathcal{S}el_n$ to get $m'_{\boldsymbol{\sigma},i,x_i}$ for all $i \in \{1,\dots,n\}$ and for $\boldsymbol{\sigma} = \mathsf{ind}(\boldsymbol{x})$. It then simulates the evaluator of the original PSM on these messages to get the output $f(x_1,\dots,x_n)$.

3 Preliminaries

3.1 NIMPC Definition

We recall the definition of NIMPC protocols from [3]. We first introduce the following notation.

Let $\mathcal{X}_1,\dots,\mathcal{X}_n$ be non-empty sets and let $\mathcal{X}$ denote their Cartesian product, namely, $\mathcal{X} := \mathcal{X}_1 \times \cdots \times \mathcal{X}_n$. We use vector notation (boldface font) to denote the elements in $\mathcal{X}$, e.g., $\boldsymbol{x} \in \mathcal{X}$ (even though $\mathcal{X}$ is not necessarily a vector space). For a subset $T = \{i_1,\dots,i_t\} \subseteq \{1,\dots,n\}$ and $\boldsymbol{x} = (x_1,\dots,x_n) \in \mathcal{X}$ we denote by $\boldsymbol{x}_T$ the t-coordinate projection vector $(x_{i_1},\dots,x_{i_t})$. For a function $f\colon \mathcal{X} \to \Omega$, we denote by $f|_{\bar{T},\boldsymbol{x}_{\bar{T}}}$ the function f with the inputs corresponding to positions $\bar{T}$ fixed to the entries of vector $\boldsymbol{x}_{\bar{T}}$.[4]

Definition 3.1 (NIMPC Protocol). *Let $\mathcal{F} = (\mathcal{F}_n)_{n \in \mathbb{N}_{>0}}$ be an ensemble of sets $\mathcal{F}_n$ of functions $f\colon \mathcal{X} \to \Omega$, where Ω is a finite set and $\mathcal{X}$ is the Cartesian product of non-empty finite sets $\mathcal{X}_1,\dots,\mathcal{X}_n$. A* non-interactive secure multiparty computation (NIMPC) protocol *for $\mathcal{F}$ is a tuple of three algorithms $\Pi = (\mathsf{Setup},\mathsf{Msg},\mathsf{Rec})$, where:*

[4] In Sect. 3.2 we slightly change notation for vectors $\boldsymbol{x}_T$.

- Setup *takes as input unary representations of* n *and of the security parameter* $\mathfrak{K}$*, and (a representation of) a function* $f \in \mathcal{F}_n$ *and outputs a tuple* $(\rho_0, \rho_1, \ldots, \rho_n)$*;*[5]
- Msg *takes as input a value* ρ_i *and an input* $x_i \in \mathcal{X}_i$*, and deterministically outputs a message* m_{i,x_i}*;*
- Rec *takes as input a value* ρ_0 *and a tuple of* n *messages* $(m_{i,x_i})_{i=1,\ldots,n}$ *and outputs an element of* Ω*.*

satisfying the following property:

- ***Correctness.*** *For any values* $n \in \mathbb{N}_{>0}$*, security parameter* $\mathfrak{K} \in \mathbb{N}$*,* $f \in \mathcal{F}_n$*,* $\boldsymbol{x} \in \mathcal{X}$ *and* $(\rho_0, \ldots, \rho_n) \xleftarrow{R} \mathsf{Setup}(f)$*:*

$$\mathsf{Rec}(\rho_0, \mathsf{Msg}(\rho_1, x_1), \ldots, \mathsf{Msg}(\rho_n, x_n)) = f(\boldsymbol{x}).$$

While the previous definition is abstract, in the sequel, we will often view NIMPC protocols as protocols with n parties $P_1, \ldots, P_n$ with respective inputs $x_1, \ldots, x_n$, and an evaluator P_0. This is actually the view adopted in the Introduction and in Sect. 2. More precisely, an NIMPC $\Pi = (\mathsf{Setup}, \mathsf{Msg}, \mathsf{Rec})$ yields a protocol in three phases as follows:

Offline preprocessing. For the security parameter $\mathfrak{K}$ and the function $f \in \mathcal{F}_n$, a trusted party generates $(\rho_0, \rho_1, \ldots, \rho_n) \xleftarrow{R} \mathsf{Setup}(1^n, 1^{\mathfrak{K}}, f)$ and gives ρ_i to party P_i (for $i \in \{1, \ldots, n\}$) and ρ_0 to the evaluator P_0.

Online messages. On input x_i, party P_i computes $m_{i,x_i} := \mathsf{Msg}(\rho_i, x_i)$ and outputs m_{i,x_i} to the evaluator P_0.

Reconstruction. After receiving m_{i,x_i} from all the parties P_i (for $i \in \{1, \ldots, n\}$), the evaluator P_0 computes and outputs $\mathsf{Rec}(\rho_0, m_{1,x_1}, \ldots, m_{n,x_n})$.

A *polynomial-time NIMPC protocol* for $\mathcal{F}$ is an NIMPC protocol (Setup, Msg, Rec) where Setup, Msg, and Rec run in polynomial time in n and $\mathfrak{K}$. In particular, functions $f \in \mathcal{F}$ should be representable by polynomial-size bit strings.

The *online communication complexity* of Π, $\mathsf{CC_{on}}(\Pi)$, is defined as the maximum of the size of the messages m_{i,x_i}. The *offline communication complexity* of Π, $\mathsf{CC_{off}}(\Pi)$, is defined as the maximum of the size of the correlated randomness ρ_i. The *communication complexity* $\mathsf{CC}(\Pi)$ is defined as the maximum of the online communication complexity and of the offline communication complexity.

Robustness. We now recall the notions of robustness for NIMPC protocols. Informally, T-robustness for a set $T \subseteq \{1, \ldots, n\}$ of colluding parties means that if $\boldsymbol{x}_{\bar{T}}$ represents the inputs of the honest parties, then an evaluator colluding with the parties in set T can compute the residual function $f|_{\bar{T}, \boldsymbol{x}_{\bar{T}}}$ on any input $\boldsymbol{x}_T$ but cannot learn anything else about the input of the honest parties. This describes the best privacy guarantee attainable in this adversarial setting. The

[5] One refers to the vector $(\rho_0, \rho_1, \ldots, \rho_n)$ as the *correlated randomness* of the parties, with ρ_0 called *public randomness*.

formal definition is stated in terms of a simulator that can generate the view of the adversary (evaluator plus the colluding parties in set T) with sole oracle access to the residual function $f|_{\bar{T},\boldsymbol{x}_{\bar{T}}}$.

All our constructions and transformations are *unconditional.* But when combined with statistically or computationally robust 0-NIMPC protocols, the resulting protocols are only statistically or computationally robust. Therefore, we also need to define statistical and computational variants of robustness.

Definition 3.2 (NIMPC Robustness). *Let $n \in \mathbb{N}_{>0}$ be a positive integer and $T \subseteq \{1,\ldots,n\}$ be a subset. An NIMPC protocol Π is perfectly (resp., statistically, computationally)* T-robust *if there exists a randomized algorithm* Sim *(called a* simulator*) such that for any $f \in \mathcal{F}_n$ and $\boldsymbol{x}_{\bar{T}} \in \mathcal{X}_{\bar{T}}$, the following distributions are perfectly (resp., statistically, computationally) indistinguishable:*

$$\{\mathsf{Sim}^{f|_{\bar{T},\boldsymbol{x}_{\bar{T}}}}(1^n,1^{\mathfrak{K}},T)\} \quad and \quad \{\mathsf{View}(1^n,1^{\mathfrak{K}},f,T,\boldsymbol{x}_{\bar{T}})\},$$

where $\mathsf{View}(1^n,1^{\mathfrak{K}},f,T,\boldsymbol{x}_{\bar{T}})$ is the view of the evaluator P_0 and of the colluding parties P_i (for $i \in T$) from running Π on inputs $\boldsymbol{x}_{\bar{T}}$ for the honest parties P_i (for $i \in \bar{T}$): namely, $((m_{i,x_{\bar{T},i}})_{i\in\bar{T}}, \rho_0, (\rho_i)_{i\in T})$ where $(\rho_0,\ldots,\rho_n) \xleftarrow{R} \mathsf{Setup}(1^n,1^{\mathfrak{K}},f)$ and $m_{i,x_{\bar{T},i}} \leftarrow \mathsf{Msg}(\rho_i, x_{\bar{T},i})$ for $i \in \bar{T}$.

Let t be an integer which is a function of n, then an NIMPC protocol Π is perfectly (resp., statistically, computationally) t-robust *if for any $n \in \mathbb{N}_{>0}$ and any subset $T \subseteq \{1,\ldots,n\}$ of size at most $t = t(n)$, Π is perfectly (resp., statistically, computationally) t-robust. It is perfectly (resp., statistically, computationally)* fully robust, *if it is perfectly (resp., statistically, computationally) n-robust.*

Computational robustness is defined non-uniformly to simplify the definition. However, it is also possible to define a uniform version with an explicit distinguisher which first chooses n, f, T, and $\boldsymbol{x}_{\bar{T}}$.

Robustness does not necessarily imply that the simulator Sim is the same for any n and T nor that it runs in polynomial time in n and $\mathfrak{K}$. Our constructions are efficient in the sense that the simulators are polynomial-time (in the communication complexity of the underlying protocols), and our transformations preserve the efficiency of the simulator.

Simplifications. In the sequel, we simplify notations as follows. The security parameter $\mathfrak{K}$ is dropped for all perfectly robust protocols. Furthermore, we suppose all the functions $f \in \mathcal{F}_n$ have the same domain $\mathcal{X}$ and the same number of parties n. The set $\mathcal{F}_n$ is simply denoted $\mathcal{F}$. We will sometimes refer to NIMPC for single functions f, to mean NIMPC for $\mathcal{F} = \{f\}$.

3.2 Group Embedding

While the definition of NIMPC is stated for arbitrary sets $\mathcal{X}_i$, for our treatment it is convenient (but not mandatory) to associate to these sets an addition operation and a neutral element 0. For this, we use the convention that each input set

$\mathcal{X}_i$ is embedded (via an arbitrary injective mapping) into a group of cardinality $\geq |\mathcal{X}_i|$ (same group for all $i \in \{1, \ldots, n\}$). Thus, hereafter, we treat the sets $\mathcal{X}_i$ as subsets of a group where these subsets always include the neutral element 0; in our applications the group is typically a field $\mathbb{F}_q$ or a ring.

With this convention we re-define vectors of the form $\boldsymbol{x}_T$ as follows:

$$\mathcal{X}_T := \{\boldsymbol{x} \in \mathcal{X} \mid \forall i \in \bar{T},\, x_i = 0\}, \qquad \mathcal{X}_{\bar{T}} := \{\boldsymbol{x} \in \mathcal{X} \mid \forall i \in T,\, x_i = 0\}.$$

Let $\boldsymbol{x} \in \mathcal{X}$ be a vector. We define the vectors $\boldsymbol{x}_T \in \mathcal{X}_T$ and $\boldsymbol{x}_{\bar{T}} \in \mathcal{X}_{\bar{T}}$ to be the only two such vectors so that $\boldsymbol{x} = \boldsymbol{x}_T + \boldsymbol{x}_{\bar{T}}$. In other words, for all $i \in \{1, \ldots, n\}$:

$$x_{T,i} = \begin{cases} x_i & \text{if } i \in T, \\ 0 & \text{otherwise,} \end{cases} \quad \text{and} \quad x_{\bar{T},i} = \begin{cases} 0 & \text{if } i \in T, \\ x_i & \text{otherwise.} \end{cases}$$

Let $\boldsymbol{x}_{\bar{T}} \in \mathcal{X}_{\bar{T}}$ be a vector. With this notation we re-define the restriction of a function $f \colon \mathcal{X} \to \Omega$ to $\bar{T}, \boldsymbol{x}_{\bar{T}}$, which we denote by $f|_{\bar{T},\boldsymbol{x}_{\bar{T}}}$, as follows:

$$f|_{\bar{T},\boldsymbol{x}_{\bar{T}}} : \boldsymbol{x}_T \in \mathcal{X}_T \mapsto f(\boldsymbol{x}_T + \boldsymbol{x}_{\bar{T}}) \in \Omega.$$

That is, $f|_{\bar{T},\boldsymbol{x}_{\bar{T}}}$ is the function f for which the inputs x_i are fixed for $i \in \bar{T}$ to $x_{\bar{T},i}$.

Finally, we define the Hamming weight of an element $\boldsymbol{x} \in \mathcal{X}$ as the number of coordinates i for which $x_i \neq 0$, and define Hamming distance between elements $\boldsymbol{x_1}$ and $\boldsymbol{x_2}$ in $\mathcal{X}$ as the Hamming weight of $\boldsymbol{x_1} - \boldsymbol{x_2}$.

4 Selectors

In this section, we introduce the notion of selectors, which are used both in our transformation from PSM to $O(1)$-robust NIMPC and in our construction of NIMPC for symmetric functions. Intuitively, a selector is an NIMPC which selects a given message in a collection of messages depending on the inputs of the parties. In our construction, the collection of messages correspond to various inputs of other PSMs or NIMPCs. In other words, selectors compose easily with other NIMPCs. That is why they play a central role in our constructions.

We start by defining general selectors, before considering and constructing two particular cases: linear selectors and NIMPC for Abelian programs. The former selectors are used in our transformation from PSM to $O(1)$-robust NIMPC, while the latter selectors are used for symmetric functions. Our constructions are perfectly fully robust. An interesting point if that these selectors are also new constructions of fully robust NIMPCs (of which very few are known, even assuming the existence of one-way functions).

4.1 Definitions

General Definition. The next definition is the general definition. Definitions of the two interesting particular cases follow.

Definition 4.1. *Let $\mathcal{X}_1, \ldots, \mathcal{X}_n, \mathcal{U}, \mathcal{M}$ be finite sets. Let $\mathcal{X} := \mathcal{X}_1 \times \cdots \times \mathcal{X}_n$. Let $\mathsf{sel}\colon \mathcal{X} \to \mathcal{U}$ be a function. A* selector *for the function* sel *and the message set $\mathcal{M}$ is an NIMPC protocol for the following set of functions $\mathcal{H} = \{h_{\mathsf{sel},\tilde{\boldsymbol{m}}}\}_{\tilde{\boldsymbol{m}} \in \mathcal{M}^{\mathcal{U}}}$, where:*

$$h_{\mathsf{sel},\tilde{\boldsymbol{m}}}\colon \boldsymbol{x} \in \mathcal{X} \mapsto \tilde{m}_{\mathsf{sel}(\boldsymbol{x})}.$$

The message set $\mathcal{M}$ is often implicitly defined. We also implicitly assume that elements of $\mathcal{M}$ can be represented by vectors of $\lceil \log_q |\mathcal{M}| \rceil$ elements in $\mathbb{F}_q$. The set $\mathcal{M}^{\mathcal{U}}$ is the set of tuples $\tilde{\boldsymbol{m}} = (\tilde{m}_{\boldsymbol{u}})_{\boldsymbol{u} \in \mathcal{U}}$ of messages in $\mathcal{M}$, indexed by elements in $\mathcal{U}$.

In this paper, we are interested in two specific types of selectors: linear selectors and NIMPC for Abelian program.

Linear Selectors. Linear selectors are used for our transformation from PSM to $O(1)$-robust NIMPC and are defined as follows.

Definition 4.2 (linear selector). *Let $\mathbb{F}_q$ be a finite field. Let k and n be positive integers. Let $M \in \mathbb{F}_q^{k \times n}$ be a matrix. A* linear selector *for M is a selector for the function* sel *defined by:*

$$\mathsf{sel} : \boldsymbol{x} \in \mathbb{F}_q^n \mapsto M \cdot \boldsymbol{x} \in \mathcal{U} := \mathbb{F}_q^k.$$

In the above definition, $\mathcal{X}_1, \ldots, \mathcal{X}_n$ are implicitly defined as $\mathbb{F}_q$. The set of messages $\mathcal{M}$ can be any finite set.

NIMPC for Abelian Programs. For our construction of NIMPC for symmetric functions, we need to introduce another type of selectors.

Abelian programs can be seen a generalization of symmetric functions introduced in [3, Sect. 4]. More precisely, we have the following definition.

Definition 4.3 (Abelian program). *Let $\mathbb{G}$ be a finite Abelian group. Let $\mathcal{X}_1, \ldots, \mathcal{X}_n$ be subsets of $\mathbb{G}$. Let $\mathcal{X} := \mathcal{X}_1 \times \cdots \times \mathcal{X}_n \subseteq \mathbb{G}^n$ denote their Cartesian product. Let Ω be some finite set. An* Abelian program *for $\mathbb{G}$, $\mathcal{X}$, and Ω is a function:*

$$\tilde{h}_{\tilde{g}}\colon \boldsymbol{x} \in \mathcal{X} \mapsto \tilde{g}(\sum_{i=1}^{n} x_i),$$

where $\tilde{g}\colon \mathbb{G} \to \Omega$ is a function.

An NIMPC for Abelian program is just an NIMPC for the class of Abelian programs for a given group $\mathbb{G}$, input set $\mathcal{X}$, and output set Ω. In this paper, we prefer to view NIMPC for Abelian programs as selectors, as follows.

Definition 4.4 (NIMPC for Abelian Programs). *Let $\mathbb{G}$ be a finite (additive) Abelian group. Let $\mathcal{X}_1, \ldots, \mathcal{X}_n$ be subsets of $\mathbb{G}$. Let $\mathcal{X} := \mathcal{X}_1 \times \cdots \times \mathcal{X}_n \subseteq \mathbb{G}^n$*

denote their Cartesian product. An NIMPC for Abelian programs *(for* $\mathcal{X}$ *and* $\mathbb{G}$*) is a selector for the function* sel *defined by:*

$$\mathsf{sel} : \boldsymbol{x} \in \mathcal{X} \mapsto \sum_{i=1}^{n} x_i \in \mathcal{U} =: \mathbb{G}.$$

The message $\mathcal{M}$ corresponds to the set Ω.

We remark that if $\mathbb{G}$ is a finite field $\mathbb{F}_q$ and $\mathcal{X}_1 = \cdots = \mathcal{X}_n = \mathbb{G}$, then an NIMPC for Abelian programs for $\mathcal{X}$ and $\mathbb{G}$ is a exactly a linear selector for the matrix $M = (1, \ldots, 1) \in \mathbb{F}_q^{1 \times n}$. However, for our constructions, the sets $\mathcal{X}_i$ are strictly included in the group $\mathbb{G}$. We therefore need to use completely different techniques for the construction of NIMPC for Abelian programs, compared to the ones used for the construction of linear selectors.

4.2 Construction of Linear Selectors

Let us now show how to construct linear selectors. As explained in Sect. 2.2, we first define and construct outputting-message NIMPC protocols.

Outputting-Message NIMPC

Definition 4.5 (outputting-message NIMPC). *Let* $\mathbb{F}_q$ *be a finite field and* $\mathcal{M}$ *be a finite set. Let* $M \in \mathbb{F}_q^{k \times n}$ *be a matrix. An outputting-message NIMPC for* M *is a NIMPC protocol for the following set of functions* $\mathcal{H}_M := \{h_{M,\boldsymbol{u},\tilde{m}}\}_{\boldsymbol{u} \in \mathbb{F}_q^k, \tilde{m} \in \mathcal{M}}$ *where:*

$$h_{M,\boldsymbol{u},\tilde{m}} : \boldsymbol{x} \in \mathbb{F}_q^n \mapsto \begin{cases} \tilde{m} & \text{if } \boldsymbol{u} = M \cdot \boldsymbol{x}, \\ \perp & \text{otherwise,} \end{cases}$$

where $\perp$ *is a fresh symbol not in* $\mathcal{M}$.

As for linear selectors, in the above definition, $\mathcal{X}_1, \ldots, \mathcal{X}_n$ are implicitly defined as $\mathbb{F}_q$.

Theorem 4.6. *Let* $\mathbb{F}_q$ *be a finite field and* $\mathcal{M}$ *be a finite message set. Let* $M \in \mathbb{F}_q^{k \times n}$ *be a matrix. There exists a perfectly fully robust outputting-message NIMPC for* M *with communication complexities:*

$$\mathsf{CC}_{\mathsf{on}}(\Pi) = (k + \lceil \log_q |\mathcal{M}| \rceil) \cdot \lceil \log q \rceil,$$
$$\mathsf{CC}_{\mathsf{on}}(\Pi) = (k + 2 \cdot \lceil \log_q |\mathcal{M}| \rceil) \cdot \lceil \log q \rceil.$$

Furthermore, the simulator for t-robustness runs in time $q^{\min(t,k)} \cdot \mathrm{poly}(q, k, n, \log |\mathcal{M}|)$. *In particular, when t or k is a constant, the simulator runs in polynomial time in q, k, n, and* $\log |\mathcal{M}|$.

Offline preprocessing (Setup). For the function $h_{M,\boldsymbol{u},\tilde{m}}$ ($M \in \mathbb{F}_q^{k\times n}$, $\boldsymbol{u} \in \mathbb{F}_q^k$, $\tilde{m} \in \mathbb{F}_q$):

1. Pick a uniform vector $\boldsymbol{s} \xleftarrow{R} \mathbb{F}_q^k$. For each $i \in \{1,\ldots,n\}$, pick a uniform scalar $r_i \xleftarrow{R} \mathbb{F}_q$ and a uniform vector $\boldsymbol{r}'_i \xleftarrow{R} \mathbb{F}_q^k$.
2. Compute:
$$\mu_0 := \tilde{m} - \boldsymbol{s}^\intercal \cdot \boldsymbol{u} - \sum_{i=1}^{n} r_i \in \mathbb{F}_q\,, \qquad \boldsymbol{\nu}_0 := \boldsymbol{u} + \sum_{i=1}^{n} \boldsymbol{r}'_i \in \mathbb{F}_q^k\,.$$
3. For each $i \in \{1,\ldots,n\}$, compute $s'_i := \boldsymbol{s}^\intercal \cdot M_{\cdot,i}$.
4. $\mathsf{Setup}_M(h_{M,\boldsymbol{u},\tilde{m}})$ outputs $(\rho_0,\ldots,\rho_n)$ where:
$$\rho_0 := (\mu_0, \boldsymbol{\nu}_0)\,, \qquad \rho_i := (s'_i, r_i, \boldsymbol{r}'_i) \qquad \text{for } i \in \{1,\ldots,n\}\,.$$

Online messages. On input x_i, party P_i computes
$$\mu_{i,x_i} := r_i + s'_i \cdot x_i \in \mathbb{F}_q\,, \qquad \boldsymbol{\nu}_{i,x_i} := \boldsymbol{r}'_i + M_{\cdot,i} \cdot x_i \in \mathbb{F}_q^k\,,$$
and outputs $\mathsf{Msg}(\rho_i, x_i) := m_{i,x_i} := (\mu_{i,x_i}, \boldsymbol{\nu}_{i,x_i})$.

Reconstruction. For $(\rho_0, m_{1,x_1},\ldots,m_{n,x_n})$, output:
$$\mathsf{Rec}(\rho_0, m_{1,x_1},\ldots,m_{n,x_n}) := \begin{cases} \mu_0 + \sum_{i=1}^n \mu_{i,x_i} & \text{if } \boldsymbol{\nu}_0 = \sum_{i=1}^n \boldsymbol{\nu}_{i,x_i}\,, \\ \bot & \text{otherwise.} \end{cases}$$

Fig. 2. Outputting-message NIMPC $(\mathsf{Setup}_M, \mathsf{Msg}_M, \mathsf{Rec}_M)$ for $M \in \mathbb{F}_q^{k\times n}$

The term $q^{\min(t,k)}$ in the simulator running time comes from the following fact. The simulator needs to enumerate all the possible input values $\boldsymbol{x}_T$ of the colluding parties P_i ($i \in T$; there are q^t such values) or all the resulting values $M \cdot \boldsymbol{x}_T$ (there are at most q^k such values) to find whether there exists $\boldsymbol{x}_T \in \mathcal{X}_T$, such that $h_{M,\boldsymbol{u},\tilde{m}}|_{\bar{T},\boldsymbol{x}_{\bar{T}}}(\boldsymbol{x}_T) \neq \bot$.

Proof Theorem (4.6). Fig. 2 describes the construction of the outputting-message NIMPC $(\mathsf{Setup}_M, \mathsf{Msg}_M, \mathsf{Rec}_M)$ for $M \in \mathbb{F}_q^{k\times n}$, when the message set is $\mathcal{M} = \mathbb{F}_q$. The security proof follows the informal presentation from Sect. 2.3 and is provided in the full version.

To construct an outputting-message NIMPC for an arbitrary message set $\mathcal{M}$ (instead of $\mathbb{F}_q$), we just split the messages in sub-messages in $\mathbb{F}_q$ (in other words, we represent a message in $\mathcal{M}$ as a vector of $\lceil \log_q |\mathcal{M}| \rceil$ elements of $\mathbb{F}_q$) and using an independent instance of the linear selector for each sub-message. To get the communication complexities of the theorem, we remark that the vectors $\boldsymbol{r}'_i$ can be the same for each sub-message. □

Construction of Linear Selectors. We can now construct linear selectors. More precisely, we have the following theorem.

Theorem 4.7. *Let $\mathbb{F}_q$ be a finite field and $\mathcal{M}$ be a finite message set. Let $M \in \mathbb{F}_q^{k\times n}$ be a matrix. There exists a perfectly fully robust linear selector for M with communication complexities:*

$$CC_{on}(\Pi) = q^k \cdot (k + \lceil \log_q |\mathcal{M}| \rceil) \cdot \lceil \log q \rceil,$$
$$CC_{off}(\Pi) = q^k \cdot (k + 2 \cdot \lceil \log_q |\mathcal{M}| \rceil) \cdot \lceil \log q \rceil.$$

Furthermore, the simulator for t-robustness runs in time $q^k \cdot \text{poly}(q, k, n, \log |\mathcal{M}|)$. *In particular, when k is a constant, the simulator runs in polynomial time in q, n, and* $\log |\mathcal{M}|$.

Proof. Fig. 3 describes the construction of a fully robust linear selector $(\mathsf{Setup}_M, \mathsf{Msg}_M, \mathsf{Rec}_M)$ for $M \in \mathbb{F}_q^{k \times n}$, from an outputting-message NIMPC. Complexities are computed assuming the outputting-message NIMPC is the one from Theorem 4.6. The security proof is provided in the full version. □

Offline preprocessing (Setup). For the function $h_{\boldsymbol{x} \mapsto M \cdot \boldsymbol{x}, \tilde{\boldsymbol{m}}}$ ($M \in \mathbb{F}_q^{k \times n}$, $\tilde{\boldsymbol{m}} \in \mathcal{M}^{\mathcal{U}}$, where $\mathcal{U} = \mathbb{F}_q^k$):

1. For each $\boldsymbol{u} \in \mathbb{F}_q^k$, compute $(\rho'_{\boldsymbol{u},0}, \ldots, \rho'_{\boldsymbol{u},n}) \xleftarrow{R} \mathsf{Setup}'_M(h_{M,\boldsymbol{u},\tilde{m}_{\boldsymbol{u}}})$.
2. Pick a random uniform permutation π of $\mathcal{U}$.
3. $\mathsf{Setup}(1^n, 1^{\kappa}, h_{M,\tilde{\boldsymbol{m}}})$ outputs $(\rho_0, \ldots, \rho_n)$ where $\rho_i = (\rho'_{\pi(\boldsymbol{u}),i})_{\boldsymbol{u} \in \mathcal{U}}$ for $i \in \{0, \ldots, n\}$.

Online messages. On input x_i, party P_i computes $m'_{\boldsymbol{u},i,x_i} := \mathsf{Msg}'_M(\rho'_{\boldsymbol{u},i}, x_i)$ for $\boldsymbol{u} \in \mathcal{U}$, and outputs $\mathsf{Msg}(\rho_i, x_i) := m_{i,x_i} := (m'_{\boldsymbol{u},i,x_i})_{\boldsymbol{u} \in \mathcal{U}}$.

Reconstruction. For $(\rho_0, m_{1,x_1}, \ldots, m_{n,x_n})$, compute for each $\boldsymbol{u} \in \mathcal{U}$:

$$\tilde{m}'_{\boldsymbol{u}} := \mathsf{Rec}'_M(\rho'_{\boldsymbol{u},0}, m'_{\boldsymbol{u},1,x_1}, \ldots, m'_{\boldsymbol{u},n,x_n}) .$$

Search for $\boldsymbol{u} \in \mathcal{U}$ such that $\tilde{m}_{\boldsymbol{u}} \neq \perp$. Abort if not exactly one such $\boldsymbol{u}$ is found. Otherwise output $\mathsf{Rec}(\rho_0, m_{1,x_1}, \ldots, m_{n,x_n}) := \tilde{m}'_{\boldsymbol{u}}$.

Fig. 3. Linear selector $\Pi_M = (\mathsf{Setup}_M, \mathsf{Msg}_M, \mathsf{Rec}_M)$ for $M \in \mathbb{F}_q^{k \times n}$ from outputting-message NIMPC $\Pi'_M = (\mathsf{Setup}'_M, \mathsf{Msg}'_M, \mathsf{Rec}'_M)$

4.3 NIMPC for Abelian Programs

In [3], Beimel et al. constructed a t-robust NIMPC for any Abelian program. But the complexity is at least $\binom{n}{t} \cdot |\mathcal{M}|$. Because of the factor $\binom{n}{t} = \omega(n^{\log \log n + \log t})$, this t-robust NIMPC protocol is not useful for our construction.

Instead, we propose a fully robust construction based on an information-theoretic variant of Yao's garbled circuits [10, 15] (for a specific circuit with gates over $\mathbb{G}$ instead of classical Boolean gates) with communication complexity $O(n \cdot |\mathbb{G}|^{\log n} \cdot (\log |\Omega| + \log |\mathbb{G}|))$. When $\mathbb{G}$ has logarithmic size in n, the communication complexity is only $n^{O(\log \log n)}$, which is only slightly quasi-polynomial.

More formally, we prove the following theorem in the full version.

Theorem 4.8. *Let* $\mathbb{G}$ *be an Abelian group and* $\Omega = \mathcal{M}$ *be a finite message set. Let* $\mathcal{X}_1, \ldots, \mathcal{X}_n$ *be subsets of* $\mathbb{G}$. *Let* $\mathcal{X} := \mathcal{X}_1 \times \cdots \times \mathcal{X}_n \subseteq \mathbb{F}_q^n$ *denote their*

Cartesian product. There exists a perfectly fully robust NIMPC Π for Abelian programs (for $\mathbb{G}$, $\mathcal{X}$, and $\mathcal{M}$), with communication complexities:

$$\mathsf{CC_{on}}(\Pi) \leq |\mathbb{G}|^{\lceil \log n \rceil} \cdot (\log |\Omega| + 2 \cdot \lceil \log |\mathbb{G}| \rceil),$$
$$\mathsf{CC_{off}}(\Pi) = O(n \cdot |\mathbb{G}|^{\lceil \log n \rceil + 2} \cdot (\log |\Omega| + \log |\mathbb{G}|)).$$

5 Admissible Linear Indexing Functions

We recall that the high level idea behind our transformation from a given PSM (or 0-robust NIMPC) protocol to a t-robust NIMPC, is to create a collection of instances (in the form of messages m_{i,x_i}) of the underlying PSM protocol and then use an indexing function that maps parties' inputs to an index that identifies one and only one of these instances. Here we describe the indexing function we use. An informal presentation of the ideas behind this function and its design are presented in Sect. 2 (more specifically, Sect. 2.1).

5.1 Definition

Definition 5.1. *Let $\mathcal{X}_1, \ldots, \mathcal{X}_n$ be subsets of $\mathbb{F}_q$ all containing 0. Let $\mathcal{X} := \mathcal{X}_1 \times \cdots \times \mathcal{X}_n \subseteq \mathbb{F}_q^n$ denote their Cartesian product. Let $\mathcal{S}$ be a finite set and $\mathsf{ind}\colon \mathcal{X} \to \mathcal{S}$ be a function. Let $T \subseteq \{1, \ldots, n\}$ be a subset and $t \in \{0, \ldots, n\}$ be an integer.*

The function ind *is a T-*admissible indexing function *if for any $\boldsymbol{x} \in \mathcal{X}_{\bar{T}}$, the values $\mathsf{ind}(\boldsymbol{x} + \boldsymbol{y})$ for $\boldsymbol{y} \in \mathcal{X}_T$ are all distinct. The function* ind *is a t-*admissible indexing function *if it is T-admissible for every subset $T \subseteq \{1, \ldots, n\}$ of size $|T| \leq t$.*

We want $\mathcal{S}$ to be as small as possible as in our transformation we need to consider $|\mathcal{S}|$ instances of the 0-robust protocol. In particular, to have polynomial communication complexity, we need $|\mathcal{S}|$ to be polynomial in n.

We focus on admissible *linear* indexing functions, of the form

$$\mathsf{ind}\colon \boldsymbol{x} \in \mathbb{F}_q^n \mapsto H \cdot \boldsymbol{x} \in \mathbb{F}_q^\ell,$$

where $H \in \mathbb{F}_q^{\ell \times n}$ is a matrix. W.l.o.g., we assume H to be full rank (if not, we replace H with a full rank sub-matrix that spans the same row-subspace of $F_q^{1 \times n}$). Note that full-rank matrices minimize the size of the indexing function's range $\mathcal{S}$ which in turn improves on the complexity of our construction.

5.2 Relation with Codes

A q-ary code of length n is a subset C of $\mathbb{F}_q^n$ and the distance δ of C is the smallest Hamming distance of two distinct vectors in C.

We have the following lemma.

Lemma 5.2. *Let $t \in \{1, \dots, n\}$ be an integer. Let $\mathcal{X}_1, \dots, \mathcal{X}_n, \mathcal{X}, \mathcal{S}$ be defined as in Definition 5.1. Then a function* $\mathsf{ind}\colon \mathcal{X} \to \mathcal{S}$ *is a t-admissible indexing function (not necessarily linear) if and only if for any $\boldsymbol{\sigma} \in \mathcal{S}$, $\mathsf{ind}^{-1}(\boldsymbol{\sigma})$ is a code of distance $\delta \geq t+1$.*

Proof. The proof follows from the fact that two vectors $\boldsymbol{x}$ and $\boldsymbol{y}$ of $\mathcal{X}$ have distance at most t if and only if $\boldsymbol{x}_{\bar{T}} = \boldsymbol{y}_{\bar{T}}$ for a subset $T \subseteq \{1, \dots, n\}$ of size at most t. □

When we restrict ourselves to linear indexing functions, the corresponding codes are either empty or shifts of the same linear code $\mathsf{ind}^{-1}(\mathbf{0})$. We recall that a q-ary linear code of length n and dimension $k = n - \ell$ is a q-ary code of length n that is also a linear subspace C of $\mathbb{F}_q^n$. It can be defined as the kernel of a full-rank matrix $H \in \mathbb{F}_q^{\ell \times n}$ where H is called the parity-check matrix of the code, namely, $C = \{\boldsymbol{x} \in \mathbb{F}_q^n \mid H \cdot \boldsymbol{x} = \mathbf{0}\}$. A q-ary linear code of length n, of dimension k, and of minimum distance δ is called a $[n,\, k,\, \delta]_q$-code.

We have the following lemma which is a specialization of Lemma 5.2 to the linear case.

Lemma 5.3. *Let $t \in \{1, \dots, n\}$ be an integer. Let $H \in \mathbb{F}_q^{\ell \times n}$ be a full-rank matrix. The function* $\mathsf{ind}\colon \boldsymbol{x} \in \mathbb{F}_q^n \mapsto H \cdot \boldsymbol{x}$ *is a t-admissible linear indexing function if and only if H is a parity-check matrix of a linear code of distance $\delta \geq t+1$.*

Proof. H is a parity-check matrix of a linear code of distance δ if and only if $\mathsf{ind}^{-1}(\mathbf{0})$, the kernel of matrix H, is a linear code of distance δ, and this holds if and only if $\mathsf{ind}^{-1}(\boldsymbol{\sigma})$ is a code of distance δ for all $\boldsymbol{\sigma} \in \mathbb{F}_q^\ell$. By Lemma 5.2 the latter condition holds if and only if ind is a t-admissible linear indexing function. □

5.3 Constructions

Constructions of t-admissible linear indexing functions can be obtained using different error correcting codes, in particular Reed-Solomon codes [13] as stated next.

Lemma 5.4. *Let $t \in \{1, \dots, n\}$ be an integer. Let $q \geq n$ be a prime power. Let $\ell = t$. Then there exists a t-admissible linear indexing function* $\mathsf{ind}\colon \boldsymbol{x} \in \mathbb{F}_q^n \mapsto H \cdot \boldsymbol{x}$*, for a matrix $H \in \mathbb{F}_q^{\ell \times n}$. In particular, H can be a parity-check of the Reed-Solomon $[n,\, n-\ell,\, \ell+1]_q$-code.*

We remark that between n and $2n$, there always exists a power of 2.[6] Therefore, the above lemma shows the existence of t-admissible linear indexing functions with $|\mathcal{S}| = q^\ell \leq (2n)^t$.

In the special case where $t = 1$, there is a more efficient construction using the parity code, i.e.:

$$H = \begin{pmatrix} 1 \dots 1 \end{pmatrix} \in \mathbb{F}_q^{1 \times n}.$$

In that case, the prime power q can be any prime power (it does not need to be at least equal to n).

[6] Better bounds for intervals containing a prime (power) exist. See [1].

5.4 Lower Bound (on the Need for Constant t)

Using the relation of t-admissible indexing functions and codes of distance $\delta \geq t+1$ (Lemma 5.2) together with a sphere-packing-like Hamming bound, we get the following lower bound on $|\mathcal{S}|$. It shows that if $t = \omega(1)$ (as a function of $n \to \infty$), $|\mathcal{S}|$ cannot be polynomial in n. It is formally proven in the full version.

Lemma 5.5. *Let $t \in \{1, \ldots, n\}$ be an integer. Let $\mathcal{X}_1, \ldots, \mathcal{X}_n, \mathcal{X}, \mathcal{S}$ be defined as in Definition 5.1. We suppose that for any $i \in \{1, \ldots, n\}$, $|\mathcal{X}_i| \geq q'$ for some integer $q' \geq 2$. (In the case of linear indexing functions, $\mathcal{X}_i = \mathbb{F}_q$ and we can take $q' = q$.) If a function $\mathsf{ind}\colon \mathcal{X} \to \mathcal{S}$ is t-admissible, then:*

$$|\mathcal{S}| \geq \sum_{k=0}^{\lfloor t/2 \rfloor} \binom{n}{k} (q'-1)^k \geq \left(\frac{n}{t}\right)^{\lfloor t/2 \rfloor}.$$

6 From 0-Robustness to $O(1)$-Robustness

Here we present the main construction and result of the paper, namely, a transformation from any PSM (i.e., 0-robust NIMPC) to a t-robust NIMPC where the latter has polynomial complexity for constant t provided the original protocol is polynomial time and the input set for each party is of polynomial size too. The transformation uses two main tools: the linear selector presented in Sect. 4.2 and admissible linear indexing functions introduced in Sect. 5. The main ideas and intuition about these tools and constructions are described in Sect. 2. The transformation is presented in Fig. 4, but first let us formally define what an NIMPC transformation is.

6.1 Definition of an NIMPC Transformation

An NIMPC transformation is a function $\mathcal{T}$ which takes as input an NIMPC protocol $\Pi' = (\mathsf{Setup}', \mathsf{Msg}', \mathsf{Rec}')$ (usually 0-robust) and outputs a new NIMPC protocol Π (usually t-robust for $t > 0$). We focus on blackbox transformations that use the original algorithms $\mathsf{Setup}', \mathsf{Msg}', \mathsf{Rec}'$ in a blackbox way (i.e., as oracles).

For convenience and without loss of generality we assume that the original NIMPC protocols Π' do not use public randomness, namely, $\rho_0 = \perp$ (indeed, if $\rho_0 \neq \perp$, ρ_0 can be appended to ρ_1 and to all the messages sent by the first party P_1).

Definition 6.1 (NIMPC transformation). *Let $\mathcal{X}_1, \ldots, \mathcal{X}_n, \Omega$ be non-empty finite sets. An NIMPC transformation is a tuple of three algorithms $\mathcal{T} =$ $(\mathsf{Setup}, \mathsf{Msg}, \mathsf{Rec})$, each with oracle access to three other algorithms $\Pi' = (\mathsf{Setup}',$ $\mathsf{Msg}', \mathsf{Rec}')$ satisfying the following property:*

Components.

- PSM protocol $\Pi' = (\mathsf{Setup}', \mathsf{Msg}', \mathsf{Rec}')$ for $\mathcal{F}$.
- A prime power $q \geq \max(|\mathcal{X}_1|, \dots, |\mathcal{X}_n|)$.
- A t-admissible linear indexing function $\mathsf{ind}\colon \boldsymbol{x} \in \mathbb{F}_q^n \mapsto H \cdot \boldsymbol{x} \in \mathbb{F}_q^\ell$.
- A linear selector $\Pi_M = (\mathsf{Setup}_M, \mathsf{Msg}_M, \mathsf{Rec}_M)$ for $M \in \mathbb{F}_q^{k \times n}$ (with $k = \ell + 1$) and for a large enough message space $\mathcal{M}$ containing at least all the possibles messages of the PSM protocol Π'.
- Matrices $M^{(i)}$ and vectors $\boldsymbol{u}^{(\boldsymbol{\sigma},v)}$ for $i \in \{1,\dots,n\}$, $\boldsymbol{\sigma} \in \mathbb{F}_q^\ell$, $v \in \mathbb{F}_q$, defined as: $M^{(i)} := \left(H^\intercal \; \boldsymbol{e}_i^\intercal\right)^\intercal$ and $\boldsymbol{u}^{(\boldsymbol{\sigma},v)} = \left(\boldsymbol{\sigma}^\intercal \; v\right)^\intercal$, where $\boldsymbol{e}_i$ is the i-th vector of the canonical basis of $\mathbb{F}_q^n$.

Offline preprocessing (Setup). For the function $f \in \mathcal{F}$:

1. For $\boldsymbol{\sigma} \in \mathbb{F}_q^\ell$, $i \in \{1,\dots,n\}$, $v \in \mathcal{X}_i$, compute $(\perp, \rho'_{\boldsymbol{\sigma},1}, \dots, \rho'_{\boldsymbol{\sigma},n}) \overset{R}{\leftarrow} \mathsf{Setup}'(1^n, 1^{\mathfrak{K}}, f)$ and $m'_{\boldsymbol{\sigma},i,v} := \mathsf{Msg}'(\rho'_{\boldsymbol{\sigma},i}, v)$.
2. For $i \in \{1,\dots,n\}$, define $\tilde{\boldsymbol{m}}^{(i)} \in \mathcal{M}^{\mathbb{F}_q^{\ell+1}}$ by: $\tilde{m}^{(i)}_{\boldsymbol{u}^{(\boldsymbol{\sigma},v)}} = m'_{\boldsymbol{\sigma},i,v}$ for $\boldsymbol{\sigma} \in \mathbb{F}_q^\ell$ and $v \in \mathcal{X}_i$ ($\tilde{m}^{(i)}_{\boldsymbol{u}}$ is arbitrary if $\boldsymbol{u}$ cannot be written as $\boldsymbol{u} = \boldsymbol{u}^{(\boldsymbol{\sigma},v)}$) and then compute $(\rho_{i,0}, \dots, \rho_{i,n}) \overset{R}{\leftarrow} \mathsf{Setup}_{M^{(i)}}(h_{\boldsymbol{x} \mapsto M^{(i)} \cdot \boldsymbol{x}}, \tilde{\boldsymbol{m}}^{(i)})$.
3. $\mathsf{Setup}(1^n, 1^{\mathfrak{K}}, f)$ outputs $(\rho_0, \dots, \rho_n)$ where $\rho_j := (\rho_{i,j})_{i \in \{1,\dots,n\}}$ for $j \in \{0,\dots,n\}$.

Online messages. On input x_j, party P_j computes $m_{i,j,x_j} := \mathsf{Msg}_{M^{(i)}}(\rho_{i,j}, x_j)$, for $i \in \{1,\dots,n\}$, and outputs $\mathsf{Msg}(\rho_j, x_j) := \boldsymbol{m}_{j,x_j} := (m_{i,j,x_j})_{i \in \{1,\dots,n\}}$.

Reconstruction. For $(\rho_0, \boldsymbol{m}_{1,x_1}, \dots, \boldsymbol{m}_{n,x_n})$, compute $m'_i := \mathsf{Rec}_{M^{(i)}}(\rho_{0,i}, m_{i,1,x_1}, \dots, m_{i,n,x_n})$ for $i \in \{1,\dots,n\}$, and output $\mathsf{Rec}'(\perp, m'_1, \dots, m'_n)$.

Fig. 4. Main NIMPC transformation $\mathcal{T} = (\mathsf{Setup}, \mathsf{Msg}, \mathsf{Rec})$

- ***Functionality preservation.*** *If* $\Pi' = (\mathsf{Setup}', \mathsf{Msg}', \mathsf{Rec}')$ *is an NIMPC protocol for some set* $\mathcal{F}$ *of functions, then* $\Pi := \mathcal{T}(\Pi') := (\mathsf{Setup}^{\Pi'}, \mathsf{Msg}^{\Pi'}, \mathsf{Msg}^{\Pi'})$[7] *is also an NIMPC protocol for the same set* $\mathcal{F}$ *of functions.*

To be useful, an NIMPC transformation also needs to be robust. We consider a very strong notion of robustness. Informally, a transformation $\mathcal{T}$ is T-robust if $\mathcal{T}(\Pi')$ can be proven T-robust for any 0-robust Π', in a black-box way. More formally, we have the following definition.

Definition 6.2 (robustness). *Let* $n \in \mathbb{N}_{>0}$ *and* $T \subseteq \{1,\dots,n\}$. *An NIMPC transformation* $\mathcal{T} = (\mathsf{Setup}, \mathsf{Msg}, \mathsf{Rec})$ *is* T*-robust if there exists a simulator* $\widetilde{\mathsf{Sim}}$ *with oracle access to four oracles* $(\mathsf{Setup}', \mathsf{Msg}', \mathsf{Rec}', O)$ *such that: if* $\Pi' = (\mathsf{Setup}', \mathsf{Msg}', \mathsf{Rec}')$ *is an NIMPC protocol, the following two distributions are indistinguishable:*

$$\{\widetilde{\mathsf{Sim}}^{\Pi', O_{n,\mathfrak{K},f,T}}(1^n, 1^{\mathfrak{K}}, T)\} \quad \text{and} \quad \{\mathsf{View}(1^n, 1^{\mathfrak{K}}, f, T, \boldsymbol{x}_{\overline{T}})\},$$

[7] The notation $\mathsf{Setup}^{\Pi'}$ is a shortcut for $\mathsf{Setup}^{\mathsf{Setup}', \mathsf{Msg}', \mathsf{Rec}'}$, i.e., Setup with the three oracles $\mathsf{Setup}', \mathsf{Msg}', \mathsf{Rec}'$.

where $O_{n,\mathfrak{K},f,T} : \boldsymbol{x}_T \in \mathcal{X}_T \mapsto \mathsf{View}'(1^n, 1^{\mathfrak{K}}, f, \emptyset, \boldsymbol{x}_{\bar{T}} + \boldsymbol{x}_T)$*, and* View *and* View' *are the views from running* $\Pi = \mathcal{T}(\Pi')$ *and* Π' *(resp.), as defined in Definition 3.2.*

Let t *be an integer, then an NIMPC transformation is* t*-robust if it is* T*-robust for any subset* $T \subseteq \{1, \ldots, n\}$ *of size at most* t*.*

The power of a T-robust NIMPC transformation for transforming 0-robustness into t-robustness, is shown in the following lemma whose proof follows directly from the above definition.

Lemma 6.3. *Let* $n \in \mathbb{N}_{>0}$*,* $T \subseteq \{1, \ldots, n\}$*. Let* $\mathcal{T} = (\mathsf{Setup}, \mathsf{Msg}, \mathsf{Rec})$ *be a* T*-robust NIMPC transformation. If* Π' *is a perfectly (resp., statistically, computationally) 0-robust NIMPC, then* $\Pi = \mathcal{T}(\Pi')$ *is perfectly (resp., statistically, computationally)* T*-robust, with the simulator* Sim *defined as follows:* $\mathsf{Sim}^{f|_{\bar{T}, \boldsymbol{x}_{\bar{T}}}}(1^n, 1^{\mathfrak{K}}, T) = \widetilde{\mathsf{Sim}}^{\Pi', O'_{n,\mathfrak{K},f,T}}(1^n, 1^{\mathfrak{K}}, T)$*, where* $O'_{n,\mathfrak{K},f,T} : \boldsymbol{x}_T \in \mathcal{X}_T \mapsto \mathsf{Sim}'^{f|_{\emptyset, \boldsymbol{x}_{\bar{T}} + \boldsymbol{x}_T}}(1^n, 1^{\mathfrak{K}}, \emptyset)$ *using notation in Definition 6.2 and where* Sim' *is a simulator for* Π'*).*

6.2 Actual Transformation

The main theorem of the paper is presented next. It proves that the transformation described in Fig. 4 is functionality preserving (Definition 6.1) and robust (Definition 6.2).

Theorem 6.4. *The NIMPC transformation* $\mathcal{T} = (\mathsf{Setup}, \mathsf{Msg}, \mathsf{Rec})$ *depicted in Fig. 4 satisfies:*

1. ***Functionality preservation.*** *For any NIMPC protocol* $\Pi' = (\mathsf{Setup}', \mathsf{Msg}', \mathsf{Rec}')$ *for a set of functions* $\mathcal{F}$ *from* $\mathcal{X} = \mathcal{X}_1 \times \cdots \times \mathcal{X}_n$*, the resulting NIMPC protocol* $\Pi = \mathcal{T}(\Pi')$ *has the following online and offline communication complexities (when the underlying linear selector is the one from Theorem 4.7):*
$$CC_{on}(\Pi) \le q^{\ell+1} \cdot n \cdot (\ell + 1 + \lceil CC_{on}(\Pi')/\log q \rceil) \cdot \lceil \log q \rceil,$$
$$CC_{off}(\Pi) \le q^{\ell+1} \cdot n \cdot (\ell + 1 + 2 \cdot \lceil CC_{on}(\Pi')/\log q \rceil) \cdot \lceil \log q \rceil,$$
where $q \ge \max(|\mathcal{X}_1|, \ldots, |\mathcal{X}_n|)$ *and* q *is a prime power, and* ℓ *is the dimension of the range of the linear indexing function* $\mathsf{ind} \colon \boldsymbol{x} \in \mathbb{F}_q^n \mapsto H \cdot \boldsymbol{x} \in \mathbb{F}_q^\ell$*.*[8]
2. ***T-robustness.*** *For any* $T \subseteq \{1, \ldots, n\}$*, if* ind *is a* T*-admissible indexing function and* Π_M *is a perfectly* T*-robust linear selector, the NIMPC transformation from Fig. 4 is* T*-robust. The corresponding simulator* $\widetilde{\mathsf{Sim}}$ *runs in polynomial time in* $n, \mathfrak{K}, q^\ell, CC_{on}(\Pi'), |\mathcal{X}_T|$ *and calls its oracle* O *once for each vector* $\boldsymbol{x}_T \in \mathcal{X}_T$*, when the underlying linear selector is the one from Theorem 4.7.*

The proof of the theorem appears in the full version. We have the following corollary.

[8] We recall that Π' is assumed not to use any public randomness: $\rho_0 = \perp$.

Corollary 6.5. *Let t be a positive integer. Let $\Pi' = (\mathsf{Setup}', \mathsf{Msg}', \mathsf{Rec}')$ be an NIMPC protocol for a set of functions $\mathcal{F}$ from $\mathcal{X} = \mathcal{X}_1 \times \cdots \times \mathcal{X}_n$. Let q be the smallest prime power at least equal to $\max(n, |\mathcal{X}_1|, \ldots, |\mathcal{X}_n|)$. We recall that $q \leq 2\max(n, |\mathcal{X}_1|, \ldots, |\mathcal{X}_n|)$.*[9] *Let $\mathsf{ind} \colon \boldsymbol{x} \in \mathbb{F}_q^n \mapsto H \cdot \boldsymbol{x} \in \mathbb{F}_q^\ell$ be the t-admissible linear indexing function defined in Lemma 5.4 (in particular $\ell = t$).*

The NIMPC protocol $\Pi = \mathcal{T}(\Pi')$ from Fig. 4 is perfectly (resp., statistically, computationally) t-robust, if Π' is perfectly (resp., statistically, computationally) 0-robust. Furthermore, if $t = O(1)$ and the communication complexity of Π' and the input size $\mathcal{X}_i$ (for all i) are all polynomial in n and $\mathfrak{K}$, then the communication complexity of Π is polynomial in n and $\mathfrak{K}$. If in addition Π' is polynomial-time, so is Π. Similarly, if the simulator for Π' is polynomial-time, so is the simulator for Π.

We point out that the simulator $\widetilde{\mathsf{Sim}}$ is uniform in T and n.

7 NIMPC for Symmetric Functions

In this section, we construct NIMPC protocols for symmetric functions with better asymptotic complexity than with our generic transformation (from an efficient 0-robust NIMPC for symmetric function which exists for any symmetric function) or with [3, Sect. 4]. The communication complexity of the latter construction is $\binom{n}{t} \cdot O(2^t \cdot n^4)$, while our new construction for symmetric functions achieve a communication complexity of $n^{\log\log n + \log t + O(1)}$. Our construction uses our new fully robust NIMPC for Abelian programs in Sect. 4.3.

7.1 Symmetric Functions

Let us first recall the definition of a symmetric function. We focus on the case where each input is a bit. But our construction can be generalized.

Definition 7.1. *Let n be a positive integer and Ω be a finite set. A function $f \colon \{0,1\}^n \to \Omega$ is symmetric if and only if for any permutation π of $\{1, \ldots, n\}$ and for any $\boldsymbol{x} \in \{0,1\}^n$, $f(x_1, \ldots, x_n) = f(x_{\pi(1)}, \ldots, x_{\pi(n)})$.*

7.2 Overview of the Construction

We remark that symmetric functions $f \colon \{0,1\}^n \to \Omega$ are Abelian programs (Definition 4.3) over any group $\mathbb{G} = \mathbb{Z}_N$ with $N > n$:

$$f \colon \boldsymbol{x} \in \{0,1\}^n \mapsto \tilde{g}(\sum_{i=1}^{n} x_i) \in \Omega,$$

where $\tilde{g} \colon \mathbb{Z}_N \to \Omega$ is some function.

[9] Better bounds for intervals containing a prime (power) exist. See [1].

If we directly use the construction of NIMPC for Abelian programs in Sect. 4.3, we would get a fully robust NIMPC for symmetric function with communication complexity $n^{\log n + O(1)} \cdot \log |\Omega|$. This is already an interesting result. However, we would like to go further. For that we use the Chinese Remainder Theorem to decompose the initial function over a large group $\mathbb{Z}_{n+1}$ or $\mathbb{Z}$ into functions over smaller groups.

Decomposition and Recombination Using CRT. Let $p_1 < \cdots < p_\ell$ be the first ℓ prime numbers, such that $N := \prod_{j=1}^{\ell} p_j \geq n + 1$. We recall that there is a ring isomorphism CRT: $\prod_{j=1}^{\ell} \mathbb{Z}_{p_j} \to \mathbb{Z}_N$. In particular $\mathrm{CRT}(y_1, \ldots, y_\ell)$ is the only integer y in $\{0, \ldots, N-1\}$ such that $y \bmod p_j = y_j$ for any $j \in \{1, \ldots, \ell\}$. By the prime number theorem, we can choose $p_j = O(\log n)$ for $j \in \{1, \ldots, \ell\}$ (and $\ell = O(\log n)$ too). The main idea is the following: we first compute some well-chosen Abelian programs over each group $\mathbb{Z}_{p_j}$ (over the original inputs $(x_1, \ldots, x_n) \in \mathcal{X}$) and then combine back the intermediate results (corresponding to some function of $\sum_{i=1}^{n} x_i \bmod p_j$) to compute $\tilde{g}(\sum_{i=1}^{n} x_i)$.

We need to combine the results in a robust way. We consider a fully robust NIMPC for the following set of functions (with ℓ parties) $\mathcal{F}' = \{f'_{\tilde{g}}\}_{\tilde{g}}$ indexed by a function $\tilde{g}\colon \mathbb{Z}_{n+1} \to \Omega$, where the function $f'_{\tilde{g}}\colon \prod_{j=1}^{\ell} \mathbb{Z}_{p_j} \to \Omega \cup \{\perp\}$ is defined by:

$$f'_{\tilde{g}}(y_1, \ldots, y_\ell) \mapsto \begin{cases} \tilde{g}(y) & \text{if } y := \mathrm{CRT}(y_1, \ldots, y_\ell) \in \{0, \ldots, n\}, \\ \perp & \text{otherwise.} \end{cases}$$

We can use the construction in [3, Sect. 3, Theorem 3.3] to get a fully robust NIMPC for $\mathcal{F}'$ of communication complexity $O(N \cdot p_\ell^2 \cdot \ell \cdot \log |\Omega|) = O(n \cdot \log |\Omega| \cdot \mathrm{polylog}(n))$. Let m'_{j,y_j} be the message that party P_j would send on input y_j in this protocol.

For each $j \in \{1, \ldots, \ell\}$, we can then use our construction for Abelian programs in Sect. 4.3 in the groups $\mathbb{Z}_{p_j}$ for the input sets $\mathcal{X}_1 = \cdots = \mathcal{X}_n = \{0, 1\}$ and the messages $\tilde{\boldsymbol{m}}_j$ defined by $\tilde{m}_{j,v} = m'_{j,v}$ (for each $v \in \mathbb{Z}_{p_j}$) to enable the computation (or selection) of m'_{j,y_j} for $y_j = \sum_{i=1}^{n} x_i \bmod p_j$. The resulting construction would have communication complexity $n^{\log\log n + O(1)} \cdot \log |\Omega|$, as $|\mathbb{Z}_{p_j}|^{\log n} = n^{\log\log n + O(1)}$.

Issues with Robustness. Unfortunately, this construction is not t-robust: the adversary might use different values x_i for $i \in T$ as input to each NIMPC for Abelian program. For example, if P_1 is colluding, the adversary can compute for any j: m_{j,y_j} and m_{j,y_j+1}, if we write $y_j = \sum_{i=2}^{n} x_i \bmod p_j$. He can then mix and match them when using them as input of the fully robust protocol for $f'_{\tilde{g}}$. In other words, he can compute:

$$\tilde{g}(\mathrm{CRT}(y_1 + b_1, \ldots, y_\ell + b_\ell))$$

for any $(b_1, \ldots, b_\ell) \in \{0,1\}^\ell$, instead of just:

$$\tilde{g}(\mathrm{CRT}(y_1, \ldots, y_\ell)) \quad \text{and} \quad \tilde{g}(\mathrm{CRT}(y_1 + 1, \ldots, y_\ell + 1)),$$

(i.e., $b_1 = \cdots = b_\ell \in \{0,1\}$).

One first solution consists in choosing p_j such that when $b_1, \ldots, b_\ell$ are not the same bit (or more generally not the same integer in $\{0, \ldots, t\}$ when t parties are colluding):

$$\mathrm{CRT}(y_1 + b_1, \ldots, y_\ell + b_\ell) > n,$$

so that $\tilde{g}(\mathrm{CRT}(y_1 + b_1, \ldots, y_\ell + b_\ell)) = \perp$. This works but makes parameters cumbersome to compute and non-optimal.

We propose a cleaner solution. Instead of working in $\mathbb{Z}_{p_j}$, we work in $\mathbb{G}_j = \mathbb{Z}_{p_j} \times \mathbb{Z}_{t+1}$. The second part z_j of an element $(y_j, z_j) \in \mathbb{G}_j$ plays a role very similar to indexes $\boldsymbol{\sigma}$ in our transformation from 0-robustness to $O(1)$-robustness. It prevents mix and matching values computed from different inputs. We consider a fully robust NIMPC protocol for the following set of functions (with ℓ parties) $\mathcal{F}' = \{f'_{\tilde{g}}\}_{\tilde{g}}$ indexed by a function $\tilde{g} \colon \mathbb{Z}_{n+1} \to \Omega$, where the function $f'_{\tilde{g}} \colon \prod_{j=1}^{\ell} \mathbb{G}_j \to \Omega \cup \{\perp\}$ is defined by:

$$f'_{\tilde{g}}((y_1, z_1), \ldots, (y_\ell, z_\ell)) = \begin{cases} \tilde{g}(y) & \text{if } y := \mathrm{CRT}(y_1, \ldots, y_\ell) \in \{0, \ldots, n\} \\ & \text{and } z_1 = \cdots = z_\ell, \\ \perp & \text{otherwise.} \end{cases}$$

Let m'_{j,y_j,z_j} be the message that party P_j would send on input (y_j, z_j) in this protocol.

For each $j \in \{1, \ldots, \ell\}$, we now use our construction for Abelian programs in Sect. 4.3 in the groups $\mathbb{G}_j$ for the input sets $\mathcal{X}_1 = \cdots = \mathcal{X}_n = \{0,1\}$ and the messages $\tilde{\boldsymbol{m}}_j$ defined by $\tilde{m}_{j,v} = m'_{j,v}$ (for each $v \in \mathbb{G}_j$), where $1 \in \{0,1\}$ is identified to $(1,1) \in \mathbb{G}_j$ and $0 \in \{0,1\}$ is identified to $(0,0) \in \mathbb{G}_j$. The communication complexity becomes $n^{\log\log n + \log t + O(1)} \cdot \log|\Omega|$.

7.3 Formal Construction

We formally prove the following theorem in the full version.

Theorem 7.2. *Let $\mathcal{F} = \{f_{\tilde{g}}\}_{\tilde{g}}$ be the set of symmetric functions $f_{\tilde{g}} \colon \boldsymbol{x} \in \{0,1\}^n \mapsto \tilde{g}(\sum_{i=1}^n x_i) \in \Omega$, where $\tilde{g} \colon \mathbb{Z}_{n+1} \to \Omega$ and Ω is some finite set. Let t be an integer. There exists a t-robust NIMPC for $\mathcal{F}$ with communication complexity $n^{\log\log n + \log t + O(1)} \cdot \log|\Omega|$. In particular, if $t = O(\log n)$, the communication complexity if $n^{O(\log\log n)} \cdot \log|\Omega|$.*

Acknowledgments. This work was supported by the Defense Advanced Research Projects Agency (DARPA) and Army Research Office (ARO) under Contract No. W911NF-15-C-0236.

References

1. Baker, R.C., Harman, G., Pintz, J.: The difference between consecutive primes, ii. Proc. Lond. Math. Soc. **83**(3), 532–562 (2001). http://www.cs.umd.edu/~gasarch/BLOGPAPERS/BakerHarmanPintz.pdf
2. Barrington, D.A.M.: Bounded-width polynomial-size branching programs recognize exactly those languages in nc^1. In: Hartmanis, J. (ed.) Proceedings of the 18th Annual ACM Symposium on Theory of Computing, 28–30 May 1986, Berkeley, California, USA, pp. 1–5. ACM (1986). http://doi.acm.org/10.1145/12130.12131
3. Beimel, A., Gabizon, A., Ishai, Y., Kushilevitz, E., Meldgaard, S., Paskin-Cherniavsky, A.: Non-interactive secure multiparty computation. In: Garay, J.A., Gennaro, R. (eds.) CRYPTO 2014. LNCS, vol. 8617, pp. 387–404. Springer, Heidelberg (2014). doi:10.1007/978-3-662-44381-1_22
4. Feige, U., Kilian, J., Naor, M.: A minimal model for secure computation (extended abstract). In: 26th ACM STOC, pp. 554–563. ACM Press, May 1994
5. Goldwasser, S., et al.: Multi-input functional encryption. In: Nguyen, P.Q., Oswald, E. (eds.) EUROCRYPT 2014. LNCS, vol. 8441, pp. 578–602. Springer, Heidelberg (2014). doi:10.1007/978-3-642-55220-5_32
6. Goldwasser, S., Rothblum, G.N.: On best-possible obfuscation. In: Vadhan, S.P. (ed.) TCC 2007. LNCS, vol. 4392, pp. 194–213. Springer, Heidelberg (2007). doi:10.1007/978-3-540-70936-7_11
7. Halevi, S., Ishai, Y., Jain, A., Kushilevitz, E., Rabin, T.: Secure multiparty computation with general interaction patterns. In: Sudan, M. (ed.) ITCS 2016, pp. 157–168. ACM, New York (2016)
8. Halevi, S., Lindell, Y., Pinkas, B.: Secure computation on the web: computing without simultaneous interaction. In: Rogaway, P. (ed.) CRYPTO 2011. LNCS, vol. 6841, pp. 132–150. Springer, Heidelberg (2011). doi:10.1007/978-3-642-22792-9_8
9. Ishai, Y., Kushilevitz, E.: Private simultaneous message protocols with applications. In: Proceedings of ISTCS, pp. 174–184 (1997)
10. Ishai, Y., Kushilevitz, E.: Perfect constant-round secure computation via perfect randomizing polynomials. In: Widmayer, P., Eidenbenz, S., Triguero, F., Morales, R., Conejo, R., Hennessy, M. (eds.) ICALP 2002. LNCS, vol. 2380, pp. 244–256. Springer, Heidelberg (2002). http://dx.doi.org/10.1007/3-540-45465-9_22
11. Karchmer, M., Wigderson, A.: On span programs. In: Proceedings of Structures in Complexity Theory, pp. 102–111 (1993)
12. Kilian, J.: Founding cryptography on oblivious transfer. In: 20th ACM STOC, pp. 20–31. ACM Press, May 1988
13. MacWilliams, F.J., Sloane, N.J.A.: The Theory of Error-correcting Codes. Elsevier, Amsterdam (1977)
14. Obana, S., Yoshida, M.: An efficient construction of non-interactive secure multiparty computation. In: Foresti, S., Persiano, G. (eds.) CANS 2016. LNCS, vol. 10052, pp. 604–614. Springer, Cham (2016). doi:10.1007/978-3-319-48965-0_39
15. Yao, A.C.C.: How to generate and exchange secrets (extended abstract). In: 27th FOCS, pp. 162–167. IEEE Computer Society Press, October 1986
16. Yoshida, M., Obana, S.: On the (in)efficiency of non-interactive secure multiparty computation. In: Kwon, S., Yun, A. (eds.) ICISC 2015. LNCS, vol. 9558, pp. 185–193. Springer, Cham (2016). doi:10.1007/978-3-319-30840-1_12

The Price of Low Communication in Secure Multi-party Computation

Juan Garay[1(✉)], Yuval Ishai[2], Rafail Ostrovsky[3], and Vassilis Zikas[4]

[1] Yahoo Research, Sunnyvale, USA
juan.a.garay@gmail.com
[2] Department of Computer Science, Technion and UCLA, Haifa, Israel
yuvali@cs.technion.ac.il
[3] Department of Computer Science, UCLA, Los Angeles, USA
rafail@cs.ucla.edu
[4] Department of Computer Science, RPI, Troy, USA
vzikas@cs.rpi.edu

Abstract. Traditional protocols for secure multi-party computation among n parties communicate at least a linear (in n) number of bits, even when computing very simple functions. In this work we investigate the feasibility of protocols with *sublinear* communication complexity. Concretely, we consider two clients, one of which may be corrupted, who wish to perform some "small" joint computation using n servers but without any trusted setup. We show that enforcing sublinear communication complexity drastically affects the feasibility bounds on the number of corrupted parties that can be tolerated in the setting of information-theoretic security.

We provide a complete investigation of security in the presence of semi-honest adversaries—static and adaptive, with and without erasures—and initiate the study of security in the presence of malicious adversaries. For semi-honest static adversaries, our bounds essentially match the corresponding bounds when there is no communication restriction—i.e., we can tolerate up to $t < (1/2 - \epsilon)n$ corrupted parties. For the adaptive case, however, the situation is different. We prove that without erasures even a small constant fraction of corruptions is intolerable, and—more surprisingly—when erasures are allowed, we prove that $t < (1 - \sqrt{0.5} - \epsilon)n$ corruptions can be tolerated, which we also show to be essentially optimal. The latter optimality proof hinges on a new treatment of probabilistic adversary structures that may be of independent interest. In the case of active corruptions in the sublinear communication setting, we prove that static "security with abort" is feasible when $t < (1/2 - \epsilon)n$, namely, the bound that is tight for semi-honest security. All of our negative results in fact rule out protocols with sublinear *message complexity*.

The full version of this paper can be found at the Cryptology ePrint Archive [28].

J. Katz and H. Shacham (Eds.): CRYPTO 2017, Part I, LNCS 10401, pp. 420–446, 2017.
DOI: 10.1007/978-3-319-63688-7_14

1 Introduction

Secure multi-party computation (MPC) allows a set of parties to compute a function on their joint inputs in a secure way. Roughly speaking, security means that even when some of the parties misbehave, they can neither disrupt the output of honest parties (correctness), nor can they obtain more information than their specified inputs and outputs (privacy). Misbehaving parties are captured by assuming an adversary that corrupts some of the parties and uses them to attack the protocol. The usual types of adversary are *semi-honest* (aka "passive"), where the adversary just observes the view of corrupted parties, and *malicious* (aka "active"), where the adversary takes full control of the corrupted parties.

The seminal results from the '80s [32,52] proved that under standard cryptographic assumption, any multi-party functionality can be securely computed in the presence of a polynomially bounded semi-honest adversary corrupting arbitrarily many parties. For the malicious case, Goldreich et al. [32] proved that arbitrarily many corruptions can be tolerated if we are willing to give up on fairness, and achieve so-called *security with abort*; otherwise, an honest majority is required.

In the information-theoretic (IT) model—where there are no restrictions on the adversary's computational power—the situation is different. Ben-Or et al. [4] and independently Chaum et al. [14] proved that IT security is possible if and only if $t < n/3$ parties are actively corrupted (or $t < n/2$ are passively corrupted, respectively). The solutions in [4] are perfectly secure, i.e., there is a zero-error probability. Rabin and Ben-Or [50] proved that if a negligible error probability is allowed, and a broadcast channel is available to the parties, then any function can be IT-securely computed if and only if $t < n/2$ parties are actively corrupted. All the above bounds hold both for a *static* adversary, who chooses which parties to corrupt at the beginning of the protocol execution, and for an *adaptive* adversary, who might corrupt more parties as the protocol evolves and depending on his view of the protocol so far.

In addition to their unconditional security and good concrete efficiency, information theoretic protocols typically enjoy strong composability guarantees. Concretely, the above conditions for the IT setting allow for universally composable (UC) protocols [10]. This is known to be impossible in the *plain model*—i.e., without assuming access to a trusted setup functionality such as a common reference string (CRS) [12], even if one settles for computational security. Given the above advantages of IT protocols, it is natural to investigate alternative models that allow for IT-secure protocols without an honest majority.

It is well known that assuming a strong setup such as *oblivious transfer* (OT) [49], we can construct IT secure protocols tolerating an arbitrary number of corruptions both in the semi-honest setting [32] and in the malicious setting [43,45]. However, these solutions require trusting (a centralized party that serves as) an OT functionality.

An alternative approach is for the parties to procure help from other servers in a network they have access to, such as the Internet. This naturally leads to the formulation of the problem in the so-called *client-server* model [16,18,19,36]. This model refines the standard MPC model by separating parties into *clients*, who wish to perform some computation and provide the inputs to and receive outputs from it, and *servers*, who help the clients perform their computation. (The same party can play both roles, as is the case in the standard model of secure computation.) The main advantage of this refinement is that it allows to decouple the number of clients from the expected "level of security," which depends on the number of servers and the security threshold, and, importantly, it allows us to address the question of how the communication complexity (CC) of the protocol increases with the number n of servers.

A direct approach to obtain security in the client/server model would be to have the clients share their input to *all* the servers (denoted by n from now on), who would perform the computation on these inputs and return to the clients their respective outputs. Using [4,14,32,50], this approach yields a protocol tolerating $t < n/2$ semi-honest corrupted servers, or, for the malicious setting, $t < n/2$ corrupted servers if broadcast is available, and $t < n/3$, otherwise. (Recall that the above bounds are required in addition to arbitrarily many corruptions of clients.)

Despite its simplicity, however, the above approach incurs a high overhead in communication when the number of clients is small in comparison to the number of servers, which is often the case in natural application scenarios. Indeed, the communication complexity of the above protocol would be polynomial in n. In this work we investigate the question of how to devise IT protocols with near-optimal resilience in the client/server model, where the communication complexity is *sublinear* in the number of servers n. As we prove, this low-communication requirement comes at a cost, inducing a different—and somewhat surprising—landscape of feasibility bounds.

Our Contributions. In this work we study the feasibility of information-theoretic MPC in the client-server model with sublinear communication complexity. We consider the case of two clients and n servers, which we refer to as the $(2, n)$-*client/server model*, and prove exact feasibility bounds on the number of corrupted servers that can be tolerated for MPC in addition to a corrupted client.[1] We provide a complete investigation of security against semi-honest adversaries—static and adaptive, with and without erasures—and also initiate the study of malicious adversaries. Our results can be summarized as follows:

- As a warmup, for the simplest possible case of static semi-honest corruptions, we confirm that the folklore protocol which has one of the clients ask a random sublinear-size server "committee" [8] to help the clients perform their computation, is secure and has sublinear message complexity against

[1] Our bounds are for the two-client case, but can be easily extended to the multi-client setting with constantly many clients, as such an extension will just incur a constant multiplicative increase in CC.

$t < (1/2 - \epsilon)n$ corrupted servers, for any given constant $0 < \epsilon < 1/2$. Further, we prove that this bound is tight. Thus, up to an arbitrarily small constant fraction, the situation is the same as in the case of MPC with unrestricted communication.

- In the case of adaptive semi-honest corruptions we distinguish between two cases, depending on whether or not the (honest) parties are allowed to erase their state. Naturally, allowing erasures makes it more difficult for the adversary to attack a protocol. However, restricting to sublinear communication complexity introduces a counterintuitive complication in providing optimally resilient protocols. Specifically, in communication-unrestricted MPC (e.g., MPC with linear or polynomial CC), the introduction of erasures does not affect the exact feasibility bound $t < n/2$ and typically makes it easier[2] to come up with a provably secure protocol against any tolerable adversary. In contrast, in the sublinear-communication realm erasures have a big effect on the feasibility bound and make the design of an optimal protocol a far more challenging task. In fact, proving upper and lower bounds for this (the erasures) setting is the most technically challenging part of this work.

  In more detail, when no erasures are assumed, we show that an adversary corrupting a constant fraction of the servers (in addition to one of the clients, say, c_1), cannot be tolerated. The reason for this is intuitive: Since there is a sublinear number of messages, there can only be a sublinear number of servers that are activated (i.e., send or receive messages) during the protocol. Thus, if the adversary has a linear corruption budget, then if he manages to find the identities of these active servers, he can adaptively corrupt all of them. Since the parties cannot erase anything (and in particular they cannot erase their communication history), the adversary corrupting c_1 can "jump" to all servers whose view depends on c_1's view, by traversing the communication graph which includes the corrupted client. Symmetrically, the adversary corrupting the other client c_2, can corrupt the remainder "protocol-relevant" parties (i.e., parties whose view depends on the joint view of the clients). Security in the presence of such an adversary contradicts classical MPC impossibility results [35], which prove that if there is a two-set partition of the party-set and the adversary might corrupt either of the sets (this is called the Q^2 condition in [35]) then this adversary cannot be tolerated for general MPC—i.e., there are functions that cannot be computed securely against such an adversary.

  Most surprising is the setting when erasures are allowed. We prove that, for any constant $\epsilon > 0$, an adversary corrupting at most $t < (1-\sqrt{0.5}-\epsilon)n$ servers can be tolerated, and moreover that this bound is essentially tight. The idea of our protocol is as follows. Instead of having the clients contact the servers for help—which would lead, as above, to the adversary corrupting too many helpers—every server probabilistically "wakes up" and volunteers to help. However, a volunteer cannot talk to both clients as with good probability the corrupted client will be the first he talks to which will result in the volunteer

[2] As opposed to requiring the use of more complex cryptographic tools such as non-committing encryption [11,21] as in the non-erasure setting.

being corrupted before erasing. Instead, each volunteer asks a random server, called *the intermediary*, to serve as his point of contact with one of the two clients. By an appropriate scheduling of message-sending and erasures, we can ensure that if the adversary jumps and corrupts a volunteer or an intermediary because he communicated with the corrupted client, then he might at most learn the message that was already sent to this client. The choice of $1-\sqrt{0.5}$ is an optimal choice that will ensure that no adaptive adversary can corrupt more than $1/2$ of the active servers set in this protocol. The intuition behind it is that if the adversary corrupts each party with probability $1-\sqrt{0.5}$, then for any volunteer-intermediary pair, the probability that the adversary corrupts both of them before they erase (by being lucky and corrupting any on of them at random) is $1/2$.

Although proving the above is far from straightforward, the most challenging part is the proof of impossibility for $t = (1-\sqrt{0.5}+\epsilon)n$ corruptions. In a nutshell, this proof works as follows: Every adaptive adversary attacking a protocol induces a probability distribution on the set of corrupted parties; this distribution might depend on the coins of the adversary and the inputs and coins of all parties. This is because the protocol's coins and inputs define the sequence of point-to-point communication channels in the protocol, which in turn can be exploited by the adversary to expand his corruption set, by for example jumping to parties that communicate with the already corrupted set. Such a probability distribution induces a *probabilistic adversary structure* that assigns to each subset of parties the probability that this subset gets corrupted.

We provide a natural definition of what it means for such a probabilistic adversary structure to be *intolerable* and define a suitable "domination" condition which ensures that any structure that dominates an intolerable structure is also intolerable. We then use this machinery to prove that the adversary that randomly corrupts (approximately) $(1-\sqrt{0.5})n$ servers and then corrupts everyone that talks to the corrupted parties in every protocol round induces a probabilistic structure that dominates an intolerable structure and is, therefore, also intolerable. We believe that the developed machinery might be useful for analyzing other situations in which party corruption is probabilistic.

- Finally, we initiate the study of actively secure MPC with sublinear communication. Here we look at static corruptions and provide a protocol which is IT secure with abort [32,42] against any adversary corrupting a client and $t < (1/2-\epsilon)n$ servers for a constant $0 < \epsilon < 1/2$. This matches the semi-honest lower bound for static security, at the cost, however, of allowing the protocol to abort, a price which seems inevitable in our setting. We leave open the questions of obtaining full security or adaptive security with erasures in the case of actively secure MPC.

We finally note that both our positive and negative results are of the strongest possible form. Specifically, our designed protocols communicate a sublinear number of *bits*, whereas our impossibility proofs apply to all protocols that communicate a sublinear number of *messages* (independently of how long these messages are).

Related Work. The literature on communication complexity (CC) of MPC is vast. To put out results in perspective, we now discuss some of the most relevant literature on IT MPC with low communication complexity. For simplicity, in our discussion we shall exclude factors that depend only on the security parameter which has no dependency on n, as well as factors that are poly-logarithmic in n.

The CC of the original protocols from the '80s was polynomial (in the best case quadratic) in n, in particular, $\mathsf{poly}(n) \cdot |C|$ where $|C|$ denotes the size of the circuit C that computes the given function. A long line of work ensued that reduced this complexity down to linear in the size of the party set by shifting the dependency on different parameters [2,3,6,17,22,24–27,37–39,43,44].

In the IT setting in particular, Damgård and Nielsen [23] achieve a CC of $O(n|C|+n^2)$ messages—i.e., their CC scales in a linear fashion with the number of parties. Their protocol is perfectly secure in the presence of $t < n/2$ semi-honest corruptions. In the malicious setting, they provide a protocol tolerating $t < n/3$ corruptions with a CC of $O(n|C| + d \cdot n^2) + \mathsf{poly}(n)$ messages, where d is the multiplicative depth of the circuit C. Beerliová-Trubíniová and Hirt [3] extended this result to perfect security, achieving CC of $O(n|C| + d \cdot n^2 + n^3)$. Later on, Ben-Sasson et al. [5] achieved CC $O(n|C| + d \cdot n^2) + \mathsf{poly}(n)$ messages against $t < n/2$ active corruptions, which was brought down to $O(n|C| + n^2)$ by Genkin *et al.* [29]. Note that with the exception of the maliciously secure protocol in [23], all the above works tolerate a number of corruptions which is tight even when there is no bound on the communication complexity.

Settling for a near-optimal resilience of $t < (1/2 - \epsilon)n$, the above bounds can be improved by a factor of n, making the communication complexity grow at most polylogarithmically with the number of parties. This was first shown for client-server protocols with a constant number of clients by Damgård and Ishai [19] (see also [43]) and later in the standard MPC model by Damgård et al. [20]. The latter protocol can in fact achieve *perfect* security if $t < (1/3 - \epsilon)n$.

We point out that all the above communication bounds include polynomial (in n) *additive* terms in their CC. This means that even for circuits that are small relative to the number of parties (e.g., even when $|C| = o(n)$), they communicate a number of bits (or, worse, messages) which is polynomial in n. Instead, in this work we are interested in achieving overall (bit) communication complexity of $o(n)|C|$ without such additive (polynomial or even linear in n) terms, and are willing to settle for statistical (rather than perfect) security.

Finally, a different line of work studies the problem of reducing the *communication locality* of MPC protocols [6,7,13]. This measure corresponds to the maximum number of neighbors/parties that any party communicates with *directly*, i.e., via a bilateral channel, throughout the protocol execution. Although these works achieve a sublinear (in n) communication locality, their model assumes each party to have an input, which requires the communication complexity to grow (at least) linearly with the number of parties. Moreover, the protocols presented in these works either assume a trusted setup or are restricted to static adversaries.

Organization of the Paper. In Sect. 2 we present the model (network, security) used in this work and establish the necessary terminology and notation. Section 3 presents our treatment of semi-honest static security, while Sect. 4 is dedicated to semi-honest adaptive corruptions, with erasures (Sect. 4.1) and without erasures (Sect. 4.2). Finally, Sect. 5 includes our feasibility result for malicious (static) adversaries.

2 Model, Definitions and Building Blocks

We consider $n+2$ parties, where two special parties, called the *clients*, wish to securely compute a function on their joint inputs with the help of the remaining n parties, called the *servers*. We denote by $\mathcal{C} = \{c_1, c_2\}$ and by $\mathcal{S} = \{s_1, \ldots, s_n\}$ the sets of clients and servers, respectively. We shall denote by $\mathcal{P}$ the set of all parties, i.e., $\mathcal{P} = \mathcal{C} \cup \mathcal{S}$. The parties are connected by a complete network of (secure) point-to-point channel as in standard unconditionally secure MPC protocols [4,14]. We call this model the $(2,n)$-*client/server model*.

The parties wish to compute a given two-party function f, described as an arithmetic circuit C_f, on inputs from the clients by invoking a synchronous protocol Π. (Wlog, we assume that f is a public-output function $f(x_1, x_2) = y$, where x_i is c_i's input; using standard techniques, this can be extended to multi-input and private-output functions—cf. [46].) Such a protocol proceeds in synchronous rounds where in each round any party might send messages to other parties and the guarantee is that any message sent in some round is delivered by the beginning of the following round. Security of the protocol is defined as security against an adversary that gets to corrupt parties and uses them to attack the protocol. We will consider both a *semi-honest* (aka *passive*) and a *malicious* (aka *active*) adversary. A semi-honest adversary gets to observe the view of parties it corrupts—and attempts to extract information from it—but allows parties to correctly execute their protocol. In contrast, a malicious adversary takes full control of corrupted parties. Furthermore, we consider both *static* and *adaptive* corruptions. A static adversary chooses the set of corrupted parties at the beginning of the protocol execution, whereas and adaptive adversary chooses this set dynamically by corrupting (additional) parties as the protocol evolves (and depending on his view of the protocol). A *threshold* (t_c, t_s)-*adversary* in the client/server model is an adversary that corrupts in total up to t_c clients and additionally up to t_s servers.

The adversary is *rushing* [9,40], i.e., in each round he first receives the messages that are sent to corrupted parties, and then has the corrupted parties send their messages for that round. For adaptive security *with erasures* we adopt the natural model in which each of the operations "send-message," "receive-message," and "erase-messages from state" is atomic and the adversary is able to corrupt after any such atomic operation. This, in particular, means that when a party sends a message to a corrupted party, then the adversary can corrupt the sender before he erases this message. In more detail, every round is partitioned into "mini-rounds," where in each mini-round the party can send a message, or receive a message, or erase a message from its state—exclusively. This is not only a natural erasure model, but ensures that one does not design protocols whose security relies on the assumption that honest parties can send and erase a message simultaneously, as an atomic operation (see [40] for a related discussion about atomicity of sending messages).

The *communication complexity* (CC) of a protocol is the number of bits sent by honest parties during a protocol execution.[3] Throughout this work we will consider sublinear-communication protocols, i.e., protocols in which the honest (and semi-honest) parties send at most $o(n)|C_f|$ number of messages, were the message size is independent of n. Furthermore, we will only consider information-theoretic security (see below).

Simulation-Based Security. We will use the standard simulation-based definition of security from [9]. At a high level, a protocol for a given function is rendered secure against a given class of adversaries if for any adversary in this class, there exists a simulator that can emulate, in an ideal evaluation experiment, the adversary's attack to the protocol. In more detail, the simulator participates in an ideal evaluation experiment of the given function, where the parties have access to a trusted third party—often referred to as the *ideal functionality*—that receives their inputs, performs the computation and returns their outputs. The simulator takes over ("corrupts") the same set of parties as the adversary does (statically or adaptively), and has the same control as the (semi-honest or malicious) adversary has on the corrupted parties. His goal is to simulate the view of the adversary and choose inputs for corrupted parties so that for any initial input distribution, the joint distribution of the honest parties' outputs and adversarial view in the protocol execution is indistinguishable from the joint distribution of honest outputs and the simulated view in an ideal evaluation of the function. Refer to [9] for a detailed specification of the simulation-based security definition.

In this work we consider information-theoretic security and therefore we will require statistical indistinguishability. Using the standard definitions of *negligible functions* [30], we say that a pair of distribution ensembles $\mathcal{X}$ and $\mathcal{Y}$ indexed by $n \in \mathbb{N}$ are *(statistically) indistinguishable* if for all (not necessarily efficient) distinguishers D the following function with domain S:

[3] Note that in the semi-honest setting this number equals the total number of bits received during the protocol. However, in the malicious setting, corrupted parties might attempt to send more bits to honest parties than what the protocol specifies, thereby flooding the network and increasing the total number of bits received. As we shall see, our malicious protocol defends even against such an attack by having the parties abort if they receive too many bits/messages.

$$\Delta_{\mathcal{X},\mathcal{Y}}(n) := |\Pr[D(\mathcal{X}_n) = 1] - \Pr[D(\mathcal{Y}_n) = 1]|$$

is negligible in s. In this case we write $\mathcal{X} \approx \mathcal{Y}$ to denote this relation. We will further use $\mathcal{X} \equiv \mathcal{Y}$ to denote the fact that $\mathcal{X}$ and $\mathcal{Y}$ are identically distributed.

The view of the adversary in an execution of a protocol consists of the inputs and randomness of all corrupted parties and all the messages sent and received during the protocol execution. We will use $\text{VIEW}_{\mathcal{A},\Pi}$ to denote the random variable (ensemble) corresponding to the view of the adversary when the parties run protocol Π. The view $\text{VIEW}_{\sigma,f}$ of the simulator σ in an ideal evaluation of f is defined analogously.

For a probability distribution Pr over a sample space $\mathcal{T}$ and for any $T \in \mathcal{T}$ we will denote by $\Pr(T)$ the probability of T. We will further denote by $T \leftarrow \Pr$ the action of sampling the set T from the distribution Pr. In slight abuse of notation, for an event E we will denote by $\Pr(E)$ the probability that E occurs. Finally, for random variables $\mathcal{X}$ and $\mathcal{Y}$ we will denote by $\Pr_{\mathcal{X}}(x)$ the probability that $\mathcal{X} = x$ and by $\Pr_{\mathcal{X}|\mathcal{Y}}(x|y)$ the probability that $\mathcal{X} = x$ conditioned on $\mathcal{Y} = y$.

Oblivious Transfer and OT Combiners. Oblivious Transfer (OT) [49] is a two-party functionality between a *sender* and a *receiver*. In its most common variant called 1-out-of-2-OT,[4] the sender has two inputs $x_0, x_1 \in \{0,1\}$ and the receiver has one bit input $b \in \{0,1\}$, called the *selection* bit. The functionality allows the sender to transmit the input x_b to the receiver so that (1) the sender does not learn which bit was transmitted (i.e., learns nothing), and (2) the receiver does not learn anything about the input $x_{\bar{b}}$.

As proved by Kilian and Goldreich et al. [32,45], the OT primitive is *complete* for secure xtwo-party computation (2PC), even against malicious adversaries. Specifically, Kilian's result shows that given the ability to call an ideal oracle/functionality f_{OT} that computes OT, two parties can securely compute an arbitrary function of their inputs with unconditional security. The efficiency of these protocols was later improved by Ishai *et al.* [43].

Beaver [1] showed how OT can be pre-computed, i.e., how parties can, in an offline phase, compute correlated randomness that allows, during the online phase, to implement OT by simply the sender sending to the receiver two messages of the same length as the messages he wishes to input to the OT hybrid (and the receiver sending no message). Thus, a trusted party which is equivalent (in terms of functionality) to OT, is one that internally pre-computes the above correlated randomness and hands to the sender and the receiver their "parts" of it. We will refer to such a correlated randomness setup where the sender receives R_s and the receiver R_r as an (R_s, R_r) *OT pair*. The size of each component in such an OT pair is the same as (or linear in) the size of the messages (inputs) that the parties would hand to the OT functionality.

A fair amount of work has been devoted to so-called *OT combiners*, namely, protocols that can access several, say, m OT protocols, out of which ℓ might be insecure, and combine them into a secure OT protocol (e.g., [33,34,47]). OT

[4] In this work we will use OT to refer to 1-out-of-2 OT.

combiners with linear rate (i.e., where the total communication of the combiner is linear in the total communication of the OT protocol) exist both for semi-honest and for malicious security as long as $\ell < m/2$. Such an OT combiner can be applied to the pre-computed OT protocol to transform m precomputed OT strings out of which ℓ are sampled from the appropriate distribution by a trusted party, into one securely pre-computed OT string, which can then be used to implement a secure instance of OT.

3 Sublinear Communication with Static Corruptions

As a warm up, we start our treatment of secure computation in the $(2, n)$-client/server model with the case of a static adversary, where, as we show, requiring sublinear communication complexity comes almost at no cost in terms of how many corrupted parties can be tolerated. We consider the case of a semi-honest adversary and confirm that using a "folklore" protocol any $(1, t)$-adversary with $t < (\frac{1}{2} - \epsilon)n$ corruptions can be tolerated, for an arbitrary constant $0 < \epsilon < \frac{1}{2}$. We further prove that this bound is tight (up to an arbitrary small constant fraction of corruptions); i.e., if for some $\epsilon > 0, t = (\frac{1}{2} + \epsilon)n$, then a semi-honest $(1, t)$-adversary cannot be tolerated.[5]

Specifically, in the static semi-honest case the following folklore protocol based on the approach of selecting a random committee [8] is secure and has sublinear message complexity. This protocol has any of the two clients, say, c_1, choose (with high probability) a random committee/subset of the servers of at most polylogarithmic size and inform the other client about his choice. These servers are given as input secret sharings of the clients' inputs, and are requested to run a standard MPC protocol that is secure in the presence of an honest majority, for example, the semi-honest MPC protocol by Ben-Or et al. [4], hereafter referred to as the "BGW" protocol. The random choice of the servers that execute the BGW protocol will ensure that, except with negligible (in n) probability, a majority of them will be honest. Furthermore, because the BGW protocol's complexity is polynomial in the party size, which in this case is polylogarithmic, the total communication complexity in this case is polylogarithmic. We denote the above protocol as Π_{stat} and state its security in Theorem 1. The proof is simple and follows the above idea. We refer to the full version [28] for details.

Theorem 1. *Protocol Π_{stat} unconditionally securely computes any given 2-party function f in the $(2, n)$-client/server model in the presence of a passive and static $(1, t)$-adversary with $t < (1/2 - \epsilon)n$, for any given constant $0 < \epsilon < 1/2$. Moreover, Π_{stat} communicates $O(\log^{\delta'}(n)|C_f|)$ messages, for a constant $\delta' > 1$.*

Next, we prove that Theorem 1 is tight. The proof idea is as follows: If the adversary can corrupt a majority of the servers, i.e., $t \geq n/2$, then no matter which subset of the servers is actually activated (i.e., sends or receives a

[5] Wlog we can assume that the semi-honest adversary just outputs his entire view [9]; hence semi-honest adversaries only differ in the set of parties they corrupt.

message) in the protocol[6], an adversary that randomly chooses the parties to corrupt has a good chance of corrupting any half of the active server set. Thus, existence of a protocol for computing, e.g., the OR function while tolerating such an adversary would contradict the impossibility result by Hirt and Maurer [35] which implies that an adversary who can corrupt a set and its complement—or supersets thereof—is intolerable for the OR function. The actual theorem statement is tighter, and excludes even adversaries that corrupt $t \geq n/2 - \delta$, for some constant $\delta \geq 0$. The proof uses the above idea with the additional observation that due to the small (sublinear) size of the set $\bar{\mathcal{S}}$ of *active* servers, i.e., servers that send or receive a message in the protocol, a random set of $\delta = O(1)$ servers has noticeable chance to include no such active server. We refer to the full version of this work [28] for a formal proof.

Theorem 2. *Assuming a static adversary, there exists no information theoretically secure protocol for computing the boolean OR of the (two) clients' inputs with message complexity $m = o(n)$ tolerating a $(1, t)$-adversary with $t \geq n/2 - \delta$, for some $\delta = O(1)$.*

4 Sublinear Communication with Adaptive Corruptions

In this section we consider an adaptive semi-honest adversary and prove corresponding tight bounds for security with erasures—the protocol can instruct parties to erase their state so as to protect information from an adaptive adversary who has not yet corrupted the party—and without erasures—everything that the parties see stays in their state.

4.1 Security with Erasures

We start with the setting where erasures of the parties' states are allowed, which prominently demonstrates that sublinear communication comes at an unexpected cost in the number of tolerable corruptions. Specifically, in this section we show that for any constant $0 < \epsilon < 1 - \sqrt{0.5}$, there exists a protocol that computes any given two-party function f in the presence of a $(1, t)$-adversary if $t < (1 - \sqrt{0.5} - \epsilon)n$ (Theorem 3). Most surprisingly, we prove that this bound is tight up to any arbitrary small constant fraction of corruptions (Theorem 4). The technique used in proving the lower bound introduces a novel treatment of (and a toolboox for) probabilistic adversary structures that we believe can be of independent interest.

We start with the protocol construction. First, observe that the idea behind protocol Π_{stat} cannot work here as an adaptive adversary can corrupt client c_1, wait for him to choose the servers in $\bar{\mathcal{S}}$, and then corrupt all of them adaptively since he has a linear corruption budget. (Note that erasures cannot help here as the adversary sees the list of all receivers by observing the corrupted

[6] Note that not all servers can be activated as the number of active servers is naturally bounded by the (sublinear) communication complexity.

sender's state.) This attack would render any protocol non-private. Instead, we will present a protocol which allows clients c_1 and c_2 to pre-compute sufficiently many 1-out-of-2 OT functionalities $f_{\mathrm{OT}}((m_0, m_1), b) = (\perp, m_b)$ in the $(2, n)$-client/server model with sublinear communication complexity. The completeness of OT ensures that this allows c_1 and c_2 to compute any given function.

A first attempt towards the above goal is as follows. Every server independently decides with probability $p = \frac{\log^\delta n}{n}$ (based on his own local randomness) to "volunteer" in helping the clients by acting as an OT dealer (i.e., acting as a trusted party that prepares and sends to the clients an OT pair). The choice of p can be such that with overwhelming probability not too many honest servers volunteer (at most sublinear in n) and the majority of the volunteers are honest. Thus, the majority of the distributed OT pairs will be honest, which implies that the parties can use an OT-combiner that is secure for a majority of good OTs (e.g., [34]) on the received OT pairs to derive a secure implementation of OT.

Unfortunately, the above idea does not quite work. To see why, consider an adversary who randomly corrupts one of the clients and as soon as any honest volunteer sends a messages to the corrupted client, the adversary corrupts him as well and reads his state. (Recall that send and erase are atomic operations.) It is not hard then to verify that even if the volunteer erases part of its state between contacting each of the two clients, with probability (at least) 1/2 such an adversary learns the entire internal state of the volunteer before he gets a chance to erase it.

So instead of the above idea, our approach is as follows. Every server, as above, decides with probability $p = \frac{\log^\delta n}{n}$ to volunteer in helping the clients by acting as an OT dealer and computes the OT pair, *but does not send it.* Instead, it first chooses another server, which we refer to as his *intermediary*, uniformly at random, and forwards him one of the components in the OT pairs (say, the one intended for the receiver); then, it erases the sent component and the identity of the intermediary along with the coins used to sample it (so that now his state only includes the sender's component of the OT pair); finally, both the volunteer and his intermediary forward their values to their intended recipient.

It is straightforward to verify that with the above strategy the adversary does not gain anything by corrupting a helping server—whether a volunteer or his associated intermediary—when he talks to the corrupted client. Indeed, at the point when such a helper contacts the client, the part of the OT pair that is not intended for that client and the identity of the other associated helper have both been erased. But now we have introduced an extra point of possible corruption: The adversary can learn any given OT pair by corrupting either the corresponding volunteer or his intermediary before the round where the clients are contacted. However, as we will show, when $t < (1-\sqrt{0.5}-\epsilon)n$, the probability that the adversary corrupts more than half of such pairs is negligible.

The complete specification of the above sketched protocol, denoted $\Pi^{\mathrm{OT}}_{\mathrm{adap}}$, and the corresponding security statement are shown below.

Protocol $\Pi^{\mathrm{OT}}_{\mathrm{adap}}(\mathcal{C} = \{c_1, c_2\}, \mathcal{S} = \{s_1, \ldots, s_n\})$

1. Every server $s_i \in \mathcal{S}$ locally decides to become active with probability $p = \frac{\log^{\delta} n}{n}$ for a publicly known constant $\delta > 1$. Let $\bar{\mathcal{S}}_1$ denote the set of parties that become active in this round. Every $s_i \in \bar{\mathcal{S}}_1$ prepares an OT pair $((m_i, r_i), \mathtt{otid}_i)$, where $\mathtt{otid}_i \in \{0,1\}^{\log^{\delta} n}$ is a uniformly chosen identifier.
2. Every $s_i \in \bar{\mathcal{S}}_1$ choses an intermediary $s_{ij} \in \mathcal{S}$ uniformly at random and sends $(r_i, \mathtt{otid}_i)$ to s_{ij}. Denote by $\bar{\mathcal{S}}_2 = \{s_{ij} | s_i \in \bar{\mathcal{S}}\}$ the set of all relayers.
3. Every $s_i \in \bar{\mathcal{S}}_1$ erases r_i, the identity of s_{ij}, and the randomness used to select s_{ij}; and every $s_{ij} \in \bar{\mathcal{S}}_2$ erases the identity of s_i.
4. Every $s_i \in \bar{\mathcal{S}}_1$ sends $(m_i, \mathtt{otid}_i)$ to c_1 and every $s_{ij} \in \bar{\mathcal{S}}_2$ sends $(r_i, \mathtt{otid}_i)$ to c_2.
5. Every $s_i \in \bar{\mathcal{S}}_1$ and every $s_{ij} \in \bar{\mathcal{S}}_2$ erase their entire internal state.
6. The clients c_1 and c_2 use the OT pairs with matching $\mathtt{otid}$'s within a (semi-honest) $(n/2, n)$ OT-combiner [34] to obtain a secure OT protocol.

Theorem 3. *Protocol* Π^{OT}_{adap} *unconditionally securely computes the function* $f_{OT}((m_0, m_1), b) = (\perp, m_b)$ *in the* $(2,n)$*-client/server model in the presence of a passive and adaptive* $(1,t)$*-adversary with* $t < (1 - \sqrt{0.5} - \epsilon)n$*, for any given constant* $0 < \epsilon < 1 - \sqrt{0.5}$ *and assuming erasures. Moreover,* Π^{OT}_{adap} *communicates* $O(\log^{\delta}(n))$ *messages, with* $\delta > 1$*, except with negligible probability.*

Proof. Every server $s \in \mathcal{S}$ is included in the set of servers that become active in the first round, i.e., $\bar{\mathcal{S}}_1$, with probability $p = \frac{\log^{\delta} n}{n}$ independent of the other servers. Thus by application of the Chernoff bound we get that for every $0 < \gamma < 1/2$:

$$\Pr[|\bar{\mathcal{S}}_1| > (1+\gamma)\log^{\delta} n] < e^{-\frac{\gamma \log^{\delta} n}{3}} \tag{1}$$

which is negligible. Moreover, each $s_i \in \bar{\mathcal{S}}_1$ chooses one additional relay-party s_{ij} which means that for any constant $1/2 < \gamma' < 1$:

$$|\bar{\mathcal{S}}| = |\bar{\mathcal{S}}_1 \cup \bar{\mathcal{S}}_2| \leq (2+\gamma')\log^{\delta} n$$

with overwhelming probability. (As in the proof of Theorem 2, $\bar{\mathcal{S}}$ denotes the set of active servers at the end of the protocol.) Since each such party communicates at most two messages, the total message complexity is $O(\log^{\delta} n)$ plus the messages exchanged in the OT combiner which are polynomial in the number of OT pairs. Thus, with overwhelming probability, the total number of messages is $O(\log^{\delta'}(n))$ for some constant $\delta' > \delta$.

To prove security, it suffices to ensure that for the uncorrupted client, the adversary does not learn at least half of the received OT setups. Assume wlog that c_2 is corrupted. (The case of a corrupted c_1 is handled symmetrically, because, wlog, we can assume that an adversary corrupting some party in $\bar{\mathcal{S}}_1$ also corrupts all parties in $\bar{\mathcal{S}}_2$ which this party sends messages to after its corruption.) We show that the probability that the adversary learns more than half of the m_i's is negligible.

First, we can assume, wlog, that the adversary does not corrupt any servers after Step 5, i.e., after the states of the servers have been erased. Indeed, for any such adversary $\mathcal{A}$ there exists an adversary $\mathcal{A}'$ who outputs a view with the same distribution as $\mathcal{A}$ but does not corrupt any of the parties that $\mathcal{A}$ corrupts after Step 5; in particular $\mathcal{A}'$ uses $\mathcal{A}$ as a blackbox and follows $\mathcal{A}$'s instructions, and until Step 5 corrupts every server that $\mathcal{A}$ requests to corrupt, but after that step, any request from $\mathcal{A}$ to corrupt a new server s is replied by $\mathcal{A}'$ simulating s without corrupting him. (This simulation is trivially perfect since at Step 5, s will have erased its local state so $\mathcal{A}'$ needs just to simulate the unused randomness.)

Second, we observe that, since the adversary does not corrupt c_1, the only way to learn some m_i is by corrupting the party in $\bar{\mathcal{S}}_1$ that sent it to c_1. Hence to prove that the adversary learns less than 1/2 of the m_i's it suffices to prove that the adversary corrupts less than 1/2 of $\bar{\mathcal{S}}_1$.

Next, we observe that the adversary does not gain any advantage in corrupting parties in $\bar{\mathcal{S}}_1$ by corrupting client c_2, since (1) parties in $\bar{\mathcal{S}}_1$ do not communicate with c_2, and (2) by the time an honest party $s_{ij} \in \bar{\mathcal{S}}_2$ communicates with c_2 he has already erased the identity of s_i. (Thus, corrupting s_{ij} after he communicates with c_2 yields no advantage in finding s_i.) Stated differently, if there is an adversary who corrupts more than 1/2 servers in $\bar{\mathcal{S}}_1$, then there exists an adversary that does the same without even corrupting c_2. Thus, to complete the proof it suffices to show that any adversary who does not corrupt c_2, corrupts less than 1/2 of the servers in $|\bar{\mathcal{S}}_1|$. This is stated in Lemma 2, which is proved using the following strategy: First, we isolate a "bad" subset $\bar{\mathcal{S}}_1'$ of $\bar{\mathcal{S}}_1$ which we call *over-connected parties,* for which we cannot give helpful guarantees on the number of corruptions. Nonetheless, we prove in Lemma 1 that this "bad" set is "sufficiently small" compared to $\bar{\mathcal{S}}_1$. By this we mean that we can bound the fraction of corrupted parties in $\bar{\mathcal{S}}_1$ sufficiently far from 1/2 so that even if give this bad set $\bar{\mathcal{S}}_1'$ to the adversary to corrupt for free, his chances of corrupting a majority in $\bar{\mathcal{S}}_1$ are still negligible. The formal arguments follow.

Let $E = \{(s, s') \mid s \in \bar{\mathcal{S}}_1 \vee s' \in \bar{\mathcal{S}}_2\}$ and let G denote the graph with vertex-set $\mathcal{S}$ and edge-set E. We say that server $s_i \in \bar{\mathcal{S}}_1$ is an *over-connected* server if the set $\{s_i, s_{ij}\}$ has neighbors in G. Intuitively, the set of over-connected servers is chosen so that if we remove these servers from G we get a perfect matching between $\bar{\mathcal{S}}_1$ and $\bar{\mathcal{S}}_2$.

Next, we show that even if we give up all over-connected servers in $\bar{\mathcal{S}}_1$ (i.e., allow the adversary to corrupt all of them for free) we still have a majority of uncorrupted servers in $\bar{\mathcal{S}}_1$. For this purpose, we first prove in Lemma 1 that the fraction of $\bar{\mathcal{S}}_1$ servers that are over-connected is an arbitrary small constant.

Lemma 1. *Let $\bar{\mathcal{S}}_1' \subseteq \bar{\mathcal{S}}_1$ denote the set of over-connected servers as defined above. For any constant $1 > \epsilon' > 0$ and for large enough n, $|\bar{\mathcal{S}}_1'| < \epsilon'|\bar{\mathcal{S}}_1|$ except with negligible probability.*

Proof. To prove the claim we make use of the generalized Chernoff bound [48]. For each $s_i \in \bar{\mathcal{S}}_1$ let $X_i \in \{0, 1\}$ denote the indicator random variable that is 1 if $s_i \in \bar{\mathcal{S}}_1'$ and 0 otherwise. As above for each $s_i \in \bar{\mathcal{S}}_1$ we denote by s_{ij} the party that s_i chooses as its intermediary in the protocol.

$$\begin{aligned}\Pr[X_i = 1] &= \Pr[(s_{ij} \in \bar{\mathcal{S}}_1) \cup (\exists s_k \in \bar{\mathcal{S}}_1 : s_{kj} \in \{s_i, s_{ij}\})] \\ &\leq \Pr[s_{ij} \in \bar{\mathcal{S}}_1] + \Pr[\exists s_k \in \bar{\mathcal{S}}_1 : s_{kj} = s_i] \\ &\qquad + \Pr[\exists s_k \in \bar{\mathcal{S}}_1 : s_{kj} = s_{ij}] \\ &\leq 3\frac{|\bar{\mathcal{S}}_1|}{n},\end{aligned}$$

where both inequalities follow by a direct union bound since s_{ij} is chosen uniformly at random, and for each of the servers s_i and s_{ij} there are at most $|\bar{\mathcal{S}}_1|$ servers that might choose them as an intermediary. But from Eq. 1, $|\bar{\mathcal{S}}_1| < (1+\gamma)\log^\delta n$ except with negligible probability. Thus, for large enough n, $\Pr[X_i = 1] < \epsilon'$.

Next, we observe that for any subset Q of indices of parties in $\bar{\mathcal{S}}_1$ and for any $i \in Q$ it holds that $\Pr[X_i = 1 \mid \bigwedge_{j \in Q \setminus \{i\}} X_j = 1] \leq \Pr[X_i = 1]$. This is the case because the number of edges (s_k, s_{kj}) is equal to the size of $\bar{\mathcal{S}}_1$ and any connected component in G with ℓ nodes must include at least ℓ such edges. Hence, for any such Q, $\Pr[\wedge_{i \in Q} X_i = 1] \leq \prod_{i \in Q} \Pr[X_i = 1] \leq \epsilon_1{}^{|Q|}$. Therefore, by an application of the generalized Chernoff bound [48], for $\delta = \epsilon_1 < \epsilon'$ and $\gamma = \epsilon'$, we obtain

$$\Pr[\sum_{i=1}^{n} X_i \geq \epsilon' n] \leq e^{-n2(\epsilon' - \epsilon_1)^2},$$

which is negligible. □

Now, let $\mathcal{A}$ be an adaptive $(1,t)$-adversary and let C be the total set of servers corrupted by $\mathcal{A}$ (at the end of Step 5). We want to prove that $|C \cap \bar{\mathcal{S}}_1| < \frac{1}{2}|\bar{\mathcal{S}}_1|$ except with negligible probability. Towards this objective, we consider the adversary $\mathcal{A}'$ who is given access to the identities of all servers in $\bar{\mathcal{S}}_1'$, corrupts all these parties and, additionally, corrupts the first $t - |\bar{\mathcal{S}}_1'|$ parties that adversary $\mathcal{A}$ corrupts. Let C' denote the set of parties that $\mathcal{A}'$ corrupts. It is easy to verify that if $|C \cap \bar{\mathcal{S}}_1| \geq \frac{1}{2}|\bar{\mathcal{S}}_1|$ then $|C' \cap \bar{\mathcal{S}}_1| \geq \frac{1}{2}|\bar{\mathcal{S}}_1|$. Indeed, $\mathcal{A}'$ corrupts all but the last $|\bar{\mathcal{S}}_1'|$ of the parties that $\mathcal{A}$ corrupts; if all these last parties end up in $\bar{\mathcal{S}}_1$ then we will have $|C' \cap \bar{\mathcal{S}}_1| = |C \cap \bar{\mathcal{S}}_1|$, otherwise, at least one of them will not be in $C \cap \bar{\mathcal{S}}_1$ in which case we will have $|C' \cap \bar{\mathcal{S}}_1| > |C \cap \bar{\mathcal{S}}_1|$. Hence, to prove that $|C \cap \bar{\mathcal{S}}_1| < \frac{1}{2}|\bar{\mathcal{S}}_1|$ it suffices to prove that $|C' \cap \bar{\mathcal{S}}_1| < \frac{1}{2}|\bar{\mathcal{S}}_1|$.

Lemma 2. *The set C' of servers corrupted by $\mathcal{A}'$ as above has size $|C' \cap \bar{\mathcal{S}}_1| < \frac{1}{2}|\bar{\mathcal{S}}_1|$, except with negligible probability.*

Proof. Consider the gaph G' which results by deleting from G the vertices/servers in $\bar{\mathcal{S}}_1'$. By construction, G' is a perfect pairing between parties in $\bar{\mathcal{S}}_1 \setminus \bar{\mathcal{S}}_1'$ and parties in $\bar{\mathcal{S}}_2 \setminus \bar{\mathcal{S}}_1'$. For each $s_i \in \bar{\mathcal{S}}_1 \setminus \bar{\mathcal{S}}_1'$, let X_i denote the Boolean random variable with $X_i = 1$ if $\{s_i, s_{ij}\} \cap (C' \setminus \bar{\mathcal{S}}_1') \neq \emptyset$ and $X_i = 0$ otherwise. When $X_i = 1$, we say that the adversary has corrupted the edge $e_i = (s_i, s_{ij})$. Clearly, the number of corrupted edges is an upper bound on the corresponding number of corrupted servers in $\bar{\mathcal{S}}_1 \setminus \bar{\mathcal{S}}_1'$. Thus, we will show that the number of corrupted edges is bounded away from 1/2.

By construction of G' the X_i's are independent, identically distributed random variables. Every edge in G' is equally likely, thus the adversary gets no information on the rest of the graph by corrupting some edge. Therefore we can assume wlog that $\mathcal{A}'$ chooses the servers in $C' \setminus \bar{S}_1'$ at the beginning of the protocol execution. In this case we get the following for $C_1' = C' \setminus \bar{S}_1'$:

$$\begin{aligned}\Pr[X_i = 1] &= \Pr[s_i \in C_1'] + \Pr[s_{ij} \in C_1'] - \Pr[\{s_i, s_{ij}\} \subseteq C_1'] \\ &= 2\frac{|C| - |\bar{S}_1'|}{n - |\bar{S}_1'|} - \left(\frac{|C| - |\bar{S}_1'|}{n - |\bar{S}_1'|}\right)^2 \\ &\leq \frac{2(1 - \sqrt{0.5} - \epsilon)n}{n - |\bar{S}_1'|} - \left(\frac{(1 - \sqrt{0.5} - \epsilon)n - |\bar{S}_1'|}{n - |\bar{S}_1'|}\right)^2.\end{aligned}$$

To make the notation more compact, let $\lambda = 1 - \sqrt{0.5} - \epsilon$. Because, from Lemma 1, $|\bar{S}_1'| \leq \epsilon' n$ (and thus $n - |\bar{S}_1'| > (1 - \epsilon')n$) except with negligible probability, we have that for large enough n and some negligible function μ:

$$\Pr[X_i = 1] \leq \frac{2\lambda n}{(1 - \epsilon')n} - \left(\frac{\lambda n - |\bar{S}_1'|}{n - |\bar{S}_1'|}\right)^2 + \mu. \tag{2}$$

Moreover,

$$\begin{aligned}\left(\frac{\lambda n - |\bar{S}_1'|}{n - |\bar{S}_1'|}\right)^2 &\geq \left(\frac{\lambda n - |\bar{S}_1'|}{n}\right)^2 = \left(\lambda - \frac{|\bar{S}_1'|}{n}\right)^2 \\ &\geq \lambda^2 - \frac{2\lambda|\bar{S}_1'|}{n}.\end{aligned} \tag{3}$$

But because, from Eq. 1, $|\bar{S}_1| = O(\log^\delta n)$ with overwhelming probability, we have that for every constant $0 < \epsilon_1 < 1$ and every negligible function μ', and for all sufficiently large n, $\frac{2\lambda|\bar{S}_1'|}{n} + \mu' < \epsilon_1$ holds. Thus, combining Eqs. 2 and 3 we get that for all such ϵ_1 and for sufficiently large n:

$$\begin{aligned}\Pr[X_i = 1] &\leq \frac{2}{(1 - \epsilon')}\lambda - \lambda^2 + \epsilon_1 \\ &= \frac{2}{(1 - \epsilon')}(1 - \sqrt{0.5} - \epsilon) - 1.5 - \epsilon^2 + 2\epsilon + 2(1 - \epsilon)\sqrt{0.5} + \epsilon_1 \\ &\leq \frac{2}{(1 - \epsilon')} - \frac{2\epsilon}{(1 - \epsilon')} - 1.5 - \epsilon^2 + 2\epsilon + \epsilon_1 \\ &\leq \frac{2}{(1 - \epsilon')} - 1.5 - \epsilon^2 + \epsilon_1.\end{aligned}$$

For $\epsilon' \leq 1 - \frac{2}{2 + \epsilon^2/4}$ and $\epsilon_1 = \epsilon^2/4$, the last equation gives

$$\Pr[X_i = 1] \leq \frac{1}{2} - \frac{\epsilon^2}{2}.$$

Furthermore, because the X_i's are independent, the assumptions in [48] are satisfied for $\delta = \frac{1}{2} - \frac{\epsilon^2}{2}$, hence,

$$\Pr[\sum_{s_i \in \bar{\mathcal{S}}_1 \setminus \bar{\mathcal{S}}_1'} X_i \geq (1/2 - \epsilon^2/3)|\bar{\mathcal{S}}_1 \setminus \bar{\mathcal{S}}_1'|] \leq e^{-n(\epsilon^2/6)},$$

which is negligible. Note that, by Lemma 1, for large enough n, with overwhelming probability $|\bar{\mathcal{S}}_1'| < \frac{2\epsilon^2}{3+2\epsilon^2}|\bar{\mathcal{S}}_1|$. Thus, with overwhelming probability the total number of corrupted servers in $\bar{\mathcal{S}}_1$ is less than $\frac{1}{2}|\bar{\mathcal{S}}_1|$. □

The above lemma ensures that the adversary cannot corrupt a majority of the OT pairs. Furthermore, with overwhelming probability, all the `otid`'s chosen by the parties in $\bar{\mathcal{S}}$ are distinct. Thus, the security of the protocol follows from the security of the OT combiner. This concludes the proof of Theorem 3. □

Next, we turn to the proof of the lower bound. We prove that there exists an adaptive $(1,t)$-adversary that cannot be tolerated when $t = (1 - \sqrt{0.5} + \epsilon)n$ for any (arbitrarily small) constant $\epsilon > 0$. To this end, we start with the observation that every adaptive adversary attacking a protocol induces a probability distribution on the set of corrupted parties, which might depend on the coins of the adversary and on the inputs and coins of all parties. Such a probability distribution induces a *probabilistic adversary structures* that assigns to each subset of parties the probability that this subset gets corrupted. Hence, it suffices to prove that this probabilistic adversary structure is what we call *intolerable*, which, roughly, means that there are functions that cannot be computed when the corrupted sets are chosen from this structure. Before sketching our proof strategy, it is useful to give some intuition about the main challenge one encounters when attempting to prove such a statement. This is best demonstrated by the following counterexample.

A Counterexample. It is tempting to conjecture that for every probabilistic adversary $\mathcal{A}$ who corrupts each party i with probability $p_i > 1/2$, there is no (general purpose) information-theoretic MPC protocol which achieves security against $\mathcal{A}$. While this is true if the corruption probabilities are independent, we show that this is far from being true in general.

Let f_k denote the boolean function $f_k : \{0,1\}^{3^k} \to \{0,1\}$ computed by a depth-k complete tree of 3-input majority gates. It follows from [15,36] that there is a perfectly secure information-theoretic MPC protocol that tolerates every set of corrupted parties T whose characteristic vector χ_T satisfies $f(\chi_T) = 0$. We show the following.

Proposition 1. *There exists a sequence of distributions X_k, where X_k is distributed over $\{0,1\}^{3^k}$, such that for every positive integer k we have (1) $f_k(X_k)$ is identically 0, and (2) each entry of X_k takes the value 1 with probability $1 - (2/3)^k$.*

Proof. Define the sequence X_k inductively as follows. X_1 is a uniformly random over $\{100, 010, 001\}$. The bit-string X_k is obtained as follows. Associate the entries of X_k with the leaves of a complete ternary tree of depth k. Randomly pick X_k by assigning 1 to all leaves of one of the three sub-trees of the root (the identity of which is chosen at random), and assigning values to each of the two other sub-trees according to X_{k-1}. Both properties can be easily proved by induction on k. □

Letting $\mathcal{A}_k$ denote the probabilistic adversary corresponding to X_k, we get a strong version of the desired counterexample, thus contradicting the aforementioned conjecture for $k \geq 2$.

The above counterexample demonstrates that even seemingly straightforward arguments when considering probabilistic adversary structures can be false, because of correlation in the corruption events. Next, we present the high-level structure of our lower bound proof.

We consider an adversary $\mathcal{A}$ who works as follows: At the beginning of the protocol, $\mathcal{A}$ corrupts each of the n servers independently with probability $1-\sqrt{0.5}$ and corrupts one of the two clients, say, c_1, at random; denote the set of initially corrupted servers by C_0 and initialize $C := C_0$. Subsequently, in every round, if any server sends or/receives a message to/from one of the servers in C, then the adversary corrupts him as well and adds him to C. Observe that $\mathcal{A}$ does *not* corrupt servers when they send or receive messages to the clients. (Such an adversary would in fact be stronger but we will show that even the above weaker adversary cannot be tolerated.) We also note that the above adversary might exceed his corruption budget $t = (1 - \sqrt{0.5} - \epsilon)n$. However, an application of the Chernoff bound shows that the probability that this happens in negligible in n so we can simply have the adversary abort in the unlikely case of such an overflow.

We next observe that because $\mathcal{A}$ corrupts servers independently at the beginning of the protocol, we can consider an equivalent random experiment where first the communication pattern (i.e., the sequence of edges) is decided and then the adversary $\mathcal{A}$ chooses his initial sets and follows the above corruption paths (where edges are processed in the given order). For each such sequence of edges, $\mathcal{A}$ defines a probability distribution on the (active) edge set that is *fully* corrupted, namely, both its end-points are corrupted at the latest when they send any message in the protocol (and before they get a chance to erase it). Shifting the analysis from probabilistic party-corruption structures to probabilistic *edge*-corruption structures yields a simpler way to analyze the view of the experiment. Moreover, we provide a definition of what it means for an edge-corruption structure to be intolerable, which allows us to move back from edge to party corruptions.

Next, we define a *domination relation* which, intuitively, says that a probabilistic structure $\Pr_{\mathcal{A}_1^E}$ dominates another probabilistic structure $\Pr_{\mathcal{A}_2^E}$ on the same set of edges, if there exist a monotone probabilistic mapping F among sets of edges—i.e., a mapping from sets to their subsets—that transforms $\Pr_{\mathcal{A}_1^E}$ into $\Pr_{\mathcal{A}_2^E}$. Conceptually, for an adversary that corrupts according to $\Pr_{\mathcal{A}_1^E}$ (hereafter referred to as a $\Pr_{\mathcal{A}_1^E}$*-adversary*), the use of F can be thought as "forgetting" some of the corrupted edges.[7] Hence, intuitively, an adversary who corrupts edge sets according to $\Pr_{\mathcal{A}_2^E}$ (or, equivalently, according to "$\Pr_{\mathcal{A}_1^E}$ with forget") is easier to simulate than a $\Pr_{\mathcal{A}_1^E}$-adversary, as if there is a simulator for the latter, we can apply the forget predicate F on the (simulated) set of corrupted edges to get a simulator for $\Pr_{\mathcal{A}_2^E}$. Thus, if $\Pr_{\mathcal{A}_2^E}$ is intolerable, then so is $\Pr_{\mathcal{A}_1^E}$.

Having such a domination relation in place, we next look for a simple probabilistic structure that is intolerable and can be dominated by the structure induced by our adversary $\mathcal{A}$. To this end, we prove intolerability of a special structure, where each edge set is sampled according to the following experiment: Let $\boldsymbol{E}$ be a collection of edge sets such that no $E \in \boldsymbol{E}$ can be derived as a union of the remaining sets; we choose to add each set from $\boldsymbol{E}$ to the corrupted-edge set independently with probability 1/2. The key feature of the resulting probabilistic corruption structure that enables us to prove intolerability and avoid missteps as in the above counterexample, is the independence of the above sampling strategy.

The final step, i.e., proving that the probabilistic edge-corruption structure induced by our adversary $\mathcal{A}$ dominates the above special structure, goes through a delicate combinatorial argument. We define a special graph traversing algorithm for the given edge sequence that yields a collection of potentially fully corruptible subsets of edges in this sequence, and prove that the maximal elements in this collection can be used to derive such a dominating probabilistic corruption structure.

The complete proof of our impossibility (stated in Theorem 4 below) can be found in [28].

Theorem 4. *Assume an adaptive passive adversary and that erasures are allowed. There exists no information theoretically secure protocol for computing the boolean OR function in the* $(2, n)$*-client/server model with message complexity* $m = o(n)$ *tolerating a* $(1, t)-$*adversary, where* $t = (1 - \sqrt{0.5} + \epsilon)n$ *for any constant* $\epsilon > 0$.

4.2 Security Without Erasures

We next turn to the case of adaptive corruptions (still for semi-honest adversaries) in a setting where parties do not erase any part of their state (and thus an adaptive adversary who corrupts any party gets to see the party's entire protocol view from the beginning of the protocol execution). This is another instance which demonstrates that requiring sublinear communication induces unexpected costs on the adversarial tolerance of MPC protocols.

In particular, when we do not restrict the communication complexity, then any $(1, t)$-adversary can be tolerated for information-theoretic MPC in the $(2, n)$-client/server model, as long as $t < n/2$ [4]. Instead, as we now show,

[7] Here, "forgetting" means removing the view of their end-points from the adversary's view.

when restricting to sublinear communication, there are functions that cannot be securely computed when any (arbitrary small) linear number of servers is corrupted (Theorem 5). If, on the other hand, we restrict the number of corruptions to be sublinear, a straightforward protocol computes any given function (Theorem 6).

The intuition behind the impossibility can be demonstrated by looking at protocol Π_{stat} from Sect. 3: An adaptive adversary can corrupt client c_1, wait for him to choose the servers in $\bar{\mathcal{S}}$, and then corrupt all of them rendering any protocol among them non-private. In fact, as we show below, this is not a problem of the protocol but an inherent limitation in the setting of adaptive security without erasures.

Specifically, the following theorem shows that if the adversary is adaptive and has the ability to corrupt as many servers as the protocols' message complexity, along with any one of the clients, then there are functions that cannot be privately computed. The basic idea is that such an adversary can wait until the end of the protocol, corrupt any of the two clients, say, c_i, and, by following the messages' paths, also corrupt all servers whose view is correlated to that of c_i. As we show, existence of a protocol tolerating such an adversary contradicts classical impossibility results in the MPC literature [4,35].

Theorem 5. *In the non-erasure model, there exists no information-theoretically secure protocol for computing the boolean OR function in the* $(2, n)$*-client/server model with message complexity* $m = o(n)$ *tolerating an adaptive* $(1, m + 1)$*-adversary.*

Proof. Assume towards contradiction that such a protocol Π exists. First we make the following observation: Let G denote the effective communication graph of the protocol defined as follows: $G = (V, E)$ is an undirected graph where the set V of nodes is the set of all parties, i.e., $V = \mathcal{S} \cup \{c_1, c_2\}$, and the set E of edge includes of pairs of parties that exchanged a message in the protocol execution; i.e., $E := \{(p_i, p_j) \in V^2$ s.t. p_i exchanged a message with p_j in the execution of $\Pi\}$.[8] By definition, the set $\bar{\mathcal{S}}$ of *active* parties is the set of nodes in G with degree $d > 0$. Let $\bar{\mathcal{S}}'$ denote the set of active parties that do not have a path to any of the two clients. (In other words, nodes in $\bar{\mathcal{S}}'$ do not belong in a connected component including c_1 or c_2.)

We observe that if a protocol is private against an adversary $\mathcal{A}$, then it remains private even if $\mathcal{A}$ gets access to the entire view of parties in $\bar{\mathcal{S}}'$ and of the inactive servers $\mathcal{S} \setminus \bar{\mathcal{S}}$. Indeed, the states of these parties are independent of the states of active parties and depend only on their internal randomness, hence they are perfectly simulatable.

Let $\mathcal{A}_1$ denote the adversary that attacks at the end of the protocol and chooses the parties A_1 to corrupt by the following greedy strategy: Initially $A_1 := \{c_1\}$, i.e., $\mathcal{A}_1$ always corrupts the first client. For $j = 1 \ldots, m$, $\mathcal{A}_1$ adds to A_1 all *servers* that are not already in A_1 and exchanged a message with

[8] Note that G is fully defined at the end of the protocol execution.

some party in A_1 during the protocol execution. (Observe that $\mathcal{A}_1$ does not corrupt the second client c_2.) Note that the corruption budget of the adversary is at least as big as the total message complexity, hence he is able to corrupt every active server (if they all happen to be in the same connected component as c_1). Symmetrically, we define the adversary $\mathcal{A}_2$ that starts with $A_2 = \{c_2\}$ and corrupts servers using the same greedy strategy. Clearly, $A_1 \cup A_2 = \bar{\mathcal{S}} \setminus \bar{\mathcal{S}}'$. Furthermore, as argued above, if Π can tolerate $\mathcal{A}_i$, then it can also tolerate $\mathcal{A}'_i$ which in addition to A_i learns the state of all servers in $\bar{\mathcal{S}}' \cup (\mathcal{S} \setminus \bar{\mathcal{S}})$; denote by A'_i the set of parties whose view $\mathcal{A}'_i$ learns. Clearly, $A'_1 \cup A'_2 = \mathcal{S}$, and thus, existence of such a Π contradicts the impossibility of computing the OR against non-Q^2 adversary structures [35]. □

Corollary 1. *In the non-erasure model, there exists no information theoretically secure protocol for computing the boolean OR function of the (two) clients' inputs with message complexity $m = o(n)$ tolerating an adaptive $(1, t)$-adversary, where $t = \epsilon n$ for some constant $\epsilon > 0$.*

For completeness, we show that if the adversary is restricted to a sublinear number t of corruptions, then there is a straightforward secure protocol with sublinear communication. Indeed, in this case we simply need to use Π_{stat}, with the modification that c_1 chooses $n' = 2t + 1$ servers to form a committee. Because $t = o(n)$, this committee is trivially of sublinear size, and because $n' > 2t$ a majority of the servers in the committee will be honest. Hence, the same argument as in Theorem 1 applies also here. This proves the following theorem; the proof uses the same structure as the proof of Theorem 1 and is therefore omitted.

Theorem 6. *Assuming $t = o(n)$, there exists an unconditionally secure (privately) protocol that computes any given 2-party function f in the $(2, n)$-client/server model in the presence of a passive adaptive $(1, t)$-adversary and communicates $o(n)|C_f|$ messages. The statement holds even when no erasures are allowed.*[9]

5 Sublinear Communication with Active (Static) Corruptions

Finally, we initiate the study of malicious adversaries in MPC with sublinear communication, restricting our attention to static security. Since the bound from Sect. 3 is necessary for semi-honest security, it is also necessary for malicious security (since a possible strategy of a malicious adversary is to play semi-honestly).

[9] A protocol that is secure when no erasures are allowed is also secure when erasures are allowed.

In this section we show that if $t < (1/2 - \epsilon)n$, then there exists a maliciously secure protocol for computing every two-party function *with abort*. To this end, we present a protocol which allows clients c_1 and c_2 to compute the 1-out-of-2 OT functionality $f_{\text{OT}}((m_0, m_1), b) = (\perp, m_b)$ in the $(2, n)$-client/server model with sublinear communication complexity. As before, the completeness of OT ensures that this allows c_1 and c_2 to compute any function.

We remark that the impossibility result from Sect. 3 implies that no *fully* secure protocol (i.e., without abort) can tolerate a malicious $(1, t)$-adversary as above. As we argue below, the ability of the adversary to force an abort seems inherent in protocols with sublinear communication tolerating an active adversary with a linear number of corruptions. It is an interesting open question whether the impossibility of full security can be extended to malicious security with abort.

Towards designing a protocol for the malicious setting, one might be tempted to think that the semi-honest approach of one of the clients choosing a committee might work here as well. This is not the case, as this client might be corrupted (and malicious) and only pick servers that are also corrupted. Instead, here we use the following idea, inspired by the adaptive protocol with erasures (but without intermediaries): Every server independently decides with probability $p = \frac{\log^{\delta} n}{n}$ (based on his own local randomness) to volunteer in helping the clients by acting as an OT dealer. The choice of p is such that with overwhelming probability not too many honest servers (at most sublinear in n) volunteer. The clients then use the OT-combiner on the received pre-computed OT pairs to implement a secure OT. Note that this solution does not require any intermediaries as we have static corruptions.

But now we have a new problem to solve: The adversary might pretend to volunteer with more parties than the honest volunteers. (The adversary can do that since he is allowed a linear number of corruptions.) If the clients listen to all of them, then they will end up with precomputed OTs a majority of which is generated by the adversary. This is problematic since no OT combiner exists that will yield a secure OT protocol when the majority of the combined OTs is corrupted (cf. [34,47]).

We solve this problem as follows: We will have each of the clients abort during the OT pre-computation phase if he receives OT pairs from more than a (sublinear) number q of parties. By an appropriate choice of q we can ensure that if the adversary attempts to contact the clients with more corrupted parties than the honest volunteers, then with overwhelming probability he will provoke an abort. As a desirable added feature, this technique also protects against adversaries that try to increase the overall CC by sending more or longer messages. We note in passing that such an abort seems inevitable when trying to block such a message overflow by the adversary as the adversary is rushing and can make sure that his messages are always delivered before the honest parties' messages. The resulting protocol, $\Pi_{\text{act}}^{\text{OT}}$, is given below along with its security statement.

Protocol $\Pi_{\mathrm{act}}^{\mathrm{OT}}(\mathcal{C} = \{c_1, c_2\}, \mathcal{S} = \{s_1, \ldots, s_n\})$

1. Every server $s_i \in \mathcal{S}$ locally decides to become active with probability $p = \frac{\log^\delta n}{n}$ for a given (public) constant $\delta > 1$. Let $\bar{\mathcal{S}}$ denote the set of active servers.
2. Every $s_i \in \bar{\mathcal{S}}$ prepares an OT pair (m_i, r_i) and sends m_i to c_1 and r_i to c_2.
3. Each c_i, $i \in \{1, 2\}$, sends $\perp$ to c_{2-i} and aborts the protocol execution if c_i was contacted by more than $(1 - 16\epsilon^4)\log^\delta n$ parties in the previous step.
4. If c_i, $i \in \{1, 2\}$, received a $\perp$ from c_{2-i} in the previous step then he aborts.
5. The clients use the ℓ received OT pairs in a malicious $(\ell/2, \ell)$ OT-combiner [34] to obtain a secure OT protocol.

Theorem 7. *Protocol Π_{act}^{OT} unconditionally securely computes the function $f_{OT}((m_0, m_1), b) = (\perp, m_b)$ with abort in the $(2, n)$-client/server model in the presence of an active and static $(1, t)$-adversary with $t \le (1/2 - \epsilon)n$, for any given $0 < \epsilon < 1/2$. Moreover, Π_{act}^{OT} communicates $O(\log^\delta(n))$ messages, for a given constant $\delta > 1$, except with negligible probability.*

Proof. Without loss of generality we can assume that adversary $\mathcal{A}$ corrupts $T = \lfloor(\frac{1}{2} - \epsilon)n\rfloor$ parties. Indeed, if the protocol can tolerate such an adversary then it can also tolerate any adversary corrupting $t \le T$ parties.

For a given execution of $\Pi_{\mathrm{act}}^{\mathrm{OT}}$ let $\bar{\mathcal{S}}$ denote the set of servers that would become active if the adversary would behave semi-honestly (i.e., allow all corrupted parties to play according to the protocol). Then, each server $s \in \mathcal{S}$ is included in the set $\bar{\mathcal{S}}$ with probability $p = \frac{\log^\delta n}{n}$ independently of the other servers. Thus, by application of the Chernoff bound we get that for any constant $1 < \gamma < 0$:

$$\Pr[|\bar{\mathcal{S}}| \le (1 - \gamma)\log^\delta n] < e^{-\frac{\gamma^2 \log^\delta n}{3}}.$$

For $\gamma = 4\epsilon^2$ he above equation implies that with overwhelming probability:

$$|\bar{\mathcal{S}}| > (1 - 4\epsilon^2)\log^\delta n. \tag{4}$$

Now let $C \subseteq \mathcal{S}$ denote the set of servers who are corrupted by the (static) adversary $\mathcal{A}$. (Recall that $\mathcal{A}$ corrupts $T = \lfloor(\frac{1}{2} - \epsilon)n\rfloor$ parties.) For each $s_i \in \bar{\mathcal{S}}$, let X_i denote the random variable which is 1 if $s_i \in C$ and 0 otherwise. Because the parties become OT dealers independently of the corruptions and the adversary corrupts T parties, $X_1, \ldots, X_{|\bar{\mathcal{S}}|}$ are i.i.d. random variables with $\Pr[X_i = 1] = T/n$. Thus, $X = \sum_{i=1}^{|\bar{\mathcal{S}}|} X_i = |\bar{\mathcal{S}} \cap C|$ with mean $\mu = \frac{|\bar{\mathcal{S}}|T}{n}$. By another application of the Chernoff bound we get that for any $0 < \epsilon_1 < 1$:

$$\Pr[|\bar{\mathcal{S}} \cap C| \ge (1 + \epsilon_1)\mu] < e^{-\frac{\epsilon_1^2 T}{3}}. \tag{5}$$

Hence, with overwhelming probability for $\epsilon_1 = 2\epsilon$:

$$|\bar{\mathcal{S}} \cap C| < (1 + \epsilon_1)\frac{T}{n}|\bar{\mathcal{S}}| \le (1 + \epsilon_1)(\frac{1}{2} - \epsilon)|\bar{\mathcal{S}}| = (\frac{1}{2} - 2\epsilon^2)|\bar{\mathcal{S}}|.$$

Therefore, again with overwhelming probability the number h of honest parties that contact each of the parties as OT dealers is:

$$h = |\bar{\mathcal{S}} \setminus C| \geq \left(\frac{1}{2} + 2\epsilon^2\right) |\bar{\mathcal{S}}| \overset{(4)}{>} \left(\frac{1}{2} + 2\epsilon^2\right) (1 - 4\epsilon^2) \log^{\delta} n. \quad (6)$$

However, unless the honest client aborts, he accepts at most $\rho = (1 + \epsilon^2) \log^{\delta} n$ offers for dealers; therefore, the fraction of honest OT dealers among these ρ dealers is

$$\frac{h}{\rho} > \frac{(\frac{1}{2} + 2\epsilon^2)(1 - 4\epsilon^2)}{1 - 16\epsilon^4} = \frac{1}{2} \cdot \frac{(1 + 4\epsilon^2)(1 - 4\epsilon^2)}{1 - 16\epsilon^4} = \frac{1}{2}.$$

Thus, at least a 1/2 fraction of the OT vectors that an honest client receives is private and correct, in which case the security of protocol $\Pi_{\text{act}}^{\text{OT}}$ follows from the security of the underlying OT-combiner used in the last protocol step. □

Acknowledgements. This work was done in part while the authors were visiting the Simons Institute for the Theory of Computing, supported by the Simons Foundation and by the DIMACS/Simons Collaboration in Cryptography through NSF grant #CNS-1523467. The second and third authors were supported in part by NSF-BSF grant 2015782 and BSF grant 2012366. The second author was additionally supported by ISF grant 1709/14, DARPA/ARL SAFEWARE award, NSF Frontier Award 1413955, NSF grants 1619348, 1228984, 1136174, and 1065276, a Xerox Faculty Research Award, a Google Faculty Research Award, an equipment grant from Intel, and an Okawa Foundation Research Grant. This material is based upon work supported by the DARPA through the ARL under Contract W911NF-15-C-0205. The third author was additionally supported by NSF grant 1619348, DARPA, OKAWA Foundation Research Award, IBM Faculty Research Award, Xerox Faculty Research Award, B. John Garrick Foundation Award, Teradata Research Award, and Lockheed-Martin Corporation Research Award. The views expressed are those of the authors and do not reflect the official policy or position of the DoD, the NSF, or the U.S. Government.

References

1. Beaver, D.: Precomputing oblivious transfer. In: Coppersmith, D. (ed.) CRYPTO 1995. LNCS, vol. 963, pp. 97–109. Springer, Heidelberg (1995). doi:10.1007/3-540-44750-4_8
2. Beerliová-Trubíniová, Z., Hirt, M.: Efficient multi-party computation with dispute control. In: Halevi, S., Rabin, T. (eds.) TCC 2006. LNCS, vol. 3876, pp. 305–328. Springer, Heidelberg (2006). doi:10.1007/11681878_16
3. Beerliová-Trubíniová, Z., Hirt, M.: Perfectly-secure MPC with linear communication complexity. In: Canetti, R. (ed.) TCC 2008. LNCS, vol. 4948, pp. 213–230. Springer, Heidelberg (2008). doi:10.1007/978-3-540-78524-8_13
4. Ben-Or, M., Goldwasser, S., Wigderson, A.: Completeness theorems for non-cryptographic fault-tolerant distributed computation (extended abstract). In: 20th ACM STOC, pp. 1–10. ACM Press, May 1988

5. Ben-Sasson, E., Fehr, S., Ostrovsky, R.: Near-linear unconditionally-secure multiparty computation with a dishonest minority. In: Safavi-Naini, R., Canetti, R. (eds.) CRYPTO 2012. LNCS, vol. 7417, pp. 663–680. Springer, Heidelberg (2012). doi:10.1007/978-3-642-32009-5_39
6. Boyle, E., Chung, K.-M., Pass, R.: Large-scale secure computation: multi-party computation for (parallel) RAM programs. In: Gennaro, R., Robshaw, M. (eds.) CRYPTO 2015. LNCS, vol. 9216, pp. 742–762. Springer, Heidelberg (2015). doi:10.1007/978-3-662-48000-7_36
7. Boyle, E., Goldwasser, S., Tessaro, S.: Communication locality in secure multiparty computation. In: Sahai, A. (ed.) TCC 2013. LNCS, vol. 7785, pp. 356–376. Springer, Heidelberg (2013). doi:10.1007/978-3-642-36594-2_21
8. Bracha, G.: An o(log n) expected rounds randomized byzantine generals protocol. J. ACM **34**(4), 910–920 (1987)
9. Canetti, R.: Security and composition of multiparty cryptographic protocols. J. Cryptol. **13**(1), 143–202 (2000)
10. Canetti, R.: Universally composable security: a new paradigm for cryptographic protocols. In: 42nd FOCS, pp. 136–145. IEEE Computer Society Press, October 2001
11. Canetti, R., Feige, U., Goldreich, O., Naor, M.: Adaptively secure multi-party computation. In: 28th ACM STOC, pp. 639–648. ACM Press, May 1996
12. Canetti, R., Fischlin, M.: Universally composable commitments. In: Kilian, J. (ed.) CRYPTO 2001. LNCS, vol. 2139, pp. 19–40. Springer, Heidelberg (2001). doi:10.1007/3-540-44647-8_2
13. Chandran, N., Chongchitmate, W., Garay, J.A., Goldwasser, S., Ostrovsky, R., Zikas, V.: The hidden graph model: communication locality and optimal resiliency with adaptive faults. In: Roughgarden, T. (ed.) ITCS 2015, pp. 153–162. ACM, January 2015
14. Chaum, D., Crépeau, C., Damgård, I.: Multiparty unconditionally secure protocols (extended abstract). In: 20th ACM STOC, pp. 11–19. ACM Press, May 1988
15. Cohen, G., Damgård, I.B., Ishai, Y., Kölker, J., Miltersen, P.B., Raz, R., Rothblum, R.D.: Efficient multiparty protocols via log-depth threshold formulae. In: Canetti, R., Garay, J.A. (eds.) CRYPTO 2013. LNCS, vol. 8043, pp. 185–202. Springer, Heidelberg (2013). doi:10.1007/978-3-642-40084-1_11
16. Cramer, R., Damgård, I., Ishai, Y.: Share conversion, pseudorandom secret-sharing and applications to secure computation. In: Kilian, J. (ed.) TCC 2005. LNCS, vol. 3378, pp. 342–362. Springer, Heidelberg (2005). doi:10.1007/978-3-540-30576-7_19
17. Cramer, R., Damgård, I., Nielsen, J.B.: Multiparty computation from threshold homomorphic encryption. In: Pfitzmann, B. (ed.) EUROCRYPT 2001. LNCS, vol. 2045, pp. 280–299. Springer, Heidelberg (2001). doi:10.1007/3-540-44987-6_18
18. Damgård, I., Ishai, Y.: Constant-round multiparty computation using a black-box pseudorandom generator. In: Shoup, V. (ed.) CRYPTO 2005. LNCS, vol. 3621, pp. 378–394. Springer, Heidelberg (2005). doi:10.1007/11535218_23
19. Damgård, I., Ishai, Y.: Scalable secure multiparty computation. In: Dwork, C. (ed.) CRYPTO 2006. LNCS, vol. 4117, pp. 501–520. Springer, Heidelberg (2006). doi:10.1007/11818175_30
20. Damgård, I., Ishai, Y., Krøigaard, M.: Perfectly secure multiparty computation and the computational overhead of cryptography. In: Gilbert, H. (ed.) EUROCRYPT 2010. LNCS, vol. 6110, pp. 445–465. Springer, Heidelberg (2010). doi:10.1007/978-3-642-13190-5_23

21. Damgård, I., Nielsen, J.B.: Improved non-committing encryption schemes based on a general complexity assumption. In: Bellare, M. (ed.) CRYPTO 2000. LNCS, vol. 1880, pp. 432–450. Springer, Heidelberg (2000). doi:10.1007/3-540-44598-6_27
22. Damgård, I., Nielsen, J.B.: Universally composable efficient multiparty computation from threshold homomorphic encryption. In: Boneh, D. (ed.) CRYPTO 2003. LNCS, vol. 2729, pp. 247–264. Springer, Heidelberg (2003). doi:10.1007/978-3-540-45146-4_15
23. Damgård, I., Nielsen, J.B.: Scalable and unconditionally secure multiparty computation. In: Menezes, A. (ed.) CRYPTO 2007. LNCS, vol. 4622, pp. 572–590. Springer, Heidelberg (2007). doi:10.1007/978-3-540-74143-5_32
24. Dani, V., King, V., Movahedi, M., Saia, J.: Brief announcement: breaking the o(nm) bit barrier, secure multiparty computation with a static adversary. In: Kowalski, D., Panconesi, A. (eds.) ACM Symposium on Principles of Distributed Computing, PODC 2012, Funchal, Madeira, Portugal, 16–18 July 2012, pp. 227–228. ACM (2012)
25. Dani, V., King, V., Movahedi, M., Saia, J.: Quorums quicken queries: efficient asynchronous secure multiparty computation. In: Chatterjee, M., Cao, J., Kothapalli, K., Rajsbaum, S. (eds.) ICDCN 2014. LNCS, vol. 8314, pp. 242–256. Springer, Heidelberg (2014). doi:10.1007/978-3-642-45249-9_16
26. Franklin, M., Haber, S.: Joint encryption and message-efficient secure computation. In: Stinson, D.R. (ed.) CRYPTO 1993. LNCS, vol. 773, pp. 266–277. Springer, Heidelberg (1994). doi:10.1007/3-540-48329-2_23
27. Franklin, M.K., Yung, M.: Communication complexity of secure computation (extended abstract). In: 24th ACM STOC, pp. 699–710. ACM Press, May 1992
28. Garay, J., Ishai, Y., Ostrovsky, R., Zikas, V.: The price of low communication in secure multi-party computation. Cryptology ePrint Archive, Report 2017/520 (2017). http://eprint.iacr.org/2017/520
29. Genkin, D., Ishai, Y., Prabhakaran, M., Sahai, A., Tromer, E.: Circuits resilient to additive attacks with applications to secure computation. In: Shmoys, D.B. (ed.) 46th ACM STOC, pp. 495–504. ACM Press, May/June 2014
30. Goldreich, O.: The Foundations of Cryptography - Volume 1, Basic Techniques. Cambridge University Press, Cambridge (2001)
31. Goldreich, O.: Foundations of Cryptography: Basic Applications, vol. 2. Cambridge University Press, Cambridge (2004)
32. Goldreich, O., Micali, S., Wigderson, A.: How to play any mental game or a completeness theorem for protocols with honest majority. In: Aho, A. (ed.) 19th ACM STOC, pp. 218–229. ACM Press, May 1987
33. Harnik, D., Ishai, Y., Kushilevitz, E., Nielsen, J.B.: OT-combiners via secure computation. In: Canetti, R. (ed.) TCC 2008. LNCS, vol. 4948, pp. 393–411. Springer, Heidelberg (2008). doi:10.1007/978-3-540-78524-8_22
34. Harnik, D., Kilian, J., Naor, M., Reingold, O., Rosen, A.: On robust combiners for oblivious transfer and other primitives. In: Cramer, R. (ed.) EUROCRYPT 2005. LNCS, vol. 3494, pp. 96–113. Springer, Heidelberg (2005). doi:10.1007/11426639_6
35. Hirt, M., Maurer, U.M.: Complete characterization of adversaries tolerable in secure multi-party computation (extended abstract). In: Burns, J.E., Attiya, H. (eds.) 16th ACM PODC, pp. 25–34. ACM, August 1997
36. Hirt, M., Maurer, U.M.: Player simulation and general adversary structures in perfect multiparty computation. J. Cryptol. **13**(1), 31–60 (2000)
37. Hirt, M., Maurer, U.: Robustness for free in unconditional multi-party computation. In: Kilian, J. (ed.) CRYPTO 2001. LNCS, vol. 2139, pp. 101–118. Springer, Heidelberg (2001). doi:10.1007/3-540-44647-8_6

38. Hirt, M., Maurer, U., Przydatek, B.: Efficient secure multi-party computation. In: Okamoto, T. (ed.) ASIACRYPT 2000. LNCS, vol. 1976, pp. 143–161. Springer, Heidelberg (2000). doi:10.1007/3-540-44448-3_12
39. Hirt, M., Nielsen, J.B.: Upper bounds on the communication complexity of optimally resilient cryptographic multiparty computation. In: Roy, B. (ed.) ASIACRYPT 2005. LNCS, vol. 3788, pp. 79–99. Springer, Heidelberg (2005). doi:10.1007/11593447_5
40. Hirt, M., Zikas, V.: Adaptively secure broadcast. In: Gilbert, H. (ed.) EUROCRYPT 2010. LNCS, vol. 6110, pp. 466–485. Springer, Heidelberg (2010). doi:10.1007/978-3-642-13190-5_24
41. Hoeffding, W.: Probability inequalities for sums of bounded random variables. J. Am. Stat. Assoc. **58**(301), 13–30 (1963)
42. Ishai, Y., Ostrovsky, R., Zikas, V.: Secure multi-party computation with identifiable abort. In: Garay, J.A., Gennaro, R. (eds.) CRYPTO 2014. LNCS, vol. 8617, pp. 369–386. Springer, Heidelberg (2014). doi:10.1007/978-3-662-44381-1_21
43. Ishai, Y., Prabhakaran, M., Sahai, A.: Founding cryptography on oblivious transfer - efficiently. In: Wagner, D. (ed.) CRYPTO 2008. LNCS, vol. 5157, pp. 572–591. Springer, Heidelberg (2008). doi:10.1007/978-3-540-85174-5_32
44. Jakobsson, M., Juels, A.: Mix and match: secure function evaluation via ciphertexts. In: Okamoto, T. (ed.) ASIACRYPT 2000. LNCS, vol. 1976, pp. 162–177. Springer, Heidelberg (2000). doi:10.1007/3-540-44448-3_13
45. Kilian, J.: Founding crytpography on oblivious transfer. In: Proceedings of the Twentieth Annual ACM Symposium on Theory of Computing, pp. 20–31, New York, NY, USA. ACM Press (1988)
46. Lindell, Y., Pinkas, B.: A proof of security of Yao's protocol for two-party computation. J. Cryptol. **22**(2), 161–188 (2009)
47. Meier, R., Przydatek, B., Wullschleger, J.: Robuster combiners for oblivious transfer. In: Vadhan, S.P. (ed.) TCC 2007. LNCS, vol. 4392, pp. 404–418. Springer, Heidelberg (2007). doi:10.1007/978-3-540-70936-7_22
48. Panconesi, A., Srinivasan, A.: Randomized distributed edge coloring via an extension of the chernoff-hoeffding bounds. SIAM J. Comput. **26**(2), 350–368 (1997)
49. Rabin, M.O.: How to exchange secrets with oblivious transfer. Technical report TR-81, Aiken Computation Lab, Harvard University (1981)
50. Rabin, T., Ben-Or, M.: Verifiable secret sharing and multiparty protocols with honest majority (extended abstract). In: 21st ACM STOC, pp. 73–85. ACM Press, May 1989
51. Shamir, A.: How to share a secret. Commun. Assoc. Comput. Mach. **22**(11), 612–613 (1979)
52. Yao, A.C.-C.: Protocols for secure computations (extended abstract). In: 23rd FOCS, pp. 160–164. IEEE Computer Society Press, November 1982

Topology-Hiding Computation on All Graphs

Adi Akavia[1](✉), Rio LaVigne[2](✉), and Tal Moran[3](✉)

[1] The Academic College of Tel-Aviv Jaffa, Tel Aviv-Yafo, Israel
akavia@mta.ac.il
[2] MIT, Cambridge, USA
rio@mit.edu
[3] IDC Herzliya, Herzliya, Israel
talm@idc.ac.il

Abstract. A distributed computation in which nodes are connected by a partial communication graph is called *topology-hiding* if it does not reveal information about the graph beyond what is revealed by the output of the function. Previous results have shown that topology-hiding computation protocols exist for graphs of constant degree and logarithmic diameter in the number of nodes [Moran-Orlov-Richelson, TCC'15; Hirt et al., Crypto'16] as well as for other graph families, such as cycles, trees, and low circumference graphs [Akavia-Moran, Eurocrypt'17], but the feasibility question for general graphs was open.

In this work we positively resolve the above open problem: we prove that topology-hiding MPC is feasible for *all* graphs under the Decisional Diffie-Hellman assumption.

Our techniques employ random-walks to generate paths covering the graph, upon which we apply the Akavia-Moran topology-hiding broadcast for chain-graphs (paths). To prevent topology information revealed by the random-walk, we design multiple random-walks that, together, are locally identical to receiving at each round a message from each neighbors and sending back processed messages in a randomly permuted order.

1 Introduction

The beautiful theory of secure multiparty computation (MPC) enables multiple parties to compute an arbitrary function of their inputs without revealing anything but the

A. Akavia—Work partly supported by the ERC under the EU's Seventh Framework Programme (FP/2007–2013) ERC Grant Agreement no. 307952.

R. LaVigne—This material is based upon work supported by the National Science Foundation Graduate Research Fellowship under Grant No. 1122374. Any opinion, findings, and conclusions or recommendations expressed in this material are those of the authors(s) and do not necessarily reflect the views of the National Science Foundation. Research also supported in part by NSF Grants CNS-1350619 and CNS-1414119, and by the Defense Advanced Research Projects Agency (DARPA) and the U.S. Army Research Office under contracts W911NF-15-C-0226 and W911NF-15-C-0236.

T. Moran—Supported by ISF grant no. 1790/13.

J. Katz and H. Shacham (Eds.): CRYPTO 2017, Part I, LNCS 10401, pp. 447–467, 2017.
DOI: 10.1007/978-3-319-63688-7_15

function's output [10,11,24]. In the original definitions and constructions of MPC, the participants were connected by a full communication graph (a broadcast channel and/or point-to-point channels between every pair of parties). In real-world settings, however, the actual communication graph between parties is usually not complete, and parties may be able to communicate directly with only a subset of the other parties. Moreover, in some cases the graph itself is sensitive information (e.g., if you communicate directly only with your friends in a social network).

A natural question is whether we can successfully perform a joint computation over a partial communication graph while revealing no (or very little) information about the graph itself. In the information-theoretic setting, in which a variant of this question was studied by Hinkelman and Jakoby [15], the answer is mostly negative. The situation is better in the computational setting. Moran et al. showed that topology-hiding computation *is* possible against static, semi-honest adversaries [21]; followed by constructions with improved efficiency that make only black-box use of underlying primitives [16]. However, all these protocol are restricted to communication graphs with *small diameter*. Specifically, these protocols address networks with diameter $D = O(\log n)$, logarithmic in the number of nodes n (where the diameter is the maximal distance between two nodes in the graph). Akavia and Moran [1] showed that topology hiding computation is feasible also for *large diameter* networks of certain forms, most notably, cycles, trees, and low circumference graphs.

However, there are natural network topologies not addressed by the above protocols [1,16,21]. They include, for example, wireless and ad-hoc sensor networks, as in [8,23]. The topology in these graphs is modeled by random geometric graphs [22], where, with high probability, the diameter and the circumference are simultaneously large [3, 9]. These qualities exclude the use of all aforementioned protocols. So, the question remained:

Is topology hiding MPC feasible for every network topology?

1.1 Our Results

In this work we prove that topology hiding MPC is feasible for *every* network topology under the Decisional Diffie-Hellman (DDH) assumption, thus positively resolving the above open problem. The adversary is static and semi-honest as in the prior works [1,16,21].[1] Our protocol also fits a stronger definition of security than that from prior works: instead of allowing the adversary to know who his neighbors are, he only gets pseudonyms; importantly, an adversary cannot tell if two nodes he controls share an honest neighbor. This stronger definition is elaborated on in the full version of this paper.

Theorem 1 (Topology-hiding broadcast for all network topologies – informal). *There exists a topology-hiding protocol realizing the broadcast functionality on every network topology (under DDH assumption and provided the parties are given an upper-bound n on the number of nodes).*

The formal theorem is stated and proved in Sect. 3.3.

[1] Moran et al. [21] consider also a fail-stop adversary for proving an impossibility result.

As in [1,16,21], given a *topology-hiding broadcast* for a point-to-point channels network, we can execute on top of it any MPC protocol from the literature that is designed for networks with broadcast channels; the resulting protocol remains topology-hiding. Put together with the existence of secure MPC for all efficiently computable functionalities (assuming parties have access to a broadcast channel and that public key encryption exist) [10,11,24], we conclude that *topology-hiding MPC* for all efficiently computable functionality and all networks topologies (assuming a certain type of public key encryption exists).

1.2 High-Level Overview of Our Techniques

Our main innovation is the use of *random walks* on the network graph for specifying a path, and then viewing this path as a chain-graph and employing the topology-hiding broadcast for chains of Akavia and Moran [1].

A challenge we face is that the walk itself may reveal topology information. For example, a party can deduce the graph commute-time from the number of rounds before a returning visit by the walk. We therefore hide the random-walk by using multiple simultaneous random-walks (details below). The combination of all our random-walks obeys a simple communication structure: at every round each node receives an incoming message from each of its neighbors, randomly permutes the messages, and sends them back.

To give more details on our protocol, let us first recall the Akavia-Moran protocol for chain-graphs. The Akavia-Moran protocol proceeds in two phases, a forward and a backward phase. In the forward phase, messages are passed forward on the chain, where each node adds its own encryption layer and computes the OR of the received message with its bit using homomorphic multiplication (with proper re-randomizing). In the backward phase, the messages are passed backward along the same path, where each node deletes its encryption layer. At the end of the protocol, the starting node receives the plaintext value for the OR of all input bits. This protocol is augmented to run n instances simultaneously; each node initiates an execution of the protocol while playing the role of the first node. So, by the end of the protocol, each node has the OR of all bits, which will be equal to the broadcast bit. Intuitively, this achieves topology-hiding because at each step, every node receives an encrypted message and public key. An encryption of zero is indistinguishable from an encryption of 1, and so each node's view is indistinguishable from every other view.

We next elaborate on how we define our multiple random walks, focusing on two viewpoints: the viewpoint of a node, and the viewpoint of a message. We use the former to argue security, and the latter to argue correctness.

From the point of view of a node v with d neighbors, the random walks on the forward-phase are specified by choosing a sequence of independent random permutations $\pi_t \colon [d] \to [d]$, where in each forward-phase round t, the node forwards messages received from neighbor i to neighbor $\pi_t(i)$ (after appropriate processing of the message, as discussed above). The backward-phase follows the reverse path, sending incoming message from neighbor j to neighbor $i = \pi_t^{-1}(j)$, where t is the corresponding round in the forward-phase. Furthermore, recall that all messages are encrypted under semantically-secure encryption. This fixed communication pattern together with the semantic security of the messages content leads to the topology-hiding property of our protocol.

From the point of view of a message, at each round of the forward-phase the message is sent to a uniformly random neighbor. Thus, the path the message goes through is a random-walk on the graph.[2] A sufficiently long random walk covers the entire graph with overwhelming probability. In this case, the output is the OR of the inputs bits of *all* graph nodes, and correctness is guaranteed.

1.3 Related Work

Topology Hiding in Computational Settings. Figure 1 compares our results to the previous results on topology hiding computation and specifies, for each protocol, the classes of graphs for which it is guaranteed to run in polynomial time.

The first result was a feasibility result and was the work of Moran et al. [21] from 2015. Their result was a broadcast protocol secure against static, semi-honest adversaries, and a protocol against failstop adversaries that do not disconnect the graph. However, their protocol is restricted to communication graphs with diameter logarithmic in the total number of parties.

Graphs families	[17,22]	[1]	[This Work]
Log diameter constant degree	+	−	+
Cycles, trees	−	+	+
Log circumference	−	+	+
Log diameter super-constant degree	−	−	+
Regular graphs	−	−	+
Arbitrary graphs	−	−	+

Fig. 1. Rows correspond to graph families; columns corresponds to prior works in the first two columns and to this work in last the column. A +/− mark for graph x and work y indicates that a topology hiding protocol is given/not-given in work y for graph x.

The main idea behind their protocol is a series of nested multiparty computations, in which each node is replaced by a secure computation in its local neighborhood that simulates that node. The drawback is that in order to get full security, this virtualization needs to extend to the entire graph, but the complexity of the MPC grows exponentially with the size of the neighborhood.

Our work is also a feasibility result, but instead builds on a protocol much more similar to the recent Akavia-Moran paper [1], which takes a different approach. They employ ideas from cryptographic voting literature, hiding the order of nodes in the cycle by "mixing" encrypted inputs before decrypting them and adding layers of public keys to the encryption at each step. In this work, we take this layer-adding approach and

[2] We remark that the multiple random-walks are not independent; we take this into account in our analysis.

apply it to random walks over all kinds of graphs instead of deterministically figuring out the path beforehand.

Other related works include a work by Hirt et al. [16], which describes a protocol that acheives better efficiency than [21], but as it uses similar tactics, is still restricted to network graphs with logarithmic diameter. Addressing a problem different from topology-hiding, the work by Chandran et al. [7] reduces communication complexity of secure MPC by allowing each party to communicate with a small (sublinear in the number of parties) number of its neighbors.

Topology Hiding in Information Theoretic Settings. Hinkelmann and Jakoby [15] considered the question of topology-hiding secure computation, but focused on the information theoretic setting. Their main result was negative: any MPC protocol in the information-theoretic setting inherently leaks information about the network graph to an adversary. However, they also show that the only information we need to leak is the routing table: if we leak the routing table beforehand, then one can construct an MPC protocol which leaks no further information.

Secure Multiparty Computation with General Interaction Patterns. Halevi et al. [13] presented a unified framework for studying secure MPC with arbitrary restricted interaction patterns, generalizing models for MPC with specific restricted interaction patterns [4,12,14]. Their goal is not topology hiding, however. Instead, they ask the question of when is it possible to prevent an adversary from learning the output to a function on several inputs. They started by observing that an adversary controlling the final players $P_i, \cdots, P_n$ in the interaction pattern can learn the output of the computed function on several inputs because the adversary can rewind and execute the protocol on any possible party values $x_i, \cdots, x_n$. This model allows complete knowledge on the underlying interaction pattern (or as in our case, the graph).

1.4 Organization of Paper

In Sect. 2 we describe our adversarial model and introduce some notation. In Sect. 2.5 we detail the special properties we require from the encryption scheme that we use in our cycle protocol, and show how it can be instantiated based on DDH. In Sect. 3, we explain our protocol for topology-hiding broadcast on general graphs and prove its completeness and security. Then, in Sect. 4, we go over a time and communication tradeoff, and explain how we can optimize our protocol with respect to certain classes of graphs. Finally, in Sect. 5, we conclude and discuss future work.

2 Preliminaries

2.1 Computation and Adversarial Models

We model a network by an undirected graph $G = (V, E)$ that is not fully connected. We consider a system with n parties denoted $P_1, \ldots, P_n$, where n is upper bounded by $\text{poly}(\kappa)$ and κ is the security parameter. We identify V with the set of parties $\{P_1, \ldots, P_n\}$.

We consider a static and computationally bounded (PPT) adversary that controls some subset of parties (any number of parties). That is, at the beginning of the protocol, the adversary corrupts a subset of the parties and may instruct them to deviate from the protocol according to the corruption model. Throughout this work, we consider only semi-honest adversaries. In addition, we assume that the adversary is rushing; that is, in each round the adversary sees the messages sent by the honest parties before sending the messages of the corrupted parties for this round. For general MPC definitions including in-depth descriptions of the adversarial models we consider, see [10].

2.2 Notation

In this section, we describe our common notation conventions for both graphs and for our protocol.

Graph Notation

Let $G = (V, E)$ be an undirected graph. For every $v \in V$, we define the neighbors of v as $\mathcal{N}(v) = \{w : (v, w) \in E\}$ and will refer to the degree of v as $d_v = |\mathcal{N}(v)|$.

Protocol Notation

Our protocol will rely on generating many public-secret key pairs, and ciphertexts at each round. In fact, each node will produce a public-secret key pair for each of its neighbors at every timestep. To keep track of all these, we introduce the following notation. Let $pk_{i \to d}^{(t)}$ represent the public key created by node i to be used for neighbor d at round t; $sk_{i \to d}^{(t)}$ is the corresponding secret key. Ciphertexts are labeled similarly: $c_{d \to i}^{(t)}$, is from neighbor d to node i.

2.3 UC Security

As in [21], we prove security in the UC model [5]. If a protocol is secure in the UC model, it can be composed with other protocols without compromising security, so we can use it as a subprotocol in other constructions. This is critical for constructing topology-hiding MPC based on broadcast—broadcast is used as a sub-protocol.

A downside of the UC model is that, against general adversaries, it requires setup. However, setup is not necessary against semi-honest adversaries that must play according to the rules of the protocol. Thus, we get a protocol that is secure in the plain model, without setup. For details about the UC framework, we refer the reader to [5].

2.4 Simulation-Based Topology Hiding Security

Here we will review the model for defining simulation-based topology hiding computation, as proposed by [21], in the UC framework.

The UC model usually assumes all parties can communicate directly with all other parties. To model the restricted communication setting, [21] define the $\mathcal{F}_{\text{graph}}$-hybrid model, which employs a special "graph party," P_{graph}. Figure 2 shows $\mathcal{F}_{\text{graph}}$'s functionality: at the start of the functionality, $\mathcal{F}_{\text{graph}}$ receives the network graph from P_{graph}, and then outputs, to each party, that party's neighbors. Then, $\mathcal{F}_{\text{graph}}$ acts as an "ideal channel" for parties to communicate with their neighbors, restricting communications to those allowed by the graph.

Since the graph structure is an input to one of the parties in the computation, the standard security guarantees of the UC model ensure that the graph structure remains hidden (since the only information revealed about parties' inputs is what can be computed from the output). Note that the P_{graph} party serves only to specify the communication graph, and does not otherwise participate in the protocol.

Participants/Notation:
This functionality involves all the parties $P_1, \ldots, P_n$ and a special graph party P_{graph}.
Initialization Phase:
Inputs: $\mathcal{F}_{\text{graph}}$ waits to receive the graph $G = (V, E)$ from P_{graph}.
Outputs: $\mathcal{F}_{\text{graph}}$ outputs $\mathcal{N}(v)$ to each P_v.
Communication Phase:
Inputs: $\mathcal{F}_{\text{graph}}$ receives from a party P_v a destination/data pair (w, m) where $w \in \mathcal{N}(v)$ and m is the message P_v wants to send to P_w.
Output: $\mathcal{F}_{\text{graph}}$ gives output (v, m) to P_w indicating that P_v sent the message m to P_w.

Fig. 2. The functionality $\mathcal{F}_{\text{graph}}$.

The initialization phase of $\mathcal{F}_{\text{graph}}$ provides local information about the graph to every corrupted party, and so both ideal-world and real-world adversaries get access to this information. This information is independent of the functionality we are trying to implement, but always present. So we will isolate it in the functionality $\mathcal{F}_{\text{graphInfo}}$ which contains only the initialization phase of $\mathcal{F}_{\text{graph}}$, and then, for any functionality $\mathcal{F}$, we compose $\mathcal{F}$ with $\mathcal{F}_{\text{graphInfo}}$, writing $(\mathcal{F}_{\text{graphInfo}}||\mathcal{F})$ as the "composed functionality." Now we can define topology-hiding MPC in the UC framework:

Definition 2. *We say that a protocol* Π *securely realizes a functionality* $\mathcal{F}$ hiding topology *if it UC-realizes* $(\mathcal{F}_{graphInfo}||\mathcal{F})$ *in the* $\mathcal{F}_{graph}$*-hybrid model.*

This definition also captures functionalities that depend on the structure of the graph, like shortest path or determining the length of the longest cycle.

Broadcast Functionality, $\mathcal{F}_{\text{Broadcast}}$

In accordance with this definition, we need to define an ideal functionality of broadcast, denoted $\mathcal{F}_{\text{Broadcast}}$, shown in Fig. 3. We will prove that a simulator only with knowledge

Participants/Notation:
This functionality involves all the parties $P_1, \ldots, P_n$.
Inputs: The broadcasting party P_i receives a bit $b \in \{0, 1\}$.
Outputs: All parties $P_1, \ldots, P_n$ receive output b.

Fig. 3. The functionality $\mathcal{F}_{\text{Broadcast}}$.

of the output of $\mathcal{F}_{\text{Broadcast}}$ and knowledge of the local topology of the adversarially chosen nodes Q can produce a transcript to nodes in Q indistinguishable from running our protocol.

2.5 Privately Key-Commutative and Rerandomizable Encryption

As in [1], we require a public key encryption scheme with the properties of being *homomorphic* (with respect to OR in our case), *privately key-commutative*, and *re-randomizable*. In this section we first formally define the properties we require, and then show how they can be achieved based on the Decisional Diffie-Hellman assumption.

We call an encryption scheme satisfying the latter two properties, i.e., privately key-commutative and re-randomizable, a *PKCR-enc*;

Required Properties

Let $\mathsf{KeyGen} : \{0,1\}^* \mapsto \mathcal{PK} \times \mathcal{SK}, \mathsf{Enc} : \mathcal{PK} \times \mathcal{M} \times \{0,1\}^* \mapsto C, \mathsf{Dec} : \mathcal{SK} \times C \mapsto \mathcal{M}$ be the encryption scheme's key generation, encryption and decryption functions, respectively, where $\mathcal{PK}$ is the space of public keys, $\mathcal{SK}$ the space of secret keys, $\mathcal{M}$ the space of plaintext messages and C the space of ciphertexts.

We will use the shorthand $[m]_k$ to denote an encryption of the message m under public-key k. We assume that for every secret key $sk \in \mathcal{SK}$ there is associated a single public key $pk \in \mathcal{PK}$ such that (pk, sk) are in the range of KeyGen. We slightly abuse notation and denote the public key corresponding to sk by $pk(sk)$.

Privately Key-Commutative

The set of public keys $\mathcal{PK}$ form an abelian (commutative) group. We denote the group operation $\circledast$. Given any $k_1, k_2 \in \mathcal{PK}$, there exists an efficient algorithm to compute $k_1 \circledast k_2$. We denote the inverse of k by k^{-1} (i.e., $k^{-1} \circledast k$ is the identity element of the group). Given a secret key sk, there must be an efficient algorithm to compute the inverse of its public key $(pk(sk))^{-1}$.

There exist a pair of algorithms $\mathsf{AddLayer} : C \times \mathcal{SK} \mapsto C$ and $\mathsf{DelLayer} : C \times \mathcal{SK} \mapsto C$ that satisfy:

1. For every public key $k \in \mathcal{PK}$, every message $m \in \mathcal{M}$ and every ciphertext $c = [m]_k$,
$$\mathsf{AddLayer}(c, sk) = [m]_{k \circledast pk(sk)} \,.$$
2. For every public key $k \in \mathcal{PK}$, every message $m \in \mathcal{M}$ and every ciphertext $c = [m]_k$,
$$\mathsf{DelLayer}(c, sk) = [m]_{k \circledast (pk(sk))^{-1}} \,.$$

We call this *privately* key-commutative since adding and deleting layers both require knowledge of the secret key.

Note that since the group $\mathcal{PK}$ is commutative, adding and deleting layers can be done in any order.

Rerandomizable

We require that there exists a ciphertexts "re-randomizing" algorithm $\mathsf{Rand} : C \times \mathcal{PK} \times \{0,1\}^* \mapsto C$ satisfying the following:

1. *Randomization:* For every message $m \in \mathcal{M}$, every public key $pk \in \mathcal{PK}$ and ciphertext $c = [m]_{pk}$, the distributions $(m, pk, c, \mathsf{Rand}(c, pk, U^*))$ and $(m, pk, c, \mathsf{Enc}_{pk}(m; U^*))$ are computationally indistinguishable.
2. *Neutrality:* For every ciphertext $c \in C$, every secret key $sk \in \mathcal{SK}$ and every $r \in \{0,1\}^*$,
$$\mathsf{Dec}_{sk}(c) = \mathsf{Dec}_{sk}(\mathsf{Rand}(c, pk(sk), r)).$$

Furthermore, we require that public-keys are "re-randomizable" in the sense that the product $k \circledast k'$ of an arbitrary public key k with a public-key k' generated using KeyGen is computationally indistinguishable from a fresh public-key generated by KeyGen.

Homomorphism

We require that the message space $\mathcal{M}$ forms a group with operation denoted $\cdot$, and require that the encryption scheme is homomorphic with respect this operation $\cdot$ in the sense that there exists an efficient algorithm $\mathsf{hMult} : C \times C \mapsto C$ that, given two ciphertexts $c = [m]_{pk}$ and $c' = [m']_{pk}$, returns a ciphertext $c'' \leftarrow \mathsf{hMult}(c, c')$ s.t. $\mathsf{Dec}_{sk}(c'') = m \cdot m'$ (for sk the secret-key associated with public-key pk).

Notice that with this operation, we can homomorphically raise any ciphertext to any power via repeated squaring. We will call this operation hPower.

Homomorphic OR

This feature is built up from the re-randomizing and the homomorphism features. One of the necessary parts of our protocol for broadcast functionality is to have a homomorphic OR. We need this operation not to reveal if it is ORing two 1's or one 1 at decryption. So, following [1], first we define an encryption of 0 to be an encryption of the identity element in $\mathcal{M}$ and an encryption of 1 to be an encryption of any other element. Then, we define HomOR so that it re-randomizes encryptions of 0 and 1 by raising ciphertexts to a random power with hPower.

```
function HomOR(c, c', pk, r = (r, r'))  // r is randomness.
    ĉ ← hPower(c, r, pk) and ĉ' ← hPower(c', r', pk)
    return Rand(hMult(ĉ, ĉ''), pk)
end function
```

Claim. Let $\mathcal{M}$ have prime order p, where $1/p$ is negligible in the security parameter, and $M, M' \in \{0,1\}$ be messages with corresponding ciphertexts c and c' under public key pk. The distribution $(c, c', pk, M, M', \mathsf{Enc}(M \vee M', pk; U^*))$ is computationally indistinguishable from $(c, c', pk, M, M', \mathsf{HomOR}(c, c', pk; U^*))$.

Proof. We will go through three cases for values of M and M': first, when $M = M' = 0$; second when $M = 1$ and $M' = 0$; and third when $M = 1$ and $M' = 1$. The case $M = 0$ and $M' = 1$ is handled by the second case.

– Consider when $M = M' = 0$. Note that $1_{\mathcal{M}}$ is the group element in $\mathcal{M}$ that encodes 0, so an encryption of 0 is represented by an encryption of the identity element,

$m = m' = 1_{\mathcal{M}}$, of $\mathcal{M}$. Consider c_0 and c'_0 both encryptions of $1_{\mathcal{M}}$. After hPower, both $\hat{c}_0$ and $\hat{c}'_0$ are still encryptions of $1_{\mathcal{M}}$. hMult then produces an encryption of $1_{\mathcal{M}} \cdot 1_{\mathcal{M}} = 1_{\mathcal{M}}$, and Rand makes that ciphertext indistinguishable to a fresh encryption of $1_{\mathcal{M}}$. We have proved our first case.

- Next, let c_0 be an encryption of 0 and c'_1 be an encryption of 1. In this case, 0 is represented again by $1_{\mathcal{M}}$, but c'_1 is represented by some $m' \overset{\$}{\leftarrow} \mathcal{M}$ (with all but negligible probability $m' \neq 1$). After hPower, $\hat{c}_0$ still encrypts $1_{\mathcal{M}}$, but $\hat{c}'_1$ encrypts $\hat{m} = m'^{r'}$ for some $r' \overset{\$}{\leftarrow} \mathbb{Z}_p$. hMult yeilds an encryption of $\hat{m}$ and Rand makes a ciphertext computationally indistinguishable from a fresh encryption of $\hat{m}$. Since $\mathcal{M}$ has prime order p and $r' \overset{\$}{\leftarrow} \mathbb{Z}_p$, as long as $m' \neq 1$, m'^{r} is uniformly distributed over $\mathcal{M}$, and so computationally has a distribution indistinguishable to a fresh encryption of the boolean message 1.
- Finally, let c_1 and c'_1 both be encryptions of 1: c_1 encrypts $m \overset{\$}{\leftarrow} \mathcal{M}$ and c'_1 encrypts $m' \overset{\$}{\leftarrow} \mathcal{M}$. We will go through the same steps to have at the end, a ciphertext computationally indistinguishable[3] from a fresh encryption of $m^r \cdot m'^{r'}$ for $r, r' \overset{\$}{\leftarrow} \mathbb{Z}_p$. Again because the order of $\mathcal{M}$ is prime, $m^r \cdot m'^{r'}$ is uniformly distributed over $\mathbb{Z}_p$, and so the resulting ciphertext looks like a fresh encryption of 1. □

This claim means that we cannot tell how many times 1 or 0 has been OR'd together during an or-and-forward type of protocol. This will be critical in our proof of security.

Instantiation of OR-Homomorphic PKCR-enc Under DDH

We use standard ElGamal, augmented by the additional required functions. The KeyGen, Dec and Enc functions are the standard ElGamal functions, except that to obtain a one-to-one mapping between public keys and secret keys, we fix the group G and the generator g, and different public keys vary only in the element $h = g^x$. Below, g is always the group generator. The Rand function is also the standard rerandomization function for ElGamal:

function RAND($c = (c_1, c_2), pk, r$)
  return $(c_1 \cdot g^r, pk^r \cdot c_2)$
end function

We use the shorthand notation of writing Rand(c, pk) when the random coins r are chosen independently at random during the execution of Rand. We note that the distribution of public-keys outputted by KeyGen is uniform, and thus the requirement for "public-key rerandomization" indeed holds. ElGamal public keys are already defined over an abelian group, and the operation is efficient. For adding and removing layers, we define:

[3] In our definition of a PKCR encryption scheme, Rand is only required to be computationally randomizing, which carries over in our distribution of homomorphically-OR'd ciphertexts. However, ElGamal's re-randomization function is distributed statistically close to a fresh ciphertext, and so our construction will end up having HomOR be identically distributed to a fresh encryption of the OR of the bits.

function AddLayer($c = (c_1, c_2), sk$)
  return $(c_1, c_2 \cdot c_1^{sk})$
end function
function DelLayer($c = (c_1, c_2), sk$)
  return $(c_1, c_2 / c_1^{sk})$
end function

Every ciphertext $[m]_{pk}$ has the form $(g^r, pk^r \cdot m)$ for some element $r \in \mathbb{Z}_{ord(g)}$. So

$$\mathsf{AddLayer}\left([m]_{pk}, sk'\right) = (g^r, pk^r \cdot m \cdot g^{r \cdot sk'}) = (g^r, pk^r \cdot (pk')^r \cdot m) = (g^r, (pk \cdot pk')^r \cdot m) = [m]_{pk \cdot pk'} .$$

It is easy to verify that the corresponding requirement is satisfied for DelLayer as well.

ElGamal message space already defined over an abelian group with homomorphic multiplication, specifically:

function hMult($c = (c_1, c_2), c' = (c'_1, c'_2)$)
  return $c'' = (c_1 \cdot c'_1, c_2 \cdot c'_2)$
end function

Recalling that the input ciphertext have the form $c = (g^r, pk^r \cdot m)$ and $c' = (g^{r'}, pk^{r'} \cdot m')$ for messages $m, m' \in \mathbb{Z}_{ord(g)}$, it is easy to verify that decrypting the ciphertext $c'' = (g^{r+r'}, pk^{r+r'} \cdot m \cdot m')$ returned from hMult yields the product message $\mathsf{Dec}_{sk}(c'') = m \cdot m'$.

Finally, to obtain a negligible error probability in our broadcast protocols, we take G a prime order group of size satisfying that $1/|G|$ is negligible in the security parameter κ. With this property and valid Rand and hMult operations, we get hPower and hence HomOR with ElGamal.

3 Topology Hiding Broadcast Protocol for General Graphs

In this section, we describe how our protocol works and prove that it is complete and secure.

The protocol (see Protocol 1) is composed of two phases: an aggregate (forward) phase and a decrypt (backward) phase. In the aggregate phase messages traverse a random walk on the graph where each of the passed-through nodes adds a fresh encryption layer and homomorphically ORs the passed message with its bit. In the decrypt phase, the random-walk is traced back where each node deletes the encryption layer it previously added. At the end of the backward phase, the node obtains the plaintext value of the OR of all input bits. The protocol executes simultaneous random walks, locally defined at each node v with d neighbors by a sequence of permutations $\pi_t \colon [d] \to [d]$ for each round t, so that at round t of the forward phase messages received from neighbor i are forwarded to neighbor $\pi_t(i)$, and at the backward phase messages received from neighbor j are sent back to neighbor $\pi_t^{-1}(j)$.

3.1 Proof of Completeness

The main idea of the protocol is that we take a random walk around the graph, or-ing bits as we go, and hopefully by the time we start walking backwards along that path

Protocol 1. Topology-hiding broadcast for general graphs. Inputs parameters: n is the number of nodes; $2^{-\tau}$ the failure probability; d_i the degree of node i; and b_i the input bit of node i. See Sect. 2.2 for an explanation of notation.

procedure BROADCAST$((n, \tau, d_i, b_i))$
    // The number of steps we take in our random walk will be T.
    $T \leftarrow \tau \cdot 8n^3$
    Generate $T \cdot d_i$ key pairs: for $t \in [T]$ and $d \in [d_i]$, generate pair $(pk^{(t)}_{i\to d}, sk^{(t)}_{i\to d}) \leftarrow$ KeyGen(1^κ).
    Generate $T-1$ random permutations on d_i elements $\{\pi_1, \cdots, \pi_{T-1}\}$. Let π_T be the identity permutation.
    // **Aggregate phase.**
    For all $d \in [d_i]$, send to neighbor d the ciphertext $[b_i]_{pk^{(1)}_{i\to d}}$ and the public key $pk^{(1)}_{i\to d}$.
    for $t = 1$ to $T-1$ **do**
        for Neighbors $d \in [d_i]$ **do**
            Wait to receive ciphertext $c^{(t)}_{d\to i}$ and public key $k^{(t)}_{d\to i}$.
            Let $d' \leftarrow \pi_t(d)$.
            Compute $k^{(t+1)}_{i\to d'} = k^{(t)}_{d\to i} \circledast pk^{(t+1)}_{i\to d'}$.
            Compute $\hat{c}^{(t+1)}_{i\to d} \leftarrow \text{AddLayer}\left(c^{(t)}_{d\to i}, sk^{(t+1)}_{i\to d'}\right)$ and $[b_i]_{k^{(t+1)}_{i\to d'}}$.
            Compute $c^{(t+1)}_{i\to d'} \leftarrow \text{HomOR}\left([b_i]_{k^{(t+1)}_{i\to d'}}, \hat{c}^{(t+1)}_{i\to d'}\right)$.
            Send $c^{(t+1)}_{i\to d'}$ and $k^{(t+1)}_{i\to d'}$ to neighbor d'.
        end for
    end for
    Wait to receive $c^{(T)}_{d\to i}$ and $k^{(T)}_{d\to i}$ from each neighbor $d \in [d_i]$.
    Compute $[b_i]_{k^{(T)}_{d\to i}}$ and let $e^{(T)}_{d\to i} \leftarrow \text{HomOR}\left(c^{(T)}_{d\to i}, [b_i]_{k^{(T)}_{d\to i}}\right)$
    // **Decrypt phase.**
    for $t = T$ to 1 **do**
        For each $d \in [d_i]$, send $e^{(t)}_{i\to d'}$ to $d' = \pi_t^{-1}(d)$. // Passing back.
        for $d \in [d_i]$ **do**
            Wait to receive $e^{(t)}_{d\to i}$ from neighbor d.
            Compute $d' \leftarrow \pi_t^{-1}(d)$.
            $e^{(t-1)}_{i\to d'} \leftarrow \text{DelLayer}\left(e^{(t)}_{d\to i}, sk^{(t)}_{i\to d'}\right)$ // If $t = 1$, DelLayer decrypts..
        end for
    end for
    // **Produce output bit.**
    $b \leftarrow \bigvee_{d\in[d_i]} e^{(0)}_{i\to d}$.
    Output b.
end procedure

we have reached all of the nodes. We will rely on the following definition and theorem from Mitzenmacher and Upfal's book (see Chap. 5) [20].

Definition 3 (Cover time). *The cover time of a graph $G = (V, E)$ is the maximum over all vertices $v \in V$ of the expected time to visit all of the nodes in the graph by a random walk starting from v.*

Theorem 4 (Cover time bound). *The cover time of any connected, undirected graph $G = (u, v)$ is bounded above by $4nm \leq 4n^3$.*

Corollary 5. *Let $\mathcal{W}(u, \tau)$ be a random variable whose value is the set of nodes covered by a random walk starting from u and taking $\tau \cdot (8n^3)$ steps. We have*

$$\Pr_{\mathcal{W}}[\mathcal{W}(u, \tau) = V] \geq 1 - \frac{1}{2^\tau}.$$

Proof. First, consider a random walk that takes t steps to traverse a graph. Theorem 4 tells us that we expect $t \leq 4n^3$, and so by a Markov bound, we have

$$\Pr\left[t \geq 2 \cdot (4n^3)\right] \leq \frac{1}{2}$$

Translating this into our notation, for any node $u \in G$, $\Pr[\mathcal{W}(u, 1) = V] \geq \frac{1}{2}$.

We can represent $\mathcal{W}(u, \tau)$ as a union of τ random walks, each of length $8n^3$: $\mathcal{W}(u_1 = u, 1) \cup \mathcal{W}(u_2, 1) \cup \cdots \cup \mathcal{W}(u_\tau, 1)$, where u_i is the node we have reached at step $i \cdot 8n^3$ (technically, u_i is a random variable, but the specific node at which we start each walk will not matter). $\mathcal{W}(u, \tau)$ will succeed in covering all nodes in G if any $\mathcal{W}(u_i, 1)$ covers all nodes.

So, we will bound the probability that all $\mathcal{W}(u_i, 1) \neq V$. Note that each $\mathcal{W}(u_i, 1)$ is independent of all other walks except for the node it starts on, but our upper bound is independent of the starting node. This means

$$\Pr[\mathcal{W}(u_i, 1) \neq V, \ \forall i \in [\tau]] = \prod_{i \in [\tau]} \Pr[\mathcal{W}(u_i, 1) \neq V] \leq \frac{1}{2^\tau}.$$

Therefore,

$$\Pr[\mathcal{W}(u, \tau) = V] = 1 - \Pr[\mathcal{W}(u, \tau) \neq V] \geq 1 - \Pr[\mathcal{W}(u, 1) \neq V]^\tau \geq 1 - \frac{1}{2^\tau}.$$

□

Theorem 6 (Completeness). *At the end of Protocol 1, which takes $2 \cdot \tau \cdot 8n^3$ rounds, every node will have $b = \bigvee_{i \in [n]} b_i$ with probability at least $1 - n/2^\tau$.*

Proof. First, we will prove that by the end of our protocol, every node along the walk OR's its bit and the resulting bit is decrypted. Then, we will prove that with all but probability $n/2^\tau$, every node has some walk that gets the output bit, meaning that with high probability, b at the end of the protocol is the output bit received by each node.

So, consider a single node, u_0, with bit b_0. Recall that $T = \tau \cdot 8n^3$. We will follow one walk that starts at u_0 with bit b_0. In the protocol, u_0's neighbors are ordered 1 to d_{u_0} and referred to by their number. Since this ordering is arbitrary, we will let u_1 identify the neighbor chosen by the protocol to send the encryption of b_0 in the first round, and, generalizing this notation, u_i will identify the ith node in the walk. For the sake of notation, pk_i will denote the public key generated by node u_i at step $i + 1$ for node u_{i+1} (so $pk_i = pk^{(i+1)}_{u_i \to u_{i+1}}$), and k_i will be the aggregate key-product at step i (so $k_i = pk_0 \circledast \ldots \circledast pk_i$).

- On the first step, u_0 encrypts b_0 with pk_0 into c_1 and sends it and public key pk_0 to one of its neighbors, u_1. We will follow c_1 on its random walk through T nodes.
- At step $i \in [T-1]$, c_i was just sent to u_i from u_{i-1} and is encrypted under the product $k_{i-1} = pk_0 \circledast pk_1 \circledast \cdots \circledast pk_{i-1}$, also sent to u_i. u_i computes the new public key $pk_0 \circledast \cdots \circledast pk_i = k_i$, adding its own public key to the product, encrypts b_i under k_i, and re-encrypts c_i under k_i via AddLayer. Then, using the homomorphic OR, u_i computes c_{i+1} encrypted under k_i. u_i sends c_{i+1} and k_i to $u_{i+1} = \pi_i^{(u_i)}(u_{i-1})$.
- At step T, node u_T receives c_T, which is the encryption of $b_0 \vee b_1 \vee \cdots b_{T-1}$ under key $pk_0 \circledast \cdots \circledast pk_{T-1} = k_{T-1}$. u_T encrypts and then OR's his own bit to get ciphertext $e_T = \mathsf{HomOR}(c_T, [b_T]_{k_{T-1}})$. u_T sends e_T back to u_{T-1}.
- Now, on its way back in the decrypt phase, for each step $i \in [T-1]$, u_i has just received e_i from node u_{i+1} encrypted under $pk_1 \circledast \cdots \circledast pk_i = k_i$. u_i deletes the key layer pk_i to get k_{i-1} and then using DelLayer, removes that key from encrypting e_i to get e_{i-1}. u_i sends e_{i-1} and k_{i-1} to $u_{i-1} = (\pi_i^{(u_i)})^{-1}(u_{i+1})$.
- Finally, node u_0 receives e_0 encrypted only under public key pk_0 on step 1. u_0 deletes that layer pk_0, revealing $e_0 = b_0 \vee \cdots \vee b_T$.

Now notice that each of these "messages" sent from every node to every neighbor takes a random walk on the graph when viewed on their own (these are correlated random walks when viewed as a whole, but independently, they can be analyzed as random walks). Let $\mathcal{W}_u$ represent some walk of the message starting at node u—even though u starts $\deg(u)$ different walks, we will only consider one walk per node.

By Corollary 5, for each $\mathcal{W}_u$, their set of traversed nodes covers the graph with probability $1 - \frac{1}{2^\tau}$ where $\tau = T/(8n^3)$. A union bound yields

$$\Pr[\exists u \in V, \mathcal{W}_u \neq V] \leq \sum_{u \in V} \Pr[\mathcal{W}_u \neq V] \leq n \cdot \frac{1}{2^n} \leq \frac{n}{2^\tau}.$$

This means that all walks cover the graph with at least the following probability

$$\Pr[\forall u \in V, \mathcal{W}_u = V] \geq 1 - \frac{n}{2^\tau},$$

and every walk will traverse the entire graph with all but negligible probability in our parameter τ. □

3.2 Proof of Soundness

We now turn to analyzing the security of our protocol, with respect to the topology-hiding security from Definition 2.

Theorem 7. *If the underlying encryption OR-homomorhpic PKCR scheme is CPA-secure, then Protocol 1 realizes the functionality of $\mathcal{F}_{\mathsf{Broadcast}}$ in a topology-hiding way against a statically corrupting, semi-honest adversary.*

Proof. First, we will describe an ideal-world simulator $\mathcal{S}$: $\mathcal{S}$ lives in a world where all honest parties are dummy parties and has no information on the topology of the graph other than what a potential adversary knows. More formally, $\mathcal{S}$ works as follows

1. Let $\mathcal{Q}$ be the set of parties corrupted by $\mathcal{A}$. $\mathcal{A}$ is a static adversary, so $\mathcal{Q}$ and the inputs of parties in $\mathcal{Q}$ must be fixed by the start of the protocol.
2. $\mathcal{S}$ sends the input for all parties in $\mathcal{Q}$ to the broadcast function $\mathcal{F}_{broadcast}$. $\mathcal{F}_{broadcast}$ outputs bit b_{out} and sends it to $\mathcal{S}$. Note $\mathcal{S}$ only requires knowledge of $\mathcal{Q}$'s inputs and the output of $\mathcal{F}_{\text{Broadcast}}$.
3. $\mathcal{S}$ gets the local neighborhood for each $P \in \mathcal{Q}$: $\mathcal{S}$ knows how many neighbors each P has and if that neighbor is also in $\mathcal{Q}$, but doesn't need to know anything else about the topology[4].
4. Consider every party $P \in \mathcal{Q}$ such $\mathcal{N}(P) \not\subset \mathcal{Q}$. $\mathcal{S}$ will need to simulate these neighbors not in $\mathcal{Q}$.
   - **Simulating messages from honest parties in Aggregate phase.** For every $Q \in \mathcal{N}(P)$ and $Q \notin \mathcal{Q}$, $\mathcal{S}$ simulates Q as follows. At the start of the algorithm, $\mathcal{S}$ creates T key pairs:

$$(pk^{(1)}_{Q\to P}, sk^{(1)}_{Q\to P}), \cdots, (pk^{(T)}_{Q\to P}, sk^{(T)}_{Q\to P}) \leftarrow \mathsf{Gen}(1^\kappa)$$

     At step $t = i$ in the for loop on line 8, $\mathcal{S}$ simulates Q sending a message to P by sending $([0]_{pk^{(i)}_{Q\to P}}, pk^{(i)}_{Q\to P})$. $\mathcal{S}$ receives the pair $(c^{(i)}_{P\to Q}, k^{(i)}_{P\to Q})$ from P at this step.
   - **Simulating messages from honest parties in the Decrypt phase.** Again, for every $P \in \mathcal{Q}$, $Q \in \mathcal{N}(P)$ and $Q \notin \mathcal{Q}$, $\mathcal{S}$ simulates Q. At $t = i$ in the for loop on line 21, $\mathcal{S}$ sends $[b_{out}]_{k^{(i)}_{Q\to P}}$ to P. $\mathcal{S}$ receives $e^{(i)}_{P\to Q}$ from P.

We will prove that any PPT adversary cannot distinguish whether he is interacting with the simulator $\mathcal{S}$ or with the real network except with negligible probability.

1. Hybrid 1. $\mathcal{S}$ simulates the real world exactly and has information on the entire topology of the graph, each party's input, and can simulate each random walk identically to how the walk would take place in the real world (Fig. 4, top).
2. Hybrid 2. $\mathcal{S}$ replaces the real keys with simulated public keys, but still knows everything about the graph (as in Hybrid 1). Formally, for every honest Q that is a neighbor to $P \in \mathcal{Q}$, $\mathcal{S}$ generates

$$(pk^{(1)}_{Q\to P}, sk^{(1)}_{Q\to P}), \cdots, (pk^{(T)}_{Q\to P}, sk^{(T)}_{Q\to P}) \leftarrow \mathsf{Gen}(1^\kappa)$$

   and instead of adding a layer to the encrypted $[b]_{pk^*}$ that P has at step t, as done in line 12 and 13, $\mathcal{S}$ computes $b' \leftarrow b_Q \vee b$ and sends $[b']_{pk^{(t)}_{Q\to P}}$ to P during the aggregate phase; it is the same message encrypted in Hybrid 1, but it is now encrypted under an unlayered, fresh public key. In the decrypt phase, each honest Q neighbor to P will get back the bit we get from the sequence of OR's encrypted under that new public key as well; the way all nodes in $\mathcal{Q}$ peel off layers of keys guarantees this.
3. Hybrid 3. $\mathcal{S}$ now simulates the ideal functionality during the aggregate phase, sending encryptions of 0. Formally, during the aggregate phase, every honest Q that is

[4] Recall that from Definition 2, $\mathcal{F}_{\text{graphInfo}}$ reveals if nodes in $\mathcal{Q}$ have neighbors in common, however all $\mathcal{S}$ needs to know is which neighbors are also in $\mathcal{Q}$; $\mathcal{S}$ does not use all of the available graph information (in the full version of the paper, we describe a stronger definition capturing this quality).

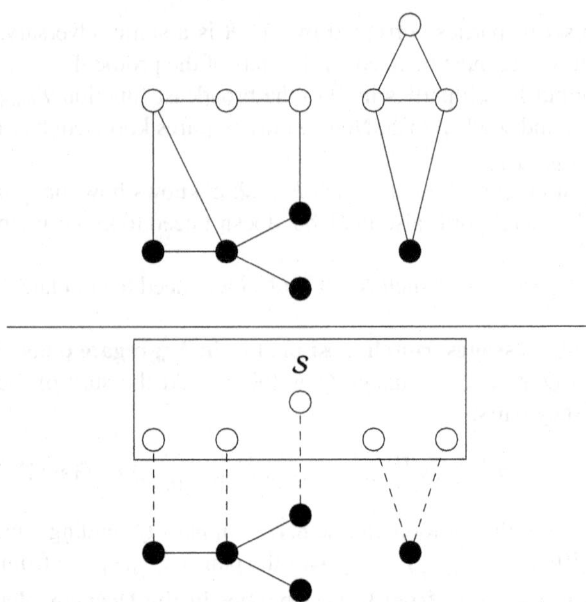

Fig. 4. An example of how the simulator works. The top shows how the graph normally looks. The bottom shows the graph topology that the simulator generates. Black nodes are nodes in Q. Notice that the simulator doesn't require knowing if nodes in Q have a common neighbor—neighbors can identify themselves with pseudonyms or edge-labels.

a neighbor to $P \in Q$ $\mathcal{S}$ sends $[0]_{pk^{(t)}_{Q\to P}}$ to P instead of sending $[b']_{pk^{(t)}_{Q\to P}}$. Nothing changes during the decrypt phase; the simulator still sends the resulting bit from each walk back and is not yet simulating the ideal functionality.

4. Hybrid 4. $\mathcal{S}$ finally simulates the ideal functionality at the during the decrypt phase, sending encryptions of b_{out}, the output of $\mathcal{F}_{\text{Broadcast}}$, under the simulated public keys. This is instead of simulating random walks through the graph and ORing only specific bits together. Notice that this hybrid is equivalent to our original description of $\mathcal{S}$ and requires no knowledge of other parties' values or of the graph topology other than local information about Q (as specified by the $\mathcal{F}_{\text{graphInfo}}$ functionality).

Now, let's say we have an adversary $\mathcal{A}$ that can distinguish between the real world and the simulator. This means $\mathcal{A}$ can distinguish between Hybrids 1 and 4. So, $\mathcal{A}$ can distinguish, with non-negligible probability, between two consecutive hybrids. We will argue that given the security of our public key scheme and the high probability of success of the algorithm, that this should be impossible.

1. First, we claim no adversary can distinguish between Hybrid 1 and 2. The difference between these Hybrids is distinguishing between AddLayer and computing a fresh encryption key. In Hybrid 1, we compute a public key sequence, multiplying public key k by a freshly generated public key. In Hybrid 2, we just use a fresh public key. Recall that the public keys in our scheme form a group. Since the key sequence

$k \circledast pk_{new}$ has a new public key that has not been included anywhere else in the transcript, $k \circledast pk_{new}$ can be thought of as choosing a new public key independently at random from k. This is the same distribution as just choosing a new public key: $\{k \circledast pk_{new}\} \equiv \{pk_{new}\}$. Therefore, any tuple of multiplied keys and fresh keys are indistinguishable from each other. So, no adversary $\mathcal{A}$ can distinguish between Hybrids 1 and 2.

2. Now we will show that no PPT adversary can distinguish between Hybrids 2 and 3. The only difference between these two hybrids is that $\mathcal{A}$ sees encryptions of the broadcast bit as it is being transmitted as opposed to seeing only encryptions of 0 from the simulator. Note that the simulator chooses a key independent of any key chosen by parties in Q in each of the aggregate rounds, and so the bit is encrypted under a key that $\mathcal{A}$ does not know. This means that if $\mathcal{A}$ can distinguish between these two hybrids, then $\mathcal{A}$ can break semantic security of the scheme, distinguishing between encryptions of 0 and 1.
3. For this last case, we will show that there should not exist a PPT adversary $\mathcal{A}$ that can distinguish between Hybrids 3 and 4.
   There are two differences between Hybrids 3 and 4. The first is that, during the decrypt phase, we send $b_{out} = \bigvee_{i \in [n]} b_i$, the OR of all of the node's bits, instead of $b_{\mathcal{W}} = \bigvee_{u \in \mathcal{W}} b_u$, the OR of all node's bits in a specific length-T walk.
   Corollary 5 tells us that a walk $\mathcal{W}$ taken during the course of the algorithm covers the graph with probability $1 - 1/2^\tau$. There are two walks starting at each edge in the graph, which is at most $2n^2$ walks. So, the probability that $b_{out} \neq b_{\mathcal{W}}$ at most $2n^2/2^\tau$, which is negligible in τ, and therefore is undetectable.
   The second difference is that our simulated encryption of b_{out} is generated by making a fresh encryption of b_{out}. But, if $b_{out} = b_{\mathcal{W}}$ (which it will with overwhelming probability), by the claim in Sect. 2.5, the encryption generated by ORing many times in the graph is computationally indistinguishable to a fresh encryption of b_{out}. Therefore, computationally, it is impossible to distinguish between Hybrids 3 and 4. □

3.3 Proof of Main Theorem

In this section, we put the pieces together: we formally state and prove Theorem 1 using Protocol 1.

Theorem 8 (Topology-hiding broadcast for all network topologies). *If there exists an OR-homomorphic PKCR, then for any network topology graph G on n nodes, there exists a polynomial-time protocol* Π *that is a topology-hiding realization of broadcast functionality* $\mathcal{F}_{broadcast}$.

Proof. Will will show that Protocol 1 is the topology-hiding realization of $\mathcal{F}_{broadcast}$. Since we assume existence of an OR-homomorphic PKCR, we are able to run our protocol. The rest of this proof is simply combining the results of Theorems 6 and 7. Now, for a security parameter κ, we let $\tau = \kappa + \log(n)$.

To show Protocol 1 is complete, Theorem 6 states that for our parameter τ, Protocol 1 outputs the correct bit for every node with probability at least $1 - n/2^\tau = 1 - 1/2^\kappa$.

This means, our protocol is correct with overwhelming probability with respect to the security parameter κ.

To show our protocol is sound, Theorem 7 states that for our input parameter τ, an adversary can distinguish a simulated transcript from a real transcript with probability negligible in τ. Since τ is strictly greater than κ, our protocol is secure with respect to κ as well. Therefore, Protocol 1 is sound against all PPT adversaries: they have only a negligible chance with respect to κ of distinguishing the simulation versus a real instantiation of the protocol. □

Corollary 9. *Under the DDH assumption, there exists polynomial-time executable, topology-hiding broadcast for any graph G.*

Proof. ElGamal, which is secure under the DDH assumption, is an OR-homomorphic PKCR by Sect. 2.5. So, applying Theorem 8, we get that there exists a protocol which is a topology-hiding realization of $\mathcal{F}_{broadcast}$. □

Because we now have topology-hiding broadcast on any graph, we can use the existence of secure MPC for all efficiently computable functionalities $\mathcal{F}$, we get topology-hiding MPC for all efficiently computable $\mathcal{F}$ (assuming we have an OR-homomorphic PKCR, or DDH).

4 Complexity and Optimizations

In this section we give an upper bound on the communication complexity of Protocol 1 and discuss optimizations for graph families where tighter cover time bounds are known.

In the following n, m are upper bounds on the number of nodes and edges; B an upper bound on the cover time; and τ an input parameter controlling the probability of incorrect output to be at most $n/2^\tau$. We point out that while in Protocol 1 we set the number of rounds to be $T = 2\tau B$ for $B = 4n^3$; our completeness and soundness proofs hold for every upper bound B on the cover time.

4.1 Communication Complexity

We show that the communication complexity is $\Theta(B\tau m)$ group elements, where B is an upper bound on the cover time of the graph (for our protocol on general graphs, we have $B = 4n^3$). We measure the communication complexity in terms of the overall number of group elements transmitted throughout the protocol (where the group elements are for the ciphertext and public-key pairs of the underlying DDH-based encryption scheme, and their size is polynomial in the security parameter).

Claim (Communication complexity). The communication complexity of Protocol 1 with $T = 2\tau B$ is $\Theta(B\tau m)$ group elements.

Proof. The random-walks in Protocol 1 are of length $T = 2B\tau$, yielding $2T$ total rounds of communication including both the forward and backwards phases. At each round, every node v sends out $\deg(v)$ messages. Summing over all $v \in V$, all of the nodes communicate $2m$ messages every round – one for each direction of each edge (for m denoting the number of edges in the network graph). By the end of the protocol, the total communication is $4Tm = \Theta(B\tau m)$. □

We conclude the communication complexity of Protocol 1 on input n, τ is $\Theta(\tau n^5)$ group elements.

Corollary 10. *On input n, τ, the communication complexity of Protocol 1 is $\Theta(\tau n^5)$ group elements.*

Proof. For a graph with at most n nodes, $B = 4n^3$ is an upper bound on the cover time (see Theorem 4), and $m = n^2$ is an upper bound on the number of edges. Assigning those B, m in the bound from Sect. 4.1, the proof follows: $\Theta(B\tau m) = \Theta(\tau \cdot n^3 \cdot n^2) = \Theta(\tau n^5)$. □

4.2 Better Bounds on Cover Time for Some Graphs

Now that we have seen how the cover time bound B controls both the communication and the round complexity, we will look at how to get a better bound than $O(n^3)$.

Cover time has been studied for various kinds of graphs, and so if we leak the kind of graph we are in (e.g. expanders), then we can use a better upper bound on the cover time, shown in Fig. 5.

For example on expander graphs (arising for example in natural applications on random regular graphs), it is known that the cover times $C_G = O(n \log n)$, much less than $O(n^3)$ [6]. This means that for expanders, we can run in $C_G = O(n \log n)$ round complexity, and $O(C_G \tau m) = O(\tau m n \log n)$ communication complexity. Even assigning the worst case bound $m \leq n^2$, we get round and communication complexity $O(n \log n)$ and $O(\tau n^3 \log n)$ respectively—much better than the general case that has $O(\tau n^5)$ communication complexity.

Type of Graph	Cover time
Arbitrary graph [21]	$O(n^3)$
Expanders [6]	$O(n \log n)$
Regular Graphs [18]	$O(n^2)$

Fig. 5. Cover times for specific graphs.

5 Conclusion and Future Work

This work showed that topology-hiding computation is feasible for *every* network topology (in the computational setting, assuming DDH), using random walks. This resolution completes a line of works on the feasibility of topology hiding computation against a static semi-honest adversary [1,16,21]. Yet, it leaves open the feasibility question against a malicious or adaptive adversary. Another intriguing question is whether our random walks could be derandomized, perhaps using *universal-traversal* [2,19] that is a deterministic walk guaranteed to cover all d-regular n-nodes graph, with explicit constructions known under some restrictions such as consistent labeling [17].

References

1. Akavia, A., Moran, T.: Topology hiding computation beyond logarithmic diametere. In: Eurocrypt (2017, to appear)
2. Aleliunas, R., Karp, R.M., Lipton, R.J., Lovász, L., Rackoff, C.: Random walks, universal traversal sequences, and the complexity of maze problems. In: 20th Annual Symposium on Foundations of Computer Science, San Juan, Puerto Rico, 29–31 October 1979, pp. 218–223 (1979)
3. Balogh, J., Bollobás, B., Krivelevich, M., Müller, T., Walters, M.: Hamilton cycles in random geometric graphs. Ann. Appl. Probab. **21**(3), 1053–1072 (2011)
4. Beimel, A., Gabizon, A., Ishai, Y., Kushilevitz, E., Meldgaard, S., Paskin-Cherniavsky, A.: Non-interactive secure multiparty computation. In: Garay, J.A., Gennaro, R. (eds.) CRYPTO 2014. LNCS, vol. 8617, pp. 387–404. Springer, Heidelberg (2014). doi:10.1007/978-3-662-44381-1_22
5. Canetti, R.: Universally composable security: a new paradigm for cryptographic protocols. In: FOCS, pp. 136–145. IEEE Computer Society (2001)
6. Chandra, A.K., Raghavan, P., Ruzzo, W.L., Smolensky, R.: The electrical resistance of a graph captures its commute and cover times. In: Proceedings of the Twenty-First Annual ACM Symposium on Theory of Computing, STOC 1989, pp. 574–586. ACM, New York (1989)
7. Chandran, N., Chongchitmate, W., Garay, J.A., Goldwasser, S., Ostrovsky, R., Zikas, V.: The hidden graph model: communication locality and optimal resiliency with adaptive faults. In: Proceedings of the 2015 Conference on Innovations in Theoretical Computer Science, ITCS 2015, pp. 153–162. ACM, New York (2015)
8. Estrin, D., Govindan, R., Heidemann, J., Kumar, S.: Next century challenges: scalable coordination in sensor networks. In: Proceedings of the 5th Annual ACM/IEEE International Conference on Mobile Computing and Networking, pp. 263–270. ACM (1999)
9. Friedrich, T., Sauerwald, T., Stauffer, A.: Diameter and broadcast time of random geometric graphs in arbitrary dimensions. Algorithmica **67**(1), 65–88 (2013)
10. Goldreich, O.: Foundations of Cryptography: Basic Applications, vol. 2. Cambridge University Press, New York (2004)
11. Goldreich, O., Micali, S., Wigderson, A.: How to play any mental game. In: Proceedings of the Nineteenth Annual ACM Symposium on Theory of Computing, STOC 1987, pp. 218–229. ACM, New York (1987)
12. Goldwasser, S., et al.: Multi-input functional encryption. In: Nguyen, P.Q., Oswald, E. (eds.) EUROCRYPT 2014. LNCS, vol. 8441, pp. 578–602. Springer, Heidelberg (2014). doi:10.1007/978-3-642-55220-5_32
13. Halevi, S., Ishai, Y., Jain, A., Kushilevitz, E., Rabin, T.: Secure multiparty computation with general interaction patterns. In: Proceedings of the 2016 ACM Conference on Innovations in Theoretical Computer Science, ITCS 2016, pp. 157–168. ACM, New York (2016)
14. Halevi, S., Lindell, Y., Pinkas, B.: Secure computation on the web: computing without simultaneous interaction. In: Rogaway, P. (ed.) CRYPTO 2011. LNCS, vol. 6841, pp. 132–150. Springer, Heidelberg (2011). doi:10.1007/978-3-642-22792-9_8
15. Hinkelmann, M., Jakoby, A.: Communications in unknown networks: preserving the secret of topology. Theor. Comput. Sci. **384**(2–3), 184–200 (2007). Structural Information and Communication Complexity (SIROCCO 2005)

16. Hirt, M., Maurer, U., Tschudi, D., Zikas, V.: Network-hiding communication and applications to multi-party protocols. In: Robshaw, M., Katz, J. (eds.) CRYPTO 2016. LNCS, vol. 9815, pp. 335–365. Springer, Heidelberg (2016). doi:10.1007/978-3-662-53008-5_12
17. Hoory, S., Wigderson, A.: Universal traversal sequences for expander graphs. Inf. Process. Lett. **46**(2), 67–69 (1993)
18. Kahn, J.D., Linial, N., Nisan, N., Saks, M.E.: On the cover time of random walks on graphs. J. Theor. Probab. **2**(1), 121–128 (1989)
19. Lovász, L.: Random walks on graphs: a survey. In: Miklós, D., Sós, V.T., Szőnyi, T. (eds.) Combinatorics, Paul Erdős is Eighty, vol. 2, pp. 353–398. János Bolyai Mathematical Society, Budapest (1996)
20. Mitzenmacher, M., Upfal, E.: Probability and Computing - Randomized Algorithms and Probabilistic Analysis. Cambridge University Press, Cambridge (2005)
21. Moran, T., Orlov, I., Richelson, S.: Topology-hiding computation. In: Dodis, Y., Nielsen, J.B. (eds.) TCC 2015. LNCS, vol. 9014, pp. 169–198. Springer, Heidelberg (2015). doi:10.1007/978-3-662-46494-6_8
22. Penrose, M.: Random Geometric Graphs. Oxford University Press, Oxford (2003). no. 5
23. Pottie, G.J., Kaiser, W.J.: Wireless integrated network sensors. Commun. ACM **43**(5), 51–58 (2000)
24. Yao, A.C.-C.: How to generate and exchange secrets. In: Proceedings of the 27th Annual Symposium on Foundations of Computer Science, SFCS 1986, pp. 162–167. IEEE Computer Society, Washington, D.C. (1986)

A New Approach to Round-Optimal Secure Multiparty Computation

Prabhanjan Ananth[1(✉)], Arka Rai Choudhuri[2], and Abhishek Jain[2]

[1] University of California, Los Angeles, USA
prabhanjan@cs.ucla.edu
[2] Johns Hopkins University, Baltimore, USA
{achoud,abhishek}@cs.jhu.edu

Abstract. We present a new approach towards constructing round-optimal secure multiparty computation (MPC) protocols against malicious adversaries without trusted setup assumptions. Our approach builds on ideas previously developed in the context of covert multiparty computation [Chandran et al., FOCS'07] even though we do not seek covert security. Using our new approach, we obtain the following results:

- A five round MPC protocol based on the Decisional Diffie-Hellman (DDH) assumption.
- A four round MPC protocol based on one-way permutations and sub-exponentially secure DDH. This result is *optimal* in the number of rounds.

Previously, no four-round MPC protocol for general functions was known and five-round protocols were only known based on indistinguishability obfuscation (and some additional assumptions) [Garg et al., EUROCRYPT'16].

1 Introduction

The notion of secure multiparty computation (MPC) [16,42] is fundamental in cryptography. Informally speaking, an MPC protocol allows mutually distrusting parties to jointly evaluate a function on their private inputs in such a manner that the protocol execution does not leak anything beyond the output of the function.

A fundamental measure of efficiency in MPC is round complexity, i.e., the number of rounds of communication between the parties. Protocols with smaller round complexity are more desirable so as to minimize the effect of network latency, which in turn decreases the time complexity of the protocol. Indeed, the round complexity of MPC has been extensively studied over the last three decades.

In this work, we study round-optimal MPC against malicious adversaries who may corrupt an arbitrary subset of parties, in the plain model without any trusted setup assumptions. We consider the traditional simultaneous message model for MPC, where in each round of the protocol, each party simultaneously broadcasts a message to the other parties.

J. Katz and H. Shacham (Eds.): CRYPTO 2017, Part I, LNCS 10401, pp. 468–499, 2017.
DOI: 10.1007/978-3-319-63688-7_16

A lower bound for this setting was established last year by Garg et al. [14] who proved that three rounds are insufficient for coin-tossing w.r.t. black-box simulation. (Their work builds on [26] who proved the necessity of five rounds for coin-tossing in the unidirectional message model.) In the positive direction, several constant-round MPC protocols were constructed in a long sequence of works, based on a variety of assumptions and techniques (see, e.g., [18,27,34,35,41]). Garg et al. [14] established an upper bound on the exact round complexity of MPC by constructing a *five* round protocol based on indistinguishability obfuscation [4,12] and some additional assumptions.[1] Their work constitutes the state of the art on this subject.

Our Goals. Presently, no constructions of indistinguishability obfuscation are known from standard assumptions. This motivates the following important question:

Does there exist a five round maliciously-secure MPC protocol for general functions based on standard polynomial-time assumptions?

Furthermore, given the gap between the lower bound (three rounds) and the upper bound (five rounds) established by [14], we ask whether their upper bound is tight:

Does there exist a four round maliciously-secure MPC protocol for general functions?

In this work, we resolve both of these questions in the affirmative.

The Main Barrier. We highlight the main conceptual barrier towards achieving our goals. Garg et al. [14] follow a natural two-step approach to obtain their positive results: in the first step, they construct a four round multiparty coin-tossing protocol. In the next step, they use their coin-tossing protocol to replace the common random string (CRS) in a two-round MPC protocol in the CRS model [11,31].

We note, however, that this approach, in general, cannot do better than five rounds. Indeed, since at least one of the rounds of the two-round MPC must depend upon the CRS, we can only hope to parallelize its first round with the coin-tossing protocol. Since coin-tossing requires four rounds, this only yields a five round protocol at best.

A New Approach. In this work, we present a new approach towards constructing round-optimal MPC protocols in the plain model. At a high level, our approach implements the classical GMW methodology [16] for constructing maliciously-secure MPC protocols, *with a crucial twist*, to minimize the number of rounds. This approach is inspired by the beautiful work of Chandran et al. [8] for constructing covert multiparty computation protocols [8,20,40].

[1] Garg et al. also construct a four-round protocol for the coin-tossing functionality. In this work, we are interested in MPC for general functions.

Recall that the GMW compiler transforms a semi-honest MPC protocol into a maliciously secure one by requiring the parties to prove (using zero-knowledge proofs [17]) that each message in the semi-honest protocol was computed "honestly." Towards our goal of minimizing round complexity, we cannot afford to prove honest behavior with every round of semi-honest MPC. Therefore, in our approach, the parties prove honest behavior only *once*.

At first, such an approach may sound completely absurd. If each party is only required to give a single proof of honest behavior, then a malicious adversary may choose to cheat in the first few rounds of the semi-honest MPC protocol. By the time the proof is completed and the honest parties are able to detect cheating, it may already be "too late." Indeed, the opportunity to cheat in even a single round may be sufficient for a malicious adversary to completely break the security of a semi-honest protocol. Therefore, it is not at all clear why such an approach can be implemented in a secure manner.

In order to tackle this problem, we design a "special-purpose" semi-honest MPC protocol that remains partially immune to malicious behavior before the last round of the protocol. Specifically, in such a protocol, an adversary can influence the protocol outcome but not learn any private information by behaving maliciously before the last round. We then "shield" the last round from being revealed to the adversary until it has proven honest behavior for all of the preceding rounds. A single proof suffices to accomplish this task. By parallelizing this proof with the semi-honest MPC, we are able to minimize the round complexity.

We note that the above idea of delaying the proof of honest behavior to the end of the computation was first developed in [8]. While they developed this technique to achieve covert security (namely, hiding protocol participation from other players), we use it in our setting to minimize round complexity.

1.1 Our Results

We present a new approach for constructing round-efficient MPC protocols that are secure against malicious adversaries in the plain model. Using this approach, we are able to achieve both of our aforementioned goals.

I. Robust Semi-honest MPC. As a first step towards obtaining our results for maliciously-secure MPC, we construct a four round *robust* semi-honest MPC protocol that remains partially immune to malicious behavior. In this protocol, at the end of the first three rounds of computation, each party receives a secret share of the function output. In the last round, the parties simply exchange their shares to reconstruct the output. The key security property of this protocol is that if the adversary cheats in the first three rounds, then it can only influence the function output, but not learn any private information.

We construct such an MPC scheme for general functions assuming the existence of low-depth pseudorandom generators (PRGs) and a two-round "covert" oblivious transfer (OT) protocol [40].[2] Both of these primitives can be instantiated from the Decisional Diffie-Hellman (DDH) assumption.

[2] We use low-depth PRGs to obtain degree-three randomizing polynomials for general functions [2].

Theorem 1. *Assuming DDH, there exists a four round robust semi-honest MPC protocol for general functions.*

The above result may be of independent interest.

II. Maliciously-secure MPC. Using Theorem 1, we next construct maliciously-secure MPC protocols in the plain model.

Our first result is a five round MPC protocol based on any four-round robust semi-honest MPC, injective one-way functions and collision-resistant hash functions (CRHFs). Since injective one-way functions and CRHFs can be built from Discrete Log, we obtain the following result:

Theorem 2 (Five Rounds). *Assuming DDH, there exists a five round maliciously-secure MPC protocol for computing general functions.*

We next modify our five round protocol to obtain a four round protocol, albeit using sub-exponential hardness. The security of our construction uses complexity leveraging between multiple primitives.

Theorem 3 (Four Rounds). *Assuming one-way permutations and sub-exponentially secure DDH, there exists a four round maliciously-secure MPC protocol for computing general functions.*

1.2 Our Techniques

As discussed earlier, the approach of Garg et al. [14] for constructing maliciously-secure MPC protocols is unsuitable for achieving our goals. Therefore, we develop a new approach for constructing round-efficient MPC against malicious adversaries.

At a high-level, our approach implements the GMW paradigm for constructing maliciously-secure MPC protocols, with a crucial twist. Recall that the GMW paradigm transforms a semi-honest MPC protocol into a maliciously secure one using the following three steps: (1) first, the parties commit to their inputs and random tapes. (2) Next, the parties perform coin-tossing to establish an unbiased random tape for each party. (3) Finally, the parties run the semi-honest MPC protocol where along with every message, each party also gives zero-knowledge proof of "honest" behavior consistent with the committed input and random tape.

Both steps (2) and (3) above introduce additional rounds of interaction, and constitute the main bottleneck towards constructing round-optimal MPC.

Main Ideas. Towards this, we develop two key modifications to the GMW compiler:

1. **"One-shot" proof**: Instead of requiring the parties to give a proof of honest behavior in each round of the underlying semi-honest protocol, we use a "delayed verification" technique where the parties prove honest behavior only *once*, towards the end of the protocol. As we explain below, this allows us to

limit the overhead of additional rounds introduced by zero-knowledge proofs in the GMW compiler.

The idea of delayed verification was previously developed in the work of Chandran et. al. [8]. Interestingly, while they used this technique to achieve security in the setting of covert computation [8,40], we use this technique to minimize the round complexity of our protocol.

2. **No coin tossing**: Second, we eliminate the coin-tossing step (i.e., step 2). Note that by removing coin-tossing, we implicitly allow the adversarial parties to potentially use "bad" randomness in the protocol. To ensure security in this scenario, we will use a special semi-honest MPC protocol that is secure against bad randomness. This idea has previously been used in many works (see, e.g., [3,31]).

We now elaborate on the first step, which constitutes the conceptual core of our work. We consider semi-honest MPC protocols with a specific structure consisting of two phases: (a) *Computation phase*: in the first phase of the protocol, the parties compute the function such that each party obtains a secret-share of the output. (b) *Output phase*: In the second phase, the parties exchange their output shares with each other to compute the final output. This phase consists of only one round and is deterministic. Note that standard MPC protocols such as [16] follow this structure.

At a high-level, we implement our delayed verification strategy as follows: the parties first run the computation phase of the semi-honest protocol "as is" without giving any proofs. At the end of this phase, each party gives a single proof that it behaved honestly throughout the computation phase (using the committed input and random tape). If all the proofs verify, then the parties execute the output phase.

Right away, one may notice a glaring problem in the above approach. If the computation phase is executed without any proof of honest behavior, the adversary may behave maliciously in this phase and potentially learn the honest party inputs even before the output phase begins! Indeed, standard semi-honest MPC protocols do not guarantee security in such a setting.

To combat this problem, we develop a special purpose semi-honest MPC protocol that remains "partially immune" to malicious behavior. Specifically, such a protocol maintains privacy against malicious adversaries *until the end of the computation phase*. However, output correctness is not guaranteed if the adversary behaved maliciously in the computation phase. We refer to such an MPC protocol as *robust* semi-honest MPC. Later, we describe a four-round construction of robust semi-honest MPC where the first three rounds correspond to the computation phase and the last round constitutes the output phase.

Note that the robustness property as described above perfectly suits our requirements because in our compiled protocol, the output phase is executed only after each party has proven that it behaved honestly during the computation phase. This ensures full security of our compiled protocol.

A New Template for Malicious MPC. Putting the above ideas together, we obtain the following new template for maliciously-secure MPC:

- First, each party commits to its input and randomness using both a three-round extractable commitment scheme[3], and a non-interactive commitment scheme. In parallel, the parties also execute the computation phase of a four-round robust semi-honest MPC.
- Next, each party proves to every other party that it behaved honestly during the first three rounds.
- Finally, the parties execute the output phase of the robust semi-honest MPC and once again prove that their message is honestly computed.

In order to obtain a five round protocol from this template, we need to parallelize the proofs with the other protocol messages. For this purpose, we use delayed-input proofs [29] where the instance is only required in the last round.[4] In particular, we use four-round delayed input zero-knowledge (ZK) proofs whose first three messages are executed in parallel with the first three rounds of the robust semi-honest MPC. This yields us a five round protocol.

We remark that during simulation, our simulator is able to extract the adversary's input only at the end of the third round. This means that we need to simulate the first three rounds of the robust semi-honest MPC without knowledge of the adversary's input (or the function output). Our robust semi-honest MPC satisfies this property; namely, the simulator for our robust semi-honest MPC needs the adversary's input and randomness (and the function output) only to simulate the output phase.

Four Rounds: Main Ideas. We next turn to the problem of constructing four-round MPC. At first, it is not clear how to obtain a four round protocol using the above template. Indeed, as argued earlier, we cannot afford to execute the output phase without verifying that the parties behaved honestly during the computation phase. In the above template, the output phase is executed *after* this verification is completed. Since three-round zero-knowledge proofs with polynomial-time simulation are not known presently, the verification process in the above protocol requires four rounds. Therefore, it may seem that that we are limited to a five round protocol.

Towards that, we note that our robust semi-honest MPC (described later) satisfies the following property: in order to simulate the view of the adversary (w.r.t. the correct output), the simulator only needs to "cheat" in the output phase (i.e., the last round). In particular, the simulation of the computation phase can be done "honestly" using random inputs for the honest parties. In this case, we do not need full-fledged ZK proofs to establish honest behavior in the computation phase; instead, we only need *strong* witness indistinguishable (WI) proofs. Recall that in a strong WI proof system, for any two indistinguishable instance distributions D_1 and D_2, a proof for $x_1 \leftarrow D_1$ using a witness w_1 is

[3] We use a variant of the extractable commitment scheme in [38] for this purpose. This variant has been used in many prior works such as [13,19,21] because it is "rewinding secure" – a property that is used in the security proofs.

[4] Note that the witness for these proofs corresponds to the adversary's input and random tape which is already fixed in the first round.

indistinguishable from a proof for $x_2 \leftarrow D_2$ using a witness w_2. This suffices for us because using strong WI, we can switch from an honest execution of the computation phase using the real inputs of the honest parties to another honest execution of the computation phase using random inputs for the honest parties.

Recently, Jain et al. [25] constructed three-round delayed-input strong WI proofs of knowledge from the DDH assumption. However, their proof system only guarantees strong WI property if the entire statement is chosen by the prover in the last round. In our case, this is unfortunately not true, and hence we cannot use their construction. Therefore, we take a different route, albeit at the cost of sub-exponential hardness assumptions. Specifically, we observe that by relying upon sub-exponential hardness, we can easily construct a three-round (delayed-input) strong WI argument by combining any three-round (delayed-input) WI proof of knowledge with a one or two-message "trapdoor phase" in our simultaneous message setting. For example, let f be a one-way permutation. The trapdoor phase can be implemented by having the verifier send $y = f(x)$ for a random x in parallel with the first prover message. The statement of the WI proof of knowledge is changed to: either the original statement is true or the prover knows x.

Now, by running in exponential time in the hybrids, we can break the one-way permutation to recover x and then prove knowledge of x. This allows us to switch from honest execution of the computation phase using the real inputs of the honest parties to another honest execution using random inputs. After this switch, we can go back to proving the honest statement which can be done in polynomial time. This ensures that our final simulator is also polynomial time.

Handling Non-malleability Issues. So far, we ignored non-malleability related issues in our discussion. However, as noted in many prior works, zero-knowledge proofs with standard soundness guarantee do not suffice in the setting of constant-round MPC. Indeed, since proofs are being executed in parallel, we need to ensure that an adversary's proofs remain sound even when the honest party's proofs are being simulated [39].

We handle such malleability issues by using the techniques developed in a large body of prior works. In our five round MPC protocol, we use a slight variant of the four-round non-malleable zero-knowledge (NMZK) argument of [9] to ensure that adversary's proofs remain sound even during simulation.[5] We make non-black-box use of their protocol in our security proof. More specifically, following prior works such as [5,13,19,21], we establish a "soundness lemma" to ensure that the adversary is behaving honestly across the hybrids. We use the extractability property of the non-malleable commitment used inside the non-malleable zero-knowledge argument to prove this property.

In our four round protocol, we use the above NMZK to prove honest behavior in the output phase. In order to prove honest behavior in the computation phase, we use a slightly modified version of the strong WI argument system described

[5] We also use the fact that argument system of [9] allows for simulating multiple proofs executed in parallel.

above which additionally uses either a three-round [22] or two-round [28] non-malleable commitment scheme with extractability to achieve the desired non-malleability properties. Unlike the five round construction, here, we rely upon complexity leveraging in several of the hybrids to argue the "soundness lemma" as well as to tackle some delicate rewinding-related issues that are commonplace in such proofs.[6] We refer the reader to the technical sections for details.

Robust Semi-honest MPC. We now briefly describe the high-level ideas in our four-round construction of robust semi-honest MPC for general functionalities. Towards this, we note that it suffices to achieve a simpler goal of constructing robust semi-honest MPC for a restricted class of functionalities, namely, for computing randomized encodings.[7] That is, in order to construct a robust MPC for a n-party functionality F, it suffices to construct a robust MPC for a n-functionality F_{rnd} that takes as input $(x_1, r_1; \cdots; x_n, r_n)$ and outputs a randomized encoding of $F(x_1, \ldots, x_n)$ using randomness $r_1 \oplus \cdots \oplus r_n$. This is because all the parties can jointly execute the protocol for F_{rnd} to obtain the randomized encoding. Each party can then individually execute the decoding algorithm of the randomized encoding to recover the output $F(x_1, \ldots, x_n)$. Note that this transformation preserves round complexity.

To construct a robust semi-honest n-party protocol for F_{rnd}, we consider a specific type of randomized encoding defined in [2]. In particular, they construct a degree 3 randomizing polynomials[8] for arbitrary functionalities based on low-depth pseudorandom generators. In their construction, every output bit of the encoding can be computed by a degree 3 polynomial on the input and the randomness. Hence, we further break down the goal of constructing a protocol for F_{rnd} into the following steps:

- Step 1: Construct a robust semi-honest MPC 3-party protocol for computing degree 3 terms. In particular, at the end of the protocol, every party who participated in the protocol get a secret share $x_1 x_2 x_3$, where x_q is the qth party's input for $q \in \{1, 2, 3\}$. The randomness for the secret sharing comes from the parties in the protocol.
- Step 2: Using Step 1, construct a robust semi-honest MPC protocol to compute degree 3 polynomials.
- Step 3: Using Step 2, construct a robust semi-honest MPC protocol for F_{rnd}.

Steps 2 and 3 can be achieved using standard transformations and these transformations are round preserving. Thus, it suffices to achieve Step 1 in four rounds.

---

6 We believe that some of the use of complexity leveraging in our hybrids can be avoided by modifications to our protocol. We leave further exploration of this direction for subsequent work.

7 A randomized encoding of function f and input x is such that, the output $f(x)$ can be recovered from this encoding and at the same time, this encoding should not leak any information about either f or x.

8 The terms randomized encodings and randomizing polynomials are interchangeably used.

Suppose P_1, P_2 and P_3 participate in the protocol. Roughly, the protocol proceeds as follows: P_1 and P_2 perform a two message covert OT protocol to receive a share of x_1x_2. Then, P_1 and P_3 perform a two message OT protocol to receive a share of $x_1x_2x_3$. We need to do more work to ensure that at the end, all of them have shares of $x_1x_2x_3$. Further, the robustness guarantee is argued using the covert security of the OT protocol. We refer the reader to the technical sections for more details.

1.3 Concurrent Work

In a concurrent and independent work, Brakerski et al. [7] construct a maliciously-secure 4-round MPC protocol based on the sub-exponential hardness of the Learning with Errors (LWE) problem and on the adaptive commitments of [33]. Their approach is very different from ours, most notably in the initial step, in that they construct and use a 3-round protocol against semi-malicious adversaries from LWE, while we construct and use a robust semi-honest MPC protocol from DDH.

1.4 Related Work

The study of constant-round protocols for MPC was initiated by Beaver et al. [6]. Their constructed constant-round MPC protocols in the presence of honest majority. Subsequently, a long sequence of works constructed constant-round MPC protocols against dishonest majority based on a variety of assumptions and techniques (see, e.g., [18,27,34,35,41]). Very recently, Garg et al. [14] constructed five round MPC using indistinguishability obfuscation and three-round parallel non-malleable commitments. They also construct a six-round MPC protocol using learning with errors (LWE) assumption and three-round parallel non-malleable commitments. All of these results are in the plain model where no trusted setup assumptions are available.

Asharov et al. [3] constructed three round MPC protocols in the CRS model. Subsequently, two-round MPC protocols in the CRS model were constructed by Garg et al. [11] using indistinguishability obfuscation, and by Mukherjee and Wichs [31] using LWE assumption.

1.5 Full Version

Due to space constraints, much of the details of the security proofs for our constructions are omitted from this manuscript. The full version of the paper is available at [1].

2 Definitions

We denote n to be the security parameter. Consider two distributions $\mathcal{D}_0$ and $\mathcal{D}_1$. We denote $\mathcal{D}_0 \approx_c \mathcal{D}_1$ if $\mathcal{D}_0$ and $\mathcal{D}_1$ are computationally indistinguishable.

2.1 Oblivious Transfer

We recall the notion of oblivious transfer [10,37] below. We require that the oblivious transfer protocol satisfies *covert security* [8,20,40]. Intuitively, we require that the receiver's messages are computationally indistinguishable from a uniform distribution to a malicious sender. Similarly, we require that the sender's messages are computationally indistinguishable from a uniform distribution to a malicious receiver.

Definition 1 (Covert Oblivious Transfer). *A 1-out-of-2 oblivious transfer (OT) protocol* OT *is a two party protocol between a sender and a receiver. A sender has two input bits* (b_0, b_1) *and the receiver has a choice bit* c. *At the end of the protocol, the receiver receives an output bit* b'. *We denote this process by* $b' \leftarrow \langle \mathsf{Sen}(b_0, b_1), \mathsf{Rec}(c) \rangle$.

We require that an OT protocol satisfies the following properties:

- **Correctness**: *For every* $b_0, b_1, c \in \{0,1\}$, *we have:*

$$\mathsf{Pr}[b_c \leftarrow \langle \mathsf{Sen}(b_0, b_1), \mathsf{Rec}(c) \rangle] = 1$$

- **Covert security against adversarial senders**: *For all PPT senders* Sen^*, *we require that the honest receiver's messages are computationally indistinguishable from uniform distribution.*
- **Covert security against adversarial receivers**: *Suppose the input of the sender* (b_0, b_1) *is sampled from a distribution on* $\{0,1\}^2$. *For all PPT receivers* Rec^*, *we require that the honest sender's messages (computed as a function of* (b_0, b_1)*) are computationally indistinguishable from uniform distribution.*

An oblivious transfer protocol satisfying the above definition was constructed in [40] using [32].

Theorem 4 [40]. *Assuming decisional Diffie Helman assumption, there exists a two message 1-out-of-2 covert oblivious transfer protocol.*

We note that for our constructions, it actually suffices if the OT protocol achieves indistinguishability security against malicious senders and receivers. (This property is satisfied by [32].) The covertness property helps to simplify the proof of our robust semi-honest MPC.

2.2 Randomizing Polynomials

We first recall the definition of randomizing polynomials [2,24]. Instead of considering the standard form of randomizing polynomials consisting of encode and decode algorithms, we instead consider a decomposable version where the circuit is first encoded as polynomials and decode algorithm gets as input evaluations of polynomials on input and randomness.

Definition 2 (Randomizing Polynomials). *A randomizing polynomials scheme* $\mathsf{RP} = (\mathsf{CktE}, \mathsf{D})$ *for a family of circuits* $\mathcal{C}$ *has the following syntax:*

- *Encoding,* $\mathsf{CktE}(C)$*: On input circuit* $C \in \mathcal{C}$*, input* x*, it outputs polynomials* $p_1, \ldots, p_m$*.*
- *Decoding,* $\mathsf{D}(p_1(x;r), \ldots, p_m(x;r))$*: On input evaluations of polynomials* $p_1(x;r), \ldots, p_m(x;r)$*, it outputs the decoded value* α*.*

RP *is required to satisfy the following properties:*

- Correctness*: For every security parameter* $n \in \mathbb{N}$*, circuit* C *and input* x*,* $C(x) = \mathsf{D}(p_1(x;r), \ldots, p_m(x;r))$*, where (i)* $(p_1, \ldots, p_m) \leftarrow \mathsf{CktE}(C)$*, (ii)* r *is randomness sampled from uniform distribution.*
- Efficiency*: The typical efficiency we require is that the degree of the polynomials* $\{p_i\}$ *should be significantly smaller than the degree of the circuit* C*, where* $(p_1, \ldots, p_m) \leftarrow \mathsf{CktE}(C)$*.*
- Security*: For every PPT adversary* $\mathcal{A}$*, for large enough security parameter* $n \in \mathbb{N}$*, circuit* C *and input* x*, there exists a simulator* Sim *such that:*

$$\{(p_1(x;r), \ldots, p_m(x;r))\} \approx_c \left\{\mathsf{Sim}(1^n, 1^{|C|}, C(x))\right\},$$

where (i) $(p_1, \ldots, p_m) \leftarrow \mathsf{CktE}(C)$*, (ii)* r *is randomness sampled from uniform distribution.*

We define the **degree** *of randomizing polynomials to be* $\max_{C \in \mathcal{C}}\{\deg(p_i) : (p_1, \ldots, p_m) \leftarrow \mathsf{CktE}(C \in \mathcal{C})\}$*.*

We have the following theorem from [2].

Theorem 5 [2]. *Assuming the existence of pseudorandom generators in* $\oplus\mathrm{L}/Poly$ *for all polynomial-time computable functions.*

2.3 Non-malleable Commitments

Let $\Pi = \langle C, R\rangle$ be a statistically binding commitment scheme. Consider MiM adversaries that are participating in one left and one right sessions in which k commitments take place. We compare between a MiM and a simulated execution. In the MiM execution, the adversary $\mathcal{A}$, with auxiliary information z, is participating in one left and one right sessions. In the left session, the MiM adversary interacts with C receiving commitments to value m using identities $\mathtt{id}$ of its choice. In the right session $\mathcal{A}$ interacts with R, attempting to commit to a related value $\tilde{m}$ again using identities $\tilde{\mathtt{id}}$ of its choice. If any the right commitment is invalid, or undefined, its value is set to $\perp$. If $\tilde{\mathtt{id}} = \mathtt{id}$, set $\tilde{m} = \perp$ (i.e., any commitment where the adversary uses the same identity as that of honest senders is considered invalid). Let $\mathsf{mim}_{\Pi}^{\mathcal{A},m}(z)$ denote the random variable that describes the values $\tilde{m}$ and the view of $\mathcal{A}$, in the above experiment.

In the simulated execution, an efficient simulator Sim directly interacts with R. Let $\mathsf{sim}_{\Pi}^{\mathsf{Sim}}(1^n, z)$ denote the random variable describing the value $\tilde{m}$ committed by Sim, and the output view of Sim; whenever the view contains the same identity as that identity of the left session, $\tilde{m}$ is set to $\perp$.

Definition 3 (non-malleable commitment scheme). *A commitment scheme is non-malleable with respect to commitment if, for every* PPT *parallel MiM adversary* $\mathcal{A}$*, there exists a* PPT *simulator* Sim *such that for all* m *the following ensembles are computationally indistinguishable:*

$$\{\mathsf{mim}_{\Pi}^{\mathcal{A},m}(z)\}_{n\in\mathbb{N},z\in\{0,1\}^*} \approx \{\mathsf{sim}_{\Pi}^{\mathsf{Sim}}(1^n,z)\}_{n\in\mathbb{N},z\in\{0,1\}^*}$$

For our construction, we will require that the non-malleable commitments are public coin and extractable. Four round non-malleable commitments based on CRHFs satisfying both the conditions are described in [23]. Similarly, three round non-malleable commitments based on quasi-polynomial injective OWFs satisfying both conditions are described in [22]. Two round (private coin) non-malleable commitments, with respect to commitment, are based on sub-exponential hardness of DDH [28]. Additionally, two round non-interactive concurrent non-malleable commitments can be based on time-lock puzzles [30].

Binding Property of the Commitments. For convenience, we assume that the first message sent by the committer in the four round non-malleable commitment scheme is statistically binding. Thus, the second message in the scheme is statistically binding. The non-malleable commitment scheme in [9] satisfies this property. But importantly, with minor modifications our proofs go through even without this assumption.

2.4 Delayed-Input Non-malleable Zero Knowledge

Let $\Pi_{\mathsf{nmzk}} = \langle P, V\rangle$ be a delayed-input interactive argument system for an NP-language L with witness relation Rel_L. Consider a PPT MiM adversary $\mathcal{A}$ that is simultaneously participating in one left session and one right session. Before the execution starts, both P, V and $\mathcal{A}$ receive as a common input the security parameter n, and $\mathcal{A}$ receives as auxiliary input $z \in \{0,1\}^*$.

In the left session $\mathcal{A}$ interacts with P using identity $\mathtt{id}$ of his choice. In the right session, $\mathcal{A}$ interacts with V, using identity $\widetilde{\mathtt{id}}$ of his choice.

In the left session, before the last round of the protocol, P gets the statement x. Also, in the right session $\mathcal{A}$, during the last round of the protocol selects the statement $\tilde{x}$ to be proved and sends it to V. Let $\mathsf{View}^{\mathcal{A}}(1^n, z)$ denote a random variable that describes the view of $\mathcal{A}$ in the above experiment.

Definition 4 (Delayed-input NMZK). *A delayed-input argument system* $\Pi_{\mathsf{nmzk}} = \langle P, V\rangle$ *for* NP*-language* L *with witness relation* $\mathsf{Rel_L}$ *is Non-Malleable Zero Knowledge (NMZK) if for any MiM adversary* $\mathcal{A}$ *that participates in one left session and one right session, there exists a* PPT *machine* $\mathsf{Sim}(1^n, z)$ *such that*

1. *The probability ensembles* $\{\mathsf{Sim}^1(1^n, z)\}_{n\in\mathbb{N},z\in\{0,1\}^*}$ *and* $\{\mathsf{View}^{\mathcal{A}}(1^n, z)\}_{\lambda\in\mathbb{N},z\in\{0,1\}^*}$ *are computationally indistinguishable over* n*, where* $\mathsf{Sim}^1(1^n, z)$ *denotes the first output of* $\mathsf{Sim}(1^n, z)$.

2. *Let* $z \in \{0,1\}^*$ *and let* $(\mathsf{View}, \tilde{w})$ *denote the output of* $\mathsf{Sim}(1^n, z)$. *Let* $\tilde{x}$ *be the right-session statement appearing in* View *and let* $\mathtt{id}$ *and* $\tilde{\mathtt{id}}$ *be the identities of the left and right sessions appearing in* View. *If the right session is accepting and* $\mathtt{id} \neq \tilde{\mathtt{id}}$, *then* $\mathsf{Rel}_{\mathsf{L}}(\tilde{x}, \tilde{w}) = 1$.

The above definition, is easily extended to parallel NMZK, where the adversary interacts with a polynomially bounded sessions on the left and right in parallel.

For our constructions, we shall use a slight variant of the 4-round NMZK protocol in [9]. The protocol is secure assuming CRFHs, and can thus be instantiated from DDH, and we refer the reader to their paper for a description of the protocol. In their protocol, in the honest setting, the internal WI proof system proves that the non-malleable commitment contains the witness to the NMZK language[9], or that it knows the trapdoor. Instead in our variant, we modify the internal proof system to prove that either the NMZK instance is true or the non-malleable commitment contains the trapdoor. We give a detailed discussion in the full version of our paper. Additionally, we note that their protocol is also parallel ZK since we can extract trapdoors of multiple executions in parallel.

2.5 Extractable Commitment Scheme

We will also use a simple challenge-response based extractable statistically-binding string commitment scheme $\langle C, R\rangle$ that has been used in several prior works, most notably [36,38]. We note that in contrast to [36] where a multi-slot protocol was used, here (similar to [38]), we only need a one-slot protocol.

Protocol $\langle C, R\rangle$. Let $\mathsf{com}(\cdot)$ denote the commitment function of a non-interactive perfectly binding string commitment scheme which requires the assumption of injective one-way functions for its construction. Let n denote the security parameter. The commitment scheme $\langle C, R\rangle$ is described as follows.

COMMIT PHASE:

1. To commit to a string $\mathtt{str}$, C chooses $k = \omega(\log(n))$ independent random pairs $\{\alpha_i^0, \alpha_i^1\}_{i=1}^k$ of strings such that $\forall i \in [k]$, $\alpha_i^0 \oplus \alpha_i^1 = \mathtt{str}$; and commits to all of them to R using com. Let $B \leftarrow \mathsf{com}(\mathtt{str})$, and $A_i^0 \leftarrow \mathsf{com}(\alpha_i^0)$, $A_i^1 \leftarrow \mathsf{com}(\alpha_i^1)$ for every $i \in [k]$.
2. R sends k uniformly random bits $v_1, \ldots, v_n$.
3. For every $i \in [k]$, if $v_i = 0$, C opens A_i^0, otherwise it opens A_i^1 to R by sending the appropriate decommitment information.

OPEN PHASE: C opens all the commitments by sending the decommitment information for each one of them.

For our construction, we require a modified extractor for the extractable commitment scheme. The standard extractor returns the value $\mathtt{str}$ that was

[9] It actually proves that the non-malleable commitment contains the masked witness, where the mask is sent separately. But we ignore this technicality for the discussion.

committed to in the scheme. Instead, we require that the extractor return i, and the openings of A_i^0 and A_i^1. This extractor can be constructed easily, akin to the standard extractor for the extractable commitment scheme.

This completes the description of $\langle C, R \rangle$.

"Rewinding secure" Commitment Scheme. Due to technical reasons, we will also use a minor variant, denoted $\langle C', R' \rangle$, of the above commitment scheme which will be rewinding secure. Protocol $\langle C', R' \rangle$ is the same as $\langle C, R \rangle$, except that for a given receiver challenge string, the committer does not "open" the commitments, but instead simply reveals the appropriate committed values (without revealing the randomness used to create the corresponding commitments). More specifically, in protocol $\langle C', R' \rangle$, on receiving a challenge string $v_1, \ldots, v_n$ from the receiver, the committer uses the following strategy: for every $i \in [k]$, if $v_i = 0$, C' sends α_i^0, otherwise it sends α_i^1 to R'. Note that C' does not reveal the decommitment values associated with the revealed shares.

The scheme is rewinding secure because we can respond to queries from the adversary (for the commitment scheme) when we need to rewind it, and the commitment scheme is exposed to an external challenger. This follows from the fact that we can send random messages in the third round when the adversary makes a different second round query.

When we use $\langle C', R' \rangle$ in our main construction, we will require the committer C' to prove the "correctness" of the values (i.e., the secret shares) it reveals in the last step of the commitment protocol. In fact, due to technical reasons, we will also require the committer to prove that the commitments that it sent in the first step are "well-formed". Below we formalize both these properties in the form of a *validity* condition for the commit phase.

Proving Validity of the Commit Phase. We say that commit phase between C' and R' is *well formed* with respect to a value $\hat{\mathtt{str}}$ if there exist values $\{\hat{\alpha}_i^0, \hat{\alpha}_i^1\}_{i=1}^k$ such that:

1. For all $i \in [k]$, $\hat{\alpha}_i^0 \oplus \hat{\alpha}_i^1 = \hat{\mathtt{str}}$, and
2. Commitments B, $\{A_i^0, A_i^1\}_{i=1}^k$ can be decommitted to $\hat{\mathtt{str}}$, $\{\hat{\alpha}_i^0, \hat{\alpha}_i^1\}_{i=1}^k$ respectively.
3. Let $\bar{\alpha}_1^{v_1}, \ldots, \bar{\alpha}_k^{v_k}$ denote the secret shares revealed by C in the commit phase. Then, for all $i \in [k]$, $\bar{\alpha}_i^{v_i} = \hat{\alpha}_i^{v_i}$.

We state a simple lemma below, that states that $\exists$ an extractor E that extracts the correct committed value with overwhelming probability if the commitment is well formed. This lemma is implicit from [36,38].

Lemma 1. *If the validity condition for the commitment protocol holds, then E fails to extract the committed value with only negligible probability.*

3 Robust Semi-honest MPC

We consider semi-honest secure multi-party computation protocols that satisfy an additional *robustness* property. Intuitively the property says that, except the final round, the messages of honest parties reveal no information about their inputs even if the adversarial parties behave *maliciously.*

Definition 5. *Let F be an n-party functionality. Let $\mathcal{A} = (\mathcal{A}^1, \mathcal{A}^2)$ represent a PPT algorithm controlling a set of parties $S \subseteq [n]$. For a t-round protocol computing F, we let $\mathsf{RealExec}^{\mathcal{A}^1}_{(t-1)}(\boldsymbol{x}, z)$ denote the view of $\mathcal{A}^1$ during the first $t-1$ rounds in the real execution of the protocol on input $\boldsymbol{x} = (x_1, \cdots, x_n)$ and auxiliary input z. We require that at the end of the first $t-1$ rounds in the real protocol, $\mathcal{A}^1$ outputs state and $(\mathsf{inp}, \mathsf{rand})$ on a special tape where either $(\mathsf{inp}, \mathsf{rand}) = (\bot, \bot)$ (if $\mathcal{A}^1$ behaved maliciously) or $(\mathsf{inp}, \mathsf{rand}) = (\{\widehat{x_i}\}_{i\in S}, \{\widehat{r_i}\}_{i\in S})$ which is consistent with the honest behavior for $\mathsf{RealExec}_{(t-1)}$ (first $t-1$ rounds).*

*A protocol is said to be a "**robust**" secure multiparty computation protocol for F if for every PPT adversary $\mathcal{A} = (\mathcal{A}^1, \mathcal{A}^2)$ controlling a set of parties S in the real world, where $\mathcal{A}^2$ is semi-honest, there exists a PPT simulator $\mathsf{Sim} = (\mathsf{Sim}^1, \mathsf{Sim}^2)$ such that for every initial input vector $\boldsymbol{x}$, every auxiliary input z*

- *If $(\mathsf{inp}, \mathsf{rand}) \neq (\bot, \bot)$, then:*

$$\left(\mathsf{RealExec}^{\mathcal{A}^1}_{(t-1)}(\boldsymbol{x}, z),\ \mathsf{RealExec}^{\mathcal{A}^2}_{t}(\boldsymbol{x}, \mathsf{state})\right)$$
$$\approx_c \left(\mathsf{RealExec}^{\mathcal{A}^1}_{(t-1)}(\boldsymbol{x}, z),\ \mathsf{Sim}^2(\{\widehat{x_i}\}_{i\in S}, \{\widehat{r_i}\}_{i\in S}, y, \mathsf{state})\right)$$
$$\approx_c \left(\mathsf{Sim}^1(z),\ \mathsf{Sim}^2\left(\{\widehat{x_i}\}_{i\in S}, \{\widehat{r_i}\}_{i\in S}, y, \mathsf{state}\right)\right).$$

  Here $y = F(\widehat{x_1}, \ldots, \widehat{x_n})$, where $\widehat{x_i} = x_i$ for $i \notin S$. And $\mathsf{RealExec}^{\mathcal{A}^2}_{t}(\boldsymbol{x}, \mathsf{state})$ is the view of adversary $\mathcal{A}^2$ in the tth round of the real protocol.
- *Else,*

$$\mathsf{RealExec}^{\mathcal{A}^1}_{(t-1)}(\boldsymbol{x}, z) \approx_c \mathsf{Sim}^1(z).$$

Note that, in general, a semi-honest MPC protocol may not satisfy this property. Below, we construct a four-round semi-honest MPC protocol with robustness property.

3.1 Four Round Robust Semi-honest MPC

We first describe the tools required for our construction. We require,

- Two message 1-out-of-2 covert oblivious transfer protocol. Denote this by OT.
- Degree 3 randomizing polynomials for arbitrary polynomial sized circuits. Denote this by $\mathsf{RP} = (\mathsf{CktE}, \mathsf{D})$.

Both the tools mentioned above can be instantiated from DDH.

Construction. Our goal is to construct an n-party MPC protocol Π_{sh}^{F} secure against semi-honest adversaries for an n-party functionality F. Moreover, we show that Π_{sh}^{F} satisfies Robust property (Definition 5). We employ the following steps:

- **Step I:** We first construct an 3-party semi-honest MPC protocol $\Pi_{\mathsf{sh}}^{\mathsf{3MULT}}$ for the functionality $\mathsf{3MULT}$ defined below. This protocol is a three round protocol. However, we view this as a four round protocol (with the last round being empty) – the reason behind doing this is because this protocol will be used as a sub-protocol in the next steps and in the proof, the programming of the simulator occurs only in the fourth round.

$$\mathsf{3MULT}((x_1, r_1); (x_2, r_2); (x_3)) \text{ outputs } (r_1;\ r_2;\ x_1x_2x_3 + r_1 + r_2)$$

- **Step II:** We use $\Pi_{\mathsf{sh}}^{\mathsf{3MULT}}$ to construct an n-party semi-honest MPC protocol $\Pi_{\mathsf{sh}}^{\mathsf{3POLY}\{p\}}$ for the functionality $\mathsf{3POLY}\{p\}$ defined below, where p is a degree 3 polynomial in $\mathbb{F}_2[\mathbf{y}_1, \ldots, \mathbf{y}_N]$. This protocol is a four round protocol and it satisfies robust property.

$$\mathsf{3POLY}\{p\}(X_1; \cdots ; X_n) \text{ outputs } p(\mathbf{y}_1, \ldots, \mathbf{y}_N),$$

  where $X_1, \ldots, X_n$ are partitions of $\mathbf{y}_1, \ldots, \mathbf{y}_N$.
- **Step III:** We use $\Pi_{\mathsf{sh}}^{\mathsf{3POLY}}$ to construct an n-party semi-honest MPC protocol Π_{sh}^{F}. This protocol is a four round protocol and it satisfies robust property.

We now describe the steps in detail.

Step I: Constructing $\Pi_{\mathsf{sh}}^{\mathsf{3MULT}}$. Denote the parties by P_1, P_2 and P_3. Denote the input of P_1 to be (x_1, r_1), the input of P_2 to be (x_2, r_2) and the input of P_3 to be (x_3). The protocol works as follows:

- **Round 1**: P_1 participates in a 1-out-of-2 oblivious transfer protocol OT_{12} with P_2. P_1 plays the role of receiver. It generates the first message of OT_{12} as a function of x_1.
  Simultaneously, P_2 and P_3 participate in a 1-out-of-2 protocol OT_{23}. P_3 takes the role of the receiver. It generates the first message of OT_{23} as a function of x_3.
- **Round 2**: P_2 sends the second message in OT_{12} as a function of $(x_2 \cdot 0 + r_2';\ x_2 \cdot 1 + r_2')$, where r_2' is sampled at random. P_2 sends the second message in OT_{23} as a function of $(0 \cdot r_2' + r_2;\ 1 \cdot r_2' + r_2)$.
  Simultaneously, P_1 and P_3 participate in a OT protocol OT_{13}. P_3 takes the role of the receiver. It sends the first message of OT_{13} as a function of x_3.
- **Round 3**: Let u be the value recovered by P_1 from OT_{12}. P_1 sends the second message to P_3 in OT_{13} as a function of $(u \cdot 0 + r_1, u \cdot 1 + r_1)$. Let α_3' recovered from OT_{13} by P_3 and let α_3'' be the output recovered from OT_{23}.

P_1 outputs $\alpha_1 = r_1$, P_2 outputs $\alpha_2 = r_2$ and P_3 outputs $\alpha_3 = \alpha_3' + \alpha_3''$ (operations performed over $\mathbb{F}_2$).

Theorem 6. *Assuming the correctness of* OT, $\Pi_{\mathsf{sh}}^{\mathsf{3MULT}}$ *satisfies correctness property.*

Theorem 7. *Assuming the security of* OT, $\Pi_{\mathsf{sh}}^{\mathsf{3MULT}}$ *is a robust semi-honest three-party secure computation protocol satisfying Definition 5.*

Step II: Constructing $\Pi_{\mathsf{sh}}^{\mathsf{3POLY}\{p\}}$. We first introduce some notation. Consider a polynomial $q \in \mathbb{F}_2[\mathbf{y}_1, \ldots, \mathbf{y}_N]$ with coefficients over $\mathbb{F}_2$. We define the set $\mathsf{MonS}\{q\}$ as follows: a term $t \in \mathsf{MonS}\{q\}$ if and only if t appears in the expansion of the polynomial q. We define $\mathsf{MonS}\{q\}_i$ as follows: a term $t \in \mathsf{MonS}\{q\}_i$ if and only if $t \in \mathsf{MonS}\{q\}$ and t contains the variable $\mathbf{y}_i$.

We now describe $\Pi_{\mathsf{sh}}^{\mathsf{3POLY}\{p\}}$.

PROTOCOL $\Pi_{\mathsf{sh}}^{\mathsf{3POLY}\{p\}}$: Let $P_1, \ldots, P_n$ be the set of parties in the protocol. Let X_i be the input set of P_i for every $i \in [n]$. We have, $\sum_{i=1}^{n} |X_i| = N$ and $X_i \cap X_j = \emptyset$ for $i \neq j$. Every $x \in X_i$ corresponds to a unique variable $\mathbf{y}_j$ for some j.

- For every $i \in [n]$, party P_i generates n additive shares $s_{i,1}, \ldots, s_{i,n}$ of 0. It sends share $s_{i,j}$ to P_j in the first round.
- In parallel, for every term t in the expansion of p, do the following:
  - If t is of the form x_i^3, then P_i computes x_i^3.
  - If t is of the form $x_i^2 x_j$ then pick $k \in [n]$ and $k \neq i, k \neq j$. Let r_i^t and r_j^t be the randomness, associated with t, sampled by P_i and P_j respectively. The parties $P_i(x_i, r_i^t), P_j(x_j, r_j^t)$ and $P_k(1)$ execute $\Pi_{\mathsf{sh}}^{\mathsf{3MULT}}$ to obtain the corresponding shares α_i^t, α_j^t and α_k^t. Note that this finishes in the third round.
  - If t is of the form $x_i x_j x_k$, then parties P_i, P_j and P_k sample randomness r_i^t, r_t^j and r_k^t respectively. Then, they execute $\Pi_{\mathsf{sh}}^{\mathsf{3MULT}}$ on inputs (x_i, r_i^t), (x_j, r_j^t) and (x_k) to obtain the corresponding shares α_i^t, α_j^t and α_k^t. Note that this finishes in the third round.
- After the third round, P_i adds all the shares he has so far (including his own shares) and he broadcasts his final share s_i to all the parties. This consumes one round.
- Finally, P_i outputs $\sum_{i=1}^{n} s_i$.

Theorem 8. *Assuming* $\Pi_{\mathsf{sh}}^{\mathsf{3MULT}}$ *satisfies correctness,* $\Pi_{\mathsf{sh}}^{\mathsf{3POLY}\{p\}}$ *satisfies correctness property.*

Theorem 9. *Assuming the security of* $\Pi_{\mathsf{sh}}^{\mathsf{3MULT}}$, $\Pi_{\mathsf{sh}}^{\mathsf{3POLY}\{p\}}$ *is a robust semi-honest MPC protcol satisfying Definition 5 as long as* $\Pi_{\mathsf{sh}}^{\mathsf{3MULT}}$ *satisfies Definition 5.*

Step III: Constructing Π_{sh}^{F}. We describe Π_{sh}^{F} below.

PROTOCOL Π_{sh}^{F}: Let C be a circuit representing F. That is, $F(x_1; \ldots, x_n) = C(x_1 || \cdots || x_n)$. Let $\mathsf{RP.CktE}(C) = (p_1, \ldots, p_m)$. Note that p_i, for every i, is a degree 3 polynomial in $\mathbb{F}_2[\mathbf{y}_1, \ldots, \mathbf{y}_n, \mathbf{r}_1, \ldots, \mathbf{r}_N]$. Construct polynomial $\hat{p_i} \in \mathbb{F}_2[\mathbf{y}_1, \ldots, \mathbf{y}_n, , \mathbf{r}_{1,1}, \ldots, \mathbf{r}_{n,N}]$ by replacing $\mathbf{r}_j$, for every $j \in [N]$, in p_i by the polynomial $\sum_{k=1}^{n} \mathbf{r}_{k,j}$. Note that $\hat{p_i}$ is still a degree 3 polynomial.

P_i samples randomness $r_{i,j}$, for every $j \in [N]$. For every $j \in [m]$, all the parties execute the protocol $\Pi_{\mathsf{sh}}^{\mathsf{3POLY}\{\hat{p_j}\}}$. The input of P_i is $(x_i, r_{i,1}, \ldots, r_{i,N})$ in this protocol. In the end, every party receives $\alpha_j = \hat{p_j}(x_1, \ldots, x_n)$, for every $j \in [m]$. Every party then executes $\mathsf{D}(\alpha_1, \ldots, \alpha_n)$ to obtain α^*. It outputs α^*.

Theorem 10. *Assuming the security of* $\Pi_{\mathsf{sh}}^{\mathsf{3POLY}\{p\}}$ *and security of* RP, Π_{sh}^{F} *is a robust semi-honest secure MPC protocol satisfying Definition 5 as long as* $\Pi_{\mathsf{sh}}^{\mathsf{3POLY}\{p\}}$ *satisfies Definition 5.*

The proofs can be found in the full version of the paper.

4 Five Round Malicious MPC

Overview. We start by giving an overview of our construction. We want to use the robust semi honest MPC as the basis for our construction, but its security is only defined in the semi-honest setting. We enforce the semi-honest setting by having the players prove, in parallel, that they computed the robust semi honest MPC honestly. Players prove that (1) they computed the first three rounds of the robust semi honest MPC honestly; and (2) they committed their input and randomness used in the robust semi honest MPC to every other party using both an extractable commitment scheme, and a non-interactive commitment scheme. To do so, we use a four round input delayed proof system, where the statement for the proof can be delayed till the final round. This lets players send the final round of their proof in the fourth round. Before proceeding, we verify each of the proofs received to ensure everyone is behaving in an honest manner. Next, to prove that the last round of the robust semi honest MPC is computed correctly, we use another instance of the four round input delayed proof system. The first three rounds run in parallel with the first three rounds of the protocol, but the last round of the proof system is delayed till the fifth round, after computing the last round of the robust semi honest MPC. This gives the total of five rounds.

Construction. For construction of the protocol, we require the following tools:

1. *A 3-round "rewinding-secure" extractable commitment scheme* $\Pi_{\mathsf{rext}} = \langle C_{\mathsf{rext}}, R_{\mathsf{rext}} \rangle$ (refer to definition in Sect. 2.5). We require the commitments to be well formed, where this property is defined in Sect. 2.5. Since there will be commitments in both directions for every pair of players, we introduce notation for individual messages of the protocol. $\pi^{\mathsf{j}}_{\mathsf{rext}_{\mathsf{k} \to \mathsf{i}}}$ refers to the j-th round of the P_{k}'s commitment to P_{i}.
   We will denote by $\tau_{\mathsf{rext}_{\mathsf{i} \to \mathsf{k}}} := \left(\pi^1_{\mathsf{rext}_{\mathsf{i} \to \mathsf{k}}}, \pi^2_{\mathsf{rext}_{\mathsf{i} \to \mathsf{k}}}, \pi^3_{\mathsf{rext}_{\mathsf{i} \to \mathsf{k}}}\right)$.
2. *A non-interactive commitment scheme* $\Pi_{\mathsf{nic}} = \langle C_{\mathsf{nic}}, R_{\mathsf{nic}} \rangle$.
3. *A 4-round robust semi honest MPC protocol* Π_{rMPC} *(refer to Definition 5)* that has a next-message function $\mathsf{nextMsg}^{\Pi_{\mathsf{rMPC}}}$ which, for player P_{i}, on input $(x_{\mathsf{i}}, r_{\mathsf{i}}, \boldsymbol{m}^1, \cdots, \boldsymbol{m}^{\mathsf{j}})$ returns $m_i^{\mathsf{j}+1}$, the message P_{i} broadcasts to all other players in the $(\mathsf{j}+1)$-*th* round as a part of the protocol. Here $\boldsymbol{m}^{\mathsf{j}} = (m_1^{\mathsf{j}}, \cdots, m_n^{\mathsf{j}})$

consists of all the messages sent during round j of the protocol. The robust semi honest MPC also consists of a function $\mathsf{Out}^{\Pi_{\mathsf{rMPC}}}$ that computes the final output y.

4. *Two 4-round delayed-input parallel non-malleable zero-knowledge protocols (refer to Definition 4).* We use the variant of the NMZK protocol in [9] described earlier. (Our proof will make non-black box use of the NMZK.) $\Pi_{\mathsf{nmzk}} = \langle P_{\mathsf{nmzk}}, V_{\mathsf{nmzk}} \rangle$ for the language

$$L = \Big\{ (\{\tau_{\mathsf{rext}_{i\to k}}, r^1_{\mathsf{rext}_{i\to k}}, \pi_{\mathsf{nic}_{i\to k}}\}_{k\in[n]\setminus\{i\}}, \mathtt{id}_i, \boldsymbol{m}_i = (\boldsymbol{m}^1, \boldsymbol{m}^2, m_i^3)) :$$
$$\exists (x_i, r_i, \{\mathsf{dec}_{\mathsf{rext}_{i\to k}}, \mathsf{dec}_{\mathsf{nic}_{i\to k}}\}_{k\in[n]}) \text{ s.t. } \Big((\forall\, k : \tau_{\mathsf{rext}_{i\to k}} \text{ is a } \textit{well formed}$$
$$\text{commitment of } ((x_i, r_i) \oplus r^1_{\mathsf{rext}_{i\to k}}) \texttt{ AND } \pi_{\mathsf{nic}_{i\to k}} \text{is a commitment of}$$
$$(x_i, r_i)) \texttt{ AND } (m_i^1 = \mathsf{nextMsg}^{\Pi_{\mathsf{rMPC}}}(x_i, r_i) \texttt{ AND } m_i^2 =$$
$$\mathsf{nextMsg}^{\Pi_{\mathsf{rMPC}}}(x_i, r_i, \boldsymbol{m}^1) \texttt{ AND } m_i^3 = \mathsf{nextMsg}^{\Pi_{\mathsf{rMPC}}}(x_i, r_i, \boldsymbol{m}^1, \boldsymbol{m}^2)\ )\Big)\Big\}$$

and $\widehat{\Pi}_{\mathsf{nmzk}} = \langle \widehat{P}_{\mathsf{nmzk}}, \widehat{V}_{\mathsf{nmzk}} \rangle$ for the language

$$\widehat{L} = \Big\{ (\{\tau_{\mathsf{rext}_{i\to k}}, r^1_{\mathsf{rext}_{i\to k}}, \pi_{\mathsf{nic}_{i\to k}}\}_{k\in[n]\setminus\{i\}}, \mathtt{id}_i, \boldsymbol{m}_i = (\boldsymbol{m}^1, \boldsymbol{m}^2, \boldsymbol{m}^3, m_i^4)) :$$
$$\exists (x_i, r_i, \{\mathsf{dec}_{\mathsf{rext}_{i\to k}}, \mathsf{dec}_{\mathsf{nic}_{i\to k}}\}_{k\in n}) \text{ s.t. } \Big((\ \forall\, k : \tau_{\mathsf{rext}_{i\to k}} \text{ is a } \textit{well formed}$$
$$\text{commitment of } ((x_i, r_i) \oplus r^1_{\mathsf{rext}_{i\to k}}) \texttt{ AND } \pi_{\mathsf{nic}_{i\to k}} \text{is a commitment of}$$
$$(x_i, r_i)) \texttt{ AND } (\ m_i^4 = \mathsf{nextMsg}^{\Pi_{\mathsf{rMPC}}}(x_i, r_i, \boldsymbol{m}^1, \boldsymbol{m}^2, \boldsymbol{m}^3)\ )\Big)\Big\}.$$

We represent by $\pi^j_{\mathsf{nmzk}_{k\to i}}$ and $\widehat{\pi}^j_{\mathsf{nmzk}_{k\to i}}$ the messages sent in the j-th round of P_k's proof to P_i for an instance of L and $\widehat{L}$ respectively.
Here L consists of instances where the player with identifier $\mathtt{id}_i$, P_i, correctly computes the first 3 rounds of the robust semi honest MPC with inputs (x_i, r_i), and commits to this input to ever other player (in both commitments). Likewise, $\widehat{L}$ consists of instances where the player with identifier $\mathtt{id}_i$, P_i, correctly computes the 4-th round of the robust semi honest MPC with inputs (x_i, r_i), and commits to this input to ever other player (in both commitments).

Let $\mathcal{P} = \{P_1, \cdots, P_n\}$ be the set of parties and $\{\mathtt{id}_1, \cdots, \mathtt{id}_n\}$ denote their corresponding unique identifiers (one can think of $\mathtt{id}_i = \mathrm{i}$). The input and randomness (x_i, r_i) to the robust semi honest MPC for player P_i is fixed in the beginning of the protocol.

The protocol instructs each player P_i to compute a message M_i^j for round j and broadcasts it over the simultaneous broadcast channel. Thus in round j, messages $(M_1^j, \cdots, M_n^j)$ are simultaneously broadcast.

The protocol is detailed below. For ease of notation, we shall assume the that security parameter n is an implicit argument to each of the functions.

Round 1. Each player P_i computes the message M_i^1 to be sent in the first round as follows:

1. Compute independently, with fresh randomness, the first (committer) message of the "rewinding secure" extractable commitment for every other player. i.e., $\forall k \in [n] \setminus \{i\}$

$$r^0_{\mathsf{rext}_{i\to k}} \leftarrow \{0,1\}^{|(x_i,r_i)|};\ (\pi^1_{\mathsf{rext}_{i\to k}}, \mathsf{dec}_{\mathsf{rext}_{i\to k}}) \leftarrow C_{\mathsf{rext}}(r^0_{\mathsf{rext}_{i\to k}})$$

   Set $\pi^1_{\mathsf{rext}_i} := (\pi^1_{\mathsf{rext}_{i\to 1}}, \cdots, \pi^1_{\mathsf{rext}_{i\to i-1}}, \perp, \pi^1_{\mathsf{rext}_{i\to i+1}}, \cdots, \pi^1_{\mathsf{rext}_{i\to n}})$.
2. Compute independently, with fresh randomness, the non-interactive commitment for every other player. i.e., $\forall k \in [n] \setminus \{i\}$

$$(\pi_{\mathsf{nic}_{i\to k}}, \mathsf{dec}_{\mathsf{nic}_{i\to k}}) \leftarrow C_{\mathsf{nic}}((x_i, r_i))$$

   Set $\pi_{\mathsf{nic}_i} := (\pi_{\mathsf{nic}_{i\to 1}}, \cdots, \pi_{\mathsf{nic}_{i\to i-1}}, \perp, \pi_{\mathsf{nic}_{i\to i+1}}, \cdots, \pi_{\mathsf{nic}_{i\to n}})$.
3. Compute independently, with fresh randomness, the first (verifier) message of both non-malleable zero-knowledge protocols for every other player. i.e., $\forall k \in [n] \setminus \{i\}$

$$\pi^1_{\mathsf{nmzk}_{k\to i}} \leftarrow V_{\mathsf{nmzk}}(\mathtt{id}_k, \ell),\ \widehat{\pi}^1_{\mathsf{nmzk}_{k\to i}} \leftarrow \widehat{V}_{\mathsf{nmzk}}(\mathtt{id}_k, \widehat{\ell})$$

   where ℓ and $\widehat{\ell}$ are the lengths of the input delayed statements for L and $\widehat{L}$ respectively.

   Set

$$\pi^1_{\mathsf{nmzk}_i} := (\pi^1_{\mathsf{nmzk}_{1\to i}}, \cdots, \pi^1_{\mathsf{nmzk}_{i-1\to i}}, \perp, \pi^1_{\mathsf{nmzk}_{i+1\to i}}, \cdots, \pi^1_{\mathsf{nmzk}_{n\to i}})$$
$$\widehat{\pi}^1_{\mathsf{nmzk}_i} := (\widehat{\pi}^1_{\mathsf{nmzk}_{1\to i}}, \cdots, \widehat{\pi}^1_{\mathsf{nmzk}_{i-1\to i}}, \perp, \widehat{\pi}^1_{\mathsf{nmzk}_{i+1\to i}}, \cdots, \widehat{\pi}^1_{\mathsf{nmzk}_{n\to i}})$$

M_i^1 is now defined as, $M_i^1 := (\pi^1_{\mathsf{rext}_i}, \pi_{\mathsf{nic}_i}, \pi^1_{\mathsf{nmzk}_i}, \widehat{\pi}^1_{\mathsf{nmzk}_i})$. Broadcast M_i^1 and receive $M_1^1, \cdots, M_{i-1}^1, M_{i+1}^1, \cdots, M_n^1$.

Round 2. Each player P_i computes the message M_i^2 to be sent in the second round as follows:

1. Compute the second message of the "rewinding secure" extractable commitment in response to the messages from the other parties. i.e., $\forall k \in [n] \setminus \{i\}$

$$\pi^2_{\mathsf{rext}_{k\to i}} \leftarrow R_{\mathsf{rext}}(\pi^1_{\mathsf{rext}_{k\to i}})$$

   where $\pi^1_{\mathsf{rext}_{k\to i}}$ can be obtained from $\pi^1_{\mathsf{rext}_k}$ in M_k^1.
   Set $\pi^2_{\mathsf{rext}_i} := (\pi^2_{\mathsf{rext}_{1\to i}}, \cdots, \pi^2_{\mathsf{rext}_{i-1\to i}}, \perp, \pi^2_{\mathsf{rext}_{i+1\to i}}, \cdots, \pi^2_{\mathsf{rext}_{n\to i}})$.

2. Compute the second message of both non-malleable zero-knowledge protocols in response to the messages from the other parties. i.e., $\forall \mathrm{k} \in [\mathrm{n}] \setminus \{\mathrm{i}\}$

$$\pi^2_{\mathsf{nmzk}_{\mathrm{i}\to\mathrm{k}}} \leftarrow P_{\mathsf{nmzk}}(\mathtt{id}_{\mathrm{i}}, \ell, \pi^1_{\mathsf{nmzk}_{\mathrm{i}\to\mathrm{k}}});\ \widehat{\pi}^2_{\mathsf{nmzk}_{\mathrm{i}\to\mathrm{k}}} \leftarrow \widehat{P}_{\mathsf{nmzk}}(\mathtt{id}_{\mathrm{i}}, \widehat{\ell}, \widehat{\pi}^1_{\mathsf{nmzk}_{\mathrm{i}\to\mathrm{k}}})$$

where $\pi^1_{\mathsf{nmzk}_{\mathrm{k}\to\mathrm{i}}}$ and $\widehat{\pi}^1_{\mathsf{nmzk}_{\mathrm{k}\to\mathrm{i}}}$ can be obtained from $\pi^1_{\mathsf{nmzk}_{\mathrm{k}}}$ and $\widehat{\pi}^1_{\mathsf{nmzk}_{\mathrm{k}}}$ respectively in M^1_{k}. Set

$$\pi^2_{\mathsf{nmzk}_{\mathrm{i}}} := (\pi^2_{\mathsf{nmzk}_{\mathrm{i}\to 1}}, \cdots, \pi^2_{\mathsf{nmzk}_{\mathrm{i}\to\mathrm{i}-1}}, \bot, \pi^2_{\mathsf{nmzk}_{\mathrm{i}\to\mathrm{i}+1}}, \cdots, \pi^2_{\mathsf{nmzk}_{\mathrm{i}\to\mathrm{n}}})$$
$$\widehat{\pi}^2_{\mathsf{nmzk}_{\mathrm{i}}} := (\widehat{\pi}^2_{\mathsf{nmzk}_{\mathrm{i}\to 1}}, \cdots, \widehat{\pi}^2_{\mathsf{nmzk}_{\mathrm{i}\to\mathrm{i}-1}}, \bot, \widehat{\pi}^2_{\mathsf{nmzk}_{\mathrm{i}\to\mathrm{i}+1}}, \cdots, \widehat{\pi}^2_{\mathsf{nmzk}_{\mathrm{i}\to\mathrm{n}}})$$

3. Compute the first message of the robust semi honest MPC,

$$m^1_{\mathrm{i}} \leftarrow \mathsf{nextMsg}^{\Pi_{\mathsf{rMPC}}}(x_{\mathrm{i}}, r_{\mathrm{i}}).$$

M^2_{i} is now defined as, $M^2_{\mathrm{i}} := (\pi^2_{\mathsf{rext}_{\mathrm{i}}}, \pi^2_{\mathsf{nmzk}_{\mathrm{i}}}, \widehat{\pi}^2_{\mathsf{nmzk}_{\mathrm{i}}}, m^1_{\mathrm{i}})$. Broadcast M^2_{i} and receive $M^2_1, \cdots, M^2_{\mathrm{i}-1}, M^2_{\mathrm{i}+1}, \cdots, M^2_{\mathrm{n}}$.

Round 3. Each player P_{i} computes the message M^3_{i} to be sent in the third round as follows:

1. Compute the final message of the "rewinding secure" extractable commitment. i.e., $\forall \mathrm{k} \in [\mathrm{n}] \setminus \{\mathrm{i}\}$

$$\pi^3_{\mathsf{rext}_{\mathrm{i}\to\mathrm{k}}} \leftarrow C_{\mathsf{rext}}(\pi^1_{\mathsf{rext}_{\mathrm{i}\to\mathrm{k}}}, \pi^2_{\mathsf{rext}_{\mathrm{i}\to\mathrm{k}}})$$

where $\pi^1_{\mathsf{rext}_{\mathrm{i}\to\mathrm{k}}}$ is as computed earlier and $\pi^2_{\mathsf{rext}_{\mathrm{i}\to\mathrm{k}}}$ is obtained from $\pi^2_{\mathsf{rext}_{\mathrm{k}}}$ in M^2_{k}. Set $\pi^3_{\mathsf{rext}_{\mathrm{i}}} := (\pi^3_{\mathsf{rext}_{\mathrm{i}\to 1}}, \cdots, \pi^3_{\mathsf{rext}_{\mathrm{i}\to\mathrm{i}-1}}, \bot, \pi^3_{\mathsf{rext}_{\mathrm{i}\to\mathrm{i}+1}}, \cdots, \pi^3_{\mathsf{rext}_{\mathrm{i}\to\mathrm{n}}})$.
2. Compute $(x_{\mathrm{i}}, r_{\mathrm{i}})$ masked with the randomness sent in the "rewinding secure" extractable commitment, i.e. $\forall \mathrm{k} \in [\mathrm{n}] \setminus \{\mathrm{i}\}$

$$r^1_{\mathsf{rext}_{\mathrm{i}\to\mathrm{k}}} := r^0_{\mathsf{rext}_{\mathrm{i}\to\mathrm{k}}} \oplus (x_{\mathrm{i}}, r_{\mathrm{i}})$$

Set $r^1_{\mathsf{rext}_{\mathrm{i}}} := (r^1_{\mathsf{rext}_{\mathrm{i}\to 1}}, \cdots, r^1_{\mathsf{rext}_{\mathrm{i}\to\mathrm{i}-1}}, \bot, r^1_{\mathsf{rext}_{\mathrm{i}\to\mathrm{i}+1}}, \cdots, r^1_{\mathsf{rext}_{\mathrm{i}\to\mathrm{n}}})$.
3. Compute the third message of both non-malleable zero-knowledge protocols. i.e., $\forall \mathrm{k} \in [\mathrm{n}] \setminus \{\mathrm{i}\}$

$$\pi^3_{\mathsf{nmzk}_{\mathrm{k}\to\mathrm{i}}} \leftarrow V_{\mathsf{nmzk}}(\mathtt{id}_{\mathrm{k}}, \pi^1_{\mathsf{nmzk}_{\mathrm{k}\to\mathrm{i}}}, \pi^2_{\mathsf{nmzk}_{\mathrm{k}\to\mathrm{i}}})$$
$$\widehat{\pi}^3_{\mathsf{nmzk}_{\mathrm{k}\to\mathrm{i}}} \leftarrow \widehat{V}_{\mathsf{nmzk}}(\mathtt{id}_{\mathrm{k}}, \widehat{\pi}^1_{\mathsf{nmzk}_{\mathrm{k}\to\mathrm{i}}}, \widehat{\pi}^2_{\mathsf{nmzk}_{\mathrm{k}\to\mathrm{i}}})$$

where $\pi^1_{\mathsf{nmzk}_{\mathrm{k}\to\mathrm{i}}}$ is as computed earlier and $\pi^2_{\mathsf{nmzk}_{\mathrm{k}\to\mathrm{i}}}$ is obtained from $\pi^2_{\mathsf{nmzk}_{\mathrm{k}}}$ in M^2_{k}. $\widehat{\pi}^1_{\mathsf{nmzk}_{\mathrm{k}\to\mathrm{i}}}$ and $\widehat{\pi}^2_{\mathsf{nmzk}_{\mathrm{k}\to\mathrm{i}}}$ are obtained similarly.
Set

$$\pi^3_{\mathsf{nmzk}_{\mathrm{i}}} := (\pi^3_{\mathsf{nmzk}_{1\to\mathrm{i}}}, \cdots, \pi^3_{\mathsf{nmzk}_{\mathrm{i}-1\to\mathrm{i}}}, \bot, \pi^3_{\mathsf{nmzk}_{\mathrm{i}+1\to\mathrm{i}}}, \cdots, \pi^3_{\mathsf{nmzk}_{\mathrm{n}\to\mathrm{i}}})$$
$$\widehat{\pi}^3_{\mathsf{nmzk}_{\mathrm{i}}} := (\widehat{\pi}^3_{\mathsf{nmzk}_{1\to\mathrm{i}}}, \cdots, \widehat{\pi}^3_{\mathsf{nmzk}_{\mathrm{i}-1\to\mathrm{i}}}, \bot, \widehat{\pi}^3_{\mathsf{nmzk}_{\mathrm{i}+1\to\mathrm{i}}}, \cdots, \widehat{\pi}^3_{\mathsf{nmzk}_{\mathrm{n}\to\mathrm{i}}})$$

4. Compute the second message of the robust semi honest MPC,

$$m_i^2 \leftarrow \mathsf{nextMsg}^{\Pi_{\mathsf{rMPC}}}(x_i, r_i, \boldsymbol{m}^1)$$

where $\boldsymbol{m}^1 := (m_1^1, \cdots, m_n^1)$.

M_i^3 is now defined as, $M_i^3 := (\pi^3_{\mathsf{rext}_i}, r^1_{\mathsf{rext}_i}, \pi^3_{\mathsf{nmzk}_i}, \widehat{\pi}^3_{\mathsf{nmzk}_i}, m_i^2)$. Broadcast M_i^3 and receive $M_1^3, \cdots, M_{i-1}^3, M_{i+1}^3, \cdots, M_n^3$.

Round 4. Each player P_i computes the message M_i^4 to be sent in the fourth round as follows:

1. Compute the third message of the robust semi honest MPC,

$$m_i^3 \leftarrow \mathsf{nextMsg}^{\Pi_{\mathsf{rMPC}}}(x_i, r_i, \boldsymbol{m}^1, \boldsymbol{m}^2)$$

where $\boldsymbol{m}^1 := (m_1^1, \cdots, m_n^1)$ and $\boldsymbol{m}^2 := (m_1^2, \cdots, m_n^2)$.

2. Compute the final message of the non-malleable zero-knowledge protocol for language L. i.e., $\forall k \in [n] \setminus \{i\}$

$$\begin{aligned} w_{\mathsf{nmzk}_i} &:= \left(x_i, r_i, \{\mathsf{dec}_{\mathsf{rext}_{i\to k}}, \mathsf{dec}_{\mathsf{nic}_{i\to k}}\}_{k\in[n]}\right) \\ \boldsymbol{m}_i &:= \left(\boldsymbol{m}^1, \boldsymbol{m}^2, m_i^3\right) \\ x_{\mathsf{nmzk}_i} &:= \left(\left\{\tau_{\mathsf{rext}_{i\to k}}, r^1_{\mathsf{rext}_{i\to k}}, \pi_{\mathsf{nic}_{i\to k}}\right\}_{k\in[n]}, \mathtt{id}_i, \boldsymbol{m}_i\right) \\ \pi^4_{\mathsf{nmzk}_{i\to k}} &\leftarrow P_{\mathsf{nmzk}}(\mathtt{id}_i, \ell, x_{\mathsf{nmzk}_i}, w_{\mathsf{nmzk}_i} \pi^1_{\mathsf{nmzk}_{i\to k}}, \pi^2_{\mathsf{nmzk}_{i\to k}}, \pi^3_{\mathsf{nmzk}_{i\to k}}) \end{aligned}$$

where $|x_{\mathsf{nmzk}_i}| = \ell$, and $\pi^1_{\mathsf{nmzk}_{i\to k}}$ is obtained from $\pi^1_{\mathsf{nmzk}_k}$ in M_k^1. Similarly, $\pi^3_{\mathsf{nmzk}_{i\to k}}$ is be obtained from $\pi^3_{\mathsf{nmzk}_k}$ in M_k^3. $\pi^2_{\mathsf{nmzk}_{i\to k}}$ is as computed earlier. Set $\pi^4_{\mathsf{nmzk}_i} := (\pi^4_{\mathsf{nmzk}_{i\to 1}}, \cdots, \pi^4_{\mathsf{nmzk}_{i\to i-1}}, \bot, \pi^4_{\mathsf{nmzk}_{i\to i+1}}, \cdots, \pi^4_{\mathsf{nmzk}_{i\to n}})$.

M_i^4 is now defined as, $M_i^4 := (\pi^4_{\mathsf{nmzk}_i}, m_i^3)$. Broadcast M_i^4 and receive $M_1^4, \cdots, M_{i-1}^4, M_{i+1}^4, \cdots, M_n^4$.

Round 5. Each player P_i computes the message M_i^5 to be sent in the fifth round as follows:

1. Check if all the proofs in the protocol are accepting. The proof from P_k to P_j is accepting if P_k has computed the first 3 rounds of the robust semi honest MPC correctly and has committed to the same inputs, used in the robust semi honest MPC, to every other player.
First, compute the statement x_{nmzk_k} for each player P_k. i.e., $\forall k \in [n] \setminus \{i\}$

$$\boldsymbol{m}_k := \left(\boldsymbol{m}^1, \boldsymbol{m}^2, m_k^3\right); \; x_{\mathsf{nmzk}_k} := \left(\left\{\tau_{\mathsf{rext}_{k\to t}}, r^1_{\mathsf{rext}_{k\to t}}, \pi_{\mathsf{nic}_{k\to t}}\right\}_{t\in[n]}, \mathtt{id}_k, \boldsymbol{m}_k\right)$$

Next, check if every proof is valid.

$$\text{if } \exists k, j \text{ s.t } \mathsf{accept} \neq V_{\mathsf{nmzk}}(\mathtt{id}_k, x_{\mathsf{nmzk}_k}, \pi^1_{\mathsf{nmzk}_{k\to j}}, \pi^2_{\mathsf{nmzk}_{k\to j}}, \pi^3_{\mathsf{nmzk}_{k\to j}}, \pi^4_{\mathsf{nmzk}_{k\to j}})$$
$$\text{then } \mathsf{output} \bot \text{ and } \mathsf{abort}$$

else continue

This can be done because the proofs are public coin. Moreover this is done to avoid the case that some honest parties continue on to the next round, but the others abort.

2. Compute the final message of the robust semi honest MPC,

$$m_i^4 \leftarrow \mathsf{nextMsg}^{\Pi_{\mathsf{rMPC}}}(x_i, r_i, \boldsymbol{m}^1, \boldsymbol{m}^2, \boldsymbol{m}^3)$$

where $\boldsymbol{m}^1 := (m_1^1, \cdots, m_n^1)$, $\boldsymbol{m}^2 := (m_1^2, \cdots, m_n^2)$ and $\boldsymbol{m}^3 := (m_1^3, \cdots, m_n^3)$.

3. Compute the final message of the non-malleable zero-knowledge protocol for language $\widehat{L}$. i.e., $\forall k \in [n] \setminus \{i\}$

$$\widehat{w}_{\mathsf{nmzk}_i} := \left(x_i, r_i, \{\mathsf{dec}_{\mathsf{rext}_{i\to k}}, \mathsf{dec}_{\mathsf{nic}_{i\to k}}\}_{k\in[n]}\right)$$
$$\boldsymbol{m}_i := \left(\boldsymbol{m}^1, \boldsymbol{m}^2, \boldsymbol{m}^3, m_i^4\right)$$
$$\widehat{x}_{\mathsf{nmzk}_i} := \left(\left\{\tau_{\mathsf{rext}_{i\to k}}, r^1_{\mathsf{rext}_{i\to k}}, \pi_{\mathsf{nic}_{i\to k}}\right\}_{k\in[n]}, \mathtt{id}_i, \boldsymbol{m}_i\right)$$
$$\widehat{\pi}^4_{\mathsf{nmzk}_{i\to k}} \leftarrow \widehat{P}_{\mathsf{nmzk}}(\mathtt{id}_i, \widehat{\ell}, \widehat{x}_{\mathsf{nmzk}_i}, \widehat{w}_{\mathsf{nmzk}_i}, \widehat{\pi}^1_{\mathsf{nmzk}_{i\to k}}, \widehat{\pi}^2_{\mathsf{nmzk}_{i\to k}}, \widehat{\pi}^3_{\mathsf{nmzk}_{i\to k}})$$

where $|\widehat{x}_{\mathsf{nmzk}_{i\to k}}| = \widehat{\ell}$, and $\widehat{\pi}^1_{\mathsf{nmzk}_{i\to k}}$ is obtained from $\widehat{\pi}^1_{\mathsf{nmzk}_k}$ in M_k^1. Similarly, $\widehat{\pi}^3_{\mathsf{nmzk}_{i\to k}}$ is obtained from $\widehat{\pi}^3_{\mathsf{nmzk}_k}$ in M_k^3. $\widehat{\pi}^2_{\mathsf{nmzk}_{k\to i}}$ is as computed earlier.
Set $\widehat{\pi}^4_{\mathsf{nmzk}_i} := (\widehat{\pi}^4_{\mathsf{nmzk}_{i\to 1}}, \cdots, \widehat{\pi}^4_{\mathsf{nmzk}_{i\to i-1}}, \bot, \widehat{\pi}^4_{\mathsf{nmzk}_{i\to i+1}}, \cdots, \widehat{\pi}^4_{\mathsf{nmzk}_{i\to n}})$

M_i^5 is now defined as, $M_i^5 := (m_i^4, \widehat{\pi}^4_{\mathsf{nmzk}_i})$. Broadcast M_i^5 and receive $M_1^5, \cdots, M_{i-1}^5, M_{i+1}^5, \cdots, M_n^5$.

Output Computation. To compute the output, P_i performs the following steps:

1. Check if all the proofs in the protocol are accepting. The proof from P_k to P_j is accepting if P_k has computed the 4-th round of the robust semi honest MPC correctly and has committed to the same inputs, used in the robust semi honest MPC, to every other party.
First, compute the statement $\widehat{x}_{\mathsf{nmzk}_k}$ for each player P_k. i.e., $\forall k \in [n] \setminus \{i\}$

$$\widehat{\boldsymbol{m}}_k := \left(\boldsymbol{m}^1, \boldsymbol{m}^2, \boldsymbol{m}^3, m_k^4\right)$$
$$\widehat{x}_{\mathsf{nmzk}_k} := \left(\left\{\tau_{\mathsf{rext}_{k\to t}}, r^1_{\mathsf{rext}_{k\to t}}, \pi_{\mathsf{nic}_{k\to t}}\right\}_{t\in[n]}, \mathtt{id}_k, \widehat{\boldsymbol{m}}_k\right)$$

Next, check if every proof is valid.

$$\text{if } \exists \mathsf{k},\mathsf{j} \text{ s.t } \mathsf{accept} \neq \widehat{V}_{\mathsf{nmzk}}(\mathtt{id}_k, \widehat{x}_{\mathsf{nmzk}_k}, \widehat{\pi}^1_{\mathsf{nmzk}_{k\to j}}, \widehat{\pi}^2_{\mathsf{nmzk}_{k\to j}}, \widehat{\pi}^3_{\mathsf{nmzk}_{k\to j}}, \widehat{\pi}^4_{\mathsf{nmzk}_{k\to j}})$$
$$\text{then output } \bot \text{ and abort}$$

else continue

2. Compute the output of the protocol as

$$y \leftarrow \mathsf{Out}^{\Pi_{\mathsf{rMPC}}}(x_i, r_i, \boldsymbol{m}^1, \boldsymbol{m}^2, \boldsymbol{m}^3, \boldsymbol{m}^4)$$

Theorem 11. *Assuming security of the "rewinding secure" extractable commitment, non-interactive commitment scheme, robust semi-honest MPC and NMZK, the above described five round protocol is secure against malicious adversaries.*

We use the standard definition of security with abort against malicious adversaries (see [15] for details).

Extractable commitments and NMZK can be instantiated from DL, while the robust semi-honest MPC can be instantiated from DDH. Thus, all the required primitives can be instantiated from DDH.

The complete proof can be found in the full version of our paper, but we give an overview of the simulator below. Before we proceed to the simulator, we discuss a few properties of the underlying primitives that we will need:

- Recall that simulator for the robust semi honest MPC consists of two parts. The first part, $\mathsf{Sim}^1_{\mathsf{rMPC}}$, simulates the first three rounds of the robust semi honest MPC without requiring inputs or outputs of the adversary. The second part, $\mathsf{Sim}^2_{\mathsf{rMPC}}$, when given the inputs, random tape and outputs a simulated transcript of the last round that is consistent with the input and randomness. Additionally, note that this simulation succeeds as long as the adversary behaved honestly in the first three rounds of the robust semi honest MPC.
- The extractor for the 3 round "rewinding secure" extractable commitment works by rewinding the second and third round polynomial number of times. From Lemma 1, we know that if the commitments are well formed, extraction fails with only negligible probability.
- The simulator of the NMZKs works by extracting a trapdoor. Specifically, it rewinds the second and third round polynomial number of times to get signatures for two distinct messages. Further, this extraction fails only with negligible probability.
- Combining the above two properties, we see that the rewindings of NMZK and the "rewinding secure" extractable commitment are "composable" because they rewind in the same rounds in our MPC protocol.

We describe the ideal world simulator Sim below. We shall denote the set of honest players by $\mathcal{H}$ and the set of corrupted players by $\mathcal{P}^{\mathcal{A}}$.

1. The first three rounds of protocol are simulated as follows:
   - For the robust semi honest MPC, since $\mathsf{Sim}^1_{\mathsf{rMPC}}$ doesn't require any input or output to simulate the first three rounds, we use it directly to obtain $\{m^1_{\mathrm{i}}, m^2_{\mathrm{i}}, m^3_{\mathrm{i}}\}_{P_{\mathrm{i}} \in \mathcal{H}}$. Since the robust semi honest MPC starts from the second round, $\{m^3_{\mathrm{i}}\}_{P_{\mathrm{i}} \in \mathcal{H}}$ is sent in the 4th round with the last round of the NMZK for L, but we group them here for simplicity.
   - For simulating proofs for the NMZKs, we deal with three different cases:
     (a) For proofs from the adversary, the honest player acts as a verifier. In this case, fix a random tape for the verifier and respond honestly to adversary queries.

(b) For proofs within honest players, we fix the random tape for the verifiers and thus can trivially compute the trapdoor in the NMZKs for both languages using the verifier's random tape.
(c) For proofs from honest players to the adversary, we run the simulators $\mathsf{Sim}_{\mathsf{nmzk}}$ and $\widehat{\mathsf{Sim}}_{\mathsf{nmzk}}$ to simulate the first three rounds. This internally rewinds polynomial many times to obtain the trapdoors. If the extractor fails, output $\bot_{\mathsf{nmzk}}$ and abort.
- For the "rewinding secure" extractable commitment, we deal with two cases:
(a) For commitments from the honest players to the adversary, we just commit to the all '0' string. We do this for commitments within the honest players as well.
(b) For commitments where the honest players are recipients, run the extractor to send responses and extract the values inside the commitments. If extractor fails, output $\bot_{\mathsf{rext}}$ and abort.
- For the non-interactive commitments, commit to the all '0' string for commitments from the honest players to the adversary.
- For the masked value in the third round, send the same random string as committed earlier in the "rewinding secure" extractable commitment.

As noted earlier, the rewinding performed within the NMZK simulator and the extractor for "rewinding secure" extractable commitments work in the same rounds and can be performed for each without affecting the other. Additionally, these extracted values along with the masked values sent by the adversary gives us its input and randomness.

2. Simulate the last round of the NMZK for L in two steps.
   - For proofs from the honest parties to the adversary, use $\mathsf{Sim}_{\mathsf{nmzk}}$ and the trapdoors obtained to compute the last round of the NMZK for L.
   - For proofs within honest parties, the trapdoor is trivially known to the simulator and thus compute the last round of the NMZK for L.

   On receiving the proofs for L from the adversary, check if all the received proofs are valid. This is equivalent to checking if all proofs in the protocol verify. If the check fails, send `abort` to the ideal functionality and exit.
3. We perform an additional check before we obtain the final round of the robust semi honest MPC. Given $\boldsymbol{m}^1, \boldsymbol{m}^2, \boldsymbol{m}^3, \{(x_k, r_k)\}_{P_k \in \mathcal{P}^{\mathcal{A}}}$, we check if the adversary has followed the computation in the first three rounds correctly. If the check fails we output $\bot^1_{\mathsf{rMPC}}$ and abort. It is implicit that the proofs for L have verified prior to this step.
4. Send the extracted inputs $\{x_k\}_{P_k \in \mathcal{P}^{\mathcal{A}}}$ to the ideal functionality to obtain the output y.

Compute the final round (of all players) of the robust semi honest MPC as

$$\{m_i^4\}_{P_i \in \mathcal{P}} \leftarrow \mathsf{Sim}^2_{\mathsf{rMPC}}\left(\boldsymbol{m}^1, \boldsymbol{m}^2, \boldsymbol{m}^3, \{x_k\}_{P_k \in \mathcal{P}^{\mathcal{A}}}, \{r_k\}_{P_k \in \mathcal{P}^{\mathcal{A}}}, y\right).$$

Additionally, simulate the last round of the NMZK for $\widehat{L}$. This is done in two steps

- For proofs from the honest parties to the adversary, use $\widehat{\mathsf{Sim}}_{\mathsf{nmzk}}$ and the trapdoors obtained to compute the last round of the NMZK for $\widehat{L}$.
- For proofs within honest parties, the trapdoor is trivially known to the adversary and thus compute the last round of the NMZK for $\widehat{L}$.

5. On receiving the proofs for $\widehat{L}$ from the adversary check if all the received proofs are valid. If the check fails, send `abort` to the ideal functionality. Otherwise, on receiving $\{m_{\mathsf{k}}^{*4}\}_{P_{\mathsf{k}} \in \mathcal{P}^{\mathcal{A}}}$ from the adversary, we check if it matches the transcript simulated by $\mathsf{Sim}^2_{\mathsf{rMPC}}$ earlier. If not, but the proofs above have verified output $\bot^2_{\mathsf{rMPC}}$ and abort. Else send `continue` to the ideal functionality.

5 Four Round Malicious MPC

Overview. We give an overview of our four round construction. At a high-level, the four round protocol is very similar to the five round protocol (from the previous section) but to compress the number of rounds we cannot have two instances of the four-round NMZK as before. Instead, we use a 3 round input-delayed strong WI argument of knowledge (with appropriate non-malleability properties), ending in the third round, to enable parties to prove their honest behavior of the first three rounds. This lets the players send the fourth message in the clear if the proof at the end of the third round verifies. For the output round, we use a four-round NMZK as before to prove honest behavior.

The three-round input-delayed proof system that we use to establish honest behavior in the first three rounds is depicted in Fig. 1. We do not argue its security separately, but within the hybrids of our overall security proof. We present the construction with 2-round non-malleable commitment for simplicity, but a 3-round non-malleable commitment can also be used. The required complexity leveraging levels for the proof are different in each case.

Proof for a language L using this proof system requires:

- Prover committing to 0 using a 2-round non-malleable commitment [28]. The relevance of this will become clear shortly.
- The verifier sends the image of the one way permutation applied on a random string r.
- An input delayed witness indistinguishable proof of knowledge (WIPoK) proving knowledge of either: (1) w such that $(x, w) \in \mathsf{Rel}_L$ and the non-malleable commitment decommits to 0; or (2) the decommitment of the non-malleable commitment to pre-image r of the one way permutation. Informally speaking, one can think of the above construction as a strong input delayed WI argument of knowledge with non-malleability properties.

Construction. For construction of the protocol, we require the tools described below. The exact security levels for each of these primitives are discussed at the end of the construction.

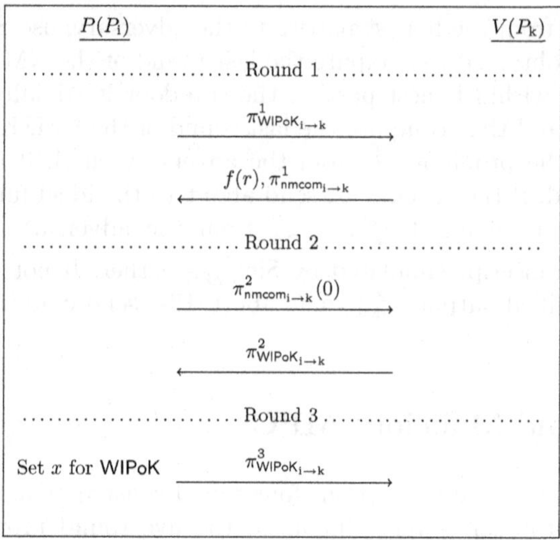

Fig. 1. Components of the proof system

1. A *one-way permutation* f.
2. *A 3-round "rewinding secure" extractable commitment scheme* $\Pi_{\mathsf{rext}} = \langle C_{\mathsf{rext}}, R_{\mathsf{rext}} \rangle$ (refer to definition in Sect. 2.5).
3. *A non-interactive commitment scheme* $\Pi_{\mathsf{nic}} = \langle C_{\mathsf{nic}}, R_{\mathsf{nic}} \rangle$.
4. An instance of *a 2-round (private coin) extractable non-malleable commitment scheme* $\Pi_{\mathsf{nmcom}} = \langle C_{\mathsf{nmcom}}, R_{\mathsf{nmcom}} \rangle$. These can be constructed from the assumption of sub-exponentially hard DDH [28].[10]
   We will use the following notation throughout the protocol for the various commitment schemes
$$\tau_{\mathsf{rext}_{i\to k}} := \left(\pi^1_{\mathsf{rext}_{i\to k}}, \pi^2_{\mathsf{rext}_{i\to k}}, \pi^3_{\mathsf{rext}_{i\to k}}\right);\ \tau_{\mathsf{nmcom}_{i\to k}} := \left(\pi^1_{\mathsf{nmcom}_{i\to k}}, \pi^2_{\mathsf{nmcom}_{i\to k}}\right)$$
5. *A 4-round robust semi-honest MPC protocol* Π_{rMPC} as described in the five round protocol.
6. A 3 round input delayed witness indistinguishable proof of knowledge (WIPoK) protocol $\Pi_{\mathsf{WIPoK}} = (P_{\mathsf{WIPoK}}, V_{\mathsf{WIPoK}})$ for the language L_{WIPoK}. We require the protocols to be public coin and instantiate them using the Lapidot-Shamir protocol [29].
   For the sake of readability and clarity, we modularize the language to obtain the final language.

[10] While in all other cases, we have required the use of public coins, we can make do with a private coin protocol here. This will become apparent in the proof.

$$L = \Big\{ (\{\tau_{\mathsf{rext}_{i\to k}}, r^1_{\mathsf{rext}_{i\to k}}, \pi_{\mathsf{nic}_{i\to k}}\}_{k\in[n]\setminus\{i\}}, \mathtt{id}_i, \boldsymbol{m}_i = (\boldsymbol{m}^1, \boldsymbol{m}^2, m^3_i)) : \exists (x_i, r_i, \{\mathsf{dec}_{\mathsf{rext}_{i\to k}}, \mathsf{dec}_{\mathsf{nic}_{i\to k}}\}_{k\in[n]}) \text{ s.t. } \Big((\forall\, k : \tau_{\mathsf{rext}_{i\to k}} \text{ is a } \textit{well formed} \text{ commitment of } ((x_i, r_i) \oplus r^1_{\mathsf{rext}_{i\to k}}) \texttt{ AND } \pi_{\mathsf{nic}_{i\to k}} \text{is a commitment of } (x_i, r_i)) \texttt{ AND } (m^1_i = \mathsf{nextMsg}^{\Pi_{\mathsf{rMPC}}}(x_i, r_i) \texttt{ AND } m^2_i = \mathsf{nextMsg}^{\Pi_{\mathsf{rMPC}}}(x_i, r_i, \boldsymbol{m}^1) \texttt{ AND } m^3_i = \mathsf{nextMsg}^{\Pi_{\mathsf{rMPC}}}(x_i, r_i, \boldsymbol{m}^1, \boldsymbol{m}^2)\ ) \Big) \Big\}$$

L is the language which consists of instances where player P_i correctly computes the first three rounds of the robust semi honest MPC with inputs (x_i, r_i), commits to $(x_i, r_i) \oplus r^1_{\mathsf{rext}_{i\to k}}$ to every other player P_k in the "rewinding secure" extractable commitment and commits to (x_i, r_i) to every other player P_k in the non-interactive commitment. Additionally, we require that the commitments in each of these "rewinding secure" extractable commitment is well formed. We define $x_{L_i} := (\{\tau_{\mathsf{rext}_{i\to k}}, r^1_{\mathsf{rext}_{i\to k}}\}_{k\in[n]\setminus\{i\}}, \mathtt{id}_i, \boldsymbol{m}_i = (\boldsymbol{m}^1, \boldsymbol{m}^2, m^3_i))$.

$$L_{\mathsf{WIPoK}} = \Big\{ (x_{L_i}, \mathtt{id}_k, \tau_{\mathsf{nmcom}_{i\to k}}, y_{k\to i}) : \exists (w, \mathsf{dec}_{\mathsf{nmcom}_{i\to k}}, \rho) \text{ s.t. } \Big((x_{L_i}, w) \in \mathsf{Rel}_L \Big) \texttt{ OR } \Big(f(\rho) = y_{k\to i} \texttt{ AND } (\ (\rho, \mathsf{dec}_{\mathsf{nmcom}_{i\to k}}, \mathtt{id}_i) \text{ is a valid decommitment of } \tau_{\mathsf{nmcom}_{i\to k}}\ ) \Big) \Big\}$$

L_{WIPoK} consists of instances where player P_i proves to player P_k that either

- it behaved honestly, i.e. it has a witness w such that $(x_{L_i}, w) \in \mathsf{Rel}_L$; or
- it possesses the trapdoor mentioned earlier, and has committed to it in the non-malleable commitment.

We define $x_{\mathsf{WIPoK}_{i\to k}} := (x_{L_i}, \mathtt{id}_k, \tau_{\mathsf{nmcom}_{i\to k}}, y_{k\to i})$.

7. *A 4-round delayed-input parallel non-malleable zero-knowledge protocols* (refer to Definition 4). We use a variant the NMZK protocol in [9] described earlier. Our proof will make non-black box use of the NMZK. $\Pi_{\mathsf{nmzk}} = \langle P_{\mathsf{nmzk}}, V_{\mathsf{nmzk}} \rangle$ for the language

$$\widehat{L} = \Big\{ (\{\tau_{\mathsf{rext}_{i\to k}}, r^1_{\mathsf{rext}_{i\to k}}, \pi_{\mathsf{nic}_{i\to k}}\}_{k\in[n]\setminus\{i\}}, \mathtt{id}_i, \boldsymbol{m}_i = (\boldsymbol{m}^1, \boldsymbol{m}^2, \boldsymbol{m}^3, m^4_i)) : \exists (x_i, r_i, \{\mathsf{dec}_{\mathsf{rext}_{i\to k}}, \mathsf{dec}_{\mathsf{nic}_{i\to k}}\}_{k\in n}) \text{ s.t. } \Big((\ \forall\, k : \tau_{\mathsf{rext}_{i\to k}} \text{ is a } \textit{well formed} \text{ commitment of } ((x_i, r_i) \oplus r^1_{\mathsf{rext}_{i\to k}}) \texttt{ AND } \pi_{\mathsf{nic}_{i\to k}} \text{is a commitment of } (x_i, r_i)) \texttt{ AND } (\ m^4_i = \mathsf{nextMsg}^{\Pi_{\mathsf{rMPC}}}(x_i, r_i, \boldsymbol{m}^1, \boldsymbol{m}^2, \boldsymbol{m}^3)\ ) \Big) \Big\}.$$

$\widehat{L}$ is the language which consists of instances where player P_i (a) correctly computed the final round of the robust MPC with inputs (x_i, r_i); (b) commits to $(x_i, r_i) \oplus r^1_{\mathsf{rext}_{i\to k}}$ to every other player P_k in the "rewinding secure" extractable commitment such that they are well formed; and (c) commits to (x_i, r_i) to every other player P_k in the non-interactive commitment. We define $\widehat{x}_{L_i} := (\{\tau_{\mathsf{rext}_{i\to k}}, r^1_{\mathsf{rext}_{i\to k}}\}_{k\in[n]\setminus\{i\}}, \mathtt{id}_i, \boldsymbol{m}_i = (\boldsymbol{m}^1, \boldsymbol{m}^2, \boldsymbol{m}^3, m^4_i))$.

We briefly describe each round of the protocol. A complete description of the protocol can be found in the full version.

Round 1. Each player P_i computes the message M_i^1 to be broadcast in the first round constituting of:

1. The first (committer) message of the "rewinding secure" extractable commitment for every other player, computed independently with fresh randomness.
2. Commit to the input and randomness to every other player independently with fresh randomness, using the non-interactive commitment.
3. The first message of the robust semi honest MPC.
4. The different components that make up the proof system for L, computed independently for every other player. This includes the image of the one-way permutation on a random string, the first (receiver) message of the non-malleable commitment and the first message for the input delayed witness indistinguishable proof of knowledge (WIPoK) for L_{WIPoK}.
5. The first (verifier) message of the non-malleable zero-knowledge protocol for every other player, computed independently with fresh randomness.

Round 2. Each player P_i computes the message M_i^2 to be broadcast in the second round consisting of:

1. The second message of the "rewinding secure" extractable commitment in response to the messages from the other parties.
2. The second message of the robust semi honest MPC,
3. The second message for the different components in the proof system for L. This includes the second message of the non-malleable commitment scheme and the second message of the input delayed WIPoK for L_{WIPoK}, in response to messages from every other player.
4. The second message of the non-malleable zero-knowledge protocols in response to the messages from the other parties.

Round 3. Each player P_i computes the message M_i^3 to be broadcast in the third round constituting of:

1. The final message of the "rewinding secure" extractable commitment.
2. (x_i, r_i) masked with the randomness sent in the "rewinding secure" extractable commitment. Here (x_i, r_i) is the input and randomness used by P_i in the robust semi honest MPC.
3. The third message of the robust semi honest MPC.
4. The final message WIPoK for language L_{WIPoK}.
5. The third message of the non-malleable zero-knowledge protocol.

Round 4. Each player P_i computes the message M_i^4 to be broadcast in the fourth round:

1. The final message of the robust semi honest MPC. Prior to computing the final message, P_i checks if proofs for L_{WIPoK} between every pair of players are accepting. This is possible since the proofs are public coin and have been previously broadcast. If the proofs fail, P_i aborts the protocol.
2. The final message of the non-malleable zero-knowledge protocol for language $\widehat{L}$.

Output Computation. To compute the output, P_i performs the following steps:

1. Check if proofs between every pair of players for $\widehat{L}_{\mathsf{WIPoK}}$ are accepting. As before, abort if the check fails.
2. Compute the output of the protocol.

In the full version of our paper [1], we prove the security of the above protocol where we rely on complexity leveraging between various primitives. Overall, our construction can be based on one-way permutation and sub-exponential DDH.

Acknowledgements. The third author would like to thank Yuval Ishai for describing ideas for constructing a four-round semi-honest MPC protocol using randomizing polynomials.

The first author was supported by grant 360584 from the Simons Foundation. The second and the third authors were supported in part by a DARPA/ARL Safeware Grant W911NF-15-C-0213.

References

1. Ananth, P., Choudhuri, A.R., Jain, A.: A new approach to round-optimal secure multiparty computation. IACR Cryptology ePrint Archive 2017, 402 (2017). http://eprint.iacr.org/2017/402
2. Applebaum, B., Ishai, Y., Kushilevitz, E.: Computationally private randomizing polynomials and their applications. Comput. Complex. **15**(2), 115–162 (2006)
3. Asharov, G., Jain, A., López-Alt, A., Tromer, E., Vaikuntanathan, V., Wichs, D.: Multiparty computation with low communication, computation and interaction via threshold FHE. In: Pointcheval, D., Johansson, T. (eds.) EUROCRYPT 2012. LNCS, vol. 7237, pp. 483–501. Springer, Heidelberg (2012). doi:10.1007/978-3-642-29011-4_29
4. Barak, B., Goldreich, O., Impagliazzo, R., Rudich, S., Sahai, A., Vadhan, S., Yang, K.: On the (im)possibility of obfuscating programs. In: Kilian, J. (ed.) CRYPTO 2001. LNCS, vol. 2139, pp. 1–18. Springer, Heidelberg (2001). doi:10.1007/3-540-44647-8_1
5. Barak, B., Prabhakaran, M., Sahai, A.: Concurrent non-malleable zero knowledge. In: 47th Annual IEEE Symposium on Foundations of Computer Science (FOCS 2006), Berkeley, California, USA, Proceedings, 21–24 October 2006, pp. 345–354 (2006)
6. Beaver, D., Micali, S., Rogaway, P.: The round complexity of secure protocols (extended abstract). In: Proceedings of the 22nd Annual ACM Symposium on Theory of Computing, Baltimore, Maryland, USA, 13–17 May 1990, pp. 503–513 (1990)

7. Brakerski, Z., Halevi, S., Polychroniadou, A.: Four round secure computation without setup. IACR Cryptology ePrint Archive 2017, 386 (2017). http://eprint.iacr.org/2017/386
8. Chandran, N., Goyal, V., Ostrovsky, R., Sahai, A.: Covert multi-party computation. In: 48th Annual IEEE Symposium on Foundations of Computer Science, FOCS 2007, pp. 238–248. IEEE (2007)
9. Ciampi, M., Ostrovsky, R., Siniscalchi, L., Visconti, I.: 4-round concurrent non-malleable commitments from one-way functions. In: Katz, J., Shacham, H. (eds.) CRYPTO 2017, Part II. LNCS, vol. 10401, pp. 127–157. Springer, Cham (2017)
10. Even, S., Goldreich, O., Lempel, A.: A randomized protocol for signing contracts. In: Advances in Cryptology: Proceedings of CRYPTO 1982, Santa Barbara, California, USA, 23–25 August 1982, pp. 205–210 (1982)
11. Garg, S., Gentry, C., Halevi, S., Raykova, M.: Two-round secure MPC from indistinguishability obfuscation. In: Lindell, Y. (ed.) TCC 2014. LNCS, vol. 8349, pp. 74–94. Springer, Heidelberg (2014). doi:10.1007/978-3-642-54242-8_4
12. Garg, S., Gentry, C., Halevi, S., Raykova, M., Sahai, A., Waters, B.: Candidate indistinguishability obfuscation and functional encryption for all circuits. In: FOCS, pp. 40–49 (2013)
13. Garg, S., Goyal, V., Jain, A., Sahai, A.: Concurrently secure computation in constant rounds. In: Pointcheval, D., Johansson, T. (eds.) EUROCRYPT 2012. LNCS, vol. 7237, pp. 99–116. Springer, Heidelberg (2012). doi:10.1007/978-3-642-29011-4_8
14. Garg, S., Mukherjee, P., Pandey, O., Polychroniadou, A.: The exact round complexity of secure computation. In: Fischlin, M., Coron, J.-S. (eds.) EUROCRYPT 2016. LNCS, vol. 9666, pp. 448–476. Springer, Heidelberg (2016). doi:10.1007/978-3-662-49896-5_16
15. Goldreich, O.: Foundations of Cryptography: Volume 2, Basic Applications, vol. 2. Cambridge University Press, Cambridge (2009)
16. Goldreich, O., Micali, S., Wigderson, A.: How to play any mental game. In: STOC (1987)
17. Goldwasser, S., Micali, S., Rackoff, C.: The knowledge complexity of interactive proof-systems. In: STOC, pp. 291–304 (1985)
18. Goyal, V.: Constant round non-malleable protocols using one way functions. In: Proceedings of the 43rd ACM Symposium on Theory of Computing, STOC 2011, San Jose, CA, USA, 6–8 June 2011, pp. 695–704 (2011)
19. Goyal, V.: Positive results for concurrently secure computation in the plain model. In: 53rd Annual IEEE Symposium on Foundations of Computer Science, FOCS 2012, New Brunswick, NJ, USA, 20–23 October 2012, pp. 41–50 (2012)
20. Goyal, V., Jain, A.: On the round complexity of covert computation. In: Proceedings of the Forty-Second ACM Symposium on Theory of Computing, pp. 191–200. ACM (2010)
21. Goyal, V., Jain, A., Ostrovsky, R.: Password-authenticated session-key generation on the internet in the plain model. In: Rabin, T. (ed.) CRYPTO 2010. LNCS, vol. 6223, pp. 277–294. Springer, Heidelberg (2010). doi:10.1007/978-3-642-14623-7_15
22. Goyal, V., Pandey, O., Richelson, S.: Textbook non-malleable commitments. In: STOC, pp. 1128–1141 (2016)
23. Goyal, V., Richelson, S., Rosen, A., Vald, M.: An algebraic approach to non-malleability. In: FOCS, pp. 41–50 (2014)
24. Ishai, Y., Kushilevitz, E.: Randomizing polynomials: a new representation with applications to round-efficient secure computation. In: 41st Annual Symposium on Foundations of Computer Science, 2000, Proceedings, pp. 294–304. IEEE (2000)

25. Jain, A., Kalai, Y.T., Khurana, D., Rothblum, R.: Distinguisher-dependent simulation in two rounds and its applications. IACR Cryptology ePrint Archive 2017, 330 (2017). http://eprint.iacr.org/2017/330
26. Katz, J., Ostrovsky, R.: Round-optimal secure two-party computation. In: Franklin, M. (ed.) CRYPTO 2004. LNCS, vol. 3152, pp. 335–354. Springer, Heidelberg (2004). doi:10.1007/978-3-540-28628-8_21
27. Katz, J., Ostrovsky, R., Smith, A.: Round efficiency of multi-party computation with a dishonest majority. In: Biham, E. (ed.) EUROCRYPT 2003. LNCS, vol. 2656, pp. 578–595. Springer, Heidelberg (2003). doi:10.1007/3-540-39200-9_36
28. Khurana, D., Sahai, A.: How to achieve non-malleability in one or two rounds. IACR Cryptology ePrint Archive 2017, 291 (2017). http://eprint.iacr.org/2017/291
29. Lapidot, D., Shamir, A.: Publicly verifiable non-interactive zero-knowledge proofs. In: Menezes, A.J., Vanstone, S.A. (eds.) CRYPTO 1990. LNCS, vol. 537, pp. 353–365. Springer, Heidelberg (1991). doi:10.1007/3-540-38424-3_26
30. Lin, H., Pass, R., Soni, P.: Two-round concurrent non-malleable commitment from time-lock puzzles. IACR Cryptology ePrint Archive 2017, 273 (2017). http://eprint.iacr.org/2017/273
31. Mukherjee, P., Wichs, D.: Two round multiparty computation via multi-key FHE. In: Fischlin, M., Coron, J.-S. (eds.) EUROCRYPT 2016. LNCS, vol. 9666, pp. 735–763. Springer, Heidelberg (2016). doi:10.1007/978-3-662-49896-5_26
32. Naor, M., Pinkas, B.: Efficient oblivious transfer protocols. In: Proceedings of the Twelfth Annual Symposium on Discrete Algorithms, Washington, DC, USA, 7–9 January 2001, pp. 448–457 (2001)
33. Pandey, O., Pass, R., Vaikuntanathan, V.: Adaptive one-way functions and applications. In: Wagner, D. (ed.) CRYPTO 2008. LNCS, vol. 5157, pp. 57–74. Springer, Heidelberg (2008). doi:10.1007/978-3-540-85174-5_4
34. Pass, R.: Bounded-concurrent secure multi-party computation with a dishonest majority. In: Proceedings of the 36th Annual ACM Symposium on Theory of Computing, Chicago, IL, USA, 13–16 June 2004, pp. 232–241 (2004)
35. Pass, R., Wee, H.: Constant-round non-malleable commitments from subexponential one-way functions. In: Gilbert, H. (ed.) EUROCRYPT 2010. LNCS, vol. 6110, pp. 638–655. Springer, Heidelberg (2010). doi:10.1007/978-3-642-13190-5_32
36. Prabhakaran, M., Rosen, A., Sahai, A.: Concurrent zero knowledge with logarithmic round-complexity. In: FOCS, pp. 366–375 (2002)
37. Rabin, M.O.: How to exchange secrets with oblivious transfer. IACR Cryptology ePrint Archive 2005, 187 (2005)
38. Rosen, A.: A note on constant-round zero-knowledge proofs for NP. In: Naor, M. (ed.) TCC 2004. LNCS, vol. 2951, pp. 191–202. Springer, Heidelberg (2004). doi:10.1007/978-3-540-24638-1_11
39. Sahai, A.: Non-malleable non-interactive zero knowledge and adaptive chosen-ciphertext security. In: 40th Annual Symposium on Foundations of Computer Science, FOCS 1999, New York, NY, USA, 17–18 October 1999, pp. 543–553 (1999)
40. von-Ahn, L., Hopper, N., Langford, J.: Covert two-party computation. In: Proceedings of the Thirty-Seventh Annual ACM Symposium on Theory of Computing, pp. 513–522. ACM (2005)
41. Wee, H.: Black-box, round-efficient secure computation via non-malleability amplification. In: FOCS, pp. 531–540 (2010)
42. Yao, A.C.C.: How to generate and exchange secrets (extended abstract). In: FOCS, pp. 162–167 (1986)

Award Papers

Watermarking Cryptographic Functionalities from Standard Lattice Assumptions

Sam Kim(✉) and David J. Wu

Stanford University, Stanford, USA
{skim13,dwu4}@cs.stanford.edu

Abstract. A software watermarking scheme allows one to embed a "mark" into a program without significantly altering the behavior of the program. Moreover, it should be difficult to remove the watermark without destroying the functionality of the program. Recently, Cohen et al. (STOC 2016) and Boneh et al. (PKC 2017) showed how to watermark cryptographic functions such as PRFs using indistinguishability obfuscation. Notably, in their constructions, the watermark remains intact even against *arbitrary* removal strategies. A natural question is whether we can build watermarking schemes from standard assumptions that achieve this strong mark-unremovability property.

We give the first construction of a watermarkable family of PRFs that satisfy this strong mark-unremovability property from standard lattice assumptions (namely, the learning with errors (LWE) and the one-dimensional short integer solution (SIS) problems). As part of our construction, we introduce a new cryptographic primitive called a translucent PRF. Next, we give a concrete construction of a translucent PRF family from standard lattice assumptions. Finally, we show that using our new lattice-based translucent PRFs, we obtain the first watermarkable family of PRFs with strong unremovability against arbitrary strategies from standard assumptions.

1 Introduction

A software watermarking scheme enables one to embed a "mark" into a program such that the marked program behaves almost identically to the original program. At the same time, it should be difficult for someone to remove the mark without significantly altering the behavior of the program. Watermarking is a powerful notion that has many applications for digital rights management, such as tracing information leaks or resolving ownership disputes. Although the concept itself is quite natural, and in spite of its numerous potential applications, a rigorous theoretical treatment of the notion was given only recently [6,7,31].

Constructing software watermarking with strong security guarantees has proven difficult. Early works on cryptographic watermarking [35,36,40] could only achieve mark-unremovability against adversaries who can only make

The full version of this paper is available at https://eprint.iacr.org/2017/380.pdf.

J. Katz and H. Shacham (Eds.): CRYPTO 2017, Part I, LNCS 10401, pp. 503–536, 2017.
DOI: 10.1007/978-3-319-63688-7_17

a *restricted* set of modifications to the marked program. The more recent works [12,21] that achieve the strongest notion of unremovability against *arbitrary* adversarial strategies all rely on heavy cryptographic tools, namely, indistinguishability obfuscation [6,23]. In this paper, we focus on constructions that achieve the stronger notion of mark-unremovability against arbitrary removal strategies.

Existing constructions of software watermarking [12,21,35,36,40] with formal security guarantees focus primarily on watermarking cryptographic functions. Following [12,21], we consider watermarking for PRFs. In this work, we give the first watermarkable family of PRFs from *standard assumptions* that provides mark-unremovability against *arbitrary* adversarial strategies. All previous watermarking constructions [12,21] that could achieve this notion relied on indistinguishability obfuscation. As we discuss in Sect. 1.2, this notion of software watermarking shares some similarities with program obfuscation, so it is not entirely surprising that existing constructions rely on indistinguishability obfuscation.

To construct our watermarkable family of PRFs, we first introduce a new cryptographic primitive we call *translucent constrained PRFs.* We then show how to use translucent constrained PRFs to build a watermarkable family of PRFs. Finally, we leverage a number of lattice techniques (outlined in Sect. 2) to construct a translucent PRF. Putting these pieces together, we obtain the first watermarkable family of PRFs with strong mark-unremovability guarantees from standard assumptions. Thus, this work broadens our abilities to construct software watermarking, and we believe that by leveraging and extending our techniques, we will see many new constructions of cryptographically-strong watermarking for new functionalities (from standard assumptions) in the future.

1.1 Background

The mathematical foundations of digital watermarking were first introduced by Barak et al. [6,7] in their seminal work on cryptographic obfuscation. Unfortunately, their results were largely negative, for they showed that assuming indistinguishability obfuscation, then certain forms of software watermarking cannot exist. Central to their impossibility result is the assumption that the underlying watermarking scheme is *perfect functionality-preserving.* This requirement stipulates that the input/output behavior of the watermarked program is identical to the original unmarked program on all input points. By relaxing this requirement to allow the watermarked program to differ from the original program on a small number (i.e., a negligible fraction) of the points in the domain, Cohen et al. [21] gave the first construction of an *approximate functionality-preserving* watermarking scheme for a family of pseudorandom functions (PRFs) using indistinguishability obfuscation.

Watermarking Circuits. A watermarking scheme for circuits consists of two algorithms: a marking algorithm and a verification algorithm. The marking algorithm is a keyed algorithm takes as input a circuit C and outputs a new circuit

C' such that on almost all inputs x, $C'(x) = C(x)$. In other words, the watermarked program preserves the functionality of the original program on almost all inputs. The verification algorithm then takes as input a circuit C' and either outputs "marked" or "unmarked." The correctness requirement is that any circuit output by the marking algorithm should be regarded as "marked" by the verification algorithm. A watermarking scheme is said to be publicly-verifiable if anyone can test whether a circuit is watermarked or not, and secretly-verifiable if only the holder of the watermarking key is able to test whether a program is watermarked.

The primary security property a software watermarking scheme must satisfy is unremovability, which roughly says that given a watermarked circuit C, the adversary cannot produce a new circuit $\tilde{C}$ whose functionality is similar to C, and yet is not considered to be marked from the perspective of the verification algorithm. The definition can be strengthened by also allowing the adversary to obtain marked circuits of its choosing. A key source of difficulty in achieving unremovability is that we allow the adversary *complete freedom* in crafting its circuit $\tilde{C}$. All existing constructions of watermarking from standard assumptions [35,36,40] constrain the output or power of the adversary (e.g., the adversary's output must consist of a tuple of group elements). In contrast, the works of Cohen et al. [21], Boneh et al. [12], and this work protect against *arbitrary* removal strategies.

A complementary security property to unremovability is unforgeability, which says that an adversary who does not possess the watermarking secret key is unable to construct a new program (i.e., one sufficiently different from any watermarked programs the adversary might have seen) that is deemed to be watermarked (from the perspective of the verification algorithm). As noted by Cohen et al. [21], unforgeability and unremovability are oftentimes conflicting requirements, and depending on the precise definitions, may not be simultaneously satisfiable. In this work, we consider a natural setting where both conditions are simultaneously satisfiable (and in fact, our construction achieves exactly that).

Watermarking PRFs. Following Cohen et al. [21] and Boneh et al. [12], we focus on watermarking cryptographic functions, specifically PRFs, in this work. Previously, Cohen et al. [21] demonstrated that many natural classes of functions, such as any efficiently learnable class of functions, cannot be watermarked. A canonical and fairly natural class of non-learnable functionalities are cryptographic ones. Moreover, watermarking PRFs already suffices for a number of interesting applications; we refer to [21] for the full details.

Building Software Watermarking. We begin by describing the high-level blueprint introduced by Cohen et al. [21] for constructing watermarkable PRFs.[1] To watermark a PRF F with key k, the marking algorithm first evaluates the PRF on several (secret) points $h_1, \ldots, h_d$ to obtain values $t_1, \ldots, t_d$. Then, the

[1] There are numerous technicalities in the actual construction, but these are not essential to understanding the main intuition.

marking algorithm uses the values $(t_1, \ldots, t_d)$ to derive a (pseudorandom) pair (x^*, y^*). The watermarked program is a circuit C that on all inputs $x \neq x^*$, outputs $F(k, x)$, while on input x^*, it outputs the special value y^*. To test whether a program C' is marked or not, the verification algorithm first evaluates C' on the secret points $h_1, \ldots, h_d$. It uses the function evaluations to derive the test pair (x^*, y^*). Finally, it evaluates the program at x^* and outputs "marked" if $C'(x^*) = y^*$; otherwise, it outputs "unmarked." For this scheme to be secure against *arbitrary* removing strategies, it must be the case that the watermarked circuit C hides the marked point x^* from the adversary. Moreover, the value y^* at the "reprogrammed" point should not be easily identifiable. Otherwise, an adversary can trivially defeat the watermarking scheme by simply producing a circuit that behaves just like C, but outputs $\perp$ whenever it is queried on the special point x^*. In some sense, security requires that the point x^* is carefully embedded within the description of the watermarked program such that no efficient adversary is able to identify it (or even learn partial information about it). This apparent need to embed a secret within a piece of code is reminiscent of program obfuscation, so not surprisingly, the existing constructions of software watermarking all rely on indistinguishability obfuscation.

Puncturable and Programmable PRFs. The starting point of our construction is the recent watermarking construction by Boneh et al. [12] (which follows the Cohen et al. [21] blueprint sketched above). In their work, they first introduce the notion of a *private puncturable* PRF. In a regular puncturable PRF [14,15,33], the holder of the PRF key can issue a "punctured" key sk_{x^*} such that sk_{x^*} can be used to evaluate the PRF everywhere except at a single point x^*. In a private puncturable PRF, the punctured key sk_{x^*} also hides the punctured point x^*. Intuitively, private puncturing seems to get us partway to the goal of constructing a watermarkable family of PRFs according to the above blueprint. After all, a private puncturable PRF allows issuing keys that agree with the real PRF almost everywhere, and yet, the holder of the punctured key cannot tell which point was punctured. Unfortunately, standard puncturable PRFs do not provide an efficient algorithm for testing whether a particular point is punctured or not, and thus, we do not have a way to determine (given just oracle access to the program) whether the program is marked or not.

To bridge the gap between private puncturable PRFs and watermarkable PRFs, Boneh et al. introduced a stronger notion called a private *programmable* PRF, which allows for *arbitrary* reprogramming of the PRF value at the punctured point. This modification allows them to instantiate the Cohen et al. blueprint for watermarking. However, private programmable PRFs seem more difficult to construct than a private puncturable PRF, and the construction in [12] relies on indistinguishability obfuscation. In contrast, Boneh et al. [10] as well as Canetti and Chen [19] have recently showed how to construct private puncturable PRFs (and in the case of [19], private constrained PRFs for NC^1) from standard lattice assumptions.

1.2 Our Contributions

While the high-level framework of Cohen et al. [21] provides an elegant approach for building watermarkable PRFs (and by extension, other cryptographic functionalities), realizing it without relying on some form of obfuscation is challenging. Our primary contribution in this work is showing that it is possible to construct a watermarkable family of PRFs (in the secret-key setting) while only relying on standard lattice assumptions (namely, on the subexponential hardness of LWE and 1D-SIS). Thus, this work gives the first construction of a mathematically-sound watermarking construction for a nontrivial family of cryptographic primitives from standard assumptions. In this section, we give a brief overview of our main construction and results. Then, in Sect. 2, we give a more detailed technical overview of our lattice-based watermarking construction.

Relaxing Programmability. The work of Boneh et al. [12] introduces two closely-related notions: private puncturable PRFs and private programmable PRFs. Despite their similarities, private programmable PRFs give a direct construction of watermarking while private puncturable PRFs do not seem sufficient. In this work, we take a "meet-in-the-middle" approach. First, we identify an intermediate notion that interpolates between private puncturable PRFs and private programmable PRFs. For reasons described below, we refer to our new primitive as a private translucent PRF. The advantages to defining this new notion are twofold. First, we show how to augment and extend the Boneh et al. [10] private puncturable PRF to obtain a private translucent PRF from standard lattice assumptions. Second, we show that private translucent PRFs still suffice to instantiate the rough blueprint in [21] for building cryptographic watermarking schemes. Together, these ingredients yield the first (secretly-verifiable) watermarkable family of PRFs from standard assumptions.[2]

Private Translucent PRFs. The key cryptographic primitive we introduce in this work is the notion of a translucent puncturable PRF. To keep the description simple, we refer to it as a "translucent PRF" in this section. As described above, private translucent PRFs interpolate between private puncturable PRFs and private programmable PRFs. We begin by describing the notion of a (non-private) translucent PRF. A translucent PRF consists of a set of public parameters pp and a secret testing key tk. Unlike standard puncturable and programmable PRFs, each translucent PRF (specified by $(\mathsf{pp}, \mathsf{tk})$) defines an entire *family* of puncturable PRFs over a domain $\mathcal{X}$ and range $\mathcal{Y}$, and which share a common set of public parameters. More precisely, translucent PRFs implement a $\mathsf{SampleKey}$ algorithm which, on input the public parameters pp, samples a PRF key k from the underlying puncturable PRF family. The underlying PRF family associated with pp is puncturable, so all of the keys k output by $\mathsf{SampleKey}$ can be punctured.

---

[2] Another approach for building a watermarkable family of PRFs is to directly construct a private programmable PRF (from standard assumptions) and then invoke the construction in [12]. We discuss this approach at the end of this section.

The defining property of a translucent PRF is that when a punctured key sk_{x^*} (derived from some PRF key k output by $\mathsf{SampleKey}$) is used to evaluate the PRF at the punctured point x^*, the resulting value lies in a specific subset $S \subset \mathcal{Y}$. Moreover, when the punctured key sk_{x^*} is used to evaluate at any non-punctured point $x \neq x^*$, the resulting value lies in $\mathcal{Y} \setminus S$ with high probability. The particular subset S is *global* to all PRFs in the punctured PRF family, and moreover, is uniquely determined by the public parameters of the overall translucent PRF. The second requirement we require of a translucent PRF is that the secret testing key tk can be used to test whether a particular value $y \in \mathcal{Y}$ lies in the subset S or not. In other words, given only the evaluation output of a punctured key sk_{x^*} on some input x, the holder of the testing key can efficiently tell whether $x = x^*$ (without any knowledge of sk_{x^*} or its associated PRF key k).

In a *private* translucent PRF, we impose the additional requirement that the underlying puncturable PRF family is privately puncturable (that is, the punctured keys also hide the punctured point). An immediate consequence of the privacy requirement is that whenever a punctured key is used to evaluate the PRF at a punctured point, the output value (contained in S) should look indistinguishable from a random value in the range $\mathcal{Y}$. If elements in S are easily distinguishable from elements in $\mathcal{Y} \setminus S$ (without tk), then an adversary can efficiently test whether a punctured key is punctured at a particular point x, thus breaking privacy. In particular, this means that S must be a sparse hidden subset of $\mathcal{Y}$ such that anyone who does not possess the testing key tk cannot distinguish elements in S from elements in $\mathcal{Y}$. Anyone who possesses the testing key, however, should be able to tell whether a particular element is contained in S or not. Moreover, all of these properties should hold even though it is *easy* to publicly sample elements from S (the adversary can always sample a PRF key k using $\mathsf{SampleKey}$, puncture k at any point x^*, and then evaluate the punctured key at x^*). Sets $S \subset \mathcal{Y}$ that satisfy these properties were referred to as "translucent sets" in the work of Canetti et al. [20] on constructing deniable encryption. In our setting, the outputs of the punctured PRF keys in a private translucent PRF precisely implement a translucent set system, hence the name "translucent PRF."

From Private Translucency to Watermarking. Once we have a private translucent PRF, it is fairly straightforward to obtain from it a family of watermarkable PRFs. Our construction roughly follows the high-level blueprint described in [21]. Take any private translucent PRF with public parameters pp and testing key tk. We now describe a (secretly-verifiable) watermarking scheme for the family of private puncturable PRFs associated with pp. The watermarking secret key consists of several randomly chosen domain elements $h_1, \ldots, h_d \in \mathcal{X}$ and the testing key tk for the private translucent PRF. To watermark a PRF key k (output by $\mathsf{SampleKey}$), the marking algorithm evaluates the PRF on $h_1, \ldots, h_d$ and uses the outputs to derive a special point $x^* \in \mathcal{X}$. The watermarked key sk_{x^*} is the key k punctured at the point x^*. By definition, this means that if the watermarked key sk_{x^*} is used to evaluate the PRF at x^*, then the resulting value lies in the hidden sparse subset $S \subseteq \mathcal{Y}$ specific to the private translucent PRF.

To test whether a particular program (i.e., circuit) is marked, the verification algorithm first evaluates the circuit at $h_1, \ldots, h_d$. Then, it uses the evaluations to derive the special point x^*. Finally, the verification algorithm evaluates the program at x^* to obtain a value y^*. Using the testing key tk, the verification algorithm checks to see if y^* lies in the hidden set S associated with the public parameters of the private translucent PRF. Correctness follows from the fact that the punctured key is functionality-preserving (i.e., computes the PRF correctly at all but the punctured point). Security of the watermarking scheme follows from the fact that the watermarked key hides the special point x^*. Furthermore, the adversary cannot distinguish the elements of the hidden set S from random elements in the range $\mathcal{Y}$. Intuitively then, the only effective way for the adversary to remove the watermark is to change the behavior of the marked program on many points (i.e., at least one of $h_1, \ldots, h_d, x^*$). But to do so, we show that such an adversary necessarily corrupts the functionality on a noticeable fraction of the domain. In Sect. 6, we formalize these notions and show that every private translucent PRF gives rise to a watermarkable family of PRFs. In fact, we show that starting from private translucent PRFs, we obtain a watermarkable family of PRFs satisfying a *stronger* notion of mark-unremovability security compared to the construction in [12]. We discuss this in greater detail in Sect. 6 (Remark 6.8).

Message-Embedding via t-Puncturing. Previous watermarking constructions [12, 21] also supported a stronger notion of watermarking called "message-embedding" watermarking. In a message-embedding scheme, the marking algorithm also takes as input a message $m \in \{0,1\}^t$ and outputs a watermarked program with the message m embedded within it. The verification algorithm is replaced with an extraction algorithm that takes as input a watermarked program (and in the secret-key setting, the watermarking secret key), and either outputs "unmarked" or the embedded message. The unremovability property is strengthened to say that given a program with an embedded message m, the adversary cannot produce a similar program on which the extraction algorithm outputs something other than m. Existing watermarking constructions [12,21] leverage reprogrammability to obtain a message-embedding watermarking scheme—that is, the program's outputs on certain special inputs are modified to contain a (blinded) version of m (which the verification algorithm can then extract).

A natural question is whether our construction based on private translucent PRFs can be extended to support message-embedding. The key barrier seems to be the fact that private translucent PRFs do not allow much flexibility in programming the actual value to which a punctured key evaluates on a punctured point. We can only ensure that it lies in some translucent set S. To achieve message-embedding watermarking, we require a different method of embedding the message. Our solution contains two key ingredients:

- First, we introduce a notion of private t-puncturable PRFs, which is a natural extension of puncturing where the punctured keys are punctured on a set of exactly t points in the domain rather than a single point. Fortunately, for small values of t (i.e., polynomial in the security parameter), our

private translucent PRF construction (Sect. 5) can be modified to support keys punctured at t points rather than a single point. The other properties of translucent PRFs remain intact (i.e., whenever a t-punctured key is used to evaluate at any one of the t punctured points, the result of the evaluation lies in the translucent subset $S \subset \mathcal{Y}$).
- To embed a message $m \in \{0,1\}^t$, we follow the same blueprint as before, but instead of deriving a single special point x^*, the marking algorithm instead derives $2 \cdot t$ (pseudorandom) points $x_1^{(0)}, x_1^{(1)}, \ldots, x_t^{(0)}, x_t^{(1)}$. The watermarked key is a t-punctured key, where the t points are chosen based on the bits of the message. Specifically, to embed a message $m \in \{0,1\}^t$ into a PRF key k, the marking algorithm punctures k at the points $x_1^{(m_1)}, \ldots, x_t^{(m_t)}$. The extraction procedure works similarly to the verification procedure in the basic construction. It first evaluates the program on the set of (hidden) inputs, and uses the program outputs to derive the values $x_i^{(b)}$ for all $i = 1, \ldots, t$ and $b \in \{0,1\}$. For each index $i = 1, \ldots, t$, the extraction algorithm tests whether the program's output at $x_i^{(0)}$ or $x_i^{(1)}$ lies within the translucent set S. In this way, the extraction algorithm is able to extract the bits of the message.

Thus, without much additional overhead (i.e., proportional to the bit-length of the embedded messages), we obtain a message-embedding watermarking scheme from standard lattice assumption.

Constructing Translucent PRFs. Another technical contribution in this work is a new construction of a private translucent PRF (that supports t-puncturing) from standard lattice assumptions. The starting point of our private translucent PRF construction is the private puncturable PRF construction of Boneh et al. [10]. We provide a detailed technical overview of our algebraic construction in Sect. 2, and the concrete details of the construction in Sect. 5. Here, we provide some intuition on how we construct a private translucent PRF (for the simpler case of puncturing). Recall first that the construction of Boneh et al. gives rise to a PRF with output space $\mathbb{Z}_p^m$. In our private translucent PRF construction, the translucent set is chosen to be a random *noisy* 1-dimensional subspace within $\mathbb{Z}_p^m$. By carefully exploiting the specific algebraic structure of the Boneh et al. PRF, we ensure that whenever an (honestly-generated) punctured key is used to evaluate on a punctured point, the evaluation outputs a vector in this random subspace (with high probability). The testing key simply consists of a vector that is essentially orthogonal to the hidden subspace. Of course, it is critical here that the hidden subspace is noisy. Otherwise, since the adversary is able to obtain arbitrary samples from this subspace (by generating and puncturing keys of its own), it can trivially learn the subspace, and thus, efficiently decide whether a vector lies in the subspace or not. Using a noisy subspace enables us to appeal to the hardness of LWE and 1D-SIS to argue security of the overall construction. We refer to the technical overview in Sect. 2 and the concrete description in Sect. 5 for the full details.

An Alternative Approach. An alternative method for constructing a watermarkable family of PRFs is to construct a private programmable PRF from standard assumptions and apply the construction in [12]. For instance, suppose we had a private puncturable PRF with the property that the value obtained when using a punctured key to evaluate at a punctured point varies depending on the randomness used in the puncturing algorithm. This property can be used to construct a private programmable PRF with a single-bit output. Specifically, one can apply rejection sampling when puncturing the PRF to obtain a key with the desired value at the punctured point. To extend to multiple output bits, one can concatenate the outputs of several single-bit programmable PRFs. In conjunction with the construction in [12], this gives another approach for constructing a watermarkable family of PRFs (though satisfying a weaker security definition as we explain below). The existing constructions of private puncturable PRFs [10, 19], however, do not naturally satisfy this property. While the puncturing algorithms in [10, 19] are both randomized, the value obtained when using the punctured key to evaluate at the punctured point is *independent* of the randomness used during puncturing. Thus, this rejection sampling approach does not directly yield a private programmable PRF, but may provide an alternative starting point for future constructions.

In this paper, our starting point is the Boneh et al. [10] private puncturable PRF, and one of our main contributions is showing how the "matrix-embedding-based" constrained PRFs in [10, 17] (and described in Sect. 2) can be used to construct watermarking.[3] One advantage of our approach is that our private translucent PRF satisfies key-injectivity (a property that seems non-trivial to achieve using the basic construction of private programmable PRFs described above). This property enables us to achieve a stronger notion of security for watermarking compared to that in [12]. We refer to Sect. 4 (Definition 4.14) and Remark 6.8 for a more thorough discussion. A similar notion of key-injectivity was also needed in [21] to argue full security of their watermarking construction. Moreover, the translucent PRFs we support allow (limited) programming at *polynomially-many* points, while the rejection-sampling approach described above supports programming of at most logarithmically-many points. Although this distinction is not important for watermarking, it may enable future applications of translucent PRFs. Finally, we note that our translucent PRF construction can also be viewed as a way to randomize the constraining algorithm of the PRF construction in [10, 17], and thus, can be combined with rejection sampling to obtain a programmable PRF.

Open Problems. Our work gives a construction of *secretly-verifiable* watermarkable family of PRFs from standard assumptions. Can we construct a *publicly-verifiable* watermarkable family of PRFs from standard assumptions? A first step might be to construct a secretly-verifiable watermarking scheme that gives the adversary access to an "extraction" oracle. The only watermarking schemes (with security against arbitrary removal strategies) that satisfy either one of these goals are due to Cohen et al. [21] and rely on indistinguishability obfuscation. Another direction is to explore additional applications of private

[3] In contrast, the Canetti-Chen constrained PRF construction [19] builds on secure modes of operation of the Gentry et al. multilinear map [26].

translucent PRFs and private programmable PRFs. Can these primitives be used to base other cryptographic objects on standard assumptions?

1.3 Additional Related Work

Much of the early (and ongoing) work on digital watermarking have focused on watermarking digital media, such as images or video. These constructions tend to be ad hoc, and lack a firm theoretical foundation. We refer to [22] and the references therein for a comprehensive survey of the field. The work of Hopper et al. [31] gives the first formal and rigorous definitions for a digital watermarking scheme, but they do not provide any concrete constructions. In the same work, Hopper et al. also introduce the formal notion of secretly-verifiable watermarking, which is the focus of this work.

Early works on cryptographic watermarking [35,36,40] gave constructions that achieved mark-unremovability against adversaries who could only make a *restricted* set of modifications to the marked program. The work of Nishimaki [36] showed how to obtain message-embedding watermarking using a bit-by-bit embedding of the message within a dual-pairing vector space (specific to his particular construction). Our message-embedding construction in this paper also takes a bit-by-bit approach, but our technique is more general: we show that any translucent t-puncturable PRF suffices for constructing a watermarkable family of PRFs that supports embedding t-bit messages.

In a recent work, Nishimaki et al. [37] show how to construct a traitor tracing scheme where arbitrary data can be embedded within a decryption key (which can be recovered by a tracing algorithm). While the notion of message-embedding traitor tracing is conceptually similar to software watermarking, the notions are incomparable. In a traitor-tracing scheme, there is a *single* decryption key and a central authority who issues the marked keys. Conversely, in a watermarking scheme, the keys can be chosen by the *user*, and moreover, different keys (implementing different functions) can be watermarked.

PRFs from LWE. The first PRF construction from LWE was due to Banerjee et al. [5]. Subsequently, [4,11] gave the first lattice-based key-homomorphic PRFs. These constructions were then generalized to the setting of constrained PRFs in [3,10,17]. Recently, Canetti and Chen [19] showed how certain secure modes of operation of the multilinear map by Gentry et al. [26] can be used to construct a private constrained PRF for the class of NC^1 constraints (with hardness reducing to the LWE assumption).

ABE and PE from LWE. The techniques used in this work build on a series of works in the areas of *attribute-based encryption* [39] and *predicate encryption* [13, 32] from LWE. These include the attribute-based encryption constructions of [1,9,16,18,28,30], and predicate encryption constructions of [2,24,29].[4]

[4] We note that the LWE-based predicate encryption constructions satisfy a weaker security property (compared to [13,32]) sometimes referred to as *weak attribute-hiding*.

2 Construction Overview

In this section, we give a technical overview of our private translucent t-puncturable PRF from standard lattice assumptions. As described in Sect. 1, this directly implies a watermarkable family of PRFs from standard lattice assumptions. The formal definitions, constructions and accompanying proofs of security are given in Sects. 4 and 5. The watermarking construction is given in Sect. 6.

The LWE Assumption. The learning with errors (LWE) assumption [38], parameterized by n, m, q, χ, states that for a uniformly random vector $\mathbf{s} \in \mathbb{Z}_q^n$ and a uniformly random matrix $\mathbf{A} \in \mathbb{Z}_q^{n \times m}$, the distribution $(\mathbf{A}, \mathbf{s}^T \mathbf{A} + \mathbf{e}^T)$ is computationally indistinguishable from the uniform distribution over $\mathbb{Z}_q^{n \times m} \times \mathbb{Z}_q^m$, where $\mathbf{e}$ is sampled from a (low-norm) error distribution χ. To simplify the presentation in this section, we will ignore the precise generation and evolution of the error term $\mathbf{e}$ and just refer to it as "noise."

Matrix Embeddings. The starting point of our construction is the recent privately puncturable PRF of Boneh, Kim, and Montgomery [10], which itself builds on the constrained PRF construction of Brakerski and Vaikuntanathan [17]. Both of these constructions rely on the matrix embedding mechanism introduced by Boneh et al. [9] for constructing attribute-based encryption. In [9], an input $x \in \{0,1\}^\rho$ is embedded as the vector

$$\mathbf{s}^T \big(\mathbf{A}_1 + x_1 \cdot \mathbf{G} \mid \cdots \mid \mathbf{A}_\rho + x_\rho \cdot \mathbf{G}\big) + \mathsf{noise} \in \mathbb{Z}_q^{m\rho}, \tag{2.1}$$

where $\mathbf{A}_1, \ldots, \mathbf{A}_\rho \in \mathbb{Z}_q^{n \times m}$ are uniformly random matrices, $\mathbf{s} \in \mathbb{Z}_q^n$ is a uniformly random vector, and $\mathbf{G} \in \mathbb{Z}_q^{n \times m}$ is a special fixed matrix (called the "gadget matrix"). Embedding the inputs in this way enables homomorphic operations on the inputs while keeping the noise small. In particular, given an input $x \in \{0,1\}^\rho$ and any polynomial-size circuit $C : \{0,1\}^\rho \to \{0,1\}$, there is a public operation that allows computing the following vector from Eq. (2.1):

$$\mathbf{s}^T \big(\mathbf{A}_C + C(x) \cdot \mathbf{G}\big) + \mathsf{noise} \in \mathbb{Z}_q^m, \tag{2.2}$$

where the matrix $\mathbf{A}_C \in \mathbb{Z}_q^{n \times m}$ depends only on the circuit C, and *not* on the underlying input x. Thus, we can define a homomorphic operation $\mathsf{Eval}_{\mathsf{pk}}$ on the matrices $\mathbf{A}_1, \ldots, \mathbf{A}_\rho$ where on input a sequence of matrices $\mathbf{A}_1, \ldots, \mathbf{A}_\rho$ and a circuit C, $\mathsf{Eval}_{\mathsf{pk}}(C, \mathbf{A}_1, \ldots, \mathbf{A}_\rho) \to \mathbf{A}_C$.

A Puncturable PRF from LWE. Brakerski and Vaikuntanathan [17] showed how the homomorphic properties in [9] can be leveraged to construct a (single-key) constrained PRF for general constraints. Here, we provide a high-level description of their construction specialized to the case of puncturing. First, let eq be the equality circuit where $\mathsf{eq}(x^*, x) = 1$ if $x^* = x$ and 0 otherwise. The public parameters[5] of the scheme in [17] consist of randomly generated matrices

[5] Since a constrained PRF is a secret-key primitive, we can always include the public parameters as part of the secret key. However, in the lattice-based constrained PRF

$\mathbf{A}_0, \mathbf{A}_1 \in \mathbb{Z}_q^{n\times m}$ for encoding the PRF input x and matrices $\mathbf{B}_1, \ldots \mathbf{B}_\rho \in \mathbb{Z}_q^{n\times m}$ for encoding the punctured point x^*. The secret key for the PRF is a vector $\mathbf{s} \in \mathbb{Z}_q^n$. Then, on input a point $x \in \{0,1\}^\rho$, the PRF value at x is defined to be

$$\mathsf{PRF}(\mathbf{s}, x) := \lfloor \mathbf{s}^T \cdot \mathbf{A}_{\mathsf{eq},x} \rceil_p \quad \text{where} \quad \mathbf{A}_{\mathsf{eq},x} := \mathsf{Eval}_{\mathsf{pk}}(\mathsf{eq}, \mathbf{B}_1, \ldots, \mathbf{B}_\rho, \mathbf{A}_{x_1}, \ldots, \mathbf{A}_{x_\rho}),$$

where $\mathbf{A}_0, \mathbf{A}_1, \mathbf{B}_1, \ldots, \mathbf{B}_\rho \in \mathbb{Z}_q^{n\times m}$ are the matrices in the public parameters, and $\lfloor\cdot\rceil_p$ is the component-wise rounding operation that maps an element in $\mathbb{Z}_q$ to an element in $\mathbb{Z}_p$ where $p < q$. By construction, $\mathbf{A}_{\mathsf{eq},x}$ is a function of x.

To puncture the key $\mathbf{s}$ at a point $x^* \in \{0,1\}^\rho$, the construction in [17] gives out the vector

$$\mathbf{s}^T \cdot \big(\mathbf{A}_0 + 0 \cdot \mathbf{G} \mid \mathbf{A}_1 + 1 \cdot \mathbf{G} \quad \mid \quad \mathbf{B}_1 + x_1^* \cdot \mathbf{G} \mid \cdots \mid \mathbf{B}_\rho + x_\rho^* \cdot \mathbf{G}\big) + \mathsf{noise}. \tag{2.3}$$

To evaluate the PRF at a point $x \in \{0,1\}^\rho$ using a punctured key, the user first homomorphically evaluates the equality circuit eq on input (x^*, x) to obtain the vector $\mathbf{s}^T\big(\mathbf{A}_{\mathsf{eq},x} + \mathsf{eq}(x^*, x) \cdot \mathbf{G}\big) + \mathsf{noise}$. Rounding down this vector yields the correct PRF value whenever $\mathsf{eq}(x^*, x) = 0$, or equivalently, whenever $x \neq x^*$, as required for puncturing. As shown in [17], this construction yields a secure (though non-private) puncturable PRF from LWE with some added modifications.

Private Puncturing. The reason the Brakerski-Vaikuntanathan puncturable PRF described here does not provide privacy (that is, hide the punctured point) is because in order to operate on the embedded vectors, the evaluator needs to know the underlying inputs. In other words, to homomorphically compute the equality circuit eq on the input (x^*, x), the evaluator needs to know both x and x^*. However, the punctured point x^* is precisely the information we need to hide. Using an idea inspired by the predicate encryption scheme of Gorbunov et al. [29], the construction of Boneh et al. [10] hides the point x^* by first encrypting it using a fully homomorphic encryption (FHE) scheme [25] before applying the matrix embeddings of [9]. Specifically, in [10], the punctured key has the following form:

$$\begin{aligned}\mathbf{s}^T \cdot \big(\mathbf{A}_0 + 0 \cdot \mathbf{G} \mid \mathbf{A}_1 + 1 \cdot \mathbf{G} \quad &\mid \quad \mathbf{B}_1 + \mathsf{ct}_1 \cdot \mathbf{G} \mid \cdots \mid \mathbf{B}_z + \mathsf{ct}_z \cdot \mathbf{G} \\ &\mid \quad \mathbf{C}_1 + \mathsf{sk}_1 \cdot \mathbf{G} \mid \cdots \mid \mathbf{C}_\tau + \mathsf{sk}_\tau \cdot \mathbf{G}\big) + \mathsf{noise},\end{aligned}$$

where $\mathsf{ct}_1, \ldots, \mathsf{ct}_z$ are the bits of an FHE encryption ct of the punctured point x^*, and $\mathsf{sk}_1, \ldots, \mathsf{sk}_\tau$ are the bits of the FHE secret key sk. Given the ciphertext ct, the evaluator can homomorphically evaluate the equality circuit eq and obtain an FHE encryption of $\mathsf{eq}(x^*, x)$. Next, by leveraging an "asymmetric multiplication property" of the matrix encodings, the evaluator is able to compute the inner

constructions [3,10,17], the public parameters can be sampled once and shared across multiple *independent* secret keys. Our construction of translucent PRFs will rely on choosing the public parameter matrices to have a certain structure that is shared across multiple secret keys.

product between the encrypted result with the decryption key sk.[6] Recall that for lattice-based FHE schemes (e.g. [27]), decryption consists of evaluating a rounded inner product of the ciphertext with the decryption key. Specifically, the inner product between the ciphertext and the decryption key results in $\frac{q}{2}+e \in \mathbb{Z}_q$ for some "small" error term e.

Thus, it remains to show how to perform the rounding step in the FHE decryption. Simply computing the inner product between the ciphertext and the secret key results in a vector

$$\mathbf{s}^T \left(\mathbf{A}_{\mathsf{FHE},\mathsf{eq},x} + \left(\frac{q}{2} \cdot \mathsf{eq}(x^*, x) + e\right) \cdot \mathbf{G}\right) + \text{noise},$$

where e is the FHE noise (for simplicity, by FHE, we always refer to the specific construction of [27] and its variants hereafter). Even though the error e is small, neither $\mathbf{s}$ nor $\mathbf{G}$ are low-norm and therefore, the noise does not simply round away. The observation made in [10], however, is that the gadget matrix $\mathbf{G}$ contains some low-norm column vectors, namely the identity matrix $\mathbf{I}$ as a submatrix. By restricting the PRF evaluation to just these columns and sampling the secret key $\mathbf{s}$ from the low-norm noise distribution, they show that the FHE error term $\mathbf{s}^T \cdot e \cdot \mathbf{I}$ can be rounded away. Thus, by defining the PRF evaluation to only take these specific column positions of

$$\mathsf{PRF}(\mathbf{s}, x) := \lfloor \mathbf{s}^T \mathbf{A}_{\mathsf{FHE},\mathsf{eq},x} \rceil_p,$$

it is possible to recover the PRF evaluation from the punctured key if and only if $\mathsf{eq}(x^*, x) = 0$.[7]

Trapdoor at Punctured Key Evaluations. We now describe how we extend the private puncturing construction in [10] to obtain a private translucent puncturable PRF where a secret key can be used to test whether a value is the result of using a punctured key to evaluate at a punctured point. We begin by describing an alternative way to perform the rounding step of the FHE decryption in the construction of [10]. First, consider modifying the PRF evaluation at $x \in \{0,1\}^\rho$ to be

$$\mathsf{PRF}(\mathbf{s}, x) := \lfloor \mathbf{s}^T \mathbf{A}_{\mathsf{FHE},\mathsf{eq},x} \cdot \mathbf{G}^{-1}(\mathbf{D}) \rceil_p,$$

[6] Normally, multiplication of two inputs requires knowledge of both of the underlying inputs. The "asymmetry" in the embedding scheme of [9] enables multiplications to be done even if only one of the values to be multiplied is known to the evaluator. In the case of computing an inner product between the FHE ciphertext and the FHE secret key, the evaluator knows the bits of the ciphertext, but not the FHE secret key. Thus, the asymmetry enables the evaluator to homomorphically evaluate the inner product without knowledge of the FHE secret key.

[7] To actually show that the challenge PRF evaluation is pseudorandom at the punctured point, additional modifications must be made such as introducing extra randomizing terms and collapsing the final PRF evaluation to be field elements instead of vectors. We refer to [10] for the full details.

where $\mathbf{D} \in \mathbb{Z}_q^{n \times m}$ is a public *binary* matrix and $\mathbf{G}^{-1}$ is the component-wise *bit-decomposition* operator on matrices in $\mathbb{Z}_q^{n \times m}$.[8] The gadget matrix $\mathbf{G}$ is defined so that for any matrix $\mathbf{A} \in \mathbb{Z}_q^{n \times m}$, $\mathbf{G} \cdot \mathbf{G}^{-1}(\mathbf{A}) = \mathbf{A}$. Then, if we evaluate the PRF using the punctured key and multiply the result by $\mathbf{G}^{-1}(\mathbf{D})$, we obtain the following:

$$\begin{aligned}\left(\mathbf{s}^T\left(\mathbf{A}_{\mathsf{FHE},\mathsf{eq},x} + \left(\frac{q}{2}\cdot \mathsf{eq}(x^*,x) + e\right)\cdot \mathbf{G}\right) + \mathsf{noise}\right)\mathbf{G}^{-1}(\mathbf{D}) \\ = \mathbf{s}^T \underbrace{\left(\mathbf{A}_{\mathsf{FHE},\mathsf{eq},x}\mathbf{G}^{-1}(\mathbf{D}) + \left(\frac{q}{2}\cdot \mathsf{eq}(x^*,x) + e\right)\cdot \mathbf{D}\right)}_{\tilde{\mathbf{A}}_{\mathsf{FHE},\mathsf{eq},x}} + \mathsf{noise}' \\ = \mathbf{s}^T \tilde{\mathbf{A}}_{\mathsf{FHE},\mathsf{eq},x} + \mathsf{noise}'\end{aligned}$$

Since $\mathbf{D}$ is a low-norm (in fact, binary) matrix, the FHE error component $\mathbf{s}^T \cdot e \cdot \mathbf{D}$ is short, and thus, will disappear when we round. Therefore, whenever $\mathsf{eq}(x^*, x) = 0$, we obtain the real PRF evaluation.

The key observation we make is that the algebraic structure of the PRF evaluation allows us to "program" the matrix $\tilde{\mathbf{A}}_{\mathsf{FHE},\mathsf{eq},x}$ whenever $\mathsf{eq}(x^*, x) = 1$ (namely, when the punctured key is used to evaluate at the punctured point). As described here, the FHE ciphertext decrypts to $q/2+e$ when the message is 1 and e when the message is 0 (where e is a small error term). In the FHE scheme of [27] (and its variants), it is possible to encrypt scalar elements in $\mathbb{Z}_q$, and moreover, to modify the decryption operation so that it outputs the encrypted scalar element (with some error). In other words, decrypting a ciphertext encrypting $w \in \mathbb{Z}_q$ would yield a value $w + e$ for some small error term e. Then, in the PRF construction, instead of encrypting the punctured point x^*, we encrypt a tuple (x^*, w) where $w \in \mathbb{Z}_q$ is used to program the matrix $\tilde{\mathbf{A}}_{\mathsf{FHE},\mathsf{eq},x}$.[9] Next, we replace the basic equality function eq in the construction with a "scaled" equality function that on input $(x, (x^*, w))$, outputs w if $x = x^*$, and 0 otherwise. With these changes, evaluating the punctured PRF at a point x now yields:[10]

$$\mathbf{s}^T \left(\mathbf{A}_{\mathsf{FHE},\mathsf{eq},x}\mathbf{G}^{-1}(\mathbf{D}) + (w \cdot \mathsf{eq}(x^*,x) + e)\cdot \mathbf{D}\right) + \mathsf{noise}.$$

Since w can be chosen arbitrarily when the punctured key is constructed, a natural question to ask is whether there exists a w such that the matrix $\mathbf{A}_{\mathsf{FHE},\mathsf{eq},x}\mathbf{G}^{-1}(\mathbf{D}) + w \cdot \mathbf{D}$ has a particular structure. This is not possible if w is a scalar, but if there are *multiple* w's, this becomes possible.

---

[8] Multiplying by the matrix $\mathbf{G}^{-1}(\mathbf{D})$ can be viewed as an alternative way to restrict the PRF to the column positions corresponding to the identity submatrix in $\mathbf{G}$.

[9] A similar construction is used in [10] to show security. In their construction, they sample and encrypt a random set of w's and use them to blind the real PRF value at the punctured point.

[10] To reduce notational clutter, we redefine the matrix $\mathbf{A}_{\mathsf{FHE},\mathsf{eq},x}$ here to be the matrix associated with homomorphic evaluation of the scaled equality-check circuit.

To support programming of the matrix $\tilde{\mathbf{A}}_{\mathsf{FHE},\mathsf{eq},x}$, we first take $N = m \cdot n$ (public) binary matrices $\mathbf{D}_\ell \in \{0,1\}^{n \times m}$ where the collection $\{\mathbf{D}_\ell\}_{\ell \in [N]}$ is a basis for the module $\mathbb{Z}_q^{n \times m}$ (over $\mathbb{Z}_q$). This means that any matrix in $\mathbb{Z}_q^{n \times m}$ can be expressed as a unique linear combination $\sum_{\ell \in [N]} w_\ell \mathbf{D}_\ell$ where $\mathbf{w} = (w_1, \ldots, w_N) \in \mathbb{Z}_q^N$ are the coefficients. Then, instead of encrypting a single element w in each FHE ciphertext, we encrypt a vector $\mathbf{w}$ of coefficients. The PRF output is then a sum of N *different* PRF evaluations:

$$\mathsf{PRF}(\mathbf{s}, x) := \left\lfloor \sum_{\ell \in [N]} \mathbf{s}^T \mathbf{A}_{\mathsf{FHE},\mathsf{eq}_\ell,x} \mathbf{G}^{-1}(\mathbf{D}_\ell) \right\rceil_p ,$$

where the ℓth PRF evaluation is with respect to the circuit eq_ℓ that takes as input a pair $(x, (x^*, \mathbf{w}))$ and outputs w_ℓ if $x = x^*$ and 0 otherwise. If we now consider the corresponding computation using the punctured key, evaluation at x yields the vector

$$\sum_{\ell \in [N]} \mathbf{s}^T \left(\mathbf{A}_{\mathsf{FHE},\mathsf{eq}_\ell,x} \mathbf{G}^{-1}(\mathbf{D}_\ell) + (w_\ell \cdot \mathsf{eq}(x^*, x) + e) \cdot \mathbf{D}_\ell \right) + \mathsf{noise} \tag{2.4}$$

The key observation is that for any matrix $\mathbf{W} \in \mathbb{Z}_q^{n \times m}$, the puncturing algorithm can choose the coefficients $\mathbf{w} \in \mathbb{Z}_q^N$ so that

$$\mathbf{W} = \left(\sum_{\ell \in [N]} \mathbf{A}_{\mathsf{FHE},\mathsf{eq}_\ell,x^*} \mathbf{G}^{-1}(\mathbf{D}_\ell) \right) + \sum_{\ell \in [N]} w_\ell \cdot \mathbf{D}_\ell. \tag{2.5}$$

Next, we choose $\mathbf{W}$ to be a lattice trapdoor matrix with associated trapdoor $\mathbf{z}$ (i.e., $\mathbf{W}\mathbf{z} = 0 \bmod q$). From Eqs. (2.4) and (2.5), we have that whenever a punctured key is used to evaluate the PRF at the punctured point, the result is a vector of the form $\lfloor \mathbf{s}^T \mathbf{W} \rceil_p \in \mathbb{Z}_p^m$. Testing whether a vector $\mathbf{y}$ is of this form can be done by computing the inner product of $\mathbf{y}$ with the trapdoor vector $\mathbf{z}$ and checking if the result is small. In particular, when $\mathbf{y} = \lfloor \mathbf{s}^T \mathbf{W} \rceil_p$, we have that

$$\left\langle \lfloor \mathbf{s}^T \mathbf{W} \rceil_p, \mathbf{z} \right\rangle \approx \lfloor \mathbf{s}^T \mathbf{W} \mathbf{z} \rceil_p = 0.$$

In our construction, the trapdoor matrix $\mathbf{W}$ is chosen independently of the PRF key $\mathbf{s}$, and included as part of the public parameters. To puncture a key $\mathbf{s}$, the puncturing algorithm chooses the coefficients $\mathbf{w}$ such that Eq. (2.5) holds. This allows us to program punctured keys associated with different secret keys $\mathbf{s}_i$ to the *same* trapdoor matrix $\mathbf{W}$. The underlying "translucent set" then is the set of vectors of the form $\lfloor \mathbf{s}_i^T \mathbf{W} \rceil_p$. Under the LWE assumption, this set is indistinguishable from random. However, as shown above, using a trapdoor for $\mathbf{W}$, it is easy to determine if a vector lies in this set. Thus, we are able to embed a noisy hidden subspace within the public parameters of the translucent PRF.

We note here that our construction is not expressive enough to give a programmable PRF in the sense of [12], because we do not have full control of the value $\mathbf{y} \in \mathbb{Z}_p^m$ obtained when using the punctured key to evaluate at the punctured point. We only ensure that $\mathbf{y}$ lies in a hidden (but efficiently testable) subspace of $\mathbb{Z}_p^m$. As we show in Sect. 6, this notion suffices for watermarking.

Puncturing at Multiple Points. The construction described above yields a translucent puncturable PRF. As noted in Sect. 1, for message-embedding watermarking, we require a translucent t-puncturable PRF. While we can trivially build a t-puncturable PRF from t instances of a puncturable PRF by xoring the outputs of t independent puncturable PRF instances, this construction does not preserve translucency. Notably, we can no longer detect whether a punctured key was used to evaluate the PRF at one of the punctured points. Instead, to preserve the translucency structure, we construct a translucent t-puncturable PRF by defining it to be the sum of multiple independent PRFs with different (public) parameter matrices, but *sharing the same secret key.* Then, to puncture at t different points we first encrypt each of the t punctured points $x_1^*, \ldots, x_t^*$, each with its own set of coefficient vectors $\mathbf{w}_1, \ldots, \mathbf{w}_t$ to obtain t FHE ciphertexts $\mathsf{ct}_1, \ldots, \mathsf{ct}_t$. The constrained key then contains the following components:

$$\begin{aligned}\mathbf{s}^T \cdot \big(\mathbf{A}_0 + 0 \cdot \mathbf{G} \mid \mathbf{A}_1 + 1 \cdot \mathbf{G} \quad &| \quad \mathbf{B}_{1,1} + \mathsf{ct}_{1,1} \cdot \mathbf{G} \mid \cdots \mid \mathbf{B}_{t,z} + \mathsf{ct}_{t,z} \cdot \mathbf{G} \\ &| \quad \mathbf{C}_1 + \mathsf{sk}_1 \cdot \mathbf{G} \mid \cdots \mid \mathbf{C}_\tau + \mathsf{sk}_\tau \cdot \mathbf{G}\big) + \mathsf{noise}.\end{aligned}$$

To evaluate the PRF at a point $x \in \{0,1\}^\rho$ using the constrained key, one evaluates the PRF on each of the t instances, that is, for all $i \in [t]$,

$$\mathbf{s}^T \left(\sum_{\ell \in [N]} \mathbf{A}_{\mathsf{FHE}, \mathsf{eq}_\ell, i, x} \mathbf{G}^{-1}(\mathbf{D}_\ell) + \mathsf{eq}(x_i^*, x) \cdot \sum_{\ell \in [N]} w_{i,\ell} \cdot \mathbf{D}_\ell \right) + \mathsf{noise}'.$$

The output of the PRF is the (rounded) sum of these evaluations:

$$\mathbf{s}^T \left(\sum_{\substack{i \in [t] \\ \ell \in [N]}} (\mathbf{A}_{\mathsf{FHE}, \mathsf{eq}_\ell, i, x} \mathbf{G}^{-1}(\mathbf{D}_\ell)) + \sum_{i \in [t]} \left(\mathsf{eq}(x_i^*, x) \cdot \sum_{\ell \in [N]} w_{i,\ell} \cdot \mathbf{D}_\ell \right) \right) + \mathsf{noise}'.$$

Similarly, the real value of the PRF is the (rounded) sum of the t independent PRF evaluations:

$$\mathsf{PRF}(\mathbf{s}, x) := \left\lfloor \mathbf{s}^T \sum_{\substack{i \in [t] \\ \ell \in [N]}} \mathbf{A}_{\mathsf{FHE}, \mathsf{eq}_\ell, i, x} \mathbf{G}^{-1}(\mathbf{D}_\ell) \right\rceil_p.$$

If the point x is not one of the punctured points, then $\mathsf{eq}(x_i^*, x) = 0$ for all $i \in [t]$ and one recovers the real PRF evaluation at x. If x is one of the punctured points (i.e., $x = x_i^*$ for some $i \in [t]$), then the PRF evaluation using the punctured key yields the vector

$$\mathbf{s}^T \left(\sum_{\substack{i \in [t] \\ \ell \in [N]}} (\mathbf{A}_{\mathsf{FHE},\mathsf{eq}_\ell,i,x} \mathbf{G}^{-1}(\mathbf{D}_\ell)) + \mathsf{eq}(x_i^*, x) \cdot \sum_{\ell \in [N]} w_{i,\ell} \cdot \mathbf{D}_\ell \right) + \mathsf{noise}'.$$

and as before, we can embed trapdoor matrices $\mathbf{W}_{i^*}$ for all $i^* \in [t]$ by choosing the coefficient vectors $\mathbf{w}_{i^*} = (w_{i^*,1}, \ldots, w_{i^*,N}) \in \mathbb{Z}_q^N$ accordingly:[11]

$$\mathbf{W}_{i^*} = \sum_{\substack{i \in [t] \\ \ell \in [N]}} \left(\mathbf{A}_{\mathsf{FHE},\mathsf{eq}_\ell,i,x_{i^*}^*} \mathbf{G}^{-1}(\mathbf{D}_\ell) \right) + \sum_{\ell \in [N]} w_{i^*,\ell} \cdot \mathbf{D}_\ell.$$

A Technical Detail. In the actual construction in Sect. 5.1, we include an additional "auxiliary matrix" $\hat{\mathbf{A}}$ in the public parameters and define the PRF evaluation as the vector

$$\mathsf{PRF}(\mathbf{s}, x) := \left\lfloor \mathbf{s}^T \left(\hat{\mathbf{A}} + \sum_{\substack{i \in [t] \\ \ell \in [N]}} \mathbf{A}_{\mathsf{FHE},\mathsf{eq}_\ell,i,x} \mathbf{G}^{-1}(\mathbf{D}_\ell) \right) \right\rceil_p.$$

The presence of the additional matrix $\hat{\mathbf{A}}$ does not affect pseudorandomness, but facilitates the argument for some of our other security properties. We give the formal description of our scheme as well as the security analysis in Sect. 5.

3 Preliminaries

We begin by introducing some of the notation we use in this work. For an integer $n \geq 1$, we write $[n]$ to denote the set of integers $\{1, \ldots, n\}$. For a distribution $\mathcal{D}$, we write $x \leftarrow \mathcal{D}$ to denote that x is sampled from $\mathcal{D}$; for a finite set S, we write $x \xleftarrow{\text{R}} S$ to denote that x is sampled uniformly from S. We write $\text{Funs}[\mathcal{X}, \mathcal{Y}]$ to denote the set of all functions mapping from a domain $\mathcal{X}$ to a range $\mathcal{Y}$. For a finite set S, we write 2^S to denote the *power set* of S, namely the set of all subsets of S.

Unless specified otherwise, we use λ to denote the security parameter. We say a function $f(\lambda)$ is negligible in λ, denoted by $\mathsf{negl}(\lambda)$, if $f(\lambda) = o(1/\lambda^c)$ for all $c \in \mathbb{N}$. We say that an event happens with overwhelming probability if its complement happens with negligible probability. We say an algorithm is efficient if it runs in probabilistic polynomial time in the length of its input. We use $\mathsf{poly}(\lambda)$ to denote a quantity whose value is bounded by a fixed polynomial in λ, and $\mathsf{polylog}(\lambda)$ to denote a quantity whose value is bounded by a fixed polynomial in $\log \lambda$ (that is, a function of the form $\log^c \lambda$ for some $c \in \mathbb{N}$). We say that a family of distributions $\mathcal{D} = \{\mathcal{D}_\lambda\}_{\lambda \in \mathbb{N}}$ is *B-bounded* if the support of

[11] For the punctured keys to hide the set of punctured points, we need a different trapdoor matrix for each punctured point. We provide the full details in Sect. 5.

$\mathcal{D}$ is $\{-B, \ldots, B-1, B\}$ with probability 1. For two families of distributions $\mathcal{D}_1$ and $\mathcal{D}_2$, we write $\mathcal{D}_1 \overset{c}{\approx} \mathcal{D}_2$ if the two distributions are computationally indistinguishable (that is, no efficient algorithm can distinguish $\mathcal{D}_1$ from $\mathcal{D}_2$, except with negligible probability). We write $\mathcal{D}_1 \overset{s}{\approx} \mathcal{D}_2$ if the two distributions are statistically indistinguishable (that is, the statistical distance between $\mathcal{D}_1$ and $\mathcal{D}_2$ is negligible).

Vectors and Matrices. We use bold lowercase letters (*e.g.*, $\mathbf{v}, \mathbf{w}$) to denote vectors and bold uppercase letter (*e.g.*, $\mathbf{A}, \mathbf{B}$) to denote matrices. For two vectors $\mathbf{v}, \mathbf{w}$, we write $\mathsf{IP}(\mathbf{v}, \mathbf{w}) = \langle \mathbf{v}, \mathbf{w} \rangle$ to denote the inner product of $\mathbf{v}$ and $\mathbf{w}$. For a vector $\mathbf{s}$ or a matrix $\mathbf{A}$, we use $\mathbf{s}^T$ and $\mathbf{A}^T$ to denote their transposes, respectively. For an integer $p \leq q$, we define the modular "rounding" function

$$\lfloor \cdot \rceil_p \colon \mathbb{Z}_q \to \mathbb{Z}_p \text{ that maps } x \to \lfloor (p/q) \cdot x \rceil$$

and extend it coordinate-wise to matrices and vectors over $\mathbb{Z}_q$. Here, the operation $\lfloor \cdot \rceil$ is the rounding operation over the real numbers.

In the full version of this paper [34], we also review the definition of a pseudorandom function and provide some background on the lattice-based techniques that we use in this work.

4 Translucent Constrained PRFs

In this section, we formally define our notion of a translucent constrained PRFs. Recall first that in a constrained PRF [14], the holder of the master secret key for the PRF can issue constrained keys which enable PRF evaluation on only the points that satisfy the constraint. Now, each translucent constrained PRF actually defines an entire *family* of constrained PRFs (see the discussion in Sect. 1.2 and Remark 4.2 for more details). Moreover, this family of constrained PRFs has the special property that the constraining algorithm embeds a hidden subset. Notably, this hidden subset is shared across *all* PRF keys in the constrained PRF family; the hidden subset is specific to the constrained PRF family, and is determined wholly by the parameters of the particular translucent constrained PRF. This means that whenever an (honestly-generated) constrained key is used to evaluate at a point that does not satisfy the constraint, the evaluation lies within this hidden subset. Furthermore, the holder of the constrained key is unable to tell whether a particular output value lies in the hidden subset or not. However, anyone who possesses a secret testing key (specific to the translucent constrained PRF) is able to identify whether a particular value lies in the hidden subset or not. In essence then, the set of outputs of all of the constrained keys in a translucent constrained PRF system defines a translucent set in the sense of [20]. We now give our formal definitions.

Definition 4.1 (Translucent Constrained PRF). *Let λ be a security parameter. A translucent constrained PRF with domain $\mathcal{X}$ and range $\mathcal{Y}$ is a tuple of algorithms Π_{TPRF} =* (TPRF.Setup, TPRF.SampleKey, TPRF.Eval, TPRF.Constrain, TPRF.ConstrainEval, TPRF.Test) *with the following properties:*

- $\mathsf{TPRF.Setup}(1^\lambda) \to (\mathsf{pp}, \mathsf{tk})$: *On input a security parameter* λ, *the setup algorithm outputs the public parameters* pp *and a testing key* tk.
- $\mathsf{TPRF.SampleKey}(\mathsf{pp}) \to \mathsf{msk}$: *On input the public parameter* pp, *the key sampling algorithm outputs a master PRF key* msk.
- $\mathsf{TPRF.Eval}(\mathsf{pp}, \mathsf{msk}, x) \to y$: *On input the public parameters* pp, *a master PRF key* msk *and a point in the domain* $x \in \mathcal{X}$, *the PRF evaluation algorithm outputs an element in the range* $y \in \mathcal{Y}$.
- $\mathsf{TPRF.Constrain}(\mathsf{pp}, \mathsf{msk}, S) \to \mathsf{sk}_S$: *On input the public parameters* pp, *a master PRF key* msk *and a set of points* $S \subseteq \mathcal{X}$, *the constraining algorithm outputs a constrained key* sk_S.
- $\mathsf{TPRF.ConstrainEval}(\mathsf{pp}, \mathsf{sk}_S, x) \to y$: *On input the public parameters* pp, *a constrained key* sk_S, *and a point in the domain* $x \in \mathcal{X}$, *the constrained evaluation algorithm outputs an element in the range* $y \in \mathcal{Y}$.
- $\mathsf{TPRF.Test}(\mathsf{pp}, \mathsf{tk}, y') \to \{0, 1\}$: *On input the public parameters* pp, *a testing key* tk, *and a point in the range* $y' \in \mathcal{Y}$, *the testing algorithm either accepts (with output* 1*) or rejects (with output* 0*).*

Remark 4.2 (Relation to Constrained PRFs). Every translucent constrained PRF defines an entire *family* of constrained PRFs. In other words, every set of parameters $(\mathsf{pp}, \mathsf{tk})$ output by the setup function $\mathsf{TPRF.Setup}$ of a translucent constrained PRF induces a constrained PRF family (in the sense of [14, Sect. 3.1]) for the same class of constraints. Specifically, the key-generation algorithm for the constrained PRF family corresponds to running $\mathsf{TPRF.SampleKey}(\mathsf{pp})$. The constrain, evaluation, and constrained-evaluation algorithms for the constrained PRF family correspond to $\mathsf{TPRF.Constrain}(\mathsf{pp}, \cdot)$, $\mathsf{TPRF.Eval}(\mathsf{pp}, \cdot, \cdot)$, and $\mathsf{TPRF.ConstrainEval}(\mathsf{pp}, \cdot, \cdot)$, respectively.

Correctness. We now define two notions of correctness for a translucent constrained PRF: evaluation correctness and verification correctness. Intuitively, evaluation correctness states that a constrained key behaves the same as the master PRF key (from which it is derived) on the allowed points. Verification correctness states that the testing algorithm can correctly identify whether a constrained key was used to evaluate the PRF at an allowed point (in which case the verification algorithm outputs 0) or at a restricted point (in which case the verification algorithm outputs 1). Like the constrained PRF constructions of [10,17], we present definitions for the computational relaxations of both of these properties.

Definition 4.3 (Correctness Experiment). *Fix a security parameter* λ, *and let* Π_{TPRF} *be a translucent constrained PRF (Definition 4.1) with domain* $\mathcal{X}$ *and range* $\mathcal{Y}$. *Let* $\mathcal{A} = (\mathcal{A}_1, \mathcal{A}_2)$ *be an adversary and let* $\mathcal{S} \subseteq 2^{\mathcal{X}}$ *be a set system. The (computational) correctness experiment* $\mathsf{Expt}_{\Pi_{\mathsf{TPRF}}, \mathcal{A}, \mathcal{S}}$ *is defined as follows:*

Experiment $\mathsf{Expt}_{\Pi_{\mathsf{TPRF}},\mathcal{A},\mathcal{S}}(\lambda)$*:*

1. $(\mathsf{pp}, \mathsf{tk}) \leftarrow \mathsf{TPRF.Setup}(1^\lambda)$
2. $\mathsf{msk} \leftarrow \mathsf{TPRF.SampleKey}(\mathsf{pp})$
3. $(S, \mathsf{st}_\mathcal{A}) \leftarrow \mathcal{A}_1(1^\lambda, \mathsf{pp})$ *where* $S \in \mathcal{S}$
4. *Output* (x, S) *where* $x \leftarrow \mathcal{A}_2(\mathsf{st}_\mathcal{A}, \mathsf{sk})$ *and* $\mathsf{sk} \leftarrow \mathsf{TPRF.Constrain}(\mathsf{pp}, \mathsf{msk}, S)$

Definition 4.4 (Correctness). *Fix a security parameter* λ*, and let* Π_{TPRF} *be a translucent constrained PRF with domain* $\mathcal{X}$ *and range* $\mathcal{Y}$*. We say that* Π_{TPRF} *is* correct *with respect to a set system* $\mathcal{S} \subseteq 2^{\mathcal{X}}$ *if it satisfies the following two properties:*

- ***Evaluation correctness:*** *For all efficient adversaries* $\mathcal{A}$ *and setting* $(x, S) \leftarrow \mathsf{Expt}_{\Pi_{\mathsf{TPRF}},\mathcal{A},\mathcal{S}}(\lambda)$*, then*

$$x \in S \text{ and } \mathsf{TPRF.ConstrainEval}(\mathsf{pp}, \mathsf{sk}_S, x) \neq \mathsf{TPRF.Eval}(\mathsf{pp}, \mathsf{msk}, x)$$

with probability $\mathsf{negl}(\lambda)$.
- ***Verification correctness:*** *For all efficient adversaries* $\mathcal{A}$ *and taking* $(x, S) \leftarrow \mathsf{Expt}_{\Pi_{\mathsf{TPRF}},\mathcal{A},\mathcal{S}}(\lambda)$*, then*

$$x \in \mathcal{X} \setminus S \text{ and } \mathsf{TPRF.Test}(\mathsf{pp}, \mathsf{tk}, \mathsf{TPRF.ConstrainEval}(\mathsf{pp}, \mathsf{sk}_S, x)) = 1$$

with probability $1 - \mathsf{negl}(\lambda)$*. Conversely,*

$$x \in S \text{ and } \mathsf{TPRF.Test}(\mathsf{pp}, \mathsf{tk}, \mathsf{TPRF.ConstrainEval}(\mathsf{pp}, \mathsf{sk}_S, x)) = 1$$

with probability $\mathsf{negl}(\lambda)$.

Remark 4.5 (Selective Notions of Correctness). In Definition 4.3, the adversary is able to choose the set $S \in \mathcal{S}$ adaptively, that is, after seeing the public parameters pp. We can define a weaker (but still useful) notion of *selective* correctness, where the adversary is forced to commit to its set S before seeing the public parameters. The formal correctness conditions in Definition 4.4 remain unchanged. For certain set systems (e.g., when all sets $S \in \mathcal{S}$ contain a polynomial number of points), *complexity leveraging* [8] can be used to boost a scheme that is selectively correct into one that is also adaptively correct, except under a possibly super-polynomial loss in the security reduction. For constructing a watermarkable family of PRFs (Sect. 6), a selectively-correct translucent PRF already suffices.

Translucent Puncturable PRFs. A special case of a translucent constrained PRF is a translucent puncturable PRF. Recall that a puncturable PRF [14,15, 33] is a constrained PRF where the constrained keys enable PRF evaluation at all points in the domain $\mathcal{X}$ except at a single, "punctured" point $x^* \in \mathcal{X}$. We can generalize this notion to a t-*puncturable* PRF, which is a PRF that can be punctured at t different points. Formally, we define the analog of a translucent puncturable and t-puncturable PRFs.

Definition 4.6 (Translucent t-Puncturable PRFs). *We say that a translucent constrained PRF over a domain $\mathcal{X}$ is a* translucent t-puncturable PRF *if it is constrained with respect to the set system $\mathcal{S}^{(t)} = \{S \subseteq \mathcal{X} : |S| = |\mathcal{X}| - t\}$. The special case of $t = 1$ corresponds to a* translucent puncturable PRF.

4.1 Security Definitions

We now introduce several security requirements a translucent constrained PRF should satisfy. First, we require that $\mathsf{Eval}(\mathsf{pp}, \mathsf{msk}, \cdot)$ implements a PRF whenever the parameters pp and msk are honestly generated. Next, we require that given a constrained key sk_S for some set S, the real PRF values $\mathsf{Eval}(\mathsf{pp}, \mathsf{msk}, x)$ for points $x \notin S$ remain pseudorandom. This is the notion of constrained pseudorandomness introduced in [14]. Using a similar argument as in [10, Appendix A], it follows that a translucent constrained PRF satisfying constrained pseudorandomness is also pseudorandom. Finally, we require that the key sk_S output by $\mathsf{Constrain}(\mathsf{pp}, \mathsf{msk}, S)$ hides the constraint set S. This is essentially the privacy requirement in a private constrained PRF [12].

Definition 4.7 (Pseudorandomness). *Let λ be a security parameter, and let Π_{TPRF} be a translucent constrained PRF with domain $\mathcal{X}$ and range $\mathcal{Y}$. We say that Π_{TPRF} is* pseudorandom *if for $(\mathsf{pp}, \mathsf{tk}) \leftarrow \mathsf{TPRF.Setup}(1^\lambda)$, the tuple $(\mathsf{KeyGen}, \mathsf{Eval})$ is a secure PRF, where $\mathsf{KeyGen}(1^\lambda)$ outputs a fresh draw $k \leftarrow \mathsf{TPRF.SampleKey}(\mathsf{pp})$ and $\mathsf{Eval}(k, x)$ outputs $\mathsf{TPRF.Eval}(\mathsf{pp}, k, x)$. Note that we implicitly assume that the PRF adversary in this case also is given access to the public parameters* pp.

Definition 4.8 (Constrained Pseudorandomness Experiment). *Fix a security parameter λ, and let Π_{TPRF} be a translucent constrained PRF with domain $\mathcal{X}$ and range $\mathcal{Y}$. Let $\mathcal{A} = (\mathcal{A}_1, \mathcal{A}_2)$ be an adversary, $\mathcal{S} \subseteq 2^{\mathcal{X}}$ be a set system, and $b \in \{0,1\}$ be a bit. The constrained pseudorandomness experiment $\mathsf{CExpt}^{(b)}_{\Pi_{\mathsf{TPRF}}, \mathcal{A}, \mathcal{S}}(\lambda)$ is defined as follows:*

Experiment $\mathsf{CExpt}^{(b)}_{\Pi_{\mathsf{TPRF}}, \mathcal{A}, \mathcal{S}}(\lambda)$*:*

1. $(\mathsf{pp}, \mathsf{tk}) \leftarrow \mathsf{TPRF.Setup}(1^\lambda)$
2. $\mathsf{msk} \leftarrow \mathsf{TPRF.SampleKey}(\mathsf{pp})$
3. $(S, \mathsf{st}_{\mathcal{A}}) \leftarrow \mathcal{A}_1^{\mathsf{TPRF.Eval}(\mathsf{pp}, \mathsf{msk}, \cdot)}(1^\lambda, \mathsf{pp})$ *where* $S \in \mathcal{S}$
4. *Output* $b' \leftarrow \mathcal{A}_2^{\mathsf{TPRF.Eval}(\mathsf{pp}, \mathsf{msk}, \cdot), \mathcal{O}_b(\cdot)}(\mathsf{st}_{\mathcal{A}}, \mathsf{sk})$ *where* $\mathsf{sk} \leftarrow \mathsf{TPRF.Constrain}(\mathsf{pp}, \mathsf{msk}, S)$ *and the challenge oracle $\mathcal{O}_b$ is defined as follows:*
   - $\mathcal{O}_0(\cdot) = \mathsf{TPRF.Eval}(\mathsf{pp}, \mathsf{msk}, \cdot)$
   - $\mathcal{O}_1(\cdot) = f(\cdot)$ *where* $f \xleftarrow{R} \mathrm{Funs}[\mathcal{X}, \mathcal{Y}]$ *is chosen (and fixed) at the beginning of the experiment.*

Definition 4.9 (Constrained Pseudorandomness [14, adapted]**).** *Fix a security parameter λ, and let Π_{TPRF} be a translucent constrained PRF with domain $\mathcal{X}$ and range $\mathcal{Y}$. We say that an adversary $\mathcal{A}$ is admissible for the constrained pseudorandomness game if all of the queries x that it makes to the* *evaluation oracle* TPRF.Eval *satisfy* $x \in S$ *and all of the queries it makes to the challenge oracle* ($\mathcal{O}_0$ *or* $\mathcal{O}_1$) *satisfy* $x \notin S$.[12] *Then, we say that* Π_{TPRF} *satisfies* constrained pseudorandomness *if for all efficient and admissible adversaries* $\mathcal{A}$,

$$\left| \Pr\left[\mathsf{CExpt}^{(0)}_{\Pi_{\mathsf{TPRF}},\mathcal{A},\mathcal{S}}(\lambda) = 1 \right] - \Pr\left[\mathsf{CExpt}^{(1)}_{\Pi_{\mathsf{TPRF}},\mathcal{A},\mathcal{S}}(\lambda) = 1 \right] \right| = \mathsf{negl}(\lambda).$$

Theorem 4.10 (Constrained Pseudorandomness Implies Pseudorandomness [10]**).** *Let* Π_{TPRF} *be a translucent constrained PRF. If* Π_{TPRF} *satisfies constrained pseudorandomness (Definition 4.9), then it satisfies pseudorandomness (Definition 4.7).*

Proof. Follows by a similar argument as that in [10, Appendix A].

Definition 4.11 (Privacy Experiment). *Fix a security parameter* λ, *and let* Π_{TPRF} *be a translucent constrained PRF with domain* $\mathcal{X}$ *and range* $\mathcal{Y}$. *Let* $\mathcal{A} = (\mathcal{A}_1, \mathcal{A}_2)$ *be an adversary,* $\mathcal{S} \subseteq 2^{\mathcal{X}}$ *be a set system, and* $b \in \{0,1\}$ *be a bit. The privacy experiment* $\mathsf{PExpt}^{(b)}_{\Pi_{\mathsf{TPRF}},\mathcal{A},\mathcal{S}}(\lambda)$ *is defined as follows:*

Experiment $\mathsf{PExpt}^{(b)}_{\Pi_{\mathsf{TPRF}},\mathcal{A},\mathcal{S}}(\lambda)$*:*

1. $(\mathsf{pp}, \mathsf{tk}) \leftarrow \mathsf{TPRF.Setup}(1^\lambda)$
2. $(S_0, S_1, \mathsf{st}_{\mathcal{A}}) \leftarrow \mathcal{A}_1(1^\lambda, \mathsf{pp})$ *where* $S_0, S_1 \in \mathcal{S}$
3. $\mathsf{sk}_b \leftarrow \mathsf{TPRF.Constrain}(\mathsf{pp}, \mathsf{msk}, S_b)$ *where* $\mathsf{msk} \leftarrow \mathsf{TPRF.SampleKey}(\mathsf{pp})$
4. *Output* $b' \leftarrow \mathcal{A}_2(\mathsf{st}_{\mathcal{A}}, \mathsf{sk}_b)$

Definition 4.12 (Privacy [12, adapted]**).** *Fix a security parameter* λ. *Let* Π_{TPRF} *to be a translucent constrained PRF with domain* $\mathcal{X}$ *and range* $\mathcal{Y}$. *We say that* Π_{TPRF} *is* private *with respect to a set system* $\mathcal{S} \subseteq 2^{\mathcal{X}}$ *if for all efficient adversaries* $\mathcal{A}$,

$$\left| \Pr\left[\mathsf{PExpt}^{(0)}_{\Pi_{\mathsf{TPRF}},\mathcal{A},\mathcal{S}}(\lambda) = 1 \right] - \Pr\left[\mathsf{PExpt}^{(1)}_{\Pi_{\mathsf{TPRF}},\mathcal{A},\mathcal{S}}(\lambda) = 1 \right] \right| = \mathsf{negl}(\lambda).$$

Remark 4.13 (Selective vs. Adaptive Security). We say that a scheme satisfying Definition 4.9 or Definition 4.12 is *adaptively* secure if the adversary chooses the set S (or sets S_0 and S_1) after seeing the public parameters pp for the translucent constrained PRF scheme. As in Definition 4.5, we can define a selective notion of security where the adversary commits to its set S (or S_0 and S_1) at the beginning of the game before seeing the public parameters.

Key Injectivity. Another security notion that becomes useful in the context of watermarking is the notion of *key injectivity*. Intuitively, we say a family of PRFs

[12] In the standard constrained pseudorandomness game introduced in [14], the adversary is also allowed to make evaluation queries on values not contained in S. While our construction can be shown to satisfy this stronger property, this is not needed for our watermarking construction. To simplify the presentation and security analysis, we work with this weaker notion here.

satisfies key injectivity if for all distinct PRF keys k_1 and k_2 (not necessarily uniformly sampled from the key-space), the value of the PRF under k_1 at any point x does not equal the value of the PRF under k_2 at x with overwhelming probability. We note that Cohen et al. [21] introduce a similar, though incomparable, notion of key injectivity[13] to achieve their strongest notions of watermarking (based on indistinguishability obfuscation). We now give the exact property that suffices for our construction:

Definition 4.14 (Key Injectivity). *Fix a security parameter λ and let Π_{TPRF} be a translucent constrained PRF with domain $\mathcal{X}$. Take $(\mathsf{pp}, \mathsf{tk}) \leftarrow \mathsf{TPRF.Setup}(1^\lambda)$, and let $\mathcal{K} = \{\mathcal{K}_\lambda\}_{\lambda \in \mathbb{N}}$ be the set of possible keys output by $\mathsf{TPRF.SampleKey}(\mathsf{pp})$. Then, we say that Π_{TPRF} is key-injective if for all keys $\mathsf{msk}_1, \mathsf{msk}_2 \in \mathcal{K}$, and any $x \in \mathcal{X}$,*

$$\Pr[\mathsf{TPRF.Eval}(\mathsf{msk}_1, x) = \mathsf{TPRF.Eval}(\mathsf{msk}_2, x)] = \mathsf{negl}(\lambda),$$

where the probability is taken over the randomness used in $\mathsf{TPRF.Setup}$.

5 Translucent Puncturable PRFs from LWE

In this section, we describe our construction of a translucent t-puncturable PRF. After describing the main construction, we state the concrete correctness and security theorems for our construction. We defer their formal proofs to the full version [34]. Our scheme leverages a number of parameters (described in detail at the beginning of Sect. 5.1). We give concrete instantiations of these parameters based on the requirements of the correctness and security theorems in Sect. 5.2.

5.1 Main Construction

In this section, we formally describe our translucent t-puncturable PRF (Definition 4.6). Let λ be a security parameter. Additionally, we define the following scheme parameters:

- (n, m, q, χ) - LWE parameters
- ρ - length of the PRF input
- p - rounding modulus
- t - the number of punctured points (indexed by i)
- N - the dimension of the coefficient vectors $\mathbf{w}_1, \ldots, \mathbf{w}_t$ (indexed by ℓ). Note that $N = m \cdot n$
- B_{test} - norm bound used by the PRF testing algorithm

Let $\Pi_{\mathsf{HE}} = (\mathsf{HE.KeyGen}, \mathsf{HE.Enc}, \mathsf{HE.Enc}, \mathsf{HE.Dec})$ be the (leveled) homomorphic encryption scheme with plaintext space $\{0,1\}^\rho \times \mathbb{Z}_q^N$. We define the following additional parameters specific to the FHE scheme:

[13] Roughly speaking, Cohen et al. [21, Definition 7.1] require that for a uniformly random PRF key k, there does not exist a key k' and a point x where $\mathsf{PRF}(k, x) = \mathsf{PRF}(k', x)$. In contrast, our notion requires that any two PRF keys do not agree at any particular point with overwhelming probability.

- z - bit-length of a fresh FHE ciphertext (indexed by j)
- τ - bit-length of the FHE secret key (indexed by k)

Next, we define the equality-check circuit $\mathsf{eq}_\ell : \{0,1\}^\rho \times \{0,1\}^\rho \times \mathbb{Z}_q^N \to \mathbb{Z}_q$ where

$$\mathsf{eq}_\ell(x, (x^*, \mathbf{w})) = \begin{cases} w_\ell & \text{if } x = x^* \\ 0 & \text{otherwise,} \end{cases} \tag{5.1}$$

as well as the circuit $C_{\mathsf{Eval}}^{(\ell)} : \{0,1\}^z \times \{0,1\}^\rho \to \{0,1\}^\tau$ for homomorphic evaluation of eq_ℓ:

$$C_{\mathsf{Eval}}^{(\ell)}(\mathsf{ct}, x) = \mathsf{HE.Eval}(\mathsf{eq}_\ell(x, \cdot), \mathsf{ct}). \tag{5.2}$$

Finally, we define the following additional parameters for the depths of these two circuits:

- d_{eq} - depth of the equality-check circuit eq_ℓ
- d - depth of the homomorphic equality-check circuit $C_{\mathsf{Eval}}^{(\ell)}$

For $\ell \in [N]$, we define the matrix $\mathbf{D}_\ell$ to be the ℓth elementary "basis matrix" for the $\mathbb{Z}_q$-module $\mathbb{Z}_q^{n \times m}$. More concretely,

$$\mathbf{D}_\ell[a, b] = \begin{cases} 1 & \text{if } am + b = \ell \\ 0 & \text{otherwise.} \end{cases}$$

In other words, each matrix $\mathbf{D}_\ell$ has its ℓth component (when viewing the matrix as a collection of $N = mn$ entries) set to 1 and the remaining components set to 0.

Translucent PRF Construction. The translucent t-puncturable PRF $\Pi_{\mathsf{TPRF}} = (\mathsf{TPRF.Setup}, \mathsf{TPRF.Eval}, \mathsf{TPRF.Constrain}, \mathsf{TPRF.ConstrainEval}, \mathsf{TPRF.Test})$ with domain $\{0,1\}^\rho$ and range $\mathbb{Z}_p^m$ is defined as follows:

- $\mathsf{TPRF.Setup}(1^\lambda)$: On input the security parameter λ, the setup algorithm samples the following matrices uniformly at random from $\mathbb{Z}_q^{n \times m}$:
  - $\hat{\mathbf{A}}$: an auxiliary matrix used to provide additional randomness
  - $\{\mathbf{A}_b\}_{b \in \{0,1\}}$: matrices to encode the bits of the input to the PRF
  - $\{\mathbf{B}_{i,j}\}_{i \in [t], j \in [z]}$: matrices to encode the bits of the FHE encryptions of the punctured points
  - $\{\mathbf{C}_k\}_{k \in [\tau]}$: matrices to encode the bits of the FHE secret key

  It also samples trapdoor matrices $(\mathbf{W}_i, \mathbf{z}_i) \leftarrow \mathsf{TrapGen}(1^n, q)$ for all $i \in [t]$. Finally, it outputs the public parameters pp and testing key tk:

$$\mathsf{pp} = \left(\hat{\mathbf{A}}, \{\mathbf{A}_b\}_{b \in \{0,1\}}, \{\mathbf{B}_{i,j}\}_{i \in [t], j \in [z]}, \{\mathbf{C}_k\}_{k \in [\tau]}, \{\mathbf{W}_i\}_{i \in [t]}\right) \quad \mathsf{tk} = \{\mathbf{z}_i\}_{i \in [t]}.$$

- $\mathsf{TPRF.SampleKey}(\mathsf{pp})$: On input the public parameters pp, the key generation algorithm samples a PRF key $\mathbf{s} \leftarrow \chi^n$ and sets $\mathsf{msk} = \mathbf{s}$.

- $\mathsf{TPRF.Eval}(\mathsf{pp}, \mathsf{msk}, x)$: On input the public parameters pp, the PRF key $\mathsf{msk} = \mathbf{s}$, and an input $x = x_1 x_2 \cdots x_\rho \in \{0,1\}^\rho$, the evaluation algorithm first computes

$$\widetilde{\mathbf{B}}_{i,\ell} \leftarrow \mathsf{Eval}_{\mathsf{pk}}\left(C_\ell, \mathbf{B}_{i,1}, \ldots, \mathbf{B}_{i,z}, \mathbf{A}_{x_1}, \ldots, \mathbf{A}_{x_\rho}, \mathbf{C}_1, \ldots, \mathbf{C}_\tau\right)$$

for all $i \in [t]$ and $\ell \in [N]$, and where $C_\ell = \mathsf{IP} \circ C_{\mathsf{Eval}}^{(\ell)}$. Finally, the evaluation algorithm outputs the value

$$\mathbf{y}_x = \left\lfloor \mathbf{s}^T \left(\hat{\mathbf{A}} + \sum_{\substack{i \in [t] \\ \ell \in [N]}} \widetilde{\mathbf{B}}_{i,\ell} \cdot \mathbf{G}^{-1}(\mathbf{D}_\ell) \right) \right\rceil_p .$$

- $\mathsf{TPRF.Constrain}(\mathsf{pp}, \mathsf{msk}, \mathsf{T})$:[14] On input the public parameters pp, the PRF key $\mathsf{msk} = \mathbf{s}$ and the set of points $\mathsf{T} = \{x_i^*\}_{i \in [t]}$ to be punctured, the constraining algorithm first computes

$$\widetilde{\mathbf{B}}_{i,i^*,\ell} \leftarrow \mathsf{Eval}_{\mathsf{pk}}(C_\ell, \mathbf{B}_{i,1}, \ldots, \mathbf{B}_{i,z}, \mathbf{A}_{x^*_{i^*,1}}, \ldots, \mathbf{A}_{x^*_{i^*,\rho}}, \mathbf{C}_1, \ldots, \mathbf{C}_\tau)$$

for all $i, i^* \in [t]$ and $\ell \in [N]$ where $C_\ell = \mathsf{IP} \circ C_{\mathsf{Eval}}^{(\ell)}$. Then, for each $i^* \in [t]$, the puncturing algorithm computes the (unique) vector $\mathbf{w}_{i^*} = (w_{i^*,1}, \ldots, w_{i^*,N}) \in \mathbb{Z}_q^N$ where

$$\mathbf{W}_{i^*} = \hat{\mathbf{A}} + \sum_{\substack{i \in [t] \\ \ell \in [N]}} \widetilde{\mathbf{B}}_{i,i^*,\ell} \cdot \mathbf{G}^{-1}(\mathbf{D}_\ell) + \sum_{\ell \in [N]} w_{i^*,\ell} \cdot \mathbf{D}_\ell.$$

Next, it samples an FHE key $\mathsf{HE.sk} \leftarrow \mathsf{HE.KeyGen}(1^\lambda, 1^{d_{\mathsf{eq}}}, 1^{\rho+N})$, and for each $i \in [t]$, it constructs the ciphertext $\mathsf{ct}_i \leftarrow \mathsf{HE.Enc}(\mathsf{HE.sk}, (x_i^*, \mathbf{w}_i))$ and finally, it defines $\mathsf{ct} = \{\mathsf{ct}_i\}_{i \in [t]}$. It samples error vectors $\mathbf{e}_0 \leftarrow \chi^m$, $\mathbf{e}_{1,b} \leftarrow \chi^m$ for $b \in \{0,1\}$, $\mathbf{e}_{2,i,j} \leftarrow \chi^m$ for $i \in [t]$ and $j \in [z]$, and $\mathbf{e}_{3,k} \leftarrow \chi^m$ for $k \in [\tau]$ and computes the vectors

$$\begin{aligned}
\hat{\mathbf{a}}^T &= \mathbf{s}^T \hat{\mathbf{A}} + \mathbf{e}_0^T \\
\mathbf{a}_b^T &= \mathbf{s}^T (\mathbf{A}_b + b \cdot \mathbf{G}) + \mathbf{e}_{1,b}^T && \forall b \in \{0,1\} \\
\mathbf{b}_{i,j}^T &= \mathbf{s}^T (\mathbf{B}_j + \mathsf{ct}_{i,j} \cdot \mathbf{G}) + \mathbf{e}_{2,i,j}^T && \forall i \in [t], \forall j \in [z] \\
\mathbf{c}_k^T &= \mathbf{s}^T (\mathbf{C}_k + \mathsf{HE.sk}_k \cdot \mathbf{G}) + \mathbf{e}_{3,k}^T && \forall k \in [\tau].
\end{aligned}$$

Next, it sets $\mathsf{enc} = \left(\hat{\mathbf{a}}, \{\mathbf{a}_b\}_{b \in \{0,1\}}, \{\mathbf{b}_{i,j}\}_{i \in [t], j \in [z]}, \{\mathbf{c}_k\}_{k \in [\tau]}\right)$. It outputs the constrained key $\mathsf{sk}_\mathsf{T} = (\mathsf{enc}, \mathsf{ct})$.
- $\mathsf{TPRF.ConstrainEval}(\mathsf{pp}, \mathsf{sk}_\mathsf{T}, x)$: On input the public parameters pp, a constrained key $\mathsf{sk}_\mathsf{T} = (\mathsf{enc}, \mathsf{ct})$, where $\mathsf{enc} = \left(\hat{\mathbf{a}}, \{\mathbf{a}_b\}_{b \in \{0,1\}}, \{\mathbf{b}_{i,j}\}_{i \in [t], j \in [z]},\right.$

[14] For notational convenience, we modify the syntax of the constrain algorithm to take in a set T of t punctured points rather than a set of allowed points.

$\{\mathbf{c}_k\}_{k\in[\tau]})$, $\mathsf{ct} = \{\mathsf{ct}_i\}_{i\in[t]}$, and a point $x \in \{0,1\}^\rho$, the constrained evaluation algorithm computes

$$\widetilde{\mathbf{b}}_{i,\ell} \leftarrow \mathsf{Eval}_{\mathsf{ct}}((\mathsf{ct}_i, x), C_\ell, \mathbf{b}_{i,1}, \ldots, \mathbf{b}_{i,z}, \mathbf{a}_{x_1}, \ldots, \mathbf{a}_{x_\rho}, \mathbf{c}_1, \ldots, \mathbf{c}_\tau)$$

for $i \in [t]$ and $\ell \in [N]$, and where $C_\ell(\mathsf{ct}, x) = \mathsf{IP} \circ C^{(\ell)}_{\mathsf{Eval}}$. Then, it computes and outputs the value

$$\mathbf{y}_x = \left\lfloor \hat{\mathbf{a}} + \sum_{\substack{i\in[t] \\ \ell\in[N]}} \widetilde{\mathbf{b}}^T_{i,\ell} \cdot \mathbf{G}^{-1}(\mathbf{D}_\ell) \right\rceil_p .$$

- $\mathsf{TPRF.Test}(\mathsf{pp}, \mathsf{tk}, \mathbf{y})$: On input the testing key $\mathsf{tk} = \{\mathbf{z}_i\}_{i\in[t]}$ and a point $\mathbf{y} \in \mathbb{Z}_p^m$, the testing algorithm outputs 1 if $\langle \mathbf{y}, \mathbf{z}_i \rangle \in [-B_{\mathsf{test}}, B_{\mathsf{test}}]$ for some $i \in [t]$ and 0 otherwise.

Correctness Theorem. We now state that under the LWE and 1D-SIS assumptions (with appropriate parameters), our translucent t-puncturable PRF Π_{TPRF} satisfies (selective) evaluation correctness and verification correctness (Definition 4.4, Remark 4.5). We give the formal proof in the full version [34].

Theorem 5.1 (Correctness). *Fix a security parameter λ, and define parameters $n, m, p, q, \chi, t, z, \tau, B_{\mathsf{test}}$ as above. Let B be a bound on the error distribution χ, and suppose $B_{\mathsf{test}} = B(m+1)$, $p = 2^{\rho^{(1+\varepsilon)}}$ for some constant $\varepsilon > 0$, and $\frac{q}{2pmB} > B \cdot m^{O(d)}$. Then, take $m' = m \cdot (3 + t \cdot z + \tau)$ and $\beta = B \cdot m^{O(d)}$. Under the $\mathsf{LWE}_{n,m',q,\chi}$ and $\mathsf{1D\text{-}SIS\text{-}R}_{m',p,q,\beta}$ assumptions, Π_{TPRF} is (selectively) correct.*

Security Theorems. We now state that under the LWE assumption (with appropriate parameters), our translucent t-puncturable PRF Π_{TPRF} satisfies selective constrained pseudorandomness (Definition 4.9), selective privacy (Definition 4.12) and weak key-injectivity (Definition 4.14). We give the formal proofs in the full version [34]. As a corollary of satisfying constrained pseudorandomness, we have that Π_{TPRF} is also pseudorandom (Definition 4.7, Theorem 4.10).

Theorem 5.2 (Constrained Pseudorandomness). *Fix a security parameter λ, and define parameters $n, m, p, q, \chi, t, z, \tau$ as above. Let $m' = m \cdot (3 + t(z + 1) + \tau)$, $m'' = m \cdot (3 + t \cdot z + \tau)$ and $\beta = B \cdot m^{O(d)}$ where B is a bound on the error distribution χ. Then, under the $\mathsf{LWE}_{n,m',q,\chi}$ and $\mathsf{1D\text{-}SIS\text{-}R}_{m'',p,q,\beta}$ assumptions, Π_{TPRF} satisfies selective constrained pseudorandomness (Definition 4.9).*

Corollary 5.3 (Pseudorandomness). *Fix a security parameter λ, and define the parameters $n, m, p, q, \chi, t, z, \tau$ as above. Under the same assumptions as in Theorem 5.2, Π_{TPRF} satisfies selective pseudorandomness (Definition 4.7).*

Theorem 5.4 (Privacy). *Fix a security parameter λ, and define parameters $n, m, q, \chi, t, z, \tau$ as above. Let $m' = m \cdot (3 + t(z+1) + \tau)$. Then, under the $\mathsf{LWE}_{n,m',q,\chi}$ assumption, and assuming the homomorphic encryption scheme Π_{HE} is semantically secure, Π_{TPRF} is selectively private (Definition 4.12).*

Theorem 5.5 (Key-Injectivity). *If the bound B on the error distribution χ satisfies $B < \hat{p}/2$ where $\hat{p}$ is the smallest prime dividing the modulus q, and $m = \omega(n)$, then the translucent t-puncturable PRF Π_{TPRF} satisfies key-injectivity (Definition 4.14).*

5.2 Concrete Parameter Instantiations

In this section, we give one possible instantiation for the parameters for the translucent t-puncturable PRF construction in Sect. 5.1. We choose our parameters so that the underlying LWE and 1D-SIS assumptions that we rely on are as hard as approximating worst-case lattice problems to within a subexponential factor $2^{\tilde{O}(n^{1/c})}$ for some constant c (where n is the lattice dimension). Fix a constant c and a security parameter λ.

- We set the PRF input length $\rho = \lambda$. Then, the depth d_{eq} of the equality check circuit eq_ℓ satisfies $d_{\mathsf{eq}} = O(\log \rho) = O(\log \lambda)$.
- We set the lattice dimension $n = \lambda^{2c}$.
- The noise distribution χ is set to be the discrete Gaussian distribution $D_{\mathbb{Z},\sqrt{n}}$. Then the FHE ciphertext length z and the FHE secret key length τ is determined by $\mathsf{poly}(\lambda, d_{\mathsf{eq}}, \rho, \log q) = \mathsf{poly}(\lambda)$. The depth of the FHE equality check circuit is $d = \mathsf{poly}(d_{\mathsf{eq}}, \log z) = \mathsf{polylog}(\lambda)$. Finally, we set $B_{\mathsf{test}} = B \cdot (m+1)$.
- We set $q > m^{O(d)}$ in order to invoke correctness and security of the leveled homomorphic encryption scheme and the matrix embeddings. We refer to the full version [34] for more details. Furthermore, for the 1D-SIS-R assumption, we need q to be the product of λ primes $p_1, \ldots, p_\lambda$. For each $i \in [\lambda]$, we set the primes $p_j = 2^{O(n^{1/2c})}$ such that $p_1 < \cdots < p_\lambda$.
- We set $p = 2^{n^{1/2c+\varepsilon}}$ for any $\varepsilon > 0$, so the condition in Theorem 5.1 is satisfied.
- We set $m = \Theta(n \log q)$, and $B_{\mathsf{test}} = B \cdot (m+1)$. For these parameter settings, $m^{O(d)} = m^{\mathsf{polylog}(\lambda)}$ and $q = 2^{\tilde{O}(n^{1/2c})} = 2^{\tilde{O}(\lambda)}$.

Under these parameter setting, the private translucent t-puncturable PRF in Sect. 5.1 is selectively secure assuming the polynomial hardness of approximating worst-case lattice problems over an n-dimensional lattice to within a subexponential approximation factor $2^{\tilde{O}(n^{1/2c})}$. Using complexity leveraging [8], the same construction is adaptively secure assuming subexponential hardness of the same worst-case lattice problems.

6 Watermarkable PRFs from Translucent PRFs

In this section, we formally introduce the notion of a watermarkable family of PRFs. Our definitions are adapted from those of [12,21]. Then, in Sect. 6.2, we show how to construct a secretly-extractable, message-embedding watermarkable family of PRFs from translucent t-puncturable PRFs. Combined with our concrete instantiation of translucent t-puncturable PRFs from Sect. 5, this gives the first watermarkable family of PRFs (with security against arbitrary removal strategies) from standard assumptions.

6.1 Watermarking PRFs

We begin by introducing the notion of a watermarkable PRF family.

Definition 6.1 (Watermarkable Family of PRFs [12, adapted]**).** *Fix a security parameter λ and a message space $\{0,1\}^t$. Then, a secretly-extractable, message-embedding watermarking scheme for a PRF $\Pi_{\mathsf{PRF}} = (\mathsf{PRF.KeyGen}, \mathsf{PRF.Eval})$ is a tuple of algorithms $\Pi_{\mathsf{WM}} = (\mathsf{WM.Setup}, \mathsf{WM.Mark}, \mathsf{WM.Extract})$ with the following properties:*

- $\mathsf{WM.Setup}(1^\lambda) \to \mathsf{msk}$: *On input the security parameter λ, the setup algorithm outputs the watermarking secret key* msk.
- $\mathsf{WM.Mark}(\mathsf{msk}, k, m) \to C$: *On input the watermarking secret key* msk, *a PRF key k (to be marked), and a message $m \in \{0,1\}^t$, the mark algorithm outputs a marked circuit C.*
- $\mathsf{WM.Extract}(\mathsf{msk}, C') \to m$: *On input the master secret key* msk *and a circuit C', the extraction algorithm outputs a string $m \in \{0,1\}^t \cup \{\perp\}$.*

Definition 6.2 (Circuit Similarity). *Fix a circuit class $\mathcal{C}$ on n-bit inputs. For two circuits $C, C' \in \mathcal{C}$ and for a non-decreasing function $f : \mathbb{N} \to \mathbb{N}$, we write $C \sim_f C'$ to denote that the two circuits agree on all but an $1/f(n)$ fraction of inputs. More formally, we define*

$$C \sim_f C' \quad \Longleftrightarrow \quad \Pr_{x \xleftarrow{R} \{0,1\}^n} [C(x) \neq C'(x)] \leq 1/f(n)$$

We also write $C \not\sim_f C'$ to denote that C and C' differ on at least a $1/f(n)$ fraction of inputs.

Correctness. The correctness property for a watermarking scheme for a PRF family consists of two requirements which we state below.

Definition 6.3 (Watermarking Correctness). *Fix a security parameter λ. We say that a watermarking scheme $\Pi_{\mathsf{WM}} = (\mathsf{WM.Setup}, \mathsf{WM.Mark}, \mathsf{WM.Extract})$ for a PRF $\Pi_{\mathsf{PRF}} = (\mathsf{PRF.KeyGen}, \mathsf{PRF.Eval})$ with domain $\{0,1\}^n$* is correct *if for all messages $m \in \{0,1\}^t$, and setting $\mathsf{msk} \leftarrow \mathsf{WM.Setup}(1^\lambda)$, $k \leftarrow \mathsf{PRF.KeyGen}(1^\lambda)$, and $C \leftarrow \mathsf{WM.Mark}(\mathsf{msk}, k, m)$, the following two properties hold:*

- ***Functionality-preserving:*** $C(\cdot) \sim_f \mathsf{PRF.Eval}(k, \cdot)$ *where* $1/f(n) = \mathsf{negl}(\lambda)$ *with overwhelming probability.*
- ***Extraction correctness:*** $\Pr[\mathsf{WM.Extract}(\mathsf{msk}, C) = m] = 1 - \mathsf{negl}(\lambda)$.

Security. Following [12,21], we introduce two different security notions for a watermarking scheme: unremovability and unforgeability. We begin by defining the watermarking experiment.

Definition 6.4 (Watermarking Experiment [12, adapted]**).** *Fix a security parameter* λ. *Let* $\Pi_{\mathsf{WM}} = (\mathsf{WM.Setup}, \mathsf{WM.Mark}, \mathsf{WM.Extract})$ *be a watermarking scheme for a PRF* $\Pi_{\mathsf{PRF}} = (\mathsf{PRF.KeyGen}, \mathsf{PRF.Eval})$ *with key-space* $\mathcal{K}$, *and let* $\mathcal{A}$ *be an adversary. Then the watermarking experiment* $\mathsf{Expt}_{\Pi_{\mathsf{WM}},\mathcal{A}}(\lambda)$ *proceeds as follows. The challenger begins by sampling* $\mathsf{msk} \leftarrow \mathsf{WM.Setup}(1^\lambda)$. *The adversary* $\mathcal{A}$ *is then given access to the following oracles:*

- ***Marking oracle.*** *On input a message* $m \in \{0,1\}^t$ *and a PRF key* $k \in \mathcal{K}$, *the challenger returns the circuit* $C \leftarrow \mathsf{WM.Mark}(\mathsf{msk}, k, m)$ *to* $\mathcal{A}$.
- ***Challenge oracle.*** *On input a message* $m \in \{0,1\}^t$, *the challenger samples a key* $k \leftarrow \mathsf{PRF.KeyGen}(1^\lambda)$, *and returns the circuit* $C \leftarrow \mathsf{WM.Mark}(\mathsf{msk}, k, m)$ *to* $\mathcal{A}$.

Finally, $\mathcal{A}$ *outputs a circuit* C'. *The output of the experiment, denoted* $\mathsf{Expt}_{\Pi_{\mathsf{WM}},\mathcal{A}}(\lambda)$, *is* $\mathsf{WM.Extract}(\mathsf{msk}, C')$.

Definition 6.5 (Unremovability [12,21]**).** *Fix a security parameter* λ. *For a watermarking scheme* $\Pi_{\mathsf{WM}} = (\mathsf{WM.Setup}, \mathsf{WM.Mark}, \mathsf{WM.Extract})$ *for a PRF* $\Pi_{\mathsf{PRF}} = (\mathsf{PRF.KeyGen}, \mathsf{PRF.Eval})$ *and an adversary* $\mathcal{A}$, *we say that* $\mathcal{A}$ *is* unremoving-admissible *if the following conditions hold:*

- *The adversary* $\mathcal{A}$ *makes exactly one query to the challenge oracle.*
- *The circuit* $\tilde{C}$ *that* $\mathcal{A}$ *outputs satisfies* $\tilde{C} \sim_f \hat{C}$, *where* $\hat{C}$ *is the circuit output by the challenge oracle and* $1/f = \mathsf{negl}(\lambda)$.

Then, we say that Π_{WM} *is* unremovable *if for all efficient and unremoving-admissible adversaries* $\mathcal{A}$,

$$\Pr[\mathsf{Expt}_{\Pi_{\mathsf{WM}},\mathcal{A}}(\lambda) \neq \hat{m}] = \mathsf{negl}(\lambda),$$

where $\hat{m}$ *is the message* $\mathcal{A}$ *submitted to the challenge oracle in* $\mathsf{Expt}_{\Pi_{\mathsf{WM}},\mathcal{A}}(\lambda)$.

Definition 6.6 (δ-Unforgeability [12,21]**).** *Fix a security parameter* λ. *For a watermarking scheme* $\Pi_{\mathsf{WM}} = (\mathsf{WM.Setup}, \mathsf{WM.Mark}, \mathsf{WM.Extract})$ *for a PRF* $\Pi_{\mathsf{PRF}} = (\mathsf{PRF.KeyGen}, \mathsf{PRF.Eval})$ *and an adversary* $\mathcal{A}$, *we say that* $\mathcal{A}$ *is* δ-unforging-admissible *if the following conditions hold:*

- *The adversary* $\mathcal{A}$ *does not make any challenge oracle queries.*
- *The circuit* $\tilde{C}$ *that* $\mathcal{A}$ *outputs satisfies* $\tilde{C} \not\sim_f C_\ell$ *for all* $\ell \in [Q]$, *where* Q *is the number of queries* $\mathcal{A}$ *made to the marking oracle,* C_ℓ *is the output of the marking oracle on the* ℓ^{th} *query, and* $1/f > \delta$. *Moreover,* $\tilde{C} \not\sim_f \mathsf{PRF.Eval}(k_\ell, \cdot)$, *where* k_ℓ *is the key the adversary submitted on its* ℓ^{th} *query to the marking oracle.*

Then, we say that Π_{WM} is δ-unforgeable *if for all efficient and δ-unforging-admissible adversaries $\mathcal{A}$,*

$$\Pr[\mathsf{Expt}_{\Pi_{\mathsf{WM}},\mathcal{A}}(\lambda) \neq \bot] = \mathsf{negl}(\lambda).$$

Remark 6.7 (Giving Access to an Extraction Oracle). As noted in [21], in the secret-key setting, the watermarking security game (Definition 6.4) can be augmented to allow the adversary oracle access to an extraction oracle (which implements $\mathsf{WM.Extract}(\mathsf{msk}, \cdot)$). It is an open problem to construct secretly-extractable watermarking from standard assumptions where the adversary is additionally given access to a extraction oracle. The only known constructions today [21] rely on indistinguishability obfuscation.

Remark 6.8 (Marking Oracle Variations). In the watermarking security game (Definition 6.4), the adversary can submit arbitrary keys (of its choosing) to the marking oracle. Cohen et al. [21] also consider a stronger notion where the adversary is allowed to submit arbitrary *circuits* (not corresponding to any particular PRF) to the marking oracle. However, in this model, they can only achieve lunch-time security (i.e., the adversary can only query the marking oracle before issuing its challenge query). In the model where the adversary can only query the marking oracle on valid PRF keys, their construction achieves full security (assuming the PRF family satisfies a key-injectivity property). Similarly, our construction achieves *full* security in this model (in the secret-key setting), and also relies on a key-injectivity property on the underlying PRF. Our notion is strictly stronger than the notion in [12]. In the Boneh et al. model [12], the adversary *cannot* choose the key for the marking oracle. Instead, the marking oracle samples a key (honestly) and gives both the sampled key as well as the watermarked key to the adversary. In contrast, in both our model as well as that in [21], the adversary is allowed to see watermarked keys on *arbitrary* keys of its choosing. The key difference in our security analysis that enables us to achieve this stronger security notion (compared to [12]) is the new key-injectivity property on the underlying translucent PRF. Instantiating the construction in [12] with a private programmable PRF satisfying key-injectivity should also yield a watermarkable family of PRFs under our strengthened definition.

In the full version of this paper [34], we further compare our correctness and security notions to those considered in previous work [12,21].

6.2 Watermarking Construction

In this section, we show how any translucent t-puncturable PRF can be used to obtain a watermarkable family of PRFs. Combined with our construction of a translucent t-puncturable PRF from Sect. 5.1, we obtain the first watermarkable family of PRFs from standard assumptions.

Construction 6.9. *Fix a security parameter λ and a positive real value $\delta < 1$ such that $d = \lambda/\delta = \mathsf{poly}(\lambda)$. Let $\{0,1\}^t$ be the message space for the watermarking scheme. Our construction relies on the following two ingredients:*

- *Let* Π_{TPRF} *be a translucent* t*-puncturable PRF (Definition 4.6) with key-space* $\mathcal{K}$*, domain* $\{0,1\}^n$*, and range* $\{0,1\}^m$*.*
- *Let* Π_{PRF} *be a secure PRF with domain* $(\{0,1\}^m)^d$ *and range* $(\{0,1\}^n)^{2t}$*.*

We require $n, m, t = \omega(\log \lambda)$*. The secretly-extractable, message-embedding watermarking scheme* $\Pi_{\mathsf{WM}} = (\mathsf{WM.Setup}, \mathsf{WM.Mark}, \mathsf{WM.Extract})$ *for the PRF associated with* Π_{TPRF} *is defined as follows:*

- $\mathsf{WM.Setup}(1^\lambda)$*: On input the security parameter* λ*, the setup algorithm runs* $(\mathsf{pp}, \mathsf{tk}) \leftarrow \mathsf{TPRF.Setup}(1^\lambda)$*. Next, for each* $j \in [d]$*, it samples* $h_j \xleftarrow{\text{R}} \{0,1\}^n$*. It also samples a key* $\mathsf{k}^* \leftarrow \mathsf{PRF.KeyGen}(1^\lambda)$*. Finally, it outputs the master secret key* $\mathsf{msk} = (\mathsf{pp}, \mathsf{tk}, h_1, \ldots, h_d, \mathsf{k}^*)$*.*
- $\mathsf{WM.Mark}(\mathsf{msk}, k, m)$*: On input the master secret key* $\mathsf{msk} = (\mathsf{pp}, \mathsf{tk}, h_1, \ldots, h_d, \mathsf{k}^*)$*, a PRF key* $k \in \mathcal{K}$ *to be marked, and a message* $m \in \{0,1\}^t$*, the marking algorithm proceeds as follows:*
  1. *For each* $j \in [d]$*, set* $y_j \leftarrow \mathsf{TPRF.Eval}(\mathsf{pp}, k, h_j)$*. Let* $\mathbf{y} = (y_1, \ldots, y_d)$*.*
  2. *Compute points* $\mathbf{x} = \left(x_1^{(0)}, x_1^{(1)}, \ldots, x_t^{(0)}, x_t^{(1)}\right) \leftarrow \mathsf{PRF.Eval}(\mathsf{k}^*, \mathbf{y})$*.*
  3. *Compute the* t*-punctured key* $\mathsf{sk}_S \leftarrow \mathsf{TPRF.Constrain}(\mathsf{pp}, k, S)$*, where the set* S *is given by* $S = \{x \in \{0,1\}^n : x \neq x_i^{(m_i)} \ \forall i \in [t]\}$*,*
  4. *Output the circuit* C *where* $C(\cdot) = \mathsf{TPRF.ConstrainEval}(\mathsf{pp}, \mathsf{sk}_S, \cdot)$*.*
- $\mathsf{WM.Extract}(\mathsf{msk}, C)$*: On input the master secret key* $\mathsf{msk} = (\mathsf{pp}, \mathsf{tk}, h_1, \ldots, h_d, k)$ *and a circuit* $C : \{0,1\}^n \to \{0,1\}^m$*, the extraction algorithm proceeds as follows:*
  1. *Compute points* $\mathbf{x} = \left(x_1^{(0)}, x_1^{(1)}, \ldots, x_t^{(0)}, x_t^{(1)}\right) \leftarrow \mathsf{PRF.Eval}(\mathsf{k}^*, C(h_1), \ldots, C(h_d))$*.*
  2. *For each* $i \in [t]$*, and* $b \in \{0,1\}$*, compute* $z_i^{(b)} = \mathsf{TPRF.Test}(\mathsf{pp}, \mathsf{tk}, C(x_i^{(b)}))$*.*
  3. *If there exists some* i *for which* $z_i^{(0)} = z_i^{(1)}$*, output* $\perp$*. Otherwise, output the message* $m \in \{0,1\}^t$ *where* $m_i = 0$ *if* $z_i^{(0)} = 1$ *and* $m_i = 1$ *if* $z_i^{(1)} = 1$*.*

Security Analysis. We now state the correctness and security theorems for our construction, but defer their formal proofs to the full version of this paper [34].

Theorem 6.10. *If* Π_{TPRF} *is a secure translucent* t*-puncturable PRF, and* Π_{PRF} *is a secure PRF, then the watermarking scheme in Construction 6.9 is correct.*

Theorem 6.11. *If* Π_{TPRF} *is a selectively-secure translucent* t*-puncturable PRF, and* Π_{PRF} *is secure, then the watermarking scheme in Construction 6.9 is unremovable.*

Theorem 6.12. *If* Π_{TPRF} *is a selectively-secure translucent* t*-puncturable PRF, and* Π_{PRF} *is secure, then the watermarking scheme in Construction 6.9 is* δ*-unforgeable.*

Acknowledgments. We thank Vinod Vaikuntanathan and Daniel Wichs for pointing out the connection between private programmable PRFs and private puncturable PRFs. We thank Yilei Chen for many helpful discussions about watermarking. This work was funded by NSF, DARPA, a grant from ONR, and the Simons Foundation. Opinions, findings and conclusions or recommendations expressed in this material are those of the authors and do not necessarily reflect the views of DARPA.

References

1. Agrawal, S., Boneh, D., Boyen, X.: Efficient lattice (H)IBE in the standard model. In: Gilbert, H. (ed.) EUROCRYPT 2010. LNCS, vol. 6110, pp. 553–572. Springer, Heidelberg (2010). doi:10.1007/978-3-642-13190-5_28
2. Agrawal, S., Freeman, D.M., Vaikuntanathan, V.: Functional encryption for inner product predicates from learning with errors. In: Lee, D.H., Wang, X. (eds.) ASIACRYPT 2011. LNCS, vol. 7073, pp. 21–40. Springer, Heidelberg (2011). doi:10.1007/978-3-642-25385-0_2
3. Banerjee, A., Fuchsbauer, G., Peikert, C., Pietrzak, K., Stevens, S.: Key-homomorphic constrained pseudorandom functions. In: Dodis, Y., Nielsen, J.B. (eds.) TCC 2015. LNCS, vol. 9015, pp. 31–60. Springer, Heidelberg (2015). doi:10.1007/978-3-662-46497-7_2
4. Banerjee, A., Peikert, C.: New and improved key-homomorphic pseudorandom functions. In: Garay, J.A., Gennaro, R. (eds.) CRYPTO 2014. LNCS, vol. 8616, pp. 353–370. Springer, Heidelberg (2014). doi:10.1007/978-3-662-44371-2_20
5. Banerjee, A., Peikert, C., Rosen, A.: Pseudorandom functions and lattices. In: Pointcheval, D., Johansson, T. (eds.) EUROCRYPT 2012. LNCS, vol. 7237, pp. 719–737. Springer, Heidelberg (2012). doi:10.1007/978-3-642-29011-4_42
6. Barak, B., Goldreich, O., Impagliazzo, R., Rudich, S., Sahai, A., Vadhan, S., Yang, K.: On the (im)possibility of obfuscating programs. In: Kilian, J. (ed.) CRYPTO 2001. LNCS, vol. 2139, pp. 1–18. Springer, Heidelberg (2001). doi:10.1007/3-540-44647-8_1
7. Barak, B., Goldreich, O., Impagliazzo, R., Rudich, S., Sahai, A., Vadhan, S.P., Yang, K.: On the (im)possibility of obfuscating programs. J. ACM **59**(2), 6 (2012)
8. Boneh, D., Boyen, X.: Efficient selective-ID secure identity-based encryption without random oracles. In: Cachin, C., Camenisch, J.L. (eds.) EUROCRYPT 2004. LNCS, vol. 3027, pp. 223–238. Springer, Heidelberg (2004). doi:10.1007/978-3-540-24676-3_14
9. Boneh, D., Gentry, C., Gorbunov, S., Halevi, S., Nikolaenko, V., Segev, G., Vaikuntanathan, V., Vinayagamurthy, D.: Fully key-homomorphic encryption, arithmetic circuit ABE and compact garbled circuits. In: Nguyen, P.Q., Oswald, E. (eds.) EUROCRYPT 2014. LNCS, vol. 8441, pp. 533–556. Springer, Heidelberg (2014). doi:10.1007/978-3-642-55220-5_30
10. Boneh, D., Kim, S., Montgomery, H.: Private puncturable PRFs from standard lattice assumptions. In: Coron, J.-S., Nielsen, J.B. (eds.) EUROCRYPT 2017. LNCS, vol. 10210, pp. 415–445. Springer, Cham (2017). doi:10.1007/978-3-319-56620-7_15
11. Boneh, D., Lewi, K., Montgomery, H., Raghunathan, A.: Key homomorphic PRFs and their applications. In: Canetti, R., Garay, J.A. (eds.) CRYPTO 2013. LNCS, vol. 8042, pp. 410–428. Springer, Heidelberg (2013). doi:10.1007/978-3-642-40041-4_23

12. Boneh, D., Lewi, K., Wu, D.J.: Constraining pseudorandom functions privately. In: Fehr, S. (ed.) PKC 2017. LNCS, vol. 10175, pp. 494–524. Springer, Heidelberg (2017). doi:10.1007/978-3-662-54388-7_17
13. Boneh, D., Waters, B.: Conjunctive, subset, and range queries on encrypted data. In: Vadhan, S.P. (ed.) TCC 2007. LNCS, vol. 4392, pp. 535–554. Springer, Heidelberg (2007). doi:10.1007/978-3-540-70936-7_29
14. Boneh, D., Waters, B.: Constrained pseudorandom functions and their applications. In: Sako, K., Sarkar, P. (eds.) ASIACRYPT 2013. LNCS, vol. 8270, pp. 280–300. Springer, Heidelberg (2013). doi:10.1007/978-3-642-42045-0_15
15. Boyle, E., Goldwasser, S., Ivan, I.: Functional signatures and pseudorandom functions. In: Krawczyk, H. (ed.) PKC 2014. LNCS, vol. 8383, pp. 501–519. Springer, Heidelberg (2014). doi:10.1007/978-3-642-54631-0_29
16. Brakerski, Z., Cash, D., Tsabary, R., Wee, H.: Targeted homomorphic attribute-based encryption. In: Hirt, M., Smith, A. (eds.) TCC 2016. LNCS, vol. 9986, pp. 330–360. Springer, Heidelberg (2016). doi:10.1007/978-3-662-53644-5_13
17. Brakerski, Z., Vaikuntanathan, V.: Constrained key-homomorphic PRFs from standard lattice assumptions. In: Dodis, Y., Nielsen, J.B. (eds.) TCC 2015. LNCS, vol. 9015, pp. 1–30. Springer, Heidelberg (2015). doi:10.1007/978-3-662-46497-7_1
18. Brakerski, Z., Vaikuntanathan, V.: Circuit-ABE from LWE: unbounded attributes and semi-adaptive security. In: Robshaw, M., Katz, J. (eds.) CRYPTO 2016. LNCS, vol. 9816, pp. 363–384. Springer, Heidelberg (2016). doi:10.1007/978-3-662-53015-3_13
19. Canetti, R., Chen, Y.: Constraint-hiding constrained PRFs for NC^1 from LWE. In: EUROCRYPT (2017)
20. Canetti, R., Dwork, C., Naor, M., Ostrovsky, R.: Deniable encryption. In: Kaliski, B.S. (ed.) CRYPTO 1997. LNCS, vol. 1294, pp. 90–104. Springer, Heidelberg (1997). doi:10.1007/BFb0052229
21. Cohen, A., Holmgren, J., Nishimaki, R., Vaikuntanathan, V., Wichs, D.: Watermarking cryptographic capabilities. In: STOC (2016)
22. Cox, I., Miller, M., Bloom, J., Fridrich, J., Kalker, T.: Digital Watermarking and Steganography. Morgan Kaufmann, Burlington (2007)
23. Garg, S., Gentry, C., Halevi, S., Raykova, M., Sahai, A., Waters, B.: Candidate indistinguishability obfuscation and functional encryption for all circuits. In: FOCS (2013)
24. Gay, R., Méaux, P., Wee, H.: Predicate encryption for multi-dimensional range queries from lattices. In: Katz, J. (ed.) PKC 2015. LNCS, vol. 9020, pp. 752–776. Springer, Heidelberg (2015). doi:10.1007/978-3-662-46447-2_34
25. Gentry, C.: Fully homomorphic encryption using ideal lattices. In: STOC (2009)
26. Gentry, C., Gorbunov, S., Halevi, S.: Graph-induced multilinear maps from lattices. In: Dodis, Y., Nielsen, J.B. (eds.) TCC 2015. LNCS, vol. 9015, pp. 498–527. Springer, Heidelberg (2015). doi:10.1007/978-3-662-46497-7_20
27. Gentry, C., Sahai, A., Waters, B.: Homomorphic encryption from learning with errors: conceptually-simpler, asymptotically-faster, attribute-based. In: Canetti, R., Garay, J.A. (eds.) CRYPTO 2013. LNCS, vol. 8042, pp. 75–92. Springer, Heidelberg (2013). doi:10.1007/978-3-642-40041-4_5
28. Gorbunov, S., Vaikuntanathan, V., Wee, H.: Attribute-based encryption for circuits. In: STOC (2013)
29. Gorbunov, S., Vaikuntanathan, V., Wee, H.: Predicate encryption for circuits from LWE. In: Gennaro, R., Robshaw, M. (eds.) CRYPTO 2015. LNCS, vol. 9216, pp. 503–523. Springer, Heidelberg (2015). doi:10.1007/978-3-662-48000-7_25

30. Gorbunov, S., Vinayagamurthy, D.: Riding on asymmetry: efficient ABE for branching programs. In: Iwata, T., Cheon, J.H. (eds.) ASIACRYPT 2015. LNCS, vol. 9452, pp. 550–574. Springer, Heidelberg (2015). doi:10.1007/978-3-662-48797-6_23
31. Hopper, N., Molnar, D., Wagner, D.: From weak to strong watermarking. In: Vadhan, S.P. (ed.) TCC 2007. LNCS, vol. 4392, pp. 362–382. Springer, Heidelberg (2007). doi:10.1007/978-3-540-70936-7_20
32. Katz, J., Sahai, A., Waters, B.: Predicate encryption supporting disjunctions, polynomial equations, and inner products. In: Smart, N. (ed.) EUROCRYPT 2008. LNCS, vol. 4965, pp. 146–162. Springer, Heidelberg (2008). doi:10.1007/978-3-540-78967-3_9
33. Kiayias, A., Papadopoulos, S., Triandopoulos, N., Zacharias, T.: Delegatable pseudorandom functions and applications. In: CCS (2013)
34. Kim, S., Wu, D.J.: Watermarking cryptographic functionalities from standard lattice assumptions. IACR Cryptology ePrint Archive 2017 (2017)
35. Naccache, D., Shamir, A., Stern, J.P.: How to copyright a function? In: Imai, H., Zheng, Y. (eds.) PKC 1999. LNCS, vol. 1560, pp. 188–196. Springer, Heidelberg (1999). doi:10.1007/3-540-49162-7_14
36. Nishimaki, R.: How to watermark cryptographic functions. In: Johansson, T., Nguyen, P.Q. (eds.) EUROCRYPT 2013. LNCS, vol. 7881, pp. 111–125. Springer, Heidelberg (2013). doi:10.1007/978-3-642-38348-9_7
37. Nishimaki, R., Wichs, D., Zhandry, M.: Anonymous traitor tracing: how to embed arbitrary information in a key. In: Fischlin, M., Coron, J.-S. (eds.) EUROCRYPT 2016. LNCS, vol. 9666, pp. 388–419. Springer, Heidelberg (2016). doi:10.1007/978-3-662-49896-5_14
38. Regev, O.: On lattices, learning with errors, random linear codes, and cryptography. In: STOC (2005)
39. Sahai, A., Waters, B.: Fuzzy identity-based encryption. In: Cramer, R. (ed.) EUROCRYPT 2005. LNCS, vol. 3494, pp. 457–473. Springer, Heidelberg (2005). doi:10.1007/11426639_27
40. Yoshida, M., Fujiwara, T.: Toward digital watermarking for cryptographic data. IEICE Trans. **94–A**(1), 270–272 (2011)

Identity-Based Encryption from the Diffie-Hellman Assumption

Nico Döttling[(✉)] and Sanjam Garg

University of California, Berkeley, Berkeley, USA
{nico.doettling,sanjamg}@berkeley.edu

Abstract. We provide the first constructions of identity-based encryption and hierarchical identity-based encryption based on the hardness of the (Computational) Diffie-Hellman Problem (without use of groups with pairings) or Factoring. Our construction achieves the standard notion of identity-based encryption as considered by Boneh and Franklin [CRYPTO 2001]. We bypass known impossibility results using garbled circuits that make a non-black-box use of the underlying cryptographic primitives.

1 Introduction

Soon after the invention of public-key encryption [20,43], Shamir [44] posed the problem of constructing a public-key encryption scheme where encryption can be performed using just the identity of the recipient. In such an identity-based encryption (IBE) scheme there are four algorithms: (1) Setup generates the global public parameters and a master secret key, (2) KeyGen uses the master secret key to generate a secret key for the user with a particular identity, (3) Encrypt allows for encrypting messages corresponding to an identity, and (4) Decrypt can be used to decrypt the generated ciphertext using a secret key for the matching identity.

The ability of IBE to "compress" exponentially many public keys into "small" global public parameters [11,19] provides a way for simplifying certificate management in e-mail systems. Specifically, Alice can send an encrypted email to Bob at bob@iacr.org by just using the string "bob@iacr.org" and the public parameters generated by a setup authority. In this solution, there is no need for Alice to obtain Bob's public key. Bob could decrypt the email using a secret key corresponding to "bob@iacr.org" that he can obtain from the setup authority.

Research supported in part from AFOSR YIP Award, DARPA/ARL SAFEWARE Award W911NF15C0210, AFOSR Award FA9550-15-1-0274, NSF CRII Award 1464397, and research grants by the Okawa Foundation, Visa Inc., and Center for Long-Term Cybersecurity (CLTC, UC Berkeley). The views expressed are those of the author and do not reflect the official policy or position of the funding agencies. Nico Döttling was supported by a postdoc fellowship of the German Academic Exchange Service (DAAD).

J. Katz and H. Shacham (Eds.): CRYPTO 2017, Part I, LNCS 10401, pp. 537–569, 2017.
DOI: 10.1007/978-3-319-63688-7_18

The more functional notion of hierarchical IBE (HIBE) [28,32] additionally allows a user with a secret key for an identity id to generate a secret key for any identity $\mathsf{id}\|\mathsf{id}'$. For instance, in the example above, Bob can use the secret key corresponding to identity "`bob@iacr.org`" to obtain a secret key corresponding to the identity "`bob@iacr.org`$\|$`2017`". Bob could then give this key to his secretary who could now decrypt all his emails tagged as being sent during the year 2017, while Bob is on vacation.

The first IBE schemes were realized by Boneh and Franklin [11] and Cocks [19]. Subsequently, significant research effort has been devoted to realizing IBE and HIBE schemes. By now, several constructions of IBE are known based on (i) various assumptions on groups with a bilinear map, e.g. [8,9,11, 16,41,48], (ii) the quadratic residuocity assumption [12,19] (in the random oracle model [6]), or (iii) the learning-with-errors (LWE) assumption [3,17,27]. On the other hand, HIBE schemes are known based on (i) various assumptions on groups with a bilinear map [8,10,25,28,32,35,45,47], or (ii) LWE [1,2,17].

On the negative side, Boneh et al. [13] show that IBE cannot be realized using trapdoor permutations or CCA-secure public-key encryption in a black-box manner. Furthermore, Papakonstantinou et al. [42] show that black-box use of a group over which DDH is assumed to be hard is insufficient for realizing IBE.

1.1 Our Results

In this work, we show a fully-secure construction of IBE and a selectively secure HIBE based just on the Computational Diffie-Hellman (CDH). In the group of quadratic residues this problem is as hard as the Factoring problem [7,38,46]. Therefore, this implies a solution based on the hardness of factoring as well.

Our constructions bypass the known impossibility results [13,42] by making a non-black-box use of the underlying cryptographic primitives. However, this non-black-box use of cryptographic primitives also makes our scheme inefficient. In Sect. 6, we suggest ideas for reducing the non-black-box of the underlying primitives thereby improving the efficiency of our scheme. Even with these optimizations, our IBE scheme is prohibitive when compared with the IBE schemes based on bilinear maps. We leave open the problem of realizing an efficient IBE scheme from the Diffie-Hellman Assumption.

Subsequent Work. In a followup paper [21] we show how the techniques from this paper can be used to obtain generic constructions of fully-secure IBE and selectively-secure HIBE starting with any selectively-secure IBE scheme.

2 Our Techniques

In this section, we give an intuitive explanation of our construction of IBE from the Decisional Diffie-Hellman (DDH) Assumption. We defer the details on constructing HIBE and obtaining the same results based on Computational Diffie-Hellman to the main body of the paper.

We start by describing a chameleon hash function [34] that supports certain encryption and decryption procedures. We refer to this new primitive as a *chameleon encryption scheme.*[1] Subsequently, we describe how chameleon encryption along with garbled circuits can be used to realize IBE.

2.1 Chameleon Encryption

As mentioned above, a chameleon encryption scheme is a chameleon hash function that supports certain encryption and decryption procedures along with. We start by describing the chameleon hash function and then the associated encryption and decryption procedures. Recall that a chameleon hash function is a collision resistant hash function for which the knowledge of a trapdoor enables collision finding.

Our Chameleon Hash. Given a cyclic group $\mathbb{G}$ of prime order p with a generator g consider the following chameleon hash function:

$$\mathsf{H}(\mathsf{k}, \mathsf{x}; r) = g^r \prod_{j \in [n]} g_{j,\mathsf{x}_j},$$

where $\mathsf{k} = (g, \{g_{j,0}, g_{j,1}\}_{j\in[n]})$, $r \in \mathbb{Z}_p$ and x_j is the jth bit of $\mathsf{x} \in \{0,1\}^n$. It is not very hard to note that this hash function is (i) collision resistant based on the hardness of the discrete-log problem, and (ii) chameleon given the trapdoor information $\{\mathsf{dlog}_g\ g_{j,0}, \mathsf{dlog}_g\ g_{j,1}\}_{j\in[n]}$—specifically, given any $\mathsf{x}, r, \mathsf{x}'$ and the trapdoor information we can efficiently compute r' such that $\mathsf{H}(\mathsf{k}, \mathsf{x}; r) = \mathsf{H}(\mathsf{k}, \mathsf{x}'; r')$.

The Associated Encryption—Abstractly. Corresponding to a chameleon hash function, we require encryption and decryption algorithms such that

1. encryption $\mathsf{Enc}(\mathsf{k}, (\mathsf{h}, i, b), \mathsf{m})$ on input a key k, a hash value h, a location $i \in [n]$, a bit $b \in \{0,1\}$, and a message $\mathsf{m} \in \{0,1\}$ outputs a ciphertext ct, and
2. decryption $\mathsf{Dec}(\mathsf{k}, (\mathsf{x}, r), \mathsf{ct})$ on input a ciphertext ct, x and coins r yields m if

$$\mathsf{h} = \mathsf{H}(\mathsf{k}, \mathsf{x}; r) \text{ and } \mathsf{x}_i = b,$$

where (h, i, b) are the values used in the generation of the ciphertext ct.

In other words, the decryptor can use the knowledge of the preimage of h as the key to decrypt m as long as the ith bit of the preimage it can supply is equal to the value b chosen at the time of encryption. Our security requirement roughly is that

$$\{\mathsf{k}, \mathsf{x}, r, \mathsf{Enc}(\mathsf{k}, (\mathsf{h}, i, 1 - \mathsf{x}_i), 0)\} \stackrel{c}{\approx} \{\mathsf{k}, \mathsf{x}, r, \mathsf{Enc}(\mathsf{k}, (\mathsf{h}, i, 1 - \mathsf{x}_i), 1)\},$$

where $\stackrel{c}{\approx}$ denotes computational indistinguishability.[2]

[1] The notion of chameleon hashing is closely related to the notion of chameleon commitment scheme [15] and we refer the reader to [34] for more discussion on this.

[2] The success of decryption is conditioned on certain requirements placed on (x, r). This restricted decryption capability is reminiscent of the concepts of witness encryption [22] and extractable witness encryption [4,14].

The Associated Encryption—Realization. Corresponding to the chameleon hash defined above our encryption procedure $\mathsf{Enc}(\mathsf{k}, (\mathsf{h}, i, b), \mathsf{m})$ proceeds as follows. Sample a random value $\rho \xleftarrow{\$} \mathbb{Z}_p$ and output the ciphertext ct where $\mathsf{ct} = (e, c, c', \{c_{j,0}, c_{j,1}\}_{j \in [n] \setminus \{i\}})$ and

$$\begin{aligned} & c := g^{\rho} && c' := \mathsf{h}^{\rho}, \\ \forall j \in [n]\setminus\{i\}, \quad & c_{j,0} := g_{j,0}^{\rho} && c_{j,1} := g_{j,1}^{\rho}, \\ & e := \mathsf{m} \oplus g_{i,b}^{\rho}. \end{aligned}$$

It is easy to see that if $\mathsf{x}_i = b$ then decryption $\mathsf{Dec}(\mathsf{ct}, (\mathsf{x}, r))$ can just output

$$e \oplus \frac{c'}{c^r \prod_{j \in [n] \setminus \{i\}} c_{j,\mathsf{x}_j}}.$$

However, if $\mathsf{x}_i \neq b$ then the decryptor has access to the value g_{i,x_i}^{ρ} but not $g_{i,b}^{\rho}$, and this prevents him from learning the message m. Formalizing this intuition, we can argue security of this scheme based on the DDH assumption.[3] In a bit more detail, we can use an adversary $\mathcal{A}$ breaking the security of the chameleon encryption scheme to distinguish DDH tuples (g, g^u, g^v, g^{uv}) from random tuples (g, g^u, g^v, g^s). Fix (adversarially chosen) $\mathsf{x} \in \{0,1\}^n$, index $i \in [n]$ and a bit $b \in \{0,1\}$. Given a tuple (g, U, V, T), we can simulate public key k, hash value h, coins r and ciphertext ct as follows. Choose uniformly random values $\alpha_{j,0}, \alpha_{j,1} \xleftarrow{\$} \mathbb{Z}_p$ and set $g_{j,0} = g^{\alpha_{j,0}}$ and $g_{j,1} = g^{\alpha_{j,1}}$ for $j \in [n]$. Now *reassign* $g_{i,1-\mathsf{x}_i} = U$ and set $\mathsf{k} := (g, \{g_{j,0}, g_{j,1}\}_{j \in [n]})$. Choose $r \xleftarrow{\$} \mathbb{Z}_p$ uniformly at random and set $\mathsf{h} := \mathsf{H}(\mathsf{k}, \mathsf{x}; r)$. Finally prepare a challenge ciphertext $\mathsf{ct} := (e, c, c', \{c_{j,0}, c_{j,1}\}_{j \in [n] \setminus \{i\}})$ by choosing

$$\begin{aligned} & c := V && c' := V^r \cdot \prod_{j \in [n]} V^{\alpha_{j,\mathsf{x}_j}}, \\ \forall j \in [n]\setminus\{i\}, \quad & c_{j,0} := V^{\alpha_{j,0}} && c_{j,1} := V^{\alpha_{j,1}}, \\ & e := \mathsf{m} \oplus T, \end{aligned}$$

where $\mathsf{m} \in \{0,1\}$. Now, if $(g, U, V, T) = (g, g^u, g^v, g^{uv})$, then a routine calculation shows that k, h, r and ct have the same distribution as in the security experiment, thus $\mathcal{A}$'s advantage in guessing m remains the same. On the other hand, if T is chosen uniformly at random and independent of g, U, V, then $\mathcal{A}$'s advantage to guess m given k, h, r and ct is obviously 0, which concludes this proof-sketch.

2.2 From Chameleon Encryption to Identity-Based Encryption

The public parameters of an IBE scheme need to encode exponentially many public keys succinctly—one per each identity. Subsequently, corresponding to

[3] In Sect. 5, we explain our constructions of chameleon encryption based on the (Computational) Diffie-Hellman Assumption, or the Factoring Assumption.

these public parameters the setup authority should be able to provide the secret key for any of the exponentially many identities. This is in sharp contrast with public-key encryption schemes for which there is only one trapdoor per public key, which if revealed leaves no security. This is the intuition behind the black-box impossibility results for realizing IBE based on trapdoor permutations and CCA secure encryption [13,42]. At a very high level, we overcome this intuitive barrier by actually allowing for exponentially many public keys which are somehow compressed into small public parameters using our chameleon hash function. We start by describing how these keys are sampled and hashed.

Arrangement of the Keys. We start by describing the arrangement of the exponentially many keys in our IBE scheme for identities of length n bits. First, imagine a fresh encryption decryption key pair for any public-key encryption scheme for each identity in $\{0,1\}^n$. We will denote this pair for identity $\mathsf{v} \in \{0,1\}^n$ by $(\mathsf{ek_v}, \mathsf{dk_v})$. Next, in order to setup the hash values, we sample n hash keys — namely, $\mathsf{k}_0, \ldots \mathsf{k}_{n-1}$. Now, consider a tree of depth n and for each node $\mathsf{v} \in \{0,1\}^{\leq n-1} \cup \{\epsilon\}$[4] the hash value $\mathsf{h_v}$ is set as:

$$\mathsf{h_v} = \begin{cases} \mathsf{H}(\mathsf{k}_i, \mathsf{ek}_{\mathsf{v}\|0}\|\mathsf{ek}_{\mathsf{v}\|1}; r_\mathsf{v}) & \mathsf{v} \in \{0,1\}^{n-1} \text{ where } i = |\mathsf{v}| \\ \mathsf{H}(\mathsf{k}_i, \mathsf{h}_{\mathsf{v}\|0}\|\mathsf{h}_{\mathsf{v}\|1}; r_\mathsf{v}) & \mathsf{v} \in \{0,1\}^{<n-1} \cup \{\epsilon\} \text{ where } i = |\mathsf{v}| \end{cases} \quad (1)$$

where r_v for each $\mathsf{v} \in \{0,1\}^{<n} \cup \{\epsilon\}$ are chosen randomly.

Generating the Tree on Demand. Note that the setup authority cannot generate and hash these exponentially many hash keys at setup time. Instead, it generates them implicitly. More specifically, the setup authority computes each $\mathsf{h_v}$ as $\mathsf{H}(\mathsf{k}_{|\mathsf{v}|}, 0^\lambda; \omega_\mathsf{v})$. Then, later on when needed, using the trapdoor $\mathsf{t}_{|\mathsf{v}|}$ for the hash key $\mathsf{k}_{|\mathsf{v}|}$ we can obtain coins r_v such that the generated value $\mathsf{h_v}$ indeed satisfies Eq. 1. Furthermore, in order to maintain consistency (in the tree and across different invocations) the randomness ω_v used for each v is chosen using a pseudorandom function. In summary, with this change the entire can be represented succinctly.

What Are the Public Parameters? Note that the root hash value h_ε somehow binds the entire tree of hash values. With this in mind, we sent the public parameters of the scheme to be the n hash keys and the root hash value, i.e.

$$\mathsf{k}_0, \ldots \mathsf{k}_{n-1}, \mathsf{h}_\epsilon.$$

Secret-Key for a Particular Identity id. Given the above tree structure the secret key for some identity id simply consists of the hash values along the path from the root to the leaf corresponding to id and their siblings along with the

[4] We use ϵ to denote the empty string.

decryption key $\mathsf{dk}_{\mathsf{id}}$.[5] Specifically, the secret key $\mathsf{sk}_{\mathsf{id}}$ for identity id consists of $(\{\mathsf{lk}_{\mathsf{v}}\}_{\mathsf{v}\in V}, \mathsf{dk}_{\mathsf{id}})$ where $V := \{\varepsilon, \mathsf{id}[1], \ldots \mathsf{id}[1 \ldots n-1]\}$ and

$$\mathsf{lk}_{\mathsf{v}} = \begin{cases} (\mathsf{h}_{\mathsf{v}}, \mathsf{h}_{\mathsf{v}\|0}, \mathsf{h}_{\mathsf{v}\|1}, r_{\mathsf{v}}) & \text{for } \mathsf{v} \in V \backslash \{\mathsf{id}[1 \ldots n-1]\} \\ (\mathsf{h}_{\mathsf{v}}, \mathsf{ek}_{\mathsf{v}\|0}, \mathsf{ek}_{\mathsf{v}\|1}, r_{\mathsf{v}}) & \text{for } \mathsf{v} = \mathsf{id}[1 \ldots n-1] \end{cases}.$$

Encryption and Decryption. Before providing details of encryption and decryption, we will briefly discuss how chameleon encryption can be useful in conjunction with garbled circuits.[6] Chameleon encryption allows an encryptor knowing a key k and a hash value h to encrypt a set of labels $\{\mathsf{lab}_{j,0}, \mathsf{lab}_{j,1}\}_j$ such that a decryptor knowing x and r with $\mathsf{H}(\mathsf{k}, \mathsf{x}; r) = \mathsf{h}$ can recover $\{\mathsf{lab}_{j,\mathsf{x}_j}\}_j$. On the other hand, security of chameleon encryption guarantees that the receiver learns nothing about the remaining labels. In summary, using this mechanism, an the generated ciphertexts enable the decryptor to feed x into a garbled circuit to be processed further.

To encrypt a message m to an identity $\mathsf{id} \in \{0,1\}^n$, the encryptor will generate a sequence of $n+1$ garbled circuits $\{\tilde{P}^0, \ldots \tilde{P}^{n-1}, \tilde{T}\}$ such that a decryptor in possession of the identity secret key $\mathsf{sk}_{\mathsf{id}} = (\{\mathsf{lk}_{\mathsf{v}}\}_{\mathsf{v}\in V}, \mathsf{dk}_{\mathsf{id}})$ will be able evaluate these garbled circuits one after another. Roughly speaking, circuit P^i for any $i \in \{0 \ldots n-1\}$ and $\mathsf{v} = \mathsf{id}[1 \ldots i]$ takes as input a hash value h_{v} and generates chameleon encryptions of the input labels of the next garbled circuit $\tilde{P}^{i+1}$ using a $\mathsf{k}_{|\mathsf{v}|}$ hardwired inside it and the hash value h given to it as input (in a manner as described above). The last circuit T will just take as input an encryption key $\mathsf{pk}_{\mathsf{id}}$ and output an encryption of the plaintext message m under $\mathsf{ek}_{\mathsf{id}}$. Finally, the encryptor provides input labels for the first garbled circuit $\tilde{P}^0$ for the input h_ε in the ciphertext.

During decryption, for each $i \in \{0 \ldots n-1\}$ and $\mathsf{v} = \mathsf{id}[1 \ldots i]$ the decryptor will use the local key lk_{v} to decrypt the ciphertexts generated by $\tilde{P}^i$ and obtain the input labels for the garbled circuits $\tilde{P}^{i+1}$ (or, T if $i = n-1$). We will now explain the first iteration of this construction in more detail, all further iterations proceed analogously. The encryptor provides garbled input labels corresponding to input h_ε for the first garbled circuit $\tilde{P}^0$ in the ciphertext. Thus the decryptor can evaluate $\tilde{P}^0$ and obtain encryptions of input labels $\{\mathsf{lab}_{j,0}, \mathsf{lab}_{j,1}\}_{j\in[\lambda]}$ for the circuit $\tilde{P}^1$, namely:

$$\{\mathsf{Enc}(\mathsf{k}_0, (\mathsf{h}_\varepsilon, \mathsf{id}[1] \cdot \lambda + j, 0), \mathsf{lab}_{j,0}), \qquad \mathsf{Enc}(\mathsf{k}_0, (\mathsf{h}_\varepsilon, \mathsf{id}[1] \cdot \lambda + j, 1), \mathsf{lab}_{j,1})\}_{j\in[\lambda]}$$

The garbled circuit has $\mathsf{id}[1]$ and the input labels $\{\mathsf{lab}_{j,0}, \mathsf{lab}_{j,1}\}_{j\in[\lambda]}$ hardwired in it. Given these encryptions the decryptor uses $\mathsf{lk}_\varepsilon = (\mathsf{h}_\varepsilon, \mathsf{h}_0, \mathsf{h}_1, r_\varepsilon)$ to learn the garbled input labels $\{\mathsf{lab}_{j,\mathsf{h}_{\mathsf{id}[1],j}}\}_{j\in[\lambda]}$ where $\mathsf{h}_{\mathsf{id}[1],j}$ is the jth bit of $\mathsf{h}_{\mathsf{id}[1]}$.

[5] We note that our key generation mechanism can be seen as an instantiation of the Naor and Yung [40] tree-based construction of signature schemes from universal one-way hash functions and one-time signatures. This connection becomes even more apparent in the follow up paper [21].

[6] For this part of the intuition, we assume familiarity with garbled circuits.

In other words, the decryptor now possesses input labels for the input $\mathsf{h}_{\mathsf{id}[1]}$ for the garbled circuit $\tilde{P}^1$ and can therefore evaluate $\tilde{P}^1$. Analogous to the previous step, the decryptor uses $\mathsf{lk}_{\mathsf{id}[1]}$ and $r_{\mathsf{id}[1]}$ to obtain input labels to $\tilde{P}^2$ and so on. The decryptor's ability to provide the local keys lk_v for $v \in V$ keeps this process going ultimately revealing an encryption of the message m under the encryption key $\mathsf{pk}_{\mathsf{id}}$. This final ciphertext can be decrypted using the decryption key $\mathsf{dk}_{\mathsf{id}}$. At a high level, our encryption method (and the use of garbled circuits for it) has similarities with garbled RAM schemes [18,23,24,26,37]. Full details of the construction are provided in Sect. 6.

Proof Sketch. The intuition behind the proof of security which follows by a sequence of hybrid changes is as follows. The first (easy) change is to replace the pseudorandom function used to generate the local keys by a truly random function something that should go undetected against a computationally bounded attacker. Next, via a sequence of hybrids we change the $n+1$ garbled circuits $\tilde{P}^0, \ldots \tilde{P}^{n-1}, \tilde{T}$ to their simulated versions one by one. Once these changes are made the simulated circuit $\tilde{T}$ just outputs an encryption of the message m under the encryption key $\mathsf{pk}_{\mathsf{id}^*}$ corresponding challenge identity id^*, which hides m based on semantic security of the encryption scheme.

The only "tricky" part of the proof is the one that involves changing garbled circuits to their simulated versions. In this intuitive description, we explain how the first garbled circuit $\tilde{P}^0$ is moved to its simulated version. The argument of the rest of the garbled circuits is analogous. This change involves a sequence of four hybrid changes.

1. First, we change how h_ε is generated. As a quick recap, recall that h_ε is generated as $\mathsf{H}(\mathsf{k}_0, 0^{2\lambda}; \omega_\varepsilon)$ and r_ε are set to $\mathsf{H}^{-1}(\mathsf{t}_0, (0^{2\lambda}, \omega_\varepsilon), \mathsf{h}_0\|\mathsf{h}_1)$. We instead generate h_ε directly to be equal to the value r_ε are set to $\mathsf{H}(\mathsf{k}_0, \mathsf{h}_0\|\mathsf{h}_1, r_\varepsilon)$ using fresh coins r_ε. The trapdoor collision and uniformity properties of the chameleon encryption scheme ensure that this change does not affect the distribution of the h_ε and r_ε, up to a negligible error.
2. The second change we make is that the garbled circuit $\tilde{P}^0$ is not generates in simulated form instead of honestly. Note that at this point the distribution of this garbled circuit depends only on its output which is $\{\mathsf{Enc}(\mathsf{k}_\varepsilon, (\mathsf{h}_\varepsilon, j, b), \mathsf{lab}_{j,b})\}_{j\in[\lambda], b\in\{0,1\}}$ where $\{\mathsf{lab}_{j,b}\}_{j\in[\lambda], b\in\{0,1\}}$ are the input labels for the garbled circuit $\tilde{P}^1$.
3. Observe that at this point the trapdoor t_ε is not being used at all and $\tilde{P}^0$ is the simulated form. Therefore, based on the security of the chameleon encryption we have that for all $j \in [\lambda]$, $\mathsf{Enc}(\mathsf{k}_\varepsilon, (\mathsf{h}_\varepsilon, j, 1-\mathsf{h}_{\mathsf{id}[1],j}), \mathsf{lab}_{j,1-\mathsf{h}_{\mathsf{id}[1],j}})$ hides $\mathsf{lab}_{j,1-\mathsf{h}_{\mathsf{id}[1],j}}$. Hence, we can change the hardcoded ciphertexts from
$$\{\mathsf{Enc}(\mathsf{k}_\varepsilon, (\mathsf{h}_\varepsilon, j, b), \mathsf{lab}_{j,b})\}_{j\in[\lambda], b\in\{0,1\}}$$
to
$$\{\mathsf{Enc}(\mathsf{k}_\varepsilon, (\mathsf{h}_\varepsilon, j, b), \mathsf{lab}_{j,\mathsf{h}_{\mathsf{id}[1],j}})\}_{j\in[\lambda], b\in\{0,1\}}$$

4. Finally, the fourth change we make is that we reverse the first change. In particular, we generate h_ε as is done in the real execution.

As a consequence, at this point only the labels $\{\mathsf{lab}_{j,\mathsf{h}_{\mathsf{id}[1],j}}\}_{j\in[\lambda]}$ are revealed in an information theoretic sense and the same sequence of hybrids can be repeated for the next garbled circuit $\tilde{P}^1$. The only change in this step is that now both h_0 and h_1 will be generated (if needed) by first sampling their children. The full proof of security is provided in Sect. 6.2.

3 Preliminaries

Let λ denote the security parameter. We use the notation $[n]$ to denote the set $\{1,\ldots,n\}$. By PPT we mean a probabilistic polynomial time algorithm. For any set S, we use $x \xleftarrow{\$} S$ to mean that x is sampled uniformly at random from the set S.[7] Alternatively, for any distribution D we use $x \xleftarrow{\$} D$ to mean that x is sampled from the distribution D. We use the operator $:=$ to represent assignment and $=$ to denote an equality check.

3.1 Computational Problems

Definition 1 (The Diffie-Hellman (DH) Problem). *Let $(\mathbb{G},\cdot)$ be a cyclic group of order p with generator g. Let a,b be sampled uniformly at random from $\mathbb{Z}_p$ (i.e., $a,b \xleftarrow{\$} \mathbb{Z}_p$). Given (g,g^a,g^b), the* $\mathsf{DH}(\mathbb{G})$ *problem asks to compute g^{ab}.*

Definition 2 (The Factoring Problem). *Given a Blum integer $N = pq$ (p and q are large primes with $p = q = 3 \mod 4$) the* FACT *problem asks to compute p and q.*

3.2 Identity-Based Encryption

Below we provide the definition of identity-based encryption (IBE).

Definition 3 (Identity-Based Encryption (IBE) [11,44]). *An* identity-based encryption *scheme consists of four PPT algorithms* (Setup, KeyGen, Encrypt, Decrypt) *defined as follows:*

- $\mathsf{Setup}(1^\lambda)$*: given the security parameter, it outputs a master public key* mpk *and a master secret key* msk.
- $\mathsf{KeyGen}(\mathsf{msk},\mathsf{id})$*: given the master secret key* msk *and an identity* $\mathsf{id} \in \{0,1\}^n$*, it outputs a decryption key* $\mathsf{sk}_{\mathsf{id}}$.
- $\mathsf{Encrypt}(\mathsf{mpk},\mathsf{id},\mathsf{m})$*: given the master public key* mpk*, an identity* $\mathsf{id} \in \{0,1\}^n$*, and a message* m*, it outputs a ciphertext* ct.

[7] We use this notion only when the sampling can be done by a PPT algorithm and the sampling algorithm is implicit.

- $\mathsf{Decrypt}(\mathsf{sk}_{\mathsf{id}}, \mathsf{ct})$: *given a secret key* $\mathsf{sk}_{\mathsf{id}}$ *for identity* id *and a ciphertext* ct, *it outputs a string* m.

The following completeness and security properties must be satisfied:

- ***Completeness:*** *For all security parameters* λ, *identities* $\mathsf{id} \in \{0,1\}^n$ *and messages* m, *the following holds:*

$$\mathsf{Decrypt}(\mathsf{sk}_{\mathsf{id}}, \mathsf{Encrypt}(\mathsf{mpk}, \mathsf{id}, \mathsf{m})) = \mathsf{m}$$

where $\mathsf{sk}_{\mathsf{id}} \leftarrow \mathsf{KeyGen}(\mathsf{msk}, \mathsf{id})$ *and* $(\mathsf{mpk}, \mathsf{msk}) \leftarrow \mathsf{Setup}(1^\lambda)$.
- ***Security:*** *For any PPT adversary* $\mathcal{A} = (\mathcal{A}_1, \mathcal{A}_2)$, *there exists a negligible function* negl(.) *such that the following holds:*

$$\Pr[IND_{\mathcal{A}}^{IBE}(1^\lambda) = 1] \leq \frac{1}{2} + \mathsf{negl}(\lambda)$$

where $IND_{\mathcal{A}}^{IBE}$ *is shown in Fig. 1, and for each key query* id *that* $\mathcal{A}$ *sends to the* KeyGen *oracle, it must hold that* $\mathsf{id} \neq \mathsf{id}^*$.

Experiment $IND_{\mathcal{A}}^{IBE}(1^\lambda)$:

1. $(\mathsf{mpk}, \mathsf{msk}) \xleftarrow{\$} \mathsf{Setup}(1^\lambda)$.
2. $(\mathsf{id}^*, \mathsf{m}_0, \mathsf{m}_1, \mathsf{st}) \xleftarrow{\$} \mathcal{A}_1^{\mathsf{KeyGen}(\mathsf{msk},.)}(\mathsf{mpk})$ *where* $|m_0| = |m_1|$ *and for each query* id *by* $\mathcal{A}_1$ *to* KeyGen(msk, .) *we have that* $\mathsf{id} \neq \mathsf{id}^*$.
3. $b \xleftarrow{\$} \{0,1\}$.
4. $\mathsf{ct}^* \xleftarrow{\$} \mathsf{Encrypt}(\mathsf{mpk}, \mathsf{id}^*, \mathsf{m}_b)$.
5. $b' \xleftarrow{\$} \mathcal{A}_2^{\mathsf{KeyGen}(\mathsf{msk},.)}(\mathsf{mpk}, \mathsf{ct}^*, \mathsf{st})$ *where for each query* id *by* $\mathcal{A}_2$ *to* KeyGen(msk, .) *we have that* $\mathsf{id} \neq \mathsf{id}^*$.
6. *Output* 1 *if* $b = b'$ *and* 0 *otherwise.*

Fig. 1. The $\mathrm{IND}_{\mathcal{A}}^{\mathrm{IBE}}$ experiment

Hierarchical Identity-Based Encryption (HIBE). A HIBE scheme is an IBE scheme except that we set $\mathsf{sk}_\varepsilon := \mathsf{msk}$ and modify the KeyGen algorithm. In particular, KeyGen takes $\mathsf{sk}_{\mathsf{id}}$ and a string id′ as input and outputs a secret key $\mathsf{sk}_{\mathsf{id}\|\mathsf{id}'}$. More formally:

- $\mathsf{KeyGen}(\mathsf{sk}_{\mathsf{id}}, \mathsf{id}')$: given the secret key $\mathsf{sk}_{\mathsf{id}}$ and an identity $\mathsf{id}' \in \{0,1\}^*$, it outputs a decryption key $\mathsf{sk}_{\mathsf{id}\|\mathsf{id}'}$.

Correctness condition for HIBE is same as it was from IBE. Additionally, the security property is analogous to $\mathrm{IND}_{\mathcal{A}}^{\mathrm{IBE}}(1^\lambda)$ except that now we only consider the notion of *selective security* for HIBE—namely, the adversary $\mathcal{A}$ is required to announce the challenge identity id* before it has seen the mpk and has made any secret key queries. This experiment $\mathrm{IND}_{\mathcal{A}}^{\mathrm{HIBE}}$ is shown formally in Fig. 2.

Experiment $\text{IND}_{\mathcal{A}}^{\text{HIBE}}(1^\lambda)$:

1. $(\mathsf{id}^*, \mathsf{m}_0, \mathsf{m}_1, \mathsf{st}) \xleftarrow{\$} \mathcal{A}_1$ where $|m_0| = |m_1|$.
2. $(\mathsf{mpk}, \mathsf{msk}) \xleftarrow{\$} \mathsf{Setup}(1^\lambda)$.
3. $b \xleftarrow{\$} \{0,1\}$.
4. $\mathsf{ct}^* \xleftarrow{\$} \mathsf{Encrypt}(\mathsf{mpk}, \mathsf{id}^*, \mathsf{m}_b)$.
5. $b' \xleftarrow{\$} \mathcal{A}_2^{\mathsf{KeyGen}(\mathsf{msk},.)}(\mathsf{mpk}, \mathsf{ct}^*, \mathsf{st})$ where for each query id by $\mathcal{A}_2$ to $\mathsf{KeyGen}(\mathsf{msk},.)$ we have that $\mathsf{id} \neq \mathsf{id}^*$.
6. Output 1 if $b = b'$ and 0 otherwise.

Fig. 2. The $\text{IND}_{\mathcal{A}}^{\text{HIBE}}$ experiment

3.3 Garbled Circuits

Garbled circuits were first introduced by Yao [49] (see Lindell and Pinkas [36] and Bellare et al. [5] for a detailed proof and further discussion). A circuit garbling scheme is a tuple of PPT algorithms (GCircuit, Eval). Very roughly GCircuit is the circuit garbling procedure and Eval the corresponding evaluation procedure. More formally:

- $(\widetilde{\mathsf{C}}, \{\mathsf{lab}_{w,b}\}_{w\in\mathsf{inp}(\mathsf{C}),b\in\{0,1\}}) \xleftarrow{\$} \mathsf{GCircuit}\left(1^\lambda, \mathsf{C}\right)$: GCircuit takes as input a security parameter λ and a circuit C. This procedure outputs a *garbled circuit* $\widetilde{\mathsf{C}}$ and labels $\{\mathsf{lab}_{w,b}\}_{w\in\mathsf{inp}(\mathsf{C}),b\in\{0,1\}}$ where each $\mathsf{lab}_{w,b} \in \{0,1\}^\lambda$.[8]
- $y := \mathsf{Eval}\left(\widetilde{\mathsf{C}}, \{\mathsf{lab}_{w,x_w}\}_{w\in\mathsf{inp}(\mathsf{C})}\right)$: Given a garbled circuit $\widetilde{\mathsf{C}}$ and a garbled input represented as a sequence of input labels $\{\mathsf{lab}_{w,x_w}\}_{w\in\mathsf{inp}(\mathsf{C})}$, Eval outputs an output y.

Correctness. For correctness, we require that for any circuit C and input $x \in \{0,1\}^m$ (here m is the input length to C) we have that:

$$\Pr\left[\mathsf{C}(x) = \mathsf{Eval}\left(\widetilde{\mathsf{C}}, \{\mathsf{lab}_{w,x_w}\}_{w\in\mathsf{inp}(\mathsf{C})}\right)\right] = 1$$

where $(\widetilde{\mathsf{C}}, \{\mathsf{lab}_{w,b}\}_{w\in\mathsf{inp}(\mathsf{C}),b\in\{0,1\}}) \xleftarrow{\$} \mathsf{GCircuit}\left(1^\lambda, \mathsf{C}\right)$.

[8] Typical definitions of garbled circuits do not require the length of each input label to be λ bits long. This additional requirement is crucial in our constructions as we chain garbled circuits. Note that input labels in any garbled circuit construction can always be shrunk to λ bits using a pseudorandom function.

Security. For security, we require that there is a PPT simulator Sim such that for any C, x, we have that

$$\left(\widetilde{\mathsf{C}}, \{\mathsf{lab}_{w,x_w}\}_{w \in \mathsf{inp}(\mathsf{C})}\right) \overset{\text{comp}}{\approx} \mathsf{Sim}\left(1^\lambda, \mathsf{C}(x)\right)$$

where $(\widetilde{\mathsf{C}}, \{\mathsf{lab}_{w,b}\}_{w \in \mathsf{inp}(\mathsf{C}), b \in \{0,1\}}) \xleftarrow{\$} \mathsf{GCircuit}\left(1^\lambda, \mathsf{C}\right)$.[9]

4 Chameleon Encryption

In this section, we give the definition of a chameleon encryption scheme.

Definition 4 (Chameleon Encryption). *A chameleon encryption scheme consists of five PPT algorithms* Gen, H, H^{-1}, Enc, *and* Dec *with the following syntax.*

- $\mathsf{Gen}(1^\lambda, n)$*: Takes the security parameter λ and a message-length n (with $n = \mathsf{poly}(\lambda)$) as input and outputs a key* k *and a trapdoor* t.
- $\mathsf{H}(\mathsf{k}, \mathsf{x}; r)$*: Takes a key* k*, a message $\mathsf{x} \in \{0,1\}^n$, and coins r and outputs a hash value* h*, where* h *is λ bits.*
- $\mathsf{H}^{-1}(\mathsf{t}, (\mathsf{x}, r), \mathsf{x}')$*: Takes a trapdoor* t*, previously used message $\mathsf{x} \in \{0,1\}^n$ and coins r, and a message $\mathsf{x}' \in \{0,1\}^n$ as input and returns r'.*
- $\mathsf{Enc}(\mathsf{k}, (\mathsf{h}, i, b), \mathsf{m})$*: Takes a key* k*, a hash value* h*, an index $i \in [n]$, $b \in \{0,1\}$, and a message $\mathsf{m} \in \{0,1\}^*$ as input and outputs a ciphertext* ct.[10]
- $\mathsf{Dec}(\mathsf{k}, (\mathsf{x}, r), \mathsf{ct})$*: Takes a key* k*, a message* x*, coins r and a ciphertext* ct*, as input and outputs a value* m *(or $\perp$).*

We require the following properties[11]

- ***Uniformity**: For $\mathsf{x}, \mathsf{x}' \in \{0,1\}^n$ we have that the two distributions $\mathsf{H}(\mathsf{k}, \mathsf{x}; r)$ and $\mathsf{H}(\mathsf{k}, \mathsf{x}'; r')$ are statistically close (when r, r' are chosen uniformly at random).*
- ***Trapdoor Collisions**: For every choice of $\mathsf{x}, \mathsf{x}' \in \{0,1\}^n$ and r it holds that if $(\mathsf{k}, \mathsf{t}) \xleftarrow{\$} \mathsf{Gen}(1^\lambda, n)$ and $r' := \mathsf{H}^{-1}(\mathsf{t}, (\mathsf{x}, r), \mathsf{x}')$, then it holds that*

  $$\mathsf{H}(\mathsf{k}, \mathsf{x}; r) = \mathsf{H}(\mathsf{k}, \mathsf{x}'; r'),$$

  i.e. $\mathsf{H}(\mathsf{k}, \mathsf{x}; r)$ *and* $\mathsf{H}(\mathsf{k}, \mathsf{x}'; r')$ *generate the same hash* h*. Moreover, if r is chosen uniformly at random, then r' is also statistically close to uniform.*

---

[9] In abuse of notation we assume that Sim knows the (non-private) circuit C. When C has (private) hardwired inputs, we assume that the labels corresponding to these are included in the garbled circuit $\tilde{C}$.

[10] ct is assumed to contain (h, i, b).

[11] Typically, Chameleon Hash functions are defined to also have the collision resilience property. This property is implied by the semantic security requirement below. However, we do not need this property directly. Therefore, we do not explicitly define it here.

- ***Correctness:*** *For any choice of* $\mathsf{x} \in \{0,1\}^n$*, coins* r*, index* $i \in [n]$ *and message* m *it holds that if* $(\mathsf{k},\mathsf{t}) \xleftarrow{\$} \mathsf{Gen}(1^\lambda, n)$*,* $\mathsf{h} := \mathsf{H}(\mathsf{k},\mathsf{x};r)$*, and* $\mathsf{ct} \xleftarrow{\$} \mathsf{Enc}(\mathsf{k},(\mathsf{h},i,\mathsf{x}_i),\mathsf{m})$ *then* $\mathsf{Dec}(\mathsf{k},\mathsf{ct},(\mathsf{x},r)) = \mathsf{m}$.
- ***Security:*** *For any PPT adversary* $\mathcal{A} = (\mathcal{A}_1,\mathcal{A}_2)$ *there exists a negligible function* $\mathsf{negl}(\cdot)$ *such that the following holds:*

$$\Pr[IND_{\mathcal{A}}^{CE}(1^\lambda) = 1] \le \frac{1}{2} + \mathsf{negl}(\lambda)$$

where $IND_{\mathcal{A}}^{CE}$ *is shown in Fig. 3.*

Experiment $IND^{CE}_{\mathcal{A}=(\mathcal{A}_1,\mathcal{A}_2)}(1^\lambda)$:

1. $(\mathsf{k},\mathsf{t}) \xleftarrow{\$} \mathsf{Gen}(1^\lambda, n)$.
2. $(\mathsf{x}, r, i \in [n], \mathsf{st}) \xleftarrow{\$} \mathcal{A}_1(\mathsf{k})$.
3. $b \xleftarrow{\$} \{0,1\}$.
4. $\mathsf{ct} \xleftarrow{\$} \mathsf{Enc}(\mathsf{k},(\mathsf{H}(\mathsf{k},\mathsf{x};r), i, 1-\mathsf{x}_i), b)$.
5. $b' \xleftarrow{\$} \mathcal{A}_2(\mathsf{k},\mathsf{ct},(\mathsf{x},r),\mathsf{st})$.
6. *Output* 1 *if* $b = b'$ *and* 0 *otherwise.*

Fig. 3. The $\mathrm{IND}_{\mathcal{A}}^{\mathrm{CE}}$ experiment

5 Constructions of Chameleon Encryption from CDH

Let $(\mathbb{G},\cdot)$ be a cyclic group of order p (not necessarily prime) with generator g. Let $\mathsf{Sample}(\mathbb{G})$ be a PPT algorithm such that its output is statistically close to a uniform element in $\mathbb{Z}_p$, where p (not necessarily prime) is the order of $\mathbb{G}$.[12] We will now describe a chameleon encryption scheme assuming that the $\mathsf{DH}(\mathbb{G})$ problem is hard.

- $\mathsf{Gen}(1^\lambda, n)$: For each $j \in [n]$, choose uniformly random values $\alpha_{j,0}, \alpha_{j,1} \xleftarrow{\$} \mathsf{Sample}(\mathbb{G})$ and compute $g_{j,0} := g^{\alpha_{j,0}}$ and $g_{j,1} := g^{\alpha_{j,1}}$. Output (k,t) where[13]

$$\mathsf{k} := \left(g, \begin{pmatrix} g_{1,0}, g_{2,0} \ldots, g_{n,0} \\ g_{1,1}, g_{2,1}, \ldots, g_{n,1} \end{pmatrix}\right) \qquad \mathsf{t} := \begin{pmatrix} \alpha_{1,0}, \alpha_{2,0} \ldots, \alpha_{n,0} \\ \alpha_{1,1}, \alpha_{2,1}, \ldots, \alpha_{n,1} \end{pmatrix}. \tag{2}$$

- $\mathsf{H}(\mathsf{k},\mathsf{x};r)$: Parse k as in Eq. 2, sample $r \xleftarrow{\$} \mathsf{Sample}(\mathbb{G})$, set $\mathsf{h} := g^r \cdot \prod_{j\in[n]} g_{j,\mathsf{x}_j}$ and output h

[12] We will later provide instantiations of $\mathbb{G}$ which are of prime order and composite order. The use of $\mathsf{Sample}(\mathbb{G})$ procedure is done to unify these two instantiations.

[13] We also implicitly include the public and secret parameters for the group $\mathbb{G}$ in k and t respectively.

- $\mathsf{H}^{-1}(\mathsf{t}, (\mathsf{x}, r), \mathsf{x}')$: Parse t as in Eq. 2, compute $r' := r + \sum_{j \in [n]} (\alpha_{j,\mathsf{x}_j} - \alpha_{j,\mathsf{x}'_j}) \mod p$. Output r'.
- $\mathsf{Enc}(\mathsf{k}, (\mathsf{h}, i, b), \mathsf{m})$: Parse k as in Eq. 2, $\mathsf{h} \in \mathbb{G}$ and $\mathsf{m} \in \{0,1\}$. Sample $\rho \xleftarrow{\$} \mathsf{Sample}(\mathbb{G})$ and proceed as follows:
  1. Set $c := g^\rho$ and $c' := \mathsf{h}^\rho$.
  2. For every $j \in [n] \backslash \{i\}$, set $c_{j,0} := g_{j,0}^\rho$ and $c_{j,1} := g_{j,1}^\rho$.
  3. Set $c_{i,0} := \perp$ and $c_{i,1} := \perp$.
  4. Set $e := \mathsf{m} \oplus \mathsf{HardCore}(g_{i,b}^\rho)$.[14]
  5. Output $\mathsf{ct} := \left(e, c, c', \begin{pmatrix} c_{1,0}, c_{2,0} \ldots, c_{n,0} \\ c_{1,1}, c_{2,1}, \ldots, c_{n,1} \end{pmatrix}\right)$.
- $\mathsf{Dec}(\mathsf{k}, (\mathsf{x}, r), \mathsf{ct})$: Parse $\mathsf{ct} := \left(e, c, c', \begin{pmatrix} c_{1,0}, c_{2,0} \ldots, c_{n,0} \\ c_{1,1}, c_{2,1}, \ldots, c_{n,1} \end{pmatrix}\right)$
  Output $e \oplus \mathsf{HardCore}\left(\frac{c'}{c^r \cdot \prod_{j \in [n] \backslash \{i\}} c_{j,\mathsf{x}_j}}\right)$.

Multi-bit Encryption. The encryption procedure described above encrypts single bit messages. Longer messages can be encrypted by encrypting individual bits.

Lemma 1. *Assuming that* $\mathsf{DH}(\mathbb{G})$ *is hard, the construction described above is a chameleon encryption scheme, i.e. it satisfies Definition 4.*

Proof. We need to argue the trapdoor collision property, uniformity property, correctness of encryption property and semantic security of the scheme above and we that below.

- **Uniformity:** Observe that for all k and x, we have that $\mathsf{H}(\mathsf{k}, \mathsf{x}; r) = g^r \cdot \prod_{j \in [n]} g_{j,\mathsf{x}_j}$ is statistically close to a uniform element in $\mathbb{G}$. This is because r is sampled statistically close to uniform in $\mathbb{Z}_p$, where p is the order of $\mathbb{G}$.
- **Trapdoor Collisions:** For any choice of $\mathsf{x}, \mathsf{x}', r, \mathsf{k}, \mathsf{t}$ the value r' is obtained as $r + \sum_{j \in [n]} (\alpha_{j,\mathsf{x}_j} - \alpha_{j,\mathsf{x}'_j}) \mod p$. It is easy to check that $\mathsf{H}(\mathsf{k}, \mathsf{x}'; r')$ is equal to $\mathsf{H}(\mathsf{k}, \mathsf{x}; r)$.
  Moreover, as r is statistically close to uniform in $\mathbb{Z}_p$, $r' := r + \sum_{j \in [n]} (\alpha_{j,\mathsf{x}_j} - \alpha_{j,\mathsf{x}'_j}) \mod p$ is also statistically close to uniform in $\mathbb{Z}_p$.
- **Correctness:** For any choice of $\mathsf{x} \in \{0,1\}^n$, coins r, index $i \in [n]$ and message $\mathsf{m} \in \{0,1\}$ if $(\mathsf{k}, \mathsf{t}) \xleftarrow{\$} \mathsf{Gen}(1^\lambda, n)$, $\mathsf{h} := \mathsf{H}(\mathsf{k}, \mathsf{x}; r)$, and $\mathsf{ct} := \mathsf{Enc}(\mathsf{k}, (\mathsf{h}, i, \mathsf{x}_i), \mathsf{m})$ then we have that $\mathsf{Dec}(\mathsf{k}, (\mathsf{x}, r), \mathsf{ct}) = e \oplus \mathsf{HardCore}\left(\frac{c'}{c^r \cdot \prod_{j \in [n] \backslash \{i\}} c_{j,\mathsf{x}_j}}\right)$ which evaluates to $e \oplus \mathsf{HardCore}(g_{i,\mathsf{x}_i}^\rho)$. Finally, this value can be seen to be equal to m.

[14] We assume that the $\mathsf{HardCore}(g^{ab})$ is a hardcore bit of g^{ab} given g^a and g^b. If a deterministic hard-core bit for the specific function is not known then we can always use the Goldreich-Levin [30] construction. We skip the details of that with the goal of keeping exposition simple.

- **Security:** For the sake of contradiction, let us assume that there exists a PPT adversary $\mathcal{A} = (\mathcal{A}_1, \mathcal{A}_2)$ and a non-negligible function $\mu(\cdot)$ such that

$$\Pr[\mathrm{IND}_{\mathcal{A}}^{\mathrm{CE}}(1^\lambda) = 1] \geq \frac{1}{2} + \mu(\lambda).$$

Now we will provide a PPT reduction $\mathcal{R}^{\mathcal{A}}$ which on input $g, U = g^u, V = g^v$ correctly computes the hardcore bit $\mathsf{HardCore}(g^{uv})$ with probability $\frac{1}{2} + \nu(\lambda)$ for some non-negligible function ν. Formally, **Reduction** $\mathcal{R}^{\mathcal{A}=(\mathcal{A}_1,\mathcal{A}_2)}(g, U, V)$ proceeds as follows:

1. For each $j \in [n]$, sample $\alpha_{j,0}, \alpha_{j,1} \xleftarrow{\$} \mathsf{Sample}(\mathbb{G})$ and set $g_{j,0} := g^{\alpha_{j,0}}$ and $g_{j,1} := g^{\alpha_{j,1}}$.
2. Sample $x \xleftarrow{\$} \{0,1\}$ and $i^* \xleftarrow{\$} [n]$ and reassign $g_{i^*,x} := U$. Finally set

$$\mathsf{k} := \left(g, \begin{pmatrix} g_{1,0}, g_{2,0} \ldots, g_{n,0} \\ g_{1,1}, g_{2,1}, \ldots, g_{n,1} \end{pmatrix}\right).$$

3. $(\mathsf{x}, r, i) \xleftarrow{\$} \mathcal{A}_1(\mathsf{k})$.
4. If $i \neq i^*$ or $\mathsf{x}_i = x$ then skip rest of the steps and output a random bit $b \xleftarrow{\$} \{0,1\}$.
5. Otherwise, set $\mathsf{h} := \mathsf{H}(\mathsf{k}, \mathsf{x}; r)$ and $\mathsf{ct} := \left(e, c, c', \begin{pmatrix} c_{1,0}, c_{2,0} \ldots, c_{n,0} \\ c_{1,1}, c_{2,1}, \ldots, c_{n,1} \end{pmatrix}\right)$ where:

$$\begin{aligned} & c := V & & c' := V^{r + \sum_{j \in [n]} \alpha_{i,\mathsf{x}_i}}, \\ \forall j \in [n] \backslash \{i\}, \quad & c_{j,0} := V^{\alpha_{j,0}} & & c_{j,1} := V^{\alpha_{j,1}}, \\ & e \xleftarrow{\$} \{0,1\}. & & \end{aligned}$$

6. $b \xleftarrow{\$} \mathcal{A}_2(\mathsf{k}, (\mathsf{x}, r), \mathsf{ct})$.
7. Output $b \oplus e$.

Let E be the event that the $i = i^*$ and $x_i \neq x$. Now observe that the distribution of k in Step 3 is statistically close to distribution resulting from Gen. This implies that (1) the view of the attacker in Step 3 is statistically close to experiment $\mathrm{IND}_{\mathcal{A}}^{\mathrm{CE}}$, and (2) $\Pr[E]$ is close to $\frac{1}{2n}$ up to a negligible additive term. Furthermore, conditioned on the fact that E occurs we have that the view of the attacker in Step 3 is statistically close to experiment $\mathrm{IND}_{\mathcal{A}}^{\mathrm{CE}}$ where ct is an encryption of $e \oplus \mathsf{HardCore}(g^{uv})$ (where $U = g^u$ and $V = g^v$). Now, if $\mathcal{A}_2$ in Step 6 correctly predicts $e \oplus \mathsf{HardCore}(g^{uv})$ then we have that the output of our reduction $\mathcal{R}$ is a correct prediction of $\mathsf{HardCore}(g^{uv})$. Thus, we conclude that $\mathcal{R}$ predicts $\mathsf{HardCore}(g^{uv})$ correctly with probability at least $\frac{1}{2} \cdot (1 - \frac{1}{2n}) + \frac{1}{2n} \cdot (\frac{1}{2} + \mu) = \frac{1}{2} + \frac{\mu}{2n}$ up to a negligible additive term.

5.1 Instantiations

Instantiating by Prime Order Groups. Our scheme can be directly instantiated in any prime order group $\mathbb{G}$ where $\mathsf{DH}(\mathbb{G})$ is assumed to be hard. Candidates are prime order multiplicative subgroups of finite fields [20] and elliptic curve groups [33,39].

Corollary 1. *Under the assumption that* $\mathsf{DH}(\mathbb{G})$ *is hard over some group* $\mathbb{G}$*, there exists a chameleon encryption scheme.*

Instantiating by Composite Order Groups and Reduction to the Factoring Assumption. Consider the group of quadratic residues $\mathbb{QR}_N$ over a Blum integer $N = PQ$ (P and Q are large safe primes[15] with $P = Q = 3$ mod 4). Let g be a random generator of $\mathbb{G}$ and $\mathsf{Sample}(\mathbb{G})$ just outputs a uniformly random number from the set $[(N-1)/4]$. Shmuely [46] and McCurley [38] proved that the $\mathsf{DH}(\mathbb{QR}_N)$ problem is at least as hard as FACT (also see [7,31]).

For this instantiation, we assume that the Gen algorithm generates a fresh Blum integer $N = PQ = (2p+1)(2q+1)$, includes N in the public key k and $|\mathbb{G}| = |\mathbb{QR}_N| = \phi(N)/4 = pq$ in the trapdoor t. Notice that only the trapdoor-collision algorithm H^{-1} needs to know the group-order $|\mathbb{G}| = pq$, while all other algorithms use the public sampling algorithm $\mathsf{Sample}(\mathbb{G})$.

Hence, using the group $\mathbb{QR}_N$ in the above described construction yields a construction of chameleon encryption based on the FACT Assumption.

Corollary 2. *Under the assumption that* FACT *is hard there exists a chameleon encryption scheme.*

6 Construction of Identity-Based Encryption

In this section, we describe our construction of IBE from chameleon encryption. Let $\mathsf{PRF} : \{0,1\}^\lambda \times \{0,1\}^{\leq n} \cup \{\varepsilon\} \to \{0,1\}^\lambda$ be a pseudorandom function, $(\mathsf{Gen}, \mathsf{H}, \mathsf{H}^{-1}, \mathsf{Enc}, \mathsf{Dec})$ be a chameleon encryption scheme and $(\mathsf{G}, \mathsf{E}, \mathsf{D})$ be any semantically secure public-key encryption scheme.[16] We let $\mathsf{id}[i]$ denote the ith-bit of id and let $\mathsf{id}[1 \dots i]$ denote the first i bits of id. Note that $\mathsf{id}[1 \dots 0]$ is the empty string denoted by ε of length 0.

$\mathsf{NodeGen}$ and $\mathsf{LeafGen}$ Functions. As explained in the introduction, we need an exponential sized tree of hash values. The functions $\mathsf{NodeGen}$ and $\mathsf{LeafGen}$ provides efficient access to the *hash value* corresponding to any node in this (exponential sized) tree. We will use these function repeatedly in our construction.

[15] A prime number $P > 2$ is called safe prime if $(P-1)/2$ is also prime.

[16] The algorithm G takes as input the security parameter 1^λ and generates encryption key and decryption key pair ek and dk respectively, where the encryption key ek is assumed to be λ bits long. The encryption algorithm $\mathsf{E}(\mathsf{ek}, \mathsf{m})$ takes as input an encryption key ek and a message m and outputs a ciphertext ct. Finally, the decryption algorithm $\mathsf{D}(\mathsf{dk}, \mathsf{ct})$ takes as input the secret key and the ciphertext and outputs the encrypted message m.

$\mathsf{NodeGen}((\mathsf{k}_0,\ldots \mathsf{k}_{n-1}),(\mathsf{t}_0,\ldots \mathsf{t}_{n-1},s),\mathsf{v})$:

1. Let $i := |\mathsf{v}|$ (length of v) and generate

$$\begin{aligned} \mathsf{h}_{\mathsf{v}} &:= \mathsf{H}(\mathsf{k}_i, 0^{2\lambda}; \mathsf{PRF}(s,\mathsf{v})),\\ \mathsf{h}_{\mathsf{v}\|0} &:= \mathsf{H}(\mathsf{k}_{i+1}, 0^{2\lambda}; \mathsf{PRF}(s,\mathsf{v}\|0)),\\ \mathsf{h}_{\mathsf{v}\|1} &:= \mathsf{H}(\mathsf{k}_{i+1}, 0^{2\lambda}; \mathsf{PRF}(s,\mathsf{v}\|1)). \end{aligned}$$

2. $r_{\mathsf{v}} := \mathsf{H}^{-1}(\mathsf{t}_{\mathsf{v}},(0^{2\lambda},\mathsf{PRF}(s,\mathsf{v})),\mathsf{h}_{\mathsf{v}\|0}\|\mathsf{h}_{\mathsf{v}\|1})$.
3. Output $(\mathsf{h}_{\mathsf{v}},\mathsf{h}_{\mathsf{v}\|0},\mathsf{h}_{\mathsf{v}\|1},r_{\mathsf{v}})$.

$\mathsf{LeafGen}(\mathsf{k}_{n-1},(\mathsf{t}_{n-1},s),\mathsf{v})$:

1. Generate

$$\begin{aligned} \mathsf{h}_{\mathsf{v}} &:= \mathsf{H}(\mathsf{k}_{n-1}, 0^{2\lambda}; \mathsf{PRF}(s,\mathsf{v}))\\ (\mathsf{ek}_{\mathsf{v}\|0},\mathsf{dk}_{\mathsf{v}\|0}) &:= \mathsf{G}(1^{\lambda}; \mathsf{PRF}(s,\mathsf{v}\|0)),\\ (\mathsf{ek}_{\mathsf{v}\|1},\mathsf{dk}_{\mathsf{v}\|1}) &:= \mathsf{G}(1^{\lambda}; \mathsf{PRF}(s,\mathsf{v}\|1)). \end{aligned}$$

2. $r_{\mathsf{v}} := \mathsf{H}^{-1}(\mathsf{t}_n,(0^{2\lambda},\mathsf{PRF}(s,\mathsf{v})),\mathsf{ek}_{\mathsf{v}\|0}\|\mathsf{ek}_{\mathsf{v}\|1})$.
3. Output $((\mathsf{h}_{\mathsf{v}},\mathsf{ek}_{\mathsf{v}\|0},\mathsf{ek}_{\mathsf{v}\|1},r_{\mathsf{v}}),\mathsf{dk}_{\mathsf{v}\|0},\mathsf{dk}_{\mathsf{v}\|1})$.

Fig. 4. Description of NodeGen and LeafGen.

The NodeGen function takes as input the hash keys $\mathsf{k}_0,\ldots \mathsf{k}_{n-1}$ and corresponding trapdoors $\mathsf{t}_0,\ldots \mathsf{t}_{n-1}$, the PRF seed s, and a node $\mathsf{v} \in \{0,1\}^{\leq n-2} \cup \{\varepsilon\}$. On the other hand, the LeafGen function takes as input the hash key k_{n-1} and corresponding trapdoor t_{n-1}, the PRF seed s, and a node $\mathsf{v} \in \{0,1\}^{n-1}$. The NodeGen and LeafGen functions are described in Fig. 4.

Construction. We describe our IBE scheme (Setup, KeyGen, Encrypt, Decrypt).

- $\mathsf{Setup}(1^\lambda, 1^n)$: Proceed as[17] follows:
  1. Sample $s \xleftarrow{\$} \{0,1\}^\lambda$ (seeds for the pseudorandom function PRF).
  2. For each $i \in \{0,\ldots n-1\}$ sample $(\mathsf{k}_i,\mathsf{t}_i) \xleftarrow{\$} \mathsf{Gen}(1^\lambda, 2\lambda)$.
  3. Obtain $(\mathsf{h}_\varepsilon,\mathsf{h}_0,\mathsf{h}_1,r_\varepsilon) := \mathsf{NodeGen}((\mathsf{k}_0,\ldots \mathsf{k}_{n-1}),(\mathsf{t}_0,\ldots \mathsf{t}_{n-1},s),\varepsilon)$
  4. Output $(\mathsf{mpk},\mathsf{msk})$ where $\mathsf{mpk} := (\mathsf{k}_0,\ldots \mathsf{k}_{n-1},\mathsf{h}_\varepsilon)$ and $\mathsf{msk} := (\mathsf{mpk},\mathsf{t}_0,\ldots \mathsf{t}_{n-1},s)$
- $\mathsf{KeyGen}(\mathsf{msk} = ((\mathsf{k}_0,\ldots \mathsf{k}_{n-1},\mathsf{h}_\varepsilon),\mathsf{t}_0,\ldots \mathsf{t}_{n-1},s),\mathsf{id} \in \{0,1\}^n)$:

  $V := \{\varepsilon,\mathsf{id}[1],\ldots \mathsf{id}[1\ldots n-1]\}$, where ε is the empty string
  For all $\mathsf{v} \subset V \backslash \{\mathsf{id}[1\ldots n-1]\}$:

[17] The IBE scheme defined in Sect. 3 does not fix the length of identities that it can be used with. However, in this section we fix the length of identities at setup time and use appropriately changed definitions. Looking ahead, the HIBE construction in Sect. 7 works for identities of arbitrary length.

$\mathsf{lk}_\mathsf{v} := \mathsf{NodeGen}((\mathsf{k}_0, \ldots \mathsf{k}_{n-1}), (\mathsf{t}_0, \ldots \mathsf{t}_{n-1}, s), \mathsf{v})$
For $\mathsf{v} = \mathsf{id}[1 \ldots n-1]$, set $(\mathsf{lk}_\mathsf{v}, \mathsf{dk}_{\mathsf{v}\|0}, \mathsf{dk}_{\mathsf{v}\|1}) := \mathsf{LeafGen}(\mathsf{k}_{n-1}, (\mathsf{t}_{n-1}, s), \mathsf{v})$
$\mathsf{sk}_\mathsf{id} := (\mathsf{id}, \{\mathsf{lk}_\mathsf{v}\}_{\mathsf{v} \in V}, \mathsf{dk}_\mathsf{id})$

- $\mathsf{Encrypt}(\mathsf{mpk} = (\mathsf{k}_0, \ldots \mathsf{k}_{n-1}, \mathsf{h}_\varepsilon), \mathsf{id} \in \{0,1\}^n, \mathsf{m})$: Before describing the encryption procedure we describe two circuits[18] that will be garbled during the encryption process.
  - $\mathsf{T}[\mathsf{m}](\mathsf{ek})$: Compute and output $\mathsf{E}(\mathsf{ek}, \mathsf{m})$.
  - $\mathsf{P}[\beta \in \{0,1\}, \mathsf{k}, \overline{\mathsf{lab}}](\mathsf{h})$: Compute and output $\{\mathsf{Enc}(\mathsf{k}, (\mathsf{h}, j + \beta \cdot \lambda, b), \mathsf{lab}_{j,b})\}_{j \in [\lambda], b \in \{0,1\}}$, where $\overline{\mathsf{lab}}$ is short for $\{\mathsf{lab}_{j,b}\}_{j \in [\lambda], b \in \{0,1\}}$.

  Encryption proceeds as follows:
  1. Compute $\tilde{T}$ as:
  $$(\tilde{T}, \overline{\mathsf{lab}}) \xleftarrow{\$} \mathsf{GCircuit}(1^\lambda, \mathsf{T}[\mathsf{m}]).$$
  2. For $i = n-1, \ldots, 0$ generate $(\tilde{P}^i, \overline{\mathsf{lab}}') \xleftarrow{\$} \mathsf{GCircuit}(1^\lambda, \mathsf{P}[\mathsf{id}[i+1], \mathsf{k}_i, \overline{\mathsf{lab}}])$ and set $\overline{\mathsf{lab}} := \overline{\mathsf{lab}}'$.
  3. Output $\mathsf{ct} := (\{\mathsf{lab}_{j,\mathsf{h}_{\varepsilon,j}}\}_{j \in [\lambda]}, \{\tilde{P}^0, \ldots, \tilde{P}^{n-1}, \tilde{T}\})$ where $\mathsf{h}_{\varepsilon,j}$ is the jth bit of h_ε.
- $\mathsf{Decrypt}(\mathsf{ct}, \mathsf{sk}_\mathsf{id} = (\mathsf{id}, \{\mathsf{lk}_\mathsf{v}\}_{\mathsf{v} \in V}), \mathsf{dk}_\mathsf{id})$: Decryption proceeds as follows:
  1. Parse ct as $(\{\mathsf{lab}_{j,\mathsf{h}_{\varepsilon,j}}\}_{j \in [\lambda]}, \{\tilde{P}^0, \ldots, \tilde{P}^{n-1}, \tilde{T}\})$.
  2. Parse lk_v as $(\mathsf{h}_\mathsf{v}, \mathsf{h}_{\mathsf{v}\|0}, \mathsf{h}_{\mathsf{v}\|1}, r_\mathsf{v})$ for each $\mathsf{v} \in V \backslash \{\mathsf{id}[1 \ldots n-1]\}$. (Recall $V = \{\varepsilon, \mathsf{id}[1] \ldots \mathsf{id}[1 \ldots n-1]\}$.)
  3. And for $\mathsf{v} = \mathsf{id}[1 \ldots n-1]$, parse lk_v as $(\mathsf{h}_\mathsf{v}, \mathsf{ek}_{\mathsf{v}\|0}, \mathsf{pk}_{\mathsf{v}\|1}, r_\mathsf{v})$.
  4. Set $y := \mathsf{h}_\varepsilon$.
  5. For each $i \in \{0, \ldots n-1\}$, set $\mathsf{v} := \mathsf{id}[1 \ldots i]$, and proceed as follows:
     (a) $\{e_{j,b}\}_{j \in [\lambda], b \in \{0,1\}} := \mathsf{Eval}(\tilde{P}^i, \{\mathsf{lab}_{j,y_j}\}_{j \in [\lambda]})$.
     (b) If $i = n-1$ then set $y := \mathsf{ek}_\mathsf{id}$ and for each $j \in [\lambda]$, compute
     $$\mathsf{lab}_{j,y_j} := \mathsf{Dec}(\mathsf{k}_\mathsf{v}, e_{j,y_j}, (\mathsf{ek}_{\mathsf{v}\|0} \| \mathsf{ek}_{\mathsf{v}\|1}, r_\mathsf{v})).$$
     (c) If $i \neq n-1$ then set $y := \mathsf{h}_\mathsf{v}$ and for each $j \in [\lambda]$, compute
     $$\mathsf{lab}_{j,y_j} := \mathsf{Dec}(\mathsf{k}_\mathsf{v}, e_{j,y_j}, (\mathsf{h}_{\mathsf{v}\|0} \| \mathsf{h}_{\mathsf{v}\|1}, r_\mathsf{v})).$$
  6. Compute $f := \mathsf{Eval}(\tilde{T}, \{\mathsf{lab}_{j,y_j}\}_{j \in [\lambda]})$.
  7. Output $\mathsf{m} := \mathsf{Dec}(\mathsf{dk}_\mathsf{id}, f)$.

A Note on Efficiency. The most computationally intensive part of the construction is the non-black box use of Enc inside garblings of the circuit P and E inside garbling of the circuit T. However, we note that not all of the computation corresponding to Enc and E needs to be performed inside the garbled circuit and it might be possible to push some of it outside of the garbled circuits.

[18] Random coins used by these circuits are hardwired in them. For simplicity, we do not mention them explicitly.

In particular, when Enc is instantiated with the DDH based chameleon encryption scheme then we can reduce each Enc to a single modular exponentiation inside the garbled circuit. Similar optimization can be performed for E. In short, this reduces the number of non-black-box modular exponentiations to 2λ for every circuit P and 1 for the circuit T. Finally, we note that additional improvements in efficiency might be possible by increasing the arity of the tree from 2 to a larger value. This would also reduce the depth of the tree and thereby reduce the number of non-black-box modular exponentiations needed.

6.1 Proof of Correctness

We will first show that our scheme is correct. For any identity id, let $V = \{\varepsilon, \mathsf{id}[1], \dots \mathsf{id}[1 \dots n-1]\}$. Then the secret key $\mathsf{sk}_{\mathsf{id}}$ consists of $(\mathsf{id}, \{\mathsf{lk}_{\mathsf{v}}\}_{\mathsf{v} \in V}, \mathsf{dk}_{\mathsf{id}})$. We will argue that a correctly generated ciphertext on decryption reveals the original message. Note that by construction (and the trapdoor collision property of the chameleon encryption scheme for the first equation below) for all nodes $\mathsf{v} \in V \backslash \{\mathsf{id}[1 \dots n-1]\}$ we have that:

$$\mathsf{H}(\mathsf{k}_{|\mathsf{v}|}, \mathsf{h}_{\mathsf{v}\|0} \| \mathsf{h}_{\mathsf{v}\|1}; r_{\mathsf{v}}) = \mathsf{h}_{\mathsf{v}}.$$

and additionally for $\mathsf{v} = \mathsf{id}[1 \dots n-1]$ we have

$$\mathsf{H}(\mathsf{k}_{n-1}, \mathsf{ek}_{\mathsf{v}\|0} \| \mathsf{ek}_{\mathsf{v}\|1}; r_{\mathsf{v}}) = \mathsf{h}_{\mathsf{v}}.$$

Next consider a ciphertext $\mathsf{ct} = (\{\mathsf{lab}_{j,\mathsf{h}_{\varepsilon,j}}\}_{j \in [\lambda]}, \{\tilde{P}^0, \dots, \tilde{P}^{n-1}, \tilde{T}\})$. We argue correctness as each step of decryption is performed. By correctness of garbled circuits, we have that the evaluation of $\tilde{P}^0$ yields correctly formed ciphertexts $e_{j,b}$ which are encryptions of labels of the next garbled circuit $\tilde{P}^1$. Next, by correctness of Dec of the chameleon encryption scheme we have that the decrypting the appropriate ciphertexts yields the correct labels $\{\mathsf{lab}_{j,\mathsf{h}_{\mathsf{id}[1],j}}\}_{j \in [\lambda]}$ for the next garbled circuit, namely $\tilde{P}^1$. Following the same argument we can argue that the decryption of the appropriate ciphertexts generated by $\tilde{P}^1$ yields the correct input labels for $\tilde{P}^2$. Repeatedly applying this argument allows us to conclude that the last garbled circuit $\tilde{P}^{n-1}$ outputs labels corresponding to $\mathsf{ek}_{\mathsf{id}}$ as input for the circuit T which outputs an encryption of m under $\mathsf{ek}_{\mathsf{id}}$. Finally, using the correctness of the public-key encryption scheme $(\mathsf{G}, \mathsf{E}, \mathsf{D})$ we have that the recovered message m is the same as the one encrypted.

6.2 Proof of Security

We are now ready to prove the security of the IBE construction above. For the sake of contradiction we proceed by assuming that there exists an adversary $\mathcal{A}$ such that $\Pr[\mathrm{IND}_{\mathcal{A}}^{\mathrm{IBE}}(1^\lambda) = 1] \geq \frac{1}{2} + \epsilon$ for a non-negligible ϵ (in λ), where $\mathrm{IND}_{\mathcal{A}}^{\mathrm{IBE}}$ is shown in Fig. 1. Assume further that q is a polynomial upper bound for the running-time of $\mathcal{A}$, and thus also an upper bound for the number of $\mathcal{A}$'s key queries. Security follows by a sequence of hybrids. In our hybrids, changes are made in how the secret key queries of the adversary $\mathcal{A}$ are answered and how the challenge ciphertext is generated. Furthermore, these changes are intertwined and need to be done carefully. Our proof consist of a sequence of $n+2$ hybrids $\mathcal{H}_{-1}, \mathcal{H}_0, \mathcal{H}_1, \ldots \mathcal{H}_{n+1}$. We next describe these hybrids.

- $\mathcal{H}_{-1}$: This hybrid corresponds to the experiment $\mathrm{IND}_{\mathcal{A}}^{\mathrm{IBE}}$ as shown in Fig. 1.
- $\mathcal{H}_0$: In this hybrid, we change how the public parameters are generated and how the adversary's requests to the KeyGen oracle are answered. Specifically, we replace all pseudorandom function calls $\mathsf{PRF}(s, \cdot)$ with a random function. The only change from $\mathcal{H}_{-1}$ to $\mathcal{H}_0$ is that calls to a pseudorandom are replaced by a random function. Therefore, the indistinguishability between the two hybrids follows directly from the pseudorandomness property of the pseudorandom function.
- $\mathcal{H}_\tau$ for $\tau \in \{0 \ldots n\}$: For every τ, this hybrid is identical to the experiment $\mathcal{H}_0$ except in how the ciphertext is generated. Recall that the challenge ciphertext consists of a sequence of $n+1$ garbled circuits. In hybrid $\mathcal{H}_\tau$, we generate the first τ of these garbled circuits using the simulator provided by the garbled circuit construction. The outputs hard-coded in the simulated circuits are set to be consistent with the output that would have resulted from the execution of honestly generated garbled circuits in there unsimulated versions. More formally, for the challenge identity id^* the challenge ciphertext is generated as follows (modifications with respect to honest ciphertext generation have been highlighted in red). Even though, the adversary never queries $\mathsf{sk_{id}}$, we can generate it locally. In particular, it contains the values $\mathsf{lk_v} = (\mathsf{h_v}, \mathsf{h_{v\|0}}, \mathsf{h_{v\|1}}, r_\mathsf{v})$ for each $\mathsf{v} \in \{\varepsilon, \ldots \mathsf{id}[1 \ldots n-2]\}$, $\mathsf{lk_v} = (\mathsf{h_v}, \mathsf{ek_{v\|0}}, \mathsf{ek_{v\|1}}, r_\mathsf{v})$ for each $\mathsf{v} = \mathsf{id}[1 \ldots n-1]$, and $\mathsf{dk_{id^*}}$.
  1. Compute $\tilde{T}$ as:
     If $\tau \neq n$
     $$(\tilde{T}, \overline{\mathsf{lab}}) \xleftarrow{\$} \mathsf{GCircuit}(1^\lambda, \mathsf{T}[\mathsf{m}])$$
     where $\overline{\mathsf{lab}} = \{\mathsf{lab}_{j,b}\}_{j\in[\lambda], b\in\{0,1\}}$. Else set $y = \mathsf{ek_{id^*}}$ and generate garbled circuit as,
     $$(\tilde{T}, \{\mathsf{lab}_{j,y_j}\}_{j\in[\lambda]}) \xleftarrow{\$} \mathsf{Sim}(1^\lambda, \mathsf{E}(y, \mathsf{m}))$$
     and set $\overline{\mathsf{lab}} := \{\mathsf{lab}_{j,y_j}, \mathsf{lab}_{j,y_j}\}_{j\in[\lambda]}$.
  2. For $i = n-1, \ldots, \tau$ generate $(\tilde{P}^i, \overline{\mathsf{lab}}') \xleftarrow{\$} \mathsf{GCircuit}(1^\lambda, \mathsf{P}[\mathsf{id}[i+1], \mathsf{k}_i, \overline{\mathsf{lab}}])$ and set $\overline{\mathsf{lab}} := \overline{\mathsf{lab}}'$.
  3. For $i = \tau - 1, \ldots, 0$, set $\mathsf{v} = \mathsf{id}^*[1 \ldots i-1]$ and generate
     $$\tilde{P}^i, \{\mathsf{lab}'_{j,\mathsf{h}_{\mathsf{v},j}}\}_{j\in[\lambda]}) := \mathsf{Sim}(1^\lambda, \{\mathsf{Enc}(\mathsf{k_v}, (\mathsf{h_v}, j, b), \mathsf{lab}_{j,b})\}_{j\in[\lambda], b\in\{0,1\}})$$
     and set $\overline{\mathsf{lab}} := \{\mathsf{lab}'_{j,\mathsf{h}_{\mathsf{v},j}}, \mathsf{lab}'_{j,\mathsf{h}_{\mathsf{v},j}}\}_{j\in[\lambda]}$.
  4. Output $\mathsf{ct} := (\{\mathsf{lab}_{j,\mathsf{h}_{\varepsilon,j}}\}_{j\in[\lambda]}, \{\tilde{P}^0, \ldots, \tilde{P}^{n-1}, \tilde{T}\})$ where $\mathsf{h}_{\varepsilon,j}$ is the jth bit of h_ε.

The computational indistinguishability between hybrids $\mathcal{H}_{\tau-1}$ and $\mathcal{H}_\tau$ is based on Lemma 2 which is proved in Sect. 6.3.

Lemma 2. *For each $\tau \in \{1 \dots n\}$ it is the case that $\mathcal{H}_{\tau-1} \overset{c}{\approx} \mathcal{H}_\tau$.*

- $\mathcal{H}_{n+1}$: This hybrid is same as $\mathcal{H}_n$ except that we change the ciphertext $\mathsf{E}(\mathsf{ek}_{\mathsf{id}^*}, \mathsf{m})$ hardwired in the simulated garbling of the circuit T to be $\mathsf{E}(\mathsf{ek}_{\mathsf{id}^*}, 0)$. Note that the adversary $\mathcal{A}$ never queries for $\mathsf{sk}_{\mathsf{id}^*}$. Therefore, it is never provided the value $\mathsf{dk}_{\mathsf{id}^*}$. Therefore, we can use an adversary distinguishing between $\mathcal{H}_n$ and $\mathcal{H}_{n+1}$ to construct an attacker against the semantic security of the public-key encryption scheme $(\mathsf{G}, \mathsf{E}, \mathsf{D})$. This allows us to conclude that $\mathcal{H}_n \overset{c}{\approx} \mathcal{H}_{n+1}$.
  Finally, note that the hybrid $\mathcal{H}_{n+1}$ is information theoretically independent of the plaintext message m.

6.3 Proof of Lemma 2

The proof follows by a sequence of sub-hybrids $\mathcal{H}_{\tau,0}$ to $\mathcal{H}_{\tau,6}$ where $\mathcal{H}_{\tau,0}$ is same as $\mathcal{H}_{\tau-1}$ and $\mathcal{H}_{\tau,6}$ is same as $\mathcal{H}_\tau$.

- $\mathcal{H}_{\tau,0}$: This hybrid is same as $\mathcal{H}_{\tau-1}$.
- $\mathcal{H}_{\tau,1}$: Skip this hybrid if $\tau = n$. Otherwise, this hybrid is identical to $\mathcal{H}_{\tau,0}$, except that we change how the values h_v and r_v for $\mathsf{v} \in \{0,1\}^\tau$ (if needed to answer a KeyGen query of the adversary) are generated.

  Recall that in hybrid $\mathcal{H}_{\tau,0}$, h_v is generated as $\mathsf{H}(\mathsf{k}_\tau, 0^{2\lambda}; \omega_\mathsf{v})$ and then

  $$r_\mathsf{v} := \begin{cases} \mathsf{H}^{-1}(\mathsf{k}_\tau, (0^{2\lambda}, \omega_\mathsf{v}), \mathsf{h}_{\mathsf{v}\|0} \| \mathsf{h}_{\mathsf{v}\|1}) & \text{if } \tau < n-1 \\ \mathsf{H}^{-1}(\mathsf{k}_\tau, (0^{2\lambda}, \omega_\mathsf{v}), \mathsf{ek}_{\mathsf{v}\|0} \| \mathsf{ek}_{\mathsf{v}\|1}) & \text{otherwise} \end{cases}.$$

  In this hybrid, we generate r_v first as being chosen uniformly. Next,

  $$\mathsf{h}_\mathsf{v} := \begin{cases} \mathsf{H}(\mathsf{k}_\tau, \mathsf{h}_{\mathsf{v}\|0} \| \mathsf{h}_{\mathsf{v}\|1}; r_\mathsf{v}) & \text{if } \tau < n-1 \\ \mathsf{H}(\mathsf{k}_\tau, \mathsf{ek}_{\mathsf{v}\|0} \| \mathsf{ek}_{\mathsf{v}\|1}; r_\mathsf{v}) & \text{otherwise} \end{cases}.$$

  Statistical indistinguishability of hybrids $\mathcal{H}_{\tau,0}$ and $\mathcal{H}_{\tau,1}$ follows from the trapdoor collision and uniformity properties of the chameleon encryption scheme.
- $\mathcal{H}_{\tau,2}$: We start with the case when $\tau < n$. For this case, in this hybrid, we change how the garbled circuit $\tilde{P}^\tau$ is generated. Let $\mathsf{v} = \mathsf{id}^*[1 \dots \tau]$ and recall that

  $$\mathsf{lk}_\mathsf{v} = \begin{cases} (\mathsf{h}_\mathsf{v}, \mathsf{ek}_{\mathsf{v}\|0}, \mathsf{h}_{\mathsf{v}\|1}, r_\mathsf{v}) & \text{if } \tau < n-1 \\ (\mathsf{h}_\mathsf{v}, \mathsf{ek}_{\mathsf{v}\|0}, \mathsf{ek}_{\mathsf{v}\|1}, r_\mathsf{v}) & \text{if } \tau = n-1 \end{cases}.$$

  In this hybrid, we change the generation process of the garbled circuit $\tilde{P}^\tau$ from

  $$(\tilde{P}^\tau, \overline{\mathsf{lab}}') \xleftarrow{\$} \mathsf{GCircuit}(1^\lambda, \mathsf{P}[\mathsf{id}[\tau+1], \mathsf{k}_\tau, \overline{\mathsf{lab}}])$$

and setting $\overline{\mathsf{lab}} := \overline{\mathsf{lab}}'$ to

$$(\tilde{P}^i, \{\mathsf{lab}'_{j,\mathsf{h}_{\mathsf{v},j}}\}_{j\in[\lambda]}) := \mathsf{Sim}(1^\lambda, \{\mathsf{Enc}(\mathsf{k}_\mathsf{v}, (\mathsf{h}_\mathsf{v}, j, b), \mathsf{lab}_{j,b})\}_{j\in[\lambda],b\in\{0,1\}})$$

and set $\overline{\mathsf{lab}} := \{\mathsf{lab}'_{j,\mathsf{h}_{\mathsf{v},j}}, \mathsf{lab}'_{j,\mathsf{h}_{\mathsf{v},j}}\}_{j\in[\lambda]}$.
For the case when $\tau = n$, then we change computation of $\tilde{T}$ from

$$(\tilde{T}, \overline{\mathsf{lab}}) \xleftarrow{\$} \mathsf{GCircuit}(1^\lambda, \mathsf{T}[\mathsf{m}])$$

where $\overline{\mathsf{lab}} = \{\mathsf{lab}_{j,b}\}_{j\in[\lambda],b\in\{0,1\}}$ to setting $y = \mathsf{ek}_{\mathsf{id}^*}$ and generating garbled circuit as,

$$(\tilde{T}, \{\mathsf{lab}_{j,y_j}\}_{j\in[\lambda]}) \xleftarrow{\$} \mathsf{Sim}(1^\lambda, \mathsf{E}(y, \mathsf{m}))$$

and setting $\overline{\mathsf{lab}} := \{\mathsf{lab}_{j,y_j}, \mathsf{lab}_{j,y_j}\}_{j\in[\lambda]}$.
For the case when $\tau < n$, computational indistinguishability of hybrids $\mathcal{H}_{\tau,1}$ and $\mathcal{H}_{\tau,2}$ follows by the security of the garbling scheme and the fact that $\{\mathsf{Enc}(\mathsf{k}_\mathsf{v}, (\mathsf{h}_\mathsf{v}, j, b), \mathsf{lab}_{j,b})\}_{j\in[\lambda],b\in\{0,1\}}$ is exactly the output of the circuit $\mathsf{P}[\mathsf{id}[\tau+1], \mathsf{k}_\tau, \overline{\mathsf{lab}}]$ on input h_v. On the other hand, for the case when $\tau = n$, then again indistinguishability of hybrids $\mathcal{H}_{n,1}$ and $\mathcal{H}_{n,2}$ follows by the security of the garbling scheme and the fact that $\mathsf{E}(\mathsf{ek}_{\mathsf{id}^*}, \mathsf{m})$ is the output of the circuit $\mathsf{T}[\mathsf{m}]$ on input $\mathsf{ek}_{\mathsf{id}^*}$.

- $\mathcal{H}_{\tau,3}$: Skip this hybrid if $\tau = n$. This hybrid is identical to $\mathcal{H}_{\tau,2}$, except that using $\mathsf{v} := \mathsf{id}[1 \ldots \tau]$ we change

$$(\tilde{P}^i, \{\mathsf{lab}'_{j,\mathsf{h}_{\mathsf{v},j}}\}_{j\in[\lambda]}) := \mathsf{Sim}(1^\lambda, \{\mathsf{Enc}(\mathsf{k}_\mathsf{v}, (\mathsf{h}_\mathsf{v}, j, b), \mathsf{lab}_{j,b})\}_{j\in[\lambda],b\in\{0,1\}})$$

to

$$\tilde{P}^i, \{\mathsf{lab}'_{j,\mathsf{h}_{\mathsf{v},j}}\}_{j\in[\lambda]}) := \mathsf{Sim}(1^\lambda, \{\mathsf{Enc}(\mathsf{k}_\mathsf{v}, (\mathsf{h}_\mathsf{v}, j, b), \mathsf{lab}_{j,\mathsf{h}_{\mathsf{id}[1\ldots\tau+1],j}})\}_{j\in[\lambda],b\in\{0,1\}})$$

Notice that t_v is not used in this experiment. Therefore computational indistinguishability of hybrids $\mathcal{H}_{\tau,2}$ and $\mathcal{H}_{\tau,3}$ follows by λ^2 invocations (one invocation for each bit of the λ labels) of the security of the chameleon encryption scheme. We now provide the reduction for one change below.
More formally, we now describe a reduction to the security of the chameleon hash function. Specifically, the challenger provides a hash key k^* and the attacker needs to submit x^*, r^*. Our reduction achieves this by setting $\mathsf{k}_\tau := \mathsf{k}^*$. It then submits the $\mathsf{x}^* := \mathsf{h}_{\mathsf{v}\|0}\|\mathsf{h}_{\mathsf{v}\|1}$ and randomly chosen coins $r_\mathsf{v} := r^*$ used in the computation of $\mathsf{h}_\mathsf{v} := \mathsf{H}(\mathsf{k}_\tau, \mathsf{x}^*; r^*)$ for the node v. Now we can use the attackers ability to distinguish the encryptions of the provided labels to break the security of the chameleon encryption scheme.

Remark: We note that the ciphertexts hardwired inside the garbled circuit only provide the labels $\{\mathsf{lab}_{j,\mathsf{h}_{\mathsf{id}[1\ldots\tau+1]},j}\}_{j\in[\lambda]}$ (in an information theoretical sense).

- $\mathcal{H}_{\tau,4}$: Skip this hybrid if $\tau = n$. In this hybrid, we undo the change made in going from hybrid $\mathcal{H}_{\tau,0}$ to hybrid $\mathcal{H}_{\tau,1}$, i.e. we go back to generating all $\mathsf{h_v}$ values using NodeGen and LeafGen.
  Computational indistinguishability of hybrids $\mathcal{H}_{\tau,3}$ and $\mathcal{H}_{\tau,4}$ follows from the trapdoor collision and uniformity properties of the chameleon encryption scheme. Observe that the hybrid $\mathcal{H}_{\tau,4}$ is the same as hybrid $\mathcal{H}_{\tau}$.

7 Construction of Hierarchical Identity-Based Encryption

In this section, we describe our construction of HIBE from chameleon encryption. Let $(\mathsf{Gen}, \mathsf{H}, \mathsf{H}^{-1}, \mathsf{Enc}, \mathsf{Dec})$ be a chameleon encryption scheme and $(\mathsf{G}, \mathsf{E}, \mathsf{D})$ be any semantically secure public-key encryption scheme. We let $\mathsf{id}[i]$ denote the ith-bit of id and $\mathsf{id}[1 \ldots i]$ denote the first i bits of id (and $\mathsf{id}[1 \ldots 0] = \varepsilon$).

Notation for the Pseudorandom Function F. Let $\mathsf{PRG} : \{0,1\}^\lambda \to \{0,1\}^{3\lambda}$ be a length tripling pseudorandom generator and $\mathsf{PRG}_0, \mathsf{PRG}_1$ and PRG_2 be the $1 \ldots \lambda$, $\lambda+1 \ldots 2\lambda$ and $2\lambda+1 \ldots 3\lambda$ bits of the output of PRG, respectively. Now define a GGM-type [29] pseudo-random function $\mathsf{F} : \{0,1\}^\lambda \times \{0,1,2\}^* \to \{0,1\}^\lambda$ such that $\mathsf{F}(s,x) := \mathsf{PRG}_{x_n}(\mathsf{PRG}_{x_{n-1}}(\ldots(\mathsf{PRG}_{x_1}(s))\ldots))$, where $n = |x|$ and for each $i \in [n]$ x_i is the ith element (from 0, 1 or 2) of string x.[19]

NodeGen and NodeGen′ Functions. As explained in the introduction, we need an exponential sized tree of local-keys. The function NodeGen provides efficient access to *local-keys* corresponding to any node in this (exponential sized) tree. We will use this function repeatedly in our construction. The function takes as input the hash key k_G (a key of the chameleon hash function from $2\ell + 2\lambda$ bits to λ bits, where ℓ is specified later), a node $\mathsf{v} \in \{0,1\}^* \cup \{\varepsilon\}$ (ε denotes the empty string), and $s = (s_1, s_2, s_3)$ seeds for the pseudo-random function PRF. This function is explained in the Fig. 5.

We also define a function NodeGen′, which is identical to NodeGen except that it additionally takes a bit β as input and outputs $\mathsf{dk}_{\mathsf{v}\|\beta}$. More formally, $\mathsf{NodeGen}'(\mathsf{k}_G, \mathsf{v}, (s_1, s_2, s_3), \beta)$ executes just like NodeGen but in Step 8 it outputs $\mathsf{dk}_{\mathsf{v}\|\beta}$.

Construction. We describe our HIBE scheme (Setup, KeyGen, Encrypt, Decrypt).

- $\mathsf{Setup}(1^\lambda)$: Proceed as follows:
  1. Sample $s \xleftarrow{\$} \{0,1\}^\lambda$ (seeds for the pseudorandom function PRF).
  2. Setup a global hash function $(\mathsf{k}_G, \cdot) := \mathsf{Gen}(1^\lambda, 2\ell + 2\lambda)$[20] where $\ell = \ell' + \lambda$ and ℓ' is the length of k generated from $\mathsf{Gen}(1^\lambda, \lambda)$.
  3. Obtain $(\mathsf{k}_\varepsilon, \mathsf{h}_\varepsilon, r_\varepsilon, \mathsf{h}'_\varepsilon, r'_\varepsilon, \mathsf{k}_0, \mathsf{h}_0, \mathsf{k}_1, \mathsf{h}_1) := \mathsf{NodeGen}(\mathsf{k}_G, \varepsilon, s)$

[19] $\mathsf{F}(s, \varepsilon)$ is set to output s.

[20] The trapdoor for the global hash function is not needed in the construction or the proof and is therefore dropped.

4. Output $(\mathsf{mpk}, \mathsf{msk})$ where $\mathsf{mpk} := (\mathsf{k}_G, \mathsf{k}_\varepsilon, \mathsf{h}_\varepsilon)$ and $\mathsf{msk} = \mathsf{sk}_\varepsilon := (\varepsilon, \emptyset, s, \bot)$

– $\mathsf{KeyGen}(\mathsf{sk}_{\mathsf{id}} = (\mathsf{id}, \{\mathsf{lk}_\mathsf{v}\}_{\mathsf{v}\in V}, s, \mathsf{dk}_{\mathsf{id}}), \mathsf{id}' \in \{0,1\}^*)$:[21]

Let $n := |\mathsf{id}'|$ and set $V' := \{\mathsf{id}\|\mathsf{id}'[1\dots j-1]\}_{j\in[n]}$
For all $\mathsf{v} \in V'$:
$\mathsf{lk}_\mathsf{v} := \mathsf{NodeGen}(\mathsf{k}_G, \mathsf{v}, (\mathsf{F}(s, \mathsf{v}\|2), \mathsf{F}(s, \mathsf{v}\|0\|2), \mathsf{F}(s, \mathsf{v}\|1\|2)))$
Let $\mathsf{v} := \mathsf{id}\|\mathsf{id}'[1\dots n-1]$
$\mathsf{dk}_{\mathsf{id}\|\mathsf{id}'} := \mathsf{NodeGen}'(\mathsf{k}_G, \mathsf{v}, (\mathsf{F}(s, \mathsf{v}\|2), \mathsf{F}(s, \mathsf{v}\|0\|2), \mathsf{F}(s, \mathsf{v}\|1\|2)), \mathsf{id}'[n])$
Output $\mathsf{sk}_{\mathsf{id}\|\mathsf{id}'} := (\mathsf{id}, \{\mathsf{lk}_\mathsf{v}\}_{\mathsf{v}\in V\cup V'}, \mathsf{F}(s, \mathsf{id}'), \mathsf{dk}_{\mathsf{id}\|\mathsf{id}'})$

$\mathsf{NodeGen}(\mathsf{k}_G, \mathsf{v}, (s_1, s_2, s_3))$:

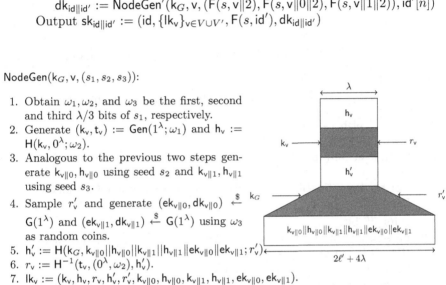

1. Obtain ω_1, ω_2, and ω_3 be the first, second and third $\lambda/3$ bits of s_1, respectively.
2. Generate $(\mathsf{k}_\mathsf{v}, \mathsf{t}_\mathsf{v}) := \mathsf{Gen}(1^\lambda; \omega_1)$ and $\mathsf{h}_\mathsf{v} := \mathsf{H}(\mathsf{k}_\mathsf{v}, 0^\lambda; \omega_2)$.
3. Analogous to the previous two steps generate $\mathsf{k}_{\mathsf{v}\|0}, \mathsf{h}_{\mathsf{v}\|0}$ using seed s_2 and $\mathsf{k}_{\mathsf{v}\|1}, \mathsf{h}_{\mathsf{v}\|1}$ using seed s_3.
4. Sample r'_v and generate $(\mathsf{ek}_{\mathsf{v}\|0}, \mathsf{dk}_{\mathsf{v}\|0}) \xleftarrow{\$} \mathsf{G}(1^\lambda)$ and $(\mathsf{ek}_{\mathsf{v}\|1}, \mathsf{dk}_{\mathsf{v}\|1}) \xleftarrow{\$} \mathsf{G}(1^\lambda)$ using ω_3 as random coins.
5. $\mathsf{h}'_\mathsf{v} := \mathsf{H}(\mathsf{k}_G, \mathsf{k}_{\mathsf{v}\|0}\|\mathsf{h}_{\mathsf{v}\|0}\|\mathsf{k}_{\mathsf{v}\|1}\|\mathsf{h}_{\mathsf{v}\|1}\|\mathsf{ek}_{\mathsf{v}\|0}\|\mathsf{ek}_{\mathsf{v}\|1}; r'_\mathsf{v})$
6. $r_\mathsf{v} := \mathsf{H}^{-1}(\mathsf{t}_\mathsf{v}, (0^\lambda, \omega_2), \mathsf{h}'_\mathsf{v})$.
7. $\mathsf{lk}_\mathsf{v} := (\mathsf{k}_\mathsf{v}, \mathsf{h}_\mathsf{v}, r_\mathsf{v}, \mathsf{h}'_\mathsf{v}, r'_\mathsf{v}, \mathsf{k}_{\mathsf{v}\|0}, \mathsf{h}_{\mathsf{v}\|0}, \mathsf{k}_{\mathsf{v}\|1}, \mathsf{h}_{\mathsf{v}\|1}, \mathsf{ek}_{\mathsf{v}\|0}, \mathsf{ek}_{\mathsf{v}\|1})$.
8. Output lk_v

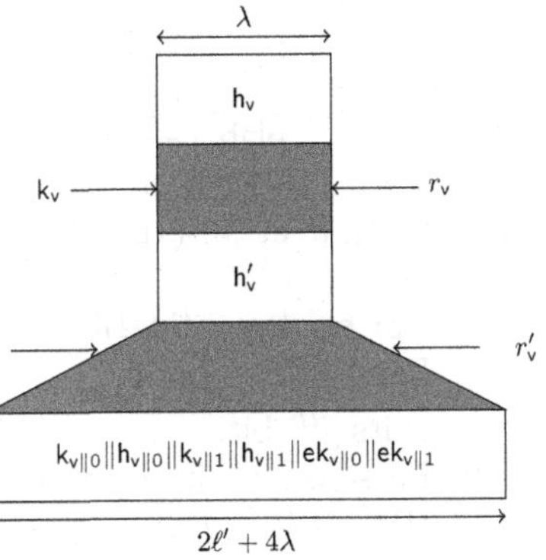

Fig. 5. Explanation on how NodeGen works. Strings ω_1, ω_2 and ω_3 are used as randomness for cryptographic functions and can be sufficiently expanded using a PRG.

Remark: We note that in our construction the secret key for any identity is unique regardless of many iterations of KeyGen operations were performed to obtain it.

– $\mathsf{Encrypt}(\mathsf{mpk} = (\mathsf{k}_G, \mathsf{k}_\varepsilon, \mathsf{h}_\varepsilon), \mathsf{id} \in \{0,1\}^n, \mathsf{m})$: Before describing the encryption procedure we describe four circuits that will be garbled during the encryption process.
  - $\mathsf{T}[\mathsf{m}](\mathsf{ek})$: Compute and output $\mathsf{E}(\mathsf{ek}, \mathsf{m})$.
  - $\mathsf{Q}_{last}[\beta \in \{0,1\}, \mathsf{k}_G, \overline{\mathsf{tlab}}](\mathsf{h})$: Compute and output $\{\mathsf{Enc}(\mathsf{k}_G, (\mathsf{h}, j + \beta\cdot\lambda + 2\ell, b), \mathsf{tlab}_{j,b})\}_{j\in[\lambda], b\in\{0,1\}}$, where $\overline{\mathsf{tlab}}$ is short for $\{\mathsf{tlab}_{j,b}\}_{j\in[\lambda], b\in\{0,1\}}$.
  - $\mathsf{Q}[\beta \in \{0,1\}, \mathsf{k}_G, \overline{\mathsf{plab}}](\mathsf{h})$: Compute and output $\{\mathsf{Enc}(\mathsf{k}_G, (\mathsf{h}, j + \beta\cdot\ell, b), \mathsf{plab}_{j,b})\}_{j\in[\ell], b\in\{0,1\}}$, where $\overline{\mathsf{plab}}$ is short for $\{\mathsf{plab}_{j,b}\}_{j\in[\ell], b\in\{0,1\}}$.

[21] HIBE is often defined to have separate KeyGen and Delegate algorithms. For simplicity, we describe our scheme with just one KeyGen algorithm that enables both the tasks of decryption and delegation. Secret-keys without delegation capabilities can be obtained by dropping the third entry (the PRG seed) from $\mathsf{sk}_{\mathsf{id}}$.

- $\mathsf{P}[\overline{\mathsf{qlab}}](\mathsf{k},\mathsf{h})$: Compute and output $\{\mathsf{Enc}(\mathsf{k},(\mathsf{h},j,b),\mathsf{qlab}_{j,b})\}_{j\in[\lambda],b\in\{0,1\}}$, where $\overline{\mathsf{qlab}}$ is short for $\{\mathsf{qlab}_{j,b}\}_{j\in[\lambda],b\in\{0,1\}}$.

Encryption proceeds as follows:

1. Compute $\tilde{T}$ as:

$$(\tilde{T},\overline{\mathsf{tlab}}) \xleftarrow{\$} \mathsf{GCircuit}(1^\lambda, \mathsf{Q}_{out}[\mathsf{k}_G,\mathsf{m}])$$

2. For $i = n,\ldots,1$ generate
   (a) If $i = n$ then

$$(\tilde{Q}^n,\overline{\mathsf{qlab}}^n) \xleftarrow{\$} \mathsf{GCircuit}(1^\lambda, \mathsf{Q}_{last}[\mathsf{id}[n],\mathsf{k}_G,\overline{\mathsf{tlab}}]),$$

   else

$$(\tilde{Q}^i,\overline{\mathsf{qlab}}^i) \xleftarrow{\$} \mathsf{GCircuit}(1^\lambda, \mathsf{Q}[\mathsf{id}[i],\mathsf{k}_G,\overline{\mathsf{plab}}^{i+1}]).$$

   (b) $(\tilde{P}^i,\overline{\mathsf{plab}}^i) \xleftarrow{\$} \mathsf{GCircuit}(1^\lambda, \mathsf{P}[\overline{\mathsf{qlab}}^i])$.
3. Set $x_\varepsilon := \mathsf{k}_\varepsilon \| \mathsf{h}_\varepsilon$.
4. Output $\mathsf{ct} := (\{\mathsf{plab}^1_{j,x_{\varepsilon,j}}\}_{j\in[\ell]}, \{\tilde{P}^i,\tilde{Q}^i\}_{i\in[n]}, \tilde{T})$ where $x_{\varepsilon,j}$ is the jth bit of x_ε.

– $\mathsf{Decrypt}(\mathsf{ct},\mathsf{sk}_{\mathsf{id}} = (\mathsf{id},\{\mathsf{lk}_\mathsf{v}\}_{\mathsf{v}\in V}), s, \mathsf{dk}_{\mathsf{id}})$: Decryption proceeds as follows:
  1. Parse ct as $(\{\mathsf{plab}^1_{j,x_{\varepsilon,j}}\}_{j\in[\ell]}, \{\tilde{P}^i,\tilde{Q}^i\}_{i\in[n]}, \tilde{T})$ where $x_\varepsilon := \mathsf{k}_\varepsilon\|\mathsf{h}_\varepsilon$ and $x_{\varepsilon,j}$ is its jth bit.
  2. Parse lk_v as $(\mathsf{h}_\mathsf{v}, r_\mathsf{v}, \mathsf{h}'_\mathsf{v}, r'_\mathsf{v}, \mathsf{k}_{\mathsf{v}\|0}, \mathsf{h}_{\mathsf{v}\|0}, \mathsf{k}_{\mathsf{v}\|1}, \mathsf{h}_{\mathsf{v}\|1}, \mathsf{ek}_{\mathsf{v}\|0}, \mathsf{ek}_{\mathsf{v}\|1})$ for each $\mathsf{v} \in V$. (Recall $V = \{\mathsf{id}[1\ldots j-1]\}_{j\in[n]}$.)
  3. For each $i \in [n]$, proceed as follows:
     (a) Set $\mathsf{v} := \mathsf{id}[1\ldots i-1]$, $x_\mathsf{v} := \mathsf{k}_\mathsf{v}\|\mathsf{h}_\mathsf{v}$, $y_\mathsf{v} := \mathsf{h}'_\mathsf{v}$, and if $i < n$ then set $z_\mathsf{v} := \mathsf{k}_{\mathsf{v}\|\mathsf{id}[i]}\|\mathsf{h}_{\mathsf{v}\|\mathsf{id}[i]}$ else set $z_\mathsf{v} := \mathsf{ek}_{\mathsf{id}}$.[22]
     (b) $\{e^i_{j,b}\}_{j\in[\lambda],b\in\{0,1\}} := \mathsf{Eval}(\tilde{P}^i, \{\mathsf{plab}^i_{j,x_{\mathsf{v},j}}\}_{j\in[\ell]})$.
     (c) For each $j \in [\lambda]$, compute $\mathsf{qlab}^i_{j,y_{\mathsf{v},j}} := \mathsf{Dec}(\mathsf{k}_\mathsf{v}, e^i_{j,y_{\mathsf{v},j}}, (\mathsf{h}'_\mathsf{v}, r_\mathsf{v}))$.
     (d) If $i < n$ then,

$$\{f^i_{j,b}\}_{j\in[\ell],b\in\{0,1\}} := \mathsf{Eval}(\tilde{Q}^i, \mathsf{qlab}^i_{j,y_{\mathsf{v},j}})$$

     and for each $j \in [\ell]$

$$\mathsf{plab}^{i+1}_{j,z_{\mathsf{v},j}} := \mathsf{Dec}(\mathsf{k}_G, f^i_{j,z_{\mathsf{v},j}}, (\mathsf{k}_{\mathsf{v}\|0}\|\mathsf{h}_{\mathsf{v}\|0}\|\mathsf{k}_{\mathsf{v}\|1}\|\mathsf{h}_{\mathsf{v}\|1}\|\mathsf{ek}_{\mathsf{v}\|0}\|\mathsf{pk}_{\mathsf{v}\|1}, r'_\mathsf{v}))$$

     (e) else,

$$\{g_{j,b}\}_{j\in[\lambda],b\in\{0,1\}} := \mathsf{Eval}(\tilde{Q}^n, \mathsf{qlab}^n_{j,y_{\mathsf{v},j}})$$

     and for each $j \in [\lambda]$

$$\mathsf{tlab}_{j,z_{\mathsf{v},j}} := \mathsf{Dec}(\mathsf{k}_G, g_{j,z_{\mathsf{v},j}}, (\mathsf{k}_{\mathsf{v}\|0}\|\mathsf{h}_{\mathsf{v}\|0}\|\mathsf{k}_{\mathsf{v}\|1}\|\mathsf{h}_{\mathsf{v}\|1}\|\mathsf{pk}_{\mathsf{v}\|0}\|\mathsf{pk}_{\mathsf{v}\|1}, r'_\mathsf{v})).$$

  4. Output $\mathsf{D}(\mathsf{dk}_{\mathsf{id}}, \mathsf{Eval}(\tilde{T}, \{\mathsf{tlab}_{j,\mathsf{ek}_{\mathsf{id},j}}\}_{j\in[\lambda]}))$.

[22] For $i < n$, z_v will become the x_v in next iteration.

7.1 Proof of Correctness

For any identity id, let $V = \{\mathsf{id}[1 \ldots j-1]\}_{j \in [n]}$ be the set of nodes on the root-to-leaf path corresponding to identity id. Then the secret key $\mathsf{sk}_{\mathsf{id}}$ consists of $\{\mathsf{lk}_{\mathsf{v}}\}_{\mathsf{v} \in V}$, $\mathsf{dk}_{\mathsf{id}}$ and a seed of the pseudorandom function F. $\{\mathsf{lk}_{\mathsf{v}}\}_{\mathsf{v} \in V}$, $\mathsf{dk}_{\mathsf{id}}$ and will be used for decryption and s is used for delegating keys. Note that by construction (and the trapdoor collision property of the chameleon encryption scheme for the first equation below) for all nodes $\mathsf{v} \in V$ we have that:

$$\mathsf{H}(\mathsf{k}_G, \mathsf{k}_{\mathsf{v}\|0} \| \mathsf{h}_{\mathsf{v}\|0} \| \mathsf{k}_{\mathsf{v}\|1} \| \mathsf{h}_{\mathsf{v}\|1} \| \mathsf{pk}_{\mathsf{v}\|0} \| \mathsf{ek}_{\mathsf{v}\|1}; r'_{\mathsf{v}}) = \mathsf{h}'_{\mathsf{v}},$$
$$\mathsf{H}(\mathsf{k}_{\mathsf{v}}, \mathsf{h}'_{\mathsf{v}}; r_{\mathsf{v}}) = \mathsf{h}_{\mathsf{v}}.$$

By correctness of garbled circuits, we have that the evaluation of $\tilde{P}^1$ yields correctly formed ciphertexts $f^1_{j,b}$. Next, by correctness of Dec of the chameleon encryption scheme we have that the decrypted values $\mathsf{qlab}^1_{j,y_{\varepsilon,j}}$ are the correct input labels for the next garbled circuit $\tilde{Q}^1$. Following the same argument we can argue that the decryption of ciphertexts generated by $\tilde{Q}^1$ yields the correct input labels for $\tilde{P}^2$. Repeatedly applying this argument allows us to conclude that the last garbled circuit $\tilde{Q}^n$ outputs correct encryptions of input labels of $\tilde{T}$. The decryption of appropriate ciphertexts among these and the execution of the garbled circuit $\tilde{T}$ using the obtained labels yields the ciphertext $\mathsf{E}(\mathsf{ek}_{\mathsf{id}}, \mathsf{m})$ which can be decrypted using the decryption key $\mathsf{dk}_{\mathsf{id}}$. Correctness of the last steps depends on the correctness of the public-key encryption scheme.

Next, the correctness of delegation follows from the fact that for every id and id'

$$\mathsf{KeyGen}(\mathsf{sk}_{\varepsilon}, \mathsf{id} \| \mathsf{id}') = \mathsf{KeyGen}(\mathsf{KeyGen}(\mathsf{sk}_{\varepsilon}, \mathsf{id}), \mathsf{id}').$$

This fact follows directly from the following property of the GGM PRF. Specifically, for every x we have that $\mathsf{F}(s, \mathsf{id} \| x) = \mathsf{F}(\mathsf{F}(s, \mathsf{id}), x)$.

7.2 Proof of Security

We are now ready to prove the selective security of the HIBE construction above. For the sake of contradiction we proceed by assuming that there exists an adversary $\mathcal{A}$ such that $\Pr[\mathrm{IND}^{\mathrm{HIBE}}_{\mathcal{A}}(1^\lambda) = 1] \geq \frac{1}{2} + \epsilon$ for a non-negligible ϵ (in λ), where $\mathrm{IND}^{\mathrm{HIBE}}_{\mathcal{A}}$ is shown in Fig. 2. Assume further that q is a polynomial upper bound for the running-time of $\mathcal{A}$, and thus also an upper bound for the number of $\mathcal{A}$'s key queries. Security follows by a sequence of hybrids. In our hybrids, changes are made in how the secret key queries of the adversary $\mathcal{A}$ are answered and how the challenge ciphertext is generated. However, unlike the IBE case these changes are not intertwined with each other. In particular, we will make changes to the secret keys first and then the ciphertext. We describe our hybrids next. Our proof consist of a sequence of hybrids $\mathcal{H}_{-3}, \mathcal{H}_{-2}, \mathcal{H}_{-1}, \mathcal{H}_0, \mathcal{H}_1, \ldots \mathcal{H}_{n+2}$. We describe these below. Since we are in the selective the case the adversary declares the challenge identity id^* before the public parameters mpk are provided to it. Also, we let V^* be the set $\{\varepsilon, \mathsf{id}^*[1] \ldots \mathsf{id}^*[1 \ldots n-1]\}$.

- $\mathcal{H}_{-3}$: This hybrid corresponds to the experiment $\mathsf{IND}_{\mathcal{A}}^{\mathrm{HIBE}}$ as shown in Fig. 2.
- $\mathcal{H}_{-2}$: In this hybrid, we change how the seed s of generated in Step 1 of Setup is used. Specifically, we sample $s \xleftarrow{\$} \{0,1\}^\lambda$ and generate
  1. For each $i \in [n]$, let $a_i := \mathsf{F}(s, \mathsf{id}^*[1 \ldots i-1] \| (1 - \mathsf{id}^*[i])$.
  2. $b := \mathsf{F}(s, \mathsf{id}^*)$.
  3. For each $i \in \{0 \ldots n-1\}$, let $c_i := \mathsf{F}(s, \mathsf{id}^*[1 \ldots i] \| 2)$.

  Now, through out the execution of the experiment we replace the use of s with the values $(\{a_i\}, b, \{c_i\})$. First, observe that (by standard properties of the GGM pseudorandom function) given these values we can generate $\mathsf{F}(s, \mathsf{v} \| 2)$ for all $\mathsf{v} \in \{0,1\}^* \cup \{\varepsilon\}$. Also, note that for the execution of the functions NodeGen and NodeGen′ only $\mathsf{F}(s, \mathsf{v} \| 2)$ needs to be generated. Therefore, all executions of NodeGen and NodeGen′ remain unaffected.
  Secondly, note that the $\mathcal{A}$ is only allowed to make KeyGen queries for identities $\mathsf{id} \notin V^* \cup \{\mathsf{id}^*\}$. Therefore, in order to answer these queries the experiment needs to generate $\mathsf{F}(s, \mathsf{v})$ for $\mathsf{v} \notin V^* \cup \{\mathsf{id}^*\}$. Observe that using $(\{a_i\}, b)$ by standard properties of the GGM pseudorandom function the experiment can compute $\mathsf{F}(s, \mathsf{v})$ for any $\mathsf{v} \notin V^*$. Therefore, all of $\mathcal{A}$'s KeyGen queries can be answered.[23]
  The hybrids $\mathcal{H}_{-3}$ and $\mathcal{H}_{-2}$ are the same distribution and the only change we have made is syntactic.
- $\mathcal{H}_{-1}$: In this hybrids, we change how each c_i is generated. In particular, we sample each c_i uniformly and independently instead of using F.
  The indistinguishability between hybrids $\mathcal{H}_{-2}$ and $\mathcal{H}_{-1}$ follows based on the pseudorandomness of the pseudorandom function F.
- $\mathcal{H}_0$: In this hybrid, we change how NodeGen and NodeGen′ behave when computed with an input $\mathsf{v} \in V^*$.[24] For all $\mathsf{v} \notin V^*$ the behavior of NodeGen and NodeGen′ remains unchanged. At a high level, the goal is to change the generating of $\{\mathsf{lk}_\mathsf{v}\}_{\mathsf{v} \in V^*}$ such that the trapdoor values $\mathsf{t}_{\mathsf{v} \in V^*}$ are unused and so that the encryption key $\mathsf{ek}_{\mathsf{id}^*}$ is sampled independent of everything else. The execution of NodeGen and NodeGen′ for every $\mathsf{v} \notin V^*$ remain unaffected. In particular, at Setup time we proceed as follows and fix the values $\{\mathsf{lk}_\mathsf{v}\}_{\mathsf{v} \in V^*}$ and $\{\mathsf{dk}_{\mathsf{v}\|0}, \mathsf{dk}_{\mathsf{v}\|1}\}_{\mathsf{v} \in V^*}$.[25]

  1. For every $\mathsf{v} \in V^*$:
     (a) Generate $(\mathsf{k}_\mathsf{v}, \mathsf{t}_\mathsf{v}) \xleftarrow{\$} \mathsf{Gen}(1^\lambda)$.
     (b) Generate $(\mathsf{ek}_{\mathsf{v}\|0}, \mathsf{dk}_{\mathsf{v}\|0}) \xleftarrow{\$} \mathsf{G}(1^\lambda)$ and $(\mathsf{ek}_{\mathsf{v}\|1}, \mathsf{dk}_{\mathsf{v}\|1}) \xleftarrow{\$} \mathsf{G}(1^\lambda)$.
     (c) Sample r'_v, r_v.
  2. Let $S^* := \{\mathsf{id}^*[1 \ldots i-1] \| (1 - \mathsf{id}^*[i])\}_{i \in [n]} \cup \{\mathsf{id}^*\}$. (Note that $S^* \cap V^* = \emptyset$.)

---

[23] The experiment can provide $\mathsf{F}(s, \mathsf{id}^*)$ even though it does not appear in any of the $\mathcal{A}$'s secret key queries. The reason is that $\mathsf{F}(s, \mathsf{id}^*)$ allows the capabilities of delegation but not decryption for ciphertexts to identity id^*.

[24] Observe that these are specifically the cases in which one or two of the values s_1, s_2 and s_3 given as input to NodeGen and NodeGen′ depend on the $\{c_i\}$ values.

[25] Note that since the adversary never makes a KeyGen query for an identity id that is a prefix of id^*. Therefore, we have that dk_v for $\mathsf{v} \in V^* \cup \{\mathsf{id}^*\}$ will not be provided to $\mathcal{A}$.

3. For all $\mathsf{v} \in S^*$ set $\mathsf{k_v}, \mathsf{h_v}$ as first two outputs of $\mathsf{NodeGen}(\mathsf{k}_G, \mathsf{v}, (\mathsf{F}(s, \mathsf{v}\|2), \mathsf{F}(s, \mathsf{v}\|0\|2), \mathsf{F}(s, \mathsf{v}\|1\|2)))$.
4. For each $i \in \{n-1 \dots 0\}$:
   (a) Set $\mathsf{v} := \mathsf{id}^*[1 \dots i]$
   (b) Generate $\mathsf{h}'_\mathsf{v} := \mathsf{H}(\mathsf{k}_G, \mathsf{k}_{\mathsf{v}\|0}||\mathsf{h}_{\mathsf{v}\|0}||\mathsf{k}_{\mathsf{v}\|1}||\mathsf{h}_{\mathsf{v}\|1}\|\mathsf{ek}_{\mathsf{v}\|0}\|\mathsf{ek}_{\mathsf{v}\|1}; r'_\mathsf{v})$.
   (c) $\mathsf{h_v} := \mathsf{H}(\mathsf{k_v}, \mathsf{h}'_\mathsf{v}; r_\mathsf{v})$.
   (d) $\mathsf{lk_v} := (\mathsf{k_v}, \mathsf{h_v}, r_\mathsf{v}, \mathsf{h}'_\mathsf{v}, r'_\mathsf{v}, \mathsf{k}_{\mathsf{v}\|0}, \mathsf{h}_{\mathsf{v}\|0}, \mathsf{k}_{\mathsf{v}\|1}, \mathsf{h}_{\mathsf{v}\|1}, \mathsf{ek}_{\mathsf{v}\|0}, \mathsf{ek}_{\mathsf{v}\|1})$.
5. Output $\{\mathsf{lk_v}\}_{\mathsf{v} \in V^*}$ and $\{\mathsf{dk}_{\mathsf{v}\|0}, \mathsf{dk}_{\mathsf{v}\|1}\}_{\mathsf{v} \in V^*}$.

Statistical indistinguishability of hybrids $\mathcal{H}_{\tau,-1}$ and $\mathcal{H}_{\tau,0}$ follows from the trapdoor collision and uniformity properties of the chameleon encryption scheme. Note that in this hybrid the trapdoor $\mathsf{t_v}$ for any node $\mathsf{v} \in V^*$ is no longer being used.

- $\mathcal{H}_\tau$ for $\tau \in \{1 \dots n\}$: This hybrid is identical to $\mathcal{H}_0$ except we change how the ciphertext is generated. Recall that the challenge ciphertext consists of a sequence of $2n+1$ garbled circuits. In hybrid $\mathcal{H}_\tau$, we generate the first 2τ of these garbled circuits (namely, $\tilde{P}^1, \tilde{Q}^1 \dots \tilde{P}^\tau, \tilde{Q}^\tau$) using the simulator provided by the garbled circuit construction. The outputs hard-coded in the simulated circuits are set to be consistent with the output that would have resulted from the execution of honestly generated garbled circuits using keys obtained from invocations of NodeGen. More formally, for the challenge identity id^* the challenge ciphertext is generated as follows (modifications with respect to honest ciphertext generation have been highlighted in red):
  1. Compute $\tilde{T}$ as:
  $$(\tilde{T}, \overline{\mathsf{tlab}}) \xleftarrow{\$} \mathsf{GCircuit}(1^\lambda, \mathsf{Q}_{out}[\mathsf{k}_G, \mathsf{m}])$$
  2. For $i = n, \dots, \tau+1$ generate
     (a) If $i = n$ then
     $$(\tilde{Q}^n, \overline{\mathsf{qlab}}^n) \xleftarrow{\$} \mathsf{GCircuit}(1^\lambda, \mathsf{Q}_{last}[\mathsf{id}[n], \mathsf{k}_G, \overline{\mathsf{tlab}}]),$$
     else
     $$(\tilde{Q}^i, \overline{\mathsf{qlab}}^i) \xleftarrow{\$} \mathsf{GCircuit}(1^\lambda, \mathsf{Q}[\mathsf{id}[i], \mathsf{k}_G, \overline{\mathsf{plab}}^{i+1}]).$$
     (b) $(\tilde{P}^i, \overline{\mathsf{plab}}^i) \xleftarrow{\$} \mathsf{GCircuit}(1^\lambda, \mathsf{P}[\overline{\mathsf{qlab}}^i])$.
  3. For $i = \tau, \dots, 1$:
     (a) Set $\mathsf{v} = \mathsf{id}^*[1 \dots i-1]$, $x_\mathsf{v} := \mathsf{k_v}\|\mathsf{h_v}$, $y_\mathsf{v} := \mathsf{h}'_\mathsf{v}$, and if $i < n$ then $z_\mathsf{v} := \mathsf{k}_{\mathsf{v}\|\mathsf{id}^*[i]}\|\mathsf{h}_{\mathsf{v}\|\mathsf{id}^*[i]}$ else $z_\mathsf{v} := \mathsf{ek}_{\mathsf{id}^*}$.
     (b) If $i = n$ then $(\tilde{Q}^n, \{\mathsf{qlab}^n_{j,y_{\mathsf{v},j}}\}_{j\in[\lambda]}) := \mathsf{Sim}(1^\lambda, \{\mathsf{Enc}(\mathsf{k}_G, (\mathsf{h}'_\mathsf{v}, j + \mathsf{id}^*[n] \cdot \lambda + 2\ell, b), \mathsf{tlab}_{j,z_{\mathsf{v},j}})\}_{j\in[\lambda], b\in\{0,1\}})$ else $(\tilde{Q}^i, \{\mathsf{qlab}^i_{j,y_{\mathsf{v},j}}\}_{j\in[\lambda]}) := \mathsf{Sim}(1^\lambda, \{\mathsf{Enc}(\mathsf{k}_G, (\mathsf{h}'_\mathsf{v}, j + \mathsf{id}^*[i] \cdot \ell, b), \mathsf{plab}^{i+1}_{j,z_{\mathsf{v},j}})\}_{j\in[\ell], b\in\{0,1\}})$.
     (c) $\overline{\mathsf{qlab}}^i := \{\mathsf{qlab}^i_{j,y_{\mathsf{v},j}}, \mathsf{qlab}^i_{j,y_{\mathsf{v},j}}\}_{j\in[\lambda]}$.
     (d) $(\tilde{P}^i, \{\mathsf{plab}^i_{j,x_{\mathsf{v},j}}\}_{j\in[\ell]}) := \mathsf{Sim}(1^\lambda, \{\mathsf{Enc}(\mathsf{k_v}, (\mathsf{h_v}, j, b), \mathsf{qlab}^i_{j,y_{\mathsf{v},j}})\}_{j\in[\lambda], b\in\{0,1\}})$.
     (e) $\overline{\mathsf{plab}}^i := \{\mathsf{plab}^i_{j,x_{\mathsf{v},j}}, \mathsf{plab}^i_{j,x_{\mathsf{v},j}}\}_{j\in[\ell]}$.
  4. Set $x_\varepsilon := \mathsf{k}_\varepsilon\|\mathsf{h}_\varepsilon$.

5. Output $\mathsf{ct} := (\{\mathsf{plab}^1_{j,x_{\varepsilon,j}}\}_{j\in[\lambda]}, \{\tilde{P}^i, \tilde{Q}^i\}_{i\in[n]}, \tilde{T})$ where $x_{\varepsilon,j}$ is the jth bit of x_ε.

The computational indistinguishability between hybrids $\mathcal{H}_{\tau-1}$ and $\mathcal{H}_\tau$ is based on Lemma 3 which is proved in Sect. 7.3.

Lemma 3. *For each $\tau \in \{1 \dots n\}$ it is the case that $\mathcal{H}_{\tau-1} \stackrel{c}{\approx} \mathcal{H}_\tau$.*

- $\mathcal{H}_{n+1}$: This hybrid is same as hybrid $\mathcal{H}_n$ except that we generate the garbled circuit $\tilde{T}$ to using the garbling simulator. More specifically, instead of generating $\tilde{T}$ as

$$(\tilde{T}, \overline{\mathsf{tlab}}) \xleftarrow{\$} \mathsf{GCircuit}(1^\lambda, \mathsf{Q}_{out}[\mathsf{k}_G, \mathsf{m}])$$

  we set $y = \mathsf{ek}_{\mathsf{id}^*}$ and generate garbled circuit as,

$$(\tilde{T}, \{\mathsf{lab}_{j,y_j}\}_{j\in[\lambda]}) \xleftarrow{\$} \mathsf{Sim}(1^\lambda, \mathsf{E}(y, \mathsf{m}))$$

  and set $\overline{\mathsf{lab}} := \{\mathsf{lab}_{j,y_j}, \mathsf{lab}_{j,y_j}\}_{j\in[\lambda]}$.
  Computational indistinguishability between hybrids $\mathcal{H}_n$ and $\mathcal{H}_{n+1}$ follows directly from the security of the gabled circuits.
- $\mathcal{H}_{n+2}$: This hybrid is same as $\mathcal{H}_n$ except that we change the ciphertext $\mathsf{E}(\mathsf{ek}_{\mathsf{id}^*}, \mathsf{m})$ hardwired in the simulated garbling of the circuit T to be $\mathsf{E}(\mathsf{ek}_{\mathsf{id}^*}, 0)$.
  Note that the adversary $\mathcal{A}$ never queries for $\mathsf{sk}_{\mathsf{id}^*}$. Therefore, it is never provided the value $\mathsf{dk}_{\mathsf{id}^*}$. Therefore, we can use an adversary distinguishing between $\mathcal{H}_{n+1}$ and $\mathcal{H}_{n+2}$ to construct an attacker against the semantic security of the public-key encryption scheme $(\mathsf{G}, \mathsf{E}, \mathsf{D})$. This allows us to conclude that $\mathcal{H}_{n+1} \stackrel{c}{\approx} \mathcal{H}_{n+2}$.
  Finally, note that the hybrid $\mathcal{H}_{n+2}$ is information theoretically independent of the plaintext message m.

7.3 Proof of Lemma 3

The proof follows by a sequence of sub-hybrids $\mathcal{H}_{\tau,0}$ to $\mathcal{H}_{\tau,4}$ where $\mathcal{H}_{\tau,0}$ is same as $\mathcal{H}_{\tau-1}$ and $\mathcal{H}_{\tau,4}$ is same as $\mathcal{H}_\tau$.

- $\mathcal{H}_{\tau,0}$: This hybrid is same as $\mathcal{H}_{\tau-1}$.
- $\mathcal{H}_{\tau,1}$: In this hybrid, we change how the garbled circuit $\tilde{P}^\tau$ is generated. Let $\mathsf{v} = \mathsf{id}^*[1 \dots \tau-1]$ and $\mathsf{lk}_\mathsf{v} = (\mathsf{k}_\mathsf{v}, \mathsf{h}_\mathsf{v}, r_\mathsf{v}, \mathsf{h}'_\mathsf{v}, r'_\mathsf{v}, \mathsf{k}_{\mathsf{v}\|0}, \mathsf{h}_{\mathsf{v}\|0}, \mathsf{k}_{\mathsf{v}\|1}, \mathsf{h}_{\mathsf{v}\|1}, \mathsf{ek}_{\mathsf{v}\|0}, \mathsf{ek}_{\mathsf{v}\|1})$ and define $x_\mathsf{v} := \mathsf{k}_\mathsf{v}\|\mathsf{h}_\mathsf{v}$. The change we make is the following. We generate

$$(\tilde{P}^\tau, \overline{\mathsf{plab}}^\tau) \xleftarrow{\$} \mathsf{GCircuit}(1^\lambda, \mathsf{P}[\overline{\mathsf{qlab}}^\tau])$$

  now as

$$(\tilde{P}^\tau, \{\mathsf{plab}^\tau_{j,x_{\mathsf{v},j}}\}_{j\in[\ell]}) \xleftarrow{\$} \mathsf{Sim}(1^\lambda, \{\mathsf{Enc}(\mathsf{k}_\mathsf{v}, (\mathsf{h}_\mathsf{v}, j, b), \mathsf{qlab}^\tau_{j,b})\}_{j\in[\lambda], b\in\{0,1\}})$$

where $x_{\mathsf{v},j}$ is the jth bit of x_{v}. Next, we set $\overline{\mathsf{plab}}^i := \{\mathsf{plab}^i_{j,x_{\mathsf{v},j}}, \mathsf{plab}^i_{j,x_{\mathsf{v},j}}\}_{j\in[\ell]}$. Computational indistinguishability of hybrids $\mathcal{H}_{\tau,0}$ and $\mathcal{H}_{\tau,1}$ follows by the security of the garbling scheme $\mathsf{GCircuit}$ and the fact that $\{\mathsf{Enc}(\mathsf{k_v}, (\mathsf{h_v}, j, b), \mathsf{qlab}^{\tau}_{j,b})\}_{j\in[\lambda],b\in\{0,1\}}$ is exactly the output of the circuit $P[\overline{\mathsf{qlab}}^{\tau}]$ on input x_{v}.

- $\mathcal{H}_{\tau,2}$: This hybrid is identical to $\mathcal{H}_{\tau,2}$, except that for $\mathsf{v} = \mathsf{id}^*[1\ldots\tau-1]$ we change

$$(\tilde{P}^{\tau}, \{\mathsf{plab}^{\tau}_{j,x_{\mathsf{v},j}}\}_{j\in[\ell]}) := \mathsf{Sim}(1^{\lambda}, \{\mathsf{Enc}(\mathsf{k_v}, (\mathsf{h_v}, j, b), \mathsf{qlab}^{\tau}_{j,b})\}_{j\in[\lambda],b\in\{0,1\}})$$

to

$$(\tilde{P}^{\tau}, \{\mathsf{plab}^{\tau}_{j,x_{\mathsf{v},j}}\}_{j\in[\ell]}) := \mathsf{Sim}(1^{\lambda}, \{\mathsf{Enc}(\mathsf{k_v}, (\mathsf{h_v}, j, b), \mathsf{qlab}^{\tau}_{j,y_{\mathsf{v},j}})\}_{j\in[\lambda],b\in\{0,1\}}),$$

where $y_{\mathsf{v}} := \mathsf{h}'_{\mathsf{v}}$.

Notice that node v is generated so that the trapdoor value $\mathsf{t_v}$ is not used in the execution of the experiment. Therefore, computational indistinguishability of hybrids $\mathcal{H}_{\tau,1}$ and $\mathcal{H}_{\tau,2}$ follows by λ^2 invocations (one invocation for each bit of the λ labels) of the security of the chameleon encryption scheme. The reduction is analogous to the reduction proving indistinguishability of hybrids $\mathcal{H}_{\tau,2}$ and $\mathcal{H}_{\tau,3}$ in the proof of Lemma 2.
Remark: We note that the ciphertexts hardwired inside the garbled circuit only provide the labels $\{\mathsf{qlab}^{\tau}_{j,y_{\mathsf{v},j}}\}_{j\in[\lambda]}$ (in an information theoretical sense).

- $\mathcal{H}_{\tau,3}$ This hybrid is identical to $\mathcal{H}_{\tau,2}$, except that for $\mathsf{v} = \mathsf{id}^*[1\ldots\tau-1]$ we change how $\tilde{Q}^{\tau}$ is generated. If $\tau = n$ then

$$(\tilde{Q}^{n}, \overline{\mathsf{qlab}}^{n}) \xleftarrow{\$} \mathsf{GCircuit}(1^{\lambda}, \mathsf{Q}_{last}[\mathsf{id}^*[n], \mathsf{k}_G, \overline{\mathsf{tlab}}]),$$

is changed to $(\tilde{Q}^{n}, \{\mathsf{qlab}^{n}_{j,y_{\mathsf{v},j}}\}_{j\in[\lambda]}) := \mathsf{Sim}(1^{\lambda}, \{\mathsf{Enc}(\mathsf{k}_G, (\mathsf{h}'_{\mathsf{v}}, j + \mathsf{id}^*[n]\cdot\lambda + 2\ell, b), \mathsf{tlab}_{j,b})\}_{j\in[\lambda],b\in\{0,1\}})$, and $\overline{\mathsf{qlab}}^{n} := \{\mathsf{qlab}^{n}_{j,y_{\mathsf{v},j}}, \mathsf{qlab}^{n}_{j,y_{\mathsf{v},j}}\}_{j\in[\lambda]}$ where $y_{\mathsf{v}} := \mathsf{h}'_{\mathsf{v}}$. Otherwise, if $\tau \neq n$ then

$$(\tilde{Q}^{\tau}, \overline{\mathsf{qlab}}^{\tau}) \xleftarrow{\$} \mathsf{GCircuit}(1^{\lambda}, \mathsf{Q}[\mathsf{id}^*[\tau], \mathsf{k}_G, \overline{\mathsf{plab}}^{\tau+1}])$$

is changed to $(\tilde{Q}^{\tau}, \{\mathsf{qlab}^{\tau}_{j,y_{\mathsf{v},j}}\}_{j\in[\lambda]}) := \mathsf{Sim}(1^{\lambda}, \{\mathsf{Enc}(\mathsf{k}_G, (\mathsf{h}'_{\mathsf{v}}, j + \mathsf{id}^*[\tau]\cdot\ell, b), \mathsf{plab}^{\tau+1}_{j,b})\}_{j\in[\ell],b\in\{0,1\}})$, and $\overline{\mathsf{qlab}}^{\tau} := \{\mathsf{qlab}^{\tau}_{j,y_{\mathsf{v},j}}, \mathsf{qlab}^{\tau}_{j,y_{\mathsf{v},j}}\}_{j\in[\lambda]}$ where $y_{\mathsf{v}} := \mathsf{h}'_{\mathsf{v}}$. Computational indistinguishability between hybrids $\mathcal{H}_{\tau,2}$ and $\mathcal{H}_{\tau,3}$ follows by the security of the garbling scheme and the fact that is the output of the circuit $\mathsf{Q}_{last}[\mathsf{id}^*[n], \mathsf{k}_G, \overline{\mathsf{tlab}}]$ is $\{\mathsf{Enc}(\mathsf{k}_G, (\mathsf{h}'_{\mathsf{v}}, j + \mathsf{id}^*[n]\cdot\lambda + 2\ell, b), \mathsf{tlab}_{j,b})\}_{j\in[\lambda],b\in\{0,1\}}$ and the output of the circuit $\mathsf{Q}[\mathsf{id}^*[\tau], \mathsf{k}_G, \overline{\mathsf{plab}}^{\tau+1}]$ is $\{\mathsf{Enc}(\mathsf{k}_G, (\mathsf{h}'_{\mathsf{v}}, j + \mathsf{id}^*[\tau]\cdot\ell, b), \mathsf{plab}^{\tau+1}_{j,b})\}_{j\in[\ell],b\in\{0,1\}}$.

- $\mathcal{H}_{\tau,4}$: This hybrid is identical to $\mathcal{H}_{\tau,4}$, except that we change generation of $\tilde{Q}^{\tau}$. Specifically, in the case $\tau = n$ then we change the generation process of $\tilde{Q}^{n}$ from $(\tilde{Q}^{n}, \{\mathsf{qlab}^{n}_{j,y_{\mathsf{v},j}}\}_{j\in[\lambda]}) := \mathsf{Sim}(1^{\lambda}, \{\mathsf{Enc}(\mathsf{k}_G, (\mathsf{h}'_{\mathsf{v}}, j + \mathsf{id}^*[n]\cdot\lambda + 2\ell, b),$

$\mathsf{tlab}_{j,b})\}_{j\in[\lambda],b\in\{0,1\}})$ to $(\tilde{Q}^n, \{\mathsf{qlab}^n_{j,y_{\mathsf{v},j}}\}_{j\in[\lambda]}) := \mathsf{Sim}(1^\lambda, \{\mathsf{Enc}(\mathsf{k}_G, (\mathsf{h}'_\mathsf{v}, j + \mathsf{id}^*[n]\cdot\lambda + 2\ell, b), \mathsf{tlab}_{j,z_{\mathsf{v},j}})\}_{j\in[\lambda],b\in\{0,1\}})$, where $z_\mathsf{v} := \mathsf{ek}_{\mathsf{id}^*}$. On the other hand, when $\tau \neq n$ then it is changed from $(\tilde{Q}^\tau, \{\mathsf{qlab}^\tau_{j,y_{\mathsf{v},j}}\}_{j\in[\lambda]}) := \mathsf{Sim}(1^\lambda, \{\mathsf{Enc}(\mathsf{k}_G, (\mathsf{h}'_\mathsf{v}, j + \mathsf{id}^*[\tau]\cdot\ell, b), \mathsf{plab}^{\tau+1}_{j,b})\}_{j\in[\ell],b\in\{0,1\}})$ to $(\tilde{Q}^\tau, \{\mathsf{qlab}^\tau_{j,y_{\mathsf{v},j}}\}_{j\in[\lambda]}) := \mathsf{Sim}(1^\lambda, \{\mathsf{Enc}(\mathsf{k}_G, (\mathsf{h}'_\mathsf{v}, j + \mathsf{id}^*[\tau]\cdot\ell, b), \mathsf{plab}^{\tau+1}_{j,z_{\mathsf{v},j}})\}_{j\in[\ell],b\in\{0,1\}})$ where $z_\mathsf{v} := \mathsf{h}_{\mathsf{v}\|\mathsf{id}^*[\tau]}\|\mathsf{k}_{\mathsf{v}\|\mathsf{id}^*[\tau]}$.
Notice that since the trapdoor for k_G is unavailable (never generated or used), computational indistinguishability of hybrids $\mathcal{H}_{\tau,3}$ and $\mathcal{H}_{\tau,4}$ follows by λ^2 invocations (one invocation per bit of the λ labels) if $\tau = n$ and by $\ell\lambda$ invocations (one invocation per bit of the ℓ labels) otherwise of the security of the chameleon encryption scheme. And the reduction to the security of the chameleon encryption scheme is analogous to the reduction described for indistinguishability between hybrids $\mathcal{H}_{\tau,1}$ and $\mathcal{H}_{\tau,2}$.
Observe that the hybrid $\mathcal{H}_{\tau,4}$ is the same as hybrid $\mathcal{H}_\tau$.

Acknowledgments. We thank the anonymous reviewers of CRYPTO 2017 for their valuable feedback.

References

1. Agrawal, S., Boneh, D., Boyen, X.: Efficient lattice (H)IBE in the standard model. In: Gilbert, H. (ed.) EUROCRYPT 2010. LNCS, vol. 6110, pp. 553–572. Springer, Heidelberg (2010). doi:10.1007/978-3-642-13190-5_28
2. Agrawal, S., Boneh, D., Boyen, X.: Lattice basis delegation in fixed dimension and shorter-ciphertext hierarchical IBE. In: Rabin, T. (ed.) CRYPTO 2010. LNCS, vol. 6223, pp. 98–115. Springer, Heidelberg (2010). doi:10.1007/978-3-642-14623-7_6
3. Agrawal, S., Boyen, X.: Identity-based encryption from lattices in the standard model. Manuscript (2009)
4. Ananth, P., Boneh, D., Garg, S., Sahai, A., Zhandry, M.: Differing-inputs obfuscation and applications. Cryptology ePrint Archive, Report 2013/689 (2013). http://eprint.iacr.org/2013/689
5. Bellare, M., Hoang, V.T., Rogaway, P.: Foundations of garbled circuits. In: Yu, T., Danezis, G., Gligor, V.D. (eds.) ACM CCS 2012, pp. 784–796. ACM Press, Raleigh, 16–18 October 2012
6. Bellare, M., Rogaway, P., Random oracles are practical: a paradigm for designing efficient protocols. In: Ashby, V. (ed.) ACM CCS 1993, pp. 62–73. ACM Press, Fairfax, 3–5 November 1993
7. Biham, E., Boneh, D., Reingold, O.: Generalized Diffie-Hellman modulo a composite is not weaker than factoring. Cryptology ePrint Archive, Report 1997/014 (1997). http://eprint.iacr.org/1997/014
8. Boneh, D., Boyen, X.: Efficient selective-ID secure identity-based encryption without random oracles. In: Cachin, C., Camenisch, J.L. (eds.) EUROCRYPT 2004. LNCS, vol. 3027, pp. 223–238. Springer, Heidelberg (2004). doi:10.1007/978-3-540-24676-3_14
9. Boneh, D., Boyen, X.: Secure identity based encryption without random oracles. In: Franklin, M. (ed.) CRYPTO 2004. LNCS, vol. 3152, pp. 443–459. Springer, Heidelberg (2004). doi:10.1007/978-3-540-28628-8_27

10. Boneh, D., Boyen, X., Goh, E.-J.: Hierarchical identity based encryption with constant size ciphertext. In: Cramer, R. (ed.) EUROCRYPT 2005. LNCS, vol. 3494, pp. 440–456. Springer, Heidelberg (2005). doi:10.1007/11426639_26
11. Boneh, D., Franklin, M.: Identity-based encryption from the weil pairing. In: Kilian, J. (ed.) CRYPTO 2001. LNCS, vol. 2139, pp. 213–229. Springer, Heidelberg (2001). doi:10.1007/3-540-44647-8_13
12. Boneh, D., Gentry, C., Hamburg, M.: Space-efficient identity based encryption without pairings. In: 48th FOCS, pp. 647–657. IEEE Computer Society Press, Providence, 20–23 October 2007
13. Boneh, D., Papakonstantinou, P.A., Rackoff, C., Vahlis, Y., Waters, B.: On the impossibility of basing identity based encryption on trapdoor permutations. In: 49th FOCS, pp. 283–292. IEEE Computer Society Press, Philadelphia, 25–28 October 2008
14. Boyle, E., Chung, K.-M., Pass, R.: On extractability obfuscation. In: Lindell, Y. (ed.) TCC 2014. LNCS, vol. 8349, pp. 52–73. Springer, Heidelberg (2014). doi:10.1007/978-3-642-54242-8_3
15. Brassard, G., Chaum, D., Crépeau, C.: Minimum disclosure proofs of knowledge. J. Comput. Syst. Sci. **37**(2), 156–189 (1988)
16. Canetti, R., Halevi, S., Katz, J.: A forward-secure public-key encryption scheme. In: Biham, E. (ed.) EUROCRYPT 2003. LNCS, vol. 2656, pp. 255–271. Springer, Heidelberg (2003). doi:10.1007/3-540-39200-9_16
17. Cash, D., Hofheinz, D., Kiltz, E., Peikert, C.: Bonsai trees, or how to delegate a lattice basis. In: Gilbert, H. (ed.) EUROCRYPT 2010. LNCS, vol. 6110, pp. 523–552. Springer, Heidelberg (2010). doi:10.1007/978-3-642-13190-5_27
18. Cho, C., Döttling, N., Garg, S., Gupta, D., Miao, P., Polychroniadou, A.: Laconic receiver oblivious transfer and its applications. In: CRYPTO (2017, to appear)
19. Cocks, C.: An identity based encryption scheme based on quadratic residues. In: Honary, B. (ed.) Cryptography and Coding 2001. LNCS, vol. 2260, pp. 360–363. Springer, Heidelberg (2001). doi:10.1007/3-540-45325-3_32
20. Diffie, W., Hellman, M.E.: New directions in cryptography. IEEE Trans. Inf. Theory **22**(6), 644–654 (1976)
21. Döttling, N., Garg, S.: From selective IBE to full IBE and selective HIBE. Manuscript (2017)
22. Garg, S., Gentry, C., Sahai, A., Waters, B.: Witness encryption and its applications. In: Boneh, D., Roughgarden, T., Feigenbaum, J. (eds.) 45th ACM STOC, pp. 467–476. ACM Press, Palo Alto, 1–4 June 2013
23. Garg, S., Lu, S., Ostrovsky, R.: Black-box garbled RAM. In: Guruswami, V. (ed.) 56th FOCS, pp. 210–229. IEEE Computer Society Press, Berkeley, 17–20 October 2015
24. Garg, S., Lu, S., Ostrovsky, R., Scafuro, A.: Garbled RAM from one-way functions. In: Servedio, R.A., Rubinfeld, R. (eds.) 47th ACM STOC, pp. 449–458. ACM Press, Portland, 14–17 June 2015
25. Gentry, C., Halevi, S.: Hierarchical identity based encryption with polynomially many levels. In: Reingold, O. (ed.) TCC 2009. LNCS, vol. 5444, pp. 437–456. Springer, Heidelberg (2009). doi:10.1007/978-3-642-00457-5_26
26. Gentry, C., Halevi, S., Lu, S., Ostrovsky, R., Raykova, M., Wichs, D.: Garbled RAM revisited. In: Nguyen, P.Q., Oswald, E. (eds.) EUROCRYPT 2014. LNCS, vol. 8441, pp. 405–422. Springer, Heidelberg (2014). doi:10.1007/978-3-642-55220-5_23
27. Gentry, C., Peikert, C., Vaikuntanathan, V.: Trapdoors for hard lattices and new cryptographic constructions. In: Ladner, R.E., Dwork, C. (eds.) 40th ACM STOC, pp. 197–206. ACM Press, Victoria, 17–20 May 2008

28. Gentry, C., Silverberg, A.: Hierarchical ID-based cryptography. In: Zheng, Y. (ed.) ASIACRYPT 2002. LNCS, vol. 2501, pp. 548–566. Springer, Heidelberg (2002). doi:10.1007/3-540-36178-2_34
29. Goldreich, O., Goldwasser, S., Micali, S.: How to construct random functions (extended abstract). In: 25th FOCS, pp. 464–479. IEEE Computer Society Press, Singer Island, 24–26 October 1984
30. Goldreich, O., Levin, L.A.: A hard-core predicate for all one-way functions. In: 21st ACM STOC, pp. 25–32. ACM Press, Seattle, 15–17 May 1989
31. Hofheinz, D., Kiltz, E.: The group of signed quadratic residues and applications. In: Halevi, S. (ed.) CRYPTO 2009. LNCS, vol. 5677, pp. 637–653. Springer, Heidelberg (2009). doi:10.1007/978-3-642-03356-8_37
32. Horwitz, J., Lynn, B.: Toward hierarchical identity-based encryption. In: Knudsen, L.R. (ed.) EUROCRYPT 2002. LNCS, vol. 2332, pp. 466–481. Springer, Heidelberg (2002). doi:10.1007/3-540-46035-7_31
33. Koblitz, N.: Elliptic curve cryptosystems. Math. Comput. **48**(177), 203–209 (1987)
34. Krawczyk, H., Rabin, T.: Chameleon hashing and signatures. Cryptology ePrint Archive, Report 1998/010 (1998). http://eprint.iacr.org/1998/010
35. Lewko, A., Waters, B.: New techniques for dual system encryption and fully secure HIBE with short ciphertexts. In: Micciancio, D. (ed.) TCC 2010. LNCS, vol. 5978, pp. 455–479. Springer, Heidelberg (2010). doi:10.1007/978-3-642-11799-2_27
36. Lindell, Y., Pinkas, B.: A proof of security of Yao's protocol for two-party computation. J. Cryptol. **22**(2), 161–188 (2009)
37. Lu, S., Ostrovsky, R.: How to garble RAM programs? In: Johansson, T., Nguyen, P.Q. (eds.) EUROCRYPT 2013. LNCS, vol. 7881, pp. 719–734. Springer, Heidelberg (2013). doi:10.1007/978-3-642-38348-9_42
38. McCurley, K.S.: A key distribution system equivalent to factoring. J. Cryptol. **1**(2), 95–105 (1988)
39. Miller, V.S.: Use of elliptic curves in cryptography. In: Williams, H.C. (ed.) CRYPTO 1985. LNCS, vol. 218, pp. 417–426. Springer, Heidelberg (1986). doi:10.1007/3-540-39799-X_31
40. Naor, M., Yung, M.: Universal one-way hash functions and their cryptographic applications. In: 21st ACM STOC, pp. 33–43. ACM Press, Seattle, 15–17 May 1989
41. Okamoto, T., Takashima, K.: Fully secure functional encryption with general relations from the decisional linear assumption. In: Rabin, T. (ed.) CRYPTO 2010. LNCS, vol. 6223, pp. 191–208. Springer, Heidelberg (2010). doi:10.1007/978-3-642-14623-7_11
42. Papakonstantinou, P.A., Rackoff, C.W., Vahlis, Y.: How powerful are the DDH hard groups? Cryptology ePrint Archive, Report 2012/653 (2012). http://eprint.iacr.org/2012/653
43. Rivest, R.L., Shamir, A., Adleman, L.M.: A method for obtaining digital signature and public-key cryptosystems. Commun. Assoc. Comput. Mach. **21**(2), 120–126 (1978)
44. Shamir, A.: Identity-based cryptosystems and signature schemes. In: Blakley, G.R., Chaum, D. (eds.) CRYPTO 1984. LNCS, vol. 196, pp. 47–53. Springer, Heidelberg (1985). doi:10.1007/3-540-39568-7_5
45. Shi, E., Waters, B.: Delegating capabilities in predicate encryption systems. In: Aceto, L., Damgård, I., Goldberg, L.A., Halldórsson, M.M., Ingólfsdóttir, A., Walukiewicz, I. (eds.) ICALP 2008. LNCS, vol. 5126, pp. 560–578. Springer, Heidelberg (2008). doi:10.1007/978-3-540-70583-3_46

46. Shmuely, Z.: Composite Diffie-hellman public-key generating systems are hard to break. Technical report no. 356, Computer Science Department, Technion, Israel (1985)
47. Waters, B.: Dual system encryption: realizing fully secure IBE and HIBE under simple assumptions. In: Halevi, S. (ed.) CRYPTO 2009. LNCS, vol. 5677, pp. 619–636. Springer, Heidelberg (2009). doi:10.1007/978-3-642-03356-8_36
48. Waters, B.: Efficient identity-based encryption without random oracles. In: Cramer, R. (ed.) EUROCRYPT 2005. LNCS, vol. 3494, pp. 114–127. Springer, Heidelberg (2005). doi:10.1007/11426639_7
49. Yao, A.C.-C.: Protocols for secure computations (extended abstract). In: 23rd FOCS, pp. 160–164. IEEE Computer Society Press, Chicago, 3–5 November 1982

The First Collision for Full SHA-1

Marc Stevens[1](✉), Elie Bursztein[2], Pierre Karpman[1], Ange Albertini[2], and Yarik Markov[2]

[1] CWI Amsterdam, Amsterdam, The Netherlands
info@shattered.io
[2] Google Research, Mountain View, USA
https://shattered.io

Abstract. SHA-1 is a widely used 1995 NIST cryptographic hash function standard that was officially deprecated by NIST in 2011 due to fundamental security weaknesses demonstrated in various analyses and theoretical attacks.

Despite its deprecation, SHA-1 remains widely used in 2017 for document and TLS certificate signatures, and also in many software such as the GIT versioning system for integrity and backup purposes.

A key reason behind the reluctance of many industry players to replace SHA-1 with a safer alternative is the fact that finding an actual collision has seemed to be impractical for the past eleven years due to the high complexity and computational cost of the attack.

In this paper, we demonstrate that SHA-1 collision attacks have finally become practical by providing the first known instance of a collision. Furthermore, the prefix of the colliding messages was carefully chosen so that they allow an attacker to forge two distinct PDF documents with the same SHA-1 hash that display different arbitrarily-chosen visual contents.

We were able to find this collision by combining many special cryptanalytic techniques in complex ways and improving upon previous work. In total the computational effort spent is equivalent to $2^{63.1}$ calls to SHA-1's compression function, and took approximately 6 500 CPU years and 100 GPU years. While the computational power spent on this collision is larger than other public cryptanalytic computations, it is still more than 100 000 times faster than a brute force search.

Keywords: Hash function · Cryptanalysis · Collision attack · Collision example · Differential path construction

1 Introduction

A cryptographic hash function $\mathrm{H} : \{0,1\}^* \rightarrow \{0,1\}^n$ is a function that computes for any arbitrarily long message M a fixed-length hash value of n bits. It is a versatile cryptographic primitive used in many applications including digital signature schemes, message authentication codes, password hashing and content-addressable storage. The security or even the proper functioning of many of these

J. Katz and H. Shacham (Eds.): CRYPTO 2017, Part I, LNCS 10401, pp. 570–596, 2017.
DOI: 10.1007/978-3-319-63688-7_19

applications rely on the assumption that it is practically impossible to *find* collisions, *i.e.* two distinct messages x, y that hash to the same value $\mathrm{H}(x) = \mathrm{H}(y)$. When the hash function behaves in a "sufficiently random" way, the expected number of calls to H (or in practice its underlying fixed-size function) to find a collision using an optimal generic algorithm is $\sqrt{\pi/2} \cdot 2^{n/2}$ (see *e.g.* [33, Appndix A]); an algorithm that is faster at finding collisions for H is then a collision attack for this function.

A major family of hash function is "MD-SHA", which includes MD5, SHA-1 and SHA-2 that all have found widespread use. This family originally started with MD4 [36] in 1990, which was quickly replaced by MD5 [37] in 1992 due to serious attacks [9,11]. Despite early known weaknesses of its underlying compression function [10], MD5 was widely deployed by the software industry for over a decade. The MD5CRK project that attempted to find a collision for MD5 by brute force was halted early in 2004, when Wang and Yu produced explicit collisions [49], found by a groundbreaking attack that pioneered new techniques. In a major development, Stevens *et al.* [45] later showed that a more powerful type of attack (the so-called *chosen-prefix collision attack*) could be performed against MD5. This eventually led to the forgery of a Rogue Certification Authority that in principle completely undermined HTTPS security [46] in 2008. Despite this, even in 2017 there are still issues in deprecating MD5 for signatures [18].

Currently, the industry is facing a similar challenge in the deprecation of SHA-1, a 1995 NIST standard [31]. It is one of the main hash functions of today, and it also has been facing important attacks since 2005. Based on previous successful cryptanalysis [3–5] of SHA-0 [30] (SHA-1's predecessor, that only differs by a single rotation in the message expansion function), Wang *et al.* [48] presented in 2005 the very first collision attack on SHA-1 that is faster than brute-force. This attack, while groundbreaking, was purely theoretical as its expected cost of 2^{69} calls to SHA-1's compression function was practically out-of-reach.

Therefore, as a proof of concept, many teams worked on generating collisions for reduced versions of the function: 64 steps [8] (with a cost of 2^{35} SHA-1 calls), 70 steps [7] (cost 2^{44} SHA-1), 73 steps [15] (cost $2^{50.7}$ SHA-1) and finally 75 steps [16] (cost $2^{57.7}$ SHA-1) using extensive GPU computation power.

In 2013, building on these advances and a novel rigorous framework for analyzing SHA-1, the current best collision attack on full SHA-1 was presented by Stevens [43] with an estimated cost of 2^{61} calls to the SHA-1 compression function. Nevertheless, a publicly known collision still remained out of reach. This was also highlighted by Schneier [38] in 2012, when he estimated the cost of a SHA-1 collision attack to be around US$ 700K in 2015, down to about US$ 173K in 2018 (using calculations by Walker based on a 2^{61} attack cost [43], Amazon EC2 spot prices and Moore's Law), which he deemed to be within the resources of criminals.

More recently, a collision for the full compression function underlying SHA-1 was obtained by Stevens *et al.* [44] using a start-from-the-middle approach and a highly efficient GPU framework (first used to mount a similar freestart attack on the function reduced to 76 steps [21]). This required only a reasonable amount of GPU computation power, about 10 days using 64 GPUs, equivalent to approximately $2^{57.5}$ calls to SHA-1 on GPU. Based on this attack, the authors projected that a collision attack on SHA-1 may cost between US$ 75K and US$ 120K by renting GPU computing time on Amazon EC2 [39] using spot-instances, which is significantly lower than Schneier's 2012 estimates. These new projections had almost immediate effect when CABForum Ballot 152 to extend issuance of SHA-1 based HTTPS certificates was withdrawn [13], and SHA-1 was deprecated for digital signatures in the IETF's TLS protocol specification version 1.3.

Unfortunately CABForum restrictions on the use of SHA-1 only apply to actively enrolled Certification Authority certificates and not on any other certificates, *e.g.* retracted CA certificates that are still supported by older systems (and CA certificates have indeed been retracted for continued use of SHA-1 certificates to serve to these older systems unchecked by CABForum regulations[1]), and certificates for other TLS applications including up to 10% of credit card payment systems [29,47]. It thus remains in widespread use across the software industry for, *e.g.*, digital signatures of software, documents, and many other applications, most notably in the GIT versioning system.

It is well worth noting that academic researchers have not been the only ones to compute (and exploit) hash function collisions. Nation-state actors [24, 25,34] have been linked to the highly advanced espionage malware "Flame" that was found targeting the Middle-East in May 2012. As it turned out, it used a forged signature to infect Windows machines via a man-in-the-middle attack on *Windows Update*. Using a new technique of *counter-cryptanalysis* that is able to expose cryptanalytic collision attacks given only one message from a colliding message pair, it was proven that the forged signature was made possible by a *then secret* chosen-prefix attack on MD5 [12,42].

2 Our Contributions

We are the first to exhibit an example collision for SHA-1, presented in Table 1, thereby proving that theoretical attacks on SHA-1 have now become practical. Our work builds upon the best known theoretical collision attack [43] with estimated cost of 2^{61} SHA-1 calls. This is an *identical-prefix collision attack*, where a given prefix P is extended with two distinct *near-collision block pairs* such that they collide for any suffix S:

$$\text{SHA-1}\left(P||M_1^{(1)}||M_2^{(1)}||S\right) = \text{SHA-1}\left(P||M_1^{(2)}||M_2^{(2)}||S\right). \tag{1}$$

The computational effort spent on our attack is estimated to be equivalent to $2^{63.1}$ SHA-1 calls (see Sect. 6). There is certainly a gap between the theoretical attack as presented in [43] and our executed practical attack that was based

[1] For instance, SHA-1 certificates are still being sold by CloudFlare at the time of writing: https://www.cloudflare.com/ssl/dedicated-certificates/.

Table 1. Colliding message blocks for SHA-1.

CV_0	4e a9 62 69 7c 87 6e 26 74 d1 07 f0 fe c6 79 84 14 f5 bf 45
$M_1^{(1)}$	7f 46 dc 93 a6 b6 7e 01 3b 02 9a aa 1d b2 56 0b
	45 ca 67 d6 88 c7 f8 4b 8c 4c 79 1f e0 2b 3d f6
	14 f8 6d b1 69 09 01 c5 6b 45 c1 53 0a fe df b7
	60 38 e9 72 72 2f e7 ad 72 8f 0e 49 04 e0 46 c2
$CV_1^{(1)}$	8d 64 d6 17 ff ed 53 52 eb c8 59 15 5e c7 eb 34 f3 8a 5a 7b
$M_2^{(1)}$	30 57 0f e9 d4 13 98 ab e1 2e f5 bc 94 2b e3 35
	42 a4 80 2d 98 b5 d7 0f 2a 33 2e c3 7f ac 35 14
	e7 4d dc 0f 2c c1 a8 74 cd 0c 78 30 5a 21 56 64
	61 30 97 89 60 6b d0 bf 3f 98 cd a8 04 46 29 a1
CV_2	1e ac b2 5e d5 97 0d 10 f1 73 69 63 57 71 bc 3a 17 b4 8a c5

CV_0	4e a9 62 69 7c 87 6e 26 74 d1 07 f0 fe c6 79 84 14 f5 bf 45
$M_1^{(2)}$	73 46 dc 91 66 b6 7e 11 8f 02 9a b6 21 b2 56 0f
	f9 ca 67 cc a8 c7 f8 5b a8 4c 79 03 0c 2b 3d e2
	18 f8 6d b3 a9 09 01 d5 df 45 c1 4f 26 fe df b3
	dc 38 e9 6a c2 2f e7 bd 72 8f 0e 45 bc e0 46 d2
$CV_1^{(2)}$	8d 64 c8 21 ff ed 52 e2 eb c8 59 15 5e c7 eb 36 73 8a 5a 7b
$M_2^{(2)}$	3c 57 0f eb 14 13 98 bb 55 2e f5 a0 a8 2b e3 31
	fe a4 80 37 b8 b5 d7 1f 0e 33 2e df 93 ac 35 00
	eb 4d dc 0d ec c1 a8 64 79 0c 78 2c 76 21 56 60
	dd 30 97 91 d0 6b d0 af 3f 98 cd a4 bc 46 29 b1
CV_2	1e ac b2 5e d5 97 0d 10 f1 73 69 63 57 71 bc 3a 17 b4 8a c5

on it. Indeed, the theoretical attack's estimated complexity does not include the inherent relative loss in efficiency when using GPUs, nor the inefficiency we encountered in actually launching a large scale computation distributed over several data centers. Moreover, the construction of the second part of the attack was significantly more complicated than could be expected from the literature.

To find the first near-collision block pair $(M_1^{(1)}, M_1^{(2)})$ we employed the open-source code from [43], which was modified to work with our prefix P given in Table 2, and for large scale distribution over several data centers. To find the second near-collision block pair $(M_2^{(1)}, M_2^{(2)})$ that leads to the collision was more challenging, as the attack cost is known to be significantly higher, but also because of additional obstacles.

In Sect. 5 we will discuss in particular the process of building the second near-collision attack. Essentially we followed the same steps as was done for the first near-collision attack [43], combining many existing cryptanalytic techniques. Yet we further employed the SHA-1 collision search GPU framework from Karpman *et al.* [21] to achieve a significantly more cost efficient attack.

We also describe two new additional techniques used in the construction of the second near-collision attack. The first allowed us to use additional differential

Table 2. Identical prefix of our collision.

25 50 44 46 2d 31 2e 33 0a 25 e2 e3 cf d3 0a 0a	%PDF-1.3.%......
0a 31 20 30 20 6f 62 6a 0a 3c 3c 2f 57 69 64 74	.1 0 obj.<</Widt
68 20 32 20 30 20 52 2f 48 65 69 67 68 74 20 33	h 2 0 R/Height 3
20 30 20 52 2f 54 79 70 65 20 34 20 30 20 52 2f	0 R/Type 4 0 R/
53 75 62 74 79 70 65 20 35 20 30 20 52 2f 46 69	Subtype 5 0 R/Fi
6c 74 65 72 20 36 20 30 20 52 2f 43 6f 6c 6f 72	lter 6 0 R/Color
53 70 61 63 65 20 37 20 30 20 52 2f 4c 65 6e 67	Space 7 0 R/Leng
74 68 20 38 20 30 20 52 2f 42 69 74 73 50 65 72	th 8 0 R/BitsPer
43 6f 6d 70 6f 6e 65 6e 74 20 38 3e 3e 0a 73 74	Component 8>>.st
72 65 61 6d 0a ff d8 ff fe 00 24 53 48 41 2d 31	ream......$SHA-1
20 69 73 20 64 65 61 64 21 21 21 21 21 85 2f ec	is dead!!!!!./.
09 23 39 75 9c 39 b1 a1 c6 3c 4c 97 e1 ff fe 01	.#9u.9...<L.....

paths around step 23 for increased success probability and more degrees of freedom without compromising the use of an early-stop technique. The second was necessary to overcome a serious problem of an unsolvable strongly over-defined system of equations over the first few steps of SHA-1's compression function that threatened the feasibility of finishing this project.

As can be deduced from Eq. 1, our example colliding files only differ in two successive random-looking message blocks generated by our attack. We exploit these limited differences to craft two colliding PDF documents containing arbitrary distinct images. Examples can be downloaded from https://shattered.io. PDFs with the same MD5 hash have previously been constructed by Gebhardt *et al.* [14] by exploiting so-called Indexed Color Tables and Color Transformation functions. However, this method is not effective for many common PDF viewers that lack support for these functionalities. Our PDFs rely on distinct parsings of JPEG images, similar to Gebhardt *et al.*'s TIFF technique [14] and Albertini *et al.*'s JPEG technique [1]. Yet we improved upon these basic techniques using very low-level "wizard" JPEG features such that these work in all common PDF viewers, and even allow very large JPEGs that can be used to craft multi-page PDFs. This overall approach and the technical details will be described in a separate article [2].

The remainder of this paper is organized as follows. We first give a brief description of SHA-1 in Sect. 3. Then, we give a high-level overview of our attack in Sect. 4, followed by Sect. 5 that details the entire process and the cryptanalytic techniques employed, where we also highlight improvements with respect to previous work. Finally, we discuss the large-scale distributed computations required to find the two near-collision block pairs in Sect. 6. The parameters used to find the second colliding block are given in the appendix, in Sect. A.

3 The SHA-1 Hash Function

We provide a brief description of SHA-1 as defined by NIST [31]. SHA-1 takes an arbitrary-length message and computes a 160-bit hash. It divides the (padded) input message into k blocks $M_1, \ldots, M_k$ of 512 bits. The 160-bit internal state CV_j of SHA-1, called the chaining value, is initialized to a predefined initial value $CV_0 = IV$. Each message block is then fed to a compression function h that updates the chaining value, *i.e.* $CV_{j+1} = h(CV_j, M_{j+1})$, for $0 \leq j < k$, where the final CV_k is output as the hash.

The compression function h takes a 160-bit chaining value CV_j and a 512-bit message block M_{j+1} as inputs, and outputs a new 160-bit chaining value CV_{j+1}. It mixes the message block into the chaining value as follows, operating on *words*, simultaneously seen as 32-bit strings and as elements of $\mathbb{Z}/2^{32}\mathbb{Z}$: the input chaining value is parsed as five words a, b, c, d, e, and the message block as 16 words $m_0, \ldots, m_{15}$. The latter are expanded into 80 words using the following recursive linear equation:

$$m_i = (m_{i-3} \oplus m_{i-8} \oplus m_{i-14} \oplus m_{i-16})^{\circlearrowleft 1}, \quad \text{for } 16 \leq i < 80.$$

Starting from $(A_{-4}, A_{-3}, A_{-2}, A_{-1}, A_0) := (e^{\circlearrowright 2}, d^{\circlearrowright 2}, c^{\circlearrowright 2}, b, a)$, each m_i is mixed into an intermediate state over 80 steps $i = 0, \ldots, 79$:

$$A_{i+1} = A_i^{\circlearrowleft 5} + \varphi_i(A_{i-1}, A_{i-2}^{\circlearrowleft 2}, A_{i-3}^{\circlearrowleft 2}) + A_{i-4}^{\circlearrowleft 2} + K_i + m_i,$$

where φ_i and K_i are predefined Boolean functions and constants:

Step i	$\varphi_i(x, y, z)$	K_i
$0 \leq i < 20$	$\varphi_{\text{IF}} = (x \wedge y) \vee (\neg x \wedge z)$	`0x5a827999`
$20 \leq i < 40$	$\varphi_{\text{XOR}} = x \oplus y \oplus z$	`0x6ed9eba1`
$40 \leq i < 60$	$\varphi_{\text{MAJ}} = (x \wedge y) \vee (x \wedge z) \vee (y \wedge z)$	`0x8f1bbcdc`
$60 \leq i < 80$	$\varphi_{\text{XOR}} = x \oplus y \oplus z$	`0xca62c1d6`

After the 80 steps, the new chaining value is computed as the sum of the input chaining value and the final intermediate state:

$$CV_{j+1} = (a + A_{80}, b + A_{79}, c + A_{78}^{\circlearrowleft 2}, d + A_{77}^{\circlearrowleft 2}, e + A_{76}^{\circlearrowleft 2}).$$

4 Overview of our SHA-1 Collision Attack

We illustrate our attack from a high level in Fig. 1. Starting from identical chaining values for two messages, we use two pairs of blocks. The differences in the first block pair cause a small difference in the output chaining value, which is canceled by the difference in the second block pair, leading again to identical chaining values and hence a collision (indicated by (2)). We employ *differential paths* that are a precise description of differences in state words and message words and of how these differences should propagate through the 80 steps.

Note that although the first five state words are fixed by the chaining value, one can freely modify message words and thus directly influence the next sixteen

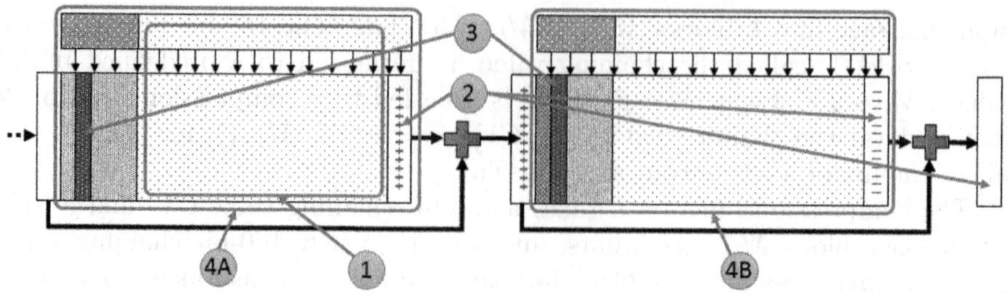

Fig. 1. Attack overview

state words. Moreover, with additional effort this can be extended to obtain limited influence over another eight state words. However, control over the remaining state words (indicated by (1)) is very hard and thus requires very sparse target differences that correctly propagate with probability as high as possible. Furthermore, these need to be compatible with differences in the expanded message words. The key solution is the concept of *local collisions* [5], where any state bit-difference introduced by a perturbation message bit-difference is to be canceled in the next five steps using correction message bit-differences.

To ensure all message word bit differences are compatible with the linear message expansion, one uses a *disturbance vector* (DV) [5] that is a correctly expanded message itself, but where every "1" bit marks the start of a local collision. The selection of a good disturbance vector has a very high impact on the overall attack cost. As previously shown by Wang *et al.* [48], the main reason of using two block pairs (*i.e.* to search for a near-collision over a first message block, that is completed to a full collision over a second) instead of only one is that this choice alleviates an important restriction on the disturbance vector, namely that there are no state differences after the last step. Similarly, it may be impossible to unite the input chaining value difference with the local collisions for an arbitrary disturbance vector. This was solved by Wang *et al.* [48] by crafting a tailored differential path (called the non-linear (NL) path, indicated by (3)) that over the first 16 steps connects the input chaining value differences to the local collision differences over the remaining steps (called the linear path, referring to the linear message expansion dictating the local collision positions).

One has to choose a good disturbance vector, then craft a non-linear differential path for each of the two near-collision attacks (over the first and second message blocks), determine a system of equations over all steps and finally find a solution in the form of a message block pair (as indicated by (4A) and (4B)). Note that one can only craft the non-linear path for the second near-collision attack once the chaining values resulting from the first block pair are known. This entire process including our improvements is described below.

5 Near-Collision Attack Procedure

This section describes the overall procedure of each of the two near-collision attacks. Since we relied on our modification of Stevens' public source-code [17,43]

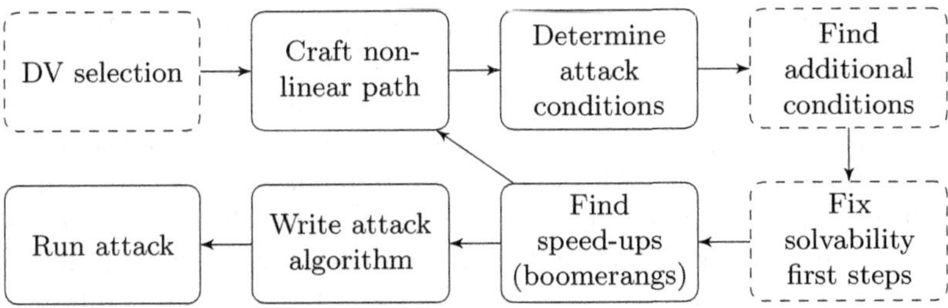

Fig. 2. The main steps for each near-collision attack.

for the first near-collision attack, we focus on our extended procedure for our second near-collision attack. As shown in Fig. 2, this involves the following steps that are further detailed below:

1. selection of the disturbance vector (same for both attacks);
2. construction of the non-linear differential path;
3. determine attack conditions over all steps;
4. find additional conditions beyond the fixed differential path for early-stop;
5. if necessary fix solvability of attack conditions over the first few steps;
6. find message modification rules to speed-up collision search;
7. write the attack algorithm;
8. finally, run the attack to find a near-collision block pair.

5.1 Disturbance Vector Selection

The selection of which disturbance vector to use is a major choice, as it directly determines many aspects of the collision attack. These include the message XOR differences, but also in theory the optimal attack choices over the linear path, including the optimal set of candidate endings for the non-linear path together with optimal linear message-bit equations that maximize the success probability over the linear part.

Historically several approaches have been used to analyze a disturbance vector to estimate attack costs over the linear part. Initially, the Hamming weight of the DV that counts the active number of local collisions was used (see *e.g.* [4,35]). For the first theoretical attack on SHA-1 with cost 2^{69} SHA-1-calls by Wang *et al.* [48] a more refined measure was used, that counts the number of bit-conditions on the state and message bits that ensure that the differential path would be followed. This was later refined by Yajima *et al.* [51] to a more precise count by exploiting all possible so-called bit compressions and interactions through the Boolean functions. However, this approach does not allow any difference in the carry propagation, which otherwise could result in alternate differential paths that may improve the overall success probability. Therefore, Mendel *et al.* [28] proposed to use the more accurate probability of single local collisions where carry propagations are allowed, in combination with known local collision interaction corrections.

The current state-of-the-art is joint-local-collision analysis (JLCA) introduced by Stevens [41,43] which given sets of allowed differences for each state word A_i and message word m_i (given by the disturbance vector) computes the exact optimal success probability over the specified steps by exhaustively evaluating all differential paths with those allowed differences. This approach is very powerful as it also provides important information for the next steps, namely the set of optimal chaining value differences (by considering arbitrary high probability differences for the last five A_is) and the set of optimal endings for the non-linear path, together with a corresponding set of message-bit equations, using which the optimal highest success probability of the specified steps can actually be achieved. The best theoretical collision attack on SHA-1 with cost 2^{61} SHA-1 calls [43] was built using this analysis. As we build upon this collision attack, we use the same disturbance vector, named II(52, 0) by Manuel [26] and originally described by Jutla and Patthak [20].

5.2 Construction of a Non-linear Differential Path

Once the disturbance vector and the corresponding linear part of the differential path have been fixed, the next step consists in finding a suitable non-linear path connecting the chaining value pair (with fixed differences) to the linear part. This step needs to be done separately for each near-collision attack of the full collision attack[2].

As explained for instance in [43], in the case of the first near-collision attack, the attacker has the advantage of two additional freedoms. Firstly, an arbitrary prefix can be included before the start of the attack to pre-fulfill a limited number of conditions on the chaining value. This allows greater freedom in constructing the non-linear path as this does not have to be restricted to a specific value of the chaining value pair, whereas the non-linear path for the second near-collision attack has to start from the specific given value of input chaining value pair. Secondly, it can use the entire set of output chaining value differences with the same highest probability. The first near-collision attack is not limited to a particular value and succeeds when it finds a chaining value difference in this set, whereas the second near-collision attack has to cancel the specific difference in the resulting chaining value pair. Theory predicts the first near-collision attack to be at least a factor six faster than the second attack [43]. For our collision attack it is indeed the second near-collision attack that dominates the overall attack complexity.

Historically, the first non-linear paths for SHA-1 were hand-crafted by Wang *et al.* Several algorithms were subsequently developed to automatically search for non-linear paths for MD5, SHA-1, and other functions of the MD-SHA family. The first automatic search for SHA-1 by De Cannière and Rechberger [8] was based on a guess-and-determine approach. This approach tracks the allowed

[2] We eventually produced two message block pair solutions for the first near-collision attack. This provided a small additional amount of freedom in the search for the non-linear path of the second block.

values of each bit pair in the two related compression function computations. It starts with no constraints on the values of these bit pairs other than the chaining value pair and the linear part differences. It then repeatedly restricts values on a selected bit pair and then propagates this information via the step function and linear message expansion relation, *i.e.*, it determines and eliminates previously-allowed values for other bit pairs that are now impossible due the added restriction. Whenever a contradiction occurs, the algorithm backtracks and chooses a different restriction on the last selected bit pair.

Another algorithm for SHA-1 was introduced by Yajima *et al.* [52] that is based on a meet-in-the-middle approach. It starts from two fully-specified differential paths; the first is obtained from a forward expansion of the input chaining value pair, whereas the other is obtained from a backward expansion of the linear path. It then tries to connect these two differential paths over the remaining five steps in the middle by recursively iterating over all solutions over a particular step.

A similar meet-in-the-middle algorithm was independently first developed for MD5 and then adapted to SHA-1 by Stevens *et al.* [17,41,45], which operates on bit-slices and is more efficient. The open-source HashClash project [17] seems to be the only publicly available non-linear path construction implementation, which we improved as follows. Originally, it expanded a large set of differential paths step by step, keeping only the best N paths after each step, for some user-specified number N. However, there might be several good differential paths that result in the same differences and conditions around the connecting five steps, where either none or all lead to fully-connected differential paths. Since we only need the best fully-connected differential path we can find, we only need to keep a best differential path from each subset of paths with the same differences and conditions over the last five steps that were extended. So to remove this redundancy, for each step we extend and keep, say, the $4N$ best paths, then we remove all such superfluous paths, and finally keep at most N paths. This improvement led to a small but very welcome reduction in the amount of differential path conditions under the same path construction parameter choices, but also allowed a better positioning of the largest density of sufficient conditions for the differential path.

Construction of a very good non-linear path for the second near-collision attack using our improved HashClash version took a small effort with our improvements, yet even allowed us to restrict the section with high density of conditions to just the first six steps. However, to find a very good non-linear differential path that is also solvable turned out to be more complicated. Our final solution is described in Sect. 5.5, which in the end did allow us to build our attack on the best non-linear path we found without any compromises. The fixed version of this best non-linear path is presented in Fig. 3, Sect. A.

5.3 Determine Attack Conditions

Having selected the disturbance vector and constructed a non-linear path that bridges into the linear part, the next step is to determine the entire system of equations for the attack. This system of equations is expressed entirely over the computation of message $M^{(1)}$, and not over $M^{(2)}$, and consists of two types of equations:

1. Linear equations over message bits. These are used to control the additive signs of the message word XOR differences implied by the disturbance vector. Since there are many different "signings" over the linear part with the same highest probability, instead of one specific choice one uses a linear hull that captures many choices to reduce the amount of necessary equations.
2. Linear equations over state bits given by a fixed differential path up to some step i (that includes the non-linear path). These control whether there is a difference in a state bit and which sign it has, furthermore they force target differences in the outputs of the Boolean functions φ_i.

We determine this entire system by employing our implementation of joint-local-collision analysis that has been improved as follows. JLCA takes input sets of allowed differences for each A_i and m_i and exhaustively analyzes the set of differential paths with those allowed differences, which originally is only used to analyze the linear part. We additionally provide it with specific differences for A_i and m_i as given by the non-linear path, so we can run JLCA over all 80 steps and have it output an optimal fixed differential path over steps $0, \ldots, 22$ together with an optimal set of linear equations over message bits over the remaining steps. These are optimal results since JLCA guarantees these lead to the highest probability that is possible using the given allowed differences, but furthermore that a largest linear hull is used to minimize the amount of equations.

Note that having a fixed differential path over more steps directly provides more state bit equations which is helpful in the actual collision search because we can apply an early-stop technique. However, this also adds further restrictions on A_i limiting a set of allowed differences to a single specific difference. In our case limiting A_{24} would result, besides a drop in degrees of freedom, in a lower overall probability, thus we only use a fixed differential path up to step 22, *i.e.*, up to A_{23}. Below in Sect. 5.4 we show how we compensated for fewer state equations that the actual collision search uses to early stop.

5.4 Find Additional State Conditions

As explained in Sect. 5.3, the system of equations consists of linear equations over (expanded) message bits and linear equations over state bits. In the actual collision search algorithm, we depend on these state bit equations to stop computation on a bad current solution as early as possible and start backtracking. These state bit equations are directly given by a fixed differential path, where every bit difference in the state and message is fixed. Starting from step 23 we allow several alternate differential paths that increase success probability, but also allow distinct message word differences that lead to a decrease in the overall number of equations. Each alternate differential path depends on its own (distinct) message word differences and leads to its own state bit equations. To find additional equations, we also consider linear equations over state *and* message bits around steps 21–25. Although in theory these could be computed by JLCA by exhaustively reconstructing all alternate differential paths and then determining the desired linear equations, we instead took a much simpler approach. We generated a large amount of random solutions of the system of equations up to step 31 using an unoptimized general collision search algorithm. We then proceeded to exhaustively test potential linear equations over at most four state bits and message bits around steps 21–25, which is quite efficient as on average only two samples needed to be checked for each bad candidate. The additional equations we found and used for the collision search are shown in Table 4, Sect. A.

5.5 Fix Solvability over the First Steps

This step is not required when there are sufficient degrees of freedom in the non-linear part, as was the case in the first-block near-collision attack. As already noted, in the case of the second-block near-collision attack, the non-linear path has to start will a fully-fixed chaining value and has significantly more conditions in the first steps. As a result, the construction of a very good *and* solvable non-linear differential path for the second near-collision attack turned out to be quite complex. Our initially constructed paths unfortunately proved to be unsolvable over the first few steps. We tried several approaches including using the guess-and-determine non-linear path construction to make corrections as done by Karpman *et al.* [21], as well as using worse differential path construction parameters, but all these attempts led to results that not only were unsatisfactory but that even threatened the feasibility of the second near-collision attack. Specifically, both approaches led to differential paths with a significantly increased number of conditions, bringing the total number of degrees of freedom critically low. Moreover, the additional conditions easily conflicted with candidate speed-up measures named "boomerangs" necessary to bring the attack's complexity down to a feasible level. Our final solution was to encode this problem into a satisfiability (SAT) problem and use a SAT solver to find a drop-in replacement differential path over the first eight steps that is solvable.

More specifically, we adapted the SHA-1 SAT system generator from Nossum[3] [32] (initially used to compute reduced-round practical preimages) to generate two independent 8-step compression function computations, which we then linked by adding constraints that set the given input chaining value pair, the message XOR differences over $m_0, \ldots, m_7$, the path differences of $A_4, \ldots, A_8$ and the path conditions of $A_5, \ldots, A_8$. In effect, we allowed complete freedom over A_1, A_2, A_3 and some freedom over A_4. All solutions were exhaustively generated by MiniSAT[4] and then converted into drop-in replacement paths, from which we kept the one with fewest conditions.

This allowed us to build our attack on the best non-linear path we found without any compromises and the corrected non-linear path is presented in Fig. 3,

[3] https://github.com/vegard/sha1-sat.

[4] http://minisat.se/.

Sect. A. Note that indeed the system of equations is over-defined: over the first five steps, there are only 15 state bits without an equation, while at the same time there are 23 message equations.

5.6 Find Message Modifications to Speed-Up Collision Search

To speed-up the collision search significantly, it is important to employ message modification rules, that make small changes in the current message block that do not affect any bit involved with the state and message-bit equations up to some step n (with sufficiently high probability). This effectively allows such a message modification rule to be applied to one solution up to step n to generate several solutions up to the same step with almost no additional cost, thereby significantly reducing the average cost to generate solutions up to step n.

The first such speed-up technique that was developed in attacks of the MD-SHA family was called *neutral bits*, introduced by Biham and Chen to improve attacks on SHA-0 [3]. A message bit is *neutral* up to a step n if flipping this bit causes changes that do not interact with differential path conditions up to step n with high probability. As the diffusion of SHA-0/SHA-1's step function is rather slow, it is not hard to find many bits that are neutral for a few steps.

A nice improvement of the original neutral bits technique was ultimately described by Joux and Peyrin as "boomerangs" [19]. It consists in carefully selecting a few bits that are all flipped together in such a way that this effectively flips, say, only one state bit in the first 16 steps, and such that the diffusion of uncontrollable changes is significantly delayed. This idea can be instantiated efficiently by flipping together bits that form a local collision for the step function. This local collision will eventually introduce uncontrollable differences through the message expansion; however, these do not appear immediately, and if all conditions for the local collision to be successful are verified, the first few steps after the introduction of its initial perturbation will be free of any difference. Joux and Peyrin then noted that sufficient conditions for the local collision can be pre-satisfied when creating the initial partial solution, effectively leading to probability-one local collisions. This leads to a few powerful message modification rules that are neutral up to very late steps.

A closely-related variant of boomerangs is named *advanced message modification* by Wang *et al.* in their attack of the MD-SHA family (see *e.g.* [48]). While the objective of this technique is also to exploit the available freedom in the message, it applies this in a distinct way by identifying ways of interacting with an isolated differential path condition with high probability. Then, if an initial message pair fails to verify a condition for which a message modification exists, the bits of the latter are flipped, so that the resulting message pair now verifies the condition with high probability.

In our attack, we used both neutral bits and boomerangs as message modification rules. This choice was particularly motivated by the ability to efficiently implement these speed-up techniques on GPUs, used to compute the second block of the collision, similar to [21,44].

Our search process for finding the neutral bits follows the one described in [44]. Potential boomerangs are selected first, one being eligible if its initial perturbation does not interact with differential path conditions and if the corrections of the local collision do not break some linear message-bit-relation (this would typically happen if an odd number of bits to be flipped are part of such a relation). The probability with which a boomerang eventually interacts with path conditions is then evaluated experimentally by activating it on about 4 000 independent partial solutions; the probability threshold used to determine up to which step a boomerang can be used is set to 0.9, meaning that it can be used to generate an additional partial solution at step n from an existing one if it does not interact with path conditions up to step n with probability more than 0.1. Once boomerangs have been selected, the sufficient conditions necessary to ensure that their corresponding local collisions occur with probability 1 are added to the differential path, and all remaining free message bits are tested for neutrality using the same process (*i.e.*, a bit is only eligible if flipping it does not trivially violate path conditions or make it impossible to later satisfy message-bit-relations, and its quality is evaluated experimentally).

The list of neutral bits and boomerangs used for the second block of the attack is given in Sect. A. There are 51 neutral bits, located on message words m_{11} to m_{15}, and three boomerangs each made of a single local collision started on m_6 (for two of them) or m_9.

5.7 Attack Implementation

A final step in the design of the attack is to implement it. This is needed for obvious reasons if the goal is to find an actual collision as we do here, but it is also a necessary step if one wishes to obtain a precise estimate of the complexity of the attack. Indeed, while the complexity of the probabilistic phase of the attack can be accurately computed using JLCA (or can also be experimentally determined by sampling many mock partial solutions), there is much more uncertainty as to "where" this phase actually starts. In other words, it is hard to exactly predict how effective the speed-up techniques can be without actually implementing them. The only way to determine the real complexity of an attack is then to implement it, measure the rate of production of partial solutions up to a step where there is no difference in the differential path for five consecutive state words, and use JLCA to compute the exact probability of obtaining a (near-) collision over the remaining steps.

The first near-collision block pair of the attack was computed with CPUs, using an adapted version of the HashClash software [17]. As the original code was not suitable to run on a large scale, a significant effort was spent to make it efficient on the hundreds of cores necessary to obtain a near-collision in reasonable time. The more expensive computation of the second block was done on GPUs, based on the framework used by Karpman *et al.* [21], which we briefly describe below.

The main structure used in this framework consists in first generating *base solutions* on CPUs that fix the sixteen free message words, and then to use GPUs to extend these to partial solutions up to a late step, by only exploiting the freedom offered by speed-up techniques (in particular neutral bits and boomerangs). These partial solutions are then sent back to a CPU to check if they result in collisions.

The main technical difficulty of this approach is to make the best use of the power offered by GPUs. Notably, their programming model differs from the one of CPUs in how diverse the computations run on their many available cores can be: on a multicore CPU, every core can be used to run an independent process; however, even if a recent GPU can feature many more cores than a CPU (for instance, the Nvidia GTX 970 used in [21, 44] and the initial implementation of this attack features 1664 cores), they can only be programmed at the granularity of *warps* made of 32 threads, which must then run the same code. Furthermore, divergence in the control flow of threads of a single warp is dealt with by serializing the diverging computations; for instance, if a single thread takes a different branch than the rest of the warp in an *if* statement, all the other threads become idle while it is taking its own branch. This limitation would make a naïve parallel implementation of the usage of neutral bits rather inefficient, and there is instead a strong incentive to minimize control-flow divergence when implementing the attack.

The approach taken by Karpman *et al.* [21] to limit the impact of the inherent divergence in neutral bit usage is to decompose the attack process step by step and to use the fair amount of memory available on recent GPUs to store partial solutions up to many different steps in shared buffers. In a nutshell, all threads of a single warp are asked to load their own partial solution up to a certain state word A_i, and they will together apply all neutral bits available at this step, each time checking if the solution can be validly extended to a solution up to A_{i+1}; if and only if this is the case, this solution is stored in the buffer for partial solutions up to A_{i+1}, and this selective writing operation is the only moment where the control flow of the warps may diverge.

To compute the second block pair of the attack, and hence obtain a full collision, we first generated base solutions consisting of partial solutions up to A_{14} on CPU, and used GPUs to generate additional partial solutions up to A_{26}. These were further probabilistically extended to partial solutions up to A_{53}, still using GPUs, and checking whether they resulted in a collision was finally done on a CPU. The probability of such a partial solution to also lead to a collision can be computed by JLCA to be equal to $2^{-27.8}$, and $2^{-48.7}$ for partial solutions up to A_{33} (these probabilities could in fact both be reduced by a factor $2^{0.6}$; however, the ones indicated here correspond to the attack we carried out). On a GTX 970, a prototype implementation of the attack produced partial solutions up to A_{33} at a rate of approximately 58 100 per second, while the full SHA-1 compression function can be evaluated about $2^{31.8}$ times per second on the same GPU. Thus, our attack has an expected complexity of $2^{64.7}$ on this platform.

Finally, adapting the prototype GPU implementation to a large-scale infrastructure suitable to run such an expensive computation also required a fair amount of work.

6 Computation of the Collision

This section gives some details about the computation of the collision and provides a few comparisons with notable cryptographic computations.

6.1 Units of Complexity

The complexity figures given in this section follow the common practice in the cryptanalysis of symmetric schemes of comparing the efficiency of an attack to the cost of using a generic algorithm achieving the same result. This can be made by comparing the time needed, with the same resources, to *e.g.* compute a collision on a hash function by using a (memoryless) generic collision search *versus* by using a dedicated process. This comparison is usually expressed by dividing the time taken by the attack, *e.g.* in core hours, by the time taken to compute the attacked primitive once on the same platform; the cost of using a generic algorithm is then left implicit. This is for instance how the figure of $2^{64.7}$ from Sect. 5.7 has been derived.

While this approach is reasonable, it is far from being as precise as what a number such as $2^{64.7}$ seems to imply. We discuss below a few of its limitations.

The Impact of Code Optimization. An experimental evaluation of the complexity of an attack is bound to be sensitive to the quality of the implementation, both of the attack itself and of the reference primitive used as a comparison. A hash function such as SHA-1 is easy to implement relatively efficiently, and the difference in performance between a reference and optimized implementation is likely to be small. This may however not be true for the implementation of an attack, which may have a more complex structure. A better implementation may then decrease the "complexity" of an attack without any cryptanalytical improvements.

Although we implemented our attack in the best way we could, one cannot exclude that a different approach or some modest further optimizations may lead to an improvement. However, barring a radical redesign, the associated gain should not be significant; the improvements brought by some of our own low-level optimizations was typically of about 15%.

The Impact of the Attack Platform. The choice of the platform used to run the attack may have a more significant impact on its evaluated complexity. While a CPU is by definition suitable to run general-purpose computations, this is not the case of *e.g.* GPUs. Thus, the gap between how fast a simple computation, such as evaluating the compression function of SHA-1, and a more complex one, such as our attack, need not be the same on the two kinds of architectures. For instance, the authors of [21] noticed that their 76-step freestart attack could be implemented on CPU (a 3.2 GHz Haswell Core i5) for a cost equivalent to $2^{49.1}$ compression function computations, while this increased to $2^{50.25}$ on their best-performing GTX 970, and $2^{50.34}$ on average.

This difference leads to a slight paradox: from an attacker's point of view, it may seem best to implement the attack on a CPU in order to be able to claim a better attack complexity. However, a GPU being far more powerful, it is actually much more efficient to run it on the latter: the attack of [21] takes only a bit more than four days to run on a single GTX 970, which is much less than the estimated 150 days it would take using a single quad-core CPU.

We did not write a CPU (resp. GPU) implementation of our own attack for the search of the second (resp. first) block, and are thus unable to make a similar comparison for the present full hash function attack. However, as we used the same framework as [21], it is reasonable to assume that the gap would be of the same order.

How to Pick the Best Generic Attack. As we pointed out above, the common methodology for measuring the complexity of an attack leaves implicit the comparison with a generic approach. This may introduce a bias in suggesting a strategy for a generic attacker that is in fact not optimal. This was already hinted in the previous paragraph, where we remarked that an attack may seem to become worse when implemented on a more efficient platform. In fact, the underlying assumption that a generic attacker would use the same platform as the one on which the cryptanalytic attack is implemented may not always be justified: for instance, even if the latter is run on a CPU, there is no particular reason why a generic attacker would not use more energy-efficient GPUs or FPGAs. It may thus be hard to precisely estimate the absolute gain provided by a cryptanalytic attack compared to the best implementation of a generic algorithm *with identical monetary and time resources*, especially when these are high.

The issues raised here could all be addressed in principle by carefully implementing, say van Oorschot and Wiener's parallel collision search on a cluster of efficient platforms [33]. However, this is usually not done in practice, and we made no exception in our case.

Despite the few shortcomings of this usual methodology used to evaluate the complexity of attacks, it remains in our opinion a reliable measure thereof, that allows to compare different attack efforts reasonably well. For want of a better one, it is also the approach used in this paper.

6.2 The Computation

The major challenge when running our near-collision attacks distributed across the world was to adapt it into a distributed computation model which pursues two goals: the geographically distributed workers should work independently without duplication of work, and the number of the wasted computational time due to worker's failures should be minimized. The first goal required storage with the ability endure high loads of requests coming from all around the globe. For the second goal, the main sources of failures we found were preemption by higher-priority workers and bugs in GPU hardware. To diminish the impact of these failures, we learned to predict failures in the early stages of computation and terminated workers without wasting significant amounts of computational time.

First Near-Collision Attack. The first phase of the attack, corresponding to the generation of first-block near collisions, was run on a heterogeneous CPU cluster hosted by Google, spread over eight physical locations. The computation was split into small jobs of expected running time of one hour, whose objectives were to compute partial solutions up to step 61. The running time of one hour proved to be the best choice to be resilient against various kind of failures (mostly machine failure, preemption by other users of the cluster, or network issues), while limiting the overhead of managing many jobs. A *MapReduce* paradigm was used to collect the solutions of a series of smaller jobs; in hindsight, this was not the best approach, as it introduced an unnecessary bottleneck in the reduce phase.

The first first-block near collision was found after spending about 3583 core years that had produced 180 711 partial solutions up to step 61. A second near collision block was then later computed; it required an additional 2987 core years and 148 975 partial solutions.

There was a variety of CPUs involved in this computation, but it is reasonable to assume that they all were roughly equivalent in performance. On a single core of a 2.3 GHz Xeon E5-2650v3, the OpenSSL implementation of SHA-1 can compute up to $2^{23.3}$ compression functions per second. Taking this as a unit, the first near-collision block required an effort equivalent to 2^{60} SHA-1 compression function calls, and the second first block required $2^{59.75}$.

Second Near-Collision Attack. The second more expensive phase of the attack was run on a heterogeneous cluster of K20, K40 and K80 GPUs, also hosted by Google. It corresponded to the generation of a second-block near-collision leading to a full collision.

The overall setup of the computation was similar to the one of the first block, except that it did not use a MapReduce approach and resorted to using simpler queues holding the unprocessed jobs. A worker would then select a job, potentially produce one or several partial solutions up to step 61, and die on completion.

The collision was found after 369 985 partial solutions had been produced[5]. The production rates of partial 61-step solutions of the different devices used in the cluster were of 0.593 per hour for the K80 (which combines two GPU chips on one card), 0.444 for the K40 and 0.368 for the K20. The time needed for a homogeneous cluster to produce the collision would then have been of 114 K20-years, 95 K40-years or 71 K80-years.

The rate at which these various devices can compute the compression function of SHA-1 is, according to our measurements, $2^{31.1}\,s^{-1}$ for the K20, $2^{31.3}\,s^{-1}$ for

[5] We were quite lucky in that respect. The expected number required is about 2.5 times more than that.

the K40, and $2^{31}\,s^{-1}$ for the K80 ($2^{30}\,s^{-1}$ per GPU). The effort of finding the second block of the collision for homogeneous clusters, measured in number of equivalent calls to the compression function, is thus equal to $2^{62.8}$ for the K20 and K40 and $2^{62.1}$ for the K80.

Although a GTX 970 was only used to prototype the attack, we can also consider its projected efficiency and measure the effort spent for the attack w.r.t. this GPU. From the measured production rate of 58 100 step 33 solutions per second, we can deduce that 0.415 step 61 solutions can be computed per hour on average. This leads to a computational effort of 102 GPU years, equivalent to $2^{63.4}$ SHA-1 compression function calls.

The monetary cost of computing the second block of the attack by renting Amazon instances can be estimated from these various data. Using a `p2.16xlarge` instance, featuring 16 K80 GPUs and nominally costing US$ 14.4 per hour would cost US$ 560K for the necessary 71 device years. It would be more economical for a patient attacker to wait for low "spot prices" of the smaller `g2.8xlarge` instances, which feature four K520 GPUs, roughly equivalent to a K40 or a GTX 970. Assuming thusly an effort of 100 device years, and a typical spot price of US$ 0.5 per hour, the overall cost would be of US$ 110K.

Finally, summing the cost of each phase of the attack in terms of compression function calls, we obtain a total effort of $2^{63.1}$, including the redundant second near-colliding first block and taking the figure of $2^{62.8}$ for the second block collision. This should however not be taken as an absolute number; depending on luck and equipment but without changing any of the cryptanalytical aspects of our attack, it is conceivable that the spent effort could have been anywhere from, say, $2^{62.3}$ to $2^{65.1}$ equivalent compression function calls.

6.3 Complexity Comparisons

We put our own result into perspective by briefly comparing its complexity to a few other relevant cryptographic computations.

Comparison with MD5 and SHA-0 Collisions. An apt comparison is first to consider the cost of computing collisions for MD5 [37], a once very popular hash function, and SHA-0 [30], identical to SHA-1 but for a missing rotation in the message expansion. The most efficient known identical-prefix collision attacks for these three functions are all based on the same series of work from Wang *et al.* from the mid-2000s [48–50], but have widely varying complexities.

The best current identical-prefix collision attacks on MD5 are due to Stevens *et al.*, and require the equivalent of about 2^{16} compression function calls [46]. Furthermore, in the same paper, *chosen-prefix* collisions are computed for a cost equivalent to about 2^{39} calls, increasing to 2^{49} calls for a three-block chosen-prefix collision as was generated on 200 PS3s for the rogue Certification Authority work.

Though very similar to SHA-1, SHA-0 is much weaker against collision attacks. The best current such attack on SHA-0 is due to Manuel and Peyrin [27], and requires the equivalent of about $2^{33.6}$ calls to the compression function.

Identical-prefix collisions for MD5 and SHA-0 can thus be obtained within a reasonable time by using very limited computational power, such as a decent smartphone.

Comparison with RSA Modulus Factorization and Prime Field Discrete Logarithm Computation. Some of the most expensive attacks implemented in cryptography are in fact concerned with establishing records of factorization and discrete logarithm computations. We believe that it is instructive to compare the resources necessary in both cases. As an example, we consider the 2009 factorization of a 768-bit RSA modulus from Kleinjung *et al.* [22] and the recent 2016 discrete logarithm computation in a 768-bit prime field from Kleinjung *et al.* [23].

The 2009 factorization required about 2000 core years on a 2.2 GHz AMD Opteron of the time. The number of single instructions to have been executed is estimated to be of the order of 2^{67} [22][6].

The 2016 discrete logarithm computation was a bit more than three times more expensive, and required about 5300 core years on a single core of a 2.2 GHz Xeon E5-2660 [23].

In both cases, the overall computational effort could have been decreased by reducing the time that was spent collecting relations [22,23]. However, this would have made the following linear-algebra step harder to manage and a longer computation in calendar time. Kleinjung *et al.* estimated that a shorter sieving step could have resulted in a discrete logarithm computation in less than 4000 core years [23].

To compare the cost of the attacks, we can estimate how many SHA-1 (compression function) calls can be performed in the 5300 core years of the more expensive discrete logarithm record [23]. Considering again a 2.3 GHz Xeon E5-2650 (slightly faster than the CPU used as a unit by Kleinjung *et al.*) running at about $2^{23.3}$ SHA-1 calls per second, the overall effort of [23] is equivalent to approximately $2^{60.6}$ SHA-1 calls. It is reasonable to expect that even on an older processor the performance of running SHA-1 would not decrease significantly; taking the same base figure per core would mean that the effort of [22] is equivalent to approximately $2^{58.9}$–$2^{59.2}$ SHA-1 calls.

In absolute value, this is less than the effort of our own attack, the more expensive discrete logarithm computation being about five times cheaper[7], and less than twice more expensive than computing a single first-block near collision. However, the use of GPUs for the computation of the second block of our attack allowed both to significantly decrease the calendar time necessary to perform the computation, and its efficiency in terms of necessary power: as an example, the peak power consumption of a K40 is only 2.5 times the one of a 10-core Xeon E5-2650, yet it is about 25 times faster at computing the compression function of

[6] Note that the comparison between factorization and discrete logarithm computation mentioned in [23] gives for the former a slightly lower figure of about 1700 core years.

[7] But now is also a good time to recall that directly comparing CPU and GPU cost is tricky.

SHA-1 than the whole CPU, and thence 10 times more energy-efficient overall. The energy required to compute a collision using GPUs is thus about twice less than the one required for the discrete logarithm computation[8]. As a conclusion, computing a collision for SHA-1 seems to need slightly more effort than 768-bit RSA factorization or prime-field discrete logarithm computation but, if done on GPUs, the amount of resources necessary to do so is slightly less.

Acknowledgements. We thank the anonymous reviewers for their helpful comments, and Michael X. Lyons for pointing out a few minor inconsistencies between the presented differential path and the actual colliding blocks.

A The Attack Parameters

The first block of the attack uses the same path and conditions as the one given in [43, Sect. 5], which we refer to for a description. This section gives the differential path, linear (message) bit-relations and neutral bits used in our second-block near-collision attack.

We use the notation of Table 3 to represent signed differences of the differential path and to indicate the position of neutral bits.

We give the differential path of the second block up to A_{23} in Fig. 3. We also give *necessary conditions* for A_{22} to A_{26} in Table 4, which are required for all alternate differential paths allowed. In order to maximize the probability, some additional conditions are also imposed on the message. These message-bit-relations are given in Table 5. The rest of the path can then be determined from the disturbance vector.

We also give the list of the neutral bits used in the attack. There are 51 of them over the seven message words m_{11} to m_{15}, distributed as follows (visualized in Fig. 4):

Table 3. Meaning of the bit difference symbols, for a symbol located on $A_t[i]$. The same symbols are also used for m.

Symbol	Condition on $(A,\widetilde{A})$	Symbol	Condition on $(A,\widetilde{A})$
·	$A_t[i] = \widetilde{A}_t[i]$	☆	$A_t[i] = \widetilde{A}_t[i] = A_{t-1}[i]$
●	$A_t[i] \neq \widetilde{A}_t[i]$	★	$A_t[i] = \widetilde{A}_t[i] \neq A_{t-1}[i]$
▲	$A_t[i] = 0, \quad \widetilde{A}_t[i] = 1$	◇	$A_t[i] = \widetilde{A}_t[i] = (A_{t-1}^{\circlearrowleft 2})[i]$
▼	$A_t[i] = 1, \quad \widetilde{A}_t[i] = 0$	◆	$A_t[i] = \widetilde{A}_t[i] \neq (A_{t-1}^{\circlearrowleft 2})[i]$
▽	$A_t[i] = \widetilde{A}_t[i] = 0$	□	$A_t[i] = \widetilde{A}_t[i] = (A_{t-2}^{\circlearrowleft 2})[i]$
△	$A_t[i] = \widetilde{A}_t[i] = 1$	■	$A_t[i] = \widetilde{A}_t[i] \neq (A_{t-2}^{\circlearrowleft 2})[i]$
*	No condition on $A_t[i]$, $\widetilde{A}_t[i]$		

[8] This is assuming that the total energy requirements scale linearly with the consumption of the processing units.

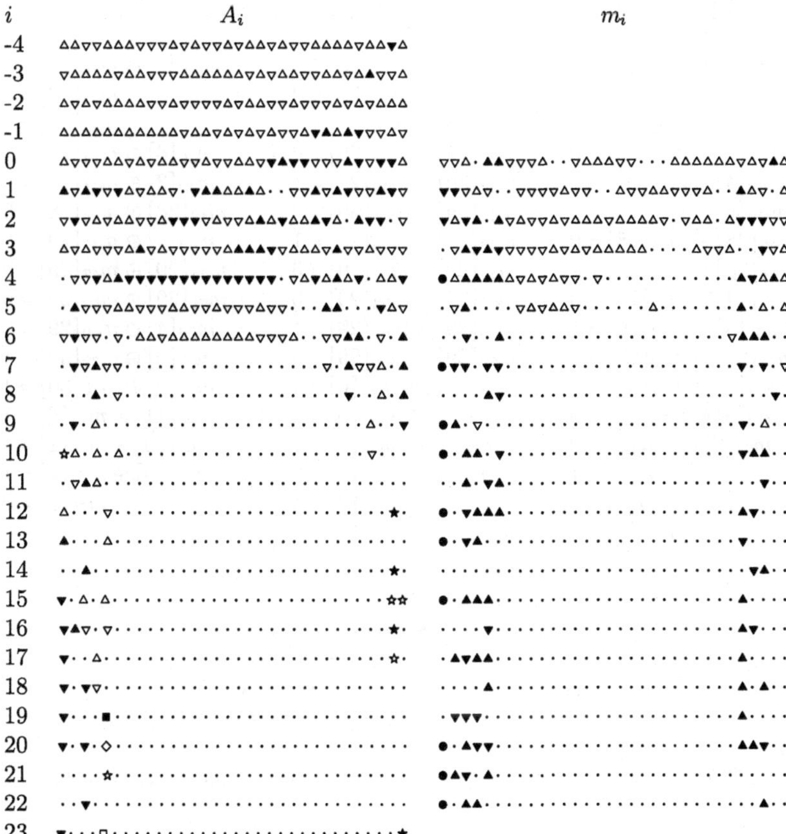

Fig. 3. The differential path of the second block up to A_{23}.

Table 4. Additional necessary conditions used for A_{22} to A_{26}.

$$A_{22}[27] \oplus m_{23}[27] = A_{21}[29] \oplus 1$$
$$A_{24}[27] \oplus m_{25}[27] = A_{23}[29]$$
$$A_{25}[28] \oplus m_{25}[27] = A_{23}[30] \oplus 1$$
$$A_{26}[27] \oplus m_{27}[27] = A_{25}[29]$$
$$\begin{cases} A_{25}[29] \oplus m_{23}[27] = A_{24}[31] & \text{if } A_{24}[30] = m_{23}[30] \\ A_{24}[31] = m_{23}[30] & \text{if } A_{24}[30] \neq m_{23}[30] \end{cases}$$

- m_{11}: bit positions (starting with the least significant bit at zero) 7, 8, 9, 10, 11, 12, 13, 14, 15
- m_{12}: positions 2, 5, 6, 7, 8, 9, 10, 11, 12, 13, 14, 15, 16, 17, 18, 19, 20
- m_{13}: positions 5, 6, 7, 8, 9, 10, 11, 12, 13, 15, 16, 30
- m_{14}: positions 4, 6, 7, 8, 9, 10
- m_{15}: positions 5, 6, 7, 8, 9, 10, 12

Table 5. Linear part message-bit-relations for the second block path.

$m_{23}[27] \oplus m_{23}[28] = 1$	$m_{23}[30] \oplus m_{24}[3] = 1$	$m_{23}[30] \oplus m_{28}[28] = 1$
$m_{23}[4] = 0$	$m_{24}[28] = 0$	$m_{24}[29] = 0$
$m_{24}[2] = 0$	$m_{26}[28] \oplus m_{26}[29] = 1$	$m_{27}[29] = 0$
$m_{28}[27] = 0$	$m_{28}[4] \oplus m_{32}[29] = 0$	$m_{36}[4] \oplus m_{44}[28] = 1$
$m_{38}[4] \oplus m_{44}[28] = 0$	$m_{39}[30] \oplus m_{44}[28] = 1$	$m_{40}[3] \oplus m_{44}[28] = 0$
$m_{40}[4] \oplus m_{44}[28] = 1$	$m_{41}[29] \oplus m_{41}[30] = 0$	$m_{42}[28] \oplus m_{44}[28] = 0$
$m_{43}[28] \oplus m_{44}[28] = 0$	$m_{43}[29] \oplus m_{44}[28] = 1$	$m_{43}[4] \oplus m_{47}[29] = 0$
$m_{44}[28] \oplus m_{44}[29] = 1$	$m_{45}[29] \oplus m_{47}[29] = 0$	$m_{46}[29] \oplus m_{47}[29] = 0$
$m_{48}[4] \oplus m_{52}[29] = 0$	$m_{50}[29] \oplus m_{52}[29] = 0$	$m_{51}[29] \oplus m_{52}[29] = 0$
$m_{54}[4] \oplus m_{60}[29] = 1$	$m_{56}[29] \oplus m_{60}[29] = 1$	$m_{56}[4] \oplus m_{60}[29] = 0$
$m_{57}[29] \oplus m_{60}[29] = 1$	$m_{59}[29] \oplus m_{60}[29] = 0$	$m_{67}[0] \oplus m_{72}[30] = 1$
$m_{68}[5] \oplus m_{72}[30] = 0$	$m_{70}[1] \oplus m_{71}[6] = 1$	$m_{71}[0] \oplus m_{76}[30] = 1$
$m_{72}[5] \oplus m_{76}[30] = 0$	$m_{73}[2] \oplus m_{78}[0] = 1$	$m_{74}[1] \oplus m_{75}[6] = 1$
$m_{74}[7] \oplus m_{78}[0] = 0$	$m_{75}[1] \oplus m_{76}[6] = 1$	$m_{76}[0] \oplus m_{76}[1] = 1$
$m_{76}[3] = 1$	$m_{77}[0] \oplus m_{77}[1] = 0$	$m_{77}[0] \oplus m_{77}[2] = 1$
$m_{77}[8] = 0$	$m_{78}[3] = 1$	$m_{78}[7] = 0$
$m_{79}[2] = 0$	$m_{79}[4] = 1$	

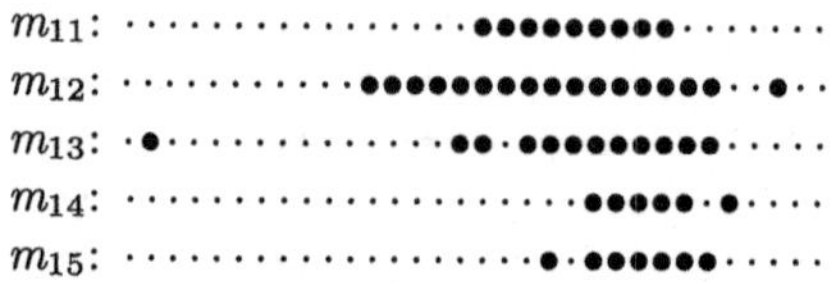

```
m11: ················●●●●●●●●●·······
m12: ···········●●●●●●●●●●●●●●●●··●··
m13: ·●·············●●·●●●●●●●●●·····
m14: ·····················●●●●●·●····
m15: ···················●·●●●●●●·····
```

Fig. 4. The 51 single neutral bits used in the second block attack.

Not all of the neutral bits of the same word (say m_{13}) are neutral up to the same point. Their repartition in that respect is as follows, a graphical representation being also given in Fig. 5.

- Bits neutral up to A_{14} (included): m_{11}[9,10,11,12,13,14,15], m_{12}[2,14,15,16,17,18,19,20], m_{13}[12,16]
- Bits neutral up to A_{15} (included): m_{11}[7,8], m_{12}[9,10,11,12,13], m_{13}[15,30]
- Bits neutral up to A_{16} (included): m_{12}[5,6,7,8], m_{13}[10,11,13]
- Bits neutral up to A_{17} (included): m_{13}[5,6,7,8,9], m_{14}[10]
- Bits neutral up to A_{18} (included): m_{14}[6,7,9], m_{15}[10,12]
- Bits neutral up to A_{19} (included): m_{14}[4,8], m_{15}[5,6,7,8,9]

A bit neutral to A_i is then used to produce partial solutions at A_{i+1}. One should also note that this list only includes a single bit per neutral bit group, and some additional flips may be necessary to preserve message-bit-relations.

Out of the three boomerangs used in the attack, one first introduced a perturbation on m_9 on bit 7, and the other two on m_6, on bit 6 and on bit 8. All three boomerangs then introduce corrections to ensure a local collision. Because these local collisions happen in the first round, where the Boolean function is φ_{IF}, only two corrections are necessary for each of them.

A_{14} : m_{11}: ················●●●●●●●·········
m_{12}: ···········●●●●●●●···········●··
m_{13}: ···············●···●············
A_{15} : m_{11}: ·······················●●·······
m_{12}: ··················●●●●●·········
m_{13}: ·●··············●···············
A_{16} : m_{12}: ·······················●●●●·····
m_{13}: ··················●·●●··········
A_{17} : m_{13}: ······················●●●●●·····
m_{14}: ·····················●··········
A_{18} : m_{14}: ······················●·●●······
m_{15}: ···················●·●··········
A_{19} : m_{14}: ·······················●···●····
m_{15}: ······················●●●●●·····

Fig. 5. The 51 single neutral bits regrouped by up to where they are neutral.

m_{06}: ·······················★·▲······
m_{07}: ··················☆·△···········
m_{08}: ································
m_{09}: ························◆·······
m_{10}: ···················◇············
m_{11}: ·························☆·△····
m_{12}: ································
m_{13}: ································
m_{14}: ··························◇·····

Fig. 6. Boomerang local collision patterns using symbols. The first perturbation difference is highlighted with a black symbol. Associated correcting differences are identified with the corresponding white symbol.

The lone boomerang introduced on m_9 is neutral up to A_{22}, and the couple introduced on m_6 are neutral up to A_{25}. The complete sets of message bits defining all of them are shown in Fig. 6, using a "difference notation".

References

1. Albertini, A., Aumasson, J.-P., Eichlseder, M., Mendel, F., Schläffer, M.: Malicious hashing: Eve's variant of SHA-1. In: Joux, A., Youssef, A. (eds.) SAC 2014. LNCS, vol. 8781, pp. 1–19. Springer, Cham (2014). doi:10.1007/978-3-319-13051-4_1
2. Albertini, A., et al.: Exploiting identical-prefix hash function collisions. Draft (2017)
3. Biham, E., Chen, R.: Near-collisions of SHA-0. In: Franklin, M. (ed.) CRYPTO 2004. LNCS, vol. 3152, pp. 290–305. Springer, Heidelberg (2004). doi:10.1007/978-3-540-28628-8_18
4. Biham, E., Chen, R., Joux, A., Carribault, P., Lemuet, C., Jalby, W.: Collisions of SHA-0 and reduced SHA-1. In: Cramer [6], pp. 36–57 (2005)

5. Chabaud, F., Joux, A.: Differential collisions in SHA-0. In: Krawczyk, H. (ed.) CRYPTO 1998. LNCS, vol. 1462, pp. 56–71. Springer, Heidelberg (1998). doi:10.1007/BFb0055720
6. Cramer, R. (ed.): EUROCRYPT. LNCS, vol. 3494. Springer, Cham (2005)
7. Cannière, C., Mendel, F., Rechberger, C.: Collisions for 70-step SHA-1: on the full cost of collision search. In: Adams, C., Miri, A., Wiener, M. (eds.) SAC 2007. LNCS, vol. 4876, pp. 56–73. Springer, Heidelberg (2007). doi:10.1007/978-3-540-77360-3_4
8. De Cannière, C., Rechberger, C.: Finding SHA-1 characteristics: general results and applications. In: Lai, X., Chen, K. (eds.) ASIACRYPT 2006. LNCS, vol. 4284, pp. 1–20. Springer, Heidelberg (2006). doi:10.1007/11935230_1
9. Boer, B., Bosselaers, A.: An attack on the last two rounds of MD4. In: Feigenbaum, J. (ed.) CRYPTO 1991. LNCS, vol. 576, pp. 194–203. Springer, Heidelberg (1992). doi:10.1007/3-540-46766-1_14
10. Boer, B., Bosselaers, A.: Collisions for the compression function of MD5. In: Helleseth, T. (ed.) EUROCRYPT 1993. LNCS, vol. 765, pp. 293–304. Springer, Heidelberg (1994). doi:10.1007/3-540-48285-7_26
11. Dobbertin, H.: Cryptanalysis of MD4. In: Gollmann, D. (ed.) FSE 1996. LNCS, vol. 1039, pp. 53–69. Springer, Heidelberg (1996). doi:10.1007/3-540-60865-6_43
12. Fillinger, M., Stevens, M.: Reverse-engineering of the cryptanalytic attack used in the flame super-malware. In: Iwata, T., Cheon, J.H. (eds.) ASIACRYPT 2015. LNCS, vol. 9453, pp. 586–611. Springer, Heidelberg (2015). doi:10.1007/978-3-662-48800-3_24
13. Cab Forum: Ballot 152 - Issuance of SHA-1 certificates through 2016. Cabforum mailing List (2015). https://cabforum.org/pipermail/public/2015-October/006081.html
14. Gebhardt, M., Illies, G., Schindler, W.: A note on practical value of single hash collisions for special file formats. In: NIST First Cryptographic Hash Workshop, October 2005
15. Grechnikov, E.: Collisions for 72-step and 73-step SHA-1: improvements in the method of characteristics. Cryptology ePrint Archive, Report 2010/413 (2010)
16. Grechnikov, E., Adinetz, A.: Collision for 75-step SHA-1: intensive parallelization with GPU. Cryptology ePrint Archive, Report 2011/641 (2011)
17. Hashclash project webpage. https://marc-stevens.nl/p/hashclash/. Accessed May 2017
18. InfoWorld: Oracle to Java devs: stop signing jar files with MD5, January 2017
19. Joux, A., Peyrin, T.: Hash functions and the (amplified) boomerang attack. In: Menezes, A. (ed.) CRYPTO 2007. LNCS, vol. 4622, pp. 244–263. Springer, Heidelberg (2007). doi:10.1007/978-3-540-74143-5_14
20. Jutla, C.S., Patthak, A.C.: A matching lower bound on the minimum weight of SHA-1 expansion code. IACR Cryptology ePrint Archive 2005, 266 (2005)
21. Karpman, P., Peyrin, T., Stevens, M.: Practical free-start collision attacks on 76-step SHA-1. In: Gennaro, R., Robshaw, M. (eds.) CRYPTO 2015. LNCS, vol. 9215, pp. 623–642. Springer, Heidelberg (2015). doi:10.1007/978-3-662-47989-6_30
22. Kleinjung, T., et al.: Factorization of a 768-bit RSA modulus. In: Rabin, T. (ed.) CRYPTO 2010. LNCS, vol. 6223, pp. 333–350. Springer, Heidelberg (2010). doi:10.1007/978-3-642-14623-7_18
23. Kleinjung, T., Diem, C., Lenstra, A.K., Priplata, C., Stahlke, C.: Computation of a 768-bit prime field discrete logarithm. In: Coron, J.-S., Nielsen, J.B. (eds.) EUROCRYPT 2017. LNCS, vol. 10210, pp. 185–201. Springer, Cham (2017). doi:10.1007/978-3-319-56620-7_7

24. CrySyS Lab: sKyWiper (a.k.a. flame a.k.a. flamer): a complex malware for targeted attacks. Laboratory of Cryptography and System Security, Budapest University of Technology and Economics, 31 May 2012
25. Kaspersky Lab: The flame: questions and answers. Securelist blog, 28 May 2012
26. Manuel, S.: Classification and generation of disturbance vectors for collision attacks against SHA-1. Des. Codes Cryptogr. **59**(1–3), 247–263 (2011)
27. Manuel, S., Peyrin, T.: Collisions on SHA-0 in one hour. In: Nyberg, K. (ed.) FSE 2008. LNCS, vol. 5086, pp. 16–35. Springer, Heidelberg (2008). doi:10.1007/978-3-540-71039-4_2
28. Mendel, F., Pramstaller, N., Rechberger, C., Rijmen, V.: The impact of carries on the complexity of collision attacks on SHA-1. In: Robshaw, M. (ed.) FSE 2006. LNCS, vol. 4047, pp. 278–292. Springer, Heidelberg (2006). doi:10.1007/11799313_18
29. Third author's mum, T.: SHA-1 is still being used. Personnal communication
30. National Institute of Standards and Technology: FIPS 180: Secure Hash Standard, May 1993
31. National Institute of Standards and Technology: FIPS 180-1: Secure Hash Standard, April 1995
32. Nossum, V.: SAT-based preimage attacks on SHA-1. Master's thesis, University of Oslo (2012)
33. van Oorschot, P.C., Wiener, M.J.: Parallel collision search with cryptanalytic applications. J. Cryptol. **12**(1), 1–28 (1999)
34. Post, T.W.: US, Israel developed flame computer virus to slow Iranian nuclear efforts, officials say, June 2012
35. Pramstaller, N., Rechberger, C., Rijmen, V.: Exploiting coding theory for collision attacks on SHA-1. In: Smart, N.P. (ed.) Cryptography and Coding 2005. LNCS, vol. 3796, pp. 78–95. Springer, Heidelberg (2005). doi:10.1007/11586821_7
36. Rivest, R.L.: The MD4 message digest algorithm. In: Menezes, A.J., Vanstone, S.A. (eds.) CRYPTO 1990. LNCS, vol. 537, pp. 303–311. Springer, Heidelberg (1991). doi:10.1007/3-540-38424-3_22
37. Rivest, R.L.: RFC 1321: The MD5 Message-Digest Algorithm, April 1992
38. Schneier, B.: When will we see collisions for SHA-1? Blog (2012)
39. Amazon Web Services: Amazon EC2 - Virtual Server Hosting. aws.amazon.com. Accessed Jan 2016
40. Shoup, V. (ed.): CRYPTO. LNCS, vol. 3621. Springer, Heidelberg (2005)
41. Stevens, M.: Attacks on hash functions and applications. Ph.D. thesis, Leiden University, June 2012
42. Stevens, M.: Counter-cryptanalysis. In: Canetti, R., Garay, J.A. (eds.) CRYPTO 2013. LNCS, vol. 8042, pp. 129–146. Springer, Heidelberg (2013). doi:10.1007/978-3-642-40041-4_8
43. Stevens, M.: New collision attacks on SHA-1 based on optimal joint local-collision analysis. In: Johansson, T., Nguyen, P.Q. (eds.) EUROCRYPT 2013. LNCS, vol. 7881, pp. 245–261. Springer, Heidelberg (2013). doi:10.1007/978-3-642-38348-9_15
44. Stevens, M., Karpman, P., Peyrin, T.: Freestart collision for full SHA-1. In: Fischlin, M., Coron, J.-S. (eds.) EUROCRYPT 2016. LNCS, vol. 9665, pp. 459–483. Springer, Heidelberg (2016). doi:10.1007/978-3-662-49890-3_18
45. Stevens, M., Lenstra, A., Weger, B.: Chosen-prefix collisions for MD5 and colliding X.509 certificates for different identities. In: Naor, M. (ed.) EUROCRYPT 2007. LNCS, vol. 4515, pp. 1–22. Springer, Heidelberg (2007). doi:10.1007/978-3-540-72540-4_1

46. Stevens, M., Sotirov, A., Appelbaum, J., Lenstra, A., Molnar, D., Osvik, D.A., Weger, B.: Short chosen-prefix collisions for MD5 and the creation of a rogue CA certificate. In: Halevi, S. (ed.) CRYPTO 2009. LNCS, vol. 5677, pp. 55–69. Springer, Heidelberg (2009). doi:10.1007/978-3-642-03356-8_4
47. ThreadPost: SHA-1 end times have arrived, January 2017
48. Wang, X., Yin, Y.L., Yu, H.: Finding collisions in the full SHA-1. In: Shoup [40], pp. 17–36 (2005)
49. Wang, X., Yu, H.: How to break MD5 and other hash functions. In: Cramer [6], pp. 19–35 (2005)
50. Wang, X., Yu, H., Yin, Y.L.: Efficient collision search attacks on SHA-0. In: Shoup [40], pp. 1–16 (2005)
51. Yajima, J., Iwasaki, T., Naito, Y., Sasaki, Y., Shimoyama, T., Peyrin, T., Kunihiro, N., Ohta, K.: A strict evaluation on the number of conditions for SHA-1 collision search. IEICE Transactions, vol. 92-A, no. 1, pp. 87–95 (2009). http://search.ieice.org/bin/summary.php?id=e92-a_1_87&category=A&year=2009&lang=E&abst=
52. Yajima, J., Sasaki, Y., Naito, Y., Iwasaki, T., Shimoyama, T., Kunihiro, N., Ohta, K.: A new strategy for finding a differential path of SHA-1. In: Pieprzyk, J., Ghodosi, H., Dawson, E. (eds.) ACISP 2007. LNCS, vol. 4586, pp. 45–58. Springer, Heidelberg (2007). doi:10.1007/978-3-540-73458-1_4

Obfuscation I

Indistinguishability Obfuscation from SXDH on 5-Linear Maps and Locality-5 PRGs

Huijia Lin(✉)

University of California, Santa Barbara, Santa Barbara, USA
rachel.lin@cs.ucsb.edu

Abstract. Two recent works [Lin, EUROCRYPT 2016, Lin and Vaikuntanathan, FOCS 2016] showed how to construct Indistinguishability Obfuscation (IO) from constant degree multilinear maps. However, the concrete degrees of multilinear maps used in their constructions exceed 30. In this work, we reduce the degree of multilinear maps needed to 5, by giving a new construction of IO from asymmetric L-linear maps and a pseudo-random generator (PRG) with output locality L and polynomial stretch. When plugging in a candidate PRG with locality-5 (*e.g.*, [Goldreich, ECCC 2010, Mossel, Shpilka, and Trevisan, FOCS 2013, O'Donnald and Wither, CCC 2014]), we obtain a construction of IO from *5-linear maps*.

Our construction improves the state-of-the-art at two other fronts: First, it relies on "classical" multilinear maps, instead of their powerful generalization of graded encodings. Second, it comes with a security reduction to (i) the SXDH assumption on algebraic multilinear maps [Boneh and Silverberg, Contemporary Mathematics, Rothblum, TCC 2013], (ii) the security of PRG, and (iii) sub-exponential LWE, all with sub-exponential hardness. The SXDH assumption is weaker and/or simpler than assumptions on multilinear maps underlying previous IO constructions. When noisy multilinear maps [Garg *et al.*, EUROCRYPT 2013] are used instead, security is based on a family of more complex assumptions that hold in the generic model.

1 Introduction

Indistinguishability obfuscation, defined first in the seminal work of Barak *et al.* [11], aims to transform programs into "unintelligible" ones while preserving functionality. IO is an extradinarily powerful object and has been used as a central tool for obtaining a plethora of new cryptographic constructions, solutions to long-standing open problems, and techniques enabling new cryptographic goals.

Unfortunately, so far, the existence of IO remain uncertain. Most known candidate IO schemes [5,7,10,17,25,27,30,33,46,49,53] are built from the so-called *graded encoding schemes* [26], a framework of complex algebraic structures that, in essence, enables evaluating *polynomial-degree* polynomials on secret encoded

H. Lin—Partially supported by NSF grants CNS-1528178, CNS-1514526, CNS-1652849 (CAREER).

J. Katz and H. Shacham (Eds.): CRYPTO 2017, Part I, LNCS 10401, pp. 599–629, 2017.
DOI: 10.1007/978-3-319-63688-7_20

values and revealing whether the output is zero or not. The security of most IO candidates are either analyzed in the ideal model or based on strong uber assumptions [49], with only one exception [33]. On the front of instantiating graded encodings from concrete mathematical objects, the state of affairs is even more worrisome: Vulnerabilities have been demonstrated in all instantiations proposed so far [21,22,26,31,39]. Of course, this does not mean that the resulting IO constructions are insecure. In fact, this has motivated the search for IO constructions that withstand all existing attacks [29].

The state-of-affairs motivates the following natural question.

How much can we narrow the gap between
objects and assumptions that imply IO and well – studied ones,
such as, asymmetric bilinear maps with the SXDH assumption?

Two recent works [41,44] have made significant progress towards answering the question: Lin [41] showed that to construct IO, we do not need full-fledged graded encodings that support evaluation of all polynomial-degree polynomials, instead, it suffices to start with graded encodings for only constant-degree polynomials, called *constant-degree graded encodings.* Following that, Lin and Vaikuntanathan [44] further weakened the assumption on constant-degree graded encodings from a uber assumption in [41] to the so-called joint-SXDH assumption, which is a stronger variant of the classical SXDH assumption. Besides from multilinear maps, their IO constructions additionally rely on *PRGs in* NC^0 and sub-exponential LWE.

The trajectory of recent developments points towards the holly grail of "building IO from bilinear maps". In this work, we make new strides in this direction: We give a new construction of IO from asymmetric L-linear maps and a PRG with output locality L (*i.e.*, every output bit depends on at most L input bits). When plugging in a candidate PRG with locality-5 in the literature [34,47,48], we obtain a construction of IO from 5-*linear maps.* This gets the degree of multilinear maps needed for IO much closer to the dream version of 2. In comparison, previous IO constructions [41,44] rely on multilinear maps with degree at least 30. On the other hand, no PRGs with locality 4 exist [23,47]. Thus, our approach hits a barrier and cannot base IO on multilinear maps with degree $L \leq 4$. This barrier is common to recent IO constructions [41,44] and suggests that we need new techniques circumventing the lower bound on locality of PRGs.

In addition to reducing the degree of multilinear maps, our IO construction improves the state-of-the-art at two other fronts. First, our construction uses the classical asymmetric multilinear maps introduced in [15,50], which are direct generalization of bilinear pairing groups to higher degree. Previous constructions rely on graded encodings, which are enhanced versions of multilinear maps with more powerful functionalities (such as, supporting complex label structures). Second, the security of our IO scheme is based on the sub-exponential SXDH assumption on L-linear maps, the sub-exponential security of PRGs, and sub-exponential LWE. The SXDH assumption on multilinear maps is much simpler and/or weaker than the assumption on graded encodings underlying previous IO constructions, for instance, the joint-SXDH assumption in [44] and the multilinear subgroup elimination assumption in [33].

1.1 Our Results

We start with defining the SXDH assumption on multilinear maps and then describe our results.

SXDH on Multilinear Maps. Asymmetric multilinear pairing groups introduced in [15,50] generalize asymmetric bilinear pairing maps to a collection of source groups $G_1, \cdots, G_D$, whose elements can be paired to produce elements in a target group G_T via a multilinear map $e(g_1^{a_1}, \cdots, g_D^{a_D}) = g_T^{a_1 \cdots a_D}$. The degree (a.k.a. multilinearity) of the multilinear map is the number of elements that can be paired together, which equals to the number of source groups D. We say that the multilinear pairing groups have *prime order* if all source groups and the target group have the same prime order, and *composite order* if all groups have the same composite order. In this work, we consider constant-degree multilinear paring groups, and in particular 5-linear pairing groups, with either prime or composite order. We omit specifying the order of groups below.

The SXDH assumption on asymmetric multilinear pairing groups is a natural generalization of the standard symmetric external Diffie-Hellman (SXDH) assumption on asymmetric bilinear pairing groups, introduced first in [50]. In short, SXDH states that the decisional Diffie-Hellman assumption holds in every source group: It postulates that the distribution of g_d^a, g_d^b, g_d^{ab} in any source group d should be indistinguishable to that of g_d^a, g_d^b, g_d^r. Formally, for all $d \in [D]$,

$$\left\{g_d^a,\ g_d^b \xleftarrow{\$} G_d :\ \{g_i\}_{i\in[D]},\ g_d^a,\ g_d^b,\ g_d^{ab}\right\}$$
$$\approx \left\{g_d^a,\ g_d^b,\ g_d^r \xleftarrow{\$} G_d\ :\ \{g_i\}_{i\in[D]},\ g_d^a,\ g_d^b,\ g_d^r\right\},$$

where $\{g_i\}$ is the set of generators in all groups. When $D = 2$, this gives the SXDH assumption on bilinear pairing groups.

Multilinear Maps v.s. Graded Encodings. The interface of (asymmetric) multilinear pairing groups is much simpler than that of graded encoding schemes introduced by [26]. First, graded encoding schemes support *graded multiplication* over a collection of groups $\{G_l\}$: Graded multiplication can pair elements of two groups G_{l_1}, G_{l_2}, indexed by two labels l_1, l_2, to produce an element in the group $G_{l_1+l_2}$, indexed by label $l_1 + l_2$[1]. In particular, the output element in $G_{l_1+l_2}$ can be further paired with elements in other groups to produce elements in group $G_{l_1+l_2+l_3+\cdots}$ and so on. In contrast, multilinear map allows only "one-shot" multiplication, where the output element belongs to the target group G_T

[1] The operation is according to some well-defined addition operation over the labels; for example, if labels are integers, + is integer addition, and if labels are sets, + is set union.

that cannot be paired anymore. Second, graded encoding schemes support the notion of "pairable groups" in the sense that only elements from groups G_{l_1}, G_{l_2} that satisfy a "pairable" relation can be paired.[2]

The support for graded multiplication between pairable groups provides powerful capabilities. In essence, GES allows one to "engineer" the labels of a set of group elements $\{g_{l_i}^{a_i}\}$, so that, only polynomials of certain specific forms can be evaluated on values in the exponent. In contrast, the simple interface of multilinear maps does not provide such capabilities.

SXDH v.s. Joint-SXDH. Lin and Vaikuntanathan introduced the joint-SXDH assumption on graded encoding schemes, and showed that IO for $\mathsf{P/poly}$ can be based on sub-exponential joint-SXDH and PRG in NC^0. Their joint-SXDH assumption strengthens the SXDH assumption as follows: It considers the joint distribution of elements $(g_l^a, g_l^b, g_l^{ab})_{l \in S}$ in a set S of groups. The intuition is that as long as *no* pairs of groups G_{l_1}, G_{l_2} in the set S are pairable, in the same spirit as SXDH, the distribution is possibly indistinguishable to the joint distribution of elements $(g_l^a, g_l^b, g_l^r)_{l \in S}$ in the same set of groups.[3] The joint-SXDH assumption is more complex and potentially stronger than the SXDH assumption.

Our Main Result: IO from SXDH on L-Linear Maps and Local-L PRG

Theorem 1 (Main Theorem). *Let L be any positive integer. Assume the sub-exponential hardness of LWE with sub-exponential modulus-to-noise ratio. Then, IO for $\mathsf{P/poly}$ is implied by the sub-exponential SXDH assumption on L-linear pairing groups, and the existence of a sub-exponentially secure locality-L PRG with polynomial $n^{1+\varepsilon}$-stretch for some $\varepsilon > 0$.*

We note that the sub-exponential hardness of SXDH and PRG required by our theorem is weaker than standard notions of sub-exponential hardness of decisional problems, in the sense that we only require the distinguishing gap to be sub-exponentially small against polynomial time adversaries, as opposed to sub-exponential time adversaries.

Our result establishes a direct and tight connection between the degree D of multilinear maps needed for constructing IO and the locality L of PRGs—*they are the same $D = L$*—assuming sub-exponential LWE. In comparison, the previous state-of-the-art [44] requires the degree of the multilinear map to be much larger, namely $D > 6L$. Thus, when plugging-in a PRG of locality-5, their construction requires at least 30-linear maps, whereas our construction relies on 5-linear maps.

Step 1: Bootstrapping IO from Locality-L PRG and Degree-L FE. We follow the same two-step approach in all previous IO constructions: First,

[2] For instance, if labels are sets, then two groups are pairable, if their label-sets l_1, l_2 are disjoint.

[3] Note that in both distributions, the same exponents, a, b, r, are used in all groups in S.

construct IO for $\mathsf{P/poly}$ from some simpler primitives—call this the *bootstrapping step*—and then instantiate the primitives needed, using graded encodings or multilinear maps. In the literature, previous bootstrapping theorems have shown that general purpose IO can be built from one of the following: *(i)* IO for NC^1 [27], *or (ii)* sub-exponentially secure FE for NC^1 [2,3,13,14], *or (iii)* sub-exponentially secure IO for constant degree computations and PRG in NC^0 [41], *or (iv)* sub-exponentially secure FE for NC^0 and PRG in NC^0 [44].[4]

In this work, we strengthen the bootstrapping theorem of [44], and show how to build IO from PRGs with locality-L and FE for computing degree L polynomials in some ring $\mathcal{R}$ (which eventually corresponds to the exponent space of multilinear maps used for instantiating the FE).

Theorem 2 (Bootstrapping Theorem). *Let L be any positive integer. Assume the sub-exponential hardness of LWE with sub-exponential modulus-to-noise ratio. IO for $\mathsf{P/poly}$ is implied by the existence of sub-exponentially secure (collusion resistant) secret-key FE schemes for computing degree-L polynomials in some ring $\mathcal{R}$ with linear efficiency, and a sub-exponentially secure locality-L PRG with $n^{1+\varepsilon}$-stretch for some $\varepsilon > 0$.*

(In the case that the FE schemes are public-key, the assumption of sub-exponential LWE is not needed.)

Above, the linear efficiency of FE schemes means that encryption time is linear in the input length $N(\lambda)$, that is, $\mathsf{Time}_{\mathsf{FE.Enc}} = N(\lambda)\mathrm{poly}(\lambda)$. In fact, we only need the FE scheme to achieve the weaker functionality of revealing whether the output of a degree-L polynomial is zero in $\mathcal{R}$. Below, we refer to such FE schemes as degree-L FE in $\mathcal{R}$ with linear efficiency.

In comparison, with locality-L PRG, the bootstrapping theorem in [44] needs to start with FE for computing polynomials with higher degree $3L + 2$. We here reduce the degree of FE to exactly L, by proposing a new pre-processing idea: At a very high-level, we let the encryptor pre-process the input to be encrypted to perform part of the degree-$(3L + 2)$ computations, and encrypt the processed values, so that later, the decryptor only need to perform a degree-L computation, and hence degree-L FE suffices. An overview of our bootstrapping step is given in Sect. 2.1.

Step 2: Degree Preserving Construction of FE. Next, we construct degree-L FE based on the SXDH assumption on L-linear maps.

Theorem 3. *Let D be any positive integer and $\mathcal{R}$ any ring. Assuming SXDH on D-linear maps over ring $\mathcal{R}$, there exist secret key FE schemes for degree-D polynomials in $\mathcal{R}$, with linear efficiency.*

This new FE scheme is our main technical contribution. Previous constructions of FE for NC^1 either relies on IO for NC^1 or high degree multilinear maps [27,28],

[4] Some bootstrapping theorems additionally assume LWE [27,41] or the existence of public key encryption [13]).

whose degree is polynomial in the circuit-size of the computations. In [44], Lin and Vaikuntanathan constructed FE for NC^0 from constant-degree graded encodings. Their construction, however, is *not* degree-preserving: To compute NC^0 functions that can be evaluated in degree D, they require degree $2D$ graded encodings. Our FE construction is the first one that supports degree-D computations using only degree-D multilinear maps.

It turns out that removing a factor of 2 in the degree requires completely new techniques for constructing FE. The reason is that the factor of 2 increase in degree allows the FE construction in [44] to evaluate instead of a degree-D computation directly, an arithmetic randomized encodings of the computation. The benefit is that they can rely on the security of randomized encoding to argue the security of FE. In our case, since the degree is exactly D, we cannot afford to "embed" any cryptographic primitives in the FE construction, and must come up with ways of encoding inputs and intermediate computation values using multilinear maps that directly guarantee security. For this reason, our construction share similar flavor with constructions of inner product encryptions based on bilinear maps. See Sects. 2.2 and 2.3 for an overview of our degree-preserving FE construction.

Additional Contributions. Along the way of designing our degree-preserving FE construction, we also construct the following primitives that are of independent interests.

Simple Function Hiding IPE Schemes from SXDH on Bilinear Maps. Without using the heavy hammers of multilinear maps or IO, the state-of-the-art collusion resistant FE schemes can only compute inner products, they are called Inner Product Encryption (IPE). In the literature, Abdalla *et al.* (ABDP) [1] came up with a public key IPE scheme based on one of a variety of assumptions, such as, DDH, Paillier, and LWE.

Bishop *et al.* [12] (BJK) constructed the first secret-key IPE scheme based on the SXDH assumption over asymmetric bilinear pairing groups. Their scheme achieves a stronger security notion, called *weak function-hiding*, and is improved by [24] to achieve full *function hiding.* Lin and Vaikuntanathan [44] further showed that any weakly function hiding IPE scheme can be generically transformed into a function hiding IPE scheme. Here, (weak) function hiding requires the FE scheme to hide *both* inputs and functions (revealing only outputs), and is much harder to achieve than standard security that hides only inputs.

While the ABDP public-key IPE scheme is simple, the secret-key (weak) function hiding IPE schemes [12,24] are much more complex. In this work, we give a *simple* construction of weak function hiding IPE from SXDH on bilinear maps, which can then be transformed to function hiding IPE using [44]. Our IPE scheme is built from the ABDP public-key IPE scheme in a modular way, and inherits its efficiency and simplicity: Ciphertexts and secret keys of length-N vectors consists of $(N + 2)$ group elements, and the construction and security proof of our scheme fits within 2 pages (reducing to the security of the ABDP IPE scheme). In addition, the new scheme satisfies certain special properties that are important for our construction of degree-L FE schemes, which are not satisfied by previous IPE schemes [12,24]. See Sect. 2.5 for an overview of our simple function hiding IPE.

High-Degree IPE. We also generalize IPE to the notion of *high-degree IPE*, or *HIPE* for short. They are *multi-input* FE schemes [35] for computing, so called, *degree-D inner product* defined as

$$\langle \mathbf{x}^1, \cdots, \mathbf{x}^D \rangle = \Sigma_{i \in [N]} x_i^1 x_i^2 \cdots x_i^D .$$

We construct HIPE for degree-D inner products from degree-D multilinear maps, which is then used to build degree-D FE schemes. We believe that this notion is interesting on its own and may have other applications. See Sect. 2.3 for an overview of HIPE.

Algebraic v.s. Noisy Multilinear Maps. Our results and proofs are described w.r.t. algebraic multilinear maps. However, finding algebraic multilinear maps with degree above 2 is still a major open problem. *Can our IO and FE schemes be instantiated with known noisy multilinear map candidates* [21,22,26,31,39]*?* The answer is nuanced: The constructions can be instantiated as-is with noisy multilinear maps and correctness holds, but the security proof fails, for (1) the SXDH assumption does not hold on known candidates, and (2) the current security reduction relies on the homomorphic scalar multiplication functionality, which is not supported by known candidates. (The latter is shared with all previous reductions that base security on a laconic and instance-independent assumption [33,44].) Nevertheless, the security proof of the degree-L FE scheme (the only component that relies on multilinear maps) can be adapted into a proof in the degree-5 ideal multilinear map model *without* homomorphic scalar multiplication. Security in the ideal model does not imply security against known cryptanalytic attacks [6,16,18–20,26,32,46]. It is unclear whether these instantiations are secure against them—we have no concrete attacks nor formal arguments that validate their security against known attacks, such as, a security proof in the weak multilinear map model [29]. See Sect. 2.6 for a more detailed discussion.

1.2 Concurrent and Independent Work

In a concurrent work, Ananth and Sahai [4] (AS) showed a similar result. Both works convey the same high-level message that "IO can be constructed from 5-linear maps and locality-5 PRG, assuming sub-exponential LWE". But, the concrete theorem statements differ. First, while our construction relies on the classical 5-linear maps, the AS construction uses degree-5 *set-based* graded encodings, which, as discussed above, is more powerful. Second, a main contribution of this paper is basing security of IO on the SXDH assumption, which is laconic and instance dependent. In comparison, the AS construction is proven secure based on two assumptions on graded encodings that are tailored to their construction and justified in the ideal model, and the security of their FE scheme follows immediately from the assumptions. In terms of techniques, both works follow the paradigm of IO construction in [44]. The two works propose different notions of FE for low-degree polynomials, and use completely different methods to construct them.

1.3 Subsequent Works

Given that locality 4 PRGs do not exist [47], the approach (in this and recent works [4,44]) of using local PRGs to reduce the degree of multilinear maps used in IO constructions hits a barrier at degree 5. In a subsequent work, Lin and Tessaro [43] overcame this barrier and further reduced the degree of multilinear maps needed to 3. More specifically, they showed that assuming sub-exponential LWE, IO can be based on the SXDH assumption on L-linear maps and PRGs with a new notion of *block-wise locality* L. Roughly speaking, a PRG has block-wise locality L if every output bit depends on at most L *input blocks*, each containing up to $\log \lambda$ bits. Their result crucially relies on our IO construction, with the modification of replacing locality L PRGs with block-wise locality L PRGs in the first bootstrapping step (the rest of the construction, such as, the low-degree FE scheme, is kept the same). They further initiated the study of block-wise local PRGs based on Goldreich's local functions and their (in)security. In particular, they showed that the security of candidates with block-wise locality $L \geq 3$ is backed by similar validation as candidates with (conventional) locality 5. Soon after their work, two exciting cryptanalytic works [9,45] showed that, unfortunately, (polynomial-stretch) PRGs with block-wise locality 2 do not exist.

Summarizing the new state-of-the-art: Assuming sub-exponential LWE, there is a construction of IO from trilinear maps and PRGs with block-wise locality 3—we are one degree away from the dream statement of "building IO from bilinear maps".

Organization. Next, we proceed to give an overview of our FE and IO constructions and their security proofs. Due to the lack of space, we leave the formal description of constructions and proofs to the full version [42]. In Sect. 2.6, we discuss in more detail issues related to instantiating our schemes with noisy multilinear maps.

2 Overview

In this work, scalars are written in normal font, such as a, b, and vectors are written in boldface, such as $\mathbf{v}, \mathbf{w}$.

2.1 Bootstrapping

Our bootstrapping theorem follows the same two step approach as [41,44]. To construct IO for $\mathsf{P/poly}$,

Step 1. First, construct sub-exponentially secure single-key FE schemes **CFE** for NC^1 that are *weakly compact*, meaning that encryption time scales polynomially in the security parameter λ and the input length N, but also scales *sublinearly* in the maximal size S of the circuits for which secret keys are generated. More precisely, a FE scheme is said to be $(1-\varepsilon)$-weakly-compact if its encryption time is $\text{poly}(\lambda, \text{N})\text{S}^{1-\varepsilon}$.

Step 2. If the FE schemes obtained from Step 1 are public-key schemes, invoke the result of [2,14] that any public-key (single-key) weakly-compact FE schemes (for any $\varepsilon > 0$) imply IO for $\mathsf{P/poly}$.
Otherwise, if the FE schemes obtained are secret-key schemes, then invoke the recent result of [13] that any secret-key weakly-compact FE schemes also imply IO for $\mathsf{P/poly}$, assuming additionally sub-exponential LWE.

The challenging task is constructing (public-key or secret-key) weakly-compact FE schemes for NC^1 from simpler primitives. In [44] (LV), they constructed such schemes from (public key or secret key respectively) *collusion resistant* FE schemes for NC^0 with *linear efficiency*, assuming the existence of a polynomial-stretch PRG in NC^0. We observe that in their construction, if the PRG has locality L, the NC^0-FE scheme is used to compute polynomials with low degree $3L + 2$. In this work, we show that the degree of the FE schemes (*i.e.*, the degree of the polynomials supported) can be reduced to L. Below, we start with reviewing the LV construction of weakly-compact FE for NC^1, and then modify their construction to reduce the degree of the underlying FE scheme. (In the exposition below, we do not differentiate public-key vs secret-key schemes, since they are handled in the same way.)

The LV Weakly-Compact FE for NC^1. To construct weakly-compact FE schemes for NC^1 from FE schemes for NC^0, LV uses Randomized Encodings (RE) [8,37] to represent every NC^1 function $f(\mathbf{x})$, as a simpler NC^0 randomized function $\hat{f}(\mathbf{x};\ \mathbf{r})$. Then, to enable computing $f(\mathbf{x})$, it suffices to publish a secret key for $\hat{f} \in \mathsf{NC}^0$, and a ciphertext of $(\mathbf{x}, \mathbf{r})$, which can be done using the NC^0-FE scheme. But, the resulting ciphertext is not compact, since the randomness $\mathbf{r}$ for computing the randomized encoding is at least of length $S(\lambda)\text{poly}(\lambda)$, where $S(\lambda)$ is the size of the circuit computing f. The key idea of LV is using a polynomial-stretch PRG $\mathbf{PRG}\colon \{0,1\}^n \to \{0,1\}^{n^{1+\alpha}}$ in NC^0 to generate pseudo-randomness for RE, that is, computing instead $g(\mathbf{x}, \mathbf{s}) = \hat{f}(\mathbf{x}; \mathbf{PRG}(\mathbf{s}))$. Now the input of the function becomes $(\mathbf{x}, \mathbf{s})$, whose length is sublinear in $S(\lambda)$ thanks to the fact that the PRG has polynomial stretch. Since the NC^0-FE scheme has linear efficiency, the ciphertext size is also sublinear in $S(\lambda)$. In addition, the function g can still be computed in NC^0.

Observe that if g can be computed by a degree-D polynomial in some ring $\mathcal{R}$, then one can instantiate the LV construction with degree-D FE schemes in $\mathcal{R}$. The question is how large is the degree D? Plug in the randomized encoding scheme by Applebaum *et al.* [8], whose encodings $\hat{f}(\mathbf{x}; \mathbf{r})$ are computable in NC^0_4 and has degree 1 in $\mathbf{x}$ and degree 3 in $\mathbf{r}$. Then, the degree of g is determined by the degree D_{PRG} of the PRG (*i.e.*, the minimal degree of polynomials that computes PRG in $\mathcal{R}$), namely, $D = 3D_{\text{PRG}} + 1$. As the degree of PRG is upper bounded by its locality $D_{\text{PRG}} \leq L$, the degree of g is bounded by $3L+1$. For the security proof to work out, the actual functions used in the LV construction are more complicated and has degree $3L + 2$. For simplicity of this overview, it is convenient to ignore this issue, as it does not affect understanding the main ideas.

A formal description of the LV weakly-compact FE scheme $\mathbf{CFE}^{N,D,S}$ for NC^1 circuits with input-length $N = N(\lambda)$, depth $D = D(\lambda)$, and size $S = S(\lambda)$ can be found in Fig. 1; it relies on the following tools:

- A (collusion resistant) FE scheme for degree-$(3D + 2)$ polynomials $\{\mathbf{FE} = (\mathsf{FE.Setup}, \mathsf{FE.KeyGen}, \mathsf{FE.Enc}, \mathsf{FE.Dec})\}$ in some ring $\mathcal{R}$ with linear efficiency.
- A pseudorandom generator **PRG** with $n^{1+\alpha}$-stretch for any $\alpha > 0$ that is computable in degree D in ring $\mathcal{R}$.
- A weak PRF F in NC^1.
- A specific randomized encoding scheme, which is the composition of Yao's garbling scheme [51,52] and the AIK randomized encoding scheme in NC^0 [8]. Denote by $\hat{C}_x = \mathsf{Yao}(C, \mathbf{x};\ \mathbf{r})$ Yao's garbling algorithm that compiles a circuit C and an input $\mathbf{x}$ into a garbled circuit $\hat{C}_x$, and by $\Pi = \mathsf{AIK}(f, \mathbf{x}\ ;\ \mathbf{r})$ the AIK encoding algorithm.

We refer the reader to [44] for the correctness and security of the scheme, and to our full version [42] for the analysis of compactness and degree.

Relying on Degree-L FE. To reduce the degree of polynomials computed using the low-degree FE, our key idea is *pre-processing* the input $(\mathbf{x}, \mathbf{s})$, so that, part of the computation of the function g is already done at *encryption time*. To illustrate the idea, recall that g is linear in $\mathbf{x}$. Thus, if one pre-computes $\mathbf{x} \otimes \mathbf{s}$ (where $\mathbf{x} \otimes \mathbf{s}$ is the tensor product of $\mathbf{x}$ and $\mathbf{s}$), then g can be computed with one degree less. More specifically, there exists another function g' that takes input $(\mathbf{x}, \mathbf{s}, \mathbf{x} \otimes \mathbf{s})$ and computes $g(\mathbf{x}, \mathbf{s})$ in degree $3L$, by replacing every monomial of form $x_i s_{i_1} s_{i_2} \cdots$ with $(x_i s_{i_1})\ s_{i_2} \cdots$, where $x_i s_{i_1}$ is taken directly from $\mathbf{x} \otimes \mathbf{s}$. Therefore, we can modify the LV construction to encrypt $(\mathbf{x}, \mathbf{s}, \mathbf{x} \otimes \mathbf{s})$, whose length is still sublinear in $S(\lambda)$, and generate keys for functions g' that have degree $3L$.

The more tricky part is how to further reduce the degree of g in $\mathbf{s}$. The naive method of pre-computing $\mathbf{s} \otimes \mathbf{s}$ at encryption time would not work, since it would make encryption time exceed $S(\lambda)$, losing compactness. To avoid this, consider a simple case where the NC^1 function f to be computed is *decomposable*, in the sense that it has $I = S(\lambda)/\text{poly}(\lambda)$ output bits, and every output bit $i \in [I]$ can be computed by a function f_i of fixed polynomial size $\text{poly}(\lambda)$. (In fact, it is w.l.o.g. to assume this, since every function f can be turned into one that is decomposable using Yao's garbled circuits.) Then, the AIK randomized encoding of f consists of $\{\hat{f}_i(\mathbf{x}, \mathbf{r}[i])\}_{i \in [I]}$, where the random tape $\mathbf{r}[i]$ for every encoding has a fixed polynomial length $Q = poly(\lambda)$, since $|f_i| = poly(\lambda)$.

In LV, all the random tapes $\{\mathbf{r}[i]\}$ are generated by evaluating a PRG on a single seed $\mathbf{r} = \mathbf{PRG}(\mathbf{s})$. We first modify how these random tapes are generated.

Parse $\mathbf{s}$ as Q equally-long seeds, $\mathbf{s}_1, \cdots \mathbf{s}_Q$, and use $\mathbf{s}_q$ to generate the qth bit in all the random tapes, that is,

$$\forall\, q \in [Q],\ i \in [I], \quad \mathbf{r}[i]_q = \mathbf{PRG}(\mathbf{s}_q)|_i = \mathbf{PRG}_i(\{s_{q,\gamma}\}_{\gamma \in \Gamma(i)})\ ,$$

where $\mathbf{PRG}_i$ is the function that computes the ith output bit of the PRG, which depends on at most L seed bits with indexes $\gamma \in \Gamma(i)$. $\mathbf{PRG}(\mathbf{s}_q)$ is a length-I

Single-key Compact FE Scheme CFE by [44]

SETUP: $\mathsf{CFE.Setup}(1^\lambda)$ samples $(\mathsf{mpk}, \mathsf{msk}) \xleftarrow{\$} \mathsf{FE.Setup}(1^\lambda)$.

KEY GENERATION: $\mathsf{CFE.KeyGen}(\mathsf{msk}, f)$ does the following:

- Sample $\mathbf{CT} \xleftarrow{\$} \{0,1\}^\ell$, where $\ell = \ell(\lambda)$ is set below.
- Define function g as follows: On input $\mathbf{x}$ of length N, a weak PRF key $\mathbf{k}$ of length poly(λ), two PRG seeds $\mathbf{s}, \mathbf{s}'$ each of length $\ell^{1/(1+\alpha)}$ and a bit b,

  $g(\mathbf{x}, \mathbf{k}, \mathbf{s}, \mathbf{s}', b)$ does the following:
  - Let $h_i(\mathbf{x}, \mathbf{k})$ denote the function that computes the ith bit in Yao's garbling of $(f, \mathbf{x})$ using pseudo-randomness generated by a weak PRF

    $$\forall i \in [I], \qquad h_i(\mathbf{x}, \mathbf{k}) := \mathsf{Yao}_i(f, \mathbf{x}\ ;\ \mathbf{r} = \{r_j = \mathsf{F}(\mathbf{k}, j)\})\ ,$$

    where I is the length of Yao's garbling of $(f, \mathbf{x})$. (Note that $h \in \mathsf{NC}^1$ since Yao's garbling algorithm and the weak PRF are both computable in NC^1.)
  - If $b = 0$, for every $i \in [I]$, compute the AIK encoding $\Pi[i]$ of computation $(h_i, (\mathbf{x}, \mathbf{k})))$, using pseudo-randomness generated by a PRG

    $$\forall\ i \in [I], \qquad \Pi[i] = \mathsf{AIK}(h_i,\ (\mathbf{x}, \mathbf{k})\ ;\ \mathbf{r}[i])\ ,\ \text{where } \mathbf{r}[i] = \mathbf{PRG}[i](\mathbf{s})$$

    where $\mathbf{PRG}[i](\mathbf{s})$ denotes the ith *portion* in the output of $\mathbf{PRG}$, and each portion has equal length poly(λ).
    Output $\Pi = \{\Pi[i]\}_i$.
  - If $b = 1$, output $\Pi = \mathbf{CT} \oplus \mathbf{PRG}(\mathbf{s}')$.

  For every $l \in [\ell = |\Pi|]$, let P_l denote the degree-$(3D+2)$ polynomial in $\mathcal{R}$ that computes the lth output bit of g. (See the full version [42] for a proof that every output bit of g can indeed be computed by a degree-$(3D+2)$ polynomial in $\mathcal{R}$.)
- For every $l \in [\ell]$, generate a secret key $\mathsf{SK}_l \xleftarrow{\$} \mathsf{FE.KeyGen}(\mathsf{msk}, P_l)$ for P_l.

Output $\mathsf{SK} = \{\mathsf{SK}_l\}_{l \in [\ell]}$.

ENCRYPTION: $\mathsf{CFE.Enc}(\mathsf{mpk}, \mathbf{x})$ samples $\mathbf{k} \xleftarrow{\$} \{0,1\}^{\text{poly}(\lambda)}$, $\mathbf{s}, \mathbf{s}' \xleftarrow{\$} \{0,1\}^{\ell^{1/(1+\alpha)}}$, and generates

$$\mathsf{CT} \xleftarrow{\$} \mathsf{FE.Enc}(\mathsf{mpk}, (\mathbf{x}, \mathbf{k}, \mathbf{s}, \mathbf{s}', 0))$$

DECRYPTION: $\mathsf{CFE.Dec}(\mathsf{SK}, \mathsf{CT})$ computes $\Pi = \{\mathsf{FE.Dec}(\mathsf{SK}_l, \mathsf{CT})\}_{l \in [\ell]}$, parses $\Pi = \{\Pi[i]\}_{i \in I}$, and decodes every $\Pi[i]$ using the AIK decoding algorithm to obtain a garbled circuit, which is further decoded to obtain the output $f(\mathbf{x})$.

Fig. 1. Single-key compact FE **CFE** by [44]

string, and hence the length $|\mathbf{s}_q|$ of each seed $\mathbf{s}_q$ is sublinear in $S(\lambda)$. Since each encoding $\hat{f}_i$ has degree 3 in its random tape $\mathbf{r}[i]$, consider an arbitrary degree 3 monomial $\mathbf{r}[i]_{q1}\mathbf{r}[i]_{q2}\mathbf{r}[i]_{q2}$.

$$\mathbf{r}[i]_{q1}\mathbf{r}[i]_{q2}\mathbf{r}[i]_{q2} = \mathbf{PRG}_i(\{s_{q1,\gamma}\}_{\gamma\in\Gamma(i)})\ \mathbf{PRG}_i(\{s_{q2,\gamma}\}_{\gamma\in\Gamma(i)})\ \mathbf{PRG}_i(\{s_{q3,\gamma}\}_{\gamma\in\Gamma(i)})$$

$$= \sum_{\substack{\text{Monomials}\\ X,Y,Z \text{ in } \mathbf{PRG}_i}} \begin{pmatrix} X(s_{q1,\gamma_1},\cdots,s_{q1,\gamma_L}) \\ \times\ Y(s_{q2,\gamma_1},\cdots,s_{q2,\gamma_L}) \\ \times\ Z(s_{q3,\gamma_1},\cdots,s_{q3,\gamma_L}) \end{pmatrix},$$

where $\Gamma(i) = \{\gamma_1,\cdots,\gamma_L\}$. Now, suppose that for every index $\gamma \in [|\mathbf{s}_q|]$ in all seeds, the encryptor pre-compute all the degree ≤ 3 monomials over the γth bits in all Q seeds; denote this set as

$$M^3(\mathbf{s},\gamma) = \{\text{ degree} \leq 3 \text{ monomials over } \{\mathbf{s}_{q,\gamma}\}_{q\in[Q]}\ \}.$$

Note that given $M^3(\mathbf{s},\gamma)$ for every $\gamma \in \Gamma(i)$, the above monomial $\mathbf{r}[i]_{q1}\mathbf{r}[i]_{q2}\mathbf{r}[i]_{q2}$ can be computed in just degree L. Therefore, given $M^3(\mathbf{s},\gamma)$ for every $\gamma \in [|\mathbf{s}_q|]$, the function g can be computed in degree L (with additionally the above-mentioned trick for reducing the degree in $\mathbf{x}$). More precisely, there exists a degree-L polynomial g'' that, on input $\mathbf{x}$, $\{M^3(\mathbf{s},\gamma)\}_\gamma$, and their tensor product, computes $g(\mathbf{x},\mathbf{s})$.

Finally, we need to make sure that the total number of such degree ≤ 3 monomials is sublinear in $S(\lambda)$, so that, encryption remains weakly-compact. Note that, for each $\gamma \in [|\mathbf{s}_q|]$, the number of degree ≤ 3 monomials over the γth bits in these Q seeds is bounded by $(Q+1)^3 = \text{poly}(\lambda)$. Moreover, the length of each seed $|s_q|$ is still sublinear in $S(\lambda)$. Thus, the total number of monomials to be pre-computed is sublinear in $S(\lambda)$.

A formal description of our weakly-compact FE scheme can be found in Fig. 2. Important difference from the LV scheme is highlighted with red underline.

2.2 Quadratic Secret-Key FE

Before proceeding to constructing degree-D FE schemes from SXDH on degree-D MMaps, we describe a self-contained construction of FE for quadratic polynomials from SXDH on bilinear maps. The degree-D scheme is a generalization of the quadratic scheme.

We start with reviewing the tool, Inner Product Encryption (IPE), for constructing quadratic FE. A (public key or secret key) IPE scheme allows to encode vectors $\mathbf{y}$ and $\mathbf{x}$ in a ring $\mathcal{R}$, in a function key $\mathsf{iSK}(\mathbf{y})$ and ciphertext $\mathsf{iCT}(\mathbf{x})$ respectively, and decryption evaluates the inner product $\langle \mathbf{y},\mathbf{x}\rangle$. In this work (like in [44]), we use specific IPEs that compute the inner product *in the exponent*, which, in particular, allows the decryptor to test whether the inner product is zero, or whether it falls into any polynomial-sized range.[5]

[5] Such IPEs should be contrasted with functional encryption for testing the orthogonality of two vectors (see, e.g., [38,40] and many others), which reveals *only* whether the inner product is zero and nothing else. In particular, they do not compute the inner product in the exponent in a way that allows for further computation, which is needed for our quadratic FE construction.

Our Single-key Compact FE Scheme CFE

SETUP: $\mathsf{CFE.Setup}(1^\lambda)$ samples $(\mathsf{mpk}, \mathsf{msk}) \xleftarrow{\$} \mathsf{FE.Setup}(1^\lambda)$.

KEY GENERATION: $\mathsf{CFE.KeyGen}(\mathsf{msk}, f)$ does the following:

- Sample $\mathbf{CT} \xleftarrow{\$} \{0,1\}^\ell$, where $\ell = \ell(\lambda)$ is set below.
- Define function g defined as follows: On input $\mathbf{x}$ of length N, a weak PRF key $\mathbf{k}$ of length $\mathrm{poly}(\lambda)$, PRG seeds $\mathbf{s}$ and $\mathbf{s}'$ of length $I^{1/(1+\alpha)} \times Q$ and $\ell^{1/1+\alpha}$ respectively, and a bit b,

  $g(\mathbf{x}, \mathbf{k}, \mathbf{s}, \mathbf{s}', b)$ does the following:
  - Let $h_i(\mathbf{x}, \mathbf{k})$ denote the function that computes the ith bit in Yao's garbling of $(f, \mathbf{x})$,

    $$\forall i \in [I], \qquad h_i(\mathbf{x}, \mathbf{k}) := \mathsf{Yao}_i(f, \mathbf{x}\ ;\ \mathbf{r} = \{r_j = \mathsf{F}(\mathbf{k}, j)\})\ ,$$

    where I is the length of Yao's garbling of $(f, \mathbf{x})$.
  - If $b = 0$, parse $\mathbf{s}$ into Q strings, $\mathbf{s} = \mathbf{s}_1 || \cdots || \mathbf{s}_Q$, of equal length $I^{1/(1+\alpha)}$, and compute

    $$\forall\ i \in [I],\ \Pi[i] = \mathsf{AIK}(h_i,\ (\mathbf{x}, \mathbf{k})\ ;\ \mathbf{r}[i])\ ,$$
    $$\text{where } Q = |\mathbf{r}[i]| \text{ and } \forall\ q \in [Q]\ ,\ \mathbf{r}[i]_q = \mathbf{PRG}_i(\mathbf{s}_q)$$

    Output $\Pi = \{\Pi[i]\}_i$.
  - If $b = 1$, output $\Pi = \mathbf{CT} \oplus \mathbf{PRG}(\mathbf{s}')$.

  For every $l \in [\ell = |\Pi|]$, let P_l denote the degree-$(3D+2)$ polynomial in $\mathcal{R}_\lambda$ that computes the lth output bit of g. Moreover, define

  $$P'_l((1||\mathbf{x}||\mathbf{k}||b) \otimes (1||\mathbf{S}), (b(\mathbf{x}||\mathbf{k})) \otimes \mathbf{S}, (1||b) \otimes (1||\mathbf{s}'))$$
  $$:= \text{ The degree } L \text{ polynomial that computes } P_l(\mathbf{x}, \mathbf{k}, \mathbf{s}, \mathbf{s}', b) \text{ in Figure 1}$$

  where L is the locality of $\mathbf{PRG}$ and $\mathbf{S} = \{(1||\mathbf{s}_{\star,\gamma}) \otimes (1||\mathbf{s}_{\star,\gamma}) \otimes (1||\mathbf{s}_{\star,\gamma})\}_{\gamma \in [I^{1/(1+\alpha)}]}$.
- For every $l \in [\ell]$, generate a secret key $\mathsf{SK}_l \xleftarrow{\$} \mathsf{FE.KeyGen}(\mathsf{msk}, P'_l)$ for P'_l.

Output $\mathsf{SK} = \{\mathsf{SK}_l\}_{l \in [\ell]}$.

ENCRYPTION: $\mathsf{CFE.Enc}(\mathsf{mpk}, \mathbf{x})$ samples $\mathbf{k} \xleftarrow{\$} \{0,1\}^{\mathrm{poly}(\lambda)}$, $\mathbf{s} \xleftarrow{\$} \{0,1\}^{I^{1/(1+\alpha)} \times Q}$, and $\mathbf{s}' \xleftarrow{\$} \{0,1\}^{\ell^{1/(1+\alpha)}}$, and generates

$$\mathsf{CT} \xleftarrow{\$} \mathsf{FE.Enc}(\mathsf{mpk}, (1||\mathbf{x}||\mathbf{k}||0) \otimes (1||\mathbf{S}),\ (0(\mathbf{x}||\mathbf{k})) \otimes \mathbf{S},\ (1||0) \otimes (1||\mathbf{s}'))$$

DECRYPTION: $\mathsf{CFE.Dec}(\mathsf{SK}, \mathsf{CT})$ computes $\Pi = \{\mathsf{FE.Dec}(\mathsf{SK}_l, \mathsf{CT})\}_{l \in [\ell]}$, parse $\Pi = \{\Pi[i]\}_{i \in I}$, and decodes every $\Pi[i]$ using the AIK decoding algorithm to obtain a garbled circuit, which is further decoded to obtain the output $f(\mathbf{x})$.

Fig. 2. Single-key compact FE **CFE** from locality-L PRG and degree-L FE

Given IPE schemes, it is trivial to implement FE for quadratic polynomials, or quadratic FE schemes for short: Simply write a quadratic function f as a linear function over quadratic monomials $f(x) = \Sigma_{i,j} c_{i,j} x_i x_j = \langle \mathbf{c}, \mathbf{x} \otimes \mathbf{x} \rangle$. Then, generate an IPE secret key $\mathsf{iSK}(\mathbf{c})$, and an IPE ciphertext $\mathsf{iSK}(\mathbf{x} \otimes \mathbf{x})$, from which the function output can be computed. However, such a scheme has encryption time quadratic in the input length $N = |\mathbf{x}|$. The key challenge is improving the encryption time to be linear in the input length under standard assumptions (*e.g.* bilinear maps).

In this work, we do so based on SXDH on bilinear maps, where the exponent space $\mathcal{R}$ of the bilinear map is the ring in which quadratic polynomials are evaluated. At a high-level, our key idea is "compressing" the encryption time of the above trivial quadratic FE schemes from quadratic to linear, by publishing some "compressed information" of linear size at encryption time, which can be expanded to an IPE ciphertext of $\mathbf{x} \otimes \mathbf{x}$ at decryption time. To make this idea work, we will use, as our basis, the public key IPE scheme by Abdalla *et al.* (ABDP) [1] based on the DDH assumption; we briefly review their scheme.

The ABDP Public Key IPE Scheme. The ABDP scheme **IPE** resembles the El Gamal encryption and is quite simple. Let G be a cyclic group of order p with generator g, in which DDH holds. A master secret key of the ABDP scheme is a random vector $\mathbf{s} = s_1, \cdots, s_N \xleftarrow{\$} \mathbb{Z}_p^N$, and its corresponding public key is $\mathsf{iMPK} = g^{s_1}, \cdots g^{s_N}$. A ciphertext encrypting a vector $\mathbf{x} = x_1, \cdots, x_N$ looks like $\mathsf{iCT} = g^{-r},\ g^{rs_1+x_1},\ \cdots,\ g^{rs_N+x_N}$, where r is the random scalar "shared" for encrypting every coordinate. It is easy to see that it follows from DDH that this encryption is semantically secure.

To turn the above scheme into an IPE, observe that given a vector $\mathbf{y} \in \mathbb{Z}_p^N$, and in addition the inner product $\langle \mathbf{y}, \mathbf{s} \rangle$ in the clear, one can homomorphically compute inner product in the exponent to obtain $g^{-r\langle \mathbf{y},\mathbf{s}\rangle} g^{r\langle \mathbf{s},\mathbf{y}\rangle + \langle \mathbf{x},\mathbf{y}\rangle} = g^{\langle \mathbf{x},\mathbf{y}\rangle}$, which reveals whether the inner product $\langle \mathbf{x}, \mathbf{y} \rangle$ is zero or not. Therefore, the ABDP scheme sets the secret key to be $\mathsf{iSK} = \langle \mathbf{s}, \mathbf{y} \rangle \,||\mathbf{y}$.

In this work, we will use the bracket notation $[x]_l = g_l^x$ to represent elements in group G_l, and omit l when there is no need to specify the group. Under this notation, the ABDP scheme can be written as,

$$\mathsf{iMSK} = \mathbf{s} \xleftarrow{\$} \mathbb{Z}_p, \quad \mathsf{iMPK} = [\mathbf{s}], \quad \mathsf{iCT} = [-r \,||\, (r\ \mathbf{s} + \mathbf{x})] \quad \mathsf{iSK} = \langle \mathbf{s}, \mathbf{y} \rangle \,||\mathbf{y}$$

where $a\mathbf{u}$ denotes coordinate-wise multiplication with a scalar a and $\mathbf{u}+\mathbf{v}$ denotes coordinate-wise addition between two vectors. We will also refer to $[x]_l$ as an encoding of x in group G_l.

Compress an ABDP Ciphertext $\mathsf{iCT}(\mathbf{x} \otimes \mathbf{x})$. The first difficulty with "compressing" a ciphertext $\mathsf{iCT} = \mathsf{iCT}(\mathbf{x} \otimes \mathbf{x}) = [-r \,||\, (r\ \mathbf{s} + \mathbf{x} \otimes \mathbf{x})]$ is that it contains information of the master secret key $\mathbf{s}$ of quadratic length, which is truely random and cannot be "compressed".

Our idea is replacing the truly random secret key $\mathbf{s}$ with the tensor product of two length-N vectors $\mathbf{s}^1 \otimes \mathbf{s}^2$, so that, the new ciphertext depends only on information, namely $(r, \mathbf{s}^1, \mathbf{s}^2, \mathbf{x})$, of linear size. The reason that we use the tensor product $\mathbf{s}^1 \otimes \mathbf{s}^2$ as the secret key is that under DDH, encodings $\left[\mathbf{s}^1 \otimes \mathbf{s}^2\right]$ is indistinguishable to encodings of N^2 truely random elements, and hence there is hope that $\mathbf{s}^1 \otimes \mathbf{s}^2$ is "as good as" a truly random master secret key. As we will see later, this hope is true, however through complicated security proof.

Now, it is information theoretically possible to compress $\mathsf{iCT}(\mathbf{x} \otimes \mathbf{x})$. However, simply publishing $(r, \mathbf{s}^1, \mathbf{s}^2, \mathbf{x})$ would blatantly violate security. We need a way to securely and succinctly encode them so that only the ciphertext iCT is revealed. Classical cryptographic tools for hiding computation like garbled circuits or randomized encodings do not help here, since the output length is quadratic, and garbled circuits or randomized encodings have at least quadratic size too. Instead, we leverage the special structure of iCT: Each of the last N^2 encodings of iCT encodes an element that is the inner product of two length-2 vectors,

$$\mathsf{iCT}[0] = [-r], \quad \left(\mathsf{iCT}[i,j] = [\ \langle\ x_i || s_i^1,\ x_j || r s_j^2\ \rangle\ ]\right)_{i \in [N], j \in [N]}$$

Here, for convenience, we use 0 and $\{(i,j)\}$ to index different encodings in iCT.

Suppose that we have a (secret key) IPE scheme **cIPE** that is function hiding (defined shortly) from bilinear maps, and has certain *canonical form*: In particular, its ciphertexts and secret keys encodes the input and function vectors in different source groups G_1, G_2 of the bilinear map, and decryption simply uses pairing to produce an *encoding of the output inner product* in the target group G_3. (Unfortunately, off-the-shelf function hiding IPEs [12,24,44] do not have the canonical form and we discuss how to construct such a scheme later.)

Then, we can use a canonical function hiding IPE, to generate the last N^2 encodings $\{\mathsf{iCT}[i,j]\}$: Publish N ciphertext $\{\mathsf{cCT}_i\}$ where each cCT_i encrypts vector $(x_i || s_i^1)$, and N secret keys $\{\mathsf{cSK}_j\}$ where each cSK_j encrypts vector $(x_j || r s_j^2)$. To obtain the $(i,j)^{\text{th}}$ encoding, one can simply decrypt the ith ciphertext using the jth secret key, which produces

$$\mathsf{iCT}[i,j] = [\ \langle\ x_i || s_i^1,\ x_j || r s_j^2\ \rangle\ ] = \mathsf{cIPE.Dec}(\mathsf{cSK}_j, \mathsf{cCT}_i)$$

In order to hide r, x_j's, and s_j^1, s_j^2's, it is necessary that the IPE scheme is function hiding, which guarantees that secret keys and ciphertexts for two sets of vectors $\{\mathbf{u}_i, \mathbf{v}_i\}$ and $\{\mathbf{u}'_i, \mathbf{v}'_i\}$ are indistinguishable if they produce identical inner products $\langle \mathbf{u}_i, \mathbf{v}_j \rangle = \langle \mathbf{u}'_i, \mathbf{v}'_j \rangle$. The hope is that function hiding is also sufficient, as, intuitively, it ensures that only the set of possible outputs $\{\mathsf{iCT}[i,j]\}$ is revealed, and all other information of $(r, \mathbf{x}, \mathbf{s}^1, \mathbf{s}^2)$ is hidden. (This intuition is not precise, as the IPE scheme is not simulation-secure, but is a good starting point.)

In summary, we now have the first version of our quadratic FE schemes.

VERSION 1 OF OUR SECRET KEY QUADRATIC FE SCHEME **qFE**

– SETUP: A master secret key msk consists of two random vectors $\mathbf{s}^1, \mathbf{s}^2$ of length N.

– KEY GENERATION: A secret key $\mathsf{SK}(\mathbf{c})$ of a function $f_{\mathbf{c}}(\mathbf{x}) = \langle \mathbf{c}, \mathbf{x} \otimes \mathbf{x} \rangle$ consists of

$$\mathsf{SK}(\mathbf{c}) = \left(\ \langle \mathbf{s}^1 \otimes \mathbf{s}^2, \mathbf{c} \rangle,\ \mathbf{c}\ \right).$$

- ENCRYPTION: Sample a random scalar $r \xleftarrow{\$} \mathbb{Z}_p$. A ciphertext $\mathsf{CT}(\mathbf{x})$ of input vector $\mathbf{x}$ contains

$$\mathsf{CT}(\mathbf{x}) = \Big([-r],\ \{\mathsf{cCT}_i(\chi_i^1),\ \mathsf{cSK}_i(\chi_i^2)\}_{i\in[N]} \Big)$$

$$\text{where } \chi_i^d = \begin{cases} x_i || s_i^1 & \text{if } d = 1 \\ x_i || r s_i^2 & \text{if } d = 2 \end{cases} \tag{1}$$

and $\{\mathsf{cSK}_j,\ \mathsf{cCT}_i\}$ are generated using a *freshly sampled* master secret key cMSK of a canonical function hiding IPE **cIPE**.
- DECRYPTION: For every $(i, j) \in [N]^2$, decrypt cCT_i using cSK_j to obtain

$$\mathsf{cIPE.Dec}(\mathsf{cSK}_j, \mathsf{cCT}_i) = [\langle \chi_i^1, \chi_j^2 \rangle] = [r s_i^1 s_j^2 + x_i x_j] = \mathsf{iCT}[i, j]. \tag{2}$$

Homomorphically compute $\Lambda_1 = \langle \mathbf{s}^1 \otimes \mathbf{s}^2, \mathbf{c} \rangle [-r] = [-r \langle \mathbf{s}^1 \otimes \mathbf{s}^2, \mathbf{c} \rangle]$, and $\Lambda_2 = \langle \{\mathsf{iCT}[i, j]\},\ \mathbf{c} \rangle$. Homomorphically add $\Lambda_1 + \Lambda_2$ to produce an encoding of the output $[f_{\mathbf{c}}(\mathbf{x})]$.

Next, we move to describing ideas for the security proof. As we develop the proof ideas, we will need to make several modifications to the above scheme.

Selective IND-Security of Our Quadratic FE Scheme. We want to show that ciphertexts of **qFE** of one set of inputs $\{\mathbf{u}_i\}$ is indistinguishable from that of another $\{\mathbf{v}_i\}$, as long as all the secret keys published are associated with functions $\{f_{\mathbf{c}_j}\}$ that do not separate these inputs, that is, $f_{\mathbf{c}_j}(\mathbf{u}_i) = f_{\mathbf{c}_j}(\mathbf{v}_i)$ for all i, j. For simplicity of this overview, we restrict our attention to the simpler case where only a single ciphertext and many secret keys are published. The security proof for the general case with many ciphertexts follows from a hybrid argument where the encrypted vectors are switched one by one from $\mathbf{u}_i$ to $\mathbf{v}_i$, and the indistinguishability of each step is proven using the same ideas to the single-ciphertext case.

Naturally, we want to reduce the security of **qFE** the security of the ABDP IPE scheme **IPE** and the function hiding of **cIPE**. Our intuition is that given a ciphertext $\mathsf{CT}(\mathbf{x})$ for $\mathbf{x} = \mathbf{u}$ or $\mathbf{v}$, the security of **cIPE** ensures that the N ciphertexts and secret keys $\{\mathsf{cCT}_i\}, \{\mathsf{cSK}_j\}$ contained in ciphertext $\mathsf{CT}(\mathbf{x})$ reveals only the output encodings $\{\mathsf{iCT}[i, j]\}$ and nothing else. Then, the security of the ABDP scheme ensures that the derived ciphertext iCT encrypting either $\mathbf{u} \otimes \mathbf{u}$ or $\mathbf{v} \otimes \mathbf{v}$ is indistinguishable, at the presence of secret keys for vectors $\{\mathbf{c}_j\}$ that do not separate them. This intuition would go through if the two building blocks **cIPE** and **IPE** provide very strong security guarantees: Naturally, **cIPE** has simulation security, so that, its ciphertexts and secret keys $\{\mathsf{cCT}_i\}, \{\mathsf{cSK}_j\}$ can be simulated from the set of output encodings $\{\mathsf{iCT}[i, j]\}$, and second, the ABDP scheme is secure even when the master secret keys are generated as a tensor product $\mathbf{s}^1 \otimes \mathbf{s}^2$ as opposed to be truely random. Unfortunately, our building blocks do not provide such strong security guarantees, which leads to the following challenges.

- *Challenge 1—Relying only on indistinguishability-based function hiding of* **cIPE**. The simulation security of **cIPE** essentially allows one to easily reduce the security of **qFE** to that of **IPE**. With only indistinguishability-based security of **cIPE**, the reduction to security of **IPE** becomes significantly harder. Typically, one build a black-box security reduction that receives from its challenger **IPE** secret keys and a ciphertext, in this case $\{\mathsf{SK}_j\}, \mathsf{iCT}$, and embeds them in the view of the adversary attacking the **qFE** scheme. However, the ciphertext CT of **qFE** has only linear size, but iCT has quadratic size—there is not enough space for embedding.[6]
  To resolve this problem, our idea is to *embed* iCT *in "piecemeal"*. Observe that the ABDP scheme encrypts its input vector *element by element* using different master secret key elements, and a shared random scalar. Thus, we can flexibly view its ciphertext iCT either as a single ciphertext, or as a list of many ciphertexts encrypting a list of vectors of shorter length. In particular, we will "cut" the ciphertext into N pieces, each of length N and indexed by $i \in [N]$.
  $$\mathsf{iCT} = [r], \quad \left\{ \mathsf{iCT}[i, \star] = \{[rs_i^1 s_j^2 + x_i x_j]\}_{j \in [N]} \right\}_{i \in [N]}.$$
  Since the ith ciphertext-piece can be viewed as an **IPE** ciphertext of vector $x_i\mathbf{x}$, generated with master secret key $s_i^1\mathbf{s}^2$ and shared random scalar r. Our idea is gradually switching the values of $x_i\mathbf{x}$ from $u_i\mathbf{u}$ to $v_i\mathbf{v}$ piece by piece in N steps. In each step, we first apply the function hiding of **cIPE** to move to a hybrid distribution where the challenge-piece $\mathsf{iCT}[i, \star]$ is directly hardwired in the **qFE** ciphertext; since $|\mathsf{iCT}[i, \star]| = N$, there is enough space for it. Then, we rely on the indistinguishability-security of **IPE** to argue that switching the plaintext-piece underlying $\mathsf{iCT}[i, \star]$ from $u_i\mathbf{u}$ to $v_i\mathbf{v}$ is indistinguishable.
- *Challenge 2—Relying on the security of the ABDP scheme under correlated randomness.* Arguing the indistinguishability of switching the vectors underlying each ciphertext-piece $\mathsf{iCT}[i, \star]$ from $u_i\mathbf{u}$ to $v_i\mathbf{v}$ turns out to be tricky. First, An acute reader might have already noticed the problem that changing pieces in the tensor product would affect the function output, which is noticeable. For example, after switching the first plaintext piece to $v_i\mathbf{v}$, the function output changes to $\langle \mathbf{c}_j, \mathbf{u} \otimes \mathbf{u} \rangle \neq \langle \mathbf{c}_j, v_1\mathbf{v} || \mathbf{u}_{\geq 1} \otimes \mathbf{u} \rangle$. To resolve this problem, we modify the scheme to build in an *offset* value Δ_j in every secret key SK_j to ensure that the function output remains the same throughout all steps.
  Second, the challenge ciphertext-piece is generated with master secret key $s_i^1\mathbf{s}^2$, which is not truly random, since the vector $\mathbf{s}^2$ is used for generating the master secret keys $s_k^1\mathbf{s}^2$ of other ciphertext-pieces for $k \neq i$. We overcome this by relying on the SXDH assumption to argue that encodings of $s_i^1\mathbf{s}^2$, given encodings of s_i^1 and $\mathbf{s}^2$, are indistinguishable to encodings of random elements, and hence as good as a truly random master secret key. Similar idea was used in [44].

---

[6] Non-black-box security reduction may get around this difficulty, but is unclear how one can design a non-black-box reduction here.

Next, we discuss in more detail how to overcome these two challenges.

Overcoming Challenge 1—Embed ABDP IPE ciphertext in piecemeal. Our goal is switching *piece by piece* the tensor product underlying the derived **IPE** ciphertext from $\mathbf{u} \otimes \mathbf{u}$ to $\mathbf{v} \otimes \mathbf{v}$, which corresponds to changing the encrypted input from $\mathbf{u}$ to $\mathbf{v}$. To do so, we build a sequence of $2N$ hybrids $\{H^b_\rho\}_{\rho\in[N],b\in\{0,1\}}$ satisfying the following desiderata:

1. In H^b_ρ, the ρth ciphertext-piece $\mathsf{iCT}[\rho, \star]$ is embedded in the **qFE** ciphertext CT,
2. The derived **IPE** ciphertext iCT encrypts the following "hybrid" vectors.

$$\begin{array}{ll} \text{In } H^0_\rho, & v_1\mathbf{v}||\cdots||v_{\rho-1}\mathbf{v}||\underline{\,u_\rho\mathbf{u}\,}||u_{\rho+1}\mathbf{u}||\cdots||u_N\mathbf{u} \\ \text{In } H^1_\rho, & v_1\mathbf{v}||\cdots||v_{\rho-1}\mathbf{v}||\underline{\,v_\rho\mathbf{v}\,}||u_{\rho+1}\mathbf{u}||\cdots||u_N\mathbf{u} \end{array}$$

To build such hybrids, we need to modify our **qFE** scheme to build in more "redundant space" in its ciphertext.

VERSION 2 OF OUR SECRET KEY QUADRATIC FE SCHEME **qFE**
– ENCRYPTION: A ciphertext $\mathsf{CT}(\mathbf{x})$ consists of

$$\mathsf{CT}(\mathbf{x}) = \Big([-r],\ \{\mathsf{cCT}_i(\underline{\,\mathbf{X}^1_i\,})\}_{i\in[N]},\ \{\mathsf{cSK}_j(\underline{\,\mathbf{X}^2_j\,})\}_{j\in[N]} \Big), \quad \text{where } \underline{\mathbf{X}^d_i = (\boldsymbol{\chi}^d_i||\mathbf{0}, 0)} \qquad (3)$$

where $\{\mathsf{cCT}_i\}$ and $\{\mathsf{cSK}_j\}$ encode vectors $\boldsymbol{\chi}^d_i$ like before, but now padded with 3 zeros.

We refer to the first 4 elements in $\mathbf{X}$'s as the first slot, which holds two vectors of length 2, and the last element as the second slot. In the honest executions, these vectors $\{\mathbf{X}^d_i\}$ are set to either $(\boldsymbol{\mu}^d||\mathbf{0}, 0)$ if $\mathbf{u}$ is encrypted, or $(\boldsymbol{\nu}^d||\mathbf{0}, 0)$ if $\mathbf{v}$ is encrypted, with $\boldsymbol{\mu}$ and $\boldsymbol{\nu}$ defined as $\boldsymbol{\chi}$ in Eq. 1 but replacing x_i with u_i or v_i respectively.

Set the Vector $\mathbf{X}$*'s in Hybrid* H^b_ρ. Hybrid H^b_ρ uses the following set of vectors $\mathbf{X}$'s, which leverages the "space" of the additional zeros to satisfy the above desiderata.

$$\mathbf{X}^1_i = \left(\begin{cases} \mathbf{0} \,||\, \boldsymbol{\nu}^1_i & \text{if } i < \rho \\ \boldsymbol{\mu}^1_i \,||\, \mathbf{0} & \text{if } i > \rho \\ \mathbf{0} \,||\, \mathbf{0} & \text{if } i = \rho \end{cases},\ \begin{cases} 0 & \text{if } i < \rho \\ 0 & \text{if } i > \rho \\ 1 & \text{if } i = \rho \end{cases} \right)$$

$$\mathbf{X}^2_j = \left(\boldsymbol{\mu}^2_j||\boldsymbol{\nu}^2_j\ ,\ \begin{cases} \langle \boldsymbol{\mu}^1_\rho, \boldsymbol{\mu}^2_j \rangle & \text{in } H^0_\rho \\ \langle \boldsymbol{\nu}^1_\rho, \boldsymbol{\nu}^2_j \rangle & \text{in } H^1_\rho \end{cases} \right)$$

Let us first see how the challenge ciphertext-piece $\mathsf{iCT}[\rho, \star]$ is hardwired. Observe that the last slots of $\mathbf{X}^2_j$'s contain exactly the values encoded in $\mathsf{iCT}[\rho, \star]$: In H^0_ρ, they are set to $\{\langle \boldsymbol{\mu}^1_\rho, \boldsymbol{\mu}^2_j \rangle = rs^1_\rho s^2_j + u_\rho u_j\}_{j\in[N]}$ (see Eq. 2), corresponding to encrypting $u_\rho \mathbf{u}$, while in H^1_ρ, they are set to $\{\langle \boldsymbol{\nu}^1_\rho, \boldsymbol{\nu}^2_j \rangle = r s^1_\rho s^2_j + v_\rho v_j\}_j$, encrypting $v_\rho \mathbf{v}$. By the fact that **cIPE** encodes its function vectors, $\mathbf{X}^2_j$'s here, in a bilinear source group, $[\mathbf{X}^2_j]$ is effectively embedded in cSK_j's and hence so is $\mathsf{iCT}[\rho, \star]$. Next, we check that the **IPE** ciphertext derived by decrypting every pair $(\mathsf{cCT}_i, \mathsf{cSK}_j)$ indeed encrypts the right hybrid vector.

$$\mathsf{cIPE.Dec}(\mathsf{cSK}_j, \mathsf{cCT}_i) = [\langle \mathbf{X}^1_i, \mathbf{X}^2_j \rangle]$$
$$= \left[\begin{cases} \langle \mathbf{0} \,||\, \boldsymbol{\nu}^1_i \,||\, 0,\ \boldsymbol{\mu}^2_j \,||\, \boldsymbol{\nu}^2_j \,||\, \star \rangle = \langle \boldsymbol{\nu}^1_i,\ \boldsymbol{\nu}^2_j \rangle & \text{if } i < \rho \\ \langle \boldsymbol{\mu}^1_i \,||\, \mathbf{0} \,||\, 0,\ \boldsymbol{\mu}^2_j \,||\, \boldsymbol{\nu}^2_j \,||\, \star \rangle = \langle \boldsymbol{\mu}^1_i,\ \boldsymbol{\mu}^2_j \rangle & \text{if } i > \rho \\ \langle\ \mathbf{0}\ \,||\, \mathbf{0} \,||\, 1,\ \boldsymbol{\mu}^2_j \,||\, \boldsymbol{\nu}^2_j \,||\, \star \rangle = \qquad \star & \text{if } i = \rho \end{cases} \right]$$

In the case $i = \rho$, $\mathsf{iCT}[\rho, \star]$ encodes exactly the values hardwired in the last slot, which as argued above encrypts $u_\rho \mathbf{u}$ in H^0_ρ and $v_\rho \mathbf{v}$ in H^1_ρ as desired. In the case $i < \rho$, the derived ciphertext-piece $\mathsf{iCT}[i, \star]$ encodes values $\{\langle \boldsymbol{\nu}^1_i, \boldsymbol{\nu}^2_j \rangle\}_j$, corresponding to encrypting $v_i \mathbf{v}$; and similarly, when $i > \rho$, the ciphertext-piece $\mathsf{iCT}[i, \star]$ encrypts $u_i \mathbf{u}$ as desired. Therefore, all desiderata above are satisfied.

Now, to show the security of **qFE**, it suffices to argue that every pair of neighboring hybrids is indistinguishable. Note that the only difference between different hybrids lies in the values of the $\mathbf{X}$ vectors encoded in the ciphertexts and secret keys of **cIPE**. Observe first that in hybrids H^1_ρ and $H^0_{\rho+1}$, every pair of vectors $(\mathbf{X}^1_i, \mathbf{X}^2_j)$ produce the *same* inner products, and hence the indistinguishability of H^1_ρ and $H^0_{\rho+1}$ follows immediately from the function hiding property of **cIPE**. This is, however, not the case in hybrids H^0_ρ and H^1_ρ, where for the special index ρ, the challenge ciphertext-piece change from encrypting $u_\rho \mathbf{u}$ to $v_\rho \mathbf{v}$. Next, we show how to reduce the indistinguishability of H^0_ρ and H^1_ρ to the security of the ABDP IPE scheme, which turns out to be quite tricky.

Overcoming Challenge 2: Indistinguishability of H^0_ρ and H^1_ρ from IPE security. The goal is relying on the security of **IPE** to argue that the embedded challenge ciphertext-pieces in H^0_ρ and H^1_ρ are indistinguishable, and hence so are the hybrids. But, we immediately encounter a problem: The function outputs obtained when decrypting the derived ciphertext iCT using secret keys SK_j's are different in H^0_ρ and H^1_ρ, namely

$$\langle v_1 \mathbf{v} || \cdots || v_{\rho-1} \mathbf{v} || \underline{\ u_\rho \mathbf{u}\ } || u_{\rho+1} \mathbf{u} || \cdots || u_N \mathbf{u},,\ \mathbf{c}_j \rangle$$
$$\neq \langle v_1 \mathbf{v} || \cdots || v_{\rho-1} \mathbf{v} || \underline{\ v_\rho \mathbf{v}\ } || u_{\rho+1} \mathbf{u} || \cdots || u_N \mathbf{u}\ ,\ \mathbf{c}_j \rangle .$$

This means the hybrids are clearly distinguishable. To fix this, we modify our **qFE** scheme to build in an offset value Δ in its secret keys, which will be added to the decryption output. In the honest execution, the offsets are set to zero, whereas in hybrid H^b_ρ, they are set to $\Delta^b_j(\rho)$ in each secret key SK_j, so that, the above inner products when added with $\Delta^0_j(\rho)$ in the left hand side and $\Delta^1_j(\rho)$ in the right hand side become equal. Clearly, whether the offset values Δ are used (set to non-zero) at all and their values must be hidden, we do so by encoding it using **cIPE**, as described below.

VERSION 3 OF OUR SECRET KEY QUADRATIC FE SCHEMES **qFE**

– SETUP: A master secret key $\mathsf{msk} = (\mathbf{s}^1, \mathbf{s}^2, \mathsf{cMSK}')$ contains additionally $\underline{\text{a master secret key } \mathsf{cMSK}' \text{ of } \mathbf{cIPE}}$.

– KEY GENERATION: In the secret key $\mathsf{SK}(\mathbf{c})$, the inner product $\langle \mathbf{s}^1 \otimes \mathbf{s}^2, \mathbf{c} \rangle$ is now encoded, together with an offset value Δ, using cMSK' of **cIPE**:

$$\mathsf{SK}(\mathbf{c}) = \left(\underline{\mathsf{cSK}'\left(\langle \mathbf{s}^1 \otimes \mathbf{s}^2, \mathbf{c} \rangle \,||\, \Delta = 0 \right)},\ \mathbf{c} \right).$$

– ENCRYPTION: In the ciphertext $\mathsf{CT}(\mathbf{x})$, the random scalar r is now encrypted, with an additional 0, using cMSK' of **cIPE**:

$$\mathsf{CT}(\mathbf{x}) = \left(\underline{\mathsf{cCT}'(-r||0)},\ \left\{\mathsf{cCT}_i(\mathbf{X}_j^2)\right\}_{i\in[N]},\ \left\{\mathsf{cSK}_j(\mathbf{X}_j^2)\right\}_{j\in[N]} \right).$$

– DECRYPTION: Decryption proceeds as before, except that now encoding Λ_1 is obtained by decrypting cCT' using cSK', which yields $\left[-r \left\langle \mathbf{s}^1 \otimes \mathbf{s}^2, \mathbf{c} \right\rangle + \Delta\right]$ as desired.

With the new offset value in secret key, we can now fix our hybrids so that the function outputs always stay the same.

Set the offsets in hybrid H_ρ^b. In hybrid H_ρ^b, not only that the vectors $\mathbf{X}$'s are set differently as above, the **cIPE** ciphertext cCT' in ciphertext CT encrypts $(0||1)$ instead of $(-r||0)$ and the corresponding **cIPE** secret key cSK_j' in SK_j encodes vector $(\langle \mathbf{s}^1 \otimes \mathbf{s}^2, \mathbf{c} \rangle \,||\, r \langle \mathbf{s}^1 \otimes \mathbf{s}^2, \mathbf{c} \rangle + \Delta_j^b(\rho))$, instead of $(\langle \mathbf{s}^1 \otimes \mathbf{s}^2, \mathbf{c} \rangle \,||0)$. At decryption time, the offset $\Delta_j^b(\rho)$ is added to the inner product between $\mathbf{c}_j$ and hybrid vector underlying iCT. Setting $\Delta_j^b(\rho)$ appropriately ensures that

$$\begin{aligned}&\langle v_1\mathbf{v}||\cdots||v_{\rho-1}\mathbf{v}||\underline{\ u_\rho \mathbf{u}\ }||u_{\rho+1}\mathbf{u}||\cdots||u_N\mathbf{u},\ ,\ \mathbf{c}_j\rangle + \Delta_j^0(\rho)\\ &\quad = \langle v_1\mathbf{v}||\cdots||v_{\rho-1}\mathbf{v}||\underline{\ v_\rho \mathbf{v}\ }||u_{\rho+1}\mathbf{u}||\cdots||u_N\mathbf{u}\ ,\ \mathbf{c}_j\rangle + \Delta_j^1(\rho) = f_{\mathbf{c}}(\mathbf{u})\ .\end{aligned}$$

Now H_ρ^0 and H_ρ^1 have the same function outputs. But, to formally reduce their indistinguishability to the security of **IPE**, we need a way to incorporate the offsets Δ's into the challenge **IPE** ciphertexts. We do so by viewing Δ_j's as extension of the plaintext. More specifically, we implicitly switch from encrypting $\mathbf{U} = u_\rho\mathbf{u}||\Delta_1^0(\rho)||\cdots||\Delta_L^0(\rho)$ to $\mathbf{V} = v_\rho\mathbf{v}||\Delta_1^1(\rho)||\cdots||\Delta_L^1(\rho)$ using master secret key $\mathbf{S} = s_\rho^1\mathbf{s}^2||t_1||\cdots||t_L$, at the presence of secret keys for vectors $\mathbf{Y}_j = \{\mathbf{c}_j[\rho,\star]||e_j\}_j$, where L is the total number of keys, t_j's are implicitly sampled secret key elements, and e_j is the unit vector of length L with a single one at index j. Observe that from such ciphertexts and secret keys, one can extract the challenge ciphertext-piece $\mathsf{iCT}[\rho,\star]$ encrypting $u_\rho\mathbf{u}$ or $v_\rho\mathbf{v}$, and obtain an encoding of $-r\langle \mathbf{s}^1 \otimes \mathbf{s}^2, \mathbf{c}\rangle + \Delta_j^b(\rho)$ embedded in each secret key cSK_j'—these are the only parts that hybrids H_ρ^0 and H_ρ^1 differ at. Given that $\langle \mathbf{U}, \mathbf{Y}_j\rangle = \langle \mathbf{V}, \mathbf{Y}_j\rangle$ for every j, we are almost done: Apply the security of **IPE** to argue that H_ρ^0 and H_ρ^1 are indistinguishable, except that we must overcome one last hurdle—the master secret key for encrypting $u_i\mathbf{u}$ or $v_i\mathbf{v}$ is not truely random.

Pseudorandomness from SXDH. The master secret key of the challenge ciphertext-piece is $s^1_\rho \mathbf{s}^2$. It is not truely random since $\mathbf{s}^2$ is also used for generating the master secret keys of other ciphertext-pieces. But, observe that both the challenge ciphertext-piece and $\mathbf{s}^2$ are embedded in secret keys $\{\mathsf{cSK}_j\}$, and hence encoded in the same bilinear map source group. Furthermore, thanks to the fact that in H^b_ρ, the ρth ciphertext cCT_ρ encrypts the vector $(\mathbf{0}||\mathbf{0},1)$, the key element s^1_ρ does not appear in the other source group. Therefore, we can apply the SXDH assumption to argue that encodings of $s^1_\rho \mathbf{s}^2$ is indistinguishable to that of a truly random vector $\mathbf{w}$—in other words, the master secret key $s^1_\rho \mathbf{s}^2$ is pseudorandom, *inside encodings*. Therefore, the security of **IPE** applies, and we conclude that hybrid H^0_ρ and H^1_ρ are indistinguishable.

2.3 Degree-D Secret-Key FE

Generalizing from quadratic FE to degree-D secret key FE, the natural idea is again starting from the trivial **IPE**-based construction that encrypts all degree-D monomials, denoted as $\mathbf{x}^{\leq D} = \otimes_{d\in[D]}\mathbf{x}$, and compressing the N^D-size ciphertext into linear size. Naturally, instead of compressing a ciphertext generated using a truly random master secret key, we will use a structured master secret key $\mathbf{s}^{\leq D} = \otimes_{d\in[D]}\mathbf{s}^i$. Thus the **IPE** ciphertext to be compressed looks like:

$$\mathsf{iCT}[0] = [-r], \qquad \mathsf{iCT}[I_1, \cdots, I_d] = \left[rs^1_{I_1}\cdots s^D_{I_D} + x_{I_1}\cdots x_{I_D}\right]$$

The challenge is how to generate the N^D encodings $\mathsf{iCT}[I]$ from just linear-sized information?

Key Tool: High-Degree IPE. We generalize IPE to the notion of high-degree IPE, or HIPE for short. More precisely, a degree-D HIPE is a *multi-input* functional encryption scheme for degree-D inner product defined as follows,

$$\left\langle \mathbf{x}^1, \cdots, \mathbf{x}^D \right\rangle = \Sigma_{i\in[N]} x^1_i x^2_i \cdots x^D_i$$

Introduced by [35], a multi-input functional encryption allows one to encrypt inputs at different coordinates, and generate secret keys associated with multi-input functions, so that, decryption computes the output of the function evaluated on inputs encrypted at different coordinates. In the context of HIPE, a degree-D HIPE encryption scheme **hIPE** allows one to generate a ciphertext $\mathsf{hCT}^d(\mathbf{x}^d)$ encrypting an input vector $\mathbf{x}^d$ at a coordinate $d \in [D-1]$, and a secret key $\mathsf{hSK}(\mathbf{x}^D)$ at coordinate D, so that, decryption reveals whether the degree-D inner product $\left\langle \mathbf{x}^1 \cdots \mathbf{x}^D \right\rangle$ is zero or not. Under this generalization, standard IPE is a special case of HIPE for degree $D = 2$.

In terms of security, the notion of function hiding also generalizes naturally, HIPE is function hiding, if ciphertexts and keys $\{\mathsf{hCT}^1_i, \cdots, \mathsf{hCT}^{D-1}_i, \mathsf{hSK}_i\}_{i\in[L]}$ encoding two sets of vectors $\{\mathbf{u}^1_i, \cdots, \mathbf{u}^{D-1}_i, \mathbf{u}^D_i\}_{i\in[L]}$ and $\{\mathbf{v}^1_i, \cdots, \mathbf{v}^{D-1}_i, \mathbf{v}^D_i\}_{i\in[L]}$ are indistinguishable, whenever all degree-D inner products that can be computed from them are identical, that is,

$$\forall I \in [L]^D, \left\langle \mathbf{u}^1_{I_1}, \cdots \mathbf{u}^D_{I_D} \right\rangle = \left\langle \mathbf{v}^1_{I_1}, \cdots \mathbf{v}^D_{I_D} \right\rangle$$

In this work, we give a construction of function hiding degree-D HIPE scheme from the SXDH assumption on degree-D multilinear maps. Our construction starts from a canonical function hiding IPE scheme (for $D = 2$), and inductively build degree-$(D+1)$ HIPE scheme, by composing a degree-D HIPE scheme and a special-purpose function hiding IPE scheme. Our HIPE schemes have *canonical form* (similar to the canonical form for standard IPE): Ciphertexts (or secret keys) at coordinate d (or D) consist of encodings in the dth (or D^{th} respectively) MMap source group, and decryption uses degree-D pairing to produce an encoding of the degree-D inner product. That is,

$$\mathsf{hIPE.Dec}(\mathsf{hSK}(\mathbf{x}^D), \mathsf{hCT}^1(\mathbf{x}^1), \cdots, \mathsf{hCT}^D(\mathbf{x}^{D-1})) = [\langle \mathbf{x}^1, \cdots, \mathbf{x}^D \rangle]$$

From Degree-D HIPE to Degree-D FE. HIPE works perfectly for our goal of compressing the ciphertext iCT. Generalizing **qFE**, our degree-D FE scheme **dFE** generates ciphertexts as follows:

$$\mathsf{CT}(\mathbf{x}) = \left(\mathsf{cCT}'(-r||0),\ \left\{ \mathsf{cCT}_i^1(\mathbf{X}_i^1),\ \cdots,\ \mathsf{cCT}_i^{D-1}(\mathbf{X}_i^{D-1}),\ \mathsf{cSK}_i(\mathbf{X}_i^D) \right\}_{i \in [N]} \right)$$

$$\text{where } \mathbf{X}_i^d = \chi_i^d||\mathbf{0} \text{ and } \chi_i^d = \begin{cases} x_i||s_i^d & \text{if } d < D \\ x_i||rs_i^D & \text{if } d = D \end{cases}.$$

From such a ciphertext, a decryptor can "expand" out a size-N^D **IPE** ciphertext iCT by decrypting every combination of HIPE ciphertexts and secret keys. Namely, for every $I \in [N]^D$,

$$\mathsf{hIPE.Dec}(\mathsf{cCT}_{I_1}^1,\ \cdots,\ \mathsf{cCT}_{I_{D-1}}^{D-1},\ \mathsf{cSK}_{I_D}) = [\langle \mathbf{X}_{I_1}^1, \cdots, \mathbf{X}_{I_D}^D \rangle]$$

$$= \left[r \prod_{d \in [D]} s_{I_d}^d + \prod_{d \in [D]} x_{I_d} \right] = \mathsf{iCT}[I]$$

where $\mathsf{iCT}[I]$ encrypts the Ith degree-D monomial $\prod_{d \in [D]} x_{I_d}$, using the Ith key element $\prod_{d \in [D]} s_{I_d}^d$.

To show security of **dFE**, we, again, switch the degree-D monomials encrypted in the **IPE** ciphertext iCT in piecemeal. In each step, we can still only embed a size-N ciphertext-piece; naturally we embed $\mathsf{iCT}[\rho, \star]$ for a prefix $\rho \in [N]^{D-1}$ of length $D-1$. Thus, the N^D encrypted monomials are changed piece by piece in N^{D-1} steps, where in the ρth step, all monomials with index I smaller than ρ (*i.e.*, $I_{\leq D-1} < \rho$) have already been switched to $\prod_{d \in [D]} v_{I_d}$, monomials with index I larger than ρ (*i.e.*, $I_{\leq D-1} > \rho$) remain to be $\prod_{d \in [D]} u_{I_d}$, and monomials with index I that agrees with ρ (*i.e.*, $I_{\leq D-1} = \rho$) are being switched from $\prod_{d \in [D]} u_{I_d}$ in H_ρ^0 to $\prod_{d \in [D]} v_{I_d}$ in H_ρ^1.

Creating a sequence of hybrids that carry out these steps is more complex than the case for degree 2. First, we need more space in the ciphertext to make sure that the right monomials are encrypted for every index I; thus, the vectors $\mathbf{X}$'s are padded to length $2D-1$. Second, it becomes significantly harder to argue that the key elements $(\prod_{d\in[D-1]} s^d_{\rho_d})\mathbf{s}^{\leq D}$ are pseudorandom, as the shares s^d_i's are encoded in different MMap source groups, and unlike the degree 2 case, we cannot eliminate the appearance of all shares $\{s^d_{\rho_d}\}$ since they are also used for generating the master secret keys of other ciphertext-pieces (whereas in the degree 2 case, s^1_ρ is only used for generating $s^1_\rho\mathbf{s}^2$). To resolve this, we apply the SXDH assumption iteratively to gradually replace every partial product $\prod_{d\in[d^\star]} s^d_{\rho_d}$ with an independent and random element w^d_ρ, so that, the master secret keys for other ciphertext-pieces are generated using independent w elements.

2.4 Construction of HIPE

We construct function hiding HIPE schemes by induction in the degree D.

- **For the base case of** $D = 2$, function hiding degree-2 HIPE is identical to function hiding IPE, which we give a new construction discussed shortly in the next subsection.
- **For the induction step**, we show that for any $D \geq 2$, if there exist a function hiding degree-D HIPE scheme, denoted as **dIPE**, from SXDH on degree-D MMap, then there exist a function-hiding degree-$(D+1)$ HIPE scheme, denoted as **hIPE**, from SXDH on degree-$(D+1)$ MMap. Our induction keeps the invariant that both **dIPE** and **hIPE** have canonical form.

In the induction step, we construct the degree-$D+1$ scheme **hIPE**, by combining the degree-D scheme **dIPE**, with a special purpose IPE scheme **sIPE**. Denote by $(\mathsf{hCT}^1, \cdots, \mathsf{hCT}^D)$ and hSK the ciphertexts and secret key of **hIPE**, $(\mathsf{dCT}^1, \cdots, \mathsf{dCT}^{D-1})$ and dSK that of **dIPE**, and sCT and sSK that of **sIPE**.

To achieve functionality, we need to specify how to generate ciphertexts and secret key for input vectors $\mathbf{x}^1, \cdots, \mathbf{x}^D$ and $\mathbf{x}^{D+1}$, so that,

$$\mathsf{hIPE.Dec}(\mathsf{hSK}, \mathsf{hCT}^1, \cdots, \mathsf{hCT}^D) = [\langle \mathbf{x}^1, \cdots, \mathbf{x}^D, \mathbf{x}^{D+1}\rangle].$$

Observe that a degree-$(D+1)$ inner product of $\mathbf{x}^1, \cdots \mathbf{x}^{D+1}$, can be computed as the inner product between $\mathbf{x}^{D+1}$ and the coordinate-wise product of the first D vectors $\prod_{d\in[D]} \mathbf{x}^d$, denoted as $\mathbf{x}^{\leq D}$, that is,

$$y = \langle \mathbf{x}^1, \cdots \mathbf{x}^{D+1}\rangle = \left\langle \prod_{d\in[D]} \mathbf{x}^d, \mathbf{x}^{D+1} \right\rangle = \langle \mathbf{x}^{\leq D}, \mathbf{x}^{D+1}\rangle$$

Therefore, if the decryptor obtains a pair of **sIPE** ciphertext and secret key $(\mathsf{sCT}, \mathsf{sSK})$ for $(\mathbf{x}^{\leq D}, \mathbf{x}^{D+1})$, he/she can decrypt to obtain $[y]$. To do so, our new scheme **hIPE** simply publishes sSK as its secret key,

$$\textbf{Secret key of hIPE:} \qquad \mathsf{hSK} = \mathsf{sSK} \leftarrow \mathsf{sIPE.KeyGen}(\mathsf{sMSK}, \mathbf{x}^{D+1}).$$

However, it cannot directly publish a ciphertext of $\mathbf{x}^{\leq D}$, as $\mathbf{x}^{\leq D}$ is the product of D input vectors, but each encryption algorithm $\mathsf{hIPE.Enc}^d$ receives only a single vector $\mathbf{x}^d$ as input and cannot compute $\mathbf{x}^{\leq D}$. The idea is to include in the D ciphertexts $\mathsf{hCT}^1, \cdots, \mathsf{hCT}^D$ of **hIPE**, ciphertexts and secret keys of the degree-D scheme, so that the decryptor can combine them to generate a ciphertext sCT of $\mathbf{x}^{\leq D}$.

Towards this end, we rely on the first property of **sIPE** that its ciphertext sCT consists of many encodings $\{\mathsf{sCT}_l\}_{l\in[L]}$. Suppose that the element encoded sct_l in every encoding sCT_l can be expressed as the inner product of D vectors

Condition C: $\quad \mathrm{sct}_l = \langle \chi_l^1, \cdots \chi_l^D \rangle$, and each χ_l^d depends only on $\mathbf{x}^d$,

Then, it suffices to encode these vectors in a tuple $(\mathsf{dCT}_l^1, \cdots \mathsf{dCT}_l^{D-1}, \mathsf{dSK}_l)$ of ciphertexts and secret key of **dIPE** using an independently sampled master secret key dMSK_l, from which the decryptor can obtain exactly sCT_l. Thus, the D ciphertexts $\mathsf{hCT}^1, \cdots, \mathsf{hCT}^D$ of our new scheme **hIPE** consists of exactly one such tuple $(\mathsf{dCT}_l^1, \cdots \mathsf{dCT}_l^{D-1}, \mathsf{dSK}_l)$ for every l, namely,

Ciphertext of hIPE:

$$\mathsf{hCT}^d = \begin{cases} \left\{\mathsf{dCT}_l^d \leftarrow \mathsf{dIPE.Enc}(\mathsf{dMSK}_l, \chi_l^d)\right\}_{l\in[L]} & \text{if } d \leq D \\ \left\{\mathsf{dSK}_l \leftarrow \mathsf{dIPE.KeyGen}(\mathsf{dMSK}_l, \chi_l^D)\right\}_{l\in[L]} & \text{if } d = D \end{cases}.$$

Given $(\mathsf{hCT}^1, \cdots, \mathsf{hCT}^D)$ and hSK as specified above, the decryptor proceeds in two steps:

1. First, decrypt for every l, the tuple $(\mathsf{dCT}_l^1, \cdots \mathsf{dCT}_l^{D-1}, \mathsf{dSK}_l)$ using the decryption algorithm of **dIPE** to obtain sCT_l; put them together to get a ciphertext sCT of $\mathbf{x}^{\leq D}$.
2. Then, decrypt the obtained ciphertext sCT using the decryption algorithm of **sIPE** and secret key $\mathsf{hSK} = \mathsf{sSK}$ of $\mathbf{x}^{D+1}$ to obtain an encoding of the final inner product y, as illustrated below.

$$\underbrace{\mathsf{hCT}^1 = \{\mathsf{dCT}_l^1\}_l, \quad \cdots, \quad \overbrace{\mathsf{hCT}^{D-1} = \{\mathsf{dCT}_l^{D-1}\}_l, \quad \mathsf{hCT}^D = \{\mathsf{dSK}_l\}_l}} \quad \mathsf{hSK} = \mathsf{sSK}$$

Decrypt to sCT

Decrypt to $[y]$

Setting Condition C – A First Attempt. We now argue that **Condition C** above indeed holds. This relies on a second property of the special-purpose IPE scheme **sIPE** that the elements $\{\mathrm{sct}_l\}$ encoded in its ciphertext sCT, depends *linearly* in the encrypted vector $\mathbf{x}^{\leq D}$ and randomness $\mathbf{r}$ of encryption. More specifically, when the master secret key sMSK is fixed, each element sct_l is the output of a linear function $h_l^{(\mathsf{sMSK})}$ on input $(\mathbf{x}^{\leq D}, \mathbf{r})$,

$$\mathsf{sCT} = \mathsf{sIPE.Enc}(\mathsf{sMSK},\ \mathbf{x}^{\leq D};\ \mathbf{r}) = \{[\mathrm{sct}_l]\}_l\,,$$
$$\text{with } \mathrm{sct}_l = h_l^{(\mathsf{sMSK})}(\mathbf{x}^{\leq D},\ \mathbf{r}) = \left\langle \mathbf{c}_l^{(\mathsf{sMSK})}, (\mathbf{x}^{\leq D}||\mathbf{r}) \right\rangle,$$

where $\mathbf{c}_l^{(\mathsf{sMSK})}$ is the coefficient vector of $h_l^{(\mathsf{sMSK})}$. Then, since $\mathbf{x}^{\leq D} = \mathbf{x}^1 \cdots \mathbf{x}^D$, we can represent sct_l as the inner product of D vectors $\chi_l^1, \cdots, \chi_l^D$, each depending on only one input vector $\mathbf{x}^D$, as follows:

$$\mathrm{sct}_l = \langle \chi_l^1, \chi_l^2, \cdots \chi_l^D \rangle \qquad \chi_l^d = \begin{cases} \mathbf{x}^1 || \underline{\mathbf{r}} & \text{if } d = 1 \\ \mathbf{x}^d || \mathbf{1} & \text{if } 1 < d < D \\ (\mathbf{x}^D || \mathbf{1}) \underline{(\mathbf{c}_l^{(\mathsf{sMSK})})} & \text{if } d = D \end{cases}.$$

Therefore, as discussed above, encrypting the vectors $\{\chi_l^d\}$ in the ciphertexts of **hIPE** guarantees that the decryptor can obtain sCT from the ciphertexts, and decrypting the ciphertext sCT further produces an encoding of the correct output y.

A Security Issue. The above way of setting the vectors $\{\chi_l^d\}_{d,l}$ achieves functionality, but, does not guarantee security. A security issue stems from the fact that the randomness $\mathbf{r}$ used for generating the ciphertext sCT is hardcoded entirely in the input vectors $\{\chi_l^1\}_l$ encrypted at the first coordinate. Consider a simple scenario where a single ciphertext of **hIPE** at the first coordinate, two ciphertexts at each other coordinate, and a single secret key, are published:

$$\begin{array}{ccccc} \mathsf{hCT}^1, & \mathsf{hCT}_0^2, & \cdots, & \mathsf{hCT}_0^D, & \mathsf{hSK} \\ & \mathsf{hCT}_1^2, & \cdots, & \mathsf{hCT}_1^D & \end{array}$$

Since the randomness $\mathbf{r}$ is embedded in hCT^1, different combinations of ciphertexts, say hCT^1 and $\mathsf{hCT}_{b_2}^2 \cdots \mathsf{hCT}_{b_D}^D$, produce **sIPE** ciphertexts encrypting different vectors, $\mathbf{x}^1\mathbf{x}_{b_2}^2 \cdots \mathbf{x}_{b_D}^D$, but using the same random coins $\mathbf{r}$. The security of **sIPE** does not hold when attackers can observe ciphertexts with shared randomness, and in particular, information of the encrypted vector $\mathbf{x}^1\mathbf{x}_{b_2}^2 \cdots \mathbf{x}_{b_D}^D$ may be revealed. On the other hand, the function hiding property requires that only the final degree-$(D+1)$ inner products $\mathbf{x}^1\mathbf{x}_{b_2}^2 \cdots \mathbf{x}_{b_D}^D \mathbf{x}^{D+1}$ are revealed, and nothing else.

Setting Condition C, Right. To address this security issue, we need to ensure that ciphertexts sCT produced by different combinations of ciphertexts of **hIPE** correspond to (at the very least) distinct randomness. To do so, we embed fresh randomness $\mathbf{r}^d$ in ciphertexts at every coordinate by modifying the encrypted vectors χ_l^d to the following:

$$\chi_l^d = \begin{cases} \mathbf{x}^d || \underline{\mathbf{r}^d} & \text{if } d < D \\ (\mathbf{x}^D || \underline{\mathbf{r}^D})(\mathbf{c}_l^{(\mathsf{sMSK})}) & \text{if } d = D \end{cases}$$

Note that the inner products of these vectors correspond to a ciphertext sCT generated using random coins $\mathbf{r}^{\leq D} = \prod_{d \in [D]} \mathbf{r}^d$. That is,

$$\langle \chi_1, \cdots, \chi_D \rangle = \left\langle \mathbf{c}_l^{(\mathsf{sMSK})}, (\mathbf{x}^{\leq D} || \mathbf{r}^{\leq D}) \right\rangle = h_l^{(\mathsf{sMSK})}(\mathbf{x}^{\leq D},\ \mathbf{r}^{\leq D}) = \mathrm{sct}_l,$$

$$\mathsf{sCT} = \{[\mathrm{sct}_l]\}_l = \mathsf{sIPE.Enc}(\mathsf{sMSK},\ \mathbf{x}^{\leq D};\ \mathbf{r}^{\leq D}).$$

In the simple scenario above, combining $\mathsf{hCT}^1, \mathsf{hCT}^2_{b_2} \cdots, \mathsf{hCT}^D_{b_D}$ now produces sCT with randomness $\mathbf{r}^1\mathbf{r}^2_{b_2} \cdots \mathbf{r}^D_{b_D}$, which is distinct for each combination.

Having distinct randomness is still not enough for applying the security of **sIPE**, which requires independently and uniformly sampled randomness. We will rely on the SXDH assumption to argue that they are indeed pseudorandom. The security analysis of the above scheme turns out to be quite complicated, and in fact for security to hold, the scheme needs to further pad the vectors χ^d_l with zeros, serving as redundant space for hardwiring information in different hybrids in the security proof.

2.5 Simple Function Hiding IPE

As described above, our construction of degree-D FE crucially relies on a *canonical* function hiding IPE. However, known secret-key IPE schemes [12,24,44] do not have the canonical form, in particular, their decryption does not produce an encoding of the output inner product $[\langle \mathbf{x}, \mathbf{y} \rangle]$, but produce the inner product masked by a scalar $[\langle \mathbf{x}, \mathbf{y} \rangle\, \theta]$ together with $[\theta]$, where the scalar θ is determined by the randomness used in key generation and encryption. In this work, we give a construction of a *canonical* function hiding IPE. Our construction is extremely simple and may be of independent interests. We now summarize the idea of the construction in one paragraph.

Lin and Vaikuntanathan [44] give a simple transformation from IPE with weak function hiding to IPE with full function hiding. Our construction starts from the ABDP public key IPE scheme, whose secret key for a vector $\mathbf{y}$ reveals $\mathbf{y}$ and its inner product with the master secret key $\langle \mathbf{s}, \mathbf{y} \rangle$ in the clear. To achieve weak function hiding, we need to hide $\mathbf{y}$. Our idea is to simply encrypt the secret key as an input vector using the ABDP scheme itself, with an independently sampled master secret key $\mathbf{s}'$ of length $N+1$, which yields the new secret key $\mathsf{iSK}' = [r'\mathbf{s}' + (\langle \mathbf{s}, \mathbf{y} \rangle \,||\, \mathbf{y})]$. Recall that decryption of the ABDP scheme simply computes (homomorphically) the inner product between its secret key and ciphertext. Now that the original secret key is encrypted, we correspondingly encode the original ciphertext in a secret key using $\mathbf{s}'$, which gives the new ciphertext $\mathsf{iCT}' = [\langle \mathbf{s}' , (r\mathbf{s} + \mathbf{x}) \rangle \,||\, (r\mathbf{s} + \mathbf{x})]$. Computing the "inner product" of iCT' and iSK' using paring simultaneously decrypts both "layers" of ABDP encryption, and produce exactly an encoding of the output inner product.

We have described ideas underlying our FE and IO constructions; due to the lack of space, we refer the reader to the full version [42] for their formal description and proofs. With a better view of the constructions and security proofs, next, we revisit the topic of instantiating our schemes with known noisy multilinear map candidates in more detail.

2.6 On Instantiation with Noisy Multilinear Maps

As mentioned in the introduction when replacing algebraic multilinear maps with noisy ones [21,22,26,31,39], the constructions work as-is, but not the security proofs. Nevertheless, the security proof can be modified into an ideal model proof, or a proof based on a family of more complex assumptions.

The FE Security Proof Fails. The only component in our IO construction that relies on MMaps is the low-degree FE scheme. When using known noisy MMap candidates, its security proofs fail for two reasons:

1. *The SXDH assumption does not hold on known noisy MMap candidates.* Roughly speaking, a noisy multilinear map scheme can encode a ring element a and a label l with some noise. Let L be a set of labels that correspond to the set of source groups in algebraic MMaps. Translating the SXDH assumption to the noisy setting would require for every label $l \in L$, the distribution of randomly sampled encodings of a, b, ab with label l to be indistinguishable to that of a, b, r, for random ring elements a, b, r, *even when low-level encodings of 1 with each label* $l \in L$ *is published.* Unfortunately, given these encodings of 1, known noisy MMap candidates can be completely broken.
2. The security reduction uses the *homomorphic scalar multiplication* functionality of algebraic MMaps, which is not support by current candidates.

The reason that encodings of 1 is needed in the assumption and homomorphic scalar multiplication is needed for the reduction is as follows. The security of the FE scheme is based on the SXDH assumption, via a security reduction that turns FE attackers to SXDH distinguishers. To do so, given a challenge sampled according to (one of the two distributions specified in) the SXDH assumption, our reduction internally simulates the view of the attacker in the FE security game, and appropriately *embeds* the challenge into the view. Since the challenge is "laconic"—containing only a constant number of encodings. To concoct the attacker's view, the reduction needs to (i) generate new encodings and (ii) randomize some encodings in the challenge for embedding. It does so using encodings of 1 in the challenge and homomorphic scalar multiplication. It seems (to us) that any reduction to a *laconic* and/or *instance-independent* assumption (*i.e.*, one that is independent of the scheme and the attacker) necessarily needs the capabilities of generating and randomizing encodings. This is indeed the case for previous such reductions [33,44] and they also require homomorphic scalar multiplication. Designing a reduction that does not rely on homomorphic scalar multiplication, or rely only on homomorphic scalar multiplication with *small* scalars is an interesting open question.

Security Proofs to Non-laconic Assumptions, and in Ideal MMap Model. Above problems can be eliminated if we give up on having a security reduction to a laconic and instance-independent assumption. In particular, our security proof presents a sequence of hybrids that gradually "morph" from one honest execution of the FE scheme to another (where the attacker receives secret keys and ciphertexts of different functions and inputs as specified in the security definition of FE). Each pair of neighboring hybrids defines an indistinguishability assumption that simply states that the attacker's views in these two hybrids are indistinguishable, and the security of FE can be based on such a family of non-laconic and instance-dependent assumptions, without using encodings of 1 and homomorphic scalar multiplication. Such a security proof is non-trivial since the assumptions only require indistinguishability of distributions that are almost identical modulo the difference induced by switching a single DDH tuple to a random tuple. Moreover, since these assumptions hold in the ideal model, such a proof also gives a proof in degree-5 ideal multilinear map model.

Instantiating the Construction with Noisy Multilinear Maps. We can instantiate our FE scheme with noisy MMaps and correctness holds. The above-discussed issues w.r.t. the security proof do not appear when instantiating the construction. This is because the secret keys and ciphertexts of our FE scheme do not contain any low-level encodings of 0 or 1, in fact, they contain only encodings of large randomized elements, and its algorithms do not rely on homomorphic scalar multiplication. We note, however, decryption may generate *top-level* encodings of 0 or 1 for correctness. It is unclear (to us) whether these instantiations are secure against known cryptanalytic attacks. We do not know whether known attacks can be adapted to break their security, nor have formal arguments that validate their security against known attacks. Obtaining a concrete attack or give some formal proof, such as, a security proof in the weak MMap model [29], are interesting open problems.

Acknowledgements. The author thanks Benny Applebaum, Nir Bitansky, Stefano Tessaro, and Vinod Vaikuntanathan for many helpful and insightful discussions.

References

1. Abdalla, M., Bourse, F., De Caro, A., Pointcheval, D.: Simple functional encryption schemes for inner products. In: Katz, J. (ed.) PKC 2015. LNCS, vol. 9020, pp. 733–751. Springer, Heidelberg (2015). doi:10.1007/978-3-662-46447-2_33
2. Ananth, P., Jain, A.: Indistinguishability obfuscation from compact functional encryption. In: Gennaro, R., Robshaw, M. (eds.) CRYPTO 2015. LNCS, vol. 9215, pp. 308–326. Springer, Heidelberg (2015). doi:10.1007/978-3-662-47989-6_15
3. Ananth, P., Jain, A., Sahai, A.: Achieving compactness generically: indistinguishability obfuscation from non-compact functional encryption. IACR Cryptology ePrint Archive, vol. 2015, p. 730 (2015)
4. Ananth, P., Sahai, A.: Projective arithmetic functional encryption and indistinguishability obfuscation from degree-5 multilinear maps. In: Coron, J.-S., Nielsen, J.B. (eds.) EUROCRYPT 2017. LNCS, vol. 10210, pp. 152–181. Springer, Cham (2017). doi:10.1007/978-3-319-56620-7_6
5. Ananth, P.V., Gupta, D., Ishai, Y., Sahai, A.: Optimizing obfuscation: avoiding Barrington's theorem. In: ACM CCS 2014, Scottsdale, AZ, USA, pp. 646–658, 3–7 November 2014
6. Apon, D., Döttling, N., Garg, S., Mukherjee, P.: Cryptanalysis of indistinguishability obfuscations of circuits over GGH 2013. In: ICALP 2017. LNCS. Springer, Heidelberg (2017)
7. Applebaum, B., Brakerski, Z.: Obfuscating circuits via composite-order graded encoding. In: Dodis, Y., Nielsen, J.B. (eds.) TCC 2015. LNCS, vol. 9015, pp. 528–556. Springer, Heidelberg (2015). doi:10.1007/978-3-662-46497-7_21

8. Applebaum, B., Ishai, Y., Kushilevitz, E.: Cryptography in nc^0. In: FOCS, pp. 166–175 (2004)
9. Barak, B., Brakerski, Z., Komargodski, I., Kothari, P.K.: Limits on low-degree pseudorandom generators (or: sum-of-squares meets program obfuscation). Cryptology ePrint Archive, Report 2017/312 (2017). http://eprint.iacr.org/2017/312
10. Barak, B., Garg, S., Kalai, Y.T., Paneth, O., Sahai, A.: Protecting obfuscation against algebraic attacks. In: Nguyen, P.Q., Oswald, E. (eds.) EUROCRYPT 2014. LNCS, vol. 8441, pp. 221–238. Springer, Heidelberg (2014). doi:10.1007/978-3-642-55220-5_13
11. Barak, B., Goldreich, O., Impagliazzo, R., Rudich, S., Sahai, A., Vadhan, S., Yang, K.: On the (im)possibility of obfuscating programs. In: Kilian, J. (ed.) CRYPTO 2001. LNCS, vol. 2139, pp. 1–18. Springer, Heidelberg (2001). doi:10.1007/3-540-44647-8_1
12. Bishop, A., Jain, A., Kowalczyk, L.: Function-hiding inner product encryption. In: Iwata, T., Cheon, J.H. (eds.) ASIACRYPT 2015. LNCS, vol. 9452, pp. 470–491. Springer, Heidelberg (2015). doi:10.1007/978-3-662-48797-6_20
13. Bitansky, N., Nishimaki, R., Passelègue, A., Wichs, D.: From cryptomania to obfustopia through secret-key functional encryption. In: Hirt, M., Smith, A. (eds.) TCC 2016. LNCS, vol. 9986, pp. 391–418. Springer, Heidelberg (2016). doi:10.1007/978-3-662-53644-5_15
14. Bitansky, N., Vaikuntanathan, V.: Indistinguishability obfuscation from functional encryption. In: IEEE 56th Annual Symposium on Foundations of Computer Science, FOCS 2015, 17–20 October 2015, Berkeley, CA, USA, pp. 171–190 (2015)
15. Boneh, D., Silverberg, A.: Applications of multilinear forms to cryptography. Contemp. Math. **324**, 71–90 (2002)
16. Boneh, D., Wu, D.J., Zimmerman, J.: Immunizing multilinear maps against zeroizing attacks. Cryptology ePrint Archive, Report 2014/930 (2014). http://eprint.iacr.org/2014/930
17. Brakerski, Z., Rothblum, G.N.: Virtual black-box obfuscation for all circuits via generic graded encoding. In: Lindell, Y. (ed.) TCC 2014. LNCS, vol. 8349, pp. 1–25. Springer, Heidelberg (2014). doi:10.1007/978-3-642-54242-8_1
18. Chen, Y., Gentry, C., Halevi, S.: Cryptanalyses of candidate branching program obfuscators. In: Coron, J.-S., Nielsen, J.B. (eds.) EUROCRYPT 2017. LNCS, vol. 10212, pp. 278–307. Springer, Cham (2017). doi:10.1007/978-3-319-56617-7_10
19. Cheon, J.H., Han, K., Lee, C., Ryu, H., Stehlé, D.: Cryptanalysis of the multilinear map over the integers. In: Oswald, E., Fischlin, M. (eds.) EUROCRYPT 2015. LNCS, vol. 9056, pp. 3–12. Springer, Heidelberg (2015). doi:10.1007/978-3-662-46800-5_1
20. Coron, J.-S., et al.: Zeroizing without low-level zeroes: new MMAP attacks and their limitations. In: Gennaro, R., Robshaw, M. (eds.) CRYPTO 2015. LNCS, vol. 9215, pp. 247–266. Springer, Heidelberg (2015). doi:10.1007/978-3-662-47989-6_12
21. Coron, J.-S., Lepoint, T., Tibouchi, M.: Practical multilinear maps over the integers. In: Canetti, R., Garay, J.A. (eds.) CRYPTO 2013. LNCS, vol. 8042, pp. 476–493. Springer, Heidelberg (2013). doi:10.1007/978-3-642-40041-4_26
22. Coron, J.-S., Lepoint, T., Tibouchi, M.: New multilinear maps over the integers. In: Gennaro, R., Robshaw, M. (eds.) CRYPTO 2015. LNCS, vol. 9215, pp. 267–286. Springer, Heidelberg (2015). doi:10.1007/978-3-662-47989-6_13
23. Cryan, M., Miltersen, P.B.: On pseudorandom generators in NC^0. In: Sgall, J., Pultr, A., Kolman, P. (eds.) MFCS 2001. LNCS, vol. 2136, pp. 272–284. Springer, Heidelberg (2001). doi:10.1007/3-540-44683-4_24

24. Datta, P., Dutta, R., Mukhopadhyay, S.: Functional encryption for inner product with full function privacy. In: Cheng, C.-M., Chung, K.-M., Persiano, G., Yang, B.-Y. (eds.) PKC 2016. LNCS, vol. 9614, pp. 164–195. Springer, Heidelberg (2016). doi:10.1007/978-3-662-49384-7_7
25. Döttling, N., Garg, S., Gupta, D., Miao, P., Mukherjee, P.: Obfuscation from low noise multilinear maps. Cryptology ePrint Archive, Report 2016/599 (2016). http://eprint.iacr.org/2016/599
26. Garg, S., Gentry, C., Halevi, S.: Candidate multilinear maps from ideal lattices. In: Johansson, T., Nguyen, P.Q. (eds.) EUROCRYPT 2013. LNCS, vol. 7881, pp. 1–17. Springer, Heidelberg (2013). doi:10.1007/978-3-642-38348-9_1
27. Garg, S., Gentry, C., Halevi, S., Raykova, M., Sahai, A., Waters, B.: Candidate indistinguishability obfuscation and functional encryption for all circuits. In: 54th Annual IEEE Symposium on Foundations of Computer Science, FOCS 2013, 26–29 October 2013, Berkeley, CA, USA, pp. 40–49 (2013)
28. Garg, S., Gentry, C., Halevi, S., Zhandry, M.: Functional encryption without obfuscation. In: Kushilevitz, E., Malkin, T. (eds.) TCC 2016. LNCS, vol. 9563, pp. 480–511. Springer, Heidelberg (2016). doi:10.1007/978-3-662-49099-0_18
29. Garg, S., Miles, E., Mukherjee, P., Sahai, A., Srinivasan, A., Zhandry, M.: Secure obfuscation in a weak multilinear map model. In: Hirt, M., Smith, A. (eds.) TCC 2016. LNCS, vol. 9986, pp. 241–268. Springer, Heidelberg (2016). doi:10.1007/978-3-662-53644-5_10
30. Garg, S., Mukherjee, P., Srinivasan, A.: Obfuscation without the vulnerabilities of multilinear maps. IACR Cryptology ePrint Archive, vol. 2016, p. 390 (2016)
31. Gentry, C., Gorbunov, S., Halevi, S.: Graph-induced multilinear maps from lattices. In: Dodis, Y., Nielsen, J.B. (eds.) TCC 2015. LNCS, vol. 9015, pp. 498–527. Springer, Heidelberg (2015). doi:10.1007/978-3-662-46497-7_20
32. Gentry, C., Halevi, S., Maji, H.K., Sahai, A.: Zeroizing without zeroes: cryptanalyzing multilinear maps without encodings of zero. Cryptology ePrint Archive, Report 2014/929 (2014). http://eprint.iacr.org/2014/929
33. Gentry, C., Lewko, A.B., Sahai, A., Waters, B.: Indistinguishability obfuscation from the multilinear subgroup elimination assumption. In: Guruswami [36], pp. 151–170 (2015)
34. Goldreich, O.: Candidate one-way functions based on expander graphs. In: Electronic Colloquium on Computational Complexity (ECCC), vol. 7, no. 90 (2000)
35. Goldwasser, S., et al.: Multi-input functional encryption. In: Nguyen, P.Q., Oswald, E. (eds.) EUROCRYPT 2014. LNCS, vol. 8441, pp. 578–602. Springer, Heidelberg (2014). doi:10.1007/978-3-642-55220-5_32
36. Guruswami, V. (ed.) IEEE 56th Annual Symposium on Foundations of Computer Science, FOCS 2015, 17–20 October 2015. IEEE Computer Society, Berkeley (2015)
37. Ishai, Y., Kushilevitz, E.: Perfect constant-round secure computation via perfect randomizing polynomials. In: Widmayer, P., Eidenbenz, S., Triguero, F., Morales, R., Conejo, R., Hennessy, M. (eds.) ICALP 2002. LNCS, vol. 2380, pp. 244–256. Springer, Heidelberg (2002). doi:10.1007/3-540-45465-9_22
38. Katz, J., Sahai, A., Waters, B.: Predicate encryption supporting disjunctions, polynomial equations, and inner products. In: Smart, N. (ed.) EUROCRYPT 2008. LNCS, vol. 4965, pp. 146–162. Springer, Heidelberg (2008). doi:10.1007/978-3-540-78967-3_9
39. Langlois, A., Stehlé, D., Steinfeld, R.: GGHLite: more efficient multilinear maps from ideal lattices. In: Nguyen, P.Q., Oswald, E. (eds.) EUROCRYPT 2014. LNCS, vol. 8441, pp. 239–256. Springer, Heidelberg (2014). doi:10.1007/978-3-642-55220-5_14

40. Lewko, A., Okamoto, T., Sahai, A., Takashima, K., Waters, B.: Fully secure functional encryption: attribute-based encryption and (hierarchical) inner product encryption. In: Gilbert, H. (ed.) EUROCRYPT 2010. LNCS, vol. 6110, pp. 62–91. Springer, Heidelberg (2010). doi:10.1007/978-3-642-13190-5_4
41. Lin, H.: Indistinguishability obfuscation from constant-degree graded encoding schemes. In: Fischlin, M., Coron, J.-S. (eds.) EUROCRYPT 2016. LNCS, vol. 9665, pp. 28–57. Springer, Heidelberg (2016). doi:10.1007/978-3-662-49890-3_2
42. Lin, H.: Indistinguishability obfuscation from DDH on 5-linear maps and locality-5 PRGs. Cryptology ePrint Archive, Report 2016/1096 (2016). http://eprint.iacr.org/2016/1096
43. Lin, H., Tessaro, S.: Indistinguishability obfuscation from trilinear maps and block-wise local PRGs. In: CRYPTO 2017 (2017, to appear)
44. Lin, H., Vaikuntanathan, V.: Indistinguishability obfuscation from DDH-like assumptions on constant-degree graded encodings. In: IEEE 57th Annual Symposium on Foundations of Computer Science, FOCS 2016, New Brunswick, NJ, USA, 9–11 October 2016
45. Lombardi, A., Vaikuntanathan, V.: On the non-existence of blockwise 2-local PRGs with applications to indistinguishability obfuscation. Cryptology ePrint Archive, Report 2017/301 (2017). http://eprint.iacr.org/2017/301
46. Miles, E., Sahai, A., Zhandry, M.: Annihilation attacks for multilinear maps: cryptanalysis of indistinguishability obfuscation over GGH13. IACR Cryptology ePrint Archive, vol. 2016, p. 147 (2016)
47. Mossel, E., Shpilka, A., Trevisan, L.: On e-biased generators in NC0. In: 44th Symposium on Foundations of Computer Science (FOCS 2003), 11–14 October 2003, Cambridge, MA, USA, Proceedings, pp. 136–145 (2003)
48. O'Donnell, R., Witmer, D.: Goldreich's PRG: evidence for near-optimal polynomial stretch. In: IEEE 29th Conference on Computational Complexity, CCC 2014, Vancouver, BC, Canada, 11–13 June 2014, pp. 1–12 (2014)
49. Pass, R., Seth, K., Telang, S.: Indistinguishability obfuscation from semantically-secure multilinear encodings. In: Garay, J.A., Gennaro, R. (eds.) CRYPTO 2014. LNCS, vol. 8616, pp. 500–517. Springer, Heidelberg (2014). doi:10.1007/978-3-662-44371-2_28
50. Rothblum, R.D.: On the circular security of bit-encryption. In: Sahai, A. (ed.) TCC 2013. LNCS, vol. 7785, pp. 579–598. Springer, Heidelberg (2013). doi:10.1007/978-3-642-36594-2_32
51. Yao, A.C.: Protocols for secure computations (extended abstract). In: 23rd Annual Symposium on Foundations of Computer Science, 3–5 November 1982, Chicago, Illinois, USA, pp. 160–164 (1982)
52. Yao, A.C.-C.: How to generate and exchange secrets (extended abstract). In: FOCS, pp. 162–167 (1986)
53. Zimmerman, J.: How to obfuscate programs directly. In: Oswald, E., Fischlin, M. (eds.) EUROCRYPT 2015. LNCS, vol. 9057, pp. 439–467. Springer, Heidelberg (2015). doi:10.1007/978-3-662-46803-6_15

Indistinguishability Obfuscation from Trilinear Maps and Block-Wise Local PRGs

Huijia Lin(✉) and Stefano Tessaro

University of California, Santa Barbara, Santa Barbara, USA
{rachel.lin,tessaro}@cs.ucsb.edu

Abstract. We consider the question of finding the lowest degree L for which L-linear maps suffice to obtain IO. The current state of the art (Lin, EUROCRYPT'16, CRYPTO '17; Lin and Vaikunthanathan, FOCS'16; Ananth and Sahai, EUROCRYPT '17) is that L-linear maps (under suitable security assumptions) suffice for IO, assuming the existence of pseudo-random generators (PRGs) with output locality L. However, these works cannot answer the question of whether $L < 5$ suffices, as no polynomial-stretch PRG with locality lower than 5 exists.

In this work, we present a new approach that relies on the existence of PRGs with *block-wise locality* L, i.e., every output bit depends on at most L (disjoint) *input blocks*, each consisting of up to $\log \lambda$ input bits. We show that the existence of PRGs with block-wise locality is plausible for any $L \geq 3$, and also provide:

- A construction of a general-purpose indistinguishability obfuscator from L-linear maps and a subexponentially-secure PRG with block-wise locality L and polynomial stretch.
- A construction of general-purpose functional encryption from L-linear maps and any slightly super-polynomially secure PRG with block-wise locality L and polynomial stretch.

All our constructions are based on the SXDH assumption on L-linear maps and subexponential Learning With Errors (LWE) assumption, and follow by instantiating our new generic bootstrapping theorems with Lin's recently proposed FE scheme (CRYPTO '17). Inherited from Lin's work, our security proof requires algebraic multilinear maps (Boneh and Silverberg, Contemporary Mathematics), whereas security when using noisy multilinear maps is based on a family of more complex assumptions that hold in the generic model.

Our candidate PRGs with block-wise locality are based on Goldreich's local functions, and we show that the security of instantiations with block-wise locality $L \geq 3$ is backed by similar validation as constructions with (conventional) locality 5. We further complement this with hardness amplification techniques that further weaken the pseudorandomness requirements.

1 Introduction

Indistinguishability obfuscation (IO), first defined in the seminal work of Barak *et al.* [16], aims to obfuscate functionally equivalent programs into indistinguish-

J. Katz and H. Shacham (Eds.): CRYPTO 2017, Part I, LNCS 10401, pp. 630–660, 2017.
DOI: 10.1007/978-3-319-63688-7_21

able ones while preserving functionality. IO is an extraordinarily powerful object that has been shown to enable a large set of new cryptographic applications. All existing IO constructions [4,5,10,15,24,36,39,41,45,52,53,56,63,65] rely on *multilinear maps* or *graded encodings*. In particular, the power of an L-linear map – first made explicit by Boneh and Silverberg [23] – stems from the fact that it essentially allows to evaluate degree-L polynomials on secret encoded values, and to test whether the output of such polynomials is zero or not.

The case $L = 2$ corresponds to bilinear maps, which can be efficiently instantiated from elliptic curves. In contrast, the instantiation of L-linear maps with $L \geq 3$ has turned to be a far more challenging problem. Garg *et al.* [38] proposed in particular *noisy* (i.e., *approximate*) versions of L-linear maps for $L \geq 3$, and gave the first candidate construction. Unfortunately, vulnerabilities [6,27,28,31,59] were later demonstrated against this and subsequent candidates [32,33,44,51]. Of course, this does not mean that the resulting constructions are insecure. In fact, this has motivated the search for IO constructions which withstand all existing attacks [41].

IO from Low-Degree Multilinear Maps. This paper addresses the problem of finding the smallest L such that degree-L mutlilinear maps are sufficient for constructing IO. This fits within the more general goal of ultimately assessing whether bilinear maps are sufficient. While first-generation IO constructions all required polynomial-degree multilinear maps, a series of recent works [4,52,53, 56] reduced the required degree to $L = 5$, assuming the existence of PRGs with output locality 5 and subexponential LWE, and under suitable assumption on the 5-linear maps. However, these works left open the question of whether multilinear maps with degree $L < 5$ are sufficient.

Further reducing the degree is important. On the one hand, *if* IO can be achieved from bilinear maps, this is going to take us one step closer. On the other hand, even if bilinear maps would not suffice, it is potentially easier to find secure algebraic instantiations for low degree multilinear maps. Moreover, we want to understand the precise power these maps would enable.

Our Contributions, in a Nutshell. This paper presents a new paradigm for IO constructions which admits instantiations with L-linear maps for $L \geq 3$, provided the SXDH assumption holds for the L-linear map. While this falls short of achieving IO from bilinear maps, our result shifts the focus on the fact that the gap between two- and three-linear maps is a seemingly fundamental barrier to be overcome. In particular, under the assumptions needed for our construction be secure, this shows that building three-linear maps is as difficult as getting full-blown IO.

We fundamentally rely on the recent line of works on building IO from constant-degree multilinear maps [4,52,53,56], which all rely on so-called *local* pseudo-random generators (PRGs) – a PRG with *locality* L has every output bit depend on L input bits. It is known that if PRGs with locality L and polynomial stretch exist, then IO can be constructed from L-linear maps [4,53]. Unfortunately, we do not even have locality-4 (polynomial stretch) PRGs [34,60], and candidate PRGs only exist starting from locality 5 [47,60,61]. To circumvent the lower bound on PRG locality, we propose a new, relaxed, notion of locality, called *block-wise locality*. We build upon Lin's [53] recent IO construction, but show that in order to obtain IO from L-linear maps, it suffices to use PRGs with block-wise locality L. As we will discuss below, such PRGs can exist for L as low as three.

Block-Wise Locality and IO. We say that a PRG mapping $n \times \ell$ input bits to m output bits has *block-wise locality* L and *block-size* ℓ, if when viewing its input (i.e., the seed) as a matrix of $n \times \ell$ bits, every output bit depends on at most L *columns* in the matrix (as opposed to L input bits), as depicted in Fig. 1. Observe that that the actual locality of such PRGs can go up to $L \times \ell$, yet, it has the special structure that all these input bits come from merely L input columns. This special structure is the key feature that allows for replacing local PRGs with block-wise-local PRGs, in the following applications.

- *Application I:* If there exists a *subexponentially-secure* PRG with block-wise-locality L, and any block-size $\ell = O(\log \lambda)$, then we can construct general-purpose IO from L-linear maps.
- *Application II:* If the block-wise local PRG is only *slightly superpolynomially secure*, we can still build special-purpose IO for circuits with super-logarithmic length inputs, which implies full-fledged Functional Encryption (FE), from L-linear maps.

All our constructions come with security reductions to (1) the security of block-wise-local PRGs, (2) the SXDH assumption on L-linear maps, and (3) the subexponential Learning With Errors (LWE), where (2) and (3) have the same level of hardness as that of the PRG.

Concurrently, we investigate the existence of block-wise local PRGs. In particular, we propose candidates following the common paradigm for candidate

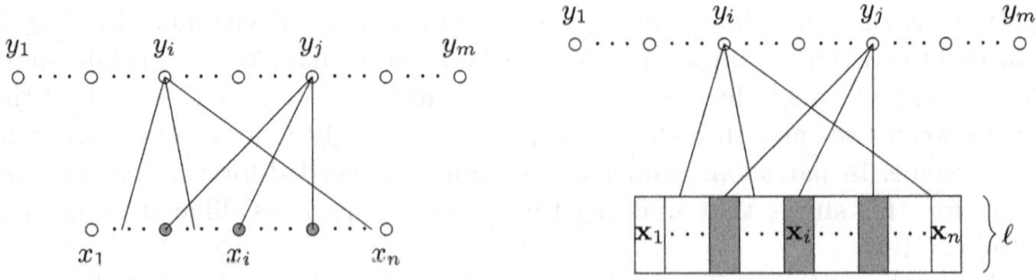

Fig. 1. Left: PRG with locality $L = 3$. Right: PRG with block-wise locality $L = 3$ and block size ℓ.

local PRGs [7,12,34,60,61], which are variants of Goldreich's functions [46]. We simply replace every PRG input bit with a column of ℓ input bits. Such a block-wise local PRG is parameterized by a bipartite expander graph and a predicate (or potentially a set of predicates) over $L \times \ell$ input bits. We discuss the security of these candidates, against known attacks, in relation to the choice of graph and predicate. Furthermore, aiming at weakening the assumption on our candidates, we present two hardness amplification techniques that amplify respectively the weaker *next-bit-unpredictability* property and *pseudo-min-entropy generation* property to different levels of pseudorandomness guarantees.

Instantiating the Underlying Multilinear Maps. We note that the results of this paper, per se, are merely new bootstrapping theorems, which do not rely, by themselves, on multilinear maps. More specifically, we show how to boostrap a FE scheme for computing degree-L polynomials to an IO scheme, using a PRG with block-wise-locality L, and then rely on Lin's [53] FE construction. Some remarks on instantiations of the underlying multilinear maps are in order.

Concretely, the FE scheme from [53] relies on algebraic L-linear maps, for which to date no candidate for $L \geq 3$ is known to exist. The alternative approach would be to instantiate them with existing noisy multilinear-map candidates. As discussed in [53, Sect. 2.6], the existing proof would however fail in this case, in addition to the SXDH assumption itself being false on exiting noisy multilinear-map candidates. Still, a proof for ideal multilinear maps would be valid, but it is not known whether (1) existing cryptanalytic attacks can be adapted to break a construction, or (2) whether a proof in a weak ideal model as in [41] is possible.

Background on Previous Versions of This Work. In a previous version of this paper, we incorrectly claimed that our approach can be extended to bilinear maps. Two subsequent works, one by Barak *et al.* [14], the other by Lombardi and Vaikuntanathan [57], have presented attacks against PRGs with block-wise locality two. Strictly speaking, these results leave a narrow window of expansion factors open where block-wise PRGs could exist, but we are not aware whether our approach could be modified to use such low-stretch PRGs, or whether the attacks can be extended. We discuss these results more in detail further below in Sect. 1.3.

In contrast, attacks for $L \geq 3$ appear out of reach, as our assumption is implied by that made by recent works in the area of local PRGs and PRFs, c.f. e.g. the pseudorandomness assumptions from the recent work by Applebaum and Raykov [13]—and in fact, our amplification results show that even less needs to be achieved by the local function.

1.1 Block-Wise Locality

A $(n \times \ell, m)$-PRG maps $n \times \ell$ input bits to m output bits. As introduced above, a PRG has block-wise locality L and block-size ℓ, if when viewing the input as a $n \times \ell$ matrix, every output bits depend on input bits in at most L columns. Such a function is fully specified by the input-output dependency graph G describing which input columns each output bit depends on, and the set of predicates $\{P_j\}_{j\in[m]}$ that each output bit is evaluated through.

In all our applications, we consider block-wise local PRGs with sufficiently large polynomial input- and output-lengths, n and m (in the security parameter λ) and logarithmic block-size $\ell = O(\log(\lambda))$. In this setting, a PRG has polynomial-stretch if $m = n^{1+\alpha}$ for some positive constant $\alpha > 0$. For convenience, below we assume such parameters are fixed in our discussion.

When compared with traditional local PRGs (which can be thought as the special case with block size $\ell = 1$), the advantage of block-wise local PRGs is that while they will still permit instantiations with L-linear maps in our applications, their output bits depend on $L \times \ell$ input bits, and hence we can use more complex, say logarithmic-degree, predicates. For this reason, known lower bounds on the locality of PRGs do not apply to block-wise locality, even when $L < 5$, when the block size satisfies $\ell = \Omega(\log(\lambda))$. Effectively, such PRGs can be seen as operating on input symbols with polynomial alphabet size. Moreover, the lower bounds in [34,60] show that for conventional locality, PRGs with polynomial stretch require $L \geq 5$, but they crucially rely on the fact that any locality-4 predicate is correlated with two of its input bits to rule out the existence of locality-4 PRGs. In contrast, a PRG with block-wise locality L can use predicates that depend on $L \log \lambda$ input bits; setting the predicate to be uncorrelated with any subset of $\log \lambda$ input bits circumvents the lower bound argument in [34,60].

Block-Wise Local PRGs via Local PRGs. Every function with block-wise locality L and block size ℓ is a function with locality $L\ell$. Therefore, the rich literature on the security of Goldreich's local functions (see Applebaum's survey [8]) provides guidelines on how to choose candidate block-wise local PRGs, more specifically, the dependency graph G and predicates $\{P_j\}$. In particular, the graph G should be (k, c)-expanding, i.e., every subset of $k' \leq k$ output bits depends on at least $c \times k'$ input columns, for appropriately large k and c. We show that for $L \geq 3$, a large $1 - o(1)$ fraction of graphs G is $(n^{1-\eta}, (1-\eta)L)$-expanding. This in turn means that we can think of this as an instance of Goldreich's function with locality $L\ell$ built from a graph which is $(n^{1-\eta}, (1-\eta)L\ell)$-expanding, thus taking us back to the classical setting studied in the literature.

Using this analogy, we can show for example that for block-wise locality 3 and block size 2, for most graphs G, the resulting function withstands all linear attacks with sub-exponential bias ϵ when using the predicate outputting $x_1^0 \oplus x_2^0 \oplus x_3^0 \oplus (x_1^1 \wedge x_2^1)$ on input three columns $(x_1^0, x_1^1), (x_2^0, x_2^1), (x_3^0, x_3^1)$. This is a criterion that has been adopted so far to validate PRG security of local functions.

Moving even one step further, Applebaum and Raykov [13] recently postulated the following (even stronger) pseudorandomness assumption on functions with logarithmic locality:

Assumption 1 (Informal). *For locality $D = O(\log \lambda)$, and arbitrarily polynomial output length $m = n^{1+\alpha}$, there exist a suitable predicate, P', such that,* *for* any *dependency graph* G' *that is* $(n^{1-\eta}, (1-\eta)D)$*-expanding for some* $0 < \eta < 1/2$*, the locality-D function specified by* P' *and* G' *is* $2^{-n^{1-\eta}}$*-pseudorandom again* $2^{n^{1-\eta}}$*-time distinguishers.*

In our setting, for block-wise locality $L \geq 3$ and block-size $\log\lambda$, we show that when choosing the dependency graph G at random, the obtained block-wise local function can be thought as a function with locality $D = L\log\lambda$ satisfying the properties specified by the Applebaum-Raykov assumption, with $1 - o(1)$ probability. In particular, such functions withstand myopic inversion attacks (cf. e.g. [30]). In fact, our applications only need pseudorandomness to hold for output length $m = n^{1+\alpha}$ for *some* arbitrarily small constant $\alpha > 0$, and against polynomial time attackers, thus a much weaker requirement than what is guaranteed by the Applebaum-Raykov assumption.

For the case $L = 2$, the assumption that a block-wise local PRG exists is not backed by any of the past results, and indeed, recent works (following up on an earlier version of this paper) show that blockwise-local PRGs with sufficient stretch do not exist. We discuss this further below in Sect. 1.3.

Amplification. In order to validate our assumptions even further, we present two transformations meant to enhance security of functions with block-wise locality. We consider two different techniques:

- Amplification Technique I: produces a PRG construction with *quasi-polynomial* indistinguishability-gap (to polynomial-time distinguishers), from any *unpredictable generator* satisfying just *polynomial next-bit unpredictability* (*i.e.*, the probability of predicting any output bit given previous output bits is at most $\frac{1}{2} + \frac{1}{\mathsf{poly}(\lambda)}$, albeit for predictors in quasi-polynomial time). Though such PRGs are not strong enough for constructing IO, it suffices for constructing FE from L-linear maps; see the next section.
- Amplification Technique II: produces a PRG construction with *sub-exponential* indistinguishability-gap, from certain special *pseudo-min-entropy-generator* whose output has sufficiently-high pseudo-min-entropy.

1.2 From Block-Wise Locality to IO and FE

We now move to an overview of our constructions from block-wise local PRGs.

IO from Subexponentially Secure Block-Wise-Local PRGs. Recent IO constructions from low-degree multilinear maps [4,53,56] follow a common two-step approach: They first implement appropriate FE schemes, and then transform them into an IO scheme; we refer to the second step as the (FE-to-IO) *bootstrapping step.* In more detail, they use locality-L PRGs in the bootstrapping step in order to start with FE schemes that support only computation of *degree-L polynomials*; they then show that such FE schemes can be constructed from L-linear maps. In this work, following the blueprint and technique in [53], we show how to replace the use of local PRGs with block-wise local PRGs within the bootstrapping step.

Theorem 1 (Bootstrapping using block-wise local PRGs). *Let L be any positive integer. There is a construction of IO for* P/poly *from the following primitives:*

- *Public-key fully-selectively-secure (collusion-resistant) FE for degree-L polynomials whose encryption time is linear in the input length (i.e., $\mathrm{poly}(\lambda)N$); or with a secret-key FE scheme with the same properties, assuming additionally the subexponential hardness of LWE with subexponential modulus-to-noise ratio.*
- *a PRG with block-wise locality L, block-size $\log\lambda$, and $n^{1+\alpha}$-stretch for some positive constant α.*

where both FE and PRG need to have subexponential security.

The type of secret-key FE schemes for degree-L polynomials needed above was constructed by Lin [53] assuming the SXDH assumption on L-linear maps.

Theorem 2 [53]. *Let L be any positive integer. Assuming the SXDH assumption on asymmetric L-linear maps, there is a construction of secret-key fully-selectively-secure (collusion-resistant) FE schemes for degree-L polynomials whose encryption time is linear in the input length (i.e., $\mathrm{poly}(\lambda)N$). Moreover, the security reduction has a polynomial security loss.*

Therefore, combining our new bootstrapping theorem with Lin's FE construction, we obtain IO from the subexponential SXDH assumption on L-linear maps, subexponentially-secure PRG with block-wise locality L, and subexponential LWE.

The Power of Super-Polynomially Secure Block-Wise Local PRGs. While constructing full-fledged IO for all polynomial-sized programs requires block-wise local PRGs with *subexponentially-security*, we ask what can be built from PRGs with weaker (slightly) *superpolynomial-security*. In particular, such PRGs can be obtained using the aforementioned *amplification technique I*, from unpredictable generator satisfying just polynomial next-bit unpredictability. To this end, we first give a parameterized version of Theorem 1 showing that if the PRG and L-linear maps are $(2^{-i\ell}\mathrm{negl})$-secure, then we can build IO schemes for circuits with $i\ell$-bit inputs.

Theorem 3 (Parameterized version of Theorem 1). *Let L be any positive integer. Then, there is a construction of IO for the class of polynomial-sized circuits with $i\ell$-bit inputs from the same primitives as in Theorem 1, and if FE and PRG are $(2^{-(i\ell+\kappa)}\mathrm{negl})$-secure, the resulting IO scheme is $(2^{-\kappa}\mathrm{negl})$-secure.*

Therefore, as discussed above, from slightly superpolynomially secure L-linear maps, a PRG with block-wise locality L, and subexponential LWE, we obtain IO for circuits with super-logarithmic, $\omega(\log \lambda)$, length inputs, and if the primitives are quasi-polynomially secure, we obtain IO for circuits with poly-logarithmic $\log^{1+\varepsilon}(\lambda)$ length inputs. Such IO schemes are already sufficient for two types of natural applications of IO:

- *Type 1:* Applications where IO is used to obfuscate a circuit with short inputs. For instance, for building FHE without relying on circular security [25], and constructing succinct randomized encoding for bounded space Turning machines [17]. In these applications, IO is used to obfuscate a circuit that receive as input an *index* from an arbitrary polynomial range.
- *Type 2:* Applications where the input length of the obfuscated circuit is determined by the security parameter of some other primitive. Then, by assuming exponential security of the other primitive, the input length can be made poly-logarithmic. For instance, as observed in [18,50], in the construction of public key encryption from one-way functions via IO, if assuming exponentially secure one-way functions, then IO for circuits with $\omega(\log \lambda)$ bit inputs suffices for the application.

We further show that IO for circuits with super-logarithmic length inputs implies full-fledged functional encryption.

Theorem 4 (Functional Encryption from $\omega(\log \lambda)$-Input IO). *Let* $\mathrm{i}\ell$ *be any super-logarithmic polynomial, that is,* $\mathrm{i}\ell = \omega(\log \lambda)$. *Assume IO for the class of polynomial-sized circuits with* $\mathrm{i}\ell$*-bit inputs and public key encryption, both with* $(2^{-\mathrm{i}\ell}\mathrm{negl})$*-security. Then, there exist collusion resistant (compact) public-key functional encryption for* P/poly, *satisfying adaptive-security.*

Combining the above two theorems, we immediately have that the existence of a PRG with block-wise locality L and L-linear maps, both with slighly super-polynomial security (and assuming subexponential LWE), implies the existence of full-fledged functional encryption, and all its applications, including, for instance, non-interactive key exchange (NIKE) for unbounded users [43], trapdoor permutations [43], PPAD hardness [19,42], publicly-verifiable delegation schemes in the CRS model [62], and secure traitor tracing scheme [22,29,39], which further implies hardness results in differential privacy [37,64].

1.3 Subsequent Works

Two recent works by Lombardi and Vaikuntanathan (LV) [57], and Barak, Brakerski, Komargodski, and Kothari (BBKK) [14] essentially rule out the existence of PRGs with block-wise locality $L = 2$, except for a very narrow window of expansion, as we explain next.

The LV Attack. The LV attack considers generators whose output bits are evaluated using the same predidate P, and whose dependency graph G is chosen at random. LV show that for any predicate P and a $1 - o(1)$ fraction of the graphs, the output can be efficiently distinguished from random, if its length reaches $\tilde{\Omega}(n2^{\ell})$, where recall that $\ell = O(\log \lambda)$ is the block size. Their attack relies on two important ingredient. The first ingredient consists of techniques for refuting random L-CSPs over large q-ary alphabets, which corresponds to PRGs with block-wise locality-L and block-size $\ell = \log q$. Allen, O'Donnell, and Witmer [1] presented an efficient algorithm for this, which succeeds when the number of constraints is roughly $\tilde{\Omega}(n^{L/2}\text{poly}(q)/\varepsilon^2)$, where ε controls the "quality" of refutation. The second ingredient is a novel structural lemma showing that any locality-2 balanced predicate P over alphabet $\mathbb{Z}_q$ must be $(1/2 + O(1)/\sqrt{q})$-correlated with a locality-2 predicate Q over the constant-sized alphabet $\mathbb{Z}_{16}$. Roughly speaking, to distinguish the output of a PRG with predicate P, they apply the refutation technique on CSPs w.r.t. the predicate Q correlated with P. This allows them to rule out PRGs with output length as short as $\tilde{\Omega}(n2^{\ell})$.

The BBKK Attack. BBKK considered the more general case where the generators use an arbitrary set of predicates $\{P_j\}$ and arbitrary dependency graph G. They show that PRGs with block-wise locality 2 and output length $\tilde{\Omega}(n2^{2\ell})$ do not exist. The bound on the output length can be improved to $\tilde{\Omega}(n2^{\ell})$ for the case where G is randomly chosen, and so is the predicate (in particular, the predicate is the same for all output bits). In fact, they proved a more general lower bound: There is no PRG whose outputs are evaluated using polynomials of degree at most d involving at most s monomials, and of output length $\tilde{O}(sn^{\lceil d/2 \rceil})$. Note that every block-wise locality L PRG can be written as such a generator, with $n2^{\ell}$ input bits, and using polynomials of degree L and at most $2^{L\ell}$ monomials. Their result is based on semidefinite programming and in particular the sum of squares (SOS) hierarchy.

BV and BBKK essentially rule out the existence of PRGs with block-wise locality 2, except for the corner case where the generator can use a set of different predicates $\{P_j\}$, a specific or random graph, and the output length is $\tilde{O}(n2^{(1+\varepsilon)\ell})$, for some $0 < \varepsilon < 1$. However, it is unclear to us whether PRGs with such small expansion is sufficient for constructing IO, or whether the attacks can be extended to cover this case.

Outline of This Paper

Section 2 discusses candidate constructions of block-wise local PRGs. Section 3 discusses our bootstrapping method using block-wise local PRGs. Finally, in Sect. 4, we discuss constructions of functional-encryption schemes in Sect. 4.

Further, the paper employs standard notation and terminology on functional encryption and IO. We refer the reader to the full version for the complete formalism [55].

2 Block-Wise Local PRGs

In this section, we introduce the notion of a block-wise local PRG. We start with formal definitions, in Sect. 2.1, which we refer to throughout the rest of the paper. Then, the remaining sub-sections will discuss a graph-based framework for block-wise local functions, and discuss candidates.

2.1 Pseudorandom Generators, Locality, and Block-Wise Locality

We review the notion of a PRG family, and its locality.

Definition 1 (Family of Pseudo-Random Generators (PRGs)). *Let n and m be polynomials. A family of $(n(\lambda), m(\lambda))$-PRG is an ensemble of distributions* $\mathbf{PRG} = \{\mathbf{PRG}_\lambda\}$ *satisfying the following properties:*

Syntax: *For every $\lambda \in \mathbb{N}$, every* PRG *in the support of* $\mathbf{PRG}_\lambda$ *defines a function mapping $n(\lambda)$ bits to $m(\lambda)$ bits.*

Efficiency: *There is a uniform Turning machine M satisfying that for every $\lambda \in \mathbb{N}$, every* PRG *in the support of* $\mathbf{PRG}_\lambda$, *and every $x \in \{0,1\}^{n(\lambda)}$,* $M(\mathrm{PRG}, x) = \mathrm{PRG}(x)$.

μ-Indistinguishability: *The following ensembles are μ-indistinguishable*

$$\{\mathrm{PRG} \xleftarrow{\$} \mathbf{PRG}_\lambda;\ s \xleftarrow{\$} \{0,1\}^{n(\lambda)} : (\mathrm{PRG}, \mathrm{PRG}(s)\}_{\lambda \in \mathbb{N}}$$

$$\approx_\mu \{\mathrm{PRG} \xleftarrow{\$} \mathbf{PRG}_\lambda;\ r \xleftarrow{\$} \{0,1\}^{m(\lambda)}\ :\ (\mathrm{PRG}, r)\}_{\lambda \in \mathbb{N}}$$

Definition 2 (Block-Wise Locality of PRGs). *Let n, m, L, and ℓ be polynomials. We say that a family of $(n(\lambda)\ell(\lambda), m(\lambda))$-PRGs has block-wise locality-$(L(\lambda), \ell(\lambda))$ if for every λ and every* PRG *in the support of* $\mathbf{PRG}_\lambda$, *inputs of* PRG *are viewed as $n(\lambda) \times \ell(\lambda)$ matrices of bits, and every output bit of* PRG *depends on input bits contained in at most $L(\lambda)$ columns.*

2.2 Graph-Based Block-Wise Local Functions

In this section, we discuss candidate PRGs with block-wise locality d, where d can be as small as two. Here, we start with the notational framework and then move on to discussing concrete assumptions on them in Sect. 2.3.

Goldreich's Function. We will consider local functions based on Goldreich's construction [46], which have been the subject for extensive study (cf. e.g. Applebaum's survey [8]).

Recall first that an $[n, m, d]$-hypergraph is a collection $G = (S_1, \ldots, S_m)$ where the *hyerpedges* S_i are elements of $[n]^d$, i.e., $S_i = (i_1, \ldots, i_d)$, where $i_j \in [n]$ (note that we allow for potential repetitions, merely for notational convenience). We use hypergraphs to build functions as follows.

Definition 3 (Goldreich's function). *Let* $\mathbf{G} = \{\mathbf{G}_\lambda\}_{\lambda \in \mathbb{N}}$ *be an ensemble such that* $\mathbf{G}_\lambda$ *is a distribution on $[n(\lambda), m(\lambda), d(\lambda)]$-hypergraphs, for polynomial functions m, n, d. Also let $P = \{P_\lambda\}_{\lambda \in \mathbb{N}} q$ be a family of predicates, where P_λ operates on $d(\lambda)$-bit strings. Then, define the function ensemble* $\mathbf{GF}^{\mathcal{G},P} = \{\mathbf{GF}_\lambda^{\mathcal{G},P}\}_{\lambda \in \mathbb{N}}$, *where* $\mathbf{GF}_\lambda^{\mathcal{G},P}$ *samples first a graph* $G = (S_1, \ldots, S_m) \xleftarrow{\$} \mathbf{G}_\lambda$, *and then outputs the function* $\mathrm{GF}_{G,P} : \{0,1\}^n \to \{0,1\}^m$ *such that for all n-bit x,*

$$\mathrm{GF}_{G,P}(x) = (y_1, \ldots, y_m), \quad y_i = P(x[S_i]),$$

where $x[S]$ denotes the d-bit sub-string obtained by concatenating the bits at positions indexed by S.[1]

Functions with Block-Wise Locality. We want to extend the notation used above to consider the case where an edge of G does not solely give a pointer to individual bits to be injected in the computation, but rather, to "chunks" consisting of ℓ-bit strings, and the predicate is applied to the concatenation of these bits. The resulting function clearly then satisfies block-wise locality d with block size ℓ.

Definition 4 (Block-wise local graph-based function). *Let $\mathbf{G} = \{\mathbf{G}_\lambda\}_{\lambda \in \mathbb{N}}$ be such that $\mathbf{G}_\lambda$ is a distribution on $[n(\lambda), m(\lambda), d(\lambda)]$-hypergraphs, for polynomial functions m, n, d. Also let $\ell(\lambda)$ be a polynomial function, and $P = \{P_\lambda\}_{\lambda \in \mathbb{N}}$ a family of predicates, where P_λ operates on $(d(\lambda) \times \ell(\lambda))$-bit strings. Then, define the function ensamble $\mathbf{GF}^{\mathcal{G},P,\ell} = \{\mathbf{GF}_\lambda^{\mathcal{G},P,\ell}\}_{\lambda \in \mathbb{N}}$, where $\mathbf{GF}_\lambda^{\mathcal{G},P,\ell}$ samples first a graph $G = (S_1, \ldots, S_m) \stackrel{\$}{\leftarrow} \mathbf{G}_\lambda$, and then outputs the function $\mathrm{GF}_{G,P,\ell} : \{0,1\}^{n \cdot \ell} \to \{0,1\}^m$ such that for all $(n \times \ell)$-bit inputs $\mathbf{x} = (\mathbf{x}[1], \ldots, \mathbf{x}[n])$, where $\mathbf{x}[1], \ldots, \mathbf{x}[n] \in \{0,1\}^\ell$,*

$$\mathrm{GF}_{G,P,\ell}(x) = (y_1, \ldots, y_m), \quad y_i = P(\mathbf{x}[S_i]),$$

where $\mathbf{x}[S]$ denotes the $d \cdot \ell$-bit sub-string obtained by concatenating ℓ-bit input chunks indexed by S.

We typically refer to the graph G describing $\mathrm{GF}_{G,P,\ell}$ as the *base graph*. This is because $\mathrm{GF}_{G,P,\ell}$ can be seen as a special case of Goldreich's function defined above, for a suitable graph. Namely, the base graph G can be extended to an $[n \cdot \ell, m, d\ell]$-hypergraph $\overline{G}$ naturally, where each edge $S_i = (i_1, \ldots, i_d)$ from G is mapped into a new hyper-edge $\overline{S}_i$ with $d \cdot \ell$ elements such that

$$\overline{S}_i = ((i_1 - 1) \cdot \ell + 1, \ldots, i_1 \cdot \ell, \cdots, (i_d - 1) \cdot \ell + 1, \ldots, i_d \cdot \ell),$$

then clearly $\mathrm{GF}_{G,P,\ell} = \mathrm{GF}_{\overline{G},P,1} = \mathrm{GF}_{\overline{G},P}$. This view will be convenient to connect back to the body of work on studying the security of Goldreich's function on suitable graphs, for which our block-wise local designs serve as a special case.

Expansion Properties. In general, we will want to instantiate our framework with functions where the base graph G is a good expander graph. Recall the following.

Definition 5. *$G = (S_1, \ldots, S_m)$ is a (k, c)-expander (or, equivalently, is (k, c)-*expanding*) if for all sets $J \subseteq [m]$ with $|J| \leq k$, we have $|\bigcup_{j \in J} S_j| \geq c \cdot |J|$.*

[1] The notion could be block-wise to the cases where predicates are drawn by a distribution, and possibly differ from each output bit. We are going to dispense with such extensions, which are straightforward but easily lead to notational overhead.

Ideally, we will want in fact $\overline{G}$ to be a good expander (in order to resort to large body of analyses for such functions). This will follow by making the base graph a good expander. In particular, the following simple fact stems from the observation that when going from G to $\overline{G}$, we have $|\overline{S}_j| = \ell|S_j|$, and hence the (relative) expansion factors of G and $\overline{G}$ are identical.

Lemma 1. *Let G be an $[n,m,d]$-hypergraph which is $(k,(1-\gamma)d)$-expanding. Then, for any block-size ℓ, the resulting $[n\cdot\ell, m, d\ell]$-hypergraph $\overline{G}$ is $(k,(1-\gamma)d\ell)$-expanding.*

In general, if we have high degree (say $O(\log\lambda)$), we can prove the existence (at least probabilistically) of very good expanders with expansion rate very close to the degree. Unfortunately, our construction of $\overline{G}$ imposes some structure, and the actual expansion factor is dictated by the graph G with much lower degree d. The following lemma establishes the existence of good expander graphs, which we summarize below in a corollary with more useful parameters. While the proof of the lemma is folklore (we take notational inspiration from the one in [9]), we give it for completeness in the full version [55].

Lemma 2 (Strong expansion lemma). *Let $d \geq 2$, and let $\gamma \in (0,1)$ and $\beta \in (0,1/2)$ be such that $d\gamma = 1+\beta$. Further, let $1 \leq \Delta \leq n^{\beta}/\log(n)$. Then, there exists a constant $\alpha > 0$ such that a random $[n, m = \Delta n, d]$-hypergraph G is a $(k = \alpha n/\Delta^{1/\beta}, d(1-\gamma))$-expander with probability $1-o(1)$.*

Corollary 1. *For every γ and d such that $1 < \gamma d < 1.5$, and every $\eta \in (0,1)$, there exists a $[n, n^{1+\zeta}, d]$-hypergraph (for some $\zeta > 0$) which is a $(n^{1-\eta},(1-\gamma)d)$-expander.*

2.3 Pseudorandom and Unpredictability Generators

We are interested in the question of finding $[n,m,d]$-hypergraphs for $m = n^{1+\alpha}$ and a constant $d \geq 2$ such that $\mathrm{GF}_{G,P,\ell}$ is a good PRG, for $\ell = O(\log\lambda)$. We consider a parameterized assumption on such functions (in terms of unpredictability), and discuss it briefly. Below, we are then going to show how strong indistinguishability follows from (potentially) weaker versions of this assumption.

Unpredictability Generator and Assumptions. Let $\mathbf{UG} = \{\mathbf{UG}_\lambda\}_{\lambda\in\mathbb{N}}$ be a function ensemble, where $\mathbf{UG}_\lambda$ is a distribution on functions from $n(\lambda)$ to $m(\lambda)$ bits, for some polynomial functions m and n.

Definition 6 (Unpredictability generator). *We say that* **UG** *is an* (s, δ)-unpredictability generator *(or (s,δ)-UG, for short) if for all (non-uniform) adversaries $A = \{A_\lambda\}_{\lambda\in\mathbb{N}}$ with size at most $s(\lambda)$ and all sequences of indices $i(\lambda) \in \{0,\ldots,i(\lambda)-1\}$, we have*

$$\Pr\left[\begin{array}{l} x \xleftarrow{\$} \{0,1\}^{n(\lambda)} \\ \mathrm{UG} \xleftarrow{\$} \mathbf{UG}_\lambda \end{array} : A_\lambda(\mathrm{UG}, \mathrm{UG}_{\leq i(\lambda)}(x)) = \mathrm{UG}_{i(\lambda)+1}(x)\right] \leq \frac{1}{2} + \delta(\lambda),$$

where $\mathrm{UG}_{\leq j}(x)$ *and* $\mathrm{UG}_j(x)$ *denote the first* j *bits and the* j*-th bit of* $\mathrm{UG}(x)$*, respectively.*

Note that by a standard argument, being a (s, δ)-UG implies being a (family of) $(s, O(m \cdot \delta))$-PRGs. We now consider the following assumption, which parametrizes the fact that $\mathrm{GF}_{G,P,\ell}$ is a good PRG.

Definition 7 (BLUG**-assumption).** *Let* $n, \ell, s : \mathbb{N} \to \mathbb{N}$*, and let* $d \geq 2$ *and* $\alpha > 0$ *be constants. Also, let* $\delta : \mathbb{N} \to [0, 1]$*. Then, the* (d, ℓ)-$\mathsf{BLUG}(n, \alpha, s, \delta)$ *assumption is the assumption that there exists a family* $G = \{G_\lambda\}_{\lambda \in \mathbb{N}}$ *of* $[n(\lambda), n(\lambda)^{1+\alpha}, d]$ *hypergraphs, and a family* $P = \{P_\lambda\}_{\lambda \in \mathbb{N}}$ *of predicates on* $(d(\lambda) \times \ell(\lambda))$*-bit strings such that* $\mathbf{GF}^{G,P,\ell}$ *is an* (s, δ)*-UG.*

We are being a bit informal here, in the sense that obviously we would like $\mathbf{GF}^{G,P,\ell}$ to additionally be efficiently computable in a uniform sense. Our candidates will not have this property, as we are only able to infer the existence of suitable G's probabilistically. There are two ways of thinking about the resulting ensemble: Either non-uniformly – the graph G_λ is given as advice for security parameter λ – but usually we actually show that a $1 - o(1)$ fraction of the $[n, n^{1+\alpha}, d]$-hypergraphs are good choices. In that case, we replace G with $\mathbf{G}$ where $\mathbf{G}_\lambda$ chooses a random $[n(\lambda), n(\lambda)^{1+\alpha}, d(\lambda)]$-hypergraph G, which is *bad* with vanishing probability $o(1)$. This is of course not good enough, yet the problem can often be by-passed in an application-dependent way, by considering the fact that the *end scheme* using $\mathbf{GF}^{\mathbf{G},P,\ell}$ will also be insecure with probability $o(1)$. One can then consider $\omega(1)$-instances of this scheme, each using an independent instance from $\mathbf{GF}^{\mathbf{G},P,\ell}$, and then combine them with a combiner, if it exists.

Our constructions below require $(d, O(\log(\lambda)))$-$\mathsf{BLUG}(n, \alpha, \mathrm{poly}(\lambda), 2^{-\omega(\log \lambda)})$ to be true for some $n(\lambda) = \mathrm{poly}(\lambda)$ and $\alpha > 0$. For stronger results, we are going to replace $2^{-\omega(\log \lambda)}$ with $2^{-\lambda^\epsilon}$ for some $\epsilon > 0$. Below, we will discuss whether this assumption can be implied by (qualitatively) weaker properties. We will show in particular that $(d, O(\log^{1-\varepsilon}(\lambda)))$-$\mathsf{BLUG}(n, \alpha, 2^{\omega(\log \lambda)}, 1/\lambda^{\Omega(1)})$ implies $(d, O(\log(\lambda)))$-$\mathsf{BLUG}(n, \alpha, \mathrm{poly}(\lambda), 2^{-\omega(\log \lambda)})$.

Here, we briefly discuss what can be expected to start with.

The case $d \geq 3$**.** For the case $d \geq 3$, a good candidate to study is the case where $\ell = O(\log(\lambda))$ and $G = \{G_\lambda\}_{\lambda \in \mathbb{N}}$ is such that G_λ is an $[n(\lambda), n(\lambda)^{1+\alpha}, d]$-hypergraph which is a good $(n^{1-\gamma}, (1-\gamma)d)$-expander where $\gamma < \frac{1}{2}$, which exists (for some suitable $\alpha > 0$) by Corollary 1. The corresponding $\overline{G}_\lambda$ are then in turn also $(n^{1-\gamma}, (1-\gamma)d\ell)$-expanders by Lemma 1.

Applebaum and Raykov [13] recently justify the assumption that for suitable predicates, P, the function family $\mathbf{GF}^{\overline{\mathcal{G}},P}$ is one way and a PRG against adversary running in time $2^{n^{1-\gamma}}$, which cannot succeed with probability larger than $2^{-n^{1-\gamma}}$. In the same paper, they also give a decision-to-search reduction for such functions, which however applies only for degrees where we can accommodate some γ with $3\gamma < 1$. In particular, such functions withstand existing attacks, such as myopic inversion attacks [30]. Also, the degree of P can be high, e.g., $O(\log(\lambda))$, and this prevents a number of attacks exploiting weakness of the predicate [21,34].

Also, as we show in the next section, it is possible to adopt the techniques from [9] to show that we can get good ϵ-biased generators (for a sub-exponential ϵ) with block-wise locality $(3, 2)$. This has been the main technique in validating PRG assumptions on graph-based local functions [9,60,61].

The special case $d = 2$. The case $d = 2$ is particularly important, as it does allow instantiations from bilinear maps in our applications. Note that algebraic attacks are mitigated here – in contrast to the case of plain locality, i.e., $\ell = 1$, we can set $\ell = O(\log \lambda)$ and achieve sufficiently high algebraic degree of the predicate P. Unfortunately, this is not sufficient to prove pseudorandomness, as shown by recent attacks [14,57], which we have discussed above in Sect. 1.3.

2.4 Block-Wise Local Small-Bias Generators

Several works [9,12,34,60] have focused on studying weaker properties achieved by local generators. In particular, a standard statement towards validating their security is that of showing that the meet the definition of being a *small-bias generator*.

Definition 8. *We say* $\mathrm{SB} : \{0,1\}^n \to \{0,1\}^m$ *is an* ϵ-small biased generator *if* $\max_{J \subseteq [n], J \neq \emptyset} \left|\Pr[x \xleftarrow{\$} \{0,1\}^n : \bigoplus_{j \in J} \mathrm{SB}_j(x) = 1] - \frac{1}{2}\right| \leq \epsilon$, *where* $\mathrm{SB}_j(x)$ *denotes the* j*-th bit of* $\mathrm{SB}(x)$.

We show that $\mathrm{GF}_{G,Q,2}$ is a good small-biased generator for a sub-exponential ϵ, where G is an $[n, m, 3]$-hypergraph, and Q is the predicate which given three 2-bit blocks $\mathbf{x}_1, \mathbf{x}_2, \mathbf{x}_3$ where $\mathbf{x}_i = (x_i^l, x_i^h)$, outputs

$$Q(\mathbf{x}_1, \mathbf{x}_2, \mathbf{x}_3) = x_1^l \oplus x_2^l \oplus x_3^l \oplus (x_1^h \wedge x_2^h).$$

Another convenient way to think about $\mathrm{GF}_{G,Q,2}$ is as

$$\mathrm{GF}_{G,Q,2}((x_1^l, x_1^h), \ldots, (x_n^l, x_n^h)) = \mathrm{GF}_{G,Q^l}(x_1^l, \ldots, x_n^l) \oplus \mathrm{GF}_{G,Q^h}(x_1^h, \ldots, x_n^j),$$

where $Q^l(x_1, x_2, x_3) = x_1 \oplus x_2 \oplus x_3$ and $Q^h(x_1, x_2, x_3) = x_1 \wedge x_2$. To show that $\mathrm{GF}_{G,Q,2}$ has small bias, the main idea is fairly straightforward. Indeed, current analyses of local small-biased generators give two separate analyses for so called "light tests" and "heavy tests", where the "weight" of a test amounts to the cardinality of $|J|$. For standard locality, withstanding both at the same time forces the graph degree to be at least five, since the predicate needs to be "non-degenerate" for the construction to withstand tests (and the theorem of [9] to apply), and all predicates up to $d = 4$ *are* degenerate (cf. e.g. [34]). This will not be a problem here, as we only target block-wise locality, and thus effectively the predicate can be non-degenerate. The proof is in the full version [55].

Lemma 3. *For all* $\delta > 0$ *and* $\alpha < \frac{1-\delta}{4}$, *for a fraction of* $1 - o(1)$ *of all* $[n, n^{1+\alpha}, 3]$*-hypergraphs* G, *and* Q *as defined above,* $\mathrm{GF}_{G,Q,2}$ *is an* $\left(e^{-\frac{n^\delta}{4}}\right)$*-biased generator.*

2.5 Hardness Amplification via the XOR Construction

In this paper, we rely on the assumption that $\mathbf{GF}^{G,P,\ell}$ is a good PRG for an appropriate family G of expanders. However, we want to add additional justification to our assumptions. Here, in particular, we discuss how weak unpredictability for graph-based block-wise local functions can be amplified to super-polynomially small unpredictability generically. This means in particular that block-wise local PRGs have strong self-amplifying properties, and that for any G and P, in order to invalidate our assumption, we need to find an attack which succeeds in predicting the next bit with large (i.e., polynomial) advantage over $\frac{1}{2}$. For otherwise, the lack of such an attack would imply that for the same G and (a related) P' and ℓ', $\mathbf{GF}^{G,P',\ell'}$ is a strong PRG.

To this end, we use a simple construction xoring the outputs of generators, which has already been studied to amplify PRG security [35,58]. Our analysis resembles the one from [35], but is given for completeness. Also, a more general construction, with xoring replaced by a general extractor, was considered by Applebaum [7]. The use of xor, however, is instrumental to preserve block-wise locality. The main drawback of this construction is that it can *at best* ensure $2^{-\Omega(\log^{1+\theta}\lambda)}$ distinguishing gap for some $\theta \in (0,1]$ while retaining block size $\ell = O(\log \lambda)$. In the full version [55], we explain a different approach which relies on a different assumption. and potentially guarantees $2^{-\lambda^{\Omega(1)}}$ distinguishing gap.

The XOR Construction. Let $\mathbf{UG} = \{\mathbf{UG}_\lambda\}_{\lambda\in\mathbb{N}}$ be an (s,δ)-UG, where $\mathbf{UG}_\lambda$ is a distribution on functions $\{0,1\}^{n(\lambda)} \to \{0,1\}^{m(\lambda)}$. For an additional parameter $k = k(\lambda) \geq 1$, we define the ensemble $\mathbf{UG}^k = \{\mathbf{UG}_\lambda^k\}_{\lambda\in\mathbb{N}}$, where $\mathbf{UG}_\lambda^k$ samples functions $\mathrm{UG}_1,\ldots,\mathrm{UG}_k \xleftarrow{\$} \mathbf{UG}_\lambda$ and output the description of a function $\mathrm{UG}^k : \{0,1\}^{n\times k} \to \{0,1\}^m$ which, on input $x = x^1 \parallel \cdots \parallel x^k$, where $x^i \in \{0,1\}^{n(\lambda)}$, outputs

$$\mathrm{UG}^k(x) = \mathrm{UG}_1(x^1) \oplus \cdots \oplus \mathrm{UG}_k(x^k).$$

We prove the following in the full version [55].

Theorem 5 (Security of the XOR Construction). *If* $\mathbf{UG}$ *is a* (s,δ)*-UG and* $k = k(\lambda)$ *is polynomial in* λ*, then* $\mathbf{UG}^k$ *is a* (s',ϵ)*-PRG, where*

$$\epsilon(\lambda) \leq (2\delta(\lambda))^{k(\lambda)}, \quad s'(\lambda) = \Theta\left(\frac{\delta(\lambda)^{2k} \cdot s(r)}{k\log(k/\delta(\lambda))}\right).$$

Block-Wise Local Instantiation. We instantiate the construction with parameter k when $\mathbf{UG} = \mathbf{GF}^{G,P,\ell}$ for a family of $[n,m,d]$-hypergraphs $G = \{G_\lambda\}_{\lambda\in\mathbb{N}}$, some $\ell = \ell(\lambda)$, and a family P of $(d\times\ell)$-bit predicates. Since the resulting function UG_λ^k uses k instances of the *same* function $\mathrm{GF}_{G_\lambda,P_\lambda,\ell}$, it can equivalently be thought as having the form (up to re-arranging the order of the input bits) $\mathrm{GF}_{G_\lambda,P_\lambda^k,\ell(\lambda)\cdot k(\lambda)}$, where the predicate P^k on input d $(k\cdot\ell)$-bit blocks $\mathbf{x}_1,\ldots,\mathbf{x}_d$, it interprets each of them as k ℓ-bit blocks $\mathbf{x}_i = \mathbf{x}_{i,1} \parallel \cdots \parallel \mathbf{x}_{i,k}$ and outputs

$$P^k(\mathbf{x}_1,\ldots,\mathbf{x}_d) = P(\mathbf{x}_{1,1},\ldots,\mathbf{x}_{d,1}) \oplus \cdots \oplus P(\mathbf{x}_{k,1},\ldots,\mathbf{x}_{k,d}).$$

To instantiate our transformation, we assume that for some $\ell(\lambda) = \Omega(\log^{1-\theta}(\lambda))$ and a family of $[n(\lambda), m(\lambda), d]$-hypergraphs $G = \{G_\lambda\}_{\lambda\in\mathbb{N}}$, the function family $\mathrm{UG} = \mathbf{GF}^{G,P,\ell}$ is a $(s(\lambda) = 2^{\log^3(\lambda)}, \delta(\lambda) = \lambda^{-\Omega(1)})$-UG. Now, set $k(\lambda) = \log^{\theta}(\lambda)$. Then, UG^k is by the above $(d, O(\log(\lambda)))$-block-wise local, and it is also (s', ϵ)-UG for $s'(\lambda) = \mathrm{poly}(\lambda)$, and

$$\epsilon(\lambda) = (2\delta(\lambda))^{k(\lambda)} = 2^{-\Omega(\log^{1+\theta}(\lambda))}.$$

In other words, we have just established the following corollary.

Corollary 2. *For any $\beta > 0$, $d \geq 2$, and $\theta \in (0,1]$, if the $(d, O(\log^{1-\theta}(\lambda)))$-$\mathsf{BLUG}(n, \beta, 2^{\log^3(\lambda)}, 1/\lambda^{\Omega(1)})$ assumption holds, then the assumption $(d, O(\log(\lambda)))$-$\mathsf{BLUG}(n, \beta, \mathrm{poly}(\lambda), 2^{-\Omega(\log^{1+\theta}(\lambda))})$ also holds true.*

3 IO from Block-Wise Locality-$(L, \log\lambda)$ PRG and L-Linear Maps

In this section, we prove the following bootstrapping theorem.

Theorem 6 (Bootstrapping via *block-wise local* PRGs). *Let $\mathcal{R} = \{\mathcal{R}_\lambda\}$ be any family of rings, ε be any positive constant, L any positive integer, n any sufficiently large polynomial, and $i\ell$ and κ any polynomials. There is a construction of $i\ell(\lambda)$-bit-input IO for $\mathsf{P/poly}$, from the following primitives:*

- *A family of $(n(\lambda) \times \log\lambda, n(\lambda)^{1+\varepsilon})$-PRGs with* block-wise locality $(L, \log\lambda)$.
- *A* public-key *FE for degree-L polynomials in $\mathcal{R}$, with linear efficiency and* $\mathsf{Full\text{-}Sel}$*-security; or with a secret-key FE with the same properties, assuming additionally LWE with subexponential modulo-to-noise ratio.*

The IO scheme is $(2^{-\kappa(\lambda)}\mathrm{negl}(\lambda))$-secure, if the PRG and FE schemes are $(2^{-i\ell(\lambda)+\kappa(\lambda)}\mathrm{negl}(\lambda))$-secure, and LWE is $(2^{-i\ell(\lambda)+\kappa(\lambda)}\mathrm{negl}(\lambda))$-hard.

Theorem 6 follows the same approach as Lin's recent bootstrapping theorem [53], but modifies it in two ways. First, it uses block-wise local PRGs to replace local PRGs. Second, it makes explicit the relation between the *security level* (more precisely, the maximal distinguishing gap) of the underlying PRG and FE, and the *input-length and security level* of the resulting IO—if the underlying primitives are $2^{-i\ell+\kappa}$negl-secure, then the resulting IO scheme is for $i\ell$-bit-input circuits and 2^{κ}negl-security. Such relations are implicit in previous works, and not as *tight* as shown here.

Overview of Proof of Theorem 6. To show the theorem, similar to previous works [53, 56], we take two steps:

Step 1. Construct a single-key public-key (or secret-key) FE schemes $\mathbf{CFE} = \{\mathbf{CFE}^{N,D,S}\}$ for P/poly, with $(1-\varepsilon)$-sublinear compactness and $2^{-i\ell+\kappa}$negl-Full-Sel-security, starting from a public-key (or secret-key) FE for degree-L polynomials in $\mathcal{R}$, with linear efficiency and Full-Sel-security.

Previously, the work of [56] showed how to achieve this transformation from a locality-L PRGs and FE for computing degree $3L+2$ polynomials. Following that, the two recent works of [4,53] used a *pre-processing technique* to relax the requirement on the underlying FE to supporting only degree-L polynomials. In this work, we extend their *pre-processing technique* even further, in order to relax the requirement on the underlying PRGs from having locality L to having *block-wise* locality $(L, \log\lambda)$. We describe this step in full detail in Sect. 3.1.

In the case that the obtained FE scheme **CFE** is a secret-key one, we invoke the result of [18] to transform it into a public key FE scheme with the same properties, assuming LWE with subexponential modulus-to-noise ratio.

Since our transformation from FE for low-degree computations to weakly-compact FE for P/poly in Sect. 3.1 incurs only a polynoimal security loss, and so does the transformation of [18], the resulting weakly-compact FE has essentially the same level of security as that of underlying primitives.

Step 2. Apply an FE-to-IO transformation to obtain $i\ell$-bit-input IO for P/poly, with $2^{-\kappa}$negl-security.

The literature already offers three FE-to-IO transformations [2,20,54] that start from a public key FE scheme $\mathbf{CFE} = \{\mathbf{CFE}^{N,D,S}\}$ as described above w.r.t. any positive constant ε. In this work, we reduce the security loss incurred in the transformation so as to start with $2^{-i\ell+\kappa}$negl-secure FE (as opposed to $2^{-O(i\ell^2)+\kappa}$negl-secure or $2^{-O(\log\lambda)i\ell+\kappa}$negl-secure FE as in previous works). To do so, we present a new FE-to-IO transformation inspired by that of [54] and present a tight analysis. We describe this step in the full version [55].

3.1 Step 1: Constructing Weakly-Compact FE

Proposition 1. *Let $\mathcal{R}$, ε, L, and n be defined as in Theorem 6, and $\bar{\kappa}$ be any polynomial. There is a construction of 1-key weakly-compact public-key FE for* P/poly *from the following primitives:*

- *A family of $(n(\lambda)\times\log\lambda, n(\lambda)^{1+\varepsilon})$-PRGs with* block-wise locality $(L, \log\lambda)$.
- Public-key *FE for degree-L polynomials in $\mathcal{R}$, with linear efficiency and* Full-Sel-*security; or secret-key FE with the same properties, assuming additionally LWE with subexponential modolus-to-noise ratio.*

*The weakly-compact FE is $(2^{-\bar{\kappa}(\lambda)}\mathrm{negl}(\lambda))$-*Full-Sel*-secure, if the underlying PRG and FE are $(2^{-\bar{\kappa}(\lambda)}\mathrm{negl}(\lambda))$-secure and LWE is $(2^{-\bar{\kappa}(\lambda)}\mathrm{negl}(\lambda))$-hard.*

It was shown in [53] that 1-key weakly-compact FE for P/poly can be constructed from locality-L PRG and (unbounded collusion) FE for degree-L polynomials. Their construction of weakly-compact FE follows from the blue-print of previous works [52,56], which uses FE for low degree polynomials to compute a randomized encoding of a computation in $\mathsf{P/poly}$, with pseudo-randomness generated through a local PRG. The locality of RE and PRG ensures that their composition can be computed in low degree. However, the straightforward composition of RE and PRG leads to a computation with degree $3L + 2$. The key idea in [53] and the concurrent work of [4] is that part of the RE computation can already be done at encryption time, that is, by asking the encryptor to pre-process the inputs (of the computation in $\mathsf{P/poly}$) and seeds of PRG, and encrypt the pre-processed values, the composition of RE and PRG can be computed in just degree L from the pre-processed values, at decryption time—This is called the *preprocessing technique.* We take this technique one step further: By also performing part of the PRG computation at encryption time, we can replace local PRG with block-wise local PRG (with appropriate parameters) at "no cost".

Below, we first briefly review the blueprint of [56], then describe the preprocessing idea of [53] and how to use it to accommodate PRG with block-wise locality.

The General Blueprint of [56]**.** To construct 1-key weakly-compact FE for $\mathsf{P/poly}$, Lin and Vaikuntanathan [56] (LV) first observed that, using the Trojan Method [26], it suffices to construct 1-key weakly-compact FE for NC^1 functions with some fixed depth $D(\lambda) = O(\log \lambda)$; denote this class of functions as NC^1_D.

Next, to bootstrap a low-degree FE scheme to FE for NC^1_D, the idea is using randomized encoding to "compress" any function $h(\mathbf{x}) \in \mathsf{NC}^1_D$ into a function $g(\mathbf{x}, \mathbf{s}) = \mathsf{REnc}(f, \mathbf{x};\ \mathrm{PRG}(\mathbf{s}))$ with small degree in $\mathcal{R}$. The reason that local PRG is used is that the locality of a Boolean function bounds the degree of computing this function in any ring. Then, plugging-in randomized encodings with small locality like that of [11] the overall degree of g is small. For the security proof to work out, the actual functions used in the LV construction are more complicated and has form

$$g(\mathbf{x}, \mathbf{s}, \mathbf{s}', b) = (1-b)(\mathsf{REnc}(f, \mathbf{x}; \mathrm{PRG}(\mathbf{s}))) + b(\mathbf{CT} \oplus \mathrm{PRG}(\mathbf{s}')),$$

where $\mathbf{CT}$ is a ciphertext hardwired in the secret key, and serves as "space" to hide values in the secret key in the security proof.

A formal description of the LV public key FE scheme $\mathbf{CFE}^{N,D,S}$ for NC^1 circuits with input-length $N = N(\lambda)$, depth $D = D(\lambda) = O(\log \lambda)$, and size $S = S(\lambda)$ is in Fig. 2. (The secret-key case has almost identical construction.) The scheme uses the following tools:

- $\mathsf{Full\text{-}Sel}$-secure (collusion resistant) FE schemes for degree-$(3L+2)$ polynomials in some $\mathcal{R}$, $\{\mathbf{FE}^{N'} = (\mathsf{FE.Setup}, \mathsf{FE.KeyGen}, \mathsf{FE.Enc}, \mathsf{FE.Dec})\}$, with linear efficiency.
- A $(n, n^{1+\alpha})$-pseudorandom generator PRG with locality L, for a sufficiently large polynomial input length $n = n(\lambda)$ and any positive constant α.
- The AIK randomized encoding scheme in NC^0 [11]; denote the encoding algorithm as $\mathsf{AIK}(f, \mathbf{x};\ \mathbf{r})$.

We refer the reader to [56] for the correctness and security of the scheme. The compactness of the scheme **CFE** follows from the following two facts:

1. The length of the input $(\mathbf{x}, \mathbf{s}, \mathbf{s}', 0)$ encrypted using **FE** is $N + 2\Gamma + 1 = N + S(\lambda)^{1/(1+\alpha)}\text{poly}(\lambda)$.
2. **FE** has linear efficiency.

Putting them together, we have,

$$\begin{aligned}\mathsf{Time}_{\mathsf{CFE.Enc}}(\mathsf{MPK}, \mathbf{x}) &= \mathsf{Time}_{\mathsf{FE.Enc}}(\mathsf{MPK}, (\mathbf{x}, \mathbf{s}, \mathbf{s}', 0)) \\ &= \text{poly}(\lambda)|(\mathbf{x}, \mathbf{s}, \mathbf{s}', 0)| = S(\lambda)^{1/(1+\alpha)}\text{poly}(\lambda, N)\end{aligned}$$

which is sublinear in the function size as desired. Furthermore, to see why degree-$(3L+2)$ FE suffices for the construction, note that the construction uses the underlying FE to generate keys computing the function g in Fig. 2, and hence it suffices to argue that g can be computed in degree $3L+2$. By definition of g, when $b = 1$, the output can be computed in degree L as the PRG can be computed in degree L in $\mathcal{R}$ (XOR with **CT** does not incur additional degree as **CT** are constants hardwired in the function g); when $b = 0$, the output can be computed in degree $3L+1$, since the AIK randomized encoding has degree 3 in the random bits (*i.e.* PRG output) and 1 in the input $\mathbf{x}$. Therefore, g has exactly degree $3L+2$, as selection by b can be done with one multiplication.

The Idea of Preprocessing in [53]. Towards reducing the degree of the underlying FE and accommodating PRGs with block-wise locality-$(L, \log\lambda)$, the idea is letting the encryptor pre-process the input $(\mathbf{x}, \mathbf{s}, \mathbf{s}', b)$ to produce certain intermediate values, from which the output of function g can be computed in exactly degree L. To see this, the output of g is viewed as corresponding to S AIK randomized encodings for functions $\{h_i\}_{i\in[S]}$. If the lth output bit belongs to the ith randomized encoding for h_i with random tape $\mathbf{r}[i]$, the function g_l computing it can be written as a sum of monomials as follows:

$$\begin{aligned}g_l(\mathbf{x}, \mathbf{s}, \mathbf{s}', b) &= (1-b)g_{l0}(\mathbf{x}, \mathbf{s}) + b g_{l1}(\mathbf{s}') \\ &= (1-b)\sum_{i_0,i_1,i_2,i_3} c_{i_0,i_1,i_2,i_3}\mathbf{x}_{i_0}\mathbf{r}[i]_{i_1}\mathbf{r}[i]_{i_2}\mathbf{r}[i]_{i_3} + b\sum_j c_j\mathbf{r}'_j \qquad (1)\end{aligned}$$

where $\mathbf{r}[i]$ is the ith portion in $\mathbf{r} = \text{PRG}(\mathbf{s})$, and $\mathbf{r}' = \text{PRG}(\mathbf{s}')$. This is because in the case of $b = 0$, the output is a bit in the AIK encoding of h_i and hence has degree 1 in the input $\mathbf{x}$ and degree 3 in $\mathbf{r}[i]$, while in the case of $b = 1$, the output has degree 1 in $\mathbf{r}'$.

When PRG has locality L, the straightforward way of computing a degree-3 monomial $\mathbf{r}[i]_{i_1}\mathbf{r}[i]_{i_2}\mathbf{r}[i]_{i_3}$ from the seed $\mathbf{s}$ requires degree $3L$. The works of [4,53] showed how to reduce the degree to just L. First, they use a different way to compute each $\mathbf{r}[i]$. View the seed $\mathbf{s}$ as a $Q \times \Gamma'$ matrix with $Q = Q(\lambda) = \text{poly}(\lambda)$ rows and $\Gamma' = S^{1/1+\alpha}$ columns; apply PRG on each row of $\mathbf{s}$ to expand the seed matrix into a $Q \times S$ matrix $\mathbf{r}$ of pseudo-random bits. That is, denote the qth

Single-key Compact FE Scheme CFE by [56]

<u>SETUP:</u> $\mathsf{CFE.Setup}(1^\lambda)$ samples $(\mathsf{MPK}, \mathsf{MSK}) \xleftarrow{\$} \mathsf{FE.Setup}(1^\lambda)$.

<u>ENCRYPTION:</u> $\mathsf{CFE.Enc}(\mathsf{MPK}, \mathbf{x})$ samples $\mathbf{s}, \mathbf{s}' \xleftarrow{\$} \{0,1\}^\Gamma$ for $\Gamma = S^{1/1+\alpha}\,\mathrm{poly}(\lambda)$, and generates

$$\mathsf{CT} \xleftarrow{\$} \mathsf{FE.Enc}(\mathsf{MPK}, (\mathbf{x}, \mathbf{s}, \mathbf{s}', 0))$$

<u>KEY GENERATION:</u> $\mathsf{CFE.KeyGen}(\mathsf{MSK}, h)$ does the following:

- Sample $\mathbf{CT} \xleftarrow{\$} \{0,1\}^\ell$, where ℓ is set below.
- Define function g as follows: On input $\mathbf{x}$ of length N, two PRG seeds $\mathbf{s}, \mathbf{s}'$ each of length Γ, and a bit b,

  $g(\mathbf{x}, \mathbf{s}, \mathbf{s}', b)$ does the following:
  - For every $i \in [S]$, let $h_i(\mathbf{x})$ denote the function that computes the ith output bit of $h(\mathbf{x})$. Since $h \in \mathsf{NC}^1_D$, h_i has depth $D(\lambda) = O(\log \lambda)$ and size $2^{D(\lambda)} = \mathrm{poly}(\lambda)$.
  - If $b = 0$, compute $\mathbf{r} = \mathrm{PRG}(\mathbf{s})$, whose output has length $\Gamma^{1+\alpha} = S\,\mathrm{poly}(\lambda)$; divide the output into S equally long portions and denote by $\mathbf{r}[i]$ the ith portion.
    For every $i \in [S]$, compute the AIK encoding $\Pi[i]$ of computation $(h_i, \mathbf{x})$ as follows:

    $$\forall\, i \in [S], \qquad \Pi[i] = \mathsf{AIK}(h_i,\ \mathbf{x}\ ;\ \ \mathbf{r}[i])\ .$$

    Output $\Pi = \{\Pi[i]\}_i$; set $\ell = |\Pi|$.
  - If $b = 1$, output $\Pi = \mathbf{CT} \oplus \mathrm{PRG}(\mathbf{s}')$.
- For every $l \in [\ell]$, generate a secret key $\mathsf{SK}_l \xleftarrow{\$} \mathsf{FE.KeyGen}(\mathsf{MSK}, g_l)$ for g_l that computes the lth output bit of g.

Output $\mathsf{SK} = \{\mathsf{SK}_l\}_{l\in[\ell]}$.

<u>DECRYPTION:</u> $\mathsf{CFE.Dec}(\mathsf{SK}, \mathsf{CT})$ computes $\Pi = \{\mathsf{FE.Dec}(\mathsf{SK}_l, \mathsf{CT})\}_{l\in[\ell]}$, parses $\Pi = \{\Pi[i]\}$, and decodes every $\Pi[i]$ using the AIK decoding algorithm to obtain the output $h(\mathbf{x})$.

Fig. 2. Single-key compact FE **CFE** by [56]

row of $\mathbf{s}$ and $\mathbf{r}$ as $\mathbf{s}_q$ and $\mathbf{r}_q$; $\mathbf{r}_q = \mathrm{PRG}(\mathbf{s}_q)$. Finally, set the random tape for computing the ith AIK encoding to be the ith column $\mathbf{r}[i]$ of $\mathbf{r}$.

In [53], they used PRGs with locality L. Let $\mathrm{PRG}[i]$ denote the function computing the ith output bit of PRG, and let $\mathsf{Nbr}(i) = \{\gamma_1, \cdots, \gamma_L\}$ be the indexes of the L seed bits that the ith output bit depends on. Therefore,

$$\begin{aligned}\mathbf{r}[i]_{i_1}\mathbf{r}[i]_{i_2}\mathbf{r}[i]_{i_3} &= \mathrm{PRG}[i](\mathbf{s}_{i_1})\ \mathrm{PRG}[i](\mathbf{s}_{i_2})\ \mathrm{PRG}[i](\mathbf{s}_{i_3}) \\ &= \sum_{\substack{\text{Monomials}\\ X,Y,Z \text{ in } \mathrm{PRG}[i]}} \begin{pmatrix} X(s_{i_1,\gamma_1}, \cdots, s_{i_1,\gamma_L}) \\ \times\, Y(s_{i_2,\gamma_1}, \cdots, s_{i_2,\gamma_L}) \\ \times\, Z(s_{i_3,\gamma_1}, \cdots, s_{i_3,\gamma_L}) \end{pmatrix}. \end{aligned} \tag{2}$$

Suppose that one has pre-computed all degree ≤ 3 monomials over bits in each column $\mathbf{s}[\gamma]$ of $\mathbf{s}$.

$$\text{Define} \qquad \mathsf{Mnml}^{\leq 3}(A) := \{a_i a_j a_k \mid a_i, a_j, a_k \in A \cup \{1\}\}$$

Given $\mathsf{Mnml}^{\leq 3}(\mathbf{s}[\gamma])$ for every $\gamma \in \mathsf{Nbr}(i)$, one can compute $\mathbf{r}[i]_{i_1}\mathbf{r}[i]_{i_2}\mathbf{r}[i]_{i_3}$ in Eq. (2) using just degree L. Similarly, given $\mathsf{Mnml}^{\leq 3}(\mathbf{s}[\gamma])$ for all $\gamma \in [\Gamma']$, one can compute *any* degree 3 monomials over bits in $\mathbf{r}[i]$ for *any* i, sufficient for the computation of g.

Furthermore, the size of each set $\mathsf{Mnml}^{\leq 3}(\mathbf{s}[\gamma])$ is bounded by $(Q+1)^3 = \text{poly}(\lambda)$, and thus the size of their union for all γ is bounded by $\Gamma'\text{poly}(\lambda) = S^{1/1+\alpha}\text{poly}(\lambda)$—only a polynomial factor (in λ) larger than the original seed $\mathbf{s}$ itself. Therefore the encryptor can afford to precompute all these monomials and encrypt them, without compromising the weak-compactness of the resulting FE for NC^1_D scheme.

This Work: Handling Block-Wise Local PRG. Our new observation is that the above technique naturally extends to accommodate block-wise local PRGs. Consider a family of $(n(\lambda) \times \log\lambda, n(\lambda)^{1+\alpha})$-PRGs with block-wise locality-$(L, \log\lambda)$. As before, we think of the seed of such PRGs as a vector $\mathbf{t}$ of length n, where every element t_i is a block of $\log\lambda$ bits, and each output bit $\text{PRG}[i](\mathbf{t})$ depends on at most L blocks.

Correspondingly, think of the seed matrix $\mathbf{s}$ described above as consisting of $Q \times \Gamma'$ blocks of $\log\lambda$ bits. When $\mathbf{r}[i]$ is computed using block-wise local PRGs, the degree-3 monomial $\mathbf{r}[i]_{i_1}\mathbf{r}[i]_{i_2}\mathbf{r}[i]_{i_3}$ in Eq. (2) now depends on a set of blocks $\{s_{i_t,\gamma_s}\}_{t\in[3],s\in[L]}$. Though the actual locality of the PRG is $L\log\lambda$, due to its special structure, we can still pre-process the seed $\mathbf{s}$ to enable computing any degree-3 monomial over $\mathbf{r}[i]$ for any i using degree L, in the following two steps.

1. Precompute all *multilinear* monomials over bits in each block $s_{q,\gamma}$ in $\mathbf{s}$.

   $$\text{Define} \qquad \mathsf{Mnml}(A) := \{a_{i_1}a_{i_2}\cdots a_{i_q} \mid q \leq |A| \ \text{ and } \forall j,k \ a_{i_j} \neq a_{i_k} \in A\}.$$

   More precisely, precompute $\mathsf{Mnml}(s_{q,\gamma})$ for all $q \in [Q]$ and $\gamma \in [\Gamma']$. Note that each set $\mathsf{Mnml}(s_{q,\gamma})$ has exactly size λ.
2. For every column $\gamma \in [\Gamma']$, take the union of monomials over blocks in column γ, that is, $\cup_q \mathsf{Mnml}(s_{q,\gamma})$. Then, precompute all degree-≤ 3 monomials over this union, that is, $\mathsf{Mnml}^{\leq 3}(\cup_q \mathsf{Mnml}(s_{q,\gamma}))$, for each γ. Observe that from $\{\mathsf{Mnml}^{\leq 3}(\cup_q \mathsf{Mnml}(s_{q,\gamma}))\}_{\gamma\in[\Gamma']}$, one can again compute *any* degree-3 monomial in $\mathbf{r}[i]$ for *any* i in just degree L.

Furthermore, since $|\mathsf{Mnml}(s_{q,\gamma})| = \lambda$ for any q, γ, the number of monomials in $\mathsf{Mnml}^{\leq 3}(\cup_q \mathsf{Mnml}(s_{q,\gamma}))$ is bounded by $(Q\lambda + 1)^3 = \text{poly}(\lambda)$. Therefore, the total size of pre-computed monomials is

$$\left|\{\mathsf{Mnml}^{\leq 3}(\cup_q \mathsf{Mnml}(s_{q,\gamma}))\}_{\gamma\in[\Gamma']}\right| \leq \Gamma'\text{poly}(\lambda) = S^{1/1+\alpha}\text{poly}(\lambda), \qquad (3)$$

which is still sublinear in the circuit size S and does not compromise the weak-compactness of the resulting FE for NC^1_D scheme.

Putting Things Together. So far, we showed how to "compress" the computation of degree 3 monomials over $\mathbf{r}[i]$, for any i, into a degree-L computation. To compute function g in Eq. (1) in degree L, we need to additionally pre-compute multiplications with $\mathbf{x}$ and b. As described in [53], this can be done easily by pre-computing the following:

$$\mathbf{V}_1 = \{\mathsf{Mnml}^{\leq 3}(\cup_q \mathsf{Mnml}(s_{q,\gamma}))\}_{\gamma \in [\Gamma']} \otimes (\mathbf{x}||b||1)$$

(where the sets of monomials are first interpreted as a vector before taking tensor product). Given the tensor product, one can compute *any* monomial with degree ≤ 3 in $\mathbf{r}[i]$ for any i, degree ≤ 1 in $\mathbf{x}$, and degree ≤ 1 in b, in just degree L, which is sufficient for computing the first additive term in g_l in Eq. (1). Similarly, to compute the second additive term in g_l, it suffices to precompute all multilinear monomials over every block in $\mathbf{s}'$ (of length Γ), and compute their tensor product with $b||1$, that is,

$$\mathbf{V}_2 = \{\mathsf{Mnml}(s'_\gamma)\}_{\gamma \in [\Gamma]} \otimes (b||1)$$

In summary, for every $l \in [\ell]$, there exists a degree-L polynomial P_l that on input $(\mathbf{V}_1, \mathbf{V}_2)$ outputs $g_l(\mathbf{x}, \mathbf{s}, \mathbf{s}', b)$.

$$\text{Define} \quad P_l := \text{the degree-}L\text{ polynomial s.t. } P_l(\mathbf{V}_1, \mathbf{V}_2) = g_l(\mathbf{x}, \mathbf{s}, \mathbf{s}', b) \quad (4)$$

Moreover, we show that both $\mathbf{V}_1$ and $\mathbf{V}_2$ have length sublinear in the circuit size. First, combining Eq. (3) with the fact that $|(\mathbf{x}||b||1)| = N+2$, we have that

$$|\mathbf{V}_1| \leq S^{1/1+\alpha}\text{poly}(\lambda) \times (N+2) = S^{1/1+\alpha}\text{poly}(\lambda, N). \quad (5)$$

The size of $\mathbf{V}_2$ is

$$|\mathbf{V}_2| = \lambda \times \Gamma \times 2 \leq S^{1/1+\alpha}\text{poly}(\lambda). \quad (6)$$

Finally, to construct a 1-key weakly-compact FE scheme for NC^1_D from FE for just degree L polynomials. We modify the LV construction as follows: (1) Instead of encrypting $(\mathbf{x}, \mathbf{s}, \mathbf{s}', b)$, the encryptor pre-computes and encrypts $\mathbf{V}_1||\mathbf{V}_2$ as described above, and (2) instead of generating secret keys for functions $\{g_l\}_{l\in[\ell]}$ which have degree $3L+2$, generate secret keys for $\{P_l\}_{l\in[\ell]}$ which have only degree L. This way, at decryption time, the decryptor computes the correct output $\{P_l(\mathbf{V}_1||\mathbf{V}_2) = g_l(\mathbf{x}, \mathbf{s}, \mathbf{s}', b)\}$. The resulting new compact FE scheme **CFE** is described in Fig. 3 (with key difference from the LV scheme highlighted). The compactness of the new scheme follows directly from the fact that the encrypted input $\mathbf{V}_1, \mathbf{V}_2$ have length sublinear in $S(\lambda)$, and that the degree-L **FE** scheme has linear efficiency. Moreover, its correctness and security follows from the same proof as that in [56]; since their security proof incur only a polynomial security loss, we conclude Proposition 1.

4 FE from $\omega(\log \lambda)$-Bit-Input IO for P/poly

In this section, we show Theorem 4, i.e., we prove via a new transformation that adaptively-secure collusion-resistant public-key functional encryption for P/poly is implied by IO for circuits with short, $\omega(\log \lambda)$-bit, inputs and public key encryption, both with slightly super-polynomial security. Note that, in contrast, previous constructions of collusion-resistant FE for P/poly either rely on multilinear maps [40], or require IO for all P/poly, including circuits with long (polynomial) inputs [39].

Our proof generically transforms any *1-key* (public key) FE scheme for any circuit class $\mathcal{C}$ into a *collusion-resistant* (public key) FE scheme for the same circuit class, using IO for circuits with $\omega(\log \lambda)$-bit inputs. The encryption time of the resulting FE schemes is polynomial in the encryption time of the original schemes, and hence if the original scheme is (non-)compact, so is the resulting FE scheme. The transformation also preserves the same type of security—namely Full-Sel- or Adap-security—and incurs a $2^{\omega(\log \lambda)}$ security loss.

More precisely, we prove the following below in Sect. 4.1.

Proposition 2. *Let $\mathcal{C}$ be any circuit class, τ be any polynomial, and $\mathsf{i}\ell$ be any polynomial such that $\mathsf{i}\ell(\lambda) = \omega(\log \lambda) \leq \lambda$. Assume the existence of an $\mathsf{i}\ell(\lambda)$-bit-input indistinguishability obfuscator $i\mathcal{O}$ for* P/poly*. Then, any* 1-key *public-key FE schemes* **OFE** *for $\mathcal{C}$ can be generically transformed into* collusion-resistant *FE schemes* **CRFE** *for $\mathcal{C}$, with the following properties:*

- *The encryption time of* **CRFE** *is polynomial in the encryption time of* **OFE**.
- *If $i\mathcal{O}$ is $2^{-(\mathsf{i}\ell(\lambda)+\tau(\lambda))}\text{negl}(\lambda)$-secure and* **OFE** *is $2^{-(\mathsf{i}\ell(\lambda)+\tau(\lambda))}\text{negl}(\lambda)$-(*Adap *or* Full-Sel*)-secure, then* **CRFE** *is $2^{-\tau(\lambda)}\text{negl}(\lambda)$-(*Adap *or* Full-Sel*)-secure.*

It is known that adaptively-secure 1-key non-compact public-key FE for P/poly can be constructed from just public key encryption [48].

Theorem 7 (1-Key Adap-Secure Public-Key FE for P/poly [48]). *Let μ be any function from $\mathbb{N}$ to $[0, 1]$. Assuming public key encryption with $\mu(\lambda)\text{negl}(\lambda)$-security, there exist $\mu(\lambda)\text{negl}(\lambda)$-*Adap*-secure 1-key non-compact public-key FE schemes for* P/poly.

Now, applying the transformation of Proposition 2 to the μnegl-Adap-secure 1-key FE schemes for P/poly with $\mu = 2^{-(\mathsf{i}\ell+\tau)}$, yields $2^{-\tau}$negl-Adap-secure *collusion-resistant* (non-compact public-key) FE for P/poly. Finally, note that it follows from [3] that collusion-resistant non-compact FE schemes implies collusion-resistant compact FE schemes with the same level of security, which yields Theorem 4.

4.1 From 1-Key to Collusion-Resistant FE, Generically

In this section, we prove Proposition 2. Let us fix any circuit class $\mathcal{C}$, and any $\mathsf{i}\ell$ such that $\mathsf{i}\ell(\lambda) = \omega(\log \lambda) \leq \lambda$. The resulting collusion-resistant FE scheme for $\mathcal{C}$, denoted **CRFE** = (CRFE.Setup, CRFE.KeyGen, CRFE.Enc, CRFE.Dec), relies on the following building blocks:

Our Single-key Compact FE Scheme CFE

SETUP: $\mathsf{CFE.Setup}(1^\lambda)$ samples $(\mathsf{MPK}, \mathsf{MSK}) \xleftarrow{\$} \mathsf{FE.Setup}(1^\lambda)$, and $\mathrm{PRG} \xleftarrow{\$} \mathrm{PRG}_\lambda$.

ENCRYPTION: $\mathsf{CFE.Enc}(\mathsf{MPK}, \mathbf{x})$ samples

- a PRG seed $\mathbf{s}$ viewed as a $Q \times \Gamma'$ matrix for $Q = \mathrm{poly}(\lambda)$ and $\Gamma' = S^{1/1+\alpha}$, where each element $s_{q,\gamma}$ in $\mathbf{s}$ is a block of $\log \lambda$ bits, and
- another PRG seed $\mathbf{s}'$ viewed as a vector of length $\Gamma = S^{1/1+\alpha}\,\mathrm{poly}(\lambda)$, where again each element s'_γ in $\mathbf{s}'$ is a block of $\log \lambda$ bits.

Pre-Compute the following for $b = 0$:

$$\mathbf{V}_1 = \left\{\mathsf{Mnml}^{\leq 3}\left(\cup_q \mathsf{Mnml}(s_{q,\gamma})\right)\right\}_{\gamma \in [\Gamma']} \otimes (\mathbf{x}||b||1) \tag{7}$$

$$\mathbf{V}_2 = \left\{\mathsf{Mnml}(s'_\gamma)\right\}_{\gamma \in [\Gamma]} \otimes (b||1) \tag{8}$$

Finally generate:

$$\mathsf{CT} \xleftarrow{\$} \mathsf{FE.Enc}(\mathsf{MPK}, (\mathbf{V}_1, \mathbf{V}_2))$$

KEY GENERATION: $\mathsf{CFE.KeyGen}(\mathsf{MSK}, h)$ does the following:

- Sample $\mathbf{CT} \xleftarrow{\$} \{0,1\}^\ell$, where ℓ is set below.
- Define function g as follows: On input $\mathbf{x}$ of length N, PRG seeds $\mathbf{s}$ and $\mathbf{s}'$ of dimensions described above, and a bit b.

  $g(\mathbf{x}, \mathbf{s}, \mathbf{s}', b)$ does the following:
  - For every $i \in [S]$, let $h_i(\mathbf{x})$ denote the function that computes the ith output bit of $h(\mathbf{x})$. Since $h \in \mathsf{NC}^1_D$, h_i has depth $D(\lambda) = O(\log \lambda)$ and size $2^{D(\lambda)} = \mathrm{poly}(\lambda)$.
  - If $b = 0$, do:
    Expand each row of $\mathbf{s}$ using PRG to obtain a $Q \times S$ matrix $\mathbf{r}$ of pseudorandom bits. That is, let $\mathbf{s}_i$ denote the ith row of $\mathbf{s}$; the ith row $\mathbf{r}_i$ of $\mathbf{r}$ is $\mathrm{PRG}(\mathbf{s}_i)$. Denote by $\mathbf{r}[i]$ the ith column of matrix $\mathbf{r}$, which has length $Q = \mathrm{poly}(\lambda)$.
    For every $i \in [S]$, compute the AIK encoding $\Pi[i]$ of computation $(h_i, \mathbf{x})$ as follows:

    $$\forall\, i \in [S], \qquad \Pi[i] = \mathsf{AIK}(h_i,\ \mathbf{x}\ ;\ \mathbf{r}[i])\ .$$

    Output $\Pi = \{\Pi[i]\}_i$; set $\ell = |\Pi|$.
  - If $b = 1$, output $\Pi = \mathbf{CT} \oplus \mathrm{PRG}(\mathbf{s}')$.
- For every $l \in [\ell]$, let P_l be the degree-L polynomial that on input $(\mathbf{V}_1, \mathbf{V}_2)$ in Equations (7) and (8) computes the lth output bit of $g(\mathbf{x}, \mathbf{s}, \mathbf{s}', b)$.
  For every l, generate a secret key $\mathsf{SK}_l \xleftarrow{\$} \mathsf{FE.KeyGen}(\mathsf{MSK}, P_l)$ for P_l.

Output $\mathsf{SK} = \{\mathsf{SK}_l\}_{l \in [\ell]}$.

DECRYPTION: $\mathsf{CFE.Dec}(\mathsf{SK}, \mathsf{CT})$ computes $\Pi = \{\mathsf{FE.Dec}(\mathsf{SK}_l, \mathsf{CT})\}_{l \in [\ell]}$, parses $\Pi = \{\Pi[i]\}$, and decodes every $\Pi[i]$ using the AIK decoding algorithm to obtain the output $h(\mathbf{x})$.

Fig. 3. Single-key compact FE **CFE** from block-wise locality-L PRG and degree-L FE

- An $i\ell$-bit-input indistinguishability obfuscator $i\mathcal{O}$ for $\mathsf{P/poly}$.
- A 1-key FE scheme **OFE** = $(\mathsf{OFE.Setup}, \mathsf{OFE.KeyGen}, \mathsf{OFE.Enc}, \mathsf{OFE.Dec})$ for $\mathcal{C}$.
- A puncturable PRF scheme $\mathsf{PPRF} = (\mathsf{PRF.Gen}, \mathsf{PRF.Punc}, \mathsf{F})$.

Given the above building blocks, to construct collusion resistant FE **CRFE** for $\mathcal{C}$, we start with the following intuition. *If efficiency were not a problem*, we could trivially construct a FE scheme that support releasing any polynomial number of secret keys, essentially by using a super-polynomial number of instances of **OFE**. Concretely, we would proceed as follows:

- *Setup:* Generate a super-polynomial number, $M = 2^{i\ell(\lambda)} = 2^{\omega(\lambda)}$, of **OFE** instances with master keys $\{(\mathsf{OMPK}_i, \mathsf{OMSK}_i) \xleftarrow{\$} \mathsf{OFE.Setup}(1^\lambda)\}_{i\in[M]}$.
- *Key Generation:* To generate a key for a function f, sample an index at random $i_f \xleftarrow{\$} [M]$ and generate a secret key using the i_f^{th} master secret key $\mathsf{OSK}_{i_f} \xleftarrow{\$} \mathsf{OFE.KeyGen}(\mathsf{OMSK}_{i_f}, f)$. Since there are at most a polynomial number of secret keys ever generated, the probability that every **OFE** instance is used to generate at most one secret key is overwhelming.
- *Encryption:* To encrypt any input x, simply encrypt the input x under all master public keys, $\{\mathsf{OCT}_i \xleftarrow{\$} \mathsf{OFE.Enc}(\mathsf{OMPK}_i, x)\}_{i\in[M]}$. Given the set of ciphertexts, one can compute the output $f(x)$ of any function f for which a secret key OSK_{i_f} has been generated, by decrypting the appropriated ciphertext OCT_{i_f} using the secret key OSK_{i_f}.

Of course, the only problem with this FE scheme is that its setup and encryption algorithms run in super-polynomial time. To address this, we follow the previously adopted idea (*e.g.* [17,25]) of using IO to "compress" these super-polynomially many **OFE** instances into "polynomial size". More precisely, instead of having the setup algorithm publish all M master public keys, let it generate an *obfuscated circuit* that on input $i \in [M]$ outputs the ith master public key. Similarly, instead of having the encryption algorithm publish M ciphertexts, let it generate an obfuscated circuit that on input $i \in [M]$ outputs the ith ciphertext under the ith master public key. Since the inputs to the obfuscated circuits are indexes from the range $[M]$, which could be represented in $i\ell$ bits, it suffices to use $i\ell$-bit-input IO. Furthermore, for "compression" to the possible, all M master public and secret keys, as well as all M ciphertexts, need to be sampled using pseudo-randomness generated by puncturable PRFs. The resulting obfuscated circuits have polynomial size, since generating individual master public keys and ciphertexts using pseudorandomness is efficient, and hence the new FE scheme becomes efficient. Finally, the security of the new FE scheme follows from the common "one-input-at-a-time" argument, which incurs a $2^{-|i|} = 2^{-i\ell}$ security loss. We formally describe the collusion-resistant FE scheme **CRFE** for $\mathcal{C}$ in Fig. 4.

We postpone the analysis of correctness, efficiency, and security of the **CRFE** scheme to the full version [55].

Collusion Resistant FE Scheme CRFE for $\mathcal{C}$

SETUP: $\mathsf{CRFE.Setup}(1^\lambda)$ does:

- Sample a PPRF key $K^s \xleftarrow{\$} \mathsf{PRF.Gen}(1^\lambda)$.
- Obfuscate the program $P_{\text{setup}}[0, K^s, \bot]$ described in Figure 5

$$\hat{P}_{\text{setup}} \xleftarrow{\$} i\mathcal{O}(1^\kappa, P_{\text{setup}}[0, K^s, \bot, \bot]) \ ,$$

  where the IO scheme is invoked with a security parameter $\kappa = \max(\lambda, |P_{\text{setup}}|)$.
- Output $\mathsf{MPK} = \hat{P}_{\text{setup}}$ and $\mathsf{MSK} = K^s$.

ENCRYPTION: $\mathsf{CRFE.Enc}(\mathsf{MPK} = \hat{P}_{\text{setup}}, x)$ does the following to encrypt an input $x \in \{0,1\}^N$:

- Sample a PPRF key $K^e \xleftarrow{\$} \mathsf{PRF.Gen}(1^\lambda)$.
- Obfuscate the program $P_{\text{enc}}[\hat{P}_{\text{setup}}, 0, K^e, x, \bot, \bot]$ described in Figure 6,

$$\mathsf{CT} = \hat{P}_{\text{enc}} \xleftarrow{\$} i\mathcal{O}(1^{\kappa'}, P_{\text{enc}}[\hat{P}_{\text{setup}}, 0, K^e, x, \bot, \bot, \bot]) \ ,$$

  where the IO scheme is invoked with a security parameter $\kappa' = \max(\lambda, |P_{\text{enc}}|)$.
- Output the obfuscated circuit as the ciphertext $\mathsf{CT} = \hat{P}_{\text{enc}}$.

KEY GENERATION: $\mathsf{CRFE.KeyGen}(\mathsf{MSK} = K^s, f)$ a key for function $f \in \mathcal{C}$ as follows:

- Sample at random an index $i_f \xleftarrow{\$} [M]$.
- Generate a secret key of f under the i_f^{th} master secret key,

$$(\mathsf{OMPK}_{i_f}, \mathsf{OMSK}_{i_f}) = \mathsf{OFE.Setup}(1^\lambda \ ; \ \mathsf{F}(K^s, i_f)) \ ,$$
$$\mathsf{OSK}_{i_f} \xleftarrow{\$} \mathsf{OFE.KeyGen}(\mathsf{OMSK}_{i_f}, f) \ .$$

- Output $\mathsf{SK} = (i_f, \mathsf{OSK}_{i_f})$.

DECRYPTION: $\mathsf{CRFE.Dec}(\mathsf{SK} = (i_f, \mathsf{OSK}_{i_f}), \mathsf{CT} = \hat{P}_{\text{enc}})$ does:

- Compute the ciphertext of x under the i_f^{th} master public key,

$$\mathsf{OCT}_{i_f} = \hat{P}_{\text{enc}}(i_f) \ .$$

- Decrypt the obtained ciphertext using OSK_{i_f},

$$y = \mathsf{OFE.Dec}(\mathsf{OSK}_{i_f}, \mathsf{OCT}_{i_f}) \ .$$

- Output y.

Fig. 4. Collusion resistant FE scheme **CRFE** for $\mathcal{C}$ from $\mathrm{i}\ell(\lambda) = \omega(\lambda)$-bit-input IO

Circuit $P_{\mathsf{setup}}[i^*, K^s, \mathsf{OMPK}^*]$

Constants: $i^* \in \{0, \cdots, M+1\}$ is an index, for $M = 2^{\mathsf{i}\ell(\lambda)}$ and $\mathsf{i}\ell = \omega(\log \lambda)$, K^s is a PPRF key, and OMPK^* is a master public key of the **OFE** scheme.
Input: Index $i \in [M]$.
Procedure:

1. If $i \neq i^*$, compute $(\mathsf{OMPK}_i, \mathsf{OMSK}_i) = \mathsf{OFE.Setup}(1^\lambda \ ; \ \mathsf{F}(K^s, i))$.
2. If $i = i^*$, output $\mathsf{OMPK}_{i^*} = \mathsf{OMPK}^*$.

Output OMPK_i.

Fig. 5. Circuit P_{setup} in the construction and analysis of **CRFE**

Circuit $P_{\mathsf{enc}}[\hat{P}_{\mathsf{setup}}, i^*, K^e, x_0, x_1, \mathsf{OCT}^*]$

Constants: $\hat{P}_{\mathsf{setup}}$ is an obfuscated program, $i^* \in \{0, \cdots, M+1\}$ is an index, for $M = 2^{\mathsf{i}\ell(\lambda)}$ and $\mathsf{i}\ell = \omega(\log \lambda)$, K^s is a PPRF key, $x_0, x_1 \in \{0,1\}^N$ are two inputs, and OCT^* is a ciphertext of **OFE**.
Input: Index $i \in [M]$.
Procedure:

1. If $i < i^*$,
   compute $\mathsf{OMPK}_i = \hat{P}_{\mathsf{setup}}(i)$ and $\mathsf{OCT}_i = \mathsf{OFE.Enc}(\mathsf{OMPK}_i, \underline{x_1};\ \mathsf{F}(K^e, i))$.
2. If $i = i^*$, output $\mathsf{OCT}_{i^*} = \mathsf{OCT}^*$.
3. If $i > i^*$,
   compute $\mathsf{OMPK}_i = \hat{P}_{\mathsf{setup}}(i)$ and $\mathsf{OCT}_i = \mathsf{OFE.Enc}(\mathsf{OMPK}_i, \underline{x_0};\ \mathsf{F}(K^e, i))$.

Output OCT_i.

Fig. 6. Circuit P_{enc} in the construction and analysis of **CRFE**

Acknowledgements. The authors thank Benny Applebaum and Vinod Vaikuntanathan for many helpful discussions and insights.

Huijia Lin was supported in part by NSF grants CNS-1528178, CNS-1514526, and CNS-1652849 (CAREER). Stefano Tessaro was supported in part by NSF grants CNS-1423566, CNS-1528178, CNS-1553758 (CAREER), and IIS-152804.

References

1. Allen, S.R., O'Donnell, R., Witmer, D.: How to refute a random CSP. In: 56th FOCS, Berkeley, CA, USA, pp. 689–708, 17–20 October 2015
2. Ananth, P., Jain, A.: Indistinguishability obfuscation from compact functional encryption. In: Gennaro, R., Robshaw, M. (eds.) CRYPTO 2015. LNCS, vol. 9215, pp. 308–326. Springer, Heidelberg (2015). doi:10.1007/978-3-662-47989-6_15
3. Ananth, P., Jain, A., Sahai, A.: Achieving compactness generically: indistinguishability obfuscation from non-compact functional encryption. IACR Cryptology ePrint Archive, vol. 2015, p. 730 (2015)
4. Ananth, P., Sahai, A.: Projective arithmetic functional encryption and indistinguishability obfuscation from degree-5 multilinear maps. Cryptology ePrint Archive, Report 2016/1097 (2016). http://eprint.iacr.org/2016/1097

5. Ananth, P.V., Gupta, D., Ishai, Y., Sahai, A.: Optimizing obfuscation: avoiding Barrington's theorem. In: ACM CCS 2014, Scottsdale, AZ, USA, pp. 646–658, 3–7 November 2014
6. Apon, D., Döttling, N., Garg, S., Mukherjee, P.: Cryptanalysis of indistinguishability obfuscations of circuits over GGH13. In: ICALP 2017. LNCS, vol. 80. Springer, Heidelberg (2017)
7. Applebaum, B.: Pseudorandom generators with long stretch and low locality from random local one-way functions. In: 44th ACM STOC, New York, NY, USA, pp. 805–816, 19–22 May 2012
8. Applebaum, B.: The cryptographic hardness of random local functions – survey. Cryptology ePrint Archive, Report 2015/165 (2015). http://eprint.iacr.org/2015/165
9. Applebaum, B., Bogdanov, A., Rosen, A.: A dichotomy for local small-bias generators. J. Cryptol. **29**, 577–596 (2016)
10. Applebaum, B., Brakerski, Z.: Obfuscating circuits via composite-order graded encoding. In: Dodis, Y., Nielsen, J.B. (eds.) TCC 2015. LNCS, vol. 9015, pp. 528–556. Springer, Heidelberg (2015). doi:10.1007/978-3-662-46497-7_21
11. Applebaum, B., Ishai, Y., Kushilevitz, E.: Cryptography in NC^0. In: FOCS, pp. 166–175 (2004)
12. Applebaum, B., Lovett, S.: Algebraic attacks against random local functions and their countermeasures. In: 48th ACM STOC, Cambridge, MA, USA, pp. 1087–1100, 18–21 June 2016
13. Applebaum, B., Raykov, P.: Fast pseudorandom functions based on expander graphs. In: Hirt, M., Smith, A. (eds.) TCC 2016. LNCS, vol. 9985, pp. 27–56. Springer, Heidelberg (2016). doi:10.1007/978-3-662-53641-4_2
14. Barak, B., Brakerski, Z., Komargodski, I., Kothari, P.K.: Limits on low-degree pseudorandom generators (or: sum-of-squares meets program obfuscation). Cryptology ePrint Archive, Report 2017/312 (2017). http://eprint.iacr.org/2017/312
15. Barak, B., Garg, S., Kalai, Y.T., Paneth, O., Sahai, A.: Protecting obfuscation against algebraic attacks. In: Nguyen, P.Q., Oswald, E. (eds.) EUROCRYPT 2014. LNCS, vol. 8441, pp. 221–238. Springer, Heidelberg (2014). doi:10.1007/978-3-642-55220-5_13
16. Barak, B., Goldreich, O., Impagliazzo, R., Rudich, S., Sahai, A., Vadhan, S., Yang, K.: On the (im)possibility of obfuscating programs. In: Kilian, J. (ed.) CRYPTO 2001. LNCS, vol. 2139, pp. 1–18. Springer, Heidelberg (2001). doi:10.1007/3-540-44647-8_1
17. Bitansky, N., Garg, S., Lin, H., Pass, R., Telang, S.: Succinct randomized encodings and their applications. In: Proceedings of 47th Annual ACM on Symposium on Theory of Computing, STOC 2015, 14–17 June 2015, Portland, OR, USA, pp. 439–448 (2015)
18. Bitansky, N., Nishimaki, R., Passelègue, A., Wichs, D.: From cryptomania to obfustopia through secret-key functional encryption. In: Hirt, M., Smith, A. (eds.) TCC 2016. LNCS, vol. 9986, pp. 391–418. Springer, Heidelberg (2016). doi:10.1007/978-3-662-53644-5_15
19. Bitansky, N., Paneth, O., Rosen, A.: On the cryptographic hardness of finding a nash equilibrium. In: Guruswami [49], pp. 1480–1498 (2015)
20. Bitansky, N., Vaikuntanathan, V.: Indistinguishability obfuscation from functional encryption. In: IEEE 56th Annual Symposium on Foundations of Computer Science, FOCS 2015, 17–20 October 2015, Berkeley, CA, USA, pp. 171–190 (2015)
21. Bogdanov, A., Qiao, Y.: On the security of Goldreich's one-way function. Comput. Complex. **21**(1), 83–127 (2012)

22. Boneh, D., Sahai, A., Waters, B.: Fully collusion resistant traitor tracing with short ciphertexts and private keys. In: Vaudenay, S. (ed.) EUROCRYPT 2006. LNCS, vol. 4004, pp. 573–592. Springer, Heidelberg (2006). doi:10.1007/11761679_34
23. Boneh, D., Silverberg, A.: Applications of multilinear forms to cryptography. Contemp. Math. **324**, 71–90 (2002)
24. Brakerski, Z., Rothblum, G.N.: Virtual black-box obfuscation for all circuits via generic graded encoding. In: Lindell, Y. (ed.) TCC 2014. LNCS, vol. 8349, pp. 1–25. Springer, Heidelberg (2014). doi:10.1007/978-3-642-54242-8_1
25. Canetti, R., Lin, H., Tessaro, S., Vaikuntanathan, V.: Obfuscation of probabilistic circuits and applications. In: Dodis, Y., Nielsen, J.B. (eds.) TCC 2015. LNCS, vol. 9015, pp. 468–497. Springer, Heidelberg (2015). doi:10.1007/978-3-662-46497-7_19
26. Caro, A., Iovino, V., Jain, A., O'Neill, A., Paneth, O., Persiano, G.: On the achievability of simulation-based security for functional encryption. In: Canetti, R., Garay, J.A. (eds.) CRYPTO 2013. LNCS, vol. 8043, pp. 519–535. Springer, Heidelberg (2013). doi:10.1007/978-3-642-40084-1_29
27. Chen, Y., Gentry, C., Halevi, S.: Cryptanalyses of candidate branching program obfuscators. In: Coron, J.-S., Nielsen, J.B. (eds.) EUROCRYPT 2017. LNCS, vol. 10212, pp. 278–307. Springer, Cham (2017). doi:10.1007/978-3-319-56617-7_10
28. Cheon, J.H., Han, K., Lee, C., Ryu, H., Stehlé, D.: Cryptanalysis of the multilinear map over the integers. In: Oswald, E., Fischlin, M. (eds.) EUROCRYPT 2015. LNCS, vol. 9056, pp. 3–12. Springer, Heidelberg (2015). doi:10.1007/978-3-662-46800-5_1
29. Chor, B., Fiat, A., Naor, M.: Tracing traitors. In: Desmedt, Y.G. (ed.) CRYPTO 1994. LNCS, vol. 839, pp. 257–270. Springer, Heidelberg (1994). doi:10.1007/3-540-48658-5_25
30. Cook, J., Etesami, O., Miller, R., Trevisan, L.: Goldreich's one-way function candidate and myopic backtracking algorithms. In: Reingold, O. (ed.) TCC 2009. LNCS, vol. 5444, pp. 521–538. Springer, Heidelberg (2009). doi:10.1007/978-3-642-00457-5_31
31. Coron, J.-S., et al.: Zeroizing without low-level zeroes: new MMAP attacks and their limitations. In: Gennaro, R., Robshaw, M. (eds.) CRYPTO 2015. LNCS, vol. 9215, pp. 247–266. Springer, Heidelberg (2015). doi:10.1007/978-3-662-47989-6_12
32. Coron, J.-S., Lepoint, T., Tibouchi, M.: Practical multilinear maps over the integers. In: Canetti, R., Garay, J.A. (eds.) CRYPTO 2013. LNCS, vol. 8042, pp. 476–493. Springer, Heidelberg (2013). doi:10.1007/978-3-642-40041-4_26
33. Coron, J.-S., Lepoint, T., Tibouchi, M.: New multilinear maps over the integers. In: Gennaro, R., Robshaw, M. (eds.) CRYPTO 2015. LNCS, vol. 9215, pp. 267–286. Springer, Heidelberg (2015). doi:10.1007/978-3-662-47989-6_13
34. Cryan, M., Miltersen, P.B.: On pseudorandom generators in NC^0. In: Sgall, J., Pultr, A., Kolman, P. (eds.) MFCS 2001. LNCS, vol. 2136, pp. 272–284. Springer, Heidelberg (2001). doi:10.1007/3-540-44683-4_24
35. Dodis, Y., Impagliazzo, R., Jaiswal, R., Kabanets, V.: Security amplification for *Interactive* cryptographic primitives. In: Reingold, O. (ed.) TCC 2009. LNCS, vol. 5444, pp. 128–145. Springer, Heidelberg (2009). doi:10.1007/978-3-642-00457-5_9
36. Döttling, N., Garg, S., Gupta, D., Miao, P., Mukherjee, P.: Obfuscation from low noise multilinear maps. Cryptology ePrint Archive, Report 2016/599 (2016). http://eprint.iacr.org/2016/599
37. Dwork, C., Naor, M., Reingold, O., Rothblum, G.N., Vadhan, S.P.: On the complexity of differentially private data release: efficient algorithms and hardness results. In: 41st ACM STOC, Bethesda, MD, USA, pp. 381–390, 31 May–2 June 2009

38. Garg, S., Gentry, C., Halevi, S.: Candidate multilinear maps from ideal lattices. In: Johansson, T., Nguyen, P.Q. (eds.) EUROCRYPT 2013. LNCS, vol. 7881, pp. 1–17. Springer, Heidelberg (2013). doi:10.1007/978-3-642-38348-9_1
39. Garg, S., Gentry, C., Halevi, S., Raykova, M., Sahai, A., Waters, B.: Candidate indistinguishability obfuscation and functional encryption for all circuits. In: 54th Annual IEEE Symposium on Foundations of Computer Science, FOCS 2013, 26–29 October 2013, Berkeley, CA, USA, pp. 40–49 (2013)
40. Garg, S., Gentry, C., Halevi, S., Zhandry, M.: Functional encryption without obfuscation. In: Kushilevitz, E., Malkin, T. (eds.) TCC 2016. LNCS, vol. 9563, pp. 480–511. Springer, Heidelberg (2016). doi:10.1007/978-3-662-49099-0_18
41. Garg, S., Miles, E., Mukherjee, P., Sahai, A., Srinivasan, A., Zhandry, M.: Secure obfuscation in a weak multilinear map model. In: Hirt, M., Smith, A. (eds.) TCC 2016. LNCS, vol. 9986, pp. 241–268. Springer, Heidelberg (2016). doi:10.1007/978-3-662-53644-5_10
42. Garg, S., Pandey, O., Srinivasan, A.: Revisiting the cryptographic hardness of finding a nash equilibrium. In: Robshaw, M., Katz, J. (eds.) CRYPTO 2016. LNCS, vol. 9815, pp. 579–604. Springer, Heidelberg (2016). doi:10.1007/978-3-662-53008-5_20
43. Garg, S., Pandey, O., Srinivasan, A., Zhandry, M.: Breaking the sub-exponential barrier in obfustopia. Cryptology ePrint Archive, Report 2016/102 (2016). http://eprint.iacr.org/2016/102
44. Gentry, C., Gorbunov, S., Halevi, S.: Graph-induced multilinear maps from lattices. In: Dodis, Y., Nielsen, J.B. (eds.) TCC 2015. LNCS, vol. 9015, pp. 498–527. Springer, Heidelberg (2015). doi:10.1007/978-3-662-46497-7_20
45. Gentry, C., Lewko, A.B., Sahai, A., Waters, B.: Indistinguishability obfuscation from the multilinear subgroup elimination assumption. In: Guruswami [49], pp. 151–170 (2015)
46. Goldreich, O.: Candidate one-way functions based on expander graphs. In: Electronic Colloquium on Computational Complexity (ECCC), vol. 7, no. 90 (2000)
47. Goldreich, O.: Foundations of Cryptography – Basic Tools. Cambridge University Press, Cambridge (2001)
48. Gorbunov, S., Vaikuntanathan, V., Wee, H.: Functional encryption with bounded collusions via multi-party computation. In: Safavi-Naini, R., Canetti, R. (eds.) CRYPTO 2012. LNCS, vol. 7417, pp. 162–179. Springer, Heidelberg (2012). doi:10.1007/978-3-642-32009-5_11
49. Guruswami, V. (ed.) IEEE 56th Annual Symposium on Foundations of Computer Science, FOCS 2015, Berkeley, CA, USA, 17–20 October 2015. IEEE Computer Society (2015)
50. Komargodski, I., Segev, G.: From minicrypt to obfustopia via private-key functional encryption. Cryptology ePrint Archive, Report 2017/080 (2017). http://eprint.iacr.org/2017/080
51. Langlois, A., Stehlé, D., Steinfeld, R.: GGHLite: more efficient multilinear maps from ideal lattices. In: Nguyen, P.Q., Oswald, E. (eds.) EUROCRYPT 2014. LNCS, vol. 8441, pp. 239–256. Springer, Heidelberg (2014). doi:10.1007/978-3-642-55220-5_14
52. Lin, H.: Indistinguishability obfuscation from constant-degree graded encoding schemes. In: Fischlin, M., Coron, J.-S. (eds.) EUROCRYPT 2016. LNCS, vol. 9665, pp. 28–57. Springer, Heidelberg (2016). doi:10.1007/978-3-662-49890-3_2
53. Lin, H.: Indistinguishability obfuscation from SXDH on 5-linear maps and locality-5 PRGs. In: CRYPTO 2017. LNCS. Springer, Heidelberg (2017)

54. Lin, H., Pass, R., Seth, K., Telang, S.: Output-compressing randomized encodings and applications. In: Kushilevitz, E., Malkin, T. (eds.) TCC 2016. LNCS, vol. 9562, pp. 96–124. Springer, Heidelberg (2016). doi:10.1007/978-3-662-49096-9_5
55. Lin, H., Tessaro, S.: Indistinguishability obfuscation from trilinear maps and block-wise local PRGs. Cryptology ePrint Archive, Report 2017/250 (2017). http://eprint.iacr.org/2017/250
56. Lin, H., Vaikuntanathan, V.: Indistinguishability obfuscation from DDH-like assumptions on constant-degree graded encodings. In: IEEE 57th Annual Symposium on Foundations of Computer Science, FOCS 2016, New Brunswick, NJ, USA, 9–11 October 2016
57. Lombardi, A., Vaikuntanathan, V.: On the non-existence of blockwise 2-local PRGs with applications to indistinguishability obfuscation. Cryptology ePrint Archive, Report 2017/301 (2017). http://eprint.iacr.org/2017/301
58. Maurer, U., Tessaro, S.: A hardcore lemma for computational indistinguishability: security amplification for arbitrarily weak PRGs with optimal stretch. In: Micciancio, D. (ed.) TCC 2010. LNCS, vol. 5978, pp. 237–254. Springer, Heidelberg (2010). doi:10.1007/978-3-642-11799-2_15
59. Miles, E., Sahai, A., Zhandry, M.: Annihilation attacks for multilinear maps: cryptanalysis of indistinguishability obfuscation over GGH13. In: Robshaw, M., Katz, J. (eds.) CRYPTO 2016. LNCS, vol. 9815, pp. 629–658. Springer, Heidelberg (2016). doi:10.1007/978-3-662-53008-5_22
60. Mossel, E., Shpilka, A., Trevisan, L.: On e-biased generators in NC0. In: 44th FOCS, Cambridge, MA, USA, pp. 136–145, 11–14 October 2003
61. O'Donnell, R., Witmer, D.: Goldreich's PRG: evidence for near-optimal polynomial stretch. In: IEEE 29th Conference on Computational Complexity, CCC 2014, 11–13 June 2014, Vancouver, BC, Canada, pp. 1–12 (2014)
62. Parno, B., Raykova, M., Vaikuntanathan, V.: How to delegate and verify in public: verifiable computation from attribute-based encryption. In: Cramer, R. (ed.) TCC 2012. LNCS, vol. 7194, pp. 422–439. Springer, Heidelberg (2012). doi:10.1007/978-3-642-28914-9_24
63. Pass, R., Seth, K., Telang, S.: Indistinguishability obfuscation from semantically-secure multilinear encodings. In: Garay, J.A., Gennaro, R. (eds.) CRYPTO 2014. LNCS, vol. 8616, pp. 500–517. Springer, Heidelberg (2014). doi:10.1007/978-3-662-44371-2_28
64. Ullman, J.: Answering $n_{2+o(1)}$ counting queries with differential privacy is hard. In: 45th ACM STOC, Palo Alto, CA, USA, pp. 361–370, 1–4 June 2013
65. Zimmerman, J.: How to obfuscate programs directly. In: Oswald, E., Fischlin, M. (eds.) EUROCRYPT 2015. LNCS, vol. 9057, pp. 439–467. Springer, Heidelberg (2015). doi:10.1007/978-3-662-46803-6_15

Lower Bounds on Obfuscation from All-or-Nothing Encryption Primitives

Sanjam Garg[1(✉)], Mohammad Mahmoody[2], and Ameer Mohammed[2]

[1] UC Berkeley, Berkeley, USA
sanjamg@berkeley.edu
[2] University of Virginia, Charlottesville, USA
{mohammad,ameer}@virginia.edu

Abstract. Indistinguishability obfuscation (IO) enables many heretofore out-of-reach applications in cryptography. However, currently all known constructions of IO are based on multilinear maps which are poorly understood. Hence, tremendous research effort has been put towards basing obfuscation on better-understood computational assumptions. Recently, another path to IO has emerged through functional encryption [Anath and Jain, CRYPTO 2015; Bitansky and Vaikuntanathan, FOCS 2015] but such FE schemes currently are still based on multi-linear maps. In this work, we study whether IO could be based on other powerful encryption primitives.

Separations for IO. We show that (assuming that the polynomial hierarchy does not collapse and one-way functions exist) IO cannot be constructed in a black-box manner from powerful all-or-nothing encryption primitives, such as witness encryption (WE), predicate encryption, and fully homomorphic encryption. What unifies these primitives is that they are of the "all-or-nothing" form, meaning either someone has the "right key" in which case they can decrypt the message fully, or they are not supposed to learn anything.

Stronger Model for Separations. One might argue that fully black-box uses of the considered encryption primitives limit their power too much because these primitives can easily lead to non-black-box constructions if the primitive is used in a *self-feeding* fashion—namely, code of the subroutines of the considered primitive could easily be fed as input to the subroutines of the primitive itself. In fact, several important results (e.g., the construction of IO from functional encryption) follow this very recipe. In light of this, we prove our impossibility results with respect to a *stronger* model than the fully black-box framework of Impagliazzo and Rudich (STOC'89) and Reingold, Trevisan, and Vadhan (TCC'04) where the non-black-box technique of self-feeding is actually allowed.

S. Garg—Research supported in part from DARPA/ARL SAFEWARE Award W911NF15C0210, AFOSR Award FA9550-15-1-0274, NSF CRII Award 1464397, AFOSR YIP Award and research grants by the Okawa Foundation and Visa Inc. The views expressed are those of the author and do not reflect the official policy or position of the funding agencies.

M. Mahmoody—Supported by NSF CAREER award CCF-1350939.

A. Mohammed—Supported by University of Kuwait.

J. Katz and H. Shacham (Eds.): CRYPTO 2017, Part I, LNCS 10401, pp. 661–695, 2017.
DOI: 10.1007/978-3-319-63688-7_22

1 Introduction

Program obfuscation provides an extremely powerful tool to make computer programs "unintelligible" while preserving their functionality. Barak et al. [11] formulated this notion in various forms and proved that their strongest formulation, called *virtual black-box* (VBB) obfuscation, is impossible for general polynomial size circuits. However, a recent result of Garg et al. [31] presented a candidate construction for a weaker notion of obfuscation, called *indistinguishability obfuscation* (IO). Subsequent work showed that IO, together with one-way functions, enables numerous cryptographic applications making IO a "cryptographic hub" [63].

Since the original work of [31] many constructions of IO were proposed [3, 5,8,10,18,31,32,53,65]. However, all these constructions are based on computational hardness assumptions on multilinear maps [27,30,37]. Going a step further, recent works of Lin [48] and Lin and Vaikunthanatan [49] showed how to weaken the required degree of the employed multilinear maps schemes to be a *constant.* Another line of work showed how to base IO on compact functional encryption [1,13]. However, the current constructions of compact functional encryption are in turn based on IO (or, multilinear maps). In summary, all currently known paths to obfuscation start from multilinear maps, which are poorly understood. In particular, many attacks on the known candidate multilinear map constructions have been shown [23,25,26,30,46,54].

In light of this, it is paramount that we base IO on well-studied computational assumptions. One of the assumptions that has been used in a successful way for realizing sophisticated cryptographic primitives is the Learning with Errors (LWE) assumption [61]. LWE is already known to imply attribute-based encryption [42] (or even predicate encryption [43]), fully homomorphic encryption [19,20,36,38][1], multi-key [17,24,55,60] and spooky homomorphic encryption [29]. One thing that all these primitives share is that they are of an "all-or-nothing" nature. Namely, either someone has the "right" key, in which case they can decrypt the message fully, or if they do not posses a right key, then they are not supposed to learn anything about the plaintext.[2] In this work, our main question is:

> **Main Question:** *Can IO be based on any powerful 'all-or-nothing' encryption primitive such as predicate encryption or fully homomorphic encryption?*

We show that the answer to the above question is essentially "no." However, before stating our results in detail, we stress that we need to be very careful in evaluating impossibility results that relate to such powerful encryption primitives and the framework they are proved in. For example, such a result

[1] Realizing full-fledged fully-homomorphic encryption needs additional circular security assumptions.

[2] This is in contrast with *functional* encryption where different keys might leak different information about the plaintext.

if proved in the fully black-box framework of [47,62] has limited value as we argue below.[3] Note that the black-box framework restricts to constructions that use the primitive and the adversary (in the security reduction) as a black-box. The reason for being cautious about this framework is that the constructions of powerful encryption primitive offer for a very natural *non*-black-box use. In fact, the construction of IO from compact functional encryption [1,2,13] is non-black-box in its use of functional encryption. This is not a coincidence (or, just one example) and many applications of functional encryption (as well as other powerful encryption schemes) and IO are non-black-box [14,33,34,36,63]. Note that the difference between these powerful primitives and the likes of one-way functions, hash functions, etc., is that these powerful primitives include subroutines that take arbitrary circuits as inputs. Therefore, it is very easy to *self-feed* the primitive. In other words, it is easy to plant gates of its own subroutines (or, subroutines of other cryptographic primitives) inside such a circuit that is then fed to it as input. For example, the construction of IO from FE plants FE's encryption subroutine as a gate inside the circuit for which it issues decryption keys. This makes FE a "special" primitive in that at least one of its subroutines takes an arbitrary circuit as input and we could plant code of its subroutines in this circuit. Consequently, the obtained construction would be non-black-box in the underlying primitive. This special aspect is present in *all* of the primitives that we study in this work. For example, one of the subroutines of predicate encryption takes a circuit as input and this input circuit is used to test whether the plaintext is revealed during the decryption or not. Along similar lines, evaluation subroutine of an FHE scheme is allowed to take as input a circuit that is executed on an encrypted message.

The above "special" aspects of the encryption functionalities (i.e. that they take as input general circuits or Turing machines and execute them) is the main reason that many of the applications of these primitives are non-black-box constructions. Therefore, any effort to prove a meaningful impossibility result, should aim for proving the result with respect to a more general framework than that of [47,62]. In particular, this more general framework should incorporate the aforementioned non-black-box techniques as part of the framework itself.

The previous works of Brakerski et al. [16] and the more recent works of Asharov and Segev [6,7] are very relevant to our studies here. All of these works also deal with proving limitations for primitives that in this work we call special (i.e. those that take general circuits as input), and prove impossibility results against constructions that use these special primitives while allowing some form of oracle gates to be present in the input circuits. A crucial point, however, is that these works still put some limitation on *what* oracle gates are allowed, and some of the subroutines are excluded. The work of [16] proved that the primitive of Witness Indistinguishable (WI) proofs for $\mathbf{NP}^O$ statements where O is a random oracle does not imply key-agreement protocols in a black-box way. However, the WI subroutines themselves are not allowed inside input circuits.

[3] Such results could still have some value for demonstrating *efficiency* limitations but not for showing infeasibility, as is the goal of this work.

The more recent works of [6,7] showed that by using IO over circuits that are *allowed* to have one-way functions gates one cannot obtain collision resistant hash functions or (certain classes of) one-way permutations families (in a black-box way). However, not all of the subroutines of the primitive itself are allowed to be planted as gates inside the input circuits (e.g., the evaluation procedure of the IO).

In this work, we revisit the models used in [6,7,16] who allowed the use of one-way function gates inside the given circuits and study a model where there is no limitation on what type of oracle gates could be used in the circuits given as input to the special subroutines, and in particular, the primitive's own subroutines could be planted as gates in the input circuits. We believe a model that captures the "gate plantation" technique without putting any limitation on the types of gates used is worth to be studied directly and at an abstract level, due to actual *positive* results that exactly benefit from this "self-feeding" non-black-box technique. For this goal, here we initiate a formal study of a model that we call *extended* black-box, which captures the above-described non-black-box technique that is commonplace in constructions that use primitives with subroutines that take arbitrary circuits as input.

More formally, suppose $\mathcal{P}$ is a primitive that is special as described above, namely, at least one of its subroutines might receive a circuit or a Turing machine C as input and executes C internally in order to obtain the answer to one of its subroutines. Examples of $\mathcal{P}$ are predicate encryption, fully homomorphic encryption, etc. An *extended* black-box construction of another primitive $\mathcal{Q}$ (e.g., IO) from $\mathcal{P}$ will be allowed to plant the subroutines of $\mathcal{P}$ inside the circuit C as gates with no further limitations. To be precise, C will be allowed to have oracle gates that call $\mathcal{P}$ itself. Some of major examples of *non-black-box* constructions that fall into this extended model are as follows.

- Gentry's bootstrapping construction [35] plants FHE's own decryption gates inside a circuit that is given as input to the evaluation subroutine. This trick falls into the extended black-box framework since planting gates inside evaluation circuits is allowed.
- The bootstrapping of IO for $\mathbf{NC}_1$ (along with FHE) to obtain IO for $\mathbf{P/poly}$ [31]. This construction uses $\mathcal{P}$ that includes both IO for $\mathbf{NC}_1$ and FHE, and it plants the FHE decryption gates inside the $\mathbf{NC}_1$ circuit that is obfuscated using IO for $\mathbf{NC}_1$. Analogously, bootstrapping methods using one-way functions [4,22] also fall in our framework.
- The construction of IO from functional encryption [1,2,13] plants the functional encryption scheme's encryption subroutine inside the circuits for which decryption keys are issued. Again, such a non-black-box technique does fall into our extended black-box framework. We note that the constructions of obfuscation based on constant degree graded encodings [48] also fit in our framework.

The above examples show the power of the "fully" extended black-box model in capturing one of the most commonly used non-black-box techniques in cryptography and especially in the context of powerful encryption primitives.

What is *not* captured by extended black-box model? It is instructive to understand the kinds of non-black-box techniques not captured by our extension to the black-box model. This model does not capture non-black-box techniques that break the computation of a primitives sub-routines into smaller parts—namely, we do not include techniques that involve partial computation of a sub-routine, save the intermediate state and complete the computation later. In other words, the planted sub-routines gates must be executed in one-shot. Therefore, in our model given just an oracle that implements a one-way function it is *not* possible to obtain garbled circuits that evaluate circuits with one-way function gates planted in them. For example, Beaver's OT extension construction cannot be realized given just oracle access to a random function.

However, a slight workaround (though a bit cumbersome) can still be used to give meaningful impossibility results that use garbled circuits (or, randomized encodings more generally) in our model. Specifically, garbled circuits must now be modeled as a special primitive that allows for inputs that can be arbitrary circuits with OWF gates planted in them. With this change the one-way function gate planted inside circuit fed to the garbled circuit construction is treated as a individual unit. With this change we can realize Beaver's OT extension construction in our model.

In summary, intuitively, our model provides a way to capture "black-box" uses of the known non-black-box techniques. While the full power of non-black-box techniques in cryptography is yet to be understood, virtually every known use of non-black-box techniques follows essentially the same principles, i.e. by plating subroutines of one primitive as gates in a circuit that is fed as input to the same (or, another) primitive. Our model captures any such non-black box use of the considered primitives.

Our Results. The main result of this paper is that several powerful encryption primitives such as predicate encryption and fully-homomorphic encryption are incapable of producing IO via an *extended* black-box construction as described above. A summery of our results is presented in Fig. 1. More specifically, we prove the following theorem.

Theorem 1 (Main Result). *Let $\mathcal{P}$ be one of the following primitives: fully-homomorphic encryption, attribute-based encryption, predicate encryption, multi-key fully homomorphic encryption, or spooky encryption. Then, assuming one-way functions exist and* $\mathbf{NP} \not\subseteq \mathbf{coAM}$, *there is no construction of IO from $\mathcal{P}$ in the extended black-box model where one is* allowed *to plant $\mathcal{P}$ gates arbitrarily inside the circuits that are given to $\mathcal{P}$ as input.*

All-or-Nothing Aspect. One common aspect of *all* of the primitives listed in Theorem 1 is that they have an all-or-nothing nature. Namely, either someone has the right key to decrypt a message, in which case they can retrieve *all* of the message, or if they do not have the right key then they are supposed to learn nothing. In contrast, in a functional encryption scheme (a primitive that does imply IO) one can obtain a key k_f for a function f that allows them to compute $f(x)$ from a ciphertext c containing the plaintext x. So, they could legitimately learn only a "partial" information about x. Even though we do not yet have a general result that handles such primitives uniformly in one shot, we still expect that other exotic encryption primitives (that may be developed in the future) that are of the all-or-nothing flavor will also not be enough for realizing IO. Additionally, we expect that our techniques will be useful in deriving impossibility results in such case.

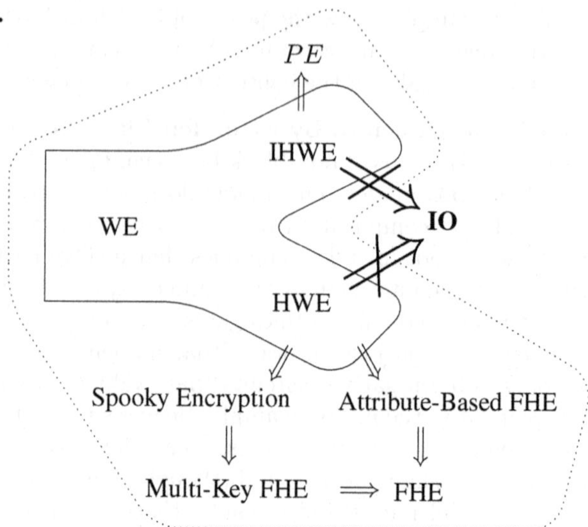

Fig. 1: Summary of our separation results. IHWE denotes instance hiding WE and HWE denotes homomorphic witness encryption.

What Does Our Results Say About LWE? Even though our separations of Theorem 1 covers most of the powerful LWE-based primitives known to date, it does not imply whether or not we can actually base IO on LWE. In fact, our result only rules out specific paths from LWE toward IO that would go through either of the primitives listed in Theorem 1. Whether or not a direct construction from LWE to IO is possible still remains as a major open problem in this area.

Key Role of Witness Encryption. Witness encryption and its variations play a key role in the proof or our impossibility results. Specifically, we consider two (incompatible) variants of WE—namely, instance hiding witness encryption and homomorphic witness encryption. The first notion boosts the security of WE and hides the statement while the second enhances the functionality of WE with some homomorphic properties. We obtain our separation results in two steps. First, we show that neither of these two primitives extended black-box imply IO. Next, we show that these two primitives extended black-box imply extended versions of all the all-or-nothing primitives listed above. The final separations follow from a specific transitivity lemma that holds in the extended black-box model.

Further Related Work. Now we describe previous work on the complexity of assumptions behind IO and previous works on generalizing the black-box framework of [47,62].

Previous Lower Bounds on Complexity of IO. The work of Mahmoody et al. [52] proved lower bounds on the assumptions that are needed for building IO in a fully black-box way.[4] They showed that, assuming $\mathbf{NP} \neq \mathbf{co\text{-}NP}$, one-way functions or even collision resistant hash functions do not imply IO in a fully black-box way.[5] Relying on the works of [21,50,58] (in the context of VBB obfuscation in idealized models) Mahmoody et al. [52] also showed that building IO from trapdoor permutations or even constant degree graded encoding oracles (constructively) implies that public-key encryption could be based on one-way functions (in a non-black-box way). Therefore, building IO from those primitives would be as hard as basing PKE on OWFs, which is a long standing open question of its own. Relying on the recent beautiful work of Brakerski et al. [15] that ruled out the existence of statistically secure *approximately correct* IO and a variant of Borel-Cantelli lemma, Mahmoody et al. [51] showed how to extend the 'hardness of constructing IO' result of [52] into conditional black-box separations.

Other Non-Black-Box Separations. Proving separations for non-black-box constructions are usually extremely hard. However, there are a few works in this area that we shall discuss here. The work of Baecher et al. [9] studied various generalizations of the black-box framework of [62] that also allow some forms of non-black-box use of primitives. The work of Pass et al. [59] showed that under (new) believable assumptions one can rule out non-black-box constructions of certain cryptographic primitives (e.g., one-way permutations, collision-resistant hash-functions, constant-round statistically hiding commitments) from one-way functions, as long as the security reductions are black-box. Pass [57] showed that the security of some well-known cryptographic protocols and assumptions (e.g., the Schnorr identification scheme) cannot be based on any falsifiable assumptions [56] as long at the security proof is black-box (even if the construction is non-black-box). The work of Genry and Wichs [39] showed that black-box security reductions (together with arbitrary non-black-box constructions) cannot be used to prove the security of any SNARG construction based on any falsifiable cryptographic assumption. Finally, the recent work of Dachman-Soled [28] showed that certain classes of constructions with some limitations, but with specific non-black-box power given to them are not capable of reducing public-key encryption to one way functions.

[4] A previous result of Asharov and Segev [6] proved lower bounds on the complexity of IO *with* oracle gates, which is a *stronger* primitive. (In fact, how this primitive is stronger is tightly related to how we define extensions of primitives. See Sect. 3 where we formalize the notion of such stronger primitives in a general way.).

[5] Note that since statistically secure IO exists if $\mathbf{P} = \mathbf{NP}$, therefore we need computational assumptions for proving lower bounds for assumptions implying IO.

Organization. Due to limited space, in this draft we only prove the separation of IO from witness encryption (in the extended black-box setting) and refer the reader to the full version of the paper for other separations. In Sect. 2 we review the needed preliminaries and also review some of the tools that are developed in previous work for proving lower bounds on IO. In Sect. 3 we discuss the extended black-box model and its relation to extended primitives in detail and give a formal definition of extended black-box constructions from witness encryption. In Sect. 4 we give a full proof of the extended black-box separation of IO from (even instance-revealing) witness encryption.

2 Preliminaries

Notation. We use "|" to concatenate strings and we use "," for attaching strings in a way that they could be retrieved. Namely, one can uniquely identify x and y from (x, y). For example $(00|11) = (0011)$, but $(0, 011) \neq (001, 1)$. When writing the probabilities, by putting an algorithm A in the subscript of the probability (e.g., $\Pr_A[\cdot]$) we mean the probability is over A's randomness. We will use n or κ to denote the security parameter. We call an efficient algorithm V a verifier for an **NP** relation R if $\mathsf{V}(w, a) = 1$ iff $(w, a) \in R$. We call $L_R = L_{\mathsf{V}} = \{a \mid \exists w, (a, w) \in R\}$ the corresponding **NP** language. By PPT we mean a probabilistic polynomial time algorithm. By an *oracle* PPT/algorithm we mean a PPT that might make oracle calls.

2.1 Primitives

In this subsection we define the primitives that we deal with in this work and are defined prior to our work. In the subsequent sections we will define variants of these primitives.

The definition of IO below has a subroutine for evaluating the obfuscated code. The reason for defining the evaluation as a subroutine of its own is that when we want to construct IO in oracle/idealized models, we allow the obfuscated circuit to call the oracle as well. Having an evaluator subroutine to run the obfuscated code allows to have such oracle calls in the framework of black-box constructions of [62] where each primitive $\mathcal{Q}$ is simply a class of acceptable functions that we (hope to) efficiently implement given oracle access to functions that implement another primitive $\mathcal{P}$ (see Definition 7).

Definition 2 (Indistinguishability Obfuscation (IO)). *An Indistinguishability Obfuscation (IO) scheme consists of two subroutines:*

- *Obfuscator iO is a PPT that takes as inputs a circuit C and a security parameter 1^κ and outputs a "circuit" B.*
- *Evaluator Ev takes as input (B, x) and outputs y.*

The completeness and soundness conditions assert that:

- *Completeness: For every C, with probability* 1 *over the randomness of iO, we get $B \leftarrow iO(C, 1^\kappa)$ such that: For all x it holds that $Ev(B, x) = C(x)$.*
- *Security: for every poly-sized distinguisher D there exists a negligible function $\mu(\cdot)$ such that for every two circuits C_0, C_1 that are of the same size and compute the same function, we have:*

$$|\Pr_{iO}[D(iO(C_0, 1^\kappa) = 1] - \Pr_{iO}[D(iO(C_1, 1^\kappa) = 1]| \leq \mu(\kappa)$$

Definition 3 (Approximate IO). *For function $0 < \epsilon(n) \leq 1$, an ϵ-approximate IO scheme is defined similarly to an IO scheme with a relaxed completeness condition:*

- *ϵ-approximate completeness. For every C and n we have:*

$$\Pr_{x, iO}[B = iO(C, 1^\kappa), Ev(B, x) = C(x)] \geq 1 - \epsilon(\kappa)$$

Definition 4 (Witness Encryption (WE) indexed by verifier V). *Let L be an* **NP** *language with a corresponding efficient relation verifier V (that takes instance x and witness w and either accepts or rejects). A* witness encryption *scheme for relation defined by V consists of two PPT algorithms* $(\mathrm{Enc}, \mathrm{Dec}_\mathsf{V})$ *defined as follows:*

- $\mathrm{Enc}(a, m, 1^\kappa)$*: given an instance $a \in \{0,1\}^*$ and a message $m \in \{0,1\}^*$, and security parameter κ (and randomness as needed) it outputs $c \in \{0,1\}^*$.*
- $\mathrm{Dec}_\mathsf{V}(w, c)$*: given ciphertext c and "witness" string w, it either outputs a message $m \in \{0,1\}^*$ or $\perp$.*

We also need the following completeness and security properties:

- ***Completeness:** For any security parameter κ, any (a, w) such that* $\mathsf{V}(a, w) = 1$*, and any m it holds that*

$$\Pr_{\mathrm{Enc}, \mathrm{Dec}_\mathsf{V}}[\mathrm{Dec}_\mathsf{V}(w, \mathrm{Enc}(a, m, 1^\kappa)) = m] = 1$$

- ***Security:** For any PPT adversary A, there exists a negligible function $\mu(.)$ such that for all $a \notin L_\mathsf{V}$ (i.e., that there is no w for which* $\mathsf{V}(a, w) = 1$*) and any $m_0 \neq m_1$ of the same length $|m_0| = |m_1|$ the following holds:*

$$|\Pr[A(\mathrm{Enc}(a, m_0, 1^\kappa)) = 1] - \Pr[A(\mathrm{Enc}(a, m_1, 1^\kappa)) = 1]| \leq \mu(\kappa)$$

When we talk about the witness encryption as a primitive (not an indexed family) we refer to the special case of the 'complete' verifier V which is a circuit evaluation algorithm and $\mathsf{V}(w, a) = 1$ if $a(w) = 1$ where a is a circuit evaluated on witness w.

The family version of WE in Definition 4 allows the verifier V to be part of the definition of the primitive. However, the standard notion of WE uses the "universal" V which allows us to obtain WE for any other efficient relation verifier V.

The following variant of witness encryption strengthens the functionality.

Definition 5 (Instance-revealing Witness Encryption (IRWE)). *A witness encryption scheme is said to be* instance-revealing *if it satisfies the properties of Definition 4 and, in addition, includes the following subroutine.*

- ***Instance-Revealing Functionality:*** Rev(c) *given ciphertext c outputs $a \in \{0,1\}^s \cup \{\bot\}$, and for every a, m, κ:*

$$\Pr_{\text{Enc},\text{Rev}}[\text{Rev}(\text{Enc}(a, m, 1^\kappa)) = a] = 1.$$

2.2 Black-Box Constructions and Separations

Impagliazzo and Rudich [47] were the first to formally study the power of "black-box" constructions that relativize to any oracle. Their notion was further explored in detail by Reingold et al. [62]. The work of Baecher et al. [9] further studied the black-box framework and studied variants of the definition of black-box constructions. We first start by recalling the definition of cryptographic primitives, and then will go over the notion of (fully) black-box constructions.

Definition 6 (Cryptographic Primitives [62]**).** *A* primitive *$\mathcal{P} = (\mathcal{F}, \mathcal{R})$ is defined as set of functions $\mathcal{F}$ and a relation $\mathcal{R}$ between functions. A (possibly inefficient) function $F \in \{0,1\}^* \to \{0,1\}^*$ is a correct implementation of $\mathcal{P}$ if $F \in \mathcal{F}$, and a (possibly inefficient) adversary A breaks an implementation $F \in \mathcal{F}$ if $(A, F) \in \mathcal{R}$.*

Definition 7 (black-box constructions [62]**).** *A* black-box *construction of a primitive $\mathcal{Q}$ from a primitive $\mathcal{P}$ consists of two PPT algorithms (Q, S):*

1. *Implementation: For any oracle P that implements $\mathcal{P}$, Q^P implements $\mathcal{Q}$.*
2. *Security reduction: for any oracle P implementing $\mathcal{P}$ and for any (computationally unbounded) oracle adversary A breaking the security of Q^P, it holds that $S^{P,A}$ breaks the security of P.*

Definition 8 (Black-box constructions of IO). *A fully-black-box construction of IO from any primitive $\mathcal{P}$ could be defined by combining Definitions 7 and 2.*

The Issue of Oracles Gates. Note that in any such construction of Definition 8 the input circuits to the obfuscation subroutine do not have any oracle gates in them, while the obfuscation algorithm and the evaluation procedure are allowed to use the oracle implementing $\mathcal{P}$. In Sect. 3 we will see that one can also define an *extended* variant of the IO primitive (as it was done in [6,7]) in which the input circuits have oracle gates.

2.3 Black-Box Separations

In this section we recall lemmas that can be used for proving black-box impossibility results (a.k.a. separations). The arguments described in this section are borrowed from a collection of recent works [15,21,50–52,58] where a framework for proving lower bounds for (assumptions behind) IO are laid out. However, the focus in those works was to prove lower bounds for IO in the (standard) black-box model rather than the extended model. We will indeed use those tools/lemmas by relating the extended black-box model to the black-box model.

Idealized Models/Oracles and Probability Measures over Them. An idealized model $\mathcal{I}$ is a randomized oracle that supposedly implements a primitive (with high probability over the choice of oracle); examples include the random oracle, random trapdoor permutation oracle, generic group model, graded encoding model, etc. An $I \leftarrow \mathcal{I}$ can (usually) be represented as a sequence $(I_1, I_2, \dots)$ of *finite* random variables, where I_n is the description of the prefix of I that is defined for inputs whose length is parameterized by (a function of) n. The measure over the actual infinite sample $I \leftarrow \mathcal{I}$ could be defined through the given finite distributions $\mathcal{D}_i$ over I_i.[6]

Definition 9 (Oracle-fixed constructions in idealized models [52]). *We say a primitive $\mathcal{P}$ has an* oracle-fixed *construction in idealized model $\mathcal{I}$ if there is an oracle-aided algorithm P such that:*

- **Completeness:** *P^I implements $\mathcal{P}$ correctly for every $I \leftarrow \mathcal{I}$.*
- **Black-box security:** *Let A be an oracle-aided adversary $A^{\mathcal{I}}$ where the* query complexity *of A is bounded by the specified complexity of the attacks for primitive $\mathcal{P}$. For example if $\mathcal{P}$ is polynomially secure (resp., quasi-polynomially secure), then A only asks a polynomial (resp., quasi-polynomial) number of queries but is computationally unbounded otherwise. Then, for any such A, with measure one over the choice of $I \xleftarrow{\$} \mathcal{I}$, it holds that A does* not *break P^I.*[7]

Definition 10 (Oracle-mixed constructions in idealized models [52]). *An* oracle-mixed *construction of a primitive $\mathcal{P}$ in idealized model $\mathcal{I}$ is defined similarly to the oracle-fixed definition, but with the difference that the correctness and soundness conditions of the construction $P^{\mathcal{I}}$ hold when the probabilities are taken over $I \leftarrow \mathcal{I}$ as well.*

Lemma 11 (Composition lemma [52]). *Suppose Q is a fully-black-box construction of primitive $\mathcal{Q}$ from primitive $\mathcal{P}$, and suppose P is an oracle-fixed*

---

[6] Caratheodory's extension theorem shows that such finite probability distributions could always be extended consistently to a measure space over the full infinite space of $I \leftarrow \mathcal{I}$. See Theorem 4.6 of [45] for a proof.

[7] For breaking a primitive, the adversary needs to 'win' with 'sufficient advantage' (this depends on what level of security is needed) over an *infinite* sequence of security parameters.

construction for primitive $\mathcal{P}$ relative to $\mathcal{I}$ (according to Definition 10). Then Q^P is an oracle-fixed implementation of $\mathcal{Q}$ relative to the same idealized model $\mathcal{I}$.

Definition 12 (Oracle-mixed constructions in idealized models [51]). *We say a primitive $\mathcal{P}$ has an* oracle-mixed *black-box construction in idealized model $\mathcal{I}$ if there is an oracle-aided algorithm P such that:*

- **Oracle-Mixed Completeness:** *P^I implements $\mathcal{P}$ correctly where the probabilities are also over $I \leftarrow \mathcal{I}$.[8] For the important case of perfect completeness, this definition is the same as oracle-fixed completeness.*
- **Oracle-mixed black-box security:** *Let A be an oracle-aided algorithm in idealized model $\mathcal{I}$ whose* query complexity *is bounded by the specified complexity of the attacks defined for primitive $\mathcal{P}$. We say that the oracle-mixed black-box security holds for $P^{\mathcal{I}}$ if for any such A there is a negligible $\mu(n)$ such that the advantage of A breaking $P^{\mathcal{I}}$ over the security parameter n is at most $\mu(n)$ where this bound is* also *over the randomness of $\mathcal{I}$.*

Using a variant of the Borel-Cantelli lemma, [51] proved that oracle-mixed attacks with *constant* advantage leads to breaking oracle-fixed constructions.

Lemma 13 [51]**.** *If there is an algorithm A that oracle-mixed breaks a construction $P^{\mathcal{I}}$ of $\mathcal{P}$ in idealized model $\mathcal{I}$ with advantage $\epsilon(n) \geq \Omega(1)$ for an infinite sequence of security parameters, then the same attacker A oracle-fixed breaks the same construction $P^{\mathcal{I}}$ over a (perhaps more sparse but still) infinite sequence of security parameters.*

The following lemmas follows as a direct corollary to Lemmas 11 and 13.

Lemma 14 (Separation Using Idealized Models). *Suppose $\mathcal{I}$ is an idealized model, and the following conditions are satisfied:*

- **Proving oracle-fixed security of $\mathcal{P}$.** *There is an oracle fixed black-box construction of $\mathcal{P}$ relative to $\mathcal{I}$.*
- **Breaking oracle-mixed security of $\mathcal{Q}$ *with* $\Omega(1)$ *advantage*.** *For any construction $Q^{\mathcal{P}}$ of $\mathcal{Q}$ relative to $\mathcal{I}$ there is a computationally-unbounded query-efficient attacker A (whose query complexity is bounded by the level of security demanded by $\mathcal{P}$) such that for an infinite sequence of security parameters $n_1 < n_2 < \dots$ the advantage of A in oracle-mixed breaking $P^{\mathcal{I}}$ is at least $\epsilon(n_i) \geq \Omega(1)$.*

Then there is no fully black-box construction for $\mathcal{Q}$ from $\mathcal{P}$.

[8] For example, an oracle-mixed construction of an ϵ-approximate IO only requires approximate correctness while the probability of approximate correctness is computed also over the probability of the input as well as the oracle.

2.4 Tools for Getting Black-Box Lower Bounds for IO

The specific techniques for proving separations for IO that is developed in [15, 21, 51, 52] aims at employing Lemma 14 by "compiling" out an idealized oracle $\mathcal{I}$ from an IO construction. Since we know that *statistically* secure IO does not exist in the *plain* model [41] this indicates that perhaps we can compose the two steps and get a query-efficient attacker against IO in the idealized model $\mathcal{I}$. The more accurate line of argument is more subtle and needs to work with *approximately correct* IO and uses a recent result of Brakerski et al. [15] who ruled out the existence of statistically secure approximate IO.

To formalize the notion of "compiling out" an oracle in more than one step we need to formalize the intuitive notion of sub oracles in the idealized/randomized context.

Definition 15 (Sub-models). *We call the idealized model/oracle $\mathcal{O}$ a sub-model of the idealized oracle $\mathcal{I}$ with subroutines $(\mathcal{I}_1, \ldots, \mathcal{I}_k)$, denoted by $\mathcal{O} \sqsubseteq \mathcal{I}$, if there is a (possibly empty) $S \subseteq \{1, \ldots, k\}$ such that the idealized oracle $\mathcal{O}$ is sampled as follows:*

- *First sample $I \leftarrow \mathcal{I}$ where the subroutines are $I = (I_1, \ldots, I_k)$.*
- *Then provide access to subroutine I_i if and only if $i \in S$ (and hide the rest of the subroutines from being called).*

If $S = \varnothing$ then the oracle $\mathcal{O}$ will be empty and we will be back to the plain model.

Definition 16 (Simulatable Compiling Out Procedures for IO). *Suppose $\mathcal{O} \sqsubset \mathcal{I}$. We say that there is a simulatable compiler from IO in idealized model $\mathcal{I}$ into idealized model $\mathcal{O}$ with correctness error ϵ if the following holds. For every implementation $P_{\mathcal{I}} = (iO_{\mathcal{P}}, Ev_{\mathcal{P}})$ of δ-approximate IO in idealized model $\mathcal{I}$ there is a implementation $P_{\mathcal{O}} = (iO_{\mathcal{O}}, Ev_{\mathcal{O}})$ of $(\delta + \epsilon)$-approximate IO in idealized model $\mathcal{O}$ such that the only security requirement for these two implementations is that they are related as follows:*
Simulation: *There is an efficient PPT simulator S and a negligible function $\mu(\cdot)$ such that for any C:*

$$\Delta(S(iO^{\mathcal{I}}(C, 1^{\kappa})), iO^{\mathcal{O}}(C, 1^{\kappa})) \leq \mu(\kappa)$$

where $\Delta(.,.)$ denotes the statistical distance between random variables.

It is easy to see that the existence of the simulator according to Definition 16 implies that $P_{\mathcal{O}}$ in idealized model $\mathcal{O}$ is "as secure as" $P_{\mathcal{I}}$ in the idealized model $\mathcal{I}$. Namely, any oracle-mixed attacker against the implementation $P_{\mathcal{O}}$ in model $\mathcal{O}$ with advantage δ (over an infinite sequence of security parameters) could be turned in to an attacker against $P_{\mathcal{I}}$ in model $\mathcal{I}$ that breaks against $P_{\mathcal{I}}$ with advantage $\delta - \text{negl}(\kappa)$ over an infinite sequence of security parameters. Therefore one can compose the compiling out procedures for a constant number of steps (but not more, because there is a polynomial blow up in the parameters in each step).

By composing a constant number of compilers and relying on the recent result of Brakerski et al. [15] one can get a general method of breaking IO in idealized models. We first state the result of [15].

Theorem 17 [15]. *Suppose one-way functions exist,* **NP** $\not\subseteq$ **coAM**, *and* $\delta, \epsilon \colon \mathbb{N} \mapsto [0,1]$ *are such that* $2\epsilon(n) + 3\delta(n) < 1 - 1/\operatorname{poly}(n)$*, then there is no* (ϵ, δ)*-approximate statistically-secure IO for all poly-size circuits.*

The above theorem implies that if we get any implementation for IO in the plain model that is $1/100$-approximately correct, then there is a computationally unbounded adversary that breaks the *statistical* security of IO with advantage at least $1/100$ over an infinite sequence of security parameters. Using this result, the following lemma shows a way to obtain attacks against IO in idealized models.

Lemma 18 (Attacking IO Using Nested Oracle Compilers). *Suppose* $\varnothing = \mathcal{I}_0 \sqsubseteq \mathcal{I}_1 \cdots \sqsubseteq \mathcal{I}_k = \mathcal{I}$ *for constant* $k = O(1)$ *are a sequence of idealized models. Suppose for every* $i \in [k]$ *there is a simulatable compiler for IO in model* $\mathcal{I}_i$ *into model* $\mathcal{I}_{i-1}$ *with correctness error* $\epsilon_i < 1/(100k)$*. Then, assuming one-way functions exist,* **NP** $\not\subseteq$ **coAM**, *any implementation* P *of IO in the idealized model* $\mathcal{I}$ *could be oracle-mixed broken by a polynomial-query adversary* A *with a* constant *advantage* $\delta > 1/100$ *for an infinite sequence of security parameters.*

Proof. Starting with our initial ideal-model construction $P_{\mathcal{I}} = P_{\mathcal{I}_k}$, we iteratively apply the simulatable compiler to get $P_{\mathcal{I}_{i-1}}$ from $P_{\mathcal{I}_i}$ for $i = \{k, ..., 1\}$. Note that the final correctness error that we get is $\epsilon_{\mathcal{I}_0} < k/(100k) < 1/100$, and thus by Theorem 17 there exists a computationally unbounded attacker $A_{\mathcal{I}_0}$ against $P_{\mathcal{I}_0}$ with constant advantage δ. Now, let S_i be the PPT simulator whose existence is guaranteed by Definition 16 for the compiler that transforms $P_{\mathcal{I}_i}$ into $P_{\mathcal{I}_{i-1}}$. We inductively construct an adversary $A_{\mathcal{I}_i}$ against $P_{\mathcal{I}_i}$ from an adversary $A_{\mathcal{I}_{i-1}}$ for $P_{\mathcal{I}_{i-1}}$ starting with $A_{\mathcal{I}_0}$. The construction of $A_{\mathcal{I}_i}$ simply takes its input obfuscation in the $\mathcal{I}_i$ ideal-model $iO^{\mathcal{I}_i}$, runs $S_i(iO^{\mathcal{I}_i})$ and feeds the result to $A_{\mathcal{I}_{i-1}}$ to get its output. Note that, after constant number k, we still get $\delta' < \delta - k\operatorname{negl}(\kappa)$ a constant advantage over infinite sequence of security parameters against $P_{\mathcal{I}_k}$.

Finally, by putting Lemmas 18 and 14 together we get a lemma for proving black-box lower bounds for IO.

Lemma 19 (Lower Bounds for IO using Oracle Compilers). *Suppose* $\varnothing = \mathcal{I}_0 \sqsubseteq \mathcal{I}_1 \cdots \sqsubseteq \mathcal{I}_k = \mathcal{I}$ *for constant* $k = O(1)$ *are a sequence of idealized models. Suppose for every* $i \in [k]$ *there is a simulatable compiler for IO in model* $\mathcal{I}_i$ *into model* $\mathcal{I}_{i-1}$ *with correctness error* $\epsilon_i < 1/(100k)$*. If primitive* $\mathcal{P}$ *can be oracle-fixed constructed in the idealized model* $\mathcal{I}$*, then there is no fully black-box construction of IO from* $\mathcal{P}$.

We will indeed use Lemma 19 to derive lower bounds for IO even in the *extended* black-box model by relating such constructions to fully black-box constructions.

3 An Abstract Extension of the Black-Box Model

In what follows, we will gradually develop an extended framework of constructions that includes the fully black-box framework of [62] and allows certain non-black-box techniques by default. This model uses steps already taken in works of Brakerski et al. [16] and the more recent works of Asharov and Segev [6,7] and takes them to the next level by allowing even non-black-box techniques involving 'self-calls' [1,2,13]. In a nutshell, this framework applies to 'special' primitives that accept generic circuits as input and run them on other inputs; therefore one can plant oracle gates to the same primitives inside those circuits. We will define such constructions using the fully black-box framework by first extending these primitives and then allowing the extensions to be used in a black-box way.

We will first give an informal discussion by going over examples of primitives that could be used in an extended black-box way. We then discuss an abstract model that allows formal definitions. We will finally give concrete and formal definitions for the case of witness encryption which is the only primitive that we will formally separate from IO in this draft. For the rest of the separations see the full version of the paper.

Special Primitives Receiving Circuits as Input. At a very high level, we call a primitive 'special', if it takes circuits as input and run those circuits as part of the execution of its subroutines, but at the same time, the exact definition depends on the execution of the input circuit only as a 'black-box' while the exact representation of the input circuits do not matter. In that case one can imagine an input circuit with oracle gates as well. We will simply call such primitives special till we give formal definitions that define those primitives as 'families' of primitives indexed by an external universal algorithm.

Here is a list of examples of special primitives.

- **Zero-knowledge proofs of circuit satisfiability (ZK-Cir-SAT).** A secure protocol for ZK-Cir-SAT is an interactive protocol between two parties, a prover and a verifier, who take as input a circuit C. Whether or not the prover can convince the verifier to accept the interaction depends on the existence of x such that $C(x) = 1$. This definition of the functionality of ZK-Cir-SAT does not depend on the specific implementation of C and only depends on executing C on x 'as a black-box'.
- **Fully homomorphic encryption (FHE).** FHE is a semantically secure public-key encryption where in addition we have an evaluation sub-routine Eval that takes as input a circuit f and ciphertexts $c_1, \ldots, c_k$ containing plaintexts $m_1, \ldots, m_k$, and it outputs a new ciphertext $c = \text{Eval}(f, c_1, \ldots, c_k)$ such that decrypting c leads to $f(m_1, \ldots, m_k)$. The correctness definition of the primitive FHE only uses the input-output behavior of the circuit f, so FHE is a special primitive.
- **Encrypted functionalities.** Primitives such as attribute, predicate, and functional encryption all involve running some generic computation at the

decryption phase before deciding what to output. There are two ways that this generic computation could be fed as input to the system:

- Key policy [44,64]: Here the circuit C is given as input to the key generation algorithm and then $C(m)$ is computed over plaintext m during the decryption.
- Ciphertext policy [12]: Here the circuit C is the actual plaintext and the input m to C is used when issuing the decryption keys.

Both of these approaches lead to special primitives. For example, for the case of predicate encryption, suppose we use a predicate verification algorithm P that takes (k, a), interprets k as a circuits and runs $k(a)$ to accept or reject. Such P would give us the key policy predicate encryption. Another P algorithm would interpret a as a circuit and runs it on k, and this gives us the ciphertext policy predicate encryption. In other words, one can think of the circuit C equivalent to $\mathsf{P}(k, \cdot)$ (with k hard coded in it, and a left out as the input) being the "input" circuit KGen subroutine, or alternatively one can think of $\mathsf{P}(\cdot, a)$ (with a hardcoded in it, and k left out as the input) to be the "input" circuit given to the Enc subroutine. In all cases, the correctness and security definitions of these primitives only depend on the input-output behavior of the given circuits.

- **Witness encryption.** The reason that witness encryption is a special primitive is very similar to the reason described above for the case of encrypted functionalities. Again we can think of $\mathsf{V}(\cdot, a)$ as the circuit given to the Enc algorithm. In this case, the definition of witness encryption (and it security) only depend on the input-output behavior of these 'input circuits' rather their specific implementations.
- **Indistinguishability Obfuscation.** An indistinguishability obfuscator takes as input a circuit C and outputs B that can be used later on the compute the same function as C does. The security of IO ensures that for any two different equally-sized and functionally equivalent circuits C_0, C_1, it is hard to distinguish between obfuscation of C_0 and those of C_1. Therefore, the correctness and security definitions of IO depend solely on the input-output behavior (and the sizes) of the input circuits.

When a primitive is special, one can talk about "extensions" of the same primitive in which the circuits that are given as input could have oracle gates (because the primitive is special and so the definition of the primitive still extends to such inputs).

3.1 An Abstract Model for Extended Primitives and Constructions

We define special primitives as 'restrictions' of a (a family of) primitives indexed by a subroutine W to the case that W is a universal circuit evaluator. We then define the extended version to be the case that W accepts oracle-aided circuits. More formally we start by defining primitives indexed by a class of functions.

Definition 20 (Indexed primitives). *Let $\mathcal{W}$ be a set of (possibly inefficient) functions. An $\mathcal{W}$-*indexed *primitive $\mathcal{P}[\mathcal{W}]$ is indeed a* set *of primitives $\{\mathcal{P}[W]\}_{W \in \mathcal{W}}$ indexed by $W \in \mathcal{W}$ where, for each $W \in \mathcal{W}$, $\mathcal{P}[W] = (\mathcal{F}[W], \mathcal{R}[W])$ is a primitive according to Definition 6.*

For the special case of $\mathcal{W} = \{W\}$ we get back the RTV definition for a primitive.

We will now define variations of indexed primitives that restrict the family to a smaller class $\mathcal{W}'$ and, for every $W \in \mathcal{W}'$, it might further restrict the set of correct implementations to be a subset of $\mathcal{F}[W]$. We first define restricted forms of indexed primitives then provide various restrictions that will be of interest to us.

Definition 21 (Restrictions of indexed primitives). *For $\mathcal{P}[\mathcal{W}] = \{(\mathcal{F}[W], \mathcal{R}[W])\}_{W \in \mathcal{W}}$ and $\mathcal{P}'[\mathcal{W}'] = \{(\mathcal{F}'[W], \mathcal{R}'[W])\}_{W \in \mathcal{W}'}$, we say $\mathcal{P}'[\mathcal{W}']$ is a* restriction *of $\mathcal{P}[\mathcal{W}]$ if the following two holds. (1) $\mathcal{W}' \subseteq \mathcal{W}$, and (2) for all $W \in \mathcal{W}'$, $\mathcal{F}'[W] \subseteq \mathcal{F}[W]$, and (3) for all $W \in \mathcal{W}'$, $\mathcal{R}'[W] = \mathcal{R}'[W]$.*

Definition 22 (Efficient restrictions). *We call a restriction $\mathcal{P}'[\mathcal{W}']$ of $\mathcal{P}[\mathcal{W}]$ an* efficient *restriction if $\mathcal{W}' = \{w\}$ where w is a polynomial time algorithm (with no oracle calls). In this case, we call $\mathcal{P}'[w]$ simply a w-restriction of $\mathcal{P}[\mathcal{W}]$.*

We are particularly interested in indexed primitives when they are indexed by the universal algorithm for circuit evaluation. This is the case for all the primitives of witness encryption, predicate encryption,[9] fully homomorphic encryption, and IO. All of the examples of the special primitives discussed in previous section fall into this category. Finally, the formal notion of what we previously simply called a 'special' primitives is defined as follows.

Definition 23 (The universal variant of indexed primitives). *We call $\mathcal{P}'[\{w\}]$ the* universal variant *of $\mathcal{P}[\mathcal{W}]$ if $\mathcal{P}'[\{w\}]$ is an efficient restriction of $\mathcal{P}[\mathcal{W}]$ for the specific algorithm $w(\cdot)$ that interprets its input as a pair (x, C) where C is a circuit, and then it simply outputs $C(x)$.*

For example, in the case of witness encryption, the relation between witness w and attribute a is verified by running a as a circuit over w and outputting the first bit of this computation. In order to define *extensions* of universal variants of indexed primitives (i.e., special primitives for short) we need the following definition.

Definition 24 ($w^{(\cdot)}$-restrictions). *For an oracle algorithm $w^{(\cdot)}$ we call $\mathcal{P}'[\mathcal{W}'] = \{(\mathcal{F}'[W], \mathcal{R}[W])\}_{W \in \mathcal{W}'}$ the $w^{(\cdot)}$-restriction of $\mathcal{P}[\mathcal{W}] = \{(\mathcal{F}[W], \mathcal{R}[W])\}_{W \in \mathcal{W}}$, if $\mathcal{P}'[\mathcal{W}']$ is constructed as follows. For all $W \in \mathcal{W}$ and F, we include $W \in \mathcal{W}'$ and $F \in \mathcal{F}'[W]$, if it holds that $W = w^F$ and $F \in \mathcal{F}[W]$.*

---

[9] Even in this case, we can imagine that we are running a circuit on another input and take the first bit of it as the predicate.

Definition 25 (The extended variant of indexed primitives). *We call $\mathcal{P}'[\mathcal{W}']$ the* extended *variant of $\mathcal{P}[\mathcal{W}]$ if $\mathcal{P}'[\mathcal{W}']$ is an $w^{(\cdot)}$-restriction of $\mathcal{P}[\mathcal{W}]$ for the specific $w^{(\cdot)}$ that interprets its input (x, C) as a pair where $C^{(\cdot)}(x)$ is an* oracle-aided *circuit, and then $w(x, C)$ outputs $C^{(\cdot)}(x)$ by forwarding all of C's oracle queries to its own oracle.*

Case of Witness Encryption. Here we show how to derive the definition of extended witness encryption as a special case. First note that witness encryption's decryption is indexed by an algorithm $V(w, a)$ that could be any predicate function. In fact, it could be any function where we pick its first bit and interpret it as a predicate. So WE is indeed indexed by $V \in \mathcal{V}$ which the set of all predicates. Then, the standard definition of witness encryption for circuit satisfiability (which is the most powerful WE among them all) is simply the universal variant of this indexed primitive WE[$\mathcal{V}$], and the following will be exactly the definition of the extended universal variant of WE[$\mathcal{V}$], which we simply call the extended WE.

In the full version of the paper we give similar definitions for other primitives of predicate encryption, fully homomorphic encrypion, etc.

Definition 26 (Extended Witness Encryption). *Let $\mathsf{V}^{(\mathrm{Enc},\mathrm{Dec})}(w, a)$ be the 'universal circuit-evaluator' Turing machine, which is simply an algorithm with oracle access to* (Enc, Dec) *that interprets a as an circuit with possible* (Enc, Dec) *gates and runs a on w and forwards any oracle calls made by a to its own orcle and forwards the answer back to the corresponding gate inside a to continue the execution. An* extended witness encryption *scheme (defined by V) consists of two PPT algorithms* $(\mathrm{Enc}, \mathrm{Dec}_{\mathsf{V}})$ *defined as follows:*

- $\mathrm{Enc}(a, m, 1^{\kappa})$*: is a randomized algorithm that given an instance $a \in \{0,1\}^*$ and a message $m \in \{0,1\}^*$, and security parameter κ (and randomness as needed) outputs $c \in \{0,1\}^*$.*
- $\mathrm{Dec}_{\mathsf{V}}(w, c)$*: given ciphertext c and "witness" string w, it either outputs a message $m \in \{0,1\}^*$ or $\perp$.*
- *Correctness and security are defined similarly to Definition 4. But the key point is that here the relation $\mathsf{V}^{(\mathrm{Enc},\mathrm{Dec})}$ is somehow recursively depending on the* $(\mathrm{Enc}, \mathrm{Dec} = \mathrm{Dec}_{\mathsf{V}})$ *on smaller input lengths (and so it is well defined).*

3.2 Extended Black-Box Constructions

We are finally ready to define our extended black-box framework. Here we assume that for a primitive $\mathcal{P}$ we have already defined what its extension $\widetilde{\mathcal{P}}$ means.

Definition 27 (Extended Black-Box Constructions – General Case). *Suppose $\mathcal{Q}$ is a primitive and $\widetilde{\mathcal{P}}$ is an extended version of the primitive $\mathcal{P}$. Any fully black-box construction for $\mathcal{Q}$ from $\widetilde{\mathcal{P}}$ (i.e. an extended version of $\mathcal{P}$) is called an* extended black-box *construction of $\mathcal{Q}$ from $\mathcal{P}$.*

Examples. Below are some examples of *non-black-box* constructions in cryptography that fall into the extended black-box framework of Definition 27.

- Gentry's bootstrapping construction [35] plants FHE's own decryption in a circuit for the evaluation subroutine. This trick falls into the extended black-box framework since planting gates inside evaluation circuits is allowed.
- The construction of IO from functional encryption by [1,13] uses the encryption oracle of the functional encryption scheme inside the functions for which decryption keys are issued. Again, such *non-black-box* technique does fall into our extended black-box framework.

Definition 28 (Formal Definition of Extended Black-Box Constructions from Witness Encryption). *Let $\mathcal{P}$ be witness encryption and $\widetilde{\mathcal{P}}$ be extended witness encryption (Definition 26). Then an extended black-box construction using $\mathcal{P}$ is a fully black-box construction using $\widetilde{\mathcal{P}}$.*

The following transitivity lemma (which is a direct corollary to the transitivity of fully black-box constructions) allows us to derive more impossibility results.

Lemma 29 (Composing extended black-box constructions). *Suppose $\mathcal{P}$, $\mathcal{Q}, \mathcal{R}$ are cryptographic primitives and $\mathcal{Q}, \mathcal{P}$ are special primitive and $\widetilde{\mathcal{Q}}$ is the extended version of $\mathcal{Q}$. If there is an extended black-box construction of $\widetilde{\mathcal{Q}}$ from $\mathcal{P}$ and if there is an extended black-box construction of $\mathcal{R}$ from $\mathcal{Q}$, then there is an extended black-box construction of $\mathcal{R}$ from $\mathcal{P}$.*

Proof. Since there is an extended black-box construction of $\mathcal{R}$ from $\mathcal{Q}$, by Definition 27 it means that there is an extension $\widetilde{\mathcal{Q}}$ of $\mathcal{Q}$ such that there is a fully black-box construction of $\mathcal{R}$ from $\widetilde{\mathcal{Q}}$. On the other hand, again by Definition 27, for any extension of $\mathcal{Q}$, and in particular $\widetilde{\mathcal{Q}}$, there is a fully black-box construction of $\widetilde{\mathcal{Q}}$ from some extension $\widetilde{\mathcal{P}}$ of $\mathcal{P}$. Therefore, since fully-black-box constructions are transitive under nested compositions, there is a fully construction of $\mathcal{R}$ from $\widetilde{\mathcal{P}}$ which (by Definition 27) means that we have an extended black-box construction of $\mathcal{R}$ from $\mathcal{P}$.

Getting More Separations. A corollary of Lemma 29 is that if one proves: (a) There is no extended black-box construction of $\mathcal{R}$ from $\mathcal{P}$ and (b) there *is* an extended black-box construction of any extended version $\widetilde{\mathcal{R}}$ (of $\mathcal{R}$) from $\mathcal{Q}$, then these two together imply that: there is no extended black-box construction of $\mathcal{Q}$ from $\mathcal{P}$. We will use this trick to derive our impossibility results from a core of two separations regarding variants of witness encryption. For example, in the full version of the paper we will use this lemma to derive separations between attribute based encryption and IO in the extended black-box model.

4 Separating IO from Instance Revealing Witness Encryption

In this section, we formally prove our first main separation theorem which states that there is no black-box constructions of IO from WE (under believable assumptions). It equivalently means that there will be no fully black-box construction of indistinguishability obfuscation from extended witness encryption scheme.

Theorem 30. *Assume the existence of one-way functions and that* **NP** $\not\subseteq$ **coAM**. *Then there exists no extended black-box construction of indistinguishability obfuscation (IO) from witness encryption (WE).*

In fact, we prove a stronger result by showing a separation of IO from a stronger (extended) version of witness encryption, which we call *extractable instance-revealing* witness encryption. Looking ahead, we require the extractability property to construct (extended) attribute-based encryption (ABE) from this form of witness encryption. By using Lemma 29, this would also imply a separation of IO from extended ABE.

Definition 31 (Extended Extractable Instance-Revealing Witness Encryption (ex-EIRWE)). *Let* V *be a universal circuit-evaluator Turing machine as defined in Definition 26. For any given security parameter* κ*, an extended* extractable instance-revealing witness encryption *scheme for* V *consists of three PPT algorithms* $P = (\text{Enc}, \text{Rev}, \text{Dec})$ *defined as follows:*

- $\text{Enc}(a, m, 1^\kappa)$: *given an instance* $a \in \{0,1\}^*$ *and a message* $m \in \{0,1\}^*$, *and security parameter* κ *(and randomness as needed) it outputs* $c \in \{0,1\}^*$.
- $\text{Rev}(c)$: *given ciphertext* c *outputs* $a \in \{0,1\}^* \cup \{\bot\}$.
- $\text{Dec}(w, c)$: *given ciphertext* c *and "witness" string* w, *it outputs a message* $m' \in \{0,1\}^*$.

An extended extractable instance-revealing witness encryption scheme satisfies the following completeness and security properties:

- ***Decryption Correctness:*** *For any security parameter* κ, *any* (w, a) *such that* $\mathsf{V}^P(w, a) = 1$, *and any* m *it holds that*

$$\Pr_{\text{Enc},\text{Dec}}[\text{Dec}(w, \text{Enc}(a, m, 1^\kappa)) = m] = 1$$

- ***Instance-Revealing Correctness:*** *For any security parameter* κ *and any* (a, m) *it holds that:*

$$\Pr_{\text{Enc},\text{Rev}}[\text{Rev}(\text{Enc}(a, m, 1^\kappa)) = a] = 1$$

Furthermore, for any c *for which there is no* a, m, κ *such that* $\text{Enc}(a, m, 1^\kappa) = c$ *it holds that* $\text{Rev}(c) = \bot$.

– ***Extractability:*** *For any PPT adversary A and polynomial* $p_1(.)$, *there exists a PPT (black-box) straight-line extractor E and a polynomial function* $p_2(.)$ *such that the following holds. For any security parameter* κ, *for all a of the same and any* $m_0 \neq m_1$ *of the same length* $|m_0| = |m_1|$, *if:*

$$\Pr\left[A(1^\kappa, c) = b \mid b \xleftarrow{\$} \{0,1\}, c \leftarrow \mathrm{Enc}(a, m_b, 1^\kappa)\right] \geq \frac{1}{2} + p_1(\kappa)$$

Then:

$$\Pr[E^A(a) = w \wedge \mathsf{V}^P(w, a) = 1] \geq p_2(\kappa)$$

Given the above definition of ex-EIRWE, we prove the following theorem, which states that there is no fully black-box construction IO from extended EIRWE.

Theorem 32. *Assume the existence of one-way functions and that* $\mathbf{NP} \not\subseteq \mathbf{coAM}$. *Then there exists no* extended *black-box construction of indistinguishability obfuscation from extractable instance-revealing witness encryption for any PPT verification algorithm* V.

Since extended EIRWE implies witness encryption as defined in Definition 4, Theorem 30 trivially follows from Theorem 32, and thus for the remainder of this section we will focus on proving Theorem 32.

4.1 Overview of Proof Techniques

To prove Theorem 32, we will apply Lemma 19 for the idealized extended IRWE model Θ (formally defined in Sect. 4.2) to prove that there is no black-box construction of IO from any primitive $\mathcal{P}$ that can be oracle-fixed constructed (see Definition 10) from Θ. In particular, we will do so for $\mathcal{P}$ that is the extended EIRWE primitive. Our task is thus twofold: **(1)** to prove that $\mathcal{P}$ can be oracle-fixed constructed from Θ and **(2)** to show a simulatable compilation procedure that compiles out Θ from any IO construction. The first task is proven in Sect. 4.3 and the second task is proven in Sect. 4.4. By Lemma 19, this would imply the separation result of IO from $\mathcal{P}$ and prove Theorem 32.

Our oracle, which is more formally defined in Sect. 4.2, resembles an idealized version of a witness encryption scheme, which makes the construction of extended EIRWE straightforward. As a result, the main challenge lies in showing a simulatable compilation procedure for IO that satisfies Definition 16 in this idealized model.

4.2 The Ideal Model

In this section, we define the distribution of our ideal randomized extended oracle.

Definition 33 (Random Instance-revealing Witness Encryption Oracle). *Let* V *be a universal circuit-evaluator Turing machine (as defined in Definition 26) that takes as input* (w, x) *where* $x = (a, m) \in \{0,1\}^n$ *and outputs* $b \in \{0,1\}$. *We define the following* random instance-revealing witness encryption *(rIRWE) oracle* $\Theta = (\mathrm{Enc}, \mathrm{Rev}, \mathrm{Dec}_{\mathsf{V}})$ *as follows. We specify the sub-oracle* Θ_n *whose inputs are parameterized by* n, *and the actual oracle will be* $\Theta = \{\Theta_n\}_{n \in \mathbb{N}}$.

- Enc: $\{0,1\}^n \mapsto \{0,1\}^{2n}$ *is a random injective function.*
- Rev: $\{0,1\}^{2n} \mapsto \{0,1\}^* \cup \perp$ *is a function that, given an input* $c \in \{0,1\}^{2n}$, *would output the corresponding attribute* a *for which* $\mathrm{Enc}(a, m) = c$. *If there is no such attribute then it outputs* $\perp$ *instead.*
- $\mathrm{Dec}_{\mathsf{V}}$: $\{0,1\}^s \mapsto \{0,1\}^n \cup \{\perp\}$: *Given* $(w, c) \in \{0,1\}^s$, $\mathrm{Dec}(w, c)$ *allows us to decrypt the ciphertext* c *and get* $x = (a, m)$ *as long as the predicate test is satisfied on* (w, a). *More formally, do as follow:*
  1. *If* $\nexists\, x$ *such that* $\mathrm{Enc}(x) = c$, *output* $\perp$. *Otherwise, continue to the next step.*
  2. *Find* x *such that* $\mathrm{Enc}(x) = c$.
  3. *If* $\mathsf{V}^{\Theta}(w, a) = 0$ *output* $\perp$. *Otherwise, output* $x = (a, m)$.

We define a query-answer pair resulting from query q *to subroutine* $T \in \{\mathrm{Enc}, \mathrm{Dec}, \mathrm{Rev}\}$ *with some answer* β *as* $(q \mapsto \beta)_T$. *The oracle* Θ *provides the subroutines for all inputs lengths but, for simplicity, and when* n *is clear from the context, we use* $\Theta = (\mathrm{Enc}, \mathrm{Rev}, \mathrm{Dec}_{\mathsf{V}})$ *to refer to* Θ_n *for a fixed* n.

Remark 34. We note that since V is a universal circuit-evaluator, the number of queries that it will ask (when we recursively unwrap all internal queries to Dec) is at most a polynomial. This is due to the fact that the sizes of the queries that V asks will be strictly less than the size of the inputs to V. In that respect, we say that V has the property of being *extended poly-query*.

4.3 Witness Encryption Exists Relative to Θ

In this section, we show how to construct a semantically-secure extended extractable IRWE for universal circuit-evaluator V relative to $\Theta = (\mathrm{Enc}, \mathrm{Rev}, \mathrm{Dec}_{\mathsf{V}})$. More formally, we will prove the following lemma.

Lemma 35. *There exists a correct and subexponentially-secure oracle-fixed implementation (Definition 10) of extended extractable instance-revealing witness encryption in the ideal* Θ *oracle model.*

We will in fact show how to construct a primitive (in the Θ oracle model) that is simpler to prove the existence of and for which we argue that it is sufficient to get the desired primitive of EIRWE. We give the definition of that primitive followed by a construction.

Definition 36 (Extended Extractable One-way Witness Encryption (ex-EOWE)). *Let* V *be a universal circuit-evaluator Turing machine (as defined in Definition 26) that takes an instance* a *and witness* w *and outputs* *a bit* $b \in \{0,1\}$. *For any given security parameter* κ, *an* extended extractable one-way witness encryption *scheme for* V *consists of the following PPT algorithms* $P = (\mathrm{Enc}, \mathrm{Rev}, \mathrm{Dec}_{\mathsf{V}})$ *defined as follows:*

- $\mathrm{Enc}(a, m, 1^\kappa)$: *given an instance* $a \in \{0,1\}^*$, *message* $m \in \{0,1\}^*$, *and security parameter* κ *(and randomness as needed) it outputs* $c \in \{0,1\}^*$.
- $\mathrm{Rev}(c)$: *given ciphertext* c *returns the underlying attribute* $a \in \{0,1\}^*$.
- $\mathrm{Dec}_{\mathsf{V}}(w, c)$: *given ciphertext* c *and "witness" string* w, *it outputs a message* $m' \in \{0,1\}^*$.

An extended extractable one-way witness encryption scheme satisfies the same correctness properties as Definition 31 but the extractability property is replaced with the following:

- ***Extractable Inversion:*** *For any PPT adversary* A *and polynomial* $p_1(.)$, *there exists a PPT (black-box) straight-line extractor* E *and a polynomial function* $p_2(.)$ *such that the following holds. For any security parameter* κ, $k = \mathrm{poly}(\kappa)$, *and for all* a, *if:*

$$\Pr\left[A(1^\kappa, c) = m \mid m \xleftarrow{\$} \{0,1\}^k, c \leftarrow \mathrm{Enc}(a, m, 1^\kappa)\right] \geq p_1(\kappa)$$

Then:

$$\Pr[E^A(a) = w \wedge \mathsf{V}^P(w, a) = 1] \geq p_2(\kappa)$$

Construction 37 (Extended Extractable One-way Witness Encryption). *For any security parameter* κ *and oracle* Θ *sampled according to Definition 33, we will implement an extended EOWE scheme* P *for the universal circuit-evaluator* V *using* $\Theta = (\mathrm{Enc}, \mathrm{Dec}_{\mathsf{V}})$ *as follows:*

- $\mathrm{WEnc}(a, m, 1^\kappa)$: *Given security parameter* 1^κ, $a \in \{0,1\}^*$, *and message* $m \in \{0,1\}^{n/2}$ *where* $n = 2\max(|a|, \kappa)$, *output* $\mathrm{Enc}(x)$ *where* $x = (a, m)$.
- $\mathrm{WDec}(w, c)$: *Given witness* w *and ciphertext* c, *let* $x' = \mathrm{Dec}_{\mathsf{V}}(w, c)$. *If* $x' \neq \perp$, *parse as* $x' = (a', m')$ *and output* m'. *Otherwise, output* $\perp$.

Remark 38 (From one-wayness to Indistinguishability). We note that the primitive ex-EOWE, which has one-way security, can be used to build an ex-EIRWE, which is indistinguishability-based, through a simple application of the Goldreich-Levin thoerem [40]. Namely, to encrypt a one-bit message b under some attribute a, we would output the ciphertext $c = (\mathrm{Enc}(a, r_1), r_2, \langle r_1, r_2 \rangle \oplus b)$ where r_1, r_2 are randomly sampled and $\langle r_1, r_2 \rangle$ is the hardcore bit. To decrypt a ciphertext $c = (y_1, r_2, y_3)$ we would run $r_1 = \mathrm{Dec}(w, y_1)$, find the hardcore bit $p = \langle r_1, r_2 \rangle$ then output $b = p \oplus y_3$. We obtain the desired indistinguishability security since, by the hardcore-bit security of the original scheme, we have $(\mathrm{Enc}(a, r_1), r_2, \langle r_1, r_2 \rangle \oplus 0) \approx (\mathrm{Enc}(a, r_1), r_2, \langle r_1, r_2 \rangle \oplus 1)$ for any fixed a.

Lemma 39. *Construction 37 is a correct and subexponentially-secure oracle-fixed implementation (Definition 10) of extended extractable one-way witness encryption in the ideal* Θ *oracle model.*

Proof. To prove the security of this construction, we will show that if there exists an adversary A against scheme P (in the Θ oracle model) that can invert an encryption of a random message with non-negligible advantage then there exists a (fixed) deterministic straight-line (non-rewinding) extractor E with access to $\Theta = (\text{Enc}, \text{Rev}, \text{Dec}_{\mathsf{V}})$ that can find the witness for the underlying instance of the challenge ciphertext.

Suppose A is an adversary in the inversion game with success probability ϵ. Then the extractor E would works as follows: given a as input and acting as the challenger for adversary A, it chooses $m \xleftarrow{\$} \{0,1\}^k$ uniformly at random then runs $A^{\Theta}(1^\kappa, c^*)$ where $c^* \leftarrow \text{WEnc}(a, m, 1^\kappa)$ is the challenge. Queries issued by A are handled by E as follows:

- To answer any query $\text{Enc}(x)$ asked by A, it forwards the query to the oracle Θ and returns some answer c.
- To answer any query $\text{Rev}(c)$ asked by A, it forwards the query to the oracle Θ and returns some answer a.
- To answer any query $\text{Dec}_{\mathsf{V}}(w, c)$ asked by A, the extractor first issues a query $\text{Rev}(c)$ to get some answer a. If $a \neq \bot$, it would execute $\mathsf{V}^{\Theta}(w, a)$, forwarding queries asked by V to Θ similar to how it does for A. Finally, it forwards the query $\text{Dec}(w, c)$ to Θ to get some answer x. If $a = \bot$, it returns $\bot$ to A otherwise it returns x.

While handling the queries made by A, if a decryption query $\text{Dec}_{\mathsf{V}}(w, c^*)$ for the challenge ciphertext is issued by A, the extractor will pass this query to Θ, and if the result of the decryption is $x \neq \bot$ then the extractor will halt execution and output w as the witness for instance x. Otherwise, if after completing the execution of A, no such query was asked then the extractor outputs $\bot$. We prove the following lemma.

Lemma 40. *For any PPT adversary A, instances a, if there exists a non-negligible function $\epsilon(.)$ such that:*

$$\Pr\left[A^{\Theta}(1^\kappa, c) = m \mid m \xleftarrow{\$} \{0,1\}^k, c \leftarrow \text{WEnc}(a, m, 1^\kappa)\right] \geq \epsilon(\kappa) \tag{1}$$

Then there exists a PPT straight-line extractor E such that:

$$\Pr\left[E^{\Theta, A}(a) = w \wedge \mathsf{V}^{\Theta}(w, a) = 1\right] \geq \epsilon(\kappa) - \text{negl}(\kappa) \tag{2}$$

Proof. Let A be an adversary satisfying Eq. (1) above and let AdvWin be the event that A succeeds in the inversion game. Furthermore, let ExtWin be the event that the extractor succeeds in extracting a witness (as in Eq. (2) above). Observe that:

$$\begin{aligned}
\Pr_{\Theta,m}[\mathsf{ExtWin}] &\geq \Pr_{\Theta,m}[\mathsf{ExtWin} \wedge \mathsf{AdvWin}] \\
&= 1 - \Pr_{\Theta,m}\left[\overline{\mathsf{ExtWin}} \vee \overline{\mathsf{AdvWin}}\right] \\
&= 1 - \Pr_{\Theta,m}\left[\overline{\mathsf{ExtWin}} \wedge \mathsf{AdvWin}\right] - \Pr_{\Theta,m}\left[\overline{\mathsf{AdvWin}}\right]
\end{aligned}$$

Since $\Pr[\mathsf{AdvWin}] \geq \epsilon$ for some non-negligible function ϵ, it suffices to show that $\Pr[\overline{\mathsf{ExtWin}} \wedge \mathsf{AdvWin}]$ is negligible. Note that, by our construction of extractor E, this event is equivalent to saying that the adversary succeeds in the inversion game but never asks a query of the form $\mathrm{Dec}_{\mathsf{V}}(w, c^*)$ for which the answer is $x \neq \perp$ and so the extractor fails to recover the witness. For simplicity of notation define $\mathsf{Win} := \overline{\mathsf{ExtWin}} \wedge \mathsf{AdvWin}$.

We will show that, with overwhelming probability over the choice of oracle Θ, the probability of Win happening is negligible. That is, we will prove the following claim:

Claim. For any negligible function δ, $\Pr_{\Theta}\left[\Pr_m[\mathsf{Win}] \geq \sqrt{\delta}\right] \leq \mathrm{negl}(\kappa)$.

Proof. Define Bad to be the event that A asks (directly or indirectly) a query of the form $\mathrm{Dec}_{\mathsf{V}}(w, c')$ for some $c' \neq c^*$ for which it has not asked $\mathrm{Enc}(x) = c$ previously. We have that:

$$\Pr_{\Theta,m}[\mathsf{Win}] \leq \Pr_{\Theta,m}[\mathsf{Win} \wedge \overline{\mathsf{Bad}}] + \Pr_{\Theta,m}[\mathsf{Bad}]$$

The probability of Bad over the randomness of Θ is at most $1/2^n$ as it is the event that A hits an image of a sparse random injective function without asking the function on the preimage beforehand. Thus, $\Pr_{\Theta,m}[\mathsf{Bad}] \leq 1/2^n$.

It remains to show that $\Pr_{\Theta,m}[\mathsf{Win} \wedge \overline{\mathsf{Bad}}]$ is also negligible. We list all possible queries that A could ask and argue that these queries do not help A in any way without also forcing the extractor to win as well. Specifically, we show that for any such A that satisfies the event $(\mathsf{Win} \wedge \overline{\mathsf{Bad}})$, there exists another adversary $\widehat{A}$ that depends on A and also satisfies the same event but does not ask any decryption queries (only encryption queries). This would then reduce to the standard case of inverting a random injective function, which is known to be hard. We define the adversary $\widehat{A}$ as follows. Upon executing A, it handles the queries issued by A as follows:

- If A asks a query of the form $\mathrm{Enc}(x)$ then $\widehat{A}$ forwards the query to Θ to get the answer.
- If A asks a query of the form $\mathrm{Rev}(c)$ then since Bad does not happen, it must be the case that $c = \mathrm{Enc}(a, m)$ is an encryption that was previously asked by A and therefore $\widehat{A}$ returns a as the answer.
- If A asks a query of the form $\mathrm{Dec}(w, c^*)$ then w must be a string for which $\mathsf{V}(w, a^*) = 0$ or otherwise the extractor wins, which contradicts that $\overline{\mathsf{ExtWin}}$ happens. If that is the case, since w is not a witness, $\widehat{A}$ would return $\perp$ to A after running $\mathsf{V}^{\Theta}(w, a^*)$ and answering its queries appropriately.
- If A asks a query of the form $\mathrm{Dec}(w, c')$ for some $c' \neq c^*$ then, since Bad does not happen, it must be the case that A has asked a (direct or indirect) visible encryption query $\mathrm{Enc}(x') = c'$. Therefore, $\widehat{A}$ would have observed this encryption query and can therefore run $\mathsf{V}^{\Theta}(w, a')$ and return the appropriate answer (x or $\perp$) depending on the answer of V.

Given that $\widehat{A}$ perfectly emulates A's view, the only possibility that A could win the inversion game is by asking $\text{Enc}(x^*) = c^*$ and hitting the challenge ciphertext, which is a negligible probability over the randomness of the oracle. By a standard averaging argument, we find that since $\Pr_{\Theta,m}[\mathsf{Win} \wedge \overline{\mathsf{Bad}}] \leq \delta(\kappa)$ for some negligible δ then $\Pr_{\Theta}[\Pr_m[\mathsf{Win} \wedge \overline{\mathsf{Bad}}] \leq \sqrt{\delta}] \geq 1 - \sqrt{\delta}$, which yields the result.

To conclude the proof of Lemma 40, we can see that the probability that the extractor wins is given by $\Pr[\mathsf{ExtWin}] \geq 1 - \Pr[\overline{\mathsf{ExtWin}} \wedge \mathsf{AdvWin}] - \Pr[\overline{\mathsf{AdvWin}}] \geq \epsilon(\kappa) - \text{negl}(\kappa)$ where ϵ is the non-negligible advantage of the adversary A.

It is clear that Construction 37 is a correct implementation. Furthermore, by Lemma 40, it satisfies the extractability property. Thus, this concludes the proof of Lemma 39.

Proof (of Lemma 35). The existence of extractable instance-revealing witness encryption in the Θ oracle model follows from Lemma 39 and Remark 38.

4.4 Compiling Out Θ from IO

In this section, we show a simulatable compiler for compiling out Θ. We adapt the approach outlined in Sect. 4.1 to the extended ideal IRWE oracle $\Theta = (\text{Enc}, \text{Rev}, \text{Dec}_{\text{V}})$ while making use of Lemma 18, which allows us to compile out Θ in two phases: we first compile out part of Θ to get an approximately-correct obfuscator $\widehat{O}^R$ in the random oracle model (that produces an obfuscation $\widehat{B}^R$ in the RO-model), and then use the previous result of [21] to compile out the random oracle R and get an obfuscator O' in the plain-model. Since we are applying this lemma only a constant number of times (in fact, just twice), security should still be preserved. Specifically, we will prove the following claim:

Lemma 41. *Let $R \sqsubseteq \Theta$ be a random oracle where "$\sqsubseteq$" denotes a sub-model relationship (see Definition 15). Then the following holds:*

- *For any IO in the Θ ideal model, there exists a simulatable compiler with correctness error $\epsilon < 1/200$ for it that outputs a new obfuscator in the random oracle R model.*
- [21] *For any IO in the random oracle R model, there exists a simulatable compiler with correctness error $\epsilon < 1/200$ for it that outputs a new obfuscator in the plain model.*

Proof. The second part of Lemma 41 follows directly by [21], and thus we focus on proving the first part of the claim. Before we start describing the compilation process, we present the following definition of canonical executions that is a property of algorithms in this ideal model and dependent on the oracle being removed.

Definition 42 (Canonical executions). *Web define an oracle algorithm A^{Θ} relative to rIRWE to be in canonical form if before asking any $\text{Dec}_{\text{V}}(w, c)$ query,*

A would first get $a \leftarrow \mathrm{Rev}(c)$ then run $\mathsf{V}^{\Theta}(w, a)$ on its own, making sure to answer any queries of V *using* Θ*. Furthermore, after asking a query* $\mathrm{Dec}_{\mathsf{V}}(w, c)$ *for which the returned answer is some message $m \neq \bot$, it would ask* $\mathrm{Enc}(x)$ *where $x = (a, m)$. Note that any oracle algorithm A can be easily modified into a canonical form by increasing its query complexity by at most a polynomial factor (since* V *is an extended poly-query algorithm).*

Definition 43 (Query Types). *For any (not necessarily canonical) oracle algorithm A with access to a rIRWE oracle Θ, we call the queries that are asked by A to Θ as* direct *queries and those queries that are asked by V^{Θ} due to a call to* Dec *as* indirect *queries. Furthermore, we say that a query is* visible *to A if this query was issued by A and thus it knows the answer that is returned by Θ. Conversely, we say a query is* hidden *from A if it is an indirect query that was not explicitly issued by A (for example, A would have asked a* $\mathrm{Dec}_{\mathsf{V}}$ *query which prompted V^{Θ} to ask its own queries and the answers returned to* V *will not be visible to A). Note that, once we canonicalize A, all indirect queries will be made visible since, by Definition 42, A will run V^{Θ} before asking* $\mathrm{Dec}_{\mathsf{V}}$ *queries and the query-answer pairs generated by* V *will be revealed to A.*

We now proceed to present the construction of the random-oracle model obfuscator that, given an obfuscator in the Θ model, would compile out and emulate queries to Dec and Rev while forwarding any Enc queries to R. Throughout this process, we assume that the obfuscators and the obfuscated circuits are all canonicalized according to Definition 42.

The New Obfuscator $\widehat{O}^R$ in the Random Oracle Model. Let $R = \{R_n\}_{n\in\mathbb{N}}$ be the (injective) random oracle where $R_n : \{0,1\}^n \to \{0,1\}^{2n}$. Given a δ-approximate obfuscator $O = (iO, Ev)$ in the rIRWE oracle model, we construct an $(\delta + \epsilon)$-approximate obfuscator $\widehat{O} = (\widehat{iO}, \widehat{Ev})$ in the random oracle model.

Subroutine $\widehat{iO}^R(C)$:

1. *Emulation phase:* Emulate $iO^{\Theta}(C)$. Let T_O be the transcript of this phase and initialize $Q_O := Q(T_O) = \varnothing$. For every query q asked by $iO^{\Theta}(C)$, call $\rho_q \leftarrow \mathtt{EmulateCall}^R(Q_O, q)$ and add ρ_q to Q_O.
   Note that, since iO is a canonical algorithm, there are no hidden queries resulting from queries asked by V (via Dec queries) since we will always run V^{Θ} before asking/emulating a Dec query.
2. *Learning phase:* Set $Q_B = \varnothing$ to be the set of query-answer pairs learned during this phase. Set $m = 2\ell_O/\epsilon$ where $\ell_O \leq |iO|$ represents the number of queries asked by iO. Choose $t \xleftarrow{\$} [m]$ uniformly at random then for $i = \{1, ..., t\}$:
   - Choose $z_i \xleftarrow{\$} \{0,1\}^{|C|}$ uniformly at random
   - Run $Ev^{\Theta}(B, z_i)$. For every query q asked by $Ev^{\Theta}(B, z_i)$, call and retrieve $\rho_q \leftarrow \mathtt{EmulateCall}^R(Q_O \cup Q_B, q)$ then add ρ_q to Q_B.

Algorithm 1. `EmulateCall`

Input: Query-answer set Q, query q
Oracle: Random Oracle R
Output: ρ_q a query-answer pair containing the answer of query q
Begin:

```
if q is a query of type Enc(x) then
|  Set ρ_q = (x ↦ R(x))_Enc
end
if q is a query of the form Rev(c) then
|  if ∃ (x ↦ c)_Enc ∈ Q where x = (a, m) then
|  |  Set ρ_q = (c ↦ a)_Rev
|  else
|  |  Set ρ_q = (c ↦ ⊥)_Rev
|  end
end
if q is a query of the form Dec_V(w, c) then
|  if ∃ (x ↦ c)_Enc ∈ Q then
|  |  Initialize Q_V = ∅ and emulate b ← V^Θ(w, x)
|  |  for each query q_V asked by V do
|  |  |  ρ_V ← EmulateCall^R(Q ∪ Q_V, q_V)
|  |  |  Q_V = Q_V ∪ ρ_V
|  |  end
|  |  if b = 1 then
|  |  |  Set ρ_q = ((w, c) ↦ x)_Dec
|  |  else
|  |  |  Set ρ_q = ((w, c) ↦ ⊥)_Dec
|  |  end
|  else
|  |  Set ρ_q = ((w, c) ↦ ⊥)_Dec
|  end
end
Return ρ_q
```

Similar to Step 1, since Ev is a canonical algorithm and Enc is a injective function, with overwhelming probability, there will be no hidden queries as a result of asking any Dec queries.

3. The output of the RO model obfuscation algorithm $\widehat{iO}^R(C)$ will be $\widehat{B} = (B, Q_B)$.

Subroutine $\widehat{Ev}^R(\widehat{B}, z)$: To evaluate $\widehat{B} = (B, Q_B)$ on a new random input z we simply emulate $Ev^\Theta(B, z)$. For every query q asked by $Ev^\Theta(B, z)$, run and set $\rho_q = \texttt{EmulateCall}^R(Q_B, q)$ then add ρ_q to Q_B.

The Running Time of $\widehat{iO}$. We note that the running time of the new obfuscator $\widehat{iO}$ remains polynomial time since we are emulating the original obfuscation once followed by a polynomial number m of learning iterations. Furthermore, while we are indeed working with an extended oracle where the PPT V can have oracle gates to subroutines of Θ, we emphasize that since V, which we are executing during `EmulateCall`, is a universal circuit evaluator, its effective running time remains to be a strict polynomial in the size of V and so the issue of exponential or infinite recursive calls is non-existent.

Proving Approximate Correctness. Consider two separate experiments (real and ideal) that construct the random oracle model obfuscator exactly as described above but differ when evaluating $\widehat{B}$. Specifically, in the real experiment, $\widehat{Ev}^R(\widehat{B}, z)$ emulates $Ev^\Theta(B, z)$ on a random input z and answers any queries by running Q_B, whereas in the ideal experiment, we execute $\widehat{Ev}^R(\widehat{B}, z)$ and answer the queries of $Ev^\Theta(B, z)$ using the actual oracle Θ instead. In essence, in the real experiment, we can think of the execution as $Ev^{\widehat{\Theta}}(B, z)$ where $\widehat{\Theta}$ is the oracle simulated by using Q_B and oracle R. We will compare the real experiment with the ideal experiment and show that the statistical distance between these two executions is at most ϵ. In order to achieve this, we will identify the events that differentiate between the executions $Ev^\Theta(B, z)$ and $Ev^{\widehat{\Theta}}(B, z)$.

Let q be a new query that is being asked by $Ev^{\widehat{\Theta}}(B, z)$ and handled by calling $\texttt{EmulateCall}^R(Q_B, q)$. The following are the cases that should be handled:

1. If q is a query of type $\mathrm{Enc}(x)$, then the answer to q will be distributed the same in both experiments.
2. If q is a query of type $\mathrm{Dec}(w, c)$ or $\mathrm{Rev}(c)$ whose answer is determined by Q_B in the real experiment then it is also determined by $Q_O \cup Q_B \supseteq Q_B$ in the ideal experiment and the answers are distributed the same.
3. If q is of type $\mathrm{Dec}(w, c)$ or $\mathrm{Rev}(c)$ that is not determined by $Q_O \cup Q_B$ in the ideal experiment then this means that we are attempting to decrypt a ciphertext for which we have not encrypted before and we will therefore answer it with $\perp$ with overwhelming probability. In that case, q will also not be determined by Q_B in the real experiment and we will answer it with $\perp$.
4. **Bad Event 1:** Suppose q is of type $\mathrm{Dec}(w, c)$ that is not determined by Q_B in the real experiment and yet is determined by $Q_O \cup Q_B$ in the ideal experiment to be some answer $x \neq \perp$. This implies that the query-answer pair $(x \mapsto c)_{\mathrm{Enc}}$ is in $Q_O \backslash Q_B$. That is, we are for the first time decrypting a ciphertext that was encrypted in Step 1 because we failed to learn the underlying x for ciphertext c during the learning phase of Step 2. In that case, in the real experiment, the answer would be $\perp$ since we do not know the corresponding message x whereas in the ideal experiment it would use the correct answer from $Q_O \cup Q_B$ and output x. However, we will show that this event is unlikely due to the learning procedure.
5. **Bad Event 2:** Suppose q is of type $\mathrm{Rev}(c)$ that is not determined by Q_B in the real experiment and yet is determined by $Q_O \cup Q_B$ in the ideal experiment. This implies that the query-answer pair $((a, m) \mapsto c)_{\mathrm{Enc}}$ is in $Q_O \setminus Q_B$. That is, we are for the first time attempting to reveal the attribute of a ciphertext that was encrypted in Step 1 because we failed to learn the answer of this

reveal query during the learning phase of Step 2. In that case, in the real experiment, the answer would be $\perp$ since we do not know the corresponding attribute a whereas in the ideal experiment it would use the correct answer from $Q_O \cup Q_B$ and output a. However, we will show that this event is unlikely due to the learning procedure.

For input x, let $E(x)$ be the event that Case 4 or 5 happen. Assuming that event $E(x)$ does not happen, both experiments will proceed identically the same and the output distributions of $Ev^{\Theta}(B, x)$ and $Ev^{\widehat{\Theta}}(B, x)$ will be statistically close. More formally, the probability of correctness for $\widehat{iO}$ is:

$$\begin{aligned}\Pr_x[Ev^{\widehat{\Theta}}(B,x) \neq C(x)] &= \Pr_x[Ev^{\widehat{\Theta}}(B,x) \neq C(x) \wedge \neg E(x)] \\ &\quad + \Pr_x[Ev^{\widehat{\Theta}}(B,x) \neq C(x) \wedge E(x)] \\ &\leq \Pr_x[Ev^{\widehat{\Theta}}(B,x) \neq C(x) \wedge \neg E(x)] + \Pr_x[E(x)]\end{aligned}$$

By the approximate functionality of iO, we have that:

$$\Pr_x[iO^{\Theta}(C)(x) \neq C(x)] = \Pr_x[Ev^{\Theta}(B,x) \neq C(x)] \leq \delta(n)$$

Therefore,

$$\Pr_x[Ev^{\widehat{\Theta}}(B,x) \neq C(x) \wedge \neg E(x)] = \Pr_x[Ev^{\Theta}(B,x) \neq C(x) \wedge \neg E(x)] \leq \delta$$

We are thus left to show that $\Pr[E(x)] \leq \epsilon$. Since both experiments proceed the same up until E happens, the probability of E happening is the same in both worlds and we will thus choose to bound this bad event in the ideal world.

Claim. $\Pr_x[E(x)] \leq \epsilon$.

Proof. For all $i \in [t]$, let $Q'_{B_i} = Q_{B_i} \cap Q_O$ be the set of query-answer pairs generated by the i'th evaluation $Ev^{\Theta}(B, z_i)$ during the learning phase (Step 2) and are also generated during the obfuscation emulation phase (Step 1). In particular, Q'_{B_i} would contain the query-answer pairs $((a, m) \mapsto c)_{\mathsf{Enc}}$ for encryptions that were generated by the obfuscation and later discovered during the learning phase. Note that, since the maximum number of learning iterations $m > \ell_O$ and $Q'_{B_i} \subseteq Q'_{B_{i+1}}$, the number of learning iterations that would increase the size of the set of learned obfuscation queries is at most $2\ell_O$ since there are at most ℓ_O obfuscation ciphertexts that can be fully discovered during the learning phase and at most ℓ_O obfuscation ciphertexts that can be partially discovered (just finding out the underlying attribute a) via Rev queries during the learning phase.

We say $t \xleftarrow{\$} [m]$ is bad if it is the case that $Q'_{B_t} \neq Q'_{B_{t+1}}$ (i.e. t is an index of a learning iteration that increases the size of the learned obfuscation queries). This would imply that after t learning iterations in the ideal world, the final evaluation $Q'_{\widehat{B}} := Q'_{B_{t+1}}$ would contain a new unlearned query-answer pair that was in Q_O. Thus, given that $m = 2\ell_O/\epsilon$, the probability (over the selection of t) that t is bad is at most $2\ell_O/m < \epsilon$.

Proving Security. To show that the resulting obfuscator is secure, it suffices to show that the compilation process represented as the new obfuscator's construction is simulatable. We show a simulator S (with access to Θ) that works as follows: given an obfuscated circuit B in the Θ ideal model, it runs the learning procedure as shown in Step 2 of the new obfuscator $\widehat{iO}$ to learn the heavy queries Q_B then outputs $\widehat{B} = (B, Q_B)$. Note that this distribution is statistically close to the output of the real execution of $\widehat{iO}$ and, therefore, security follows.

Acknowledgements. We thank the anonymous reviewers of Crypto 2017 for their useful comments.

References

1. Ananth, P., Jain, A.: Indistinguishability obfuscation from compact functional encryption. In: Gennaro, R., Robshaw, M. (eds.) CRYPTO 2015. LNCS, vol. 9215, pp. 308–326. Springer, Heidelberg (2015). doi:10.1007/978-3-662-47989-6_15
2. Ananth, P., Jain, A., Sahai, A.: Indistinguishability obfuscation from functional encryption for simple functions. Cryptology ePrint Archive, Report 2015/730 (2015). http://eprint.iacr.org/2015/730
3. Ananth, P.V., Gupta, D., Ishai, Y., Sahai, A.: Optimizing obfuscation: avoiding Barrington's theorem. In: Ahn, G.-J., Yung, M., Li, N. (eds.) ACM CCS 2014, pp. 646–658. ACM Press, November 2014
4. Applebaum, B.: Bootstrapping obfuscators via fast pseudorandom functions. In: Sarkar, P., Iwata, T. (eds.) ASIACRYPT 2014. LNCS, vol. 8874, pp. 162–172. Springer, Heidelberg (2014). doi:10.1007/978-3-662-45608-8_9
5. Applebaum, B., Brakerski, Z.: Obfuscating circuits via composite-order graded encoding. In: Dodis, Y., Nielsen, J.B. (eds.) TCC 2015. LNCS, vol. 9015, pp. 528–556. Springer, Heidelberg (2015). doi:10.1007/978-3-662-46497-7_21
6. Asharov, G., Segev, G.: Limits on the power of indistinguishability obfuscation and functional encryption. In: 2015 IEEE 56th Annual Symposium on Foundations of Computer Science (FOCS), pp. 191–209. IEEE (2015)
7. Asharov, G., Segev, G.: On constructing one-way permutations from indistinguishability obfuscation. In: Kushilevitz, E., Malkin, T. (eds.) TCC 2016. LNCS, vol. 9563, pp. 512–541. Springer, Heidelberg (2016). doi:10.1007/978-3-662-49099-0_19
8. Badrinarayanan, S., Miles, E., Sahai, A., Zhandry, M.: Post-zeroizing obfuscation: the case of evasive circuits. Cryptology ePrint Archive, Report 2015/167 (2015). http://eprint.iacr.org/2015/167
9. Baecher, P., Brzuska, C., Fischlin, M.: Notions of black-box reductions, revisited. In: Sako, K., Sarkar, P. (eds.) ASIACRYPT 2013. LNCS, vol. 8269, pp. 296–315. Springer, Heidelberg (2013). doi:10.1007/978-3-642-42033-7_16
10. Barak, B., Garg, S., Kalai, Y.T., Paneth, O., Sahai, A.: Protecting obfuscation against algebraic attacks. In: Nguyen, P.Q., Oswald, E. (eds.) EUROCRYPT 2014. LNCS, vol. 8441, pp. 221–238. Springer, Heidelberg (2014). doi:10.1007/978-3-642-55220-5_13
11. Barak, B., Goldreich, O., Impagliazzo, R., Rudich, S., Sahai, A., Vadhan, S., Yang, K.: On the (im)possibility of obfuscating programs. In: Kilian, J. (ed.) CRYPTO 2001. LNCS, vol. 2139, pp. 1–18. Springer, Heidelberg (2001). doi:10.1007/3-540-44647-8_1

12. Bethencourt, J., Sahai, A., Waters, B.: Ciphertext-policy attribute-based encryption. In: 2007 IEEE Symposium on Security and Privacy, pp. 321–334. IEEE Computer Society Press, May 2007
13. Bitansky, N., Vaikuntanathan, V.: Indistinguishability obfuscation from functional encryption. In: Guruswami, V. (ed.) 56th FOCS, pp. 171–190. IEEE Computer Society Press, October 2015
14. Boneh, D., Zhandry, M.: Multiparty key exchange, efficient traitor tracing, and more from indistinguishability obfuscation. In: Garay, J.A., Gennaro, R. (eds.) CRYPTO 2014. LNCS, vol. 8616, pp. 480–499. Springer, Heidelberg (2014). doi:10.1007/978-3-662-44371-2_27
15. Brakerski, Z., Brzuska, C., Fleischhacker, N.: On statistically secure obfuscation with approximate correctness. Cryptology ePrint Archive, Report 2016/226 (2016). http://eprint.iacr.org/
16. Brakerski, Z., Katz, J., Segev, G., Yerukhimovich, A.: Limits on the power of zero-knowledge proofs in cryptographic constructions. In: Ishai, Y. (ed.) TCC 2011. LNCS, vol. 6597, pp. 559–578. Springer, Heidelberg (2011). doi:10.1007/978-3-642-19571-6_34
17. Brakerski, Z., Perlman, R.: Lattice-based fully dynamic multi-key FHE with short ciphertexts. Cryptology ePrint Archive, Report 2016/339 (2016). http://eprint.iacr.org/2016/339
18. Brakerski, Z., Rothblum, G.N.: Virtual black-box obfuscation for all circuits via generic graded encoding. In: Lindell, Y. (ed.) TCC 2014. LNCS, vol. 8349, pp. 1–25. Springer, Heidelberg (2014). doi:10.1007/978-3-642-54242-8_1
19. Brakerski, Z., Vaikuntanathan, V.: Efficient fully homomorphic encryption from (standard) LWE. In: Ostrovsky, R. (ed.) 52nd FOCS, pp. 97–106. IEEE Computer Society Press, October 2011
20. Brakerski, Z., Vaikuntanathan, V.: Fully homomorphic encryption from ring-LWE and security for key dependent messages. In: Rogaway, P. (ed.) CRYPTO 2011. LNCS, vol. 6841, pp. 505–524. Springer, Heidelberg (2011). doi:10.1007/978-3-642-22792-9_29
21. Canetti, R., Kalai, Y.T., Paneth, O.: On obfuscation with random oracles. Cryptology ePrint Archive, Report 2015/048 (2015). http://eprint.iacr.org/
22. Canetti, R., Lin, H., Tessaro, S., Vaikuntanathan, V.: Obfuscation of probabilistic circuits and applications. In: Dodis, Y., Nielsen, J.B. (eds.) TCC 2015. LNCS, vol. 9015, pp. 468–497. Springer, Heidelberg (2015). doi:10.1007/978-3-662-46497-7_19
23. Cheon, J.H., Han, K., Lee, C., Ryu, H., Stehlé, D.: Cryptanalysis of the multilinear map over the integers. In: Oswald, E., Fischlin, M. (eds.) EUROCRYPT 2015. LNCS, vol. 9056, pp. 3–12. Springer, Heidelberg (2015). doi:10.1007/978-3-662-46800-5_1
24. Clear, M., McGoldrick, C.: Multi-identity and multi-key leveled FHE from learning with errors. In: Gennaro, R., Robshaw, M. (eds.) CRYPTO 2015. LNCS, vol. 9216, pp. 630–656. Springer, Heidelberg (2015). doi:10.1007/978-3-662-48000-7_31
25. Coron, J.-S., Gentry, C., Halevi, S., Lepoint, T., Maji, H.K., Miles, E., Raykova, M., Sahai, A., Tibouchi, M.: Zeroizing without low-level zeroes: new MMAP attacks and their limitations. In: Gennaro, R., Robshaw, M. (eds.) CRYPTO 2015. LNCS, vol. 9215, pp. 247–266. Springer, Heidelberg (2015). doi:10.1007/978-3-662-47989-6_12
26. Coron, J.-S., Lee, M.S., Lepoint, T., Tibouchi, M.: Cryptanalysis of GGH15 multilinear maps. Cryptology ePrint Archive, Report 2015/1037 (2015). http://eprint.iacr.org/2015/1037

27. Coron, J.-S., Lepoint, T., Tibouchi, M.: Practical multilinear maps over the integers. In: Canetti, R., Garay, J.A. (eds.) CRYPTO 2013. LNCS, vol. 8042, pp. 476–493. Springer, Heidelberg (2013). doi:10.1007/978-3-642-40041-4_26
28. Dachman-Soled, D.: Towards non-black-box separations of public key encryption and one way function. In: Hirt, M., Smith, A. (eds.) TCC 2016. LNCS, vol. 9986, pp. 169–191. Springer, Heidelberg (2016). doi:10.1007/978-3-662-53644-5_7
29. Dodis, Y., Halevi, S., Rothblum, R.D., Wichs, D.: Spooky encryption and its applications. In: Robshaw, M., Katz, J. (eds.) CRYPTO 2016. LNCS, vol. 9816, pp. 93–122. Springer, Heidelberg (2016). doi:10.1007/978-3-662-53015-3_4
30. Garg, S., Gentry, C., Halevi, S.: Candidate multilinear maps from ideal lattices. In: Johansson, T., Nguyen, P.Q. (eds.) EUROCRYPT 2013. LNCS, vol. 7881, pp. 1–17. Springer, Heidelberg (2013). doi:10.1007/978-3-642-38348-9_1
31. Garg, S., Gentry, C., Halevi, S., Raykova, M., Sahai, A., Waters, B.: Candidate indistinguishability obfuscation and functional encryption for all circuits. In: 54th FOCS, pp. 40–49. IEEE Computer Society Press, October 2013
32. Garg, S., Miles, E., Mukherjee, P., Sahai, A., Srinivasan, A., Zhandry, M.: Secure obfuscation in a weak multilinear map model. Cryptology ePrint Archive, Report 2016/817 (2016). http://eprint.iacr.org/2016/817
33. Garg, S., Pandey, O., Srinivasan, A.: Revisiting the cryptographic hardness of finding a nash equilibrium. In: Robshaw, M., Katz, J. (eds.) CRYPTO 2016. LNCS, vol. 9815, pp. 579–604. Springer, Heidelberg (2016). doi:10.1007/978-3-662-53008-5_20
34. Garg, S., Pandey, O., Srinivasan, A., Zhandry, M.: Breaking the sub-exponential barrier in obfustopia. Cryptology ePrint Archive, Report 2016/102 (2016). http://eprint.iacr.org/2016/102
35. Gentry, C.: A fully homomorphic encryption scheme. Ph.D. thesis, Stanford University (2009). crypto.stanford.edu/craig
36. Gentry, C.: Fully homomorphic encryption using ideal lattices. In: Mitzenmacher, M. (ed.) 41st ACM STOC, pp. 169–178. ACM Press, May/June 2009
37. Gentry, C., Gorbunov, S., Halevi, S.: Graph-induced multilinear maps from lattices. In: Dodis, Y., Nielsen, J.B. (eds.) TCC 2015. LNCS, vol. 9015, pp. 498–527. Springer, Heidelberg (2015). doi:10.1007/978-3-662-46497-7_20
38. Gentry, C., Sahai, A., Waters, B.: Homomorphic encryption from learning with errors: conceptually-simpler, asymptotically-faster, attribute-based. In: Canetti, R., Garay, J.A. (eds.) CRYPTO 2013. LNCS, vol. 8042, pp. 75–92. Springer, Heidelberg (2013). doi:10.1007/978-3-642-40041-4_5
39. Gentry, C., Wichs, D.: Separating succinct non-interactive arguments from all falsifiable assumptions. In: Fortnow, L., Vadhan, S.P. (eds.) STOC. ACM (2011)
40. Goldreich, O., Levin, L.A.: A hard-core predicate for all one-way functions. In: Proceedings of the 21st Annual ACM Symposium on Theory of Computing (STOC), pp. 25–32 (1989)
41. Goldwasser, S., Rothblum, G.N.: On best-possible obfuscation. In: Vadhan, S.P. (ed.) TCC 2007. LNCS, vol. 4392, pp. 194–213. Springer, Heidelberg (2007). doi:10.1007/978-3-540-70936-7_11
42. Gorbunov, S., Vaikuntanathan, V., Wee, H.: Attribute-based encryption for circuits. In: Boneh, D., Roughgarden, T., Feigenbaum, J. (eds.) 45th ACM STOC, pp. 545–554. ACM Press, June 2013
43. Gorbunov, S., Vaikuntanathan, V., Wee, H.: Predicate encryption for circuits from LWE. In: Gennaro, R., Robshaw, M. (eds.) CRYPTO 2015. LNCS, vol. 9216, pp. 503–523. Springer, Heidelberg (2015). doi:10.1007/978-3-662-48000-7_25

44. Goyal, V., Pandey, O., Sahai, A., Waters, B.: Attribute-based encryption for fine-grained access control of encrypted data. In: Juels, A., Wright, R.N., di Vimercati, S.C. (eds.) ACM CCS 2006, pp. 89–98. ACM Press, October/November 2006. Cryptology ePrint Archive Report 2006/309
45. Holenstein, T.: Complexity theory (2015). http://www.complexity.ethz.ch/education/Lectures/ComplexityFS15/skript_printable.pdf
46. Yupu, H., Jia, H.: Cryptanalysis of GGH map. Cryptology ePrint Archive, Report 2015/301 (2015). http://eprint.iacr.org/2015/301
47. Impagliazzo, R., Rudich, S.: Limits on the provable consequences of one-way permutations. In: 21st ACM STOC, pp. 44–61. ACM Press, May 1989
48. Lin, H.: Indistinguishability obfuscation from constant-degree graded encoding schemes. In: Fischlin, M., Coron, J.-S. (eds.) EUROCRYPT 2016. LNCS, vol. 9665, pp. 28–57. Springer, Heidelberg (2016). doi:10.1007/978-3-662-49890-3_2
49. Lin, H., Vaikuntanathan, V.: Indistinguishability obfuscation from DDH-like assumptions on constant-degree graded encodings. Cryptology ePrint Archive, Report 2016/795 (2016). http://eprint.iacr.org/2016/795
50. Mahmoody, M., Mohammed, A., Nematihaji, S.: More on impossibility of virtual black-box obfuscation in idealized models. Cryptology ePrint Archive, Report 2015/632 (2015). http://eprint.iacr.org/
51. Mahmoody, M., Mohammed, A., Nematihaji, S., Pass, R., Shelat, A.: A note on black-box separations for indistinguishability obfuscation. Cryptology ePrint Archive, Report 2016/316 (2016). http://eprint.iacr.org/2016/316
52. Mahmoody, M., Mohammed, A., Nematihaji, S., Pass, R., Shelat, A.: Lower bounds on assumptions behind indistinguishability obfuscation. In: Kushilevitz, E., Malkin, T. (eds.) TCC 2016. LNCS, vol. 9562, pp. 49–66. Springer, Heidelberg (2016). doi:10.1007/978-3-662-49096-9_3
53. Miles, E., Sahai, A., Weiss, M.: Protecting obfuscation against arithmetic attacks. Cryptology ePrint Archive, Report 2014/878 (2014). http://eprint.iacr.org/2014/878
54. Miles, E., Sahai, A., Zhandry, M.: Annihilation attacks for multilinear maps: cryptanalysis of indistinguishability obfuscation over GGH13. Cryptology ePrint Archive, Report 2016/147 (2016). http://eprint.iacr.org/2016/147
55. Mukherjee, P., Wichs, D.: Two round multiparty computation via multi-key FHE. In: Fischlin, M., Coron, J.-S. (eds.) EUROCRYPT 2016. LNCS, vol. 9666, pp. 735–763. Springer, Heidelberg (2016). doi:10.1007/978-3-662-49896-5_26
56. Naor, M.: On cryptographic assumptions and challenges. In: Boneh, D. (ed.) CRYPTO 2003. LNCS, vol. 2729, pp. 96–109. Springer, Heidelberg (2003). doi:10.1007/978-3-540-45146-4_6
57. Pass, R.: Limits of provable security from standard assumptions. In: Proceedings of the Forty-Third Annual ACM Symposium on Theory of Computing, pp. 109–118. ACM (2011)
58. Pass, R., Shelat, A.: Impossibility of VBB obfuscation with ideal constant-degree graded encodings. Cryptology ePrint Archive, Report 2015/383 (2015). http://eprint.iacr.org/
59. Pass, R., Tseng, W.-L.D., Venkitasubramaniam, M.: Towards non-black-box separations in cryptography. In: TCC (2011)
60. Peikert, C., Shiehian, S.: Multi-key FHE from LWE, revisited. Cryptology ePrint Archive, Report 2016/196 (2016). http://eprint.iacr.org/2016/196
61. Regev, O.: On lattices, learning with errors, random linear codes, and cryptography. In: Gabow, H.N., Fagin, R. (eds.) 37th ACM STOC, pp. 84–93. ACM Press, May 2005

62. Reingold, O., Trevisan, L., Vadhan, S.: Notions of reducibility between cryptographic primitives. In: Naor, M. (ed.) TCC 2004. LNCS, vol. 2951, pp. 1–20. Springer, Heidelberg (2004). doi:10.1007/978-3-540-24638-1_1
63. Sahai, A., Waters, B.: How to use indistinguishability obfuscation: deniable encryption, and more. In: Shmoys, D.B. (ed.) 46th ACM STOC, pp. 475–484. ACM Press, May/June 2014
64. Sahai, A., Waters, B.: Fuzzy identity-based encryption. In: Cramer, R. (ed.) EUROCRYPT 2005. LNCS, vol. 3494, pp. 457–473. Springer, Heidelberg (2005). doi:10.1007/11426639_27
65. Zimmerman, J.: How to obfuscate programs directly. In: Oswald, E., Fischlin, M. (eds.) EUROCRYPT 2015. LNCS, vol. 9057, pp. 439–467. Springer, Heidelberg (2015). doi:10.1007/978-3-662-46803-6_15

Structure vs. Hardness Through the Obfuscation Lens

Nir Bitansky, Akshay Degwekar(✉), and Vinod Vaikuntanathan

MIT, Cambridge, USA
{nirbitan,akshayd,vinodv}@csail.mit.edu

Abstract. Much of modern cryptography, starting from public-key encryption and going beyond, is based on the hardness of structured (mostly algebraic) problems like factoring, discrete log or finding short lattice vectors. While structure is perhaps what enables advanced applications, it also puts the hardness of these problems in question. In particular, this structure often puts them in low complexity classes such as $\mathsf{NP} \cap \mathsf{coNP}$ or statistical zero-knowledge (SZK).

Is this structure really necessary? For some cryptographic primitives, such as one-way permutations and homomorphic encryption, we know that the answer is *yes*—they imply hard problems in $\mathsf{NP} \cap \mathsf{coNP}$ and SZK, respectively. In contrast, one-way functions do *not* imply such hard problems, at least not by *fully black-box reductions*. Yet, for many basic primitives such as public-key encryption, oblivious transfer, and functional encryption, we do not have any answer.

We show that the above primitives, and many others, do *not* imply hard problems in $\mathsf{NP} \cap \mathsf{coNP}$ or SZK via fully black-box reductions. In fact, we first show that even the very powerful notion of Indistinguishability Obfuscation (IO) does *not* imply such hard problems, and then deduce the same for a large class of primitives that can be constructed from IO.

Keywords: Indistinguishability obfuscation · Statistical zero-knowledge · $\mathsf{NP} \cap \mathsf{coNP}$ · Structured hardness · Collision-resistant hashing

1 Introduction

The last four decades of research in cryptography has produced a host of fantastic objects, starting from one-way functions and permutations to public-key encryption [DH76, RSA78, GM82] and zero-knowledge proofs [GMR85] in the

MIT CSAIL. Research supported in part by NSF Grants CNS-1350619 and CNS-1414119, Alfred P. Sloan Research Fellowship, Microsoft Faculty Fellowship, the NEC Corporation, a Steven and Renee Finn Career Development Chair from MIT. This work was also sponsored in part by the Defense Advanced Research Projects Agency (DARPA) and the U.S. Army Research Office under contracts W911NF-15-C-0226.

J. Katz and H. Shacham (Eds.): CRYPTO 2017, Part I, LNCS 10401, pp. 696–723, 2017.
DOI: 10.1007/978-3-319-63688-7_23

1980s, all the way to fully homomorphic encryption [RAD78,Gen09,BV11] and indistinguishability obfuscation [BGI+01,GGH+13a] in the modern day.

The existence of all these objects requires at the very minimum that $\mathsf{NP} \not\subseteq \mathsf{BPP}$, but that is hardly ever enough. While one-way functions (OWFs), the most basic cryptographic object, does not seem to require much structure, as we advance up the ranks, we seem to require that certain *structured problems are hard.* For example, conjectured hard problems commonly used in cryptography (especially the public-key kind), such as factoring, discrete logarithms, and shortest (or closest) vectors on lattices all have considerable algebraic structure. On the one hand, it is this structure that enables strong applications such as public-key and homomorphic encryption. On the other hand, this structure is also what puts their hardness in question, and is exactly what algorithms may try to exploit in order to solve these problems. There is of course the fear that this structure will (eventually, if not today) deem these problems *easy.* Or, as Barak says more eloquently [Bar13]:

> [...] *based on the currently well studied schemes, structure is strongly associated with (and perhaps even implied by) public key cryptography. This is troubling news, since it makes public key crypto somewhat of an "endangered species" that could be wiped out by a surprising algorithmic advance. Therefore the question of whether structure is inherently necessary for public key crypto is not only of mathematical interest but also of practical importance as well.*

Thus, a fundamental question in cryptography is *what type of structure is necessary for different primitives?* Indeed, the answer to this question may be crucial to our understanding of what are the minimal assumptions required to construct these primitives. While there may be different ways of approaching this question, one main approach, which is also taken in this work, has been through the eyes of complexity theory. That is, we wish to understand which cryptographic primitives require hardness in low (and so called structured) complexity classes such as $\mathsf{NP} \cap \mathsf{coNP}$, TFNP (the class of total NP search problems), or SZK (the class of problems with statistical zero-knowledge proofs).

Aiming to answer this question, one line of research demonstrates that, for some cryptographic primitives, hardness in structured complexity classes is indeed necessary. The existence of one-way permutations (OWPs) requires a hard problem in $\mathsf{NP} \cap \mathsf{coNP}$ [Bra79]; the same holds for restricted cases of public-key encryption schemes satisfying specific structural properties (e.g. ciphertext certification) [Bra79,GG98]; homomorphic encryption schemes and non-interactive computational private information retrieval schemes imply hard problems in SZK [BL13,LV16]; and indistinguishability obfuscation schemes imply a hard problem in $\mathsf{PPAD} \subseteq \mathsf{TFNP}$ (assuming $\mathsf{NP} \not\subseteq \mathsf{ioBPP}$) [BPR15].

Yet, for many primitives such hardness is not known to be inherent. While this is perhaps expected for OWFs, it is also the case for seemingly structured primitives such as collision-resistant hash functions, oblivious transfer, and general public-key encryption schemes. *Do these primitives require hardness in structured complexity classes? Can we prove that they do or that they don't?*

Black-Box Separations. Formalizing this question in a meaningful way requires care. Indeed, it may be easy to formalize a statement of the form "the existence of crypto primitive $\mathcal{P}$ *implies* hardness in a complexity class $\mathcal{C}$": one just needs to show a reduction from breaking $\mathcal{P}$ to solving problems in $\mathcal{C}$. However, it is not clear how to prove statements of the form "the existence of crypto primitive $\mathcal{P}$ does *not* imply hardness in a complexity class $\mathcal{C}$". For example, it is commonly believed that $\mathsf{NP} \cap \mathsf{coNP}$ *does* contain hard problems. So in a trivial logical sense the existence of such problems is implied by any primitive $\mathcal{P}$. Instead, we follow the methodology of black-box separations, whose study in cryptography was pioneered by Impagliazzo and Rudich [IR89]. Faced with a similar problem of how to show that a primitive $\mathcal{P}$ (OWFs) cannot be used to construct another primitive $\mathcal{P}'$ (public-key encryption), they prove this cannot be shown through *black-box reductions*—cryptography's de facto technique for showing such implications.

A bit more elaborately, a *fully black-box reduction* [RTV04] of a primitive (or, in our case, a problem) $\mathcal{P}'$ to a primitive $\mathcal{P}$ consists of a black-box *construction* and a black-box *security reduction.* The construction of $\mathcal{P}'$ from $\mathcal{P}$ does not exploit the actual implementation of primitive $\mathcal{P}$, but rather just its input-output interface. The security reduction can use any adversary that breaks (or, in our case, solves) $\mathcal{P}'$ to break $\mathcal{P}$, and is oblivious to the implementation of the adversary (as well as of that of $\mathcal{P}$).

Following [IR89], there has been a rich study of black-box separations in cryptography (see, e.g., [Rud91, Sim98, KST99, GKM+00, GT00, GMR01, BT03, RTV04, HR04, GGKT05, Pas06, GMM07, BM09, HH09, BKSY11, DLMM11, KSS11, GKLM12, DHT12, BBF13, Fis12, Pas13, BB15, HHRS15] and many others). Most of this study has been devoted to establishing separations between different cryptographic primitives. (In particular, the most relevant to us are the recent works of Asharov and Segev [AS15, AS16] that study black-box separations for indistinguishability obfuscation, which we elaborate on below.) Some of this study puts limitations on basing cryptographic primitives on NP-hardness [GG98, AGGM06, MX10, HMX10, BL13, BB15, LV16].

Going back to our main question of which primitives require structured hardness, we know the following.

- As described above, OWPs imply a hard problem in $\mathsf{NP} \cap \mathsf{coNP}$ [Bra79], homomorphic encryption and PIR imply hard problems in SZK [BL13, LV16] and IO (with OWFs) implies a hard problem in PPAD [BPR15] via *black-box reductions.*
- On the flip side, we know that there are no black-box reductions from hard problems in $\mathsf{NP} \cap \mathsf{coNP}$ to OWFs [BI87, Rud88], and from hard-on-average problems in SZK to OWPs (corollary from [Ost91, OV08, HHRS15]).

For more advanced primitives, most notably (general) public-key encryption, we do not have results in either direction. In fact, many existing constructions are based on problems in $\mathsf{NP} \cap \mathsf{coNP}$ or SZK. We are thus left with (quite basic) primitives at an unclear state; as far as we know, they may very well imply hard problems in structured complexity classes, even by black-box reductions.

1.1 Our Results

We revisit the relationship between two structured complexity classes, statistical zero-knowledge (SZK) and NP ∩ coNP, and cryptographic primitives. In broad strokes, we show that there are no fully black-box reductions of hard problems in these classes to any one of a variety of cryptographic primitives, including (general) public-key encryption, oblivious transfer, deniable encryption, and functional encryption. More generally, we separate SZK and NP ∩ coNP from indistinguishability obfuscation (IO). Then, leveraging on the fact that IO can be used to construct a wide variety of cryptographic primitives in a black-box way, we derive corresponding separations for these primitives.[1] One complexity-theoretic corollary of this result is a separation between SZK and NP ∩ coNP from the class PPAD [MP91] that captures the complexity of computing Nash Equilibria.

On the positive side, we construct collision-resistant hash functions from a strong form of SZK-hardness and IO. It was previously known [AS15] that IO by itself does not imply collision-resistant hashing in a black-box way; we show that it does if one adds SZK-hardness as a "catalyst".

We now go into more detail on each of the results.

Statistical Zero-Knowledge and Cryptography. The notion of statistical zero-knowledge proofs was introduced in the seminal work of Goldwasser et al. [GMR85]. The class of *promise problems* with statistical zero-knowledge proofs (SZK) can be characterized by several complete problems, such as *statistical difference* [SV03] and *entropy difference* [GV99]. SZK hardness is known to follow from various number-theoretic problems that are commonly used in cryptography, such as Discrete Logarithms [GK93], Quadratic Residuosity [GMR85], Lattice Problems [GG98, MV03] as well as problems like Graph Isomorphism [GMW91]. As mentioned, we also know that a handful of cryptographic primitives such as homomorphic encryption [BL13], private information retrieval [LV16] and rerandomizable encryption imply hardness in SZK. (On the other hand, SZK ⊆ AM ∩ coAM [For89, AH91], and thus, SZK cannot contain NP-hard problems, unless the polynomial hierarchy collapses [BHZ87].)

We ask more generally which cryptographic primitives can be shown to imply such hardness, with the intuition that such primitives are *structured* in a certain way. In particular, whereas one may not expect a seemingly unstructured object like OWFs to imply such hardness, what can we say for instance about OWPs, public-key encryption, or even IO (which has proven to be powerful enough to yield almost any known cryptographic goal)?

We prove that none of these primitives imply such hardness through black-box reductions.

[1] More accurately, these primitives follow from IO and OWFs (OWFs), and accordingly our separation addresses IO and OWFs in conjunction. The concept of a black-box reduction from IO and OWF requires clarification and discussion. Here we will follow the framework of Asharov and Segev [AS15]. We elaborate below.

Theorem 1.1 (Informal). *There is no fully black-box reduction of any (even worst-case) hard problem in* SZK *to IO and OWPs.*

Corollary 1.2 (from *[SW14, Wat15]*, **Informal).** *There is no such reduction to (general) public-key encryption, oblivious transfer, deniable encryption, functional encryption, or any other object that has a black-box reduction to IO and OWPs.*

We would like to elaborate a bit more on what a black-box construction of a hard problem in SZK means. We shall focus on the characterization of SZK by the *statistical difference* promise problem [SV03]. In this problem, an instance is a pair of circuit samplers $C_0, C_1 : \{0,1\}^n \rightarrow \{0,1\}^m$ which induce distributions $\boldsymbol{C}_0$ and $\boldsymbol{C}_1$ where the distribution $\boldsymbol{C}_b$ obtained by evaluating the circuit C_b on a uniformly random input. The promise is that the statistical distance $s = \Delta(\boldsymbol{C}_0, \boldsymbol{C}_1)$ of the corresponding distributions is either large (say, $s \geq 2/3$) or small (say, $s \leq 1/3$). The problem, named $\mathbf{SD}^{1/3,2/3}$ (or just **SD**), is to decide which is the case.

Let us look at a specific example of the construction of such a problem from *rerandomizable encryption.* In a (say, symmetric-key) rerandomizable encryption scheme, on top of the usual encryption and decryption algorithms $(\mathsf{Enc}, \mathsf{Dec})$ there is a ciphertext rerandomization algorithm ReRand that can statistically refresh ciphertexts. Namely, for any ciphertext CT encrypting a bit b, $\mathsf{ReRand}(\mathsf{CT})$ produces a ciphertext that is statistically close to a fresh encryption $\mathsf{Enc}_{\mathsf{sk}}(b)$. This immediately gives rise to a hard statistical difference problem [BL13]: given a pair of ciphertexts $(\mathsf{CT}_0, \mathsf{CT}_1)$, decide whether the corresponding rerandomized distributions given by the circuits $(C_0(\cdot), C_1(\cdot)) := (\mathsf{ReRand}(\mathsf{CT}_0; \cdot), \mathsf{ReRand}(\mathsf{CT}_1; \cdot))$ are statistically far or close. Indeed, this corresponds to whether they encrypt the same bit or not, which is hard to decide by the security of the encryption scheme.

A feature of this reduction of hard statistical difference instances to rerandomizable encryption is that, similarly to most reductions in cryptography, it is *fully black-box* [RTV04] in the sense that the circuits C_0, C_1 only make black-box use of the encryption scheme's algorithms, and can in fact be represented as oracle-aided circuits $(C_0^{\mathsf{ReRand}(\cdot)}, C_1^{\mathsf{ReRand}(\cdot)})$. Furthermore, "hardness" can be shown by a black-box security proof that can use any decider for the problem in a black-box way to break the underlying encryption scheme. More generally, one can consider the statistical difference problem relative to different oracles implementing different cryptographic primitives and ask when can hardness be shown based on a black-box reduction. Theorem 1.1 rules out such reductions relative to IO and OWPs (and everything that follows from these in a fully black-box way). For more details, see Sect. 1.2 and the full version.

$\mathsf{NP} \cap \mathsf{coNP}$ *and Cryptography.* Hard (on average) problems in $\mathsf{NP} \cap \mathsf{coNP}$ are known to follow based on several number-theoretic problems in cryptography, such as Discrete Log, Factoring and Lattice Problems [Has88, LLJS90, AR04]. As in the previous section for SZK, we are interested in understanding which cryptographic primitives would imply such hardness, again with the intuition that this implies structure. For instance, it is known [Bra79] that any OWP $f : \{0,1\}^n \to \{0,1\}^n$ implies a hard problem in $\mathsf{NP} \cap \mathsf{coNP}$, e.g. given an index $i \in [n]$ and an image $f(x)$ find the ith preimage bit x_i. In contrast, Blum and Impagliazzo [BI87] and Rudich [Rud88] proved that seemingly unstructured objects like OWFs do not imply hardness in $\mathsf{NP} \cap \mathsf{coNP}$ by fully black-box reductions. In this context, a fully black-box reduction essentially means that the non-deterministic verifiers only make black-box use of the OWF (or OWP in the previous example) and the reduction establishing the hardness is also black-box (in both the decider and the OWF).[2]

But what about more structured primitives such as public-key encryption, oblivious transfer, or even IO? We rule out fully black-box reductions from OWFs (or even *injective OWFs*) and IO to hard problems in $\mathsf{NP} \cap \mathsf{coNP}$. Hence, also for the other primitives, which can be constructed from IO (with OWFs) in a fully black-box way.

Theorem 1.3 (Informal). *There is no fully black-box reduction of any (even worst-case) hard problem in* $\mathsf{NP} \cap \mathsf{coNP}$ *to IO and OWFs.*

Corollary 1.4 (from [SW14, Wat15] **Informal).** *There is no such reduction to (general) public-key encryption, oblivious transfer, deniable encryption, functional encryption, or any other object that has a black-box reduction to IO and OWFs.*

Our approach also gives a new (rather different) proof to the original separation between OWFs and $\mathsf{NP} \cap \mathsf{coNP}$ [BI87, Rud88]. For more details, see Sect. 1.2 and the full version.

We remark that unlike our result for SZK (which ruled out hard *promise problems*), the above result only rules out hard *languages* in $\mathsf{NP} \cap \mathsf{coNP}$. Indeed, Even et al. [ESY84] demonstrated promise problems in $\mathsf{NP} \cap \mathsf{coNP}$ that are NP-hard. Hence even the assumption $\mathsf{P} \neq \mathsf{NP}$ (let alone OWFs) gives us hard promise problems in $\mathsf{NP} \cap \mathsf{coNP}$. (See [Gol06] for further reading.)

Relation to the Work of Asharov and Segev. The flood of IO applications following, starting from [GGH+13b, SW14], has lead many to conjecture that IO may be "complete for cryptography" (assuming also OWFs, or just $\mathsf{NP} \not\subseteq \mathsf{ioBBP}$ [KMN+14]). Nevertheless, some cryptographic goals could not be constructed based on IO.

Asharov and Segev [AS15, AS16] were the first to initiate a formal study to understand *the limits of IO.* Our separations for IO are based on their framework [AS15]. We aim to draw the complexity-theoretic boundaries of IO. Indeed, black-box separations from IO require some care, given that the typical use of

[2] Roughly speaking, [BI87] rule out *perfectly correct constructions*, where the $\mathsf{NP} \cap \mathsf{coNP}$ structure is guaranteed for any implementation of the OWF oracle. In [Rud88], this is generalized also to *almost perfectly correct constructions* that only work for an overwhelming fraction of OWF oracles. We also rule out constructions that are perfectly correct.

IO makes non-black-box use of the circuits it obfuscates and thus any associated cryptographic primitive such as OWFs. The Asharov-Segev framework considers obfuscators that take as input circuits with OWF (or OWP) gates. They observe, most known IO-based constructions fall into this category. Thus, a separation in this model allows deriving the corresponding separations between SZK or NP ∩ coNP and a wide variety of cryptographic primitives. See Sect. 1.2 for more details.

In terms of results, they show that collision-resistant hashing and (domain invariant) OWPs do not have black-box reductions to IO (and OWFs). Our separation of IO and NP ∩ coNP is more general and implies their previous result for OWPs (and gives a rather different proof for this fact). Their result for collision-resistant hashing is not captured by our results (indeed collision-resistance is not known to imply hardness in either SZK or NP ∩ coNP). We also stress that our separation of SZK from IO and OWPs does not follow from their results; indeed, SZK-hardness is not known to imply collision-resistance.[3]

Indistinguishability Obfuscation: Perspective. Since the breakthrough of [GGH+13b], the notion of IO has been extensively studied. While we already understand that IO has far reaching implications, our understanding of how it can be constructed and under what assumptions is still at an early stage. Indeed, basing IO on solid foundations is one of cryptography's greatest challenges today. In this context, we stress that the results presented in this work hold regardless of the state of existing candidates. In fact, even if it turned out that there is no secure realization of IO, the separation of SZK and NP ∩ coNP from primitives such as public-key encryption, which follow from IO, still holds. The expressiveness of IO (established in [GGH+13b,SW14] and onwards) allows us to prove many separations in one shot. (Indeed, three years ago we would have probably addressed each primitive separately.)

As for the search for candidates itself, while at this point candidates are based on lattice-related problems that do break in SZK, our work suggests the theoretical possibility that IO candidates may not require such structure. A similar conclusion is true of course for the much more basic and long-studied question of public-key encryption. Almost all known public-key encryption candidates rely on very algebraic assumptions (that do break in SZK or NP ∩ coNP). Constructing public key encryption from less structured assumptions remains a fascinating open question. While there has been initial steps trying to diverge from such structure [Ale03,ABW10], there is yet a long way to go.

On TFNP *vs.* NP ∩ coNP. One of the corollaries of our result is a separation between SZK and NP ∩ coNP from the complexity class PPAD. PPAD, a subclass

[3] We note that previous work [Ost91,OV08] does imply that constant-round statistically-hiding commitments have a black-box reduction to any *hard-on-average* SZK problem. However, [AS15] do not rule these out (but only collision-resistant hashing). We also note that in any case, our result also rules out constructions of worst-case hard SZK problems (rather than average-case hard problems).

of total NP search problems called TFNP [MP91], was defined by Papadimitriou [Pap94] and has been shown to capture the complexity of computing Nash equilibria [DGP06,CDT09]. It was recently shown [BPR15] that IO and injective OWFs can be used (in a black-box way) to construct hard problems in PPAD. Put together with our separation, we get that there is no black-box construction of an SZK (resp. NP ∩ coNP) hard problem from PPAD-hardness.[4]

Given that TFNP, which contains PPAD, is commonly thought of as a search version of NP∩coNP, it is interesting to note that the result shows that hardness in NP ∩ coNP (of decisional problems) does not follow from hardness in TFNP (aka, hardness of search problems) in a black-box way. Namely, there is no black-box "search-to-decision reduction" between these classes.

The Positive Result: Collision-Resistant Hashing from Strong SZK*-Hardness.* We end our paper with a positive result. While most of our focus has been on showing that hardness in SZK and NP ∩ coNP does *not* follow from cryptography, here we ask the "inverse question", namely whether certain cryptographic primitives can be built from other cryptographic primitives together with hardness in certain structured complexity classes. Little is known in this direction with the exception of the beautiful work of Ostrovsky [Ost91] which constructs a OWF from average-case SZK-hardness, and the recent work of Applebaum and Raykov [AR16] who showed that average-case hardness in the subclass PRE ⊆ SRE ⊆ SZK of languages with a perfect randomized encoding gives us collision-resistant hashing.

We construct collision-resistant hashing from a strong form of SZK-hardness and IO. It was previously known [AS15] that IO by itself does not imply collision-resistant hashing in a black-box way; we show that it does if one adds SZK-hardness as a "catalyst". Slightly more precisely, in the SZK-complete problem $\mathbf{SD}^{1/3,2/3}$ is required to distinguish between distributions that are 1/3-close from ones that are 2/3-far. We show that IO together with average-case hardness of $\mathbf{SD}^{0,1}$ (a stronger assumption) implies collision-resistant hashing.

Theorem 1.5 (Informal). *Assuming average-case hardness of* $\mathbf{SD}^{0,1}$ *and the existence of IO, there is a collision-resistant hashing scheme.*

Organization. Due to the paucity of space, most of the proofs are deferred to the full version. We give an overview of the methodology and techniques used in the following Sect. 1.2. The black-box separation between SZK and IO (plus OWPs) is stated in Sect. 2. The separation between NP ∩ coNP and IO (plus injective OWFs) is described in Sect. 3.

1.2 Overview of Techniques

We now give an overview of our approach and main ideas. We start by discussing how to capture fully black-box constructions in the context of indistinguishabil-

[4] We note that in concurrent and independent work, Rosen et al. [RSS16] show that one-way functions do not have black-box reductions to PPAD-hardness, which combined with [Ost91], also yields a separation between SZK and PPAD.

ity obfuscation following [AS15]. We then recall the common methodology for ruling out black-box constructions [IR89, RTV04, BBF13], and explain the main ideas behind our impossibility results for SZK and NP ∩ coNP. In the last part of this section, we outline the construction of collision-resistant hashing from indistinguishability obfuscation and SZK-hardness and the main ideas behind it.

Indistinguishability Obfuscation and Black-Box Constructions. Traditionally, when thinking about a *black-box construction* of one cryptographic primitive $\mathcal{P}'$ (e.g., a pseudo-random generator) from a primitive $\mathcal{P}$ (e.g., a one-way function), we mean that all algorithms in the construction of $\mathcal{P}'$ invoke $\mathcal{P}$ as a black-box, oblivious of its actual implementation. This is hardly the case in constructions based on indistinguishability obfuscation where circuits that explicitly invoke the primitive $\mathcal{P}$ may be obfuscated.

Nonetheless, as observed by Asharov and Segev [AS15], in almost all existing constructions, the code implementing $\mathcal{P}$ is used in a very restricted manner. Typically, obfuscated circuits can be implemented as oracle aided circuits $C^{\mathcal{P}}$ that are completely black-box in $\mathcal{P}$, where $\mathcal{P}$ is some low-level primitive, such as a one-way function. Indeed, in most cases the circuits obfuscated are symmetric-key primitives, such as puncturable pseudo-random functions [SW14], which can be constructed in a black-box way from one-way functions (in some constructions more structured low-level primitives may be used, like injective one-way functions, or one-way permutations). Furthermore, in these constructions, the obfuscator $i\mathcal{O}$ itself is also treated as a black-box.

Accordingly, almost all existing constructions based on indistinguishability obfuscation can be cast into a model in which indistinguishability obfuscation exists for oracle-aided circuits $C^{\mathcal{P}}$, where $\mathcal{P}$ is say a one-way function, and both $\mathcal{P}$ and the obfuscator $i\mathcal{O}$ can only be accessed as black-boxes. On top of that, they can be proven secure in this model by a *black-box reduction* that makes black-box use of $(\mathcal{P}, i\mathcal{O})$ and any attacker against the constructed primitive $\mathcal{P}'$. Such constructions where both the construction itself and the reduction are black-box are called *fully black-box constructions* [RTV04]. Following Asharov and Segev [AS15, AS16], we shall prove our results in this model, ruling out black-box constructions of hard problems in SZK and NP ∩ coNP based on indistinguishability obfuscation for oracle-aided circuits. Further details follow.

Ruling out Black-Box Reductions. We prove our results in the model described above following the methodology of oracle separations (see e.g. [IR89, Sim98, RTV04, HR04]). Concretely, to prove that there is no fully black-box construction of a primitive $\mathcal{P}'$ from primitive $\mathcal{P}$, we demonstrate oracles $(\Psi, \mathcal{A})$ such that:

- relative to Ψ, there exists a construction $C^{\Psi}_{\mathcal{P}}$ realizing $\mathcal{P}$ that is secure in the presence of $\mathcal{A}$,
- but *any* construction $C^{\Psi}_{\mathcal{P}'}$ realizing $\mathcal{P}'$ can be broken in the presence of $\mathcal{A}$.

Indeed, if such oracles $(\Psi, \mathcal{A})$ exist, then no efficient reduction will be able to use (as a black-box) the attacker $\mathcal{A}$ against $\mathcal{P}'$ to break $\mathcal{P}$ (as the construction of $\mathcal{P}$ is secure in the presence of $\mathcal{A}$). In our case, we would like to apply this paradigm rule out black-box constructions of hard instances in either SZK or $\mathsf{NP} \cap \mathsf{coNP}$ from a low-level primitive (e.g. a one-way function) indistinguishability obfuscation for oracle-aided circuits. We next outline the main ideas behind the construction and analysis of the oracles $(\Psi, \mathcal{A})$ in each of the two cases.

Ruling out Black-Box Constructions of Hard SZK *Problems.* As explained in the previous section, we focus on the characterization of SZK by its complete problem: the statistical difference problem **SD** [SV03]. We demonstrate oracles $(\Psi, \mathcal{A})$ such that relative to Ψ there exist constructions of one-way permutations (OWPs) and IO for circuits with OWP gates, and these constructions are secure in the presence of $\mathcal{A}$. At the same time, $\mathcal{A}$ will decide (in the worst-case) $\mathbf{SD}^{\Psi}$. Since **SD** is complete for SZK in a relativizing manner, deciding $\mathbf{SD}^{\Psi}$ suffices to break SZK^{Ψ}. That is, $\mathcal{A}$ will decide *all* instances (C_0^{Ψ}, C_1^{Ψ}) of circuit samplers that only use the IO and OWPs realized by Ψ in a black-box manner. We next explain how each of the two are constructed.

The construction of Ψ follows a general recipe suggested in [AS15,AS16]. The oracle consists of three parts $(f, \mathcal{O}, \mathsf{Eval}^{f,\mathcal{O}})$ where:

1. f is a random permutation, realizing the one-way permutation primitive.
2. $\mathcal{O}$ is a random injective function, realizing the obfuscation algorithm. It takes as input an oracle-aided circuit $C^{(\cdot)}$ along with randomness r and outputs an obfuscation $\widehat{C} = \mathcal{O}(C, r)$.
3. $\mathsf{Eval}^{\mathcal{O},f}$ realizes evaluation of obfuscated circuits. On input $(\widehat{C}, x)$, it inverts $\mathcal{O}$ to find (C, r), and outputs $C^f(x)$. If $\widehat{C}$ is not in the image of $\mathcal{O}$, it returns $\perp$.

The above construction readily satisfies the syntactic (or "functionality") requirements of one-way permutations and indistinguishability obfuscation. Furthermore, using standard techniques, it is not hard to show that relative to Ψ, the function f is one-way and $\mathcal{O}$ satisfies IO indistinguishability requirement. The challenge is to now come up with an oracle $\mathcal{A}$ that, on one hand, will decide $\mathbf{SD}^{\Psi}$, but on the other, will not compromise the security of the latter primitives.

Recall that deciding $\mathbf{SD}^{\Psi}$ means that given two oracle-aided circuit samplers (C_0, C_1) such that the statistical distance of the corresponding distributions $(\boldsymbol{C}_0^{\Psi}, \boldsymbol{C}_1^{\Psi})$ is $s = \Delta(\boldsymbol{C}_0^{\Psi}, \boldsymbol{C}_1^{\Psi}) \in [0, \frac{1}{3}] \cup [\frac{2}{3}, 1]$, the oracle $\mathcal{A}$ must decide in which of the two intervals s lies, whereas if the promise is not satisfied and $s \in (\frac{1}{3}, \frac{2}{3})$, there is no requirement whatsoever. With this in mind, a first naive attempt would be the following. $\mathcal{A}$ will have unbounded access to Ψ, give a query (C_0, C_1), it would compute $s = \Delta(\boldsymbol{C}_0, \boldsymbol{C}_1)$, and simply say whether $s < \frac{1}{2}$ or $s \geq \frac{1}{2}$. While such an oracle would definitely decide $\mathbf{SD}^{\Psi}$, it is not too hard to show that it is simply too powerful, and would not only break IO and OWPs, but would, in fact, allow solving any problem in NP^{Ψ} (or even in PP^{Ψ}). Other naive attempts such as refusing to answer outside the promise intervals, encounter a similar problem.

At high-level, the problem with such oracles is that solutions to hard problems can be easily correlated with "tiny" differences in the statistical distance of the two input circuits, whereas the above oracle may reflect tiny changes when the statistical distance is close to some threshold (1/2 in the above example) on which the oracle changes its behaviour. This motivates our actual definition of $\mathcal{A}$ as a *noisy oracle* that produces its answer, not according to some fixed threshold, but according to a random threshold, chosen afresh for each and every query. Concretely, the oracle, which we call StaDif^{Ψ}, for any query (C_0, C_1), chooses a uniformly random threshold $t \leftarrow (\frac{1}{3}, \frac{1}{3})$, and answers accordingly:

$$\mathsf{StaDif}^{\Psi}(C_0, C_1) = \begin{cases} Y & \text{if } s \geq t \text{ (far distributions)} \\ N & \text{if } s < t \text{ (similar distributions)} \end{cases}.$$

The main challenge in proving that the security of the IO and OWPs realized by $\mathcal{A}$ is not compromised by this oracle is that StaDif^{Ψ} has the power to query Ψ on exponentially many points in order to compute s. For instance, it may query Ψ on the preimage of a OWP challenge $f(x)$ or of a given obfuscation $\mathcal{O}(C, r)$. The key observation behind the proof is that the oracle's final answer still does not reflect how Ψ behaves locally on random points.

Intuitively, choosing the threshold t at random, for each query (C_0, C_1), guarantees that with high probability t is "far" from the corresponding statistical distance $s = \Delta(C_0^{\Psi}, C_1^{\Psi})$. Thus, changing the oracle Ψ on, say, a single input x, such as the preimage of an OWP challenge $f(x)$, should not significantly change s and will not affect the oracle's answer; that is, unless the circuits query Ψ on x with high probability to begin with. We give a reduction showing that we can always assume that (C_0, C_1) are "smooth", in the sense that they do not make any specific query to Ψ with too high probability.

Following this intuition, we are able to show that through such local changes that go undetected by StaDif^{Ψ}, we can move to an ideal world where inverting the OWP or breaking IO can be easily shown to be impossible. We refer the reader to the full version for further details.

Ruling out Black-Box Constructions of Hard $\mathsf{NP} \cap \mathsf{coNP}$ *Problems.* As mentioned earlier, a fully black-box construction of hard problems in $\mathsf{NP} \cap \mathsf{coNP}$ is actually known assuming one-way permutations (OWPs), and cannot be ruled out as in the case of SZK. Instead, we rule out constructions from (non-surjective) injective one-way functions (IOWFs) and IO for circuits with IOWF gates. This generalizes several previous results by Blum and Impagliazzo [BI87] and Rudich [Rud88], showing that OWFs do not give hardness in $\mathsf{NP} \cap \mathsf{coNP}$, by Matsuda and Matsuura [MM11], showing that IOWFs do not give OWPs (which are a special case of hardness $\mathsf{NP} \cap \mathsf{coNP}$), and by Asharov and Segev [AS16], showing that OWFs and IO for circuits with OWF gates do not give OWPs. In fact, our approach yields a new (and rather different) proof for each one of these results.

We follow a similar methodology to one we used for the case of SZK. That is, we would like to come up with oracles $(\Psi, \mathcal{A})$ such that Ψ realizes IOWFs and IO for circuits with IOWFs gates, which are both secure in the presence of $\mathcal{A}$, whereas black-box constructions of problems in $\mathsf{NP} \cap \mathsf{coNP}$ from these primitives can be easily solved by $\mathcal{A}$. By black-box constructions here we mean a pair of efficient oracle-aided non-deterministic verifiers $V_0^{(\cdot)}, V_1^{(\cdot)}$ that for every oracle Ψ implementing IOWFs and IO, yield co-languages $\overline{L}^{\Psi}, L^{\Psi}$ in $\mathsf{NP} \cap \mathsf{coNP}[\Psi]$.

The requirement that V_0, V_1 give a language in $\mathsf{NP} \cap \mathsf{coNP}$ for *every* oracle implementing IOWFs and IO follows previous modeling [BI87],[5] and aligns with how we usually think about *correctness* of black-box constructions of cryptographic primitives. For instance, the construction of public-key encryption from trapdoor permutations is promised to be correct, for all oracles implementing the trapdoor permutation. Similarly, the construction of hard $\mathsf{NP} \cap \mathsf{coNP}$ languages from one-way permutations, give an $\mathsf{NP} \cap \mathsf{coNP}$ language for any oracle implementing a permutation.[6]

We stress that a construction where correctness is only guaranteed for particular (even if natural) oracles may definitely exist. This is for example the case if we only consider implementations of IO similar to those presented above in the context of SZK. Indeed, in that construction the implementation of IO has an additional property—it allows identifying *invalid obfuscations* (the Eval oracle would simply return $\perp$ on such obfuscations). This "verifiability" property coupled with the injectivity of obfuscators actually imply a hard problem in $\mathsf{NP} \cap \mathsf{coNP}$ in a black-box way.[7] Our separation thus leverages the fact that IO need not necessarily be verifiable, and rules out constructions that are required to be correct for any implementation of IO, even a non-verifiable one.

Accordingly, the oracles $\Psi = (f, \mathcal{O}, \mathsf{Eval}^{f,\mathcal{O}})$ that we consider are a tweaked version of the oracles considered in the SZK case. Now f is a random injective function that is expanding, rather than a permutation, the oracle $\mathcal{O}$ is defined as before, and the oracle $\mathsf{Eval}^{f,\mathcal{O}}$ is defined as before for valid obfuscations $\widehat{C} \in \mathrm{Image}(\mathcal{O})$ *but is allowed to act arbitrarily for invalid obfuscations.* As for $\mathcal{A}$, this time it is trivially implemented by an oracle Decide^{Ψ} that, given input x, simply returns the unique bit b such that $V_b(x) = 1$, namely it just decides the corresponding language L^{Ψ}.

In the results mentioned above [Rud88, MM11, AS16], it is actually shown that any query to such an oracle can be completely simulated with a small number of queries to Ψ.[8] We do not show such a simulation process. Instead, we take a different approach inspired by our proof for the SZK setting described above. Roughly speaking, we show that somewhat similarly to our statistical difference oracle StaDif^{Ψ}, the oracle Decide^{Ψ} is also rather robust to random local changes. The main observation here is that for any fixed yes-instance $x \in L^{\Psi}$, tweaking Ψ at a random input into a new oracle Ψ', it is likely that x will still

---

[5] Rudich [Rud88] also considered a slight relaxation of constructions that are correct for an overwhelming fraction of oracles rather than all.

[6] We note that this issue does not come up for black-box constructions of SZK *promise* problems, because the construction is allowed to yield instances that do not obey the promise; there correctness is always guaranteed, and the only question is whether the instances that do satisfy the promise are hard to decide.

[7] E.g. the language of all valid obfuscations and indices i, such that the ith bit of the obfuscated circuit is 1.

[8] More accurately, this is the case for Rudich's result for $\mathsf{NP} \cap \mathsf{coNP}$, whereas for the other results that rule out constructions of one-way permutations, one can simulate an analog of Decide that inverts the permutation.

be a yes-instance in $L^{\Psi'}$, as long as Ψ' is in our allowed family of oracles and $L^{\Psi'}$ is indeed in $\mathsf{NP} \cap \mathsf{coNP}[\Psi']$ (and the same is true for no-instances).

In slightly more detail, fixing a witness w such that $V_1^{\Psi}(x, w) = 1$, we can show that since V_1 makes a small number of oracle calls, with high probability tweaking the oracle Ψ at a random place will not affect these oracle calls and thus $V_1^{\Psi'}(x, w) = V_1^{\Psi}(x, w) = 1$. Then, assuming $L^{\Psi'}$ is guaranteed to be in $\mathsf{NP} \cap \mathsf{coNP}$, we can deduce that x must still a yes-instance (other witnesses for this fact may be added or disappear, but this does not change the oracle's answer). In the body, we argue that indeed $L^{\Psi'} \in \mathsf{NP} \cap \mathsf{coNP}[\Psi']$, where we strongly rely on the fact that arbitrary behavior of Eval is permitted on invalid obfuscations.

Once again, we show that through local changes that go undetected by Decide^{Ψ}, we can move to an ideal world where inverting the IOWF or breaking IO can be easily shown to be impossible. We refer the reader to Sect. 3 for further details.

Implied Separations. As a result of the two separations discussed above, we can rule out black-box constructions of hard problems in SZK or $\mathsf{NP} \cap \mathsf{coNP}$ from various cryptographic primitives or complexity classes. This essentially includes all primitives that have fully black-box constructions from OWPs (or IOWFs) and IO for circuits with OWP (or IWOF) gates. This includes public-key encryption, oblivious transfer, deniable encryption [SW14], functional encryption [Wat15], delegation, [BGL+15,CHJV15,KLW15], hard (on-average) PPAD instances [BPR15], and more.

We note that there a few applications of IO that do not fall under this characterization. For instance, the construction of IO for Turing machines from IO-based succinct randomized encodings [BGL+15,CHJV15,KLW15] involves obfuscating a circuit that itself outputs (smaller) obfuscated circuits. To capture this, we would need to extend the above model to IO for circuits that can also make IO oracle calls (on smaller circuits). Another example is the construction of non-interactive witness indistinguishable proofs from IO [BP15]. There an obfuscated circuit may get as input another obfuscated circuit and would have to internally run it; furthermore, in this application, the code of the obfuscator is used in a (non-black-box) ZAP. Extending the above model to account for this type of IO applications is an interesting question that we leave for future exploration.

The Positive Result: Collision-Resistance from IO and SZK*-Hardness.* We now described the main ideas behind our construction of collision-resistant hash functions. The starting point for the construction is the work of Ishai et al. [IKO05] that shows how to construct collision-resistant hash functions from commitments that are additively homomorphic (for simplicity, say over $\mathbb{F}_2$). The idea is simple: we can hash ℓ bits to m bits, where m is the size of a single bit commitment and ℓ can be arbitrarily longer, as follows. The hash key is a commitment $\gamma := (\mathsf{com}(\beta_1), \ldots, \mathsf{com}(\beta_\ell))$ to a random vector $\beta \in \mathbb{F}_2^\ell$, and hashing $x \in \mathbb{F}_2^\ell$, is done by homomorphically computing a commitment to the inner product

$\mathsf{CRH}_\gamma(x) = \mathsf{com}(\langle\beta, x\rangle)$. Intuitively, the reason this works is that any collision in CRH_γ reveals a vector that is orthogonal to β and thus leaks information about it and violating the hiding of the commitment.

At a high-level, we aim to mimic the above construction based on obfuscation. As a key for the collision-resistant hash we can obfuscate a program Π_β associated with a random vector β that given x outputs a commitment $\mathsf{com}(\langle\beta, x\rangle)$, where the commitment is derandomized using a PRF.[9] The obfuscation $i\mathcal{O}(\Pi_\beta)$ can be thought of as the commitment to β, and evaluating this program at x, corresponds to homomorphic evaluation. Despite the clear intuition behind this construction, it is not clear how to prove its security based on IO. In fact, by the work of Asharov and Segev [AS15], it cannot be proven based on a black-box reduction as long as plain statistically-binding commitments are used, as these can be constructed from OWPs in a fully black-box manner, and [AS15] rule out black-box constructions of collision-resistant hashing from OWPs and IO for circuits with OWP gates.

We show, however, that relying on a relaxed notion of perfectly-hiding commitments, as well as subexponential hardness of IO and puncturable PRFs, the construction can be proven secure. The perfect hiding of the commitment is leveraged in a probabilistic IO argument [CLTV15] that involves a number of hybrids larger than the overall number of commitments. We then observe that these relaxed commitments follow from average-case hardness of the polar statistical difference problem $\mathbf{SD}^{0,1}$.[10]

2 One-Way Permutations, Indistinguishability Obfuscation, and Hardness in SZK

In this section, we ask which cryptographic primitives imply hardness in the class statistical zero-knowledge (SZK). Roughly speaking, we show that one-way permutations (OWPs) and indistinguishability obfuscation (IO), for circuits with OWP-gates, do not give rise to a black-box construction of hard problems in SZK. This, in turn implies that many cryptographic primitives (e.g., public-key encryption, functional encryption, and delegation), and hardness in certain low-level complexity classes (e.g. PPAD), also do not yield black-box constructions of hard problems in SZK.

We first motivate and define a framework of SZK relative to oracles, define fully black-box constructions of hard SZK problems, and then move on to the actual separation.

2.1 SZK and Statistical Difference

The notion of statistical zero-knowledge proofs was introduced in the seminal work of Goldwasser et al. [GMR85]. The class of promise problems with

[9] In the body, we describe a slightly more abstract construction where inner product is replaced by an arbitrary 2-universal hash function.

[10] Similar SZK-hardness is known to imply statistically-hiding commitments against malicious receivers, but with a larger (constant) number of rounds [OV08].

statistical zero-knowledge proofs (SZK) can be characterized by several complete problems, such as *statistical difference* [SV03] and *entropy difference* [GV99] (see also [Vad99] and references within). We shall focus on the characterization of SZK by the statistical difference problem. Here an instance is a pair of circuit samplers $C_0, C_1 : \{0,1\}^n \rightarrow \{0,1\}^m$ with the promise that the statistical distance $s = \Delta(C_0, C_1)$ of the corresponding distributions is either large (say, $s \geq 2/3$) or small (say, $s \leq 1/3$). The problem is to decide which is the case.

Hard Statistical Difference Problems from Cryptography: Motivation. SZK hardness, and in particular hard statistical difference problems, are known to follow from various number-theoretic and lattice problems that are commonly used in cryptography, such as Decision Diffie-Hellman, Quadratic Residuosity, and Learning with Errors. We ask more generally which cryptographic primitives can be shown to imply such hardness, with the intuition that such primitives are *structured* in a certain way. In particular, whereas one would not expect a completely unstructured object like one-way functions to imply such hardness, what can we say for instance about public-key encryption, or even indistinguishability obfuscation (which has proven to be structured enough to yield almost any known cryptographic goal).

We prove that none of these primitives imply such hardness through the natural class of black-box constructions and security reductions. To understand what a black-box construction of a hard statistical difference problem means, let us look at a specific example of the construction of such a problem from *rerandomizable encryption*. In a (say, symmetric-key) rerandomizable encryption scheme, on top of the usual encryption and decryption algorithms $(\mathsf{Enc}, \mathsf{Dec})$ there is a ciphertext rerandomization algorithm ReRand that can statistically refresh ciphertexts. Namely, for any ciphertext CT encrypting a bit b, $\mathsf{ReRand}(\mathsf{CT})$ produces a ciphertext that is statistically close to a fresh encryption $\mathsf{Enc}(b)$. Note that this immediately gives rise to a hard statistical difference problem: given a pair of ciphertexts $(\mathsf{CT}, \mathsf{CT}')$, decide whether the corresponding rerandomized distributions given by the circuits $(C_0(\cdot), C_1(\cdot)) := (\mathsf{ReRand}(\mathsf{CT}; \cdot), \mathsf{ReRand}(\mathsf{CT}'; \cdot))$ are statistically far or close. Indeed, this corresponds to whether they encrypt the same bit or not, which is hard to decide by the security of the encryption scheme.

A feature of this construction of hard statistical difference instances is that, similarly to most constructions in cryptography, it is *fully black-box* [RTV04] in the sense that the circuits C_0, C_1 only make black-box use of the encryption scheme's algorithms, and can in fact be represented as oracle-aided circuits $(C_0^{\mathsf{ReRand}(\cdot)}, C_1^{\mathsf{ReRand}(\cdot)})$. Furthermore, "hardness" can be shown by a black-box reduction that can use any decider for the problem in a black-box way to break the underlying encryption scheme. More generally, one can consider the statistical difference problem relative to different oracles implementing different cryptographic primitives and ask when can hardness be shown based on a black-box reduction. We will rule out such reductions relative to IO and OWPs (and everything that follows from these in a fully black-box way).

2.2 Fully Black-Box Constructions of Hard SD Problems from IO and OWPs

We start by defining statistical difference problem relative to oracles. In the following definition, for an oracle-aided (sampler) circuit $C^{(\cdot)}$ with n-bit input and an oracle Ψ, we denote by $\boldsymbol{C}^{\Psi}$ the output distribution $C^{\Psi}(r)$ where $r \leftarrow \{0,1\}^n$. For two distributions $\mathbf{X}$ and $\mathbf{Y}$ we denote their statistical distance by $\Delta(\mathbf{X}, \mathbf{Y})$.

Definition 2.1 (Statistical difference relative to oracles). *For an oracle Ψ, the statistical difference promise problem relative to Ψ, denoted as $\mathbf{SD}^{\Psi} = (\mathbf{SD}^{\Psi}_{Y}, \mathbf{SD}^{\Psi}_{N})$, is given by*

$$\mathbf{SD}^{\Psi}_{Y} = \left\{ (C_0, C_1) \,\middle|\, \Delta(\boldsymbol{C}^{\Psi}_0, \boldsymbol{C}^{\Psi}_1) \geq \frac{2}{3} \right\},$$

$$\mathbf{SD}^{\Psi}_{N} = \left\{ (C_0, C_1) \,\middle|\, \Delta(\boldsymbol{C}^{\Psi}_0, \boldsymbol{C}^{\Psi}_1) \leq \frac{1}{3} \right\}.$$

We now formally define the class of constructions and reductions ruled out. That is, *fully black-box* constructions of hard statistical distance problems from OWPs and IO for OWP-aided circuits. The definition is similar in spirit to those in [AS15, AS16], adapted to our context of SZK-hardness.

Definition 2.2. *A fully black-box construction of a hard statistical distance problem from OWPs and IO for the class $\mathcal{C}$ of circuits with OWP-gates consists of a collection of oracle-aided circuit pairs $\Pi^{(\cdot)} = \left\{ \Pi^{(\cdot)}_n = \left\{ (C^{(\cdot)}_0, C^{(\cdot)}_1) \in \{0,1\}^{n \times 2} \right\} \right\}_{n \in \mathbb{N}}$ and a probabilistic oracle-aided reduction $\mathcal{R}$ that satisfy:*

- ***Black-box security proof:*** *There exist functions $q_{\mathcal{R}}(\cdot), \varepsilon_{\mathcal{R}}(\cdot)$ such that the following holds. Let f be any distribution on permutations and let $i\mathcal{O}$ be any distribution on functions such that $\widehat{C}^f \equiv C^f$ for any $C^{(\cdot)}$ and r, where $\widehat{C}^{(\cdot)} := i\mathcal{O}(C^{(\cdot)}, r)$. Then for any probabilistic oracle-aided $\mathcal{A}$ that* decides Π in the worst-case, *namely, for all $n \in \mathbb{N}$*

$$\Pr_{f, i\mathcal{O}, \mathcal{A}} \left[\mathcal{A}^{f, i\mathcal{O}}(C_0, C_1) = B \quad \textit{for all} \quad \begin{matrix} (C_0, C_1) \in \Pi_n, B \in \{Y, N\} \\ \textit{such that } (C_0, C_1) \in \mathbf{SD}^{f, i\mathcal{O}}_{B} \end{matrix} \right] = 1$$

the reduction breaks either f or $i\mathcal{O}$, *namely, for infinitely many $n \in \mathbb{N}$ either*

$$\Pr_{\substack{x \leftarrow \{0,1\}^n \\ f, i\mathcal{O}, \mathcal{A}}} \left[\mathcal{R}^{\mathcal{A}, f, i\mathcal{O}}(f(x)) = x \right] \geq \varepsilon_{\mathcal{R}}(n),$$

or

$$\left| \Pr\left[\mathsf{Exp}^{\mathsf{iO}}_{(f, i\mathcal{O}), i\mathcal{O}, \mathcal{C}, \mathcal{R}^{\mathcal{A}}}(n) = 1 \right] - \frac{1}{2} \right| \geq \varepsilon_{\mathcal{R}}(n),$$

where in both $\mathcal{R}$ makes at most $q_{\mathcal{R}}(n)$ queries to any of its oracles $(\mathcal{A}, f, i\mathcal{O})$, and any query $(C_0^{(\cdot)}, C_1^{(\cdot)})$ it makes to $\mathcal{A}$ consists of circuits that also make at most $q_{\mathcal{R}}(n)$ queries to their oracles $(f, i\mathcal{O})$. The random variable $\mathsf{Exp}^{\mathsf{iO}}_{(f,i\mathcal{O}),i\mathcal{O},\mathcal{C},\mathcal{R}^{\mathcal{A}}}(n)$ represents the reductions winning probability in the IO security game relative to $(f, i\mathcal{O})$.

We make several remarks about the definition:

- **Correctness.** Typically, we also require certain *correctness* from the black-box construction. For instance, in the next section, we shall require that the construction always satisfies the $\mathsf{NP} \cap \mathsf{coNP}$ structure. In the above definition, the construction is allowed to yield instances $(C_0^{f,i\mathcal{O}}, C_1^{f,i\mathcal{O}})$ that do not satisfy the SZK promise; namely $(C_0^{f,i\mathcal{O}}, C_1^{f,i\mathcal{O}}) \notin \mathbf{SD}_Y^{f,i\mathcal{O}} \cup \mathbf{SD}_N^{f,i\mathcal{O}}$. It is natural to think of more stringent definitions that require that the corresponding problem $\Pi^{f,i\mathcal{O}}$ is non-trivial, in the sense that $\Pi^{f,i\mathcal{O}} \cap \mathbf{SD}_Y^{f,i\mathcal{O}} \neq \emptyset$ and $\Pi^{f,i\mathcal{O}} \cap \mathbf{SD}_N^{f,i\mathcal{O}} \neq \emptyset$ (which is the case for known constructions of SZK hardness from cryptographic primitives). Our impossibility is more general and would, in particular, rule out such definitions as well.
- **Worst-Case vs. Average-Case Hardness.** In the above, we address *worst-case hardness*, in the sense that the reduction $\mathcal{R}$ has to break the underlying primitives only given a decider $\mathcal{A}$ that is always correct. One could further ask whether IO and OWPs even imply average-case hardness in SZK (as do many of the algebraic hardness assumptions in cryptography). Ruling out worst-case hardness (as we will do shortly) in particular rules out such average-case hardness as well.
- **IO for Oracle-Aided Circuits.** Following [AS15, AS16], we consider indistinguishability obfuscation for oracle-aided circuits C^f that can make calls to the one-way permutation oracle. This model captures constructions where IO is applied to circuits that use pseudo-random generators, puncturable pseudo-random functions, or injective one-way functions as all of those have fully black-box constructions from one-way permutations (see further discussion in [AS15]). This includes almost all known constructions from IO, including public-key encryption, deniable encryption [SW14], functional encryption [Wat15], delegation [BGL+15, CHJV15, KLW15], and hard (on-average) PPAD instances [BPR15]. Accordingly, separating SZK from IO and OWPs in this model, results in a similar separation between SZK and any one of these primitives.

  We note that there a few applications though that do not fall under this model. The first is in applications where the obfuscated circuit might itself output (smaller) obfuscated circuit, for instance in the construction of IO for Turing machines from IO-based succinct randomized encodings [BGL+15, CHJV15, KLW15]. To capture such applications, one would have to extend the model to also account for circuits with IO gates (and not only OWP gates). A second example is the construction of non-interactive witness indistinguishable proofs from IO [BP15]. There an obfuscated circuit may get as input another obfuscated circuit and would have to internally run it;

furthermore, in this application, the code of the obfuscator is used in a (non-black-box) ZAP. Extending our results (and those of [AS15, AS16]) to these models is an interesting question, left for future work.
- **Security Loss.** In the above definition the functions $q_{\mathcal{R}}$ and $\varepsilon_{\mathcal{R}}$ capture the *security loss* of the reduction. Most commonly in cryptography, the query complexity is polynomial $q_{\mathcal{R}}(n) = n^{O(1)}$ and the probability of breaking the underlying primitive is inverse polynomial $\varepsilon_{\mathcal{R}}(n) = n^{-O(1)}$. Our lower-bounds will in-fact apply for *exponential* $q_{\mathcal{R}}, \varepsilon_{\mathcal{R}}^{-1}$. This allows capturing also constructions that rely on subexponentially secure primitives (e.g., [BGL+15, CHJV15, KLW15, BPR15, BPW16]).

Ruling Out Fully Black-Box Constructions: A Road Map. Our main result in this section is that a fully black-box construction of a hard statistical difference problem from IO and OWPs does not exist. Furthermore, this holds even if the latter primitives are exponentially secure.

Theorem 2.3. *Any fully black-box construction of a statistical difference problem Π from OWPs and IO for circuits with OWP gates has an exponential security loss:* $\max(q_{\mathcal{R}}(n), \varepsilon_{\mathcal{R}}^{-1}(n)) \geq \Omega(2^{n/12})$.

The proof of the theorem follows a common methodology (applied for instance in [HR04, HHRS15, AS15]). We exhibit two (distributions on) oracles $(\Psi, \mathsf{StaDif}^{\Psi})$, where Ψ realizes OWPs and IO for circuits with OWP gates, and StaDif^{Ψ} that decides $\mathbf{SD}^{\Psi}$, the statistical difference problem relative to Ψ, in the worst case. Since $\mathbf{SD}$ is complete for SZK in a relativizing manner, solving $\mathbf{SD}^{\Psi}$ suffices to break SZK^{Ψ}. We then show that the primitives realized by Ψ are (exponentially) secure even in the presence of StaDif^{Ψ}. Then viewing StaDif as a worst-case decider $\mathcal{A}$ (as per Definition 2.2) directly implies Theorem 2.3, ruling out fully black-box constructions with a subexponential security loss. We defer the oracle description and the proof to the full version.

3 One-Way Functions, Indistinguishability Obfuscation, and Hardness in $\mathsf{NP} \cap \mathsf{coNP}$

In this section, we show that injective one-way functions (IOWFs) and indistinguishability obfuscation (IO), for circuits with IOWF-gates, do not give rise to a black-box construction of hard problems in $\mathsf{NP} \cap \mathsf{coNP}$. This can be seen as a generalization of previous separations by Rudich [Rud88], showing that OWFs do not give hardness in $\mathsf{NP} \cap \mathsf{coNP}$, by Matsuda and Matsuura [MM11], showing that IOWFs do not give one-way permutations (which are a special case of hardness $\mathsf{NP} \cap \mathsf{coNP}$), and by Asharov and Segev [AS16], showing that OWFs and IO do not give one-way permutations. As in the previous section, the result implies that many cryptographic primitives and hardness in PPAD, also do not yield black-box constructions of hard problems in $\mathsf{NP} \cap \mathsf{coNP}$.

We first define the framework of $\mathsf{NP} \cap \mathsf{coNP}$ relative to oracles, define fully black-box constructions of hard $\mathsf{NP} \cap \mathsf{coNP}$ problems, and then move on to the actual separation.

3.1 NP ∩ coNP

Throughout, we shall canonically represent languages $L \in \mathsf{NP} \cap \mathsf{coNP}$ by their corresponding non-deterministic poly-time verifiers V_1, V_0, where

$$L = \{x \in \{0,1\}^\star \mid \exists w : V_1(x,w) = 1\},$$
$$\overline{L} = \{x \in \{0,1\}^\star \mid \exists w : V_0(x,w) = 1\} = \{0,1\}^\star \setminus L.$$

Hardness in NP ∩ coNP *from Cryptography - Motivation.* Hard (on average) problems in NP ∩ coNP are known to follow based on certain number-theoretic problems in cryptography, such as Discrete Log and Factoring. As in the previous section for SZK, we are interested in understanding which cryptographic primitives would imply such hardness, again with the intuition that these should be appropriately structured. For instance, it is known [Bra79] that any one-way permutation $f : \{0,1\}^n \to \{0,1\}^n$ implies a hard problem in NP ∩ coNP, e.g. given an index $i \in [n]$ and an image $f(x)$ find the i-th pre-image bit x_i. In contrast, in his seminal work, Rudich [Rud88] proved that completely unstructured objects like one-way functions cannot construct even worst-case hard instances by fully black-box constructions. Here a fully black-box construction essentially means that the non-deterministic verifiers only make black-box use of the OWF (or OWP in the previous example) and the reduction establishing the hardness is also black-box (in both the adversary and the OWF).

But what about more structured primitives such as public-key encryption, oblivious transfer, or even indistinguishability obfuscation. Indeed, IO (plus OWFs) has-been shown to imply hardness in PPAD and more generally in the class TFNP of total search problems, which is often viewed as the search analog of NP ∩ coNP [MP91]. We will show, however, that fully black-box constructions do not give rise to a hard problem in NP ∩ coNP from OWFs (or even injective OWFs) and IO for circuits with OWF gates.

3.2 Fully Black-Box Constructions of Hardness in NP ∩ coNP from IO and IOWFs

We start by defining NP ∩ coNP relative to oracles [Rud88]. This, in particular, captures black-box constructions of such languages from cryptographic primitives, such as one-way functions in [Rud88] or indistinguishability obfuscation, which we will consider in this work.

Definition 3.1 (**NP∩coNP relative to oracles**). *Let $\mathfrak{S}$ be a family of oracles and let $V_1^{(\cdot)}, V_0^{(\cdot)}$ be a pair of oracle-aided non-deterministic polynomial-time verifiers. We say that V_1, V_0 define a collection of languages $L^{\mathfrak{S}} = \{L^\Gamma \mid \Gamma \in \mathfrak{S}\}$ in* NP ∩ coNP *relative to $\mathfrak{S}$ if for any $\Gamma \in \mathfrak{S}$, the machines V_1^Γ, V_0^Γ define a language $L^\Gamma \in \mathsf{NP}^\Gamma \cap \mathsf{coNP}^\Gamma$. That is*

$$L^\Gamma = \{x \in \{0,1\}^\star \mid \exists w : V_1^\Gamma(x,w) = 1\},$$
$$\overline{L}^\Gamma = \{x \in \{0,1\}^\star \mid \exists w : V_0^\Gamma(x,w) = 1\} = \{0,1\}^\star \setminus L.$$

We now formally define the class of constructions and reductions ruled out. That is, *fully black-box* constructions of hard problems in $\mathsf{NP} \cap \mathsf{coNP}$ from injective one-way functions (IOWFs) and IO for IOWF-aided circuits. The definition is similar in spirit to those in [AS15, AS16] and in the Sect. 2, adapted to the context of $\mathsf{NP} \cap \mathsf{coNP}$ hardness.

Definition 3.2. *A fully black-box construction of a hard* $\mathsf{NP} \cap \mathsf{coNP}$ *problem* L *from IOWFs and IO for the class* $\mathcal{C}$ *of circuits with IOWF-gates is given by two oracle aided poly-time machines* (V_0, V_1) *and a probabilistic oracle-aided reduction* $\mathcal{R}$ *that satisfy:*

1. ***Structure:*** *Let* $\mathfrak{S}$ *be the family of all oracles* $(f, i\mathcal{O})$ *such that* f *is injective and* $i\mathcal{O}$ *is a function such that* $\widehat{C}^f \equiv C^f$ *for any* $C^{(\cdot)} \in \mathcal{C}$, r, *and* $\widehat{C}^{(\cdot)} := i\mathcal{O}(C, r)$. *Then* (V_0, V_1) *define a language* $L^{f,i\mathcal{O}} \in \mathsf{NP}^{f,i\mathcal{O}} \cap \mathsf{coNP}^{f,i\mathcal{O}}$ *relative to any oracle* $(f, i\mathcal{O}) \in \mathfrak{S}$ *(as per Definition 3.1).*
2. ***Black-box security proof:*** *There exist functions* $q_{\mathcal{R}}(\cdot), \varepsilon_{\mathcal{R}}(\cdot)$ *such that the following holds. Let* $(f, i\mathcal{O})$ *be any distribution supported on the family* $\mathfrak{S}$ *defined above. Then for any probabilistic oracle-aided* $\mathcal{A}$ *that* decides $L^{f,i\mathcal{O}}$ in the worst-case, *namely, for all* $n \in \mathbb{N}$
$$\Pr_{f,i\mathcal{O},\mathcal{A}}\left[\mathcal{A}^{f,i\mathcal{O}}(x) = b \quad \textit{for all} \quad \begin{matrix} x \in \{0,1\}^n, b \in \{0,1\} \\ \textit{such that } V_b(x) = 1 \end{matrix}\right] = 1$$
the reduction breaks either f or $i\mathcal{O}$, *namely, for infinitely many* $n \in \mathbb{N}$ *either*
$$\Pr_{\substack{x \leftarrow \{0,1\}^n \\ f,i\mathcal{O},\mathcal{A}}}\left[\mathcal{R}^{\mathcal{A},f,i\mathcal{O}}(f(x)) = x\right] \geq \varepsilon_{\mathcal{R}}(n),$$
or
$$\left|\Pr\left[\mathsf{Exp}^{\mathsf{iO}}_{(f,i\mathcal{O}),i\mathcal{O},\mathcal{C},\mathcal{R}^{\mathcal{A}}}(n) = 1\right] - \frac{1}{2}\right| \geq \varepsilon_{\mathcal{R}}(n),$$
where in both $\mathcal{R}$ *makes at most* $q_{\mathcal{R}}(n)$ *queries to any of its oracles* $(\mathcal{A}, f, i\mathcal{O})$, *and for any query* x *made to* $\mathcal{A}$, *the non-deterministic verifiers* $V_0^{f,i\mathcal{O}}(x), V_1^{f,i\mathcal{O}}(x)$ *make at most* $q_{\mathcal{R}}(n)$ *queries to their oracles (for any non-deterministic choice of a witness* w*). The random variable* $\mathsf{Exp}^{\mathsf{iO}}_{(f,i\mathcal{O}),i\mathcal{O},\mathcal{C},\mathcal{R}^{\mathcal{A}}}(n)$ *represents the reductions winning probability in the IO security game relative to* $(f, i\mathcal{O})$.

Remark about Correct Structure. We note that here we explicitly do put a *correctness* requirement, which we refer to as *structure*; namely, that the construction yields a language in $\mathsf{NP} \cap \mathsf{coNP}$ for any implementation of OWPs and IO. This is different from the setting from Definition 2.2 where we considered *promise problems* and allowed the construction not to satisfy the promise occasionally.

Concretely, we require that V_0, V_1 give a language in $\mathsf{NP} \cap \mathsf{coNP}$ for *every* oracle implementing IOWFs and IO. This follows the modeling of [BI87],[11] and

[11] Rudich [Rud88] also considered a slight relaxation of constructions that are correct for an overwhelming fraction of oracles rather than all.

aligns with how we usually think about *correctness* of black-box constructions of cryptographic primitives. For instance, the construction of public-key encryption from trapdoor permutations is promised to be correct, for all oracles implementing the trapdoor permutation. Similarly, the construction of hard $\mathsf{NP} \cap \mathsf{coNP}$ languages from one-way permutations, give an $\mathsf{NP} \cap \mathsf{coNP}$ language for any oracle implementing a permutation.

We also note that as in Definition 2.2, our definition addresses *worst-case hardness*, which makes our impossibility result stronger. See further discussion after Definition 2.2.

Ruling out Fully Black-Box Constructions: A Road Map. Our main result in this section is that fully black-box constructions of a hard $\mathsf{NP} \cap \mathsf{coNP}$ problem from IO and IOWFs do not exist. Furthermore, this holds even if the latter primitives are exponentially secure.

Theorem 3.3. *Any fully black-box construction of an* $\mathsf{NP} \cap \mathsf{coNP}$ *problem* L *from IOWFs and IO for circuits with IOWF gates has an exponential security loss:*

$$\max(q_{\mathcal{R}}(n), \varepsilon_{\mathcal{R}}^{-1}(n)) \geq \Omega(2^{n/6})$$

The proof of the theorem follows a similar methodology to the proof of Theorem 2.3. We exhibit two (distributions on) oracles $(\Psi, \mathsf{Decide}^{\Psi})$, where Ψ realizes IOWFs and IO for circuits with IOWF gates, and Decide^{Ψ} that decides $L^{\Psi} \in \mathsf{NP}^{\Psi} \cap \mathsf{coNP}^{\Psi}$ in the worst case. We then show that the primitives realized by Ψ are (exponentially) secure even in the presence of Decide^{Ψ}. Then viewing Decide as a worst-case decider $\mathcal{A}$ (as per Definition 3.2) directly implies Theorem 3.3, ruling out fully black-box constructions with a subexponential security loss.

We defer the formal treatment to the full version.

4 Collision-Resistance from IO and SZK-Hardness

Asharov and Segev [AS15] showed that collision-resistant hashing cannot be constructed from (even subexponentially hard) indistinguishability obfuscation (IO) and one-way permutations (OWPs) relying on common IO techniques. Slightly more accurately, they rule out fully black-box constructions where (as in previous sections) IO is defined with respect to circuits with OWP oracle gates. In this section, we show that, assuming IO and a strong form of SZK-hardness, there is indeed a construction of collision-resistant hashing (CRH).

The High-Level Idea Behind the Construction. The starting point for our construction is the work of Ishai et al. [IKO05] that shows how to construct collision-resistant hash functions from commitments that are additively homomorphic (for simplicity, say over $\mathbb{F}_2$). The idea is simple: we can hash ℓ bits to m bits, where m is the size of a single bit commitment and ℓ can be arbitrarily longer, as follows. The hash key is a commitment $\gamma := (\mathsf{com}(\beta_1), \ldots, \mathsf{com}(\beta_\ell))$ to a random vector $\beta \in \mathbb{F}_2^\ell$, and hashing $x \in \mathbb{F}_2^\ell$, is done by homomorphically computing a commitment to the inner product $\mathsf{CRH}_\gamma(x) = \mathsf{com}(\langle \beta, x \rangle)$.

This idea can, in fact, be abstracted to work with any commitment scheme wherein given a commitment $\mathsf{com}(\beta)$ for a random key for a 2-universal hash allows to homomorphically compute a commitment $\mathsf{com}(\mathsf{2UH}_\beta(x))$ to the hash at any point x, so that the resulting commitment is compact in the sense that it depends only on the size of $\mathsf{2UH}_\beta(x)$ and not on the size of x. Intuitively, the reason this works is that any collision in CRH_γ implies a collision in the underlying 2-universal hash $\mathsf{2UH}_\beta$, which leaks information about the hash key β (concretely, any fixed x, x' form a collision in a random hash function with small probability) thereby violating the hiding of the commitment.

At a high-level, we aim to mimic the above construction based on obfuscation. As a key for the collision-resistant hash we can obfuscate a program Π_β associated with a secret hash key β that given x outputs a commitment $\mathsf{com}(\mathsf{2UH}_\beta(x))$, where the commitment is derandomized using a PRF. The obfuscation $i\mathcal{O}(\Pi_\beta)$ can be thought of as the commitment to β, and evaluating this program at x, corresponds to homomorphic evaluation. Despite the clear intuition behind this construction, it is not clear how to prove its security based on IO. In fact, by [AS15], it cannot be proven based on a black-box reduction as long as plain statistically-binding commitments are used, as these can be constructed from OWPs in a fully black-box manner.

We show, however, that relying on a relaxed notion of perfectly-hiding commitments, as well as subexponential hardness of IO and puncturable PRFs, the construction can be proven secure. The perfect hiding of the commitment is leveraged in a probabilistic IO argument [CLTV15] that involves a number of hybrids larger than the overall number of commitments. We then observe that these relaxed commitments follow from appropriate average-case hardness of SZK.[12]

Acknowledgements. We thank Gil Segev, Iftach Haitner and Mohammad Mahmoody for elaborately answering our questions regarding existing separation results in cryptography. We also thank the anonymous reviewers for their valuable comments.

References

[ABW10] Applebaum, B., Barak, B., Wigderson, A.: Public-key cryptography from different assumptions. In: Proceedings of 42nd ACM Symposium on Theory of Computing, STOC 2010, USA, 5–8 June 2010, Cambridge, Massachusetts, pp. 171–180 (2010)

[AGGM06] Akavia, A., Goldreich, O., Goldwasser, S., Moshkovitz, D.: On basing one-way functions on NP-hardness. In: Kleinberg [Kle06], pp. 701–710 (2006)

[12] Similar SZK-hardness is known to imply statistically-hiding commitments against malicious receivers, but with a larger (constant) number of rounds [OV08].

[AH91] Aiello, W., Hastad, J.: Statistical zero-knowledge languages can be recognized in two rounds. J. Comput. Syst. Sci. **42**(3), 327–345 (1991)

[Ale03] Alekhnovich, M., More on average case vs approximation complexity. In: 44th Symposium on Foundations of Computer Science (FOCS 2003), 11–14 October 2003, Cambridge, MA, USA, Proceedings [DBL03], pp. 298–307 (2003)

[AR04] Aharonov, D., Regev, O.: Lattice problems in NP cap coNP. In: 45th Symposium on Foundations of Computer Science (FOCS 2004), 17–19 October 2004, Rome, Italy, Proceedings, pp. 362–371. IEEE Computer Society (2004)

[AR16] Applebaum, B., Raykov, P.: From private simultaneous messages to zero-information arthur-merlin protocols and back. In: Kushilevitz, E., Malkin, T. (eds.) TCC 2016. LNCS, vol. 9563, pp. 65–82. Springer, Heidelberg (2016). doi:10.1007/978-3-662-49099-0_3

[AS15] Asharov, G., Segev, G.: Limits on the power of indistinguishability obfuscation and functional encryption. In: Symposium on the Foundations of Computer Science (2015)

[AS16] Asharov, G., Segev, G.: On constructing one-way permutations from indistinguishability obfuscation. In: Kushilevitz, E., Malkin, T. (eds.) TCC 2016. LNCS, vol. 9563, pp. 512–541. Springer, Heidelberg (2016). doi:10.1007/978-3-662-49099-0_19

[Bar13] Barak, B.: Structure vs. combinatorics in computational complexity (2013). http://windowsontheory.org/2013/10/07/structure-vs-combinatorics-in-computational-complexity/

[BB15] Bogdanov, A., Brzuska, C.: On basing size-verifiable one-way functions on NP-hardness. In: Dodis, Y., Nielsen, J.B. (eds.) TCC 2015. LNCS, vol. 9014, pp. 1–6. Springer, Heidelberg (2015). doi:10.1007/978-3-662-46494-6_1

[BBF13] Baecher, P., Brzuska, C., Fischlin, M.: Notions of black-box reductions, revisited. In: Sako, K., Sarkar, P. (eds.) ASIACRYPT 2013. LNCS, vol. 8269, pp. 296–315. Springer, Heidelberg (2013). doi:10.1007/978-3-642-42033-7_16

[BGI+01] Barak, B., Goldreich, O., Impagliazzo, R., Rudich, S., Sahai, A., Vadhan, S., Yang, K.: On the (im)possibility of obfuscating programs. In: Kilian, J. (ed.) CRYPTO 2001. LNCS, vol. 2139, pp. 1–18. Springer, Heidelberg (2001). doi:10.1007/3-540-44647-8_1

[BGL+15] Bitansky, N., Garg, S., Lin, H., Pass, R., Telang, S.: Succinct randomized encodings and their applications. In: Symposium on Theory of Computing, STOC 2015 (2015)

[BHZ87] Boppana, R.B., Hastad, J., Zachos, S.: Does co-NP have short interactive proofs? Inf. Process. Lett. **25**(2), 127–132 (1987)

[BI87] Blum, M., Impagliazzo, R.: Generic oracles and oracle classes. In: Proceedings of 28th Annual Symposium on Foundations of Computer Science, SFCS 1987, pp. 118–126. IEEE Computer Society, Washington (1987)

[BKSY11] Brakerski, Z., Katz, J., Segev, G., Yerukhimovich, A.: Limits on the power of zero-knowledge proofs in cryptographic constructions. In: Ishai [Ish11], pp. 559–578 (2011)

[BL13] Bogdanov, A., Lee, C.H.: Limits of provable security for homomorphic encryption. In: Canetti, R., Garay, J.A. (eds.) CRYPTO 2013. LNCS, vol. 8042, pp. 111–128. Springer, Heidelberg (2013). doi:10.1007/978-3-642-40041-4_7

[BM09] Barak, B., Mahmoody-Ghidary, M.: Merkle puzzles are optimal—an $O(n^2)$-query attack on any key exchange from a random oracle. In: Halevi, S. (ed.) CRYPTO 2009. LNCS, vol. 5677, pp. 374–390. Springer, Heidelberg (2009). doi:10.1007/978-3-642-03356-8_22

[BP15] Bitansky, N., Paneth, O.: ZAPs and non-interactive witness indistinguishability from indistinguishability obfuscation. In: Dodis, Y., Nielsen, J.B. (eds.) TCC 2015. LNCS, vol. 9015, pp. 401–427. Springer, Heidelberg (2015). doi:10.1007/978-3-662-46497-7_16

[BPR15] NBitansky, ., Paneth, O., Rosen, A.: On the cryptographic hardness of finding a nash equilibrium. In: Guruswami, V. (ed.) IEEE 56th Annual Symposium on Foundations of Computer Science, FOCS 2015, 17–20 October 2015, Berkeley, CA, USA, pp. 1480–1498. IEEE Computer Society (2015)

[BPW16] Bitansky, N., Paneth, O., Wichs, D.: Perfect structure on the edge of chaos. In: Kushilevitz, E., Malkin, T. (eds.) TCC 2016. LNCS, vol. 9562, pp. 474–502. Springer, Heidelberg (2016). doi:10.1007/978-3-662-49096-9_20

[Bra79] Brassard, G.: Relativized cryptography. In: 20th Annual Symposium on Foundations of Computer Science, 29–31 October 1979, San Juan, Puerto Rico, pp. 383–391. IEEE Computer Society (1979)

[BT03] Bogdanov, A., Trevisan, L.: On worst-case to average-case reductions for NP problems. In: 44th Symposium on Foundations of Computer Science (FOCS 2003), 11–14 October 2003, Cambridge, MA, USA, Proceedings [DBL03], pp. 308–317 (2003)

[BV11] Brakerski, Z., Vaikuntanathan, V.: Efficient fully homomorphic encryption from (standard) LWE. In: Ostrovsky, R. (ed.) FOCS, pp. 97–106. IEEE (2011). (Invited to SIAM Journal on Computing)

[CDT09] Chen, X., Deng, X., Teng, S.-H.: Settling the complexity of computing two-player nash equilibria. J. ACM **56**(3), 14 (2009)

[CHJV15] Canetti, R., Holmgren, J., Jain, A., Vaikuntanathan, V.: Succinct garbling and indistinguishability obfuscation for RAM programs. In: Proceedings of 47th Annual ACM on Symposium on Theory of Computing, STOC 2015, 14–17 June 2015, Portland, OR, USA, pp. 429–437 (2015)

[CLTV15] Canetti, R., Lin, H., Tessaro, S., Vaikuntanathan, V.: Obfuscation of probabilistic circuits and applications. In: Dodis, Y., Nielsen, J.B. (eds.) TCC 2015. LNCS, vol. 9015, pp. 468–497. Springer, Heidelberg (2015). doi:10.1007/978-3-662-46497-7_19

[Cra12] Cramer, R. (ed.): Theory of Cryptography - 9th Theory of Cryptography Conference, TCC 2012, 19–21 March 2012, Taormina, Sicily, Italy, Proceedings. LNCS vol. 7194. Springer, Heidelberg (2012)

[DBL00] Prceedings of 41st Annual Symposium on Foundations of Computer Science, FOCS 2000: 12–14 November 2000. IEEE Computer Society, Redondo Beach (2000)

[DBL03] Prceedings of 44th Symposium on Foundations of Computer Science (FOCS 2003: 11–14 October 2003. IEEE Computer Society, Cambridge (2003)

[DGP06] Daskalakis, C., Goldberg, P.W., Papadimitriou, C.H.: The complexity of computing a nash equilibrium. In: Kleinberg [Kle06], pp. 71–78 (2006)

[DH76] Diffie, W., Hellman, M.E.: New directions in cryptography. IEEE Trans. Inf. Theory **22**(6), 644–654 (1976)

[DHT12] Dodis, Y., Haitner, I., Tentes, A.: On the instantiability of hash-and-sign RSA signatures. In: Cramer [Cra12], pp. 112–132 (2012)

[DLMM11] Dachman-Soled, D., Lindell, Y., Mahmoody, M., Malkin, T.: On the black-box complexity of optimally-fair coin tossing. In: Ishai [Ish11], pp. 450–467 (2011)

[ESY84] Even, S., Selman, A.L., Yacobi, Y.: The complexity of promise problems with applications to public-key cryptography. Inf. Control **61**(2), 159–173 (1984)

[Fis12] Fischlin, M.: Black-box reductions and separations in cryptography. In: Mitrokotsa, A., Vaudenay, S. (eds.) AFRICACRYPT 2012. LNCS, vol. 7374, pp. 413–422. Springer, Heidelberg (2012). doi:10.1007/978-3-642-31410-0_26

[For89] Fortnow, L.J.: Complexity-theoretic aspects of interactive proof systems. Ph.D. thesis, Massachusetts Institute of Technology (1989)

[Gen09] Gentry, C.: Fully homomorphic encryption using ideal lattices. In: STOC, pp. 169–178 (2009)

[GG98] Goldreich, O., Goldwasser, S.: On the possibility of basing cryptography on the assumption that $p \neq NP$. IACR Cryptology ePrint Archive, 1998:5 (1998)

[GGH+13a] Garg, S., Gentry, C., Halevi, S., Raykova, M., Sahai, A., Waters, B.: Candidate indistinguishability obfuscation and functional encryption for all circuits. In: 54th Annual IEEE Symposium on Foundations of Computer Science, FOCS 2013, 26–29 October 2013, Berkeley, CA, USA, pp. 40–49. IEEE Computer Society (2013)

[GGH+13b] Garg, S., Gentry, C., Halevi, S., Sahai, A., Raikova, M., Waters, B.: Candidate indistinguishability obfuscation and functional encryption for all circuits. In: FOCS (2013)

[GGKT05] Gennaro, R., Gertner, Y., Katz, J., Trevisan, L.: Bounds on the efficiency of generic cryptographic constructions. SIAM J. Comput. **35**(1), 217–246 (2005)

[GK93] Goldreich, O., Kushilevitz, E.: A perfect zero-knowledge proof system for a problem equivalent to the discrete logarithm. J. Cryptol. **6**(2), 97–116 (1993)

[GKLM12] Goyal, V., Kumar, V., Lokam, S.V., Mahmoody, M.: On black-box reductions between predicate encryption schemes. In: Cramer [Cra12], pp. 440–457 (2012)

[GKM+00] Gertner, Y., Kannan, S., Malkin, T., Reingold, O., Viswanathan, M.: The relationship between public key encryption and oblivious transfer. In: 41st Annual Symposium on Foundations of Computer Science, FOCS 2000, 12–14 November 2000, Redondo Beach, California, USA [DBL00], pp. 325–335 (2000)

[GM82] Goldwasser, S., Micali, S.: Probabilistic encryption and how to play mental poker keeping secret all partial information. In: Lewis, H.R., Simons, B.B., Burkhard, W.A., Landweber, L.H. (eds.) Proceedings of 14th Annual ACM Symposium on Theory of Computing, 5–7 May 1982, San Francisco, California, USA, pp. 365–377. ACM (1982)

[GMM07] Gertner, Y., Malkin, T., Myers, S.: Towards a separation of semantic and CCA security for public key encryption. In: Vadhan, S.P. (ed.) TCC 2007. LNCS, vol. 4392, pp. 434–455. Springer, Heidelberg (2007). doi:10.1007/978-3-540-70936-7_24

[GMR85] Goldwasser, S., Micali, S., Rackoff, C.: The knowledge complexity of interactive proof-systems (extended abstract). In: Sedgewick, R. (ed.) Proceedings of 17th Annual ACM Symposium on Theory of Computing, 6–8 May 1985, Providence, Rhode Island, USA, pp. 291–304. ACM (1985)

[GMR01] Gertner, Y., Malkin, T., Reingold, O.: On the impossibility of basing trapdoor functions on trapdoor predicates. In: 42nd Annual Symposium on Foundations of Computer Science, FOCS 2001, 14–17 October 2001, Las Vegas, Nevada, USA, pp. 126–135. IEEE Computer Society (2001)

[GMW91] Goldreich, O., Micali, S., Wigderson, A.: Proofs that yield nothing but their validity for all languages in NP have zero-knowledge proof systems. J. ACM **38**(3), 691–729 (1991)

[Gol06] Goldreich, O.: On promise problems: a survey. In: Goldreich, O., Rosenberg, A.L., Selman, A.L. (eds.) Theoretical Computer Science. LNCS, vol. 3895, pp. 254–290. Springer, Heidelberg (2006). doi:10.1007/11685654_12

[GT00] Gennaro, R., Trevisan, L.: Lower bounds on the efficiency of generic cryptographic constructions. In: 41st Annual Symposium on Foundations of Computer Science, FOCS 2000, 12–14 November 2000, Redondo Beach, California, USA [DBL00], pp. 305–313 (2000)

[GV99] Goldreich, O., Vadhan, S.P.: Comparing entropies in statistical zero knowledge with applications to the structure of SZK. In: Proceedings of 14th Annual IEEE Conference on Computational Complexity, Atlanta, Georgia, USA, 4–6 May 1999, p. 54 (1999)

[Has88] Hastad, J.: Dual vectors and lower bounds for the nearest lattice point problem. Combinatorica **8**(1), 75–81 (1988)

[HH09] Haitner, I., Holenstein, T.: On the (im)possibility of key dependent encryption. In: Reingold, O. (ed.) TCC 2009. LNCS, vol. 5444, pp. 202–219. Springer, Heidelberg (2009). doi:10.1007/978-3-642-00457-5_13

[HHRS15] Haitner, I., Hoch, J.J., Reingold, O., Segev, G.: Finding collisions in interactive protocols—tight lower bounds on the round and communication complexities of statistically hiding commitments. SIAM J. Comput. **44**(1), 193–242 (2015)

[HMX10] Haitner, I., Mahmoody, M., Xiao, D.: A new sampling protocol and applications to basing cryptographic primitives on the hardness of NP. In: 2010 IEEE 25th Annual Conference on Computational Complexity (CCC), pp. 76–87. IEEE (2010)

[HR04] Hsiao, C.-Y., Reyzin, L.: Finding collisions on a public road, or do secure hash functions need secret coins? In: Franklin, M. (ed.) CRYPTO 2004. LNCS, vol. 3152, pp. 92–105. Springer, Heidelberg (2004). doi:10.1007/978-3-540-28628-8_6

[IKO05] Ishai, Y., Kushilevitz, E., Ostrovsky, R.: Sufficient conditions for collision-resistant hashing. In: Kilian, J. (ed.) TCC 2005. LNCS, vol. 3378, pp. 445–456. Springer, Heidelberg (2005). doi:10.1007/978-3-540-30576-7_24

[IR89] Impagliazzo, R., Rudich, S.: Limits on the provable consequences of one-way permutations. In: Proceedings of 21st Annual ACM Symposium on Theory of Computing, pp. 44–61. ACM (1989)

[Ish11] Ishai, Y. (ed.): Theory of Cryptography - 8th Theory of Cryptography Conference, TCC 2011, Providence, RI, USA. LNCS, 28–30 March 2011. Proceedings, vol. 6597. Springer, Heidelberg (2011)

[Kle06] Kleinberg, J.M. (ed.): Proceedings of 38th Annual ACM Symposium on Theory of Computing, Seattle, WA, USA, 21–23 May 2006. ACM (2006)

[KLW15] Koppula, V., Lewko, A.B., Waters, B.: Indistinguishability obfuscation for turing machines with unbounded memory. In: Proceedings of 47th Annual ACM on Symposium on Theory of Computing, STOC 2015, 14–17 June 2015, Portland, OR, USA, pp. 419–428 (2015)

[KMN+14] Komargodski, I., Moran, T., Naor, M., Pass, R., Rosen, A., Yogev, E.: One-way functions and (im)perfect obfuscation. In: 55th IEEE Annual Symposium on Foundations of Computer Science, FOCS 2014, 18–21 October 2014, Philadelphia, PA, USA, pp. 374–383. IEEE Computer Society (2014)

[KSS11] Kahn, J., Saks, M.E., Smyth, C.D.: The dual BKR inequality and rudich's conjecture. Comb. Probab. Comput. **20**(2), 257–266 (2011)

[KST99] Kim, J.H., Simon, D.R., Tetali, P.: Limits on the efficiency of one-way permutation-based hash functions. In: 40th Annual Symposium on Foundations of Computer Science, FOCS 1999, 17–18 October 1999, New York, NY, USA, pp. 535–542. IEEE Computer Society (1999)

[LLJS90] Lagarias, J.C., Lenstra Jr., H.W., Schnorr, C.-P.: Korkin-zolotarev bases and successive minima of a lattice and its reciprocal lattice. Combinatorica **10**(4), 333–348 (1990)

[LV16] Liu, T., Vaikuntanathan, V.: On basing private information retrieval on NP-hardness. In: Kushilevitz, E., Malkin, T. (eds.) TCC 2016. LNCS, vol. 9562, pp. 372–386. Springer, Heidelberg (2016). doi:10.1007/978-3-662-49096-9_16

[MM11] Matsuda, T., Matsuura, K.: On black-box separations among injective one-way functions. In: Ishai, Y. (ed.) TCC 2011. LNCS, vol. 6597, pp. 597–614. Springer, Heidelberg (2011). doi:10.1007/978-3-642-19571-6_36

[MP91] Megiddo, N., Papadimitriou, C.H.: On total functions, existence theorems and computational complexity. Theor. Comput. Sci. **81**(2), 317–324 (1991)

[MV03] Micciancio, D., Vadhan, S.P.: Statistical zero-knowledge proofs with efficient provers: lattice problems and more. In: Boneh, D. (ed.) CRYPTO 2003. LNCS, vol. 2729, pp. 282–298. Springer, Heidelberg (2003). doi:10.1007/978-3-540-45146-4_17

[MX10] Mahmoody, M., Xiao, D.: On the power of randomized reductions and the checkability of sat. In: 2010 IEEE 25th Annual Conference on Computational Complexity (CCC), pp. 64–75. IEEE (2010)

[Ost91] Ostrovsky, R.: One-way functions, hard on average problems, and statistical zero-knowledge proofs. In: Proceedings of 6th Annual Structure in Complexity Theory Conference, pp. 133–138. IEEE (1991)

[OV08] Ong, S.J., Vadhan, S.: An equivalence between zero knowledge and commitments. In: Canetti, R. (ed.) TCC 2008. LNCS, vol. 4948, pp. 482–500. Springer, Heidelberg (2008). doi:10.1007/978-3-540-78524-8_27

[Pap94] Papadimitriou, C.H.: On the complexity of the parity argument and other inefficient proofs of existence. J. Comput. Syst. Sci. **48**(3), 498–532 (1994)

[Pas06] Pass, R.: Parallel repetition of zero-knowledge proofs and the possibility of basing cryptography on NP-hardness. In: 21st Annual IEEE Conference on Computational Complexity (CCC 2006), 16–20 July 2006, Prague, Czech Republic, pp. 96–110. IEEE Computer Society (2006)

[Pas13] Pass, R.: Unprovable security of perfect NIZK and non-interactive non-malleable commitments. In: Sahai, A. (ed.) TCC 2013. LNCS, vol. 7785, pp. 334–354. Springer, Heidelberg (2013). doi:10.1007/978-3-642-36594-2_19

[RAD78] Rivest, R., Adleman, L., Dertouzos, M.: On data banks and privacy homomorphisms. In: Foundations of Secure Computation, pp. 169–177. Academic Press (1978)

[RSA78] Rivest, R.L., Shamir, A., Adleman, L.M.: A method for obtaining digital signatures and public-key cryptosystems. Commun. ACM **21**(2), 120–126 (1978)

[RSS16] Rosen, A., Segev, G., Shahaf, I.: Can PPAD hardness be based on standard cryptographic assumptions? In: Electronic Colloquium on Computational Complexity (ECCC), vol. 23, p. 59 (2016)

[RTV04] Reingold, O., Trevisan, L., Vadhan, S.: Notions of reducibility between cryptographic primitives. In: Naor, M. (ed.) TCC 2004. LNCS, vol. 2951, pp. 1–20. Springer, Heidelberg (2004). doi:10.1007/978-3-540-24638-1_1

[Rud88] Rudich, S.: Limits on the provable consequences of one-way functions. Ph.D. thesis, University of California, Berkeley (1988)

[Rud91] Rudich, S.: The use of interaction in public cryptosystems. In: Feigenbaum, J. (ed.) CRYPTO 1991. LNCS, vol. 576, pp. 242–251. Springer, Heidelberg (1992). doi:10.1007/3-540-46766-1_19

[Sim98] Simon, D.R.: Finding collisions on a one-way street: can secure hash functions be based on general assumptions? In: Nyberg, K. (ed.) EUROCRYPT 1998. LNCS, vol. 1403, pp. 334–345. Springer, Heidelberg (1998). doi:10.1007/BFb0054137

[SV03] Sahai, A., Vadhan, S.: A complete problem for statistical zero knowledge. J. ACM (JACM) **50**(2), 196–249 (2003)

[SW14] Sahai, A., Waters, B.: How to use indistinguishability obfuscation: deniable encryption, and more. In: Shmoys, D.B. (ed.) Symposium on Theory of Computing, STOC 2014, New York, NY, USA, 31 May–03 June 2014, pp. 475–484. ACM (2014)

[Vad99] Vadhan, S.P.: A study of statistical zero-knowledge proofs. Ph.D. thesis, Massachusetts Institute of Technology (1999)

[Wat15] Waters, B.: A punctured programming approach to adaptively secure functional encryption. In: Gennaro, R., Robshaw, M. (eds.) CRYPTO 2015. LNCS, vol. 9216, pp. 678–697. Springer, Heidelberg (2015). doi:10.1007/978-3-662-48000-7_33

Conditional Disclosure of Secrets

Conditional Disclosure of Secrets: Amplification, Closure, Amortization, Lower-Bounds, and Separations

Benny Applebaum[1(✉)], Barak Arkis[1], Pavel Raykov[1], and Prashant Nalini Vasudevan[2]

[1] Tel Aviv University, Tel Aviv, Israel
{bennyap,barakark,pavelraykov}@post.tau.ac.il
[2] MIT, Cambridge, USA
prashvas@mit.edu

Abstract. In the *conditional disclosure of secrets* problem (Gertner et al. J. Comput. Syst. Sci. 2000) Alice and Bob, who hold inputs x and y respectively, wish to release a common secret s to Carol (who knows both x and y) if and only if the input (x, y) satisfies some predefined predicate f. Alice and Bob are allowed to send a single message to Carol which may depend on their inputs and some joint randomness and the goal is to minimize the communication complexity while providing information-theoretic security.

Following Gay et al. (Crypto 2015), we study the communication complexity of CDS protocols and derive the following positive and negative results.

- (**Closure**): A CDS for f can be turned into a CDS for its complement $\bar{f}$ with only a minor blow-up in complexity. More generally, for a (possibly non-monotone) predicate h, we obtain a CDS for $h(f_1, \ldots, f_m)$ whose cost is essentially linear in the formula size of h and polynomial in the CDS complexity of f_i.
- (**Amplification**): It is possible to reduce the privacy and correctness error of a CDS from constant to 2^{-k} with a multiplicative overhead of $O(k)$. Moreover, this overhead can be amortized over k-bit secrets.
- (**Amortization**): Every predicate f over n-bit inputs admits a CDS for multi-bit secrets whose amortized communication complexity per secret bit grows linearly with the input length n for sufficiently long secrets. In contrast, the best known upper-bound for single-bit secrets is exponential in n.
- (**Lower-bounds**): There exists a (non-explicit) predicate f over n-bit inputs for which any perfect (single-bit) CDS requires communication of at least $\Omega(n)$. This is an exponential improvement over the previously known $\Omega(\log n)$ lower-bound.
- (**Separations**): There exists an (explicit) predicate whose CDS complexity is exponentially smaller than its randomized communication complexity. This matches a lower-bound of Gay et al., and, combined with another result of theirs, yields an exponential separation between the communication complexity of linear CDS and non-linear

J. Katz and H. Shacham (Eds.): CRYPTO 2017, Part I, LNCS 10401, pp. 727–757, 2017.
DOI: 10.1007/978-3-319-63688-7_24

CDS. This is the first provable gap between the communication complexity of linear CDS (which captures most known protocols) and non-linear CDS.

1 Introduction

Consider a pair of computationally-unbounded parties, Alice and Bob, each holding an n-bit input, x and y respectively, to some public predicate $f : \{0,1\}^n \times \{0,1\}^n \to \{0,1\}$. Alice and Bob also hold a joint secret $s \in \{0,1\}$ and have access to a joint source of randomness $r \xleftarrow{R} \{0,1\}^\rho$. The parties wish to disclose the secret s to a third party, Carol, if and only if the predicate $f(x,y)$ evaluates to 1. To this end, Alice (resp., Bob) should send to Carol a single message $a = a(x,s;r)$ (resp., $b = b(y,s;r)$). Based on the transcript (a,b) and the inputs (x,y), Carol should be able to recover the secret s if and only if $f(x,y) = 1$. (Note that Carol is assumed to know x and y.) That is, we require two properties:

- *Correctness:* There exists a decoder algorithm Dec that recovers s from (x,y,a,b) with high probability whenever (x,y) is a 1-input (i.e., $f(x,y) = 1$);
- *Privacy:* There exists a simulator Sim that, given a 0-input (x,y) (for which the predicate evaluates to 0), samples the joint distribution of the transcript (x,y,a,b) up to some small deviation error.

The main goal is to minimize the communication complexity of the protocol which is taken to be the total bit-length of the messages a and b. (See Sect. 3 for formal definitions.)

This form of *Conditional Disclosure of Secrets* (CDS) was introduced by Gertner et al. [18] as a tool for adding data privacy to information-theoretically private information retrieval (PIR) protocols [14] and was later used in the computational setting as a light-weight alternative to zero-knowledge proofs (cf. [2]). Apart from these applications, CDS plays a central role in the design of secret sharing schemes for graph-based access structures (cf. [10,11,37]) and in the context of attribute-based encryption [21,35]. In fact, CDS can be *equivalently formulated* under any of these frameworks as discussed below.

Secret Sharing for Forbidden Graphs. CDS can also be viewed as a special form of secret sharing for graph-based access structures (cf. [10,11,37]). Specifically, consider a secret-sharing scheme whose parties are the nodes of a bipartite graph $G = (X \cup Y, E)$ and a pair of parties $(x,y) \in X \times Y$ should be able to recover the secret s if and only if they are connected by an edge. (It is also required that singletons are not authorized, but other than that we do not require any privacy/correctness condition for other subsets of parties). Then, we can represent the secret-sharing problem as the problem of realizing a CDS for the predicate $f_G(x,y) = 1 \Leftrightarrow (x,y) \in E$ and vice-versa by setting the share of the x-th node (resp., y-th node) to be the message $a(x,s;r)$ (resp., $b(y,s;r)$). The communication complexity of the CDS protocol therefore corresponds to the size of shares.

Attribute-Based Encryption. CDS can be further viewed as a limited form of private-key attribute-based encryption [21,35] which offers one-time information-theoretic security. In such an encryption scheme both the decryption key a_x of a receiver and the ciphertext b_y of a sender are associated with some public attributes x and y, respectively. The receiver should be able to decrypt the plaintext m from the ciphertext b_y using the key a_x only if the attributes x and y "match" according to some predefined policy, i.e., satisfy some predicate $f(x, y)$. Using CDS for f, we can derive such a one-time secure scheme by letting the decryption key be Alice's message, $a_x = a(x, s; r)$, for a random secret s, and taking the ciphertext to be Bob's message $b_y = b(y, s; r)$ together with a padded-version of the message $m \oplus s$. (Here we can think of (r, s) as the sender's private-key.) In fact, it was shown by Attrapadung [8] and Wee [38] that even in the computational setting of public-key (multi-user) attribute-based encryption (ABE), *linear CDS schemes* (in which the computation of Alice and Bob can be written as a linear function in the secret an the randomness) form a central ingredient. As a result, the ciphertext size and secret key of the ABE directly depend on the communication complexity of the underlying CDS.

The Communication Complexity of CDS. In light of the above, it is interesting to understand the communication complexity of CDS. Unfortunately, not much is known. Gertner et al. [18] showed that any predicate f that can be computed by a s-size Boolean formula admits a perfect linear CDS (with zero correctness/privacy error) with communication complexity of $O(s)$. This result was extended by Ishai and Wee [26] to s-size (arithmetic) branching programs and by Applebaum and Raykov [7] to s-size (arithmetic) span programs (though in the latter case correctness is imperfect). Beimel et al. [9] proved that the CDS complexity of the *worst* predicate $f : \{0,1\}^n \times \{0,1\}^n \to \{0,1\}$ over n-bit inputs is at most $O(2^{n/2})$. A similar upper-bound was later established by Gay et al. [17] for the case of linear CDS, where a matching (non-explicit) lower-bound follows from the work of Mintz [31]. Very recently, Liu et al. [29] improved the worst-case complexity of (non-linear) CDS to $2^{O(\sqrt{n \log n})}$. Gay et al. [17] also initiated a systematic treatment of the communication complexity of CDS and established the first lower-bounds on the communication complexity of general CDS. Their main result relates the CDS communication of a predicate f to its randomized communication complexity. Roughly speaking, it is shown that a general CDS for f must communicate at least $\Omega(\log((\mathsf{R}(f)))$ bits, and a linear CDS must communicate at least $\Omega(\sqrt{\mathsf{R}(f)})$, where $\mathsf{R}(f)$ denotes the number of bits communicated in a randomized protocol that need to be exchanged between Alice and Bob in order to compute f with constant error probability.[1] This yields (explicit) lower-bounds of $\Omega(\log(n))$ and $\Omega(\sqrt{n})$, respectively, for concrete n-bit predicates. Overall, for general CDS, there is an almost double-exponential

[1] More precisely, $\mathsf{R}(f)$ can be replaced with the communication complexity of one-message protocol from Alice to Bob plus the communication complexity of one-message protocol from Bob to Alice.

gap between the best known (logarithmic) lower-bound and the best known ($2^{O(\sqrt{n \log n})}$) upper bound.

2 Our Results

Following Gay et al. [17], we conduct a systematic study of the complexity of CDS. Unlike previous works, we focus on *manipulations* and *transformations* of various forms of CDS. Our approach yields several positive and negative results regarding the complexity of CDS, and answers several open problems posed in previous works. We proceed with a statement of our results.

2.1 Closure Properties

We begin by asking whether one can generally combine CDS for basic predicates $f_1, \ldots, f_m$ into a CDS for a more complicated predicate $h(f_1, \ldots, f_m)$. Using standard secret sharing techniques, one can derive such a transformation when h is a monotone function (with overhead proportional to the monotone formula size of h). However, these techniques fail to support non-monotone operations. Our first observation asserts that linear CDS for f can be easily transformed into a linear CDS for its complement $\overline{f} \equiv 1 - f$. (A similar observation was recently made by Ambrona et al. [4] in the related context of "linear predicate encodings".[2])

Theorem 1 (Linear CDS is closed under complement). *Suppose that f has a linear* CDS *with randomness complexity of ρ and communication complexity of t, then $\overline{f}$ has a linear* CDS *scheme with randomness complexity of $t + \rho + 1$ and communication complexity of $2(\rho + 1)$.*

The theorem generalizes to arbitrary finite field $\mathbb{F}$. (See Sect. 4.1.) Roughly speaking, we rely on the following observation. It can be shown that, for a fixed input (x, y), the parties jointly compute some linear operator $T_{x,y}$ that has a high rank whenever $f(x, y) = 0$, and low rank when $f(x, y) = 1$. We "reverse" the CDS by essentially moving to the dual $T^*_{x,y}$ of $T_{x,y}$ whose rank is high when $f(x, y) = 1$, and low when $f(x, y) = 0$. One still has to find a way to distributively compute the mapping $T^*_{x,y}$. We solve this technicality by using a private simultaneous message protocol (PSM) [15] that allows Alice and Bob to securely release an image of $T^*_{x,y}$ to Carol without leaking any additional information.

Next, we show that a similar "reversing transformation" exists for general (non-linear and imperfect) CDS protocols.

Theorem 2 (CDS is closed under complement). *Suppose that f has a* CDS *with randomness complexity of ρ and communication complexity of t and privacy/correctness errors of 2^{-k}. Then $\overline{f} \equiv 1 - f$ has a* CDS *scheme with similar privacy/correctness errors and randomness/communication complexity of $O(k^3 \rho^2 t + k^3 \rho^3)$.*

[2] We thank the anonymous referee for bringing out this result to our attention.

Imitating the argument used for the case of linear CDS, we consider, for an input (x, y) and secret s, the probability distribution $D^s_{x,y}$ of the messages (a, b) induced by the choice of the common random string. Observe that the distributions $D^0_{x,y}$ and $D^1_{x,y}$ are statistically far when $f(x) = 1$ (due to correctness), and are statistically close when $f(x, y) = 0$ (due to privacy). Therefore, to prove Theorem 2 we should somehow *reverse* statistical distance, i.e., construct a CDS whose corresponding distributions $E^0_{x,y}$ and $E^1_{x,y}$ are close when $D^0_{x,y}$ and $D^1_{x,y}$ are far, and vice versa. A classical result of Sahai and Vadhan [34] (building on Okamoto [32]) provides such a reversing transformation for efficiently-samplable distributions (represented by their sampling circuits). As in the case of linear CDS, this transformation cannot be used directly since the resulting distributions do not "decompose" into an x-part and a y-part. Nevertheless, we can derive a decomposable version of the reversing transformation by employing a suitable PSM protocol. (See Sect. 4.2 for details.)

Theorems 1 and 2 can be used to prove stronger closure properties for CDS. Indeed, exploiting the ability to combine CDS's under AND/OR operations, we can further show that CDS is "closed" under (non-monotone) formulas, i.e., one can obtain a CDS for $h(f_1, \ldots, f_m)$ whose cost is essentially linear in the formula size of h and polynomial in the CDS complexity of f_i. (See Sect. 4.3 for details.)

2.2 Amplification

We move on to the study the robustness of CDS with respect to privacy and correctness errors. Borrowing tools from Sahai and Vadhan [34], it can be shown that CDS with constant correctness and privacy error of, say 1/3, can be boosted into a CDS with an error of 2^{-k} at the expense of increasing the communication by a factor of $O(k^5)$. We show that in the context of CDS one can reduce the overhead to $O(k)$ and amortize it over long secrets.

Theorem 3 (Amplification). *A CDS F for f which supports a single-bit secret with privacy and correctness error of 1/3, can be transformed into a CDS G for k-bit secrets with privacy and correctness error of $2^{-\Omega(k)}$ and communication/randomness complexity which are larger than those of F by a multiplicative factor of $O(k)$.*

The proof relies on constant-rate ramp secret sharing schemes. (See Sect. 5.)

2.3 Amortizing CDS over Long Secrets

The above theorem suggests that there may be non-trivial savings when the secrets are long. We show that this is indeed the case, partially resolving an open question of Gay et al. [17].

Theorem 4 (Amortization over long secrets). *Let $f : \{0,1\}^n \times \{0,1\}^n \rightarrow \{0,1\}$ be a predicate. Then, for sufficiently large m, there exists a perfect linear CDS which supports m-bit secrets with total communication complexity of $O(nm)$.*

Recall that for a single-bit secret, the best known upper-bound for a general predicate is $O(2^{n/2})$ [9,17]. In contrast, Theorem 4 yields an amortized complexity of $O(n)$ per each bit of the secret. The constant in the big-O notation is not too large (can be taken to be 12). Unfortunately, amortization kicks only when the value of m is huge (double exponential in n). Achieving non-trivial savings for shorter secrets is left as an interesting open problem.

The proof of Theorem 4 is inspired by a recent result of Potechin [33] regarding amortized space complexity.[3] Our proof consists of two main steps.

We begin with a *batch-CDS* scheme in which Alice holds a single input x, Bob holds a single input y, and both parties hold $2^{2^{2n}}$ secrets, one for each predicate in $\mathcal{F}_n = \{f : \{0,1\}^n \times \{0,1\}^n \to \{0,1\}\}$. The scheme releases the secret s_f if and only if f evaluates to 1 on (x, y). Using a recursive construction, it is not hard to realize such a CDS with communication complexity of $O(n|\mathcal{F}_n|)$.

Next, we use batch-CDS to get a CDS for a (single) predicate f and a vector s of $m = |\mathcal{F}_n|$ secrets, which is indexed by predicates $p \in \mathcal{F}_n$. We secret-share each bit s_p into two parts α_p, β_p and collectively release all α_p's via batch-CDS (where α_p is associated with the predicate p). Finally, we collectively release all β_p's via batch-CDS where β_p is associated with the predicate h_p that outputs 1 on (x, y) if and only if h and the target function f agree on (x, y). The key-observation is that α_p and β_p are released if only if f and p evaluates to 1. As a result we get perfect privacy and *semi-correctness*: For 1-inputs (x, y), exactly half of the secrets s_p are released (the ones for which p evaluates to 1). The latter property can be upgraded to perfect correctness by adding redundancy to the secrets (via a simple pre-encoding). See Sect. 6 for full details.

2.4 Linear Lower-Bound

We change gears and move from upper-bounds to lower-bounds. Specifically, we derive the first linear lower-bound on the communication complexity of general CDS.

Theorem 5 (Lower-bound). *There exists a predicate $f : \{0,1\}^n \times \{0,1\}^n \to \{0,1\}$ for which any perfect (single-bit) CDS requires communication of at least $0.99n$.*

Previously the best known lower-bound for general CDS (due to [17]) was logarithmic in n. As noted by [17], an "insecure" realization of CDS requires a single bit, and so Theorem 5 provides a rare example of a provable linear gap in communication complexity between secure and insecure implementation of a natural task. (As argued in [17], even super-constant gaps are typically out of reach.)

[3] In fact, Theorem 4 can be derived from Potechin's theorem by extending the connection between space-limited computation and CDS to the setting of multiple secrets. Instead, we present a self-contained proof which directly manipulates CDS and does not go through other computational models. This proof is arguably simpler, more instructive and yields (slightly) better amortized complexity.

The proof of the lower-bound (given in Sect. 7) relies, again, on CDS manipulations. Consider a generalized version of CDS where the parties wish to release some Boolean function $f(x, y, s)$ defined over x, y and the secret s. We show that one can construct such a "generalized CDS" for a function f based on a standard CDS for a related predicate $g : \{0,1\}^n \times \{0,1\}^n \to \{0,1\}$. In particular, we use a standard CDS to release the value of s only if the residual function $f(x, y, \cdot)$ depends on s (i.e., $g(x, y) = f(x, y, 0) \oplus f(x, y, 1)$). This way the output $f(x, y, s)$ can be always computed, either trivially, based on x, y alone, or based on the additional knowledge of s, which is leaked when its value matters. Moreover, privacy is preserved since s is leaked only when its value matters, which means that it can be derived anyway from $f(x, y, s)$ and (x, y). We conclude that a lower-bound on CDS follows from a lower-bound on generalized-CDS. We then note that such a lower-bound essentially appears in the work of Feige et al. [15]. Indeed, "generalized-CDS" can be equivalently viewed as a weakened version of private simultaneous message protocols for which the lower-bound of [15] applies.[4]

2.5 CDS vs. Linear CDS vs. Communication Complexity

Let us denote by $\mathsf{CDS}(f)$ the minimal communication complexity of CDS for f with a single bit of secret and constant privacy/correctness error (say 0.1). We define $\mathsf{linCDS}(f)$ similarly with respect to linear CDS protocols.

We re-visit the connection between CDS-complexity and randomized communication complexity, and show that the former can be exponentially smaller than the latter. Since linear CDS complexity is at least polynomial in the communication complexity ($\mathsf{linCDS}(f) \geq \Omega(\sqrt{\mathsf{R}(f)})$), as shown by [17], we also conclude that general CDS can have exponentially-smaller communication than linear CDS.

Theorem 6 (Separation). *There exists an (explicit) partial function f for which (1) $\mathsf{CDS}(f) \leq O(\log \mathsf{R}(f))$ and (2) $\mathsf{CDS}(f) \leq O(\log \mathsf{linCDS}(f))$.*

The first part of the theorem matches the lower-bound $\mathsf{CDS}(f) \geq \Omega(\log \mathsf{R}(f))$ established by [17].[5] The second part provides the first separation between linear CDS and general (non-linear) CDS, resolving an open question of [17].

The proof of Theorem 6 can be viewed as the communication complexity analog of Aaronson's [1] oracle separation between the complexity class **SZK** of problems admitting *statistical-zero knowledge proofs* [19], and the class **QMA** of problems admitting Quantum Merlin Arthur proofs. (See Sect. 8 for details.)

2.6 Discussion: The Big Picture

CDS vs. SZK. Our results highlight an important relation between conditional disclosure of secrets to statistical-zero knowledge protocols. A CDS protocol

[4] CDS, generalized CDS, and PSM, can be all captured under the framework of partial garbling studied by Ishai and Wee [26].

[5] The original lower-bound, which is stated for perfect CDS and for total functions, readily generalizes to partial functions and imperfect CDS. See Appendix A.

reduces the computation of $f(x, y)$, to an estimation of the statistical distance between a pair of "2-decomposable" distributions $D^0 = (a(x, 0; r), b(y, 0; r))$ and $D^1 = (a(x, 1; r), b(y, 1; r))$, similarly to the way that languages that admit a statistical zero-knowledge proofs are reduced to the analogous problem of estimating the statistical distance between a pair of efficiently-samplable distributions [34]. This simple insight has turned to be extremely useful for importing techniques from the domain of SZK to the CDS world.

CDS: The Low-End of Information-Theoretic Protocols. Determining the communication complexity of information-theoretic secure protocols is a fundamental research problem. Despite much efforts, we have very little understanding of the communication complexity of simple cryptographic tasks, and for most models, there are exponentially-large gaps between the best known upper-bounds to the best known lower-bounds. In an attempt to simplify the problem, one may try to focus on the most basic settings with a minimal non-trivial number of players (namely, 3) and the simplest possible communication pattern (e.g., single message protocols). Indeed, in this minimal communication model, conditional disclosure of secrets captures the notion of secret-sharing, just like private simultaneous message protocols (PSM) capture the notion of secure computation, and zero-information Arthur-Merlin games (ZAM) [20] capture the notion of (non-interactive) zero-knowledge. Of all three variants, CDS is the simplest one: For any given predicate f the CDS communication of f is essentially upper-bounded by its ZAM complexity which is upper-bounded by its PSM complexity [7]. Hence, CDS should be the easiest model for obtaining upper-bounds (protocols) whereas PSM should be the easiest model for proving lower-bounds.

Our results, however, demonstrate that the current techniques for proving PSM lower-bounds [15] also apply to the CDS model. The situation is even worse, since, by Theorem 4, the amortized communication complexity of CDS is indeed linear (per bit). We therefore conclude that proving a super-linear lower-bound in the PSM model requires a method that fails to lower-bound the amortized communication of CDS. Put differently, lower-bounds techniques which do not distinguish between PSM complexity and amortized CDS complexity cannot prove super-linear lower-bounds. This "barrier" provides a partial explanation for the lack of strong (super-linear) lower-bounds for PSM. It will be interesting to further formalize this argument and present some syntactic criteria that determines whether a lower-bound technique is subject to the CDS barrier.

3 Preliminaries

Through the paper, real numbers are assumed to be rounded up when being typecast into integers ($\log n$ always becomes $\lceil \log n \rceil$, for instance). The *statistical distance* between two discrete random variables, X and Y, denoted by $\Delta(X; Y)$ is defined by $\Delta(X; Y) := \frac{1}{2} \sum_z |\Pr[X = z] - \Pr[Y = z]|$. We will also use statistical distance for probability distributions, where for a probability distribution D the value $\Pr[D = z]$ is defined to be $D(z)$.

3.1 Conditional Disclosure of Secrets

We define the notion of Conditional Disclosure of Secrets [18].

Definition 1 (CDS). *Let $f : \mathcal{X} \times \mathcal{Y} \to \{0,1\}$ be a predicate. Let $F_1 : \mathcal{X} \times \mathcal{S} \times \mathcal{R} \to \mathcal{T}_1$ and $F_2 : \mathcal{Y} \times \mathcal{S} \times \mathcal{R} \to \mathcal{T}_2$ be deterministic encoding algorithms, where $\mathcal{S}$ is the secret domain. Then, the pair (F_1, F_2) is a* CDS *scheme for f if the function $F(x,y,s,r) = (F_1(x,s,r), F_2(y,s,r))$ that corresponds to the joint computation of F_1 and F_2 on a common s and r, satisfies the following properties:*

1. *(δ-Correctness) There exists a deterministic algorithm* Dec, *called a decoder, such that for every 1-input (x,y) of f and any secret $s \in \mathcal{S}$ we have that:*

$$\Pr_{r \xleftarrow{R} \mathcal{R}} [\mathsf{Dec}(x,y,F(x,y,s,r)) \neq s] \leq \delta$$

2. *(ε-Privacy) There exists a simulator* Sim *such that for every 0-input (x,y) of f and any secret $s \in \mathcal{S}$: it holds that*

$$\Delta_{r \xleftarrow{R} \mathcal{R}} (\mathsf{Sim}(x,y);\ F(x,y,s,r)) \leq \varepsilon$$

The communication complexity *of the* CDS *protocol is* $(\log|\mathcal{T}_1| + \log|\mathcal{T}_2|)$ *and its* randomness complexity *is* $\log|\mathcal{R}|$. *If δ and ε are zeros, such a* CDS *scheme is called* perfect.

By default, we let $\mathcal{X} = \mathcal{Y} = \{0,1\}^n$, $\mathcal{S} = \{0,1\}^s$, $\mathcal{R} = \{0,1\}^\rho$, $\mathcal{T}_1 = \{0,1\}^{t_1}$, and $\mathcal{T}_2 = \{0,1\}^{t_2}$ for positive integers n, s, ρ, t_1, and t_2.

Linear CDS. We say that a CDS scheme (F_1, F_2) is *linear* over a finite field $\mathbb{F}$ (or simply linear) if, for any fixed input (x,y), the functions $F_1(x,s,r)$ and $F_2(y,s,r)$ are linear over $\mathbb{F}$ in the secret s and in the randomness r, where the secret, randomness, and messages are all taken to be vectors over $\mathbb{F}$, i.e., $\mathcal{R} = \mathbb{F}^\rho$, $\mathcal{S} = \mathbb{F}^s$, $\mathcal{T}_1 = \mathbb{F}^{t_1}$ and $\mathcal{T}_2 = \mathbb{F}^{t_2}$. (By default, we think of $\mathbb{F}$ as the binary field, though our results hold over general fields.) Such a linear CDS can be canonically represented by a sequence of matrices $(M_x)_{x \in \mathcal{X}}$ and $(M_y)_{y \in \mathcal{Y}}$ where $M_x \in \mathbb{F}^{t_1 \times (1+\rho)}$ and $M_y \in \mathbb{F}^{t_2 \times (1+\rho)}$ and $F_1(x,s,r) = M_x \cdot \begin{pmatrix} s \\ \boldsymbol{r} \end{pmatrix}$ and $F_2(x,s,r) = M_y \cdot \begin{pmatrix} s \\ \boldsymbol{r} \end{pmatrix}$. It is not hard to show that any linear CDS with non-trivial privacy and correctness errors (smaller than 1) is actually perfect. Moreover, the linearity of the senders also implies that the decoding function is linear in the messages (cf. [17]).[6]

Definition 2. *We denote by* $\mathsf{CDS}(f)$ *the least communication complexity of a* CDS *protocol for f with $\frac{1}{10}$-correctness and $\frac{1}{10}$-privacy.* $\mathsf{linCDS}(f)$ *is defined analogously for linear* CDS *protocols.*

---

6 One can further consider a seemingly weaker form of linearity in which only the decoder is linear [17]. Indeed, our separation between linear CDS and standard CDS applies to this setting as well.

3.2 Private Simultaneous Message Protocols

We will also need the following model of information-theoretic non-interactive secure computation that was introduced by [15], and was later named as *Private Simultaneous Message* (PSM) protocols by [23].

Definition 3 (PSM). *Let $f : \mathcal{X} \times \mathcal{Y} \rightarrow \mathcal{Z}$ be a function. We say that a pair of deterministic encoding algorithms $F_1 : \mathcal{X} \times \mathcal{R} \rightarrow \mathcal{T}_1$ and $F_2 : \mathcal{Y} \times \mathcal{R} \rightarrow \mathcal{T}_2$ are* PSM *for f if the function $F(x, y, r) = (F_1(x, r), F_2(y, r))$ that corresponds to the joint computation of F_1 and F_2 on a common r, satisfies the following properties:*

1. *(δ-Correctness) There exists a deterministic algorithm* Dec*, called decoder, such that for every input (x, y) we have that:*
$$\Pr_{r \xleftarrow{R} \mathcal{R}} [\mathsf{Dec}(F(x, y, r)) \neq f(x, y)] \leq \delta.$$
2. *(ε-Privacy) There exists a randomized algorithm (simulator)* Sim *such that for any input (x, y) it holds that:*
$$\Delta_{r \xleftarrow{R} \mathcal{R}} (\mathsf{Sim}(f(x, y)); F(x, y, r)) \leq \varepsilon.$$

The communication complexity *of the* PSM *protocol is defined as the total encoding length* $(\log |\mathcal{T}_1| + \log |\mathcal{T}_2|)$*, and the* randomness complexity *of the protocol is defined as the length* $\log |\mathcal{R}|$ *of the common randomness. If δ and ε are zeros, such a* PSM *scheme is called* perfect*. The scheme is* balanced [6] *if the simulator maps the uniform distribution over $\mathcal{Z}$ to the uniform distribution over $\mathcal{T} = \mathcal{T}_1 \times \mathcal{T}_2$ and the decoder maps the uniform distribution over $\mathcal{T}$ to the uniform distribution over $\mathcal{Z}$.*

3.3 Randomized Encoding and CDS Encoding

When talking about PSM protocols, we will use $F(x, y, r)$ as abbreviation for $(F_1(x, r), F_2(y, r))$, and analogously for CDS. When we do not need to explicitly argue about the common randomness, we will suppress it as an argument to F – that is, we will use $F(x, y)$ to denote the random variable produced by $F(x, y, r)$ for uniformly random r. Moreover, observe that the correctness and privacy conditions of both PSM and CDS are phrased as properties of the joint mapping F. One can therefore consider a *non-decomposable* CDS/PSM F which respects privacy and correctness, but (possibly) fails to decompose into an x-part and a y-part (i.e., some of its outputs depend both on x and y). In this case, we can ignore the partition of the input into x, y and parse them as a single argument $w = (x, y)$. Following [6,24] we refer to this generalization of PSM as *randomized encoding* of f, and to the generalized version of CDS as a CDS-encoding of f. The notion of perfect and balanced PSM and perfect and linear CDS carry naturally to this setting as well. These non-decomposable variants can be trivially realized (for PSM set $F(x, y) = f(x, y)$ and for CDS take

$F(x, y, s) = f(x, y) \wedge s)$. Nevertheless, they offer a useful abstraction. In particular, we will use these non-decomposable notions as a useful stepping stone towards obtaining a decomposable realization.

4 Closure Properties

In this section, we establish several closure properties of CDS. We begin with closure under complement for linear CDS, then, extend the result to general CDS, and finally, prove that general and linear CDS are closed under $\mathbf{NC}^1$ circuits (or equivalently under Boolean formulas).

4.1 Reversing Linear CDS

We begin by proving Theorem 1 (restated here for the convenience of the reader).

Theorem 7 (Linear CDS is closed under complement). *Let f be a function that has a linear* CDS *scheme F with randomness complexity of ρ field elements and communication complexity of t field elements. Then, the complement function $\overline{f} \equiv 1-f$ has a linear* CDS *scheme with randomness complexity of $(t+\rho+1)$ field elements and communication complexity of $2(\rho+1)$ field elements.*

Proof. Let F_1, F_2 be a linear CDS scheme for f with randomness complexity ρ and total communication complexity $t = t_1 + t_2$, where t_1 is the output length of F_1 and t_2 is the output length of t_2. Due to linearity, we can assume that $F_1(x, s, \boldsymbol{c})$ and $F_2(y, s, \boldsymbol{c})$ are computed by applying matrices M_x and M_y to the vector $\begin{pmatrix} s \\ \boldsymbol{c} \end{pmatrix}$, respectively. We parse $M_x = (\boldsymbol{v}_x | T_x)$ and $M_y = (\boldsymbol{v}_y | T_y)$, i.e., $\boldsymbol{v}_x$ (resp., $\boldsymbol{v}_y$) denotes the first column of M_x (resp., M_y), and T_x (resp., T_y) denotes the remaining columns. In the following we fix x, y to be some inputs and let $\boldsymbol{v} = \begin{pmatrix} \boldsymbol{v}_x \\ \boldsymbol{v}_y \end{pmatrix}$, $T = \begin{pmatrix} T_x \\ T_y \end{pmatrix}$, $M = (\boldsymbol{v}|T)$.

One can observe that due to the linearity of CDS, it holds that $f(x, y) = 0$ if and only if $\boldsymbol{v} \in \mathsf{colspan}(T)$. Indeed, the joint distribution of the messages, $M \begin{pmatrix} s \\ \boldsymbol{c} \end{pmatrix}$, is uniform over the subspace $\mathcal{U}_s = \mathsf{colspan}(T) + s\boldsymbol{v}$. If $\boldsymbol{v} \in \mathsf{colspan}(T)$ the subspace $\mathcal{U}_s$ collapses to $\mathsf{colspan}(T)$ regardless of the value of s (and so we get perfect privacy), whereas for $\boldsymbol{v} \notin \mathsf{colspan}(T)$, different secrets $s \neq s'$ induce disjoint subspaces $\mathcal{U}_s$ and $\mathcal{U}_{s'}$, and so the secret can be perfectly recovered.

Based on this observation, one can construct a *non-decomposable* CDS for $\overline{f}$ (in which Alice and Bob are viewed as a single party) as follows. Compute a random mask $\boldsymbol{\alpha}^T \boldsymbol{v}$ (where $\boldsymbol{\alpha}$ is a random vector), and output the masked secret bit $d = s + \boldsymbol{\alpha}^T \boldsymbol{v}$ together with the row vector $\boldsymbol{\gamma} = \boldsymbol{\alpha}^T T$. The decoding procedure starts by finding a vector $\boldsymbol{z}$ such that $\boldsymbol{v} = T\boldsymbol{z}$ (such a vector always exists since $\boldsymbol{v} \in \mathsf{colspan}(T)$ if $f(x, y) = 0$), and then outputs $d - \boldsymbol{\gamma}\boldsymbol{z} = s + \boldsymbol{\alpha}^T \boldsymbol{v} - (\boldsymbol{\alpha}^T T)\boldsymbol{z} = s$. Of course, the resulting scheme is not decomposable, however, we can fix this problem by letting Alice and Bob compute a PSM of it. We proceed with a formal description.

We construct CDS scheme $G = (G_1, G_2)$ for $\overline{f}$ as follows: Alice and Bob get shared randomness $q = (u, \boldsymbol{w}, \boldsymbol{\alpha}_1, \boldsymbol{\alpha}_2)$, where $u \in \mathbb{F}$, $\boldsymbol{w} \in \mathbb{F}^{\rho}$, and $\boldsymbol{\alpha}_1 \in \mathbb{F}^{t_1}, \boldsymbol{\alpha}_2 \in \mathbb{F}^{t_2}$. Then they compute

$$G_1(x, s, q) = (\boldsymbol{\alpha}_1^T T_x + \boldsymbol{w}^T, \boldsymbol{\alpha}_1^T \cdot \boldsymbol{v}_x + u + s)$$

and

$$G_2(y, s, q) = (\boldsymbol{\alpha}_2^T T_y - \boldsymbol{w}^T, \boldsymbol{\alpha}_2^T \cdot \boldsymbol{v}_y - u).$$

The decoder on input $(\boldsymbol{m}_1, b_1)$ from Alice and $(\boldsymbol{m}_2, b_2)$ from Bob does the following: it finds a vector $\boldsymbol{z}$ such that $\boldsymbol{v} = T\boldsymbol{z}$ and outputs $b_1 + b_2 - (\boldsymbol{m}_1 + \boldsymbol{m}_2) \cdot \boldsymbol{z}$.

We now prove that the pair (G_1, G_2) is a CDS for $\overline{f}$ starting with correctness. Fix an input (x, y) for which $f(x, y) = 0$. Recall that in this case $\boldsymbol{v} \in \mathsf{colspan}(T)$, and so the decoder can find $\boldsymbol{z}$ as required. It is not hard to verify that in this case the decoding formula recovers the secret. Indeed, letting $\boldsymbol{\alpha} = \begin{pmatrix} \boldsymbol{\alpha}_1 \\ \boldsymbol{\alpha}_2 \end{pmatrix}$, we have

$$b_1 + b_2 - (\boldsymbol{m}_1 + \boldsymbol{m}_2) \cdot \boldsymbol{z} = s + \boldsymbol{\alpha}^T \cdot \boldsymbol{v} - (\boldsymbol{\alpha}^T \cdot T) \cdot \boldsymbol{z} = s + \boldsymbol{\alpha}^T \cdot \boldsymbol{v} - \boldsymbol{\alpha}^T \cdot \boldsymbol{v} = s.$$

We now turn to proving the perfect privacy of the protocol. Consider any (x, y) such that $f(x, y) = 1$ and let $M = (\boldsymbol{v}|T)$ be the joint linear mapping. To prove privacy, it suffices to show that, for random $\boldsymbol{\alpha} \xleftarrow{R} \mathbb{F}^t$, the first entry of the vector $\boldsymbol{\alpha}^T M$ is uniform conditioned on the other entries of the vector. To see this, first observe that $\boldsymbol{\alpha}^T M$ is distributed uniformly subject to the linear constraints $\boldsymbol{\alpha}^T M \cdot \boldsymbol{r} = \boldsymbol{0}$ induced by all vectors $\boldsymbol{r}$ in the Kernel of M. Therefore, $\boldsymbol{\alpha}^T \boldsymbol{v}$ is uniform conditioned on $\boldsymbol{\alpha}^T T$ if and only if all $\boldsymbol{r}$'s in the Kernel of M have 0 as their first entry. Indeed, if this is not the case, then $\boldsymbol{v} \in \mathsf{colspan}(T)$, and so (x, y) cannot be 1-input of f.

Finally, observe that the protocol consumes $(t + \rho + 1)$ field elements for the joint randomness, and communicates a total number of $2\rho + 2$ field elements. □

4.2 Reversing General CDS

We continue by proving Theorem 2 (restated below).

Theorem 8 (CDS is closed under complement). *Suppose that f has a* CDS *with randomness complexity of ρ and communication complexity of t and privacy/correctness errors of 2^{-k}. Then $\overline{f} \equiv 1 - f$ has a* CDS *scheme with similar privacy/correctness errors and randomness/communication complexity of $O(k^3\rho^2 t + k^3\rho^3)$.*

We begin with the following reversing transformation of Sahai and Vadhan [34, Corollary 4.18].

Construction 9 (Statistical Distance Reversal). *Let $D^0, D^1 : Q \to L$ be a pair of functions where $Q = \{0,1\}^\rho$ and $L = \{0,1\}^t$. For a parameter k, let $m = k^3\rho^2$, and let $\mathcal{H} = \{h : \{0,1\}^m \times Q^m \times L^m \to S\}$ be a family of 2-universal hash functions where $S = \{0,1\}^{(\rho+1)m-2(m/k)-k}$. The functions C^0 and C^1 take an input $(\boldsymbol{b}, \boldsymbol{r}, \boldsymbol{b}', \boldsymbol{r}', h, u) \in (\{0,1\}^m \times Q^m)^2 \times \mathcal{H} \times U$, and output the tuple*

$$(D^{\boldsymbol{b}}(\boldsymbol{r}), \boldsymbol{b}, h, z)$$

where $D^{\boldsymbol{b}}(\boldsymbol{r}) =: (D^{b_1}(r_1), \ldots, D^{b_m}(r_m))$, and

$$z = \begin{cases} h(\boldsymbol{b}, \boldsymbol{r}, D^{\boldsymbol{b}'}(\boldsymbol{r}')) & \text{for } C^0 \\ u & \text{for } C^1 \end{cases}.$$

In the following, we denote by D^0 (resp., D^1, C^0, C^1) the probability distributions induced by applying the function D^0 (resp., D^1, C^0, C^1) to a uniformly chosen input.

Fact 10 (Corollary 4.18 in [34]). *In the set-up of Construction 9, the following holds for every parameter k.*

1. *If $\Delta(D^0, D^1) < 2^{-k}$ then $\Delta(C^0, C^1) > 1 - 2^{-k}$.*
2. *If $\Delta(D^0, D^1) > 1 - 2^{-k}$, then $\Delta(C^0, C^1) < 2^{-k}$.*

Fact 10 allows to transform a CDS $F(x, y, s, r) = (F_1(x, s; r), F_2(y, s; r))$ for the function f, into a *CDS encoding* C for $\overline{f}$. For inputs x, y and secret s, the CDS encoding C samples a message from the distribution C^s_{xy} obtained by applying Construction 9 to the distributions $D^0_{xy} = F(x, y, 0, r)$ and $D^1_{xy} = F(x, y, 1, r)$.

Unfortunately, the resulting CDS encoding is not decomposable since the hash function is applied jointly to the x-th and y-th components of the distributions D^0_{xy} and D^1_{xy}. We fix the problem by using a PSM of h. Let us begin with the following more general observation that shows that h can be safely replaced with its randomized encoding.

Lemma 1. *Under the set-up of Construction 9, for every $h \in \mathcal{H}$ let $\hat{h}$ be a perfect balanced randomized encoding of h with randomness space V and output space $\hat{S}$. The function E^0 (resp., E^1) is defined similarly to C^0 (resp., C^1) except that the input is $(\boldsymbol{b}, \boldsymbol{r}, \boldsymbol{b}', \boldsymbol{r}', h, v, \hat{s}) \in (\{0,1\}^m \times Q^m)^2 \times \mathcal{H} \times V \times \hat{S}$ and the output is identical except for the z-part which is replaced by*

$$\hat{z} = \begin{cases} \hat{h}(\boldsymbol{b}, \boldsymbol{r}, D^{\boldsymbol{b}'}(\boldsymbol{r}'); v) & \text{for } E^0 \\ \hat{s} & \text{for } E^1 \end{cases}.$$

Then, the conclusion of Fact 10 holds for E^0 and E^1 as well. Namely, for every parameter k,

1. *if $\Delta(D^0, D^1) < 2^{-k}$ then $\Delta(E^0, E^1) > 1 - 2^{-k}$;*
2. *if $\Delta(D^0, D^1) > 1 - 2^{-k}$, then $\Delta(E^0, E^1) < 2^{-k}$.*

Proof. Fix D^0 and D^1. We prove that $\Delta(E^0, E^1) = \Delta(C^0, C^1)$ and conclude the lemma from Fact 10. Indeed, consider the randomized mapping T which maps a tuple (a, b, h, z) to $(a, b, h, \mathsf{Sim}(z))$ where Sim is the simulator of the encoding $\hat{h}$. Then, by the perfect privacy and the balanced property, T takes C^0 to E^0 and C^1 to E^1. Since statistical distance can only decrease when the same probabilistic process is applied to two random variables, it follows that $\Delta(C^0, C^1) \leq \Delta(T(C^0), T(C^1)) = \Delta(E^0, E^1)$. For the other direction, consider the mapping T' which maps a tuple $(a, b, h, \hat{z})$ to $(a, b, h, \mathsf{Dec}(\hat{z}))$ where Dec is the decoder of the encoding. Then, by the perfect correctness and by the balanced property, T takes E^0 to C^0 and E^1 to C^1. It follows that $\Delta(E^0, E^1) \leq \Delta(T'(E^0), T'(E^1)) = \Delta(C^0, C^1)$, and the lemma follows. □

We can now prove Theorem 8.

Proof (Proof of Theorem 8). Let $F = (F_1, F_2)$ be a CDS for the function f with randomness complexity ρ, communication t and privacy/correctness error of 2^{-k}. For inputs x, y and secret σ, the CDS for $\overline{f}$ will be based on the functions E^σ defined in Lemma 1 where $D^0(r) = F(x, y, 0; r)$ and $D^1(r) = F(x, y, 1; r)$. In particular, we will instantiate Lemma 1 as follows.

Let

$$\alpha = (\boldsymbol{b}, \boldsymbol{r}, D^{\boldsymbol{b}}_{xy}(\boldsymbol{r})), \quad \text{where } D^{\boldsymbol{b}}_{xy}(\boldsymbol{r}) := (F(x, y, b_1; r_1), \ldots, F(x, y, b_m; r_m))$$

be the input to the hash function h. Let $n_0 = m(1 + \rho + t)$ denote the length of α. Observe that each bit of α depends either on x or on y but not in both (since F is a CDS). Let $A \subset [n_0]$ denote the set of entries which depend on x and let $B = [n_0] \setminus A$ be its complement. Let $n_1 = (\rho+1)m - 2m/k - k$ denote the output length of the hash function family $\mathcal{H}$. We implement $\mathcal{H} = \{h\}$ by using Toeplitz matrices. That is, each function is defined by a binary Toeplitz matrix $M \in \mathbb{F}_2^{n_1 \times n_0}$ (in which each descending diagonal from left to right is constant) and a vector $w \in \mathbb{F}_2^{n_1}$, and $h(\alpha) = M\alpha + w$. Let us further view the hash function $h(\alpha)$ as a two-argument function $h(\alpha_A, \alpha_B)$ and let

$$\hat{h}(\alpha_A, \alpha_B; v) = (M_A \alpha_A + w + v, M_B \alpha_B - v),$$

where $v \in \mathbb{F}_2^{n_1}$ and M_A (resp. M_B) is the restriction of M to the columns in A (resp., columns in B). It is not hard to verify that $\hat{h}$ is a perfect balanced PSM for h. (Indeed decoding is performed by adding Alice's output to Bob's output, and simulation is done by splitting an output β of h into two random shares $c_1, c_2 \in \mathbb{F}_2^{n_1}$ which satisfy $c_1 + c_2 = \beta$.)

Consider the randomized mapping E^σ_{xy} obtained from Lemma 1 instantiated with $D^s(r) = D^s_{xy}(r) = F(x, y, s; r)$ and the above choices of $\hat{h}$. We claim that E^σ_{xy} is a CDS for $\overline{f}$ with privacy and correctness error of 2^{-k}. To see this first observe that, by construction, the output of E^σ_{xy} can be decomposed into an x-component $E_1(x, \sigma)$ and a y-component $E_2(y, \sigma)$. (All the randomness that is used as part of the input to E is consumed as part of the joint randomness of the CDS.)

To prove privacy, fix some 0-input (x, y) of $\overline{f}$ and note that $f(x, y) = 1$ and therefore, by the correctness of the CDS F, it holds that $\Delta(D^0_{xy}, D^1_{xy}) > 1-2^{-k}$. We conclude, by Lemma 1, that $\Delta(E^0_{xy}, E^1_{xy}) < 2^{-k}$ and privacy holds. For correctness, fix some 1-input (x, y) of $\overline{f}$ and note that $f(x, y) = 0$ and therefore, by the privacy of the CDS F, it holds that $\Delta(D^0_{xy}, D^1_{xy}) < 2^{-k}$. We conclude, by Lemma 1, that $\Delta(E^0_{xy}, E^1_{xy}) > 1 - 2^{-k}$ and so correctness holds (by using the optimal distinguisher as a decoder). Finally, since the description length of h is $n_0 + 2n_1$ the randomness complexity of $\hat{h}$ is n_1 and the communication complexity of $\hat{h}$ is $2n_1$, the overall communication and randomness complexity of the resulting CDS is $O(k^3\rho^2 t + k^3\rho^3)$. □

4.3 Closure Under Formulas

Closure under formulas can be easily deduced from Theorems 7 and 8.

Theorem 11. *Let g be a Boolean function over m binary inputs that can be computed by a σ-size formula. Let $f_1, \ldots, f_m$ be m boolean functions over $\mathcal{X} \times \mathcal{Y}$ each having a* CDS *with t communication and randomness complexity, and 2^{-k} privacy and correctness errors. Then, the function $h : \mathcal{X} \times \mathcal{Y} \to \{0, 1\}$ defined by $g(f_1(x, y), \ldots, f_m(x, y))$ has a* CDS *scheme with $O(\sigma k^3 t^3)$ randomness and communication complexity, and $\sigma 2^{-k}$ privacy and correctness errors. Moreover, in the case of linear CDS, the communication and randomness complexity are only $O(\sigma t)$ and the resulting CDS is also linear.*

Proof. Without loss of generality, assume that the formula g is composed of AND and OR gates and all the negations are at the bottom (this can be achieved by applying De Morgan's laws) and are not counted towards the formula size. We prove the theorem with an upper-bound of $\sigma \cdot Ck^3t^3$ where C is the constant hidden in the big-O notation in Theorem 8 (the upper-bound on the communication/randomness complexity of the complement of a CDS).

The proof is by induction on σ. For $\sigma = 1$, the formula g is either $f_i(x, y)$ or $\overline{f}_i(x, y)$ for some $i \in [m]$, in which case the claim follows either from our assumption on the CDS for f_i or from Theorem 8. To prove the induction step, consider a σ-size formula $g(f_1, \ldots, f_m)$ of the form $g_1(f_1, \ldots, f_m) \diamond g_2(f_1, \ldots, f_m)$ where $\diamond$ is either AND or OR, g_1 and g_2 are formulas of size σ_1 and σ_2, respectively, and $\sigma = \sigma_1 + \sigma_2 + 1$. For the case of an AND gate, we additively secret share the secret s into random s_1 and s_2 subject to $s_1 + s_2 = s$ and use a CDS for g_1 with secret s_1 and for g_2 for the secret s_2. For the case of OR gate, use a CDS for g_1 with secret s and for g_2 for the secret s. By the induction hypothesis, the communication and randomness complexity are at most $\sigma_1 \cdot Ck^3t^3 + \sigma_2 \cdot Ck^3t^3 + 1 \leq \sigma Ck^3t^3$, and the privacy/correctness error grow to $\sigma_1 2^{-k} + \sigma_2 2^{-k} \leq \sigma 2^{-k}$, as required.

The extension to the linear case follows by plugging the upper-bound from Theorem 7 to the basis of the induction, and by noting that the construction preserves linearity. □

5 Amplifying Correctness and Privacy of CDS

In this section we show how to simultaneously reduce the correctness and privacy error of a CDS scheme F. Moreover, the transformation has only minor cost when applied to long secrets.

Theorem 12. *Let $f : X \times Y \to \{0,1\}$ be a predicate and let F be a CDS for f which supports 1-bit secrets with correctness error $\delta_0 = 0.1$ and privacy error $\varepsilon_0 = 0.1$. Then, for every integer k there exists a CDS G for f with k-bit secrets, privacy and correctness errors of $2^{-\Omega(k)}$. The communication (resp., randomness) of G larger than those of F by a multiplicative factor of $O(k)$.*

Proof. Let ε be some constant larger than ε_0. Let E be a randomized mapping that takes k-bit message s and $O(k)$-bit random string into an encoding c of length $m = \Theta(k)$ with the following properties:

1. If one flips every bit of $\mathsf{E}(s)$ independently at random with probability δ_0 then s can be recovered with probability $1 - \exp(-\Omega(k))$.
2. For any pair of secrets s and s' and any set $T \subset [m]$ of size at most εm, the T-restricted encoding of s is distributed identically to the T-restricted encoding of s', i.e., $(\mathsf{E}(s)_i)_{i \in T} \equiv (\mathsf{E}(s')_i)_{i \in T}$.

That is, E can be viewed as a ramp secret-sharing scheme with 1-bit shares which supports robust reconstruction.[7] Such a scheme can be based on any linear error-correcting code with good dual distance [13]. In particular, by using a random linear code, we can support $\varepsilon_0 = \delta_0 = 0.1$ or any other constants which satisfy the inequality $1 - H_2(\delta_0) > H_2(\varepsilon_0)$.

Given the CDS $F = (F_1, F_2)$ we construct a new CDS $G = (G_1, G_2)$ as follows. Alice and Bob jointly map the secret $s \in \{0,1\}^k$ to $c = \mathsf{E}(s; r_0)$ (using joint randomness r_0). Then, for every $i \in [m]$, Alice outputs $F_1(x, c_i; r_i)$ and Bob outputs $F_2(y, c_i; r_i)$, where $r_1, \ldots, r_m$ are given as part of the shared randomness.

Let us analyze the correctness of the protocol. Fix some x, y for which $f(x,y) = 1$. Consider the decoder which given $(v_1, \ldots, v_m)$ and x, y applies the original decoder of F to each coordinate separately (with the same x, y), and passes the result $\hat{c} \in \{0,1\}^m$ to the decoding procedure of E, promised by Property (1) above. By the correctness of F, each bit $\hat{c}_i$ equals to c_i with probability of at least $1 - \delta_0$. Therefore, the decoder of E recovers c with all but $1 - \exp(-\Omega(k))$ probability.

Consider the simulator which simply applies G to the secret $s' = 0^k$. Fix x and y and a secret s. To upper-bound the statistical distance between $G(x, y, s')$ and $G(x, y, s)$, we need the following standard "coupling fact" (cf. [30, Lemma 5] for a similar statement).

[7] In a ramp secret sharing there may be a gap between the privacy bound (the number of parties for which privacy hold) and the reconstruction bound (the number of parties which can reconstruct the secret) and one does not care if there are sets of size in between these bounds whose joint shares reveal partial information about the secret.

Fact 13. *Any pair of distributions, (D_0, D_1) whose statistical distance is ε can be coupled into a joint distribution (E_0, E_1, b) with the following properties:*

1. *The marginal distribution of E_0 (resp., E_1) is identical to D_0 (resp., D_1).*
2. *b is an indicator random variable which takes the value 1 with probability ε.*
3. *Conditioned on $b = 0$, the outcome of E_0 equals to the outcome of E_1.*

Define the distributions $D_0 := F(x, y, 0)$ and $D_1 := F(x, y, 1)$, and let (E_0, E_1, b) be the coupled version of D_0, D_1 derived from Fact 13. Let $c = \mathsf{E}(s)$ and $c' = \mathsf{E}(s')$. Then,

$$G(x, y, s) = (E^1_{c_1}, \dots, E^m_{c_m}),$$

and

$$G(x, y, s') = (E^1_{c'_1}, \dots, E^m_{c'_m}),$$

where for each $i \in [m]$ the tuple (E^i_0, E^i_1, b^i) is sampled jointly and independently from all other tuples. Let $T = \{i \in [m] : b_i \neq 0\}$. Then, it holds that

$$\begin{aligned}\Delta(G(x, y, s); G(x, y, s')) &\leq \Delta((T, (E^i_{c_i})_{i\in T}); (T, (E^i_{c'_i})_{i\in T})) \\ &\leq \Pr[|T| > \varepsilon m] \leq \exp(-\Omega(k)),\end{aligned}$$

where the first inequality follows from Fact 13, the second inequality follows from the second property of E and the last inequality follows from a Chernoff bound (recalling that $\varepsilon - \varepsilon' > 0$ is a constant and $m = \Theta(k)$). The theorem follows. □

Remark 1 (Optimization). The polarization lemma of Sahai and Vadhan [34] provides an amplification procedure which works for a wider range of parameters. Specifically, their transformation can be applied as long as the initial correctness and privacy errors satisfy the relation $\delta_0^2 > \varepsilon_0$. (Some evidence suggest that this condition is, in fact, necessary for any amplification procedure [22].) Unfortunately, the communication overhead in their reduction is polynomially larger than ours and does not amortize over long secrets. It is not hard to combine the two approaches and get the best of both worlds. In particular, given a CDS with constant correctness and privacy errors which satisfy $\delta_0^2 > \varepsilon_0$, use the polarization lemma with constant security parameter k_0 to reduce the errors below the threshold needed for Theorem 12, and then use the theorem to efficiently reduce the errors below 2^{-k}. The resulting transformation has the same asymptotic tradeoff between communication, error, and secret length, and can be used for a wider range of parameters. (This, in particular, yields the statement of Theorem 3 in the introduction in which δ_0 and ε_0 are taken to be 1/3.)

Remark 2 (Preserving efficiency). Theorem 12 preserves efficiency (of the CDS senders and decoder) as long as the encoding E, and its decoding algorithm are efficient. This can be guaranteed by replacing the random linear codes (for which decoding is not know to be efficient) with an Algebraic Geometric Codes (as suggested in [13]; see also Claim 4.1 in [25] and [12,16]). This modification requires to start with smaller (yet constant) error probabilities δ_0, ε_0. As in Remark 1, this limitation can be easily waived. First use the inefficient transformation (based on random binary codes) with constant amplification $k_0 = O(1)$ to reduce the privacy/correctness error below the required threshold, and then use the efficient amplification procedure (based on Algebraic Geometric Codes).

6 Amortizing the Communication for Long Secrets

In this section we show that, for sufficiently long secrets, the amortized communication cost of CDS for n-bit predicates is $O(n)$ bits per each bit of the secret. As explained in the introduction, in order to prove this result we first amortize CDS over many different predicates (applied to the same input (x, y)). We refer to this version of CDS as *batch-CDS*, formally defined below.

Definition 4 (batch-CDS). *Let $\mathcal{F} = (f_1, \ldots, f_m)$ be an m-tuple of predicates over the domain $\mathcal{X} \times \mathcal{Y}$. Let $F_1 : \mathcal{X} \times \mathcal{S}^m \times \mathcal{R} \to \mathcal{T}_1$ and $F_2 : \mathcal{Y} \times \mathcal{S}^m \times \mathcal{R} \to \mathcal{T}_2$ be deterministic encoding algorithms, where $\mathcal{S}$ is the secret domain (by default $\{0,1\}$). Then, the pair (F_1, F_2) is a batch-*CDS *scheme for $\mathcal{F}$ if the function $F(x, y, s, r) = (F_1(x, s, r), F_2(y, s, r))$, that corresponds to the joint computation of F_1 and F_2 on a common s and r, satisfies the following properties:*

1. *(Perfect correctness)*[8] *There exists a deterministic algorithm* Dec, *called a decoder, such that for every $i \in [m]$, every 1-input (x, y) of f_i and every vector of secrets $s \in \mathcal{S}^m$, we have that:*

$$\Pr_{r \xleftarrow{R} \mathcal{R}} [\mathsf{Dec}(i, x, y, F(x, y, s, r)) = s_i] = 1.$$

2. *(Perfect privacy) There exists a simulator* Sim *such that for every input (x, y) and every vector of secrets $s \in \mathcal{S}^m$, the following distributions are identical*

$$\mathsf{Sim}(x, y, \hat{s}) \qquad \textit{and} \qquad F(x, y, s, r),$$

where $r \xleftarrow{R} \mathcal{R}$ and $\hat{s}$ is an m-long vector whose i-th component equals to s_i if $f_i(x, y) = 1$, and $\bot$ otherwise.

The communication complexity *of the* CDS *protocol is* $(\log|\mathcal{T}_1| + \log|\mathcal{T}_2|)$.

In the following, we let $\mathcal{F}_n$ denote the $2^{2^{2n}}$-tuple which contains all predicates $f : \{0,1\}^n \times \{0,1\}^n \to \{0,1\}$ defined over pairs of n-bit inputs (sorted according to some arbitrary order).

Lemma 2. *$\mathcal{F}_n$-batch CDS can be implemented with communication complexity of $3|\mathcal{F}_n|$. Moreover the protocol is linear.*

[8] For simplicity, we consider only perfectly correct and perfectly private batch-CDS, though the definition can be generalized to the imperfect case as well.

Proof. The proof is by induction on n. For $n = 1$, it is not hard to verify that any predicate $f : \{0,1\} \times \{0,1\} \to \{0,1\}$ admits a CDS with a total communication complexity of at most 2 bits. Indeed, there are 16 such predicates, out of which, six are trivial in the sense that the value of f depends only in the inputs of one of the parties (and so they admit a CDS with 1 bit of communication), and the other ten predicates correspond, up to local renaming of the inputs, to AND, OR, and XOR, which admit simple linear 2-bit CDS as follows. For AND, Alice and Bob send $s \cdot x + r$ and $r \cdot y$; for OR, they send $x \cdot s$ and $y \cdot s$; and, for XOR, they send $s + x \cdot r_1 + (1-x)r_2$ and $y \cdot r_2 + (1-y)r_1$ (where r and (r_1, r_2) are shared random bits and addition/multiplication are over the binary field). It follows, that $\mathcal{F}_1$-batch CDS can be implemented with total communication of at most $2|\mathcal{F}_1|$. (In fact, this bound can be improved by exploiting the batch mode.)

Before proving the induction step. Let us make few observations. For $(\alpha, \beta) \in \{0,1\}^2$, consider the mapping $\phi_{\alpha,\beta} : \mathcal{F}_{n+1} \to \mathcal{F}_n$ which maps a function $f \in \mathcal{F}_{n+1}$ to the function $g \in \mathcal{F}_n$ obtained by restricting f to $x_{n+1} = \alpha$ and $y_{n+1} = \beta$. The mapping $\phi_{\alpha,\beta}$ is onto, and is D-to-1 where $D = |\mathcal{F}_{n+1}|/|\mathcal{F}_n|$. We can therefore define a mapping $T_{\alpha,\beta}(f)$ which maps $f \in \mathcal{F}_{n+1}$ to $(g, i) \in \mathcal{F}_n \times [D]$ such that f is the i-th preimage of g under $\phi_{\alpha,\beta}$ with respect to some fixed order on $\mathcal{F}_{n+1}$. By construction, for every fixed (α, β), the mapping $T_{\alpha,\beta}$ is one-to-one.

We can now prove the induction step; That is, we construct $\mathcal{F}_{n+1}$-batch CDS based on D copies of $\mathcal{F}_n$-batch CDS. Given input $x \in \{0,1\}^{n+1}$ for Alice, $y \in \{0,1\}^{n+1}$ for Bob, and joint secrets $(s_f)_{f \in \mathcal{F}_{n+1}}$, the parties proceed as follows.

1. Alice and Bob use D copies of $\mathcal{F}_n$-batch CDS with inputs $x' = (x_1, \ldots, x_n)$ and $y' = (y_1, \ldots, y_n)$. In the i-th copy, for every predicate $g \in \mathcal{F}_n$, a random secret $r_{g,i} \in \{0,1\}$ is being used. (The $r_{g,i}$'s are taken from the joint randomness of Alice and Bob.)
2. For every $f \in \mathcal{F}_{n+1}$ and $(\alpha, \beta) \in \{0,1\}^2$, Alice and Bob release the value $\sigma_{f,\alpha,\beta} = s_f + r_{g,i}$ where $(g, i) = T_{\alpha,\beta}(f)$ iff the last bits of their inputs, x_{n+1} and y_{n+1}, are equal to α and β, respectively. This step is implemented as follows. For each f, Alice sends a pair of bits

$$c_{f,0} = \sigma_{f,x_{n+1},0} + r'_{f,0}, \quad \text{and} \quad c_{f,1} = \sigma_{f,x_{n+1},1} + r'_{f,1},$$

   and Bob sends $r'_{f,y_{n+1}}$ where $r'_{f,0}, r'_{f,1}$ are taken from the joint randomness.

The decoding procedure is simple. If the input $(x, y) \in \{0,1\}^{n+1} \times \{0,1\}^{n+1}$ satisfies $f \in \mathcal{F}_{n+1}$, the decoder does the following: (1) Computes $(g, i) = T_{x_{n+1},y_{n+1}}(f)$ and retrieves the value of $r_{g,i}$ which is released by the batch-CDS since $g(x', y') = f(x, y) = 1$; (2) Collects the values $c_{f,x_{n+1}}$ and $r'_{f,y_{n+1}}$ sent during the second step, and recovers the value of s_f by computing $c_{f,x_{n+1}} - r'_{f,y_{n+1}} - r_{g,i}$.

In addition, it is not hard to verify that perfect privacy holds. Indeed, suppose that $(x, y) \in \{0,1\}^{n+1} \times \{0,1\}^{n+1}$ does not satisfy f. Then, the only s_f-dependent value which is released is $s_f \oplus r_{g,i}$ where g is the restriction of f to (x_{n+1}, y_{n+1}). However, since (x, y) fails to satisfy f, its prefix does not satisfy

g and therefore $r_{g,i}$ remains hidden from the receiver. Formally, we can perfectly simulate the view of the receiver as follows. First simulate the first step using D calls to the simulator of $\mathcal{F}_n$-batch CDS with random secrets $r_{g,i}$. Then simulate the second step by sampling, for each f, three values $c_{f,0}, c_{f,1}$ and r' which are uniform if $f(x,y) = 0$, and, if $f(x,y) = 1$, satisfy the linear constraint $s_f = c_{f,x_{n+1}} - r'_{f,y_{n+1}} - r_{g,i}$ where $(g,i) = T_{\alpha,\beta}(f)$.

Finally the communication complexity equals to the complexity of D copies of batch CDS for $\mathcal{F}_n$ (communicated in the first step) plus $3|\mathcal{F}_{n+1}|$ bits (communicated at the second step). Therefore, by the induction hypothesis, the overall communication, is $3|\mathcal{F}_{n+1}|+3Dn|\mathcal{F}_n|$. Recalling that $D = |\mathcal{F}_{n+1}|/|\mathcal{F}_n|$, we derive an upper-bound of $3(n+1)|\mathcal{F}_{n+1}|$, as required. □

We use Lemma 2 to amortize the complexity of CDS over long secrets.

Theorem 14. *Let $f : \{0,1\}^n \times \{0,1\}^n \to \{0,1\}$ be a predicate. Then, for $m = |\mathcal{F}_n|/2 = 2^{2^{2n}}/2$, there exists a perfect linear CDS which supports m-bit secrets with total communication complexity of* 12 nm.

The case of longer secrets of length $m > |\mathcal{F}_n|/2$ (as in Theorem 4) can be treated by partitioning the secret to $|\mathcal{F}_n|/2$-size blocks and applying the CDS for each block separately. The overall communication complexity is upper-bounded by 13 nm.

Proof. Given a vector S of $m = |\mathcal{F}_n|/2$ secrets, we duplicate each secret twice and index the secrets by predicates $p \in \mathcal{F}_n$ such that $s_p = s_{\bar{p}}$ (i.e., a predicate and its complement index the same secret). On inputs x, y, Alice and Bob make two calls to $\mathcal{F}_n$-batch CDS (with the same inputs x, y). In the first call the secret associated with a predicate $p \in \mathcal{F}_n$ is a random values r_p. In the second call, for every predicate $h \in \mathcal{F}_n$, we release the secret $s_p \oplus r_p$ where p is the unique predicate for which $p = f + h + 1$ (where addition is over the binary field).

Correctness. Suppose that $f(x,y) = 1$. Recall that each of the original secrets S_i appears in two copies $(s_p, s_{\bar{p}})$ for some predicate p. Since one of these copies is satisfied by (x,y), it suffices to show that, whenever $p(x,y) = 1$, the secret s_p can be recovered. Indeed, for such a predicate p, the value r_p is released by the first batch-CDS, and the value $s_p \oplus r_p$ is released by the second batch-CDS. The latter follows by noting that the predicate h which satisfies $p = f+h+1$ is also satisfied, since $h(x,y) = p(x,y) + f(x,y) + 1 = 1$. It follows that s_p can be recovered for every p which is satisfied by (x,y), as required.

Privacy. Suppose that $f(x,y) = 0$. We show that all the "virtual secrets" s_p remain perfectly hidden in this case. Indeed, for h and p which satisfy $p = f + h + 1$, it holds that, whenever $f(x,y) = 0$, either $h(x,y) = 0$ or $p(x,y) = 0$, and therefore, for any p, either r_p or $s_p \oplus r_p$ are released, but never both.

Finally, using Lemma 2, the total communication complexity of the protocol is $2 \cdot 3 \cdot n \cdot |\mathcal{F}_n| = 12\,nm$, as claimed. □

7 A Linear Lower Bound on CDS

Here we show that the lower bound on the communication complexity of PSM protocols proven in [15] can be extended to apply for CDS as well. We do this by showing how to use CDS protocols to construct PSM protocols that are only required to hide a certain small pre-specified set of input bits (as opposed to the whole input). We define this notion of PSM below.

Definition 5 (**b-bit PSM**). *Consider a function $f : (\mathcal{W} \times \mathcal{X}) \times \mathcal{Y} \rightarrow \mathcal{Z}$, with $\log |\mathcal{W}| \geq b$ for some $b > 0$. We say that a pair of deterministic encoding algorithms $F_1 : \mathcal{W} \times \mathcal{X} \times \mathcal{R} \rightarrow \mathcal{T}_1$ and $F_2 : \mathcal{Y} \times \mathcal{R} \rightarrow \mathcal{T}_2$ constitute a b-bit* PSM *for f if the function $F((w,x), y, r) = (F_1(w,x,r), F_2(y,r))$ satisfies the following properties:*

1. *(δ-Correctness): There exists a deterministic algorithm* Dec, *called the* decoder, *such that for every input $((w,x),y)$ we have that:*

$$\Pr_{r \xleftarrow{R} \mathcal{R}} [\mathsf{Dec}(F((w,x),y,r)) \neq f((w,x),y)] \leq \delta.$$

2. *(b-bit ε-Privacy): There exists a randomized algorithm* Sim *such that for any input $((w,x),y)$ it holds that:*

$$\Delta_{r \xleftarrow{R} \mathcal{R}} (\mathsf{Sim}(f((w,x),y),x,y); F((w,x),y,r)) \leq \varepsilon.$$

The communication complexity of the protocol is defined as the total encoding length ($\log |\mathcal{T}_1| + \log |\mathcal{T}_2|$), and the randomness complexity of the protocol is defined as $\log |\mathcal{R}|$.

By default, the above sets are to be taken to be $\mathcal{W} = \{0,1\}^b$, $\mathcal{X} = \mathcal{Y} = \{0,1\}^n$, $\mathcal{Z} = \{0,1\}$, $\mathcal{R} = \{0,1\}^\rho$, $\mathcal{T}_1 = \{0,1\}^{t_1}$, and $\mathcal{T}_2 = \{0,1\}^{t_2}$ for some positive integers b, n, ρ, t_1, and t_2.

Lemma 3 (**CDS to 1-bit PSM**). *If every Boolean function on $\mathcal{X} \times \mathcal{Y}$ has a* CDS *protocol with communication complexity t, then every Boolean function on $(\{0,1\} \times \mathcal{X}) \times \mathcal{Y}$ has a 1-bit* PSM *protocol with communication complexity $(t + 1 + \log |\mathcal{X}| + \log |\mathcal{Y}|)$, with the same correctness and privacy guarantees.*

Proof. Suppose we want to construct a 1-bit PSM protocol for a function $f : (\{0,1\} \times \mathcal{X}) \times \mathcal{Y} \rightarrow \{0,1\}$. Let $(G_1, G_2, \mathsf{Dec}_{\mathsf{CDS}})$ be a CDS protocol for the function $g(x,y) = f((0,x),y) \oplus f((1,x),y)$ with communication complexity t.

We use this to construct our 1-bit PSM protocol (F_1, F_2, Dec) for f. Let s be a bit from the common randomness. F_1 is now defined as $F_1((w,x),(s,r)) = (G_1(x,s,r), w \oplus s, x)$, and F_2 is defined as $F_2(y,(s,r)) = (G_2(y,s,r), y)$.

Dec, on input $((g_1, w \oplus s, x), (g_2, y))$, works by first checking whether given x and y, the value of f still depends on w. If not, it simply computes f using x and y. If it does depend on w, this implies that $f((0,x),y) \neq f((1,x),y)$, and $g(x,y) = 1$, and so $\mathsf{Dec}_{\mathsf{CDS}}(x,y,g_1,g_2)$ outputs s, which can be used to retrieve w from $(w \oplus s)$, and now the whole input is known and f can be computed.

This argues correctness, and the error here is at most that in the CDS protocol. The communication is also seen to be at most $(t + \log|\mathcal{X}| + \log|\mathcal{Y}| + 1)$.

Let $\mathsf{Sim}_{\mathsf{CDS}}$ be the simulator for the CDS protocol for g. The simulator $\mathsf{Sim}(f((w,x),y),x,y)$ works by first checking whether $f((0,x),y) = f((1,x),y)$. If it isn't, then the value of w is determined by x, y, and the value of f and, knowing w, Sim can compute F_1 and F_2 by itself, thus simulating them perfectly. If not, this implies that $g(x,y) = 0$. In this case, Sim first computes $(g_1^*, g_2^*) \leftarrow \mathsf{Sim}_{\mathsf{CDS}}(x,y)$, picks a random bit s^*, and outputs $((g_1^*, s^*, x), (g_2^*, y))$. The simulation error is:

$$\begin{aligned}\Delta(&\mathsf{Sim}(f((w,x),y),x,y); F(x,y,c))\\ &= \Delta((\mathsf{Sim}_{\mathsf{CDS}}(x,y), s^*, x, y); (G(x,y,s), w \oplus s, x, y))\\ &= \Delta((\mathsf{Sim}_{\mathsf{CDS}}(x,y), s^*); (G(x,y,s), w \oplus s))\end{aligned}$$

Note that here s^* and $(w \oplus s)$ have the same marginal distribution, which is the uniform distribution over $\{0,1\}$. Also, $\mathsf{Sim}_{\mathsf{CDS}}(x,y)$ is independent of s^*. Writing out the expansion of Δ in terms of differences in probabilities and using Bayes' Theorem along with the above observation gives us the following:

$$\begin{aligned}\Delta(&(\mathsf{Sim}_{\mathsf{CDS}}(x,y), s^*); (G(x,y,s), w \oplus s))\\ &= \frac{1}{2} \sum_{m \in T_1 \times T_2, b \in \{0,1\}} \Big| \Pr[(\mathsf{Sim}_{\mathsf{CDS}}(x,y), s^*) = (m,b)]\\ &\qquad\qquad - \Pr[(G(x,y,s), w \oplus s) = (m,b)] \Big|\\ &= \frac{1}{2} \sum_{m \in T_1 \times T_2, b \in \{0,1\}} \Big| \Pr[s^* = b] \Pr[\mathsf{Sim}_{\mathsf{CDS}}(x,y) = m]\\ &\qquad\qquad - \Pr[w \oplus s = b] \Pr[G(x,y,b \oplus w) = m] \Big|\\ &= \frac{1}{2} \sum_{b \in \{0,1\}} \frac{1}{2} \sum_{m \in T_1 \times T_2} \Big| \Pr[\mathsf{Sim}_{\mathsf{CDS}}(x,y) = m] - \Pr[G(x,y,b \oplus w) = m] \Big|\\ &= \frac{1}{2} [\Delta(\mathsf{Sim}_{\mathsf{CDS}}(x,y); G(x,y,0)) + \Delta(\mathsf{Sim}_{\mathsf{CDS}}(x,y); G(x,y,1))]\end{aligned}$$

By the ε-privacy of the CDS scheme (since the value of $g(x,y)$ is 0), each summand in the right-hand side above is at most ε. Hence the total simulation error is at most ε. □

In [15] it was shown that there exists a Boolean function on $\{0,1\}^n \times \{0,1\}^n$ such that any perfect 1-bit PSM for it requires at least $2.99n$ bits of communication. Using Lemma 3 along with this lower bound, we have the following theorem.

Theorem 15. *There is a Boolean function on* $\{0,1\}^n \times \{0,1\}^n$ *such that any perfect* CDS *protocol for it has communication complexity at least* $0.99n$.

We can generalise the above approach to construct b-bit PSM protocols for larger values of b as follows.

Lemma 4 (CDS to b-bit PSM). *If every Boolean function on $\mathcal{X} \times \mathcal{Y}$ has a CDS protocol with communication complexity t then, for any $b > 0$, every Boolean function on $(\{0,1\}^b \times \mathcal{X}) \times \mathcal{Y}$ has a b-bit PSM protocol with communication complexity $(2^{2^b}(t+1) + \log|\mathcal{X}| + \log|\mathcal{Y}|)$, with the same correctness guarantee and with privacy that is degraded by a factor of 2^{2^b}.*

Proof (Proof sketch). The idea behind the construction is that the function $f_{x,y}(w) = f((w,x),y)$, where w is b bits long, can be one of only 2^{2^b} functions – call this set of functions $\mathcal{H} = \{h_i\}$. For each of these h_i's, we define a function $g_i(x,y)$ that indicates whether $f_{x,y} \equiv h_i$. Note that once the PSM decoder knows x and y, the information that the value of f reveals to it about w is exactly $f_{x,y}(w)$, which is the same as $h_i(w)$ if $g_i(x,y) = 1$.

In our construction, first we have F_1 reveal x and F_2 reveal y. Now we wish to, for each i, reveal $h_i(w)$ if and only if $g_i(x,y) = 1$. To do this, for each i, we choose a random bit s_i from the common randomness, reveal $h_i(w) \oplus s_i$, and run the CDS protocol for g_i with s_i as the secret.

The correctness is preserved because whenever the CDS for the "correct" value of i is correct, our protocol is correct.

The simulator, given x, y and $f((w,x),y)$, first outputs x and y. It then finds the i' such that $g_{i'}(x,y) = 1$. For every other i, it publishes a random s_i^* and the output of the CDS simulator for the function g_i with inputs x, y and secret 0. For i', it publishes $(f((w,x),y) \oplus s_{i'}^*)$ for a random $s_{i'}^*$ and the messages of the CDS protocol for $g_{i'}$ with inputs x, y and secret $s_{i'}^*$. Privacy error goes from ε to $2^{2^b}\varepsilon$ because of arguments similar to those in the proof of Lemma 3 being applied to each invocation of the CDS protocol, all of which are mutually independent. □

8 Separating CDS and Insecure Communication

Here we show an explicit function whose randomized communication complexity is much higher than its CDS communication complexity. For simplicity, assume that n below is a power of 2; the statements made here can be shown to be true for a general n along the same lines.

Definition 6 (Communication Complexity). *Consider a function $f : \mathcal{X} \times \mathcal{Y} \to \mathcal{Z}$. A protocol between two parties (with shared randomness) who are given inputs $x \in \mathcal{X}$ and $y \in \mathcal{Y}$, respectively, is said to compute f if for every $(x,y) \in \mathcal{X} \times \mathcal{Y}$, the parties arrive at the correct value of f at the end of it with probability at least $2/3$.*

The communication cost of a protocol is the most number of bits exchanged by the parties over all possible inputs and all values of shared randomness. The Randomized Communication Complexity *of f, denoted $\mathsf{R}(f)$, is the least communication cost of any protocol computing f.*

Gay et al. [17] showed that if a function has a CDS protocol with communication complexity t then, roughly, $\log \mathsf{R}(f) \leq 2t$. Moreover, this upper-bound can be achieved by a one-way communication protocol (in which only one party sends a message). We show that this bound is optimal (up to constant factors) by exhibiting a function that has a CDS protocol with low communication, but has high randomized communication complexity (even for fully interactive protocols).[9] Towards this, we first introduce the following problem.

Definition 7 (The Collision Problem). *The* Collision Problem (Col_n) *is a promise problem defined over a subset of* $\{0,1\}^{n \log n}$ *as follows. For an input* $x \in \{0,1\}^{n \log n}$, *divide* x *into* n *blocks of* $\log n$ *bits each. Each such* x *can now be used to define a function* $f_x : \{0,1\}^{\log n} \to \{0,1\}^{\log n}$, *where* $f_x(i)$ *is the* i^{th} *block of* x *(when* i *is interpreted as an integer in* $[n]$*).* $\mathsf{Col}_n(x)$ *is defined to be* 1 *if* f_x *is a permutation,* 0 *if* f_x *is 2-to-1, and is undefined otherwise.*

We use the above problem in conjunction with Sherstov's Pattern Matrix method [36] for proving communication complexity lower bounds. We define the following function that corresponds to what would be called a "pattern matrix" of Col_n.

Definition 8. *The promise problem* $\mathsf{PCol}_n : \{0,1\}^{4n \log n} \times [4]^{n \log n} \to \{0,1\}$ *is defined as follows. On an input* (x, y), *first divide* x *into* $n \log n$ *blocks of size* 4 *bits each. From the* i^{th} *block, select the bit* x_{i,y_i} *that is specified by the* i^{th} *coordinate of* y *(which is an element of* $\{1,2,3,4\}$*) to get the string* x_y *of length* $n \log n$*. The output of the function is* $\mathsf{Col}_n(x_y)$.

The pattern matrix method gives us a way to lower bound the randomized communication complexity of a function constructed in this manner using lower bounds on the approximate degree (denoted by $\widetilde{\mathsf{deg}}$ and which we do not define here) of the underlying function. We use known results to derive the following Corollary 1.

Corollary 1. $\mathsf{R}(\overline{\mathsf{PCol}_n}) = \mathsf{R}(\mathsf{PCol}_n) \geq \Omega(n^{1/3})$

Proof. It follows from [36] that $\mathsf{R}(\mathsf{PCol}_n) \geq \Omega(\widetilde{\mathsf{deg}}(\mathsf{Col}_n))$. Combined with the fact that $\widetilde{\mathsf{deg}}(\mathsf{Col}_n) \geq \Omega(n^{1/3})$ (which follows from [3,27]), we derive the corollary. □

Next we show that $\overline{\mathsf{PCol}_n}$ has a very efficient CDS protocol.

Lemma 5. *There is a* CDS *protocol for* $\overline{\mathsf{PCol}_n}$ *with* $\frac{1}{3}$*-completeness, perfect privacy, and communication complexity* $O(\log n)$.

In order to prove this lemma, we will need the following simple lemma which shows how to simulate messages generated by applying a PSM protocol to a set of inputs that are distributed jointly. It says that these can be simulated by sampling the corresponding distribution over the function outputs and running the PSM simulator on these sampled outputs.

[9] In fact, our separation holds even for quantum communication complexity – see [36] for relevant definitions and explanations.

Lemma 6. *Consider any function* $f : \mathcal{X} \times \mathcal{Y} \to \mathcal{Z}$, *and a* PSM *protocol* (F_1, F_2) *for it with* ϵ*-privacy realized by a simulator* Sim. *For any integer* $k > 0$ *and any joint distribution* $\overline{(X,Y)}$ *over* $(\mathcal{X} \times \mathcal{Y})^k$, *let* $\overline{Z}$ *be the distribution over* $\mathcal{Z}^k$ *obtained by sampling* $\overline{(x,y)} = ((x_1, y_1), \dots, (x_k, y_k))$ *from* $\overline{(X,Y)}$ *and then computing* $(f(x_1, y_1), \dots, f(x_k, y_k))$. *Then,*

$$\Delta\left((\mathsf{Sim}(z_1), \dots, \mathsf{Sim}(z_k)); (F(x_1, y_1), \dots, F(x_k, y_k))\right) \leq k\epsilon,$$

where $\overline{(x,y)} \leftarrow \overline{(X,Y)}, \overline{z} \leftarrow \overline{Z}$. *In particular, if the* PSM *is perfect, the above statistical distance is zero.*

The proof (which is standard) appears in the full version [5]. We can now prove Lemma 5.

Proof (Proof of Lemma 5). Given input $(x, y) \in \{0,1\}^{4n \log n} \times [4]^{n \log n}$ and secret bit s, the idea behind the CDS protocol is to convey through the messages a uniformly random element from the range of f_{x_y} if $s = 1$, and a uniformly random element from $\{0,1\}^{\log n}$ if $s = 0$. If $\overline{\mathsf{PCol}}_n(x,y) = 0$, f_{x_y} is a permutation, and hence the distributions in the two cases are identical. If $\overline{\mathsf{PCol}}_n(x,y) = 1$, f_{x_y}'s range covers only half the co-domain and so the two cases can be distinguished.

We now construct a CDS protocol (F_1, F_2) that functions as above. Let $G = (G_1, G_2)$ be the perfect PSM protocol for the finite function $\mathsf{ind} : \{0,1\}^4 \times [4] \to \{0,1\}$ that takes (a, b) as input and outputs the bit in a that is pointed to by b. Let $\mathsf{Dec}_{\mathsf{PSM}}$ be a perfect decoder for G. The CDS protocol (F_1, F_2) works as follows.

- First an index $i \in [n]$ is sampled from the common randomness. (In the case of $s = 1$, $f_{x_y}(i)$ is the information that will be output jointly by F_1 and F_2.)
- Note that the value $f_{x_y}(i)$ consists of $\log n$ bits, each of which is encoded by 4 bits in x and a value in [4] in y – let the relevant parts of x and y be $(x_i^1, \dots, x_i^{\log n})$ and $(y_i^1, \dots, y_i^{\log n})$ respectively, where $x_i^j \in \{0,1\}^4$ and $y_i^j \in [4]$.
- If $s = 1$, for each $j \in [\log n]$, F_1 outputs $g_1^j = G_1(x_i^j, r_j)$, and F_2 outputs $g_2^j = G_2(y_i^j, r_j)$, where r_j is from the common randomness.
- If $s = 0$, for each $j \in [\log n]$, F_1 outputs $g_1^j = G_1(w^j, r_j)$, and F_2 outputs $g_2^j = G_2(y_i^j, r_j)$, where each w^j is chosen at random from $\{0,1\}^4$.

The CDS decoding procedure Dec works as follows.

- Input: $(x, y, (g_1^1, \dots, g_1^{\log n}), (g_2^1, \dots, g_2^{\log n}))$.
- For each $j \in [\log n]$, compute $z_j \leftarrow \mathsf{Dec}_{\mathsf{PSM}}(g_1^j, g_2^j)$ to get the string z.
- If there exists an i such that $f_{x_y}(i) = z$, output 1, else output 0.

If $\overline{\mathsf{PCol}}_n(x,y) = 1$, f_{x_y} is 2-to-1. By the perfect correctness of the PSM protocol, if $s = 1$, $z = f_{x_y}(i)$ for the i chosen by (F_1, F_2), and so Dec always outputs 1. If $s = 0$, z is a random string in $\{0,1\}^{\log n}$, and Dec outputs 0 exactly when z falls outside the range of f_{x_y}; this happens with probability 1/2 as f_{x_y} is 2-to-1, and Dec outputs 1 otherwise.

This gives only $\frac{1}{2}$-correctness but this error is only one-sided, and so by repeating the protocol once more and checking whether z lies in the range of f_{x_y} both times, this error can be reduced, giving $\frac{1}{4}$-correctness. This repetition does not degrade privacy which, as shown below, is perfect.

If $\overline{\mathsf{PCol}}_n(x, y) = 0$, f_{x_y} is a permutation. The output of F_1 and F_2 is simulated as follows using $\mathsf{Sim}_{\mathsf{PSM}}$, the simulator for the perfect PSM protocol used above. Our simulator Sim, given (x, y) as input, first picks random bits $z_1^*, \ldots, z_{\log n}^*$. It then outputs $(\mathsf{Sim}_{\mathsf{PSM}}(z_1^*), \ldots, \mathsf{Sim}_{\mathsf{PSM}}(z_{\log n}^*))$.

The simulation error is:

$$\Delta((\mathsf{Sim}_{\mathsf{PSM}}(z_1^*), \ldots, \mathsf{Sim}_{\mathsf{PSM}}(z_{\log n}^*)); ((g_1^1, g_2^1), \ldots, (g_1^{\log n}, g_2^{\log n})))$$

where the (g_1^j, g_2^j)'s are the PSM messages in the protocol description.

First we consider the case $s = 1$. Recall that the (g_1^j, g_2^j)'s are computed by first selecting $i \in [n]$ at random and computing the PSM messages for $\mathsf{ind}(x_i^j, y_i^j)$, which is the jth bit of $f_{x_y}(i)$. As the range of f_{x_y} is uniform over $\{0,1\}^{\log n}$, over the randomness of i each $\mathsf{ind}(x_i^j, y_i^j)$ is a uniformly random bit independent of all the other $\mathsf{ind}(x_i^{j'}, y_i^{j'})$'s. Thus, $(\mathsf{ind}(x_i^1, y_i^1), \ldots, \mathsf{ind}(x_i^{\log n}, y_i^{\log n}))$ is distributed the same as $(z_1^*, \ldots, z_{\log n}^*)$, and so by Lemma 6, the above simulation error is zero as we are using a perfect PSM protocol.

Similarly, when $s = 0$, the (g_1^j, g_2^j)'s are computed by first selecting $i \in [n]$ at random and computing the PSM messages for $\mathsf{ind}(w^j, y_i^j)$ for uniformly random $w^1, \ldots, w^j \in \{0,1\}^4$. So again each $\mathsf{ind}(w^j, y_i^j)$ is a uniformly random bit independent of all the other $\mathsf{ind}(w^{j'}, y_i^{j'})$'s, and by Lemma 6, the simulation error is again zero.

The PSM for each bit of z is for a finite-sized function and its communication complexity is some constant, so the total communication is $\Theta(\log n)$. □

Gay et al. [17] showed the following relationships between the randomized communication complexity of a Boolean function and the complexity of general and linear CDS protocols for it with single-bit secrets. While they originally showed these for perfect protocols, we extend their proof to work for imperfect ones in Appendix A.

Theorem 16 [17]. *For any (partial or total) Boolean function f,*

$$\mathsf{CDS}(f) \geq \frac{1}{2} \log \mathsf{R}(f) \quad \textit{and} \quad \mathsf{linCDS}(f) \geq \frac{1}{10}\sqrt{\mathsf{R}(f)}$$

The following corollary of Lemma 5 and Corollary 1 shows that the above bound on CDS in general is tight up to constant factors.

Corollary 2. *There exists a partial Boolean function f such that:*

$$\mathsf{CDS}(f) \leq O(\log \mathsf{R}(f))$$

Following from Corollary 2 and Theorem 16, the next corollary says that there are functions for which general CDS protocols can do much better than linear CDS protocols.

Corollary 3. *There exists a partial Boolean function f such that:*

$$\mathsf{CDS}(f) \leq O(\log \mathsf{linCDS}(f))$$

Remark 3. In fact, [17] showed that Theorem 16 holds even for "weakly-linear" CDS protocols in which only the decoding process is assumed to be linear (and the senders are allowed to be non-linear). Corollary 3 therefore generalizes to this case as well.

Acknowledgements. We would like to thank Amos Beimel and Hoteck Wee for useful discussions. We also thank Amos Beimel for pointing out a flaw in an earlier version of this manuscript. We also thank the anonymous referees for their useful comments. Research supported by the European Union's Horizon 2020 Programme (ERC-StG-2014-2020) under grant agreement no. 639813 ERC-CLC, by an ICRC grant and by the Check Point Institute for Information Security. This work was done in part while the fourth author was visiting Tel Aviv University, and he was also supported by NSF Grants CNS-1350619 and CNS-1414119, and by the Defense Advanced Research Projects Agency (DARPA) and the U.S. Army Research Office under contracts W911NF-15-C-0226 and W911NF-15-C-0236.

A Communication Complexity and Imperfect CDS Protocols

In this section, we extend the relationships between CDS and randomised communication complexity shown by Gay et al. [17] to include imperfect CDS protocols. We prove the following theorem. (The terms involved are defined in Sects. 3 and 8.)

Theorem 17. *For any (partial or total) Boolean function f,*

$$\mathsf{CDS}(f) \geq \frac{1}{2} \log \mathsf{R}(f)$$

$$\mathsf{linCDS}(f) \geq \frac{1}{10} \sqrt{\mathsf{R}(f)}$$

Recall that $\mathsf{CDS}(f)$ is the least communication complexity of any CDS protocol for f with $\{0,1\}$ as the secret domain that has $\frac{1}{10}$ correctness and privacy. And that $\mathsf{linCDS}(f)$ is the same, but for linear protocols. We will prove Theorem 17 using the following more general lemma that we prove afterward.

Lemma 7. *Consider any function $f : \mathcal{X} \times \mathcal{Y} \rightarrow \{0,1\}$. Suppose f has a CDS protocol (F_1, F_2, Dec) with $\frac{1}{10}$-correctness and $\frac{1}{10}$-privacy, with domains as follows: $F_1 : \mathcal{X} \times \{0,1\} \times \mathcal{R} \rightarrow \mathcal{T}_1$, $F_2 : \mathcal{X} \times \{0,1\} \times \mathcal{R} \rightarrow \mathcal{T}_2$, and $\mathsf{Dec} : \mathcal{X} \times \mathcal{Y} \times \mathcal{T}_1 \times \mathcal{T}_2 \rightarrow \{0,1\}$. Let $\mathcal{H}$ be any superset of all possible functions $\{h : \mathcal{T}_1 \times \mathcal{T}_2 \rightarrow \{0,1\}\}$ that $\mathsf{Dec}(x, y, \cdot, \cdot)$ could possibly be for any $x \in \mathcal{X}$ and $y \in \mathcal{Y}$. Then,*

$$\mathsf{R}(f) \leq 100 \log |\mathcal{H}| \left(\log |\mathcal{T}_1| + \log |\mathcal{T}_2|\right)$$

Proof (Proof of Theorem 17). A lower bound for a CDS protocol for f with $\frac{1}{10}$ correctness and privacy can be obtained by taking $\mathcal{H}$ to be the set of all possible functions from $\mathcal{T}_1 \times \mathcal{T}_2 \to \{0,1\}$. There are $2^{|\mathcal{T}_1||\mathcal{T}_2|}$ of these. We then have from Lemma 7:

$$\begin{aligned} \mathsf{R}(f) &\leq 100\,|\mathcal{T}_1|\,|\mathcal{T}_2|\,(\log|\mathcal{T}_1| + \log|\mathcal{T}_2|) \\ \implies \log \mathsf{R}(f) &\leq \log 100 + (\log|\mathcal{T}_1| + \log|\mathcal{T}_2|) + \log(\log|\mathcal{T}_1| + \log|\mathcal{T}_2|) \\ &\leq 2(\log|\mathcal{T}_1| + \log|\mathcal{T}_2|) \end{aligned}$$

This is true for any such CDS protocol. Note that $(\log|\mathcal{T}_1| + \log|\mathcal{T}_2|)$ is the communication complexity of the CDS protocol in question. So this implies that $\log \mathsf{R}(f) \leq 2\mathsf{CDS}(f)$.

The lower bound on $\mathsf{linCDS}(f)$ is similarly obtained by taking $\mathcal{H}$ to be the set of all linear functions over vectors spaces that may be contained in $\mathcal{T}_1 \times \mathcal{T}_2$, as linear CDS protocols always have linear reconstruction. In this case, $\mathcal{T}_1$ and $\mathcal{T}_2$ would have to be of the form $\mathbb{F}^{t_1}$ and $\mathbb{F}^{t_2}$ for some t_1, t_2, and $\mathcal{H}$ would then contain $\mathbb{F}^{t_1+t_2} = |\mathcal{T}_1|\,|\mathcal{T}_2|$ functions. Lemma 7 now immediately gives us the following:

$$\begin{aligned} \mathsf{R}(f) &\leq 100(\log|\mathcal{T}_1| + \log|\mathcal{T}_2|)^2 \\ \implies \sqrt{\mathsf{R}(f)} &\leq 10 \cdot \mathsf{linCDS}(f) \end{aligned}$$

□

Proof (Proof of Lemma 7). Given a CDS protocol (F_1, F_2, Dec) as in the hypothesis, we construct a single message protocol (with shared randomness) for parties A, who is given an $x \in \mathcal{X}$, and B, who is given a $y \in \mathcal{Y}$, to compute $f(x,y)$ as follows.

- For an integer N that shall be determined later, the shared randomness is used to sample N random bits $s_1, \ldots, s_N$, and also $r_1, \ldots, r_N \in \mathcal{R}$.
- For each $i \in [N]$, A computes and sends $a_i = F_1(x, s_i, r_i)$ to B.
- For each $i \in [N]$, B computes, in order, $b_i = F_2(y, s_i, r_i)$ and, for each $h \in H$, $s_i^h = h(a_i, b_i)$.
- If there is an $h \in H$ such that for more than 3/4 values of $i \in [N]$, $s_i^h = s_i$, then B decides that $f(x,y) = 1$, else 0.

If $f(x,y) = 1$, by the $\frac{1}{10}$-correctness of the CDS protocol, we know that there exists an $h^* \in H$, namely $\mathsf{Dec}(x, y, \cdot, \cdot)$, such that $\Pr[h^*(a_i, b_i) = s_i] \geq 9/10$. By the Chernoff bound, the probability that the communication protocol is wrong in this case can be bounded as follows:

$$\Pr\left[\left|\left\{i : s_i^{h^*} = s_i\right\}\right| \leq \frac{3}{4}N\right] \leq e^{-N/80}$$

If $f(x,y) = 0$, by the $\frac{1}{10}$-privacy of the CDS protocol and the triangle inequality, the statistical distance between the distributions $F(x,y,0)$ and $F(x,y,1)$ is at most 2/10. This implies that for any function h, if s_i is chosen at random, $\Pr[h(a_i, b_i) = s_i] \leq 6/10$. Using the union bound and the Chernoff bound, in order, the probability that the communication protocol is wrong in this case can be bounded as follows:

$$\Pr\left[\exists h \in \mathcal{H} : \left|\left\{i : s_i^h = s_i\right\}\right| \geq \frac{3}{4}N\right] \leq |\mathcal{H}| \Pr\left[\left|\left\{i : s_i^h = s_i\right\}\right| \geq \frac{3}{4}N\right]$$
$$\leq |\mathcal{H}|\, e^{-N/80}$$

So if N is chosen to be, say, $(100 \log |\mathcal{H}|)$, the error probability in both cases would be much less than 1/3, and this would be a valid communication protocol computing f.

The total communication involved is $N \log |\mathcal{T}_1| \leq 100 \log |\mathcal{H}| (\log |\mathcal{T}_1| + \log |\mathcal{T}_2|)$, as required. □

References

1. Aaronson, S.: Impossibility of succinct quantum proofs for collision-freeness. Quantum Inf. Comput. **12**(1–2), 21–28 (2012)
2. Aiello, B., Ishai, Y., Reingold, O.: Priced oblivious transfer: how to sell digital goods. In: Pfitzmann, B. (ed.) EUROCRYPT 2001. LNCS, vol. 2045, pp. 119–135. Springer, Heidelberg (2001). doi:10.1007/3-540-44987-6_8
3. Ambainis, A.: Polynomial degree and lower bounds in quantum complexity: collision and element distinctness with small range. Theory Comput. **1**(1), 37–46 (2005)
4. Ambrona, M., Barthe, G., Schmidt, B.: Generic transformations of predicate encodings: constructions and applications. In: To appear in CRYPTO 2017 (2017). http://eprint.iacr.org/2016/1105
5. Applebaum, B., Arkis, B., Raykov, P., Vasudevan, P.N.: Conditional disclosure of secrets: amplification, closure, amortization, lower-bounds, and separations. Cryptology ePrint Archive, Report 2017/164 (2017). Full version of this paper: http://eprint.iacr.org/2017/164
6. Applebaum, B., Ishai, Y., Kushilevitz, E.: Cryptography in NC^0. In: 45th Symposium on Foundations of Computer Science (FOCS 2004), 17–19 October 2004, Rome, Italy, Proceedings, pp. 166–175. IEEE Computer Society (2004)
7. Applebaum, B., Raykov, P.: From private simultaneous messages to zero-information Arthur-Merlin protocols and back. In: Kushilevitz, E., Malkin, T. (eds.) TCC 2016. LNCS, vol. 9563, pp. 65–82. Springer, Heidelberg (2016). doi:10.1007/978-3-662-49099-0_3
8. Attrapadung, N.: Dual system encryption via doubly selective security: framework, fully secure functional encryption for regular languages, and more. In: Nguyen, P.Q., Oswald, E. (eds.) EUROCRYPT 2014. LNCS, vol. 8441, pp. 557–577. Springer, Heidelberg (2014). doi:10.1007/978-3-642-55220-5_31
9. Beimel, A., Ishai, Y., Kumaresan, R., Kushilevitz, E.: On the cryptographic complexity of the worst functions. In: Lindell [28], pp. 317–342 (2014)
10. Brickell, E.F., Davenport, D.M.: On the classification of ideal secret sharing schemes. J. Cryptol. **4**(2), 123–134 (1991)
11. Capocelli, R.M., De Santis, A., Gargano, L., Vaccaro, U.: On the size of shares for secret sharing schemes. J. Cryptol. **6**(3), 157–167 (1993)

12. Chen, H., Cramer, R.: Algebraic geometric secret sharing schemes and secure multi-party computations over small fields. In: Dwork, C. (ed.) CRYPTO 2006. LNCS, vol. 4117, pp. 521–536. Springer, Heidelberg (2006). doi:10.1007/11818175_31
13. Chen, H., Cramer, R., Goldwasser, S., de Haan, R., Vaikuntanathan, V.: Secure computation from random error correcting codes. In: Naor, M. (ed.) EUROCRYPT 2007. LNCS, vol. 4515, pp. 291–310. Springer, Heidelberg (2007). doi:10.1007/978-3-540-72540-4_17
14. Chor, B., Kushilevitz, E., Goldreich, O., Sudan, M.: Private information retrieval. J. ACM **45**(6), 965–981 (1998)
15. Feige, U., Kilian, J., Naor, M.: A minimal model for secure computation (extended abstract). In: Leighton, F.T., Goodrich, M.T. (eds.) Proceedings of 26th Annual ACM Symposium on Theory of Computing, 23–25 May 1994, Montréal, Québec, Canada, pp. 554–563. ACM (1994)
16. Garcia, A., Stichtenoth, H.: On the asymptotic behavior of some towers of function fields over finite fields. J. Num. Theory **61**(2), 248–273 (1996)
17. Gay, R., Kerenidis, I., Wee, H.: Communication complexity of conditional disclosure of secrets and attribute-based encryption. In: Gennaro, R., Robshaw, M. (eds.) CRYPTO 2015. LNCS, vol. 9216, pp. 485–502. Springer, Heidelberg (2015). doi:10.1007/978-3-662-48000-7_24
18. Gertner, Y., Ishai, Y., Kushilevitz, E., Malkin, T.: Protecting data privacy in private information retrieval schemes. J. Comput. Syst. Sci. **60**(3), 592–629 (2000)
19. Goldwasser, S., Micali, S., Rivest, R.L.: A digital signature scheme secure against adaptive chosen-message attacks. SIAM J. Comput. **17**(2), 281–308 (1988)
20. Göös, M., Pitassi, T., Watson, T.: Zero-information protocols and unambiguity in Arthur-Merlin communication. In: Roughgarden, T. (ed.) Proceedings of 2015 Conference on Innovations in Theoretical Computer Science, ITCS 2015, Rehovot, Israel, 11–13 January 2015, pp. 113–122. ACM (2015)
21. Goyal, V., Pandey, O., Sahai, A., Waters, B.: Attribute-based encryption for fine-grained access control of encrypted data. In: Juels, A., Wright, R.N., De Capitani di Vimercati, S. (eds.) Proceedings of 13th ACM Conference on Computer and Communications Security, CCS 2006, Alexandria, VA, USA, 30 October–3 November 2006, pp. 89–98. ACM (2006)
22. Holenstein, T., Renner, R.: One-way secret-key agreement and applications to circuit polarization and immunization of public-key encryption. In: Shoup, V. (ed.) CRYPTO 2005. LNCS, vol. 3621, pp. 478–493. Springer, Heidelberg (2005). doi:10.1007/11535218_29
23. Ishai, Y., Kushilevitz, E.: Private simultaneous messages protocols with applications. In: ISTCS, pp. 174–184 (1997)
24. Ishai, Y., Kushilevitz, E.: Randomizing polynomials: a new representation with applications to round-efficient secure computation. In: 41st Annual Symposium on Foundations of Computer Science, FOCS 2000, 12–14 November 2000, Redondo Beach, California, USA, pp. 294–304. IEEE Computer Society (2000)
25. Ishai, Y., Kushilevitz, E., Ostrovsky, R., Sahai, A.: Extracting correlations. In: 50th Annual IEEE Symposium on Foundations of Computer Science, FOCS 2009, 25–27 October 2009, Atlanta, Georgia, USA, pp. 261–270. IEEE Computer Society (2009)
26. Ishai, Y., Wee, H.: Partial garbling schemes and their applications. In: Esparza, J., Fraigniaud, P., Husfeldt, T., Koutsoupias, E. (eds.) ICALP 2014. LNCS, vol. 8572, pp. 650–662. Springer, Heidelberg (2014). doi:10.1007/978-3-662-43948-7_54
27. Kutin, S.: Quantum lower bound for the collision problem with small range. Theory Comput. **1**(1), 29–36 (2005)

28. Lindell, Y. (ed.): Theory of Cryptography - 11th Theory of Cryptography Conference, TCC 2014, San Diego, CA, USA, February 24–26, 2014. Proceedings, LNCS, vol. 8349. Springer, Heidelberg (2014)
29. Liu, T., Vaikuntanathan, V., Wee, H.: New protocols for conditional disclosure of secrets (and more). In: To appear in CRYPTO 2017 (2017). http://eprint.iacr.org/2017/359
30. Maurer, U., Pietrzak, K., Renner, R.: Indistinguishability amplification. In: Menezes, A. (ed.) CRYPTO 2007. LNCS, vol. 4622, pp. 130–149. Springer, Heidelberg (2007). doi:10.1007/978-3-540-74143-5_8
31. Mintz, Y.: Information ratios of graph secret-sharing schemes. Master's thesis, Department of Computer Science, Ben Gurion University (2012)
32. Okamoto, T.: On relationships between statistical zero-knowledge proofs. In: Miller, G.L. (ed.) Proceedings of 28th Annual ACM Symposium on the Theory of Computing, Philadelphia, Pennsylvania, USA, 22–24 May 1996, pp. 649–658. ACM (1996)
33. Potechin, A.: A note on amortized space complexity. CoRR, abs/1611.06632 (2016)
34. Sahai, A., Vadhan, S.P.: A complete problem for statistical zero knowledge. J. ACM **50**(2), 196–249 (2003)
35. Sahai, A., Waters, B.: Fuzzy identity-based encryption. In: Cramer, R. (ed.) EUROCRYPT 2005. LNCS, vol. 3494, pp. 457–473. Springer, Heidelberg (2005). doi:10.1007/11426639_27
36. Sherstov, A.A.: The pattern matrix method. SIAM J. Comput. **40**(6), 1969–2000 (2011)
37. Sun, H.-M., Shieh, S.-P.: Secret sharing in graph-based prohibited structures. In: Proceedings of IEEE INFOCOM 1997, The Conference on Computer Communications, Sixteenth Annual Joint Conference of the IEEE Computer and Communications Societies, Driving the Information Revolution, Kobe, Japan, 7–12 April 1997, pp. 718–724. IEEE (1997)
38. Wee, H.: Dual system encryption via predicate encodings. In: Lindell [28], pp. 616–637 (2014)

Conditional Disclosure of Secrets via Non-linear Reconstruction

Tianren Liu[1(✉)], Vinod Vaikuntanathan[1], and Hoeteck Wee[2]

[1] MIT, Cambridge, USA
liutr@mit.edu, vinodv@csail.mit.edu
[2] CNRS and ENS, Paris, France
wee@di.ens.fr

Abstract. We present new protocols for conditional disclosure of secrets (CDS), where two parties want to disclose a secret to a third party if and only if their respective inputs satisfy some predicate.

- For general predicates $\mathsf{P} : [N] \times [N] \to \{0, 1\}$, we present two protocols that achieve $o(N^{1/2})$ communication: the first achieves $O(N^{1/3})$ communication and the second achieves sub-polynomial $2^{O(\sqrt{\log N \log\log N})} = N^{o(1)}$ communication.
- As a corollary, we obtain improved share complexity for forbidden graph access structures. Namely, for every graph on N vertices, there is a secret-sharing scheme for N parties in which each pair of parties can reconstruct the secret if and only if the corresponding vertices in G are connected, and where each party gets a share of size $2^{O(\sqrt{\log N \log\log N})} = N^{o(1)}$.

Prior to this work, the best protocols for both primitives required communication complexity $\tilde{O}(N^{1/2})$. Indeed, this is essentially the best that all prior techniques could hope to achieve as they were limited to so-called "linear reconstruction". This is the first work to break this $O(N^{1/2})$ "linear reconstruction" barrier in settings related to secret sharing. To obtain these results, we draw upon techniques for non-linear reconstruction developed in the context of information-theoretic private information retrieval.

We further extend our results to the setting of private simultaneous messages (PSM), and provide applications such as an improved attribute-based encryption (ABE) for quadratic polynomials.

T. Liu—Research supported in part by NSF Grants CNS-1350619 and CNS-1414119, and by the Defense Advanced Research Projects Agency (DARPA) and the U.S. Army Research Office under contracts W911NF-15-C-0226 and W911NF-15-C-0236.
V. Vaikuntanathan—Research supported in part by NSF Grants CNS-1350619 and CNS-1414119, Alfred P. Sloan Research Fellowship, Microsoft Faculty Fellowship, the NEC Corporation, a Steven and Renee Finn Career Development Chair from MIT. This work was also sponsored in part by the Defense Advanced Research Projects Agency (DARPA) and the U.S. Army Research Office under contracts W911NF-15-C-0226 and W911NF-15-C-0236.
H. Wee—Research supported in part by ERC Project aSCEND (H2020 639554) and NSF Award CNS-1445424.

J. Katz and H. Shacham (Eds.): CRYPTO 2017, Part I, LNCS 10401, pp. 758–790, 2017.
DOI: 10.1007/978-3-319-63688-7_25

1 Introduction

We revisit a fundamental question in the foundations of cryptography: *What is the communication overhead of privacy in computation?* This question has been considered in several different models and settings (see, e.g., [CK91, OS08, ACC+14, DPP14]). In this work, we address this question in two, arguably minimalistic, models for communication in the setting of information-theoretic security, namely the conditional disclosure of secrets (CDS) model [GIKM00] and the private simultaneous messages (PSM) model [FKN94, IK97], with a focus on the former.

Conditional Disclosure of Secrets (CDS). Two-party conditional disclosure of secrets (CDS) [GIKM00] (c.f. Fig. 1) is a generalization of secret sharing [Sha79, ISN89]: two parties want to disclose a secret to a third party if and only if their respective inputs satisfy some fixed predicate $\mathsf{P} : [N] \times [N] \to \{0, 1\}$. Concretely, Alice holds x, Bob holds y and in addition, they both hold a secret $\mu \in \{0, 1\}$ (along with some additional private randomness w). Charlie knows both x and y but not μ; Alice and Bob want to disclose μ to Charlie iff $\mathsf{P}(x, y) = 1$. How many bits do Alice and Bob need to communicate to Charlie?

This is a very simple and natural model where non-private computation requires very little communication (just a single bit), whereas the best upper bound for private computation is exponential. Indeed, in the non-private setting, Alice or Bob can send μ to Charlie, upon which Charlie computes $\mathsf{P}(x, y)$ and decides whether to output μ or $\perp$. This trivial protocol with one-bit communication is not private because Charlie learns μ even when the predicate is false. In contrast, in the private setting, we have a big gap between upper and lower-bounds. The best upper bound we have for CDS for general predicates P requires that Alice and Bob each transmits $O(N^{1/2})$ bits [BIKK14, GKW15], and the best known lower bound is $\Omega(\log N)$ [GKW15, AARV17]. A central open problem is to narrow this gap, namely:

> *Do there exist CDS protocols for general predicates* $\mathsf{P} : [N] \times [N] \to \{0, 1\}$ *with* $o(N^{1/2})$ *communication?*

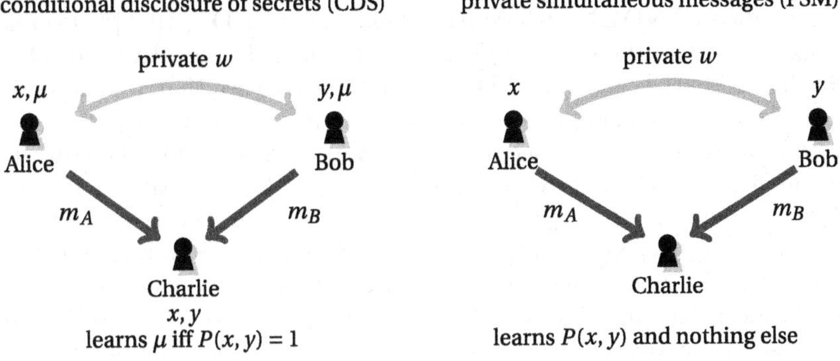

Fig. 1. Pictorial representation of CDS and PSM.

In this work, we address this question in the affirmative, giving two protocols with $o(N^{1/2})$ communication, including one with sub-polynomial $N^{o(1)}$ communication. Before describing our results in more detail, we need to place this question in a broader context.

First, the existing exponential gap between upper and lower bounds for CDS is analogous to a long-standing open question in information-theoretic cryptography, namely, the study of secret-sharing schemes for general access structures [ISN89]. For general secret-sharing schemes, the best upper bounds on the (individual) share size are exponential in the number of parties n, namely $2^{\Theta(n)}$, whereas the best lower bounds are nearly linear [Csi97], namely $\Omega(n/\log n)$ (see Beimel's survey [Bei11] for more details).

It turns out that we do have a more nuanced understanding of this gap, both for CDS and for secret-sharing. This understanding comes from looking at the complexity of the "reconstruction function": in CDS, this refers to the function that Charlie computes on Alice's and Bob's messages to recover μ, and in secret-sharing, the function used to recover the secret from the shares, and by complexity, we refer to the degree of the reconstruction function when expressed as a multivariate polynomial in its inputs, namely Alice's and Bob's messages or the shares.

On the Importance of Reconstruction Degree. Most known CDS and secret-sharing schemes have *linear* reconstruction functions (which is necessary for some applications), and for linear reconstruction, the existing upper bounds for both CDS and secret-sharing are essentially optimal [BGP95, RPRC16, GKW15]. Therefore, to narrow the exponential gap between upper and lower bounds for CDS, we need to turn to general, *non-linear* reconstruction functions, as will be the case for our new CDS protocols.

Starting from the work of Beimel and Ishai, we know of a few specific (artificial) access structures with non-linear secret sharing schemes (which are unlikely to have efficient linear secret sharing schemes) [BI01, VV15]. More recently, [AARV17] showed a specific (contrived) predicate with a non-linear CDS scheme that is exponentially more efficient than the best linear CDS scheme. Unfortunately, none of these works yield any techniques that work with general predicates.

Henceforth, instead of referring to general predicates, we will focus on a specific predicate $\mathbf{INDEX}_n$ where Alice holds a vector $\mathbf{D} \in \{0,1\}^n$, Bob holds an index $i \in [n]$ and the predicate is $\mathbf{D}, i \mapsto \mathbf{D}_i$, namely the i-th bit of $\mathbf{D}$; that is, Charlie learns the secret μ iff $\mathbf{D}_i = 1$. It is easy to see that we can derive a CDS protocol for the class of general predicates $\mathsf{P} : [N] \times [N] \to \{0,1\}$ – which we denote by $\mathbf{ALL}_N$ – from one for $\mathbf{INDEX}_N$, by considering the truth table of the predicate as the database and the input to the predicate as the index. Via this connection, our central open problem reduces to constructing CDS for $\mathbf{INDEX}_n$ with $o(\sqrt{n})$ communication. The best known CDS protocol for INDEX (regardless of the reconstruction degree) has communication $O(\sqrt{n})$; and this protocol indeed has linear reconstruction, for which there is a matching lower bound. More generally, Gay et al. [GKW15] show that any CDS for $\mathbf{INDEX}_n$ with degree k reconstruction requires communication $\Omega(n^{\frac{1}{k+1}})$.

1.1 Our Results and Techniques

The main results of this work are two CDS protocols for $\mathbf{INDEX}_n$ achieving $o(\sqrt{n})$ communication via *non-linear* reconstruction, namely:

- a CDS protocol with $O(n^{1/3})$ communication with quadratic reconstruction, which is optimal;
- a CDS protocol with $2^{O(\sqrt{\log n \log\log n})} = n^{o(1)}$ with general reconstruction.

These immediately imply CDS protocols for general predicates $\mathbf{ALL}_N$ with $O(N^{1/3})$ communication and quadratic reconstruction, and $2^{O(\sqrt{\log N \log\log N})} = N^{o(1)}$ and general reconstruction. Our CDS protocols also yield similar improvements for secret-sharing schemes for the so-called "forbidden graph access structures" [SS97] via a generic transformation in [BIKK14]; in particular, we present the first schemes that achieve $o(\sqrt{N})$ share sizes for graphs on N nodes. Overall, this is first work to break the "linear reconstruction" barrier for general predicates in settings related to secret sharing.

To obtain these results, we draw upon techniques for non-linear reconstruction developed in the context of information-theoretic *private information retrieval* (PIR) [CKGS98, WY05, Yek08, Efr09, DGY11, BIKO12, DG15]. Our $O(n^{1/3})$ protocol exploits partial derivatives of polynomials, whereas our $2^{O(\sqrt{\log n \log\log n})}$ uses matching vector families [Gro00], first invented in the context of explicit Ramsey graph constructions. While techniques from PIR have been used to improve communication complexity for information-theoretic cryptography e.g. [BIKK14], we do not know of any work that uses these techniques to improve communication complexity beyond the "linear reconstruction" barrier as we do.

Along the way, we also present new CDS protocols for low-degree polynomials (testing whether the polynomial evaluates to non-zero), along with an application to a new attribute-based encryption (ABE) scheme [SW05, GPSW06] for quadratic functions.

Finally, we show protocols in the stronger private simultaneous messages (PSM) model with optimal communication-degree tradeoffs. We summarize our CDS and PSM protocols in Fig. 2, and describe our results in more detail in the sequel.

1.2 Our CDS Protocols

As mentioned earlier, our CDS protocols draw upon techniques for non-linear reconstruction developed in the context of information-theoretic PIR. Our starting point is a recent work of Beimel, Ishai, Kumaresan and Kushilevitz (BIKK) [BIKK14], showing how to use PIR to improve PSM and information-theoretic two-party computation in several different models. While BIKK applies general transformations to variants of PIR, our constructions exploit the techniques used in a PIR in a more non-black-box manner, and along the way, we improve upon and simplify some of the constructions in BIKK. For this reason, we will first provide an overview of our CDS protocols without referring to PIR, and then explain the connection to PIR after.

Primitives	Alice's CC	Bob's CC	Reconstruction	Reference
CDS	$cc_A \cdot (cc_A + cc_B)^k = \Omega(n)$		degree k	[GKW15]
	$O(n/t)$	$t \in [n]$	degree 1	[GKW15] & Sec. 3.3
	$O(n/t^2)$	$t \in [n^{1/3}]$	degree 2	This Work (Sec. 3.3)
	$2^{O(\sqrt{\log n \log\log n})}$	$2^{O(\sqrt{\log n \log\log n})}$	general	This Work (Sec. 4)
PSM	$cc_A = \Omega(n)$, $cc_B = \Omega(\log n)$		general	folklore via [Nay99, KNR99]
	—	$\Omega(n^{1/k})$	degree k	This Work (Sec. A.3)
	$O(n)$	$O(n)$	degree 2	folklore
	$O(n)$	$O(\log n)$	degree $O(\log n)$	folklore
	$O(n)$	$O(kn^{1/k})$	degree $k+1$	This Work (Sec. 5.1)

Fig. 2. Summary of upper and lower bounds of $\mathbf{INDEX}_n$ for CDS and PSM, where Alice holds $\mathbf{D} \in \{0,1\}^n$ and Bob holds $i \in [n]$, and the columns correspond to the number of bits sent by Alice and by Bob, along with the complexity of the reconstruction function.

CDS for INDEX. Recall that in CDS for $\mathbf{INDEX}_n$, Alice holds $\mathbf{D} \in \{0,1\}^n$, Bob holds $i \in [n]$ and $\mu \in \{0,1\}$, and Charlie should learn μ iff $\mathbf{D}_i = 1$. Intuitively, the protocol proceeds by having Charlie "securely compute" $\mu\mathbf{D}_i$, so that if $\mathbf{D}_i = 0$, Charlie learns nothing about μ. To do this, we will relate $\mu\mathbf{D}_i$ to some function $F_{\mathbf{D},i}(\cdot)$, which would form part of the construction function.

Our protocols have the following high-level structure:

- Alice and Bob share randomness $\mathbf{b}, \mathbf{c}$.
- Bob deterministically encodes $i \in [n]$ as a vector $\mathbf{u}_i \in \{0,1\}^\ell$ and sends $\mathbf{m}_B^1 := \mu\mathbf{u}_i + \mathbf{b}$;
- We construct a function $F_{\mathbf{D},i}$ such that
$$\mu\mathbf{D}_i = F_{\mathbf{D},i}(\mu\mathbf{u}_i + \mathbf{b}) + \langle \mathbf{u}_i, \mathbf{y}_{\mathbf{D},\mathbf{b}} \rangle \quad (1)$$
where $\mathbf{y}_{\mathbf{D},\mathbf{b}} \in \{0,1\}^\ell$ is completely determined given $\mathbf{D}, \mathbf{b}$ and $\langle \cdot, \cdot \rangle$ corresponds to inner product. Note that Charlie can compute $F_{\mathbf{D},i}(\mu\mathbf{u}_i + \mathbf{b})$ given $\mathbf{D}, i, \mu\mathbf{u}_i + \mathbf{b}$.
- In order for Charlie to also "securely" compute $\langle \mathbf{u}_i, \mathbf{y}_{\mathbf{D},\mathbf{b}} \rangle$, Alice sends $\mathbf{m}_A^1 := \mathbf{y}_{\mathbf{D},\mathbf{b}} + \mathbf{c}$ and Bob sends $m_B^2 := \langle \mathbf{u}_i, \mathbf{c} \rangle$.
- Charlie can now compute $\mu\mathbf{D}_i$ (and thus μ) given $\mathbf{D}, i, (\mathbf{m}_A^1, \mathbf{m}_B^1, m_B^2)$ by computing
$$F_{\mathbf{D},i}(\mathbf{m}_B^1) - \langle \mathbf{u}_i, \mathbf{m}_A^1 \rangle + m_B^2.$$

Note that the total communication is $O(\ell)$, whereas the complexity of reconstruction is dominated by that of computing $F_{\mathbf{D},i}$. Privacy follows fairly readily from the fact that the joint distribution of $(\mathbf{m}_A^1, \mathbf{m}_B^1)$ is uniformly random, and that m_B^2 is completely determined given $(\mathbf{m}_A^1, \mathbf{m}_B^1)$ and $\mu\mathbf{D}_i$ along with $\mathbf{D}, i$.

Realizing $\mathbf{u}_i$ *and* $F_{\mathbf{D},i}$. We sketch how to realize the encodings $i \mapsto \mathbf{u}_i$ and $F_{\mathbf{D},i}$ by drawing upon 2-server PIR protocols from the literature (respectively [WY05] and [DG15]):

- Our CDS with $O(n^{1/3})$ communication uses degree 3 polynomials. Roughly speaking, we encode $i \in [n]$ as $\mathbf{u}_i \in \mathbb{F}_2^{O(n^{1/3})}$ (i.e., $\ell = O(n^{1/3})$) and $\mathbf{D}$ as a vector $\mathbf{p} \in \mathbb{F}_2^{O(n)}$ so that $\mathbf{D}_i = \langle \mathbf{p}, \mathbf{u}_i \otimes \mathbf{u}_i \otimes \mathbf{u}_i \rangle$. Then, $F_{\mathbf{D},i}$ is (roughly) defined to be

$$\begin{aligned} F_{\mathbf{D},i}(\mu\mathbf{u}_i + \mathbf{b}) = &\langle \mathbf{p}, (\mu\mathbf{u}_i + \mathbf{b}) \otimes (\mu\mathbf{u}_i + \mathbf{b}) \otimes \mathbf{u}_i \rangle + \langle \mathbf{p}, (\mu\mathbf{u}_i + \mathbf{b}) \otimes \mathbf{u}_i \otimes (\mu\mathbf{u}_i + \mathbf{b}) \rangle \\ &+ \langle \mathbf{p}, \mathbf{u}_i \otimes (\mu\mathbf{u}_i + \mathbf{b}) \otimes (\mu\mathbf{u}_i + \mathbf{b}) \rangle \end{aligned}$$

This means

$$\begin{aligned} F_{\mathbf{D},i}(\mu\mathbf{u}_i + \mathbf{b}) = &\, 3\mu\langle \mathbf{p}, \mathbf{u}_i \otimes \mathbf{u}_i \otimes \mathbf{u}_i \rangle \\ &+ \underbrace{2\mu(\langle \mathbf{p}, \mathbf{u}_i \otimes \mathbf{u}_i \otimes \mathbf{b} \rangle + \langle \mathbf{p}, \mathbf{u}_i \otimes \mathbf{b} \otimes \mathbf{u}_i \rangle + \langle \mathbf{p}, \mathbf{b} \otimes \mathbf{u}_i \otimes \mathbf{u}_i \rangle)}_{=0} \\ &+ \underbrace{\langle \mathbf{p}, \mathbf{u}_i \otimes \mathbf{b} \otimes \mathbf{b} \rangle + \langle \mathbf{p}, \mathbf{b} \otimes \mathbf{u}_i \otimes \mathbf{b} \rangle + \langle \mathbf{p}, \mathbf{b} \otimes \mathbf{b} \otimes \mathbf{u}_i \rangle}_{=\langle \mathbf{u}_i, \mathbf{y}_{\mathbf{D},\mathbf{b}} \rangle} \\ = &\, \mu\mathbf{D}_i + \langle \mathbf{u}_i, \mathbf{y}_{\mathbf{D},\mathbf{b}} \rangle \end{aligned}$$

where in the last equality, we use the fact that we are working over $\mathbb{F}_2$. Using this technique, we can in fact obtain communication-efficient CDS for degree 3 polynomials. Using an additional balancing technique, we can also obtain optimal trade-offs between the length of Alice's and Bob's messages.
- Our CDS with $2^{O(\sqrt{\log n \log\log n})}$ communication uses a matching vector family, namely a collection of vectors $\{(\mathbf{v}_i, \mathbf{u}_i)\}_{i \in [n]}$ such that all vectors $\mathbf{u}_i, \mathbf{v}_i \in \mathbb{Z}_6^\ell$ where $\ell = 2^{O(\sqrt{\log n \log\log n})}$ and:

$$\begin{aligned} &\langle \mathbf{v}_i, \mathbf{u}_i \rangle = 0, \\ &\langle \mathbf{v}_i, \mathbf{u}_j \rangle \in \{1, 3, 4\} \quad \text{for } i \neq j. \end{aligned}$$

Here, the inner product computations are done mod 6. Such a matching vector family was originally constructed by Grolmusz [Gro00] and improved by Dvir et al. [DGY11]. We omit precise description of $F_{\mathbf{D},i}$ but note that it is closely related to the functions G, G' defined in Sect. 4 (which are the same as those used in [DG15]).

In particular, the PIR in [DG15] matches the following high level description: The user's queries are $\mathbf{u}_i + \mathbf{b}$ and $\mathbf{b}$, the servers' answers are vectors $H_{\mathbf{D}}(\mathbf{u}_i + \mathbf{b})$ and $H_{\mathbf{D}}(\mathbf{b})$ such that

$$\langle H_{\mathbf{D}}(\mathbf{u}_i + \mathbf{b}), \mathbf{u}_i \rangle - \langle H_{\mathbf{D}}(\mathbf{b}), \mathbf{u}_i \rangle = \mathbf{D}_i. \tag{2}$$

We observe that the following relation also holds:

$$\underbrace{\langle H_{\mathbf{D}}(\mu\mathbf{u}_i + \mathbf{b}), \mathbf{u}_i \rangle}_{F_{\mathbf{D},i}(\mu\mathbf{u}_i + \mathbf{b})} - \langle \underbrace{H_{\mathbf{D}}(\mathbf{b})}_{\mathbf{y}_{\mathbf{D},\mathbf{b}}}, \mathbf{u}_i \rangle = \mu\mathbf{D}_i. \tag{3}$$

from which we may derive $F_{\mathbf{D},i}$. This technique can be further generalized to construction a CDS from any 2-server PIR with linear reconstruction.

Relation to PIR. A 2-server PIR protocol allows a user who holds an index $i \in [n]$ to retrieve an arbitrary bit $\mathbf{D}_i$ from a database $\mathbf{D} \in \{0,1\}^n$ which is held by 2 servers, while hiding the index i from each individual server:

- The user wants to learn $\mathbf{D}_i$ instead of $\mu\mathbf{D}_i$, and again, $\mathbf{D}_i$ is written as an expression related to the same function $F_{\mathbf{D},i}$, but the expression itself is different. (Roughly speaking, this is analogous to the difference between Eqs. 2 and 3 above).
- Bob's message $\mu\mathbf{u}_i + \mathbf{b}$ corresponds roughly to the user's query to the first server; note that Bob's message perfectly hides the index i.
- In PIR, one difficulty lies in jointly computing the quantity corresponding to $F_{\mathbf{D},i}(\mu\mathbf{u}_i + \mathbf{b})$ because no single party knows $\mathbf{D}$ and i, whereas this is easy in CDS. In PIR, computing the quantity corresponding to $\langle \mathbf{u}_i, \mathbf{y}_{\mathbf{D},\mathbf{b}} \rangle$ is easy as the server can send $\mathbf{y}_{\mathbf{D},\mathbf{b}}$ to the user; in PIR, Alice cannot send $\mathbf{y}_{\mathbf{D},\mathbf{b}}$ as is to Charlie as it would leak information about $\mathbf{b}$ and thus μ.

1.3 Our PSM Protocols

We consider the 2-party Private Simultaneous Message (PSM) model [FKN94] (c.f. Fig. 1): Alice holds x, Bob holds y and they both share some private randomness. Each of them sends a message to Charlie, upon which Charlie should learn $\mathsf{P}(x, y)$ for some public function P but otherwise learns nothing else about x, y. While the inputs involved in a computation (namely x and y) are not hidden in the CDS setting, they are in PSM and thus this is a harder model to design protocols in.

The state of the art in known constructions is as follows: (i) For information-theoretic security, the length of both Alice's message and Bob's message are both quadratic in the size of the branching program representation of f [FKN94, IK00,IK02]; this holds for both the Boolean and arithmetic settings. (ii) For computational security, the length of Alice's and Bob's messages are optimal up to a multiplicative overhead by the security parameter; this is the celebrated Yao's garbled circuits and requires only one-way functions.

In this work, we describe such a protocol for the class of multi-variate polynomials of total degree k, where Alice holds a degree-d polynomial $\mathbf{p}$ in n variables, Bob holds an input $\mathbf{x} \in \mathbb{F}_q^n$ and Charlie learns $\mathbf{p}(\mathbf{x})$ and nothing else. In our protocol, Alice sends $O(n^k)$ bits and Bob sends $O(kn)$ bits. This gives us a protocol for INDEX with degree-k reconstruction with the same communication profile, which is nearly optimal (up to the factor of k in Bob's communication). We refer the reader to Fig. 2 for details.

We also give a PSM for degree 4 polynomials, where the polynomial $\mathbf{p}$ (over $GF(2)$) is public, Alice and Bob hold $\mathbf{x} \in \{0,1\}^n$ and $\mathbf{y} \in \{0,1\}^n$ respectively, and Charlie gets $\mathbf{p}(\mathbf{x}, \mathbf{y})$. This in turn gives a simpler and more direct $O(\sqrt{N})$ PSM for the predicate $\mathbf{ALL}_N$, first shown in [BIKK14], along with an explicit bound on the degree of reconstruction. In $\mathbf{ALL}_N$, there is a public predicate P, Alice and Bob hold $\mathbf{x}$ and $\mathbf{y}$ respectively, and Charlie gets $\mathsf{P}(\mathbf{x}, \mathbf{y})$.

1.4 Discussion

Additional Related Work. We mention some additional related works.

Secret Sharing. The complexity of secret sharing for graph-based access structures was extensively studied in a setting where the edges of the graph represent the only minimal authorized sets, that is, any set of parties that does not contain an edge should learn nothing about the secret. The notion of forbidden graph access structures we study, originally introduced in [SS97], can be viewed as a natural "promise version" of this question, where one is only concerned about sets of size 2. The best upper bound for the total share size for every graph access structure is $O(N^2/\log N)$ [Bub86, BSGV96, EP97] whereas the best lower bounds are (i) $\Omega(N \log N)$ for general secret-sharing schemes [vD95, BSSV97, Csi05] and (ii) $\Omega(N^{3/2})$ for linear secret-sharing schemes [BGP95].

Attribute-Based Encryption. Attribute-based encryption (ABE) [SW05, GPSW06] is a new paradigm for public-key encryption that enables fine-grained access control for encrypted data. In attribute-based encryption, ciphertexts are associated with descriptive values x in addition to a plaintext, secret keys are associated with values y, and a secret key decrypts the ciphertext if and only if $\mathsf{P}(x, y) = 1$ for some boolean predicate P. Note that x and y are public given the respective ciphertext and secret key. The security requirement for attribute-based encryption enforces resilience to collusion attacks, namely any group of users holding secret keys for different values learns nothing about the plaintext if none of them is individually authorized to decrypt the ciphertext.

In [Wat09], Waters introduced the powerful *dual system encryption* methodology for building adaptively secure IBE in bilinear groups; this has since been extended to obtain adaptively secure ABE for a large class of predicates [LW10, LOS+10, OT10, LW11, Lew12, OT12]. In recent works [Att14, Wee14] (with extensions in [CGW15]), Attrapadung and Wee presented a unifying framework for the design and analysis of dual system ABE schemes, which decouples the predicate P from the security proof. Specifically, the latter work puts forth the notion of *predicate encoding*, a private-key, one-time, information-theoretic primitive similar to conditional disclosure of secrets, and provides a compiler from predicate encoding for a predicate P into an ABE for the same predicate using the dual system encryption methodology. Moreover, the parameters in the predicate encoding scheme and in CDS correspond naturally to ciphertext and key sizes in the ABE. In particular, Alice's message corresponds to the ciphertext, and Bob's message to the secret key. These applications do require linear construction over $\mathbb{Z}_q$, where q is the order of the underlying bilinear group. Note that while the parameters for ABE schemes coming from predicate encodings are not necessarily the best known parameters, they do match the state-of-the-art in terms of ciphertext and secret key sizes for many predicates such as inner product, index, and read-once formula.

Open Problems. We conclude with a number of open problems:

- Two questions related to CDS for $\mathbf{INDEX}_n$: (i) can we realize degree 2 reconstruction and communication $(\mathsf{cc}_A, \mathsf{cc}_B) = (1, \sqrt{n})$ (this would yield the full

$(n/t^2, t)$ trade-off for all t); (ii) how about total communication $O(n^{1/4})$ and degree 3 reconstruction, and more generally,$O(n^{\frac{1}{k+1}})$ and degree k reconstruction for $k \geq 3$?
- Broadcast encryption schemes for n parties with $O(n^{1/3})$ ciphertext and secret key sizes from bilinear maps, by possibly exploiting our CDS for $\mathbf{INDEX}_n$ with quadratic reconstruction.
- PSM for $\mathbf{ALL}_N$ with $o(\sqrt{N})$ total communication.
- Secret-sharing for general graph access structures with $N^{3/2}$ total share size, or even $N^{1+o(1)}$ total share size? A natural starting point would be to extend the connection between CDS and secret-sharing for forbidden graph access structures in [BIKK14] to that of general graph access structures.

Organization. We present our CDS protocols in Sects. 3 and 4, along with applications to secret-sharing and ABE in Sects. 4.2 and 3.4. We present our PSM protocols in Sect. 5. In Sect. A, we present further extensions (both upper and lower bounds) to a relaxation of PSM with a one-sided security guarantee.

2 Preliminaries

Notations. We denote by $s \leftarrow_{\mathrm{R}} S$ the fact that s is picked uniformly at random from a finite set S or from a distribution. Throughout this paper, we denote by log the logarithm of base 2.

2.1 Conditional Disclosure of Secrets

We recall the notion of conditional disclosure of secrets (CDS), c.f., Fig. 2. The definition we give here is for two parties Alice and Bob and a referee Charlie, where Alice and Bob share randomness w and want to conditionally disclose a secret α to Charlie. The general notion of conditional disclosure of secrets has first been investigated in [GIKM00]. Two-party CDS is closely related to the notions of predicate encoding [Wee14, CGW15] and pairing encoding [Att14]; in particular, the latter two notions imply two-party CDS with linear reconstruction.

Definition 2.1 (conditional disclosure of secrets (CDS) [GIKM00]**).** *Fix a predicate* $\mathsf{P} : \mathcal{X} \times \mathcal{Y} \rightarrow \{0,1\}$. *An* $(\mathsf{cc_A}, \mathsf{cc_B})$-conditional disclosure of secrets (CDS) *protocol for* P *is a triplet of deterministic functions* $(\mathsf{A}, \mathsf{B}, \mathsf{C})$

$$\mathsf{A} : \mathcal{X} \times \mathcal{W} \times \mathcal{D} \rightarrow \{0,1\}^{\mathsf{cc}_A}, \quad \mathsf{B} : \mathcal{Y} \times \mathcal{W} \times \mathcal{D} \rightarrow \{0,1\}^{\mathsf{cc}_B},$$
$$\mathsf{C} : \mathcal{X} \times \mathcal{Y} \times \{0,1\}^{\mathsf{cc_A}} \times \{0,1\}^{\mathsf{cc_B}} \rightarrow \mathcal{D}$$

satisfying the following properties:

(reconstruction.) *For all* $(x, y) \in \mathcal{X} \times \mathcal{Y}$ *such that* $\mathsf{P}(x, y) = 1$, *for all* $w \in \mathcal{W}$, *and for all* $\alpha \in \mathcal{D}$:

$$\mathsf{C}(x, y, \mathsf{A}(x, w, \alpha), \mathsf{B}(y, w, \alpha)) = \alpha$$

(privacy.) *For all* $(x, y) \in \mathcal{X} \times \mathcal{Y}$ *such that* $\mathsf{P}(x, y) = 0$*, and for all* $\mathsf{C}^* : \{0,1\}^{\mathsf{cc_A}} \times \{0,1\}^{\mathsf{cc_B}} \to \mathcal{D}$*,*

$$\Pr_{w \leftarrow \mathcal{W}, \alpha \leftarrow_{\mathrm{R}} \mathcal{D}} \left[\mathsf{C}^* \left(\mathsf{A}(x, w, \alpha), \mathsf{B}(y, w, \alpha) \right) = \alpha \right] \leq \frac{1}{|\mathcal{D}|}$$

Note that the formulation of privacy above with uniformly random secrets is equivalent to standard indistinguishability-based formulations.

A useful measure for the complexity of a CDS is the complexity of reconstruction as a function of the outputs of A, B, as captured by the function C, with (x, y) hard-wired.

Definition 2.2 ($\mathcal{C}$-reconstruction). *Given a set* $\mathcal{C}$ *of functions from* $\{0,1\}^{\mathsf{cc_A}} \times \{0,1\}^{\mathsf{cc_B}}$ *to* $\mathcal{D}$*, we say that a CDS* $(\mathsf{A}, \mathsf{B}, \mathsf{C})$ *admits* $\mathcal{C}$*-reconstruction if for all* (x, y) *such that* $\mathsf{P}(x, y) = 1$, $\mathsf{C}(x, y, \cdot, \cdot) \in \mathcal{C}$*.*

Two examples of $\mathcal{C}$ of interest are:

- $\mathcal{C}_{\mathrm{all}}$ is the set of all functions from $\{0,1\}^{\mathsf{cc_A}} \times \{0,1\}^{\mathsf{cc_B}} \to \mathcal{D}$; that is, we do not place any restriction on the complexity of reconstruction. Note that $|\mathcal{C}_{\mathrm{all}}| = |\mathcal{D}|^{2^{\mathsf{cc_A} + \mathsf{cc}_B}}$.
- $\mathcal{C}_{\mathrm{lin}}$ is the set of all *linear* functions over $\mathbb{Z}_2$ from $\{0,1\}^{\mathsf{cc_A}} \times \{0,1\}^{\mathsf{cc_B}} \to \mathcal{D}$; that is, we require the reconstruction to be linear as a function of the outputs of A and B as bit strings (but may depend arbitrarily on x, y). This is the analogue of linear reconstruction in linear secret sharing schemes and is a requirement for the applications to attribute-based encryption [Wee14, Att14, CGW15]. Note that $|\mathcal{C}_{\mathrm{linear}}| \leq |\mathcal{D}|^{\mathsf{cc_A} + \mathsf{cc}_B}$ for $|\mathcal{D}| \geq 2$.

Remark 2.3. Note that while looking at $\mathcal{C}$, we consider $\mathsf{C}(x, y, \cdot, \cdot)$, which has (x, y) hard-wired, and takes an input of total length $\mathsf{cc_A} + \mathsf{cc_B}$. In particular, it could be that C runs in time linear in $|x| = |y| = n$, and yet $\mathsf{cc_A} = \mathsf{cc_B} = O(\log n)$ so C has "exponential" complexity w.r.t. $\mathsf{cc_A} + \mathsf{cc_B}$.

Definition 2.4 (linear CDS). *We say that a CDS* $(\mathsf{A}, \mathsf{B}, \mathsf{C})$ *is linear if it admits* $\mathcal{C}_{\mathrm{lin}}$*-reconstruction.*

2.2 Private Simultaneous Message

Definition 2.5 (private simultaneous message (PSM)). *Fix a functionality* $f : \mathcal{X} \times \mathcal{Y} \to \mathcal{D}$*. An* $(\mathsf{cc_A}, \mathsf{cc_B})$-private simultaneous message (PSM) *protocol for* f *is a triplet of deterministic functions* $(\mathsf{A}, \mathsf{B}, \mathsf{C})$

$$\mathsf{A} : \mathcal{X} \times \mathcal{W} \to \{0,1\}^{\mathsf{cc}_A}, \quad \mathsf{B} : \mathcal{Y} \times \mathcal{W} \to \{0,1\}^{\mathsf{cc}_B}, \quad \mathsf{C} : \{0,1\}^{\mathsf{cc_A}} \times \{0,1\}^{\mathsf{cc_B}} \to \mathcal{D}$$

satisfying the following properties:

(reconstruction.) *For all* $(x, y) \in \mathcal{X} \times \mathcal{Y}$*:*

$$\mathsf{C}(\mathsf{A}(x, w), \mathsf{B}(y, w)) = f(x, y)$$

(privacy.) *There exists a randomized simulator* S*, such that for any* $(x, y) \in \mathcal{X} \times \mathcal{Y}$ *the joint distribution* $(\mathsf{A}(x, w), \mathsf{B}(y, w))$ *is perfectly indistinguishable from* $\mathsf{S}(f(x, y))$*, where the distributions are taken over* $w \leftarrow \mathcal{W}$ *and the coin tosses of* S*.*

2.3 Predicates and Reductions

Predicates. We consider the following predicates:

- Index $\mathbf{INDEX}_n$: $\mathcal{X} := \{0,1\}^n, \mathcal{Y} := [n]$ and

$$\mathsf{P}_{\mathbf{INDEX}}(\mathbf{D}, i) = 1 \text{ iff } \mathbf{D}_i = 1$$

  Here, $\mathbf{D}_i$ denotes the i'th coordinate of $\mathbf{D}$. Note that we can also interpret $\mathbf{D}$ as the characteristic vector of a subset of $[n]$.
- Multi-linear Polynomials $\mathbf{MPOLY}^k_{n_1,\ldots,n_k}$: $\mathcal{X} := \mathbb{F}_q^{n_1 \cdots n_k}, \mathcal{Y} := \mathbb{F}_q^{n_1} \times \cdots \times \mathbb{F}_q^{n_k}$ and

$$\mathsf{P}_{\mathbf{MPOLY}}(\mathbf{p}, (\mathbf{x}_1, \ldots, \mathbf{x}_k)) = 1 \text{ iff } \langle \mathbf{p}, \mathbf{x}_1 \otimes \cdots \otimes \mathbf{x}_k \rangle \neq 0$$

  This captures homogeneous multi-linear polynomials of total degree k in $n_1 + \cdots + n_k$ variables over $\mathbb{F}_q$; concretely, the variables are encoded as k vectors $\mathbf{x}_1, \ldots, \mathbf{x}_k$, each monomial is a product of k variables one from each of the k vectors, and $\mathbf{p}$ is the vector of coefficients. In addition, our protocols work with *inhomogeneous* multi-linear polynomials as well. Simply observe that any (even non-homogeneous) multi-linear polynomial p in n variables of total degree at most k is captured by the class $\mathbf{MPOLY}^k_{n+1,\ldots,n+1}$.[1]
- All ("worst") functions $\mathbf{ALL}_N$: a fixed function $F : [N] \times [N] \to \{0,1\}$, $\mathcal{X} = \mathcal{Y} := [N]$

$$\mathsf{P}_{\mathbf{ALL}}(x, y) = F(x, y)$$

Reductions. We have the following reductions from prior works:

- $\mathbf{MPOLY}^k_{n_1,\ldots,n_k} \Rightarrow \mathbf{INDEX}_{n_1 \cdots n_k}$. On input $\mathbf{D} \in \{0,1\}^n, i \in [n]$ where $n = \prod_{j=1}^k n_j$, we map i to $(\mathbf{e}_{i_1}, \ldots, \mathbf{e}_{i_k})$ so that $\mathbf{e}_i = \mathbf{e}_{i_1} \otimes \cdots \otimes \mathbf{e}_{i_k}$ and $\mathbf{D}$ to $\mathbf{p}$; this way, $\langle \mathbf{p}, \mathbf{e}_{i_1} \otimes \cdots \otimes \mathbf{e}_{i_k} \rangle = \langle \mathbf{D}, \mathbf{e}_i \rangle = \mathbf{D}_i$.
- $\mathbf{INDEX}_N \Rightarrow \mathbf{ALL}_N$. Fix $F : [N] \times [N] \to \{0,1\}$. We use the "truth table" reduction that maps $(x, y) \in [N] \times [N]$ to $F(x, \cdot) \in \{0,1\}^N, y \in [N]$.

2.4 Secret Sharing

Secret Sharing for Forbidden Graph Access Structure on N Parties. Consider a graph $G = (V, E)$, where $|V| = N$. Each vertex denotes a party. The sets that can reconstruct the secret are: (1) all sets of 3 or more parties, (2) all pairs of parties that correspond to vertexes that are not adjacent. The access structure is called *forbidden graph* as each edge indicates a pair of parties who can not jointly reconstruct the secret.

[1] There are two reasons why we work with multi-linear polynomials with the tensor product notation: first, it yields a cleaner and more efficient reduction for $\mathbf{MPOLY}^k_{n_1,\ldots,n_k} \Rightarrow \mathbf{INDEX}_{n_1 \cdots n_k}$ (saving a factor of k), and second, it is easier to work with for our CDS schemes in Sects. 3.1 and 3.2.

Secret Sharing for Forbidden Bipartite Graph Access Structure on 2N Parties. Consider a graph $G = (L, R, E)$ where $|L| = |R| = N$. Each vertex denotes a party. The sets that can reconstruct the secret are: (1) all pairs of parties that correspond to vertexes from the same side of the graph; (2) all pairs of parties that correspond to vertexes from different sides that are not adjacent.

Secret Sharing from PSM and CDS. As shown in [BIKK14, Sect. 7], a PSM scheme for $\mathbf{ALL}_N$ where Alice and Bob sends at most $\ell = \ell(N)$ bits yields secret-sharing schemes for every forbidden bipartite graph access structure on $2N$ nodes where the share size is $O(\ell)$ bits. This further implies secret sharing schemes for every forbidden graph access structure on $2N$ nodes where the share size is $O(\ell \log N)$ bits [BIKK14, Sect. J]. The technique can be generalized to a transformation from a CDS scheme – a weaker object – to a secret sharing scheme for forbidden graph structures.

Theorem 2.6 [BIKK14]. *A CDS scheme for $\mathbf{ALL}_{N+1}$ where Alice and Bob sends at most $\ell = \ell(N)$ bits yields secret sharing schemes for forbidden bipartite graph access structure on $2N$ nodes.*

Proof. Given any bipartite graph $G = (L, R, E)$, let $(\mathsf{A}, \mathsf{B}, \mathsf{C})$ be a CDS for predicate $\mathsf{P} : [N+1] \times [N+1] \to \{0, 1\}$ such that

$$\mathsf{P}(i,j) = \begin{cases} 1, & \text{if } i, j \leq N \text{ and } (i,j) \notin E, \\ 0, & \text{otherwise.} \end{cases}$$

Let $\alpha \in \mathscr{D}$ denotes the secret. We construct a secret sharing scheme for G by dealing with the two types of authorized sets. First, the secret is shared among each side with Shamir's 2-out-of-N threshold secret sharing. Next, sample random $w \leftarrow \mathscr{W}$, let the i-th party on the left hold $\mathsf{A}(i, w, \alpha)$, let the j-th party on the right hold $\mathsf{B}(j, w, \alpha)$.

Correctness is straight-forward: 2 parties on the same side can reconstruct the secret from Shamir's 2-out-of-N threshold secret sharing; the i-th party on the left and the j-th party on the right can reconstruct the secret using the reconstruction function of CDS for $\mathbf{ALL}_{n+1}$ if $(i, j) \notin E$. Privacy follows from the following:

- If $(i, j) \in E$, the i-th party on the left and the j-th party on the right hold $\mathsf{A}(i, w, \alpha)$, $\mathsf{B}(j, w, \alpha)$, whose joint distribution is independent from secret α by the definition of CDS.
- The i-party on the left holds $\mathsf{A}(i, w, \alpha)$. By the definition of CDS, $\mathsf{A}(i, w, \alpha)$, $\mathsf{B}(N+1, w, \alpha)$ jointly leak no information about secret α. □

3 CDS for Degree-2 and 3 Polynomials with Applications to INDEX and ABE

In this section, we present CDS for the class of multi-linear polynomials $\mathbf{MPOLY}^k_{n_1,\ldots,n_k}$ of degree $k = 2, 3$ in Sects. 3.1 and 3.2, along with applications to $\mathbf{INDEX}_n$ and ABE in Sects. 3.3 and 3.4.

3.1 Degree-2 Polynomials $\mathbf{MPOLY}^2_{n_1,n_2}$ over $\mathbb{F}_q$

Recall that in $\mathbf{MPOLY}^2_{n_1,n_2}$ over $\mathbb{F}_q$, Alice holds $\mathbf{p} \in \mathbb{F}_q^{n_1 n_2}$, Bob holds $(\mathbf{x}_1, \mathbf{x}_2) \in \mathbb{F}_q^{n_1} \times \mathbb{F}_q^{n_2}$ and $\mu \in \mathbb{F}_q$, and Charlie learns μ iff $\langle \mathbf{p}, \mathbf{x}_1 \otimes \mathbf{x}_2 \rangle \neq 0$. (In Sect. B, we present a protocol for the "negated" setting where Charlie learns μ iff $\langle \mathbf{p}, \mathbf{x}_1 \otimes \mathbf{x}_2 \rangle = 0$).

Protocol Overview. The shared randomness comprises $(\mathbf{b}, \mathbf{c}) \in \mathbb{F}_q^{n_1} \times \mathbb{F}_q^{n_2}$. Bob sends $\mathbf{m}_B^1 := \mu \mathbf{x}_1 + \mathbf{b}$. Now, Charlie knows $\mathbf{p}, \mathbf{x}_1, \mathbf{x}_2, \mu \mathbf{x}_1 + \mathbf{b}$, and could compute

$$\langle \mathbf{p}, (\mu \mathbf{x}_1 + \mathbf{b}) \otimes \mathbf{x}_2 \rangle = \mu \langle \mathbf{p}, \mathbf{x}_1 \otimes \mathbf{x}_2 \rangle + \underbrace{\langle \mathbf{p}, \mathbf{b} \otimes \mathbf{x}_2 \rangle}_{\langle \mathbf{p}'_{\mathbf{b}}, \mathbf{x}_2 \rangle}$$

where $\mathbf{p}'_{\mathbf{b}} \in \mathbb{F}_q^{n_2}$ depends on $\mathbf{p}$ and $\mathbf{b}$. In order for Charlie to compute $\langle \mathbf{p}'_{\mathbf{b}}, \mathbf{x}_2 \rangle$, and thus $\mu \langle \mathbf{p}, \mathbf{x} \otimes \mathbf{x} \rangle$, the following needs to be done:

- Alice sends $\mathbf{m}_A^1 := \mathbf{p}'_{\mathbf{b}} + \mathbf{c}$,
- Bob sends $m_B^2 := \langle \mathbf{c}, \mathbf{x}_2 \rangle$

Now Charlie can recover $\langle \mathbf{p}'_{\mathbf{b}}, \mathbf{x}_2 \rangle = \langle \mathbf{m}_A^1, \mathbf{x}_2 \rangle - m_B^2$. Concretely, Charlie recovers μ using

$$\mu \langle \mathbf{p}, \mathbf{x}_1 \otimes \mathbf{x}_2 \rangle = \langle \mathbf{p}, \mathbf{m}_B^1 \otimes \mathbf{x}_2 \rangle + m_B^2 - \langle \mathbf{m}_A^1, \mathbf{x}_2 \rangle$$

This protocol is described in detail in Fig. 3.

CDS for Degree-2 Polynomials $\mathbf{MPOLY}^2_{n_1,n_2}$ (over $\mathbb{F}_q$)

Alice's Input: A degree-2 polynomial (expressed as a vector) $\mathbf{p} \in \mathbb{F}_q^{n_1 n_2}$.
Bob's Input: $(\mathbf{x}_1, \mathbf{x}_2) \in \mathbb{F}_q^{n_1} \times \mathbb{F}_q^{n_2}$ and $\mu \in \mathbb{F}_q$.
Carol's Output: μ if $\langle \mathbf{p}, \mathbf{x}_1 \otimes \mathbf{x}_2 \rangle \neq 0$.
Shared Randomness: $(\mathbf{b}, \mathbf{c}) \in \mathbb{F}_q^{n_1} \times \mathbb{F}_q^{n_2}$.

- Alice computes a vector $\mathbf{p}'_{\mathbf{b}} \in \mathbb{F}_q^{n_2}$ such that for any $\mathbf{y} \in \mathbb{F}_q^{n_2}$, $\langle \mathbf{p}, \mathbf{b} \otimes \mathbf{y} \rangle = \langle \mathbf{p}'_{\mathbf{b}}, \mathbf{y} \rangle$. She sends $\mathbf{m}_A^1 := \mathbf{p}'_{\mathbf{b}} + \mathbf{c} \in \mathbb{F}_q^{n_2}$ to Charlie.
- Bob sends $\mathbf{m}_B^1 := \mu \mathbf{x}_1 + \mathbf{b} \in \mathbb{F}_q^{n_1}$ and $m_B^2 := \langle \mathbf{c}, \mathbf{x}_2 \rangle \in \mathbb{F}_q$ to Charlie.
- Charlie outputs $\perp$ if $\langle \mathbf{p}, \mathbf{x}_1 \otimes \mathbf{x}_2 \rangle = 0$ and

$$(\langle \mathbf{p}, \mathbf{x}_1 \otimes \mathbf{x}_2 \rangle)^{-1} \cdot (\langle \mathbf{p}, \mathbf{m}_B^1 \otimes \mathbf{x}_2 \rangle + m_B^2 - \langle \mathbf{m}_A^1, \mathbf{x}_2 \rangle)$$

otherwise.

Fig. 3. The CDS protocol for degree-2 polynomials with $(\mathsf{cc}_A, \mathsf{cc}_B) = (n_2 \log q, (n_1 + 1) \log q)$.

Theorem 3.1 (CDS for $\mathbf{MPOLY}^2_{n_1,n_2}$). *There is a CDS protocol for degree-2 polynomials over $\mathbb{F}_q$ (shown in Fig. 3) where Alice sends n_2 elements of $\mathbb{F}_q$, Bob sends n_1+1 elements of $\mathbb{F}_q$ and Charlie applies an $\mathbb{F}_q$-linear reconstruction function.*

Proof. Correctness is straight-forward and follows from the computation above. Namely,

$$\begin{aligned}\langle \mathbf{p}, \mathbf{m}_B^1 \otimes \mathbf{x}_2\rangle + m_B^2 - \langle \mathbf{m}_A^1, \mathbf{x}_2\rangle &= \langle \mathbf{p}, (\mu\mathbf{x}_1 + \mathbf{b}) \otimes \mathbf{x}_2\rangle + \langle \mathbf{c}, \mathbf{x}_2\rangle - \langle \mathbf{p}'_{\mathbf{b}} + \mathbf{c}, \mathbf{x}_2\rangle \\ &= \mu\langle \mathbf{p}, \mathbf{x}_1 \otimes \mathbf{x}_2\rangle + \langle \mathbf{p}, \mathbf{b} \otimes \mathbf{x}_2\rangle - \langle \mathbf{p}'_{\mathbf{b}}, \mathbf{x}_2\rangle \\ &= \mu\langle \mathbf{p}, \mathbf{x}_1 \otimes \mathbf{x}_2\rangle\end{aligned}$$

since, by definition of $\mathbf{p}'_{\mathbf{b}}$, $\langle \mathbf{p}, \mathbf{b} \otimes \mathbf{x}_2\rangle = \langle \mathbf{p}'_{\mathbf{b}}, \mathbf{x}_2\rangle$.

It is also easy to see that the degree of reconstruction is 1. Privacy follows from the following observations:

- The joint distribution of $\mathbf{m}_B^1$ and $\mathbf{m}_A^1$ is uniformly random, since we are using $(\mathbf{b}, \mathbf{c})$ as one-time pads; and
- $m_B^2 = \mu\langle \mathbf{p}, \mathbf{x} \otimes \mathbf{x}_2\rangle - \langle \mathbf{p}, \mathbf{m}_B^1 \otimes \mathbf{x}_2\rangle + \langle \mathbf{m}_A^1, \mathbf{x}_2\rangle$

Putting the two together, we can simulate $\mathbf{m}_A^1, \mathbf{m}_B^1$ and m_B^2 given just $\mathbf{x}_1, \mathbf{x}_2, \mathbf{p}$, $\mu\langle \mathbf{p}, \mathbf{x}_1 \otimes \mathbf{x}_2\rangle$. This finishes the proof. □

The total communication is $\mathsf{cc}_A = n_2$ elements of $\mathbb{F}_q$ and $\mathsf{cc}_B = n_1 + 1$ elements of $\mathbb{F}_q$ for a total of $n_1 + n_2 + 1$. We will use this generalization later in this section to design a CDS protocol for the INDEX functionality with a general communication tradeoff between Alice and Bob.

3.2 Degree 3 Polynomials $\mathbf{MPOLY}^3_{n_1,n_2,n_3}$ over $\mathbb{F}_2$

In $\mathbf{MPOLY}^3_{n_1,n_2,n_3}$ over $\mathbb{F}_2$, Alice holds $\mathbf{p} \in \mathbb{F}_2^{n_1 n_2 n_3}$, Bob holds $(\mathbf{x}_1, \mathbf{x}_2, \mathbf{x}_3) \in \mathbb{F}_2^{n_1} \times \mathbb{F}_2^{n_2} \times \mathbb{F}_2^{n_3}$ and $\mu \in \mathbb{F}_2$, and Charlie learns μ iff $\langle \mathbf{p}, \mathbf{x}_1 \otimes \mathbf{x}_2 \otimes \mathbf{x}_3\rangle \neq 0$. In contrast to Sect. 3.1, we can only handle polynomials over $\mathbb{F}_2$ here, yet this will be sufficient for our CDS protocol for INDEX in Sect. 3.3.

Protocol Overview. The shared randomness comprises $(\mathbf{b}_1, \mathbf{b}_2, \mathbf{b}_3, \mathbf{c}) \in \mathbb{F}_2^{n_1} \times \mathbb{F}_2^{n_2} \times \mathbb{F}_2^{n_3} \times \mathbb{F}_2^{n_1+n_2+n_3}$. Bob sends $\mathbf{m}_B^1 := \mu\mathbf{x}_1 + \mathbf{b}_1$. Now, Charlie knows $\mathbf{p}, \mathbf{x}_1, \mathbf{x}_2, \mathbf{x}_3, \mu\mathbf{x}_1 + \mathbf{b}_1, \mu\mathbf{x}_2 + \mathbf{b}_2, \mu\mathbf{x}_3 + \mathbf{b}_3$, and could compute

$$\begin{aligned}&\langle \mathbf{p}, (\mu\mathbf{x}_1 + \mathbf{b}_1) \otimes (\mu\mathbf{x}_2 + \mathbf{b}_2) \otimes \mathbf{x}_3\rangle + \langle \mathbf{p}, (\mu\mathbf{x}_1 + \mathbf{b}_1) \otimes \mathbf{x}_2 \otimes (\mu\mathbf{x}_3 + \mathbf{b}_3)\rangle \\ &\quad + \langle \mathbf{p}, \mathbf{x}_1 \otimes (\mu\mathbf{x}_2 + \mathbf{b}_2) \otimes (\mu\mathbf{x}_3 + \mathbf{b}_3)\rangle \\ &= 3\mu^2\langle \mathbf{p}, \mathbf{x}_1 \otimes \mathbf{x}_2 \otimes \mathbf{x}_3\rangle \\ &\quad + 2\mu(\langle \mathbf{p}, \mathbf{b}_1 \otimes \mathbf{x}_2 \otimes \mathbf{x}_3\rangle + \langle \mathbf{p}, \mathbf{x}_1 \otimes \mathbf{b}_2 \otimes \mathbf{x}_3\rangle + \langle \mathbf{p}, \mathbf{x}_1 \otimes \mathbf{x}_2 \otimes \mathbf{b}_3\rangle) \\ &\quad + \underbrace{\langle \mathbf{p}, \mathbf{b}_1 \otimes \mathbf{b}_2 \otimes \mathbf{x}_3\rangle + \langle \mathbf{p}, \mathbf{b}_1 \otimes \mathbf{x}_2 \otimes \mathbf{b}_3\rangle + \langle \mathbf{p}, \mathbf{x}_1 \otimes \mathbf{b}_2 \otimes \mathbf{b}_3\rangle}_{\langle \mathbf{p}'_{\mathbf{b}_1,\mathbf{b}_2,\mathbf{b}_3}, \mathbf{x}_1 \| \mathbf{x}_2 \| \mathbf{x}_3\rangle} \\ &= \mu\langle \mathbf{p}, \mathbf{x}_1 \otimes \mathbf{x}_2 \otimes \mathbf{x}_3\rangle + \langle \mathbf{p}'_{\mathbf{b}_1,\mathbf{b}_2,\mathbf{b}_3}, \mathbf{x}_1 \| \mathbf{x}_2 \| \mathbf{x}_3\rangle \end{aligned} \tag{4}$$

where in the last equality, we use the fact that we are working over $\mathbb{F}_2$.

CDS for Degree-3 Polynomials $\mathrm{MPOLY}^3_{n_1,n_2,n_3}$ (over $\mathbb{F}_2$)

Alice's Input: A degree-3 polynomial (expressed as a vector) $\mathbf{p} \in \mathbb{F}_2^{n_1 n_2 n_3}$.
Bob's Input: $\mathbf{x}_1 \in \mathbb{F}_2^{n_1}, \mathbf{x}_2 \in \mathbb{F}_2^{n_2}, \mathbf{x}_3 \in \mathbb{F}_2^{n_3}$ and $\mu \in \mathbb{F}_2$.
Carol's Output: μ if $\langle \mathbf{p}, \mathbf{x}_1 \otimes \mathbf{x}_2 \otimes \mathbf{x}_3 \rangle \neq 0$.
Shared Randomness: $(\mathbf{b}_1, \mathbf{b}_2, \mathbf{b}_3, \mathbf{c}) \in \mathbb{F}_2^{n_1} \times \mathbb{F}_2^{n_2} \times \mathbb{F}_2^{n_3} \times \mathbb{F}_2^{n_1+n_2+n_3}$.

- Alice computes a vector $\mathbf{p}'_{\mathbf{b}_1,\mathbf{b}_2,\mathbf{b}_3} \in \mathbb{F}_2^{n_1+n_2+n_3}$ such that for any $(\mathbf{y}_1, \mathbf{y}_2, \mathbf{y}_3) \in \mathbb{F}_2^{n_1} \times \mathbb{F}_2^{n_2} \times \mathbb{F}_2^{n_3}$,

$$\langle \mathbf{p}, \mathbf{b}_1 \otimes \mathbf{b}_2 \otimes \mathbf{y}_3 + \mathbf{b}_1 \otimes \mathbf{y}_2 \otimes \mathbf{b}_3 + \mathbf{y}_1 \otimes \mathbf{b}_2 \otimes \mathbf{b}_3 \rangle = \langle \mathbf{p}'_{\mathbf{b}_1,\mathbf{b}_2,\mathbf{b}_3}, \mathbf{y}_1 \| \mathbf{y}_2 \| \mathbf{y}_3 \rangle$$

  She sends $\mathbf{m}_A^1 := \mathbf{p}'_{\mathbf{b}_1,\mathbf{b}_2,\mathbf{b}_3} + \mathbf{c} \in \mathbb{F}_2^{n_1+n_2+n_3}$ to Charlie.
- Bob sends

$$(\mathbf{m}_B^1, \mathbf{m}_B^2, \mathbf{m}_B^3, m_B^4) := (\mu \mathbf{x}_1 + \mathbf{b}_1, \mu \mathbf{x}_2 + \mathbf{b}_2, \mu \mathbf{x}_3 + \mathbf{b}_3, \langle \mathbf{c}, \mathbf{x}_1 \| \mathbf{x}_2 \| \mathbf{x}_3 \rangle) \in \mathbb{F}_2^{n_1} \times \mathbb{F}_2^{n_3} \times \mathbb{F}_2^{n_3} \times \mathbb{F}_2$$

  to Charlie.
- Charlie outputs $\perp$ if $\langle \mathbf{p}, \mathbf{x}_1 \otimes \mathbf{x}_2 \otimes \mathbf{x}_3 \rangle = 0$ and

$$\langle \mathbf{p}, \mathbf{m}_B^1 \otimes \mathbf{m}_B^2 \otimes \mathbf{x}_3 + \mathbf{m}_B^1 \otimes \mathbf{x}_2 \otimes \mathbf{m}_B^3 + \mathbf{x}_1 \otimes \mathbf{m}_B^2 \otimes \mathbf{m}_B^3 \rangle + m_B^4 - \langle \mathbf{m}_A^1, \mathbf{x}_1 \| \mathbf{x}_2 \| \mathbf{x}_3 \rangle$$

  otherwise.

Fig. 4. The CDS protocol for degree-3 polynomials. with $(\mathsf{cc}_A, \mathsf{cc}_B) = (n_1 + n_2 + n_3, n_1 + n_2 + n_3 + 1)$.

As in the degree-2 case, Alice then sends $\mathbf{m}_A^1 := \mathbf{p}'_{\mathbf{b}_1,\mathbf{b}_2,\mathbf{b}_3} + \mathbf{c}$ and Bob also sends $m_B^4 := \langle \mathbf{c}, \mathbf{x}_1 \| \mathbf{x}_2 \| \mathbf{x}_3 \rangle$. From these, Charlie can recover $\langle \mathbf{p}'_{\mathbf{b}_1,\mathbf{b}_2,\mathbf{b}_3}, \mathbf{x}_1 \| \mathbf{x}_2 \| \mathbf{x}_3 \rangle$ and thus $\mu \langle \mathbf{p}, \mathbf{x}_1 \otimes \mathbf{x}_2 \otimes \mathbf{x}_3 \rangle$. Thus, he recovers μ if and only if $\langle \mathbf{p}, \mathbf{x}_1 \otimes \mathbf{x}_2 \otimes \mathbf{x}_3 \rangle \neq 0$. This protocol is described in detail in Fig. 4.

Theorem 3.2 (CDS for $\mathrm{MPOLY}^3_{n_1,n_2,n_3}$). *There is a CDS protocol for degree-3 polynomials over $\mathbb{F}_2$ (shown in Fig. 4) where Alice sends $n_1 + n_2 + n_3$ bits Bob sends $n_1 + n_2 + n_3 + 1$ bits, and Charlie applies a degree-2 reconstruction function (over $\mathbb{F}_2$).*

Proof. Correctness is straight-forward and follows from the computation above. Namely, from (4), we know that

$$\begin{aligned}\langle \mathbf{p}, \mathbf{m}_B^1 \otimes \mathbf{m}_B^2 \otimes \mathbf{x}_3 + \mathbf{m}_B^1 \otimes \mathbf{x}_2 \otimes \mathbf{m}_B^3 + \mathbf{x}_1 \otimes \mathbf{m}_B^2 \otimes \mathbf{m}_B^3 \rangle \\ = \mu \langle \mathbf{p}, \mathbf{x}_1 \otimes \mathbf{x}_2 \otimes \mathbf{x}_3 \rangle + \langle \mathbf{p}'_{\mathbf{b}_1,\mathbf{b}_2,\mathbf{b}_3}, \mathbf{x}_1 \| \mathbf{x}_2 \| \mathbf{x}_3 \rangle\end{aligned}$$

Charlie computes

$$\begin{aligned}
&\langle \mathbf{p}, \mathbf{m}_B^1 \otimes \mathbf{m}_B^2 \otimes \mathbf{x}_3 + \mathbf{m}_B^1 \otimes \mathbf{x}_2 \otimes \mathbf{m}_B^3 + \mathbf{x}_1 \otimes \mathbf{m}_B^2 \otimes \mathbf{m}_B^3 \rangle \\
&\quad + m_B^4 - \langle \mathbf{m}_A^1, \mathbf{x}_1 \| \mathbf{x}_2 \| \mathbf{x}_3 \rangle \\
&= \mu \langle \mathbf{p}, \mathbf{x}_1 \otimes \mathbf{x}_2 \otimes \mathbf{x}_3 \rangle + \langle \mathbf{p}'_{\mathbf{b}_1,\mathbf{b}_2,\mathbf{b}_3}, \mathbf{x}_1 \| \mathbf{x}_2 \| \mathbf{x}_3 \rangle \\
&\quad + \langle \mathbf{c}, \mathbf{x}_1 \| \mathbf{x}_2 \| \mathbf{x}_3 \rangle - \langle \mathbf{p}'_{\mathbf{b}_1,\mathbf{b}_2,\mathbf{b}_3} + \mathbf{c}, \mathbf{x}_1 \| \mathbf{x}_2 \| \mathbf{x}_3 \rangle \\
&= \mu \langle \mathbf{p}, \mathbf{x}_1 \otimes \mathbf{x}_2 \otimes \mathbf{x}_3 \rangle
\end{aligned}$$

It is also easy to see that Alice sends $n_1 + n_2 + n_3$ bits in total, Bob sends $n_1 + n_2 + n_3 + 1$ bits, and that the degree of reconstruction is 2.

Privacy follows from the following observations:

- The joint distribution of $\mathbf{m}_B^1, \mathbf{m}_B^2, \mathbf{m}_B^3$ and $\mathbf{m}_A^1$ is uniformly random, since we are using $(\mathbf{b}_1, \mathbf{b}_2, \mathbf{b}_3, \mathbf{c})$ as one-time pads;
- The last bit of Bob's message, namely m_B^4, is uniquely defined given $\mathbf{m}_A^1$, $\mathbf{m}_B^1, \mathbf{m}_B^2, \mathbf{m}_B^3$ and $\mu\langle \mathbf{p}, \mathbf{x}_1 \otimes \mathbf{x}_2 \otimes \mathbf{x}_3 \rangle$. In particular,

$$\begin{aligned}
m_B^4 &= \langle \mathbf{c}, \mathbf{x}_1 \| \mathbf{x}_2 \| \mathbf{x}_3 \rangle \\
&= \langle \mathbf{m}_A^1, \mathbf{x}_1 \| \mathbf{x}_2 \| \mathbf{x}_3 \rangle - \langle \mathbf{p}'_{\mathbf{b}_1,\mathbf{b}_2,\mathbf{b}_3}, \mathbf{x}_1 \| \mathbf{x}_2 \| \mathbf{x}_3 \rangle \\
&= \langle \mathbf{m}_A^1, \mathbf{x}_1 \| \mathbf{x}_2 \| \mathbf{x}_3 \rangle + \mu \langle \mathbf{p}, \mathbf{x}_1 \otimes \mathbf{x}_2 \otimes \mathbf{x}_3 \rangle \\
&\quad - \langle \mathbf{p}, \mathbf{m}_B^1 \otimes \mathbf{m}_B^2 \otimes \mathbf{x}_3 + \mathbf{m}_B^1 \otimes \mathbf{x}_2 \otimes \mathbf{m}_B^3 + \mathbf{x}_1 \otimes \mathbf{m}_B^2 \otimes \mathbf{m}_B^3 \rangle
\end{aligned}$$

Putting the two together, we can simulate $\mathbf{m}_A^1, \mathbf{m}_B^1, \mathbf{m}_B^2, \mathbf{m}_B^3, m_B^4$ given just $\mathbf{x}_1, \mathbf{x}_2, \mathbf{x}_3, \mathbf{p}$ and $\mu\langle \mathbf{p}, \mathbf{x}_1 \otimes \mathbf{x}_2 \otimes \mathbf{x}_3 \rangle$. □

Remark 3.3 (Beyond degree 3). For degree d, the above approach yields communication complexity $O(n^{d-2})$, which is no better than $O(n^{\lceil d/2 \rceil})$ for $d \geq 4$. To get to $O(n^{d-3})$ with the above approach, we would want to pick a field and a in the field such that $da^{d-1} \neq 0, (d-1)a^{d-2}, (d-2)a^{d-3} = 0$. This is impossible since $a^{d-2} = (d-1)a^{d-2} - a \cdot (d-2)a^{d-3} = 0$.

3.3 CDS for $\mathbf{INDEX}_n$

Recall that in $\mathbf{INDEX}_n$, Alice holds $\mathbf{D} \in \{0,1\}^n$, Bob holds $i \in [n]$ and $\mu \in \mathbb{F}_q$, and Charlie learns μ iff $\mathbf{D}_i = 1$. We obtain several CDS protocols for $\mathbf{INDEX}_n$ by combining the reductions in Sect. 2.3 and our CDS protocols from Sects. 3.1 and 3.2.

Theorem 3.4. *There are CDS protocols for* $\mathbf{INDEX}_n$ *with:*

- $(\mathsf{cc}_A, \mathsf{cc}_B) = (\lceil n/t \rceil, t+1)$ *and degree-1 reconstruction, for* $1 \leq t \leq n$*; and*
- $(\mathsf{cc}_A, \mathsf{cc}_B) = (\lceil n/t^2 \rceil, 3t+1)$ *and degree-2 reconstruction, for* $1 \leq t \leq n^{1/3}$.

As a corollary, we obtain a CDS for $\mathbf{INDEX}_n$ *with total communication* $O(n^{1/2})$ *and degree-1 reconstruction, and one with total communication* $O(n^{1/3})$ *and degree-2 reconstruction.*

We note that the first bullet was already shown in prior works [GKW15], but we provide an alternative, more algebraic construction here.

Proof. The first bullet follows readily from combining the $\mathbf{MPOLY}^2_{n/t,t} \Rightarrow \mathbf{INDEX}_n$ reduction in Sect. 2.3 with our CDS for $\mathbf{MPOLY}^2_{n/t,t}$ in Theorem 3.1. This immediately yields a CDS for $\mathbf{INDEX}_n$ with $(\mathsf{cc}_A, \mathsf{cc}_B) = (n/t, t+1)$ and degree-1 reconstruction.

For the second bullet, we start by observing that combining the $\mathbf{MPOLY}^3_{t,t,t} \Rightarrow \mathbf{INDEX}_{t^3}$ reduction in Sect. 2.3 with our CDS for $\mathbf{MPOLY}^3_{t,t,t}$ in Theorem 3.2. This immediately yields a CDS for $\mathbf{INDEX}_{t^3}$ with $(\mathsf{cc}_A, \mathsf{cc}_B) = (3t, 3t+1)$ and degree-2 reconstruction.

To go from $\mathbf{INDEX}_{t^3}$ to $\mathbf{INDEX}_n$, fix any $t \in [n^{1/3}]$ and run $\frac{n}{t^3}$ copies of CDS for $\mathbf{INDEX}_{t^3}$. That is,

- Alice breaks up $\mathbf{D}$ into n/t^3 databases $\mathbf{D}^1, \ldots, \mathbf{D}^{n/t^3} \in \{0,1\}^{t^3}$, and runs n/t^3 copies of CDS for $\mathbf{INDEX}_{t^3}$, each of which incurs $O(t)$ communication.
- Bob parses his input $i \in [n]$ as $(j, i') \in [n/t^3] \times [t^3]$ so that $\mathbf{D}^j_{i'} = \mathbf{D}_i$. Then, Bob just needs to send a message for the CDS corresponding to $\mathbf{D}^j$ and with input $i' \in [t^3]$. This means that Bob only sends $3t+1$ bits.

Altogether, Alice sends $\frac{n}{t^3} \cdot 3t$ bits and Bob sends $3t+1$ bits. □

Remark 3.5 (balancing communication in CDS). The idea of constructing a CDS for $\mathbf{INDEX}_n$ from n/t copies of CDS for $\mathbf{INDEX}_t$ works well on any CDS protocol for **INDEX**. It's also implicitly used in the previous $(\mathsf{cc}_A, \mathsf{cc}_B) = (n/t, t+1)$ CDS for $\mathbf{INDEX}_n$ (e.g. [GKW15]). In general, a CDS protocols for $\mathbf{INDEX}_n$ with communication complexity $(\mathsf{cc}_A, \mathsf{cc}_B)$ implies CDS protocols for $\mathbf{INDEX}_n$ with communication communication $(\mathsf{cc}'_A, \mathsf{cc}'_B) = (\lceil \frac{n}{t} \rceil \mathsf{cc}_A(t), \mathsf{cc}_B(t))$ for any $t \in [n]$.

3.4 Attribute-Based Encryption for Degree-2 Polynomials

We obtain a new ABE scheme for degree-2 polynomials, by essentially combining the framework of Chen, Gay and Wee (CGW) [CGW15] with our CDS schemes for $\mathbf{MPOLY}^2_{n_1,n_2}$. In the ABE, ciphertexts are associated $\mathbf{p} \in \mathbb{F}_q^{n_1 n_2}$, secret keys with $(\mathbf{x}_1, \mathbf{x}_2) \in \mathbb{F}_q^{n_1} \times \mathbb{F}_q^{n_2}$, and decryption is possible whenever $\langle \mathbf{p}, \mathbf{x}_1 \otimes \mathbf{x}_2 \rangle \neq 0$. We obtain an adaptively secure ABE under the standard k-linear assumption in prime-order bilinear groups, where ciphertext contains $O(n_2)$ group elements, and the secret key contains $O(n_1)$ group elements. This achieves a quadratic savings over the naive approach of encoding degree-2 polynomials as an inner product, where the total ciphertext and secret key size will be $O(n_1 n_2)$ group elements.

Formally, the CGW framework requires CDS with additional structure (e.g. Alice's and Bob's messages are linear in the shared randomness), which our schemes do satisfy with some straight-forward modifications. In the ABE scheme, the master public key, secret key and ciphertext are of the form:

$$\begin{aligned}\mathsf{mpk} &:= \left(g_1,\ g_1^{\mathbf{b}}, g_1^{\mathbf{c}},\ e(g_1,g_1)^{\alpha}\right)\\ \mathsf{ct}_{\mathbf{p}} &:= \left(g_1^{s},\ g_1^{s(\mathbf{p}'_{\mathbf{b}}+\mathbf{c})},\ e(g_1,g_1)^{\alpha s}\cdot m\right)\\ \mathsf{sk}_{\mathbf{x}_1,\mathbf{x}_2} &:= \left(g_1^{r},\ g_1^{\alpha\mathbf{x}_1+r\mathbf{b}}, g_1^{\langle\mathbf{c},\mathbf{x}_2\rangle r}\right)\end{aligned} \tag{5}$$

where $\mathbf{p}'_{\mathbf{b}}$ is defined as in Fig. 3. Decryption relies on the fact that

$$s\cdot(\langle\mathbf{p},(\alpha\mathbf{x}_1+r\mathbf{b})\otimes\mathbf{x}_2\rangle+\langle\mathbf{c},\mathbf{x}_2\rangle r)-\langle s(\mathbf{p}'_{\mathbf{b}}+\mathbf{c})\rangle\cdot r=\alpha s\cdot\langle\mathbf{p},\mathbf{x}_1\otimes\mathbf{x}_2\rangle$$

4 CDS for INDEX from Matching Vector Families

Recall that in $\mathbf{INDEX}_n$, Alice holds $\mathbf{D}\in\{0,1\}^n$, Bob holds $i\in[n]$ and $\mu\in\mathbb{F}_q$, and Charlie learns μ iff $\mathbf{D}_i=1$. In this section, we will construct a CDS protocol for $\mathbf{INDEX}_n$ with communication complexity $2^{O(\sqrt{\log n\log\log n})}$. The key tool in the construction is matching vector families first constructed by Grolmusz [Gro00] and introduced to cryptography in the context of PIR [Yek08, Efr09, DGY11, DG15].

Lemma 4.1 (Matching vector family [Gro00]). *For every sufficiently large $n\in\mathbb{N}$, there exists a collection of vectors $\{(\mathbf{v}_i,\mathbf{u}_i)\}_{i\in[n]}$ such that $\mathbf{u}_i,\mathbf{v}_i\in\mathbb{Z}_6^{\ell}$ where $\ell=2^{O(\sqrt{\log n\log\log n})}=n^{o(1)}$ and:*

$$\begin{aligned}&\langle\mathbf{v}_i,\mathbf{u}_i\rangle=0,\\ &\langle\mathbf{v}_i,\mathbf{u}_j\rangle\in\{1,3,4\}\quad \textit{for } i\neq j.\end{aligned}$$

Moreover, the collection of vectors is computable in time $\mathsf{poly}(n)$.

Such a collection of vectors is known in the literature as a *matching vector family*; the statement above corresponds to the special case where the underlying modulus is 6. Our CDS for $\mathbf{INDEX}_n$ uses the above matching vector family in a way similar to the 2-server PIR in [DG15].

4.1 CDS for $\mathbf{INDEX}_n$ with $n^{o(1)}$ communication

Protocol Overview. The shared randomness consists of $(\mathbf{b},\mathbf{c},c')\in\mathbb{Z}_6^{\ell}\times\mathbb{Z}_3^{\ell}\times\mathbb{Z}_3$. Following [DG15], we consider the following functions $G,G':\{0,1\}\to\mathbb{Z}_3$ (which depend on both inputs i and $\mathbf{D}$ and randomness $\mathbf{b}$) given by[2]

$$G(t):=\sum_{j\in[n]}D_j\cdot(-1)^{\langle t\mathbf{u}_i+\mathbf{b},\mathbf{v}_j\rangle},\quad G'(t):=\sum_{j\in[n]}\langle\mathbf{u}_i,\mathbf{v}_j\rangle\cdot D_j\cdot(-1)^{\langle t\mathbf{u}_i+\mathbf{b},\mathbf{v}_j\rangle} \tag{6}$$

[2] Note that the sums in G,G' are performed over $\mathbb{Z}_3$, whereas the computation in the exponents of -1 are performed over $\mathbb{Z}_2$. This means that we will treat elements of $\mathbb{Z}_6$ (as used in the matching vector family) as elements of $\mathbb{Z}_2$ and $\mathbb{Z}_3$.

CDS for INDEX from Matching Vector Families

Public Knowledge: Matching vector family $\mathbf{v}_1, \mathbf{u}_1, \ldots, \mathbf{v}_n, \mathbf{u}_n \in \mathbb{Z}_6^\ell$
Alice's Input: $\mathbf{D} \in \{0,1\}^n$ and $\mu \in \mathbb{F}_2$.
Bob's Input: $i \in [n]$ and $\mu \in \mathbb{F}_2$.
Shared Randomness: $\mathbf{b} \in \mathbb{Z}_6^\ell, \mathbf{c} \in \mathbb{F}_3^\ell, c' \in \mathbb{F}_3$

- Alice sends $m_A^1 := (2\mu - 1)\sum_j D_j(-1)^{\langle \mathbf{b}, \mathbf{v}_j \rangle} - c' \in \mathbb{F}_3$, $\mathbf{m}_A^2 := \mathbf{c} + (2\mu - 1)\sum_j \mathbf{v}_j D_j (-1)^{\langle \mathbf{b}, \mathbf{v}_j \rangle} \in \mathbb{F}_3^\ell$
- Bob sends $\mathbf{m}_B^1 := \mu \mathbf{u}_i + \mathbf{b} \in \mathbb{Z}_6^\ell$, $m_B^2 := \langle \mathbf{u}_i, \mathbf{c} \rangle + c' \in \mathbb{F}_3$
- Charlie outputs 1 if

$$\langle \mathbf{u}_i, \mathbf{m}_A^2 \rangle - m_A^1 - m_B^2 - \sum_j D_j (-1)^{\langle \mathbf{m}_B^1, \mathbf{v}_j \rangle} + \sum_{j \in [n]} \langle \mathbf{u}_i, \mathbf{v}_j \rangle \cdot D_j \cdot (-1)^{\langle \mathbf{m}_B^1, \mathbf{v}_j \rangle} \neq 0,$$

and 0 otherwise.

Fig. 5. The $2^{O(\sqrt{\log n \log \log n})}$-bit CDS protocol for $\mathbf{INDEX}_n$ using matching vector families.

where D_j is the jth entry of the vector $\mathbf{D}$. Our protocol crucially exploits the identity

$$(2\mu - 1)G'(0) - (2\mu - 1)G(0) - G(\mu) + G'(\mu) = \mu \cdot D_i \cdot (-1)^{\langle \mathbf{b}, \mathbf{v}_i \rangle} \tag{7}$$

which relies on both the properties of the matching vector family and the structure of the underlying ring $\mathbb{Z}_3$ (we defer the proof to the end of this section). To compute the left hand side of Eq. 7, namely $(2\mu - 1)G'(0) - (2\mu - 1)G(0) - G(\mu) + G'(\mu)$ (and therefore recover μ if $D_i = 1$), we observe that

- Bob sends $\mathbf{m}_B^1 := \mu \mathbf{u}_i + \mathbf{b}$ to Charlie.
- Charlie knows $i, \mathbf{D}$ and $\mu \mathbf{u}_i + \mathbf{b}$ and could therefore compute $G(\mu)$ and $G'(\mu)$.
- Alice can compute $G(0) = \sum_j D_j (-1)^{\langle \mathbf{b}, \mathbf{v}_j \rangle}$ since it does not depend on i. Alice then sends $m_A^1 = (2\mu - 1)G(0) - c'$.
- We can write $G'(0) = \sum_j \langle \mathbf{u}_i, \mathbf{v}_j \rangle D_j (-1)^{\langle \mathbf{b}, \mathbf{v}_j \rangle}$ as

$$\langle \mathbf{u}_i, \sum_j \mathbf{v}_j D_j (-1)^{\langle \mathbf{b}, \mathbf{v}_j \rangle} \rangle$$

  Alice would send $\mathbf{m}_A^2 := \mathbf{c} + (2\mu - 1)\sum_j \mathbf{v}_j D_j (-1)^{\langle \mathbf{b}, \mathbf{v}_j \rangle}$ and Bob would send $m_B^2 := \langle \mathbf{u}_i, \mathbf{c} \rangle + c'$. Note that we have $(2\mu - 1)G'(0) - (2\mu - 1)G(0) = -m_A^1 + \langle \mathbf{u}_i, \mathbf{m}_A^2 \rangle - m_B^2$.
- Charlie outputs 1 if $(2\mu - 1)G'(0) - (2\mu - 1)G(0) - G(\mu) + G'(\mu) \neq 0$, and 0 otherwise.

Theorem 4.2. *There is a CDS protocol for* $\mathbf{INDEX}_n$ *(given in Fig. 5) with* $\mathsf{cc}_A, \mathsf{cc}_B = 2^{O(\sqrt{\log n \log \log n})}$.

Analysis. Correctness is straight-forward. It is also easy to see that the total communication complexity is $O(\ell) = 2^{O(\sqrt{\log n \log\log n})}$. Privacy follows from the following observations:

- the joint distribution of $\mathbf{m}_B^1, m_A^1, \mathbf{m}_A^2$ is uniformly random, since we are using $(\mathbf{b}, \mathbf{c}, c')$ as one-time pads;
- when $D_i = 0$, we have $(2\mu-1)G'(0) - (2\mu-1)G(0) - G(\mu) + G'(\mu) = 0$. This means that $m_B^2 = \langle \mathbf{u}_i, \mathbf{m}_A^2 \rangle - m_A^1 - G(\mu) + G'(\mu)$. Recall that $G(\mu), G'(\mu)$ can in turn be computed from $\mathbf{D}, i, \mathbf{m}_B^1$.

Putting these together, we can simulate $m_A^1, \mathbf{m}_A^2, \mathbf{m}_B^1, m_B^2$ given just $\mathbf{D}, i$ when $D_i = 0$.

Completing the Proof. It remains to prove the identity described in (7). Fix $i \in [n], \mathbf{D} \in \{0,1\}^n$ and $\mathbf{b} \in \mathbb{Z}_6^\ell$. For $\sigma \in \{0,1,3,4\}$, we define

$$S_\sigma := \{j : \langle \mathbf{u}_i, \mathbf{v}_j \rangle = \sigma\} \subseteq [n]$$
$$c_\sigma := \sum_{j \in S_\sigma} D_j (-1)^{\langle \mathbf{b}, \mathbf{v}_j \rangle} \in \mathbb{Z}_3$$

We can then rewrite $G(t), G'(t)$ as

$$G(t) = \sum_\sigma \Big(\sum_{j \in S_\sigma} D_j (-1)^{\langle \mathbf{b}, \mathbf{v}_j \rangle} \Big) \cdot (-1)^{t\sigma}$$
$$G'(t) = \sum_\sigma \sigma \Big(\sum_{j \in S_\sigma} D_j (-1)^{\langle \mathbf{b}, \mathbf{v}_j \rangle} \Big) \cdot (-1)^{t\sigma}$$

and thus

$$G(t) = c_0 + c_1(-1)^t + c_3(-1)^{3t} + c_4(-1)^{4t}, \quad G'(t) = c_1(-1)^t + c_4(-1)^{4t}$$

This means

$$\begin{bmatrix} G(0) \\ G'(0) \\ G(1) \\ G'(1) \end{bmatrix} = \begin{bmatrix} 1 & 1 & 1 & 1 \\ & 1 & & 1 \\ 1 & -1 & -1 & 1 \\ & -1 & & 1 \end{bmatrix} \begin{bmatrix} c_0 \\ c_1 \\ c_3 \\ c_4 \end{bmatrix} \tag{8}$$

It is then easy to see that

$$G(0) - G'(0) = c_0 + c_3$$
$$G(1) - G'(1) = c_0 - c_3$$
$$G(\mu) - G'(\mu) = c_0 + (1 - 2\mu)c_3$$

Therefore,

$$(G(\mu) - G'(\mu)) - (1-2\mu)(G(0) - G'(0)) = 2\mu \cdot c_0 = -\mu \cdot c_0$$

The identity in (7) then follows readily from the fact that $c_0 = D_i \cdot (-1)^{\langle \mathbf{b}, \mathbf{v}_i \rangle}$.

Comparison with Dvir and Gopi. Dvir and Gopi considered the ring $\mathbb{Z}_6[X]/(X^6 - 1)$ which has a generator X, but we use $\mathbb{Z}_3$ and -1 as suggested there-in. The definitions of $G(t), G(t'), c_0, c_1, c_3, c_4$ are the same as those in DG, and the relation in (8) is a simplification of that in DG.

Remark 4.3 (From PIR to CDS). In Sect. 1.2, we informally construct a CDS for $\mathbf{INDEX}_n$ from any 2-server PIR scheme whose reconstruction function has good structure (as in formula (2)). We claimed that [DG15] has similar structure so that the construction is possible.

Let $\tilde{\mathbf{u}}_i := (\mathbf{u}_i \| 1)$, $\tilde{\mathbf{v}}_j := (\mathbf{v}_j \| -1)$, $\tilde{\mathbf{b}} := (\mathbf{b} \| 0)$. Define $H_{\mathbf{D}}(\mathbf{y}) = \sum_j \tilde{\mathbf{v}}_j \cdot D_j \cdot (-1)^{\langle \mathbf{y}, \tilde{\mathbf{v}}_j \rangle}$, then $\langle H_{\mathbf{D}}(t\tilde{\mathbf{u}}_i + \tilde{\mathbf{b}}), \tilde{\mathbf{u}}_i \rangle = \sum_j (\langle \mathbf{v}_j, \mathbf{u}_i \rangle - 1) \cdot D_j \cdot (-1)^{\langle t\mathbf{u}_i + \mathbf{b}, \mathbf{v}_j \rangle - t} = (G'(t) - G(t)) \cdot (-1)^{-t}$. Finally,

$$\langle H_{\mathbf{D}}(\tilde{\mathbf{u}}_i + \tilde{\mathbf{b}}), \tilde{\mathbf{u}}_i \rangle - \langle H_{\mathbf{D}}(\tilde{\mathbf{b}}), \tilde{\mathbf{u}}_i \rangle = -G'(t) + G(t) + G'(0) - G(0) = D_j \cdot (-1)^{\langle \mathbf{b}, \mathbf{v}_i \rangle},$$

which is similar to the property mentioned in Sect. 1.2.

4.2 Applications to $\mathbf{ALL}_N$ and Secret-Sharing

Corollary 1. *There exist CDS schemes for $\mathbf{ALL}_N$ with $\mathsf{cc}_A = \mathsf{cc}_B = 2^{O(\sqrt{\log N \log\log N})}$.*

Corollary 2. *There are secret sharing schemes for forbidden graph access structures on N nodes where the share size for each node is $2^{O(\sqrt{\log N \log\log N})}$ bits and total share size is $N \cdot 2^{O(\sqrt{\log N \log\log N})} = N^{1+o(1)}$.*

Combining Theorem 4.2 and reduction for $\mathbf{INDEX}_N \Rightarrow \mathbf{ALL}_N$ in Sect. 2.3 yields Corollary 1 immediately. Further combining Corollary 1 with the construction of secret sharing schemes for forbidden graph access structures from CDS for **ALL** (Theorem 2.6) yields Corollary 2.

5 PSM for Polynomials with Applications to INDEX

5.1 Degree-k Polynomials $\mathbf{MPOLY}^k_{n_1,\ldots,n_k}$

We start with a PSM protocol for degree-k polynomials, which is "essentially optimal" in the sense that the communication complexity is roughly the same as that for sending the inputs in the clear. Our protocol uses the standard "random shift" technique in information-theoretic cryptography, but to the best of our knowledge, the protocol has not appeared in the literature.

Warm-up. Suppose Alice holds multi-variate polynomial p in n variables over $\mathbb{F}_q$ of total degree at most k, Bob holds an input $\mathbf{x} \in \mathbb{F}_q^n$, and we want Charlie to learn $p(\mathbf{x})$ and nothing else. Here is a simple protocol:

- the shared randomness is $\mathbf{w} \in \mathbb{F}_q^n$ along with a random polynomial g of total degree k;

– Alice sends $(\mathbf{x}', u) := (\mathbf{x} + \mathbf{w}, g(\mathbf{x} + \mathbf{w}))$; Bob sends the polynomial h where $h(\mathbf{y}) := p(\mathbf{y} - \mathbf{w}) + g(\mathbf{y})$; Charlie outputs $h(\mathbf{x}') - u$.

Correctness is straight-forward. Privacy follows readily from the fact that we can simulate the view of Charlie given $p(\mathbf{x})$ by picking a random $\mathbf{x}', h$ and outputting $(\mathbf{x}', h(\mathbf{x}') - f(\mathbf{x})), h$. Alice only sends a polynomial, thus her communication complexity cc_A matches the information lower bound.

This warm-up PSM relies on the fact that for any degree-k polynomial $p(\mathbf{x})$, after shifting the input by a vector $\mathbf{w}$, the resulting polynomial $p(\mathbf{x} - \mathbf{w})$ is still a degree-k polynomial. This is not true for homogeneous polynomial (e.g. $\mathbf{MPOLY}^k_{n_1,\ldots,n_k}$). Therefore, when we apply the technique from this warm-up PSM to $\mathbf{MPOLY}^k_{n_1,\ldots,n_k}$, the one-time pad polynomial g is chosen from a class larger than $\mathbf{MPOLY}^k_{n_1,\ldots,n_k}$. A naïve solution is to sample random n-variate degree-k polynomial g. This makes Alice's message ($\geq \frac{(n_1+\ldots+n_k+1)^k}{k!}$ bits) much longer than her input ($\prod_j n_j$ bits). In order to overcome this difficult and preserve close-to-optimal communication complexity, we sample g from a more subtle polynomial class.

Functionality. The functionality $\mathbf{MPOLY}^k_{n_1,\ldots,n_k}$ is defined as: Alice holds a homogeneous multi-linear polynomial $\mathbf{p} \in \mathbb{F}_q^{n_1 \cdots n_k}$ and Bob holds $\overline{\mathbf{x}} := (\mathbf{x}_1, \ldots, \mathbf{x}_k) \in \mathbb{F}_q^{n_1} \otimes \ldots \otimes \mathbb{F}_q^{n_k}$. Charlie learns $\mathbf{p}(\overline{\mathbf{x}}) := \langle \mathbf{p}, \mathbf{x}_1 \otimes \ldots \otimes \mathbf{x}_k \rangle$.

Protocol Overview. The shared randomness comprises $\overline{\mathbf{b}} = (\mathbf{b}_1, \ldots, \mathbf{b}_k) \in \mathbb{F}_q^{n_1} \times \ldots \times \mathbb{F}_q^{n_k}$ and a random polynomial g. Bob sends $\overline{\mathbf{m}}_B^1 := \overline{\mathbf{x}} + \overline{\mathbf{b}}$ and Alice sends a polynomial h such that $h(\overline{\mathbf{y}}) := \langle \mathbf{p}, (\mathbf{y}_1 - \mathbf{b}_1) \otimes \ldots \otimes (\mathbf{y}_k - \mathbf{b}_k) \rangle + g(\overline{\mathbf{y}})$. Now Charlie knows, $\overline{\mathbf{x}} + \overline{\mathbf{b}}, h$, and can compute

$$h(\overline{\mathbf{x}} + \overline{\mathbf{b}}) = \langle \mathbf{p}, \mathbf{x}_1 \otimes \ldots \otimes \mathbf{x}_k \rangle + g(\overline{\mathbf{x}} + \overline{\mathbf{b}}).$$

Charlie could learns $f(\overline{\mathbf{x}})$ if Bob sends $m_B^2 := g(\overline{\mathbf{x}} + \overline{\mathbf{b}})$.

When we compose homogeneous polynomial $\mathbf{p}(\overline{\mathbf{y}}) := \langle \mathbf{p}, \mathbf{y}_1 \otimes \ldots \otimes \mathbf{y}_k \rangle$ with an input shift, the resulting polynomial $\langle \mathbf{p}, (\mathbf{y}_1 - \mathbf{b}_1) \otimes \ldots \otimes (\mathbf{y}_k - \mathbf{b}_k) \rangle$ is not homogeneous. Let $\mathbf{y}_1 \| 1$ denote the vector obtained by padding constant 1 at the end of $\mathbf{y}$. There exists $\mathbf{p}'_{\mathbf{b}_1,\ldots,\mathbf{b}_k} \in \mathbb{F}_q^{(n_1+1)\ldots(n_k+1)}$ such that

$$\langle \mathbf{p}, (\mathbf{y}_1 - \mathbf{b}_1) \otimes \ldots \otimes (\mathbf{y}_k - \mathbf{b}_k) \rangle = \langle \mathbf{p}'_{\mathbf{b}_1,\ldots,\mathbf{b}_k}, (\mathbf{y}_1 \| 1) \otimes \ldots \otimes (\mathbf{y}_k \| 1) \rangle.$$

Therefore, to hide polynomial $\langle \mathbf{p}, (\mathbf{y}_1 - \mathbf{b}_1) \otimes \ldots \otimes (\mathbf{y}_k - \mathbf{b}_k) \rangle$ using a one-time pad, Alice pick a random polynomial g that

$$g(\overline{\mathbf{x}}) := \langle \mathbf{g}, (\mathbf{y}_1 \| 1) \otimes \ldots \otimes (\mathbf{y}_k \| 1) \rangle, \tag{9}$$

where $\mathbf{g} \in \mathbb{F}_q^{(n_1+1)\ldots(n_k+1)}$.

Theorem 5.1. *There is a PSM protocol for degree k polynomials over $\mathbb{F}_q$ (shown in Fig. 6) where Alice sends $\prod_j (n_j + 1)$ elements of $\mathbb{F}_q$, Bob sends $\sum_j n_j + 1$ elements of $\mathbb{F}_q$ and Charlie applies a degree-$(k + 1)$ reconstruction function over $\mathbb{F}_q$.*

PSM for Polynomials (over $\mathbb{F}_q$)

Alice's Input: $\mathbf{p} \in \mathbb{F}_q^{n_1 \dots n_k}$
Bob's Input: $\overline{\mathbf{x}} := (\mathbf{x}_1, \dots, \mathbf{x}_k) \in \mathbb{F}_q^{n_1} \otimes \dots \otimes \mathbb{F}_q^{n_k}$
Carol's Output: $\langle \mathbf{p}, \mathbf{x}_1 \otimes \dots \otimes \mathbf{x}_k \rangle$.
Shared Randomness: $\overline{\mathbf{b}} = (\mathbf{b}_1, \dots, \mathbf{b}_k) \in \mathbb{F}_q^{n_1} \times \dots \times \mathbb{F}_q^{n_k}$ and a random degree-k multilinear polynomial $g : \mathbb{F}_q^{n_1} \times \dots \times \mathbb{F}_q^{n_k} \to \mathbb{F}_q$;

- Alice sends the polynomial h where $h(\overline{\mathbf{y}}) := \langle \mathbf{p}, (\mathbf{y}_1 - \mathbf{b}_1) \otimes \dots \otimes (\mathbf{y}_k - \mathbf{b}_k) \rangle + g(\overline{\mathbf{y}})$ for all $\overline{\mathbf{y}} = (\mathbf{y}_1, \dots, \mathbf{y}_k) \in \mathbb{F}_q^{n_1} \otimes \dots \otimes \mathbb{F}_q^{n_k}$;
- Bob sends $(\overline{\mathbf{m}}_B^1, m_B^2) := (\overline{\mathbf{x}} + \overline{\mathbf{b}}, g(\overline{\mathbf{x}} + \overline{\mathbf{b}}))$;
- Charlie outputs $h(\overline{\mathbf{m}}_B^1) - m_B^2$.

Fig. 6. The PSM protocol for degree-k polynomials with $(\mathsf{cc}_A, \mathsf{cc}_B) = (\prod_j (n_j + 1) \log q, (\sum_j n_j + 1) \log q)$.

Proof. The correctness is straight-forward, as

$$h(\overline{\mathbf{m}}_B^1) - m_B^2 = h(\overline{\mathbf{x}} + \overline{\mathbf{b}}) - g(\overline{\mathbf{x}} + \overline{\mathbf{b}}) = \langle \mathbf{p}, \mathbf{x}_1 \otimes \dots \otimes \mathbf{x}_k \rangle.$$

It takes $\prod_j (n_j + 1)$ elements of $\mathbb{F}_q$ to encode a non-homogeneous degree-k polynomial over $\mathbb{F}_q$. Thus the communication complexity is $\mathsf{cc}_A = \prod_j (n_j + 1) \cdot \log q$, $\mathsf{cc}_B = (\sum_j n_j + 1) \log q$. Privacy follows from the following observations:

- the joint distribution of $\overline{\mathbf{m}}_B^1, h$ is uniformly random, since we are using $(\overline{\mathbf{b}}, g)$ as one-time pads;
- we have $m_B^2 = h(\overline{\mathbf{m}}_B) - f(\overline{\mathbf{x}})$.

Putting the two together, we can simulate $h, \overline{\mathbf{m}}_B^1, m_B^2$ given just $f(\overline{\mathbf{x}})$. The reconstruction is of degree $k + 1$. □

Generalization. The technique of this PSM protocol (shown in Fig. 6) can be generalized to the following functionality: Alice holds $f \in \mathscr{F}$, Bob holds $\mathbf{x} \in \mathscr{X}$ and Charlie learns $f(\mathbf{x}) \in \mathscr{D}$, where $\mathscr{F}$ is a public set of functions from finite group $\mathscr{X}$ to finite group $\mathscr{D}$ satisfying

- **Closure under group operation:** for any $f, f' \in \mathscr{F}$, the function $f + f'$, defined as $(f + f')(\mathbf{x}) = f(\mathbf{x}) + f'(\mathbf{x})$, is in $\mathscr{F}$ as well;
- **Closure under input shift:** for any $f \in \mathscr{F}, \mathbf{s} \in \mathscr{X}$, the function $f_{\mathbf{s}}$, defined as $f_{\mathbf{s}}(\mathbf{x}) = f(\mathbf{x} - \mathbf{s})$, is also in $\mathscr{F}$.

The resulting PSM has nearly optimal communication complexity, $\mathsf{cc}_A = \log |\mathscr{F}|$ which matches information theoretical lower bound and $\mathsf{cc}_B = \log |\mathscr{X}| + \log |\mathscr{D}|$ which is higher than the optimal by at most $\log |\mathscr{D}|$.

Inner Product. The inner product problem, where Alice and Bod hold $\mathbf{x}, \mathbf{y} \in \mathbb{F}_p^n$ respectively and Charlie learns $\langle \mathbf{x}, \mathbf{y} \rangle$, is an alias of $\mathbf{MPOLY}_n^1$. Thus there is an efficient PSM protocol for inner product.

Corollary 3. *There exists a PSM protocol for inner product with* $\mathsf{cc}_A = \mathsf{cc}_B = n + 1$ *and degree-2 reconstruction.*

5.2 Degree-4 Functions

Here, we present a PSM for degree 4 functions with linear communication, which we then use to derive a PSM for $\mathbf{ALL}_N$ in the next section.

Functionality. There is a fixed public function $\mathbf{p} \in \mathbb{F}_q^{n^4}$. Alice holds $\mathbf{x}_1, \mathbf{x}_2 \in \mathbb{F}_q^n$ and Bob holds $\mathbf{y}_1, \mathbf{y}_2 \in \mathbb{F}_q^n$. Charlie learns $\langle \mathbf{p}, \mathbf{x}_1 \otimes \mathbf{x}_2 \otimes \mathbf{y}_1 \otimes \mathbf{y}_2 \rangle$.

Protocol Overview. Alice sends $\mathbf{x}_1 + \mathbf{b}_1, \mathbf{x}_2 + \mathbf{b}_2$, Bob sends $\mathbf{y}_1 + \mathbf{c}_1, \mathbf{y}_2 + \mathbf{c}_2$. Then Charlie can computes

$$
\begin{aligned}
&\langle \mathbf{p}, (\mathbf{x}_1 + \mathbf{b}_1) \otimes (\mathbf{x}_2 + \mathbf{b}_2) \otimes (\mathbf{y}_1 + \mathbf{c}_1) \otimes (\mathbf{y}_2 + \mathbf{c}_2) \rangle \\
= &\underbrace{\langle \mathbf{p}, (\mathbf{x}_1 + \mathbf{b}_1) \otimes (\mathbf{x}_2 + \mathbf{b}_2) \otimes (\mathbf{y}_1 \otimes \mathbf{c}_2 + \mathbf{c}_1 \otimes \mathbf{y}_2 + \mathbf{c}_1 \otimes \mathbf{c}_2) \rangle}_{\text{affine in } \mathbf{y}_1 \| \mathbf{y}_2} \\
&+ \underbrace{\langle \mathbf{p}, (\mathbf{x}_1 \otimes \mathbf{b}_2 + \mathbf{b}_1 \otimes \mathbf{x}_2 + \mathbf{b}_1 \otimes \mathbf{b}_2) \otimes \mathbf{y}_1 \otimes \mathbf{y}_2 \rangle}_{\text{affine in } \mathbf{x}_1 \| \mathbf{x}_2} \\
&+ \langle \mathbf{p}, \mathbf{x}_1 \otimes \mathbf{x}_2 \otimes \mathbf{y}_1 \otimes \mathbf{y}_2 \rangle \\
= &\langle \mathbf{p}'_{\mathbf{b}_1, \mathbf{b}_2, \mathbf{c}_1, \mathbf{c}_2, \mathbf{x}_1, \mathbf{x}_2}, \mathbf{y}_1 \| \mathbf{y}_2 \| 1 \rangle + \langle \mathbf{p}''_{\mathbf{b}_1, \mathbf{b}_2, \mathbf{c}_1, \mathbf{c}_2, \mathbf{y}_1, \mathbf{y}_2}, \mathbf{x}_1 \| \mathbf{x}_2 \| 1 \rangle \\
&+ \langle \mathbf{p}, \mathbf{x}_1 \otimes \mathbf{x}_2 \otimes \mathbf{y}_1 \otimes \mathbf{y}_2 \rangle
\end{aligned} \tag{10}
$$

The key insight is that the two terms that are linear in either in $\mathbf{x}_1 \| \mathbf{x}_2$ or $\mathbf{y}_1 \| \mathbf{y}_2$ and can be computed using a PSM for inner product with $O(n)$ communication.

Theorem 5.2. *This is a PSM protocol for degree-4 functions over* $\mathbb{F}_q$ *(shown in Fig. 7) where both Alice and Bob send* $(4n + 3)$ *elements of* $\mathbb{F}_q$ *and Charlie applies a degree-4 reconstruction function over* $\mathbb{F}_q$.

Proof. Correctness is straight-forward from Eq. (10), as

$$
\begin{aligned}
&\langle \mathbf{p}, \mathbf{m}_A^1 \otimes \mathbf{m}_A^2 \otimes \mathbf{m}_B^1 \otimes \mathbf{m}_B^2 \rangle - a \\
= &\langle \mathbf{p}, \mathbf{m}_A^1 \otimes \mathbf{m}_A^2 \otimes \mathbf{m}_B^1 \otimes \mathbf{m}_B^2 \rangle \\
&- \langle \mathbf{p}'_{\mathbf{b}_1, \mathbf{b}_2, \mathbf{c}_1, \mathbf{c}_2, \mathbf{x}_1, \mathbf{x}_2}, \mathbf{y}_1 \| \mathbf{y}_2 \| 1 \rangle - \langle \mathbf{p}'_{\mathbf{b}_1, \mathbf{b}_2, \mathbf{c}_1, \mathbf{c}_2, \mathbf{y}_1, \mathbf{y}_2}, \mathbf{x}_1 \| \mathbf{x}_2 \| 1 \rangle \\
= &\langle \mathbf{p}, \mathbf{x}_1 \otimes \mathbf{x}_2 \otimes \mathbf{y}_1 \otimes \mathbf{y}_2 \rangle.
\end{aligned}
$$

Privacy follows from the following observations:

- the joint distribution of $\mathbf{m}_A^1, \mathbf{m}_A^2, \mathbf{m}_B^1, \mathbf{m}_B^2$ is uniformly random, since we are using $(\mathbf{b}_1, \mathbf{b}_2, \mathbf{c}_1, \mathbf{c}_2)$ as one-time pads;

- a is determined by $\mathbf{p}, \mathbf{m}_A^1, \mathbf{m}_A^2, \mathbf{m}_B^1, \mathbf{m}_B^2$ and $\langle \mathbf{p}, \mathbf{x}_1 \otimes \mathbf{x}_2 \otimes \mathbf{y}_1 \otimes \mathbf{y}_2 \rangle$ as $a = \langle \mathbf{p}, \mathbf{m}_A^1 \otimes \mathbf{m}_A^2 \otimes \mathbf{m}_B^1 \otimes \mathbf{m}_B^2 \rangle - \langle \mathbf{p}, \mathbf{x}_1 \otimes \mathbf{x}_2 \otimes \mathbf{y}_1 \otimes \mathbf{y}_2 \rangle$. The messages in the underlying PSM for inner product can be simulated given just a.

Putting the two together, we can simulate Charlie's view, consisting of $\mathbf{m}_A^1, \mathbf{m}_A^2, \mathbf{m}_B^1, \mathbf{m}_B^2$ and the messages in PSM for inner product, given $\langle \mathbf{p}, \mathbf{x}_1 \otimes \mathbf{x}_2 \otimes \mathbf{y}_1 \otimes \mathbf{y}_2 \rangle$.

The reconstruction is of degree 4. Communication complexity is $\mathsf{cc}_A = \mathsf{cc}_B = (4n+3)\log q$, each party sends $2n$ elements as one-time pads of its input, and $2n+3$ elements for computing the inner product. □

5.3 Applications to $\mathbf{INDEX}_n$ and $\mathbf{ALL}_N$

Theorem 5.3. *For any integer $k \geq 1$, there are PSM protocols for $\mathbf{INDEX}_n$ with: $(\mathsf{cc}_A, \mathsf{cc}_B) = (O(n), k \cdot n^{1/k} + 1)$ and degree-$(k+1)$ reconstruction.*

Note that setting $k = 1$ and $k = \log n$ yields the folklore constructions described in Fig. 2.

Proof. It follows from combining the $\mathbf{MPOLY}^k_{n^{1/k},\ldots,n^{1/k}} \Rightarrow \mathbf{INDEX}_n$ reduction in Sect. 2.3 with our PSM for $\mathbf{MPOLY}^k$ in Theorem 5.1. This immediately yields a PSM for $\mathbf{INDEX}_n$ with $(\mathsf{cc}_A, \mathsf{cc}_B) = ((\lceil n^{1/k} \rceil + 1)^k, k\lceil n^{1/k} \rceil + 1)$ and degree-$(k+1)$ reconstruction.

$$\mathsf{cc}_A(n) \leq (\lceil n^{1/k} \rceil + 1)^k \leq (n^{1/k} + 2)^k = n + 2kn^{1-1/k} + \ldots = O(n) \qquad \square$$

Theorem 5.4. *There are PSM protocols for $\mathbf{ALL}_N$ with: $(\mathsf{cc}_A, \mathsf{cc}_B) = (\sqrt{N}, \sqrt{N})$ and degree-4 reconstruction.*

Note that such PSM protocols were already shown in [BIKK14] via the use of a 4-server PIR; our construction is simpler, and we provide an explicit bound on the complexity of reconstruction.

Proof. The predicate $\mathbf{ALL}_N$ can be reduced to degree-4 function problem defined in Fig. 7.

- $\mathbf{p} \in \mathbb{F}_2^{N^2}$ is the true table of the fixed function F, such that for any $x, y \in [N]$, $\langle \mathbf{p}, \mathbf{e}_x \otimes \mathbf{e}_y \rangle = F(x, y)$
- Alice holds $\mathbf{x}_1 := \mathbf{e}_{i_1} \in \mathbb{F}_2^{\sqrt{N}}, \mathbf{x}_2 := \mathbf{e}_{i_2} \in \mathbb{F}_2^{\sqrt{N}}$ such that $\mathbf{e}_{i_1} \otimes \mathbf{e}_{i_2} = \mathbf{e}_x$.
- Bob holds $\mathbf{y}_1 := \mathbf{e}_{i_1} \in \mathbb{F}_2^{\sqrt{N}}, \mathbf{y}_2 := \mathbf{e}_{i_2} \in \mathbb{F}_2^{\sqrt{N}}$ such that $\mathbf{e}_{i_1} \otimes \mathbf{e}_{i_2} = \mathbf{e}_y$.

Under such reduction, $\langle \mathbf{p}, \mathbf{x}_1 \otimes \mathbf{x}_2 \otimes \mathbf{y}_1 \otimes \mathbf{y}_2 \rangle = \langle \mathbf{p}, \mathbf{e}_x \otimes \mathbf{e}_y \rangle = F(x, y)$. Combining with the PSM protocol for degree-4 function in Sect. 5.2, there are PSM protocols for $\mathbf{ALL}_N$ with $(\mathsf{cc}_A, \mathsf{cc}_B) = O(\sqrt{N}, \sqrt{N})$ and degree-4 reconstruction. □

PSM for Degree-4 Functions (over $\mathbb{F}_q$)

Public knowledge: Function $\mathbf{p} \in \mathbb{F}_q^{n^4}$
Alice's Input: $(\mathbf{x}_1, \mathbf{x}_2) \in \mathbb{F}_q^{n_1} \times \mathbb{F}_q^{n_2}$
Bob's Input: $(\mathbf{y}_1, \mathbf{y}_2) \in \mathbb{F}_q^{n_1} \times \mathbb{F}_q^{n_2}$
Carol's Output: $\langle \mathbf{p}, \mathbf{x}_1 \otimes \mathbf{x}_2 \otimes \mathbf{y}_1 \otimes \mathbf{y}_2 \rangle$.
Shared Randomness: $\mathbf{b}_1, \mathbf{b}_2, \mathbf{c}_1, \mathbf{c}_2 \in \mathbb{F}_q^n$ and randomness of PSM for inner product.

- Alice computes a vector $\mathbf{p}'_{\mathbf{b}_1,\mathbf{b}_2,\mathbf{c}_1,\mathbf{c}_2,\mathbf{x}_1,\mathbf{x}_2} \in \mathbb{F}_q^{2n+1}$ such that for any $\mathbf{z}_1, \mathbf{z}_2 \in \mathbb{F}_q^n$

$$\langle \mathbf{p}'_{\mathbf{b}_1,\mathbf{b}_2,\mathbf{c}_1,\mathbf{c}_2,\mathbf{x}_1,\mathbf{x}_2}, \mathbf{z}_1 \| \mathbf{z}_2 \| 1 \rangle = \langle \mathbf{p}, (\mathbf{x}_1 + \mathbf{b}_1) \otimes (\mathbf{x}_2 + \mathbf{b}_2) \otimes (\mathbf{z}_1 \otimes \mathbf{c}_2 + \mathbf{c}_1 \otimes \mathbf{z}_2 + \mathbf{c}_1 \otimes \mathbf{c}_2) \rangle.$$

  She sends $(\mathbf{m}_A^1, \mathbf{m}_A^2) := (\mathbf{x}_1 + \mathbf{b}_1, \mathbf{x}_2 + \mathbf{b}_2)$ to Charlie.
- Bob computes a vector $\mathbf{p}''_{\mathbf{b}_1,\mathbf{b}_2,\mathbf{c}_1,\mathbf{c}_2,\mathbf{y}_1,\mathbf{y}_2} \in \mathbb{F}_q^{2n+1}$ such that for any $\mathbf{z}_1, \mathbf{z}_2 \in \mathbb{F}_q^n$

$$\langle \mathbf{p}'_{\mathbf{b}_1,\mathbf{b}_2,\mathbf{c}_1,\mathbf{c}_2,\mathbf{y}_1,\mathbf{y}_2}, \mathbf{z}_1 \| \mathbf{z}_2 \| 1 \rangle = \langle \mathbf{p}, (\mathbf{z}_1 \otimes \mathbf{b}_2 + \mathbf{b}_1 \otimes \mathbf{z}_2 + \mathbf{b}_1 \otimes \mathbf{b}_2) \otimes \mathbf{y}_1 \otimes \mathbf{y}_2 \rangle.$$

  He sends $(\mathbf{m}_B^1, \mathbf{m}_B^2) := (\mathbf{y}_1 + \mathbf{c}_1, \mathbf{y}_2 + \mathbf{c}_2)$ to Charlie.
- Let Charlie learns $a := \langle \mathbf{p}'_{\mathbf{b}_1,\mathbf{b}_2,\mathbf{c}_1,\mathbf{c}_2,\mathbf{x}_1,\mathbf{x}_2}, \mathbf{y}_1 \| \mathbf{y}_2 \| 1 \rangle + \langle \mathbf{p}'_{\mathbf{b}_1,\mathbf{b}_2,\mathbf{c}_1,\mathbf{c}_2,\mathbf{y}_1,\mathbf{y}_2}, \mathbf{x}_1 \| \mathbf{x}_2 \| 1 \rangle$ using a PSM protocol for inner product (Corollary 3).
- Charlie outputs $\langle \mathbf{p}, \mathbf{m}_A^1 \otimes \mathbf{m}_A^2 \otimes \mathbf{m}_B^1 \otimes \mathbf{m}_B^2 \rangle - a$.

Fig. 7. The PSM protocol for degree-4 functions with $\mathsf{cc}_A = \mathsf{cc}_B = (4n+3)\log q$.

A PSM with One-Sided Privacy (1/2-PSM)

A.1 Private Simultaneous Message with One-Sided Privacy

Definition A.1 (private simultaneous message with one-sided privacy (1/2-PSM)). *Fix a functionality $f : \mathcal{X} \times \mathcal{Y} \to \mathcal{D}$. An* $(\mathsf{cc_A}, \mathsf{cc_B})$-private simultaneous message with one-sided privacy (1/2-PSM) *protocol for functionality f is a triplet of deterministic functions* $(\mathsf{A}, \mathsf{B}, \mathsf{C})$

$$\mathsf{A} : \mathcal{X} \times \mathcal{W} \to \{0,1\}^{\mathsf{cc}_A}, \quad \mathsf{B} : \mathcal{Y} \times \mathcal{W} \to \{0,1\}^{\mathsf{cc}_B}, \quad \mathsf{C} : \mathcal{X} \times \{0,1\}^{\mathsf{cc_A}} \times \{0,1\}^{\mathsf{cc_B}} \to \mathcal{D}$$

satisfying the following properties:

(reconstruction.) *For all $(x, y) \in \mathcal{X} \times \mathcal{Y}$:*

$$\mathsf{C}(x, \mathsf{A}(x, w), \mathsf{B}(y, w)) = f(x, y)$$

(one-sided privacy.) *There exists a randomized simulator* S, *such that for any $(x, y) \in \mathcal{X} \times \mathcal{Y}$ the joint distribution* $(\mathsf{A}(x, w), \mathsf{B}(y, w))$ *is perfectly indistinguishable from* $\mathsf{S}(x, f(x, y))$, *where the distributions are taken over randomness $w \leftarrow \mathcal{W}$ and the coin tosses of* S.

A.2 Degree 2 Polynomials

For degree-2 polynomials, we show a 1/2-PSM protocol where Alice and Bob both communicate $O(n)$ bits.

Functionality. Alice holds $\mathbf{p} \in \mathbb{F}_p^{n^2}$, Bob holds $\mathbf{x} \in \mathbb{F}_p^n$ and Charlie learns $\langle \mathbf{p}, \mathbf{x} \otimes \mathbf{x} \rangle$.

Protocol Overview. The shared randomness comprises $(\mathbf{b}, b', \mathbf{c}) \in \mathbb{F}_p^n \times \mathbb{F}_p \times \mathbb{F}_p^n$. Bob sends $\mathbf{m}_B^1 = \mathbf{x} + \mathbf{b}$. Now, Charlie knows $\mathbf{p}$ and $\mathbf{x} + \mathbf{b}$, and could compute

$$\begin{aligned} &\langle \mathbf{p}, (\mathbf{x} + \mathbf{b}) \otimes (\mathbf{x} + \mathbf{b}) \rangle \\ &= \langle \mathbf{p}, \mathbf{x} \otimes \mathbf{x} \rangle + \underbrace{\langle \mathbf{p}, \mathbf{b} \otimes \mathbf{x} \rangle + \langle \mathbf{p}, \mathbf{x} \otimes \mathbf{b} \rangle}_{\langle \mathbf{p}'_{\mathbf{b}}, \mathbf{x} \rangle} + \underbrace{\langle \mathbf{p}, \mathbf{b} \otimes \mathbf{b} \rangle}_{c'} \end{aligned}$$

where $c' := \langle \mathbf{p}, \mathbf{b} \otimes \mathbf{b} \rangle$ and $\mathbf{p}'_{\mathbf{b}} \in \mathbb{F}_2^n$ depends on $\mathbf{p}$ and $\mathbf{b}$.

In a nutshell, now, Alice and Bob run a PSM protocol to compute the linear function $\langle \mathbf{p}'_{\mathbf{b}}, \mathbf{x} \rangle + c'$ where Alice has $\mathbf{p}'_{\mathbf{b}}$ and c' whereas Bob has $\mathbf{x}$. Since there is such a protocol where Alice and Bob both send $n + 1$ bits, the total communication complexity for Alice is $O(n)$, and that for Bob is $O(n)$ as well. The degree of reconstruction is 2, which follows from the fact that Charlie computes the bilinear form described above and the fact that the PSM protocol for linear functions has degree 2.

Concretely, Alice sends $\mathbf{m}_A^1 = \mathbf{p}'_{\mathbf{b}} + \mathbf{c}, m_A^2 = \langle \mathbf{m}_A^1, \mathbf{b} \rangle - c' - b'$, Bob sends $m_B^2 = \langle \mathbf{c}, \mathbf{x} \rangle + b'$. Charlie recover $\langle \mathbf{p}, \mathbf{x} \otimes \mathbf{x} \rangle$ by

$$\begin{aligned} \langle \mathbf{p}, \mathbf{x} \otimes \mathbf{x} \rangle &= \langle \mathbf{p}, (\mathbf{x} + \mathbf{b}) \otimes (\mathbf{x} + \mathbf{b}) \rangle - \langle \mathbf{p}'_{\mathbf{b}} + \mathbf{c}, \mathbf{x} + \mathbf{b} \rangle + \langle \mathbf{p}'_{\mathbf{b}} + \mathbf{c}, \mathbf{b} \rangle + \langle \mathbf{c}, \mathbf{x} \rangle - c' \\ &= \langle \mathbf{p}, \mathbf{m}_B^1 \otimes \mathbf{m}_B^1 \rangle - \langle \mathbf{m}_A^1, \mathbf{m}_B^1 \rangle + m_A^2 + m_B^2 \end{aligned}$$

Theorem A.2. *There is a PSM protocol with one-sided privacy for n-variable quadratic polynomial over $\mathbb{F}_q$, where Alice and Bob each sends $n+1$ elements of $\mathbb{F}_q$, Charlie applies a reconstruction function of degree-2.*

Proof. Correctness is straight-forward.

Privacy follows from the following observations:

- the joint distribution of $\mathbf{m}_B^1, m_B^2, \mathbf{m}_A^1$ is uniformly random, since we are using $(\mathbf{b}, b', \mathbf{c})$ as one-time pads;
- we have $m_A^2 = \langle \mathbf{p}, \mathbf{x} \otimes \mathbf{x} \rangle - \langle \mathbf{p}, \mathbf{m}_B^1 \otimes \mathbf{m}_B^1 \rangle + \langle \mathbf{m}_A^1, \mathbf{m}_B^1 \rangle - m_B^2$.

Putting the two together, we can simulate $\mathbf{m}_B^1, m_B^2, \mathbf{m}_A^1, m_A^2$ given just $\mathbf{p}, \langle \mathbf{p}, \mathbf{x} \otimes \mathbf{x} \rangle$. □

A degree-k polynomial $\langle \mathbf{p}, \mathbf{x} \otimes \ldots \otimes \mathbf{x} \rangle$ can be naturally reduced to a degree-2 polynomial with $O(n^{\lceil k/2 \rceil})$ variables:

$$\langle \mathbf{p}, \underbrace{\mathbf{x} \otimes \ldots \otimes \mathbf{x}}_{\text{viewed as size-}O(n^{\lceil k/2 \rceil})\text{ input}} \otimes \underbrace{\mathbf{x} \otimes \ldots \otimes \mathbf{x}}_{\text{viewed as size-}O(n^{\lfloor k/2 \rfloor})\text{ input}} \rangle.$$

Corollary 4. *There is a PSM protocol with one-sided privacy for n-variable degree-k polynomial over $\mathbb{F}_q$, where Alice and Bob each sends $O(n^{\lceil k/2 \rceil})$ elements of $\mathbb{F}_q$, Charlie applies a reconstruction function of degree-2.*

A.3 One-Side PSM Lower Bounds for $\mathbf{INDEX}_n$

In this section, we present lower bounds on both cc_A and cc_B. Let $\mathbf{m}_A = \mathsf{A}(\mathbf{D}, \mathbf{w}) \in \mathbb{F}_q^{\ell_A}, \mathbf{m}_B = \mathsf{B}(i, \mathbf{w}) \in \mathbb{F}_q^{\ell_B}$ denote the messages sent by Alice and Bob respectively. Here $\ell_A = \mathsf{cc}_A / \log q, \ell_B = \mathsf{cc}_B / \log q$.

Theorem A.3. *In any one-sided PSM protocol for* $\mathbf{INDEX}_n$ *with a linear reconstruction function over* $\mathbb{F}_q$*, Bob's communication complexity* $\mathsf{cc}_B \geq n - 2$.

Proof. The reconstruction function can be written as

$$\mathsf{C}(\mathbf{D}, \mathbf{m}_A, \mathbf{m}_B) = \langle \mathbf{a}_\mathbf{D}, \mathbf{m}_A \rangle + \langle \mathbf{b}_\mathbf{D}, \mathbf{m}_B \rangle + c.$$

Based on this one-sided PSM, a 2-server PIR can be constructed:

- The client choose random $\mathbf{w} \in \mathscr{W}$. The first query is $\mathbf{w}$. Receive 1-bit response $\langle \mathbf{a}_\mathbf{D}, \mathsf{A}(\mathbf{D}, \mathbf{w}) \rangle$.
- The second query is $\mathbf{m}_B = \mathsf{B}(i, \mathbf{w})$. Receive 1-bit response $\langle \mathbf{b}_\mathbf{D}, \mathbf{m}_B \rangle$.
- The client recovers D_i using $D_i = \langle \mathbf{a}_\mathbf{D}, \mathbf{m}_A \rangle + \langle \mathbf{b}_\mathbf{D}, \mathsf{B}(\mathbf{D}, \mathbf{w}) \rangle + c$.

The correctness of the 2-server PIR is a direct corollary from the correctness of one-sided PSM $(\mathsf{A}, \mathsf{B}, \mathsf{C})$. Privacy follows from the following two observations:

- The first query is fresh randomness $\mathbf{w}$, which is independent from i.
- The second query is one-sided PSM message $\mathbf{m}_B = \mathsf{B}(i, \mathbf{w})$. Consider the zero database $\mathbf{0}$, by the privacy of one-sided PSM protocol, the joint distribution of $\mathsf{A}(\mathbf{0}, \mathbf{w}), \mathsf{B}(i, \mathbf{w})$ is independent from i.

In a 2-server 1-round information-theoretic PIR scheme, if the servers' responses are 1-bit, then the queries to each server must be at least $n - 2$ bit [BFG06]. Therefore, $\mathsf{cc}_B \geq n - 2$ and $\log |\mathscr{W}| \geq n - 2$. □

Theorem A.4. *In any one-sided PSM protocol for* $\mathbf{INDEX}_n$ *with a linear reconstruction function over* $\mathbb{F}_q$*, Bob's communication complexity* $\mathsf{cc}_B \geq O(n^{1/k}) \log q$.

Proof. In order to prove a lower bound of Alice's communication complexity, we construct a PSM for $\mathbf{INDEX}_n$ problem based on a one-sided PSM scheme for the same problem.

The reconstruction function C is a degree-k polynomial. By the correctness guarantee,

$$\mathsf{C}(\mathsf{A}(\mathbf{D}, \mathbf{w}), \mathsf{B}(i, \mathbf{w})) = D_i$$

for any $\mathbf{D}, i, \mathbf{w}$. Define a degree-$k$ polynomial $p_{\mathbf{D},\mathbf{w}}$ as

$$p_{\mathbf{D},\mathbf{w}}(\mathbf{y}) = \mathsf{C}(\mathsf{A}(\mathbf{D}, \mathbf{w}), \mathbf{y}).$$

Then a PSM scheme for $\mathbf{INDEX}_n$ is to let Alice compute $p_{\mathbf{D},\mathbf{w}}$, let Bob compute $\mathbf{y} = \mathsf{B}(i, \mathbf{w})$, then let Charlie learn $T_{\mathbf{D},\mathbf{w}}(\mathbf{y})$ using the PSM scheme for polynomial. In such PSM scheme, Bob's communication complexity is no more than $(\mathsf{cc}_B + 1)\log|\mathbb{F}_q|$, Alice's communication complexity is no more than $(\mathsf{cc}_B+1)^k \cdot \log|\mathbb{F}_q|$. Then by the communication complexity lower bound of PSM protocol for $\mathbf{INDEX}_n$,

$$(\mathsf{cc}_B + 1)^k \cdot \log q \geq n \cdot \log q. \qquad \square$$

Theorem A.4 proves an $\Omega(n^{1/k})$ lower bound of Bob's communication complexity in one-sided PSM for $\mathbf{INDEX}_n$, it matches the $O(n^{1/k})$ upper bound of PSM $\mathbf{INDEX}_n$ (Theorem 5.3).

The proof of Theorem A.4 only uses the fact that the reconstruction function is a degree-k polynomial on Bob's message. It doesn't use the privacy guarantee of one-sided PSM for $\mathbf{INDEX}_n$ that Bob's message hides index i.

B CDS for Degree-2 Polynomials $\neg\mathbf{MPOLY}^2_{n_1,n_2}$

In this section, we describe a CDS protocol for $\neg\mathbf{MPOLY}^2_{n_1,n_2}$. Alice holds degree-2 polynomial $\mathbf{p} \in \mathbb{F}_q^{n_1 n_2}$, Bob holds $(\mathbf{x}_1, \mathbf{x}_2) \in \mathbb{F}_q^{n_1} \times \mathbb{F}_q^{n_2}$ and secret $\mu \in \mathbb{F}_q$ and Charlie learns μ if and only if $\langle \mathbf{p}, \mathbf{x}_1 \otimes \mathbf{x}_2 \rangle = 0$. This predicate is a negation of the predicate in CDS for $\mathbf{MPOLY}^2_{n_1,n_2}$.

Theorem B.1. *There is a CDS protocol for* $\neg\mathbf{MPOLY}^2_{n_1,n_2}$ *over* $\mathbb{F}_q$ *(given in Fig. 8) where Alice sends* n_2 *elements of* $\mathbb{F}_q$*, Bob sends* $n_1 + 1$ *elements of* $\mathbb{F}_q$ *and Charlie applies an* $\mathbb{F}_q$*-linear reconstruction function.*

Proof. Charlie's output equals

$$\begin{aligned}
&\langle \mathbf{p}, \mathbf{m}_B^1 \otimes \mathbf{x}_2 \rangle + m_B^2 - \langle \mathbf{m}_A^1, \mathbf{x}_2 \rangle \\
&= \langle \mathbf{p}, (a\mathbf{x}_1 + \mathbf{b}) \otimes \mathbf{x}_2 \rangle + \mu + \langle \mathbf{c}, \mathbf{x}_2 \rangle - \langle \mathbf{p}'_{\mathbf{b}} + \mathbf{c}, \mathbf{x}_2 \rangle \\
&= a\langle \mathbf{p}, \mathbf{x}_1 \otimes \mathbf{x}_2 \rangle + \mu
\end{aligned}$$

When $\langle \mathbf{p}, \mathbf{x}_1 \otimes \mathbf{x}_2 \rangle = 0$, Charlie's output equals μ. This proves correctness.

Privacy follows from the following observations:

- the joint distribution of $\mathbf{m}_B^1, \mathbf{m}_A^1$ is uniformly random, since we are using $(\mathbf{b}, \mathbf{c})$ as one-time pads;
- we have

$$m_B^2 = a\langle \mathbf{p}, \mathbf{x}_1 \otimes \mathbf{x}_2 \rangle + \mu - \langle \mathbf{p}, \mathbf{m}_B^1 \otimes \mathbf{x}_2 \rangle + \langle \mathbf{m}_A^1, \mathbf{x}_2 \rangle$$

  when $\langle \mathbf{p}, \mathbf{x}_1 \otimes \mathbf{x}_2 \rangle \neq 0$, the distribution of m_B^2 is uniformly random conditional on $\mathbf{m}_B^1, \mathbf{m}_A^1$, since a acts as a one-time pad.

Putting the two together, the joint distribution of $\mathbf{m}_A^1, \mathbf{m}_B^1, m_B^2$ is uniformly random when $\langle \mathbf{p}, \mathbf{x}_1 \otimes \mathbf{x}_2 \rangle \neq 0$. $\square$

CDS for Degree-2 Polynomials $\neg\mathbf{MPOLY}^2_{n_1,n_2}$ (over $\mathbb{F}_q$)

Alice's Input: A degree-2 polynomial (expressed as a vector) $\mathbf{p} \in \mathbb{F}_q^{n_1 n_2}$.
Bob's Input: $(\mathbf{x}_1, \mathbf{x}_2) \in \mathbb{F}_q^{n_1} \times \mathbb{F}_q^{n_2}$ and $\mu \in \mathbb{F}_q$.
Carol's Output: μ if $\langle \mathbf{p}, \mathbf{x}_1 \otimes \mathbf{x}_2 \rangle = 0$.
Shared Randomness: $(a, \mathbf{b}, \mathbf{c}) \in \mathbb{F}_q \times \mathbb{F}_q^{n_1} \times \mathbb{F}_q^{n_2}$.

- Alice computes a vector $\mathbf{p}'_{\mathbf{b}} \in \mathbb{F}_q^{n_2}$ such that for any $\mathbf{y} \in \mathbb{F}_q^{n_2}$, $\langle \mathbf{p}, \mathbf{b} \otimes \mathbf{y} \rangle = \langle \mathbf{p}'_{\mathbf{b}}, \mathbf{y} \rangle$. She sends $\mathbf{m}_A^1 := \mathbf{p}'_{\mathbf{b}} + \mathbf{c} \in \mathbb{F}_q^{n_2}$ to Charlie.
- Bob sends $\mathbf{m}_B^1 := a\mathbf{x}_1 + \mathbf{b} \in \mathbb{F}_q^{n_1}$ and $m_B^2 := \mu + \langle \mathbf{c}, \mathbf{x}_2 \rangle \in \mathbb{F}_q$ to Charlie.
- Charlie outputs $\perp$ if $\langle \mathbf{p}, \mathbf{x}_1 \otimes \mathbf{x}_2 \rangle \neq 0$ and

$$\langle \mathbf{p}, \mathbf{m}_B^1 \otimes \mathbf{x}_2 \rangle + m_B^2 - \langle \mathbf{m}_A^1, \mathbf{x}_2 \rangle$$

otherwise.

Fig. 8. The CDS protocol for degree-2 polynomials with $(\mathsf{cc}_A, \mathsf{cc}_B) = (n_2 \log q, (n_1 + 1) \log q)$.

Connection with CDS for $\mathbf{MPOLY}^2_{n_1,n_2}$. On closer examination, the CDS for $\mathbf{MPOLY}^2_{n_1,n_2}$ (given in Fig. 3) allows Charlie to learn $\mu \cdot \mathsf{P}_{\mathbf{MPOLY}}(\mathbf{p}, (\mathbf{x}_1, \mathbf{x}_2))$ using a linear reconstruction function, where $\mathsf{P}_{\mathbf{MPOLY}}$ denotes the predicate defined in Sect. 2.3. Upon this protocol that computes $\mu \cdot \mathsf{P}_{\mathbf{MPOLY}}(\mathbf{p}, (\mathbf{x}_1, \mathbf{x}_2))$, we can construct a CDS protocol for $\neg\mathbf{MPOLY}^2_{n_1,n_2}$.

Concretely, Fig. 3 is a protocol for following functionality: Alice holds degree-2 polynomial $\mathbf{p} \in \mathbb{F}_q^{n_1 n_2}$, Bob holds $(\mathbf{x}_1, \mathbf{x}_2) \in \mathbb{F}_q^{n_1} \times \mathbb{F}_q^{n_2}$ and secret $\mu \in \mathbb{F}_q$, Charlie holds $\mathbf{p}, \mathbf{x}_1, \mathbf{x}_2$ and learns $\mu \cdot \mathsf{P}_{\mathbf{MPOLY}}(\mathbf{p}, (\mathbf{x}_1, \mathbf{x}_2))$. The reconstruction functionality is linear in $\mathbb{F}_q$. Assume Bob deviates from the protocol: whenever he is supposed use secret μ, he feed the protocol with a random value $a \in \mathbb{F}_q$ picked from the random string: he also shift his message so that the value recovered by Charlie is shifted by μ (it's possible as Charlie applies a linear reconstruction). As the result, Charlie learns $a \cdot \mathsf{P}_{\mathbf{MPOLY}}(\mathbf{p}, (\mathbf{x}_1, \mathbf{x}_2)) + \mu$. This is exactly a CDS for $\neg\mathbf{MPOLY}^2_{n_1,n_2}$. Charlie recovers μ if $\mathsf{P}_{\mathbf{MPOLY}}(\mathbf{p}, (\mathbf{x}_1, \mathbf{x}_2)) = 0$, and Charlie recovers a random value otherwise.

This explains the similarity between the CDS for $\mathbf{MPOLY}^2_{n_1,n_2}$ (given in Fig. 3) and the CDS for $\neg\mathbf{MPOLY}^2_{n_1,n_2}$ (given in Fig. 8). Similar transformation can be applied to CDS for $\mathbf{MPOLY}^3_{n_1,n_2,n_3}$ over $\mathbb{F}_2$, the resulting CDS for $\neg\mathbf{MPOLY}^3_{n_1,n_2,n_3}$ over $\mathbb{F}_2$ has communication complexity $\mathsf{cc}_A = n_1 + n_2 + n_3$, $\mathsf{cc}_B = n_1 + n_2 + n_3 + 1$ and a degree-2 reconstruction function.

References

[AARV17] Applebaum, B., Arkis, B., Raykov, P., Vasudevan, P.N.: Conditional disclosure of secrets: amplification, closure, amortization, lower-bounds, and separations. IACR Cryptology ePrint Archive 2017:164 (2017)

[ACC+14] Ada, A., Chattopadhyay, A., Cook, S.A., Fontes, L., Koucký, M., Pitassi, T.: The hardness of being private. TOCT **6**(1), 1:1–1:24 (2014)

[Att14] Attrapadung, N.: Dual system encryption via doubly selective security: framework, fully secure functional encryption for regular languages, and more. In: Nguyen, P.Q., Oswald, E. (eds.) EUROCRYPT 2014. LNCS, vol. 8441, pp. 557–577. Springer, Heidelberg (2014). doi:10.1007/978-3-642-55220-5_31

[Bei11] Beimel, A.: Secret-sharing schemes: a survey. In: Chee, Y.M., Guo, Z., Ling, S., Shao, F., Tang, Y., Wang, H., Xing, C. (eds.) IWCC 2011. LNCS, vol. 6639, pp. 11–46. Springer, Heidelberg (2011). doi:10.1007/978-3-642-20901-7_2

[BFG06] Beigel, R., Fortnow, L., Gasarch, W.I.: A tight lower bound for restricted pir protocols. Comput. Complex. **15**(1), 82–91 (2006)

[BGP95] Beimel, A., Gál, A., Paterson, M.: Lower bounds for monotone span programs. In: FOCS, pp. 674–681 (1995)

[BI01] Beimel, A., Ishai, Y.: On the power of nonlinear secret-sharing. In: Proceedings of the 16th Annual IEEE Conference on Computational Complexity, Chicago, Illinois, USA, 18–21 June 2001, pp. 188–202. IEEE Computer Society (2001)

[BIKK14] Beimel, A., Ishai, Y., Kumaresan, R., Kushilevitz, E.: On the cryptographic complexity of the worst functions. In: Lindell, Y. (ed.) TCC 2014. LNCS, vol. 8349, pp. 317–342. Springer, Heidelberg (2014). doi:10.1007/978-3-642-54242-8_14

[BIKO12] Beimel, A., Ishai, Y., Kushilevitz, E., Orlov, I.: Share conversion and private information retrieval. In: Proceedings of the 27th Conference on Computational Complexity, CCC 2012, Porto, Portugal, 26–29 June 2012, pp. 258–268. IEEE Computer Society (2012)

[BSGV96] Blundo, C., De Santis, A., Gargano, L., Vaccaro, U.: On the information rate of secret sharing schemes. Theor. Comput. Sci. **154**(2), 283–306 (1996)

[BSSV97] Blundo, C., De Santis, A., De Simone, R., Vaccaro, U.: Tight bounds on the information rate of secret sharing schemes. Des. Codes Crypt. **11**(2), 107–122 (1997)

[Bub86] Bublitz, S.: Decomposition of graphs and monotone formula size of homogeneous functions. Acta Inf. **23**(6), 689–696 (1986)

[CGW15] Chen, J., Gay, R., Wee, H.: Improved dual system ABE in prime-order groups via predicate encodings. In: Oswald, E., Fischlin, M. (eds.) EUROCRYPT 2015. LNCS, vol. 9057, pp. 595–624. Springer, Heidelberg (2015). doi:10.1007/978-3-662-46803-6_20

[CK91] Chor, B., Kushilevitz, E.: A zero-one law for boolean privacy. SIAM J. Discrete Math. **4**(1), 36–47 (1991)

[CKGS98] Chor, B., Kushilevitz, E., Goldreich, O., Sudan, M.: Private information retrieval. J. ACM **45**(6), 965–981 (1998)

[Csi97] Csirmaz, L.: The size of a share must be large. J. Cryptol. **10**(4), 223–231 (1997)

[Csi05] Csirmaz, L.: Secret sharing schemes on graphs. IACR Cryptology ePrint Archive 2005:59 (2005)

[DG15] Dvir, Z., Gopi, S.: 2-server PIR with sub-polynomial communication. In: STOC, pp. 577–584 (2015)

[DGY11] Dvir, Z., Gopalan, P., Yekhanin, S.: Matching vector codes. SIAM J. Comput. **40**(4), 1154–1178 (2011)

[DPP14] Data, D., Prabhakaran, M.M., Prabhakaran, V.M.: On the communication complexity of secure computation. In: Garay, J.A., Gennaro, R. (eds.) CRYPTO 2014. LNCS, vol. 8617, pp. 199–216. Springer, Heidelberg (2014). doi:10.1007/978-3-662-44381-1_12

[Efr09] Efremenko, K.: 3-query locally decodable codes of subexponential length. In: STOC, pp. 39–44 (2009)

[EP97] Erdös, P., Pyber, L.: Covering a graph by complete bipartite graphs. Discrete Math. **170**(1–3), 249–251 (1997)

[FKN94] Feige, U., Kilian, J., Naor, M.: A minimal model for secure computation (extended abstract). In: Leighton, F.T., Goodrich, M.T. (eds.) Proceedings of the Twenty-Sixth Annual ACM Symposium on Theory of Computing, 23–25 May 1994, Montréal, Québec, Canada, pp. 554–563. ACM (1994)

[GIKM00] Gertner, Y., Ishai, Y., Kushilevitz, E., Malkin, T.: Protecting data privacy in private information retrieval schemes. J. Comput. Syst. Sci. **60**(3), 592–629 (2000)

[GKW15] Gay, R., Kerenidis, I., Wee, H.: Communication complexity of conditional disclosure of secrets and attribute-based encryption. In: Gennaro, R., Robshaw, M. (eds.) CRYPTO 2015. LNCS, vol. 9216, pp. 485–502. Springer, Heidelberg (2015). doi:10.1007/978-3-662-48000-7_24

[GPSW06] Goyal, V., Pandey, O., Sahai, A., Waters, B.: Attribute-based encryption for fine-grained access control of encrypted data. In: ACM Conference on Computer and Communications Security, pp. 89–98 (2006)

[Gro00] Grolmusz, V.: Superpolynomial size set-systems with restricted intersections mod 6 and explicit ramsey graphs. Combinatorica **20**(1), 71–86 (2000)

[IK97] Ishai, Y., Kushilevitz, E.: Private simultaneous messages protocols with applications. In: ISTCS, pp. 174–184 (1997)

[IK00] Ishai, Y., Kushilevitz, E.: Randomizing polynomials: a new representation with applications to round-efficient secure computation. In: 41st Annual Symposium on Foundations of Computer Science, FOCS 2000, 12–14 November 2000, Redondo Beach, California, USA, pp. 294–304. IEEE Computer Society (2000)

[IK02] Ishai, Y., Kushilevitz, E.: Perfect constant-round secure computation via perfect randomizing polynomials. In: Widmayer, P., Eidenbenz, S., Triguero, F., Morales, R., Conejo, R., Hennessy, M. (eds.) ICALP 2002. LNCS, vol. 2380, pp. 244–256. Springer, Heidelberg (2002). doi:10.1007/3-540-45465-9_22

[ISN89] Ito, M., Saito, A., Nishizeki, T.: Secret sharing scheme realizing general access structure. Electron. Commun. Jpn (Part III: Fundam. Electron. Sci.) **72**(9), 56–64 (1989)

[KNR99] Kremer, I., Nisan, N., Ron, D.: On randomized one-round communication complexity. Comput. Complex. **8**(1), 21–49 (1999)

[Lew12] Lewko, A.: Tools for simulating features of composite order bilinear groups in the prime order setting. In: Pointcheval, D., Johansson, T. (eds.) EUROCRYPT 2012. LNCS, vol. 7237, pp. 318–335. Springer, Heidelberg (2012). doi:10.1007/978-3-642-29011-4_20

[LOS+10] Lewko, A.B., Okamoto, T., Sahai, A., Takashima, K., Waters, B.: Fully secure functional encryption: attribute-based encryption and (hierarchical) inner product encryption. In: Gilbert, H. (ed.) EUROCRYPT 2010. LNCS, vol. 6110, pp. 62–91. Springer, Heidelberg (2010). doi:10.1007/978-3-642-13190-5_4

[LW10] Lewko, A.B., Waters, B.: New techniques for dual system encryption and fully secure HIBE with short ciphertexts. In: Micciancio, D. (ed.) TCC 2010. LNCS, vol. 5978, pp. 455–479. Springer, Heidelberg (2010). doi:10.1007/978-3-642-11799-2_27

[LW11] Lewko, A.B., Waters, B.: Decentralizing attribute-based encryption. In: Paterson, K.G. (ed.) EUROCRYPT 2011. LNCS, vol. 6632, pp. 568–588. Springer, Heidelberg (2011). doi:10.1007/978-3-642-20465-4_31

[Nay99] Nayak, A.: Optimal lower bounds for quantum automata and random access codes. In: FOCS, pp. 369–377 (1999)

[OS08] Ostrovsky, R., Skeith III, W.E.: Communication complexity in algebraic two-party protocols. In: Wagner, D. (ed.) CRYPTO 2008. LNCS, vol. 5157, pp. 379–396. Springer, Heidelberg (2008). doi:10.1007/978-3-540-85174-5_21

[OT10] Okamoto, T., Takashima, K.: Fully secure functional encryption with general relations from the decisional linear assumption. In: Rabin, T. (ed.) CRYPTO 2010. LNCS, vol. 6223, pp. 191–208. Springer, Heidelberg (2010). doi:10.1007/978-3-642-14623-7_11

[OT12] Okamoto, T., Takashima, K.: Adaptively attribute-hiding (hierarchical) inner product encryption. In: Pointcheval, D., Johansson, T. (eds.) EUROCRYPT 2012. LNCS, vol. 7237, pp. 591–608. Springer, Heidelberg (2012). doi:10.1007/978-3-642-29011-4_35. Also, Cryptology ePrint Archive, Report 2011/543

[RPRC16] Robere, R., Pitassi, T., Rossman, B., Cook, S.A.: Exponential lower bounds for monotone span programs. In: FOCS, pp. 406–415 (2016)

[Sha79] Shamir, A.: How to share a secret. Commun. ACM **22**(11), 612–613 (1979)

[SS97] Sun, H.-M., Shieh, S.-P.: Secret sharing in graph-based prohibited structures. In: INFOCOM, pp. 718–724 (1997)

[SW05] Sahai, A., Waters, B.: Fuzzy identity-based encryption. In: Cramer, R. (ed.) EUROCRYPT 2005. LNCS, vol. 3494, pp. 457–473. Springer, Heidelberg (2005). doi:10.1007/11426639_27

[vD95] van Dijk, M.: On the information rate of perfect secret sharing schemes. Des. Codes Crypt. **6**(2), 143–169 (1995)

[VV15] Vaikuntanathan, V., Vasudevan, P.N.: Secret sharing and statistical zero knowledge. In: Iwata, T., Cheon, J.H. (eds.) ASIACRYPT 2015. LNCS, vol. 9452, pp. 656–680. Springer, Heidelberg (2015). doi:10.1007/978-3-662-48797-6_27

[Wat09] Waters, B.: Dual system encryption: realizing fully secure IBE and HIBE under simple assumptions. In: Halevi, S. (ed.) CRYPTO 2009. LNCS, vol. 5677, pp. 619–636. Springer, Heidelberg (2009). doi:10.1007/978-3-642-03356-8_36

[Wee14] Wee, H.: Dual system encryption via predicate encodings. In: Lindell, Y. (ed.) TCC 2014. LNCS, vol. 8349, pp. 616–637. Springer, Heidelberg (2014). doi:10.1007/978-3-642-54242-8_26

[WY05] Woodruff, D.P., Yekhanin, S.: A geometric approach to information-theoretic private information retrieval. In: CCC, pp. 275–284 (2005)

[Yek08] Yekhanin, S.: Towards 3-query locally decodable codes of subexponential length. J. ACM **55**(1), 1:1–1:16 (2008)

Author Index

Printed in the United States
By Bookmasters

Printed in the United States
By Bookmasters